THE ENCYCLOPEDIA OF
ANIMATED CARTOONS

THE ENCYCLOPEDIA OF
ANIMATED CARTOONS

Jeff Lenburg

Foreword by Gary Owens

Facts On File
New York • Oxford

To my wife, Debby,
for her love and devotion, this book is for you.

The Encyclopedia of Animated Cartoons
Copyright © 1991 by Jeff Lenburg

Facts On File, Inc.   Facts On File Limited
460 Park Avenue South   Collins Street
New York NY 10016   Oxford OX4 1XJ
USA   United Kingdom

Library of Congress Cataloging-in-Publication Data
Lenburg, Jeff.
    The encyclopedia of animated cartoons / Jeff Lenburg.
      p. cm.
    Rev. ed. of: The encyclopedia of animated cartoon series. c1981.
    Includes index.
    ISBN 0-8160-2252-6 (hardcover)
    ISBN 0-8160-2775-7 (paperback)
    1. Animated films—United States—History and criticism.
I. Lenburg, Jeff. Encyclopedia of animated cartoon series.
II. Title.
NC1766.U5L46   1990
791.43'75'0973—dc20   90-21182

A British CIP catalogue record for this book is available from the British Library.

Facts On File books are available at special discounts when purchased in bulk quantities for businesses, associations, institutions or sales promotions. Please call our Special Sales Department in New York at 212/683-2244 (dial 800/322-8755 except in NY, AK or HI) or in Oxford at 865/728399.

Text design by Donna Sinisgalli
Jacket design by James Victore
Composition by the Maple-Vail Book Manufacturing Group
Manufactured by the Maple-Vail Book Manufacturing Group
Printed in the United States of America

10 9 8 7 6 5 4 3 2 1

This book is printed on acid-free paper.

CONTENTS

FOREWORD
BY GARY OWENS

From beautiful downtown Burbank, the Nurgle Capitol of the World, greetings to animated cartoons fans everywhere!

My friend, Jeff Lenburg, has done it again. I've enjoyed every book he's ever written, from his tomes on Dudley Moore, Steve Martin, Dustin Hoffman and the Three Stooges to his previous books on animation history. His ability to research day and night, week and month, Burke and Hare proves that he is a virtuoso of frightening perfection. That's why I love his *Encyclopedia of Animated Cartoons*.

Cartoons have always meant a lot to me. When I was 12 years old, I loved to draw and had the good fortune to win a scholarship to an Art Correspondence School in Minneapolis. The instructor who chose my drawings was a gentleman named Charles Schulz, the same rascal who later moved to California and created Charlie Brown and Snoopy. (Somehow in my life, a giant magnet seems to drift me toward great people. My economics professor in college was Joe Robbie, who went on to own the Miami Dolphins and Joe Robbie Stadium. My history teacher was George McGovern, who ran for president of the United States. My childhood idol was Walt Disney. One of the happiest moments came when they put my star on Hollywood's Walk of Fame next to Walt's.)

This was just the beginning of my wonderful love affair with cartoons. Although I began as a writer for Jay Ward Productions, my first cartoon speaking series was Roger Ramjet (the lovable oafish super hero) for 162 Pantomime Pictures episodes in 1965. Since the 1960s, I've worked for Disney Studios doing narrative and voices on short subjects, specials and the like with Mickey Mouse, Donald Duck and Goofy (including being the announcer of the "Wonderful World of Disney" for six years).

I can't imagine having a more joyful experience than my association with many of the great animators and voice people from the world of animated cartoons. Joe Barbera and Bill Hanna are among those in the animation industry who have been very helpful in my career of animation vox. They alone have chosen me for hundreds of cartoons. By lifting the Hanna-Barbera cornucopia, some of those series have included: "Space Ghost," "The Perils of Penelope Pit-stop," "Scooby Doo's All-Star Laff-A-Lympics," "Dynomutt, Dog Wonder," "Jonny Quest," "Captain Caveman" and "Yogi's Space Race" and others. For the great cartoonist Jim Davis, I've been the announcer for "Garfield And His Friends" and the super hero Captain Squash on "Bobby's World" with Howie Mandell.

These magic moments have meant a strong sense of personal destiny for me. I've been lucky enough to be a featured voice on more than 1,500 cartoon episodes!

A friend whom I miss dearly is the late great Mel Blanc. Mel and his creative son, Noel, and I worked together as friends in radio for many years. As you look in this Encyclopedia, you can see that Mel was "the star" of Warner Brothers cartoons for over 50 years. We must thank Mel for the innovative change that he brought about in our business. Because of his actions, he got all voice stars their names on the screen.

In the late '30s, with his wife Estelle pregnant and baby son on the way, he needed a raise. Mel asked Warner Brothers' cartoon chief Leon Schlesinger for a pay boost. Those were the days of querulous uncertainty (and his orchestra). Leon did not want to give Mel a raise but did allow that he would give Mel credit on the screen for his marvelous voice characterizations. No one had ever received that before. Mel accepted and within three years he was clearing more than $2,000 a week doing 18 coast-to-coast radio shows! His identity finally became known.

This was not a time of pitiless elitism. That was more money over a year's period of time than Joe Louis got in 1942 defending his world championship boxing title against Abe Simon.

What this has to do with cartoons, I'm not sure. But I am certain about one thing. You'll find fascinating moments galore in this volume, thanks to Jeff Lenburg's superhuman research, chronicling virtually every cartoon since the invention of the Vort (a machine invented in 1908 by Oveta Culp Feckle enabling a person to send tapioca through the telephone wires).

Congratulations, Jeff!

Your chum,
Gary Owens

PREFACE

More than a decade ago, I penned what was intended to be the most complete book on animated cartoon series ever, *The Encyclopedia of Animated Cartoon Series*. The book was born out of the dream that there be a major reference on animated cartoons.

The book was the first to document hundreds of cartoon series—silent cartoons, theatrical cartoons and television cartoons. It was an exhausting accomplishment and one which I swore I would never do again.

In recent years, I have received hundreds of letters from fans in response to my original book asking for an updated and expanded edition. While this seemed like a simple enough task to them, I could only recall the horrors of writing that first edition: retyping an entire 800–page manuscript five times on a rickety Smith–Corona typewriter and the complete exhaustion that followed.

Well, due to a variety of circumstances, I have decided with this year marking the 10th anniversary of my original edition that it was time to try again, making one last effort to deliver to the world what I set out to accomplish a decade ago—the most comprehensive, authoritative volume on cartoons ever imagined.

This book is designed as the ultimate cartoon fan's guide. It features detailed information on every animated cartoon production, series or program exhibited theatrically or broadcast on television—on networks and cable—in the United States (foreign cartoon imports from Japan, Canada and elsewhere are included) from 1911 through the 1989–1990 television season—more than 80 years' worth of 'toons!

Every attempt has been made to provide the most complete account possible of each cartoon production listed, culling the information from studio production records, motion picture trade paper listings, television program guides, movie and television reviews, film vaults and movie warehouses, and, in many cases, from credits listed on the films themselves. This information was then cross–referenced with countless reliable sources to ensure its accuracy.

The book is divided into six sections: silent cartoon series, theatrical sound cartoon series, full–length animated features, animated television specials, television cartoon series (including Saturday–morning, syndicated and cable–produced programs) and Academy Award and Emmy Award listings, featuring winners and nominees in the area of cartoon animation since the honors first began.

For easy reference, each entry provides the following: series history, voice credits (except silent cartoons, of course) and year produced or broadcast, with complete filmographies (titles of each cartoon produced) for nearly every silent, theatrical sound and television series featured.

Silent cartoon entries include a complete historical account of each series and, where available, director and producer credits, and release dates (month, day and year) of each cartoon in the series. For theatrical sound cartoon series, director credits (overall and for each cartoon), voice credits, release dates (month, day and year), reissue dates (abbreviated as "re:"), episode co–stars (example: w/ Porky Pig), Academy Award nominations (listed as A.A. nominee or A.A. winner) and special film format (i.e., Cinecolor, CinemaScope, Technicolor, etc.) are listed under the respective series.

In the full–length animated feature section, complete summaries have been provided for each entry, as well as technical credits and side notes about the production (listed under "PN," for "production notes"). The section contains only feature films which received wide distribution in this country, whether produced domestically or overseas.

As for television specials and television series, premiere dates and rebroadcast dates have been included and, wherever possible, episode titles have been listed under the season (example: 1960–61) in which they were originally produced. In many cases, background information and reminiscences of the animators or producers have been incorporated into the entries, painting a vivid picture of the production and its characters, and providing insight into the filmmaking process.

In addition, the book has been carefully indexed for easy reference.

Enjoy!

Jeff Lenburg
Rancho Mirage, California

© Joe Oriolo Productions.

ACKNOWLEDGMENTS

In tackling a project so broadly scoped as this one, few people could ever possibly imagine the hours involved in compiling a definitive reference with one single purpose: to offer the most informative, nostalgic reference on nearly every animated cartoon since man first invented the art.

Well, the truth of the matter is that most of the information contained in this volume took more years than I would personally like to remember to research, write and cross–check in order to present the most accurate account possible for each production listed. Studios, distributors, directors, producers, animators, cartoon collectors and even curators of film vaults were consulted in the course of compiling this book. The result was hundreds of letters, phone calls, FAXes (thank God for this technological wonder) and other means of correspondence in the United States and abroad to corroborate facts and acquire information necessary to make this wonderful celebration of animated cartoons complete.

Fortunately, a great many people shared with me the importance of documenting the history of this popular medium, all willing to share one more bit of information or render a few more hours of their precious time to make this "dream book" a reality.

First and foremost, I would like to thank the many producers, directors and animators, many of whom I have admired for their ingenuity and talent, who, over the years, supplied information, materials and their personal support of this project. They include Joe Barbera, Bill Hanna, Friz Freleng, David H. DePatie, Chuck Jones, Walter Lantz, Bob Clampett, Arthur Rankin, Jules Bass, Joe Ruby, Ken Spears, Lou Scheimer, Jay Ward, Bill Hurtz, Fred Calvert, Hal Seeger, Joe Oriolo, Bill Melendez, Shamus Culhane, Fred Ladd, Dick Brown, Faith Hubley, Norman Maurer and Rudy Zamora.

Much of the information featured in this volume would not have been possible without the generous support of many production companies and their staffs. In this instance, I would like to extend my personal thanks to David R. Smith, Paula Sigman, Derek Westervelt and Nancy Battele, Walt Disney Productions; Nina Skahan, Bill Melendez Productions; William Ruiz, Eric Stein and George Robertson, DIC Enterprises; Trudi Takamatsu, Murakami–Wolf–Swenson Films; Monika Weiss, Nelvana Limited; Henry Saperstein and Helen Newbury, United Productions of America (UPA); Kelly Irwin and Star Kaplan, Marvel Productions; Stanley Stunell and Jacki Yaro, Lone Ranger Television; Ken Snyder and Tish Gainey, Ken Snyder Productions; Art Scott, Jean Rich, Guyla Toth, Sarah Baisley, Mark Hoffmeier and Maggie Roberts, Hanna–Barbera Productions; Janie Fields and Jan Albright, DePatie–Freleng Productions; and Loretta High, Ruby–Spears Productions.

I would also like to acknowledge Joanne McQueen, Rankin–Bass Productions; Robert Miller, Walter Lantz Productions; Herbert A. Nusbaum, Metro–Goldwyn–Mayer; Tod Roberts and Sari DeCesare, National Broadcasting Company (NBC); Jenny Trias and Joyce Loeb, Filmation; John Cawley, Film Roman Productions; Gloria Foster, ZIV International; Lee Polk and Laurie Tritini, King Features Entertainment; Leon Harvey and Evelyn Johnson, Harvey Films; William Weiss and Charles Tolep, Terrytoons Productions; Ann Pulley, Royal Productions; Deborah Fine,

LucasFilm; Janis Diamond, Farmhouse Films; James Stabile and Lee Orgel, Metromedia Producers Corporation; Elizabeth Shaw, MCA; Bart Farber, Virginia Brown and Maury Oken, United Artists'; Hal Geer, Ahuva Rabani and Edward A. Hoffman, Warner Brothers; Robert L. Rosen, RLR Associates; Laura Ramsay, Bob Keeshan Enterprises; Jodi Berman, Ruby–Spears Productions; Loretta Petersohn, Thea Flaum Productions; C. J. Grant, Saban International; Stephen Worth, Bagdasarian Productions; Rosalind Goldberg, Larry Harmon Pictures; and Michael Hack, TMS Entertainment.

The support of the following individuals and companies was also most appreciated: Tiffany Fegley, Hearst Entertainment; Pam Bobbitt–Daniel, Lightyear Entertainment; Valerie Delafoy, Parafrance Communication; Adrian Woolery, Playhouse Pictures; Keven Reher, Premavision; Liz Foster and Claire Wilmut, Evergreen Productions; Joyce Irby, 20th Century–Fox Television; Peggy Ray, Republic Pictures Corporation; Anita Kelso, World Events Productions; Leslie Maryon–LaRose, Scholastic Productions; and Allan Migram, Marvel Comics Group.

Television networks, local television stations and television program distributors also played significant roles in contributing material to this book. Among those who helped were Jerry Westfeldt, TV Cinema Sales; Sandy Frank, Sandy Frank Film Syndication; Lonnie D. Halouska, Rex Waggoner and Phyllis Kirk, National Telefilm Associates (NTA); Tom Hatten, KTLA–TV; Lisa Mateas, Dick O'Connell, Michelle Couch and Mike Lazzo, Turner Network Television; Lee Nash, Worldvision; Barry Kluger, March 5; Caroline Ansell, Viacom International; Robert Ferson, The Right Stuf; Donita J. Delzer, Evangelical Lutheran Church in America; Ann B. Cody, Westchester Films; Nancy Allen, Thames Taffner; Priscilla French, Harmony Gold; Joe Adelman and Elise Sugar, Color Systems Technology; Lisa Schiradli and Fran Brochstein, Nickelodeon; Holly Grieve, MG Perin, Inc.; Amy Sauertieg, SFM Entertainment; Daniel Mulholland, Muller Media, Inc.; Yolanda Cortez, Alice Communications; Sara Fitzsimmons, HBO; Joyce Nishihira, CBS Entertainment; Farrell Meisel, WWOR–TV; and William Cayton, Radio and Television Packagers.

Many historians, cartoon collectors and buffs (some of them experts in their own field of interest) provided information critical to the successful completion of numerous entries in this book. I would like to pay special tribute to Jerry Beck, Al Bigley, Dan Brown, John Cawley, Karl Cohen, Greg Duffel, Mark Evanier, James Gauthier, Ronnie James, Mark Kausler, Ken Layton, Mike Lefebvre, Greg Lenburg, Bob Miller, David Moore, Brian Pearce, Doug Ranney (of Whole Toon Access), Randy Skretvedt, Anthony Specian Jr. and Charles Wagner.

In the area of Japanese cartoons, perhaps the most difficult to document, I would like to thank the following for their time in furnishing vital information and materials to me for the many entries listed: Barbara Edmunds, Meg Evans, Tom Hamilton, James Long, Lorraine Savage and Scott Wheeler.

Naturally, I cannot forget the tremendous support that I received from the following libraries and their staffs in tracking down background information, reviews, production listings, special collections and illustrations to make this project as authoritative as possible. They are Howard H. Prouty, The Academy of Motion Pictures Arts and Sciences Library; The Museum of Modern Art; Alan Braun, The Louis B. Mayer Library of The American Film Institute; The Cerritos Public Library; The Anaheim Public Library; and The College of The Desert Library.

Much of the information contained in this book was dependent upon not only studio records and private collections, but also on material culled from the pages of several major Hollywood motion picture and television journals. To this end, I would like to offer my personal thanks to the men and women of the following publications whose diligence in recording weekly production logs and other technical information made this book what it is today: *Box Office, Daily Variety, Hollywood Reporter, Motion Picture Herald* and *Motion Picture News.*

The following publications were also invaluable sources for facts and information contained in this book: *American Film, Animania* (formerly *Mindrot*), *Broadcast Information Bureau— TV Series Source Book, Broadcasting Magazine, The Los Angeles Times, Millimeter Magazine, The New York Times, Radio/TV Age* and *TV Guide.*

I would also like to tip my hat to other devotees of animation who through their own personal interest and commitment have provided the basis for reseach on various cartoon characters, their films or programs through their own labors of love. They are Jerry Beck and

Will Friedwald, co–authors of *The Looney Tunes/Merrie Melodies Book;* Leonard Maltin, author of *Of Mice and Magic;* Leslie Cabarga, author of *The Fleischer Story;* George Woolery, author of *Children's Television: The Animated Cartoons;* Joe Adamson, author of *Tex Avery: King of Cartoons* and *The Walter Lantz Story;* and Donald Crafton, author of *Before Mickey.*

Last but not least, I want to thank God for providing me with the patience and fortitude to cope with the challenges that greeted me at every turn—especially in typing the 1,900–plus paged manuscript—and to complete the task at hand. And, of course, to my wife, Debby, for her love and encouragement every step of the way.

A NUTSHELL HISTORY OF THE AMERICAN ANIMATED CARTOON

For more than 80 years, the animated cartoon has been entertaining people, young and old, in movie theaters and on television with countless works of art and a virtual calvacade of cartoon characters that have captured the hearts and imaginations of fans in every corner of the globe. This legion of animated heroes and vast array of cartoon productions still produce wild cheers and uncontrollable laughter, whether it be through television reruns of old favorites or the debut of new, original characters who create enchanting and memorable moments that endure forever.

Why this long–running love affair with cartoons? Why do so many people still watch their favorite cartoon characters in countless television reruns? And why do new characters and new ideas still turn on audiences today? The reason for this amazing phenomenon is simple: Animated cartoons are the embodiment of a fantasy world worth treasuring, worth enjoying and, most of all, worth remembering over and over again, no matter what place in time or what changes have occurred in the real world around it.

It is funny, in a strange sort of way, but animated cartoons were not always viewed with such high esteem. In the days of silent cartoons, the industry experienced a tremendous backlash of criticism from film critics, movie fans and even studio executives who felt the new medium lacked congruent stories and consistent animation quality to be taken seriously in the world of entertainment. Maybe so. But, like any untested product, it was just a matter of time before the technique of animation would be mastered, creating a visually perfect running machine with plenty of mileage still ahead.

The beginning was 1906, with the debut of the first animated film in this country, *Humorous Phases of Funny Faces*. Released by Vitagraph, cartoonist James Stuart Blackton, who sold his first cartoon to the *New York World* and co–founded Vitagraph, entered the animation business with this first effort six years after his non–animated triumph, *The Enchanted Drawing*, a short Edison film based on the newspaper cartoonist's "chalk–talk" vaudeville act.

By today's standards of animation, *Humorous Phases of Funny Faces* is rudimentary at best. The film is comprised of a series of scenes featuring letters, words and faces drawn by an "unseen" hand. For the era in which it was made, the simplistically–styled one–reel short, if anything, was an important first step. The film demonstrated the tremendous promise of cartoon animation and served as inspiration for other cartoonists to follow with equally fascinating and entertaining works of art.

The concept of animated cartoons in this country ultimately took root thanks to two other farsighted pioneers: French cartoonist Emil Cohl and American newspaper cartoonist Winsor McCay.

Cohl followed Blackton with a stick–figure animated short presented in a series of comic vignettes, entitled, *Drame Chez Les Fantoches* (1908). The film was everything that an animated cartoon was supposed to be— funny, sophisticated and well–conceived. While Cohl's work was strikingly different, McCay surpassed even Cohl's landmark effort with his first entry, *Little Nemo*, the first fully animated cartoon. Based on McCay's beloved *New York Herald* strip "Little Nemo in Slumberland," McCay reportedly spent four years animating the production.

While the films of all three men were important to

the growth of the cartoon industry, McCay may have done more for the art of animation than his predecessors when he created what many historians consider to be the first genuine American cartoon star in *Gertie the Dinosaur* (1914). The first film to feature frame–by–frame animation and fluid, sophisticated movement, it took McCay approximately 10,000 drawings to animate the five–minute production. The one–reel short was animated on six–by–eight inch sheets of translucent rice paper, with the drawings lightly penciled first and then detailed in Higgins black ink. (McCay animated his first three films in this manner.)

It was a tremendous technical achievement, but surprisingly most critics felt the production lost audiences with its storyline. In the film, the animator (McCay) is seen drawing the cartoon, in live action, slowly bringing Gertie into existence and into the real world to then try and tame the beast.

Audiences did not share the critics' opinion. They were reportedly awed by the dinosaur's lifelike movements, unaware that what they had seen would positively change the course of animation's young history.

The late Paul Terry, the father of *Terrytoons,* often credited McCay for arousing interest in animated cartoons, when most people did not fully grasp the potential of the medium. As he once said, "Together with more than a hundred other artists, I attended a dinner in 1914 at which McCay spoke. He showed us his cartoon, *Gertie the Dinosuar.* It was the first animated cartoon we had ever seen, and as McCay told us his ideas about animation as a great coming medium of expression, we really hardly knew what he was talking about, he was so far ahead of his time."

McCay's imprint on the cartoon industry was widespread, but another early pioneer was responsible for establishing a mechanism like McCay's that improved the consistency of animation and the health of the industry overall. John Randolph (J. R.) Bray was perhaps the country's most prolific producer of cartoon shorts. In 1913, following his career as an American newspaper cartoonist, Bray produced his first animated short, *The Artist's Dream* (or *The Dachsund and the Sausage*), which quickly established him in the medium.

Bray followed this celluloid feat with his first of many successful cartoon series, *Colonel Heeza Liar,* based on the tale–spinning adventures of Baron Munchausen. (Walter Lantz, the father of Woody Woodpecker, was one of the series' chief animators.) The series spawned other successes for Bray, among them, *Bobby Bumps* (1915), *Otto Luck* (1915), *Police Dog* (1915) and *Quacky Doodles* (1917). By 1916, his studio was so successful that he began producing one cartoon per week.

In 1914, Bray revolutionized the business of anima-tion with his patented invention of a labor–saving animation process in which backgrounds were printed on translucent paper to facilitate the positioning of moving objects in successive drawings. (This economy of drawings is evident in many of Bray's early cartoons, including *Colonel Heeza Liar, Hobo* (1916), which used only a few more than a hundred basic arrangements of the cels in 1,600 frames of footage.) During the next year, he would patent two other methods to enhance the quality of animation. The first was a technique that enabled animators to affix solid cutouts to the back of drawings so they were visible from the front of the drawing; the second, a process which used a translucent sheet that was laid over a piece of paper on which characters and objects could be animated.

Other pioneer animators followed Bray with patented techniques of their own. Earl Hurd patented the first cel animation process, probably one of the most significant of the early animation patents, while Max and Dave Fleischer, of Ko–Ko the Clown and later Betty Boop fame, developed a fascinating process called Rotoscope, which enabled animators to trace figures seen on projected film.

During the teens, Bray was not the only major cartoon studio producing animated films. Two others came into existence: Raoul Barrē and Hearst International. Barrē was an established cartoonist whose caricatures of Indians and the life–style of French Canadian women were published as *En Rolant Ma Boule.* Turning his energies to animation, he produced several noteworthy animated series. His first was *Animated Grouch Chasers* (1915–16), an intriguing use of live action openings and animated segues that won him widespread acclaim. He went on to develop one of the most successful comic strip cartoon adaptations, *Mutt and Jeff* (1918), based on Bud Fisher's popular strip characters.

In 1916, newspaper mogul William Randolph Hearst realized the promise of animation by opening his own studio, International Film Service. Hearst hired talented animators Gregory LaCava, Frank Moser and Bill Nolan away from Raoul Barrē's studio to bring many of his newspaper syndicate's cartoon properties to the screen. In short order, Hearst's company produced animated versions of such comic–page favorites as *Krazy Kat* (1916), *The Katzenjammer Kids* (1916) and *Happy Hooligan* (1917).

Other comic strip artists brought their strip creations to the screen to capitalize on the success of the new medium. Henry (Hy) Mayer, a prolific illustrator, drew comics on the screen for the Universal Weekly newsreel in 1913. He ultimately produced a series of screen magazines known as *Travelaughs.* Rube Goldberg briefly pursued a career in animation by signing up with Pathé Films to produce a newsreel spoof called,

Boob Weekly. Other animated versions of popular strips included George McManus' *Bringing Up Father* (1918), Walter Hoban's *Jerry On The Job* (1917), Jimmy Swinnerton's *Little Jimmy* (1916) and Tom E. Powers' *Phables* (1916).

Paul Terry, who first started working as an animator for Bray in 1916–1917, also became an important figure during this period. After he opened his own studio, Terry became the first to prefigure the visual style of the Hollywood cartoons of the 1930s and 1940s by giving characters more depth and dimension, as is evident in a handful of early titles, including *Farmer Al Falfa's Catastrophe* (1916) and *Farmer Al Falfa's Wayward Pup* (1917).

In general, production staffs for most of these studios were minimal at best. On the average, producers turned out one new cartoon short a week which was often animated by one person. (Hearst was known to enlist the services of well–known artists who sketched strips for his syndicate to contribute animated ideas to his weekly newsreel.) In most cases, the cartoonist was the animator, director, gagman and artist. Toward week's end, the animator's sketchings were collected, photographed and wound onto a single reel before being distributed to theaters throughout the country.

As a direct result, stories and production values often suffered, prompting critics to denounce animated works. As one film critic stated, the major problem inherent in the cartoons was that "the artist was merely sketching his ideas on film."

Walter Lantz, who wrote and directed many cartoons for J. R. Bray, discussed the storyline difficulties he and other animators encountered. "We had a makeshift stu-

The farmer's true identity is unmasked in this scene from *Aesop's Amateur Night On The Ark* (1923). (Courtesy: Blackhawk Films)

Model sheet for Max and Dave Fleischer's Ko–Ko the Clown.

dio on the top floor of a loft building in Fordham, New York," he recalled. "There weren't enough people in the organization to make the story department of a cartoon studio today. But we didn't bother with stories. Our only object was to turn out five to six hundred feet of film!"

Because animators overlooked story transitions, the films often confused theater audiences. (Some confusion was due to the inconsistent use of cartoon balloons over the subject's head to describe dialogue or action.) Sometimes when studios churned out five to six hundred feet of cartoon film, that's exactly what the audience got—just film, with no real story. "Most audiences would rather flee from the theater than sit through a screening of these cartoons," commented one reviewer.

Dick Huemer, who animated *Mutt and Jeff*, had this to say about the reaction of moviegoers to silent cartoons: "They didn't get it. I swear, they didn't get what we were doing. For one thing, our timing was way off or nonexistent. And we didn't have sound. Sound was the great savior of the animated cartoon."

At this same time, however, there were several animators who set new standards for the industry through their unique storytelling ability, among them were Max and Dave Fleischer, Walt Disney and Walter Lantz. All four men blazed new trails in animation and achieved great success through instinct and imagination, as evidenced in their work.

The Fleischers turned heads with their inventive series, *Out of the Inkwell* (1916), which combined live–action and animation, and featured the antics of Koko the Clown (later hyphenated as "Ko–Ko"). The films are technical marvels—beautifully blending animation and live scenes of the animator (Max) bringing Koko to life as well as the entire story on the drawing board at the animator's table. This feat was equalled by Disney and Lantz who employed the process of live–ac-

Animator Walter Lantz looks on as cartoon star Colonel Heeza Liar takes on a menacing bull in a studio publicity still to promote the classic silent cartoon series. (Courtesy: Walter Lantz)

tion/animation in similar fashion with successful results.

Disney mastered the art with his series of cartoon fables, *Alice Comedies* (1924), shot in Los Angeles at various outdoor locations. The films starred a young girl—played mostly by billboard star–turned–child actor Virginia Davis—who was joined by animated characters in telling each story. The films were extremely popular vehicles, as was Lantz's *Dinky Doodle* (1924), which he wrote and directed for Bray.

Lantz starred as the comic straight man in these films alongside his cartoon counterparts Dinky, a young boy, and his faithful dog, Weakheart, in comical exploits that were often as funny as the best of the era's silent film comedies. (Lantz admitted his source of inspiration was the work of several silent film comedians, including Charlie Chaplin, Harry Langdon and Chester Conklin.)

One reason for Lantz's success may have been his understanding of his role as an animator. In an interview, he defined his job thusly: "An animator is like an actor going before the camera, only he has to act out his feelings and interpret the scene with that pencil,"

Lantz recalled. "Also he has to know how to space characters because the spacing of their movements determines the tempo; he must know expression; he must know feeling; he has to know the character, and make him walk with a funny action."

The advent of sound changed the whole method of making animated cartoons and, if anything, enabled the industry to prosper at a time when the silent film industry was stagnating. The first sound cartoons were produced in 1924 by the Fleischers. *Song Car–Tunes,* a series of "bouncing ball singalongs," were synchronized to popular music by a revolutionary DeForest Phonofilm system. The films had one major disadvantage that prevented the concept from flourishing: Many of the theaters were "unwired" and thus were unable to project the films accompanied by 18–piece orchestrations.

The first "talking" motion picture, Al Jolson's musical feature *The Jazz Singer* (1927), helped popularize the use of sound in the film industry and inspired theaters to accommodate this innovation.

Walt Disney introduced the first widely distributed

Mickey Mouse starred in the first synchronized sound cartoon, Steamboat Willie *(1928). © Walt Disney Productions*

synchronized sound cartoon in 1928, Mickey Mouse's *Steamboat Willie.* With this creation began another chapter in animation history. Sound gave cartoons a dimension that was not possible in silent form. It enabled animators to create better stories, more life–like characters and fuller animation. The process did not come cheaply, however. Production costs skyrocketed from the normal $6,000 budgets for silent cartoons, yet the all–around quality improved and was worth the price.

During the 1930s, as animators explored the virtues of sound, many new characters burst onto the screen in productions featuring popular musical tunes of the day. Warner Brothers introduced several cartoon stars, many of them influenced by vaudeville and radio. The studio's first real star was Bosko, a black sambo character, who spoke for the first time in the 1930s *Sinkin' In The Bathtub.* Created by former Disney animators Hugh Harman and Rudolf Ising, Bosko became enormously popular and was soon joined by a handful of other characters in the studio's *Looney Tunes* series, among them, Foxy, Piggy and Goopy Geer.

Meanwhile, MGM contributed its own series of musical cartoons, *Happy Harmonies,* directed by Harman and Ising, who left Warner to open the Metro's cartoon department. Walt Disney continued making his Oscar–winning *Silly Symphony* (1928) series, the forerunner to the musical cartoon concept, while Ub Iwerks, Disney's former protege, set up shop to produce his musically inclined *Flip the Frog* (1931) series. Van Beuren Studios also joined the competition with its popular *Aesop's Fables* (1928) series, initially released by Pathé and then RKO Radio Pictures.

While many of the early sound cartoons had merit, most of these productions—outside of a few that had

name stars—lacked distinguishable personalities but instead featured a myriad of characters appearing in a single setting.

More than any individual, Warner Brothers director Chuck Jones credits Walt Disney for establishing the concept of cartoon "pesonalities" and inspiring the rest of the industry to develop their own unique characters. As Jones explained:

> Anybody who knows anything about animation knows that the things that happened at Disney Studio were the backbone that upheld everything else. Disney created a climate that enabled us all to exist. Everyone in animation considered themselves behind Disney. We all did. Strange thing: that was probably healthy for us all. Perhaps the biggest thing Disney contributed was that he established the idea of individual personality. We would look at his stuff and say, "No matter what we do, Disney is going to be a little ahead of us, particularly in technique." He created the idea that you could make an animated cartoon character who had personality and wasn't just leaping in the air like "Terrytoons." So without thinking he forced us into evolving our own style.

Thus, from the mid–1930s on, animators began to develop sound cartoon era's first bonafide stars—characters with heart and soul and mass appeal. Many of the characters people remember today emerged during this period. Walt Disney added to his stable of stars the likes of Donald Duck (1934) and Goofy (1932), while studio rival Warner Brothers introduced several "superstars": Porky Pig (1936), Daffy Duck (1938) and Bugs

Walt Disney introduced the first three–strip Technicolor cartoon in 1932, Flowers and Trees, *which won an Academy Award. © Walt Disney Productions*

Sexy screen star Betty Boop is joined by sidekicks Bimbo and Ko–Ko the Clown in 1932's A Hunting We Will Go, *produced by Max Fleischer.*

Bunny (1940). Metro–Goldwyn–Mayer's famed cat–and–mouse tandem Tom and Jerry (1940) turned on audiences, as did Walter Lantz's Andy Panda (1940) and Woody Woodpecker (1941). Meanwhile, Paul Terry, of Terrytoons fame, unveiled his most promising creations, Dinky Duck (1939) and Mighty Mouse (1942).

These solidly constructed characterizations together with tightly written scripts captured in animated form the crazy appeal of Laurel and Hardy, the Marx Brothers, Buster Keaton, Abbott and Costello, and Charlie Chaplin, and became important factors in the success of sound cartoons.

One other important element in their success was physical action. Unlike silent cartoons, sound cartoons were fast–paced, full of slapstick and punctuated by violence. Combined, these qualities generated a terrific response from moviegoers whose sides often ached from fits of laughter before the main feature was even introduced (cartoons, newsreels and live–action shorts were shown prior to the feature–length attraction, appropriately called "curtain–raisers" in their day).

"We found that you can get terrific laughs out of someone just getting demolished, as long as you clean up and bring him back to life again," the late Tex Avery told biographer Joe Adamson. "It's exaggeration to the point where we hope it's funny."

The successful cartoon formula of transitions, action and sound was further improved in 1932 when Walt Disney produced the first true Technicolor cartoon, a *Silly Symphony* short called, *Flowers and Trees.* (The production cost $27,500 to make, two–thirds more than black–and–white cartoons.)* Disney was not the first to experiment with color by any means. There were others who toyed with the process as far back as the early 1920s by "tinting" the films. (In 1930, Walter Lantz animated the first two–color Technicolor cartoon, a four–minute opening segment for Paul Whiteman's *King of Jazz.*) Disney's introduction of color to animated cartoons brought a whole new dimension to the screen that had never before been realized. It was a gamble that paid off not only for his studio, but one which took the cartoon industry into a whole new era of filmmaking.

In the beginning, because of Disney's exclusive contract to use the Technicolor process, several studios were forced to use a less effective two–strip color method, Cinecolor. The results were not as vivid as the three–strip color process, but it did not prevent several rival studios from competing.

Ub Iwerks was among the first to use Cinecolor for his 1933 ComiColor cartoon, *Jack and the Beanstalk.* Warner Brothers offered two Cinecolor releases in the 1934–1935 season, *Honeymoon Hotel* and *Beauty and the Beast,* both Merrie Melodies. Walter Lantz countered with *The Jolly Elves* (1933), which received an Oscar nomination the same year Disney's *Flowers and Trees* (1932) won Best Short Subject honors. Max Fleischer also employed the Cinecolor technique in his *Color Classics* series, beginning with *Poor Cinderella* (1934).

The most spectacular use of color was yet to come, however. In 1937, Walt Disney again paved the way when he produced the first full–length feature, *Snow White and the Seven Dwarfs.* It was a monumental undertaking for his studio, costing a tiny fortune to produce (more than six times its original budget of $250,000). Fortunately, it was well worth the price as

---

*Technicolor was a three-color process that encompassed all the colors of the rainbow. The process replaced the two-color process which used only the colors of red and green to give the illusion of color.

Opening title sequence from Ub Iwerks' ComiColor cartoon, Jack Frost (1934). (Courtesy: Blackhawk Films)

the film became a tremendous box office hit, earning $8 million in revenue following its release. With this newfound success, Disney opened many animator's eyes to the full potential of color to animated cartoons, no matter what their length.

Max Fleischer shared the same vision as Disney. He gave Disney perhaps his strongest competition in the feature film arena when he produced his studio's first fully animated feature, *Gulliver's Travels* (1939), two years after Disney's Technicolor extravaganza. The film did compare in quality to Disney's full−length production but unfortunately, never produced the same financial and critical success.

Nonetheless, Fleischer would produce one more fea-

An electrified musician rings out new vibrant sounds on his old harp for the onlooking conductor in a scene from Hugh Harman's Mad Maestro (1939). © Turner Entertainment

ture, *Mr. Bug Goes to Town* (1941), before abandoning cartoon features altogether and leaving the field to his contemporary, Walt Disney, who became the sole producer of feature−length cartoons for the next two decades.

The outbreak of World War II unified the cartoon industry in a patriotic sort of way. Studios showed their allegiance by producing propaganda training films and cartoons satirizing the war, with obvious anti−German and anti−Japanese overtones, to boost the public's morale.

The effort resulted in a number of flag−waving sendups which are still funny today, among them, Donald Duck's *Der Fuehrer's Face* (Disney, 1943), an Oscar−winning short−subject; Tex Avery's *Blitz Wolf* (MGM, 1942); and *Daffy's Draftee* (Warner, 1944). Warner Brothers also produced a topical war bond short, *Bugs Bunny's Bond Rally* (1943), with Bugs Bunny, Daffy Duck and Porky Pig urging Americans to buy war bonds, as well as its own share of animated training films, namely *Private Snafu*, directed by Frank Tashlin, the noted comedy film director, and *Hook*, which dealt with the misadventures of a navy sailor.

While the war proved to be a timely subject, Hollywood animators continued to display their affection for the actors, actresses and comedians of Hollywood's Golden Age. Caricatured versions of many celebrities have made their way to the screen in one cartoon or another since the early 1930s. Some of the most notable appearances by movie stars in animated form include *Hollywood Steps Out* (Warner, 1941), featuring Clark Gable, Harpo Marx, Buster Keaton, Joan Crawford, the Three Stooges and others; *A Tale of Two Mice* (Warners, 1942), depicting Abbott and Costello as mice ("Babbit and Catstello"); *Bacall To Arms* (Warner, 1946), with Humphrey Bogart and Lauren Bacall as cartoon characters; and *Popeye's 25th Anniversary* (Paramount, 1948), with Dean Martin and Jerry Lewis, Bob Hope and Jimmy Durante.

The measure of success that cartoons had attained in the 1930s and 1940s continued into the 1950s. During this decade, the cartoon industry experienced several important achievements. In 1953, with 3−D becoming the rage, several studios began turning out three−dimensional feature films and short−subjects to the delight of moviegoing audiences. The technique was used in cartoons as well. In 1953, Paramount's Famous Studios created two three−dimensional cartoons, *Popeye, The Ace of Space* and *Book Man*, starring Casper the Friendly Ghost. The following year, Warner Brothers added its own 3−D favorite, *Lumber Jack Rabbit* (1954), starring Bugs Bunny.

Perhaps more important than 3−D was the unveiling of a new style of animation four years earlier, which

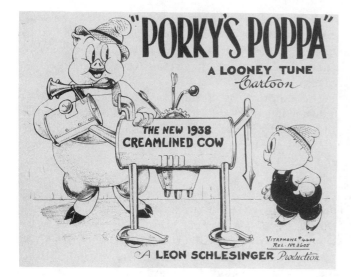

Lobby card from Bob Clampett's 1938 Looney Tune cartoon, Porky's Poppa. © Warner Brothers

used fewer cartoon cels to tell a complete story. The method—called "limited animation"—was the brainchild of United Productions of America (UPA), producers of Mr. Magoo and Gerald McBoing Boing cartoons. The concept presented an economical way for producers to animate cartoons while still achieving a wide range of motion and believability on screen. Bill Scott, a former UPA animator, recalls the new process "proved that cartoonists could use fewer drawings and still do an excellent job telling their story."

Economically, the new system of animation made sense, as the cost to produce fully animated cartoons became more and more prohibitive. As costs rose, many of the major cartoon producers would adopt this method of animation long before the double-feature invaded movie theaters in 1959 (the same style of animation was later employed by television cartoon producers). It was the only way theatrical cartoons became economically feasible.

MGM animators used this cartoon model sheet for guidelines when drawing Tex Avery's Droopy in Senor Droopy (1949). Turner Entertainment

Popeye gets the best of Bluto in the first Popeye two—reeler, Popeye The Sailor Meets Sinbad The Sailor (1936).

"People began to care less about going to the movies," remarked Norm Prescott, co—founder of Filmation Studios. "As a consequence, it took four or five years for studios to recoup their cartoon costs."

For years it was believed that television brought about the demise of the animated cartoon short. This is true to some extent. But what actually killed the cartoon short was a 1949 U.S. Supreme Court ruling forcing studios to abandon "block bookings." Under this method, theater owners were offered hit feature films as long as they agreed to book a cartoon, newsreel or live—action short as part of the package. A percentage of the rental fee is what usually helped finance the cartoon production.

After this ruling, theater owners refused to pay more than nominal fees for cartoons. As a result, the animated short couldn't earn back its production costs on its initial release. It often took several re—releases before most cartoons turned a profit, if any. The impact of this ruling and the birth of television ultimately resulted in many Hollywood cartoon studios closing their doors during the late 1950s and early 1960s. Walter Lantz, who was the last to stop production in 1972, said, "We didn't stop producing cartoons because their popularity died out, it was because we couldn't afford to make them."

In essence, television replaced movie theaters as a place to showcase animated productions. The growth of this medium clearly undermined the success of movie theaters in this country, as witnessed in a strong decline in box office receipts. (In 1950, the number of television sets in use jumped from one million at the beginning of the year to four million by the end of the year.) With many programs accessible on the "tube" for free, American moviegoers had little incentive to go to the theater.

Viewing television as fertile ground, several film distributors of vintage cartoons kept in well—guarded film vaults took advantage of this new and thriving medium by syndicating the films to local television stations. The first cartoons to appear were black—and—white treasures made by Van Beuren Studios in the 1930s, seen on DuMont's WABD—TV, New York, in 1947 on "Mov-

Max Fleischer's attempt to compete with Walt Disney by producing full—length features ended with the release of his second feature, Mister Bug Goes To Town (1940). (Courtesy: Republic Pictures)

Daffy Duck meets up with Sherlock Holmes in a scene from Bob Clampett's 1946 cartoon, The Great Piggy Bank Robbery. (Courtesy: Bob Clampett Animation Art) © Warner Brothers

ies for Small Fry." The program was broadcast Tuesday evenings and inspired "The Small Fry Club," a network continuation of the show in January 1948, hosted by Big Brother Bob Emery. The latter continued through the 1950–1951 season, screening Van Beuren's *Cubby* cartoon series and several early Walter Lantz cartoons before the program was cancelled. (The Van Beuren films also appeared on "TV Tots Time" on WENR, Chicago, and on the ABC network between 1950 and 1952.)

This did not mark the first time cartoons were used on television. Chad Grothkopf, a Disney employee in his 20s, went East in 1938 to work for NBC on "the very first animated show on the network." Only 50 television sets were in use at the time when Grothkopf produced "Willie the Worm," a low–budget, eight–minute black–and–white cartoon that aired in April, 1938. The film was full of cutout animation, plus a small amount of cel animation, to illustrate the popular chil-

Walter Lantz reviews the storyboard to a cartoon that is under production. (Courtesy: Citizen–News)

Studio one–sheet from the 1947 Mighty Mouse cartoon, Dead End Cats. © 20th Century Fox.

dren's poem ("Willie Worm has taken a wife, to live and to love the rest of his life").

One year later, in May 1939, when NBC presented its first full schedule of evening programming on experimental station W2XBS (now WNBC), New York, the station previewed Walt Disney's Donald Duck cartoon, "Donald's Cousin," for viewers.

In the early 1950s, many classic cartoons, previously released to theaters, made their way to the tiny screen, almost exclusively shown on children's shows hosted by local television station personalities. Cartoons were the cornerstone of such popular programs as the "Captain Bob Show," Buffalo, New York; "Uncle Willie's Cartoon Show," Beaumount, Texas; and scores of others.

In 1953, 20 to 25 stations were regularly broadcasting cartoons throughout the country, garnering high ratings from a predominantly juvenile audience. And by January, 1955, more than 400 television stations were programming animated cartoons.

The influx of stations that aired cartoons was largely due to a high number of cartoon packages that became available for the first time. Warner Brothers, Paramount–Fleischer–Famous Studios, and Terrytoons all released cartoons to television, joined by MGM's "Tom and Jerry" package and spot broadcasts of various Walt Disney cartoons on ABC's "Disneyland."

With the availability of new films, the movement among television stations throughout the country was to launch their own afternoon children's shows hosted by a virtual army of "sea captains, space commanders, Western sodbusters and neighborhood policemen." Officer Joe Bolton hosted cartoons and comedy short–subjects in New York. In Los Angeles, Tom Hatten en-

Early animated cartoon broadcasts occurred on after-noon children's programs hosted by local television sta-tion personalities. Tom Hatten (in sailor outfit) introduced "Popeye" cartoons on his weekday show, "Pier 5 Club," for Los Angeles' KTLA-TV. (Courtesy: Tom Hatten)

tertained youngsters with "Popeye" cartoons in his "Pier 5 Club" on KTLA-TV Channel 5.

Other stations devised clever titles to inform children when "cartoon time" aired on their local station. Philadelphia's WFIL added "Funny Flickers," while WGRB in Schenectady ran "Kartoon Karnival" to attract young viewers with large doses of cartoon entertainment. Networks joined the cartoon craze. CBS segmented an assortment of "Terrytoons" cartoons on "The CBS Cartoon Theatre," a three-month long series hosted by newcomer comedian Dick Van Dyke. Meanwhile, ABC countered with ventriloquist Paul Winchell headlining "Cartoonsville" (later retitled "Cartoonies").

These programs only whetted viewers' appetites, however. What was vitally missing from television logs was newly produced cartoon programs to keep viewers interested. Since producers could not afford to produce theatrical-styled cartoons that were fully animated, the medium had to settle for a less expensive process.

"Full animation was very, very expensive," recalled Norm Prescott. "Television, in turn, could not support full animation. The economics just wouldn't jive unless somebody could come up with a way of doing animation with fewer drawings."

The UPA-style of animation thus came to television. Early animated fare reflected this cost-efficient or "cookie-cutter" method. The process enabled producers to use a variety of angles, cuts and camera moves to imply motion, while using the fewest number of cels possible to tell their story. For television, the format fit

like a glove and audiences never noticed the difference.

The technique was officially introduced to viewers in the first made-for-television series, the cliff-hanging, serialized adventures of Crusader Rabbit, co-invented by Rocky and Bullwinkle creator Jay Ward. In 1949, the series was test marketed before making its debut one year later. Ward produced the program expressly for the new medium, animating the series out of his makeshift studio in San Francisco and sending his sketches to Hollywood film producer Jerry Fairbanks to film, edit and add sountracks to complete each story for broadcast.

"When Jay did 'Crusader Rabbit,' it was still axiomatic that no one could produce a cartoon series for television," remembered Bill Scott, who created UPA's Gerald McBoing Boing and was the voice of Bullwinkle J. Moose. "Jay refused to believe that."

As was the case with other cartoon programs that followed, the cost of the "Crusader Rabbit" series is what made it attractive for television sales. One complete 19½ minute story cost approximately $2,500 to produce. "We would simply plan a story so we reused some of the animation with a different background," recalled series producer Jerry Fairbanks.

Ward was followed into the television arena by two veteran animators who, accustomed to producing high quality theatrical cartoons, decided to turn their energies towards television. Bill Hanna and Joe Barbera are two individuals who were most responsible for giving limited animation its biggest boost. They perpetuated the art form in a number of highly successful series for television. The seven-time Academy Award-winning directors, who invented the hilarious hijinks of MGM's Tom and Jerry, entered television's animated age eight years after Ward with "Ruff and Reddy" (NBC, 1957), the first hosted cartoon series for Saturday morning. (Between 1958 and 1963, with their package of "Huckleberry Hound," "Quick Draw McGraw" and "Yogi Bear" cartoons, they were the first to introduce the half-hour all-cartoon program.) The series used only 12,000 cels to animate 30 minutes of cartoon entertainment (in this case, roughly three cartoons per show).

For television, this style of animation seemed most effective. "When we first started limited animation, it disturbed me," admitted Hanna in an interview. "Then when I saw some of the old cartoons on TV, I saw that actually limited animation came off better on the dimly lit television screen than the old fully animated things."

The biggest adjustment for Barbera was not conforming to the new style of animation but to the prices television paid for his and Hanna's animated productions. "We received about $2,700 (per show) and that was after great negotiating and pleading," he once said.

To retain a tidy profit, Hanna and Barbera effectively did away with production items that usually resulted in higher costs. They trimmed most schedule–delaying procedures, eliminated many preliminary sketches and recorded soundtracks in one setting.

By producing cartoons at such rock–bottom prices, the marketplace for made–for–television cartoons blossomed overnight. In 1959, Jay Ward returned to television with a new series, the misadventures of a moose and a flying squirrel, better known as "Rocky and His Friends." (Ward originated the characters years earlier for a never–produced series entitled, "The Frostbite Falls Follies.") Pat Sullivan produced a new litter of "Felix the Cat" cartoons, bearing the trademark limited animation style that had become so suitable for the medium. (Animator Chuck Jones has often called this style of animation "illustrated radio" because it's like "a radio script with a minimum of drawings in front of it, and if you turn off the picture, you can still tell what's happening because you hear it.")

Consequently, during the next 10 years, the syndicated marketplace would be deluged with other all–

Charlie Brown (left), Lucy and Linus dance around their beagle–topped tree in "A Charlie Brown Christmas" (1965), the first prime–time animated special based on Charles Schulz's popular comic strip. (Courtesy: CBS)

One of the most popular cartoon shows to appear on prime–time television was "The Flintstones." The series was a cartoon version of the classic television sitcom, "The Honeymooners." © Hanna–Barbera Productions, Inc.

cartoon series, aimed at attracting adults and children with characters and situations that appealed to both segments of the population. Other characters to barnstorm the "tube" during its early days of animation included Quick Draw McGraw (1959), Spunky and Tadpole (1960), Q.T. Hush (1960), Lippy the Lion (1962), Wally Gator (1962) and Magilla Gorilla (1964).

Japanese cartoon producers also began to import fully animated fantasy/adventure series that were re–edited and re–dubbed in English for broadcast, many of which have cult followings today. Some popular titles were "Astro Boy" (1964), "Eighth Man" (1965), "Gigantor" (1966) and "Speed Racer" (1967).

Many of television's earliest concepts for animated shows were derived from successful characters or formats that worked well in many popular live–action shows. "The Flintstones" (ABC, 1960) featuring television's "modern stone–age family," was actually based on the classic television sitcom, "The Honeymooners." "Top Cat" (ABC, 1961), another Hanna–Barbera Production, mirrored the antics of Sergeant Bilko and his platoon of misfits from "The Phil Silvers Show." "Calvin and the Colonel" (ABC, 1961) patterned after radio's "Amos 'n' Andy," featured the voices of the original radio team, Freeman Gosden and Charles Correll, who created the animated spin–off. Like television sitcoms, several programs even featured studio–recorded laugh-tracks to provoke laughter in the home.

Producers later turned to other bankable properties to attract viewers. Comic strips and comics gave television characters with built–in followings. Chester Gould's "Dick Tracy" (1961), caricatured in a series of cheaply produced five–minute cartoons, headed a legion of renowned comic characters in cartoon versions for television. Superheroes were included in this menagerie, flying onto television screens in countless action/adventure shows like "Marvel Superheroes" (1966), featuring the extraordinary feats of Spider–Man, The Incredible Hulk, Captain America and The Mighty Thor. "The New Adventures of Superman" (CBS, 1966) was the first fully animated network show based on a superhero character.

Motion picture and recording stars were also naturals for animated cartoons. Hanna–Barbera was the first to get into the act by producing cartoon versions of "Abbott and Costello" (1965), featuring the voice of straight man Bud Abbott, and "Laurel and Hardy" (1966). The Three Stooges (Moe Howard, Larry Fine and Curly Joe DeRita) brought their zany brand of slapstick to animation in "The New Three Stooges," a live–action/animated series for syndication. Musical artists who gave animation a new beat in cartoon form included Ross Bagdasarian's "Alvin and the Chipmunks" in "The Alvin Show" (CBS, 1961) and Liverpool's Fab Four "The Beatles" (ABC, 1965), the last musical group to be given animated life until Motown's "The Jackson 5ive" (ABC, 1971) and teenage rock sensations "The Osmonds" (ABC, 1972) burst onto the musical scene.

Holiday themes became a popular forum for animated network specials in the 1960s. Here Frosty leads a merry parade in a scene from the animated musical special, "Frosty the Snowman." © Rankin–Bass Productions

SIZE COMPARISON CHART
FELIX THE CAT CREATIONS 4/12/60

Model sheet from Pat Sullivan's syndicated cartoon series, "Felix the Cat." Pictured: Rock Bottom, the Professor, Felix and Poindexter. © Joe Oriolo Productions

With so many programs eventually flooding the market, however, even film and television critics wondered just how long cartoons could last in the medium. In reviewing television animation, Charles Champlin, *Los Angeles Times* critic, wrote: "Operating on the adage 'if it works, copy it,' networks went so cartoon happy there was talk of animating the 'Huntley–Brinkley Report.'"

One recurring criticism of television animation was that the work often appeared rushed, thus dramatically undermining the quality. Animators had little control over the quality because "the pressures of television are greater than the pressures of producing films for theatres," noted Bill Hanna. "Back when we made the MGM cartoons, we worked at a more leisurely, almost relaxed pace. There was definitely more care put into the drawing, timing, sound effects and the recording of the music. Much more time was taken to discuss stories and to design characters; pictures were reviewed in pencil test form, and changes were made before they were inked and painted. It was an elaborate process. Every phase of production was handled much more carefully than it is today. We just don't have the time today to put in all that effort."

Friz Freleng, who created several successful cartoon series for television for his company, DePatie–Freleng Enterprises, offered his own perspective of television cartoons. "I used to turn out 11 or 12 theatrical cartoons a year. At six minutes per cartoon, that was a little over an hour's worth. Here, in one week, they'll turn out four shows. They do at least one and a half hours of new animation a week," he said. "The networks go for the numbers (or viewers). They don't care what the quality of the show is—I don't think they even watch the shows. As long as it's got high numbers, it doesn't matter whether the show is good or not."

Former Disney animator Don Bluth, the genius behind such full–length cartoon treasures as *The Secret of NIMH* (1982) and *Land Before Time* (1988), shared Freleng's frustration. "They cut corners on Saturday morning animation and when they cut corners, they kill the product," he said. "The networks say, 'A kid will watch cartoons that cost $90,000 a half hour, so why spend $300,000?'"

While the quality of most cartoons was suspect, most viewers welcomed the glut of animated cartoon fare that infiltrated Saturday mornings and prime–time television, long before "The Simpsons," cartoon programs demonstrated they could attract nighttime audiences.

In 1958, CBS pioneered the concept of airing the all–cartoon show in prime–time for the very first time. The network reran that summer "The Gerald McBoing Boing Show," featuring the first–ever newly produced cartoons for network television (the series actually debuted two years earlier).

Networks did not fully pick up on the idea of slotting fully animated cartoons during the family viewing hour until the turn of the decade. ABC did the most with cartoons in prime–time. In September 1960, it began airing "The Flintstones" on its nighttime schedule, followed by "The Bugs Bunny Show" one month later. In 1962, the network also spotted "The Jetsons" on Sunday evenings, with "The Adventures of Jonny Quest" (1964) to make its debut in prime–time two years later, also on ABC. CBS ran a distant second in the prime–time cartoon derby. During the 1961–1962 season, it aired "Alvin and the Chipmunks" during the evening hours, as well as "Calvin and the Colonel."

In 1962, after networks won big ratings with prime–time cartoon programs, NBC aired the first made–for–television special, sponsored by Timex, "Mr. Magoo's Christmas Carol," starring the near–sighted codger of theatrical cartoon fame. The program, which was also the first animated television musical, was an hour–long adaptation of Charles Dickens' classic holiday story. This program marked the illustrious beginning of the prime–time holiday special and the animated special in general.

Although this charming animated rendering produced explosive ratings, it took three years before television viewers were treated to their second prime–time special, "A Charlie Brown Christmas" (CBS, 1965), based on Charles M. Schulz's beloved "Peanuts" comic strip characters. (The special remained on the shelf for one year, with no takers, before Coca–Cola agreed to sponsor the show.) The program garnered a huge audience, nearly half of the nation's prime–time viewers.

Resulting from the show's impressive performance, CBS made "Peanuts" an annual attraction on the network, since becoming the longest–running series of

Japanese cartoon offerings were staples of 1960s television. One syndicated favorite was "Kimba, the White Lion." (Courtesy: NBC)

cartoon specials in television history. Runner–up "Dr. Seuss" inspired the first of several specials beginning with 1966's "Dr. Seuss' How the Grinch Stole Christmas," produced by Chuck Jones and children's book author Ted Geisel. The show also premiered on CBS.

During the 1960s, many other made–for–television cartoon specials were produced, most notably by television innovators Arthur Rankin Jr. and Jules Bass, who presented a string of perennial cartoon classics in prime–time. They created such memorable half hours as "Rudolph, The Red–Nosed Reindeer" (NBC, 1964), "The Ballad of Smokey the Bear" (NBC, 1964), narrated by James Cagney, "Frosty the Snowman" (CBS, 1969), and "The Little Drummer Boy" (ABC, 1968). The pair's first prime–time entry was the hour–long animated special, "Return to Oz," which debuted on NBC in February, 1964.

Not all of these shows used conventional animation, however. Many were filmed using a lifelike stop–motion puppet process created by Rankin and Bass called "Animagic," a technique they initiated in their 1961 children's series, "Tales of The Wizard of Oz."

Until 1963, the Saturday–morning lineup on all three networks was mostly comprised of reruns of theatrical cartoons and popular children's programs, including "My Friend Flicka," "Sky King" and others. For the 1963–1964 season, CBS took the first step towards creating an all–cartoon Saturday morning schedule by offering a two–hour blend of cartoons.

Attracting national sponsors like Kellogg's and General Mills, the network's new Saturday morning lineup included the new "Tennessee Tuxedo and His Tales," "Quick Draw McGraw," which had previously premiered in syndication, and network returnees "The Alvin Show" and "Mighty Mouse Playhouse." (By the following season, CBS expanded the schedule by another hour, adding "Linus the Lionhearted" and then "The Tom and Jerry Show" during the following season.)

CBS daytime programmer Fred Silverman, who was only 26 years old, was responsible for new Saturday morning programming. He recognized that adults, like children, love animated cartoons and could attract a larger viewing audience. Silverman's assumption proved correct. Ratings skyrocketed and by the 1966–1967 season, after restructuring Saturday morning with nine back–to–back half–hour cartoon shows, CBS rocketed into first place in the Saturday morning ratings derby.

Taking notice of CBS's success, runners–up NBC and ABC soon began their Saturday–morning cartoon scheduling in earnest. ABC followed CBS in 1964 by adding cartoons to its Saturday–morning schedule, while NBC did the same in 1965.

In the late 1960s, Saturday morning became known as "a jungle of competition" and rightfully so. New cartoons were delivering the largest network audience ever and network bidding for programs became intensely competitive. The average price for a half–hour cartoon show ranged from $48,000 to $62,000, climbing to $70,000 and $100,000 by the 1970s. Financially, these figures were nothing compared to the revenues Saturday morning cartoons generated. By 1970, the combined network take was $66.8 million in advertising revenue from their respective Saturday–morning line-ups.

By 1968, however, the success of television cartoons was somewhat diminished by one factor: the public outcry against television violence. The aftermath of the shocking assasinations of Dr. Martin Luther King and Senator Robert Kennedy brought about tremendous unrest among the public when it came to violence, whether in their neighborhood streets or on television.

In a recent survey, *The Christian Science Monitor* recorded 162 threats or acts of violence on Saturday morning, the majority occurring between 7:30 and 9:30 A.M. when an estimated 26.7 million children, aged two to 17, were tuned in. The issue of violence on television was seconded by a report prepared by the National Commission on the Causes and Prevention of Violence (Kerner Commission), which ultimately forced networks to make changes in policy with respect to children's programming.

Network censors were hired to sit in on script meetings, approve storyboards and veto subject matter right up to airtime in an effort to control the violent or suggestive content of cartoons. The policy remains in force today.

In addition to instituting in–house control, the three major networks removed most of the objectionable shows and characters that were the subject of parental protests. Action–adventure shows were thus replaced by comedy series that de–emphasized violence. The new aim of children's programming would be to "entertain, stimulate and educate." However, not all animators agreed that censorship was the right thing.

"Cartoon characters never die—they never bleed," remarked veteran animator Walter Lantz. "They get blown up or run over and the next scene there they are, hale and hearty. That's part of their magic, their fantasy. These so–called critics say kids can't separate fantasy from reality. They're looking at things they, as adults, consider harmful to the child. The critics don't look at cartoons through the eyes of a child. I always considered our type of humor as being slapstick, not violent."

Director Friz Freleng, of Warner Brothers fame, supported Lantz's theory that home audiences would rather be watching slapstick comedies. "The adult audience today has been robbed of a certain amount of entertainment," he said. "Kids keep getting it [cartoons] on TV, but you won't find an adult sitting down and watching a kid's show. I believe they miss it, and I believe there's a neglected audience."

Freleng and others had reason to be concerned. In many instances, the network's decisions on what to censor could often be questioned. Lou Scheimer, cartoon producer for Filmation Studios, related that he had run into trouble when he was animating "Superboy." One sequence called for Superboy to stop an oncoming train with his hands. "It was thought that it might tempt kids to try the same," Scheimer said. The scene was changed.

In one episode of CBS's "Josie and the Pussycats" (CBS, 1970), a script called for one of the pussycats to escape from a science fiction menace by taking refuge in a dish of spaghetti. Former producer and comic–book artist Norman Maurer, who wrote the scene, once recalled, "CBS disallowed it. They said, 'Kids will put their cats in spaghetti.' I was told to rewrite the scene."

Also frustrating for most animators during this time was the audience response at early screenings of the fall shows. In the late 1970s, during a screening of Filmation's "Fat Albert" and "Space Academy" shows, more than half the audience walked out, prompting producer Joe Barbera, who was on hand to measure the audience response to his own Hanna–Barbera cartoons, to remark that he yearned for a return to the old days so that "when a cat chases a mouse, he doesn't have to stop and teach him how to blow glass or weave a bas-

Characters with built–in appeal were given animated series of their own. NBC's television sitcom "Alf" inspired an animated spin–off which proved highly successful on Saturday mornings. © Alien Productions (Courtesy: DIC Enterprises)

ket. My wish for Christmas is they would leave education to the schools and entertainment to us."

While many animators might disagree, network censorship, in its earliest form, brought forth stronger values that were necessary in cartoons. The action/adventure shows had their place in history, as much as their replacements, teenage mystery and rock 'n' roll group programs, which served a vital purpose to educate and entertain children in a manner that reflected new attitudes in society and the world.

This was the crux of the new wave of network cartoon shows that received airplay on Saturday mornings

The dark comedy feature "Beetlejuice" made its way to television as a hit Saturday morning series in 1989. © Warner Brothers, Inc. (Courtesy: Nelvana Limited)

by the late 1960s and during the 1970s. In the theatrical cartoon marketplace, it was a completely different story. Producers tread forbidden turf by producing animated works that were largely more adult. One principal reason for this was the increase of grown–ups and young adults lining up to see cartoon features.

The one film that changed the visual and commercial style of the cartoon feature more than any single production was *Yellow Submarine* (1968), an animated odyssey featuring The Beatles (John, Paul, George and Ringo) that incorporated psychedelic images and stylized movement. Audiences were most receptive to the film, proving there was indeed room for animated films that were less Disney–esque.

Another film that revolutionized the cartoon feature industry was Ralph Bakshi's *Fritz The Cat* (1971), the first X–rated full–length cartoon based on Robert Crumb's underground comic strip. Like *Yellow Submarine*, this departure from mainstream animation was full of topical statements—this time about life in the 1960s, including the sexual and political revolution of the decade.

The landmark accomplishments of both films marked a new beginning for the animated feature film business that for several years was stifled by the lack of other innovators in the field taking chances with full–length cartoons in this high–risk area. As a result, more feature–length cartoons were produced than ever before and, for the first time in years, Disney had actually to compete in an ever–crowded marketplace.

Some of the new and original concepts, from here and abroad, that followed included *A Boy Named Charlie Brown* (1969), *Charlotte's Web* (1972), *Fantastic Planet* (1973), *Hugo the Hippo* (1976), *Raggedy Ann and Andy* (1977), and *Watership Down* (1978).

In the 1980s, the success of the animated feature continued, spawning new ideas to meet the increased demand of baby–boomer families. While most of the films' characters were based on greeting card and action–toy figures (this was also true in television animation), one film renewed hope in the animation business that original characters and stories still sold audiences: *Who Framed Roger Rabbit?* (1988), a splendidly conceived comedy/mystery produced by Walt Disney whose style harkened back to Hollywood's golden age of animation. The blockbuster film, which grossed more than $100 million, renewed interest in creating quality animated films for adults and children, and pumped new life into the cartoon industry.

As a ripple effect, the public's insatiable appetite for new cartoon product only increased. More cartoon feature projects than ever were announced. Theaters witnessed the return of the theatrical cartoon short, absent as a regular program feature in the cinema for almost 20 years. In 1990, Warner Brothers released 130 original *Looney Tunes* and *Merrie Melodies* cartoons, starring Bugs Bunny, Daffy Duck, Porky Pig and others, to hundreds of theaters nationwide. Meanwhile, Disney released the second in a series of *Roger Rabbit* theatrical cartoon shorts, with a new Mickey Mouse cartoon being readied for release. In all, six new cartoon features were produced that year and the profitability of animation was no longer questioned.

Animation also gained respect as an art form. Special historical exhibits on animation's history were promoted at museums and universities. Celebrations of Hollywood's glory days of animation included film festival tributes to Warner Brothers animators Chuck Jones, Friz Freleng and Tex Avery as well as former MGM greats Bill Hanna and Joe Barbera. Even commemorative videocassette editions of such favorites as Bugs Bunny, Daffy Duck, Porky Pig, Tom and Jerry and Droopy were popular sellers.

With this renewed interest, the animated cartoon is headed towards an enterprising new decade of productivity and imagination. At no time in its cinematic life—outside of Hollywood's golden age of animation—did things seem better. The underlying element, consistent throughout animation's rich history, continues to be a force behind its success. That is, the animated cartoon will last as long as people thirst for the flicker of action, the ingenius blend of characters and well–conceived original stories that only cartoons can offer. If this holds true, the next 80 years should be worth watching.

SILENT CARTOON SERIES

ABIE THE AGENT

Based on the popular comic strip by Harry Hershfield. *Directed by Gregory La Cava. An International Film Service Production.*

1917: *Iska Worreh* (Aug. 5) and *Abie Kabibble Outwitting His Rival* (Sept. 23).

AESOP'S FABLES

After forming his own studio near the end of World War I, pioneer animator Paul Terry brought this series of popular fables to the screen in 1921, using animal characters in the roles of humans to depict their improprieties without offending audiences. (The series was also known simply as *Fables.*) Each picture in the series concluded with an Aesop–type moral. While most of the films were enacted by animals, others starred Farmer Al Falfa, Terry's best known character at the time.

During the first eight years of the series' run, Terry's staff wrote, animated and produced one complete Aesop's cartoon a week. Five director–animators shared the workload—men like Frank Moser, Harry Bailey, John Foster, Fred Anderson and Jerry Shields, each instrumental in the series success. Mannie Davis and Bill Tytla, two other animation veterans, joined Terry's team of director–animators in the late 1920s.

Terry devised the basic stories for most of the films, borrowing many of his "morals" from a short-subject series entitled, *Topics of the Day,* in addition to others he dreamed up himself.

The Keith–Albee Theatre circuit, one of the largest vaudeville/movie theater chains in the country, bankrolled the series, setting up Terry in business as Fable Pictures Inc. (The name was later changed to Fables Studio.) His deal with Keith–Albee guaranteed that his cartoons played in each of the chain's theaters throughout the country, earning him the distinction of becoming "the first [animator] to really make money in the business," as animator Dick Huemer, who worked on the rival *Mutt and Jeff* series, remarked.

In 1928, following the arrival of sound, Fable Studios was taken over by Amadee J. Van Beuren, who purchased the studio from Keith–Albee and under his Van Beuren Productions successfully revived the series by adding soundtracks to the product. Van Beuren had actually served as president of Fables Studios prior to buying the studio, so he was already familiar with the series.

Terry went on to start his famed Terrytoons studio, where he created such cartoon notables as Mighty Mouse and Heckle and Jeckle. *A Paul Terry Production released by Pathé Film Exchange, Inc.*

1921: *The Cat And The Canary* (May 13), *The Country Mouse And City Mouse* (May 13), *The Donkey In Lion's Skin* (May 13), *The Fashionable Fox* (May 13), *The Fox And The Crow* (May 13), *The Fox And The Goat* (May 13), *The Goose That Laid The Golden Egg* (May 13), *The Hare And Frogs* (May 13), *The Hare And The Tortoise* (May 13), *The Hermit And The Bear* (May 13), *The Lioness And The Bugs* (May 13), *Mice At War* (May 13), *Mice In Council* (May 13), *The Wolf And The Crane* (May 13), *The Rooster And The Eagle* (May 13), *Cats At Law* (May 13), *The Cat And The Monkey* (Oct. 15), *The Dog And The Bone* (Oct. 15), *The Frog And The Ox* (Oct. 15), *The Fly And The Ant* (Oct. 15), *The Owl And The Grasshopper* (Nov. 13), *Venus And The Cat* (Nov. 15), *The Woman And The Hen* (Nov. 20), *The Frogs That Wanted A King* (Nov. 27), *The Conceited Donkey* (Dec. 6), *The Wolf And The Kid* (Dec. 6), *The Wayward Dog* (Dec. 10), *The Cat And The Mice* (Dec. 13) and *The Dog And The Flea* (Dec. 31).

1922: *The Bear And The Bees* (Jan. 26), *The Miller And His Donkey* (Jan. 26), *The Tiger And The Donkey* (Jan. 26), *The Cat And The Swordfish* (Jan. 26), *The Dog And The Thief* (Jan. 26), *The Fox And The Grapes* (Jan. 26), *The Spendthrift* (Jan. 26), *The Villain In Disguise* (Jan. 26), *The Farmer And The Ostrich* (Jan. 26), *The Dissatisfied Cobbler* (Feb. 8), *The Lion And The Mouse* (Feb. 21), *The Rich Cat And The Poor Cat* (Feb. 21), *The Wicked Cat* (Mar. 4), *The Wolf in Sheep's Clothing* (Mar. 4), *The Boy And The Dog* (Apr. 3), *The Eternal Triangle* (Apr. 3), *The Model Diary* (Apr. 11), *Love At First Sight* (Apr. 11), *The Hunter And His Dog* (Apr. 27), *The Dog And The Wolves* (Apr. 27), *The Maid And The Millionaire* (Apr. 27), *The Farmer And His Cat* (May 17), *The Cat And*

The farmer conspires to rid himself of a pesky cat in a scene from the Aesop's Fable, The Farmer and His Cat (1922). (Courtesy: Blackhawk Films)

The Pig (May 17), *Crime In A Big City* (May 29), *The Country Mouse And City Cat* (June 22), *The Brewing Trouble* (June 22), *The Boastful Cat* (June 22), *The Dog And The Fish* (June 22), *The Mischievous Cat* (June 22), *The Worm That Turned* (June 22), *The Farmer And The Mice* (June 26), *The Fearless Fido* (July 20), *The Mechanical Horse* (Aug. 9), *The Dog And The Mosquito* (Aug. 12), *The Two Explorers* (Aug. 12), *The Two Slick Traders* (Aug. 12), *The Henpecked Henry* (Sept. 27), *The Hated Rivals* (Sept. 27), *The Romantic Mouse* (Sept. 27), *The Elephant's Trunk* (Sept. 27), *The Two Of A Trade* (Sept. 27), *The Enchanged Fiddle* (Sept. 27), *The Rolling Stone* (Oct. 9), *Friday The Thirteenth* (Nov. 11), *Henry's Busted Romance* (Nov. 11), *The Fortune Hunters* (Nov. 11), *The Man Who Laughs* (Nov. 11), *The Frog And The Catfish* (Dec. 1), *Two Trappers* (Dec. 1), *The Dog's Paradise* (Dec. 1), *A Stone Age Romeo* (Dec. 14) and *Cheating The Cheaters* (Dec. 14).

1923: *A Fisherman's Jinx* (Feb. 17), *A Raisin And A Cake* (Feb. 17), *The Alley Cat* (Feb. 17), *Troubles On The Ark* (Feb. 17), *The Gliders* (Feb. 17), *The Mysterious Hat* (Feb. 17), *The Sheik* (Feb. 17), *The Spider And The Fly* (Feb. 17), *The Traveling Salesman* (Feb. 17), *Day By Day In Every Day* (Mar. 22), *One Hard Pull* (Mar. 22), *The Jolly Rounders* (Mar. 22), *Pharoah's Tomb* (Mar. 22), *The Gamblers* (Mar. 22), *The Mouse Catcher* (Apr. 27), *Amateur Night On The Ark* (Apr. 27), *A Fishy Story* (Apr. 27), *Spooks* (Apr. 27), *The Stork's Mistake* (May 12), *Springtime* (May 12), *The Burglar Alarm* (June 6), *The Beauty Parlor* (June 6), *The Covered Pushcart* (June 6), *Do Women Pay?* (June 7), *The Pace That Kills* (June 7), *The Great Explorers* (July 19), *The Bad Bandit* (July 19), *The Marathon Dancers* (July 19), *Mysteries Of The Seas* (July 19), *The Pearl Divers* (July 19), *The Nine of Spades* (Aug. 2), *The Cat That Failed* (Aug. 7), *The Cat's Revenge* (Aug. 11), *The Walrus Hunters* (Aug. 11), *Love In A Cottage* (Sept. 1), *Derby Day* (Sept. 1), *The Cat's Whiskers* (Sept. 1), *Aged In The Wood* (Sept. 29), *The High Flyers* (Sept. 29), *The*

Circus (Sept. 29), *Thoroughbred* (Sept. 29), *The Best Man Wins* (Nov. 9), *Happy Go Luckies* (Nov. 9), *The Five Fifteen* (Nov. 9), *A Dark Horse* (Nov. 9), *Farmer Al Falfa's Pet Cat* (Nov. 9), *The Cat That Came Back* (Nov. 16), *The Morning After* (Nov. 16), *The Animals' Fair* (Dec. 14), *Five Orphans Of The Storm* (Dec. 22) and *Good Old Days* (Dec. 24).

1924: *The Black Sheep* (Jan. 9), *Good Old College Days* (Jan. 26), *The Rat's Revenge* (Jan. 26), *A Rural Romance* (Jan. 26), *The All-Star Cast* (Feb. 20), *Captain Kidder* (Feb. 20), *From Rags To Riches* (Feb. 20), *Herman The Great Mouse* (Feb. 20), *Why Mice Leave Home* (Feb. 20), *The Champion* (Mar. 20), *Runnin' Wild* (Mar. 20), *Homeless Pups* (Apr. 22), *An Ideal Farm* (Apr. 22), *If Noah Lived Today* (Apr. 22), *The Jealous Fisherman* (Apr. 22), *A Trip To The Pole* (Apr. 22), *When Winter Comes* (Apr. 22), *The Jolly Jail Bird* (May 12), *The Organ Grinder* (May 29), *That Old Can Of Mine* (June 14), *Home Talent* (June 28), *One Good Turn* (June 30), *The Body In The Bag* (July 5), *Desert Sheiks* (July 12), *A Woman's Honor* (July 19), *The Sport Of The Kings* (July 26), *Amelia Comes Back* (Aug. 2), *Flying Fever* (Aug. 2), *The Prodigal Pup* (Aug. 2), *House Cleaning* (Aug. 2), *The Barnyard Olympics* (Sept. 5), *A Message From The Sea* (Sept. 5), *In The Good Old Summer Time* (Sept. 13), *The Mouse That Turned* (Sept. 20), *A Lighthouse By The Sea* (Sept. 25), *Hawks Of The Sea* (Sept. 25), *Noah's Outing* (Sept. 25), *Black Magic* (Oct. 29), *The Cat And The Magnet* (Oct. 29), *Monkey Business* (Oct. 29), *She Knew Her Man* (Oct. 29), *Good Old Circus Days* (Nov. 22), *Lumber Jacks* (Nov. 22), *Sharp Shooters* (Dec. 3), *She's In Again* (Dec. 3), *On The Ice* (Dec. 3), *Mysteries of Old Chinatown* (Dec. 3), *Down On The Farm* (Dec. 3), *African Huntsmen* (Dec. 11), *One Game Pup* (Dec. 11), *Hold That Thought* (Dec. 26), and *Biting The Dust* (Dec. 31).

1925: *Bigger And Better Jails* (Jan. 19), *Fisherman's Luck* (Jan. 19), *Transatlantic Flight* (Jan. 19), *Clean Up Week* (Feb. 19), *In Dutch* (Feb. 13), *Jungle Bike Riders* (Feb. 13), *The Pie Man* (Feb. 13), *At The Zoo* (Mar. 5), *Housing Shortage* (Mar. 26), *S.O.S.* (Mar. 26), *The Adventures of Adenoid* (Apr. 10), *Permanent Waves* (Apr. 10), *Darkest Africa* (May 4), *Runaway Balloon* (May 8), *When Men Were Men* (May 18), *Wine, Women And Song* (May 18), *Bugville Field Day* (June 11), *Office Help* (June 11), *Over The Plate* (June 23), *Bubbles* (July 6), *Yarn About Yarn* (July 6), *Barnyard Follies* (July 20), *Deep Stuff* (Aug. 10), *Hungry Hounds* (Aug. 28), *The Lion And The Monkey* (Aug. 28), *Nuts And Squirrels* (Aug. 28), *Ugly Duckling* (Aug. 28), *Air-Cooled* (Sept. 28), *Closer Than A Brother* (Sept. 28), *The Hero Wins* (Sept. 28), *The Honor System* (Sept. 28), *Wild Cats Of Paris* (Sept. 28), *Laundry Man* (Oct. 26), *The Great Open Spaces* (Nov. 6), *On The Links* (Nov. 10), *The Bonehead Age* (Dec. 17), *Day's Outing* (Dec. 17), *The English Channel Swim* (Dec. 17), *The Haunted House* (Dec. 17), *More Mice Than Brains* (Dec. 17), and *Noah Had His Troubles* (Dec. 17).

1926: *Hunting in 1950* (Jan. 23), *The June Bride* (Jan. 23), *Lighter Than Air* (Jan. 23), *Little Brown Jug* (Jan. 23), *Three Blind Mice* (Jan. 23), *Wicked City* (Jan. 23), *The Wind Jammers* (Jan. 23), *The Mail Coach* (Feb. 6), *The Merry*

Blacksmith (Mar. 2), *Fire Fighters* (Mar. 26), *Big Hearted Fish* (Apr. 20), *Hearts And Showers* (Apr. 20), *Rough And Ready Romeo* (Apr. 20), *Farm Hands* (Apr. 20), *The Shootin' Fool* (Apr. 20), *An Alpine Flapper* (May 16), *Liquid Dynamite* (May 17), *A Bumper Crop* (May 26), *Chop Suey And Noodle* (July 6), *Jungle Sports* (July 6), *The Land Boom* (July 6), *Plumber's Life* (July 6), *Pirates Gold* (July 22), *The Last Ha Ha* (July 26), *Little Parade* (July 26), *A Knight Out* (Sept. 17), *Pests* (Sept. 17), *Scrambled Eggs* (Sept. 17), *Charleston Queen* (Sept. 17), *Phoney Express* (Oct. 22), *Buck Fever* (Oct. 26), *Hitting The Rails* (Oct. 26), *Home Sweet Home* (Oct. 26), *In Vaudeville* (Oct. 26), *Radio Controlled* (Oct. 26), *Thru Thick And Thin* (Oct. 26), *Bars And Stripes* (Dec. 31), *Musical Parrot* (Dec. 31), *School Days* (Dec. 31) and *Where Friendship Ceases* (Dec. 31).

1927: *Chasing Rainbows* (Jan. 13), *Plow Boy's Revenge* (Jan. 13), *Tit for Tat* (Jan. 13), *The Mail Pilot* (Feb. 14), *All For A Bride* (Mar. 4), *Cracked Ice* (Mar. 4), *Taking The Air* (Mar. 4), *The Honor Man* (Apr. 1), *Bubbling Over* (May 6), *When Snow Flies* (May 6), *A Fair Exchange* (May 6), *Pie-Eyed Piper* (May 6), *Horses, Horses, Horses* (May 10), *Big Reward* (May 12), *Crawl Stroke Kid* (May 12), *Died In The Wool* (May 12), *Digging For Gold* (May 12), *A Dog's Day* (May 12), *One Man Dog* (May 12), *Hard Cider* (May 12), *Riding High* (May 12), *Ant Life As It Isn't* (June 20), *Red Hot Sands* (July 8), *Cutting A Melon* (July 22), *Line And Sinker* (July 22), *The Small-Town Sheriff* (July 22), *All Bull and Yard Wide* (Aug. 16), *Human Fly* (Aug. 16), *In Again, Out Again* (Aug. 16), *River Of Doubt* (Aug. 16), *The Big Tent* (Sept. 2), *Lindy's Cat* (Sept. 2), *Brave Heart* (Sept. 17), *The Fox Hunt* (Oct. 13), *Saved By A Keyhole* (Oct. 13) and *Flying Hunters* (Oct. 26).

1928: *Flying Age* (Terry, Foster/Apr. 20), *War Bride* (Terry, Bailey/Apr. 20), *Alaska Or Bust* (Terry, Moser/Aug. 16), *Static* (Aug. 4), *Sunday On The Farm* (Terry, Foster/Aug. 16), *Monkey Love* (Terry, Davis/Sept. 24), *Big Game* (Terry, Bailey/Oct. 2), *Laundry Man* (Oct. 26), *On The Links* (Nov. 10), *Day Off* (Terry, Foster/Nov. 24), *Barnyard Politics* (Terry, Shields/Nov. 26), *Flying Hoofs* (Terry, Bailey/Dec. 3), *Gridiron Demons* (Terry, Moser/Dec. 4), *Mail Man* (Terry, Davis/Dec. 12), *White Elephant* (Terry, Shields/Dec. 27) and *Land O' Cotton* (Terry, Moser/Dec. 28).

1929: *Break Of The Day* (Terry, Davis/Jan. 2), *Snapping The Whip* (Terry, Moser/Jan. 6), *Wooden Money* (Terry, Foster/Jan. 6), *Sweet Adeline* (Terry, Moser/Jan. 8), *Queen Bee* (Terry, Shields/Jan. 30), *Grandma's House* (Terry/Feb. 11), *Back To The Soil* (Terry/Feb. 12), *Lad And His Lamp* (Mar. 2), *Underdog* (Mar. 13), *Fight Game* (Apr. 26), *Homeless Cats* (Apr. 26), *Little Game Hunter* (May 5), *Custard Pies* (May 9), *Ball Park* (May 19), *Fish Day* (May 26), *Skating Hounds* (May 27), *Polo Match* (June 2), *Snow Birds* (June 3), *Kidnapped* (June 23), *In His Cups* (June 30), *The Cold Steel* (July 7), *House Cleaning Time* (July 21), *A Midsummer's Day* (July 28), *Farmer's Goat* (July 29), *3 Game Guys* (Aug. 4), *Enchanted Flute* (Aug. 11), *Fruitful Farm* (Aug. 22) and *The Cabaret* (Aug 25).

ALICE COMEDIES

Walt Disney produced this series featuring animated characters and a live-action girl, employing similar techniques popularized earlier by Max Fleischer in his *Out of the Inkwell* series. Alice was portrayed by several girls, primarily Virginia Davis and Margie Gay, who interacted with animated friends on screen in various episodes.

Distributor M. J. Winkler financed the series, which was Disney's second, and enabled the mustached animator to establish a studio in Los Angeles (near the corner of Vermont and Hollywood Boulevard) to animate these imaginative productions. Along with animators Ub Iwerks, Rudolf Ising and Hugh Harman, Disney turned out these films at a rate of one every two or three weeks. For the era in which these were made, the productions were clearly ingenious, with the interplay between the live and cartoon figures proving to be magical on screen.

"We'd film in a vacant lot," said Virginia "Gini" McGhee, formerly Virginia Davis, who fondly remembered her days playing Alice. "Walt would drape a white tarpaulin over the back of a billboard and along the ground, and I'd have to work in pantomime. They would add the animation around me later. It was such fun. Kids in the neighborhood would act as extras, and Walt paid them fifty cents apiece."

As Disney's first star, Davis appeared in 14 *Alice* shorts, featured in roles ranging from cowgirl to big-game hunter. Disney brought Davis with him from Kansas to star in the pictures. He selected her for the part after spotting her face on a billboard advertisement for Warneker's bread.

How Disney got the series off the ground is noteworthy. When a bankrupt distributor forced him to shut down his Laugh-O-Grams studio, laying off his entire staff, he raised fare to Los Angeles and, with the financial support of brother Roy, finished the sample reel for what became the series pilot. After relentless attempts to find a distributor, he nearly gave up until noted film distributor M. J. Winkler offered him $1,500 a reel to produce the *Alice* series. (The venture became quite profitable for Walt, since the first film cost him only $750.)

In 1927, Disney dropped the series when his distributor encouraged him to start a new series. It starred a floppy-eared character, dubbed Oswald the Rabbit, which was immediately successful with moviegoing audiences. *Directed by Walt Disney. A Walt Disney Production released by M. J. Winkler.*

1924: *Alice's Day At Sea* (Mar. 1), *Alice's Spooky Adventure* (Apr. 1), *Alice's Wild West Show* (May 1), *Alice's Fishy Story* (June 1), *Alice And The Dog Catcher* (July 1), *Alice The Peacemaker* (Aug. 1), *Alice Gets In Dutch* (Nov. 1), *Alice Hunting In Africa* (Nov. 15), *Alice And The Three Bears* (Dec. 1) and *Alice The Piper* (Dec. 15).

1925: *Alice Cans The Cannibals* (Jan. 1), *Alice The Toreador* (Jan. 15), *Alice Gets Stung* (Feb. 1), *Alice Solves The Puzzle* (Feb. 15), *Alice's Egg Plant, Alice Loses Out, Alice Stage Struck, Alice Wins The Derby, Alice Picks The Champ, Alice's Tin Pony, Alice Chops The Suey, Alice The Jail Bird* (Sept. 15), *Alice Plays Cupid* (Oct. 15), *Alice Rattled By Rats* (Nov. 15) and *Alice In The Jungle* (Dec. 15).

1926: *Alice On The Farm* (Jan. 1), *Alice's Balloon Race* (Jan. 15), *Alice's Ornery Orphan*, *Alice's Little Parade* (Feb. 1), *Alice's Mysterious Mystery* (Feb. 15), *Alice Charms The Fish* (Sept. 6), *Alice's Monkey Business* (Sept. 20), *Alice In The Wooly West* (Oct. 4), *Alice The Fire Fighter* (Oct. 18), *Alice Cuts The Ice* (Nov. 1), *Alice Helps The Romance* (Nov. 15), *Alice's Spanish Guitar* (Nov. 29), *Alice's Brown Derby* (Dec. 13) and *Alice The Lumber Jack* (Dec. 27).

1927: *Alice The Golf Bug* (Jan. 10), *Alice Foils The Pirates* (Jan. 24), *Alice At the Carnival* (Feb. 7), *Alice At The Rodeo* (Feb. 21/originally *Alice's Rodeo*), *Alice The Collegiate* (Mar. 7), *Alice In The Alps* (Mar. 21), *Alice's Auto Race* (Apr. 4), *Alice's Circus Daze* (Apr. 18), *Alice's Knaughty Knight* (May 2), *Alice's Three Bad Eggs* (May 16), *Alice's Picnic* (May 30), *Alice's Channel Swim* (June 13), *Alice In The Klondike* (June 27), *Alice's Medicine Show* (July 11), *Alice The Whaler* (July 25), *Alice The Beach Nut* (Aug. 8) and *Alice In The Big League* (Aug. 22).

ANIMATED GROUCH CHASERS

French–Canadian cartoonist Raoul Barré produced this series of thematically related films for Edison Company in New York. Employing the technique of animation on paper, the films featured a burlesque introduction by live actors followed by a comic book title, *The Grouch Chasers,* signaling the beginning of the animation program.

The series starred a group of insects—the most notable being Ferdinand the fly and his "flyancee"—and three of Barré's other prized creations: Kid Kelly and his larcenous sidekick dog, Jip; Hercules Hicks, a henpecked little man who escaped his overbearing wife by means of dreaming; and Silas Bunkum, a potbellied teller of tales. *A Gaumount Studios release.*

1915: *The Animated Grouch Chaser* (Mar. 4), *Cartoons In The Kitchen* (Apr. 21), *Cartoons In The Barber Shop* (May 22), *Cartoons In The Parlor* (June 5), *Cartoons In The Hotel* (June 21), *Cartoons In The Laundry* (July 8), *Cartoons On Tour* (Aug. 6), *Cartoons On The Beach* (Aug. 25), *Cartoons In A Seminary* (Sept. 9), *Cartoons In The Country* (Oct. 9), *Cartoons On a Yacht* (Oct. 29), *Cartoons In A Sanitarium* (Nov. 12) and *Black's Mysterious Box And Hicks In Nightmareland* (Dec. 4).

ANIMATED HAIR

Celebrity caricatures evolved (out of "a strand of hair") in this series of line drawn cartoons by noted caricaturist Marcus, a former *Life* magazine cartoonist. The series ran from November 1924 to 1925, and was distributed by Max Fleischer's distribution company, Red Seal Pictures. *A Red Seal Pictures release.*

B.D.F. CARTOONS

Paul Fenton produced, directed and animated this series of advertising cartoons. *A B.D.F. Film Company Production.*

1918: *Old Tire Man Diamond Cartoon Film* (July 13).

1919: *Re-Blazing The '49 Trail In A Motor Car Train* (Sept. 10), *Tire Injury* (Sept. 13) and *Paradental Anesthesia* (Sept. 13).

1921: *A Movie Trip Through Film Land* (Dec. 17).

1922: *For Any Occasion* (Nov. 20) and *In Hot Weather* (Nov. 20).

1923: *The Champion* (Sept. 30) and *Land Of The Unborn Children* (Nov. 1).

1924: *Some Impressions On The Subject of Thrift.*

1925: *Live And Help Live* (May 22).

1926: *The Carriage Awaits* (June 15), *Family Album* (June 15), *What Price Noise* (June 16) and *For Dear Life* (Dec. 30).

BERTLEVYETTES

This series combined live action and animation, produced and written by Bert Levy and directed by Sidney Olcott. *A World Film Corporation Production.*

1915: *Great Americans Past and Present* (Jan. 4), *Famous Men Of Today* (Jan. 11), *Famous Rulers Of The World* (Jan. 18) and *New York And Its People* (Jan. 25).

BOBBY BUMPS

Pioneer animator Earl Hurd created this mischievous little boy, inspired by R. F. Outcault's well-known comic strip character Buster Brown. (Like Buster, Bobby was given a bulldog companion, only his is named Fido.) These humorous and delightfully sympathetic adventures of a boy's life were first produced in 1915 by J. R. Bray's studio following the success of his *Colonel Heeza Liar* series. The idea of producing a figure "out of the inkwell" was a key element in the films—Bumps was introduced by Hurd's hand—foreshadowing Max Fleischer's technique by several years. Early stories were shaped around Bobby's pranks, often played on his parents or friends *Directed by Earl Hurd. A Bray Production released by Paramount Pictures.*

1915: *Bobby Bumps Gets Pa's Goat* (July 3) and *Bobby Bumps' Adventures.*

1916: *Bobby Bumps And His Pointer Pup* (Feb. 24), *Bobby Bumps Gets a Substitute* (Mar. 30), *Bobby Bumps And His Goatmobile* (Apr. 30), *Bobby Bumps Goes Fishing* (June 1), *Bobby Bumps' Fly Swatter* (June 29), *Bobby Bumps And The Detective Story* (July 27), *Bobby Bumps Loses His Pup* (Aug. 17), *Bobby Bumps And The Stork* (Sept. 7), *Bobby Bumps Starts A Lodge* (Sept. 28), *Bobby Bumps Helps Out A Book Agent* (Oct. 23), *Bobby Bumps Queers A Choir* (Oct. 26) and *Bobby Bumps At The Circus* (Nov. 11).

1917: *Bobby Bumps In The Great Divide* (Feb. 5), *Bobby Bumps Adopts A Turtle* (Mar. 5), *Bobby Bumps, Office Boy* (Mar. 26), *Bobby Bumps Outwits The Dogsnatcher* (Apr. 16), *Bobby Bumps Volunteers* (May 7), *Bobby Bumps Daylight*

Camper (May 28), *Bobby Bumps Submarine Chaser* (June 18), *Bobby Bumps' Fourth* (July 9), *Bobby Bumps' Amusement Park* (Aug. 6), *Bobby Bumps, Surf Rider* (Aug. 27), *Bobby Bumps Starts For School* (Sept. 17), *Bobby Bumps' World Serious* (Oct. 8), *Bobby Bumps, Chef* (Oct. 29), *Bobby Bumps Fido's Birthday* (Nov. 18), *Bobby Bumps Early Shopper* (Dec. 9) and *Bobby Bumps' Tank* (Dec. 30).

1918: *Bobby Bumps' Disappearing Gun* (Jan. 21), *Bobby Bumps At The Dentist* (Feb. 25), *Bobby Bumps' Fight* (Mar. 25), *Bobby Bumps On The Road* (Apr. 15), *Bobby Bumps Caught In The Jamb* (May 13), *Bobby Bumps Out West* (June 10), *Bobby Bumps Films A Fire* (June 24), *Bobby Bumps Becomes An Ace* (July 15), *Bobby Bumps On The Doughnut Trail* (Aug. 19), *Bobby Bumps And The Speckled Death* (Sept. 30), *Bobby Bumps Incubator* (Oct. 8), *Bobby Bumps In Before And After* (Nov. 20) and *Bobby Bumps Puts A Beanery On The Bum* (Dec. 4).

1919: *Bobby Bumps' Last Smoke* (Jan. 24), *Bobby Bumps' Lucky Day* (Mar. 19), *Bobby Bumps' Night Out With Some Night Owls* (Apr. 16), *Bobby Bumps' Pup Gets The Flea-enza* (Apr. 23), *Bobby Bumps' Eel-ectric Launch* (Apr. 30), *Bobby Bumps And The Sand Lizard* (May 21), *Bobby Bumps And The Hypnotic Eye* (June 25) and *Bobby Bumps Throwing The Bull* (July 16).

Paramount Magazine
1920: *Bobby Bumps The Cave Man* (Aug. 8) and *Bobby Bumps' Orchestra* (Dec. 19).

1921: *Bobby Bumps Checkmated* (Mar. 20).

Paramount Cartoons
1921: *Bobby Bumps Working On An Idea* (May 8), *Bobby Bumps In Shadow Boxing* (July 9) and *Bobby Bumps In Hunting And Fishing* (Aug. 21).

1922: *Bobby Bumps At School* (Dec. 16/Bray Magazine) and *Railroading* (Dec. 2/Earl Hurd Comedies).

1923: *The Movie Daredevil* (Apr. 1/Earl Hurd Comedies) and *Their Love Growed Cold* (June 2/Earl Hurd Comedies).

Educational Pictures Release
1925: *Bobby Bumps And Company* (Sept. 22/Pen and Ink Vaudeville).

THE BOOB WEEKLY

Rube Goldberg wrote and directed this series of newsreel spoofs, which were animated by George Stallings at Barré Studios in 1916. Goldberg was actually contracted by Pathé Films to produce the series as part of a lucrative contract that netted him $75,000 a year for his efforts. *A Rube Goldberg/Barré Studios Production released by Pathé Films.*

1916: *The Boob Weekly* (May 8), *Leap Year* (May 22), *The Fatal Pie* (June 5), *From Kitchen Mechanic To Movie Star* (June 19), *Nutty News* (July 3), *Home Sweet Home* (July 17) and *Losing Weight* (July 31).

BOOMER BILL

Along with his series of Felix the Cat and Charlie Chaplin cartoons, pioneer animator Pat Sullivan also produced and directed this series of comic misadventures. Unfortunately, no records could be found to describe the character or the films at length. *A Pat Sullivan Cartoon released through Universal Pictures.*

1917: *Boomer Bill's Awakening* (Jan. 3) and *Boomer Bill Goes to Sea* (Mar. 31).

BOX CAR BILL

Following his widely acclaimed two-reel comic short, *Twenty Thousand Laughs Under the Sea,* a spoof of the Jules Verne classic *Twenty Thousand Leagues Under the Sea,* Pat Sullivan produced and directed this short-lived series for Universal in 1917. Little else is known about the production and content of the films. *A Pat Sullivan Cartoon released through Universal.*

1917: *Box Car Bill Falls In Luck* (July 10).

BRINGING UP FATHER

Most early silent cartoon series were comic strip adaptations. This series was similarly based on a long-running weekly strip, featuring henpecked Jiggs and his society wife, Maggie, created by cartoonist George McManus in 1912. *An International Films Production released by Pathé Film Exchange.*

1916: *Father Gets Into The Movies* (Nov. 21) and *Just Like A Woman* (Dec. 14).

1917: *The Great Hansom Cab Mystery* (Apr. 26), *A Hot Time In The Gym* (Apr. 26), *Music Hath Charms* (June 7) and *He Tries His Hand At Hypnotism* (Aug. 8).

1918: *Second, The Stimulating Mrs. Barton* (Apr. 16), *Second, Father's Close Shave* (May 16) and *Third, Jiggs And The Social Lion* (June 27).

BUD AND SUSIE

Frank Moser, who supervised George McManus' *Bringing Up Father* series, animated this series of husband–and–wife stories shaped around the madcap adventures of henpecked husband, Bud, and his overbearing wife, Susie. The films were released by Paramount in 1919, the year they were produced. *A Bray Production released by Paramount.*
(Filmography lists known titles only.)

1920: *Handy Mandy's Goat* (Mar. 21), *The Kids Find Candy's Catching* (Apr. 11), *Bud Takes The Cake* (May 2), *The New Cook's Debut* (May 23), *Mice And Money* (June 13), *Down The Mississippi* (July 25), *Play Ball* (Aug. 15), *Romance And Rheumatism* (Aug. 29), *Bud And Tommy Take A Day Off* (Sept. 5), *The North Pole* (Oct. 3), *The Great Clean Up* (Oct. 31), *Bud And Susie Join The Tecs* (Nov. 28) and *Fifty-Fifty* (Dec. 5).

1921: *Getting Theirs* (Jan. 2), *Ma's Wipe Your Feet Campaign* (Feb. 27), *Circumstantial Evidence* (Apr. 3), *By The*

Sea (May 29), *$10,000 Under A Pillow* (June 26), *Dashing North* (July 31), *Kitchen, Bedroom And Bath* (Aug. 28) and *The Wars Of Mice And Men* (Sept.).

CANIMATED NOOZ PICTORIAL

Wallace A. Carlson, of *Goodrich Dirt* fame, unveiled this innovative series of caricatured drawings described as "photographic heads on pen and ink bodies." Premiering in 1916, Carlson produced and directed the series for Essanay Pictures until mid–1917 when he left the studio to pursue other interests. *An Essanay Pictures release.*

CINEMA LUKE

This live–action and animated series was produced for the *Universal Screen Magazine.* Leslie Elton served as writer, animator and director of the series, which Carl Laemmle produced. *A Universal Pictures Production.*

1919: *Cinema Luke* (Dec. 6).

1920: *Cinema Luke* (Mar. 11) and *Cinema Luke* (May 28).

CHARLIE CARTOONS

Comedian Charlie Chaplin's Little Tramp character inspired several animated cartoon series based on his comical film exploits. As early as 1915, European filmgoers were treated to animated adventures when Gaumont released its series of animated facsimiles. In July of that year, Kinema Exchange launched its own series of Chaplin cartoons—known as *Charlot*—which supposedly were authorized by the great comedian himself. Otto Messmer, who animated *Felix The Cat,* animated another series, *Charlie et l'elephant blanc,* for Beaumont Films.

One year after these series were made, Pat Sullivan contracted with Chaplin to produce a new animated series simply titled, *Charlie.* In all, 12 films were made in 1916, each drawing ideas from films and photographs supplied by Chaplin. *A Gaumont/Kinema Exchange/Pat Sullivan release.* (Following titles are from the Pat Sullivan series.)

1916: *Charlie In Carmen* (May 15), *Charlie's White Elephant, Charlie Has Some Wonderful Adventures in India, Charlie In Cuckoo Land, Charlie The Blacksmith, Charlie's Busted Romance, Charlie Across The Rio Grande, The Rooster's Nightmare, Charlie's Barnyard Pets* and *Charlie Throws The Bull.*

COLONEL HEEZA LIAR

After working on *Mutt and Jeff* at Barrĕ/Bowers Studios for a year, Walter Lantz joined the J. R. Bray Studios and his first assignment was to animate this series of misadventures starring a short, middle-aged fibbing army colonel created by J. R. Bray himself.

Bray originally created the character 10 years earlier to illustrate gags in magazines. The colonel is said to have been a lampoon of Teddy Roosevelt, noted for telling stories that seemed like "tall tales." (The character was also modeled after Baron von Munchausen, another teller of tales.)

Producer J. R. Bray and animator Walter Lantz introduced the accomplished liar Colonel Heeza Liar in 1915. (Courtesy: The Museum of Modern Art/Film Stills Archive)

As with most Bray cartoons, the early Colonel Heeza Liar films illustrate a remarkable sense of economy in both animation and production values. Only 100 basic arrangements of cels were used for each film, so animation was quite limited. In several episodes, the colonel's small stature was played for laughs, pitting him against his domineering wife who was three times his size!

In the 1920s Bray assigned Vernon Stallings to direct the series. *A Bray Company Production released by Pathé Film Exchange and Hodkinson and Selznick Pictures.*

1913: *Col. Heeza Liar In Africa* (Nov. 29).

1914: *Col. Heeza Liar's African Hunt* (Jan. 10), *Col. Heeza Liar Shipwrecked* (Mar. 14), *Col. Heeza Liar In Mexico* (Apr. 18), *Col. Heeza Liar, Farmer* (May 18), *Col. Heeza Liar, Explorer* (Aug. 15), *Col. Heeza Liar In The Wilderness* (Sept. 26) and *Col. Heeza Liar, Naturalist* (Oct. 24).

1915: *Col. Heeza Liar, Ghost Breaker* (Feb. 6), *Col. Heeza Liar In The Haunted Castle* (Feb. 20), *Col. Heeza Liar Runs The Blockade* (Mar. 20), *Col. Heeza Liar And The Torpedo* (Apr. 3), *Col. Heeza Liar And The Zeppelin* (Apr. 10), *Col. Heeza Liar Signs The Pledge* (May 8), *Col. Heeza Liar In The Trenches* (May 13), *Col. Heeza Liar At The Front* (May 16), *Col. Heeza Liar, Aviator* (May 22), *Col. Heeza Liar Invents A New King Of Shell* (June 5), *Col. Heeza Liar, Dog Fancier* (July 10), *Col. Heeza Liar Foils The Enemy* (July 31), *Col. Heeza Liar, War Dog* (Aug. 21), *Col. Heeza Liar At The Bat* (Sept. 4), *Col. Heeza Liar, Nature Faker* (Dec. 28).

1916: *Col. Heeza Liar's Waterloo* (Jan. 6), *Col. Heeza Liar And The Pirates* (Mar. 5), *Col. Heeza Liar Wins The Pennant* (Apr. 27), *Col. Heeza Liar Captures Villa* (May 25), *Col. Heeza Liar And The Bandits* (June 22), *Col. Heeza Liar's Courtship* (July 20), *Col. Heeza Liar On Strike* (Aug. 17), *Col. Heeza Liar Plays Hamlet* (Aug. 24), *Col. Heeza Liar Bachelor Quarters* (Sept. 14), *Col. Heeza Liar Gets Married* (Oct. 11), *Col. Heeza Liar, Hobo* (Nov. 15) and *Col. Heeza Liar At The Vaudeville Show* (Dec. 21).

1917: *Col. Heeza Liar On The Jump* (Feb. 4), *Col. Heeza Liar, Detective* (Feb. 25), *Col. Heeza Liar, Spy Dodger* (Mar. 19) and *Col. Heeza Liar's Temperance Lecture* (Aug. 20).

1922: *Colonel Heeza Liar's Treasure Island* (Stallings/Dec. 17).

1923: *Colonel Heeza Liar And The Ghost* (Stallings/Jan. 14), *Colonel Heeza Liar, Detective* (Stallings/Feb. 1), *Colonel Heeza Liar's Burglar* (Stallings/Mar. 11), *Col. Heeza Liar In The African Jungles* (Stallings/June 3), *Col. Heeza Liar In Uncle Tom's Cabin* (July 8), *Col. Heeza Liar's Vacation* (Aug. 5), *Col. Heeza Liar's Forbidden Fruit* (Nov. 1) and *Col. Heeza Liar, Strikebreaker* (Dec. 1).

Selznick Pictures
1924: *Col. Heeza Liar, Nature Faker* (Jan. 1), *Col. Heeza Liar's Mysterious Case* (Feb. 1), *Col. Heeza Liar's Ancestors* (Mar. 1), *Col. Heeza Liar's Knighthood* (Apr. 1), *Col. Heeza Liar, Sky Pilot* (May 1), *Col. Heeza Liar, Daredevil* (June 1), *Col. Heeza Liar's Horseplay* (July 1), *Col. Heeza Liar, Cave Man* (Aug. 1), *Col. Heeza Liar, Bull Thrower* (Sept. 1), *Col. Heeza Liar The Lyin' Tamer* (Oct. 1) and *Col. Heeza Liar's Romance* (Nov. 1).

DINKY DOODLE

Walter Lantz, best known for his creation of Woody Woodpecker, was writer, animator and director of this live action/animated series for J. R. Bray Studios featuring the adventures of a young button–eyed boy Dinky and his faithful dog, Weakheart.

Like Max Fleischer's *Out Of The Inkwell* series, this production placed a live character (Lantz) in situations with the animated stars. However, several differences existed between the two series. Lantz used an entirely different process than Fleischer to blend the live–action sequences with animation.

Animator Walter Lantz is joined at the animator's table by cartoon stars Dinky Doodle and Weakheart the Dog. (Courtesy: Walter Lantz)

After filming the scenes, he took the negative and made eight–by–ten stills of every frame—three to four thousand of them. The stills were then punched like animation paper and re-photographed with each cel of character animation overlapping the live–action scenes. (Character drawings were done on onionskin paper then duly inked and painted on cels before being shot in combination with the live–action enlargements.)

Lantz's job of acting in the live–action scenes was therefore difficult because he had to act without knowing how the characters were going to appear opposite him in each scene. "If Walt was supposed to duel a cartoon villain, he would first duel a live person, like Gerry Geronimi, one of his chief animators," recalled James "Shamus" Culhane, an assistant on the series. "The cartoon characters were added later and the final result was Walt dueling merrily with an animated cartoon."

Lantz took many of his live–action sequences outside the studio to be filmed in a variety of locations, unlike Fleischer who always opened his Inkwell cartoons seated behind an animator's table. "We never opened a cartoon with the same setting," Lantz remembered in an interview. "We went outside to do our stories. We went to a large field, or to the beach or to Buckhill Falls in upstate New York. We went all over."

As the live actor in these films, Lantz's aim wasn't to upstage his cartoon contemporaries. "I was short and not especially funny looking, so I imitated Harold Lloyd's prop–eye glasses. All the comedians in those days used something—Chaplin had his tramp outfit; Conklin a walrus mustache; Langdon that ill–fitting peaked cap. The glasses weren't too good of a trademark for me, but then I wasn't aiming to be a full–time comedian."

Even so Lantz's work in the leading role was tested in the same manner as most of these great comedians. Most of the comic moments placed heavy emphasis on chase scenes, and in this sense Lantz had to do more than resemble a comedian to make the segments work.

Incredibly, Lantz completed a cartoon for release about every two weeks, at a cost of $1,800 apiece, for producing 700 feet of live action and animated film. "I had no idea what the cartoons were costing," he admitted, "so this figure didn't frighten me."

Most stories were based on classic fairy tales and standard everyday situations. Lantz's personal series favorites were *Cinderella* and *Little Red Riding Hood*, both based on popular children's fairy tales. Unfortunately, few examples of this great series remain since most of the films were destroyed in a warehouse fire.

In addition to Lantz, the series chief animators were Clyde Geronimi and David Hand, who both became key animators at Walt Disney Studios in the 1930s. *A Bray Production and Standard Cinema Corporation release.*

1924: *The Magic Lamp* (Sept. 15), *The Giant Killer* (Oct. 15) and *The Pied Piper* (Dec. 1).

1925: *Little Red Riding Hood* (Jan. 4), *The House That Dinky Built* (Feb. 1), *Cinderella* (Mar. 1), *Peter Pan Handled* (Apr. 26), *Magic Carpet* (May 24), *Robinson Crusoe* (June 21), *Three Bears* (July 19), *Just Spooks* (Sept. 13), *Dinky*

Doodle And The Bad Man (Sept. 20), *Dinky Doodle In The Hunt* (Nov. 1), *Dinky Doodle In The Circus* (Nov. 29) and *Dinky Doodle In The Restaurant* (Dec. 27).

1926: *Dinky Doodle In Lost And Found* (Feb. 19), *Dinky Doodle In Uncle Tom's Cabin* (Feb. 21), *Dinky Doodle In The Arctic* (Mar. 21), *Dinky Doodle In Egypt* (Apr. 8), *Dinky Doodle In The Wild West* (May 12), *Dinky Doodle's Bed Time Story* (June 6), *Dinky Doodle And The Little Orphan* (July 4) and *Dinky Doodle In The Army* (Aug. 29).

DOC YAK

Created by newspaper cartoonist Sidney Smith, Doc Yak originally ran as a regular strip in the *Chicago Herald* and *New York Daily News* newspapers. Like so many other cartoonists, Smith adapted this middle–aged character to the screen in a series of cartoon calamities. Smith produced a few experimental reels which were released by Selig–Polyscope in July 1913. In May 1914, he launched a second series, which was as successful as the first. *A Sidney Smith Production released by Selig–Polyscope.*

1913: *Old Doc Yak* (July 11), *Old Doc Yak And The Artist's Dream* (Oct. 29) and *Old Doc Yak's Christmas* (Dec. 30).

1914: *Doc Yak, Moving Picture Artist* (Jan. 22), *Doc Yak Cartoonist* (Mar. 14), *Doc Yak The Poultryman* (Apr. 11), *Doc Yak's Temperance Lecture* (May 2), *Doc Yak The Marksman* (May 9), *Doc Yak Bowling* (May 23), *Doc Yak's Zoo* (May 30), *Doc Yak And The Limited Train* (June 6), *Doc Yak's Wishes* (June 11), *Doc Yak's Bottle* (Sept. 16), *Doc Yak's Cats* (Oct. 15), *Doc Yak Plays Golf* (Oct. 24) and *Doc Yak And Santa Claus* (Dec. 8).

Chicago Tribune Animated Weekly
1915: *Doc In The Ring* (Sept. 18) and *Doc The Ham Actor* (Oct. 16).

DREAMS OF A RAREBIT FIEND

Winsor McCay wrote, produced, directed and co-animated this series based on his popular comic strip. *A Rialto Production.*

1921: *Bug Vaudeville* (Sept. 26), *The Pet* (Sept. 26), *The Flying House* (Sept. 26), *The Centaurs, Flip's Circus* and *Gertie On Tour.*

DREAMY DUD

Essanay Studios commissioned renowned animator Wallace A. Carlson to direct and animate this series of tall tales starring his Walter Mittyish lad whose daydreams—often a result of boredom and loneliness—lead him into trouble. Carlson projected Dreamy into all kinds of heroic situations and other feats of valor that often included his loyal dog, Wag. *An Essanay Pictures release.*

1915: *A Visit To The Zoo* (May 15), *An Alley Romance* (May 15), *Lost In The Jungle* (June 1), *Dreamy Dud In The Swim* (June 7), *Dreamy Dud Resolves Not To Smoke* (June 22), *Dreamy Dud In King Koo Koo's Kingdom* (June 30), *He Goes Bear Hunting* (July 17), *A Visit To Uncle Dudley's Farm* (July 26), *Dreamy Dud Sees Charlie Chaplin* (Aug. 9), *Dreamy Dud Cowboy* (Aug. 31), *Dreamy Dud At The Old Swimmin' Hole* (Sept. 17), *Dreamy Dud In The Air* (Oct. 14) and *Dreamy Dud In Love* (Nov. 29).

1916: *Dreamy Dud Lost At Sea* (Jan. 22), *Dreamy Dud Has A Laugh On The Boss* (Sept. 20), *Dreamy Dud In The African War Zone* (Oct. 13) and *Dreamy Dud Joyriding With Princess Zlim* (Nov. 21).

EBENEZER EBONY

A Sering D. Wilson & Company Production.

1925: *The Flying Elephant* (Apr. 22), *An Ice Boy* (May 22), *Gypping The Gypsies* (June 22), *Fire In A Brimstone* (July 1), *High Moon* (Aug. 1), *Love Honor And Oh Boy* (Sept. 1), *Foam Sweet Foam* (Oct. 1), and *Fisherman's Luck* (Oct. 31).

ECLAIR JOURNAL

Pioneer animator Emile Cohl wrote, directed and animated this series of animated cartoon items for a weekly newsreel. *An Eclair Company Production.*

1913: *War In Turkey* (Jan.), *Castro In New York* (Jan.), *Rockefeller* (Jan.), *Confidence* (Jan.), *Milk* (Feb.), *Coal* (Feb.), *The Subway* (Feb.), *Graft* (Feb.), *The Two Presidents* (Mar.), *The Auto* (Mar.), *Wilson And The Broom* (Mar.), *The Police Women* (Mar.), *Wilson And The Hats* (Mar.), *Poker* (Mar.), *Gaynor And The Night Clubs* (Mar.), *Universal Trade Marks* (Mar.), *Wilson And The Tariffs* (Apr.), *The Masquerade* (Apr.), *The Brand Of California* (Apr.), *The Safety Pin* (May), *The Two Suffragettes* (May), *The Mosquito* (May), *The Red Balloons* (May), *The Cubists* (June), *Uncle Sam And His Suit* (June), *The Polo Boat* (June), *The Artist* (June), *Wilson's Row Row* (July), *The Hat* (Aug.), *Thaw And The Lasso* (Aug.), *Bryant And The Speeches* (Aug.), *Thaw And The Spider* (Sept.), *Exhibition Of Caricatures* (Nov.) and *Pickup Is A Sportsman* (Dec.).

1914: *The Bath* (Jan.), *The Future Revealed By The Lines Of The Feet* (Jan.), *The Social Group* (Nov.), *The Greedy Neighbor, What They Eat, The Anti-Neurasthenic Trumpet, His Ancestors, Serbia's Card* and *The Terrible Scrap Of Paper.*

FARMER AL FALFA

Animator Paul Terry developed this bald, white–bearded farmer shortly after becoming a staff animator for J. R. Bray Studios, first bringing him to the screen in 1916. Most of the early films cast this popular hayseed in a continuing series of barnyard skirmishes with animals. The series later focused on his attempts to make "modern improvements" to the farm.

Terry's work on the series was briefly interrupted when he was inducted into the Army in 1917. At the end of the war, he returned to New York and formed a company with fellow animators Earl Hurd, Frank Moser, Hugh (Jerry) Shields, Leighton Budd and brother John Terry, but it lasted only for a short time. He continued making Farmer Al Falfa cartoons for release through Paramount until 1923, later to revive the character when sound was introduced.

Paul Terry produced and directed the series. *A Paul Terry cartoon released by J. R. Bray, Thomas Edison Inc. and Pathé Film Exchange.*

1916: *Farmer Al Falfa's Catastrophe* (Feb. 3), *Farmer Al Falfa Invents A New Kite* (Mar. 12), *Farmer Al Falfa's Scientific Diary* (Apr. 14), *Farmer Al Falfa And His Tentless Circus* (June 3), *Farmer Al Falfa's Watermelon Patch* (June 29), *Farmer Al Falfa's Egg-Citement* (Aug. 4), *Farmer Al Falfa's Revenge* (Aug. 25), *Farmer Al Falfa's Wolfhound* (Sept. 16), *Farmer Al Falfa Sees New York* (Oct. 9), *Farmer Al Falfa's Prune Plantation* (Nov. 3) and *Farmer Al Falfa's Blind Pig* (Dec. 1).

Thomas Edison, Inc.
1917: *Farmer Al Falfa's Wayward Pup* (May 7).

Paramount Magazine
1920: *The Bone Of Contention* (Mar. 14).

Pathé Film Exchange
1922: *The Farmer And The Ostrich* (Jan. 26) and *The Farmer And His Cat* (May 17).

1923: *Farmer Al Falfa's Bride* (Feb. 23) and *Farmer Al Falfa's Pet Cat* (Nov. 9).

FELIX THE CAT

The public loved this clever feline long before the 1960s syndicated cartoon revival. Australian-born artist Pat Sullivan (b. 1888; d. February 5, 1963) originated the character for the silent screen. The devil–eared cat headlined in more than 80 one–reel cartoon shorts. He had no bag of tricks as in the television–made cartoons, but through intelligent, spontaneous gags overcame obstacles and awkward situations (in early cartoons, Felix was known to transform his "tail" into assorted objects to help him out of jams).

The origin of Felix's name came from the word "felicity," meaning "great happiness," and he was made black for practical reasons. "It saves making a lot of outlines, and the solid black moves better," explained pioneer animator Otto Messmer, who brought Sullivan's character to life on screen.

Oddly, Felix was more popular overseas than in the United States, resulting in assorted merchandise bearing his name. In this country, adoration of the character took a different form. In 1922, Felix appeared as the New York Yankees lucky mascot and, three years later, a song was written in his honor called, "Felix Kept Walking." By 1927, a Felix doll became Charles Lindbergh's companion on his famed flight across the Atlantic. The following year, he became the first image ever to appear on television when the first experimental television broadcast took place, the subject being a Felix doll. A popular item in the United Kingdom remains a pet food affectionately named after the sly cat.

The downfall of the silent series was Sullivan's refusal to add sound to his pictures following the birth of "talkies." Consequently, series revenue fell off dramatically and he was forced to lay off his staff. In 1936, Felix was revived in a short–lived series of sound cartoons produced by RKO-Van Beuren. *Directed by Pat Sullivan. A Pat Sullivan Production released by Pathé Film Exchange Inc. and M. J. Winkler.*

(Note: The early 1920s cartoons had no titles but were simply referred to as *Felix* in trade paper listings. The 1921 and 1924 filmography contains only those which were given titles.)

Paramount Magazine
1920: *Feline Follies* (Mar. 28), *Felix The Landlord* (Oct. 24) and *My Hero* (Dec. 26).

1921: *The Hypnotist* (Mar. 13), *Free Lunch* (Apr. 17), *Felix Goes On Strike* (May 15), *Felix In The Love Punch* (June 5), *Felix Out Of Luck* (July 3), *Felix Left At Home* (July 17) and *Felix The Gay Dog* (Oct. 30).

Winkler Productions
1922: *Felix Saves The Day* (Jan. 22), *Felix At The Fair* (Feb.), *Felix Makes Good* (Mar.), *Felix All At Sea* (Apr.), *Felix In Love* (May), *Felix In The Swim* (June) and *Felix Wakes Up* (Nov. 25).

1923: *Felix Turns The Tide* (Jan. 1), *Felix On The Trail* (Jan. 15), *Felix Lends A Hand* (Feb. 1), *Felix In The Bone Age* (Mar. 1), *Felix The Ghost Breaker* (Mar. 15), *Felix Wins Out* (Apr. 1), *Felix Tries For Treasure* (Apr. 15), *Felix Revolts* (May 1), *Felix Calms HIs Conscience* (May 15), *Felix The Globe Trotter* (June 1), *Felix Gets Broadcasted* (Sept. 1), *Felix Strikes It Rich* (Sept. 15), *Felix In Hollywood* (Oct. 1), *Felix In Fairyland* (Oct. 15), *Felix Laughs Last* (Nov. 1), *Felix Fills A Shortage* (Nov. 15), *Felix The Goat Getter* (Dec. 1) and *Felix Goes A-Hunting* (Dec. 15).

1924: *Felix Out Of Luck* (Jan. 1), *Felix Loses Out* (Jan. 15), *Felix Hypes The Hippo* (Feb. 1), *Felix Crosses The Crooks* (Feb. 15), *Felix Tries To Rest* (Apr. 1), *Felix Baffled By Banjos* (Aug. 15), *Felix Pinches The Pole* (Sept. 15), *Felix Puts It Over* (Oct. 1) and *Felix A Friend In Need* (Oct. 15).

1925: *Felix Wins and Loses* (Jan. 1), *Felix All Puzzled* (Jan. 15), *Felix Follows The Swallows* (Feb. 1), *Felix Rests In Peace* (Feb. 15), *Felix Gets His Fill* (Mar. 1), *Felix Full Of Fight* (Apr. 13), *Felix Outwits Cupid* (Apr. 27), *Felix Monkeys With Magic* (May 8), *Felix Cops The Prize* (May 25) and *Felix Gets The Can* (June 8).

Pat Sullivan Productions
1925: *Felix Uses His Head* (July 13), *Felix Trifles With Time* (Aug. 23), *Felix Busts Into The Business* (Sept. 6), *Felix Trips Thru Toyland* (Sept. 20), *Felix On The Farm* (Oct. 4), *Felix On The Job* (Oct. 18), *Felix In The Cold Rush* (Nov. 1), *Felix In Eats Are West* (Nov. 15), *Felix Tries The Trades* (Nov.

29), *Felix At Rainbow's End* (Dec. 13) and *Felix Kept On Walking* (Dec. 27).

1926:   *Felix Spots The Spook* (Jan. 30), *Felix Flirts With Fate* (Mar. 2), *Felix In Blunderland* (Mar. 7), *Felix Fans The Flames* (Mar. 20), *Felix Laughs It Off* (Mar. 20), *Felix Weathers The Weather* (Mar. 20), *Felix Misses The Cue* (May 8), *Felix Braves The Briny* (June 12), *Felix In A Tale Of Two Kitties* (June 26), *Felix Scoots Thru Scotland* (July 3), *Felix Rings The Ringer* (July 17), *Felix In Gym Gems* (Aug. 8), *Felix Seeks Solitude* (Aug. 8), *Felix In Two-Lip Time* (Aug. 22), *Felix Miss His Swiss* (Aug. 28), *Felix In Scrambled Yeggs* (Sept. 5), *Felix Shatters The Shriek* (Sept. 19), *Felix Hunts The Hunter* (Nov. 8), *Felix In Reverse English* (Nov. 14), *Felix In Land O'Fancy* (Nov. 19), *Felix Trumps The Ace* (Nov. 28), *Felix Butts A Bubble* (Nov. 30), *Felix Collars In The Button* (Dec. 12) and *Felix In Zoo Logic* (Dec. 26).

1927:   *Felix Dines And Pines* (Jan. 18), *Felix In Icy Eyes* (Feb. 2), *Felix In Pedigreedy* (Feb. 8), *Felix Stars In Stripes* (Feb. 20), *Felix Sees 'Em In Season* (Mar. 6), *Felix In Barn Yarns* (Mar. 20), *Felix In Germ Mania* (Apr. 4), *Felix In Sax Appeal* (Apr. 17), *Felix In Eye Jinks* (May 1), *Felix As Roameow* (May 15), *Felix Ducks His Duty* (May 29), *Felix In*

Otto Messemer created Pat Sullivan's malicious, inventive adventures of Felix the Cat. The character was one of the most popular cartoon stars of the silent film era. (Courtesy: The Museum of Modern Art/Film Stills Archive)

Dough Nutty (June 12), *Felix In Loco Motive* (June 26), *Felix In Art For Heart's Sake* (July 27), *Felix In The Travel-Hog* (Aug. 10), *Felix In Jack From All Trades* (Aug. 17), *Felix In Non-Stop Fright* (Sept. 20), *Felix In Film Flam Films* (Nov. 3), *Felix Switches Witches* (Nov. 7), *Felix In No Fuelin'* (Nov. 16), *Felix In Daze And Knights* (Nov. 28), *Felix In Uncle Tom's Crabbin'* (Nov. 28), *Felix Behind In Front* (Dec. 12), *Felix Hits The Deck* (Dec. 19) and *Felix In Whys And Other-Whys* (Dec. 27).

1928:   *Felix In The Smoke Screen* (Jan. 8), *Felix In Draggin' the Dragon* (Jan. 22), *Felix In The Oily Bird* (Feb. 5), *Felix In Ohm Sweet Ohm* (Feb. 19), *Felix In Japanicky* (Mar. 14), *Felix In Polly-tics* (Mar. 18), *Felix In Sure Locked Homes* (Apr. 15), *Felix In Eskimotive* (Apr. 29), *Felix In Comicalamities* (May 7), *Felix In Arabianatics* (May 13), *Felix In In And Outlaws* (May 27), *Felix In Outdoor Indore* (June 10), *Felix In Futuritzy* (June 24), *Felix In Astronomeows* (July 8), *Felix In Jungle Bungles* (July 22) and *Felix In The Last Life* (Aug. 5).

FULLER PEP

Like Paul Terry's Farmer Al Falfa character, Pat Powers introduced this series of animated films about a benign farmer, Fuller Pep, drawn by F. M. Follett in 1916–17. The series appeared in some Hollywood trade paper listing as "Mr. Fuller Pep." *A Pat Powers Production released through Universal.*

1916:   *He Tries Mesmerism* (May 11), *He Dabbles In The Pond* (May 17) and *He Breaks For The Beach* (May 31).

1917:   *He Celebrates His Wedding Anniversary* (Jan. 14), *He Goes To The Country* (Jan. 21), *His Wife Goes For A Rest* (Feb. 4), *He Does Some Quick Moving* (Feb. 18), *An Old Bird Pays Him A Visit* (Mar. 14) and *His Day Of Rest* (Mar. 11).

FUN FROM THE PRESS

In 1923, Max Fleischer produced this series of animated sequences adapted from *The Literary Digest.* The series was directed by Max's brother, Dave Fleischer. *An Out of the Inkwell Films Production.*

GAUMONT REEL LIFE

This series of technical cartoons appeared in a weekly magazine film series in 1917. *A Gaumont Company Production.*

1917:   *A One Man Submarine* (Apr. 5), *A Flying Torpedo* (Apr. 12), *Cargo Boats Of Tomorrow* (Apr. 26) and *The Liberty Loan* (June 7).

GLACKENS CARTOONS

Famed painter/illustrator W. L. Glackens animated and directed this series of beautifully executed humorous drawings comparing modern customs with those of bygone days. *A Bray Production.*

1916: *Stone Age Roost Robber, My, How Times Have Changed, Yes, Times Have Changed, When Knights Were Bold* and *A Stone Age Adventure.*

GOODRICH DIRT

In the tradition of legendary film tramp Charlie Chaplin, Wallace A. Carlson animated these skillfully drawn adventures of a cheerful hobo and his optimistic dog in pursuit of a good meal or a dishonest buck. Carlson, who started in animation in 1915, ended the series two years after its debut. He went on to direct an animated version of *The Gumps. A Bray Production released by Paramount.*

1917: *Goodrich Dirt At The Seashore* (Sept. 3), *Goodrich Dirt Lunch Detective* (Oct. 1), *Goodrich Dirt At The Training Camp* (Nov. 5), *Goodrich Dirt's Amateur Night* (Dec. 2) and *Goodrich Dirt And The $1000 Reward* (Dec. 23).

1918: *Goodrich Dirt And The Duke De Whatanob* (Jan. 6), *Goodrich Dirt's Bear Hunt* (Feb. 11), *Goodrich Dirt In The Barber Business* (Mar. 18), *Goodrich Dirt Mat Artist* (Apr. 6), *Goodrich Dirt Bad Man Tamer* (May 6), *Goodrich Dirt In Darkest Africa* (May 27), *Goodrich Dirt King Of Spades* (June 17), *Goodrich Dirt The Cop* (July 8), *Goodrich Dirt In The Dark And Stormy Knight* (Aug. 5), *Goodrich Dirt Coin Collector* (Aug. 26), *Goodrich Dirt Millionaire* (Sept. 30), *Goodrich Dirt When Wishes Come True* (Oct. 29) and *Goodrich Drit Cowpuncher* (Dec. 4).

1919: *Goodrich Dirt In Spot Goes Romeoing* (Jan. 6), *Goodrich Dirt In A Difficult Delivery* (Jan. 22) and *Goodrich Dirt Hypnotist* (Feb. 26).

THE GUMPS

Harry Grossman of Celebrated Players contracted this series of 13 episodes based on cartoonist Sidney Smith's nationally syndicated strip. Mostly comprised of live action, the films also featured animated sequences by Wallace Carlson, who previously animated and directed the Dreamy Dud series for Essanay. *A Celebrated Film Players Corp. release.*

1920: *Andy's Dancing Lesson* (June 5), *Flat Hunting* (June 5), *Andy Visits His Mama-In-Law* (June 5), *Andy Spends A Quiet Day At Home* (June 26), *Andy Plays Golf* (June 26), *Andy's Wash Day* (June 26), *Andy On Skates* (June 26), *Andy's Mother-In-Law Pays Him A Visit* (June 26), *Andy On A Diet* (July 3), *Andy's Night Out* (July 3), *Andy And Min At The Theatre* (Aug. 14), *Andy Visits The Osteopath* (Aug. 14), *Andy's Inter-Ruben Guest* (Oct. 23), *Andy Redecorates His Flat* (Oct. 23), *Andy The Model* (Oct. 23), *Accidents Will Happen* (Oct. 23), *Andy Fights The High Cost Of Living* (Oct. 23), *Militant Min* (Oct. 23), *Ice Box Episodes* (Oct. 23), *Wim And Wigor* (Oct. 23), *Equestrian Andy* (Oct. 23), *Andy The Hero* (Oct. 23), *Andy's Picnic* (Oct. 23), *Andy The Chicken Farmer* (Oct. 23), *Andy The Actor* (Oct. 23), *Andy*

At Shady Rest (Oct. 23), *Andy On The Beach* (Oct. 23), *Andy On Pleasure Bent* (Oct. 23), *Howdy Partner* (Oct. 23), *There's A Reason* (Nov. 27), *Ship Ahoy* (Nov. 27), *The Toreador* (Nov. 27), *The Broilers* (Nov. 27), *Flicker Flicker Little Star* (Nov. 27), *Mixing Business With Pleasure* (Nov. 27), *Up She Goes* (Nov. 27), *A-Hunting We Will Go* (Nov. 27) and *Get To Work* (Nov. 27).

1921: *The Best Of Luck* (Feb. 12), *The Promoters* (Feb. 12), *The Masked Ball* (Feb. 12), *Giver 'Er The Gas* (Feb. 12), *Chester's Cat* (Feb. 12), *Rolling Around* (Feb. 12), *Andy's Holiday* (Feb. 12), *Andy Has A Caller* (Feb. 12), *Le Cuspidoree* (Feb. 12), *Andy's Cow* (Feb. 26), *Jilted And Jolted* (Mar. 19), *A Terrible Time* (Mar. 19), *A Quiet Little Game* (May 14), *Andy's Dog Day* (May 14), *Fatherly Love* (June) and *The Chicken Thief* (June).

HAPPY HOOLIGAN

Once a week, the Hearst newspaper syndicate produced new installments of its ever popular Hearst-Vitagraph News Pictorial, which highlighted the week's news and were screened before the main feature at movie theaters across the country. At the end of each production were alternating adventures based on many of Hearst's comic strip favorites: Judge Rummy, Maud the Mule, Jerry On The Job, the Katzenjammer Kids and Tad's Daffydils.

Happy Hooligan was another Hearst strip to gain national exposure via these weekly productions. Like the strip, Jiggs and Miggs appeared as supporting characters in the film series. Episodes generally ran three minutes in length.

Gregory La Cava, who later graduated to the rank of feature film director, directed the series until William C. Nolan and Ben Sharpsteen assumed this responsibility in the 1920s. *An International Film Service Production released by Educational Film Corp. and Goldwyn-Bray.*

1916: *He Tries The Movies Again* (Oct. 9).

1917: *Ananias Has Nothing On Hooligan* (Jan. 20), *Happy Hooligan, Double-Cross Nurse* (Mar. 25), *The New Recruit* (Apr. 8), *Three Strikes You're Out* (Apr. 26), *Around The World In Half An Hour* (June 9), *The Great Offensive* (July 1), *The White Hope* (July 29), *Happy Gets The Razoo* (Sept. 2), *Happy Hooligan In The Zoo* (Sept. 9), *The Tanks* (Sept. 16), *Happy Hooligan In Soft* (Oct. 7), *Happy Hooligan At The Picnic* (Oct. 16), *The Tale Of A Fish* (Oct. 16), *The Tale Of A Monkey* (Nov. 25), *Happy Hooligan At The Circus* (Dec. 8) and *Bullets And Bull* (Dec. 16).

1918: *Hearts And Horses* (Jan. 13) and *All For The Ladies* (Feb. 10).

Educational Film Corp. Releases
1918: *Doing His Bit* (Apr. 19), *Throwing The Bull* (June 17), *Mopping Up A Million* (July 22), *His Dark Past* (Aug. 5), *Tramp Tramp Tramp* (Aug. 12), *A Bold Bad Man* (Sept.), *The Latest In Underwear* (Oct.) and *Where Are The Papers* (Dec.).

1919: *Der Wash On Der Line* (Jan.) *Knocking The "H" Out Of Heine* (Feb.), *A Smash-Up In China* (Mar. 22), *The Tale Of A Shirt* (June 22), *A Wee Bit O' Scotch* (June 29), *Transatlantic Flight* (July 20), *The Great Handicap* (Aug. 24), *Jungle Jumble* (Sept. 7), *After The Ball* (Sept. 28) and *Business Is Business* (Nov. 23).

Goldwyn-Bray Comic
1920: *The Great Umbrella Mystery* (Apr. 17), *Turn To The Right Leg* (June 2), *All For The Love Of A Girl* (June 18), *His Country Cousin* (July 3), *Cupid's Advice* (Aug.), *Happy Hooldini* (Sept. 11), *Apollo* (Sept. 18), *A Doity Deed* (Nolan/Oct. 25), *The Village Blacksmith* (Sharpsteen/Oct. 27), *A Romance Of '76* (Nov. 22), *Dr. Jekyll And Mr. Zip* (Dec. 8) and *Happy Hooligan In Oil* (Nolan/Dec. 23).

1921: *Fatherly Love* (Nolan/Jan. 3), *Roll Your Own* (Jan. 3) and *A Close Shave* (Apr. 29).

HARDROCK DOME

Assorted calamities were the end result for this eccentric detective, who appeared briefly in this series produced by J. R. Bray. *Directed by Pat Sullivan. A Bray Production.*

1917: *Hardrock Dome, The Great Detective* (Jan. 29), *Episode 2* (Feb. 5), *Episode 3* (Feb. 12) and *Origin Of The Shinny.*

HESANUT

A Kalem Company Production.

1914: *Hesanut Hunts Wild Game* (Sept. 25), *Hesanut Buys An Auto* (Oct. 10), *Hesanut Builds A Skyscraper* (Nov.) and *Hesanut At A Vaudeville Show* (Dec.).

1915: *A Night In New Jersey* (Jan. 16).

HISTORICAL CARTOONS

This timely, short-lived series propagandized World War I through related stories which were both topical and political in nature. *Produced by J. R. Bray. A Bray Production.*

1917–18: *The Bronco Buster, Stung!, Awakening Of America, Evolution Of The Dachsund, Sic 'Em Cat, Uncle Sam's Dinner Party, Peril Of Prussiaism, Putting Friz On The Water Wagon, Von Loon's 25,000-Mile Gun, Kaiser's Surprise Party, The Watched Pot, Von Loon's Non-Capturable Gun, The Greased Pole, Long Arm Of Law And Order, A German Trick That Failed, Uncle Sam's Coming Problem, Pictures In The Fire* and *Private Bass: His Pass.*

HISTORIETS

A series of animated cartoons in color. *A Reel Colors Inc. Production.*

1924: *The Teapot Dome* (May), *Famous Sayings Of Famous Americans* (May), *Witty Sayings Of Witty Frenchmen* (May) and *Witty Naughty Thoughts* (May).

HODGE PODGE

No main characters starred in this series of animated sequences based on specific themes, such as pioneering the movie business, which was distributed with live–action magazine films. *Produced by Lyman H. Howe. A Lyman H. Howe Films Company Production released by Educational Films Corporation.*

1922: *King Winter* (Oct. 8), *Sea Elephants* (Nov. 1) and *The Garden Of Geysers* (Dec. 8).

1923: *Hot Shots* (Jan. 23), *Mrs. Hippo* (Jan. 6), *Fishing For Tarpon* (Mar. 14), *Speed Demons* (May 2), *Shooting The Earth* (May 17), *A Flivver Elopement* (July 18), *The Cat And The Fiddle* (July 18), *Dipping In The Deep* (Aug. 11), *Why The Globe Trotter Trots* (Sept. 29), *Speedville* (Oct. 16), *The Bottom Of The Sea* (Nov. 19) and *Liquid Love* (Dec. 17).

1924: *A Sailor's Life* (Jan. 16), *Movie Pioneer* (Feb. 9), *Jumping Jacks* (Mar. 13), *The Realm Of Sport* (Apr. 19), *A Tiny Tour Of The U.S.A.* (May 1), *Snapshots Of The Universe* (June 12), *Frozen Water* (July 26), *Hazardous Hunting* (Aug. 29), *A Crazy Quilt Of Travel* (Sept. 18), *Whirligigs* (Oct. 16), *Earth's Oddities* (Nov. 28) and *Hi-Flyers* (Dec. 28).

1925: *Topsy Turvy Travel* (Jan. 25), *Lots Of Knots* (Feb. 16), *Movie Morsels* (Mar. 27), *The Village School* (Apr. 19), *Earth's Other Half* (May 26), *Mexican Melody* (June 16), *Travel Treasures* (June 30), *Pictorial Proverbs* (Aug. 1), *The Story Teller* (Aug. 22), *Knicknacks Of Knowledge* (Oct. 18), *Magical Movies* (Nov. 16) and *A Mythical Monster* (Dec. 21).

1926: *Mother Goose's Movies* (Jan. 20), *Criss Cross Cruise* (Feb. 16), *Congress Of Celebrities* (Mar. 20), *Neptune's Domain* (Apr. 12), *From A To Z Thru Filmdom* (May 23), *Peeking At The Planets* (June 22), *Chips Off The Old Block* (July 25), *Alligator's Paradise* (Aug. 22), *A Merrygoround Of Travel* (Sept. 19), *Figures Of Fancy* (Nov. 28) and *Movie Medley* (Dec. 26).

1927: *A Cluster Of Kings* (Jan. 6), *The Wise Old Owl* (Feb. 13), *Climbing Into Cloudland* (Mar. 13), *A Bird Of Flight* (Apr. 17), *A Scenic Treasure Chest* (May 22), *Tales Of A Traveler* (June 16), *Capers Of A Camera* (July 17), *Bubbles Of Geography* (Aug. 8), *Delving Into The Dictionary* (Aug. 30), *Here And There In Travel Land* (Oct. 16), *Models In Mud* (Nov. 13) and *A Whirl Of Activity* (Dec. 11).

1928: *Recollections Of A Rover* (Jan. 8), *Star Shots* (Jan. 28), *How To Please The Public* (Mar. 31), *Nicknames* (Apr. 8), *The Wandering Toy* (May 19), *Pictorial Tidbits* (June 19), *Conquering The Colorado* (July 3), *The Peep Show* (Aug. 7), *On The Move* (Sept. 28), *Glorious Adventure* (Nov. 2) and *A Patchwork Of Pictures* (Nov. 30).

1929: *Shifting Scenes* (Jan. 11), *Question Marks* (Jan 25) and *A Dominion Of Diversity* (Mar. 15).

INK-RAVINGS

Milt Gross wrote, animated and directed this brief series of cartoons for the *Bray Magazine. A Bray Production.*

1922: *Scrap Hangers* (Dec. 16) and *Taxes* (Dec. 30).

1923: *If We Reversed* (Jan.).

INKLINGS

Max Fleischer produced this series featuring different types of animation between 1924 and 1925. Films were not released until three years later. *Directed by Dave Fleischer. A Red Seal Pictures Production.*

INKWELL IMPS

Ko-Ko the Clown, who first starred in Max Fleischer's *Out Of The Inkwell* series, reappeared in this 1927 Paramount series produced by Alfred Weiss and Out of the Inkwell Films. Weiss was removed from the role of producer after his company went bankrupt, and Paramount contracted the Fleischer Studios to take over production of the series (due to copyright changes, the character's name was hyphenated for the series). In 1929, the series was converted to sound and became known as *Talkartoons. An Out of the Inkwell Films, Inc. and Fleischer Studios Production released by Paramount Pictures.*

1927: (Dates listed are copyright dates.) *Ko-Ko Makes 'Em Laugh, Ko-Ko Plays Pool* (Aug. 6), *Ko-Ko's Kane* (Aug. 20), *Ko-Ko The Knight* (Sept. 3), *Ko-Ko Hops Off* (Sept. 17), *Ko-Ko The Kop* (Oct. 1), *Ko-Ko Explores* (Oct. 15), *Ko-Ko Chops Suey* (Oct. 29), *Ko-Ko's Klock* (Nov. 26), *Ko-Ko's Quest* (Dec. 10), *Ko-Ko The Kid* (Dec. 24), *Ko-Ko Back Tracks* and *Ko-Ko Needles The Boss.*

1928: *Ko-Ko's Kink* (Jan. 7), *Ko-Ko's Kozy Korner* (Jan. 21), *Ko-Ko's Germ Jam* (Feb. 4), *Ko-Ko's Bawth* (Feb. 18), *Ko-Ko Smokes* (Mar. 3), *Ko-Ko's Tattoo* (Mar. 17), *Ko-Ko's Earth Control* (Mar. 31), *Ko-Ko's Hot Dog* (Apr. 14), *Ko-Ko's Haunted House* (Apr. 28), *Ko-Ko's Lamps Aladdin* (May 12), *Ko-Ko Squeals* (May 26), *Ko-Ko's Field Daze* (June 9), *Ko-Ko Goes Over* (June 23), *Ko-Ko's Catch* (July 7), *Ko-Ko's War Dogs* (July 21), *Ko-Ko's Chase* (Aug. 11), *Ko-Ko Heaves Ho* (Aug. 25), *Ko-Ko's Big Pull* (Sept. 7), *Ko-Ko Cleans Up* (Sept. 21), *Ko-Ko's Parade* (Oct. 8), *Ko-Ko's Dog Gone* (Oct. 22), *Ko-Ko In The Rough* (Nov. 3), *Ko-Ko's Magic* (Nov. 16), *Ko-Ko On The Track* (Dec. 4), *Ko-Ko's Act* (Dec. 17) and *Ko-Ko's Courtship* (Dec. 28).

1929: *No Eyes Today* (Jan. 11), *Noise Annoys Ko-Ko* (Jan. 25), *Ko-Ko Beats Time* (Feb. 8), *Ko-Ko's Reward* (Feb. 23), *Ko-Ko's Hot Ink* (Mar. 8), *Ko-Ko's Crib* (Mar. 23), *Ko-Ko's Saxophonies* (Apr. 5), *Ko-Ko's Knock Down* (Apr. 19), *Ko-Ko's Signals* (May 3), *Ko-Ko's Conquest* (May 31), *Ko-Ko's Focus* (May 17), *Ko-Ko's Harem Scarum* (June 14), *Ko-Ko's Big Sale* (June 28), *Ko-Ko's Hypnotism* (July 12) and *Chemical Ko-Ko* (July 26).

JERRY ON THE JOB

At the ripe age of 18, Walter Lantz was assigned to animate this series, spotlighting the adventures of a diminutive but exceedingly active and resourceful office boy named Jerry. Created by Walter Hoban, *Jerry On The Job* originated as a daily strip in the *New York Journal.* Like other Hearst cartoons, this animated version appeared at the tail end of weekly Hearst-Vitagraph News Pictorials.

In the animated episodes, stories often revolved around Jerry's ineptitude. (In one film, his attempt to soothe his boss's aching tooth results in his successfully uprooting the tooth—and the train station after stringing the tooth to the outbound train.) Two supporting characters rounded the series: Fred Blink, a young rival for Jerry's job, and his younger brother, Herman. *Directed by Vernon Stallings and Gregory La Cava. A Bray Production released by International Film Service.*

1916: *Jerry Ships A Circus* (Nov. 13) and *On The Cannibal Isle* (Dec. 18).

1917: *A Tankless Job* (Jan. 21), *Jerry Saves The Navy* (Feb. 18), *Quinine* (May 20), *Love And Lunch* (July 5) and *On The Border* (Aug. 19).

Goldwyn-Bray Pictographs

1919: *Where Has My Little Coal Bin* (La Cava/Sept. 6), *Pigs In Clover* (La Cava/Nov. 10), *How Could William Tell* (La Cava/Nov. 26), *Sauce For The Goose* (Stallings/Dec. 9) and *Sufficiency* (Stallings/Dec. 23).

1920: *The Chinese Question* (Jan. 6), *A Warm Reception* (Feb. 10), *The Wrong Track* (Feb. 27), *The Tale Of A Wag* (Mar. 9), *A Very Busy Day* (La Cava/Mar. 23), *Spring Fever* (La Cava/Apr. 21), *Swinging His Vacation* (La Cava/May 29),

Max and Dave Fleischer's most popular silent cartoon character, Ko—Ko the Clown, ardently watches his musical note—eating friend co—orchestrate the melody in In The Good Old Summertime (1929). (Courtesy: Blackhawk Films)

A Punk Piper (Stallings/June 12), *A Quick Change* (Stallings/ July 16), *The Trained Horse* (Stallings/July 27), *Dots And Dashes* (Stallings/Aug. 26), *Water Water Everywhere* (Stallings/Sept. 14), *Jerry And The Five Fifteen Train* (Stallings/Oct. 2), *Beated By A Hare* (Stallings/Oct. 7), *A Tough Pull* (Stallings/Oct. 7), *The Bomb Idea* (Stallings/Nov. 6), *A Thrilling Drill* (Stallings/Dec. 14) and *Without Coal* (Stallings/Dec. 28).

JOE BOKO

Wallace Carlson wrote, produced and directed this short—lived series. *A Historic Feature Film Co./Essanay Film/Powers-Universal release.*

1914: *Joe Boko Breaking Into The Big League* (Oct. 10).

1915: *Joe Boko In A Close Shave* (June 1) and *Joe Boko In Saved By Gasoline* (Aug. 27).

1916: *Joe Boko* (Apr. 4/Canimated Nooz Pictorial) and *Joe Boko's Adventures* (Feb. 9).

JOYS AND GLOOM

Controversial series covering topical news events in a satirical manner based on the newspaper strip by Tom E. Powers. *Directed by Gregory La Cava. An International Film Service Production.*

1916: *Bang Go The Rifles* (Jan. 4), *Old Doc Gloom* (Feb. 11) and *The Joys Elope* (Mar. 1).

1916–17: *Adventures of Mr. Nobody Holme, Cooks Versus Chefs, Feet Is Feet, Never Again, A Newlywed Phable, Parcel Post Pete: Not All His Troubles Are Little Ones, Parcel Post Pete's Nightmare, Phable Of A Busted Romance, Phable Of A Phat Woman, Phable Of Sam And Bill, 'Twas But A Dream* and *Who Said They Never Come Back?*

JUDGE RUMMY

Created as a Hearst comic strip by Tad Dorgan, originator of the term "hot dog," this series featured the misadventures of a dog court justice, whose passion for upholding the law was equalled by his love for cigars. The series was one of several to utilize strip characters originally syndicated by the Hearst newspaper syndicate and transformed into animated series. *Directed by Gregory La Cava, Jack King, Burt Gillett and Grim Natwick. An International Film Service Production released by Goldwyn-Bray.*

1918: *Judge Rummy's Off Day* (Aug. 19), *Hash And Hypnotism* (Oct.) and *Twinkle Twinkle* (Dec.).

1919: *Snappy Cheese* (Mar. 22), *The Sawdust Trail* (June 22), *The Breath Of A Nation* (June 29), *Good Night Nurse* (Aug. 24), *Judge Rummy's Miscue* (Sept.), *Rubbing It In* (Oct.) and *A Sweet Pickle* (Nov.).

Goldwyn-Bray Comic
1920: *Shimmie Shivers* (Apr. 21), *A Fitting Gift* (May 7), *His Last Legs* (May 25), *Smokey Smokes* (La Cava/June 6),

Doctors Should Have Patience (June 19), *A Fish Story* (July 3), *The Last Rose Of Summer* (July 17), *The Fly Guy* (Aug. 26), *Shedding The Profiteer* (Sept. 5), *The Sponge Man* (Sept. 22) and *The Prize Dance* (Oct. 3).

International Cartoons
1920: *Hypnotice Hooch* (Oct. 26), *The Hooch Ball* (Nov. 3), *Kiss Me* (King/Nov. 3), *Snap Judgement* (Gillett/Nov. 22), *Why Change Your Husband* (King/Nov. 22), *Bear Facts* (La Cava/Dec. 10) and *Yes Dear* (Natwick/Dec. 12).

1921: *Too Much Pep* (King/Jan. 4), *The Chicken Thief* (Natwick/Jan. 17) and *The Skating Fool* (Mar. 15).

JUDGE'S CROSSWORD PUZZLES

John Colman Terry produced, directed and animated this series of animated crossword puzzles for Educational Pictures. *A Crossword Film Company Production released by Educational Pictures Corporation.*

1925: *No. 1* (Jan. 31), *No. 2* (Mar. 8), *No. 3* (Mar. 15), *No. 4* (Mar. 22), *No. 5* (Mar. 29), *No. 6* (Apr. 5), *No. 7* (Apr. 12), *No. 8* (Apr. 19), *No. 9* (Apr. 26) and *No. 10* (May 3).

KARTOON KOMICS

This series of animated creations was produced, written and directed by Harry S. Palmer. *A Gaumont Company Production released by Mutual Pictures.*

1916: *Our National Vaudeville* (Mar. 4), *The Trials of Thoughtless Thaddeus* (Mar. 12), *Signs Of Spring* (Mar. 26), *Nosey Ned* (Apr. 2), *The Greatest Show On Earth* (Apr. 5), *Watchful Waiting* (Apr. 12), *Nosey Ned* (Apr. 26), *Estelle And The Movie Hero* (May 3), *The Escapes of Estelle* (May 10), *As An Umpire Nosey Ned Is An Onion* (May 17), *Nosey Ned And His New Straw Lid* (May 24), *The Gnat Gets Estelle's Goat* (May 31), *The Escapades Of Estelle* (June 7), *Johnny's Stepmother And The Cat* (June 14), *Johnny's Romeo* (June 28), *Scrambled Events* (July 5), *Weary's Dog Dream* (July 12), *Old Pfool Pfancy At The Beach* (July 26), *Music As A Hair Restorer* (Aug. 2), *Kuring Korpulent Karrie* (Aug. 16), *Mr. Jocko From Jungletown* (Aug. 23), *The Tale Of A Whale* (Sept. 6), *Nosey Ned Commandeers An Army Mule* (Sept. 13), *Pigs* (Sept. 20), *Golf* (Sept. 27), *Abraham And The Oppossum* (Oct. 4), *Babbling Bess* (Oct. 11), *Inspiration* (Oct. 18), *I'm Insured* (Oct. 25), *Babbling Bess* (Nov. 8), *Haystack Horace* (Nov. 15), *What's Home Without A Dog* (Nov. 22), *Diary Of A Murderer* (Nov. 29), *Our Forefathers* (Dec. 6), *Curfew Shall Not Ring* (Dec. 13), *Twas Ever Thus* (Dec. 20) and *Mr. Bonehead Gets Wrecked* (Dec. 27).

1917: *Miss Catnip Goes To The Movies* (Jan. 3), *The Gourmand* (Jan. 1), *Mr. Common Peepful Investigates* (Jan. 17), *Absent Minded Willie* (Jan. 24), *Never Again* (Jan. 31), *The Old Roue Visualizes* (Feb. 7), *Taming Tony* (Feb. 14), *Polly's Day At Home* (Feb. 21), *The Elusive Idea* (Feb. 28), *Ratus Runs Amuck* (Mar. 7) and *They Say Pigs Is Pigs* (July 14).

THE KATZENJAMMER KIDS

Cartoonist Rudolph Dirk first developed this well-known newspaper strip about the life of a German family in 1897, later adapting it into an animated cartoon series of its own. Spaghetti–bearded Captain, who spoke broken English, commanded this cartoon troupe comprised of the Inspector, Mamma and squat, wavy–haired sons, Hans and Fritz.

Filmmaker Gregory La Cava produced and directed the series under the International Film Service banner. Production was halted because of anti–German feelings that spread throughout the United States during World War I. The series was later revived in sound shorts at MGM in 1938 but renamed *The Captain And The Kids. An International Film Service Production released by Pathé Film Exchange Inc. and Educational Pictures.*

Pathé Film Exchange
1916: *The Captain Goes 'A-Swimming* (Dec. 11).

1917: *Der Great Bear Hunt* (Jan. 8), *Der Captain Is Examined For Insurance* (Feb. 11), *Der Captain Goets A-Flivvering* (Apr. 1), *Robbers And Thieves* (Apr. 12), *Sharks Is Sharks* (Apr. 26), *Down Where The Limburger Blows* (June 9), *20,000 Legs Under The Sea* (June 9), *Der Captain Discovers The North Pole* (July 8), *Der Captain's Valet* (Aug. 25), *Der End Of Der Limit* (Oct. 14), *By The Sad Sea Waves* (Oct. 16), *The Mysterious Yarn* (Nov. 11), *Der Last Straw* (Nov. 18), *A Tempest In A Paint Pot* (Dec. 8), *Fast And Furious* (Dec. 23) and *Peace And Quiet* (Dec. 30).

1918: *Der Captain's Birthday* (Jan. 6), *Rub-A-Dud-Dud* (Jan. 20), *Rheumatics* (Jan. 27), *Policy And Pie* (Feb. 10), *Burglars* (Feb. 24), *Too Many Cooks* (Mar. 3), and *Spirits* (Mar. 10).

Educational Pictures
1918: *Vanity And Vengeance* (Apr. 22), *The Two Twins* (May 6), *His Last Will* (May 13), *Der Black Mitt* (May 20), *Fisherman's Luck* (May 27), *Up In The Air* (June 3), *Swat The Fly* (June 10), *The Best Man Loses* (June 24), *Crabs Is Crabs* (July 1), *A Picnic For Two* (July 8), *A Heathen Benefit* (July 15), *Pep* (July 19) and *War Gardens* (Aug.).

KEEN CARTOONS

Henry W. Zippy and Jerry McDub were central characters in this animated series written, animated and directed by Charles F. Howell, Lee Connor and H. M. Freck. *A Keen Cartoon Corporation Production.*

1916: *Henry W. Zippy Buys A Motor Boat* (Howell/Oct.), *Slinky The Yegg* (Connor/Oct.), *Jerry McDub Collects Some Accidental Insurance* (Freck/Oct.), *Henry W. Zippy Buys A Pet Pup* (Howell/Dec.) and *Dr. Zippy Opens A Sanatorium* (Howell/Dec.).

1917: *Mose Is Cured* (Jan. 1), *The Old Forty-niner* (Jan. 8), *Jeb Jenkins The Village Genius* (Jan. 15), *Zoo-illogical Studies* (Feb. 5), *A Dangerous Girl* (Feb. 12), *The Fighting Blood Of Jerry McDub* (Freck/Feb. 28), *Mr. Coon* (Mar.) and *When Does A Hen Lay* (Howell/May 9).

KEEPING UP WITH THE JONESES

A series of cartoons based on the comic strip by Arthur "Pop" Momand. *Directed by Harry S. Palmer. A Gaumont Company Production.*

1915: *The Dancing Lesson* (Sept. 13), *The Reelem Moving Picture Co.* (Oct. 6), *The Family Adopt A Camel* (Oct. 13), *Pa Feigns Sickness* (Oct. 20), *The Family's Taste In Modern Furniture* (Oct. 27), *Moving Day* (Nov. 3), *The Family In Mexico* (Nov. 10), *Pa Takes A Flier In Stocks* (Nov. 17), *Pa Buys A Flivver* (Nov. 24), *Pa Lectures On The War* (Dec. 1), *The Skating Craze* (Dec. 7), *Pa Sees Some New Styles* (Dec. 14), *Ma Tries To Reduce* (Dec. 21) and *Pa Dreams He Wins The War* (Dec. 28).

1916: *The Pet Parrot* (Jan. 4), *Ma Drives A Car* (Jan. 11), *The Family Visits Florida* (Jan. 23), *Pa Fishes In An Alligator Pond* (Jan. 30), *Pa Tries To Write* (Feb. 6), *Pa Dreams He Is Lost* (Feb. 13), *Pa And Ma Have Their Fortunes Told* (Feb. 20) and *Pa Rides A Goat* (Feb. 27).

KRAZY KAT

Originally conceived as a daily syndicated Hearst newspaper strip, love–sick Krazy Kat and pesky Ignatz the Mouse headlined their own animated series under the guidance of their creator, George Herriman. Like Pat Sullivan's *Felix The Cat,* Krazy's onscreen trials and tribulations centered around intellectual fantasies.

In transferring the strip to the screen, however, the Hearst animators were not completely faithful to the original concept of the strip. Krazy Kat bore no resemblance to Herriman's drawing, and Offisa Bull Pup, a primary character in the comic panel, was rarely used. Even the humor was diluted. Animator James "Shamus" Culhane, a series inker, once wrote: "The stories were heavy–handed chases and primitive acting. Every gag was automatically repeated three times."

Small budgets played a major factor in the poor production values of these cartoons. Most films were grounded out at a cost of $900, so "the animation department was obliged to bat out animation footage at breakneck speed . . . time only for breathing," noted series animator I. Klein.

The series might have benefited greatly if Herriman had been more involved. He nominally supervised the series, and instead the animation was chiefly produced by Klein, Leon Searl, William C. Nolan, Bert Green, Frank Moser, Art Davis, Al Rose and Sid Marcus, all top–notch animators, with little creative input from him. As a result, the series was given a different direction by directors H. E. Hancock, William C. Nolan, Manny Gould and Ben Harrison, who supervised the cartoons.

Initial production of the series was performed in conjunction with Hearst's International Film Service. After a short–lived association with International, the series was later distributed by R–C Pictures and the Paramount–Famous Lasky

Corporation. *An International Film Service/Bray Productions/Winkler Pictures Production.*

The Hearst-Vitagraph News Pictorial
1916: *Introducing Krazy Kat And Ignatz Mouse* (Feb. 18), *Krazy Kat And Ignatz Mouse Believe In Signs* (Feb. 21), *Krazy Kat And Ignatz Mouse Discuss The Letter G* (Feb. 25), *Kratz Kat A-Wooing* (Feb. 29), *Krazy Kat And Ignatz Mouse: A Duet, He Made Me Love Him* (Mar. 3), *Krazy Kat And Ignatz Mouse In Their One-Act Tragedy, The Tale Of The Nude Tail* (Mar. 6), *Krazy Kat, Bugologist* (Mar. 13), *Krazy Kat And Ignatz Mouse At The Circus* (Mar. 17), *Krazy Kat Demi-Tasse* (Mar. 21), *Krazy Kat To The Rescue* (Mar. 24), *Krazy Kat Invalid* (Mar. 27), *Krazy Kat At The Switchboard* (Apr. 3), *Krazy Kat The Hero* (Apr. 7) and *A Tale That Is Knot* (Apr. 14).

International Film Service Cartoons
1916: *Krazy Kat At Looney Park* (June 17), *A Tempest In A Paint Pot* (July 3), *A Grid–Iron Hero* (Oct. 9), *The Missing One* (Nov. 27) and *Krazy Kat Takes Little Katrina For An Airing* (Dec. 23).

1917: *Throwing The Bull* (Feb. 4), *Roses And Thorns* (Mar. 11), *Robbers And Thieves* (Apr. 12), *The Cook* (Apr. 29), *Moving Day* (May 27), *All Is Not Gold That Glitters* (June 24) and *A Krazy Katastrophe* (Aug. 5).

Bray Productions
1920: *The Great Cheese Robbery* (Jan. 16), *Love's Labor Lost* (Stallings/Jan. 30), *The Best Mouse Loses* (Stallings/Mar. 3), *A Tax From The Rear* (Stallings/Apr. 14), *Kats Is Kats* (Stallings/June 4), *The Chinese Honeymoon* (July 3) and *A Family Affair* (Oct. 25).

1921: *The Hinges On The Bar Room Door* (Stallings/Jan. 8), *How I Became Krazy* (Stallings/Jan. 26), *The Awful Spook* (Jan. 21), *Scrambled Eagles* (Stallings/Jan. 28) and *The Wireless Wire-Walkers* (Stallings/Feb. 26).

Winkler Pictures (released by R.C. Pictures Corp.)
1925: *Hot Dogs* (Oct. 1), *The Smoke Eater* (Oct. 15), *A Uke-Calamity* (Nov. 1), *The Flight That Failed* (Nov. 15), *Hair Raiser* (Nov. 15), *The New Champ* (Nov. 30), *James And Gems* (Dec. 1) and *Monkey Business* (Dec. 15).

1926: *Battling For Barleycorn* (Jan. 1), *A Picked Romance* (Jan. 15), *The Ghost Fakir* (Feb. 1), *Sucker Game* (Feb. 15), *Back To Backing* (Mar. 1), *Double Crossed* (Mar. 15), *Invalid* (Mar. 28), *Scents And Nonsense* (Apr. 1), *Feather Pushers* (Apr. 15), *Cops Suey* (May 1), *The Chicken Chaser* (Nolan/Sept. 2), *East Is Best* (Nolan/Sept. 22), *Shore Enough* (Nolan/Oct. 11), *Watery Gravey* (Nolan/Oct. 25), *Cheese It* (Nov. 8), *Dots And Dashes* (Nov. 22) and *Gold Struck* (Dec. 10).

1927: *Horse Play* (Jan. 3), *Busy Birds* (Jan. 17), *Sharp Flats* (Jan. 31), *Kiss Crossed* (Feb. 14), *A Fool's Errand* (Feb. 28), *Stomach Trouble* (Mar. 14), *The Rug Fiend* (Mar. 28), *Hire A Hall* (Apr. 11), *Don Go On* (Apr. 23), *Burnt Up* (May 9), *Night Owl* (May 23), *On The Trail* (June 6), *Passing The Hat* (June 20), *Best Wishes* (July 4), *Black And White* (July 10) and *Wild Rivals* (July 18).

Paramount–Famous–Lasky
1927: *Sealing Whacks* (Aug. 1), *Tired Wheels* (Aug. 13), *Bee Cause* (Aug. 15), *Web Feet* (Aug. 27), *Skinny* (Aug. 29), *School Daze* (Sept. 10), *Rail Rode* (Sept. 24), *Aero Nuts* (Oct. 8), *Topsy Turvy* (Oct. 22), *Pie Curs* (Nov. 5), *For Crime's Sake* (Harrison, Gould/Nov. 19), *Milk Made* (Dec. 3), *Stork Exchange* (Dec. 17) and *Grid Ironed* (Harrison, Gould/Dec. 31).

1928: *Pig Styles* (Jan. 14), *Shadow Theory* (Jan. 28), *Ice Boxed* (Feb. 11), *A Hunger Stroke* (Feb. 25), *Wire And Fired* (Mar. 10), *Love Sunk* (Mar. 24), *Tong Tied* (Apr. 7), *A Bum Steer* (Apr. 21), *Gold Bricks* (May 5), *The Long Count* (May 19), *The Patent Medicine Kid* (June 2), *Stage Coached* (June 16), *The Rain Dropper* (June 30), *A Companionate Mirage* (July 14), *News Reeling* (Aug. 4), *Baby Feud* (Aug. 16), *Sea Sword* (Sept. 5), *The Show Vote* (Sept. 15), *The Phantom Trail* (Sept. 29), *Come Easy, Go Slow* (Oct. 15), *Beaches And Scream* (Oct. 29), *Nicked Nags* (Nov. 9), *Liar Bird* (Nov. 23), *Still Waters* (Dec. 7) and *Night Owls* (Dec. 22).

1929: *Cow Belles* (Jan. 5), *Hospitalities* (Jan. 18), *Reduced Weights* (Feb. 1), *Flying Yeast* (Feb. 15), *Vanishing Screams* (Mar. 1), *A Joint Affair* (Mar. 15), *Sheep Skinned* (Mar. 19), *The Lone Shark* (Apr. 12), *Golf Socks* (May 10), *Petting Larceny* (May 24), *Hat Aches* (June 7), *A Fur Peace* (June 22), *Auto Suggestion* (July 6) and *Sleepy Holler* (July 19).

KRITERION KOMIC KARTOONS
Harry S. Palmer wrote, produced, directed and animated this series of comic drawn cartoons. *A Pyramid Film Company Production.*

1915: *No. 1* (Feb. 12/*Taft Playing Golf*), *No. 2* (Feb. 15/*Professor Dabbler*), *No. 3* (Feb. 26/*Hotel de Gink*), *No. 4* (Mar. 5/*Industrial Investigation*), *No. 5* (Mar. 19) and *No. 6* (Mar. 26).

LAMPOONS
Burt Gillett animated and directed this series of joke cartoons redrawn from the magazines of *Judge* and *Leslie's Weekly* for producer J. R. Bray. *A Bray Production released by Goldwyn Pictures.*

LAUGH-O-GRAMS
Walt Disney, at age 18, produced a series of short films satirizing topics of the day. Subjects ranged from police corruption to ladies' fashions.

The first batch of cartoons was made while Disney worked days for the Kansas City Film Ad Company, which produced advertisements for local businesses that were shown in motion

A scene from the Walt Disney Laugh–O–Grams adventure, Puss In Boots (1922).

picture theaters in the area. The animation was primitive and crude in its style—figures were cut out of paper and animated—yet the short films were so successful that local theater owners clamored for more.

Disney sold the series to the owner of the Newman Theatre, located in town. (The series was appropriately re-named *Newman Laugh–O–Grams.*) Figuring demand for commercials was great enough in the Kansas City area, he then quit his job and set up his own company, Laugh–O–Grams Films, retaining the series' original name.

After raising enough collateral, Disney proceeded to animate six cartoons, each modernized versions of standard fairy tales. In the process, he expanded his staff to include several animators, namely Hugh Harman and Walker Harman, Rudolf Ising and Max Maxwell, in addition to Ub Iwerks, who served as Disney's partner on the early ad company *Laugh–O–Grams.*

While the first Newman *Laugh–O–Grams* were produced in 1920, when Walt was a member of the Kansas City Film Ad Company, titles and release dates of these cartoons do not exist. Only titles for films made after 1922 are available. *Directed by Walt Disney. A Walt Disney Cartoon.*

1922: *The Four Musicians Of Bremen, Little Red Riding Hood, Puss In Boots, Jack And The Beanstalk, Goldie Locks And The Three Bears* and *Cinderella.*

(Note: Non-fairy tale cartoons made during the same period were *Tommy Tucker's Tooth* and in 1923 *Martha [A Song–O–Reel]* and *Alice's Wonderland* [a pilot for the *Alice Comedies*].)

LEAVES FROM LIFE

This series featured cartoons from *Life* magazine produced as animated sequences for magazine film series. *A Gaumont Company Production.*

1917: *No. 62* (July 5), *No. 63* (July 12/A *Hasty Pudding*), *No. 64* (July 19), *No. 65* (July 26), *No. 66* (Aug. 2), *No. 67* (Aug. 9/*Not A Shadow Of Doubt*), *No. 68* (Aug. 16/*The Absent Minded Dentist*), *No. 69* (Aug. 23), *No. 70* (Aug. 30/*The*

March of Science), *No. 71* (Sept. 6/*Fresh Advances*), *No. 73* (Sept. 20/*When A Big Car Goes By*), *No. 74* (Sept. 27/*So Easy*), *No. 75* (Oct. 4), *No. 77* (Oct. 18), *No. 78* (Oct. 25), *No. 79* (Oct. 31/*Had Your Missing Stock Panned Out*) and *No. 80* (Nov. 8/*It Was Not the Colic*).

LEDERER CARTOONS

Carl Francis Lederer wrote, produced, directed and animated this short–lived series of cartoons. *A Lubin/Vitagraph release.*

1915: *Bunny In Bunnyland* (May 1) and *When They Were 21* (May 27), *Ping Pong Woo* (June 26) and *Wandering Bill* (Sept. 9).

LIFE CARTOON COMEDIES

Technical credits and production information could not be found for this series. *A Sherwood-Wadsworth Pictures Production released by Educational Pictures.*

1926: *Red Hot Rails* (Sept. 18), *Flaming Ice* (Sept. 25), *Missing Links* (Sept. 25), *The Yellow Pirate* (Oct. 5), *Cut Price Glory* (Oct. 11), *The Mighty Smithy* (Nov. 7), *Barnum Was Right* (Nov. 21), *Balloon Tired* (Dec. 5) and *Why Women Pay* (Dec. 16).

1927: *The Peaceful City* (Jan. 2), *Mike Wins A Medal* (Jan. 18), *Soft Soap* (Jan. 30), *A Heavy Date* (Feb. 8), *Hitting The Trail* (Feb. 23), *Local Talent* (Mar. 8), *Ruling The Rooster* (Mar. 27), *The Prince Of Whales* (Apr. 10), *Racing Fever* (Apr. 24) and *North Of Nowhere* (May 8).

LITTLE EBONY

An L. B. Cornwell Inc. Production.

1925: *Ebony Cleans Up* (Oct. 15), *The Stowaway* (Nov. 1) and *A Drop In The Bucket* (Dec. 30).

LITTLE JIMMY

Since its inception in mid–December 1915, Hearst's International Film Service planned to produce animated subjects for its weekly newsreel, the Hearst–Vitagraph News Pictorial. Initially, animated cartoons based on Tom Powers' and George Herriman's characters were featured until April 1916 when other comic–strip artists joined the studio's lineup. One of the new faces who later joined the roster was star cartoonist Jimmy Swinnerton, who contributed this animated series shaped around the comic misadventures of a mischievous little boy. The series was based on Swinnerton's popular weekday strip, which he developed in 1905. *An International Films Production.*

M-IN-A CARTOONS

This series of cartoons featuring different themes was written, animated and directed by Harry S. Palmer and produced by David S. Horley. *A M-in-A Films (Made in America Films) Production.*

1915: *The Siege Of Liege* (Jan. 9), *Great Americans* (Feb. 6), *The Dove Of Peace* (Mar. 6) and *Doctor Monko* (May 29).

MacDONO CARTOONS

J. J. MacManus and R. E. Donahue served as producers, directors, animators and writers of this animated series. *A MacDono Cartoons Inc. Production released by Affiliated Distributors. Affiliated Distributors.*

1921: *Mr. Ima Jonah's Home Brew* (June 4) and *Skipping The Pen* (June 4).
Mastodon Films.

1922: *Burr's Novelty Review No. 1* (Mar. 1), *Burr's Novelty Review No. 2* (Apr. 1), *Burr's Novelty Review No. 3* (May 1), *Burr's Novelty Review No. 4* (June 1), *Burr's Novelty Review No. 5* (July 1) and *Burr's Novelty Review No. 6* (Aug. 1).

MAUD THE MULE

William Randolph Hearst produced this series based on the comic strip *And Her Name Was Maud* by Frederick Burr Opper. *Directed by Gregory La Cava. An International Film Service Production.*

1916: *Poor Si Keeler* (Feb. 4), *A Quiet Day In The Country* (June 5), *Maud The Educated Mule* (July 3) and *Round And Round Again* (Oct. 2).

MERKEL CARTOONS

Topical issues of the day were turned into animated commentaries in this series produced by Arno Merkel. Kenneth M. Anderson wrote, directed and animated the series. *A Merkel Film Company Production.*

1918: *Me And Gott* (Feb.), *Power Pro And Con* (Feb.), *The Girth Of A Nation* (Apr.), *Truths On The War In Slang* (Apr.), *Oh What A Beautiful Dream* (Apr.) and *Hocking The Kaiser* (Apr.).

MILE-A-MINUTE MONTY

Animator Leon Searl wrote, produced and directed this series. *A Lubin Company/Essanay release.*

1915: *Mile-A-Minute Monty* (Aug. 25), *Monty The Missionary* (Sept. 14) and *Mile-A-Minute Monty* (Dec. 22).

MILT GROSS

Along with George McManus and Sidney Smith, Milt Gross was another famous comic strip artist who tried his hand at animation. In 1920, following his stint at Barré–Bowers Studios, where he animated the Mutt and Jeff series, Gross animated this short–lived series for J. R. Bray. The films burlesqued the foibles and frailities of people. *A Bray Production.*

1920: *We'll Say They Do, Tumult In Toy Town, Frenchy Discovers America, Ginger Snaps* and *The Cow Milker.*

MISS NANNY GOAT

An overzealous goat starred in this series produced by J. R. Bray. *A J. R. Bray Production released by Paramount.*

1916: *Miss Nanny Goat Becomes An Aviator* (Feb. 17) and *Miss Nanny Goat On The Rampage* (May 14).

1917: *Miss Nanny Goat At The Circus* (Apr. 6).

MUTT AND JEFF

Archibald J. Mutt was first sketched by newspaper cartoonist Bud Fisher in 1907. Within a year, partner Edgar Horace Jeff appeared. Mutt, a tall, lanky, mustachioed man, and Jeff, his short, wide–bristle mustachioed, bald–headed partner replete with tuxedo hat and attire, entered films in 1916.

The series reached the screen thanks in part to Raoul Barré, a French-Canadian artist who turned to animation following a successful career as a newspaper cartoonist. Barré joined forces with another cartoonist, Charles Bowers, who had acquired the screen rights to the "Mutt and Jeff" strip. Bowers was in charge of the Mutt and Jeff Company, which Fisher launched to handle production of the cartoon shorts. Distribution of these early films was handled by Fox Films.

Oddly, neither Barré's nor Bowers' name was ever mentioned in the screen credits of these films. Fisher denied them credit, wanting only his name to appear in connection with the characters.

World War I served as a primary backdrop for early series' storylines, pairing off the characters in spy invasions and other entanglements with the Germans. Additional stories dealt with typical daily situations—working as hospital orderlies to running a pawn shop—but with catastrophic results.

Staff animators completed these films at a rate of one a week. Consequently, not every cartoon made its mark. Animator Dick Huemer remarked in an interview: "Very often they [theater managers] didn't even run the cartoons. If the exhibitor hated them, he didn't run them. That's how interested they were."

Gag development suffered in the process, with cartoons being cranked out so quickly. "We used to look at our own work and laugh like hell. We thought it was great. But in the theaters they didn't," said Huemer.

In 1921, production of the series was continued under the Jefferson Film Corporation banner, headed by animator Dick Friel. The series flourished through 1926, ending production two years before the arrival of sound. *Directed by Bud Fisher. A Pathé Frères/Mutt and Jeff Films/Bud Fisher Film Corporation Production released by Pathé Film Exchange, Celebrated Players, Fox Film Corporation and Short Film Syndicate.*

Pathé Film Exchange
1913: *Mutt And Jeff* (Feb. 10), *Mutt And Jeff* (Feb. 17), *Mutt And Jeff* (Feb. 24), *Mutt And Jeff At Sea* (Part 1) (Mar. 3), *Mutt and Jeff At Sea* (Part 2) (Mar. 10), *Mutt And Jeff In Constantinople* (Mar. 17), *The Matrimonial Agency* (Mar. 24), *Mutt And Jeff In Turkey* (Mar. 31), *Mutt's Moneymaking Scheme* (Apr. 7), *The Sultan's Harem* (Apr. 14), *Mutt And*

Jeff In Mexico (Apr. 21), *The Sandstorm* (Apr. 28), *Mutt Puts One Over* (May 5), *Mutt And Jeff* (May 12), *Mutt and Jeff* (May 19), *Pickaninni's G-String* (May 26), *Mutt And Jeff* (June 2), *Baseball* (June 9), *The California Alien Land Law* (June 23), *The Merry Milkmaid* (June 30), *The Ball Game* (July 7), *Mutt And Jeff* (July 24), *Mutt's Marriage* (Aug. 4), *Johnny Reb's Wooden Leg* (Aug. 11), *A Substitute For Peroxide* (Aug. 18), *Mutt And Jeff* (Aug. 25), *The Hypnotist* (Sept. 1), *The Mexican Problem* (Sept. 8), *Mutt And Jeff* (Sept. 29), *Mutt And Jeff* (Oct. 13), *Mutt And Jeff* (Oct. 20), *Mutt And Jeff* (Oct. 27), *Mutt And Jeff* (Oct. 30), *Mutt And Jeff* (Nov. 13), *Whadya Mean You're Contended* (Nov. 20) and *Mutt and Jeff* (Dec. 4).

Celebrated Players

1916: *Jeff's Toothache* (Apr. 1), *Mutt And Jeff In The Submarine* (Apr. 8), *The Indestructible Hats* (Aug. 12), *Cramps, The Promoters, Two For Hire, The Dog Pound, The Hock Shop* and *Wall Street.*

1917: *The Submarine Chasers* (July 9), *The Cheese Tamers, Cows And Caws, The Janitors, A Chemical Calamity, The Prospectors, The Bell Hops, In The Theatrical Business, The Boarding House, The Chamber of Horrors, A Day In Camp, A Dog's Life, The Interpreters, Preparedness* and *Revenge Is Sweet.*

Fox Film Corporation

1918: *The Decoy* (Mar. 24), *Back To The Balkans* (Mar. 31), *The Leak* (Apr. 7), *Freight Investigation* (Apr. 14), *On Ice* (Apr. 21), *Helping McAdoo* (Apr. 28), *A Fisherless Cartoon* (May 5), *Occultism* (May 12), *Superintendents* (May 19), *Tonsorial Artists* (May 26), *The Tale Of A Pig* (June 2), *Hospital Orderlies* (June 9), *Life Savers* (June 16), *Meeting Theda Bara* (June 23), *The Seventy-Mile Gun* (June 30), *The Burglar Alarm* (July 7), *The Extra-Quick Lunch* (July 14), *Hunting The U-Boats* (July 21), *Hotel De Mutt* (July 28), *Joining The Tanks* (Aug. 4), *An Ace And A Joker* (Aug. 11), *Landing A Spy* (Aug. 18), *Efficiency* (Aug. 25), *The Accident Attorney* (Sept. 1), *At The Front* (Sept. 8), *To The Rescue* (Sept. 15), *The Kaiser's New Dentist* (Sept. 22), *Bulling The Bolshevik* (Sept. 29), *Our Four Days In Germany* (Oct. 6), *The Side Show* (Oct. 13), *A Lot Of Bull* (Nov. 10), *The Doughboy* (Nov. 17), *Around The World In Nine Minutes* (Nov. 24), *Pot Luck In The Army* (Dec. 1), *Hitting The High Sports* (Dec. 15), *The Draft Board* (Dec. 22) and *Throwing The Bull* (Dec. 29).

1919: *The Lion Tamers* (Jan. 5), *Here And There* (Jan. 19), *The Hula Hula Cabaret* (Jan. 19), *Dog-Gone Tough Luck* (Jan. 26), *Landing An Heiress* (Feb. 2), *The Bearded Lady* (Feb. 9), *500 Miles On A Gallon Of Gas* (Feb. 16), *The Pousse Cafe* (Feb. 25), *Fireman Save My Child* (Mar. 2), *Wild Waves And Angry Woman* (Mar. 9), *William Hohenzollern Sausage Maker* (Mar. 16), *Out An' In Again* (Mar. 23), *The Cow's Husband* (Mar. 30), *Mutt The Mutt Trainer* (Apr. 6), *Subbing For Tom Mix* (Apr. 13), *Pigtails And Peaches* (Apr. 20), *Seeing Things* (Apr. 27), *The Cave Man's Bride* (May 4), *Sir Sidney* (May 11), *Left At The Post* (May 18), *The Shell Game* (May 25), *Oh Teacher* (June 1), *Hands Up* (June 15), *Sweet Papa* (June 15), *Pets And Pests* (June 22), *A Prize Fight* (June 29), *Look Pleasant Please* (July 6), *Downstairs And Up* (July 13), *A Tropical Eggs-pedition* (July 20), *West Is East* (July 27), *Sound Your 'A'* (Aug. 24), *Hard Lions* (Aug. 31), *Mutt And Jeff In Paris* (Sept. 7), *Mutt And Jeff In Switzerland* (Sept. 7), *All That Glitters Is Not Goldfish* (Sept. 14), *Everybody's Doing It* (Sept. 21), *Mutt And Jeff In Spain* (Sept. 28), *The Honest Book Agent* (Oct. 5), *Bound In Spaghetti* (Oct. 19), *In The Money* (Oct. 26), *The Window Cleaners* (Nov. 2), *Confessions Of A Telephone Girl* (Nov. 9), *The Plumbers* (Nov. 16), *The Chambermaid's Revenge* (Nov. 23), *Why Mutt Left The Village* (Nov. 30), *Cutting Out His Nonsense* (Dec. 7), *For Bitter Or For Verse* (Dec. 14), *He Ain't Done Right By Our Nell* (Dec. 21) and *Another Man's Wife* (Dec. 28).

1920: *A Glutton For Punishment* (Jan.), *His Musical Soup* (Jan.), *A Rose By Any Other Name* (Jan.), *Mutt And Jeff In Iceland* (Jan.), *Fisherman's Luck* (Jan.), *The Latest In Underwear* (Jan.), *On Strike* (Jan.), *Shaking The Shimmy* (Jan.), *The Rum Runners* (Jan.), *The Berth Of A Nation* (Jan.), *Mutt And Jeff's Nooze Weekly* (Jan.), *Pretzel Farming* (Jan.), *I'm Ringing Your Party* (Feb.), *Fishing* (Feb.), *Dead Eye Jeff* (Feb.), *The Soul Violin* (Feb.), *The Mint Spy* (Feb.), *The Pawnbrokers* (Feb.), *The Chemists* (Feb.), *Putting On The Dog* (Feb.), *The Plumbers* (Feb.), *The Great Pickle Robbery* (Mar.), *The Price Of A Good Sneeze* (Mar.), *The Chewing Gum Industry* (Mar.), *Hula Hula Town* (Mar.), *The Beautiful Model* (Mar.), *The Honest Jockey* (Mar.), *The Bicycle Race* (Apr.), *The Bowling Alley* (Apr.), *Nothing But Girls* (Apr.), *The Private Detectives* (Apr.), *The Wrestlers* (Apr.), *The Paper Hangers* (Apr.), *The Toy Makers* (May), *The Tango Dancers* (May), *One Round Jeff* (May), *A Trip To Mars* (May), *Three Raisins And A Cake Of Yeast* (June), *Departed Spirits* (June), *The Mystery Of Galvanized Iron Ash Can* (June), *The Breakfast Food Industry* (June), *The Bare Idea* (July), *The Merry Cafe* (Aug.), *In Wrong* (Aug.), *Hot Dogs* (Aug.), *The Politicians* (Aug.), *The Yacht Race* (Aug.), *The Cowpunchers* (Sept.), *Home Sweet Home* (Sept.), *Napoleon* (Sept.), *The Song Birds* (Sept.), *The Tailor Shop* (Oct.), *The Brave Toreador* (Oct.), *The High Cost Of Living* (Oct.), *Flapjacks* (Oct.), *The League Of Nations* (Oct.), *A Tightrope Romance* (Oct.), *Farm Efficiency* (Nov.), *The Medicine Man* (Nov.), *Home Brew* (Nov.), *Gum Shoe Work* (Nov.), *A Hard Luck Santa Claus* (Nov.), *All Stuck Up* (Nov.), *Sherlock Hawkshaw And Company* (Dec.), *The North Woods* (Dec.), *On The Hop* (Dec.), *The Papoose* (Dec.), *The Hypnotist* (Dec.), *Cleopatra* (Dec.) and *The Parlor Bolshevist* (Dec.).

1921: *The Lion Hunters* (Feb. 26), *The Ventriloquist* (Feb. 27), *Dr. Killjoy* (Mar. 18), *Factory To Consumer* (Mar. 20), *A Crazy Idea* (Apr.), *The Naturalists* (Apr. 17), *Mademoiselle Fifi* (May 7), *Gathering Coconuts* (May 7), *It's A Bear* (May 7), *The Far North* (May 7), *A Hard Shell Game* (May 14), *The Vacuum Cleaner* (May 7), *A Rare Bird* (May 21), *Flivvering* (May 21), *The Lion Hunters* (June 11), *The Glue Factory* (June 11), *Cold Tea* (June 11), *The Gusher* (June 12), *Watering The Elephants* (June 26), *A Crazy Idea* (July), *The Far East* (July), *Training Woodpeckers* (Aug.), *A Shocking Idea* (Aug.), *Touring* (Aug.), *Darkest Africa* (Sept. 17),

Not Wedded But A Wife (Sept. 17), *Crows And Scarecrows* (Sept. 17), *The Painter's Frolic* (Sept. 17), *The Stampede* (Sept. 17), *The Tong Sandwich* (Sept. 17), *Shadowed* (Oct. 18), *The Turkish Bath* (Oct. 18), *The Village Cutups* (Nov. 26), *A Messy Christmas* (Nov. 26), *Fast Freight* (Nov. 26), *The Stolen Snooze* (Dec. 11), *Getting Ahead* (Dec. 18) and *Bony Parts* (Dec. 25).

1922: *A Ghostly Wallop* (Jan.), *Beside The Cider* (Jan.), *Long Live The King* (Jan.), *The Last Laugh* (Jan.), *The Hole Cheese* (Feb.), *The Phoney Focus* (Feb.), *The Crystal Gazer* (Feb.), *Stuck In The Mud* (Feb.), *The Last Shot* (Feb. 27), *The Cashier* (Mar.), *Any Ice Today* (Mar.), *Too Much Soap* (Mar. 12), *Hoot Mon* (Apr.), *Golfing* (Apr.), *Tin Foiled* (Apr.), *Around The Pyramids* (Apr.), *Getting Even* (Apr.), *Hop, Skip And Jump* (May 15), *Modern Fishing* (May), *Hither And Thither* (May), *Court Plastered* (Aug.), *Falls Ahead* (Aug.), *Riding The Goat* (Sept. 17), *The Fallen Archers* (Oct. 1), *Cold Turkey* (Oct. 8), *The Wishing Duck* (Nov. 12), *Bumps And Things* (Nov. 26), *Nearning The End* (Dec. 10), *The Chewing Gum Industry* (Dec. 23) and *Gym Jams* (Dec. 30).

1923: *Down In Dixie* (Feb. 4).

Short Film Syndicate
1925: *Accidents Won't Happen* (Aug.), *Soda Clerks* (Aug.), *Invisible Revenge* (Sept.), *Where Am I?* (Sept.), *The Bear Facts* (Oct.), *Mixing In Mexico* (Oct. 17), *All At Sea* (Nov. 14), *Oceans Of Trouble* (Nov.), *Thou Shalt Not Pass* (Dec. 5) and *A Link Missing* (Dec. 12).

1926: *Bombs and Boobs* (Jan.), *On Thin Ice* (Feb. 20), *When Hell Froze Over* (Mar. 6), *Westward Whoa* (Apr.), *Slick Sleuths* (Aug. 1), *Ups And Downs* (Aug. 15), *Playing With Fire* (Sept. 1), *Dog Gone* (Sept. 15), *The Big Swim* (Oct. 1), *Mummy O' Mine* (Oct. 15), *A Roman Scandal* (Nov. 1), *Alona Of The South Seas* (Nov. 15) and *The Globe Trotters* (Dec. 1).

NERVY NAT

Animator Pat Sullivan, who created Felix the Cat, produced and animated this 1916 screen adaptation of James Montgomery Flagg's bulbous–nosed tramp which first appeared as a comic strip in national magazines. Not as innocent as Happy Hooligan or Charlie Chaplin, Nat had adventures that involved frequent encounters with the law and others who fell prey to his well–planned schemes. *A Pat Sullivan Cartoon release.*

THE NEWLYWEDS

Emile Cohl animated and directed this series based on the comic strip by George McManus. *A Eclair Films Production.*

1913: *When He Wants A Dog He Wants A Dog* (Jan. 18), *Business Must Not Interfere* (Mar. 15), *He Wants What He Wants When He Wants It* (Mar. 29), *Poor Little Chap He Was Only Dreaming* (Apr. 20), *He Loves To Watch The Flight Of Time* (May 18), *He Ruins His Family's Reputation* (June 1), *He Slept Well* (June 15), *He Was Not Ill Only Unhappy* (June 19), *It Is Hard To Please Him But It Is Worth It* (July 13) and *He Poses For His Portrait* (July 27).

NEWSLAFFS

William C. Nolan, who was head animator of the *Felix The Cat* series, wrote, produced, directed and animated this series of humorous news commentaries between 1927 and 1928. *A Film Booking Offices release.*

1927: *No. 1* (Sept. 4), *No. 2* (Sept. 18), *No. 3* (Oct. 2), *No. 4* (Oct. 16), *No. 5* (Oct. 30), *No. 6* (Nov. 13), *No. 7* (Nov. 27), *No. 8* (Dec. 11) and *No. 9* (Dec. 25).

1928: *No. 10* (Jan. 8), *No. 11* (Jan.), *No. 12* (Feb. 5), *No. 13* (Feb. 19), *No. 14* (Mar. 2), *No. 15* (Mar. 2), *No. 16* (Mar. 5), *No. 17* (Apr. 17), *No. 18* (Apr. 30), *No. 19* (May 14), *No. 20* (May 28), *No. 21* (June 11), *No. 22* (June 25), *No. 23* (July 9) and *No. 24* (July 23).

NORBIG CARTOONS

Joseph Cammer served as producer and animator of this series, which premiered in 1915. *A Norbig Company Production released by Powers-Universal.*

1915: *Professor Wiseguy's Trip To The Moon* (June 6).

OSWALD THE LUCKY RABBIT

The floppy-eared rabbit resembled Walt Disney's Mickey Mouse in attire, wearing short pants. Disney took on the series when his distributor suggested dropping the *Alice* series and launching something new instead.

The Oswald series became an immediate success, with producer Charles Mintz and his brother-in-law, George Winkler, releasing the cartoons through Universal. The films paid big dividends for Disney, too. He earned as much as $2,500 a short.

Walt Disney's Oswald Rabbit (right) gallops ahead in a scene from Ride 'Em Plowboy (1928). © Walt Disney Productions

Ub Iwerks assisted Walt on the animation, along with several other young animation stalwarts, including Isadore "Friz" Freleng, who replaced Rollin "Ham" Hamilton, later a prominent Warner Brothers animator. Story ideas were derived from "bull sessions" convened by Disney, during which members of his animation staff made suggestions for gags and ideas to integrate into storylines.

After the second year of production, Disney felt certain he could negotiate a raise during contract negotiations with Mintz. Much to his surprise, Mintz had something else in mind. He wanted to reduce Disney's box-office share from each short to $1,800 a reel! He, too, realized the tremendous profit potential of the series and was determined to keep a larger percentage for himself. As it turned out, Disney found Mintz's offer completely unacceptable, and rejected the proposal even though Mintz threatened to take the series away from him.

Mintz kept his word. He eventually hired animator Walter Lantz to supervise a new Oswald series. Dejected, Disney returned with an even bigger hit—a cartoon series featuring a lovable mouse named Mickey. *Directed by Walt Disney. A Walt Disney Production released by Universal Pictures.*

1927: *Trolley Troubles* (Sept. 5), *Oh, Teacher!* (Sept. 19), *The Mechanical Cow* (Oct. 3), *Great Guns* (Oct. 17), *All Wet* (Oct. 31), *The Ocean Hop* (Nov. 14), *The Banker's Daughter* (Nov. 28), *Empty Socks* (Dec. 12) and *Rickety Gin* (Dec. 26).

1928: *Harem Scarem* (Jan. 9), *Neck 'N Neck* (Jan. 23), *Ol' Swimmin' 'Ole* (Feb. 6), *Africa Before Dark* (Feb. 20), *Rival Romeos* (Mar. 5), *Bright Lights* (Mar. 19), *Sagebrush Sadie* (Apr. 2), *Ride 'Em Plow Boy* (Apr. 16), *Ozzie Of The Mounted* (Apr. 30), *Hungry Hoboes* (May 14), *Oh, What A Knight* (May 28), *Poor Papa* (June 11), *The Fox Chase* (June 25), *Tall Timber* (July 9), *Sleigh Bells* (July 23), *Hot Dogs* (Aug. 20) and *Sky Scrappers* (Sept. 3).

OTTO LUCK

J. R. Bray produced this short—lived series following the adventures of a romantic young man who persistently creates the impression that there is a screw loose in the mental machinery. *Written, directed and animated by Wallace A. Carlson. A Bray Production released by Paramount.*

1915: *Otto Luck In The Movies* (June 4), *Otto Luck To The Rescue* (June 25), *Otto Luck And The Ruby Of Rasmataz* (July 16) and *Otto Luck's Flivvered Romance* (Aug. 13).

OUT OF THE INKWELL

Animator Max Fleischer created this series starring Koko the Clown (the name was not hyphenated at this time), one of the first to combine live action and animation. The technique was accomplished through a process called Rotoscope, which Max and brother Dave Fleischer developed for the screen.

The Fleischers invented the technique after being unsatisfied with the results of other cartoonists' animated films. They first employed this new technical marvel in the pilot film that launched the series. Rotoscope was simply a drawing board

and film projector combined, enabling animators to retrace frame—by—frame projected film images of human characters to achieve lifelike animation.

The pilot resulted in the birth of Koko, actually Dave Fleischer dressed in a puffy sleeved clown suit with large white buttons. He performed sommersaults and other acrobatics before the camera, then brought to the screen with some exaggeration in the final animation.

This initial film, appropriately called *Out Of The Inkwell*, was so well received that Max Fleischer decided to produce additional films right away. He sold cartoon magnate J. R. Bray on the idea of handling distribution and he animated one Inkwell cartoon a month. The films appeared as part of Bray's *Paramount Pictograph* screen magazine.

Response to the cartoons was overwhelming to say the

Animator Dave Fleischer, dressed in a clown suit, was actually Koko the Clown, filmed live and transposed into animated sketchings for the Fleischers' Out Of The Inkwell *series.*

least. As one critic for the *New York Times* noted: "One's first reflection after seeing this bit of work is, 'Why doesn't Mr. Fleischer do more?'"

Such raves were not uncommon for the series. Koko enthralled audiences with his fluid movement and the novelty of blending live footage with animation saved these films. The stock opening had Koko materialize out of a cartoonist's inkwell or pen point, only to harrass the animator before being placed in some type of animated situation. The animator seen in the opening sequence was Max Fleischer, who played both Koko's master and nemesis.

By 1923, Max Fleischer stopped animating the series and brother Dave took over the series direction. Some of the animators who worked on the series included Burt Gillett, Dick Huemer, Mannie Davis, Ben Sharpensteen and Roland "Doc" Crandall. Between Inkwell films, Koko also starred in sing–a–long cartoons called *Koko Songs*, animated versions using a bouncing ball set to popular tunes of the day. *My Bonnie September* was the first production under this series banner in 1925. *A Bray and Out Of The Inkwell Films Production released by Warner Brothers, Paramount, Rodner Productions, Winkler Pictures and Red Seal Pictures.*

Paramount-Bray Pictographs
1916: *Out Of The Inkwell.*

1918: *Experiment No. 1* (June 10).
Goldwyn-Bray Pictographs.

1919: *Experiment No. 2* (Mar. 5), *Experiment No. 3* (Apr. 2), *The Clown's Pup* (Aug. 30), *The Tantalizing Fly* (Oct. 4) and *Slides* (Dec. 3).

1920: *The Boxing Kangaroo* (Feb. 2), *The Chinaman* (Mar. 19), *The Circus* (May 6), *The Ouija Board* (June 4), *The Clown's Little Brother* (July 6), *Poker* (Oct. 2), *Perpetual Motion* (Oct. 2) and *The Restaurant* (Nov. 6).

1921: *Cartoonland* (Feb. 2) and *The Automobile Ride* (June 20).

Out Of The Inkwell Films Inc.
1921: *Modelling* (Oct.), *Fishing* (Nov. 21) and *Invisible Ink* (Dec. 3).

1922: (released by Warner Brothers) *The Fish* (Jan. 7), *The Dresden Doll* (Feb. 7) and *The Mosquito* (Mar. 6).

1922: (released by Winkler Pictures) *Bubbles* (Apr. 20), *Flies* (May), *Pay Day* (July 8), *The Hypnotist* (July 26), *The Challenge* (Aug. 29), *The Show* (Sept. 21), *The Reunion* (Oct. 27), *The Birthday* (Nov. 4) and *Jumping Beans* (Dec. 15).

1923: (released by Rodner Productions) *Modeling* (Feb. 3), *Surprise* (Mar. 15), *The Puzzle* (Apr. 15), *Trapped* (May 15), *The Battle* (July 1), *False Alarm* (Aug. 1), *Balloons* (Sept. 1), *The Fortune Teller* (Oct. 1), *Shadows* (Nov. 1) and *Bed Time* (Dec. 1).

1924: (released by Red Seal Pictures) *The Laundry* (Jan. 1), *Masquerade* (Feb. 1), *The Cartoon Factory* (Feb. 21), *Mother Gooseland* (Mar. 21), *A Trip To Mars* (Apr. 1), *A Stitch In Time* (May 1), *Clay Town* (May 28), *The Runaway*

(June 25), *Vacation* (July 23), *Vaudeville* (Aug. 20), *League Of Nations* (Sept. 17), *Sparring Partners* (Oct.) and *The Cure* (Dec. 13).

1925: *Koko The Hot Shot* (Jan.), *Koko The Barber* (Feb. 25), *Big Chief Koko* (Mar. 2), *The Storm* (Mar. 21), *Koko Trains 'Em* (May 9), *Koko Sees Spooks* (June 13), *Koko Celebrates The Fourth* (July 4), *Koko Nuts* (Sept. 5), *Koko On The Run* (Sept. 26), *Koko Packs 'Em* (Oct. 17), *Koko Eats* (Nov. 15), *Koko's Thanksgiving* (Nov. 21), *Koko Steps Out* (Nov. 21) and *Koko In Toyland* (Dec. 12).

1926: *Koko's Paradise* (Feb. 27), *Koko Baffles The Bulls* (Mar. 6), *It's The Cats* (May 1), *Koko At The Circus* (May 1), *Toot Toot* (June 5), *Koko Hot After It* (June 12), *The Fade-away* (Sept. 1), *Koko's Queen* (Oct. 1), *Koko Kidnapped* (Oct.), *Koko The Convict* (Nov. 1) and *Koko Gets Egg-Cited* (Dec. 1).

1927: *Koko Back Tracks* (Jan. 1), *Koko Makes 'Em Laugh* (Feb. 10), *Koko in 1999* (Mar. 10), *Koko The Kavalier* (Apr. 10) and *Koko Needles The Boss* (May 10).

PEANUT COMEDIES
Produced as part of the *Paramount Magazine*, this series combined live action and animation. The series was produced, directed, written and animated by Harry D. Leonard. *A Paramount Pictures release.*

1920: *One Hundred Per Cent Proof* (Nov. 21).

1921: *Some Sayings Of Benjamin Franklin* (Jan. 9) and *The Sheriff* (Mar. 20).

1921: *Spaghetti For Two* (May 15), *In Old Madrid* (June 5) and *School Days* (Aug. 8).

PEN AND INK VAUDEVILLE
These absurd cartoons feature an animator on a vaudeville stage sketching various outlandish drawings and editorial cartoons which miraculously come to life onscreen. *A Earl Hurd Production released by Educational Film Corp.*

1924: *Boneyard Blues* (Aug. 31), *The Hoboken Nightingale* (Oct. 5), *The Sawmill Four* (Nov. 2), *The Artist's Model* (Nov. 15) and *Broadcasting* (Dec. 20).

1925: *He Who Gets Socked* (Feb. 7), *Two Cats And A Bird* (Mar. 7), *The Mellow Quartette* (Apr. 4), *Monkey Business* (May 2), *Two Poor Fish* (May 30), *Props' Dash For Cash* (June 20), *Bobby Bumps And Company* (July 4) and *Props And The Spirits* (Sept. 5).

PETE THE PUP
This series starred one of Walter Lantz's last silent cartoon characters, a lovable but pesky pup and his jocular tramp sidekick. Each cartoon was shaped around live segments of Lantz at his animator's table, a la Max Fleischer's *Out Of The Inkwell*, while his star characters looked on. The series was also billed as *Hot Dog Cartoons*.

Lantz animated and directed the series. It lasted two years. *A Bray Production released by Pathé Film Exchange Inc.*

1926:   *For The Love O' Pete* (Oct. 2), *Pete's Haunted House* (Oct. 5) and *Pete's Party* (Oct. 26).

1927:   *Dog Gone It* (Jan. 4), *Along Came Fido* (Jan. 31), *The Puppy Express* (Feb. 4), *Petering Out* (Feb. 16), *S'matter, Pete?* (Mar. 15), *Lunch Hound* (Apr. 8), *Jingle Bells* (Apr. 26), *Bone Dry* (May 14) and *The Farm Hand* (May 27).

PHABLES

Raoul Barré, who was associated with William Randolph Hearst's International Film Service, produced this series of films based on Tom E. Powers' clever comic drawings in 1916, which were packed with witty social commentary as well as sticklike figures. Barré quit after making only seven films to accept an offer to adapt the *Mutt And Jeff* strip into a series. *An International Film Service Production.*

1915:   *The Phable Of Sam And Bill* (Dec. 17), *The Phable of A Busted Romance* (Dec. 24) and *Feet Is Feet: A Phable* (Dec. 31).

1916:   *A Newlywed Phable* (Jan. 7), *The Phable Of A Phat Woman* (Jan. 14) and *Cooks Vs. Chefs: The Phable of Olaf And Louie* (Jan. 21).

POLICE DOG

Extremely funny stories of the amazing achievements of a friendly and most precocious dog which has attached himself to the policeman on the beat. Drawn by gifted comic–strip artist Carl Anderson (who also directed), it was the only animal series to emerge from the J. R. Bray Studios. *A Bray Production released by Pathé Film Exchange.*

1914:   *The Police Dog* (Nov. 21).

1915:   *The Police Dog Gets Piffles In Bad* (July 24) and *The Police Dog To The Rescue* (Sept. 25).

1916:   *Police Dog On The Wire* (Jan. 27), *Police Dog Turns Nurse* (Apr. 2), *Police Dog In The Park* (May 7) and *Working Out With The Police Dog* (June 6).

POPULAR SONG PARODIES

Like Max Fleischer's *Song Car-Tunes* series, this series used popular music as the basis for storylines. Produced by Louis Weiss. *An Artclass Pictures Production released by Film Booking Offices.*

1926:   *Alexander's Ragtime Band* (May), *Annie Laurie, The Sheik Of Araby, In My Harem, When I Lost You, Margie, When That Midnight Choochoo Leaves For Alabam, Oh What A Pal Was Mary, Everybody's Doing It, My Wife's Gone To The Country, Oh How I Hate To Get Up In The Morning, Just Try To Picture Me, I Love To Fall Asleep, For Me And My Gal, Yak-A-Hula-Hick-A-Doola, My Sweetie, Old Pal, Tumble-*

down Shack In Athlone, The Rocky Road To Dublin, When I Leave This World Behind, Finiculee Finicula, When The Angelus Was Ringing, Beautiful Eyes, Call Me Up Some Rainy Afternoon, Micky and *Oh I Wish I Was In Michigan.*

QUACKY DOODLES

Cartoonist Johnny B. Gruelle, founder of the *Raggedy Ann* comic strip among others, created this series showcasing a family of ducks: Quacky Doodles, the mother; Danny Doodles, the father; and the little Doodles. They appeared at regular intervals with J. R. Bray's Colonel Heeza Liar, Bobby Bumps and his dog Fido as part of Bray's weekly *Paramount Pictograph* screen magazine. *A Bray Production released by Paramount Pictures.*

1917:   *Quacky Doodles' Picnic* (Feb. 18), *Quacky Doodles' Food Crisis* (Mar. 12), *Quacky Doodles The Early Bird* (Apr. 1), *Quacky Doodles Soldiering For Fair* (Apr. 23), *Quacky Doodles Sings The Pledge* (Sept. 10) and *Quacky Doodles The Cheater* (Oct. 15).

RED HEAD COMEDIES

This series of cartoons, which spoofed noted figures in world history, was produced in color. The series was written, produced, directed and animated by Frank A. Nankivell, Richard M. Friel, "Hutch" and W. E. Stark. *A Lee-Bradford Corporation Production.*

1923:   *Robinson Crusoe Returns On Friday* (Sept.), *Cleopatra And Her Easy Mark* (Sept.), *Napoleon Not So Great* (Sept.), *Kidding Captain Kidd* (Sept.), *Rip Without A Wink* (Sept.), *Columbus Discovers A New Whirl* (Sept.), *Why Sitting Bull Stood Up* (Dec.), *What Did William Tell* (Dec.), *A Whale Of A Story* (Dec.), *How Troy Was Collared* (Dec.) and *The Jones Boys' Sister* (Dec.).

RHYME REELS

Walt Mason wrote, produced and directed this series which combined live action with animated sequences. *A Filmcraft Corporation Production.*

1917:   *Bunked And Paid For* (Aug. 18), *The Dipper* (Aug. 18), *True Love And Fake Money* (Aug.) and *Hash* (Aug.).

ROVING THOMAS

This series of adventures, featuring a cat named Roving Thomas, combined live action and animation. *Produced by Charles Urban. A Kineto Films Production released by Vitagraph.*

1922:   *Roving Thomas Sees New York* (Sept. 17), *Roving Thomas On An Aeroplane* (Oct. 22) and *Roving Thomas On A Fishing Trip* (Dec. 10).

1923:   *Roving Thomas At The Winter Carnival* (Feb.) and *Roving Thomas In Chicago* (Oct. 27).

SAMMIE JOHNSIN

Inheriting the rights to comic strips penned by the great William F. Marriner, Pat Sullivan turned one of them, "Sambo and his Funny Noses," into an animated cartoon series in 1916, called *Sammie Johnsin*. The films centered around the adventures of this Little Black Sambo character. Sullivan reportedly photographed the films at Universal's studio in Fort Lee, New Jersey. *A Pat Sullivan Cartoon released through Powers-Universal Pictures.*

1916: *Sammie Johnsin Hunter* (Jan. 19), *Sammie Johnsin Strong Man* (Mar. 3), *Sammie Johnsin Magician* (June 20), *Sammie Johnsin Gets A Job* (July 3), *Sammie Johnsin In Mexico* (Aug. 10), *Sammie Johnsin Minds The Baby* (Oct. 23), *Sammie Johnsin At The Seaside* (Nov. 18), *Sammie Johnsin's Love Affair* (Nov. 24), *Sammie Johnsin And His Wonderful Lamp* (Dec. 8) and *Sammie Johnsin Slumbers Not* (Dec. 21).

SCAT CAT

The success of Pat Sullivan's *Felix The Cat* inspired several other animators to create cat characters of their own. Frank Moser's series followed the exploits of Scat Cat, which alternated with Sullivan's *Felix The Cat* on Paramount's *Paramount Magazine* newsreel. The series was produced in 1920. *A Paramount Pictures release.*

SCENIC SKETCHOGRAPHS

Following the success of his *Travelaughs* series, Henry (Hy) Mayer wrote, produced, directed and animated this series for Pathé Exchange. *A Mayer Production released by Pathé Exchange.*

1926: *The Family Album* (July 26), *Tripping The Rhine* (July 26), *A Pup's Tale* (July 26) and *Nurenberg The Toy City* (July 26).

SCREEN FOLLIES

Animators Luis Seel and F. A. Dahne wrote, produced, directed and animated this series for which little else is known. *A Capital Film Company.*

1920: *No. 1* (Jan. 4) and *No. 2* (Jan 4).

THE SHENANIGAN KIDS

Based on the comic strip by Rudolph Dirks, this series continued the adventures of Dirks' *The Katzenjammer Kids*. Directed by Gregory La Cava, Burt Gillett and Grim Natwick. *An International Film Service/Goldwyn-Bray Comic Production.*

1920: *Knock On The Window, The Door Is A Jamb* (Apr. 17), *One Good Turn Deserves Another* (June 17), *The Dummy* (June 27), *The Rotisserie Brothers* (Natwick/July 24) and *Hunting Big Game* (Gillett/Oct. 9).

SILLIETTES

Issued as part of film magazine series, this series consisted of animated silhouettes to tell a story. Herbert M. Dawley produced, directed and animated the series. *A Herbert M. Dawley Production released by Pathé Exchange.*

1923: *Silliettes* (Mar. 24), *The Lobster Nightmare* (Apr. 7), *The Absent Minded Poet* (June 9) and *The Classic Centaur* (July 7).

1924: *Pan The Piper* (Feb. 9), *Thumbelina* (Sept. 27), *Jack And The Beanstalk, Cinderella, Sleeping Beauty, Tattercoats* and *Aladdin And The Wonderful Lamp.*

1925: *Jack The Giant Killer* (May 9).

SILHOUETTE FANTASIES

In the mid–1900s, movie shadow plays were among the realm of popular entertainment. J. R. Bray teamed up with his associate C. Allan Gilbert to produce a series of animated films based on this archaic art form. The films turned out to be "serious" adaptations of Greek myths, staged in art nouveau arabesque tableaux. Bray had plans to create a five–reel feature using the same technique. However, Gilbert left the studio in 1916 and the series was instead abandoned. *A Bray-Gilbert Films Production released by Paramount Pictures.*

1916: *Inbad The Sailor* (Jan. 20), *Haunts For Rent* (Feb. 10), *The Chess Queen* (Mar. 7), *In The Shadows* (Mar. 15), *Inbad The Sailor Gets Into Deep Water* (Apr 8) and *The Toyland Paper Chase* (May 10).

SKETCHOGRAFS

Social and topical issues were among the themes covered in this series which was included in weekly magazine film series, written, produced, directed and animated by Julian Ollendorff. *An Ollendorff Production released by Educational Pictures and Pathé Exchange.*

Educational Pictures
1921: *Play Ball* (Aug. 7), *Just For Fun* (Sept. 16), *Eve's Leaves* (Oct.), *Seeing Greenwich Village* (Nov.) and *What's The Limit* (Dec. 24).

Pathé Exchange
1921: *Jiggin' On The Old Sod* (Sept. 18).

Educational Pictures
1922: *Famous Men* (Oct. 21), *Athletics And Women* (Oct. 28), *Champions* (Nov. 4), *Animals And Humans* (Nov. 11), *Mackerel Fishing* (Dec. 2) and *The Coastguard* (Dec. 16).

1923: *Family Album* (Jan. 8).

Cranfield and Clarke
1926: *Beauty And The Beach* (Sept. 1), *Everybody Rides* (Sept. 15), *Fair Weather* (Oct. 1), *The Big Show* (Oct. 15).

Watch Your Step (Nov. 1), *Revolution Of The Sexes* (Nov. 15) and *Tin Pan Alley* (Dec. 1).

SONG CAR-TUNES

Before the advent of sound, theaters were known to project song slides onto the movie screen showing lyrics of well–known tunes, often accompanied by a live singer or musician, to commit audiences into singing along. Animator Max Fleischer took this simple concept and illustrated lyrics with drawings and live–action footage in a series of cartoons, first shown in 1924, called, *Song Car–Tunes.*

In the beginning of most films, on–camera talent—usually a Fleischer employee—highlighted the lyrics using a long stick with a luminescent white ball at the end. Films then often cut away to Fleischer cartoon stars—Koko the Clown, Fritz the dog and others—in ingenious visual gags to lead the second or third chorus of the song.

Some sing–a–long cartoons were synchronized using Dr. Lee DeForest's Phonofilm sound process, but theaters were ill–equipped to project these musical novelties employing this then–revolutionary technique. *A Out of the Inkwell Film Production released by Arrow Film Corp. and Red Seal Pictures.*

Arrow Film Corp.
1924:   *Mother Pin A Rose On Me* (Mar. 9/released in sound in June), *Come Take A Trip In My Airship* (Mar. 9/released in sound in June) and *Goodbye My Lady Love* (Mar. 9/released with sound in June).

Red Seal Pictures
1925:   *Come Take A Trip In My Airship* (Jan. 15), *The Old Folks At Home* (Feb. 1), *Mother, Mother Pin A Rose On Me* (Mar. 1), *I Love A Lassie* (Mar. 20), *The Swanee River* (Apr. 25), *Daisy Bell* (May 30), *Nutcracker Suite* (Sept./unconfirmed title), *My Bonnie Lies Over The Ocean* (Sept. 15/first bouncing ball cartoon), *Ta-Ra-Ra-Boom-De-A* (Oct. 15), *Dixie* (Nov. 15) and *Sailing, Sailing* (Dec. 15).

1926:   *Dolly Gray* (Feb. 6), *Has Anybody Here Seen Kelly* (Feb. 21/released with sound), *My Old Kentucky Home* (Mar. 13/released with sound), *Sweet Adeline* (May 1), *Tramp, Tramp, Tramp The Boys Are Marching* (May 8), *Goodbye My Lady Love* (May 22), *Coming Through The Rye* (June 1), *Pack Up Your Troubles* (July 17), *The Trail Of The Lonesome Pine* (July 17/released with sound), *By The Light Of The Silvery Moon* (Aug. 21/released with sound), *In The Good Old Summer Time* (Sept./released with sound), *Oh You Beautiful Doll* (Sept./released with sound) and *Old Black Joe* (Nov. 1/released with sound).

1927:   *Jingle Bells* (Apr. 1), *Waiting For The Robert E. Lee* (Apr. 15) and *Old Black Joe* (July/released with sound).

1924–26:   (Following are undated titles from the series.) *Dear Old Pal, When The Midnight Choo-Choo Comes To Alabama, Yaka-Hula-Hickla-Ooola, When I Lost You, Oh, Suzanna, My Wife's Gone to The Country, Margie, Annie Laurie, Oh, How I Hate To Get Up In The Morning* and *East Side, West Side.*

SUCH IS LIFE

Henry (Hy) Mayer created—he also wrote, produced, directed and animated—this series of humorous perspectives on life in New York and in Europe. *A Hy Mayer Production released by Pathé Exchange, R. C. Pictures and Film Booking Offices.*

Pathé Exchange
1920:   *Such Is Life Among The Dogs* (Oct. 2), *Such Is Life At The Zoo* (Oct. 16), *Such Is Life At Coney Island* (Nov. 6), *Such Is Sporting Life* (Nov. 13), *Such Is Life In Greenwich Village* (Dec. 4) and *Such Is Life In East Side New York.*

1921:   *Such Is Life In The Land Of Fancy* (Jan. 30), *Such Is Life At A County Fair* (Feb. 19), *Such Is Life In Summer* (Mar. 12), *Such Is Life In Ramblerville* (Apr. 10), *Such Is Life At The Race Track* (July 3), *Such Is Life At The Zoo* (July 17) and *Such is Life In New York* (Nov. 20).

1922:   *Such Is Life* (Feb. 27).

R. C. Pictures/Film Booking Offices
1922:   *Such Is Life In London's West End* (Apr. 15), *Such Is Life In Vollendam* (May 7), *Such Is Life In Monte Carlo* (May 31), *Such Is Life In Mon Petit Paris* (June 4), *Such Is Life Among The Children Of France* (June 18), *Such Is Life In Munich* (July 22), *Such Is Life In Montemártre* (July 22), *Such Is Life On The Riviera* (Aug. 12), *Such Is Life Among The Paris Shoppers* (Aug. 12), *Such Is Life Near London* (Aug. 19), *Such Is Life In Amsterdam And Alkmaar* (Aug. 27), *Such Is Life Among The Idlers Of Paris* (Oct.), *Such Is Life In Busy London* (Nov. 4), *Such Is Life In A Dutch County Fair* (Nov.) and *Such Is Life In Italy* (Dec.).

TAD'S CAT

In 1919, as many as two films were possibly made for this Universal cartoon series, produced and animated by popular American newspaper cartoonist Tad Dorgan. The films starred a tall, lanky cat whose creation was spurred by the success of Pat Sullivan's own cat series, *Felix The Cat. A Universal Picture release.*

TECHNICAL ROMANCES

Produced by J. R. Bray, this series was written, directed and animated by J. A. Norling, Ashley Miller and F. Lyle Goldman. *A Bray Production released by Hodkinson.*

1922:   *The Mystery Box* (Nov. 25) and *The Sky Splitter* (Dec. 9).

1923:   *Gambling With The Gulf Stream* (Feb. 4), *The Romance Of Life* (Mar. 1), *The Immortal Voice* (June 10) and *Black Sunlight* (Dec. 1).

TERRY FEATURE BURLESQUES

Paul Terry wrote, produced and directed this series of witty satires. *A Paul Terry Production released by A. Kay Company.*

1917: *20,000 Feats Under The Sea* (Apr. 23), *Golden Spoon Mary* (Apr. 30), *Some Barrier* (July) and *His Trial* (July).

TERRY HUMAN INTEREST REELS

This series shaped storylines around the qualities of human characteristics. *Produced and directed by Paul Terry. A Paul Terry Production released by A. Kay Company.*

1917: *Character As Revealed By The Nose* (June), *Character As Revealed By The Eye* (July), *Character As Revealed By The Mouth* (Aug.) and *Character As Revealed By The Ear* (Sept.).

TOM AND JERRY

No information could be found for this series—its starring characters or production staff. *An Arrow Film Corporation Production.*

1923: *The Gasoline Trail* (Aug. 1) and *Tom's First Flivver* (Sept. 1).

TONY SARG'S ALMANAC

Famed illustrator Tony Sarg, who toured vaudeville with a marionette routine, wrote and animated this series of marionette sequences (called, *Shadowgraphs*). The series was co-written and co–animated by Herbert M. Dawley, who also produced. *A Herbert M. Dawley Production released by Rialto Productions and Educational Pictures.*

Rialto Productions
1921: *The First Circus* (May 21), *The First Dentist* (June), *Why They Love Cave Men* (July 2), *When The Whale Was Jonahed* (Aug. 20) and *Fireman Save My Child* (Sept. 10).

1922: *The Original Golfer* (Jan. 7), *Why Adam Walked The Floor* (Feb. 5), *The Original Movie* (Apr. 9), *The First Earful* (May 29) and *Noah Put The Cat Out* (July 9).

Educational Pictures
1922: *The First Flivver* (July 29), *The First Degree* (July 29), *The First Barber* (Aug. 19), *Baron Bragg And The Devilish Dragon* (Sept. 9), *The Ogling Ogre* (Nov. 19) and *Baron Bragg And The Haunted Castle* (Dec. 17).

1923: *The Terrible Tree* (Jan. 6).

TOYLAND

This series featured animated dolls and toys and was produced by the team of R. F. Taylor and W. W. Wheatley. *Directed by Horace Taylor. A Taylor and Wheatley Production released by Powers.*

1916: *A Romance Of Toyland* (Mar. 9), *A Toyland Mystery* (Mar. 15), *The Toyland Villain* (Apr. 12) and *A Toyland Robbery* (May 10).

TRAVELAUGHS

Henry (Hy) Mayer, a prolific caricaturist and illustrator, was the mastermind behind this series of tastefully done satires on travelogues, combining drawings with live footage. Films appeared as part of screen magazines, and were distributed to theaters nationwide. Otto Messmer, who later animated Felix the Cat, served as Mayer's assistant on the series. In 1920, the series shifted to Pathé. Episodes which appear in the filmography are the only titles available through research. *A Keen Cartoon Production released by Universal Pictures.*

1915: *To 'Frisco By The Cartoon Route* (Aug. 9).

1916: *Globe Trotting With Hy Mayer* (Apr. 14), *Such Is Life In China* (June 22), *Pen And Inklings In And Around Jerusalem* (Oct. 5), *High Life On A Farm* (Nov. 9), *A Pen Trip To Palestine* (Nov. 9) and *Such Is Life In Alaska* (Dec. 19).

1917: *Such Is Life In South Algeria* (Apr. 28), *China Awakened* (June 26), *Seeing Ceylon With Hy Mayer* (Aug. 6) and *Seeing New York With Hy Mayer* (Oct. 15).

1918: *New York By Heck* (May 1).

Pathé Review
1921: *Behind The Scenes Of The Circus* (Jan. 15), *Water Stuff* (Mar. 5), *Spring Hats* (Mar. 26), *All The Merry Bow-Wows* (Apr. 30), *In The Silly Summertime* (May 29), *The Door That Has No Lock* (June 26), *A Ramble Through Provincetown* (July 31), *The Little City Of Dreams* (Sept. 4), *Day Dreams* (Sept. 18), *Down To The Fair* (Oct. 2), *Summer Scenes* (Oct. 16), *All Aboard* (Oct. 30) and *Puppies* (Dec. 25).

1922: *How It Feels* (Sept. 24), *In The Dear Old Summertime* (Oct. 14) and *Sporting Scenes* (Nov. 25).

1923: *Faces* (Jan. 6).

THE TRICK KIDS

J. R. Bray produced this series of films, consisting of animated dolls and toys, for the *Paramount Pictographs. A Bray Studios Production released by Paramount Pictures.*

1916: *The Birth Of The Trick Kids* (Feb. 20), *The Strange Adventures Of The Lamb's Tail* (Mar. 12), *Happifat's New Playmate* (Mar. 19), *The Magic Pail* (Apr. 19), *Happifat Does Some Spring Planting* (Apr. 23), *Happifat And Flossy Fisher's Unexpected Buggy Ride* (Apr. 30), *Happifat's Fishing Trip* (May 7), *Happifat's Interrupted Meal* (May 21), *Happifat Becomes An Artist And Draws A Bear* (May 28) and *Everybody's Uncle Sam* (June).

UN-NATURAL HISTORY

In true Aesopian style, Walter Lantz introduced this series of outlandish history fables, becoming his fourth series for J. R. Bray Studios. Beginning in 1925, the series alternated with *Dinky Doodles* and was distributed by FBO until September 1926, at which time Bray resumed distribution of the series himself.

Two former Disney directors, Dave Hand and Clyde Geronimi, later supervised and helped animate the series, which used child actors to play opposite animal characters in moralistic stories. Anita Louis, later a contract player at 20th Century-Fox, was one of the actors to appear in the series.

Like earlier productions, Lantz's staff was limited to seven people—including the inker, painter, background artist and cameraman—to produce each new installment. He therefore wrote, directed and animated almost every cartoon. Along with *Pete The Pup*, the series marked the end for the Bray Studios, which closed its doors in 1927. *A Bray Production released by Standard Cinema Corporation and Film Booking Offices.*

1925: *How The Elephant Got His Trunk* (Lantz/Oct. 4), *How The Bear Got His Short Tail* (Lantz/Oct. 18), *How The Camel Got His Hump* (Geronimi/Nov. 15) and *The Leopard's Spots* (Dec. 13).

1926: *The Goat's Whiskers* (Jan. 10), *How The Giraffe Got His Long Neck* (Feb. 7), *The Stork Brought It* (Mar. 7), *The King Of The Beasts* (Apr. 4), *The Ostrich's Plumes* (Apr. 19), *The Pelican's Bill* (Lantz/May 30), *The Cat's Whiskers* (Lantz/June 20), *The Mule's Disposition* (Lantz/July 18), *The Pig's Curly Tail* (Lantz/Aug. 15) and *The Tail Of The Monkey* (Lantz, Hand/Dec. 29).

1927: *The Cat's Nine Lives* (Lantz, Hand, Geronimi/Jan. 15) and *The Hyena's Laugh* (Lantz, Geronimi/Jan. 18).

US FELLERS

Cartoonist Wallace A. Carlson wrote and directed these cartoon reminiscences seen through the eyes of a young lad who dreams about the events and mishaps of his boyhood days. *A Bray Production released by Paramount Pictures. Paramount-Bray Pictographs.*

1919: *Dud Perkins Gets Mortified* (Apr. 12), *The Parson* (Apr. 26), *Wounded By The Beauty* (Apr. 26), *Dud The Circus Performer* (May 29), *Dud's Greatest Circus On Earth* (June 21) and *At The "Ol' Swimmin' Hole* (Aug. 7). *Goldwyn-Bray Pictographs.*

1919: *Dud's Home Run* (Sept. 23), *Dud Leaves Home* (Oct. 9), *Dud's Geography Lesson* (Nov. 17) and *A Chip Off The Old Block* (Dec. 31).

1920: *Dud's Haircut* (Feb. 16) and *Dud The Lion Tamer* (Sept. 9).

VERNON HOWE BAILEY'S SKETCHBOOK

This sketchbook travel series was written, produced and directed by Vernon Howe Bailey. *An Essanay Film Production.*

1915: *Vernon Howe Bailey's Sketchbook* (Nov. 13).

1916: *. . . Of Chicago* (Jan. 29), *. . . Of London* (Mar. 1), *. . . Of Philadelphia* (Mar. 14), *. . . Of Paris* (Mar. 27), *. . . Of Boston* (Apr. 14), *. . . Of Rome* (Apr. 26), *. . . Of San Francisco* (May 20), *. . . Of Berlin* (June 9), *. . . Of St. Louis* (June 19), *. . . Of New Orleans* (July 10), *. . . Of Petrograd* (July 27) and *. . . Of Washington.*

VINCENT WHITMAN CARTOONS

Vincent Whitman served as writer, director and animator of this animated series. *Produced by Sigmund Lubin. A Lubin Manufacturing Company Production.*

1914: *A Trip To The Moon* (Mar. 14), *The Bottom Of The Sea* (Mar. 21), *A Strenuous Ride* (Apr. 11), *Another Tale* (Apr. 25), *A Hunting Absurdity* (Oct. 3), *An Interrupted Nap* (Oct. 23) and *The Troublesome Cat* (Dec. 15).

1915: *Curses Jack Dalton* (Apr. 24), *A Hot Time In Punkville* (May 3), *His Pipe Dreams* (May 21), *Studies In Clay* (July 6), *A Barnyard Mixup* (July 12), *An African Hunt* (July 15), *A One Reel Feature* (July 26), *Relentless Dalton* (Aug. 2) and *The Victorious Jockey* (Aug. 16).

THE WHOZIT WEEKLY

This series of burlesque cartoon items was produced for the *Universal Screen Magazine*, written, directed and animated by Leslie Elton. *Produced by Carl Laemmle. A Universal Pictures Production.*

1919: *No. 115* (Mar. 23), *No. 123* (May 18), *No. 124* (May 25), *No. 126* (June 8), *No. 129* (June 29), *No. 131* (July 13), *No. 131* (July 13), *No. 134* (Aug. 3), *No. 137* (Aug. 24), *No. 143* (Oct. 4) and *No. 144* (Oct. 11).

1920: *No. 164* (Feb. 28).

WINSOR McCAY

A superb storyteller and cartoonist, Winsor McCay is often credited with producing the first animated cartoon in history. Actually, he is one of several pioneers who helped shape the industry during its formative years.

McCay honed his talent as an artist and illustrator for the *Cincinnati Commercial Tribune* in 1897 before finding fame with a weekly comic strip, "Little Nemo in Slumberland," appearing in the *New York Herald* and other newspapers in 1905. He became interested in making animated films when his son picked up several "flip books" and brought them home to him. The tiny books produced an illusion of movement

Winsor McCay's Gertie the Dinosaur (1914). The cartoon used only 10,000 pencil sketchings to produce the action. (Courtesy: The Museum of Modern Art/Film Stills Archive)

when flipping the pages. McCay became so imbued with this technique that he decided to utilize the same concept only using animated characters.

It has been said that McCay's first cartoon resulted from a friendly bet with cartoonist cronies George McManus, Tad Dorgan and Tom Powers. As part of the wager, he claimed he would produce enough line drawings to sustain a four— or five—minute cartoon making the film a special feature of his already popular vaudeville act. (He traveled the circuit giving what he called "chalk talks.")

In 1911, McCay released his first animated cartoon based on his popular syndicated strip. The film was masterful in more ways than style and craftsmanship. It did so much with so little, using only 4,000 penciled drawings to animate five minutes of film. In recalling his work, the famed animator once stated, "Not until I drew 'Gertie the Dinosaur' did the audience understand that I was making drawings move."

McCay finally achieved real success in 1914 with *Gertie The Dinosaur* (also called *Gertie The Trained Dinosaur*), generally regarded as the first "cartoon star." The cartoon became quite a novelty for McCay, who built on this success and continued making animated films for seven more years. *A Winsor McCay Production released by Vitagraph Film Corp., Box Office Attractions and Jewel Productions/Universal.*

1911: *Little Nemo* (first in a series).

1912: *The Story Of A Mosquito* (Jan.).

1914: *Gertie The Dinosaur* (Sept. 15).

1916: *Bug Vaudeville, The Pet* and *Winsor McCay And His Jersey Skeeters.*

1917: *Gertie On Tour* (second in a series) and *The Adventures Of Rarebit Eater* (first in a series).

1918: *The Sinking Of The Lusitania* (May 18).

1920: *The Flying House.*

THEATRICAL SOUND CARTOON SERIES

AESOP'S FABLES

When Walt Disney released the first synchronized sound cartoon in 1928, most animated film producers followed suit. Paul Terry was no exception. He made the conversion to sound with his *Aesop's Fables* series, first popular during the silent era.

Terry directed the series for his new boss, Amadee J. Van Beuren of Van Beuren Productions, which, in November, 1928, announced every animated series would be made with sound. The first *Aesop* entry to have sound was *Dinner Time*, featuring synchronized soundtracks—music but no voices—added to the silent product.

Terry continued to direct most of the films until 1929, when he left Van Beuren to form his own studio. Several other animators shared the directorial duties from that year forth: John Foster, Harry Bailey, J. J. McManus, George Stallings and George Rufle. Black–and–white. *A Pathé Film and RKO Van Beuren release. (Copyright dates are marked by ©)*

1928: *Dinner Time* (Terry/© Dec. 17).

1929: *The Faithful Pup* (Terry/May 4), *Concentrate* (Terry/May 4), *The Jail Breakers* (Terry/May 6), *Woodchoppers* (Terry/May 9), *Presto Chango* (Terry/May 20), *Skating Hounds* (Terry/May 27), *Stage Struck* (Terry/July 23), *House Cleaning Time* (Foster/July 23), *A Stone Age Romance* (Aug. 1), *The Big Scare* (Terry/Aug. 15), *Jungle Fool* (Foster, Davis/Sept. 15), *Fly's Bride* (Foster/Sept. 21), *Summer Time* (Foster/Oct. 11), *Mill Pond* (Foster/Oct. 18), *Barnyard Melody* (Foster/Nov. 1), *Tuning In* (Nov. 7), *Night Club* (Foster, Davis/Dec. 1) and *Close Call* (Bailey/Dec. 1).

1930: *The Iron Man* (Foster/Jan. 4), *Ship Ahoy* (Foster/Jan. 7), *Singing Saps* (Foster, Davis/Feb. 7), *Sky Skippers* (Foster, Bailey/Mar. 7), *Good Old Schooldays* (Foster, Davis/Mar. 7), *Foolish Follies* (Foster, Bailey/Mar. 7), *Dixie Days* (Foster, Davis/Apr. 8), *Western Whoopee* (Foster, Bailey/Apr. 10), *The Haunted Ship* (Foster, Davis/Apr. 27), *Noah Knew His Ark* (Foster, Davis/May 25), *Oom Pah Pah* (Foster, Bailey/May 30), *A Romeo Robin* (Foster, Davis/June 22), *Jungle Jazz* (Foster, Bailey/July 6), *Snow Time* (Foster, Davis/July 20), *Hot Tamale* (Foster/Aug. 3), *Laundry Blues* (Foster, Davis/Aug. 17), *Frozen Frolics* (Foster, Bailey/Aug. 31), *Farm Foolery* (Foster/Sept. 14), *Circus Capers* (Foster, Bailey/Sept. 28), *Midnight* (Foster, Davis/Oct. 12), *The Big Cheeze* (Foster/Oct. 26), *Gypped In Egypt* (Foster, Davis/Nov. 9), *The Office Boy* (Foster, Bailey/Nov. 23), *Stone Age Stunts* (Foster/Dec. 7) and *King Of The Bugs* (Foster, Bailey/Dec. 21).

RKO Pathé Film Exchange Releases

1931: *Toy Town* (Foster, Davis/Jan. 4), *Red Riding Hood* (Foster, Bailey/Jan. 18), *The Animal Fair* (Foster, Davis/Feb. 1), *Cowboy Blues* (Foster, Bailey/Feb. 15), *Radio Racket* (Foster/Mar. 1), *College Capers* (Foster, Bailey/Mar. 15), *Old Hokum Bucket* (Mar. 29), *Cinderella Blues* (Foster, Bailey/Apr. 12), *Mad Melody* (Foster, Davis/Apr. 26), *The Fly Guy* (Foster, Bailey/May 10), *Play Ball* (Foster, Davis/May 24), *Fisherman's Luck* (Foster, Bailey/June 13), *Pale Face Pup* (Foster, Davis/June 22), *Making 'Em Move* (Foster, Bailey/July 5), *Fun On The Ice* (Foster, Davis/July 19), *Big Game* (Aug. 3), *Love In A Pond* (Foster, Davis/Aug. 17), *Fly Hi* (Foster, Bailey/Aug. 31), *The Family Shoe* (Foster, Davis/Sept. 14), *Fairyland Follies* (Foster, Bailey/Sept. 28), *Horse Cops* (Foster, J. J. McManus/Oct. 12), *Cowboy Cabaret* (Foster, Davis/Oct. 26), *In Dutch* (Foster, Bailey/Nov. 9) and *The Last Dance* (Nov. 23).

1932: *Toy Time* (Foster, Bailey/Jan. 27), *A Romeo Monk* (Foster, Davis/Feb. 20), *Fly Frolic* (Foster, Bailey/Mar. 5), *The Cat's Canary* (Foster, Davis/Mar. 26), *Magic Art* (Foster, Bailey/Apr. 25), *Happy Polo* (May 14), *Spring Antics* (Foster, Davis/May 21), *Farmerette* (June 11), *Stone Age Error* (Foster, Davis/July 9), *Chinese Jinks* (Foster, Davis/July 23), *The Ball Game* (Foster, Rufle/July 30), *Wild Goose Chase* (Foster, Davis/Aug. 12), *Nursery Scandal* (Foster, Bailey/Aug. 26), *Bring 'Em Back Half–Shot* (Foster, Davis/Sept. 9), *Down In Dixie* (Foster, Bailey/Sept. 23), *Catfish Romance* (Foster, Davis/Oct. 7), *Feathered Follies* (Oct. 21), *Venice Vamp* (Foster, Davis/Nov. 4), *Hokum Hotel* (Foster, Bailey/Nov. 18), *Pickaninny Blues* (Foster, Davis/© Dec. 12), *A Yarn Of Wool*

(Foster, Bailey/© Dec. 16) and *Bugs And Books* (Foster, Davis/© Dec. 30).

1933: *Silvery Moon* (Foster, Davis/© Jan. 13), *A.M. To P.M.* (© Jan. 20), *Tumble Down Town* (Foster, Bailey/© Jan. 27), *Love's Labor Won* (Foster, Davis/© Mar. 10), *A Dizzy Day* (Bailey/© May 5), *Barking Dogs* (Davis/© May 18), *The Bully's End* (Bailey/© June 16), *Indian Whoopee* (Davis/© July 7), *Fresh Ham* (© July 12) and *Rough On Rats* (Bailey/© July 14).

AMOS 'N' ANDY

Van Beuren Studios, creators of the *Little King and Cubby* cartoon series, bolstered its roster of stars by signing actors Freeman Gosden and Charles Correll to reprise the roles of Amos Jones and Andy Brown, characters from their popular radio program, in a series of cartoon shorts. Gosden and Correll provided their own voices for the series, which, unfortunately, never caught on with moviegoers. The series was dropped from the studio's production schedule after the first year. *Directed by George Stallings. Black–and–white. A RKO Van Beuren Corporation release.*

Voices:

Amos: Freeman Gosden, **Andy:** Charles Correll

1934: *The Rasslin' Match* (Jan. 5) and *The Lion Tamer* (Feb. 2).

ANDY PANDA

Created by Walter Lantz, the cuddly cartoon panda made his film debut in 1939 and proved so successful that Lantz contracted for four or five one–reelers a year. Lantz originated the idea for the character following a national news story he read about a panda being donated to the Chicago Zoo.

The series opener was called, *Life Begins With Andy Panda,* a play on words on the title of a popular Andy Hardy feature of the same name. Three cartoons later, Andy Panda marked another historical event in his young career—the first appearance of Lantz's wood–beating bird, Woody Woodpecker, in *Knock Knock* (1940).

Sarah Berner, who was better known as the switchboard operator on the Jack Benny radio program, was the second actor to voice the character until Bernice Hansen assumed that role for the balance of the series. *Directors were Walter Lantz, Dick Lundy, Alex Lovy and James "Shamus" Culhane. Technicolor. A Walter Lantz Production released through Universal Pictures.*

Voices:

Andy Panda: Bernice Hansen, Sarah Berner, Walter Tetley

1939: *Life Begins With Andy Panda* (Lovy/Sept. 9).

1940: *Andy Panda Goes Fishing* (Gillett/Jan. 22), *100 Pygmies And Andy Panda* (Lovy/Apr. 22), *Crazy House* (Lantz/Sept. 2) and *Knock Knock* (Woody Woodpecker's debut/Lantz/Nov. 25).

1941: *Mouse Trappers* (Lantz/Jan. 27), *Dizzy Kitty* (Lantz/May 26) and *Andy Panda's Pop* (Lantz/July 28).

1942: *Under The Spreading Blacksmith Shop* (Lovy/Jan. 12), *Goodbye Mr. Moth* (Lantz/May 11), *Nutty Pine Cabin* (Lovy/June 1) and *Andy Panda's Victory* (Lovy/Sept. 7).

1943: *Meatless Tuesday* (Culhane/Oct. 25).

1944: *Fish Fry* (Culhane/June 19) and *The Painter And The Pointer* (Culhane/Dec. 18).

1945: *Crow Crazy* (Lundy/July 9).

1946: *The Poet And Peasant* (Lundy/Mar. 18/Musical Miniature), *Mousie Come Home* (Culhane/Apr. 15), *Apple Andy* (Lundy/May 20) and *The Wacky Weed* (Lundy/Dec. 16).

1947: *Musical Moments From Chopin* (with Woody Woodpecker/Lundy/Feb. 24/Musical Miniature) and *The Band Master* (Lundy/Dec.).

1948: *Banquet Busters* (with Woody Woodpecker/Lundy/Mar. 2), *Playful Pelican* (Lundy/Oct. 8) and *Dog Tax Dodgers* (Lundy/Nov. 19).

1949: *Scrappy's Birthday* (Lundy/Feb. 11).

ANIMATED ANTICS

This series evolved from Max Fleischer's *Gulliver's Travels* (1939), testing various supporting characters from the classic animated feature in a new animated series. Films spotlighted character favorites, such as Twinkletoes and Sneak, Snoop and Snitch, in animated adventures. *Director and voice credits unknown. Black–and–white. A Fleischer Studios Production released through Paramount Pictures.*

1940: *The Dandy Lion* (Sept. 20), *Sneak, Snoop and Snitch* (Oct. 25), *Mommy Loves Puppy* (Nov. 29) and *Bring Himself Back Alive* (Dec. 20).

1941: (Copyright dates are marked by a ©) *Zero, The Hound* (© Feb 14), *Twinkletoes Gets The Bird* (Mar. 14), *Sneak, Snoop and Snitch In Triple Trouble* (May 9), *Twinkletoes—Where He Goes Nobody Knows* (June 27), *Copy Cat* (July 18), *The Wizard Of Ants* (Aug. 8) and *Twinkletoes In Hat Stuff* (Aug. 29).

THE ANT AND THE AARDVARK

The misadventures of a purple, vacuumed–nosed aardvark in constant pursuit of his meal: a tiny red ant. In his ill–fated attempts to sniff out the ant, the aardvark instead picks up gunpowder, tacks, dynamite and virtually every object imaginable during its prowl. Episodes were later featured as part of the television series, "The New Pink Panther Show." *Directors were Gerry Chiniquy, Art Davis, George Gordon and Hawley Pratt. Technicolor. A Mirisch-DePatie-Freleng Production released through United Artists.*

Voices:

The Ant/The Aardvark: John Byner

Additional Voices:

Athena Lorde, Marvin Miller

1966: *Never Bug An Ant* (Chiniquy/Feb. 2/pilot cartoon).

1969: *The Ant And The Aardvark* (Gordon/Mar. 5), *Hasty But Tasty* (Chiniquy/Mar. 6), *The Ant From UNCLE* (Gordon/Apr. 2), *I've Got Ants In My Plans* (Chiniquy/May 14), *Technology Phooey* (Chiniquy/June 25), *Mumbo Jumbo* (Davis/Sept. 27), *Dune Bug* (Davis/Oct. 29) and *Isle Of Caprice* (Chiniquy/Dec. 18).

1970: *Scratch A Tiger* (Pratt/Jan. 28), *Odd Ant Out* (Chiniquy/Apr. 29), *Ants In The Pantry* (Pratt/June 10), *Science Friction* (Chiniquy/June 28), *The Froze Nose Knows* (Chiniquy/Nov. 18) and *Don't Hustle An Ant With Muscle* (Davis/Dec. 27).

1971: *Rough Bunch* (Davis/Jan. 3) and *From Bed To Worse* (Davis/May 16).

ASTRONUT

This friendly, outer–space gremlin first appeared in a *Deputy Dawg* episode before starring in a theatrical series of his own. Each adventure followed Astronut's frolics across Earth with his friend and companion, Oscar Mild. *Directors were Connie Rasinski, Dave Tendlar, Arthur Bartsch and Cosmo Anzilotti. Technicolor. A Terrytoons Production released through 20th Century–Fox.*

Voices:
Astronut: Dayton Allen, Lionel Wilson, Bob McFadden, **Oscar:** Bob McFadden

1964: *Brother From Outer Space* (Rasinski/Mar.), *Kisser Plant* (Rasinski/June), *Outer Space Gazette* (Rasinski/Sept.) and *Molecular Mixup* (Tendlar/Dec.).

1965: *The Sky's The Limit* (Tendlar/Feb.), *Weather Magic* (Anzilotti/May), *Robots In Toyland* (Rasinski/Aug.) and *Twinkle, Twinkle Little Telestar* (Bartsch/Nov.).

1966: *Gems From Gemini* (Tendlar/Jan.) and *Haunted Housecleaning* (Rasinski/May).

1969: *Space Pet* (Mar.), *Scientific Sideshow* (June) and *Balloon Snatcher* (Sept.).

1970: *Going Ape* (Jan.) and *Martian Moochers* (May).

1971: *Oscar's Birthday Present* (Jan.), *Oscar's Thinking Cap* (May) and *No Space Like Home* (Oct.).

BABBIT AND CATSTELLO

Bob Clampett created this pair of loquacious cats based on the antics of the movie comedy greats, Abbott and Costello. Originally designed as one–shot characters, the funny felines first appeared in 1942's *A Tale of Two Kitties,* which marked the debut of Tweety Bird (who was unofficially called Orson in the cartoon). Three years after their screen debut, Babbit and Catstello were redrawn as mice, and returned to star in Frank Tashlin's *A Tale of Two Mice* (1945) and then, the following year, in Robert McKimson's *The Mouse–Merized Cat* (1946) before the characters were retired. *Directed by*

Abbott and Costello inspired a series of cartoons produced by Warner Brothers. As Babbit and Catstello, the pair appeared in several cartoon shorts. From A Tale Of Two Mice (1945). © Warner Brothers, Inc.

Bob Clampett, Frank Tashlin and Robert McKimson. Technicolor. A Warner Brothers release.

Voices:
Babbit: Mel Blanc, **Catstello:** Mel Blanc

Merrie Melodies
1942: *A Tale of Two Kitties* (with Tweety/Clampett/Nov. 21).

1946: *The Mouse–Merized Cat* (McKimson/Oct. 19).

Looney Tunes
1945: *A Tale of Two Mice* (Tashlin/June 30).

BABY FACE MOUSE

In the late 1930s, Walter Lantz introduced a flurry of new characters to the screen in one–shot cartoons and potential series. Baby Face Mouse was among the lot, featured in a short–lived series of his own, who bore some resemblance to Warner Brothers' Sniffles the Mouse and was introduced to moviegoers that same year. *Directed by Alex Lovy and Les Kline. Black–and–white. A Walter Lantz Production released through Universal Pictures.*

1938: *Cheese Nappers* (Lovy/July 14), *The Big Cat And The Little Mousie* (Aug. 15), *The Cat And The Bell* (Oct. 3), *The Sailor Mouse* (Lovy/Nov. 7) and *Disobedient Mouse* (Kline/Nov. 28).

BABY HUEY

Baby Huey was the inspiration of Paramount/Famous Studios, which also brought the likes of Casper the Friendly Ghost, Little Audrey and Herman and Katnip to the screen. The

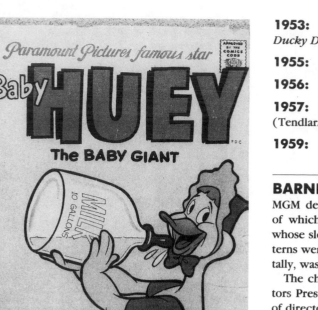

The cherubic, musclebound Baby Huey created havoc everywhere he went in a series of cartoons produced by Paramount's Famous Studios. © Harvey Cartoons

studio was formed in 1942, following Paramount's removal of Max and Dave Fleischer from control of its animation studio, thereafter re–named and enlisted with new personnel.

Like his cohorts, Baby Huey's cartoons can be best described as "formula" with little room for imagination. The premise: a husky, strong baby duck whose complete naïvete makes him a prime target for one hungry fox who is repeatedly thwarted by Huey's immense strength, rendering him virtually indestructible in a clumsy sort of way. Comedian Syd Raymond, who created the voice of Katnip, also provided the voice characterization for Huey. *Directed by Isadore Sparber, Seymour Kneitel and Dave Tendlar. Technicolor. A Famous Studios Production released through Paramount Pictures.*

Voices:
Baby Huey: Syd Raymond

1951: (Each listed below were from the *Noveltoons* series) *One Quack Mind* (Sparber/Jan. 12), *Party Smarty* (Kneitel/Aug. 3) and *Scout Fellow* (Kneitel/Dec. 21).

1952: *Clown On The Farm* (Kneitel/Aug. 22/*Noveltoon*).

1953: *Starting From Hatch* (Kneitel/Mar. 6) and *Huey's Ducky Daddy* (Sparber/Nov. 20).

1955: *Git Along Lil' Duckie* (Tendlar/Mar. 25).

1956: *Swab The Duck* (Tendlar/May 11).

1957: *Pest Pupil* (Tendlar/Jan. 25) and *Jumping With Toy* (Tendlar/Oct. 4).

1959: *Huey's Father's Day* (Kneitel/May 8).

BARNEY BEAR

MGM developed several promising animated film stars, one of which starred the lumbering but lovable Barney Bear, whose slowburn reactions, sympathetic nature and vocal patterns were reminiscent of actor Wallace Beery, who, incidentally, was an MGM star in the 1930s.

The character was redesigned in the late 1940s by animators Preston Blair and Michael Lah, the latter an understudy of director Tex Avery. Lah also directed the series following Rudolf Ising's departure in 1943. *Directed by Preston Blair, George Gordon, Rudolf Ising, Dick Lundy and Michael Lah. Technicolor. A Metro–Goldwyn–Mayer release.*

Voices:
Barney Bear: Billy Bletcher, Rudolf Ising, Paul Frees

1939: *The Bear That Couldn't Sleep* (Ising/June 10).

1940: *The Fishing Bear* (Ising/Jan. 20).

1941: *The Prospecting Bear* (Ising/Mar. 8), *Rookie Bear* (Ising/May 17) and *The Flying Bear* (Ising/Nov 1).

1942: *The Bear And The Beavers* (Ising/Mar. 28), *Wild Honey* (Ising/Nov. 7/formerly *How To Get Along Without A Ration Book*) and *Barney Bear's Victory Garden* (Ising/Dec. 26).

1943: *Bah Wilderness* (Ising/Feb. 13) and *The Uninvited Pest* (Ising/July/re: Apr. 29, 1950).

A flustered, shocked Barney Bear encounters problems with a fish in MGM's The Fishing Bear (1949). © Turner Entertainment

1944: *Bear Raid Warden* (Gordon/Sept. 9) and *Barney Bear's Polar Pest* (Gordon/Dec. 30/originally *Bedtime For Barney*).

1945: *Unwelcome Guest* (Gordon/Feb. 17/originally *Skunk Story*).

1948: *The Bear And The Bean* (Blair, Lah/Jan. 31) and *The Bear And The Hare* (Blair, Lah/June 26/originally *Snowshoe Baby*).

1949: *Goggle Fishing Bear* (Blair, Lah/Jan. 15/originally *Goggle Fishing*).

1952: *Little Wise Quacker* (Lundy/Nov. 8) and *Busybody Bear* (Lundy/Dec. 20).

1953: *Barney's Hungry Cousin* (Lundy/Jan. 31), *Cobs and Robbers* (Lundy/Mar. 14), *Heir Bear* (Lundy/May 30), *Wee Willie Wildcat* (Lundy/June 20) and *Half Pint Palomino* (Lundy/Sept. 26).

1954: *Impossible Possum* (Lundy/Mar. 28), *Sleepy–Time Squirrel* (Lundy/June 19) and *Bird–Brain Bird Dog* (Lundy/July 30).

BARNEY GOOGLE

Producer Charles Mintz, who wanted another established star in Columbia Pictures' cartoon stable, brought this popular comic strip character to the screen by special arrangement with its creator, Billy DeBeck. Unfortunately, the character had little audience appeal on the big screen, appearing in only four films before the series was abandoned. *Director and voice credits unknown. Technicolor. A Columbia Pictures release.*

1935: *Tetched In the Head* (Oct. 24) and *Patch Mah Britches* (Dec. 19).

1936: *Spark Plug* (Apr. 12) and *Major Google* (May 24).

BEAKY BUZZARD

Bob Clampett dreamed up this misfit buzzard who was literally as stupid as he looked. Beaky, a shy, Mortimer Snerd–type, first appeared in 1942's *Bugs Bunny Gets the Boid*, which Clampett directed. He re–appeared three years later in 1945's *The Bashful Buzzard*. The character was voiced in these earlier adventures by an actor named Kent Rogers. After Clampett left Warner in 1946, Beaky's career remained dormant until Friz Freleng resurrected him four years later in *The Lion's Busy*. By then, Rogers was replaced by veteran Warner Brothers voice artist Mel Blanc as the voice of Beaky. *Directed by Bob Clampett, Friz Freleng and Robert Mc-Kimson. Technicolor. A Warner Brothers release.*

Voice:
Beaky Buzzard: Kent Rogers, Mel Blanc

Looney Tunes
1945: *The Bashful Buzzard* (Clampett/Sept. 5).

Bugs Bunny surprises Beaky Buzzard by tickling his Adam's apple in Bob Clampett's Bugs Bunny Gets The Boid (1942). Beaky was inspired by Edgar Bergen's Mortimer Snerd character. © Warner Brothers, Inc. (Courtesy: Bob Clampett Animation Art)

1950: *The Lion's Busy* (Freleng/Feb. 18) and *Strife With Father* (McKimson/Apr. 1).

Merrie Melodies
1942: *Bugs Bunny Gets the Boid* (Clampett/July 11).

BEANS

One of Warner Brothers' earliest cartoon stars, this mischievous black cat was primarily used as a supporting character in *Looney Tunes* cartoons produced in mid–1930s. Created by Bob Clampett, Beans' first appearance was in the 1935 *Merrie Melodies* cartoon, *I Haven't Got a Hat*, which also marked the debut of Porky Pig. *Directed by Jack King, Tex Avery and Friz Freleng. Black–and–white. A Warner Brothers release.*

Looney Tunes
1935: *A Cartoonist's Nightmare* (King/Sept. 21) and *Hollywood Capers* (King/Oct. 19).

1936: *Gold Diggers Of '49* (with Porky/Avery/Jan. 6), *The Phantom Ship* (with Ham and Ex/King/Feb. 1), *Boom Boom* (with Porky/King/Feb. 29), *Alpine Antics* (King/Mar. 9), *The Fire Alarm* (with Ham and Ex/King/Mar. 9) and *Westward Whoa* (King/Apr. 25).

Merrie Melodies
1935: *I Haven't Got a Hat* (with Porky/Freleng/Mar. 9).

THE BEARY FAMILY

Modern cave–life situations run amuck when father Charlie, children Junior and Suzy, and wife Bessie battle everyday problems of a bear's life. The series was inspired by TV's "Life of Riley" starring William Bendix, and lasted nine years.

Walter Lantz, who created the series, once described the basic formula of the series thusly: "Charlie is the type of character who won't pay to have anything done, but will try to fix it himself, and end up blowing up the house. This is the basis for all Beary pictures." *Former Disney director Jack Hannah and veteran Lantz animator Paul J. Smith directed the series. Technicolor. A Walter Lantz Production released through Universal Pictures.*

Voices:
Charlie Beary: Paul Frees, **Bessie Beary:** Grace Stafford, **Junior:** Paul Frees, **Suzy:** Grace Stafford

1962: *Fowled–Up Birthday* (Hannah/Mar. 27) and *Mother's Little Helper* (Hannah/June 12).

1963: *Charlie's Mother–In–Law* (Smith/Apr. 16), *Goose In The Rough* (Smith/July 30) and *The Goose Is Wild* (Smith/Nov. 12).

1964: *Rah, Rah, Ruckus* (Smith/May 5) and *Rooftop Razzle Dazzle* (Smith/Sept. 29).

1965: *Guest Who?* (Smith/Feb. 1) and *Davey Cricket* (Smith/June 1).

1966: *Foot Brawl* (Smith/Jan. 1).

1967: *Window Pains* (Smith/Jan. 1) and *Mouse On The House* (Smith/Apr. 1).

1968: *Jerkey Turkey* (Smith), *Paste Makes Waste* (Smith) and *Bugged By A Rug* (Smith).

1969: *Gopher Broke* (Smith), *Charlie's Campout* (Smith) and *Cool It, Charlie* (Smith).

1970: *Charlie In Hot Water* (Smith), *Charlie's Golf Classic* (Smith) and *The Unhandy Man* (Smith).

1971: *Charlie The Rainmaker* (Smith), *The Bungling Builder* (Smith) and *Moochin' Pooch* (Smith).

1972: *Let Charlie Do It* (Smith), *A Fish Story* (Smith), *Rain, Rain, Go Away* (Smith), and *Unlucky Potluck* (Smith).

BETTY BOOP

In *Dizzy Dishes,* the sixth cartoon of Max Fleischer's *Talkartoon* series, this bubbling beauty of the cartoon world was first introduced. Initially she was nothing like the femme fatale who later seduced a nation of filmgoers with her cute button nose, wide–sparkling eyes, flapper–style dress and saucy "Boop–Boop–a–Doop" tagline.

Grim Natwick, who later animated for Ub Iwerks and Walt Disney, fashioned Betty after singer/actress Helen Kane, who happened to be a Paramount star. (The Betty Boop cartoons were released by the same studio.) Natwick based Betty's looks on Kane, after seeing the singer's face on a song sheet cover. He took Kane's own physical features and blended them with a French poodle. Thus, in her screen debut, Betty looks more like a hybrid of a dog, sporting long floppy ears

and other characteristics which were more dog–like in manner.

By 1932, Betty's character was completely modified and she returned with her new look in a number of cartoons under the *Talkartoon* banner. She was actually without a name until her appearance in *Stopping the Show,* billed as the first official Betty Boop cartoon, that same year. Stardom was instantaneous for Betty, who became known as "the first top–billed female cartoon character of any significance" and was given a daily newspaper comic strip of her own.

Dave Fleischer, Max Fleischer's brother, was responsible for standardizing Betty's appearance, making her feminine. Consequently, she exhibited the true Betty Boop personality for the first time in *Minnie the Moocher,* featuring Cab Calloway and his orchestra. (Calloway was rotoscoped as a ghost walrus who dances to the sounds of the orchestra.)

The film's sexual themes ultimately became the series' downfall. By the mid–1930s, with stricter censorship laws enforced against cartoons, Betty underwent substantial changes again. Her garter, short skirt, and decolletage were soon gone, undermining her appeal. Cast members Bimbo and Ko–Ko the Clown, who had come out of retirement, were given pink slips as well.

National Television Associates (NTA) bought the package of Betty Boop one–reelers in the late 1950s to distribute the series to television. *Directed by Dave Fleischer. Black–and–white. A Fleischer Studios Production released through Paramount Pictures.*

Voices:
Betty Boop: Mae Questel, Ann Rothschild, Margie Heinz, Kate Wright, Bonnie Poe

1930: *Dizzy Dishes* (Aug. 9/Talkartoon).

1931: *Silly Scandals* (May 23/Talkartoon), *Bimbo's Initiation* (July 24/Talkartoon), *Bimbo's Express* (Aug 22/Talkartoon), *Minding the Baby* (Sept. 26/Talkartoon), *Mask–A–Raid* (Nov. 7/Talkartoon), *Jack And The Beanstalk* (Nov. 21/Talkartoon) and *Dizzy Red Riding Hood* (Dec. 12).

1932: *Any Rags* (Jan. 2/Talkartoon), *Boop–Oop–A–Doop* (Jan. 16/Talkartoon), *Minnie the Moocher* (with Cab Calloway/Mar. 1), *Crazy Town* (Mar. 25/Talkartoon), *The Dancing Fool* (Apr. 18/Talkartoon), *A Hunting We Will Go* (Apr. 28), *Admission Free* (June 10/Talkartoon), *The Betty Boop Limited* (July 1/Talkartoon), *Rudy Vallee Melodies* (Aug. 5/Screen Song), *Stopping The Show* (Aug. 12), *Betty Boop Bizzy Bee* (Aug. 19), *Betty Boop, M.D.* (Sept. 2), *Betty Boop's Bamboo Isle* (with Royal Samoans with Miri/Sept. 23), *Betty Boop's Ups And Downs* (Oct. 14), *Betty Boop For President* (Nov. 4), *I'll Be Glad When You're Dead You Rascal You* (with Louis Armstrong/Nov. 25) and *Betty Boop's Museum* (Dec. 16).

1933: *Betty Boop's Ker–Choo* (Jan. 6), *Betty Boop's Crazy Inventions* (Jan. 27), *Is My Palm Red?* (Feb. 17), *Betty Boop's Penthouse* (Mar. 10), *Snow White* (Mar. 31), *Betty Boop's Birthday Party* (Apr. 21), *Betty Boop's May Party* (May 12), *Betty Boop's Big Boss* (June 2), *Mother Goose Land* (June 23), *Popeye The Sailor* (Popeye's debut/July 14), *The Old*

Man Of The Mountain (with Cab Calloway/Aug. 4), *I Heard* (with Don Redman/Sept. 1), *Morning, Noon And Night* (with Rubinoff/Oct. 6), *Betty Boop's Halloween Party* (Nov. 3) and *Parade Of the Wooden Soldiers* (with Rubinoff/Dec. 1).

1934: *She Wronged Him Right* (Jan. 5), *Red Hot Mama* (Feb. 2), *Ha! Ha! Ha!* (Mar. 2), *Betty in Blunderland* (Apr. 6), *Betty Boop's Rise To Fame* (May 18), *Betty Boop's Trial* (June 15), *Betty Boop's Lifeguard* (July 13), *There's Something About A Soldier* (Aug. 17), *Betty Boop's Little Pal* (Sept. 21), *Betty Boop's Prize Show* (Oct. 19), *Keep In Style* (Nov. 16) and *When My Ship Comes In* (Dec. 21).

1935: *Baby Be Good* (Jan. 18), *Taking The Blame* (Feb. 25), *Stop that Noise* (Mar. 15), *Swat The Fly* (Apr. 19), *No! No! A Thousand Times No!* (May 24), *A Little Soap And Water* (June 21), *A Language All My Own* (July 19), *Betty Boop And Grampy* (Aug. 16) *Judge For A Day* (Sept. 20), *Making Stars* (Oct. 18), and *Betty Boop, With Henry, The Funniest Living American* (Nov. 22).

1936: *Little Nobody* (Jan. 27), *Betty Boop And The Little King* (Jan. 31), *Not Now* (Feb. 28), *Betty Boop And Little Jimmy* (Mar. 27), *We Did It* (Apr. 24), *A Song A Day* (May 22), *More Pep* (June 19), *You're Not Built That Way* (July 17), *Happy You And Merry Me* (Aug. 21), *Training Pigeons* (Sept. 18), *Grampy's Indoor Outing* (Oct. 16), *Be Human* (Nov. 20) and *Making Friends* (Dec. 18).

1937: *House Cleaning* (Jan. 15), *Whoops! I'm A Cowboy* (Feb. 12), *The Hot Air Salesman* (Mar. 12), *Pudgy Takes A Bow—Wow* (Apr. 19), *Pudgy Picks A Fight* (May 14), *The Impractical Joker* (June 18), *Ding Dong Doggie* (July 23), *The Candid Candidate* (Aug. 27), *Service With A Smile* (Sept. 23), *The New Deal Show* (Oct. 22), *The Foxy Hunter* (Nov. 26) and *Zula Hula* (Dec. 24).

1938: *Riding The Rails* (Jan. 28), *Be Up To Date* (Feb. 25), *Honest Love And True* (Mar. 25), *Out Of The Inkwell* (Apr. 22), *Swing School* (May 27), *Pudgy And The Lost Kitten* (June 24), *Buzzy Boop* (July 29), *Pudgy The Watchman* (Aug. 12), *Buzzy Boop At The Concert* (Sept. 16), *Sally Swing* (Oct. 14), *On With The New* (Dec. 2) and *Pudgy In Thrills And Chills* (Dec. 23).

1939: *My Friend The Monkey* (Jan. 27), *So Does An Automobile* (Mar. 31), *Musical Mountaineers* (May 12), *The Scared Crows* (June 9), *Rhythm On The Reservation* (July 7) and *Yip, Yip, Yippy* (Aug. 11/officially released as a Betty Boop cartoon even though she does not appear).

BLACKIE THE LAMB

Innocent—looking Blackie the Lamb was always the target of a lamb—hungry Wolf, whose level of frustration mounted every time his attempt to capture the wool—skinned creature failed, in this series of cartoon shorts released under the *Noveltoons* banner. The series' first entry was *No Mutton For Nuttin'* (1943). The director of this first entry is unknown. *Directed by Isadore Sparber. Technicolor. A Famous Studios Production released by Paramount Pictures.*

1943: *No Mutton For Nuttin'* (Nov. 26).

1945: *A Lamb In A Jam* (Sparber/May 4).

1946: *Sheep Shape* (Sparber/June 28).

THE BLUE RACER

In the tradition of the Road Runner and Coyote cartoons, this series followed a similar "chase" premise in each episode, with the fast moving sissy blue snake (self-billed as "the fastest little ol' snake west of the Pecos") pursuing the ever-elusive Japanese beetle, a self-proclaimed black belt karate champion who is always one step ahead in outwitting the sly reptile. *Directed by Friz Freleng, Hawley Pratt, Bob McKimson, Sid Marcus, Gerry Chiniquy, Art Leonardi, Art Davis and Dave Detiege. Technicolor. A DePatie—Freleng/Mirisch Cinema Company Production released through United Artists.*

Voices:
The Blue Racer Larry D. Mann, **Japanese Beetle** Tom Holland

1972: *Hiss and Hers* (July 3), *Support Your Local Serpent* (July 9), *Punch and Judo* (Davis/July 23), *Love And Hisses* (Aug. 3), *Camera Bug* (Aug. 6), *Yokahama Mamma* (Dec. 24) and *Blue Racer Blues* (Dec. 31).

1973: *The Boa Friend* (Feb. 11), *Wham And Eggs* (Feb. 18), *Blue Aces Wild* (May 16), *Fowl Play* (June 1), *Freeze A Jolly Good Fellow* (June 1), *Aches And Snakes* (Aug. 10) and *Snake Preview* (Aug. 10).

1974: *Little Boa Peep* (Jan. 16).

BOBO

Bobo, a sorrowful—looking baby pink elephant, finds success in the big city in this short—lived *Looney Tunes* series, directed by Warner Brothers veteran Robert McKimson. *Directed by Robert McKimson. Technicolor. A Warner Brothers release.*

Voices: Mel Blanc

Looney Tunes
1947: *Hobo Bobo* (May 17).

1954: *Gone Batty* (Sept. 4).

BOSKO

In 1929, Hugh Harman and Rudolf Ising, formerly Disney veterans, turned to animating independent productions. That summer, they completed a three—minute pilot starring a black minstrel character they hoped to develop into a series. Called *Bosko the Talkink Kid*, the film's lead character resembled a humanized Mickey Mouse who favored a derby and spoke in a Southern Negro dialect.

Animator Friz Freleng cartooned the pilot one—reeler, with animator Hugh Harman making the first drawing of Bosko, who he had "behave like a little boy." The film was previewed

Warner Brothers' first legitimate cartoon star, Bosko, premiered on movie screens in 1930. Animators Hugh Harman and Rudolf Ising created the series. © Warner Brothers, Inc.

for several distributors in hopes of selling the package, but initially no offers were made.

Leon Schlesinger, president of Pacific Arts and Titles, next viewed the short with interest and used his connections at Warner Brothers to have the series contracted by the studio, with the three men co–producing it. The first Bosko cartoon for Warner was also the first *Looney Tunes* cartoon, called *Sinkin' in the Bathtub.* (The title was a play on the popular song title introduced in a Warner feature, *The Show of Shows.*)

Opening in New York with *Song of the Flames,* a Warner Brothers feature film attraction, the cartoon featured musical interludes and gags that had all the earmarks of Disney, Harman and Ising's former employer. In fact, as evidenced in this series, both animators tried to copy Disney's famed style verbatim in several ways. Bosko's girlfriend, Honey, for instance, was a thinly disguised Minnie Mouse, while their dog, Bruno, had Pluto overtones.

Regardless, Bosko became a mainstay at Warner for several years. The black–and–white animation had a distinct flavor of its own, populated by visual puns and other exaggerations set to popular tunes of the day, recorded by the studio's orchestra. (Abe Lyman Brunswick Record Orchestra played on several of the first releases before relinquishing his duties.)

In 1932, Ising, the idea man of the two, left the series to work on the studio's fledgling *Merrie Melodies* cartoons. As a result, the Bosko series was never the same. A year later, he and Harman departed Warner for good, taking Bosko with them to MGM, where they revived the series two years later but with little success.

Besides Freleng, the series' animators included Rollin Hamilton, Paul J. Smith and Carmen Maxwell, who also supplied the voice of Bosko. *Directed by Hugh Harman, Rudolf Ising and Friz Freleng. Black–and–white. A Vitaphone Production released through Warner Brothers.*

Voices:

Bosko: Carmen Maxwell, **Honey,** his girlfriend: Rochelle Hudson

1930: *Sinkin' In The Bathtub* (with Honey/Harman, Ising/Sept.), *Congo Jazz* (Harman, Ising/Oct.), *Hold Anything* (with Honey/Harman, Ising/Nov.) and *The Booze Hangs High* (Harman, Ising/Dec.).

1931: *Box Car Blues* (Harman, Ising/Jan.), *Big Man From The North* (Harman, Ising/Feb.), *Ain't Nature Grand?* (Harman, Ising/Mar.), *Ups 'N Downs* (Harman, Ising), *Dumb Patrol* (Harman, Ising/May), *Yodelling Yokels* (Harman, Ising/June), *Bosko's Holiday* (Harman, Ising/July), *The Tree's Knees* (Harman, Ising/Aug.), *Bosko Shipwrecked* (Harman/Sept. 19), *Bosko The Doughboy* (Harman/Oct. 17), *Bosko's Soda Fountain* (with Honey/Harman/Nov. 14) and *Bosko's Fox Hunt* (Harman/Dec. 12).

1932: *Bosko At The Zoo* (with Honey/Harman/Jan. 9), *Battling Bosko* (with Honey/Harman/Feb. 6), *Big–Hearted Bosko* (with Bruno/Harman, Ising/Mar. 5/originally *Bosko's Orphans*), *Bosko's Party* (with Honey/Harman/Apr. 2), *Bosko And Bruno* (with Bruno/Harman/Apr. 30), *Bosko's Dog Race* (Harman/June 25), *Bosko At The Beach* (Harman/July 23), *Bosko's Store* (Harman/Aug. 13) and *Bosko The Lumberjack* (with Honey/Harman/Sept. 3).

1933: *Ride Him, Bosko* (Harman/Jan. 16), *Bosko's Dizzy Date* (with Honey/Harman/Feb. 6/uses footage from the unreleased *Bosko And Honey*), *Bosko The Drawback* (Harman/Feb. 24), *Bosko The Speed King* (with Honey/Harman/Mar. 22), *Bosko's Woodland Daze* (Harman/Mar. 22), *Bosko In Dutch* (with Goopy Geer/Freleng/Mar. 22), *Bosko In Person* (with Honey/Freleng/Apr. 10), *Bosko's Knight–Mare* (Harman/June 8), *Bosko The Sheep–Herder* (Harman/June 14), *Beau Bosko* (Freleng/July 1), *Bosko The Musketeer* (with Honey/Harman/Sept. 16), *Bosko's Picture Show* (Freleng/Sept. 18) and *Bosko's Mechanical Man* (Harman/Sept. 27).

MGM Bosko Cartoons Released as Happy Harmonies
1934: (in Technicolor) *Bosko's Parlor Pranks* (Harman/Nov. 24).

1935: *Hey, Hey Fever* (Harman/Jan. 9) and *Run, Sheep, Run* (Harman/Dec. 14).

1936: *The Old House* (Harman/May 2).

1937: *Circus Daze* (Harman/Jan. 16), *Bosko's Easter Eggs* (Harman/Mar. 17), *Bosko And The Pirates* (Harman/May 1) and *Bosko And The Cannibals* (Harman/Aug. 28).

1938: *Bosko In Baghdad* (Harman/Jan. 1).

BUDDY

As a replacement for Bosko, producer Leon Schlesinger unveiled Buddy, a nondescript, wide–eyed boy, as the new lead in the *Looney Tunes* series. A pale imitation at best, Buddy was "Bosko in whiteface" and had little impact on moviegoers, proving to be "a nothing," recalled Bob Clampett, a series' animator.

The Disney influence was apparent again in this series, the third for Warner Brothers' young animation studio. Like Bosko, Buddy had Disney–ish co–stars: a flapper girlfriend, Cookie

(Minnie Mouse in costume) and, later, a dog named Towser (yet another Pluto–like clone).

Chuck Jones, a young inbetweener at the time, graduated to animator on the series and as he recalled, "Nothing in the way of bad animation could make Buddy worse than he was anyway."

Surprisingly, with such internal unrest over the character, Buddy lasted two years in 23 cartoon adventures released from 1933 to 1935.

Additional series' animators were Jack King, Robert Mc-Kimson, Frank "Tish Tash" Tashlin (all of whom became Warner directors besides Clampett and Jones), Paul J. Smith, Sandy Walker and Don Williams. *Series direction was handled by Earl Duvall, Ben Hardaway, Friz Freleng, Tom Palmer and Jack King. Black–and–white. A Vitaphone Production released through Warner Brothers.*

Voices:
Buddy: Jack Carr

1933: *Buddy's Day Out* (Palmer/Sept. 9), *Buddy's Beer Garden* (Duvall/Nov. 11) and *Buddy's Show Boat* (Duvall/Dec. 9).

1934: *Buddy The Gob* (with Shanghai Lil/Freleng/Jan. 13), *Buddy And Towser* (Freleng/Feb. 24), *Buddy's Garage* (Duvall/Apr. 14), *Buddy's Trolley Trouble* (Freleng/May 5), *Buddy Of the Apes* (Hardaway/May 26), *Buddy's Bearcats* (King/June 23), *Buddy The Woodsman* (with Cookie/King/Oct. 20), *Buddy The Detective* (King/Oct. 17), *Buddy's Circus* (King/Nov. 8) and *Viva Buddy* (King/Dec. 12).

1935: *Buddy's Theatre* (Hardaway/Feb. 16), *Buddy's Adventures* (with Cookie/Hardaway/Mar. 5), *Buddy's Pony Express* (Hardaway/Mar. 9), *Buddy Of The Legion* (Hardaway/Apr. 4), *Buddy's Lost World* (King/May 18), *Buddy's Bug Hunt* (King/June 22), *Buddy In Africa* (Hardaway/July 6), *Buddy Steps Out* (King/July 20), *Buddy The Gee Man* (King/Aug. 24) and *Buddy The Dentist* (Hardaway/Dec. 15).

BUGS BUNNY

Long a staple of the Warner Brothers cartoon roster, Bugs Bunny still remains one of the most popular cartoon characters in animation history. The long–eared, screwy rabbit who chomped on carrots and uttered in Brooklynese the famous words of "Eh, What's up Doc?" starred in 150 cartoons during his 25 years on screen, the most of any character in Warner Brothers' cartoon history.

First appearing in cartoons in a formative stage between 1938–1939, Bugs' characterization became the basis for ridiculous situations that were offbeat and outrageously funny. Often, the humor was pointed and self–serving, with the brunt of the situational gags taken by a handful of supporting characters, including Elmer Fudd, Daffy Duck, Yosemite Sam and others.

The story behind Bugs' origin has gone through several versions over the years, mostly due to several animators' attempts to claim credit for his creation. For a long time the most accepted version was that Ben "Bugs" Hardaway, who was directing a second rabbit picture, enlisted a fellow by the

Hollywood trade paper advertisement for Warner Brothers "new" Bugs Bunny cartoon series. © Warner Brothers, Inc.

name of Charlie Thorson to make a drawing of a crazy rabbit like Woody Woodpecker. When Thorson sent the drawing back to Hardaway, he labeled the corner of the page "Bugs' bunny"—and that's how Bugs supposedly got his name.

New research has revealed otherwise. Bugs did not receive his name until two years after the first model sheet was drawn. He first appeared as an "unnamed rabbit" in three cartoons: *Porky's Hare Hunt* (1938), *Prest–O Change–O* (1939) and *Hare–Um Scare–Um* (1939).

Bob Clampett wrote the story for the first cartoon, *Porky's Hare Hunt,* using some leftover gags from *Porky's Duck Hunt* and reshaping them for the rabbit. In this first appearance, several key aspects of Bugs' character emerged: chomping on a carrot; the fake dying act ("You got me!"); and the Groucho Marx line of "Of course, you know this means war!" When Clampett's story timed short, Hardaway added a few other touches, like having Bugs bounce across the scene a la studio contemporary, Daffy Duck. (By the second cartoon, Bugs was portrayed as more high–strung in the fashion of Woody Woodpecker in both voice and actions.)

Bugs' creation initially stirred some controversy, however. Some people at Walt Disney Studios cried foul as he resembled Disney's own rabbit character, Max Hare, who made his cartoon debut in *The Tortoise and the Hare* (1935), which won an Academy Award.

Ah, yes—the name. In 1940, animator Tex Avery took over the series. He directed the first official Bugs Bunny cartoon and also helped the studio decide on what to call the rascally rabbit. The studio was getting nervous since the rabbit was fast becoming a rising star. It was before producing *A Wild Hare* that the studio opened discussions on naming the character.

Tex wanted to call the character "Jack Rabbit," but the idea didn't stick. Finally it was suggested that he be named "Bugsy" after famed West Coast mobster Bugsy Siegel. Producer Leon Schlesinger nixed the idea of naming the rabbit after a reputed gangster. Instead another round of discussions ensued before the issue was settled. The name that won out over all the others was, "Bugs Bunny."

During production of this first Bugs Bunny cartoon, Avery created the character's trademark phrase, "What's up, Doc?," partly inspired by an idea given to him by Bob Clampett, Tex's key gag man from the *Termite Terrace* days, who suggested the line of "What's up, Duke?" (used in the screwball comedy, *My Man Godfrey*) and from Avery's own recollection of expressions used in his native Texas—"Hey, Doc? Whaddya, know?" and "How ya been today, Doc?"

Introduced during the cartoon's first confrontation between Bugs and Elmer Fudd, the befuddled hunter ("I'm hunting wabbit! Heh–heh–heh–heh–heh!"), Avery believes the phrase was the key to Bugs' success while giving audiences something they never expected.

"We decided he [Bugs] was going to be a smart–aleck rabbit, but casual about it. That opening line of 'Eh, What's up, Doc?' in the very first picture floored them [the audience]," Avery told biographer Joe Adamson. "They expected the rabbit to scream, or anything but make a casual remark. For here's a guy pointing a gun in his face! It got such a laugh that we said, 'Boy, we'll do that every chance we get.'"

Besides his long–running feud with Elmer Fudd, Bugs developed several other rivalries with his co–stars Yosemite Sam, a pint–sized Westerner (his classic line, "I'm the roughest, toughest, meanest hombre ever to terrorize the West") and Daffy Duck, the ever–malevolent wise–quacker, who was always jealous of Bugs stealing the spotlight from him. (The most popular gag between both characters was "Duck Season! Rabbit Season!" instrumented by Chuck Jones in several cartoons).

Bugs' final cartoon appearance was in 1964, a year after Warner Brothers closed its animation department and made special arrangements with Friz Freleng's new company, De-Patie–Freleng Enterprises to produce a series of new *Looney Tunes* and *Merrie Melodies*. (Warner re–opened its department in 1967, hiring a new staff to head its productions.)

In 1990, Bugs returned to the screen in an all–new theatrical short, *Box Office Bunny*, the studio's first Bugs Bunny cartoon in 26 years. The film premiered nationwide with the Warner Brothers feature *Reversal of Fortune*. Jeff Bergman took over as the voice of Bugs Bunny and his co-stars Elmer Fudd and Daffy Duck, succeeding Mel Blanc who died that year. *Series directors included Friz Freleng, Ben Hardaway, Robert McKimson, Bob Clampett, Frank Tashlin, Charles (Chuck) M. Jones, Abe Levitow, Dave Detiege, Tex Avery, Gerry Chiniquy, Cal Dalton, Art Davis, Ken Harris, Maurice Noble and Darrel Von Citters. Black–and–white. Technicolor. A Warner Brothers release.*

Voices:
Bugs Bunny: Mel Blanc, Jeff Bergman

Looney Tunes
1938: *Porky's Hare Hunt* (with Porky Pig/Hardaway/Apr. 30).

1940: *Patient Porky* (With Porky Pig/Clampett/Aug. 24).

1943: *Porky Pig's Feat* (with Porky Pig/Tashlin/July 17).

1944: *Buckaroo Bugs* (Clampett/Aug. 26).

1945: *Hare Conditioned* (Jones/Aug. 11) and *Hare Tonic* (with Elmer Fudd/Jones/Nov. 10).

1946: *Baseball Bugs* (Freleng/Feb. 2), *Hair–Raising Hare* (Jones/May 25), *Acrobatty Bunny* (McKimson/June 29), *Racketeer Rabbit* (with Edward G. Robinson, Peter Lorre characters/Freleng/Sept. 14) and *The Big Snooze* (with Elmer Fudd/Clampett/Oct. 5).

1947: *Easter Yeggs* (with Elmer Fudd/McKimson/June 28).

1948: *Gorilla My Dreams* (McKimson/Jan. 3), *A Feather In His Hare* (Jones/Feb. 7), *Buccaneer Bunny* (with Yosemite Sam/Freleng/May 8), *Haredevil Hare* (with Marvin Martian/Jones/July 24) and *A–Lad–In His Lamp* (McKimson/Oct. 23).

1949: *Mississippi Hare* (Jones/Feb. 26), *High Diving Hare* (with Yosemite Sam/Freleng/Apr. 30), *Long–Haired Hare* (Jones/June 25), *The Grey–Hounded Hare* (McKimson/Aug. 6) and *The Windblown Hare* (McKimson/Aug. 27).

1950: *Mutiny On The Bunny* (with Yosemite Sam/Freleng/Feb. 11), *What's Up, Doc?* (with Elmer Fudd/McKimson/June 17), *8 Ball Bunny* (with Penguin, Humphrey Bogart/Jones/July 8), *Bushy Hare* (McKimson/Nov. 11) and *Rabbit Of Seville* (with Elmer Fudd/Jones/Dec. 16).

1951: *Rabbit Every Monday* (with Yosemite Sam/Freleng/Feb. 10), *The Fair Haired Hare* (with Yosemite Sam/Freleng/Apr. 4), *Rabbit Fire* (with Daffy Duck, Elmer Fudd/Jones/May 19), and *His Hare Raising Tale* (with Clyde Rabbit, Bugs' nephew/Freleng/Aug. 11).

1952: *Operation Rabbit* (with Wile E. Coyote/Jones/Jan. 19), *14 Carrot Rabbit* (with Yosemite Sam/Freleng/Feb. 16), *Water, Water, Every Hare* (Jones/Apr. 19), *The Hasty Hare* (with Marvin Martian/Jones/June 7) and *Hare Lift* (with Yosemite Sam/Freleng/Dec. 20).

1953: *Forward March Hare* (Jones/Feb. 4), *Bully For Bug* (Jones/Aug. 8), *Robot Rabbit* (with Elmer Fudd/Freleng/Dec. 12) and *Punch Trunk* (Jones/Dec. 19). *

1954: *Captain Hareblower* (with Yosemite Sam/Freleng/Feb. 16), *Bugs and Thugs* (with Rocky, Mugsy/McKimson/Mar. 2), *No Parking Hare* (McKimson/May 1), *Dr. Jekyll's Hide* (with Spike and Chester/Freleng/May 8), *Devil May Hare* (with Tasmanian Devil/McKimson/June 19), *Bewitched Bunny* (with Witch Hazel/Jones/July 24), *Yankee Doodle Bugs* (with Clyde/Freleng/Aug. 28) and *Lumberjack Rabbit* (in 3–D/Jones/Nov. 13).

1955: *Sahara Hare* (with Yosemite Sam/Freleng/Mar. 26), *Hare Brush* (with Elmer Fudd/Freleng/May 7), *Rabbit Rampage* (Jones/June 11), *Hyde And Hare* (Freleng/Aug. 27) and *Roman Legion Hare* (with Yosemite Sam/Freleng/Nov. 12).

1956: *Broom–Stick Bunny* (with Witch Hazel/Jones/Feb. 25), *Rabbitson Crusoe* (with Yosemite Sam/Freleng/Apr. 28), *Barbary Coast Bunny* (Jones/July 21) and *A Star Is Bored* (with Elmer Fudd, Yosemite Sam/Freleng/Sept. 15).

1957: *Piker's Peak* (with Yosemite Sam/Freleng/May 25), *Bugsy And Mugsy* (Freleng/Aug. 31) and *Show Biz Bugs* (with Daffy Duck/Freleng/Nov. 2).

1958: *Hare–Way To The Stars* (Jones/Mar. 29), *Now Hare This* (McKimson/May 31), *Knighty–Knight Bugs* (with Yosemite Sam/Freleng/Aug. 23/A.A. winner) and *Pre–Hysterical Hare* (with Elmer Fudd/McKimson/Nov. 1).

1959: *Baton Bunny* (Jones, Levitow/Jan. 10), *Wild And Wooly Hare* (with Yosemite Sam/Freleng/Aug. 1) and *A Witch's Tangled Hare* (with Witch Hazel/Levitow/Oct. 31).

1960: *Horse Hare* (with Yosemite Sam/Freleng/Feb. 13).

1961: *Prince Violent* (with Yosemite Sam/Freleng/Sept. 2).

1962: *Wet Hare* (McKimson/Jan. 20).

1963: *The Million Hare* (McKimson/Apr. 6) and *Hare–Breadth Hurry* (with Wile E. Coyote/Jones, Noble/June 8).

DePatie–Freleng Enterprises Releases
1964: *Dumb Patrol* (with Yosemite Sam/Chiniquy/Jan. 18) and *False Hare* (McKimson/July 16).

Warner Brothers Releases
1990: *Box Office Bunny* (with Elmer Fudd, Daffy Duck/Van Citters/Nov.).

Merrie Melodies
1939: *Prest–O Change–O* (with formative Bugs Bunny/Jones/Mar. 25) and *Hare–Um Scare–Um* (with formative Bugs Bunny/Hardaway, Dalton/Aug. 12).

1940: *Elmer's Candid Camera* (first Elmer Fudd cartoon/Jones/Mar. 2) and *A Wild Hare* (first official Bugs Bunny cartoon/ with Elmer Fudd/Avery/July 27/A.A. nominee).

1941: *Elmer's Pet Rabbit* (with Elmer Fudd/Jones/Jan. 4), *Tortoise Beats Hare* (Avery/Mar. 25), *Hiawatha's Rabbit Hunt* (Freleng/June 7/A.A. nominee), *The Heckling Hare* (Avery/July 5), *All This And Rabbit Stew* (Avery/Sept. 13) and *Wabbit Twouble* (with Elmer Fudd/Clampett/Dec. 20).

1942: *The Wabbit Who Came To Supper* (with Elmer Fudd/Freleng/Mar. 28), *The Wacky Wabbit* (with Elmer Fudd/Clampett/May 2), *Hold The Lion, Please!* (Jones/June 13), *Bugs Bunny Gets The Boid* (with Beaky Buzzard/Clampett/June 11), *Fresh Hare* (with Elmer Fudd/Freleng/Aug. 22), *The Hare–Brained Hypnotist* (with Elmer Fudd/Freleng/Oct. 31) and *Case Of The Missing Hare* (Jones/Dec. 22).

1943: *Tortoise Wins By A Hare* (Clampett/Feb. 20), *Super Rabbit* (Jones/Apr. 3), *Jack–Wabbit And The Beanstalk* (Freleng/June 12), *Wackiki Wabbit* (Jones/July 3), *A Corny Concerto* (with Elmer Fudd, Porky Pig/Clampett/Sept. 18) and *Falling Hare* (with Grelim/Clampett/Oct. 30).

1944: *Little Red Riding Rabbit* (Freleng/Jan. 1), *What's Cooking, Doc?* (Clampett/Jan. 8), *Bugs Bunny And The Three Bears* (with Papa, Mamma and Junior/Jones/Feb. 26), *Bugs Bunny Nips The Nips* (Freleng/Apr. 22), *Hare Ribbin'* (Clampett/June 24), *Hare Force* (Freleng/July 22), *The Old Grey Hare* (with Elmer Fudd/Clampett/Oct. 28) and *Stage Door Cartoon* (with Elmer/Freleng/Dec. 30).

1945: *Herr Meets Hare* (Freleng/Jan. 13), *The Unruly Hare* (with Elmer Fudd/Tashlin/Feb. 10) and *Hare Trigger* (with Yosemite Sam/Freleng/May 5).

1946: *Hare Remover* (with Elmer/Tashlin/Mar. 23) and *Rhapsody Rabbit* (Freleng/Nov. 9).

1947: *Rabbit Transit* (Freleng/May 10), *A Hare Grows In Manhattan* (Freleng/May 22) and *Slick Hare* (Freleng/Nov. 1).

1948: *Rabbit Punch* (Jones/ Apr. 10), *Bugs Bunny Rides Again* (with Yosemite Sam/Freleng/June 12), *Hot Cross Bunny* (McKimson/Aug. 21), *Hare Splitter* (Freleng/Sept. 25) and *My Bunny Lies Over The Sea* (Jones/Dec. 4).

1949: *Hare Do* (with Elmer Fudd/Freleng/Jan. 15), *Rebel Rabbit* (McKimson/Apr. 9), *Bowery Bugs* (Davis/June 4), *Knights Must Fall* (Freleng/July 16), *Frigid Hare* (Jones/Oct. 7) and *Rabbit Hood* (Jones/Dec. 24).

1950: *Hurdy–Gurdy Hare* (McKimson/Jan. 21), *Homeless Hare* (Jones/Mar. 11), *Hillbilly Hare* (McKimson/Aug. 12) and *Bunker Hill Bunny* (with Yosemite Sam/Freleng/Sept. 23).

1951: *Hare We Go* (McKimson/Jan. 6), *Bunny Hugged* (Jones/Mar. 10), *French Rarebit* (McKimson/June 30), *Ballot Box Bunny* (with Yosemite Sam/Freleng/Oct. 6) and *Big Top Bunny* (McKimson/Dec. 12).

1952: *Foxy By Proxy* (Freleng/Feb. 23), *Oily Hare* (McKimson/July 26), *Rabbit Seasoning* (with Elmer Fudd, Daffy Duck/Jones/Sept. 20) and *Rabbit's Kin* (McKimson/Nov. 15).

1953: *Upswept Hare* (with Elmer Fudd/McKimson/Mar. 14), *Southern Fried Rabbit* (with Elmer Fudd/Freleng/May 2), *Hare Trimmed* (with Yosemite Sam/Freleng/June 20) and *Duck! Rabbit! Duck!* (with Daffy Duck/Elmer Fudd/Jones/Oct. 3).

1954: *Baby Buggy Bunny* (Jones/Dec. 18).

1955: *Beanstalk Bunny* (with Elmer Fudd, Daffy Duck/Jones/Feb. 12), *This Is A Life?* (with Daffy Duck, Yosemite Sam/Freleng/July 9) and *Knight–Mare Hare* (Jones/Oct. 1).

1956: *Bugs Bonnets* (with Elmer Fudd/Jones/Jan. 14), *Napoleon Bunny–Part* (Freleng/June 16), *Half Fare Hare* (McKimson/Aug. 18), *Wideo Wabbit* (with Elmer Fudd/McKimson/Oct. 27) and *To Hare Is Human* (with Wile E. Coyote/Jones/Dec. 15).

1957: *Ali Baba Bunny* (with Daffy Duck/Jones/Feb. 9), *Bedeviled Rabbit* (with Tasmanian Devil/Jones/Apr. 13), *What's Opera, Doc?* (with Elmer Fudd/Jones/July 6) and *Rabbit Romeo* (with Elmer Fudd/McKimson/Dec. 14).

1958: *Hare–Less Wolf* (Freleng/Feb. 1).

1959: *Hare–Abian Knights* (with Yosemite Sam/Harris/Feb. 28), *Apes Of Wrath* (Freleng/Apr. 18), *Backwoods Bunny* (McKimson/June 13), *Bonanza Bunny* (McKimson/Sept. 5) and *People Are Bunny* (with Daffy Duck/McKimson/Dec. 19).

1960: *Person To Bunny* (with Daffy Duck, Elmer Fudd/Freleng/Apr. 1), *From Hare To Heir* (with Yosemite Sam/Freleng/Sept. 3) and *Lighter Than Hare* (with Yosemite Sam/Freleng/Dec. 17).

1961: *Compressed Hare* (with Wile E. Coyote/Jones/July 29).

1962: *Bill Of Hare* (with Tasmanian Devil/McKimson/June 9).

1963: *Devil's Feud Cake* (with Yosemite Sam/Freleng/Feb. 9), *The Unmentionables* (with Rocky, Mugsy/Freleng/Sept. 7), *Mad As A Mars Hare* (with Marvin Martian/Jones, Noble/Oct. 19) and *Transylvania 6–5000* (Jones, Noble/Nov. 30).

DePatie-Freleng Enterprises Releases
1964: *Dr. Devil And Mr. Hare* (with Tasmanian Devil/McKimson/Mar. 28).

BUNNY AND CLAUDE

One of Warner Brothers' last cartoon series, this one featured two outlaw rabbits, Bunny and Claude, who steal carrots for a living, hotly pursued by a mean redneck sheriff in comical misadventures inspired by the hit Warner feature, *Bonnie and Clyde. Directed by Robert McKimson. Technicolor. A Warner Brothers release.*

Voices:
Bunny: Pat Wodell, **Clyde:** Mel Blanc, **Sheriff:** Mel Blanc

1968: *Bunny And Claude (We Rob Carrot Patches)* (Nov. 9/*Merrie Melodies*).

1969: *The Great Carrot Train Robbery* (Jan. 25/*Merrie Melodies*).

Wise–cracking, fast–talking Buzzy the Crow, always on the lookout for a sucker, starred in a series of cartoons for Paramount's Famous Studios. © Harvey Cartoons

BUZZY THE CROW

Buzzy the Crow was the star of several *Noveltoons* cartoons in which his fast–talking, double–talking ways resulted in a series of mishaps. The character debuted in 1947's *Stupidstitious Cat*, directed by Paramount cartoon veteran Seymour Kneitel. *Directed by Seymour Kneitel and Isadore Sparber. Technicolor. A Famous Studios Production released by Paramount Pictures.*

1947: *Stupidstitious Cat* (Kneitel/Apr. 25).

1950: *Sock–A–Bye Kitty* (with Katnip/Kneitel/Dec. 2).

1951: *As The Crow Lies* (Kneitel/June 1) and *Cat–Choo* (with Katnip/Kneitel/Oct. 12).

1952: *The Awful Tooth* (Kneitel/May 2).

1953: *Better Bait Than Never* (Kneitel/June 5).

1954: *Hair Today, Gone Tomorrow* (Kneitel/Apr. 16) and *No Ifs, And Or Butts* (Sparber/Dec. 17).

CAPTAIN AND THE KIDS

United Features Syndicate and MGM reached an agreement in the late 1930s to co–produce a sound cartoon series of Rudolf Dirks' famous "Katzenjammer Kids" comic strip, retitling the series and featuring most of the same cast of characters as the silent version.

Fred Quimby, MGM's cartoon studio head, produced the series, while former Warner Brothers director Friz Freleng joined forces with the studio to help direct. Freleng's association with the series resulted from some crafty manipulation on the part of Quimby, who "painted a beautiful picture for me, telling me I could hire anyone I wanted, that money was no object, and I could use any character I saw fit."

Convinced, Freleng broke his contract with Warner (it ran out in October of that year), and joined MGM in August to launch what he thought was going to be a new cartoon series of his own. He had planned to create a character with some staying power, along the lines of Porky Pig, but instead, once he arrived, he found the picture Quimby had painted was indeed different. The studio's board of directors had already struck a deal with United Features to produce the Captain and the Kids series, eliminating Freleng's opportunity to invent something original.

"I went over to MGM because they offered me a lot more money than I was making at Warners," remembered Freleng. "But I knew the Katzenjammer Kids wouldn't sell. They were humanoid characters. Humanoids were not selling, only animal pairs like Tom and Jerry were."

As Freleng feared, the series turned into an unmemorable experience. The budgets were much larger than the Warner Brothers cartoons, but "it didn't help much since the audience didn't recognize that."

The series did fail, surviving less than two full seasons. Freleng returned to Warner Brothers the same year of the series demise, while co–directors William Hanna, of Hanna and Barbera fame, and Robert Allen remained. *Black–and–white. Technicolor. A Metro–Goldwyn–Mayer release.*

Voices:
Captain: Billy Bletcher

1938: (All produced in sepiatone unless otherwise noted) *Cleaning House* (Allen/Feb. 19), *Blue Monday* (Hanna/Apr. 2), *Poultry Pirates* (Freleng/Apr. 16), *Captain's Pup* (Allen/Apr. 30), *A Day At The Beach* (Freleng/June 25), *What A Lion!* (Hanna/July 16), *The Pygmy Hunt* (Freleng/Aug. 6), *Old Smokey* (Hanna/Sept. 3), *Buried Treasure* (Allen/Sept. 17/formerly *Treasure Hunt*), *The Winning Ticket* (Oct. 1), *Honduras Hurricane* (Oct. 15/formerly *He Couldn't Say No*) and *The Captain's Christmas* (Dec. 17/formerly *The Short Cut*/Technicolor).

1939: *Petunia National Park* (Jan. 14), *Seal Skinners* (Jan. 28) and *Mamma's New Hat* (Feb. 11).

CASPER, THE FRIENDLY GHOST

His appearance frequently met by shrieks of "It's a g–g–ghost!", Casper, the Friendly Ghost became a huge money-maker for Paramount Pictures' Famous Studio, the same studio responsible for cartoon stalwarts like Baby Huey and others. Producer/animator Joseph Oriolo, who later revived Felix the Cat on television, created the friendly ghost, who in each adventure wished he had "someone to play with me."

Oriolo lost out on millions of dollars in revenue the studio earned in merchandise and other licensed products, including a long–running comic book series based on the character. He was paid by Paramount Pictures the paltry sum of $175 for the initial pilot in 1945, never making another dime.

"It's a shame that I never held onto the Casper series," explained Oriolo, "for Paramount and the Harvey people have made literally millions of dollars from the series from which made mere pennies."

Since then, several animators have claimed credit for masterminding Casper, but the first story, *The Friendly Ghost*, was actually drafted by Seymour Wright. The character did not appear again on screen until 1948, and after the 1949 cartoon, *A–Haunting We Will Go*, he was finally given his name.

Made into a regular series in 1950, Casper scored a bigger hit on television in the 1960s, when a new series of films were commissioned, aimed strictly at children. Like the theatrical series, the new cartoons were built around the same premise: Casper's eternal search for a friend. *Directed by Isadore Sparber, Bill Tytla, and Seymour Kneitel. A Famous Studios Production released through Paramount Pictures.*

Voices:
Casper: Mae Questel, Norma McMillan, Gwen Davies, Cecil Roy

1945: *The Friendly Ghost* (Sparber/Nov. 16/*Noveltoon*).

1948: *There's Good Boos Tonight* (Sparber/Apr. 23/*Noveltoon*).

1949: *A–Haunting We Will Go* (Kneitel/May 13/*Noveltoon*).

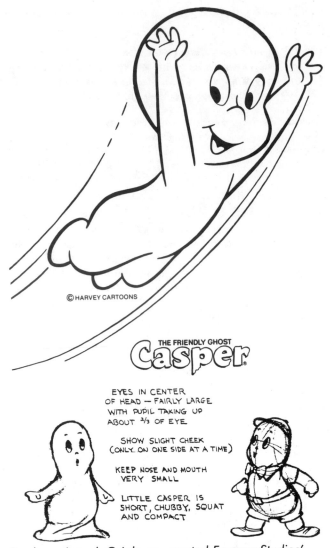

Producer Joseph Oriolo co–created Famous Studios' popular friendly ghost, Casper, in 1946. Oriolo was paid a paltry $175 for the idea. Pictured: (top) Casper, in standard form; (bottom) original concept drawings of the character. © Harvey Cartoons

1950: *Casper's Spree Under The Sea* (Tytla/Oct. 13) and *Once Upon A Rhyme* (Sparber/Dec. 20).

1951: *Boo–Boo Baby* (Kneitel/Mar. 30), *To Boo Or Not To Boo* (Sparber/June 8), *Boo Scout* (Sparber/July 27), *Casper Comes To Clown* (Sparber/Aug. 10) and *Casper Takes A Bow––Wow* (Sparber/Dec. 7).

1952: *Deep Boo Sea* (Kneitel/Feb. 15), *Ghost Of The Town* (Sparber/Apr. 11), *Spunky Skunky* (Sparber/May 30), *Cage Fright* (Kneitel/Aug. 8), *Pig–A–Boo* (Sparber/Sept. 12) and *True Boo* (Sparber/Oct. 24).

1953: *Frightday The 13th* (Sparber/Feb. 13), *Spook No Evil* (Kneitel/Mar. 13), *North Pal* (Sparber/May 29), *By The Old Mill Scream* (Kneitel/July 3), *Little Boo Peep* (Kneitel/Aug.

28), *Do Or Diet* (Sparber/Oct. 16) and *Boo's And Saddles* (Sparber/Dec. 25).

1954: *Boo Moon* (Kneitel/Jan. 1/first released in 3–D; re–released in flat prints on Mar. 5), *Zero The Hero* (Kneitel/Mar. 26), *Casper Genie* (Kneitel/May 28), *Puss 'N' Boos* (Kneitel/July 16), *Boos And Arrows* (Kneitel/Oct. 15) and *Boo Ribbon Winner* (Sparber/Dec. 3).

1955: *Hide And Shriek* (Kneitel/Jan. 28), *Keep Your Grin Up* (Sparber/Mar. 4), *Spooking With A Brogue* (Kneitel/May 27), *Bull Fright* (Kneitel/July 15), *Red, White And Boo* (Sparber/Oct. 21) and *Boo Kind To Animals* (Sparber/Dec. 23).

1956: *Ground Hog Play* (Kneitel/Feb. 10), *Dutch Treat* (Sparber/Apr. 20), *Penguin For Your Thoughts* (Kneitel/June 15), *Line of Screammage* (Kneitel/Aug. 17) and *Fright From Wrong* (Kneitel/Nov. 2).

1957: *Spooking About Africa* (Kneitel/Jan. 4), *Hooky Spooky* (Sparber/Mar. 1), *Peekaboo* (Kneitel/May 24), *Ghost Of Honor* (Sparber/July 19), *Ice Scream* (Kneitel/Aug. 30) and *Boo Bop* (Kneitel/Nov. 11).

1958: *Heir Restorer* (Sparber/Jan. 24), *Spook And Span* (Kneitel/Feb. 28), *Ghost Writers* (Kneitel/Apr. 25), *Which Is Witch?* (Kneitel/May 2) and *Good Scream Fun* (Kneitel/Sept. 12).

1959: *Doing What's Fright* (Kneitel/Jan. 16), *Down To Mirth* (Kneitel/Mar. 20), *Not Ghoulty* (Kneitel/June 5) and *Casper's Birthday Party* (Kneitel/July 31).

THE CAT

This series features a feline British super–sleuth whose voice is patterned after Cary Grant. Each time the cat escapes trouble he happily sings, "When you're wearing a new kind of hat." *Directed by Seymour Kneitel. Technicolor. A Famous Studios Production released through Paramount Pictures.*

Voices:
The Cat: Dayton Allen

1960: *Top Cat* (July) and *Shootin' Stars* (Aug./Modern Madcap).

1961: *Cool Cat Blues* (Jan.), *Bopin' Hood* (Aug. 15) and *Cane And Able* (Oct. 1).

CHARLIE DOG

Chuck Jones invented this wise–guy, orphan dog in stories shaped around his relentless search for a home. Charlie was introduced to moviegoers in 1947's *Little Orphan Airedale*, starring Porky Pig. *Directed by Chuck Jones. Technicolor. A Warner Brothers release.*

Voices:
Charlie Dog: Mel Blanc

Looney Tunes
1947: *Little Orphan Airedale* (with Porky Pig/Oct. 4).

1949: *Often An Orphan* (Aug. 13).

1951: *A Hound For Trouble* (Apr. 28).

Merrie Melodies
1949: *Awful Orphan* (with Porky Pig/Jan. 29).

1950: *Dog Gone South* (Aug. 26).

CHILLY WILLY

Chilly Willy, a mute penguin, was one of Walter Lantz's most productive film series, next to Woody Woodpecker. The character was Chaplinesque in nature, scooting around corners using Chaplin's famed one–legged stand, to elude his enemies in sticky situations.

The series was initiated in 1953 in a film bearing the character's own name, directed by Paul J. Smith, whom Lantz once described as "a competent director and fantastic animator."

Unfortunately, Chilly was not well received, and Lantz brought in Tex Avery, of Warner Brothers and MGM fame, to redesign the character, which he was determined to make into a star. As Avery told biographer Joe Adamson: "The penguin wasn't funny. There was nothing to it, no personality, no nothing."

In 1954, Avery's direction of Chilly Willy in *I'm Cold* made a splash with critics and theatergoers alike. The film even earned an Academy Award nomination for *Best Short–Subject* of that year.

Avery remained on the series only for a short time, however. He left over a salary dispute in 1955, at which time Alex Lovy took over as the series' director. The series was terminated in 1960, having amassed 35 cartoons during its lifetime. *Directed by Paul J. Smith, Alex Lovy, Jack Hannah, Tex Avery*

© 1977 Walter Lantz

Mute penguin Chilly Willy, who displayed Charlie Chaplin's famous stiff legged walk, outwitted his adversaries in a host of Walter Lantz cartoons. © Walter Lantz Productions

and Sid Marcus. Technicolor. A Walter Lantz Production released through Universal Pictures.

Voices:
Chilly Willy: Daws Butler

1953: *Chilly Willy* (Smith/Dec. 21).

1954: *I'm Cold* (Avery/Nov. 29/A.A. nominee).

1955: *The Legend Of Rock–A–Bye Point* Avery/Apr. 11) and *Hot And Cold* (Lovy/Oct. 24).

1956: *Room And Wrath* (Lovy/June 4), *Hold That Rock* (Lovy/July 30) and *Operation Cold Feet* (Lovy/Dec. 24).

1957: *The Big Snooze* (Lovy/Aug. 30) and *Swiss Miss–Fit* (Lovy/Dec. 2).

1958: *Polar Pests* (Lovy/May 19), *A Chilly Reception* (Lovy/June 16) and *Little Televillain* (Lovy/Dec. 8).

1959: *Robinson Gruesome* (Smith/Feb. 2) and *Yukon Have It* (Lovy/Mar. 30).

1960: *Fish Hooked* (Smith/Aug.10).

1961: *Clash And Carry* (Hannah/Apr. 25), *St. Moritz Blitz* (Smith/May. 16) and *Tricky Trout* (Smith/Sept. 5).

1962: *Mackerel Moocher* (Hannah/Apr. 10).

1963: *Fish And Chips* (Hannah/Jan. 8), *Salmon Loafer* (Marcus/May 28) and *Pesky Pelican* (Marcus/Sept. 24).

1964: *Deep–Freeze Squeeze* (Marcus/Mar. 1).

1965: *Fractured Friendship* (Marcus/Mar. 1), *Half–Baked Alaska* (Marcus/Apr. 1) and *Pesty Guest* (Marcus/June 1).

1966: *Snow Place Like Home* (Smith/Feb. 1), *South Pole Pals* (Smith/Mar. 1), *Polar Fright* (Smith/Apr. 1) and *Teeny Weeny Meany* (Marcus/May 1).

1967: *Operation Shanghai* (Smith/Jan. 1), *Vicious Viking* (Smith/Feb. 1), *Hot Time On Ice* (Smith/Mar. 1), *Chilly And The Woodchopper* (Smith/May 1), *Chilly Chums* (Smith/June 1) and *Chiller Dillers* (Smith/Dec. 1).

1968: *Undersea Dogs* (Smith) and *Hiway Hecklers* (Smith/Sept. 1).

1969: *Project Reject* (Smith/May 1), *Chilly And Looney Gooney* (Smith/July 1) and *Sleepytime Bear* (Smith/Dec. 1).

1970: *Gooney's Goofy Landing* (Smith/Mar. 2), *Chilly's Ice Folly* (Smith/June 8) and *Chilly's Cold War* (Smith/Nov. 2).

1971: *A Gooney Is Born* (Smith/Jan. 1), *Airlift A La Carte* (Smith) and *Chilly's Hide–Away* (Smith).

1972: *The Rude Intruder* (Smith).

CHIP AN' DALE

These two pesty, buck–toothed chipmunks were mainly supporting characters in cartoons for Walt Disney, usually as a source of irritation to the irascible Donald Duck. Formative versions of the characters first appeared in 1943's *Private Pluto* and *Squatter's Rights,* also with Pluto, which was nominated for an Academy Award. The squeaky–voiced duo were given their rightful names in the Donald Duck cartoon, *Chip An' Dale,* in 1947. They appeared in several more Donald Duck one–reelers before the studio featured the characters in their own series. The first series entry was 1951's *Chicken in the Rough. Directed by Jack Hannah and Jack Kinney. Technicolor. A Walt Disney Production.*

Voices:
Chip/Dale: Dessie Miller, Helen Silbert (Cartoons listed are from the *Chip 'An Dale* series only.)

1951: *Chicken In The Rough* (Hannah/Jan. 19).

1952: *Two Chips And A Miss* (Hannah/Mar. 21).

1954: *The Lone Chipmunks* (Kinney/Apr. 7).

CHUCK JONES MGM CARTOONS

Director Chuck Jones' prolific career was footnoted at Warner Brothers for his direction of cartoon stars Bugs Bunny, Pepe Le Pew and the Road Runner. In the 1960s, he co–produced MGM's Tom and Jerry cartoons, besides directing several miscellaneous one–reelers for the studio, one winning an Academy Award. *Technicolor. A Metro–Goldwyn–Mayer release.*

1965: *The Dot And The Line* (Dec. 31/A.A. winner).

1967: *The Bear That Wasn't* (Dec. 31).

CLAUDE CAT

Created by Chuck Jones, this paranoid yellow cat was usually menaced by mice adversaries, Hubie and Bertie, in a series of Warner Brothers cartoons. Claude first appeared in 1949's *Mouse Wreckers,* which was nominated for an Academy Award. *Directed by Chuck Jones. Technicolor. A Warner Brothers release.*

Voices:
Claude Cat: Mel Blanc

Looney Tunes
1949: *Mouse Wreckers* (with Hubie and Bertie/Apr. 23/A.A. nominee).

1952: *Mouse Warming* (with Hubie and Bertie/Sept. 8).

1954: *Feline Frame–Up* (with Marc Antony, Pussyfoot/Feb. 13).

Merrie Melodies
1950: *The Hypo–Chondri–Cat* (with Hubie and Bertie/Jones/Apr. 28).

1951: *Cheese Chasers* (with Hubie and Bertie/McKimson/Aug. 25).

1952: *Terrier Stricken* (Jones/Nov. 29).

CLINT CLOBBER

Fully named DeWitt Clinton Clobber, this bombastic superintendent of the Flamboyant Arms apartments was reminiscent of comedian Jackie Gleason, especially the famed comedian's gruff demeanor. The series was one of several new Terrytoons creations made during the reign of the studio's creative director Gene Deitch in the late 1950s. *Directed by Connie Rasinski and Dave Tendlar. Technicolor and CinemaScope. A Terrytoons Production released through 20th Century–Fox.*

1957: *Clint Clobber's Cat* (Rasinski/July).

1958: *Springtime For Clobber* (Rasinski/Jan.), *Camp Clobber* (Tendlar/July), *Old Mother Clobber* (Rasinski/Sept.) and *Signed, Sealed and Clobbered* (Rasinski/Nov.).

1959: *Clobber's Ballet Ache* (Rasinski/Jan.) and *The Flamboyant Arms* (Rasinski/Apr.).

COLOR CLASSICS

Max Fleischer followed Walt Disney into the color cartoon arena with this series of charming fables produced in two–strip and then three–strip Technicolor. Betty Boop was featured in the series opener, a fairytale spoof called, *Poor Cinderella*, released in 1934. *Technicolor. A Fleischer Studios Production released through Paramount Pictures.*

1934: *Poor Cinderella* (with Betty Boop/Aug. 3) and *Little Dutch Mill* (Oct. 26).

1935: (Copyright dates are marked with a ©) *An Elephant Never Forgets* (© Jan. 2), *The Song Of The Birds* (© Feb. 27), *The Kids In The Shoe* (May 19), *Dancing On The Moon* (July 12), *Time For Love* (Sept. 6) and *Musical Memories* (Nov. 8).

1936: *Somewhere In Dreamland* (Jan. 17), *The Little Stranger* (Mar. 13), *The Cobweb Hotel* (May 15), *Greedy Humpty Dumpty* (July 10), *Hawaiian Birds* (Aug. 28), *Play Safe* (Oct. 16) and *Christmas Comes But Once A Year* (Dec. 4).

1937: *Bunny Mooning* (Feb. 12), *Chicken A La King* (Apr. 16), *A Car–Tune Portrait* (June 26), *Peeping Penguins* (Aug. 26), *Educated Fish* (Oct. 29) and *Little Lamby* (Dec. 31).

1938: *The Tears Of An Onion* (Feb. 26), *Hold It!* (Apr. 29), *Hunky And Spunky* (June 24), *All's Fair At The Fair* (Aug. 26) and *The Playful Polar Bears* (Oct. 28).

1939: *Always Kickin'* (Jan. 26), *Small Fry* (Apr. 21), *Barnyard Brat* (June 30) and *The Fresh Vegetable Mystery* (Sept. 29).

1940: (Copyright dates are marked by a ©) *Little Lambkin* (© Feb. 2), *Ants In the Plants* (Mar. 15), *A Kick In Time* (May 17), *Snubbed By A Snob* (July 19) and *You Can't Shoe A Horsefly* (Aug. 23).

COLOR RHAPSODIES

In an effort to emulate Walt Disney's *Silly Symphonies*, Columbia Pictures' cartoon division created a similar fairy tale series using the same commercial format of storyboarding music, children's tales and various cartoon calamities.

The cartoons were initially produced using a two–strip color process over the three–strip Technicolor, for which Disney had exclusive rights at the time. (Later full Technicolor films were produced after Disney lost his exclusivity.)

The series remained popular until Columbia's animation department closed in 1948. *Produced by Charles Mintz, Dave Fleischer and Ray Katz. Directed by Ub Iwerks, Ben Harrison, Art Davis, Sid Marcus, Paul Fennell, Frank Tashlin, Alec Geiss, Bob Wickersham, Paul Sommer, John Hubley, Dun Roman, Howard Swift and Alex Lovy. Technicolor. A Columbia Pictures release.*

1934: *Holiday Land* (with Scrappy/Nov. 9/A.A. nominee) and *Babes At Sea* (Nov. 30).

1935: *The Shoemaker And The Elves* (Jan. 20), *The Make Believe Revue* (Mar. 22), *A Cat, A Mouse, And A Bell* (May 10), *Little Rover* (June 28), *Neighbors* (Aug. 15), *Monkey Love* (Sept. 12) and *Bon Bon Parade* (Dec. 5).

1936: *Doctor Bluebird* (Feb. 5), *Football Bugs* (Apr. 29), *Glee Worms* (June 24), *The Untrained Seal* (July 26), *The Novelty Shop* (Aug. 15), *In My Gondola* (with Scrappy/Sept. 3), *Merry Mutineers* (Oct. 2), *Birds In Love* (Oct. 28), *Two Lazy Crows* (Iwerks/Nov. 26) and *A Boy And His Dog* (Dec. 23).

1937: *Gifts From The Air* (Jan. 1), *Skeleton Frolic* (Iwerks/Jan. 29), *Merry Mannequins* (Iwerks/Jan. 19), *Let's Go* (Apr. 10), *Mother Hen's Holiday* (May 7), *The Foxy Pup* (Iwerks/May 21), *The Stork Takes A Holiday* (June 11), *Indian Serenade* (July 16), *Spring Festival* (Aug. 6), *Scary Crows* (Aug. 20), *Swing Monkey Swing* (Sept. 10), *The Air Hostess* (Oct. 22), *Little Match Girl* (Nov. 5) and *Hollywood Panic* (Dec. 18).

1938: *Bluebird's Baby* (Jan. 21), *The Horse On The Merry–Go–Round* (Iwerks/Feb. 17), *The Foolish Bunny* (Davis/Mar. 26), *Snowtime* (Iwerks/Apr. 14), *The Big Birdcast* (May 13), *Window Shopping* (Marcus/June 3), *Poor Little Butterfly* (Harrison/July 4), *Poor Elmer* (Marcus/July 22), *The Frog Pond* (Iwerks/Aug. 12), *Hollywood Graduation* (Davis/Aug. 26), *Animal Cracker Circus* (Harrison/Sept. 23), *Little Moth's Big Flame* (Marcus/Nov. 3), *Midnight Frolics* (Iwerks/Nov. 24) and *The Kangaroo Kid* (Harrison/Dec. 23).

1939: *Peaceful Neighbors* (Marcus/Jan. 26), *The Gorilla Hunt* (Iwerks/Feb. 24), *Happy Tots* (Harrison/Mar. 31), *The House That Jack Built* (Marcus/Apr. 14), *Lucky Pigs* (Harrison/May 26), *Nell's Yells* (Iwerks/June 30), *Hollywood Sweepstakes* (Harrison/July 28), *Jitterbug Knights* (Marcus/Aug. 11), *Crop Chasers* (Iwerks/Sept. 22), *Dreams On Ice* (Marcus/Oct. 20), *Mountain Ears* (Gould/Nov. 3) and *Mother Goose In Swingtime* (Gould/Dec. 18).

1940: *A Boy, A Gun And Birds* (Harrison/Jan. 12), *Happy Tots' Expedition* (Harrison/Feb. 9), *Blackboard Revue* (Iwerks/Mar. 15), *The Greyhound And The Rabbit* (Marcus/Apr. 19), *The Egg Hunt* (Iwerks/May 31), *Ye Old Swap Shoppe* (Iwerks/June 28), *The Timid Pup* (Harrison/Aug. 1), *Tangled Television* (Marcus/Aug. 30), *Mr. Elephant Goes To Town* (Davis/Oct. 4), *The Mad Hatter* (Marcus/Nov. 3) and *Wise Owl* (Iwerks/Dec. 6).

1941: *A Helping Paw* (Marcus/Jan. 7), *Way Of All Pests* (Davis/Feb. 28), *The Carpenters* (Fennell/Mar. 14), *Land Of Fun* (Marcus/Apr. 18), *Tom Thumb's Brother* (Marcus/June 12), *The Cuckoo I.Q.* (Marcus/July 24), *Who's Zoo In Hollywood* (Davis/Nov. 15), *The Fox And The Grapes* (with Fox and the Crow/Tashlin/Dec. 5) and *Red Riding Hood Rides Again* (Marcus/Dec. 5).

1942: *A Hollywood Detour* (Tashlin/Jan. 23), *Wacky Wigwams* (Geiss/Feb. 22), *Concerto In B–Flat Minor* (Tashlin/Mar. 20), *Cinderella Goes To A Party* (Tashlin/May 3), *Woodman Spare That Tree* (Wickersham/June 19), *Song Of A Victory* (Wickersham/Sept. 4), *Tito's Guitar* (with Tito/Wickersham/Oct. 30), *Toll Bridge Troubles* (with Fox and the Crow/Wickersham/Nov. 27) and *King Midas Junior* (Sommer, Hubley/Dec. 18).

1943: *Slay It With Flowers* (with Fox and the Crow/Wickersham/Jan. 8), *There's Something About A Soldier* (Geiss/Feb. 26), *Professor Small And Mister Tall* (Sommer, Hubley/Mar. 26), *Plenty Below Zero* (with Fox and the Crow/Wickersham/May 14), *Tree For Two* (with Fox and the Crow/Wickersham/June 21), *He Can't Make It Stick* (Sommer, Hubley/June 11), *A Hunting We Won't Go* (with Fox and the Crow/Wickersham/Aug. 23), *The Rocky Road To Ruin* (Sommer/Sept. 16), *Imagination* (Wickersham/Oct. 29/A.A. nominee) and *The Herring Murder Mystery* (Roman/Dec. 30).

1944: *Disillusioned Bluebird* (Swift/May 26).

1945: *Dog, Cat And Canary* (with Flippy/Swift/Jan. 5), *Rippling Romance* (Wickersham/June 21), *Fiesta Time* (with Tito/Wickersham/July 12), *Hot Foot Lights* (Swift/Aug. 2), *Carnival Courage* (with Willoughby Wren/Swift/Sept. 6) and *River Ribber* (with Professor Small and Mr. Tall/Sommer/Oct. 4).

1946: *Polar Playmates* (Swift/Apr. 25), *Picnic Panic* (Wickersham/June 20), *Cagey Bird* (with Flippy/Swift/July 18) and *Loco Lobo* (Swift/Oct. 31).

1947: *Cockatoos For Two* (Wickersham/Feb. 13), *Big House* (with Flippy/Swift/Mar. 6), *Mother Hubba–Hubba–Hubba–Hubbard* (Wickersham/May 29), *Up 'N' Atom* (Marcus/July 10), *Swiss Teaser* (Marcus/Sept. 1) and *Boston Beany* (Marcus/Dec. 4).

1948: *Flora* (Lovy/Mar. 18), *Pickled Puss* (Swift/Sept. 2) and *Lo, The Poor Buffalo* (Lovy/Nov. 14).

1949: *Coo–Coo Bird Dog* (Marcus/Feb. 3), *Grape Nutty* (with Fox and the Crow/Lovy/Apr. 14) and *Cat–Tastrophy* (Marcus/June 30).

Porky Pig orders Daffy Duck to sit on and hatch a mysterious egg in a scene from Bob Clampett's 1946 cartoon, *Baby Bottleneck.* © Warner Brothers, Inc. (Courtesy: Bob Clampett Animation Art)

COMIC KINGS

The series starred the kings of Sunday comic strips, from Krazy Kat to Beetle Bailey, in madcap animated adventures simultaneously released to television and theaters. *Directed by Seymour Kneitel and Gene Deitch. Technicolor. A Famous Studios Production released through Paramount Pictures.*

1962: *Frog's Legs* (with Little Lulu/Kneitel/Jan. 1), *Home Sweet Swampy* (with Beetle Bailey/Kneitel/Jan. 1), *Hero's Reward* (with Beetle Bailey/Kneitel/May 1), *Psychological Testing* (with Beetle Bailey/Kneitel/May 1), *Snuffy's Song* (with Snuffy Smith/Kneitel/June 1), *The Hat* (with Snuffy Smith/Kneitel/July 1), *The Method And The Maw* (with Snuffy Smith/Kneitel/Aug. 1), *A Tree Is A Tree Is A Tree?* (with Beetle Bailey/Kneitel/Aug. 1), *Et Tu Otto* (with Beetle Bailey/Kneitel/Sept. 1), *Take Me To Your Gen'rul* (with Snuffy Smith, Barney Google/Kneitel/Sept. 1), *Keeping Up With Krazy* (with Krazy Kat/Deitch/Oct.) and *Mouse Blanche* (with Krazy Kat/Deitch/Nov. 1).

COMICOLOR CARTOONS

Veteran animator Ub Iwerks, a former Disney protege, directed these cartoon fables from 1933 to 1936. They were formula–type adventures using music and fanciful storylines in the Disney mold. The films were produced in Cinecolor, a two–color process combining red and blue hues, which was the forerunner to three–strip Technicolor.

The series' first entry, *Jack And The Beanstalk* premiered in 1933, and the following year Iwerks broadened the scope of these films by adding his most prestigious invention: multiplane animation, a technique Max Fleischer later used in Paramount's two–reel Popeye cartoons.

A scene from Ub Iwerks' ComicColor cartoon, Tom Thumb *(1936).* (Courtesy: Blackhawk Films)

In 1934, Iwerks unveiled the process in *The Headless Horseman,* based on Washington Irving's *The Legend of Sleepy Hollow.* The technique added a three—dimensional foreground and background to cartoons by using a multiplane camera, capable of shooting through layers of animated background, moving either forward or backward, to project on film elaborate backgrounds and a greater feeling of depth.

Not all ComiColor cartoons were produced using the multiplane camera, but all had the highest quality animation and stories.

The last cartoon of the series, *Happy Days* (1936), was also the pilot for a new series Iwerks wanted to animate based on Gene Byrnes' widely syndicated strip, "Reg'lar Fellers." Plans for the series, scheduled for the 1936—1937 season, never materialized.

Musical director Carl Stalling, long at Warner Brothers, scored the ComiColor series. *Directed by Ub Iwerks. Cinecolor. A Celebrity Pictures release.*

1933: *Jack And The Beanstalk* (Nov. 30).

1934: *The Little Red Hen* (Feb. 16), *The Brave Tin Soldier* (Apr. 7), *Puss In Boots* (May 17), *The Queen Of Hearts* (June 25), *Aladdin And The Wonderful Lamp* (Aug. 10), *The Headless Horseman* (Oct. 1), *The Valiant Tailor* (Oct. 29), *Don Quixote* (Nov. 26) and *Jack Frost* (Dec. 24).

1935: *Little Black Sambo* (Feb. 6), *Bremen Town Musicians* (Mar. 6), *Old Mother Hubbard* (Apr. 3), *Mary's Little Lamb* (May 1), *Summertime* (June 15/originally *In The Good Ol' Summertime*), *Sinbad The Sailor* (July 30), *The Three Bears* (Aug. 30), *Balloonland* (Sept. 30/aka: *The Pincushion Man*) and *Humpty Dumpty* (Dec. 30).

1936: *Ali Baba* (Jan. 30), *Tom Thumb* (Mar. 30), *Dick Whittington's Cat* (May 30), *Little Boy Blue* (July 30) and *Happy Days* (Sept. 30).

CONRAD CAT

Dim—witted Conrad Cat was created for the screen by Warner Brothers veteran Chuck Jones. The character first starred as an errand boy for the Arctic Palm Company in *The Bird Came C.O.D.,* a *Merrie Melodies* cartoon. *Directed by Chuck Jones. Technicolor. A Warner Brothers release.*

Voices:
Conrad Cat: Mel Blanc

Merrie Melodies
1942: *The Bird Came C.O.D.* (Jan. 17) and *Conrad The Sailor* (with Daffy Duck/Feb. 28).

COOL CAT

This series, one of the last at Warner Brothers, starred a hip kind of tiger created by Alex Lovy, who was hired in 1967 to direct a new series of Speedy Gonzales and Daffy Duck cartoons for the studio's newly formed animation department. Actor Larry Storch of TV's "F Troop" provided the character's "coool" voice. *Directed by Alex Lovy and Robert McKimson. Technicolor. A Warner Brothers release.*

Voices:
Cool Cat: Larry Storch

1967: *Cool Cat* (Lovy/Oct. 14/*Looney Tunes*).

1968: *Big Game Haunt* (Lovy/Feb. 10/*Merrie Melodies*), *Hippydrome Tiger* (Lovy/Mar. 30/*Merrie Melodies*) and *3—Ring Wing—Ding* (Lovy/July 13/*Looney Tunes*).

1969: *Bugged By A Bee* (McKimson/July 26/*Merrie Melodies*).

CUBBY THE BEAR

In 1933, George Stallings was appointed director of Van Beuren's animation department. Studio chief Amadee J. Van Beuren's first request was for Stallings to develop a lead character that brought life to the studio's sagging cartoon productions.

Animator Mannie Davis suggested a portly bear with round ears and impish grin, animated in the same style as Mickey Mouse. Davis submitted a sketching to Stallings for consideration. Named Cubby, the character won immediate approval and Davis directed the series' opener, *Opening Night,* released in February of that year.

Unfortunately, the series never caught on, so, in 1934, Van Beuren laid off personnel and to save costs sub—contracted animators Rudolf Ising and Hugh Harman to animate three cartoons for the series: *Cubby's World Flight, Gay Gaucho,* and *Mischievous Mice,* animated by the pair's production company. *Mischievous Mice* was never released because Van Beuren broke off relations with the famed animators after its completion. *Directed by Eddie Donnelly, Steve Muffati, George Stallings, Mannie Davis, Rollin Hamilton, Tom McKimson, Rudolf Ising and Hugh Harman. Black—and—white. A Van Beuren Production released through RKO—Radio Pictures.*

1933: (Copyright dates are marked by a ©) *Opening Night* (© Feb. 10), *The Last Mail* (© Mar. 24), *Runaway Blackie* (© Apr. 7), *Bubbles And Troubles* (© Apr. 28), *The Nut Factory* (Davis/Aug. 11), *Cubby's Picnic* (Muffati, Donnelly/ Oct. 6), *The Gay Gaucho* (Hamilton, McKimson/Nov. 3), *Galloping Fanny* (Muffati, Donnelly/Dec. 1) and *Croon Crazy* (Muffati/Dec. 29).

1934: *Sinister Stuff* (Muffati/Jan. 26), *Goode Knight* (Stallings/Feb. 23), *How's Crops?* (Stallings/Mar. 23), *Cubby's Stratosphere Flight* (Stallings/Apr. 20), *Mild Cargo* (Stallings/May 18) and *Fiddlin' Fun* (Stallings/June 15).

DAFFY DITTIES

John Sutherland Productions, the same company which produced industrial cartoons for MGM, produced this series. Most of these were regular animated cartoons, with a few done in stop–motion animation using "plastic and clay" figures a la George Pal's *Puppetoons. Directors and voice credits are unknown. Technicolor. A John Sutherland Production released through United Artists.*

1945: *The Cross–Eyed Bull.*

1946: *The Lady Said No* (Apr. 26), *Pepito's Serenade* (July 5), *Choo Choo Amigo* (Aug. 16) and *The Flying Jeep* (Aug. 20).

1947: *The Fatal Kiss* (Nov. 7).

DAFFY DUCK

Daffy was a wisecracking duck whose screen antics originated at Warner Brothers in the late 1930s. The web–footed looney, who first appeared as a co–star in Tex Avery's 1937 cartoon, *Porky's Duck Hunt,* was not officially christened until his second cartoon appearance, *Daffy Duck and Egghead,* the following year.

At first, Daffy was nothing like the character audiences grew to love. He was more screwloose than the later witty sophisticate who spouted verbal gems in his adversarial sparrings with Bugs Bunny, Porky Pig and Elmer Fudd. Instead, cross–eyed with a squat and round physique, he made the quick, jerky movements of a lunatic on the loose, performing hand-stands, sommersaults and other acrobatics that underscored his manic "Woo–hoo! Woo–hoo!" laugh (reportedly inspired by comedian Hugh Herbert's famous "Hoo–hoo! Hoo–hoo!" tagline).

Daffy's unique personality proved infectious, winning support to cast him in additional cartoons of his own. As director Bob Clampett, who animated Daffy's first screen appearance, recalled in an interview: "At the time, audiences weren't accustomed to seeing a cartoon character do these things. And so, when it hit the theatres it was like an explosion. People would leave the theatres talking about this 'daffy duck.' "

Through the 1940s, Daffy's character remained "out–of–control" in the films that followed under the effective direction of Clampett, who streamlined Daffy's design, making him taller, skinnier and thin–limbed. Daffy showed signs of screw-

ballness in his first star–billed effort, *Daffy and the Dinosaur* (1939), directed by Chuck Jones, but Clampett took the character to greater extremes in such notable efforts as *Draftee Daffy* (1945), *The Great Piggy Bank Robbery* (1946), *Book Revue* (1946) and *Baby Bottleneck* (1946).

By the 1950s, Daffy became more malevolent in nature, and was transformed into a hilarious cartoon foil for Warner cartoon stars, Bugs Bunny and Porky Pig, in a host of cartoons. It was during this period that Daffy's speech impediment evolved—he was unable to pronounce words having an "s" sound (thus "despicable" became "desthpicable"). In the 1960s, with DePatie–Freleng as his producer, Daffy's character became even more hard–edged when he was cast as a villain of sorts opposite Speedy Gonzales in a series of cartoons.

According to Chuck Jones, the successful formula for Daffy was having him victimized by his own ego: "Daffy was insane. He never settled down. His personality was very self–serving, as if to say, 'I may be mean, but at least I'm alive.' "

Perhaps the most memorable cartoons in the series include the Bugs Bunny/Daffy Duck pairings about duck/rabbit season—*Rabbit Fire* (1951), *Rabbit Seasoning* (1952), and *Duck! Rabbit! Duck!* (1953)—as well as the science-fiction favorite, *Duck Dodgers In The 24½th Century* (1953), each directed by Jones (in 1977, Jones directed a sequel, "The Return of Duck Dodgers In The 24½th Century," intended for theatrical release but instead broadcast as the centerpiece of a TV special, "Daffy Duck's Thanks–For–Giving Special" in 1981). *Directed by Tex Avery, Bob Clampett, Norm McCabe, Charles M. Jones, Frank Tashlin, Friz Freleng, Robert McKimson, Phil Monroe, Art Davis, Rudy Larriva, Alex Lovy, Maurice Noble, Ted Bonnicksen, Greg Ford and Terry Lennon. Black–and–white. Technicolor. A Warner Brothers release.*

Voices:
Daffy Duck: Mel Blanc

Looney Tunes
1937: *Porky's Duck Hunt* (with Porky Pig/Avery/Apr. 7).

1938: *What Price Porky* (Clampett/Feb. 26), *Porky And Daffy* (Clampett/Aug. 6) and *The Daffy Doc* (with Porky Pig/ Clampett/Nov. 26).

1939: *Scalp Trouble* (with Porky Pig/Clampett/June 24) and *Wise Quacks* (with Porky Pig/Clampett/Aug. 5).

1940: *Porky's Last Stand* (with Porky Pig/Clampett/Jan. 6) and *You Ought To Be In Pictures* (with Porky Pig/Freleng/ May 18).

1941: *A Coy Decoy* (with Porky Pig/McCabe/June 7) and *The Henpecked Duck* (with Porky Pig/Clampett/Aug. 30).

1942: *Daffy's Southern Exposure* (McCabe/May 2), *The Impatient Patient* (McCabe/Sept. 5), *Daffy Duckaroo* (Mc-Cabe/Oct. 24) and *My Favorite Duck* (with Porky Pig/Jones/ Dec. 5).

1943: *To Duck Or Not To Duck* (with Elmer Fudd/Jones/ Mar. 6), *The Wise Quacking Duck* (Clampett/May 1), *Yankee Doodle Daffy* (with Porky Pig/Freleng/July 3), *Porky Pig's Feat* (with Porky Pig, Bugs Bunny/Tashlin/July 17), *Scrap Happy*

Daffy (Tashlin/Aug. 21) and *Daffy—The Commando* (Freleng/Nov. 28).

1944: *Tom Turk And Daffy* (with Porky Pig/Jones/Feb. 12), *Tick Tock Tuckered* (with Porky Pig/Clampett/Apr. 8), *Duck Soup To Nuts* (with Porky Pig/Freleng/May 27), *Plane Daffy* (Tashlin/Sept. 16) and *The Stupid Cupid* (with Elmer Fudd/Tashlin/Nov. 25).

1945: *Draftee Daffy* (Clampett/Jan. 27) and *Ain't That Ducky* (Freleng/May 19).

1946: *Book Revue* (Clampett/Jan. 5), *Baby Bottleneck* (with Porky Pig/Clampett/Mar. 16), *Daffy Doodles* (with Porky Pig/McKimson/Apr. 6) and *The Great Piggy Bank Robbery* (Clampett/July 20).

1947: *Birth Of A Notion* (with Peter Lorre, Joe Besser—like goose/McKimson/Apr. 12), *Along Came Daffy* (with Yosemite Sam/Freleng/June 4), *The Up–Standing Sitter* (McKimson/July 13) and *Mexican Joy Ride* (Davis/Nov. 29).

1948: *What Makes Daffy Duck?* (with Elmer Fudd/Davis/Feb. 14/Cinecolor) and *The Stupor Salesman* (Davis/Nov. 20).

1949: *Wise Quackers* (with Elmer Fudd/Freleng/Jan. 1) and *Daffy Duck Hunt* (with Porky Pig/McKimson/Mar. 26).

1950: *Boobs In Woods* (with Porky Pig/McKimson/Jan. 28), *The Scarlet Pumpernickel* (with Porky Pig, Sylvester the Cat, Elmer Fudd, Momma Bear/Jones/Mar. 4) and *The Ducksters* (with Porky Pig/Jones/Sept. 2).

1951: *Rabbit Fire* (with Bugs Bunny, Elmer Fudd/Jones/May 19).

1952: *Thumb Fun* (with Porky Pig/McKimson/Mar. 1), *The Super Snooper* (McKimson/Nov. 1) and *Fool Coverage* (with Porky Pig/McKimson/Dec. 13).

1954: *Design For Leaving* (with Elmer Fudd/McKimson/Mar. 27).

1955: *Dime To Retire* (with Porky Pig/McKimson/Sept. 3).

1956: *The High And The Flighty* (with Foghorn Leghorn/McKimson/Feb. 18), *Stupor Duck* (McKimson/July 17), *A Star Is Bored* (with Elmer Fudd, Bugs Bunny/Freleng/Sept. 15) and *Deduce, You Say* (with Porky Pig/Jones/Sept. 29).

1957: *Boston Quackie* (with Porky Pig/McKimson/June 22) and *Show Biz Bugs* (with Bugs Bunny/Freleng/Nov. 2).

1959: *China Jones* (with Porky Pig/McKimson/Feb. 14).

1961: *The Abominable Snow–Rabbit* (with Bugs Bunny/Jones/May 20) and *Daffy's Inn Trouble* (with Porky Pig/McKimson/Sept. 23).

1962: *Good Noose* (McKimson/Nov. 10).

DePatie–Freleng Enterprises Releases
1964: *The Iceman Ducketh* (with Bugs Bunny/Monroe, Noble/May 16).

1965: *Moby Duck* (with Speedy Gonzales/McKimson/Mar. 27), *Well Worn Daffy* (with Speedy Gonzales/McKimson/May 22) and *Tease For Two* (with Goofy Gophers/McKimson/Aug. 28).

1966: *The Astroduck* (with Speedy Gonzales/McKimson/Jan. 1), *Daffy Rents* (with Speedy Gonzales/McKimson/Apr. 29), *A Haunting We Will Go* (with Speedy Gonzales, Witch Hazel/McKimson/Apr. 16) and *Swing Ding Amigo* (with Speedy Gonzales/McKimson/Sept. 17).

Warner Brothers Releases
1967: *Quacker Tracker* (with Speedy Gonzales/Larriva/Apr. 29), *The Spy Swatter* (with Speedy Gonzales/Larriva/June 24), *Rodent To Stardom* (with Speedy Gonzales/Lovy/Sept. 23), and *Fiesta Fiasco* (Lovy/Dec. 9/originally *The Rain Maker*).

1968: *See Ya Later, Gladiator* (with Speedy Gonzales/Lovy/June 29).

1987: *The Duckorcist* (Ford, Lennon/Nov. 20).

Merrie Melodies
1938: *Daffy Duck And Egghead* (with Egghead/Avery/Jan. 1) and *Daffy Duck In Hollywood* (Avery/Dec. 3).

1939: *Daffy Duck And The Dinosaur* (Jones/Apr. 22).

1942: *Conrad The Sailor* (with Conrad Cat/Jones/Feb. 28).

1944: *Slightly Daffy* (with Porky Pig/Freleng/June 17).

1945: *Nasty Quacks* (Tashlin/Dec. 1).

1946: *Hollywood Daffy* (with Bette Davis, Johnny Weissmuller, Charlie Chaplin, Jimmy Durante, Jack Benny, Bing Crosby, Joe Besser caricatures/Freleng/June 22).

1947: *A Pest In The House* (with Elmer Fudd/Jones/Aug. 3).

1948: *Daffy Duck Slept Here* (with Porky Pig/McKimson/Mar. 6), *You Were Never Duckier* (with Henery Hawk/Jones/Aug. 7), *Daffy Dilly* (Jones/Oct. 21/Cinecolor) and *Riff Raffy Daffy* (with Porky Pig/Davis/Nov. 7/Cinecolor).

1949: *Holiday For Drumsticks* (Davis/Jan. 22/Cinecolor).

1950: *His Bitter Half* (Freleng/May 20) and *Golden Yeggs* (with Porky Pig/Freleng/Aug. 5).

1951: *Dripalong Daffy* (with Porky Pig/Jones/Nov. 17) and *The Prize Pest* (with Porky Pig/McKimson/Dec. 22).

1952: *Cracked Quack* (with Porky Pig/Freleng/July 5) and *Rabbit Seasoning* (with Elmer Fudd, Bugs Bunny/Jones/Sept. 20).

1953: *Duck Amuck* (Jones/Feb. 28), *Muscle Tussle* (McKimson/Apr. 18), *Duck Dodgers In The 24½th Century* (with Porky Pig, Marvin Martian/Jones/July 25) and *Duck! Rabbit! Duck!* (with Bugs Bunny, Elmer Fudd/Jones/Oct. 3).

1954: *Quack Shot* (with Elmer Fudd/McKimson/Oct. 30) and *My Little Duckaroo* (with Porky Pig/Jones/Nov. 27).

1955: *Beanstalk Bunny* (with Bugs Bunny, Elmer Fudd/Jones/Feb. 12), *Stork Naked* (Freleng/Feb. 26) and *This Is A Life?* (with Elmer Fudd, Bugs Bunny, Yosemite Sam/Freleng/July 9).

1956: *Rocket Squad* (with Porky Pig/Jones/Mar. 10).

1957: *Ali Baba Bunny* (with Bugs Bunny/Jones/Feb. 9) and *Ducking The Devil* (with Tasmanian Devil/McKimson/Aug. 17).

1958: *Don't Axe Me* (with Elmer Fudd/McKimson/Jan. 4) and *Robin Hood Daffy* (with Porky Pig/Jones/Mar. 8).

1959: *People Are Bunny* (McKimson/Dec. 19).

1960: *Person To Bunny* (with Bugs Bunny, Elmer Fudd/Freleng/Apr. 1).

1962: *Quackodile Tears* (Davis/Mar. 31).

1963: *Fast Buck Duck* (McKimson, Bonnicksen/Mar. 9) and *Aqua Duck* (McKimson/Sept. 28).

DePatie–Freleng Enterprises Releases
1965: *Assault And Peppered* (with Speedy Gonzales/McKimson/Apr. 24), *Suppressed Duck* (McKimson/June 26) and *Go Go Amigo* (with Speedy Gonzales/McKimson/Nov. 20).

1966: *Mexican Mousepiece* (with Speedy Gonzales/McKimson/Feb. 26), *Snow Excuse* (with Speedy Gonzales/McKimson/May 21), *Feather Finger* (with Speedy Gonzales/McKimson/Aug. 20) and *Taste Of Catnip* (with Speedy Gonzales/McKimson/Dec. 3).

Warner Brothers Releases
1967: *Daffy's Diner* (with Speedy Gonzales/McKimson/Jan. 21), *Speedy Ghost To Town* (with Speedy Gonzales/Lovy/July 29) and *Go Away Stowaway* (with Speedy Gonzales/Lovy/Sept. 30).

1968: *Skyscraper Caper* (with Speedy Gonzales/Lovy/Mar. 9).

1988: *Night Of The Living Duck* (Ford, Lennon/Sept. 23).

DEPUTY DAWG

Spurned by the success of "The Deputy Dawg Show," which premiered on television in 1960, 20th Century–Fox released a number of these made–for–TV cartoons, featuring a not–so–bright lawman trying to maintain law and order in Mississippi, to theaters nationwide. The series was one of Terrytoons' most successful in the 1960s. *Directed by Bob Kuwahara and Dave Tendlar. Technicolor. A Terrytoons Production released through 20th Century–Fox.*

Voices:
Deputy Dawg: Dayton Allen

1962: *Where There's Smoke* (Kuwahara/Feb.), *Nobody's Ghoul* (Tendlar/Apr.), *Rebel Trouble* (Tendlar/June) and *Big Chief, No Treaty* (Kuwahara/Sept.).

1963: *Astronut (with Deputy Dawg/Rasinski).*

DIMWIT

As the character's name implies, Dimwit was anything but smart in this early 1950s series of Terrytoon cartoon adventures. *Directed by Connie Rasinski. Technicolor. A Terrytoons Production released through 20th Century-Fox.*

1953: *How To Keep Cool* (Oct.).

1954: *How To Relax* (Feb.).

1957: *Daddy's Little Darling* (Apr.).

DINKY DUCK

Various studios had a duck star. Walt Disney had Donald Duck and Warner Brothers had Daffy Duck. Terrytoons producer Paul Terry developed his own duck character to compete with his cartoon rivals: Dinky Duck. Dinky splashed onto the silver screen to the delight of millions of moviegoers in *The Orphan Duck* (1939). The character managed to endure despite the competition, continuing to entertain audiences in new adventures until 1957. *Directed by Eddie Donnelly, Connie Rasinski, Mannie Davis, and Win Hoskins. Black–and–white. Technicolor. A Terrytoons Production released through 20th Century–Fox.*

1939: *The Orphan Duck* (Rasinski/Oct. 6).

1940: *Much Ado About Nothing* (Rasinski/Mar. 22) and *The Lucky Ducky* (Rasinski/Sept. 6/Technicolor).

1941: *Welcome Little Stranger* (Rasinski/Oct. 3).

1942: *Life With Fido* (Rasinski/Aug. 21).

1946: (All cartoons in Technicolor) *Dinky Finds A Home* (Donnelly/June 7).

1950: *The Beauty Shop* (Donnelly/Apr. 28).

1952: *Flat Foot Fledgling* (Davis/Jan. 25), *Foolish Duckling* (Davis/May 16) and *Sink Or Swim* (Rasinski/Aug. 29).

1953: *Wise Quacks* (Davis/Feb.), *Featherweight Champ* (Donnelly/Feb. 6), *The Orphan Egg* (Donnelly/Apr. 24) and *The Timid Scarecrow* (Donnelly/Aug. 28).

1957: *It's A Living* (Hoskins/Nov. 15).

DOC

Walter Lantz first introduced this highly sophisticated cat, replete with bow tie, top hat and spindly cane, opposite two troublesome mice, Hickory and Dickory, in 1959's *Mouse Trapped,* directed by Alex Lovy. The character starred in six additional cartoons through 1962.

Director Alex Lovy left the series in 1960, with Jack Hannah, a former Disney veteran, succeeding him in that role. *Directed by Alex Lovy and Jack Hannah. Technicolor. A Walter Lantz Production released through Universal Pictures.*

Voices:
Doc: Paul Frees, **Hickory:** Dal McKennon, **Dickory:** Dal McKennon

1959: *Mouse Trapped* (with Hickory and Dickory/Lovy/Dec. 8).

The Dogfather gives directions to his henchmen in the cartoon series spoof of Marlon Brando's The Godfather, called The Dogfather. © DePatie–Freleng Enterprises

1960: *Witty Kitty* (Lovy/Jan. 5) and *Freeloading Feline* (with Cecil/Hannah/June 15/Walter Lantz Cartune Special).

1961: *Doc's Last Stand* (with Champ/Hannah/Dec. 19)

1962: *Pest Of Show* (with Champ/Hannah/Feb. 13), *Punchy Pooch* (with Champ/Hannah/Sept. 4) and *Corny Concerto* (with Champ/Hannah/Oct. 30).

THE DOGFATHER

Spoofing Marlon Brando's role in *The Godfather*, Dogfather and his canine subordinates Louie and Pugg, carry out heists and other jobs which run amuck. *Directed by Friz Freleng, Hawley Pratt, Bob McKimson, Sid Marcus, Gerry Chiniquy, Art Leonardi, Art Davis and Dave Detiege. Technicolor. A DePatie–Freleng/Mirish Company Production released through United Artists.*

Voices:
Dogfather: Bob Holt, **Louie:** Daws Butler, **Pugg:** Daws Butler

1974: *The Dogfather* (June 27), *The Goose That Laid A Golden Egg* (Oct. 4), *Heist And Seek* (Oct. 4), *The Big House Ain't A Home* (Oct. 31), *Mother Dogfather* (Oct. 31), *Bows And Errors* (Dec. 29) and *Deviled Yeggs* (Dec. 29).

1975: *Watch The Birdie* (Mar. 20), *Saltwater Tuffy* (Leonardi, Mar. 20), *M–o–n–e–y Spells Love* (Apr. 23), *Rock–A–Bye. . .Maybe* (Apr. 23), *Eagle Beagles* (May 5), *From Nags To Riches* (May 5), *Haunting Dog* (May. 2), *Goldilox And The Three Hoods* (Aug. 28) and *Rockhounds* (Nov. 20).

1976: *Medicur* (Apr. 30).

DONALD DUCK

The ill–tempered Donald Duck made his debut in 1934 in Walt Disney's *Silly Symphony* cartoon, *The Wise Little Hen*. Like Warners' Daffy Duck, Donald's features were greatly exaggerated in the beginning: he featured a longer bill, a skinnier neck, a fatter body and overly webbed feet highlighted by a tailor–made navy blue jacket. (Donald's initial design was by studio animator Dick Lundy.) By the 1940s, Donald's physique was modified into the figure which is known and recognized worldwide today.

Though Donald's first appearance won the unanimous acceptance of moviegoers, it wasn't until his second appearance in *Orphan's Benefit* that his true personality was revealed—that of "a cocky, show off with a boastful attitude that turns into anger as soon as he is crossed," according to animator Fred Spencer, who later animated MGM's *Tom and Jerry* cartoons.

Donald's success onscreen was largely due to his distinctive voice, which broke into non–descriptive jibberish when he became angry. Actor Clarence Nash was the talented individual who created Donald's voice. An Oklahoma native, Nash started at age 13 imitating animal sounds for friends down on the farm, never dreaming he would voice cartoons professionally.

Walt Disney discovered Nash one evening while listening to a Los Angeles radio show. Nash was a local milk company spokesman. "I was talking duck talk on the radio one night when Disney just happened to tune in," Nash once explained. Disney immediately had the studio's personnel director set up a voice audition for Nash and from there everything fell into place.

"When I was thirteen, I used to recite, 'Mary Had a Little Lamb,' to my friends, and they'd just cut up," remembered Nash, prior to his death in 1985. "When I got there [the studio], I stuck my tongue into the left side of my mouth and recited the same old 'Mary Had a Little Lamb.' I didn't know it, but the engineer had flipped the switch and my voice was being piped over an intercom into Walt's office."

Midway through Nash's recital, Walt ran out of his office declaring, "That's our duck! You're Donald Duck!"

Frank Thomas, a long–time Disney animator, has said Donald Duck's success was assured from the moment Nash opened his mouth. "We had many fine actors come and do voices, but I couldn't visualize anything. Clarence, with his crazy quack . . . you really believed it."

Nash's most difficult voice challenge was presented in dubbing Donald Duck cartoons in foreign languages for theatrical release abroad. "Words were written out for me phonetically," he once recalled. "I learned to quack in French, Spanish, Portuguese, Japanese, Chinese, and German."

Among Nash's favorite cartoons were *The Band Concert*, in which Mickey Mouse's attempt to play the "William Tell Overture" is marred by Donald's spiteful insistence at playing "Turkey in the Straw" on a piccolo, and the TV show, "A Day in the Life of Donald Duck," made in the 1950s, in which he appears with his alter–ego.

As the series blossomed, so did Donald's supporting cast. In 1937's *Don Donald*, Donald was paired with a young, attractive senorita named Donna, who later became Daisy Duck, Donald's girlfriend. A year later, Huey, Dewey and Louie, Donald's hellion nephews, were cast as regulars in the series.

Donald's meteoric rise led to roles in more than 150 cartoon shorts as well as appearances in several memorable feature films, among them: *The Reluctant Dragon* and *The Three Caballeros*. In 1983, he appeared in a featurette cartoon with pals Mickey Mouse and Goofy, entitled, *Mickey's Christmas Carol*.

Jack King, formerly of Warner Brothers, directed the series from 1937 to 1947. King was joined by Jack Hannah and Jack Kinney, who shared assignments with King until his retirement. Kinney is best remembered for directing the 1943 Academy Award–winning Donald Duck wartime short, *Der Fuehrer's Face,* winner in the "Best Short Films (Cartoons)" of the year category. *Additional series directors included Clyde Geronimi, Ben Sharpsteen, Dick Lundy, Riley Thomson, Wilfred Jackson, Bob Carlson, Charles Nichols, Hamilton Luske and Bill Roberts. Technicolor. A Walt Disney Production released through United Artists, RKO–Radio Pictures and later Buena Vista.*

Voices:
Donald Duck: Clarence Nash

United Artists Releases
1934: *The Wise Little Hen* (Jackson/June 9/*Silly Symphony*).

1936: *Donald And Pluto* (Sharpsteen/Sept. 12/Mickey Mouse cartoon).

1937: *Don Donald* (Sharpsteen/Jan. 9/Mickey Mouse cartoon), *Modern Inventions* (King/May 29).

RKO–Radio Pictures Releases
1937: *Donald's Ostrich* (King/Dec. 10).

1938: *Self Control* (King/Feb. 11), *Donald's Better Self* (King/Mar. 11), *Donald's Nephews* (King/Apr. 15), *Polar Trappers* (with Goofy/Sharpsteen/June 17), *Good Scouts* (King/July 8/A.A. nominee), *The Fox Hunt* (with Goofy/Sharpsteen/July 29) and *Donald's Golf Game* (King/Nov. 4).

1939: *Donald's Lucky Day* (King/Jan. 13), *Hockey Champ* (King/Apr. 28), *Donald's Cousin Gus* (King/May 19), *Beach Picnic* (with Pluto/Geronimi/June 9), *Sea Scouts* (Lundy/June 30), *Donald's Penguin* (King/Aug. 11), *The Autograph Hound* (King/Sept. 1) and *Officer Duck* (Geronimi/Oct. 10).

1940: *The Riveter* (Lundy/Mar. 15), *Donald's Dog Laundry* (with Pluto/King/Apr. 5), *Billposters* (with Goofy/Geronimi/May 17), *Mr. Duck Steps Out* (King/June 7), *Put–Put Troubles* (with Pluto/Thomson/July 19), *Donald's Vacation* (King/Aug. 9), *Window Cleaners* (with Pluto/King/Sept. 20) and *Fire Chief* (King/Dec. 3).

1941: *Timber* (King/Jan. 10), *Golden Eggs* (Jackson/Mar. 7), *A Good Time For A Dime* (Lundy/May 9), *Early To Bed* (King/July 11), *Truant Officer Donald* (King/Aug. 1/A.A. nominee), *Old MacDonald Duck* (King/Sept. 12), *Donald's Camera* (Lundy/Oct. 24) and *Chef Donald* (King/Dec. 5).

1942: *The Village Smithy* (Lundy/Jan. 16), *The New Spirit* (Jackson, Sharpsteen/Jan. 23), *Donald's Snow Fight* (King/Apr. 10), *Donald Gets Drafted* (King/May 1), *Donald's Garden* (Lundy/June 12), *Donald's Gold Mine* (Lundy/July 24), *The Vanishing Private* (King/Sept. 25), *Sky Trooper* (King/Nov. 6) and *Bellboy Donald* (King/Dec. 18).

1943: *Der Fuehrer's Face* (Kinney/Jan. 1/A.A. winner), *The Spirit Of '43* (King/Jan. 7), *Donald's Tire Trouble* (Lundy/Jan. 29), *Flying Jalopy* (Lundy/Mar. 12), *Fall Out, Fall In* (King/Apr. 23), *The Old Army Game* (King/Nov. 5) and *Home Defense* (King/Nov. 26).

1944: *Trombone Trouble* (King/Feb. 18), *Donald Duck And The Gorilla* (King/Mar. 31), *Contrary Condor* (King/Apr. 21), *Commando Duck* (King/June 2), *The Plastics Inventor* (King/Sept. 1) and *Donald's Off Day* (Hannah/Dec. 8).

1945: *The Clock Watcher* (King/Jan. 26), *The Eyes Have It* (with Pluto/Hannah/Mar. 30), *Donald's Crime* (King/June 29/A.A. nominee), *Duck Pimples* (Kinney/Aug. 10), *No Sail* (with Goofy/Hannah/Sept. 7), *Cured Duck* (King/Oct. 26) and *Old Sequoia* (King/Dec. 21).

1946: *Donald's Double Trouble* (King/June 28), *Wet Paint* (King/Aug. 9), *Dumb Bell Of The Yukon* (King/Aug. 30), *Lighthouse Keeping* (Hannah/Sept. 20) and *Frank Duck Brings 'em Back Alive* (with Goofy/Hannah/Nov. 1).

1947: *Straight Shooters* (Hannah/Apr. 18), *Sleepy Time Donald* (King/May 9), *Clown Of The Jungle* (Hannah/June 20), *Donald's Dilemma* (King/July 11), *Crazy With The Heat* (with Goofy/Carlson/Aug. 1), *Bootle Beetle* (Hannah/Aug. 22), *Wide Open Spaces* (King/Sept. 12) and *Chip An' Dale* (with Chip and Dale/Hannah/Nov. 28/A.A. winner).

1948: *Drip Dippy Donald* (King/Mar. 5), *Daddy Duck* (Hannah/Apr. 16), *Donald's Dream Voice* (King/May 21), *The Trial Of Donald Duck* (King/July 30), *Inferior Decorator* (Hannah/Aug. 27), *Soup's On* (Hannah/Oct. 15), *Three For Breakfast* (with Chip and Dale/Hannah/Nov. 5) and *Tea For Two Hundred* (Hannah/Dec. 24/A.A nominee).

1949: *Donald's Happy Birthday* (Hannah/Feb. 11), *Sea Salts* (Hannah/Apr. 8), *Winter Storage* (with Chip and Dale/Hannah/June 3), *Honey Harvester* (Hannah/Aug. 5), *All In A Nutshell* (with Chip and Dale/Hannah/Sept. 2), *The Greener Yard* (Hannah/Oct. 14), *Slide, Donald, Slide* (Hannah/Nov. 25), and *Toy Tinkers* (with Chip and Dale/Hannah/Dec. 16/A.A. nominee).

1950: *Lion Around* (Hannah/Jan. 20), *Crazy Over Daisy* (with Chip and Dale/Hannah/Mar. 24), *Trailer Horn* (with Chip and Dale/Hannah/Apr. 28), *Hook, Lion and Sinker* (Hannah/Sept. 1), *Bee At The Beach* (Hannah/Oct. 13) and *Out On A Limb* (with Chip and Dale/Hannah/Dec. 15).

1951: *Dude Duck* (Hannah/Mar. 2), *Corn Chips* (with Chip and Dale/Hannah/Mar. 23), *Test Pilot Donald* (with Chip and Dale/Hannah/June 8), *Lucky Number* (Hannah/July 20), *Out Of Scale* (with Chip and Dale/Hannah/Nov. 2) and *Bee On Guard* (Hannah/Dec. 14).

1952: *Donald Applecore* (with Chip and Dale/Hannah/Jan. 18), *Let's Stick Together* (Hannah/Apr. 25), *Uncle Donald's Ants* (Hannah/July 18) and *Trick Or Treat* (Hannah/Oct. 10).

1953: *Don's Fountain Of Youth* (Hannah/May 30), *The New Neighbor* (Hannah/Aug. 1), *Rugged Bear* (Hannah/Oct. 23/A.A. nominee), *Working For Peanuts* (with Chip and Dale/Hannah/Nov. 11/3–D) and *Canvas Back Duck* (Hannah/Dec. 25).

1954: *Spare The Rod* (Hannah/Jan. 15), *Donald's Diary* (Kinney/Mar. 5), *Dragon Around* (with Chip and Dale/Hannah/July 16), *Grin And Bear It* (Hannah/Aug. 13), *The Flying Squirrel* (Hannah/Nov. 12) and *Grand Canyonscope* (Nichols/Dec. 23/CinemaScope; Buena Vista release).

RKO–Radio Releases
1955: *No Hunting* (Hannah/Jan. 24/A.A. nominee/CinemaScope), *Lake Titicaca* (Roberts/Feb. 18/segment from *Saludos Amigos* feature), *Blame It On The Samba* (Geronimi/Apr. 1/from *Melody Time* feature), *Bearly Asleep* (Hannah/Aug. 19/CinemaScope), *Beezy Bear* (Hannah/Sept. 2/CinemaScope) and *Up A Tree* (with Chip and Dale/Hannah/Sept. 23).

1956: *Chips Ahoy* (with Chip and Dale/Kinney/Feb. 24/CinemaScope) and *How To Have An Accident In The Home* (Nichols/July 8/CinemaScope/Buena Vista release).

Buena Vista Releases
1959: *Donald In Mathmagic Land* (Luske/June 26) and *How To Have An Accident at Work* (Nichols/Sept. 2).

1961: *Donald And The Wheel* (Luske/June 21) and *The Litterbug* (Luske/June 21).

DROOPY
Dwarfed, sad–eyed, unflappable bloodhound Droopy had a Buster Keaton physique and comedy style. His creator, Tex Avery, who directed the series until he left MGM in 1954, based the character on Wallace Wimple, a supporting character in radio's "The Fibber McGee and Molly Show," played by Bill Thompson, who also voiced Droopy. (Thompson was later replaced by veteran voice artists Daws Butler and Don Messick in succession.)

Most adventures followed Avery's trademark "survival of the fittest" theme, pitting the tiny basset hound against a scene–stealing Wolf, featured between 1949 and 1952, and pesky bulldog, Spike, in situational duels with meek, low–key Droopy always emerging victorious. Situations were often earmarked by imaginative sight gags and hyperboles, complementing Droopy's notorious deadpan, which, like Keaton, convulsed audiences into laughter often without ever uttering a line of dialogue.

Michael Lah was named Avery's successor, directing five cartoons in all, including *One Droopy Knight* (1957), which was nominated for an Academy Award. (Lah actually co-directed several of Avery's last films before he was given full reign.) Dick Lundy, an MGM cartoon veteran, also directed occasional episodes. *Technicolor. CinemaScope. A Metro–Goldwyn–Mayer release.*

Voices:
Droopy: Bill Thompson, Daws Butler, Don Messick

1943: *Dumb Hounded* (Avery/Mar. 20).

1945: *Shooting Of Dan McGoo* (Avery/Mar. 3/re: Apr. 14, 1951/originally *The Shooting Of Dan McScrew*, a takeoff of MGM's feature *Dan McGrew*) and *Wild And Wolfy* (Avery/Nov. 3/re: Oct. 4, 1952/formerly *Robinson's Screwball*).

1946: *Northwest Hounded Police* (Avery/Aug. 13/re: Sept. 19, 1953/formerly *The Man Hunt*).

1949: *Senor Droopy* (Avery/Apr. 9/re: Dec. 7, 1956), *Wags To Riches* (with Spike/Avery/Aug. 13/formerly *From Wags To Riches*) and *Out–Foxed* (Avery/Oct. 12).

1950: *The Chump Champ* (with Spike/Avery/Nov. 4).

1951: *Daredevil Droopy* (with Spike/Avery/Mar. 31), *Droopy's Good Deed* (Avery/May 5) and *Droopy's Double Trouble* (Avery/Nov. 17)

1952: *Caballero Droopy* (Lundy/Sept. 27).

1953: *Three Little Pups* (Avery/Dec. 26).

1954: *Drag–Along Droopy* (Avery/Feb. 20), *Homesteader Droopy* (Avery/July 10) and *Dixieland Droopy* (Avery/Dec. 4/first in CinemaScope).

1955: *Deputy Droopy* (Avery/Oct. 28).

1956: (All in CinemaScope) *Millionaire Droopy* (Avery/Sept. 21).

1957: *Grin And Share It* (Lah/May 17/produced by William Hanna and Joseph Barbera), *Blackboard Jumble* (Lah/Oct. 4/produced by William Hanna and Joseph Barbera) and *One Droopy Knight* (Lah/Dec. 6/produced by William Hanna and Joseph Barbera).

1958: *Sheep Wrecked* (Lah/Feb. 7/produced by William Hanna and Joseph Barbera), *Mutts About Racing* (Lah/Apr. 4/produced by William Hanna and Joseph Barbera) and *Droopy Leprechaun* (Lah/July 4/produced by William Hanna and Joseph Barbera).

DR. SEUSS
Based on the Dr. Seuss children stories and written by Irving A. Jacoby. Musical score by Phillip Sheib. *Black–and–white. A Warner Brothers release.*

1931: *'Neath The Bababa Tree* (June 1) and *Put On The Spout* (June 1).

ELMER FUDD
A "wabbit hunter" by trade, his comic adventures onscreen often involved his relentless pursuit of his adversarial co–star, Bugs Bunny, who successfully outwitted the likes of one Elmer J. Fudd ("Be vew–wy quiet, I'm hunting wabbits!") in numerous animated film triumphs.

" ELMER FUDD "

© WARNER BROS. PICTURES INC.

Elmer Fudd strikes a standard pose as he prepares for "rabbit season." © Warner Brothers Inc.

The plump, chipmunk–cheeked hunter originally debuted in a different body and face as Egghead, a comic relief character in early Warner Brothers cartoons, replete with brown derby and a nose the color of wine. Patterned after famed radio/film comedian Joe Penner, whose trademark phrase was "Wanna buy a Duck?," Cliff Nazzaro supplied the character's voice through 1939's *Believe It or Else,* directed by Tex Avery.

After 11 cartoons, Warner Brothers animators decided to change the character to Elmer Fudd, appearing as such for the first time in *Dangerous Dan McFoo* (1939), again supervised by Avery. (Avery also directed Bugs Bunny's first official screen appearance, *A Wild Hare* (1940), in which Fudd also starred.)

Even with a new name and face, Elmer went through several additional design changes, beginning with Bob Clampett's *Wabbit Twouble* (1941) and three subsequent cartoons in which he appeared exceedingly portly. According to Clampett, Elmer was redesigned because "we artists were never satisfied with the way he looked—he didn't look funny."

By now, Elmer resembled his alter ego, Arthur Q. Bryan, a radio actor who played Elmer until Mel Blanc assumed the role after Bryan's death in 1958. (Bryan was well–known as Doc Gamble on "The Fibber McGee and Molly Show" and for various bit parts in movies, including the cult classic, Bela

Lugosi's *The Devil Bat*). By Friz Freleng's *The Hare–Brained Hypnotist* (1942), Elmer appeared in the style and form filmgoers would remember, including his most memorable trait—his inability to pronounce his "r's." *Directed by Tex Avery, Frank Tashlin, Ben Hardaway, Cal Dalton, Bob Clampett, Charles M. Jones, Friz Freleng and Bob McKimson. Black–and–white. Technicolor. A Warner Brothers release.*

Voices:
Egghead: Cliff Nazarro, **Elmer J. Fudd:** Arthur Q. Bryan, Mel Blanc

Merrie Melodies
1937: *Egghead Rides Again* (Avery/July 17) and *Little Red Walking Hood* (Avery/Nov. 6).

1938: *Daffy Duck And Egghead* (with Daffy Duck/Avery/Jan. 1), *The Isle Of Pingo–Pongo* (Avery/May 28), *Cinderella Meets Fella* (Avery/July 23), *A Feud There Was* (Avery/Sept. 24), *Johnny Smith And Poker Huntas* (Avery/Oct. 22) and *Count Me Out* (Hardaway, Dalton/Dec. 17).

1939: *Hamateur Nite* (Avery/Jan. 28), *A Day At The Zoo* (Avery/Mar. 11), *Believe It Or Else* (Avery/June 25) and *Dangerous Dan McFoo* (character's name changed to Elmer Fudd/Avery/July 15).

1940: *Elmer's Candid Camera* (with Bugs Bunny/Jones/Mar. 2), *A Wild Hare* (with Bugs Bunny/Avery/July 27/A.A. nominee) and *Good Night Elmer* (Jones/Oct. 26).

1941: *Elmer's Pet Rabbit* (with Bugs Bunny/Jones/Jan. 4), *All This And Rabbit Stew* (with Bugs Bunny/Avery/Sept. 13) and *Wabbit Twouble* (with Bugs Bunny/Clampett/Dec. 20).

1942: *The Wabbit Who Came To Supper* (with Bugs Bunny/Freleng/Mar. 28), *The Wacky Wabbit* (with Bugs Bunny/Clampett/May 2), *Fresh Hare* (with Bugs Bunny/Freleng/Aug. 22), and *The Hare–Brained Hypnotist* (with Bugs Bunny/Freleng/Oct. 31).

1943: *A Corny Concerto* (with Porky Pig, Bugs Bunny/Clampett/Sept. 18) and *An Itch In Time* (Clampett/Dec. 4).

1944: *The Old Grey Hare* (with Bugs Bunny/Clampett/Oct. 28) and *Stage Door Cartoon* (with Bugs Bunny/Freleng/Dec. 30).

1945: *The Unruly Hare* (with Bugs Bunny/Tashlin/Feb. 10).

1946: *Hare Remover* (with Bugs Bunny/Tashlin/Mar. 23) and *Bacall To Arms* (with Bugs Bunny/Clampett/Aug. 3).

1947: *A Pest In The House* (with Daffy Duck/Jones/Aug. 2).

1948: *Back Alley Oproar* (with Sylvester the Cat/Freleng/Mar. 27).

1949: *Hare Do* (with Bugs Bunny/Freleng/Jan. 15) and *Each Dawn I Crow* (Freleng/Sept. 23).

1952: *Rabbit Seasoning* (with Bugs Bunny, Daffy Duck/Jones/Sept. 20).

1953: *Duck! Rabbit! Duck!* (with Bugs Bunny/Jones/Oct. 3).

1954: *Quack Shot* (with Daffy Duck/McKimson/Oct. 30).

1955: *Pest For Guests* (Freleng/Jan. 29), *Beanstalk Bunny* (with Daffy Duck, Bugs Bunny/Jones/Feb. 12) and *Jumpin' Jupiter* (with Porky Pig, Sylvester the Cat/Jones/Aug. 6).

1956: *Bugs Bonnets* (with Bugs Bunny/Jones/Jan. 14), *Yankee Dood It* (with Sylvester the Cat/Freleng/Oct. 13) and *Wideo Wabbit* (with Bugs Bunny/McKimson/Oct. 27).

1957: *What's Opera, Doc?* (with Bugs Bunny/Jones/July 16) and *Rabbit Romeo* (with Bugs Bunny/McKimson/Dec. 14).

1958: *Don't Axe Me* (with Daffy Duck/McKimson/Jan. 4).

1960: *Person To Bunny* (with Bugs Bunny, Daffy Duck/Freleng/Apr. 1) and *Dog Gone People* (McKimson/Nov. 12).

Looney Tunes
1938: *The Daffy Doc* (with Porky Pig, Daffy Duck/Clampett/Nov. 26).

1943: *Confusions Of A Nutzy Spy* (McCabe/Jan. 23).

1944: *Booby Hatched* (Tashlin/Oct. 14) and *The Stupid Cupid* (with Daffy Duck/Tashlin/Nov. 25).

1945: *Hare Tonic* (with Bugs Bunny/Jones/Nov. 10).

1946: *The Big Snooze* (with Bugs Bunny/Clampett/Oct. 5).

1947: *Easter Yeggs* (with Bugs Bunny/McKimson/June 28).

1948: *Kit For Cat* (with Sylvester the Cat/Freleng/Nov. 6).

1949: *Wise Quackers* (with Daffy Duck/Freleng/Jan. 1).

1950: *The Scarlet Pumpernickel* (with Daffy Duck, Porky Pig, Sylvester the Cat, Momma Bear/Jones/Mar. 4), *What's Up, Doc?* (with Bugs Bunny/McKimson/June 17) and *Rabbit Of Seville* (with Bugs Bunny/Jones/Dec. 16).

1951: *Rabbit Fire* (with Daffy Duck, Bugs Bunny/Jones/May 19).

1953: *Ant Pasted* (Freleng/May 9) and *Robot Rabbit* (with Bugs Bunny/Freleng/Dec. 12).

1954: *Design For Living* (with Daffy Duck/McKimson/Mar. 27).

1955: *Hare Brush* (with Bugs Bunny/Freleng/May 7).

1956: *Heir-Conditioned* (with Sylvester the Cat/Freleng/Nov. 26).

1958: *Pre-Hysterical Hare* (with Bugs Bunny/McKimson/Nov. 1).

1959: *A Mutt In A Rut* (McKimson/May 23).

1961: *What's My Lion?* (McKimson/Oct. 21).

FABLES

In addition to *Color Rhapsodies*, producer Charles Mintz, who began his career producing silent cartoons, produced another series based on popular children's tales called *Fables*.

Directors included Sid Marcus, Ben Harrison, John Hubley, Lou Lilly, Frank Tashlin, Alec Geiss, Bob Wickersham and Art Davis. Technicolor. A Columbia Pictures release.

1939: *The Little Lost Sheep* (with Krazy Kat/Oct. 6) and *Park Your Baby* (with Scrappy/Dec. 22).

1940: *Practice Makes Perfect* (with Scrappy/Apr. 5), *Barnyard Babies* (Marcus/June 14), *Pooch Parade* (with Scrappy/July 19), *A Peep In The Deep* (with Scrappy/Aug. 23), *Farmer Tom Thumb* (Sept. 21), *Mouse Meets Lion* (Oct. 25) and *Paunch 'N' Judy* (Harrison/Dec. 13).

1941: *The Streamlined Donkey* (Marcus/Jan. 17), *It Happened To Crusoe* (Mar. 14), *Kitty Gets The Bird* (June 13), *Dumb Like A Fox* (July 18), *Playing The Pied Piper* (Lilly/Aug. 18), *The Great Cheeze Mystery* (Davis/Oct. 27) and *The Tangled Angler* (Tashlin/Dec. 26).

1942: *Under The Shedding Chestnut Tree* (Wickersham/Feb. 2), *Wolf Chases Pig* (Tashlin, Hubley/Apr. 30) and *The Bulldog And The Baby* (Geiss/July 3).

FARMER AL FALFA

The white-bearded hayseed who first appeared in the silent days returned to star in new sound cartoon adventures under the *Terrytoons* banner for creator Paul Terry. Later adventures co-starred two other Terrytoons stars, Kiko the Kangaroo and Puddy the Pup. *Directed by Paul Terry, Frank Moser, Mannie Davis, George Gordon and Jack Zander. Black-and-white. Voice credits unknown. A Terrytoons Production released through 20th Century-Fox.*

1931: *Club Sandwich* (Terry, Moser/Jan. 25), *Razzberries* (Terry, Moser/Feb. 8), *The Explorer* (Terry, Moser/Mar. 22), *The Sultan's Cat* (Terry, Moser/May 17), *Canadian Capers* (Terry, Moser/Aug. 23) and *The Champ* (Terry, Moser/Sept. 20).

1932: *Noah's Outing* (Terry, Moser/Jan. 24), *Ye Olde Songs* (Terry, Moser/Mar. 20), *Woodland* (Terry, Moser/May 1), *Farmer Al Falfa's Bedtime Story* (Terry, Moser/June 12), *Spring Is Here* (Terry, Moser/July 24), *Farmer Al Falfa's Ape Girl* (Terry, Moser/Aug. 1) and *Farmer Al Falfa's Birthday Party* (Terry, Moser/Oct. 2).

1933: *Tropical Fish* (Terry, Moser/May 14), *Pick-Necking* (Terry, Moser/Sept. 22), *The Village Blacksmith* (Terry, Moser/Nov. 3), *Robinson Crusoe* (Terry, Moser/Sept. 17/copyrighted as *Shipwrecked Brothers*).

1934: *The Owl And The Pussycat* (Terry, Moser/Mar. 9) and *Why Mules Leave Home* (Terry, Moser/Sept. 7).

1935: *What A Night* (Terry, Moser/Jan. 25), *Old Dog Tray* (Terry, Moser/Mar. 21), *Moans And Groans* (Terry, Moser/June 28) and *A June Bride* (Terry, Moser/Nov. 1).

1936: *The 19th Hole Club* (Terry, Moser/Jan. 24), *Home Town Olympics* (Terry, Moser/Feb. 7), *The Alpine Yodeler* (Terry, Moser/Feb. 21), *Barnyard Amateurs* (Terry, Moser/Mar. 6), *The Western Trail* (Terry, Moser/Apr. 3), *Rolling*

Stones (Terry, Moser/May 1), *The Runt* (Terry, Moser/May 15), *The Hot Spell* (with Puddy the Pup/Davis, Gordon/July 10), *Puddy The Pup And The Gypsies* (with Puddy the Pup/July 24), *Farmer Al Falfa's Prize Package* (with Kiko the Kangaroo/July 31), *The Health Farm* (Davis, Gordon/Sept. 4) and *Farmer Al Falfa's Twentieth Anniversary* (Davis, Gordon/Nov. 27).

1937: *The Tin Can Tourist* (Davis, Gordon/Jan. 22), *The Big Game Haunt* (Davis, Gordon/Feb. 19), *Flying South* (Davis, Gordon/Mar. 19), *The Mechanical Cow* (Zander/June 25), *Trailer Life* (Aug. 20), *A Close Shave* (with Ozzie/Davis/Oct. 1) and *The Dancing Bear* (Oct. 15).

FELIX THE CAT

Clever feline Felix the Cat briefly appeared in a series of sound cartoons, which were accompanied by a musical soundtrack, in which he acted in pantomime in stories that were throwbacks to the silent days of filmmaking. The cartoons were produced as part of Burt Gillett's *Rainbow Parades. Directed by Burt Gillett and Tom Palmer. Black–and–white. A Van Beuren Production released through RKO Radio Pictures.*

1936: *Felix The Cat And The Goose That Laid The Golden Eggs* (Feb. 7), *Neptune Nonsense* (Mar. 20) and *Bold King Cole* (May 29).

FIGARO

This series starred the mischief–making cat, Figaro, formerly of Walt Disney's *Pinocchio* (1940), in his eternal quest to catch the ever–elusive, Cleo the goldfish, who likewise debuted in the feature film classic. Figaro also appeared separately as a supporting player in Pluto cartoons. *Directed by Jack Kinney and Charles Nichols. Technicolor. A Walt Disney Production released through RKO–Radio Pictures.*

Voices:
Figaro: Clarence Nash, Kate–Ellen Murtagh

1943: *Figaro And Cleo* (Kinney/Oct. 15).

1946: *Bath Day* (Nichols/Oct. 11).

1947: *Figaro And Frankie* (Nichols/May 30).

FLIPPY

The "chase" formula, so popular in Terrytoons and MGM's *Tom and Jerry,* was the basis of this series that revolved around the adventures of a thin yellow canary, Flippy, who is chased by an adversary cat, Flop. That's until Sam the Dog, the neighborhood watchdog, intervenes. Flippy in some ways resembles Warner Brothers Tweety bird. The series later inspired its own comic book series. *Directed by Howard Swift and Bob Wickersham. Technicolor. A Columbia Pictures release.*

1945: *Dog, Cat And Canary* (Swift/Jan. 5/*Color Rhapsody*).

1946: *Cagey Bird* (Swift/July 18) and *Silent Treatment* (Wickersham/Sept. 19).

1947: *Big House Blues* (Swift/Mar. 6/*Color Rhapsody*).

FLIP THE FROG

The star of Ub Iwerks' first Celebrity Pictures animated series, this web–footed amphibian was featured in 38 cartoon adventures released by Metro–Goldwyn–Mayer. Each film had a ragtime musical soundtrack and other vocal effects, as none of the characters in the films ever talked.

Originally to be called "Tony the Frog," Flip's debut was in the 1930 cartoon *Fiddlesticks,* made in two–strip Cinecolor two years before Walt Disney produced the first Technicolor short, *Flowers and Trees.* With the aid of a small staff, Iwerks animated most of the cartoons himself.

After two cartoons, Flip's character was modified at the request of Iwerks' producer Pat Powers, making him "less froglike" with more human qualities. (Taller, he was dressed in plaid pants, white shoes and hand mittens.) The changes to his character were apparent in the 1930 release, *The Village Barber,* which enabled Powers to sell the series to MGM for distribution.

The *Flip the Frog* series was MGM's first animated venture and attained minimal success, lasting four seasons. Carl Stalling, who first scored Walt Disney's *Silly Symphony* series and later Warner Brothers *Merrie Melodies* and *Looney Tunes,* served as the series musical director. Additional series animators included Irv Spence, Grim Natwick, Max Fleischer, Rudy Zamora, Al Eugster and James "Shamus" Culhane.

Most cartoons were produced in black–and–white with a few filmed in the then–experimental Cinecolor. *Directed by Ub Iwerks. A Celebrity Pictures Production released through Metro–Goldwyn–Mayer.*

1930: *Fiddlesticks* (Aug. 16/Cinecolor), *Flying Fists* (Sept. 6), *The Village Barber* (Sept. 27), *Little Orphan Willie, Cuckoo Murder Case* (Oct. 18) and *Puddle Pranks.*

1931: *The Village Smithie* (Jan. 31), *The Soup Song* (Jan. 31), *Laughing Gas* (Mar. 14), *Ragtime Romeo* (May 2), *The New Car* (July 25), *Movie Mad* (Aug. 29), *The Village Spe-*

Flip the Frog in a scene from Techno–Cracked (1933), filmed in Cinecolor. (Courtesy: Blackhawk Films)

cialist (Sept. 12), *Jail Birds* (Sept. 26), *Africa Squeaks* (Oct. 17) and *Spooks* (Dec. 21).

1932: *The Milkman* (Feb. 20), *Fire! Fire!* (Mar. 5), *What A Life* (Mar. 26), *Puppy Love* (Apr. 30), *School Days* (May 14), *Bully* (June 18), *The Office Boy* (July 16), *Room Runners* (Aug. 13), *Stormy Seas* (Aug. 22), *Circus* (Aug. 27), *Goal Rush* (© Oct. 3), *Phoney Express* (© Oct. 27), *The Music Lesson* (Oct. 29), *Nurse Maid* (Nov. 26) and *Funny Face* (Dec. 24).

1933: *Cuckoo The Magician* (Jan. 21), *Flip's Lunch Room* (Apr. 3), *Techno–Cracked* (May 8/Cinecolor), *Bulloney* (May 30), *Chinaman's Chance* (June 24), *Pale–Face* (Aug. 12) and *Soda Squirt* (Oct. 12).

FOGHORN LEGHORN

A loudmouthed Southern rooster known for his boisterous babblings on ("Pay attention, boy . . . now listen here!"), Foghorn Leghorn was another popular character in Warner Brothers' stable of cartoon stars. The by–nature braggart was first featured in Warner's 1946 release, *Walky Talky Hawky*, appearing opposite a precocious chicken hawk named Henery Hawk, whose single greatest ambition is to "catch chickens."

Surprisingly, the cartoon won an Academy Award nomination for "Best Short Subject" that year. It also won Foghorn a permanent spot on the Warner's cartoon roster, afterwards being cast in his own starring cartoon series for the next 16 years.

Originally considered a parody of the Senator Claghorn character from Fred Allen's radio show, Warner's animator Robert McKimson actually modeled Foghorn after a sheriff character from an earlier radio program, "Blue Monday Jamboree." It was from this broadcast that McKimson adapted many of Foghorn's distinctive traits, among them, his overstated repartee and other standard lines for which he became famous.

Mel Blanc, the man of a thousand cartoon voices, was the voice of Foghorn Leghorn. Blanc derived the idea for the character's voice from a 1928 vaudeville show he attended as a teenager. "When I was just a youngster, I had seen a vaudeville act with this hard–of–hearing sheriff. And the fellow would say, 'Say! P–pay attenshun. I'm talkin' to ya, boy. Don't ya know what I'm ah talkin' about.' I thought, 'Gee, this might make a good character if I made a big Southern rooster out of him.' And that's how I happened to get the voice of Foghorn Leghorn," Blanc recalled prior to his death in 1989.

Since pairing Henery Hawk with Foghorn was so successful the first time around, McKimson made the character a regular in the series, alternating him in a supporting role with Br'er Dog, a grumpy backyard dog, as Foghorn's chief nemesis. For romantic interest, Miss Prissy, the husband–seeking hen, was later featured in several films, along with her son, Junior, a bookwormish child prodigy whose intelligence was vastly superior to that of Foghorn's. *Directed by Robert McKimson and Art Davis. Technicolor. A Warner Brothers release.*

Voices:
Foghorn Leghorn: Mel Blanc, **Henery Hawk:** Mel Blanc, **Miss Prissy:** Mel Blanc, Bea Benadaret, June Foray, Julie Bennett

Merrie Melodies
1946: *Walky Talky Hawky* (with Henery Hawk/McKimson/Aug. 31/A.A. nominee).

1948: *The Foghorn Leghorn* (with Henery Hawk/McKimson/Oct. 9).

1950: *A Fractured Leghorn* (McKimson/Sept. 16).

1951: *Leghorn Swoggled* (with Henery Hawk/McKimson/July 28).

1952: *The Egg–Cited Rooster* (with Henery Hawk/McKimson/Oct. 4).

1955: *Feather Dusted* (McKimson/Jan. 15).

1957: *Fox Terror* (McKimson/May 11).

1958: *Feather Bluster* (McKimson/May 10) and *Weasel While You Work* (McKimson/Aug. 6).

1960: *Crockett–Doodle–Doo* (McKimson/June 25) and *The Dixie Fryer* (McKimson/Sept. 24).

1961: *Strangled Eggs* (with Henery Hawk/McKimson/Mar. 18).

1962: *Mother Was A Rooster* (McKimson/Oct. 20).

1963: *Banty Raids* (McKimson/June 29).

Looney Tunes
1947: *Crowing Pains* (with Sylvester the Cat, Henery Hawk/McKimson/July 12).

1948: *The Rattled Rooster* (Davis/June 26).

1950: *The Leghorn Blows At Midnight* (with Henery Hawk/McKimson/May 6).

1951: *Lovelorn Leghorn* (with Miss Prissy/McKimson/Sept. 8).

1952: *Sock–A–Doodle–Do* (McKimson/May 10).

1954: *Little Boy Boo* (with Widow Hen, Junior/McKimson/June 5).

1955: *All Fowled Up* (with Henery Hawk/McKimson/Feb. 19).

1956: *The High And The Flighty* (with Daffy Duck/McKimson/Feb. 18).

1959: *A Broken Leghorn* (McKimson/Sept. 26).

1962: *The Slick Chick* (with Widow Hen, Junior/McKimson/July 21).

FOOFLE

Directed by Dave Tendlar. Technicolor and CinemaScope. A Terrytoons Production released through 20th Century–Fox.

1959: *Foofle's Train Ride* (May).

1960: *Foofle's Picnic* (March/CinemaScope) and *The Wayward Hat* (July/CinemaScope).

FOOLISH FABLES

Spoofs of popular children's fables had been done before to various degrees. That same formula inspired this short–lived series by Walter Lantz Production, which faltered after only two cartoons. *Directed by Paul J. Smith. Technicolor. Voice credits unknown. A Walter Lantz Production released through Universal Pictures.*

1953: *The Mouse And The Lion* (May 11) and *The Flying Turtle* (June 29).

FOX AND THE CROW

The slick–talking black crow and gluttonous bow–tied fox were the most flamboyant Columbia Pictures cartoon characters to appear on movie screens. The brainchild of director Frank Tashlin, who wrote and directed the first cartoon, *The Fox And The Grapes* (1941), the characters' wild pursuits of each other served as inspiration for Chuck Jones' blackout-styled humor (a series of gags joined together by one common theme) in his Road Runner and Coyote series for Warner Brothers.

Charles Mintz initially produced the series, with Dave Fleischer and Ray Katz later succeeding him as the series producer.

When Columbia Pictures closed its cartoon department, United Productions of America (UPA) picked up the series and continued its production. The characters received two Academy Award nominations. *Series directors were Bob Wickersham, Frank Tashlin, Howard Swift and John Hubley. Technicolor. A Columbia Pictures and UPA Productions release.*

Voices:
Fox: Frank Graham, **Crow:** Paul Frees

Columbia Pictures
1941: *The Fox And The Grapes* (Tashlin/Dec. 5/*Color Rhapsody*).

1942: *Woodman Spare That Tree* (Wickersham/July 2/*Color Rhapsody*) and *Toll Bridge Troubles* (Wickersham/Nov. 27/*Color Rhapsody*).

1943: *Slay It With Flowers* (Wickersham/Jan. 8), *Plenty Below Zero* (Wickersham/May 14), *Tree For Two* (Wickersham/June 21), *A Hunting We Won't Go* (Wickersham/Aug. 23), *Room And Bored* (Wickersham/Sept. 30) and *Way Down Yonder In The Corn* (Wickersham/Nov. 25).

1944: *The Dream Kids* (Wickersham/Jan. 5/last cartoon produced by Fleischer), *Mr. Moocher* (Wickersham/Sept. 8), *Be Patient, Patient* (Wickersham/Oct. 27) and *The Egg Yegg* (Wickersham/Dec. 8).

1945: *Ku–Kunuts* (Wickersham/Mar. 30), *Treasure Jest* (Wickersham/Aug. 30) and *Phoney Baloney* (Wickersham/Sept. 13).

1946: *Foxey Flatfoots* (Wickersham/Apr. 11), *Unsure Rents* (Swift/May 16) and *Mysto Fox* (Wickersham/Aug. 29).

1947: *Tooth Or Consequences* (Swift/June 5/*Phantasy* cartoon).

UPA Productions
1948: *Robin Hoodlum* (Hubley/Dec. 23/produced by Steve Bosustow/A.A. nominee).

1949: *The Magic Fluke* (Hubley/Mar. 27/produced by Steve Bosustow).

1950: *Punchy De Leon* (Hubley/Jan. 12/*Jolly Frolics*).

FOXY

Foxy, who resembled Mickey Mouse with pointy ears and a bushy tale, was an early *Merrie Melodies* star who headlined three series entries in 1931. The character was featured in episodes which were shaped around popular songs of the day.

Aesop's characters the Fox and the Crow found fame in Columbia and UPA cartoons produced in the 1940s. (Courtesy: Mark Kausler)

Frank Marsales, who was Warner's first musical director for animation, directed Foxy's screen debut. *Black–and–white. Voice credits unknown. A Warner Brothers release.*

1931: *Lady Play Your Mandolin* (Marsales/Sept.), *Smile, Darn Ya, Smile* (Sept. 5) and *One More Time* (Oct. 3).

FRACTURED FABLES

A series of outlandish tall tales directed by Ralph Bakshi, of *Lord of the Rings* and *Fritz the Cat* fame, and James "Shamus" Culhane. *Technicolor. A Famous Studios Production released through Paramount Pictures.*

1967: *My Daddy The Astronaut* (Culhane/Apr. 1), *The Stuck–Up Wolf* (Culhane/Sept. 1) and *The Stubborn Cowboy* (Culhane/Oct. 1).

1968: *The Mini–Squirts* (Bakshi/Feb. 1), *The Fuz* (Bakshi/Mar. 1) and *Mouse Trek* (Bakshi/Mar. 1).

GABBY

Gabby first appeared as a town crier in the animated feature, *Gulliver's Travels* (1939), produced by Max Fleischer. After his film debut, he starred in his own cartoon series. Stories were shaped around Gabby's inability to do anything right.

Gabby, a character in the Max Fleischer feature Gulliver's Travels (1939), starred in his own cartoon series shaped around his incompetence in doing anything right. (Courtesy: Republic Pictures)

He tried everything from diapering a baby to cleaning a castle, with predictably disastrous results.

Pinto Colvig, the original voice of Walt Disney's Goofy, provided the voice of Gabby. *Directed by Dave Fleischer. Technicolor. A Fleischer Studios Production released through Paramount Pictures.*

Voices:
Gabby: Pinto Colvig

1940: *King For A Day* (Oct. 18) and *The Constable* (Nov. 15).

1941: *All's Well* (Jan. 17), *Two For The Zoo* (Feb. 21), *Swing Cleaning* (Apr. 11), *Fire Cheese* (June 20), *Gabby Goes Fishing* (July 18) and *It's A Hap–Hap–Happy Day* (Aug. 15).

GANDY GOOSE

Inspired by comedian Ed Wynn's fluttery voice and mannerisms, sweet–nurtured Gandy was another Terrytoons attempt at copying the success of a noted personality in animated form. Unlike other attempts, this character proved to be a major disappointment after it was first introduced to filmgoers in 1938's *Gandy The Goose*. There was no real chemistry or magic to the early films.

Rather than scrap Gandy altogether, the studio resurrected a one–shot cat character, Sourpuss, from an earlier cartoon, *The Owl And The Pussycat,* to pair with Gandy in future escapades. The teaming saved the series, with the cat's offbeat personality, which was reminiscent of comedian Jimmy Durante, sparking more interest from theater audiences. The series became so successful that studio animators repeated the Gandy–Sourpuss formula for 10 years until the series ended in 1955.

Several Terrytoons veterans were responsible for directing the series. They included John Foster, Eddie Donnelly, Connie Rasinski, Volney White and Mannie Davis. *Black–and–white. Technicolor. A Terrytoons Production released through 20th Century–Fox.*

Voices:
Gandy/Sourpuss: Arthur Kay

1938: (black–and–white) *Gandy The Goose* (Foster/Mar. 4), *Goose Flies High* (Foster/Sept. 9), *Doomsday* (Rasinski/Dec. 16) and *The Frame–Up* (Rasinski/Dec. 30).

1939: *G–Man Jitters* (Donnelly/Mar. 10), *A Bully Romance* (Donnelly/June 16), *Barnyard Baseball* (Davis/July 14), *Hook, Line And Sinker* (Donnelly/Sept. 8/first Technicolor) and *The Hitchhiker* (Donnelly/Dec. 1).

1940: *It Must Be Love* (Rasinski/Apr. 5) and *The Magic Pencil* (White/Nov. 15).

1941: (All in Technicolor except noted otherwise) *Fishing Made Easy* (Donnelly/Feb. 21/black–and–white), *The Home Guard* (Davis/Mar. 7), *The One Man Navy* (Davis/Sept. 5), *Slap Happy Hunters* (Donnelly/Oct. 31) and *Flying Fever* (Davis/Dec. 26/black–and–white).

1942: *Sham Battle Shenanigans* (Rasinski/Mar. 20), *The Night* (Apr. 17), *Lights Out* (Donnelly/Apr. 17), *Tricky Business* (Donnelly/May 1/black–and–white), *The Outpost* (Davis/July 10/black–and–white), *Tire Trouble* (Donnelly/July 24/black–and–white) and *Night Life In The Army* (Davis/Oct. 12).

1943: *Camouflage* (Donnelly/Aug. 27), *Somewhere In Egypt* (Davis/Sept. 17) and *Aladdin's Lamp* (Donnelly/Oct. 22).

1944: *The Frog And The Princess* (Donnelly/Apr. 7), *The Ghost Town* (Davis/Sept. 22) and *Gandy's Dream Girl* (Davis/Dec. 8).

1945: *Post–War Inventions* (Rasinski/Mar. 23), *Fisherman's Luck* (Donnelly/Mar. 23), *Mother Goose Nightmare* (Rasinski/May 4), *Aesop Fable: The Mosquito* (Davis/June 29), *Who's Who In The Jungle* (Donnelly/Oct. 19) and *The Exterminator* (Donnelly/Nov. 23).

1946: *Fortune Hunters* (Rasinski/Feb. 8), *It's All In The Stars* (Rasinski/Apr. 12), *The Golden Hen* (Davis/May 24) and *Peace–Time Football* (Davis/July 19).

1947: *Mexican Baseball* (Davis/Mar. 14).

1948: *Gandy Goose And The Chipper Chipmunk* (Davis/Mar. 9).

1949: *Dingbat Land* (with Sourpuss/June 9), *The Covered Pushcart* (with Sourpuss/Davis/Aug. 26) and *Comic Book Land* (Davis/Dec. 23).

1950: *Dream Walking* (Rasinski/June 9) and *Wide Open Spaces* (Donnelly/Nov. 1).

1951: *Songs Of Erin* (Rasinski/Feb. 25) and *Spring Fever* (Davis/Mar. 18).

1955: *Barnyard Actor* (Rasinski/Jan. 25).

GASTON LE CRAYON

Part of several new Terrytoons series launched in the late 1950s, this talented French artist made his drawings come to life in assorted misadventures. Screen debut: *Gaston Is Here,* released in CinemaScope in 1957. *Directed by Connie Rasinski and Dave Tendlar. Technicolor. CinemaScope. A Terrytoons Production released through 20th Century–Fox.*

1957: *Gaston Is Here* (Rasinski/May).

1958: *Gaston's Baby* (Rasinski/Mar.), *Gaston, Go Home* (Rasinski/May) and *Gaston's Easel Life* (Tendlar/Oct.).

1959: *Gaston's Mama Lisa* (Rasinski/June).

George and Junior, the Abbott and Costello of cartoons, starred in riotous misadventures directed by Tex Avery for MGM. © Turner Entertainment (Courtesy: Mark Kausler)

GEORGE AND JUNIOR

Parodying characters George and Lenny from John Steinbeck's novel *Of Mice and Men*, this short—lived series featured stupid, overweight George and his clever straight-man bear, Junior. They were an uproarious and destructive pair, fashioned by Tex Avery, who also directed the series. *Technicolor. A Metro—Goldwyn—Mayer release.*

Voices:

George: Frank Graham, **Junior:** Tex Avery

1946: *Henpecked Hoboes* (Avery/Oct. 26).

1947: *Red Hot Rangers* (Avery/May 31) and *Hound Hunters* (Avery/Apr. 12).

1948: *Half—Pint Pygmy* (Avery/Aug. 7).

GEORGE PAL PUPPETOONS

While not animated cartoons in the true sense, director George Pal, noted for producing such science fiction classics as *War of the Worlds* and *When Worlds Collide*, created this widely acclaimed stop—action animation series starring the wide-eyed little black boy, Jasper, and his constant companions, Professor Scarecrow and Black Crow, in Huckleberry Finn–like tales shaped around black folklore.

The characters, which were actually wooden puppets, had flexible limbs that enabled them to move realistically. Pal and his 45 staff members, whom he credits for the series' success, diligently prepared background sets and other movable miniatures before filming each eight—minute one—reel short. A typical production cost about $25,000 to create.

According to Pal, "We had all these creative people bouncing ideas around. We were our own masters. We didn't have to get this approval and that approval, the way you do in feature motion pictures. All I had to do was pick up the phone to Paramount and tell them we had an idea, and they said, 'Go ahead.' "

Paramount was far from disappointed. The series won five Academy Award nominations in the Best Short—Subject category and critical acclaim from film industry officials who were amazed by the dexterity of Pal's creations. *Directed by George Pal. Narration by Rex Ingram and Victor Jory. Technicolor. A Paramount Pictures release.*

1941: *Western Daze* (Jan. 7/*Madcap Model* cartoon), *Dipsy Gypsy* (Apr. 4), *Hoola Boola* (June 27), *The Gay Knighties* (Aug. 22) and *Rhythm In The Ranks* (Dec. 26/A.A. nominee).

1942: *Jasper And The Watermelons* (Feb. 26/*Madcap Model* cartoon), *Sky Princess* (Mar. 27) and *Jasper And The Haunted House* (Oct. 23).

1943: *Jasper And The Choo—Choo* (Jan. 1/*Madcap Model* cartoon), *Tulips Shall Grow* (Jan. 26/A.A. nominee), *Bravo Mr. Strauss* (Feb. 26), *The 500 Hats Of Bartholomew Cubbins* (Apr. 30/A.A. nominee), *Mr. Strauss Takes A Walk* (May 8), *Jasper's Music Lesson* (May 21), *The Truck That Flew* (Aug. 6), *The Little Broadcast* (Sept. 25), *Jasper Goes Fishing* (Oct. 8) and *Good Night Rusty* (Dec. 3).

1944: *Package For Jasper* (Jan. 28), *Say, Ah Jasper* (Mar. 10), *And To Think I Saw It On Mulberry Street, Jasper Goes Hunting* (July 28), *Jasper's Paradise* (Oct. 13) and *Two—Gun Rusty* (Dec. 1).

1945: *Hot Lisp Jasper* (Jan. 5), *Jasper Tell* (Mar. 23), *Jasper's Minstrels* (May 25), *A Hatful Of Dreams* (July 6), *Jasper's Close Shave* (Sept. 28), *Jasper And The Beanstalk* (Oct. 9/A.A. nominee) and *My Man Jasper* (Dec. 14).

1946: *Olio For Jasper* (Jan. 25), *Together In The Weather* (Mar. 22), *John Henry And The Inky Poo* (Sept. 6/A.A. nominee), *Jasper's Derby* (Sept. 20) and *Jasper In A Jam* (Oct. 18).

1947: *Shoe Shine Jasper* (Feb. 28), *Wilbur The Lion* (Apr. 18), *Tubby The Tuba* (July 11), *Date With Duke* (Oct. 31) and *Rhapsody In Wood* (Dec. 29).

GERALD McBOING BOING

Based on a Dr. Seuss children's record, Gerald McBoing Boing, a curly—topped, mute boy, uttered only the sound of "Boing—Boing" when communicating with his parents and friends. Introduced in 1951, the first cartoon, titled after the character, was released to theaters under the *Jolly Frolics* series pro-

© 1975 UPA Pictures Inc.

UPA's award—winning character, Gerald McBoing Boing, was featured in a handful of cartoon shorts in the 1950s. He later starred in his own weekly television series.
© UPA Productions, Inc.

duced by United Productions of America (UPA). The film garnered an Academy Award for "Best Short Subject" of the year.

Three years later, the series was distributed under the Gerald McBoing Boing name, with the final series release, *Gerald McBoing Boing On The Planet Moo* (1956), winning the series' second Oscar in five years. *Directed by Bob Cannon. Narrated by Hal Peary. Technicolor. A UPA Productions release through Columbia Pictures.*

Voices:
Gerald McBoing Boing: Howard Morris

1951: *Gerald McBoing Boing* (Cannon/Jan. 25/A.A. winner/ *Jolly Frolics* cartoon).

1953: *Gerald McBoing Boing's Symphony* (Cannon/July 15/*Jolly Frolics* cartoon).

1954: *How Now Boing Boing* (Cannon/Sept. 9).

1956: *Gerald McBoing Boing On The Planet Moo* (Cannon/Feb. 9/A.A. winner).

GO–GO TOONS

One of Famous Studios' last cartoon series, it features a wide assortment of outlandish cartoon tales, each starring various characters. *Directed by Ralph Bakshi, James "Shamus" Culhane and Chuck Harriton. Technicolor. A Famous Studios Production released through Paramount Pictures.*

1967: *The Space Squid* (Culhane/Jan. 1), *The Plumber* (Culhane/May 1), *The Squaw Path* (Culhane/May 1), *A Bridge Grows In Brooklyn* (Harriton/Oct. 1), *The Opera Caper* (Culhane, Bakshi/Nov. 1) and *Marvin Digs* (Bakshi/Dec. 1).

GOOD DEED DAILY

The name of this character, whose lifeblood was performing "good deeds," defined the plotline of this short-lived Terrytoons series. *Directed by Connie Rasinski. Technicolor and CinemaScope. A Terrytoons Production released through 20th Century–Fox.*

1956: *Scouts To The Rescue* (Apr.) and *Cloak And Stagger* (Aug./CinemaScope).

GOODIE THE GREMLIN

Famous Studios introduced this lovable gremlin, who tries fitting into Earthly situations, in a series of *Noveltoons.* The character's career was short–lived, however; he only appeared in two cartoons altogether. *Directed by Seymour Kneitel. Technicolor. A Famous Studios Production released through Paramount Pictures.*

1961: *Goodie The Gremlin* (Apr.).

1962: *Good And Guilty* (Feb.).

GOOFY

A cross between Mortimer Snerd and Snuffy Smith, Walt Disney's hayseed Goofy lit up the screen with his apologetic laugh, "Uh–hyulk, uh–hyulk . . . yep . . . uh–hyulk," in a series of misadventures which played up his silly but harmless nature.

Affectionately nicknamed the "Goof" by studio animators, Goofy first appeared in the early 1930s as a stringbean character, Dippy Dawg, in a Disney cartoon adventure. Later renamed, his actual personality never came into focus until studio animator Art Babbitt molded Goofy into "a composite of an everlasting optimist, a gullible Good Samaritan, a halfwit and a hick with a philosophy of the barber shop variety," who seldom completes his objectives or what he has started.

Babbitt, who first worked for Paul Terry in New York in 1932, became the studio expert at animating Goofy, with director Jack Kinney, who directed the most memorable cartoons in the series, using the character to good measure. Kinney's *How To Play Football* (1944), one in a series of classic Goofy sports "how–tos," received the series' only Academy Award nomination. *Directors were Dick Huemer, Jack Kinney, Jack Hannah, Bob Carlson, Clyde Geronimi, Les Clark and Woolie Reitherman. Technicolor. A Walt Disney Production released through RKO–Radio Pictures and later Buena Vista.*

Voices:
Goofy: Pinto Colvig (1931–1939, 1944–1967), George Johnson (1933–1944), Bob Jackman (1950–1951)

RKO–Radio Pictures Releases
1939: *Goofy And Wilbur* (Huemer/Mar. 17).

1940: *Goofy's Glider* (Kinney/Nov. 22).

1941: *Baggage Buster* (Kinney/Apr. 18), *The Art Of Skiing* (Kinney/Nov. 14) and *The Art Of Self Defense* (Kinney/Dec. 26).

1942: *How To Play Baseball* (Kinney/Sept. 4), *The Olympic Champ* (Kinney/Oct.9), *How To Swim* (Kinney/Oct. 23) and *How To Fish* (Kinney/Dec. 4).

1943: *Victory Vehicles* (with Pluto/Kinney/July 30).

1944: *How To Be A Sailor* (Kinney/Jan. 28), *How To Play Golf* (Kinney/Mar. 10) and *How To Play Football* (Kinney/Sept. 15/A.A. nominee).

1945: *Tiger Trouble* (Kinney/Jan. 5), *African Diary* (Kinney/Apr. 20), *Californy 'Er Bust* (Kinney/July 15) and *Hockey Homicide* (Kinney/Sept. 21).

1946: *A Knight For A Day* (Hannah/Mar. 8) and *Double Dribble* (Hannah/Dec. 20).

1947: *Crazy With The Heat* (with Donald Duck/Carlson/ Aug. 1) and *Foul Hunting* (Hannah/Oct. 31).

1948: *They're Off* (Hannah/Jan. 23) and *The Big Wash* (Geronimi/Feb. 6).

1949: *Tennis Racquet* (Kinney/Aug. 26) and *Goofy Gymnastics* (Kinney/Sept. 23).

1950: *How To Ride A Horse* (Kinney/Feb. 24/part of *The Reluctant Dragon* feature), *Motor Mania* (Kinney/June 30) and *Hold That Pose* (Kinney/Nov. 3).

1951: *Lion Down* (Kinney/Jan. 5), *Home Made Home* (Kinney/Mar. 23), *Cold War* (Kinney/Apr. 27), *Tomorrow We Diet* (Kinney/June 29), *Get Rich Quick* (Kinney/Aug. 31), *Fathers Are People* (Kinney/Oct. 21) and *No Smoking* (Kinney/Nov. 23).

1952: *Father's Lion* (Kinney/Jan. 4), *Hello, Aloha* (Kinney/Feb. 29), *Man's Best Friend* (Kinney/Apr. 4), *Two–Gun Goofy* (Kinney/May 16), *Teachers Are People* (Kinney/June 27), *Two Weeks Vacation* (Kinney/Oct. 31) and *How To Be A Detective* (Kinney/Dec. 12).

1953: *Father's Day Off* (Kinney/Mar. 28), *For Whom The Bulls Toil* (Kinney/May 9), *Father's Week End* (Kinney/June 20), *How To Dance* (Kinney/July 11) and *How To Sleep* (Kinney/Dec. 25).

1955: *El Gaucho Goofy* (Kinney/June 10/part of *Saludos Amigos*).

Buena Vista Releases
1961: *Aquamania* (Reitherman/Dec. 20).

1965: *Freewayphobia No. 1* (Clark/Feb. 13) and *Goofy's Freeway Trouble* (Clark/Sept. 22).

GOOFY GOPHERS

This pair of polite, swift–talking gophers vaguely resembled Walt Disney's popular *Chip An' Dale* characters, not only in voice but in facial and body features.

Introduced in a 1947 cartoon of the same name, Warner's director Bob Clampett designed the gophers' rather effeminate demeanor after two well–mannered character actors of the time, Edward Everett Horton and Franklin Pangborn. (The gophers appeared earlier in a 1941 Warner cartoon, *Gopher Goofy*, but were dissimilar to Clampett's version.) Clampett wrote the story for the first cartoon, which was directed by Art Davis, Clampett's successor. Clampett left Warner after completing the story to join Columbia Pictures' animation department.

The gophers' inquisitive ways land them in a half–dozen cartoons. They were often cast in situations which enabled them to display exaggerated politeness towards one another to resolve their differences. The characters acquired the nicknames of "Mac and Tosh" when they later appeared on television's "The Bugs Bunny Show." *Directors included Robert McKimson, Friz Freleng and Arthur Davis. Cinecolor. Technicolor. A Warner Brothers release.*

Voices:
Mac: Mel Blanc, **Tosh:** Stan Freberg

Looney Tunes
1947: *Goofy Gophers* (with Bugs Bunny/Davis/Jan. 25).

1949: *A Ham In A Role* (McKimson/Dec. 31).

1951: *A Bone For A Bone* (Freleng/Apr. 7).

1955: *Lumber Jerks* (Freleng/June 25).

1958: *Gopher Broke* (McKimson/Nov. 15).

Merrie Melodies
1948: *Two Gophers From Texas* (Davis/Dec. 27/Cinecolor).

1954: *I Gopher You* (Freleng/Jan. 30).

1955: *Pests For Guests* (with Elmer Fudd/Freleng/Jan. 29).

GOOPY GEER

Considered the first *Merrie Melodies* star, Goopy is a consummate performing dog—he sings, dances and plays the piano—who appeared in a number of music–and–dance shorts for Warner Brothers. Unfortunately, Goopy's stardom was short–lived as he only appeared in three *Merrie Melodies* cartoons. *Directors unknown. Black–and–white. Voice credits unknown. A Warner Brothers release.*

1932: *Goopy Geer* (Apr. 16), *Moonlight For Two* (June 11) and *The Queen Was In The Parlor* (July 9).

GRAN' POP MONKEY

This was one of animator Ub Iwerks' last cartoon series, a British–financed production produced by Cartoons Limited, an animation studio headed by Walt Disney veteran Paul Fennell. The short-lived series featured Gran' Pop, an artful and ancient ape created by noted British painter/illustrator Lawson Wood. Wood actually drew many of the key drawings for the series starring this cheerful old chimp in a handful of full–color cartoon shorts. *Produced and directed by Ub Iwerks. Technicolor. A Cartoons Limited Production released through Monogram Pictures.*

1940: *A Busy Day, Beauty Shoppe* and *Baby Checkers*.

HAM AND EX

This pair of troublesome pups was first featured as part of an ensemble cast in 1935's *I Haven't Got a Hat*, in which Porky Pig made his first official appearance. The characters were later paired with Beans, a mischievous cat, in several *Looney Tunes* cartoons. *Directed by Friz Freleng and Jack King. Black–and–white. Voice credits unknown. A Warner Brothers release.*

Merrie Melodies
1935: *I Haven't Got A Hat* (with Porky Pig, Beans/Freleng/Mar. 9).

Looney Tunes
1936: *The Phantom Ship* (with Beans/King/Feb. 1) and *The Fire Alarm* (with Beans/King/Mar. 9).

HAM AND HATTIE

In UPA's last theatrical series, Ham and Hattie made their screen debut in the 1948 release, *Trees and Jamaica Daddy*,

© 1958 UPA PICTURES, INC.

"HAM and HATTIE"

A NEW IDEA IN SHORTS
PRODUCED BY U.P.A. • RELEASED BY COLUMBIA

*: nominated for Academy Award

UPA's last theatrical series, Ham And Hattie, paired two separate cartoons shaped around the adventures of Ham Hamilton (left) and a girl named Hattie (right). © UPA Productions

which received the studio's final Academy Award nomination. Each episode paired two three–and–a–half minute cartoons, the first featuring the adventures of a little girl named Hattie, with the second shaped around the music of Hamilton Ham. *Directed by Lew Keller. Technicolor. A UPA Production released through Columbia Pictures.*

1958: *Trees And Jamaica Daddy* (Jan. 30/A.A. nominee), *Sailing And Village Band* (Feb. 27) and *Spring And Saganaki* (Oct. 16).

1959: *Picnics Are Fun And Dino's Serenade* (Jan. 16).

HAPPY HARMONIES

Another attempt by former Disney animators Hugh Harman and Rudolf Ising to rival Walt Disney's "personality animation," this series of musical cartoons is similar in both formula and style to Disney's celebrated *Silly Symphony* series. This type of cartoon had been mastered before by both animators, who had directed the Warner Brothers *Merrie Melodies* series.

Happy Harmonies resulted after the pair left Warner Brothers in 1933. They formed their own production company in conjunction with MGM to produce cartoons for theatrical

release by the studio. Metro developed its own cartoon studio four years later, spurred by Harman's and Ising's inability to keep their films under budget. Animated by MGM's new animation department, the series continued through 1938. *Directed by Rudolf Ising, Hugh Harman and William Hanna. Technicolor. A Metro–Goldwyn–Mayer release.*

1934: *The Discontented Canary* (Ising/Sept. 1), *The Old Pioneer* (Ising/Sept. 29), *A Tale Of The Vienna Woods* (Harman/Oct. 27) and *Toyland Broadcast* (Ising/Dec. 22).

1935: *Hey, Hey Fever* (Harman/Jan. 9), *When The Cat's Away* (Ising/Feb. 16), *The Lost Chick* (Harman/Mar. 9), *The Calico Dragon* (Ising/Mar. 30), *The Good Little Monkeys* (Harman/Apr. 13), *The Chinese Nightmare* (Harman/Apr. 27), *Poor Little Me* (Harman/May 11), *Barnyard Babies* (Ising/May 25), *The Old Plantation* (Ising/Sept. 21), *Honeyland* (Ising/Oct. 19), *Alias St. Nick* (Ising/Nov. 16) and *Run, Sheep, Run* (Harman/Dec. 14).

1936: *Bottles* (Harman/Jan. 11), *The Early Bird And The Worm* (Ising/Feb. 8), *The Old Mill Pond* (Harman/Mar. 7), *Two Little Pups* (Ising/Apr. 4), *The Old House* (Harman/May 2), *Pups Picnic* (Ising/May 30), *To Spring* (Hanna/June 4), *Little Cheezer* (Ising/July 11) and *The Pups' Christmas* (Ising/Dec. 12).

1937: *Swing Wedding* (Harman/Feb. 13), *The Hound And The Rabbit* (Ising/May 29) and *Wayward Pups* (Ising/July 10).

1938: *Pipe Dream* (Harman/Feb. 5) and *Little Bantamweight* (Ising/Mar. 12).

HASHIMOTO

Created by Terrytoons animator Bob Kuwahara, Japanese house mouse Hashimoto, a judo expert, was launched in the 1959 Terrytoons, *Hashimoto San.* The series pilot and subsequent adventures dealt with Hashimoto's reminiscences about the legends of his country, its romantic tradition and numerous other aspects of Japanese lore for American newspaper correspondent, G. I. Joe. The cartoon shorts co–starred his wife, Hanako, and his children, Yuriko and Saburo. A series of new cartoons were produced as part of NBC's "The Hector Heathcote Show" in the 1960s. *Directors were Bob Kuwahara, Dave Tendlar, Connie Rasinski, Mannie Davis and Art Bartsch. A Terrytoons Production released through 20th Century–Fox.*

Voices:
Hashimoto: John Myhers, **Hanako, his wife:** John Myhers, **Yuriko** John Myhers, **Saburo** John Myhers

1959: *Hashimoto–San* (Kuwahara, Tendlar/Sept. 6).

1960: *House of Hashimoto* (Rasinski/Nov. 30).

1961: *Night Life In Tokyo* (Davis/Feb.), *So Sorry, Pussycat* (Bartsch/Mar.), *Son Of Hashimoto* (Rasinski/Apr. 12), *Strange Companion* (Davis/May 12) and *Honorable Cat Story* (Rasinski/Nov.).

1962: *Honorable Family Problem* (Kuwahara/Mar. 30), *Loyal Royalty* (Kuwahara/May 18) and *Honorable Paint In The Neck* (Kuwahara/Aug. 22).

1963: *Tea House Mouse* (Kuwahara/Jan.), *Pearl Crazy* (Kuwahara/May), *Cherry Blossom Festival* (Kuwahara/June 17) and *Spooky–Yaki* (Kuwahara/Nov. 13).

HECKLE AND JECKLE

Conniving, talking magpies Heckle and Jeckle were popular cartoon stars through the mid–1960s. Paul Terry, head of Terrytoons, instituted the characters' creation after dreaming of starting a series featuring cartoon twins or lookalikes. Terry's idea came to fruition in *The Talking Magpies,* the first Heckle and Jeckle cartoon, released in 1946.

The comical pair were identical, yet featured contrasting accents—Brooklyn and British respectively. The characters became Terry's answer to the bombastic stars of rival Warner Brothers and MGM, becoming his most popular characters next to Mighty Mouse. The cartoons revitalized the "chase" formula characteristic of most of the Terrytoons cartoons.

Heckle and Jeckle experienced a brief revival when their films were syndicated to television in the 1960s. *Directors were Mannie Davis, Connie Rasinski, Eddie Donnelly, Martin B. Taras, Dave Tendlar, George Bakes and Al Chiarito. Technicolor. A Terrytoons Production released through 20th Century–Fox.*

Voices:

Heckle: Dayton Allen, Ned Sparks, Roy Halee, **Jeckle:** Dayton Allen, Ned Sparks, Roy Halee

1946: *The Talking Magpies* (Davis/Jan. 4) and *The Uninvited Pest* (Rasinski/Nov. 29).

Paul Terry's talking magpies Heckle and Jeckle lasted 20 years on screen as mischief makers for Terrytoons.
© Viacom International

1947: *McDougal's Rest Farm* (Davis/Jan. 31), *Happy Go Lucky* (Rasinski/Feb. 28), *Cat Trouble* (Rasinski/Apr. 11), *The Intruders* (Donnelly/May 9), *Flying South* (Davis/Aug. 15), *Fishing By The Sea* (Rasinski/Sept. 19), *Super Salesman* (Donnelly/Oct. 24) and *Hitch Hikers* (Rasinski/Dec. 12).

1948: *Taming The Cat* (Rasinksi/Jan.), *Sleepless Night* (Rasinski/June), *Magpie Madness* (Donnelly/July), *Out Again, In Again* (Rasinski/Nov. 1), *Free Enterprise* (Davis/Nov. 23), *Gooney Golfers* (Rasinski/Dec. 1) and *Power Of Thought* (Donnelly/Dec. 31).

1949: *Lion Hunt* (Donnelly/Mar.), *Stowaways* (Rasinski/Apr.), *Happy Landing* (June), *Hula Lula Land* (Davis/July) and *Dancing Shoes* (Davis/Dec.).

1950: *Fox Hunt* (Rasinski/Feb. 17), *Merry Chase* (Davis/May) and *King Tut's Tomb* (Davis/Aug.).

1951: *Rival Romeos* (Donnelly/Jan.), *Bulldozing The Bull* (Donnelly/Mar. 11), *The Rain Makers* (Rasinski/June), *Steeple Jacks* (Rasinski/Sept.) and *Sno' Fun* (Donnelly/Nov.).

1952: *Movie Madness* (Rasinski/Jan.), *Seaside Adventure* (Davis/Feb.), *Off To The Opera* (Rasinski/May), *House Busters* (Rasinski/Aug.) and *Moose On The Loose* (Davis/Nov.).

1953: *Hair Cut–Ups* (Donnelly/Feb.), *Pill Peddlers* (Rasinski/Apr.), *Ten Pin Terrors* (Rasinski/June), *Bargain Daze* (Davis/Aug.) and *Log Rollers* (Davis/Nov.).

1954: *Blind Date* (Donnelly/Feb.), *Satisfied Customers* (Rasinski/May) and *Blue Plate Symphony* (Rasinski/Oct. 29).

1956: *Miami Maniacs* (Rasinski/Feb.).

1957: *Pirate's Gold* (Donnelly/Jan.).

1959: *Wild Life* (Taras/Sept.).

1960: *Thousand Smile Checkup* (Taras/Jan.), *Mint Men* (Tendlar/June 23), *Trapeze Please* (Rasinski/June 12), *Deep Sea Doodle* (Tendlar/Sept. 16) and *Stunt Men* (Taras/Nov. 23).

1961: *Sappy New Year* (Nov. 10).

1966: *Messed Up Movie Makers* (Bakes, Chiarito/Mar.).

HECTOR HEATHCOTE

As with Deputy Dawg, this series was originally produced for the theatres. It focused on the adventures of this good–natured, revolutionary war–era boy who plays an integral part in the events of this country's history. (George Washington would have never crossed the Delaware River if Hector hadn't built the rowboat.)

Ed Bower, a Terrytoons designer, is credited with creating the character. Cartoons produced for television in the early 1960s also received theatrical distribution, thus explaining the series' long run. *Directed by Arthur Bartsch, Dave Tendlar, Connie Rasinski, Bill Tytla and Bob Kuwahara. Technicolor. CinemaScope. A Terrytoons Production released through 20th Century–Fox.*

Voices:

Hector Heathcote: John Myhers

1959: *The Minute And A Half Man* (Tendlar/July/CinemaScope).

1960: *The Famous Ride* (Rasinski/Apr./CinemaScope) and *Daniel Boone, Jr.* (Tendlar/Dec./CinemaScope).

1961: *Railroaded To Fame* (Tendlar/May). *The First Fast Mail* (Tendlar/May), *Crossing The Delaware* (Bartsch/June/CinemaScope) and *Unsung Hero* (July).

1962: *Klondike Strikes Out* (Tendlar/Jan.), *He—Man Seaman* (Bartsch/Mar.), *Riverboat Mission* (Tendlar/May), *First Flight Up* (Tytla/Oct.) and *A Flight To The Finish* (Tendlar/Dec.).

1963: *Tea Party* (Tendlar/Apr.), *A Bell For Philadelphia* (Kuwahara/July) and *The Big Clean—Up* (Tendlar/Sept.).

1970: *Land Grab* (Feb.), *Lost And Foundation* (June) and *Belabout Thy Neighbor* (Oct.).

1971: *Train Terrain* (Feb.).

HERMAN AND KATNIP

The idea of a cat—and—mouse team already proved successful for MGM with Tom and Jerry. What worked for one studio seemed liked it could work again, so Famous Studios unveiled their own feuding tandem in 1947: Herman, a slick city mouse, and Katnip, a country—bumpkin cat. For 12 years, the pair starred in a series of misadventures with Herman being the target of Katnip's desires to nab him as his personal prize. Like MGM's Jerry, Herman emerged unscathed through his sheer inventiveness and ability to outwit the cat. The pair also appeared independently of each other in a series of Paramount *Noveltoons*. *Directors were Isadore Sparber, Seymour Kneitel, Bill Tytla and Dave Tendlar. Technicolor. A Famous Studios Production released through Paramount Pictures.*

Voices:

Herman: Arnold Stang, **Katnip:** Syd Raymond

1947: *Naughty But Mice* (Kneitel/Oct. 10/*Noveltoon*).

1950: *Mice Meeting You* (Kneitel/Nov. 10/*Noveltoon*).

1951: *Mice Paradise* (Sparber/Mar. 9/*Noveltoon*) and *Cat Tamale* (Kneitel/Nov. 9/*Noveltoon*).

1952: *Cat Carson Rides Again* (Kneitel/Apr. 4/*Noveltoon*) and *Mice—Capades* (Kneitel/Oct. 3/first cartoon in the *Herman and Katnip* series).

1953: *Of Mice And Magic* (Sparber/Feb. 20), *Herman The Cartoonist* (Sparber/May 15), *Drinks On The Mouse* (Tendlar/Aug. 28) and *Northwest Mousie* (Kneitel/Dec. 28).

1954: *Surf And Sound* (Tendlar/Mar. 5), *Of Mice And Menace* (Kneitel/June 25), *Ship A—Hooey* (Sparber/Aug. 20) and *Rail—Rodents* (Tendlar/Nov. 26).

Country—bumpkin cat Katnip and slick—city mouse Herman often feuded onscreen, with, naturally, the cat always on the losing end. © Harvey Cartoons

1955: *Robin Rodenthood* (Tendlar/Feb. 25), *A Bicep Built For Two* (Kneitel/Apr. 8), *Mouse Trapeze* (Sparber/Aug. 5) and *Mousier Herman* (Tendlar/Nov. 25).

1956: *Mouseum* (Kneitel/Feb. 24), *Will Do Mousework* (Kneitel/June 29), *Mousetro Herman* (Sparber/Aug. 10) and *Hide And Peak* (Tendlar/Dec. 7).

1957: *Cat In The Act* (Tendlar/Feb. 22), *Sky Scrappers* (Tendlar/June 14), *From Mad To Worse* (Kneitel/Aug. 16) and *One Funny Knight* (Tendlar/Nov. 22).

1958: *Frighty Cat* (Sparber/Mar. 14) and *You Said a Mouseful* (Kneitel/Aug. 29).

1959: *Owly To Bed* (Kneitel/Jan. 2), *Felineous Assault* (Kneitel/Feb. 20), *Fun On The Furlough* (Kneitel/Apr. 3) and *Katnip's Big Day* (Kneitel/Oct. 30).

Herman By Himself
1944: *Henpecked Rooster* (with Hector the Rooster/Kneitel/Feb. 18).

1945: *Scrappily Married* (with Hector the Rooster/Kneitel/Mar. 30).

1946: *Cheese Burglar* (Sparber/Feb. 22).

1949: *Campus Capers* (Tytla/July 1).

Katnip By Himself
1950: *Sock–A–Bye Kitty* (with Buzzy the Crow/Kneitel/Dec. 22).

1952: *City Kitty* (Sparber/July 18) and *Feast and Furious* (with Finny the Goldfish/Sparber/Dec. 26).

1953: *Better Bait Than Never* (Kneitel/June 5).

HIPPETY HOPPER

The high–jumping kangaroo was originally created by Robert McKimson as a running gag in a cartoon with lisping Sylvester the Cat. Resembling an overgrown mouse, Hippety became more than a one–shot joke. He lasted for 16 years as a non–talking co–star in a dozen cartoons with Sylvester, with his actions speaking louder than words.

In 1950, McKimson added another character to play off Hippety: Sylvester's son, Sylvester Jr., who encounters the kangaroo in situations where he questions his father's knowledge of animals. (Sylvester often mistakens Hippety for a "mouse.") *Directed by Robert McKimson. Technicolor. A Warner Brothers release.*

Looney Tunes
1948: *Hop Look And Listen* (with Sylvester the Cat/McKimson/Apr. 17).

1950: *Pop 'Em Pop!* (with Sylvester the Cat, Sylvester Jr./McKimson/Oct. 28).

1952: *Hoppy Go Lucky* (with Sylvester the Cat/McKimson/Aug. 9).

1956: *Too Hop To Handle* (with Sylvester the Cat, Sylvester Jr./McKimson/Jan. 28).

1961: *Hoppy Daze* (with Sylvester the Cat/McKimson/Feb. 11).

DePatie–Freleng Enterprises Release
1964: *Freudy Cat* (McKimson/Mar. 14).

Merrie Melodies
1949: *Hippety Hopper* (with Sylvester the Cat/McKimson/Nov. 19).

1953: *Cat's Aweigh* (with Sylvester the Cat, Sylvester Jr./McKimson/Nov. 28).

1954: *Bell Hoppy* (with Sylvester the Cat/McKimson/Apr. 17).

1955: *Lighthouse Mouse* (with Sylvester the Cat/McKimson/Mar. 12).

1956: *The Slap–Hoppy Mouse* (with Sylvester the Cat/McKimson/Sept. 1).

1957: *Mouse–Taken Identity* (with Sylvester the Cat, Sylvester Jr./McKimson/Nov. 16).

HOMER PIGEON

A 1940s addition to Walter Lantz's cartoon gallery, this rube–like country bird was based on comedian Red Skelton's famed radio character, Clem Kadiddlehopper. The straw hatted bird, who was originally cast as comic relief in a number of films, first appeared in the Walter Lantz Cartune Special, *Pigeon Patrol,* in 1942. His only other starring appearance came 14 years later before retiring from the screen. *Directed by Alex Lovy. Technicolor. A Walter Lantz Production released through Universal Pictures.*

Voices:
Homer Pigeon: Dal McKennon

1942: *Pigeon Patrol* (Aug. 3).

1956: *Pigeon Holed* (Jan. 16).

HONEY HALFWITCH

In an attempt to come up with something different, Famous Studios, producers of Casper and Herman and Katnip, launched this series featuring Honey Halfwitch, a sweet–natured apprentice who manages to escape trouble through the power of witchcraft. The series' theme song was composed by Winston Sharples, the studio's musical director. *Directors were Howard Post, James "Shamus" Culhane and Chuck Harriton. Technicolor. A Famous Studios Production released through Paramount Pictures.*

1965: *Shoeflies* (Post/Oct.).

1966: *Baggin' The Dragon* (Post/Feb.), *From Nags To Witches* (Post/Feb.), *Trick Or Cheat* (Post/Mar.), *The Rocket Racket* (Mar.), *The Defiant Giant* (Post/June), *Throne For A Loss* (Post/July) and *Potions And Notions* (Culhane/Aug.).

1967: *Alter Egotist* (Culhane/Apr.), *Clean Sweep* (Harriton/June), *High But Not Dry* (Culhane/Aug.) and *Brother Rat* (Culhane/Aug.).

THE HONEY–MOUSERS

What began as a one–shot parody of television's classic comedy series "The Honeymooners" turned into a brief series of hilarious spoofs featuring Ralph (Ralph Crumden), Alice (Alice Crumden), Norton (Ned Morton) and Trixie (Trixie Morton) as mice. Warner Brothers veteran Robert McKimson brought the characters to the screen for the first time in 1956's *The Honey–Mousers.* The film inspired two sequels, *Cheese It, The Cat* (1957) and *Mice Follies* (1960). *Directed by Robert McKimson. Technicolor. A Warner Brothers release.*

Voices:
Ralph Crumden: Mel Blanc, **Ned Morton:** Mel Blanc, **Alice Crumden:** June Foray, **Trixie Morton:** June Foray

Television's "The Honeymooners" was turned into a series of successful Warner Brother cartoons, featuring the cast as mice. © Warner Brothers Inc.

Looney Tunes
1956:   *The Honey–Mousers* (Dec. 8).

1957:   *Cheese It, The Cat* (May 4).

1960:   *Mice Follies* (Aug. 20).

HOOT KLOOT

A redneck, fat–bellied sheriff maintains law and order with the help of his silly but faithful horse, Confederate, in cartoon

Fat–bellied Sheriff Hoot Kloot prepares for trouble in a scene from DePatie–Freleng's cartoon series spoofing the Old West. © DePatie–Freleng Enterprises

adventures lampooning the Wild West. *Directors were Bob Balsar, Durward Bonaye, Gerry Chiniquy, Arthur Leonardi, Sid Marcus, Roy Morita and Hawley Pratt. Technicolor. A DePatie–Freleng Enterprises Production released through United Artists.*

Voices:
Hoot Kloot: Bob Holt, **Confederate:** Larry D. Mann

Additional Voices:
Joan Gerber, Allen Mehin

1973:   *Kloot's Kounty* (Pratt/Jan. 19), *Apache On The County Seat* (Pratt/June 16), *The Shoe Must Go On!* (Chiniquy/June 16), *A Self–Winding Side–Winder* (Morita/Oct. 9), *Pay Your Buffalo Bill* (Chiniquy/Oct. 9), *Ten Miles To The Gallop* (Leonardi/Oct. 15) and *Stirrups And Hiccups* (Chiniquy/Oct. 15).

1974:   *Phoney Express* (Chiniquy/Jan. 4), *Giddy–Up Woe!* (Marcus/Jan. 9), *Gold Struck* (Morita/Jan. 16), *As The Tumbleweed Turns* (Chiniquy/Apr. 8), *The Badge And The Beautiful* (Balsar/Apr. 17), *Strange On The Range* (Bonaye/Apr. 17), *Big Beef At The O. K. Corral* (Balsar/Apr. 17), *By Hoot Or By Crook* (Balsar/Apr. 17), *Mesa Trouble* (Marcus/May 16) and *Saddle Soap Opera* (Chiniquy/May 16).

HUBIE AND BERTIE

Chuck Jones created these two troublesome mice, Hubie and Bertie, who were added to the Warner Brothers cartoon roster in 1943. In subsequent adventures they were paired with a mouse–hungry cat, Claude Cat. The short–lived series produced one Academy Award nomination for the 1949 release, *Mouse Wreckers,* the pair's second cartoon. *Directed by Chuck Jones. Technicolor. A Warner Brothers release.*

Voices:
Hubie: Mel Blanc, **Bertie:** Mel Blanc, Stan Freberg

Merrie Melodies
1943:   *The Aristo Cat* (June 12).

1948:   *House–Hunting Mice* (Oct. 7).

1949:   *Mouse Wreckers* (with Claude Cat/Apr. 23/A.A. nominee).

1950:   *The Hypo–Chondri Cat* (with Claude Cat/Apr. 15).

1951:   *Cheese Chasers* (with Claude Cat/Aug. 28).

Looney Tunes
1946:   *Roughly Speaking* (Nov. 23).

1952:   *Mouse Warming* (with Claude Cat/Sept. 8).

HUGH HARMAN CARTOONS

In the early 1930s, Hugh Harman and partner Rudolph Ising moved from Warner Brothers to MGM to produce cartoons independently for their new studio. In 1939, after a brief departure, Harman returned to Metro following overtures from Fred Quimby, head of the studio's new cartoon department. Quimby hired Harman to develop a fresh, new cartoon series that would help establish the studio as a leader in the field of cartoon animation.

Using a familiar formula, Harman produced and directed a series of musical cartoons similar to his former *Merrie Melodies* for Warner Brothers, featuring various animated characters as the stars. His finest effort came during the first year back at the studio, when his *Peace On Earth,* a timely war–themed cartoon released that year, won an Academy Award nomination for "Best Short Subject" and a *Parents Magazine* medal of distinction.

Veteran animator Friz Freleng, who briefly defected to MGM from Warner Brothers, directed one cartoon under the series. *Directed Hugh Harman and Friz Freleng. Technicolor. A Metro–Goldwyn–Mayer release.*

1939: *Art Gallery* (Harman/May 13), *Goldilocks And The 3 Bears* (Harman/July 15/re: Nov. 22, 1947), *Bear Family* (Abandoned), *The Bookworm* (Freleng/Aug. 26), *The Blue Danube* (Harman/Oct. 28), *Peace On Earth* (Harman/Dec. 9/ A.A. nominee) and *The Mad Maestro* (Harman/Dec. 30).

1940: *A Rainy Day* (Harman/Apr. 20), *Tom Turkey And His Harmonica Humdingers* (Harman/June 8), *The Bookworm Turns* (Harman/July 20), *Papa Gets The Bird* (Harman/ Sept. 7) and *Lonesome Stranger* (Harman/Nov. 23).

1941: *Abdul The Bulbul Ameer* (Harman/Feb. 22), *The Little Mole* (Harman/Apr. 5), *The Alley Cat* (Harman/July 5) and *Field Mouse* (Harman/Dec. 27).

1942: *The Hungry Wolf* (Harman/Feb. 21).

INKI

Paired with a pesty mynah bird, Inki, a little black jungle boy with a bone in his hair, was sporadically used in a number of Warner Brothers cartoons directed by creator Chuck Jones. Inki first appeared in 1939's *The Little Lion Hunter.* He remained absent from the screen until 1943 when Jones cast him in *Inki And The Mynah Bird,* a *Merrie Melodies* cartoon. Two more cartoons followed until the series folded. *Directed by Chuck Jones. Technicolor. A Warner Brothers release.*

Voices:
Mel Blanc

Merrie Melodies
1939: *Little Lion Hunter* (Oct. 7).

1943: *Inki And The Mynah Bird* (Nov. 6).

1947: *Inki At The Circus* (June 21).

Looney Tunes
1950: *Caveman Inki* (Nov. 25).

THE INSPECTOR

The blundering French sleuth of *Pink Panther* fame, Inspector Clouseau starred in a series of cartoon shorts based on Blake Edwards' film character, played by actor–comedian Peter

Sellers in several feature films throughout the 1960s and 1970s.

In 1965, the animated character, who bears more than a fleeting resemblance to Sellers, made his animated debut along with his equally lamebrained aide, Sergeant Deudeux, when United Artists simultaneously released the James Bond thriller *Thunderball* and the cartoon *The Great de Gaulle Stone Operation.*

As in the successful feature film series, the animated adventures dealt with Clouseau's inherent ability to solve important cases despite his obvious ineptitude. Blake Edwards was actually responsible for suggesting the idea for the series. *Directors were Gerry Chiniquy, Friz Freleng, Robert McKimson and George Singer. Technicolor. A Mirisch–Geoffrey–De-Patie–Freleng Production released through United Artists.*

Voices:
The Inspector: Pat Harrington Jr., **Sergeant Deudeux:** Pat Harrington Jr., **The Chief:** Paul Frees, Marvin Miller

Additional Voices:
June Foray, Helen Gerald, Joan Gerber, Diana Maddox, Mark Skor, Hal Smith, Larry Storch, Lennie Weinrib

1965: *The Great De Gaulle Stone Operation* (Freleng, Chiniquy/Dec. 21).

1966: *Napoleon Blown–Aparte* (Chiniquy/Feb. 2), *Cirrhosis Of The Louvre* (Chiniquy/Mar. 9), *Plastered In Paris* (Chiniquy/Apr. 5), *Cock–A–Doodle Deux Deux* (McKimson/June 15), *Ape Suzette* (Chiniquy/June 24), *Le Escape Goat* (Chiniquy/June 29), *The Pique Poquette Of Paris* (Singer/Aug. 24), *Sicque! Sicque! Sicque!* (Singer/Sept. 23), *That's No Lady— That's Notre Dame* (Singer/Oct. 6), *Unsafe And Seine* (Singer/ Nov. 9), and *Toulouse La Trick* (McKimson/Dec. 30).

1967: *Reaux Reaux Reaux Your Boat* (Chiniquy/Feb. 1), *Sucre Bleu Cross* (Chiniquy/Feb. 1), *London Derriere* (Chiniquy/Feb. 7), *Le Quiet Squad* (McKimson/May 17), *Bomb Voyage* (McKimson/May 22), *Le Pig–Al Patrol* (Chiniquy/May 24), *Le Bowser Bagger* (Chiniquy/May 30), *Le Cop On Le Rocks* (Singer/July 3), *Crow De Guerre* (Chiniquy/Aug. 16), *Tour De Farce* (Chiniquy/Oct. 25), *Canadian Can Can* (Chiniquy/Dec. 20) and *The Shooting Of Caribou Lou* (Chiniquy/ Dec. 20).

1968: *Les Miserbots* (Chiniquy/Mar. 21), *Transylvania Mania* (Chiniquy/Mar. 26), *Bear De Guerre* (Chiniquy/Apr. 26), *La Great Dane Robbery* (Chiniquy), *Cherche Le Phantom* (Chiniquy/June 13), *La Feet's De Feat* (Chiniquy/July 24) and *Le Ball And Chain Gang* (Chiniquy/July 24).

1969: *French Freud* (Chiniquy/Jan. 22), *Pierre & Cottage Cheese* (Chiniquy/Feb. 26) and *Carte Blanched* (Chiniquy/ May 14).

INSPECTOR WILLOUGHBY

Believing the time was ripe for a new cartoon character to grace the screen, Walter Lantz enlisted former Disney director Jack Hannah to develop story ideas for a new series. Hannah responded with a revised version of a character from his

Disney days, named Ranger Willoughby. Making a few minor alterations, he gave the character a new identity and new profession as a burly mustachioed secret agent, 6–7/8. Willoughby's low–key demeanor and speaking voice were humanized versions of Tex Avery's popular basset–hound, Droopy.

Hannah directed the premiere episode of the series, *Hunger Strife,* in 1960. Afterwards he turned the series over to Lantz veteran Paul J. Smith, who directed the balance of the series until its demise in 1965. *Directed by Jack Hannah and Paul J. Smith. Technicolor. A Walter Lantz Production released through Universal Pictures.*

Voices:
Inspector Willoughy: Dal McKennon

1960: *Hunger Strife* (with Windy/Hannah/Oct. 5).

1961: *Rough And Tumbleweed* (Smith/Jan. 31), *Eggnapper* (Hannah/Feb. 14), *Mississippi Slow Boat* (Smith/July) and *Case Of The Red–Eyed Ruby* (Smith/Nov. 28).

1962: *Phoney Express* (Smith/May 15) and *Hyde And Sneak* (Smith/July 24).

1963: *Coming–Out Party* (Smith/Feb.), *Case Of The Cold–Storage Yegg* (Smith/Mar.) and *Hi–Seas Hi–Jacker* (Smith/May).

1964: *The Case Of The Maltese Chicken* (Smith/Feb. 4).

1965: *The Case Of The Elephant's Trunk* (Smith/Jan. 1).

JAMES HOUND

Inspired by Ian Fleming's fictional James Bond character, Terrytoons introduced this canine counterpart of the famed super sleuth in animated escapades featuring international spies and farfetched gadgets on a smaller scale. Ralph Bakshi, who made his Terrytoons directorial debut in 1964, directed the series. *Directed by Ralph Bakshi. Technicolor. A Terrytoons Production released through 20th Century–Fox.*

Voices:
James Hound: Dayton Allen

1966: *Dr. Ha Ha Ha* (Feb.), *The Monster Maker* (July), *Rain Drain* (Sept.), *Dream–Napping* (Nov.) and *The Phantom Skyscraper* (Dec. 31).

1967: *A Voodoo Spell* (Jan.), *Mr. Win Lucky* (Feb.), *It's For The Birds* (Mar.), *The Heat's Off* (Apr.), *Traffic Trouble* (May), *Bugged By A Bug* (June), *Fancy Plants* (July), *Give Me Liberty* (Aug.), *Which Is Witch?* (Sept.), *Dr. Rhinestone's Theory* (Oct.), *Frozen Sparklers* (Nov.) and *Baron Von Go–Go* (Dec.)

JEEPERS AND CREEPERS

This brief series starred a comic pair of dogs, Jeepers and Creepers, who were the original version of another Paramount cartoon team, Swifty and Shorty, who debuted two years later. *Directed by Seymour Kneitel. Technicolor. A Famous Studios Production released through Paramount Pictures.*

Voices:
Jeepers: Eddie Lawrence, **Creepers:** Eddie Lawrence

1960: *The Boss Is Always Right* (Jan. 15), *Trouble Date* (Mar. 11), *Buzy Buddies* (June) and *Scouting For Trouble* (Sept.).

JERKY JOURNIES

Two years after Republic Pictures released animator Bob Clampett's experimental TruColor cartoon, *It's a Grand Old Nag,* starring Charlie Horse and Hay–dy LaMare, the studio produced this series of animated travelogue spoofs without the guidance of Clampett, who left the studio after producing his single effort. Studio president Herbert Yates proposed making the series to further exploit its new color process in the same manner Disney made Technicolor into a success with his *Silly Symphony* cartoons.

The series became Republic's first and only cartoon series. Technical and voice credits are unknown. *TruColor. A Republic Pictures release.*

1949: *Beyond Civilization* (Mar. 15), *The Three Minnies* (Apr. 15), *Bungle In The Jungle* (May 15) and *Romantic Rumbolia* (June 15).

JOHN DOORMAT

The ups–and–downs of suburban life in the 1950s is comically portrayed in this Terrytoons series featuring John Doormat, a poor soul whose encounters deal with a variety of everyday issues. Writer Jules Feiffer later joined the series, changing the direction of the cartoons to a more Thurberish outlook on life. *Directed by Connie Rasinski and Al Kouzel. Technicolor. CinemaScope. A Terrytoons Production released through 20th Century–Fox.*

Voices:
John Doormat: Lionel Wilson

1957: *Topsy Turvy* (Rasinski/Jan.) and *Shove Thy Neighbor* (Rasinski/June).

1958: *Dustcap Doormat* (Kouzel/June).

JOLLY FROLICS

When Columbia Pictures' animation department closed down, United Productions of America (UPA) independently produced new cartoons for distribution through the studio to replace the *Phantasy* color classics series. The first cartoon to launch the series was 1949's *Ragtime Bear,* starring the myopic Mr. Magoo.

Magoo, Gerald McBoing Boing and other stalwarts from UPA's cartoon gallery appeared in several episodes of this new series. *Directors were John Hubley, Art Babbitt, Steve Bosustow, Bob Cannon, Pete Burness and Ted Parmelee. Technicolor. A UPA Production released through Columbia Pictures.*

1949: *Ragtime Bear* (with Mr. Magoo/Hubley/Sept. 8).

1950: *Spellbound Hound* (Hubley/Mar. 16), *The Miner's Daughter* (Cannon/May 25), *Giddyap* (Babbitt/July 27) and *The Popcorn Story* (Babbitt/Nov. 30).

1951: *Gerald McBoing Boing* (Cannon/Jan. 25), *The Family Circus* (Babbitt/Jan. 25), *Georgie The Dragon* (Cannon/Sept. 27) and *Wonder Gloves* (Cannon/Nov. 29).

1952: *The Oompahs* (Cannon/Jan. 24), *Rooty Tooty Toot* (Hubley/Mar. 27/A.A. winner), *Pete Hothead* (Parmelee/Sept. 25) and *Madeline* (Cannon/Nov. 27/A.A. nominee).

1953: *Little Boy With A Big Horn* (Cannon/Mar. 26), *The Emperor's New Clothes* (Parmelee/Apr. 30) and *Christopher Crumpet* (Cannon/June 25/A.A. nominee).

KARTUNES

In the early 1950s, Paramount's Famous Studios resurrected a familiar formula—themed stories with no–named stars—when it introduced *Kartunes,* animated in the same style and manner as its former success, *Noveltoons.*

Kartunes never equalled the success of *Noveltoons* in terms of popularity and longevity. The series only lasted three years. *Directed by Isadore Sparber and Seymour Kneitel. A Famous Studios Production released through Paramount Pictures.*

1951: *Vegetable Vaudeville* (Sparber/Nov. 9) and *Snooze Reel* (Kneitel/Dec. 28).

1952: *Off We Glow* (Sparber/Feb. 29), *Fun At The Fair* (Sparber/May 9), *Dizzy Dinosaurs* (Kneitel/July 4), *Gag And Baggage* (Sparber/Aug. 8) and *Forest Fantasy* (Kneitel/Nov 14).

1953: *Hysterical History* (Kneitel/Jan. 23), *Philharmaniacs* (Kneitel/Apr. 3), *Aero–Nutics* (Kneitel/May 8), *Invention Convention* (Sparber/June 10) and *No Place Like Rome* (Sparber/July 31).

KIKO THE KANGAROO

First appearing in Farmer Al Falfa cartoons, Kiko was a playful kangaroo cast in numerous misadventures. The character was created by Paul Terry, who featured the character in his own series of animated shorts beginning in 1936. *Directed by Mannie Davis and George Gordon. Black–and–white. Voice credits unknown. A Terrytoons Production released through 20th Century–Fox.*

1936: *Kiko And The Honey Bears* (Davis, Gordon/Aug. 21), *Kiko Foils A Fox* (Davis, Gordon/Oct. 2) and *Skunked Again* (Davis, Gordon/Dec. 25).

1937: *Red Hot Music* (Davis, Gordon/Mar. 5), *Ozzie Ostrich Comes To Town* (Davis, Gordon/May 28), *Play Ball* (Davis/June 11) and *Kiko's Cleaning Day* (Gordon/Sept. 17).

KRAZY KAT

The advent of sound revived many silent film favorites, including George Herriman's popular animated feline, Krazy Kat. Krazy had previously gained fame by starring in more than 80 silent cartoons. He was brought back to life when Columbia Pictures, wanting to become a major force in the cartoon industry, agreed to distribute this proven property in a series of new cartoons produced by Charles Mintz.

The sound cartoons had the same basic stories as the silent adventures, with some dialogue and musical soundtrack accompaniment. Krazy's soft–speaking voice was like Mickey Mouse, who inspired several other soundalike characters, among them, Warner Brothers' Bosko and Buddy.

As had happened in the silent series, the series suffered several setbacks because of creative differences in bringing Krazy's innate style of humor to the screen. No attempt was made to stay true to creator George Herriman's style or storylines. Consequently, Offisa Pup was rarely used and the romance between Ignatz and Krazy, ever popular in the comic strip series, was virtually ignored.

Instead, the series was based primarily on "heavy–handed chases and primitive acting, with every gag automatically repeated three times," recalled animator James "Shamus" Culhane, an inker for the series.

At the same time Mintz produced the series for Columbia, Walt Disney supplied cartoons for the studio for release. In 1932, after Disney parted company with Columbia, Mintz became the studio's sole supplier of cartoons, with Krazy leading the pack. (Coincidentally, Mintz was the same producer responsible for taking the *Oswald the Rabbit* series from Disney years earlier.)

Manny Gould and Ben Harrison, who wrote most of the cartoon stories, jointly directed and supervised the animation of each cartoon. Series animators included Allen Rose, Sid Marcus, Harry Love, Jack Carr and Art Davis. Music was supplied by Joe De Nat, a former New York pianist, whose peppy musical scores enlivened each film. *Directed by Manny Gould and Ben Harrison. Black–and–white. Technicolor. A Columbia Pictures release. Voice credits unknown.*

1929: *Ratskin* (Aug. 15), *Canned Music* (Sept. 12), *Port Whines* (Oct. 10), *Sole Mates* (Nov. 7) and *Farm Relief* (Dec. 30).

1930: *The Cat's Meow* (Jan. 2), *Spook Easy* (Jan. 30), *Slow Beau* (Feb. 27), *Desert Sunk* (Mar. 27), *An Old Flame* (Apr. 24), *Alaskan Knights* (May 23), *Jazz Rhythm* (June 19), *Honolulu Wiles* (July 17), *Cinderella* (Aug. 14), *The Bandmaster* (Sept. 8), *The Apache Kid* (Oct. 9), *Lambs Will Gamble* (Nov. 1) and *The Little Trail* (Dec. 3).

1931: *Take For A Ride* (Jan.), *Rodeo Dough* (Feb. 13), *Swiss Movements* (Apr. 4), *Disarmament Conference* (Apr. 27), *Soda Poppa* (May 29), *Stork Market* (July 11), *Svengarlic* (Aug. 3), *The Weenie Roast* (Sept. 14), *Bars And Stripes* (Oct. 15), *Hash House Blues* (Nov. 2) and *The Restless Sax* (Dec. 1).

1932: *Piano Mover* (Jan. 4), *Love Krazy* (Jan. 25), *Hollywood Goes Krazy* (Feb. 13), *What A Knight* (Mar. 14), *Soldier Old Man* (Apr. 2), *Birth Of Jazz* (Apr. 13), *Ritzy Hotel* (May 9), *Hic–Cups The Champ* (May 28), *The Paper Hanger* (June 21), *Lighthouse Keeping* (Aug. 15), *Seeing Stars* (Sept. 12), *Prosperity Blues* (Oct. 8), *The Crystal Gazebo* (Nov. 7), *The Minstrel Show* (Nov. 21) and *Show Time* (Nov. 30).

1933: *Wedding Bells* (Jan. 10), *The Medicine Show* (Feb. 7), *Wooden Shoes* (Feb. 25), *Bunnies And Bonnets* (Mar. 29), *The Broadway Malady* (Apr. 18), *Russing Dressing* (May 1), *House Cleaning* (June 1), *Antique Antics* (June 14), *Out Of The Ether* (Sept. 5), *Whacks Museum* (Sept. 29), *Krazy Spooks* (Oct. 13), *Stage Krazy* (Nov. 13), *The Bill Poster* (Nov. 24) and *The Curio Shop* (Dec. 15).

1934: *The Autograph Hunter* (Jan. 5), *Southern Exposure* (Feb. 5), *Tom Thumb* (Feb. 16), *Cinder Alley* (Mar. 9), *Bowery Daze* (Mar. 30), *Busy Bus* (Apr. 20), *Masquerade Party* (May 11), *The Trapeze Artist* (Sept. 1), *Katnips of 1940* (Oct. 12), *Krazy's Waterloo* (Nov. 16) and *Goofy Gondolas* (Dec. 21).

1935: (Technicolor) *The Bird Man* (Feb. 1), *Hotcha Melody* (Mar. 15), *The Peace Conference* (Apr. 26), *The King Jester* (May 20), *Garden Gaieties* (Aug. 1), *A Happy Family* (Sept. 27) and *Kannibal Kapers* (Dec. 27).

1936: *The Bird Stuffer* (Feb. 1), *Lil' Ainjil* (Mar. 19), *Highway Snobbery* (Aug. 9), *Krazy's Newsreel* (Oct. 24) and *Merry Cafe* (Dec. 26).

1937: *The Lyin' Hunter* (Feb. 12), *Krazy's Race Of Time* (May 6), *The Masque Raid* (June 25) and *Railroad Rhythm* (Nov. 20).

1938: *Sad Little Guinea Pigs* (Feb. 22), *The Auto Clinic* (Mar. 4), *Little Buckaroo* (Apr. 11), *Krazy Magic* (May 20), *Krazy's Travel Squawks* (July 4), *Gym Jams* (Sept. 9), *Hot Dogs On Ice* (Oct. 21) and *The Lone Mountie* (Dec. 10).

1939: *Krazy's Bear Tale* (Jan. 27), *Golf Chumps* (Apr. 6), *Krazy's Shoe Shop* (May 12) and *Little Lost Sheep* (Oct. 6/*Fables* cartoon).

1940: *The Mouse Exterminator* (Jan. 26/*Phantasy* cartoon).

LAND OF THE LOST

The popular children's radio show "The Insgrigs" inspired this series of fantasy cartoons produced as part of Famous Studios' *Noveltoons* series. *Directed by Isadore Sparber and Seymour Kneitel. Technicolor. A Famous Studios Production released through Paramount Pictures.*

1948: *Lana Of The Lost* (Sparber/June 7).

1950: *Last Of The Lost Jewels* (Sparber/Jan. 6).

1951: *Land Of Lost Watches* (Kneitel/May 4).

LIL' ABNER

Few comic–strip characters were ever successful in an animated cartoon environment. Columbia Pictures had learned this before with Krazy Kat and Barney Google, the latter an earlier comic strip–to–film adaptation that failed. Yet the studio tried again, this time with a short–lived series of cartoon shorts based on Al Capp's hillbilly character.

Movie critics panned the few episodes which were released, much to the dismay of the studio who had hoped for different results this time around. The series was dropped after only five films, actually pleasing news to creator Al Capp, who repeatedly expressed his disdain with the studio's simplifications of the characters and situations from his nationally syndicated strip. *Directors were Sid Marcus, Bob Wickersham and Howard Swift. Technicolor. A Columbia Pictures release.*

1944: *Amoozin But Confoozin* (Marcus/Mar. 3), *Sadie Hawkins Day* (Wickersham/May 4), *A Peekoolyar Sitcheeyshun* (Marcus/Aug. 11), *Porkulia Piggy* (Wickersham/Oct. 13) and *Kickapoo Juice* (Swift/Dec. 1).

LIL' EIGHTBALL

Former Disney protege Burt Gillett was responsible for creating this stereotyped black youngster who, after a brief opportunity at movie stardom, resurfaced in Walter Lantz's comic books of the 1940s. *Directed by Burt Gillett. Black–and–white. Voice credits unknown. A Walter Lantz Production released through Universal Pictures.*

When Paramount lost rights to Little Lulu, the studio introduced as its replacement a new series revolving around the life and loves of another sweet little girl, Little Audrey. © Harvey Cartoons

1939: *Stubborn Mule* (July 3) and *Silly Superstition* (Aug. 28).

LITTLE AUDREY

When Paramount lost the rights to *Little Lulu* in late 1947, the studio produced a series of Little Audrey cartoons as her replacement. This series revolved around the life and loves of a sweet little girl who earlier claimed fame as a Harvey comic book character. Stories depict her matching wits with a prank–loving boy, Melvin, tracking down hoodlums and lending a helping hand to anyone needing assistance.

Mae Questel, who did most of the female and children voices for the studio, was Audrey in the series. The first Little Audrey comic book was published four months before the series' first cartoon. *Directed by Isadore Sparber, Seymour Kneitel and Bill Tytla. Technicolor. A Famous Studios Production released through Paramount Pictures.*

Voices:

Little Audrey: Mae Questel

(All series cartoons released under the "Noveltoons" banner)
1948: *Butterscotch And Soda* (Tytla/July 16).

1949: *The Lost Dream* (Tytla/Mar. 18) and *Song Of The Birds* (Tytla/Nov. 18).

1950: *Tarts And Flowers* (Tytla/May 26) and *Goofy Goofy Gander* (Tytla/Aug. 18).

1951: *Hold The Lion Please* (Sparber/Aug. 27) and *Audrey The Rainmaker* (Sparber/Oct. 26).

1952: *Law And Audrey* (Sparber/May 23) and *The Case Of The Cockeyed Canary* (Kneitel/Dec. 19).

1953: *Surf Bored* (Sparber/July 17).

1954: *The Seapreme Court* (Kneitel/Jan. 29).

1955: *Dizzy Dishes* (Sparber/Feb. 4) and *Little Audrey Riding Hood* (Kneitel/Oct. 14).

1957: *Fishing Tackler* (Sparber/Mar. 29).

1958: *Dawn Gawn* (Kneitel/Dec. 12).

LITTLE CHEEZER

Rudolph Ising created this cute, cuddly mouse who briefly appeared on the screen in two cartoons of his own. Little Cheezer's first appearance was in a *Happy Harmonies* cartoon bearing his name. *Ising also directed the series. Black–and–white. A Metro-Goldwyn-Mayer Release.*

Voice:

Little Cheezer: Bernice Hansen

1936: *Little Cheezer* (July 11/*Happy Harmonies*).

1937: *Little Buck Cheezer* (Dec. 15).

LITTLE KING

Based on the popular comic–strip character penned by cartoonist Oscar E. Soglow, this animated version marked yet another attempt by Van Beuren Studios to find a successful screen character to upgrade the studio's image in the already crowded cartoon marketplace.

Unfortunately, audiences had become too sophisticated by the time this series was introduced, and it never quite lived up to the studio's advance expectations as a "cartoon saviour." The king never talked but acted out his response in pantomime, which may have been part of the reason for the series' failure. (Strangely, the king later appeared in several Paramount Betty Boop cartoons and was given a speaking voice for those appearances.) *Directed by Jim Tyer and George Stallings. Black–and–white. A Van Beuren Production released through RKO–Radio Pictures.*

1933: *The Fatal Note* (Sept. 29), *Marching Along* (Tyer/Mar. 27), *On The Pan* (Nov. 24) and *Pals* (Tyer/Dec. 22).

1934: *Jest Of Honor* (Stallings/Jan. 19), *Jolly Good Felons* (Stallings/Feb. 16), *Sultan Pepper* (Stallings/Mar. 16), *A Royal Good Time* (Stallings/Apr. 13), *Art For Art's Sake* (Stallings/May 11) and *Cactus King* (Stallings/June 8).

LITTLE LULU

Animator Max Fleischer adapted the Marjorie H. Bell comic–strip character, Little Lulu, to stories that relate the activities and frustrations of a mischievous little girl trying to show her

Marjorie H. Buell's popular comic–strip character, Little Lulu, was turned into a theatrical cartoon series by Max Fleischer in 1944. The series lasted five years. (Courtesy: National Telefilm Associates)

parents how grown up she can be. Already a favorite in *Saturday Evening Post* cartoon panels, Fleischer added the series to the Paramount/Famous Studios 1943–1944 roster.

As he had hoped, Lulu's childish mischief spelled success for his studio, with adventures pitting her against next–door neighbor Tubby, who always harrasses her but is avenged by Lulu's childlike wit.

The series' theme song was written by Fred Wise, Sidney Lippman and Buddy Kaye, becoming as successful a hit as the cartoon series itself.

Paramount dropped the series in 1948 when it was unable to re–negotiate the rights to continue with the character. Lulu was ultimately replaced by a new little girl character, Little Audrey, whose inspiration was clear by her Lulu–like voice and manner. *Directors were Isadore Sparber, Seymour Kneitel and Bill Tytla. Technicolor. A Famous Studios Production released through Paramount Pictures.*

Voices:

Little Lulu: Mae Questel, Cecil Roy

1943: *Eggs Don't Bounce* (Sparber/Dec. 24).

1944: *Hullaba–Lulu* (Kneitel/Feb. 25), *Lulu Gets The Birdie* (Sparber/Mar. 31), *Lulu In Hollywood* (Sparber/May 19), *Lucky Lulu* (Kneitel/June 30), *It's Nifty To Be Thrifty* (Kneitel/Aug. 18) *I'm Just Curious* (Kneitel/Sept. 8), *Indoor Outing* (Sparber/Sept. 29), *Lulu At The Zoo* (Sparber/Nov. 17) and *Birthday Party* (Sparber/Dec. 29).

1945: *Magicalulu* (Kneitel/Mar. 2), *Beau Ties* (Kneitel/Apr. 20), *Daffidilly Daddy* (Kneitel/May 25), *Snap Happy* (Tytla/June 22) and *Man's Pest Friend* (Kneitel/Nov. 30).

1946: *Bargain Counter Attack* (Sparber/Jan. 11), *Bored Of Education* (Tytla/Mar. 1) and *Chick And Double Chick* (Kneitel/Aug. 16).

1947: *Musica–Lulu* (Sparber/Jan. 24), *A Scout With The Gout* (Tytla/Mar. 24), *Loose In The Caboose* (Kneitel/May 23), *Cad And Caddy* (Sparber/July 18), *A Bout With A Trout* (Sparber/Oct. 10), *Super Lulu* (Tytla/Nov. 21) and *The Baby Sitter* (Kneitel/Nov. 28).

1948: *The Dog Show–Off* (Kneitel/Jan. 30).

LITTLE ROQUEFORT

MGM's Tom and Jerry and Famous Studios' Herman and Katnip preceded this cat–and–mouse tandem—a pesky, pint–sized mouse, Little Roquefort, and nemesis cat, Percy—who starred in assorted Terrytoons cartoon "chases" reminiscent of the style and humor first popularized in the Tom and Jerry series. Unfortunately, most comparisons of the two series end here. The Terrytoons version ran its course in five years, while MGM's cat–and–mouse stars remained popular for 26 years, winning seven Academy Awards in the process. *Directed by Connie Rasinski, Mannie Davis, and Ed Donnelly. Technicolor. A Terrytoons Production released through 20th Century–Fox.*

Voices:

Little Roquefort: Tom Morrison, **Percy the Cat:** Tom Morrison

1950: *Cat Happy* (Rasinski/Sept.) and *Mouse Garden* (Davis/Oct.).

1951: *Three Is A Crowd* (Rasinski/Feb.), *Musical Madness* (Donnelly/May), *Seasick Sailors* (Davis/July), *Pastry Panic* (Davis/Oct.) and *The Haunted Cat* (Donnelly/Dec.).

1952: *City Slicker* (Davis/Feb.), *Hypnotized* (Davis/June), *Good Mousekeeping* (Davis/Oct.) and *Flop Secret* (Donnelly/Dec.).

1953: *Mouse Meets Bird* (Rasinski/Mar.), *Playful Puss* (Davis/May), *Friday The 13th* (Davis/July) and *Mouse Menace* (Donnely/Sept.).

1954: *Runaway Mouse* (Davis/Jan.), *Prescription For Percy* (Davis/Apr.) and *Cat's Revenge* (Davis/Sept.).

1955: *No Sleep For Percy* (Rasinski/Mar. 1).

LOONEY TUNES

Looney Tunes were cartoon specials originally produced and animated in the style of Walt Disney's *Silly Symphony* cartoons, featuring popular music and assorted characters to tell a story. By the late 1930s, following structural changes, the series became a stamping ground for many of Warner Brothers' most renowned characters, including Bugs Bunny, Daffy Duck and Porky Pig.

From 1930 to 1933, the series was directed by Rudolph Ising and Hugh Harman, two ex–Disney animators who later joined MGM to head up its new cartoon department. After Harman and Ising's departure, producer Leon Schlesinger named Friz Freleng head director of the series. Freleng had worked alongside both directors since the inception of Warner's cartoon department. He served as chief animator on Harman's and Ising's *Bosko* series which, incidentally, was the *Looney Tunes* series' first regular cartoon star.

Beside Bosko, cartoons featured such studio favorites as Babbit and Catstello, Beaky Buzzard, Beans, Bobo, Buddy, Bugs Bunny, Claude Cat, Conrad Cat, Daffy Duck, Elmer Fudd, Foghorn Leghorn, Goofy Gophers, Hippety Hopper, The Honey–Mousers, Hubie and Bertie, Marc Antony, Pepe Le Pew, Ralph Wolf and Sam Sheepdog, Road Runner, Speedy Gonzales, Sylvester and Tweety. (See individual entries for series episode titles.) *Other series directors included Jack King, Bob Clampett, Norm McCabe, Frank Tashlin, Chuck Jones, Art Davis, Abe Levitow, Maurice Noble, Hawley Pratt, Alex Lovy and Robert McKimson. Black–and–white. Technicolor. A Warner Brothers release.*

Voices:

Mel Blanc, June Foray and Stan Freberg.
(Following filmography is comprised of *Looney Tunes* featuring non–starring cartoons).

1941: *The Haunted Mouse* (Avery/Feb. 15) and *Joe Glow, The Firefly* (Jones/Mar. 8).

1942: *Saps In Chaps* (Freleng/Apr. 11), *Nutty News* (Clampett/May 23), *Hobby Horse–Laffs* (McCabe/June 6), *Gopher Goofy* (McCabe/June 27), *Wacky Blackout* (Clampett/July 11), *The Ducktator* (McCabe/Aug. 11), *Eatin' On The Cuff*

(Clampett/Aug 22) and *The Hep Cat* (Clampett/Oct. 3/first Technicolor *Looney Tunes*).

1943: *Hop And Go* (McCabe/Mar. 27), *Tokio Jokio* (McCabe/May 15) and *Puss N' Booty* (Tashlin/Dec. 11/last black–and–white *Looney Tunes*).

1944: (All in Technicolor) *I've Got Plenty Of Mutton* (Tashlin/Mar. 11), *Angel Puss* (Jones/June 3) and *From Hand To Mouse* (Jones/Aug. 5).

1945: *Behind The Meat Ball* (Tashlin/Apr. 7).

1946: *Of Thee I Sting* (Freleng/Aug. 17), *Mouse Menace* (Davis/Nov. 2) and *Roughly Speaking* (Jones/Nov. 23).

1947: *House Hunting Mice* (Jones/Sept. 6).

1948: *The Rattled Rooster* (Davis/June 26), *The Shell Shocked Egg* (McKimson/July 10) and *A Horse Fly Fleas* (McKimson/Dec. 13).

1949: *Swallow The Leader* (McKimson/Oct. 14).

1950: *It's Hummer Time* (McKimson/July 22).

1951: *Chowhound* (Jones/June 16).

1952: *Who's Kitten Who* (McKimson/Jan. 5).

1953: *A Peck O' Trouble* (McKimson/Mar. 28), *There Auto Be A Law* (McKimson/Jones/June 6), *Easy Peckins* (McKimson/Oct. 17) and *Punch Trunk* (Jones/Dec. 19).

1954: *From A To Z–Z–Z–Z–Z* (Jones/Oct. 16).

1955: *The Hole Idea* (McKimson/July 16).

1956: *Mixed Master* (McKimson/Apr. 14).

1957: *Three Little Bops* (Freleng/Jan. 5/voice by Stan Freberg) and *Go Fly A Kit* (Jones/Feb. 23).

1958: *A Waggily Tale* (Freleng/Apr. 26) and *Dog Tales* (McKimson/July 26).

1959: *Mouse–Placed Kitten* (McKimson/Jan. 24).

1960: *High Note* (Jones/Dec. 3/A.A. nominee).

1962: *Martian Through Georgia* (Jones, Levitow/co–director: Noble/Dec. 29).

1963: *Now Hear This* (Jones/co–director: Noble/Apr. 27/A.A. nominee).

DePatie–Freleng Enterprises Releases
1964: *Senorella And The Glass Huarache* (Pratt/Aug. 1).

Warner Brothers Releases
1968: *Flying Circus* (Lovy/Sept. 14).

LOOPY DE LOOP

The indomitable French wolf's broken English caused unending communications gaffes which usually resulted in chaos. Loopy was the first theatrical cartoon series produced by William Hanna and Joseph Barbera for their studio, Hanna–Barbera Productions, which they co–founded after leaving MGM in 1957. Loopy later found new life through syndication of the old shorts to television in the 1960s. *Directed by William Hanna and Joseph Barbera. Technicolor. A Hanna–Barbera Production released through Columbia Pictures.*

Voices:
Loopy De Loop: Daws Butler

1959: *Wolf Hounded* (Nov. 5) and *Little Bo Bopped* (Dec. 3).

1960: *Tale Of A Wolf* (Mar. 3), *Life With Loopy* (Apr. 7), *Creepy Time Pal* (May 19), *Snoopy Loopy* (June 16), *The Do–Good Wolf* (July 14), *Here, Kiddie, Kiddie* (Sept. 1) and *No Biz Like Shoe Biz* (Sept. 8).

1961: *Count Down Clown* (Jan. 5), *Happy Go Lucky* (Mar. 2), *Two Faced Wolf* (Apr. 6), *This My Ducky Day* (May 4), *Fee Fie Foes* (June 9), *Zoo Is Company* (July 6), *Child Sock–Cology* (Aug. 10), *Catch Meow* (Sept. 14), *Kooky Loopy* (Nov. 16) and *Loopy's Hare–Do* (Dec. 14).

1962: *Bungle Uncle* (Jan. 18), *Beef For And After* (Mar. 1), *Swash Buckled* (Apr. 5), *Common Scents* (May 10), *Bearly Able* (June 28), *Slippery Slippers* (Sept. 7), *Chicken Fraca–See* (Oct. 11), *Rancid Ransom* (Nov. 15) and *Bunnies Abundant* (Dec. 13).

1963: *Just A Wolf At Heart* (Feb. 14), *Chicken Hearted Wolf* (Mar. 14), *Whatcha Watchin* (Apr. 18), *A Fallible Fable* (May 16), *Sheep Stealers Anonymous* (June 13), *Wolf In Sheep Dog's Clothing* (July 11), *Not In Nottingham* (Sept. 5), *Drum–Sticked* (Oct. 3), *Bear Up!* (Nov. 7), *Crook Who Cried Wolf* (Dec. 12) and *Habit Rabbit* (Dec. 31).

1964: *Raggedy Rug* (Jan. 2), *Elephantastic* (Feb. 6), *Bear Hug* (Mar. 5), *Trouble Bruin* (Sept. 17), *Bear Knuckles* (Oct. 15) and *Habit Troubles* (Nov. 19).

1965: *Horse Shoo* (Jan. 7), *Pork Chop Phooey* (Mar. 18), *Crow's Fete* (Apr. 14) and *Big Mouse Take* (June 17).

LUNO

The flying horse Luno and his young master Tim relive history and fairy tales through transcendental powers of the great white stallion. *Directed by Connie Rasinski and Arthur Bartsch. Technicolor. A Terrytoons Production released through 20th Century–Fox.*

Voices:
Luno, the white stallion: Bob McFadden, **Tim, his companion:** Bob McFadden

1963: *The Missing Genie* (Rasinski/Apr. 1) and *Trouble In Baghdad* (Rasinski/Sept. 13).

1964: *Roc–A–Bye Sinbad* (Bartsch/Jan.), *King Rounder* (Rasinski), *Adventure By The Sea* (Bartsch/July 15) and *The Gold Dust Bandit* (Bartsch/Sept.).

MAGGIE AND SAM

Domestic trouble was the basis for comedy misadventures of this husband–and–wife pair who starred briefly in this Walter

Lantz series. *Directed by Alex Lovy. Technicolor. A Walter Lantz Production released through Paramount Pictures.*

Voices:
Maggie: Grace Stafford, **Sam:** Daws Butler

1956: *The Ostrich And I* (Apr. 9) and *Talking Dog* (Aug. 27).

1957: *Fowled–Up Party* (Jan. 14).

MARC ANTONY

A ferocious bulldog is reduced to a softie by a tiny pussycat, Pussyfoot, in this Warner Brothers cartoon series. The characters were created by Chuck Jones. *Directed by Chuck Jones. Technicolor. A Warner Brothers release.*

Merrie Melodies
1952: *Feed The Kitty* (Feb. 2).

Looney Tunes
1953: *Kiss Me Cat* (Feb. 21).

MARVIN MARTIAN

This dwarf, super–intelligent being, whose face was kept hidden under an oversized space helmet, zapped his way into the hearts of filmgoers in the 1948 Bugs Bunny cartoon, *Haredevil Hare.* Warner's animator Chuck Jones created Marvin for the screen, along with his Commander Flyer Saucer X–2 spacecraft, featuring the character in several command performances. Marvin's most memorable appearance was opposite Daffy Duck and Porky Pig in the 1953 classic, *Duck Dodgers In The 24½th Century. Directed by Chuck Jones and Maurice Noble. Technicolor. A Warner Brothers release.*

Voices:
Marvin Martian: Mel Blanc

Looney Tunes
1948: *Haredevil Hare* (with Bugs Bunny/Jones/July 24).

1952: *The Hasty Hare* (with Bugs Bunny/Jones/June 7).

1958: *Hare–Way To The Stars* (with Bugs Bunny/Jones/Mar. 29).

Merrie Melodies
1953: *Duck Dodgers In The 24½th Century* (with Daffy Duck, Porky Pig/Jones/July 25).

1963: *Mad As A Mars Hare* (with Bugs Bunny/Jones, Noble/Oct. 19).

MAW AND PAW

The pug–nosed hillbilly Maw was half the size of her lean, bald husband, Paw. The two characters bore striking resemblances to Marjorie Main and Percy Kilbride, stars of Universal's long–running *Ma and Pa Kettle* film series, on which the cartoon series was based.

Grace Stafford, Walter Lantz's wife and voice of Woody Woodpecker, supplied the voice of Maw. *Directed by Paul J.*

© 1977 Walter Lantz

Universal's successful Ma and Pa Kettle feature film series inspired this cartoon spinoff, Maw And Paw, created by Walter Lantz. © Walter Lantz Productions

Smith. Technicolor. A Walter Lantz Production released through Universal Pictures.

Voices:
Maw: Grace Stafford, **Paw:** Dal McKennon

1953: *Maw and Paw* (Smith/Aug. 10) and *Plywood Panic* (Smith/Sept. 28).

1954: *Pig–In A Pickle* (Smith/Aug. 30).

1955: *Paw's Night Out* (Smith/Aug. 1).

MEANY, MINY AND MOE

Walter Lantz first introduced these three circus–dressed monkeys as supporting players in an Oswald Rabbit cartoon, *Monkey Wretches,* in 1935. The characters were so well–received that Lantz starred the trio in their own series, his fourth for Universal. Each episode incorporated broad comedy gags that made the Three Stooges popular, only with the trio acting out stories in pantomime.

"We didn't need any dialogue," recalled Lantz, "because they were doing the kind of pantomime like Charlie Chaplin and Harry Langdon. They didn't need to talk to be funny."

Thirteen cartoons were produced between 1936 and 1937, with the first official Meany, Miny and Moe cartoon being *Turkey Dinner,* released in November 1936. Lantz cut the number of Oswald cartoons he usually produced in half so he could start production of this new series, costing roughly $8,250 for each episode.

Lantz discontinued the series in late 1937. "There just wasn't much else we could do with the characters," he said. *Directed by Walter Lantz. Black–and–white. A Walter Lantz Production released through Universal Pictures.*

1936: *Turkey Dinner* (Nov. 30) and *Knights For A Day* (Dec. 25).

1937: *The Golfers* (Jan. 11), *House Of Magic* (Feb. 8), *The Big Race* (Mar. 3), *Lumber Camp* (Mar. 15), *Steel Workers* (Apr. 26), *The Stevedores* (May 24), *Country Store* (July 5), *Fireman's Picnic* (Aug. 16), *Rest Resort* (Aug. 23), *Ostrich Feathers* (Sept. 6) and *Air Express* (Sept. 20).

MERLIN THE MAGIC MOUSE

Reminiscent of W. C. Fields—even sounding like the great bulbous–nosed comedian—Merlin the Magic Mouse was the second new cartoon creation by Alex Lovy for Warner Brothers' new animation department after its re–opening in 1967. Stories were based on the globe–trotting adventures of the mouse, who never made a lasting impression on filmgoers and was quickly retired after only five film appearances. *Directed by Alex Lovy and Robert McKimson. Technicolor. A Warner Brothers release.*

Voices:
Merlin the Magic Mouse: Larry Storch

Merrie Melodies
1967: *Merlin The Magic Mouse* (Lovy/Nov. 18).

1968: *Feud With A Dude* (Lovy/ May 25).

1969: *Shamrock And Roll* (McKimson/June 28).

Looney Tunes
1968: *Hocus Pocus Pow Wow* (Lovy/Jan. 13).

1969: *Fistic Mystic* (McKimson/Mar. 29).

MERRIE MELODIES

Directors Rudolf Ising and Hugh Harman, two former Disney animators, produced independently through Warner Brothers a series based on popular melodies of that era. Leon Schlesinger later served as producer when Harman and Ising left Warner in 1933 to lend their talent to studio rival MGM, which was entering the cartoon field for the first time.

The earliest picture in the series made use of Abe Lyman's Recording Orchestra on soundtracks, playing "whoopee tunes" of the day, like "Smile, Darn Ya Smile" and "Freddie the Freshman." Other initial series entries revolved around "period" subjects—the vaudeville stage, the college football craze, etc.—and spot references to popular culture and current trends.

In the beginning, the closest thing to a star in the series was Goopy Geer, a wisecracking entertainer—"part comedian, part musician and part dancer"—inspsired by vaudeville showmen of that period. Throughout its history, the series featured a vast array of major and less notable cartoon stars and miscellaneous one–shot characters.

The series' stars were Babbit and Catstello, Beaky Buzzard, Bobo, Bunny and Claude, Bugs Bunny, Charlie Dog, Claude Cat, Conrad Cat, Daffy Duck, Elmer Fudd, Foxy, Goofy Gophers, Goopy Geer, Hippety Hopper, Hubie and Bertie, Inki, Marc Antony, Pepe Le Pew, Piggy, Ralph Phillips, Ralph Wolf

and Sam Sheepdog, the Road Runner and Coyote, Speedy Gonzales, Sylvester, The Three Bears, and Tweety (see individual entries for aforementioned characters for episodic listings). *Besides Harman and Ising, series directors included Frank Marsales, Bernard Brown, Friz Freleng, Tom Palmer, Earl Duvall, Ben Hardaway, Tex Avery, Frank Tashlin, Cal Dalton, Chuck Jones, Bob Clampett, Robert McKimson, Art Davis, Abe Levitow, Ken Mundie and Alex Lovy. Black–and–white. Technicolor. A Warner Brothers release.*

Voices:
Mel Blanc

(Following filmography is comprised of *Merrie Melodies* featuring non–starring cartoons.)

1931: *Red-Headed Baby* (Ising/Dec. 26).

1932: *Pagan Moon* (Ising/Jan. 31), *Freddy The Freshman* (Ising/Feb. 20), *Crosby, Columbo and Vallee* (Ising/Mar. 19), *It's Got Me Again* (Ising/May 14/A.A. nominee), *I Love A Parade* (Ising/Aug. 6) *You're Too Careless With Your Kisses* (Ising/Sept. 10), *I Wish I Had Wings* (Ising/Oct. 15) and *A Great Big Bunch of You* (Ising/Nov. 12).

1933: *The Shanty Where Santa Lives* (Ising/Jan 7.) *Three's A Crowd* (Ising/Jan. 17), *One Step Ahead Of My Shadow* (Ising/Feb. 4), *Young And Healthy* (Ising/Mar. 4), *The Organ Grinder* (Ising/Apr. 8), *Wake Up The Gypsy In Me* (Ising/May 13), *I Like Mountain Music* (Ising/June 13), *Shuffle Off To Buffalo* (Freleng/July 8), *We're In The Money* (Ising/Aug. 26), (The following *Merrie Melodies* were Leon Schlesinger Productions) *I've Got To Sing A Torch Song* (Palmer/Sept. 23), *The Dish Ran Away With The Spoon* (Ising/Sept. 24) and *Sittin' On A Backyard Fence* (Duvall/Sept. 16).

1934: *Pettin' In The Park* (Brown/Jan. 27), *Honeymoon Hotel* (Duvall/Feb. 17/Cinecolor), *Beauty And The Beast* (Freleng/Apr. 14/Cinecolor), *Those Were Wonderful Days* (Brown/Apr. 26), *Goin' To Heaven On A Mule* (Freleng/May 19/black–and–white), *How Do I Know It's Sunday* (Freleng/June 9/black–and–white), *Why Do I Dream Those Dreams?* (Freleng/June 30/black–and–white), *The Girl At The Ironing Board* (Freleng/Augs. 23/black–and–white), *The Miller's Daughter* (Freleng/Oct. 13), *Shake Your Powder Puff* (Freleng/Oct. 17/black–and–white), *Those Beautiful Dames* (Freleng/Nov. 10/two–strip color) and *Pop Goes My Heart* (Freleng/Dec. 18).

1935: *Mr. and Mrs. Is The Name* (Freleng/Jan. 19/two–strip color), *Rhythm In Bow* (Hardaway/Feb. 1/last *Merrie Melodies* in black–and–white; the following were all produced in two–strip color), *The Country Boy* (with Peter Rabbit/Freleng/Feb. 9), *Along Flirtation Walk* (Freleng/Apr. 6), *My Green Fedora* (with Peter Rabbit/Freleng/May 4), *Into Your Dance* (Freleng/June 8), *The Country Mouse* (Freleng/July 13), *The Merry Old Soul* (Freleng/Aug. 17), *The Lady In Red* (Freleng/Sept. 21), *Little Dutch Plate* (Freleng/Oct. 19), *Billboard Frolics* (Freleng/Nov. 9) and *Flowers For Madame* (Freleng/Nov. 20).

1936: (All in Technicolor) *I Wanna Play House* (Freleng/Jan. 11), *The Cat Came Back* (Freleng/Feb. 8), *I'm A Big Shot*

Now (Freleng/Apr. 11), *Miss Glory* (Avery/Mar. 7), *Let It Be Me* (Freleng/May 2), *I Love To Take Orders From You* (Avery/May 18), *Bingo Crosbyana* (Freleng/May 30), *When I Yoo Hoo* (Freleng/June 27), *I Love To Singa* (Avery/July 18), *Sunday Go To Meetin' Time* (Freleng/Aug. 8), *At Your Service Madame* (Freleng/Aug. 29), *Toytown Hall* (Freleng/Sept. 19), *Boulevardier From The Bronx* (Freleng/Oct. 10), *Don't Look Now* (Avery/Nov. 7) and *The Coo Coo Nut Grove* (Freleng/Nov. 28).

1937: *He Was Her Man* (Freleng/Jan. 2), *Pigs Is Pigs* (Freleng/Jan. 30), *I Only Have Eyes For You* (Avery/Mar. 6), *The Fella With The Fiddle* (Freleng/Mar. 27), *She Was An Acrobat's Daughter* (Freleng/Apr. 10), *Ain't We Got Fun* (Avery/Apr. 27), *Clean Pastures* (Freleng/May 22), *Uncle Tom's Bungalow* (Avery/June 5), *Streamlined Greta Green* (Freleng/June 19), *Sweet Sioux* (Freleng/June 26), *Plenty Of Money And You* (Freleng/July 31), *A Sunbonnet Blue* (Avery/Aug. 21), *Speaking Of The Weather* (Tashlin/Sept. 4), *Dog Daze* (Freleng/Sept. 18), *I Wanna Be A Sailor* (Avery/Sept. 25), *The Lyin' Mouse* (Freleng/Oct. 16), *The Woods Are Full Of Cuckoos* (Tashlin/Dec. 4) and *September In The Rain* (Freleng/Dec. 18).

1938: *My Little Buckaroo* (Freleng/Jan. 29), *Jungle Jitters* (Freleng/Feb. 19), *The Sneazin' Weasel* (Avery/Mar. 12), *A Star Is Hatched* (Freleng/Apr. 2), *The Penguin Parade* (Avery/Apr. 16) *Now That Summer Is Gone* (Tashlin/May 4), *The Isle Of Pingo—Pongo* (Avery/May 28), *Katnip Kollege* (Hardaway, Dalton/June 11), *Have You Got Any Castles?* (Tashlin/June 25), *Love And Curses* (Hardaway, Dalton/July 9), *The Major Lied Till Dawn* (Tashlin/Aug. 13), *Cracked Ice* (Tashlin/Sept. 10), *Little Pancho Vanilla* (Tashlin/Oct. 8), *You're An Education* (Tashlin/Nov. 5) and *The Mice Will Play* (Avery/Dec. 31).

1939: *Dog Gone Modern* (Jones/Jan. 14), *Robin Hood Makes Good* (Jones/Feb. 11), *Gold Rush Daze* (Hardaway,

Lobby card from the Merrie Melodies cartoon *Have You Got Any Castles?* © Warner Brothers, Inc.

Dalton/Feb. 25), *Bars And Stripes Forever* (Hardaway, Dalton/Apr. 8), *Thugs With Dirty Mugs* (Avery/May 6), *Hobo Gadget Band* (Hardaway, Dalton/June 17), *Snow Man's Land* (Jones/July 29), *Detouring America* (Avery/Aug. 26/A.A. nominee), *Sioux Me* (Hardaway, Dalton/Sept. 9), *Land Of The Midnight Fun* (Avery/Sept. 23), *The Good Egg* (Jones/Oct. 21), *Little Lion Hunter* (Jones/Oct. 7), *Fresh Fish* (Avery/Nov. 4), *Fagin's Freshman* (Hardaway, Dalton/Nov. 18), *Screwball Football* (Avery/Dec. 16) and *Curious Puppy* (Jones/Dec. 30).

1940: *The Early Worm Gets the Bird* (Avery/Jan 13.), *The Mighty Hunters* (Jones/Jan. 27), *Busy Bakers* (Hardaway, Dalton/Feb. 10), *Cross Country Detours* (Avery/Apr. 13), *A Gander At Mother Goose* (Avery/May 25), *Tom Thumb In Trouble* (Jones/June 8), *Circus Today* (Avery/June 22), *Little Blabbermouse* (Freleng/July 6), *Ghost Wanted* (Jones/Aug. 10), *Ceiling Hero* (Avery/Aug. 24), *Malibu Beach Party* (Freleng/Sept. 14), *Stage Fright* (Jones/Sept. 28), *Wacky Wildlife* (Avery/Nov. 9), *Of Fox And Hounds* (Avery/Dec. 7) and *Shop, Look And Listen* (Freleng/Dec. 21).

1941: *The Fighting 69th ½* (Freleng/Jan. 18), *The Crackpot Quail* (Avery/Feb. 15), *The Cat's Tale* (Freleng/Mar. 1), *Goofy Groceries* (Clampett/Mar. 29), *The Trial Of Mister Wolf* (Freleng/Apr. 26), *Farm Frolics* (Clampett/May 10), *Hollywood Steps Out* (with 3 Stooges, Clark Gable, Bing Crosby, Jimmy Stewart, William Powell, Peter Lorre, Groucho Marx, Harpo Marx, and Buster Keaton caricatures/Avery/May 24), *The Wacky Worm* (Freleng/June 21), *Aviation Vacation* (Avery/Aug. 2), *Sport Chumpions* (Freleng/Aug. 16), *Snowtime For Comedy* (Jones/Aug. 30), *The Bug Parade* (Avery/Oct. 11), *Rookie Revue* (Freleng/Oct. 25), *Saddle Silly* (Jones/Nov. 8), *the Cagey Canary* (Avery, Clampett/Nov. 22) and *Rhapsody In Rivets* (Freleng/Dec. 6).

1942: *Hop, Skip, And Chump* (with Laurel and Hardy portrayed as crows/Freleng/Jan. 3), *Aloha Hooey* (Avery/Jan. 30), *Crazy Cruise* (Avery, Clampett/Mar. 14), *Horton Hatches The Egg* (Clampett/Apr. 11), *Dog Tired* (Jones/Apr. 25), *The Draft Horse* (Jones/May 9), *Lights Fantastic* (Freleng/May 23), *Double Chase* (Freleng/June 27), *Foney Fables* (Freleng/Aug. 1), *The Squawkin' Hawk* (with Henery Hawk/Jones/Aug. 8), *Fox Pop* (Jones/Sept. 5), *The Dover Boys* (Jones/Sept. 10), *The Sheepish Wolf* (Freleng/Oct. 17) and *Ding Dog Daddy* (Freleng/Dec. 5).

1943: *Coal Black And De Sebben Dwarfs* (Clampett/Jan. 16), *Pigs In A Polka* (Freleng/Feb. 2/A.A. nominee), *Fifth Column Mouse* (Freleng/Mar. 6), *Flop Goes The Weasel* (Jones/Mar. 20), *Greetings Bait* (Freleng/May 15/A.A. nominee), *Tin Pan Alley Cats* (Clampett/July 3), *Hiss And Make Up* (Freleng/Sept. 11) and *Fin N' Catty* (Jones/Oct. 23).

1944: *Meatless Flyday* (Freleng/Jan. 29), *The Weakly Reporter* (Jones/Mar. 25), *Russian Rhapsody* (Clampett/May 20) and *Goldilocks And The Jivin' Bears* (Freleng/Sept. 2).

1945: *Fresh Airedale* (Jones/Aug. 25).

1946: *Holiday For Shoestrings* (with Laurel and Hardy elves/Freleng/Feb. 23), *Quentin Quail* (Jones/Mar. 2), *Hollywood Canine Canteen* (with Edward G. Robinson, Jimmy

Durante, Laurel and Hardy, Bing Crosby, Bob Hope, Jerry Colonna, Abbott and Costello, Blondie and Dagwood, Joe Besser and Harry James caricatures in the images of dogs/ McKimson/Apr. 20), *The Eager Beaver* (Jones/July 13) and *Fair And Worm—er* (Jones/Sept. 28).

1947: *The Gay Anties* (Freleng/Feb. 15) and *The Foxy Duckling* (Davis/Aug. 23).

1948: *Bone Sweet Bone* (Davis/May 22), *Dough Ray Me—ow* (Davis/Aug. 14), *A Horse Fly Fleas* (McKimson/Dec. 13/ Cinecolor) and *A Hide, A Slick, And A Chick* (Davis/Dec. 27).

1951: *A Fox In A Fix* (McKimson/Jan. 20), *Corn Plastered* (McKimson/Mar. 3), *Early To Bet* (McKimson/May 12) and *Sleepy Time Possum* (McKimson/Nov. 3).

1952: *Feed The Kitty* (Jones/Feb. 2), *Kiddin' The Kitten* (McKimson/Apr. 5) and *The Turn—Tale Wolf* (McKimson/ June 28).

1953: *Much Ado About Nutting* (Jones/May 23).

1954: *Wild Wife* (McKimson/Feb. 20), *The Oily American* (McKimson//July 10) and *Goo Goo Goliath* (Freleng/Sept. 18).

1955: *Pizzicato Pussycat* (Freleng/Jan. 1) and *One Froggy Evening* (Jones/Dec. 31).

1956: *Rocket-Bye Baby* (Jones/Aug. 4) and *Two Crows From Tacos* (Freleng/Nov. 24).

1958: *To Itch His Own* (Jones/June 28).

1959: *Mouse—Placed Kitten* (McKimson/Jan. 24), *The Mouse That Jack Built* (with Jack Benny, Rochester mice/McKimson/ Apr. 4) and *Unnatural History* (Levitow/Nov. 14).

1960: *Wild Wild World* (McKimson//Feb. 27).

1961: *The Mouse On 57th Street* (Jones/Feb. 25) and *Nelly's Folly* (with Nelly the Giraffe/Jones/Dec. 30/A.A. nominee).

1963: *I Was A Teenage Thumb* (with Ralph K., Merlin Jr./ Jones/Jan. 19).

DePatie—Freleng Enterprises Releases
1964: *Bartholomew Versus The Wheel* (McKimson/Feb. 29).

Warner Brothers Release
1968: *Chimp And Zee* (Lovy/Oct. 12).

1969: *Rabbit Stews and Rabbits Too* (with Rapid Rabbit/ McKimson/June 7).

MERRY MAKERS

This was the last cartoon series launched by Paramount's Famous Studios. James "Shamus" Culhane produced and directed each production, shaped around everyday situations and starring various animated characters. Paramount shut down its cartoon department after the 1967 season, the same year *Merry Makers* was created. *Directed by James "Shamus'*

Culhane. Technicolor. A Famous Studios Production released through Paramount Pictures.

1967: *Think Or Sink* (Mar.), *Halt, Who Grows There?* (May), *From Orbit To Obit* (June) and *Forget—Me—Nuts* (Aug.).

MGM CARTOONS

The Metro—Goldwyn—Mayer lot was known for more than producing its share of big—budget musicals and epic films. The studio also produced a number of quality, theatrical sound cartoons, first in the early 1930s with Hugh Harman— and Rudolf Ising—produced and directed cartoons, and in the 1940s a series of cartoons featuring major stars like Tom and Jerry, Droopy and Barney Bear. During the cartoon division's halcyon days it also produced an assortment of cartoons featuring an all—star cast and no—name characters which, for the most part, were equally entertaining. The following is a listing of the studio's miscellaneous cartoons which were released under the studio's trademark MGM lion logo. For MGM series entries, see Barney Bear, Bosko, Droopy, George and Junior, Tom and Jerry, Screwy Squirrel and Tex Avery, Hugh Harman and Rudolph Ising listings. *Directed by Milt Gross, George Gordon, Joseph Barbera, William Hanna, Robert Allen and Jerry Brewer. Black—and—white. Technicolor. A Metro—Goldwyn—Mayer release.*

1939: (Sepia—tone) *Jitterbug Follies* (with J. R. the Wonder Dog, Count Screwloose/Gross/Feb. 25) and *Wanted: No Master* (with J. R. the Wonder Dog, Count Screwloose/Gross/ Mar. 18).

1940: (Technicolor) *Swing Social* (Hanna, Barbera/May 18) and *Gallopin' Gals* (Hanna, Barbera/Oct. 26).

1941: *The Goose That Goes South* (Hanna, Barbera/Apr. 26), *Little Caesario* (Allen/Aug. 30) and *Officer Pooch* (Hanna, Barbera/Sept. 6).

1942: *The First Swallow* (Brewer/July 4) and *Chips Off The Old Block* (Allen/Sept. 12).

1943: *War Dogs* (Hanna, Barbera/Oct. 9) and *Stork's Holiday* (Gordon/Oct. 23).

1944. *Innertube Antics* (Jan. 22/formerly *Strange Innertube* and *Innertube Interlude*) and *The Tree Surgeon* (Gordon/ June 3).

1948: *Make Mine Freedom* (Hanna, Barbera/Feb. 25).

1950: *Why Play Leapfrog?* (produced by John Sutherland for Harding College).

1951: *Meet King Joe* (produced by John Sutherland for Harding College/Sept. 13), *Inside Cackle Corners* (produced by John Sutherland for Harding College/Nov. 13) and *Fresh Laid Plans* (produced by John Sutherland for Harding College/ Dec. 11).

1955: *Good Will To Men* (Hanna, Barbera/Dec. 23/A.A. nominee).

MICKEY MOUSE

Button—eyed, mischieveous Mickey Mouse has been a lovable world—renowned character for more than 60 years. New generations of television viewers continue to rediscover the superstar rodent through reruns of "The Mickey Mouse Club" and Mickey Mouse cartoons.

In the early cartoons, Mickey displayed some of the same physical features of Walt Disney's Oswald the Rabbit character: he wore short, button—down pants and pure—white, four—finger gloves. Disney and veteran animator Ub Iwerks first drew the soft-talking Mickey, and Disney himself supplied the voice through the late 1940s.

In 1928, inspired by the enormous success of *The Jazz Singer,* the first talking picture released the previous year, Disney cashed in on the opportunity by providing something unique—the first synchronized sound cartoon, *Steamboat Willie,* starring Mickey as the captain of his own steamboat.

The cartoon came about following initial tests by Disney and his staff. He first screened a scene using synchronized sound—a process renovated by animator Ub Iwerks—when the film was half—finished. The effect of the screening was "nothing less than electric," Disney once said. The reaction was duplicated months later when audiences witnessed this latest innovation for the first time on theater screens across the country.

This landmark film changed the course of cartoon animation, and Disney immediately added soundtracks to two previously produced silent Mickey Mouse cartoons, *Plane Crazy* and *Gallopin' Gaucho,* releasing both films with music arranged and composed by Carl Stalling who later became Warner Brothers' musical director.

Mickey experienced unprecedented worldwide fame in the years ahead, spawning hundreds of thousands of licensed merchandise items, such as games and toys. (The first Mickey Mouse stuffed doll was designed by animator Bob Clampett, then a high school student, and his enterprising aunt Charlotte Clark.) In fact, in 1932, Disney even received a special Academy Award in recognition of Mickey's creation and resulting impact on the cartoon industry.

In 1990, Mickey Mouse starred along with pals Goofy, Donald Duck and Pluto in an all-new 35-minute short-subject, *The Prince And The Pauper,* which was simultaneously released with the full-length Disney feature *The Rescuers Down Under.*

Supporting characters in the series were Minnie Mouse, Peg Leg Pete, Horace Horsecollar and Clarabelle Cow, each appearing in several episodes during the life of the series. *Directors were Walt Disney, Wilfred Jackson, Bert Gillett, David Hand, Ben Sharpsteen, Hamilton Luske, Pinto Colvig, Walt Pfeiffer, Ed Penner, Jack King, Dick Huemer, Bill Roberts, Clyde Geronimi, Riley Thomson, Charles Nichols, Jack Hannah, Milt Schaffer, George Scribner and Burny Mattinson. Black—and—white. Technicolor. A Walt Disney Production released through Celebrity Pictures, Columbia Pictures, United Artists, RKO—Radio Pictures and later Buena Vista.*

Voices:

Mickey Mouse: Walt Disney (to 1947), Jim MacDonald (1947–1983), Wayne Allwine (1983–), **Minnie Mouse:** Marcellite Garner (to 1940), Thelma Boardman (1940), Ruth Clifford (after 1942)

Celebrity Pictures

1928: *Plane Crazy* (Disney/never released silent/released in 1929 in sound), *Gallopin' Gaucho* (Disney/released in 1929 in sound) and *Steamboat Willie* (Disney/Nov. 18/first sound cartoon).

1929: *The Barn Dance* (Disney/Mar. 14), *The Opry House* (Disney/Mar. 28), *When The Cat's Away* (Disney/Apr. 11), *The Barnyard Battle* (Disney/Apr. 25), *The Plow Boy* (Disney/May 9), *The Karnival Kid* (Disney/May 23), *Mickey's Follies* (Jackson/June 26), *Mickey's Choo—Choo* (Disney/June 20), *The Jazz Fool* (Disney/July 5), *The Haunted House* (Disney/Aug. 1), *Wild Waves* (Gillett/Aug. 15) and *Jungle Rhythm* (Disney/Nov. 15).

Columbia Pictures

(The studio took over distributorship of all previous films as well as new releases.)

1930: *The Barnyard Concert* (Disney/Mar. 3), *Just Mickey* (Disney/Mar. 14/formerly *Fiddlin' Around*), *The Cactus Kid* (Disney/Apr. 11), *The Shindig* (Gillett/July 11), *The Fire Fighters* (Gillett/Aug. 6), *The Chain Gang* (with Pluto/Gillett/Aug. 18), *The Gorilla Mystery* (Gillett/Oct. 1), *The Picnic* (with Pluto/Gillett/Nov. 14) and *Pioneer Days* (with Pluto/Gillett/Dec. 10).

1931: *The Birthday Party* (Gillett/Jan. 6), *Traffic Troubles* (Gillett/Mar. 20), *The Castaway* (Jackson/Apr. 6), *The Moose Hunt* (with Pluto/Gillett/May 8), *The Delivery Boy* (Gillett/June 15), *Mickey Steps Out* (with Pluto/Gillett/June 22), *Blue Rhythm* (Gillett/Aug. 18), *Fishin' Around* (with Pluto/Gillett/Sept. 14), *The Barnyard Broadcast* (Gillett/Oct. 19), *The Beach Party* (with Pluto/Gillett/Nov. 4), *Mickey Cuts Up* (with Pluto/Gillett/Dec. 2) and *Mickey's Orphans* (with Pluto/Gillett/Dec. 14/A.A. nominee).

1932: *The Duck Hunt* (with Pluto/Gillett/Jan. 28), *The Grocery Boy* (with Pluto/Jackson/Feb. 3), *The Mad Dog* (with Pluto/Gillett/Mar. 5), *Barnyard Olympics* (with Pluto/Jackson/Apr. 18), *Mickey's Review* (with Pluto, Goofy/Jackson/May 2), *Musical Farmer* (Jackson/July 11) and *Mickey In Arabia* (Jackson/July 20).

United Artists.

1932: *Mickey's Nightmare* (with Pluto/Gillett/Aug. 13.), *Trader Mickey* (with Pluto/Hand/Aug. 20), *The Whoopee Party* (with Goofy/Jackson/Sept. 17), *Touchdown Mickey* (Jackson/Oct. 5), *The Wayward Canary* (with Pluto/Gillett/Nov. 12), *The Klondike Kid* (with Pluto/Jackson/Nov. 12) and *Mickey's Good Deed* (with Pluto/Gillett/Dec. 17).

1933: *Building A Building* (Hand/Jan. 7/A.A. nominee), *The Mad Doctor* (with Pluto/Hand/Jan. 21), *Mickey's Pal Pluto* (with Pluto/Hand/Feb. 18), *Ye Olden Days* (with Goofy/Gillett/Apr. 8), *The Mail Pilot* (Hand/May 13), *Mickey's Mechanical Man* (Jackson/June 17), *Mickey's Gala Premiere* (with Pluto, Goofy/Gillett/July 1), *Puppy Love* (with Pluto/Jackson/Sept. 2), *The Steeplechase* (Gillett/Sept. 30), *The Pet Store* (Jackson/Oct. 28) and *Giantland* (Gillett/Nov. 25).

1934: *Shanghaied* (Gillett/Jan. 13), *Camping Out* (Hand/Feb. 17), *Playful Pluto* (with Pluto/Gillett/Mar. 3), *Gulliver Mickey* (Gillett/May 19), *Mickey's Steam Roller* (Hand/June 16), *Orphan's Benefit* (with Donald Duck, Goofy/Gillett/Aug. 11), *Mickey Plays Papa* (with Pluto/Gillett/Sept. 29), *The Dognapper* (with Donald Duck/Hand/Nov. 17) and *Two–Gun Mickey* (Sharpsteen/Dec. 15).

1935: *Mickey's Man Friday* (Hand/Jan. 19), *The Band Concert* (with Donald Duck, Goofy/Jackson/Feb. 23/first color), *Mickey's Service Station* (with Donald Duck, Goofy/Sharpsteen/Mar. 16), *Mickey's Kangaroo* (with Pluto/Hand/Apr. 13/last black–and–white Mickey Mouse cartoon), *Mickey's Garden* (with Pluto/Jackson/July 13), *Mickey's Fire Brigade* (with Donald Duck, Goofy/Sharpsteen/Aug. 3), *Pluto's Judgement Day* (with Pluto/Hand/Aug. 31) and *On Ice* (with Donald Duck, Goofy, Pluto/Sharpsteen/Sept. 28).

1936: *Mickey's Polo Team* (with Donald Duck, Goofy/Hand/Jan. 4), *Orphan's Picnic* (with Donald Duck/Sharpsteen/Feb. 15), *Mickey's Grand Opera* (with Donald Duck, Pluto/Jackson/Mar. 7), *Thru The Mirror* (Hand/May 30), *Moving Day* (with Donald Duck, Goofy/Sharpsteen/June 20), *Mickey's Rival* (Jackson/June 20), *Alpine Climbers* (with Donald Duck, Pluto/Hand/July 25), *Mickey's Circus* (with Donald Duck/Sharpsteen/Aug. 1) and *Mickey's Elephant* (with Pluto/Luske/Oct. 10).

1937: *The Worm Turns* (with Pluto/Sharpsteen/Jan. 2), *Magician Mickey* (with Donald Duck/Hand/Feb. 6), *Moose Hunters* (with Donald Duck, Goofy/Sharpsteen/Feb. 20) and *Mickey's Amateurs* (with Donald Duck/Colvig, Pfeiffer, Penner/Apr. 17).

RKO–Radio Pictures
1937: *Hawaiian Holiday* (with Donald Duck, Goofy, Pluto/Sharpsteen/Sept. 24), *Clock Cleaners* (with Donald Duck, Goofy/Sharpsteen/Oct. 15) and *Lonesome Ghosts* (with Donald Duck, Goofy/Gillett/Dec. 24).

1938: *Boat Builders* (with Donald Duck, Goofy/Sharpsteen/Feb. 25), *Mickey's Trailer* (with Donald Duck, Goofy/Sharpsteen/May 6), *The Whalers* (with Donald Duck, Goofy/Huemer/Aug. 19), *Mickey's Parrot* (with Pluto/Roberts/Sept. 9) and *Brave Little Tailor* (Gillett/Sept. 23/A.A. nominee).

1939: *Society Dog Show* (with Pluto/Roberts/Feb. 3) and *The Pointer* (with Pluto/Geronimi/July 21/A.A. nominee).

1940: *Tugboat Mickey* (with Donald Duck, Goofy/Geronimi/Apr. 26), *Pluto's Dream House* (with Pluto/Geronimi/Aug. 30) and *Mr. Mouse Takes A Trip* (with Pluto/Geronimi/Oct. 1).

1941: *The Little Whirlwind* (Thomson/Feb. 14), *The Nifty Nineties* (with Donald Duck, Goofy/Thomson/June 20) and *Orphan's Benefit* (with Donald Duck, Goofy/Thomson/Aug. 12).

1942: *Mickey's Birthday Party* (with Donald Duck, Goofy/Thomson/Feb. 7) and *Symphony Hour* (with Donald Duck, Goofy/Thomson/Mar. 20).

1947: *Mickey's Delayed Date* (with Pluto/Nichols/Oct. 3).

1948: *Mickey Down Under* (with Pluto/Nichols/Mar. 19) and *Mickey And The Seal* (Nichols/Dec. 3/A.A. nominee).

1951: *Plutopia* (with Pluto/Nichols/May 18) and *R'coon Dawg* (with Pluto/Nichols/Aug. 10).

1952: *Pluto's Party* (Schaffer/Sept. 19) and *Pluto's Christmas Tree* (with Chip and Dale, Donald Duck, Goofy/Hannah/Nov. 21).

1953: *The Simple Things* (with Pluto/Nichols/Apr. 18).

1983: *Mickey's Christmas Carol* (Mattinson/Dec. 16/A.A. nominee).

1990: *The Prince And The Pauper* (with Goofy, Donald Duck, Pluto/Scribner/Nov. 16).

THE MIGHTY HEROES

Under the supervision of animator Ralph Bakshi, this series emerged in response to the growing craze for superhero cartoons, only this time poking fun at the idea. Episodes featured five defenders of justice—Diaper Man, Tornado Man, Rope Man, Strong Man and Cuckoo Man—a group of half–witted superheroes who battle evil doings of such notorious villains as the Stretcher, the Shrinker and, of course, the Enlarger.

Originally, 26 episodes were made for television, with a scant few actually released to theaters nationwide in the late 1960s and early 1970. Bakshi was named supervising director of Terrytoons in 1966, the same year the series was first broadcast on television. *Directed by Ralph Bakshi and Bob Taylor. Technicolor. A Terrytoons Production released through 20th Century–Fox.*

Voices:
The Mighty Heroes: Herschel Benardi, Lionel Wilson

1969: *The Stretcher* (Apr.), *The Frog* (Oct.) and *The Toy Man* (Dec.).

1970: *The Ghost Monster* (Apr.), *The Drifter* (Aug.), *The Proton Pulsator* (Sept.) and *The Shocker* (Dec.).

1971: *The Enlarger* (Apr.), *The Duster* (Aug.) and *The Big Freeze* (Dec.).

MIGHTY MOUSE

Combining the power of Superman and the body of Mickey Mouse, Mighty Mouse was animator Paul Terry's most popular cartoon star. For more than 15 years, the character defended the rights of mice in need of his super strength to stave off trouble and restore order.

I. Klein, a Terrytoons storyman, originated the Mighty Mouse character several years after joining the studio in the spring of 1940. Since most animated characters at that time were humanized animals and insects, Klein initially sketched a "super fly," replete with a red Superman–like cape. The sketches quickly attracted Terry's attention.

"We were putting up ideas for a cartoon at the start of a new cartoon story. It crossed my mind that a 'takeoff' of the

Model sheet for the redesigned version of Paul Terry's Mighty Mouse

new comic–strip sensation, 'Superman,' could be a subject for a Terrytoons cartoon," Klein once recalled.

Terry changed Klein's super fly to a mouse, dubbing him "Supermouse," as the character was so billed in four cartoons beginning in 1942 with *The Mouse of Tomorrow*. (He was actually more like a super rat than super mouse in this film.) The cartoon series ultimately saved Terrytoons from losing its distributor's contract with 20th Century–Fox, which had considered dropping the studio's cartoons from its roster. With the success of the Mighty Mouse series, the studio immediately changed its mind and signed a new deal with Terrytoons to continue releasing its cartoons to theaters.

A year after his debut, Terry changed the name of the character, not because of possible legal action from D. C. Comics, the license holder of Superman, for copyright infringement, as reported elsewhere. A former Terrytoons employee had contributed his own version of the character to a new comic book called, "Coo Coo Comics," with the first issue appearing the same month that *The Mouse of Tomorrow* was officially released. Terry decided he didn't want to compete with a character that was so similar in nature, so he renamed his super rodent "Mighty Mouse."

As a result of the name change, the early Supermouse cartoons were retitled before the films were syndicated to television. The films re–appeared on television as part of CBS' "The Mighty Mouse Playhouse" in 1955. *Directors were Mannie Davis, Connie Rasinksi, Eddie Donnelly, Bill Tytla and Dave Tendlar. Technicolor. A Terrytoons Production released through 20th Century–Fox.*

Voices:
Mighty Mouse: Tom Morrison

1942: *The Mouse of Tomorrow* (Donnelly/Oct. 16) and *Frankenstein's Cat* (Davis/Nov. 27).

1943: *He Dood It Again* (Donnelly/Feb. 5), *Pandora's Box* (Rasinski/June 11), *Super Mouse Rides Again* (Davis/Aug. 6/ aka *Mighty Mouse Rides Again*), *Down With Cats* (Rasinski/ Oct. 7) and *Lion And The Mouse* (Davis/Nov. 12).

1944: *Wreck of Hesperus* (Davis/Feb. 11/first cartoon billed as Mighty Mouse), *The Champion Of Justice* (Davis/Mar. 17), *Mighty Mouse Meets Jekyll And Hyde Cat* (Davis/Apr. 28), *Eliza On Ice* (Rasinski/June 16), *Wolf! Wolf!* (Davis/June 22), *The Green Line* (Donnelly/July 7), *The Two Barbers* (Donnelly/Sept. 1), *Sultan's Birthday* (Tytla/Oct. 13) and *At The Circus* (Donnelly/Nov. 17).

1945: *Mighty Mouse And The Pirates* (Rasinski/Jan. 12), *Port Of Missing Mice* (Donnelly/Feb. 2), *Raiding The Raiders* (Rasinski/Mar. 9), *Mighty Mouse And The Kilkenny Cats* (Davis/Apr. 13), *The Silver Streak* (Donnelly/June 8), *Mighty Mouse And The Wolf* (Donnelly/July 20), *Gypsy Life* (Rasinski/Aug. 3/A.A. nominee), *Mighty Mouse Meets Bad Bill Bunion* (Davis/Nov. 9) and *Mighty Mouse In Krakatoa* (Rasinski/Dec. 14).

1946: *Svengali's Cat* (Donnelly/Jan. 18), *The Wicked Wolf* (Davis/Mar. 8), *My Old Kentucky Home* (Donnelly/Mar. 29), *Throwing The Bull* (Rasinski/May 3), *The Johnstown Flood* (Rasinski/June 28), *The Trojan Horse* (Davis/July 26), *Winning The West* (Donnelly/Aug. 16), *The Electronic Mouse Trap* (Davis/Sept. 6), *The Jail Break* (Davis/Sept. 20), *The Crackpot King* (Donnelly/Nov. 15) and *The Hep Cat* (Davis/Dec. 6).

1947: *Crying Wolf* (Rasinski/Jan. 10), *Deadend Cats* (Donnelly/Feb. 14), *Aladdin's Lamp* (Donnelly/Mar. 28), *The Sky Is Falling* (Davis/Apr. 25), *Mighty Mouse Meets Deadeye Dick* (Rasinski/May 30), *A Date For Dinner* (Donnelly/Aug. 29), *The First Show* (Davis/Oct. 10), *A Fight To The Finish* (Rasinski/Nov. 14), *Swiss Cheese Family Robinson* (Davis/Dec. 19) and *Lazy Little Beaver* (Donnelly/Dec. 26).

1948: *Mighty Mouse And The Magician* (Donnelly/Mar.), *The Feuding Hillbillies* (Rasinski/Apr.), *The Witch's Cat* (Davis/July), *Love's Labor Won* (Davis/Sept.), *The Mysterious Stranger* (Davis/Oct.), *Triple Trouble* (Davis/Nov.) and *Magic Slipper* (Davis/Dec.).

1949: *Racket Buster* (Davis/Feb.), *Cold Romance* (Davis/Apr.), *The Catnip Gang* (Donnelly/July), *Perils Of Pearl Pureheart* (Donnelly/Oct.) and *Stop, Look And Listen* (Donnelly/Dec.).

1950: *Anti-Cats* (Davis/Mar.), *Law And Order* (Donnelly/June 23), *Beauty On The Beach* (Rasinski/Nov.) and *Mother Goose's Birthday Party* (Rasinski/Dec.).

1951: *Sunny Italy* (Rasinski/Mar.), *Goons From The Moon* (Rasinski/Apr. 1), *Injun Trouble* (Donnelly/June), *A Swiss Miss* (Davis/Aug.) and *A Cat's Tale* (Davis/Nov.)

1952: *Prehistoric Perils* (Rasinski/Mar.), *Hansel And Gretel* (Rasinski/June) and *Happy Holland* (Donnelly/Nov.).

1953: *Soapy Opera* (Rasinski/Jan.), *Hero For A Day* (Davis/Apr.), *Hot Rods* (Donnelly/June) and *When Mousehood Was In Flower* (Rasinski/July).

1954: *Spare The Rod* (Rasinski/Jan.), *Helpless Hippo* (Rasinski/Mar.) and *Reformed Wolf* (Rasinski/Oct.).

1959: *Outer Space Visitor* (Tendlar/Nov.).

1961: *The Mysterious Package* (Davis/Dec. 15) and *Cat Alarm* (Rasinski/Dec. 31).

MODERN MADCAPS

This series was a lame attempt by Paramount's cartoon department to provide a launch for other potential cartoon series. *Directed by Seymour Kneitel, James "Shamus" Culhane, Howard Post and Gene Deitch. Gene Deitch and Allen Swift were series producers. Technicolor. A Famous Studios Production released through Paramount Pictures.*

1958: *Right Off The Bat* (Kneitel/Nov. 7).

1959: *Fit To Be Toyed* (Kneitel/Feb. 6), *La Petite Parade* (Kneitel/Mar. 6), *Spooking Of Ghosts* (Kneitel/June 12), *Talking Horse Sense* (Kneitel/Sept. 11) and *T.V. Fuddlehead* (Kneitel/Oct. 16).

1960 *Mike The Masquerader* (Kneitel/Jan. 1), *Fiddle Faddle* (Kneitel/Feb. 26), *From Dime To Dime* (Kneitel/Mar. 25), *Trigger Treat* (Kneitel/Apr.), *The Shoe Must Go On* (Kneitel/Aug.), *Disguise The Limit* (Kneitel/Sept.), *Galaxia* (Kneitel/Oct.), *Bouncing Benny* (Kneitel/Nov.) and *Terry The Terror* (Kneitel/Dec.).

1961: *Phantom Moustacher* (Kneitel/Jan.), *The Kid From Mars* (Kneitel/Feb.), *The Mighty Thermite* (Kneitel/Apr.), *In The Nicotine* (Kneitel/June), *The Inquisit Visit* (Kneitel/July) and *The Plot Sickens* (Kneitel/Dec.).

1962: *Crumley Cogwell* (Kneitel/Jan.), *Popcorn And Politics* (Kneitel/Feb.), *Hi-Fi Jinx* (Kneitel/Mar.), *Giddy Gadgets* (Kneitel/Mar.), *Funderful Suburbia* (Kneitel/Mar.), *Samson Scrap* (Deitch/Mar.), *Penny Pals* (Kneitel/Oct.), *Robot Ringer* (Kneitel/Nov.) and *One Of The Family* (Kneitel/Dec.).

1963: *Ringading Kid* (Kneitel/Jan.), *Drump Up A Tenant* (Kneitel/Feb.), *One Weak Vacation* (Kneitel/Mar.), *Trash Program* (Kneitel/Apr.), *Harry Happy* (Kneitel/Sept.), *Tell Me A Badtime Story* (with Goodie the Gremlin/Kneitel/Oct.), *The Pig's Feat* (Kneitel/Oct.), *Sour Gripes* (Kneitel/Oct.), *Goodie's Good Deed* (with Goodie the Gremlin Kneitel/Nov.) and *Muggy-Doo Boycat* (Kneitel/Dec.)

1964: *Robot Rival* (Kneitel/Sept.), *And So Tibet* (Kneitel/Oct.), *Near-Sighted And Far Out* (Kneitel/Nov.) and *Readin', Writhing and 'Rithmetic* (Kneitel/Nov.).

1965: *Cagey Business* (Post/Feb.), *Poor Little Witch Girl* (with Honey Halfwitch/Post/Apr.), *The Itch* (Post/May) and *Solitary Refinement* (Post/Sept.) and *The Outside Dope* (Post/Nov.).

1966: *Two By Two* (Post/Jan.), *I Want My Mummy* (Post/Mar.), *A Balmy Knight* (Culhane/June) and *A Wedding Knight* (Post/Aug.).

1967: *Blacksheep Blacksmith* (Post/Jan.).

MR. MAGOO

For a long time UPA cartoon producer John Hubley wanted to get away from "funny" cartoon animals and try something different—a human character with a distinct personality of his own. Columbia Pictures, UPA's distributor, reluctantly approved Hubley's new concept: a near–sighted, crotchety old man named Mr. Magoo.

The studio bought the idea when Hubley added an animal character—a bear—to the first cartoon, *Ragtime Bear,* released in 1949. Success was immediate and soon after the studio requisitioned more Magoo cartoon shorts which became UPA's top moneymaking short–subject series during its long, award–winning run.

Milfred Kaufman, who wrote the story for *Ragtime Bear,* was the person most responsible for Magoo's creation. Hubley handled the series from the beginning, producing and directing two more cartoons until he assigned Pete Burness to direct the series. Under Burness, the Magoo series received four Academy Award nominations, winning twice for *When Magoo Flew* (1954) and *Magoo's Puddle Jumper* (1956) as "Best Short Subjects" of the year.

Magoo's character was actually derived from several real–life figures—a bullheaded uncle of Hubley's and bulbous–nosed comedian W. C. Fields among others. Jim Backus, the voice of Magoo, also drew from remembrances of his businessman father for the character's crinkly voice.

Backus was hired to voice Magoo at the recommendation of Jerry Hausner, who played Magoo's nephew, Waldo, in the series. According to Hausner, Backus "invented a lot of things and brought to the cartoons a fresh, wonderful approach."

By the 1950s, Magoo's personality was softened and made into a more sentimental character. Director Pete Burness contends that the character "would have been stronger if he had continued crotchety, even somewhat nasty." Nonetheless, Magoo continued to charm moviegoers with his slapdash humor until 1959, when the series ended. The character later experienced a re–birth in popularity when UPA produced a brand new series of cartoons for television in the early 1960s. *Directors were John Hubley, Pete Burness, Robert Cannon, Rudy Larriva, Tom McDonald, Gil Turner, Chris Ishii and Bill Hurtz. Technicolor. CinemaScope. A UPA Production released through Columbia Pictures.*

Voices:
Mr. Magoo: Jim Backus, **Waldo:** Jerry Hausner, Daws Butler

1949: *Ragtime Bear* (Hubley/Sept. 8/*Jolly Frolics* cartoon).

1950: *Spellbound Hound* (Hubley/Mar. 16/first official Mr. Magoo cartoon in the series), *Trouble Indemnity* (Burness/Sept. 4/A.A. nominee) and *Bungled Bungalow* (Burness/Dec. 28).

1951: *Bare Faced Flatfoot* (Burness/Apr. 26), *Fuddy Duddy Buddy* (Hubley/Oct. 18) and *Grizzly Golfer* (Burness/Dec. 20).

1952: *Sloppy Jalopy* (Burness/Feb. 21), *Dog Snatcher* (Burness/May 29), *Pink And Blue Blues* (Burness/Aug. 28/A.A. nominee/originally *Pink Blue Plums*), *Hotsy Footsy* (Hurtz/Oct. 23) and *Captain's Outrageous* (Burness/Dec. 25).

1953: *Safety Spin* (Burness/May 21), *Magoo's Masterpiece* (Burness/July 30) and *Magoo Slept Here* (Burness/Nov. 19).

1954: *Magoo Goes Skiing* (Burness/Mar. 11), *Kangaroo Courting* (Burness/July 1) and *Destination Magoo* (Burness/Dec. 16).

1955: *When Magoo Flew* (Burness/Jan. 6/A.A. winner), *Magoo's Check–Up* (Burness/Feb. 24), *Madcap Magoo* (Burness/June 23), *Stage Door Magoo* (Burness/Oct. 6) and *Magoo Makes News* (Burness/Dec. 15/CinemaScope).

1956: *Magoo's Caine Mutiny* (Burness/Mar. 8/originally *Canine Mutiny*), *Magoo Goes West* (Burness/Apr. 19/CinemaScope), *Calling Dr. Magoo* (Burness/May 24/CinemaScope), *Magoo Beats The Heat* (Burness/June 21/CinemaScope), *Magoo's Puddle Jumper* (Burness/July 26/A.A. winner/CinemaScope), *Trailblazer Magoo* (Burness/Sept. 13/CinemaScope), *Magoo's Problem Child* (Burness/Oct. 18/CinemaScope) and *Meet Mother Magoo* (Burness/Dec. 27/CinemaScope).

1957: *Magoo Goes Overboard* (Burness/Feb. 21/CinemaScope), *Matador Magoo* (Burness/May 30/CinemaScope), *Magoo Breaks Par* (Burness/June 27/CinemaScope), *Magoo's Glorious Fourth* (Burness/July 25/CinemaScope), *Magoo's Masquerade* (Larriva/Aug. 15/CinemaScope), *Magoo Saves The Bank* (Burness/Sept. 26), *Rock Hound Magoo* (Burness/Oct. 24), *Magoo's House Hunt* (Cannon/Nov. 28) and *Magoo's Private War* (Larriva/Dec. 19).

1958: *Magoo's Young Manhood* (Burness/Mar. 13/originally *The Young Manhood of Mr. Magoo*), *Scoutmaster Magoo* (Cannon/Apr. 10), *The Explosive Mr. Magoo* (Burness/May 8), *Magoo's Three–Point Landing* (Burness/June 5), *Magoo's Cruise* (Larriva/Sept. 11), *Love Comes To Magoo* (McDonald/Oct. 2) and *Gumshoe Magoo* (Turner/Nov.).

1959: *Bwana Magoo* (McDonald/Jan. 9)), *Magoo's Homecoming* (Turner/Mar. 5), *Merry Minstrel Magoo* (Larriva/Apr. 9), *Magoo's Lodge Brother* (Larriva/May 7) and *Terror Faces Magoo* (Ishii/July 9).

MUSICAL MINIATURES

Putting music to animation took new direction with this animated series by Walter Lantz, which used classical music as a backdrop for story elements and character development on screen. Music was performed by a 50–piece orchestra which Universal Pictures, the series' distributor, loaned out to Lantz. Woody Woodpecker's *The Poet and Peasant* inaugurated the series in 1946, held over by some theaters for four to six weeks. The films cost more than $30,000 a piece to produce—the most expensive pictures Lantz ever made. *Directed by Dick Lundy. Technicolor. A Walter Lantz Production released through Universal Pictures.*

1946: *The Poet And Peasant* (with Woody Woodpecker, Andy Panda/Lundy/Mar. 18).

1947: *Musical Moments From Chopin* (with Andy Panda, Woody Woodpecker/Lundy/Feb. 24) and *Overture To William Tell* (with Wally Walrus/Lundy/June 16).

1948: *Pixie Picnic* (Lundy/May).

Classical music and other popular melodies were given a new twist in the Walter Lantz cartoon series, Musical Miniatures. © Walter Lantz Productions

NANCY AND SLUGGO

Breaking tradition, Paul Terry purchased the rights to an established comic–strip character, in this case Ernie Bushmiller's "Nancy," which he turned into a short–lived cartoon series. *Technicolor. A Terrytoons Production released through 20th Century–Fox.*

1942: *School Daze* (Sept. 18) and *Doing Their Bit* (Oct. 30).

NOVELTOONS

A stalwart array of familiar and lesser–known cartoon stars appeared in these full–color productions, created by Paramount's Famous Studios. Characters like Tommy Tortoise, Blackie the Lamb, Moe Hare, Baby Huey and Little Audrey were among the series' featured players. Additional one–shot cartoons were based on noted commodities, such as fairy tale favorite Raggedy Ann and "The Insgrigs," a popular kid's radio show. The studio had used this formula successfully before and found it worth repeating, especially for characters that did not warrant series of their own. *Directors were Seymour Kneitel, Isadore Sparber, Bill Tytla, Dave Tendlar, Howard Post, James "Shamus" Culhane, Jack Mendelsohn and Gene Deitch. Cinecolor. Technicolor. A Famous Studios Production released through Paramount Pictures..*

Voices:
Syd Raymond, Arnold Stang and Jackson Beck.

1943: *No Mutton For Nuttin'* (with Blackie the Lamb/Nov. 26).

1944: *Henpecked Rooster* (with Herman the Mouse, Hector the Rooster/Kneitel/Feb. 18), *Cilly Goose* (with Goose that laid golden eggs/Kneitel/Mar. 24), *Suddenly It's Spring!* (with Raggedy Ann/Kneitel/Apr. 28) and *Yankee Doodle Donkey* (with Spunky and Doc/Nov. 27).

1945: *A Lamb In A Jam* (with Blackie the Lamb/Sparber/May 4), *A Self–Made Mongrel* (with Dog Face/June 29), *The Friendly Ghost* (Sparber/Nov. 16/first Casper cartoon) and *Old MacDonald Had A Farm* (Kneitel/June 7).

1946: *Cheese Burglar* (with Herman the Mouse/Sparber/Feb. 22), *Sheep Shape* (with Blackie the Lamb/Sparber/June 28), *Goal Rush* (Sept. 27), *Sudden Fried Chicken* (Tytla/Oct. 18) and *Spree For All* (with Snuffy Smith/Kneitel/Oct. 18/Cinecolor.

1947: *Stupidstitious Cat* (Kneitel/Apr. 25/first Buzzy the Crow cartoon), *The Enchanted Square* (with Raggedy Ann/Kneitel/May 9), *Madhattan Island* (June 27), *Much Ado About Mutton* (with Blackie the Lamb/Sparber/July 25), *The Wee Men* (Tytla/Aug. 8), *The Mild West* (Kneitel/Aug. 22), *Naughty But Mice* (Kneitel/Oct. 10) and *Santa's Surprise* (Kneitel/Dec.5).

1948: *Cat O' Nine Ails* (Kneitel/Jan. 9), *Flip Flap* (with the Seal/Sparber/Feb. 13), *We're In The Honey* (Mar. 19), *The Bore Cuckoo* (Tytla/Apr. 19), *There's Good Boos Tonite* (with Casper/Sparber/Apr. 23), *The Land Of The Lost* (Sparber/June 7/first Insgrigs cartoon; based on kids' radio show), *Butterscotch And Soda* (June 4/first Little Audrey cartoon), *The Mite Makes Right* (with Tom Thumb/Tytla/Oct. 15), *Hector's Hectic Life* (with Hector the Dog at Christmas/Tytla/Nov. 19) and *The Old Shell Game* (with Wolf, Turtle/Kneitel/Dec. 17).

1949: *The Little Cutup* (Sparber/Jan. 21), *Hep Cat Symphony* (Kneitel/Feb. 4), *The Lost Dream* (with Little Audrey/Tytla/Mar. 18), *Little Red Schoolmouse* (Apr. 15), *A–Haunting We Will Go* (with Casper/Kneitel/May 13), *A Mutt In A Rut* (Sparber/May 27), *Campus Capers* (with Herman the Mouse/Tytla/July 1), *Leprechaun's Gold* (Tytla/Oct. 14) and *Song Of The Birds* (with Little Audrey/Tytla/Nov. 18).

1950: *Land Of the Lost Jewels* (Sparber/Jan. 6/second *Land of the Lost* cartoon), *Quack A Doodle Doo* (Sparber/Mar. 3), *Teacher's Pest* (with Owly the Owl/Sparber/Mar. 31), *Tarts And Flowers* (with Little Audrey/Tytla/May 26), *Ups And Downs Derby* (with Lightning/Kneitel/June 9), *Please To Eat You* (Sparber/July 21), *Goofy Goofy Gander* (with Little Audrey/Tytla/Aug. 18), *Saved By The Bell* (Kneitel/Sept. 15), *Voice Of The Turkey* (with turkey voiced by Arnold Stang/Tytla/Oct. 13), *Mice Meeting You* (with Herman and Katnip/Kneitel/Nov. 10) and *Sock–A–Bye Kitty* (with Buzzy, Katnip/Kneitel/Dec. 22).

1951: *One Quack Mind* (with Baby Huey/Sparber/Jan. 12), *Mice Paradise* (Sparber/Mar. 9), *Hold The Lion Please* (with

Little Audrey/Sparber/Apr. 27), *Land Of Lost Watches* (Kneitel/May 4/third *Land of Lost* cartoon), *As The Crow Lies* (with Buzzy/Kneitel/June 1), *Slip Us Some Redskin* (with Hep Indians/ Kneitel/July 6), *Party Smarty* (with Baby Huey/Kneitel/Aug. 3), *Cat'Choo* (with Buzzy, Katnip/Kneitel/Oct. 12), *Audrey The Rainmaker* (with Little Audrey/Sparber/Oct. 26), *Cat Tamale* (Kneitel/Nov. 9), *By Leaps And Hounds* (with Herbert the Dog/Sparber/Dec. 14) and *Scout Fellow* (with Baby Huey/Kneitel/Dec. 28).

1952: *Cat Carson Rides Again* (with Herman and Katnip/Kneitel/Apr. 4), *The Awful Tooth* (Kneitel/May 2), *Law And Audrey* (with Little Audrey/Sparber/May 23), *City Kitty* (with Katnip/Sparber/July 18), *Clown On The Farm* (with Baby Huey/Kneitel/Aug. 22), *The Case Of The Cockeyed Canary* (with Little Audrey/Kneitel/Dec. 19) and *Feast and Furious* (with Finny the Goldfish, Katnip/Sparber/Dec. 26).

1953: *Starting From Hatch* (with Baby Huey/Kneitel/Mar. 6), *Winner By A Hare* (with Tommy Tortoise, Moe Hare/Sparber/Apr. 17), *Better Bait Than Never* (with Buzzy, Katnip/Kneitel/June 5), *Surf Bored* (with Little Audrey/Sparber/July 17) and *Huey's Ducky Daddy* (with Baby Huey/Sparber/Nov. 20).

1954: *The Seapreme Court* (with Little Audrey/Kneitel/Jan. 29), *Crazy Town* (a gag anthology/Sparber/Feb. 26), *Hare Today, Gone Tomorrow* (with Buzzy/Sparber/Apr. 16), *Candy Cabaret* (Tendlar/June 11), *The Oily Bird* (with Inchy the Worm/Sparber/July 30), *Fido Beta Kappa* (with Martin Kanine/Sparber/Oct. 29) and *No Ifs, And Or Butts* (with Buzzy/Sparber/Dec. 17).

1955: *Dizzy Dishes* (with Little Audrey/Sparber/Feb. 4), *Git Along Lil' Duckie* (with Baby Huey/Tendlar/Mar. 25), *News Hound* (with Snapper the Dog/Sparber/June 10), *Poop Goes The Weasel* (with Wishbone Duck and Waxey Weasel/Tendlar/July 8), *Rabbit Punch* (with Tommy Tortoise, Moe Hare/Tendlar/Sept. 30), *Little Audrey Riding Hood* (with Little Audrey/Kneitel/Oct. 14) and *Kitty Cornered* (with Kitty Cuddles/Tendlar/Dec. 30).

1956: *Sleuth But Sure* (with Tommy Tortoise, Moe Hare/Tendlar/Mar. 23), *Swab The Duck* (with Baby Huey/Tendlar/May 11), *Pedro And Lorenzo* (Tendlar/July 13), *Sir Irving And Jeames* (Kneitel/Oct. 19) and *Lion In The Roar* (with Louis the Lion/Kneitel/Dec. 21).

1957: *Pest Pupil* (with Baby Huey/Tendlar/Jan. 25), *Fishing Tackler* (Sparber/Mar. 29), *Mr. Money Gags* (with Tommy Tortoise, Moe Hare/Sparber/June 7), *L'Amour The Merrier* (Kneitel/July 5), *Possum Pearl* (Kneitel/Sept. 20), *Jumping With Toy* (with Baby Huey/Tendlar/Oct. 4), *Jolly The Clown* (Kneitel/Oct. 25) and *Cock–A–Doodle Dino* (with Danny Dinosaur, Mother Hen/Sparber/Dec. 6).

1958: *Dante Dreamer* (with Little Boy, Dragon/Sparber/Jan. 3), *Sporticles* (Kneitel/Feb. 14), *Grateful Gus* (with an obnoxious man/Tendlar/Mar. 7), *Finnegan's Flea* (Sparber/Apr. 4), *Okey Dokey Donkey* (with Spunky/Sparber/May 16), *Chew Chew Baby* (Sparber/Aug. 15), *Travelaffs* (Kneitel/Aug. 22), *Stork Raving Mad* (Kneitel/Oct. 3) and *Dawg Gawn* (with Little Audrey/Kneitel/Dec. 12).

1959: *The Animal Fair* (Kneitel/Jan. 30), *Houndabout* (Kneitel/Apr. 10), *Huey's Father's Day* (with Baby Huey/Kneitel/May 8) and *Out Of This Whirl* (Kneitel/Nov. 13).

1960: (All films are directed by Seymour Kneitel, unless noted otherwise.) *Be Mice To Cats* (with Skit and Skat/Feb. 5), *Monkey Doodles* (Apr.), *Silly Science* (May), *Peck Your Own Home* (May), *The Shoes Must Go On* (June), *Counter Attack* (July), *Turning The Fables* (Aug.), *Fine Feathered Fiend* (Sept.), *Space Conditioning* (Sept.), *Planet Mouseola* (Nov.), *Northern Mites* (Nov.) and *Miceniks* (Dec.).

1961: *The Lion's Busy* (Feb.), *Goodie The Gremlin* (Apr./first Goodie the Gremlin cartoon), *Alvin's Solo Flight* (with Little Lulu/Apr.), *Hound About That* (Apr.), *Trick Or Tree* (July), *Cape Kidnaveral* (Aug.), *Munro* (Deitch/Sept./A. A. Winner) *Turtle Scoop* (with Hare, Tortoise/Oct.) and *Kozmo Goes To School* (Nov.).

1962: *Perry Popgun* (Jan.), *Without Time Or Reason* (with Swifty and Shorty/Jan.), *Good And Guilty* (with Goodie the Gremlin/Feb.), *T.V. Or Not T.V.* (with Swifty and Shorty/Mar.), *Yule Laff* (Oct.), *It's For The Birdies* (Nov.) and *Fiddlin' Around* (Dec.).

1963: *Ollie The Owl* (Jan.), *Good Snooze Tonight* (Feb.), *A Sight For Squaw Eyes* (Mar.), *Gramps To The Rescue* (Sept.), *Hobo's Holiday* (Oct.), *Hound For Hound* (Oct.), *The Sheepish Wolf* (Nov.) and *Hiccup Hound* (Nov.).

1964: *Whiz Quiz Kid* (Feb.), *Laddy And His Lamp* (Sept.), *A Tiger's Tail* (Dec.) and *Homer On The Range* (Dec.).

1965: *A Hair–Raising Tale* (Jan.), *Horning In* (Post/Jan.), *The Story Of George Washington* (Mendelsohn/Feb.), *A Leak In The Dike* (Mendelsohn/Apr.), *Tally–Hokum* (Post/Oct.) and *Geronimo And Son* (Post/Dec.).

1966: *Space Kid* (Post/Feb.), *Op Pop Wham And Bop* (Post/Apr.) and *Sick Transit* (Post/Apr.).

1967: *The Trip* (Culhane/Apr.) and *Robin Hoodwinked* (Culhane/June).

NUDNIK

By the early 1960s, Paramount began distributing cartoon properties produced overseas, including this series featuring a galactic alien named Nudnik, animated in the fashion of Terrytoon's Astronut.

Nudnik was based on a character named Foofles, who won critical acclaim in a Terrytoons cartoon short. Its creator was William Snyder, who produced the Academy Award–winnng cartoon, *Munro,* also released by Paramount.

Storylines centered on Nudnik's problems communicating with Earthlings. Narration and sound effects were used in place of dialogue as the character did not speak. *Directed by Gene Deitch. Technicolor. A Rembrandt Films Production released through Parmount Pictures.*

1965: *Here's Nudnik* (Aug.) and *Drive On, Nudnik* (Dec.).

1966: *Home Sweet Nudnik* (Mar.), *Welcome Nudnik* (May), *Nudnik On The Roof* (July) and *From Nudnik With Love* (Sept.).

1967: *Who Needs Nudnik* (May), *Nudnik On The Beach* (May), *Good Neighbor Nudnik* (June), *Nudnik's Nudnickel* (Aug.), *I Remember Nudnik* (Sept.) and *Nudnik On A Shoestring* (Oct.).

OSWALD THE RABBIT

Originally a silent cartoon star, Oswald the Rabbit made the transition to sound, unlike many other characters from that era. Walt Disney originated the series, but lost the rights to the character in 1927 after holding out for more money. His partnership with series producer Charles Mintz came to an abrupt end as a result.

Mintz contracted his brother–in–law, George Winkler, to set up a cartoon studio to animate new Oswalds. Universal Pictures, which owned the rights to Oswald, intervened and awarded the series to animator Walter Lantz. Mintz and Winkler were thus put out of business, and Lantz was put in charge of the studio's first cartoon department.

Lantz's first job was to staff his animation department. He hired several former Disney animators, like Hugh Harman, Rudolf Ising and Friz Freleng. He then added sound to six unreleased Oswald cartoons Winkler had completed, the first called *Ozzie of the Circus.*

"It was funny how we did it," Lantz once said, remembering how he struck sound to the cartoons. "We had a bench with all the props on it—the bells, and so. And we'd project the cartoon on the screen and all of us would stand there in front of the cartoon. As the action progressed, we'd make the sound effects, dialogue, and all. We never prescored these films. We did everything as we watched the picture. It was the only way we knew how to add sound."

Lantz also changed Oswald's character, giving him a cuter look. He shortened the ears and humanized Oswald to resemble a Mickey Mouse–type character. "The Disney stories were great, mind you . . . very funny," he said, "but I didn't like the rabbit. He was just black and white. He wouldn't have any appeal for commercial items like comic books, or that sort of thing. So I redesigned him."

Mickey Rooney, who was nine–years–old at the time and went under the name of Mickey McGuire, was the first person to voice Oswald. Lantz hired him because "he had the right squealing voice for Oswald." Rooney had previously starred in a series of Mickey McGuire comedy two–reel shorts. Bernice Hansen, also the voice of Warner Brothers' Sniffles, replaced Rooney when he left the series.

Aside from regular cartoon shorts, Lantz animated the first two–strip Technicolor sequence for Universal's all–talking extravaganza, *The King Of Jazz Revue,* featuring an animated Oswald and famed bandleader Paul Whiteman.

Lantz directed most cartoons in the series. William C. Nolan co–directed with Lantz from 1931 to 1934, with additional films supervised by Friz Freleng, Alex Lovy, Fred Kopietz,

Lester Kline, Rudy Zamora and Elmer Perkins during the series' last years of production. *Black–and–white. A Walter Lantz Production released through Universal Pictures.*

Voices:
Oswald the Rabbit: Mickey McGuire, Bernice Hansen

1929: *Ozzie Of The Circus* (Lantz/Jan. 5), *Stage Stunt* (Lantz/May 13), *Stripes And Stars* (Lantz/May 27), *Wicked West* (Freleng/June 10), *Nuts And Bolts* (Lantz/June 24), *Ice Man's Luck* (Lantz/July 8), *Jungle Jingles* (Lantz/July 22), *Weary Willies* (Lantz/Aug. 5), *Saucy Sausages* (Lantz/Aug. 19), *Race Riot* (Lantz/Sept. 2), *Oil's Well* (Lantz/Sept. 16), *Permanent Wave* (Lantz/Sept. 30), *Cold Turkey* (Lantz/Oct. 14), *Pussy Willie* (Lantz/Oct. 14), *Amateur Night* (Lantz/Nov. 11), *Hurdy Gurdy* (Lantz/Nov. 24), *Snow Use* (Lantz/Nov. 25), *Nutty Notes* (Lantz/Dec. 9) and *Kounty Fair* (Lantz/Dec. 17).

1930: *Chile Con Carmen* (Lantz/Jan. 15), *Kisses And Kurses* (Lantz/Feb. 17), *Broadway Folly* (Lantz/Mar. 3), *Bowery Bimbos* (Lantz/Mar. 18/originally *Bowling Bimboes*), *Hash Shop* (Lantz/Apr. 12/originally *The Hash House*), *Prison Panic* (Lantz/Apr. 30), *Tramping Tramps* (Lantz/May 6), *Hot For Hollywood* (Lantz/May 19/originally *Hollywood*), *Hell's Heels* (Lantz/June 2), *My Pal Paul* (Lantz/June 16), *Song Of The Caballero* (Lantz/June 29), *Not So Quiet* (Lantz/June 30), *Spooks* (Lantz/July 14), *Sons Of The Saddle* (Lantz/July 20), *Cold Feet* (Lantz/Aug. 13), *Snappy Salesman* (Lantz/Aug. 18), *Henpecked* (Lantz/Aug. 20/formerly *Hen Fruit*), *Singing Sap* (Lantz/Sept. 8), *Fanny The Mule* (Lantz/Sept. 15), *Detective* (Lantz/Sept. 22), *Strange As It Seems* (Lantz/Oct. 27), *The Fowl Ball* (Lantz/Oct. 13), *The Navy* (Lantz/Nov. 3), *Mexico* (Lantz/Nov. 17), *Africa* (Lantz/Dec.1), *Alaska* (Lantz/Dec. 15) and *Mars* (Lantz/Dec. 29).

1931: *China* (Lantz, Nolan/Jan. 12), *College* (Lantz, Nolan/Jan. 27), *Shipwreck* (Lantz, Nolan/Feb. 9), *The Farmer* (Lantz, Nolan/Mar. 23), *Fireman* (Lantz, Nolan/Apr. 6), *Sunny South* (Lantz, Nolan/Apr. 20), *Country School* (Lantz, Nolan/May 5), *The Bandmaster* (Lantz, Nolan/May 18), *North Woods* (Lantz, Nolan/June 1), *Stone Age* (Lantz, Nolan/July 13), *Radio Rhythm* (Lantz, Nolan/July 27), *Kentucky Belle* (Lantz, Nolan/Sept. 2/originally *Horse Race*), *Hot Feet* (Lantz, Nolan/Sept. 14), *The Hunter* (Lantz, Nolan/Oct. 12), *In Wonderland* (Lantz, Nolan/Oct. 26), *Trolley Troubles* (Lantz, Nolan/Nov. 23), *Hare Mail* (Lantz, Nolan/Nov. 30), *Fisherman* (Lantz, Nolan/Dec. 7) and *The Clown* (Lantz, Nolan/Dec. 21).

1932: *Grandma's Pet* (Lantz, Nolan/Jan. 18), *Oh, Teacher* (Lantz, Nolan/Feb. 1), *Mechanical Man* (Lantz, Nolan/Feb. 15), *Great Guns* (Lantz, Nolan/Feb. 29), *Wins Out* (Lantz, Nolan/Mar. 14), *Beaus And Arrows* (Lantz, Nolan/Mar. 28), *Making Good* (Lantz, Nolan/Apr. 11), *Let's Eat* (Lantz, Nolan/Apr. 21/originally *Foiled*), *Winged Horse* (Lantz, Nolan/May 9), *To The Rescue* (Lantz, Nolan/May 23), *Catnipped* (Lantz, Nolan/May 23), *A Wet Knight* (Lantz, Nolan/June 20), *A Jungle Jumble* (Lantz, Nolan/July 4), *Day Nurse* (Lantz, Nolan/Aug. 1), *Busy Barber* (Lantz, Nolan/Sept. 12), *Carnival Capers* (Lantz, Nolan/Oct. 10), *Wild And Woolly* (Lantz, Nolan/Nov. 21) and *Teacher's Pest* (Lantz, Nolan/Dec. 19)

1933: *Oswald The Plumber* (Lantz, Nolan/Jan. 16), *The Shriek* (Lantz, Nolan/Feb. 27), *Going To Blazes* (Lantz, Nolan/Apr. 10), *Beau Best* (Lantz, Nolan/May 22), *Ham And Eggs* (Lantz, Nolan/June 19), *A New Deal* (Lantz, Nolan/July 17), *Confidence* (Lantz, Nolan/July 31), *Five And Dime* (Lantz, Nolan/Sept. 18), *In The Zoo* (Lantz, Nolan/Nov. 6), *Merry Old Soul* (Lantz, Nolan/Nov. 27/A.A. nominee) and *Parking Space* (Lantz, Nolan/Dec. 18).

1934: *Chicken Reel* (Lantz, Nolan/Jan. 1), *The Candy House* (Lantz, Nolan/Jan 15), *County Fair* (Lantz, Nolan/Feb. 5), *The Toy Shoppe* (Lantz, Nolan/Feb. 19), *Kings Up* (Lantz, Nolan/Mar. 12), *Wolf, Wolf* (Lantz, Nolan/Apr. 12), *Gingerbread Boy* (Lantz, Nolan/Apr. 16), *Goldielocks And The Three Bears* (Lantz, Nolan/May 14), *Annie Moved Away* (Lantz, Nolan/May 28), *The Wax Works* (Lantz, Nolan/June 25), *William Tell* (Lantz, Nolan/July 9), *Chris Columbus, Jr.* (Lantz/July 23), *Dizzy Dwarf* (Nolan/Aug. 6), *Happy Pilgrims* (Lantz/Sept. 3/originally *Ye Happy Pilgrims*), *Sky Larks* (Lantz/Oct. 22) and *Spring In The Park* (Nolan/Nov. 12).

1935: *Robinson Crusoe Isle* (Lantz/Jan. 7), *Hill Billys* (Lantz, Feb. 1), *Two Little Lambs* (Lantz/Mar. 11), *Do A Good Deed* (Lantz/Mar. 25), *Elmer The Great Dane* (Lantz/Apr. 29), *Gold Dust Oswald* (Lantz/May), *Towne Hall Follies* (Lantz/June 3), *At Your Service* (Lantz/July 8), *Bronco Buster* (Lantz/Aug. 5), *Amateur Broadcast* (Lantz/Aug. 26), *Quail Hunt* (Lantz/Sept. 23/Technicolor), *Monkey Wretches* (Lantz/Nov. 11), *Case Of The Lost Sheep* (Lantz/Dec. 9) and *Doctor Oswald* (Lantz/Dec. 30).

1936: *Softball Game* (Lantz/Jan. 27), *Alaska Sweepstakes* (Lantz/Feb. 7), *Slumberland Express* (Lantz/Mar. 9), *Beauty Shoppe* (Lantz/Mar. 20), *Barnyard Five* (Lantz/Apr. 20), *The Fun House* (Lantz/May 4), *Farming Fools* (Lantz/May 25), *Battle Royal* (Lantz/June 22), *Music Hath Charms* (Lantz/Sept. 7), *Kiddie Revue* (Lantz/Sept. 21), *Beachcombers* (Lantz/Oct. 5), *Nightlife Of The Bugs* (Lantz/Oct. 19), *Puppet Show* (Lantz/Nov. 2), *Unpopular Mechanic* (Lantz/Nov. 6) and *Gopher Trouble* (Lantz/Nov. 30).

1937: *Everybody Sings* (Lantz/Feb. 22), *Duck Hunt* (Lantz/Mar. 8), *The Birthday Party* (Lantz/Mar. 29), *Trailer Thrills* (Lantz/May 3), *The Wily Weasel* (June 7), *The Playful Pup* (July 12), *Love Sick* (Oct. 4), *Keeper Of The Lions* (Lantz/Oct. 18), *Mechanical Handyman* (Nov. 8), *Football Fever* (Lantz/Nov. 15), *The Mysterious Jug* (Nov. 29) and *The Dumb Cluck* (Dec. 20).

1938: *The Lamplighter* (Jan. 10), *Man Hunt* (Feb. 7), *Yokel Boy Makes Good* (Lantz/Feb. 21), *Trade Mice* (Feb. 28), *Feed The Kitty* (Lovy/Mar. 14), *Nellie, The Sewing Machine Girl* (Lovy/Apr. 11), *Tail End* (Kline/Apr. 25/*Cartune Special*), *Problem Child* (Zamora/May 16), *Movie Phoney News* (Lovy/May 30), *Nellie, The Indian Chief's Daughter* (June 6/Cartune Special), *Happy Scouts* (Kopietz/June 20), *Voodoo In Harlem* (Zamora/July 18/*Cartune Special*), *Silly Seals* (Kline/July 25), *Queen's Kittens* (Kline/Aug. 8), *Ghost Town Frolics* (Sept. 5) and *Pixieland* (Perkins/Sept. 12/originally *The Busy Body*).

PEPE LE PEW

Warner Brothers' storyman Michael Maltese created and refined Pepe Le Pew, the suave French skunk who charmed moviegoers for more than a decade with his aromatic adventures.

Pepe's unctuous accent and irresistible personality were based on actor Charles Boyer and other French actors. (Its name was derived from Boyer's Pepe Le Moke character in the 1938 film classic, *Algiers*). The character first appeared in Chuck Jones' 1945 *Looney Tunes* cartoon *The Odor–Able Kitty* but not as Pepe Le Pew. (On model sheets he was called "Stinky".) Two years later, the character was so named and it starred in the first "official" Pepe Le Pew film, *Scent–Imental Over You.*

In 1949, after just three cartoons, Pepe won an Academy Award for his starring role in *For Scent–Imental Reasons,* which Jones also directed. The award marked the second such honor for Jones, who won three Academy Awards during his career.

In an interview, Jones once remarked that he had no problem identifying with Pepe's romantic foibles: "Pepe was everything I wanted to be romantically. Not only was he quite sure of himself but it never occurred to him that anything was wrong with him. I always felt there must be great areas of me that were repugnant to girls, and Pepe was quite the opposite of that."

The series remained a popular Warner Brothers entry through 1962, when *Louvre Come Back To Me,* the final Pepe Le Pew cartoon, was released to theaters nationwide. *In addition to Jones, series directors were Abe Levitow and Art Davis. Technicolor. A Warner Brothers release.*

Voices:
Pepe Le Pew: Mel Blanc

Looney Tunes

1945: *The Odor–Able Kitty* (Jones/Jan. 6).

1947: *Scent–Imental Over You* (Jones/Mar. 8).

1949: *For Scent–Imental Reasons* (Jones/Nov. 12/A.A. winner).

Merrie Melodies
1951: *Scenti–Imental Romeo* (Jones/Mar. 24).

1952: *Little Beau Pepe* (Jones/Mar. 29).

1953: *Wild Over You* (Jones/July 11).

1954: *Cat's Bah* (Jones/Mar. 20).

1955: *Past Perfumance* (Jones/May 21) and *Two Scent's Worth* (Jones/Oct. 15).

1956: *Heaven Scent* (Jones/Mar. 31).

1957: *Touche And Go!* (Jones/Oct. 12).

1959: *Really Scent* (Levitow/July 27).

1960: *Who Scent You?* (Jones/June 24).

1962: *Louvre Come Back To Me* (Jones/Aug. 18).

PHANTASY CARTOONS

In addition to Krazy Kat and Scrappy, its two major cartoon stars, Columbia Pictures' cartoon department produced several catchall series featuring no–name animated characters. The *Phantasy* cartoons was the last of these series, comprised of black–and–white and Technicolor oddities. The series was discontinued in 1948 when Columbia's animation department closed down. United Productions of America (UPA) later replaced the series with *Jolly Frolics. Producers were Charles Mintz, Dave Flesicher, Raymond Katz and Henry Binder. Directors were Frank Tashlin, Alec Geiss, Paul Sommer, Howard Swift, Allen Rose, John Hubley, Sid Marcus, Bob Wickersham and Alex Lovy. Black–and–white. Technicolor. A Columbia Pictures release.*

1939:   *The Charm Bracelet* (with Scrappy/Sept. 1) and *Millionaire Hobo* (with Scrappy/Nov. 24).

1940:   *The Mouse Exterminator* (with Krazy/Jan. 26), *Man Of Tin* (with Scrappy/Feb. 23), *Fish Follies* (May 10), *News Oddities* (July 19), *Schoolboy Dreams* (with Scrappy/Sept. 24) and *Happy Holidays* (Oct. 25).

1941:   *The Little Theatre* (with Scrappy/Feb. 7), *There's Music In Your Hair* (Mar. 28), *The Cute Recruit* (May 2), *The Wall Flower* (July 3), *The Merry Mouse Cafe* (Aug. 15) and *The Crystal Gazer* (Sept. 26).

1942:   *Dog Meets Dog* (Tashlin/Mar. 6), *The Wild And Woozy West* (Rose/Apr. 30), *A Battle For A Bottle* (Tashlin/May 29), *Old Blackout Joe* (Sommer/Aug. 27), *The Gullible Canary* (Geiss/Sept. 18), *The Dumb Conscious Mind* (Sommer, Hubley/Oct. 23), *Malice In Slumberland* (Geiss/Nov. 20) and *Cholly Polly* (Geiss/Dec. 18).

1943:   *The Vitamin G Man* (Sommer, Hubley/Jan. 22), *Kindly Scram* (Geiss/Mar. 5), *Willoughby's Magic Hat* (with Willoughby Wren/Wickersham/Apr. 30), *Duty And The Beast* (Geiss/May 28), *Mass Mouse Meeting* (Geiss/June 25), *The Fly In The Ointment* (Sommer/July 23), *Dizzy Newsreel* (Geiss/Aug. 27), *Nursery Crimes* (Geiss/Oct. 8), *The Cocky Bantam* (Sommer/Nov. 12) and *The Playful Pest* (Sommer/Dec. 3).

1944:   *Polly Wants A Doctor* (Swift/Jan. 6), *Magic Strength* (Wickersham/Feb. 4), *Lionel Lion* (Sommer/Mar. 3), *Giddy Yapping* (Swift/Apr. 7), *Tangled Travels* (Geiss/June 9), *Mr. Fore By Fore* (Swift/July 7), *Case Of The Screaming Bishop* (Aug. 4), *Mutt 'N' Bones* (Sommer/Aug. 25) and *As The Fly Flies* (Swift/Nov. 17).

1945:   *Goofy News Views* (Marcus/Apr. 27), *Booby Socks* (Swift, Wickersham/July 12) and *Simple Siren* (Sommer/Sept. 20).

1946:   *Kongo–Roo* (Swift/Apr. 18), *Snap Happy Traps* (Wickersham/June 6) and *The Schooner The Better* (Swift/July 14).

1947:   *Fowl Brawl* (Swift/Jan. 9), *Uncultured Vulture* (Wickersham/Feb. 6), *Wacky Quacky* (Lovy/Mar. 20), *Leave Us Chase It* (Swift/May 15), *Tooth Or Consequences* (with Fox and the Crow/Swift/June 5) and *Kitty Caddy* (Marcus/Nov. 6).

1948:   *Topsy Turkey* (Marcus/Feb. 5) and *Short Snort On Sports* (Lovy/June 3).

1949:   *Coo–Coo Bird Dog* (Marcus/Feb. 3).

PHONEY BALONEY

Stretching the truth a bit, Phoney Baloney, a teller of tall tales, was a lesser–known character cast in a brief series of one–reel shorts under the *Terrytoons* banner. *Directed by Connie Rasinski. Technicolor. A Terrytoons Production released through 20th Century–Fox.*

1954:   *Tall Tale Teller* (May).

1957:   *African Jungle Hunt* (Mar.).

PIGGY

Called "Patty Pig" on studio model sheets, Warner Brothers introduced this happy–go–lucky musical pig in a series of musical *Merrie Melodies* cartoon shorts. *Black–and–white. A Warner Brothers release. Merrie Melodies.*

1931:   *You Don't Know What You're Doin'* (Oct. 21) and *Hittin' The Trail To Hallelujah Land* (Nov. 28).

THE PINK PANTHER

The egocentric panther was first introduced during the credits of Blake Edwards' popular spy spoof, *The Pink Panther,* named after the jewel in the movie. Edwards contracted DePatie–Freleng Enterprises, headed by David H. DePatie and Friz Freleng, to animate titles for the movie of the sly panther being hotly pursued by a cartoon version of Inspector Clouseau.

The film's clever title sequence set the stage for a series of Pink Panther cartoons that followed, produced by DePatie–Freleng for United Artists. The studio unanimously approved the idea after witnessing the widespread attention the character received for its brief appearance in the Blake Edwards feature.

The first "official" Pink Panther cartoon, *The Pink Phink,* premiered in 1964 with Billy Wilder's feature, *Kiss Me, Stupid,* at Grauman's Chinese Theatre in Hollywood. The cartoon was a huge success in more ways than one. It garnered the coveted Oscar statuette for Best Short Subject, and DePatie–Freleng was commissioned to produce a new cartoon per month following the success of their first effort in order to satisfy the public's thirst for more.

The non-speaking panther did break his silence in two cartoons. In 1965's *Sink Pink,* Paul Frees, in a Rex Harrison-type voice, spoke the first lines of dialogue in the character's history ("Why can't man be more like animals?") at the end of the film in which he outsmarts a big-game hunter who tries capturing animals of every species by building an ark. He spoke again in *Super Pink* (1966).

Silent film comedies of the 1920s served as a source of inspiration for the series' brand of humor. Many films reenact visual bits first made famous by Charlie Chaplin and Buster Keaton, two of filmdon's greatest slapstick comedians. Even a lively ragtime musical score accompanied the cartoons, similar to the music organists played in theaters to back silent film comedies as they were screened for audiences.

Friz Freleng, who found his niche at Warner Brothers, first directed the series before turning it over to his longtime assistant Hawley Pratt. Storyman John Dunn is credited with writing the wildly innovative and clever stories for the series. *Directed by Friz Freleng, Brad Case, Gerry Chiniquy, Art Davis, Dave Detiege, Cullen Houghtaling, Art Leonardi, Sid Marcus, Robert McKimson, Hawley Pratt and Bob Richardson. Technicolor. A Mirisch-Geoffrey-DePatie-Freleng Production released through United Artists.*

1964: *Suspense Account* (Freleng/pilot cartoon never released), *The Pink Phink* (Freleng, Pratt/Dec. 18/A.A. winner) and *Pink Pajamas* (Pratt/Dec. 25).

1965: *We Gave Pink Stamps* (Pratt/Feb. 12), *Dial 'P' For Pink* (Pratt/Mar. 17), *Sink Pink* (Pratt/Apr. 12), *Pickled Pink* (Pratt/May 12), *Shocking Pink* (Pratt/May 13), *Pinkfinger* (Pratt/May 13), *Pink Ice* (Pratt/June 10), *The Pink Tail Fly* (Pratt/Aug. 25), *Pink Panzer* (Pratt/Sept. 15), *An Ounce Of Pink* (Pratt/Oct. 20), *Reel Pink* (Pratt/Nov. 16) and *Bully For Pink* (Pratt/Dec. 14).

1966: *Pink Panic* (Pratt/Jan. 11), *Pink Punch* (Pratt/Feb. 21), *Pink Piston* (Pratt/Mar. 16), *Vitamin Pink* (Pratt/Apr. 21), *Smile Pretty, Say Pink* (Pratt/May 25), *The Pink Blueprint* (Pratt/May 25), *Pink, Plunk, Plink* (Pratt/May 25), *Pink-A-Boo* (Pratt/June 26), *Genie With The Light Pink Fur* (Pratt/Sept. 14), *Super Pink* (Pratt/Oct. 12) and *Rock-A-By Pinky* (Pratt/Dec. 23).

1967: *Pinknic* (Pratt/Jan. 6), *Pink Posies* (Pratt/Apr. 26), *Pink Of The Litter* (Pratt/May 17), *In The Pink* (Pratt/May 18), *Pink Paradise* (Chiniquy/June 21), *Jet Pink* (Chiniquy/June 13), *Pinto Pink* (Pratt/July 19), *Congratulations! It's Pink* (Pratt/Oct. 27), *Prefabricated Pink* (Pratt/Nov. 22) and *The Hand Is Pinker Than The Eye* (Pratt/Dec. 20).

1968: *Sky Blue Pink* (Pratt/Jan. 3), *Pinkadilly Circus* (Pratt/Feb. 21), *Psychedelic Pink* (Pratt/Mar. 13), *Come On In! The Water's Pink* (Pratt/Apr. 10), *Put-Put-Pink* (Chiniquy/Apr. 24), *G. I. Pink* (Pratt/May 1), *Lucky Pink* (Pratt/May 7), *The Pink Quarterback* (Pratt/May 22), *Twinkle, Twinkle Little Pink* (Pratt/June 30), *Pink Valiant* (Pratt/July 10), *The Pink Bill* (Chiniquy/Sept. 18), *Prehistoric Pink* (Pratt/Aug. 7), *Pink In The Clink* (Chiniquy/Sept. 18), *Tickled Pink* (Chiniquy/Oct. 6), *Little Beaux Pink* (Pratt/Oct. 20), *The Pink Sphinx* (Pratt/Oct. 23), *Pink Is A Many Splintered Thing* (Chiniquy/Nov. 20), *The Pink Package Plot* (Davis/Dec. 11) and *Pink-come Tax* (Davis/Dec. 20).

1969: *Pink-A-Rella* (Pratt/Jan. 8), *Pink Pest Control* (Chiniquy/Feb. 12), *Think Before You Pink* (Chiniquy/Mar. 19), *Slink Pink* (Freleng/Apr. 2), *In The Pink Of The Night* (Davis/May 18), *Pink On The Cob* (Pratt/May 29) and *Extinct Pink* (Pratt/June 20).

1971: *Fly In The Pink* (Pratt/June 23), *Pink Blue Plate* (Chiniquy/July 18), *Pink Tuba-Dore* (Davis/Aug. 4), *Pink Pranks* (Freleng/Aug. 18), *Psst Pink* (Davis/Sept. 5), *The Pink Flea* (Pratt/Sept. 15), *Gong With The Pink* (Pratt/Oct. 20) and *Pink-In* (Davis/Oct. 20).

1972: *Pink 8-Ball* (Pratt/Feb. 6).

1974: *Pink Aye* (Chiniquy/May 16) and *Trail Of The Lonesome Pink* (June 27).

1975: *Pink Da Vinci* (McKimson/July 23), *Pink Streaker* (Chiniquy/July 25), *Salmon Pink* (Chiniquy/July 25), *Forty Pink Winks* (Chiniquy/Aug. 8), *Pink Plasma* (Leonardi/Aug. 28), *Pink Elephant* (Chiniquy/Oct. 20), *Keep Our Forests Pink* (Chiniquy/Nov. 20), *Pink Campaign* (Leonardi/Dec. 30), *Bobolink Pink* (Chiniquy/Dec. 30), *It's Pink But Is It Mink* (McKimson/Dec. 30), and *Scarlet Pinkernel* (Chiniquy/Dec. 30).

1976: *Mystic Pink* (McKimson/Jan.6), *The Pink Arabee* (Chiniquy/Mar. 13), *The Pink Pro* (McKimson/Apr. 12), *The Pink Piper* (Houghtaling/Apr. 30), *Pinky Doodle* (Marcus/May 28), *Sherlock Pink* (McKimson/June 29) and *Rocky Pink* (Leonardi/July 9).

1977: *Therapeutic Pink* (Chiniquy/Apr. 1).

1978: *Pink Arcade* (Marcus), *Pink Lightning* (Case), *Pink In The Drink* (Marcus) and *Pink Swat* (Marcus).

1979: *String Along In Pink* (Chiniquy), *Pink Bananas* (Davis), *Pinktails For Two* (Davis), *Pink Quackers* (Case), *Pink And Shovel* (Chiniquy), *Pink Breakfast* (Case), *Toro Pink* (Marcus), *Pink In The Woods* (Case), *Pink Pull* (Marcus), *Spark Plug Pink* (Case), *Pink Lemonade* (Chiniquy) and *Supermarket Pink* (Case).

1980: *Pink Daddy* (Chiniquy), *Pink Pictures* (Chiniquy), *Pink Suds* (Davis), *Pink Trumpet* (Davis), *Sprinkle Me Pink* (Richardson), *Cat And The Pinkstalk* (Detiege), *Doctor Pink* (Marcus), *Dietetic Pink* (Marcus), *Pink Z-Z-Z* (Marcus), *Pink UFO* (Detiege), *Star Pink* (Davis) and *Pink Press* (Davis).

1981: *Yankee Doodle Pink* (Marcus/Jan.), *Pet Pink Pebbles* (Chiniquy/Feb.), *Pink of Baghdad* (Davis/Mar.) and *Pinkologist* (Chiniquy/Apr.).

PLUTO

His lovable, mischievous nature spelled instant stardom for Mickey Mouse's playful pet in a number of memorable Walt Disney cartoons. By contrast to other cartoon stars of this era, his popularity was somewhat surprising since he displayed few human characteristics and didn't even talk. Nonetheless, film audiences fell in love with this canine creation following his first screen appearance in the 1930 Mickey Mouse cartoon, *The Chain Gang.*

Norman Ferguson, who animated Pluto in his first cartoon,

was mostly responsible for establishing him as a major star. He embellished the dog's personality, adding exaggerated facial expressions and pantomime to his repertoire. Audiences were so taken by Pluto's screen presence that by the 1940s he actually outranked his mentor Mickey Mouse in popularity.

In 1937, Pluto starred in his own series, lasting 15 consecutive years before it was discontinued. *Directors were Ben Sharpsteen, Jack Kinney, Norman Ferguson, Clyde Geronimi, Charles Nichols, Jack Hannah and Milt Schaffer. Technicolor. A Walt Disney Production released through RKO–Radio Pictures.*

1937: *Pluto's Quin–Puplets* (Sharpsteen/Nov. 26).

1940: *Bone Trouble* (Kinney/June 28) and *Pantry Pirate* (Geronimi/Dec. 27).

1941: *Pluto's Playmate* (Ferguson/Jan. 24), *A Gentleman's Gentleman* (Geronimi/Mar. 28), *Canine Caddy* (Geronimi/May 30) and *Lend A Paw* (Geronimi/Oct. 3/A.A. winner).

1942: *Pluto Junior* (Geronimi/Feb. 28), *The Army Mascot* (Geronimi/May 22), *The Sleepwalker* (Geronimi/July 3), *T–Bone For Two* (Geronimi/Aug. 14) and *Pluto At The Zoo* (Geronimi/Nov. 20).

1943: *Pluto And The Armadillo* (with Mickey Mouse/Geronimi/Feb. 19) and *Private Pluto* (with formative Chip and Dale/Geronimi/Apr. 2).

1944: *Springtime For Pluto* (Nichols/June 23) and *First Aiders* (Nichols/Sept. 22).

1945: *Dog Watch* (Nichols/Mar. 16), *Canine Casanova* (Nichols/July 27), *The Legend Of Coyote Rock* (Nichols/Aug. 24) and *Canine Patrol* (Nichols/Dec. 7).

1946: *Pluto's Kid Brother* (Nichols/Apr. 12), *In Dutch* (Nichols/May 10), *Squatter's Rights* (with Chip and Dale, Mickey Mouse/Hannah/June 7/A.A. nominee) and *The Purloined Pup* (Nichols/July 19).

1947: *Pluto's Housewarming* (Nichols/Feb. 21), *Rescue Dog* (Nichols/Mar. 21), *Mail Dog* (Nichols/Nov. 14) and *Pluto's Blue Note* (Nichols/Dec. 26/A.A. nominee).

1948: *Bone Bandit* (Nichols/Apr. 30), *Pluto's Purchase* (with Mickey Mouse/Nichols/July 9), *Cat Nap Pluto* (Nichols/Aug. 13) and *Pluto's Fledgling* (Nichols/Sept. 10).

1949: *Pueblo Pluto* (with Mickey Mouse/Nichols/Jan. 14), *Pluto's Surprise Package* (Nichols/Mar. 4), *Pluto's Sweater* (Nichols/Apr. 29), *Bubble Bee* (Nichols/June 24) and *Sheep Dog* (Nichols/Nov. 4).

1950: *Pluto's Heart Throb* (Nichols/Jan. 6), *Pluto And The Gopher* (Nichols/Feb. 10), *Wonder Dog* (Nichols/Apr. 7), *Primitive Pluto* (Nichols/May 19), *Puss–Cafe* (Nichols/June 9), *Pests Of The West* (Nichols/July 21), *Food For Feudin'* (with Chip and Dale/Nichols/Aug. 11) and *Camp Dog* (Nichols/Sept. 22).

1951: *Cold Storage* (Kinney/Feb. 9), *Plutopia* (with Mickey Mouse/Nichols/May 18) and *Cold Turkey* (Nichols/Sept. 21).

Animator Walter Lantz displays his latest creation, Pooch the Pup, circa 1930s. © Walter Lantz Productions

POOCH THE PUP

A cuddly canine, whose happy disposition was typical of other 1930s cartoon stars, was the central figure in this series launched by creator Walter Lantz. The series was short–lived despite its strong characterizations and storylines based on familiar children's fairy tales and everyday themes, closing with strong morals. *Directed and animated by Walter Lantz and William Nolan. No voice credits. Black–and–white. A Walter Lantz Production released through Universal Pictures.*

1932: *The Athlete* (Aug. 29), *The Butcher Boy* (Sept. 26), *The Crowd Snores* (Oct. 24), *The Underdog* (Nov. 7) and *Cats And Dogs* (Dec. 5).

1933: *Merry Dog* (Jan. 2), *The Terrible Troubador* (Jan. 30), *The Lumber Champ* (Mar. 13), *S.O.S. Icicle* (May 8), *Pin–Feathers* (July 3), *Hot And Cold* (Aug. 14), *King Klunk* (Sept. 4) and *She Done Him Right* (Oct. 9).

POPEYE THE SAILOR

The most loved sailor of all time, Popeye came into the cartoon world in 1919 when Elzie Segar, a world–famous comic strip artist, first conceived the musclebound sailor, originally known as Ham Gravy, for the classic strip, "Thimble Theatre."

Gravy was featured in the strip along with his stick–like girlfriend, Olive Oyl. The strip became enormously popular and Segar experimented with the Gravy character, later changing his name to "Popeye" on January 17, 1929.

Even then, Popeye displayed many of the same traits that moviegoers became accustomed to in later cartoons: a gruff, straight–talking, hard–hitting sailor whose main source of energy was his can of spinach. The sailor's initial appearance was so well–received that Segar made him a regular in the strip. Then, in 1932, Max Fleischer bought the film rights to the character from King Features, which syndicated the strip nationally, to produce a series of Popeye cartoons.

Popeye's first film appearance was in a Betty Boop cartoon, *Popeye The Sailor* (1933). Fleischer chose to feature him opposite a known star like Betty to measure public reaction before starring him in his own series, which began in earnest that same year. Early titles were derived from many of Popeye's popular catch lines, like *Blow Me Down, I Eats My Spinach* and others.

Through the years Popeye's voice changed—from gruff to even solemn—due to the switchover in voice artists who played him. William Costello was the first man to do Popeye (he won the job after Fleischer heard a recording of songs from his nightclub act as Red Pepper Sam) but was let go after "success went to his head." Costello was succeeded by another man, who Dave Fleischer, Max's younger brother, overheard talking while buying a newspaper at a street corner. Fleischer hired the gentleman on the spot. His name was Jack Mercer, who, ironically, was an inbetweener at the Fleischer Studios.

Mercer remained the voice of Popeye for more than 45 years altogether, counting cartoons later produced for television. He gave the character greater dimension through memorable mutterings and other under–his–breath throwaway lines during recording sessions that added to the infectious humor of the series. A singer named Gus Wickie was the original voice of Bluto, who never appeared in the "Thimble Theatre" strip. (He was adapted from a one–shot villain in the strip "Bluto the Terrible.") As for Olive Oyl, Mae Questel, also the voice of Betty Boop, lent her voice for Popeye's lovestruck girlfriend. Questel demonstrated her versatility throughout the series, even doing the voice of Popeye for a handful of cartoons when Mercer was sent overseas during World War II.

Many early cartoons were built around songs by lyricist Sammy Lerner and musician Sammy Timberg, who wrote the original "Popeye The Sailor Man" song for the first Paramount cartoon. In time, various co–stars were added to the series, among them, the hamburger–mooching Wimpy, Swee'pea and other Segar creations, like the Jeep, Poopdeck Pappy and the Goon. In the 1940s, the series introduced Popeye's nephews: Peep–eye, Pip–eye, Pup–eye and Poop–eye, obviously inspired by Donald Duck's own nephews of Hewey, Dewey and Louie.

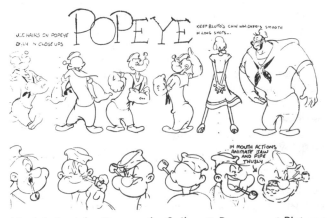

Model sheet for Popeye the Sailor. © Paramount Pictures

Besides starring in hundreds of one–reel shorts, Popeye and his cast of regulars appeared in a series of two–reel Technicolor "featurettes" before Walt Disney's breakthrough *Snow White and the Seven Dwarfs.* Adventures included *Popeye The Sailor Meets Sinbad The Sailor* (1936) and *Popeye The Sailor Meets Ali Baba His Forty Thieves* (1937).

In all, the Popeye series lasted 24 consecutive years, becoming the longest–running cartoon series in motion picture history. *Produced by Max Fleischer. Directors were Dave Fleischer, Isadore Sparber, Dan Gordon, Seymour Kneitel, Bill Tytla and Dave Tendlar. Black–and–white. Technicolor. A Fleischer Studios and Famous Studios release through Paramount Pictures.*

Voices:

Popeye: William Costello (to 1933), Jack Mercer, Mae Questel, **Olive Oyl:** Mae Questel, **Bluto:** Gus Wickie, Pinto Colvig, William Pennell, Jackson Beck, **Swee'pea:** Mae Questel, **Poopdeck Pappy:** Jack Mercer, **Peep–eye:** Jack Mercer, **Pip–eye:** Jack Mercer, **Pup–eye:** Jack Mercer, **Poop–eye:** Jack Mercer, **Wimpy:** Jack Mercer, **Shorty:** Arnold Stang
(The following cartoons are black–and–white unless indicated otherwise.)

1933: *Popeye The Sailor* (Fleischer/July 14), *I Yam What I Yam* (Fleischer/Sept. 29), *Blow Me Down* (Fleischer/Oct. 27), *I Eats My Spinach* (Fleischer/Nov. 17), *Season's Greetinks* (Fleischer/Dec. 17) and *Wild Elephinks* (Fleischer/Dec. 29).

1934: *Sock–A–Bye Baby* (Fleischer/Jan. 19), *Let's You And Him Fight* (Fleischer/Jan. 16), *The Man On The Flying Trapeze* (Fleischer/May 16), *Can You Take It* (Fleischer/Apr. 27), *Shoein' Hosses* (Fleischer/June 1), *Strong To The Finich* (Fleischer/June 29), *Shiver Me Timbers* (Fleischer/July 27), *Axe Me Another* (Fleischer/Aug. 30), *A Dream Walking* (Fleischer/Sept. 28), *The Two–Alarm Fire* (Fleischer/Oct. 26), *The Dance Contest* (Fleischer/Nov. 23) and *We Aim To Please* (Fleischer/Dec. 28).

1935: *Beware Of Barnacle Bill* (Fleischer/Jan. 25), *Be Kind To Animals* (Fleischer/Feb. 22), *Pleased To Meet Cha!* (Fleischer/Mar. 22), *The Hyp–Nut–Tist* (Fleischer/Apr. 26), *Choose Your Weppins* (Fleischer/May 31), *For Better For Worser* (Fleischer/June 28), *Dizzy Divers* (Fleischer/July 26), *You Gotta Be A Football Hero* (Fleischer/Aug. 30), *King Of The Mardi Gras* (Fleischer/Sept. 27), *Adventures Of Popeye* (Fleischer/Oct. 25) and *The Spinach Overture* (Fleischer/Dec. 7).

1936: *Vim, Vigor And Vitaliky* (Fleischer/Jan. 3), *A Clean Shaven Man* (Fleischer/Feb. 7), *Brotherly Love* (Fleischer/Mar. 6), *I–Ski Love–Ski You–Ski* (Fleischer/Apr. 3), *Bridge Ahoy* (Fleischer/May 1), *What, No Spinach* (Fleischer/May 7), *I Wanna Be A Lifeguard* (Fleischer/June 26), *Let's Get Movin'* (Fleischer/July 24), *Never Kick A Woman* (Fleischer/Aug. 28), *Little Swee' Pea* (Fleischer/Sept. 25), *Hold The Wire* (Fleischer/Oct. 23), *The Spinach Roadster* (Fleischer/Nov. 26), and *I'm In The Army Now* (Fleischer/Dec. 25).

1937: *The Paneless Window Washer* (Fleischer/Jan. 22), *Organ Grinders Swing* (Fleischer/Feb. 19), *My Artistical Tem-*

perature (Fleischer/Mar. 19), *Hospitaliky* (Fleischer/Apr. 16), *The Twisker Pitcher* (Fleischer/May 21), *Morning, Noon And Nightclub* (Fleischer/June 18), *Lost And Foundry* (Fleischer/July 16), *I Never Changes My Altitude* (Fleischer/Aug. 20), *I Like Babies And Infinks (Fleischer/Sept. 18), The Football Toucher Downer* (Fleischer/Oct. 15), *Proteck The Weakerist* (Fleischer/Nov. 19) and *Fowl Play* (Fleischer/Dec. 17).

1938: *Let's Celebrake* (Fleischer/Jan. 21), *Learn Polikness* (Fleischer/Feb. 18), *The House Builder Upper* (Fleischer/Mar. 18), *Big Chief Ugh–Amugh–Ugh* (Fleischer/Apr. 25), *I Yam Love Sick* (Fleischer/May 29), *Plumbin' Is A Pipe* (Fleischer/June 17), *The Jeep* (Fleischer/July 15), *Bulldozing The Bull* (Fleischer/Aug. 19), *Mutiny Ain't Nice* (Fleischer/Sept. 23), *Goonland* (Fleischer/Oct. 21), *A Date To Skate* (Fleischer/Nov. 18) and *Cops Is Always Right* (Fleischer/Dec. 29).

1939: *Customers Wanted* (Fleischer/Jan. 27), *Leave Well Enough Alone* (Fleischer/Apr. 28), *Wotta Nightmare* (Fleischer/May 19), *Ghosks Is The Bunk* (Fleischer/June 14), *Hello, How Am I?* (Fleischer/July 14), *It's The Natural Thing To Do* (Fleischer/July 30) and *Never Sock A Baby* (Fleischer/Nov. 3).

1940: *Shakespearian Spinach* (Fleischer/Jan. 19), *Females Is Fickle* (Fleischer/Mar. 8), *Stealin' Ain't Honest* (Fleischer/Mar. 22), *Me Feelin's Is Hurt* (Fleischer/Apr. 12), *Onion Pacific* (Fleischer/May 24), *Wimmen Is A Myskery* (Fleischer/June 7), *Nurse Mates* (Fleischer/June 21), *Fightin' Pals* (Fleischer/July 12), *Doing Impossikible Stunts* (Fleischer/Aug. 2), *Wimmin Hadn't Oughta Drive* (Fleischer/Aug. 16), *Puttin' On The Act* (Fleischer/Aug. 30), *Popeye Meets William Tell* (Fleischer/Sept. 20), *My Pop, My Pop* (Fleischer/Oct. 18), *With Poopdeck Pappy* (Fleischer/Nov. 15) and *Popeye Presents Eugene The Jeep* (Fleischer/Dec. 13).

1941: *Problem Pappy* (Fleischer/Jan. 10), *Quiet! Please* (Fleischer/Feb. 7/uses footage from *Sock–A–Bye Baby*), *Olive's Sweepstakes Ticket* (Fleischer/Mar. 7), *Flies Ain't Human* (Fleischer/Apr. 4), *Popeye Meets Rip Van Winkle* (Fleischer/May 9), *Olive's Boithday Presink* (Fleischer/June 13), *Child Psykolojiky* (Fleischer/July 11), *Pest Pilot* (Fleischer/Aug. 8), *I'll Never Grow Again* (Fleischer/Sept. 19), *The Mighty Navy* (Fleischer/Nov. 14) and *Nix On Hypnotricks* (Fleischer/Dec. 19).

1942: *Kickin' The Conga 'Round* (Fleischer/Jan. 16), *Blunder Below* (Fleischer/Feb. 13), *Fleets Of Stren'th* (Fleischer/Mar. 13), *Pip–Eye, Pup–Eye, Poop–Eye And Peep–Eye* (Fleischer/Apr. 10), *Olive Oyl And Water Don't Mix* (Fleischer/May 8), *Many Tanks* (Fleischer/May 15), *Baby Wants A Bottleship* (Fleischer/July 3/last cartoon directed by Fleischer), *You're A Sap, Mr. Jap* (Gordon/Aug. 7), *Aloha On The Sarong Seas* (Sparber/Sept. 4), *A Hull Of A Mess* (Sparber/Oct. 16), *Scrap The Japs* (Kneitel/Nov. 20) and *Me Musical Nephews* (Kneitel/Dec. 25).

1943: *Spinach Fer Britain* (Sparber/Jan. 22), *Seein' Red White 'N' Blue* (Gordon/Feb. 19), *Too Weak To Work* (Sparber/Mar. 19), *A Jolly Good Furlough* (Gordon/Apr. 23), *Ration For The Duration* (Kneitel/May 28), *The Hungry Goat* (Gordon/June 25), *Happy Birthdaze* (Gordon/July 16), *Wood Peckin'* (Sparber/Aug. 6), *Cartoons Ain't Human* (Kneitel/

Aug. 27/last black–and–white cartoon), *Her Honor The Mare* (Sparber/Nov. 26/re: Oct. 6, 1950/first Technicolor) and *Marry–Go–Round* (Kneitel/Dec. 31).

(The following cartoons are in Technicolor unless indicated otherwise.)

1944: *We're On Our Way To Rio* (Sparber/Apr. 21/re: Oct. 20, 1950), *Anvil Chorus Girl* (Sparber/May 26/re: Oct. 6, 1951/remake of *Shoein' Hosses*), *Spinach–Packin' Popeye The Sailor* (Sparber/July 21/re: Oct. 5, 1951/uses footage from *Popeye Meets Ali Baba And His Forty Thieves* and *Popeye The Sailor Meets Sinbad The Sailor*), *Puppet Love* (Kneitel/Aug. 11/re: Oct. 3, 1952), *Pitching Woo At The Zoo* (Sparber/Sept. 1/re: Oct. 3, 1953), *Moving Aweigh* (Sept. 22) and *She–Sick Sailors* (Kneitel/Dec. 8/re: Oct. 5, 1951).

1945: *Pop–Pie A La Mode* (Sparber/Jan. 26/re: Nov. 3, 1950), *Tops In The Big Top* (Sparber/Mar. 16), *Shape Ahoy* (Sparber/Apr. 27/re: Nov. 17, 1950), *For Better Or Nurse* (Sparber/June 8/re: Oct. 5, 1951/remake of *Hospitaliky*) and *Mess Production* (Kneitel/Aug. 24/re: Oct. 3, 1952).

1946: *House Tricks* (Kneitel/Mar. 15/re: Oct. 5, 1952/remake of *House Builder Uppers*), *Service With A Guile* (Tytla/Apr. 19), *Klondike Casanova* (Sparber/May 31), *Peep In The Deep* (Kneitel/June 7/Cinecolor/remake of *Dizzy Divers*), *Rocket To Marts* (Tytla/Aug. 9/Cinecolor), *Rodeo Romeo* (Sparber/Aug. 16/Cinecolor), *The Fistic Mystic* (Kneitel/Nov. 29) and *The Island Fling* (Tytla/Dec. 27).

1947: *Abusement Park* (Sparber/Apr. 25/Cinecolor), *I'll Be Skiing Ya* (Sparber/June 13), *Popeye And The Pirates* (Kneitel/Sept. 12), *Royal Four Flusher* (Kneitel/Sept. 12), *Wotta Knight* (Sparber/Oct. 24), *Safari So Good* (Sparber/Nov. 7) and *All's Fair At The Fair* (Sparber/Dec. 19/Cinecolor).

1948: *Olive Oyl For President* (Sparber/Jan. 30/Cinecolor), *Wigwam Whoopee* (Sparber/Feb. 27/Polacolor), *Pre–Hysterical Man* (Kneitel/Mar. 26/Polacolor), *Popeye Meets Hercules* (Tytla/June 18/Polacolor), *Wolf In Shiek's Clothing* (Sparber/July 30), *Spinach Vs. Hamburgers* (Kneitel/Aug. 27/footage used from *Anvil Chorus Girl*, *She–Sick Sailors* and *Pop–Pie A La Mode*), *Snow Place Like Home* (Kneitel/Sept. 3/Polacolor), *Robin Hood Winked* (Kneitel/Nov. 12/Polacolor) and *Symphony In Spinach* (Kneitel/Dec. 31/Polacolor).

1949: *Popeye's Premiere* (Mar. 25/footage used from *Popeye The Sailor Meets Aladdin And His Wonderful Lamp*), *Lumber Jack And Jill* (Kneitel/May 27/Polacolor), *Hot Air Aces* (Sparber/June 24/Polacolor), *A Balmy Swami* (Sparber/July 22), *Tar With A Star* (Tytla/Aug. 12), *Silly Hillbilly* (Sparber/Sept. 9), *Barking Dogs Don't Fite* (Sparber/Oct. 28/remake of *Proteck The Weakerist*) and *The Fly's Last Flight* (Kneitel/Dec. 23).

1950: *How Green Is My Spinach* (Kneitel/Jan. 27), *Gym Jam* (Sparber/Mar. 17/remake of *Vim, Vigor And Vitaliky*), *Beach Peach* (Kneitel/May 12), *Jitterbug Jive* (Tytla/June 23), *Popeye Makes A Movie* (Kneitel/Aug. 11/footage used from *Popeye The Sailor Meets Ali Baba And His Forty Thieves*), *Baby Wants Spinach* (Kneitel/Sept. 29), *Quick On The Vigor*

(Kneitel/Oct. 6), *Riot In Rhythm* (Kneitel/Nov. 10/remake of *Me Musical Nephews*) and *Farmer And The Belle* (Kneitel/Dec. 11).

1951: *Vacation With Play* (Kneitel/Jan. 26), *Thrill Of Fair* (Kneitel/Apr. 20/remake of *Li'l Swee' Pea*), *Alpine For You* (Sparber/May 18/remake of *I–Ski Love–Ski You–Ski*), *Double Cross Country Race* (Kneitel/June 15), *Pilgrim Popeye* (Sparber/July 13), *Let's Talk Spinach* (Kneitel/Oct. 19/remake of *Popeye And The Beanstalk*) and *Punch And Judo* (Sparber/Nov. 16).

1952: *Popeye's Pappy* (Kneitel/Jan. 25), *Lunch With A Punch* (Sparber/Mar. 14), *Swimmer Takes All* (Kneitel/May 16), *Friend Or Phony* (Sparber/June 30), *Tots Of Fun* (Kneitel/Aug. 15), *Popalong Popeye* (Kneitel/Aug. 29), *Shuteye Popeye* (Kneitel/Oct. 3) and *Big Bad Sinbad* (Kneitel/Dec. 12).

1953: *Ancient History* (Kneitel/Jan. 30), *Child Sockology* (Sparber/Mar. 27), *Popeye's Mirthday* (Kneitel/May 22), *Toredorable* (Kneitel/June 12), *Baby Wants A Battle* (Kneitel/July 24), *Fireman's Brawl* (Sparber/Aug. 21), *Popeye, The Ace Of Space* (Kneitel/Oct. 2/in 3–D) and *Shaving Mugs* (Kneitel/Oct. 9/remake of *A Clean Shaven Man*).

1954: *Flour Flushers* (Sparber/Jan. 1/remake of *Plumbing Is A Pipe*), *Popeye's 20th Anniversary* (Sparber/Apr. 2), *Taxi–Turvy* (Kneitel/June 4), *Bride And Gloom* (Sparber/July 2), *Greek Mirthology* (Kneitel/Aug. 13), *Private–Eye Popeye* (Kneitel/Nov. 12) and *Gopher Spinach* (Kneitel/Dec. 10).

1955: *Cooking With Gags* (Sparber/Jan. 14), *Nurse To Meet Ya* (Sparber/Feb. 11), *Penny Antics* (Kneitel/Mar. 11/footage used from *Silly Hillbilly* and *Wotta Knight*), *Beaus Will Be Beaus* (Sparber/May 20), *Gift Of Gag* (Kneitel/May 27), *Car–Razy Drivers* (Kneitel/July 22), *Mister And Mistletoe* (Sparber/Sept. 30), *Cops Is Tops* (Sparber/Nov. 4) and *A Job For A Gob* (Kneitel/Dec. 9).

1956: *Hillbilling And Cooling* (Kneitel/Jan. 13), *Popeye For President* (Mar. 30), *Out To Punch* (Kneitel/June 8), *Assault And Flattery* (Sparber/July 6), *Insect To Injury* (Tendlar/Aug. 10), *Parlez–Vouz Woo* (Sparber/Sept. 12), *I Don't Scare* (Sparber/Nov. 16) and *A Haul In One* (Kneitel/Dec. 14/remake of *Let's Get Movin'*).

1957: *Nearly Weds* (Kneitel/Feb. 8), *The Crystal Brawl* (Kneitel/Apr. 5/footage used from *Alpine For You* And *Fistic Mystic*), *Patriotic Popeye* (Sparber/May 10), *Spree Lunch* (Kneitel/June 21), *Spooky Swabs* (Sparber/Aug. 9) and *Tops In The Big Top* (Sept. 6).

Popeye two–reel featurettes
1936: *Popeye The Sailor Meets Sinbad The Sailor* (Fleischer/Nov. 27/A.A. nominee).

1937: *Popeye Meets Ali Baba And His 40 Thieves* (Fleischer/Nov. 26/Technicolor).

1939: *Popeye The Sailor Meets Aladdin And His Wonderful Lamp* (Fleischer/Apr. 7/Technicolor).

PORKY PIG

When Warner Brothers began testing several characters as replacements for Hugh Harman's *Buddy* series, director Friz Freleng introduced this timid, simpleminded pig who spoke with a stutter in 1935's *I Haven't Got A Hat,* an animal version of Hal Roach's *Our Gang* series (The idea for the film was suggested by producer Leon Schlesinger, who liked the classic short–subject series.) Created as part of a team called "Pork and Beans" (named after a can of Campbell's Pork & Beans) by animator Bob Clampett, Freleng renamed the pig Porky after a childhood playmate he recalled from his youth who was "very fat."

While the other characters had their moments, Porky's recital of "Mary Had A Little Lamb" was the most memorable. Warner Brothers agreed. Afterwards, they gave the stammering pig his own starring series and, as they say, the rest is history.

Actor Joe Dougherty, a Warner Brothers bit player whose credits included *The Jazz Singer* and *Ziegfeld Girl,* was first hired to do the voice of Porky. Dougherty got the job because he actually stammered when he spoke, which turned out to be a problem as the series progressed since recording his lines of dialogue was difficult. Dougherty lasted in the role for only two years, because, according to Freleng, "When he delivered his lines, he used up excessive amounts of soundtrack film since he couldn't control his stammerings. It just became too expensive to keep him so we finally let him go."

At the advice of Warner story editor Treg Brown, actor Mel Blanc was auditioned as Dougherty's replacement. He was so convincing that Freleng hired him on the spot and Blanc not only became the voice of Porky but practically every Warner Brothers cartoon character until the demise of the animation department in 1963. Blanc created Porky's famous sign–off line of "Th–th–th–th–that's all, folks!" often used at the end of every Warner Brothers cartoon.

Porky remained a headliner in his series throughout the '30s and '40s. During the '30s, Clampett almost exclusively directed Porky in such early classics as *Porky's Hero Agency* (1937), *Porky In Wackyland* (1938) and *The Lone Stranger And Porky* (1939), a Grand Shorts Award winner, plus two key 1940s films, *Baby Bottleneck* (1946) and *Kitty Kornered* (1946).

Although Porky was a major star, the studio often used him in supporting roles to play off other characters on the studio roster. He was a supporting character for the first appearances of Daffy Duck in *Porky's Duck Hunt* (1937) and of Bugs Bunny in *Porky's Hare Hunt* (1938) and, at various times, he played other comic relief roles. His most notable performances in this realm were under director Chuck Jones, who made Porky more adult–looking, and cast him opposite Daffy Duck in a series of misadventures. Their most memorable appearance together still remains the space–age encounter, *Duck Dodgers In The 24½th Century* (1953), which Jones directed. By the 1950s, Porky seemed so well–suited as a "second banana" that the studio eventually utilized him more often in this capacity for the remainder of his career.

Porky did not remain completely indifferent to members of the opposite gender. In the late 1930s, he was given a girlfriend who appeared in a handful of cartoon shorts. Her name: Petunia Pig. *Series directors were Friz Freleng, Tex Avery, Jack King, Frank Tashlin, Ub Iwerks, Bob Clampett, Cal Dalton, Cal Howard, Ben Hardaway, Norm McCabe, Chuck Jones, Art Davis, Robert McKimson and Irv Spector. Black–and–white. Technicolor. A Warner Brothers release.*

Voices:
Porky Pig: Joe Dougherty (to 1937), Mel Blanc

Looney Tunes
1936: *Gold Diggers Of '49* (with Beans/Avery/Jan. 6), *Boom Boom* (with Beans/King/Feb. 29), *The Blow Out* (Avery/Apr. 4), *Westward Whoa* (with Beans/King/Apr. 25), *Plane Dippy* (Avery/Apr. 30), *Fish Tales* (King/May 23), *Shanghaiied Shipmates* (King/June 26), *Porky's Pet* (King/July 11), *Porky The Rainmaker* (Avery/Aug. 1), *Porky's Poultry Plant* (Tashlin/Aug. 22), *Milk And Money* (Avery/Oct. 3), *Porky's Moving Day* (King/Oct. 7), *Little Beau Porky* (Tashlin/Nov. 14), *The Village Smithy* (Avery/Dec. 5) and *Porky Of The Northwoods* (Tashlin/Dec. 19).

1937: *Porky The Wrestler* (Avery/Jan. 9), *Porky's Road Race* (Tashlin/Feb. 6), *Picador Porky* (Avery/Feb. 27), *Porky's Romance* (with Petunia Pig/Tashlin/Apr. 3), *Porky's Duck Hunt* (with Daffy Duck; his first appearance/Avery/Apr. 17), *Porky And Gabby* (with Gabby Goat/Iwerks/May 15), *Porky's Building* (Tashlin/June 19), *Porky's Super Service* (Iwerks/July 3), *Porky's Badtime Story* (with Gabby Goat/Clampett/July 24), *Porky's Railroad* (Tashlin/Aug. 7), *Get Rich Quick Porky* (Clampett/Aug. 28), *Porky's Garden* (Avery/Sept. 11), *Rover's Rival* (Clampett/Oct. 9), *The Case Of The Stuttering Pig* (with Petunia Pig/Tashlin/Oct. 30).

1938: *Porky's Poppa* (Clampett/Jan. 15), *Porky At The Crocadero* (Tashlin/Feb. 5), *What Price Porky* (Clampett/Feb. 26), *Porky's Phoney Express* (Dalton, Howard/Mar. 19), *Porky's Five And Ten* (Clampett/Apr. 6), *Porky's Hare Hunt* (Hardaway/Apr. 30), *Injun Trouble* (Clampett/May 21), *Porky The Fireman* (Tashlin/June 4), *Porky's Party* (Clampett/June 25), *Porky's Spring Planting* (Tashlin/July 25), *Porky And Daffy* (with Daffy Duck/Clampett/Aug. 6), *Wholly Smoke* (Tashlin/Aug. 27), *Porky In Wackyland* (Clampett/Sept. 24), *Porky's Naughty Nephew* (Clampett/Oct. 15), *Porky In Egypt* (Clampett/Nov. 5), *The Daffy Doc* (with Daffy Duck/Clampett/Nov. 26) and *Porky The Gob* (Hardaway, Dalton/Dec. 17).

1939: *The Lone Stranger And Porky* (with Daffy Duck/Clampett/Jan. 7), *It's An Ill Wind* (Hardaway, Dalton/Jan. 28), *Porky's Tire Trouble* (Clampett/Feb. 18), *Porky's Movie Mystery* (Clampett/Mar. 11), *Chicken Jitters* (Clampett/Apr. 1), *Porky And Teabiscuit* (Hardaway, Dalton/Apr. 22), *Kristopher Kolumbus, Jr.* (Clampett/May 13), *Polar Pals* (Clampett/June 3), *Scalp Trouble* (with Daffy Duck/Clampett/June 24), *Porky's Picnic* (with Petunia Pig/Clampett/July 15), *Wise Quacks* (with Daffy Duck/Clampett/Aug. 5), *Porky's Hotel* (Clampett/Sept. 2), *Jeepers Creepers* (Clampett/Sept. 23), *Naughty Neighbors* (Clampett/Oct. 7), *Pied Piper Porky* (Clampett/Nov. 4), *Porky The Giant Killer* (Hardaway, Dalton/Nov. 18) and *The Film Fan* (Clampett/Dec. 16).

Porky Pig encounters a strange bunch of characters, including a Do–Do bird, in Bob Clampett's Porky In Wackyland (1938). © Warner Brothers, Inc. (Courtesy: Bob Clampett Animation Art)

1940: *Porky's Last Stand* (with Daffy Duck/Clampett/Jan. 6), *Africa Squeaks* (Clampett/Jan. 27), *Ali–Baba Bound* (Clampett/Feb. 17), *Pilgrim Porky* (Clampett/Mar. 16), *Slap–Happy Porky* (Clampett/Apr. 13), *You Ought To Be In Pictures* (with Daffy Duck/Freleng/May 19), *Porky's Poor Fish* (Clampett/Apr. 27), *The Chewin' Bruin* (Clampett/June 9), *Porky's Baseball Broadcast* (Freleng/July 6), *Patient Porky* (with Bugs Bunny/Clampett/Sept. 14), *Calling Dr. Porky* (Freleng/Sept. 21), *Prehistoric Porky* (Clampett/Oct. 12), *The Sour Puss* (Clampett/Nov. 2), *Porky's Hired Hand* (Freleng/Nov. 30) and *The Timid Toreador* (McCabe, Clampett/Dec. 21).

1941: *Porky's Snooze Reel* (McCabe, Clampett/Jan. 11), *Porky's Bear Facts* (Freleng/Mar. 29), *Porky's Preview* (Avery/Apr. 19), *Porky's Ant* (Jones/Apr. 10), *A Coy Decoy* (with Daffy Duck/Clampett/June 7), *Porky's Prize Pony* (Jones/June 21), *Meet John Doughboy* (Clampett/July 5), *We, The Animals Squeak* (Clampett/Aug. 9), *The Henpecked Duck* (with Daffy Duck/Clampett/Aug. 30), *Notes To You* (Freleng/Sept. 20), *Robinson Crusoe, Jr.* (McCabe/Oct. 25), *Porky's Midnight Matinee* (Jones/Nov. 22) and *Porky's Pooch* (Clampett/Dec. 27).

1942: *Porky's Pastry Pirates* (Freleng/Jan. 27), *Who's Who In The Zoo* (McCabe/Feb. 14), *Porky's Cafe* (with Conrad Cat/Jones/Feb. 21), and *My Favorite Duck* (Jones/Dec. 5).

1943: *Confusions Of A Nutzy Spy* (McCabe/Jan. 23), *Yankee Doodle Daffy* (with Daffy Duck/Freleng/July 3) and *Porky Pig's Feat* (with Daffy Duck/Tashlin/July 17).

1944: *Tom Turk And Daffy* (with Daffy Duck/Jones/Feb. 12), *Tick Tock Tuckered* (with Daffy/Clampett/Apr. 8), *The Swooner Crooner* (Tashlin/May 6/A.A. nominee), *Duck Soup Nuts* (with Daffy Duck/Freleng/May 27) and *Brother Brat* (Tashlin/July 15).

1945: *Trap Happy Porky* (Jones/Feb. 24).

1946: *Baby Bottleneck* (with Daffy Duck/Clampett/Mar. 16), *Daffy Doodles* (with Daffy Duck/McKimson/Apr. 16), *Kitty Kornered* (Clampett/June 8) and *Mouse Menace* (Davis/Nov. 2).

1947: *Little Orphan Airedale* (with Charlie Dog/Jones/Oct. 4).

1948: *The Pest That Came To Dinner* (Davis/Sept. 11).

1949: *Porky's Chops* (Davis/Feb. 12), *Paying The Piper* (McKimson/Mar. 12), *Daffy Duck Hunt* (with Daffy Duck/McKimson/Mar. 26), *Curtain Razor* (Freleng/May 21) and *Often An Orphan* (with Charlie Dog/Jones/Aug. 13).

1950: *Boobs In The Woods* (with Daffy Duck/McKimson/Jan. 28), *The Scarlet Pumpernickel* (with Daffy Duck, Sylvester the Cat, Elmer Fudd, Momma Bear/Jones/Mar. 4) and *The Ducksters* (with Daffy/Jones/Sept. 2).

1951: *The Wearing Of The Grin* (Jones/July 14).

1952: *Thumb Fun* (with Daffy Duck/McKimson/Mar. 1) and *Fool Coverage* (with Daffy Duck/McKimson/Dec. 13).

1955: *Dime To Retire* (with Daffy Duck/McKimson/Sept. 3).

1956: *Deduce, You Say* (with Daffy Duck/Jones/Sept. 29).

1957: *Boston Quackie* (with Daffy Duck/McKimson/June 22).

1959: *China Jones* (with Daffy Duck/Jones/Feb. 14).

1961: *Daffy's Inn Trouble* (McKimson/Sept. 23).

DePatie–Freleng Enterprises Releases
1965: *Corn On The Cop* (Spector/July 24).

Merrie Melodies
1935: *I Haven't Got A Hat* (first Porky/Freleng/Mar. 2) and *Into Your Dance* (Freleng/June 8).

1936: *The Phantom Ship* (with Beans, Ham and Ex/King/Feb. 1), *Alpine Antics* (with Beans/King/Mar. 9), *The Fire Alarm* (with Ham and Ex, Beans/King/Mar. 9) and *When I Yoo Hoo* (Freleng/June 27).

1938: *My Little Buckaroo* (Freleng/Jan. 29).

1939: *Old Glory* (Jones/July 1).

(The following cartoons are in Technicolor unless indicated otherwise.)

1943: *A Corny Concerto* (with Elmer Fudd, Bugs Bunny/Clampett/Sept. 18).

1944: *Slightly Daffy* (with Daffy Duck/Freleng/June 17).

1945: *Wagon Heels* (Clampett/July 28).

1947: *One Meat Brawl* (McKimson/Jan. 18).

1948: *Daffy Duck Slept Here* (McKimson/Mar. 6), *Nothing But The Tooth* (Davis/May 1), *Riff Raffy Daffy* (with Daffy Duck/Davis/Nov. 7/Cinecolor) and *Scaredy Cat* (with Sylvester the Cat/Jones/Dec. 18).

1949: *Awful Orphan* (with Charlie Dog/Jones/Jan. 29), *Dough For The Do–Do* (Freleng/Sept. 3/remake of *Porky In Wackyland*) and *Bye–Bye Bluebeard* (Davis/Oct. 21).

1950: *An Egg Scramble* (with Miss Prissy/McKimson/May 27) and *Golden Yeggs* (Freleng/Aug. 5).

1951: *Dripalong Daffy* (with Daffy Duck/Jones/Nov. 17), *Dog Collared* (McKimson/Dec. 2) and *The Prize Pest* (with Daffy Duck/McKimson/Dec. 22).

1952: *Cracked Quack* (with Daffy Duck/Freleng/July 5).

1953: *Duck Dodgers In The 24½th Century* (with Daffy Duck, Marvin Martian/Jones/July 25).

1954: *Claws Alarm* (with Sylvester the Cat/Jones/May 22) and *My Little Duckaroo* (with Daffy Duck/Jones/Nov. 27).

1956: *Rocket Squad* (with Daffy Duck/Jones/Mar. 10).

1958: *Robin Hood Daffy* (with Daffy Duck/Jones/Mar. 18).

POSSIBLE POSSUM

Set in the tiny populous of Happy Hollow, this series spinoff from Terrytoons' *Deputy Dawg* was comprised of more Southern–flavored tales, this time featuring the carefree, guitar–playing Possible Possum and his loyal swamp friends, Billy the Bear, Owlawishus Owl and Macon Mouse. *The cartoons were animated and directed by Terrytoons veterans Connie Rasinski, Art Bartsch, Bob Kuwahara, Cosmo Anzilotti and Dave Tendlar. Technicolor. A Terrytoons Production released through 20th Century–Fox.*

Voices:
Possible Possum: Lionel Wilson, **Billy Bear:** Lionel Wilson, **Owlawishus Owl:** Lionel Wilson, **Macon Mouse:** Lionel Wilson

1965: *Freight Fright* (Rasinski/Mar.), *Darn Barn* (Rasinski/June), *Get That Guitar* (Bartsch/Sept.) and *The Toothless Beaver* (Rasinski/Dec.).

1966: *Watch The Butterfly* (Tendlar/Oct.).

1968: *Big Bad Bobcat* (Anzilotti/Apr.), *Surprisin' Exercisin'* (Anzilotti/July), *The Rock Hounds* (Tendlar/Oct.) and *Mount Piney* (Bartsch/Dec.).

1969: *The General's Little Helper* (Feb.), *The Red Swamp Fox* (May), *The Bold Eagle* (May) and *Swamp Snapper* (Nov.).

1970: *Surface Surf Aces* (Mar.), *Swamp Water Taffy* (July) and *Slinky Minky* (Nov.).

1971: *Berry Funny* (Mar.) and *Big Mo* (July).

PROFESSOR SMALL AND MR. TALL

This capricious pair, who were complete opposites of their names—the "tall" Professor Small and "small" Mr. Tall—appeared in a short–lived cartoon series for Columbia Pictures. Situations revolved around the twosome's clumsy attempts to refute various superstitions of life. *Directed by John Hubley and Paul Sommer. Technicolor. Voice credits unknown. A Columbia Pictures release.*

1943: *Professor Small And Mister Tall* (Sommer, Hubley/ Mar. 26/Color Rhapsody).

1945: *River Ribber* (Sommer/Oct. 4/Color Rhapsody).

PUDDY THE PUP

Paul Terry created this frisky little pup who first appeared opposite Farmer Al Falfa before starring in a theatrical sound series of his own. *Directed by Mannie Davis, George Gordon and Connie Rasinski. Black–and–white. Voice credits unknown. A Terrytoons Production released through 20th Century–Fox.*

1936: *The Hot Spell* (with Farmer Al Falfa/Davis, Gordon/ July 10), *Puddy The Pup And The Gypsies* (with Farmer Al Falfa/July 24), *Sunken Treasure* (Davis, Gordon/Oct. 16) and *Cats In The Bag* (Davis, Gordon/Dec. 11).

1937: *The Book Shop* (Davis, Gordon/Feb. 5), *Puddy's Coronation* (Davis, Gordon/May 14), *The Homeless Pup* (Gordon/July 23) and *The Dog And The Bone* (Gordon/Nov. 12).

1938: *His Off Day* (Rasinski/Feb. 4), *Happy And Lucky* (Rasinski/Mar. 18) and *The Big Top* (Davis/May 12).

RAGGEDY ANN AND RAGGEDY ANDY

Three years after Max Fleischer's two–reel special *Raggedy Ann And Raggedy Andy*, based on the characters and stories created by Johnny Gruelle, Famous Studios produced this short–lived series of one–reel shorts, which premiered with 1944's *Suddenly It's Spring*. The cartoons were released as part of the studio's *Noveltoons* series. *Directed by Seymour Kneitel. Technicolor. A Famous Studios Production released through Paramount Pictures.*

1941: *Raggedy Ann And Raggedy Andy* (Apr. 11)

1944: *Suddenly It's Spring* (Apr. 28).

1947: *The Enchanted Square* (May 9).

RAINBOW PARADES

Former Disney director Burt Gillett, who won Academy Awards for his Walt Disney classics, *Flower And Trees* (1932) and *The Three Little Pigs* (1933), created and directed this series of musical children's fables for Van Beuren Studios, whose stars were generally lesser–knowns. Gillett, who had joined the studio in 1933, launched the idea following completion of his first series for the studio, *Toddle Tales*, which combined live–action sequences with animated characters and plotlines.

Unlike his former series, *Rainbow Parades* became the first color series for Van Beuren, initially filmed in a two–color

process and then in three–strip Technicolor. The cartoons alternated between one–shot stories and episodes with continuing characters, becoming popular installments for the studio.

The series was released to television in the 1950s after Official Films purchased Van Beuren's entire cartoon library to distribute to this thriving medium. *Other series directors were Ted Eshbaugh, Steve Muffati, Tom Palmer, James "Shamus" Culhane and Dan Gordon. Voice credits unknown. Technicolor. A RKO–Radio Pictures release.*

1934: *Pastry Town Wedding* (Gillett, Eshbaugh/July 27) and *The Parrotville Fire Department* (Gillett, Eshbaugh/Sept. 14).

1935: *The Sunshine Makers* (Gillett, Eshbaugh/Jan. 11), *Parrotville Old Folks* (Gillett, Palmer/Jan. 25), *Japanese Lanterns* (Gillett, Eshbaugh/Mar. 8), *Spinning Mice* (Gillett, Palmer/Apr. 5), *Picnic Panic* (Gillett, Palmer/May 3), *The Merry Kittens* (Gillett, Culhane/May 15), *The Foxy Terrier* (Gillett/ May 31), *Parrotville Post Office* (Gillett, Palmer/June 28), *Rag Dog* (Gillett/July 19), *Putting On The Dog* (Gillett/July 19), *The Hunting Season* (Gillett/Aug. 9), *Bird Scouts* (Gillett, Palmer/Sept. 20), *Molly Moo Cow And The Butterflies* (Gillett, Palmer/Nov. 15), *Molly Moo Cow And The Indians* (Gillett, Palmer/Nov. 15), *Molly Moo Cow And Rip Van Wrinkle* (Gillett, Palmer/Nov. 17).

1936: *Toonerville Trolley* (Gillett, Palmer/Jan. 17), *Felix The Cat And The Goose That Laid The Golden Egg* (Gillett, Palmer/Feb. 7), *Molly Moo Cow And Robinson Crusoe* (Gillett, Palmer/Feb. 28), *Neptune Nonsense* (Gillett, Palmer/Mar. 20), *Bold King Cole* (with Felix the Cat/Gillett/May 29), *A Waif's Welcome* (Palmer/June 19), *Trolley Ahoy* (Gillett/July 3/Toonerville Trolley cartoon), *Cupid Gets His Man* (Palmer/ July 24), *It's A Greek Life* (Gordon/Aug. 2) and *Toonerville Picnic* (Gillett/Oct. 2/Toonerville Trolley cartoon).

RALPH PHILLIPS

Chuck Jones brought this young boy with an overactive imagination who daydreams in the fashion of Walter Mitty, to the screen in 1954's *From A To Z–Z–Z–Z*, which was nominated for an Academy Award. Ralph appeared in only two cartoons altogether, his second being *Boyhood Daze* (1957), a *Merrie Melodies* cartoon. *Directed by Chuck Jones. Technicolor. A Warner Brothers release.*

Voices:
Ralph Phillips: Dick Beals

Looney Tunes
1954: *From A To Z–Z–Z–Z* (Oct. 16/A.A. nominee). *Merrie Melodies.*

1957: *Boyhood Daze* (Apr. 20).

RALPH WOLF AND SAM SHEEPDOG

Ralph, a scheming wolf who resembles Wile E. Coyote, tries everything possible to steal sheep under the nose of one clever sheepdog, Sam—only during working hours—in this Warner Brothers cartoon rib–tickling series created by Chuck Jones. The battling pair first starred in 1953's *Don't Give Up the Sheep. Directed by Chuck Jones. Technicolor. A Warner Brothers release.*

Voices:
Mel Blanc

Looney Tunes
1953: *Don't Give Up The Sheep* (Jan. 3).

1955: *Double Or Mutton* (July 23).

1957: *Steal Wool* (June 8).

Merrie Melodies
1954: *Sheep Ahoy* (Dec. 11).

1960: *Ready Woolen And Able* (July 30).

1962: *A Sheep In The Deep* (Feb.).

1963: *Woolen Under Where* (May).

The Coyote's never–ending pursuit of the Road Runner is about to end in disaster in the long–running Warner Brothers cartoon series created by Chuck Jones. © Warner Brothers, Inc.

ROAD RUNNER AND COYOTE

Director Chuck Jones and storyman Michael Maltese created the incredibly speedy ostrich–necked Road Runner ("Beep! Beep!") and his relentless pursuer Wile E. Coyote in what became known as the "longest chase" in cartoon history.

Jones had always aspired to animate a series using "black-outs" and sound effects in classic fashion. He admits to having been influenced by a series of a similar nature, Columbia Pictures' *Fox And The Crow* cartoons, which was based on the same chase formula but to a different extreme.

As for the Road Runner's voice, Jones recalls he and Maltese got the idea from, of all places, the hallways of Warner Brothers cartoon studio. "Curiously enough, Mel Blanc didn't come up with the 'Beep! Beep!' That was done by a fellow named Paul Julian. He was walking down the hall carrying a load of backgrounds and couldn't see where he was going," Jones recalled. "He had about sixty drawings in front of him and he kept going 'Beep! Beep!' as he went by to keep people out of his way. Mike and I were laying out the first picture when Paul went by our door making that sound. We looked at each other and thought that must have been the sound the Road Runner makes. Mike looked up and said, 'O.K. God, we'll take it from here.' "

The characters were first introduced in the 1948 Techni-color release, *Fast And Furry–Ous,* featuring the type of lunacy which became a staple of the series. Jones imposed certain disciplines when animating the series: The Road Run-ner always stayed on the road. He was never injured; the Coyote injured himself instead. The same Arizona desert locale was used in each picture. Sympathy always fell in favor of the Coyote. No dialogue was furnished for either character, with the exception of the Road Runner's traditional "Beep! Beep!" sound, which sound–effects man Treg Brown made by using an electronic horn called a claxon. (Mel Blanc mimiced the sound vocally for the second cartoon, *Beep Beep!* (1952), when the instrument got lost. Blanc's sound was used

for each and every cartoon thereafter.) The splash technique of the Coyote falling off the cliff was incorporated into almost every film. And, lastly, the Coyote never catches the Road Runner.

Jones has said that he recognized certain elements of him-self in other characters but found Wile E. Coyote was his true alter ego. "The coyote is victimized by his own ineptitude. I never understood how to use tools, and that's really the coyote's problem. He's not at war with the gods, but with the miniscule things of every day life. It is out of this mounting frustration that the comedy develops," he said.

Such contraptions were an assortment of ACME industrial devices and every do–it–yourself kit imaginable. Invariably the Coyote found himself the victim of his machinery; thus the joke was always on him.

Jones directed the most cartoons in the series. After Warner Brothers shut down its animation department, the series re-sumed under DePatie–Freleng Enterprises, which produced a new series of Warner cartoons before the studio re–opened its animation division in 1967. *Other series directors were Maurice Noble, Rudy Larriva, Ave Levitow and Robert Mc-Kimson. Technicolor. A Warner Brothers release.*

Voices:
Road Runner: Mel Blanc

Looney Tunes

1949: *Fast And Furry–Ous* (Jones/Sept. 17/first Road Run-ner cartoon).

1955: *Ready, Set, Zoom!* (Jones/Apr. 30).

1956: *Gee Whiz–z–z* (Jones/May 5) and *There They Go–Go–Go* (Jones/Nov. 10).

1957: *Scramble Aches* (Jones/Jan. 26) and *Zoom And Bored* (Jones/Sept. 14).

1958: *Hook, Line And Stinker* (Jones/Oct. 11).

1959: *Hot Rod And Reel!* (Jones/May 9).

1960: *Fastest With The Mostest* (Jones/Jan. 19) and *Hop-along Casualty* (Jones/Oct. 8).

1961: *Lickey Splat* (Jones, Levitow/June 3).

DePatie–Freleng Enterprises Releases
1964: *War And Pieces* (Jones, Noble/June 6).

1965: *Tired And Feathered* (Larriva/Sept. 18) and *Highway Runnery* (Larriva/Dec. 11).

1966: *Shot And Bothered* (Larriva/Jan. 8), *The Solid Tin Coyote* (Larriva/Feb. 29), *Clippety Clobbered* (Larriva/Mar. 12) and *Sugar And Spies* (McKimson/Nov. 5).

Merrie Melodies

1952: *Beep, Beep* (Jones/May 24) and *Going! Going! Gosh!* (Jones/Aug. 23).

1953: *Zipping Along* (Jones/Sept. 10).

1954: *Stop, Look And Hasten* (Jones/Aug. 14).

1958: *Hip Hip—Hurry* (Jones/Dec. 6).

1959: *Wild About Hurry* (Jones/Oct. 10).

1961: *Zip 'N' Snort* (Jones/Jan. 21) and *Beep Prepared* (Jones/Nov. 11).

1962: *Zoom At The Top* (Jones, Noble/June 30).

1963: *To Beep Or Not To Beep* (Jones, Noble/Dec. 28).

DePatie–Freleng Enterprises Releases
1965: *Rushing Roulette* (McKimson/July 31), *Run, Run, Sweet Roadrunner* (Larriva/Aug. 21), *Boulder Wham* (Larriva/Oct. 9), *Just Plane Beep* (Larriva/Oct. 30), *Harried And Hurried* (Larriva/Nov. 13) and *Chaser On The Rocks* (Larriva/Dec. 25).

1966: *Out And Out Rout* (Larriva/Jan. 29).

ROGER RABBIT

Following up on the success of *Who Framed Roger Rabbit?*, Walt Disney Studios launched this series of fast–paced, funny tributes to Hollywood cartoons of the '40s reuniting the film's principal cartoon stars, the zany Roger Rabbit, his voluptuous wife Jessica Rabbit and the temper–tantrum throwing Baby Herman.

Under the Maroon Cartoons banner—the fictional studio which employed Roger in the box–office smash cartoon feature—Disney released its first theatrical animated short in 25 years—the 1989 madcap adventure, *Tummy Trouble*, double–billed with the studio's feature–length *Honey, I Shrunk The Kids,* which grossed more than $87 million at the box office in the first five weeks.

Like the movie, it again paired Roger Rabbit and Baby Herman, who has been left in Roger's less–than–adroit care. When Baby swallows a rattle, Roger rushes the tyke to the hospital—St. Nowhere—and bedlam ensues. Roger's sexy, curvacious wife, Jessica, plays a nurse in the film (again voiced by Kathleen Turner) and MGM's sorrowful bloodhound Droopy makes a cameo appearance as an elevator operator.

In 1990, Disney again tied the release of the series' second short, *Rollercoast Rabbit,* with the nationwide premiere of Warren Beatty's long–awaited feature–length comic–strip adaptation, *Dick Tracy. Directed by Rob Minkoff (animation) and Frank Marshall (live action). Technicolor. A Walt Disney/Amblin Entertainment Production released through Touchstone Pictures.*

Voices:

Roger Rabbit: Charles Fleischer, **Jessica Rabbit:** Kathleen Turner, **Young Baby Herman:** April Winchell, **Adult Baby Herman:** Lou Hirsch, **Droopy:** Richard Williams

1989: *Tummy Trouble* (July 23).

1990: *Rollercoaster Rabbit* (June 15).

ROLAND AND RATTFINK

DePatie–Freleng Enterprises seemingly took over where the Warner Brothers animation department left off, producing new cartoon series mirroring the style and humor of the classic Warner cartoons only with new stars in the leading roles. Produced in the late 1960s, Roland and Rattfink was based on the idea of good versus evil. The series paired Roland, a blond, good–looking upholder of justice, against Rattfink, that all–around sleazy, dastardly, good–for–nothing bad guy who always seems to be on the wrong side of the law. *Series directors were Gerry Chiniquy, Art Davis and Hawley Pratt. Voice credits unknown. Technicolor. A DePatie–Freleng/Mirisch Films Production released through United Artists.*

Voices:

Roland: Leonard Weinrib, Dave Barry, **Rattfink:** Leonard Weinrib, John Byner

Good–looking champion of justice Roland makes peace with all–around sleaze Rattfink in the DePatie–Freleng Enterprises theatrical cartoon series, Roland And Rattfink. © DePatie–Freleng Enterprises

Additional Voices:
June Foray, Peter Halton, Athena Lorde

1968: *Hawks And Doves* (Pratt/Dec. 18).

1969: *Hurts And Flowers* (Pratt/Feb. 11), *Flying Feet* (Chiniquy/Apr. 10), *The Deadwood Thunderball* (Pratt/June 6), *Sweet & Sourdough* (Davis/June 25) and *A Pair Of Sneakers* (Davis/Sept. 17)).

1970: *Say Cheese Please* (Davis/June 7), *A Taste Of Money* (Davis/June 24), *The Foul–Kin* (Aug. 5), *Bridgework* (Davis/Aug. 26), *Robin Goodhood* (Sept. 9), *War & Pieces* (Davis/Sept. 20) and *Gem Dandy* (Chiniquy/Oct. 25).

1971: *Trick Or Retreat* (Davis/Mar. 3), *The Great Continental Overland Cross–Country Race* (May 23), *A Fink In The Rink* (Davis/July 4) and *Cattle Battle* (Davis/Aug. 4).

RUDOLF ISING CARTOONS

Producer/animator Rudolf Ising, a former Disney animator, produced and directed this series of musical cartoons, starring miscellaneous characters, on his return visit to MGM in the late 1930s. Ising felt right at home, having worked for the studio previously in 1933 after a brief stint at Warner Brothers. Following his arrival, he was responsible for directing MGM's Barney Bear series and the studio's first Academy Award–winning cartoon, *Milky Way* (1940).

For additional Ising cartoons, see Barney Bear series entry. *Directed by Rudolf Ising. Voice credits unknown. Technicolor. A Metro–Goldwyn–Mayer release.*

1939: *The Little Goldfish* (Ising/Apr. 15/re: Nov. 10, 1948), *The Bear That Couldn't Sleep* (Ising/June 10/re: Dec. 5, 1953) and *One Mother's Family* (Ising/Sept. 30).

1940: *Home On The Range* (Ising/Mar. 23), *The Milky Way* (Ising/June 22/re: Feb. 14, 1948/A.A. winner), *Romeo Rhythm* (Ising/Aug. 10), *The Homeless Flea* (Ising/Oct. 12) and *Mrs. Lady Bug* (Ising/Dec. 21/re: Jan. 17, 1958).

1941: *Dance Of The Weed* (Ising/June 7).

1942: *The Bear And The Beavers* (Ising/Mar. 28) and *Little Gravel Voice* (Ising/May 16).

1943: *Bah Wilderness* (Ising/Feb. 23), *The Boy And The Wolf* (Ising/Apr. 24) and *The Uninvited Pest* (Ising/July 17).

SAD CAT

Ralph Bakshi, after being elevated to the role of director at Terrytoons, created and directed this series about a scraggly–haired, droopy–eyed cat and his friends, Gadmouse, Impresario, Letimore and Fenimore, in numerous backwoods adventures. Following two seasons, Bakshi turned over the directorial reins to Arthur Bartsch, another Terrytoons veteran. *Directed by Ralph Bakshi and Arthur Bartsch. Technicolor. A Terrytoons Production released through 20th Century–Fox.*

Voices:
Sad Cat: Bob McFadden, **Impresario:** Bob McFadden, **Letimore:** Bob McFadden, **Fenimore:** Bob McFadden

1965: *Gadmouse The Apprentice Good Fairy* (Bakshi/Jan.), *Don't Spill The Beans* (Bakshi/Apr.), *Dress Reversal* (Bakshi/July) and *The Third Musketeer* (Bakshi/Oct.).

1966: *Scuba Duba Do* (Bakshi/June).

1968: *Dribble Drabble* (Bartsch/Jan.), *Big Game Fishing* (Bartsch/Feb.), *Grand Prix Winner* (Bartsch), *Commander Great Guy* (Bartsch/May), *All Teed Off* (Bartsch/June), *Judo Kudos* (Bartsch/Aug.), *The Abominable Mountaineers* (Bartsch/Sept.) and *Loops And Swoops* (Bartsch/Nov.).

SAM SMALL

This British–made cartoon series was the only foreign animated series to be distributed theatrically in the United States—outside of Gene Deitch's Czechoslovakian–produced cartoons for MGM and Paramount in the 1960s—and starred this defiant soldier of the King's army who was also a teller of tall tales. Sam was created by famed British comedian Stanley Holloway and English cartoonist Anson Dyer. Astor Pictures distributed the series in America. *Narrated by Stanley Holloway. Technicolor. An Astor Pictures Corporation release.*

1937: *Halt, Who Goes There* (Apr. 15), *Carmen* (May), *Sam And His Musket* (June), *Sam's Medal* (July), *Beat The Retreat* (Aug.) and *Drummed Out* (Sept.).

SCRAPPY

Produced as a companion to Columbia's Krazy Kat, Dick Huemer devised this curly–topped, button–eyed boy and his faithful dog, Yippy, in plots associated with childhood themes and encounters with juvenile nemeses, Vonsey and Oopie. When Huemer left the series in 1933 to join Walt Disney Studios, Art Davis and Sid Marcus, who contributed most of the series' stories, continued with production of the series. *Directed by Dick Huemer, Ub Iwerks, Sid Marcus, Art Davis and Ben Harrison. Produced by Charles Mintz. Voice credits unknown. Black–and–white. Technicolor. A Columbia Pictures release.*

1931: *Yelp Wanted* (Huemer/July 16), *The Little Pest* (Huemer/Aug. 15), *Sunday Clothes* (Huemer/Sept. 15), *The Dog Snatcher* (Huemer/Oct. 15), *Showing Off* (Huemer/Nov. 11) and *Minding The Baby* (Huemer/Nov. 16).

1932: *Chinatown Mystery* (Huemer/Jan. 4), *Treasure Runt* (Huemer/Feb. 25), *Railroad Wretch* (Huemer/Mar. 23), *The Pet Shop* (Huemer/Apr. 28), *Stepping Stones* (Huemer/May 17), *Battle Of The Barn* (Huemer/May 31), *Fare–Play* (Huemer/July 2), *Camping Out* (Huemer/Aug. 10), *The Black Sheep* (Huemer/Sept. 17), *The Great Bird Mystery* (Huemer/Oct. 20/formerly *The Famous Bird Case*), *Flop House* (Huemer/Nov. 9), *The Bad Genius* (Huemer/Dec. 1) and *The Wolf At The Door* (Huemer/Dec. 29).

Scrappy shares a moment with faithful companion, Yippy, in a scene from the popular Columbia Pictures cartoon series. © Columbia Pictures Inc.

1933: *Sassy Cats* (Huemer/Jan. 25), *Scrappy's Party* (Huemer/Feb. 13), *The Beer Parade* (Huemer/Mar. 4), *The False Alarm* (Huemer/Apr. 22), *The Match Kid* (Huemer/May 9), *Technocracket* (Huemer/May 20), *The World's Affair* (Huemer/June 5), *Movie Struck* (Huemer/Sept. 8), *Sandman Tales* (Huemer/Oct. 6), *Hollywood Babies* (Huemer/Nov. 10) and *Auto Show* (Huemer/Dec. 8).

1934: *Scrappy's Art Gallery* (Jan. 12), *Scrappy's Television* (Jan. 29), *Aw, Nurse* (Mar. 9), *Scrappy's Toy Shop* (Apr. 13), *Scrappy's Dog Show* (May 18), *Scrappy's Theme Song* (June 15), *Scrappy's Relay Race* (July 7), *The Great Experiment* (July 27), *Scrappy's Expedition* (Aug. 27), *Concert Kid* (Nov. 2), *Holiday Land* (Nov. 9/*Color Rhapsody*/A.A. nominee) and *Happy Butterfly* (Dec. 20).

1935: *The Gloom Chasers* (Jan. 18), *The Gold Getters* (Mar. 1), *Graduation Exercises* (Apr. 12), *Scrappy's Ghost Story* (May 24), *The Puppet Murder Case* (June 21), *Scrappy's Big Moment* (July 28), *Scrappy's Trailer* (Aug. 29), and *Let's Ring Doorbells* (Nov. 7).

1936: *Scrappy's Boy Scouts* (Jan. 2), *Scrappy's Pony* (Mar. 16), *Scrappy's Camera Troubles* (June 5), *Playing Politics* (July 8/*Color Rhapsody*), *The Novelty Shop* (Aug. 16/*Color Rhapsody*), *In My Gondola* (Sept. 3/*Color Rhapsody*), *Looney Balloonists* (Sept. 24), *Merry Mutineers* (Oct. 2/*Color Rhapsody*), *Birds In Love* (Oct. 28/*Color Rhapsody*) and *A Boy And His Dog* (Dec. 23/*Color Rhapsody*).

1937: *Skeleton Frolic* (Iwerks/Jan. 29/*Color Rhapsody*), *Merry Mannequins* (Iwerks/Mar. 19/*Color Rhapsody*), *Puttin'*

Out The Kitten (Mar. 26), *Let's Go* (Apr. 10/*Color Rhapsody*), *Scrappy's Band Concert* (Apr. 29), *Mother Hen's Holiday* (May 7/*Color Rhapsody*), *The Foxy Pup* (Iwerks/May 21/*Color Rhapsody*), *Scrappy's Music Lesson* (June 4), *I Want To Be An Actress* (July 18), *Spring Festival* (Aug. 6/*Color Rhapsody*), *Scary Crows* (Aug. 20/*Color Rhapsody*), *Swing Monkey Swing* (Sept. 10/*Color Rhapsody*), *The Air Hostess* (Oct. 22), *The Little Match Girl* (Nov. 5/*Color Rhapsody*), *The Clock Goes Round And Round* (Nov. 6), *Dizzy Ducks* (Nov. 18) and *Scrappy's News Flashes* (Dec. 8).

1938: *Bluebird's Baby* (Jan. 21/*Color Rhapsody*), *Scrappy's Trip To Mars* (Feb. 4), *The Horses On The Merry—Go—Round* (Iwerks/Feb. 17/*Color Rhapsody*), *The Foolish Bunny* (Davis/Mar. 26/*Color Rhapsody*), *Scrappy's Playmates* (Mar. 27), *Showtime* (Iwerks/Apr. 14/*Color Rhapsody*), *The Big Birdcast* (May 13/*Color Rhapsody*), *Window Shopping* (Marcus/June 3/*Color Rhapsody*), *Poor Little Butterfly* (Harrison/July 4/*Color Rhapsody*), *The Frog Pond* (Iwerks/Aug. 12/*Color Rhapsody*), *Hollywood Graduation* (Davis/Aug. 26/*Color Rhapsody*), *The Early Bird* (Sept. 16), *Animal Cracker Circus* (Harrison/Sept. 23/*Color Rhapsody*), *Happy Birthday* (Oct. 7/*Color Rhapsody*), *Midnight Frolics* (Iwerks/Nov. 24/*Color Rhapsody*) and *Kangaroo Kid* (Harrison/Dec. 23/*Color Rhapsody*).

1939: *Scrappy's Added Attraction* (Jan. 13), *Peaceful Neighbors* (Marcus/Jan. 26/*Color Rhapsody*), *The Gorilla Hunt* (Iwerks/Feb. 24/*Color Rhapsody*), *Scrappy's Side Show* (Mar. 3), *The Happy Tots* (Harrison/Mar. 31/*Color Rhapsody*), *The House That Jack Built* (Marcus/Apr. 14/*Color Rhapsody*), *A Worm's Eye View* (Apr. 28), *Lucky Pigs* (Harrison/May 26/*Color Rhapsody*), *Nell's Yells* (Iwerks/June 30/*Color Rhapsody*), *Scrappy's Rodeo* (June 2), *Hollywood Sweepstakes* (Harrison/July 28/*Color Rhapsody*), *The Charm Bracelet* (Sept. 1/*Phantasy* cartoon), *Millionaire Hobo* (Nov. 24/*Phantasy* cartoon) and *Park Your Baby* (Dec. 22/*Fable* cartoon).

1940: *Man Of Tin* (Feb. 23/*Phantasy* cartoon), *Practice Makes Perfect* (Apr. 5/*Fable* cartoon), *Pooch Parade* (July 19/*Fable* cartoon), *A Peep In The Deep* (Aug. 23/*Fable* cartoon) and *Schoolboy Dreams* (Sept. 24/*Phantasy* cartoon).

SCREEN SONGS

Animator Seymour Kneitel created the *Follow the Bouncing Ball* series, which was first produced in the late 1920s and was later revived in the late 1940s by Famous Studios. The cartoons worked on the concept popularized in movie theaters of song—slides showing lyrics of well—known tunes to invite audiences to sing—a—long with live singers or musicians. Max and Dave Fleischer adapted the idea, committing it to animated drawings with live—action footage featuring the talents of famous musical personalities within the context of the films.

The early series installments were actually filmed without sound; the dialogue and sound were synchronized later. In the late 1940's series revival, the animated stars led the sing—a—longs, this time in Technicolor. As before, the bouncing ball was incorporated into the onscreen lyrics. *Isadore Spar-*

ber also directed the series. Black–and–white. Technicolor. A Fleischer Studios and Famous Studios release through Paramount Pictures.

Voices:
Jack Mercer and Mae Questel.

1929: *The Sidewalks Of New York* (Feb. 5), *Yankee Doodle Boy* (Mar. 1), *Old Black Joe* (Apr. 5), *Ye Old Melodies* (© May 3), *Daisy Bell* (May 31), *Chinatown My Chinatown* (Aug. 2), *Dixie* (Aug. 17), *Goodbye My Lady Love* (© Aug. 21), *My Pony Boy* (© Sept. 13), *Smiles* (Sept. 27), *Oh, You Beautiful Doll* (Oct. 14), *After The Ball* (Nov. 8), *Put On Your Old Grey Bonnet* (Nov. 22) and *I've Got Rings On My Fingers* (Dec. 17).

1930: *Bedilia* (Jan. 3), *In The Shade Of The Old Apple Tree* (Jan. 18), *I'm Afraid To Come Home In The Dark* (Jan. 30), *Prisoner's Song* (Mar. 1), *La Paloma* (Mar. 20), *I'm Forever Blowing Bubbles* (Mar. 30), *Yes! We Have No Bananas* (Apr. 25), *Come Take A Trip In My Airship* (May 23), *In The Good Old Summer Time* (June 6), *A Hot Time In The Old Town Tonight* (Aug. 1), *The Glow Worm* (Aug. 18), *The Stein Song* (with Rudy Vallee/Sept. 6), *Strike Up The Band* (Sept. 26), *My Gal Sal* (Oct. 18), *Mariutch* (Nov. 15), *On A Sunday Afternoon* (Nov. 25) and *Row, Row, Row* (Dec. 19).

1931: *Please Go 'Way And Let Me Sleep* (Jan. 9), *By The Beautiful Sea* (Jan. 23), *I Wonder Who's Kissing Her Now* (Feb. 13), *I'd Climb The Highest Mountain* (Mar. 7), *Somebody Stole My Gal* (Mar. 20), *Any Little Girl That's A Nice Little Girl* (Apr. 16), *Alexander's Ragtime Band* (May 9), *And The Green Grass Grew All Around* (June 1), *My Wife's Gone To The Country* (© June 12), *That Old Gang Of Mine* (© July 9), *Betty Go–Ed* (with Rudy Vallee/Aug. 1), *Mr. Gallagher And Mr. Shean* (Aug. 29), *You're Driving Me Crazy* (Sept. 19), *Little Annie Rooney* (Oct. 10), *Kitty From Kansas City* (with Rudy Vallee/Nov. 1), *By The Light Of The Silvery Moon* (Nov. 14), *My Baby Cares For Me* (Dec. 5) and *Russian Lullaby* (with Arthur Tracy/Dec. 26).

1932: *Sweet Jenny Lee* (Jan. 9), *Show Me The Way To Go Home* (Jan. 30), *When The Red Red Robin Comes Bob Bob Bobbin' Along* (Feb. 19), *Wait Till The Sun Shines, Nellie* (Mar. 4), *Just One More Chance* (Apr. 1), *Oh! How I Hate To Get Up In The Morning* (Apr. 22), *Shine On Harvest Moon* (with Alice Joy/May 6), *Let Me Call You Sweetheart* (with Ethel Merman/May 20), *It's Ain't Got Nobody* (with The Mills Brothers/June 17), *You Try Somebody Else* (with Ethel Merman/July 29), *Rudy Vallee Melodies* (with Betty Boop/Aug. 5), *Down Along The Sugar Cane* (with Lillian Roth/Aug. 26), *Just A Gigolo* (with Irene Bordini/Sept. 9), *School Days* (with Gus Edwards/Sept. 30), *Romantic Melodies* (with Arthur Tracy/Oct. 21), *When It's Sleepy Time Down South* (with The Boswell Sisters/Nov. 11), *Sing A Song* (with James Melton/Dec. 2) and *Time On My Hands* (with Ethel Merman/Dec. 23).

1933: *Dinah* (with The Mills Brothers/Jan. 13), *Ain't She Sweet* (with Lillian Roth/Feb. 3), *Reaching For The Moon* (with Arthur Tracy/Feb. 24), *Aloha Oe* (with The Royal Sa-

moans/Mar. 17), *Popular Melodies* (with Arthur Jarrett/Apr. 7), *The Peanut Vendor* (with Armida/Apr. 28), *Song Shopping* (with Ethel Merman, Johnny Green/May 19), *Boilesk* (with The Watson Sisters/June 9), *Sing, Sisters, Sing!* (with The Three X Sisters/June 30), *Down By The Old Mill Stream* (with The Funny Boners/July 21), *Stoopnocracy* (with Stoopnagle and Budd/Aug. 18), *When Yuba Plays The Rumba On The Tuba* (with The Mills Brothers/Sept. 15), *Boo, Boo, Theme Song* (with The Funny Boners/Oct. 3), *I Like Mountain Music* (with The Eton Boys/Nov. 10) and *Sing, Babies, Sing* (with Baby Rose Marie/Dec. 15).

1934: *Keeps Rainin' All The Time* (with Gertrude Niesen/Jan. 12), *Let's All Sing Like The Birdies Sing* (with Reis and Dunn/Feb. 9), *Tune Up And Sing* (with Lanny Ross/Mar. 9), *Lazy Bones* (with Borrah Minevitch and His Harmonica Rascals/Apr. 13), *This Little Piggie Went To The Market* (with Singin' Sam/May 25), *She Reminds Me Of You* (with Eton Boys/June 22) and *Love Thy Neighbor* (with Mary Small/July 20).

1935: *I Wished On The Moon* (with Abe Lyman and His Orchestra/Sept. 20) and *It's Easy To Remember* (with Richard Himber and His Orchestra/Nov. 29).

1936: *No Other One* (with Hal Kemp and His Orchestra/Jan. 24), *I Feel Like A Feather In The Breeze* (with Jack Denny and His Orchestra/Mar. 27), *I Don't Want To Make History* (with Vincent Lopez and His Orchestra/May 22), *The Hills Of Old Wyomin'* (with The Westerners/July 31), *I Can't Escape From You* (with Joe Reichman and His Orchestra/Sept. 25) and *Talking Through My Heart* (with Dick Stable and His Orchestra, Gracie Barrie/Nov. 27).

1937: *Never Should Have Told You* (with Nat Bradywine and His Orchestra, Marine Tappen/Jan. 29), *Twilight On The Trail* (with The Westerners/Mar. 26), *Please Keep Me In Your Dreams* (with Henry King and His Orchestra/May 28), *You Came To My Rescue* (with Shep Fields and His Orchestra/July 30), *Whispers In The Dark* (with Gus Arnheim and His Orchestra/Sept. 24) and *Magic On Broadway* (with Jay Freeman and His Orchestra/Nov. 26).

1938: *You Took The Words Right Out Of My Heart* (with Jerry Blaine and His Orchestra/Jan. 28), *Thanks For The Memory* (with Bert Block and His Orchestra/Mar. 25), *You Leave Me Breathless* (with Jimmy Dorsey and His Orchestra/May 27) and *Beside A Moonlit Stream* (with Frank Dailey and His Orchestra/July 29).

Famous Studios
1947: *The Circus Comes To Town* (Sparber/Dec. 26).

1948: *Base Brawl* (Jan. 23), *Little Brown Jug* (Kneitel/Feb. 20), *The Golden State* (Mar. 12), *Winter Draws On* (Mar. 19), *Sing Or Swim* (Kneitel/June 16), *Camptown Races* (Kneitel/July 30), *The Lone Star State* (Sparber/Aug. 20) and *Readin', Ritin', and Rhythmetic* (Kneitel/Oct. 22).

1949: *The Funshine State* (Kneitel/Jan. 7), *The Emerald Isle* (Kneitel/Feb. 25), *Comin' Round The Mountain* (Sparber/Mar. 11), *The Stork Market* (Kneitel/Apr. 8), *Spring Song*

(Sparber/June 3), *The Ski's The Limit* (Sparber/June 24), *Toys Will Be Toys* (Kneitel/July 15), *Farm Foolery* (Kneitel/Aug. 5), *Our Funny Finny Friends* (Kneitel/Aug. 26), *Marriage Wows* (Sparber/Sept. 16), *The Big Flame–Up* (Sparber/Sept. 30), *Strolling Thru The Park* (Kneitel/Nov. 4), *The Big Drip* (Sparber/Nov. 25/song: *Ain't Gonna Rain No More*) and *Snow Foolin'* (Sparber/Dec. 16/song: *Jingle Bells*).

1950: *Blue Hawaii* (Kneitel/Jan. 13), *Detouring Thru Maine* (Kneitel/Feb. 17/song: *Maine Stein Song*), *Shortenin' Bread* (Sparber/Mar. 24), *Win, Place And Showboat* (Sparber/Apr. 28/song: *Waitin' For The Robert E. Lee*), *Jingle, Jangle, Jungle* (Kneitel/May 9/song: *Civilization—Bongo Bongo Bongo*), *Heap Hep Injuns* (Sparber/June 30/song: *My Pony Boy*), *Gobs Of Fun* (Sparber/July 28/song: *Strike Up The Band*) *Helter Swel-ter* (Kneitel/Aug. 25/song: *In The Good Old Summertime*), *Boos In The Night* (Sparber/Sept. 22/song: *Pack Up Your Troubles*), *Fiesta Time* (Kneitel/Nov. 17/song: *El Rancho Grande*) and *Fresh Yeggs* (Kneitel/Nov. 17/song: *Give My Regards To Broadway*).

1951: *Tweet Music* (Sparber/Feb. 9/song: *Let's All Sing Like The Birdies Sing*), *Drippy Mississippi* (Kneitel/Apr. 13/song: *M–i–s–s–i–s–s–i–p–p–i*), *Miners Forty–Niners* (Sparber/May 18/song: *Clementine*) and *Sing Again Of Michigan* (Sparber/June 29/song: *I Wanted To Go Back To Michigan Down On The Farm*).

SCREWY SQUIRREL

The bushy–tailed squirrel was a short–lived MGM character who manifested on screen animator/creator Tex Avery's wild and brash humor. During the planning stages of the first cartoon, MGM animators simply dubbed the character "the squirrel" before he was actually named. Nonetheless, MGM made quite an effort to sell the new character, releasing three cartoons in the first year. Unfortunately, Screwy was a bit too wild for filmgoers' tastes. Exhibiting the same brashness of Bugs Bunny and Woody Woodpecker, in the eyes of the public, he lacked the endearing qualities that were necessary to make him a "likeable" star. *Directed by Tex Avery. Technicolor. Voice credits unknown. A Metro–Goldwyn–Mayer release.*

1944: *Screwball Squirrel* (Apr. 1), *Happy Go Nutty* (June 24) and *Big Heel Watha* (Oct. 21/formerly *Buck Of The North*).

1945: *Screwy Truant* (Jan. 13).

1946: *Lonesome Lenny* (Mar. 9).

SIDNEY THE ELEPHANT

The final creation of Gene Deitch's regime as creative director for Terrytoons, this series helped restore the studio's image as a major cartoon producer. Deitch, who joined the studio in 1965, developed a number of starring characters after revamping the animation department. Sidney was by far his most likeable character, a neurotic, frustrated elephant who sucks on his trunk for security and feels ill–suited for life in

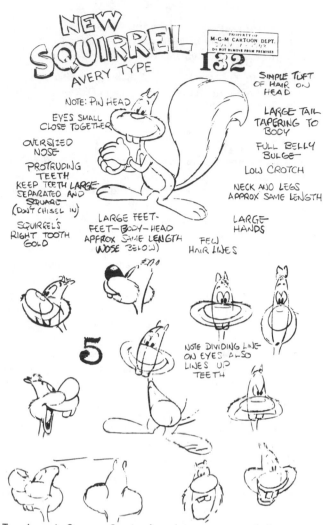

Tex Avery's Screwy Squirrel underwent several changes before appearing in his first cartoon, Screwball Squirrel. This was the second model sheet for the character who, up to this point, was nameless. © Turner Entertainment

the jungle. Pals Stanley the Lion and Cleo the Giraffe were always on hand to protect him from serious danger.

The series' second cartoon, *Sidney's Family Tree*, marked another breakthrough for the studio: It won the first Academy Award nomination for Terrytoons in 13 years. Episodes later found television exposure as part of "The Hector Heathcote Show." *Directors were Arthur Bartsch, Martin B. Taras, Dave Tendlar and Connie Rasinski. Technicolor. CinemaScope. A Terrytoons Production released through 20th Century–Fox.*

Voices:

Sidney the Elephant: Lionel Wilson, Dayton Allen, **Stanley the Lion:** Dayton Allen, **Cleo the Giraffe:** Dayton Allen

1958: *Sick, Sick Sidney* (Bartsch/Aug.).

1960: *Hide And Go Sidney* (Bartsch/Jan./CinemaScope), *Tusk Tusk* (Taras/Apr. 3), *The Littlest Bully* (Taras/Aug. 9/CinemaScope) and *Two Ton Baby Sitter* (Tendlar/Sept. 4/CinemaScope).

1962: *Peanut Battle* (Rasinski/Apr. 25/CinemaScope), *Send Your Elephant To Camp* (Bartsch/July 4/CinemaScope) and *Home Life* (Rasinski/CinemaScope).

1963: *To Be Or Not To Be* (Rasinski/CinemaScope), *Sidney's White Elephant* (Bartsch/May 1) and *Driven To Extraction* (Bartsch/June 28).

SILLY SYMPHONIES

Long wanting a series in the form of *Aesop's Fables*, Walt Disney fulfilled his dream by producing this series of non-standard character cartoons that evoked settings, seasons and events. The series was actually proposed by musical director Carl Stalling, who had composed and arranged music for Mickey Mouse's historic *Steamboat Willie* (1928).

The first cartoon officially to launch the series was entitled, *The Skeleton Dance*, animated by Disney's long–time associate, Ub Iwerks. The series went on to introduce the first three–strip Technicolor cartoon, *Flowers and Trees*, perhaps the most imaginatively drawn cartoon from this era. (The film appropriately won an Academy Award for Best Short Film (Cartoon).)

The addition of color ensured the success of the *Silly Symphony* series which lasted six more years and produced more classic cartoons like *Three Little Pigs*. *Directors were Walt Disney, Ub Iwerks, Burt Gillett, Wilfred Jackson, David Hand, Ben Sharpsteen, Dick Lundy, Hugh Harman, Rudolf Ising, Jack Cutting and Graham Heid. Black–and–white. Technicolor. A Walt Disney Production released through Columbia Pictures, United Artists and RKO–Radio Pictures.*

Columbia Pictures Releases
1928–1929: *The Skeleton Dance* (Disney), *El Terrible Toreador* (Disney), *Springtime* (Iwerks), *Hell's Bell's* (Iwerks) and *The Merry Dwarfs* (Disney).

1930: *Summer* (Iwerks/Jan. 6), *Autumn* (Iwerks/Feb. 13), *Cannibal Capers* (Gillett/Mar. 13), *Frolicking Fish* (Gillett/May 8), *Arctic Antics* (Iwerks/June 5), *In A Toy Shop* (Gillett/July 3/copyrighted as *Midnight In A Toy Shop*), *Night* (Disney/July 31), *Monkey Melodies* (Gillett/Aug. 10), *Winter* (Gillett/Nov. 5) and *Playful Pan* (Gillett/Dec. 28).

1931: *Birds Of A Feather* (Gillett/Feb. 10), *Mother Goose Melodies* (Apr. 17), *The China Plate* (Jackson/May 25), *The Busy Beavers* (Jackson/June 22), *The Cat's Out* (Jackson/July 28/originally *The Cat's Nightmare*), *Egyptian Melodies* (Jackson/Aug. 21), *The Clock Store* (Jackson/Sept. 30/originally *In A Clock Store*), *The Spider And The Fly* (Jackson/Oct. 16), *The Fox Hunt* (Jackson/Nov. 18) and *The Ugly Duckling* (Jackson/ Dec. 16).

1932: *The Bird Store* (Jackson/Jan. 16).

United Artists Releases
1932: *The Bears And The Bees* (Jackson/July 9), *Just Dogs* (Gillett/July 30), *Flowers And Trees* (Gillett/Sept. 30/first color *Silly Symphony* cartoon), *King Neptune* (Gillett/Sept. 10), *Bugs In Love* (Gillett/Oct. 1), *Babes In The Woods* (Gillett/Nov. 19/all *Silly Symphony* cartoons in color from this point on) and *Santa's Workshop* (Jackson/Dec. 10).

1933: *Birds In The Spring* (Hand/Mar. 11), *Father Noah's Ark* (Jackson/Apr. 8), *Three Little Pigs* (Gillett/May 27/A.A. winner), *Old King Cole* (Hand/July 29), *Lullaby Land* (Jackson/Aug. 19), *The Pied Piper* (Jackson/Sept. 16) and *The Night Before Christmas* (Jackson/Dec. 9).

1934: *The China Shop* (Jackson/Jan. 13), *Grasshopper And The Ants* (Jackson/Feb. 10), *Funny Little Bunnies* (Jackson/Mar. 24), *The Big Bad Wolf* (Gillett/Apr. 14), *The Wise Little Hen* (Jackson/June 9/first appearance of Donald Duck), *The Flying Mouse* (Hand/July 14), *Peculiar Penguins* (Jackson/Sept. 1) and *The Goddess Of Spring* (Jackson/Nov. 3).

1935: *The Tortoise And The Hare* (Jackson/Jan. 5/A.A. winner), *The Golden Touch* (Disney/Mar. 22), *The Robber Kitten* (Hand/Apr. 20), *Water Babies* (Jackson/May 11), *The Cookie Carnival* (Sharpsteen/May 25), *Who Killed Cock Robin?* (Hand/June 29/A.A. nominee), *Music Land* (Jackson/Oct. 5), *Three Orphan Kittens* (Hand/Oct. 26/A.A. winner), *Cock O' The Walk* (Sharpsteen/Nov. 30) and *Broken Toys* (Sharpsteen/Dec. 14).

1936: *Elmer Elephant* (Jackson/Mar. 28), *Three Little Wolves* (Hand/Apr. 18), *Toby Tortoise Returns* (Jackson/Aug. 22), *Three Blind Mouseketeers* (Hand/Sept. 26), *The Country Cousin* (Jackson/Oct. 31/A.A. winner), *Mother Pluto* (Nov. 14) and *More Kittens* (Hand/Dec. 19).

1937: *Woodland Cafe* (Jackson/Mar. 13) and *Little Hiawatha* (Hand/May 15).

RKO–Radio Pictures Releases
1937: *The Old Mill* (Jackson/Nov. 5/A.A. winner).

1938: *Moth And The Flame* (Gillett/Apr. 1), *Wynken, Blynken, And Nod* (Heid/May 27), *Farmyard Symphony* (Cutting/Oct. 14), *Merbabies* (supervised by Disney, Sharpsteen, Hand, Englander; directed by Rudolf Ising for Harman–Ising Studios/Dec. 9) and *Mother Goose Goes Hollywood* (Jackson/Dec. 23/A.A. nominee).

1939: *The Ugly Duckling* (Cutting/Apr. 7/A.A. winner).

SNIFFLES

Director Chuck Jones created this naive, bewhiskered mouse who spoke with a squealing dialect and constantly found himself in precarious situations. Sniffles personified the "cute" personalities that launched the careers of animators Hugh Harman and Rudolf Ising at the same studio. In fact, in some respects, Jones' character bore a striking resemblance to Harman's Little Buck Cheeser.

Introduced in 1939's *Naughty But Mice*, even Jones admitted the Sniffles cartoons were "often too long. When I had extra time, I'd tend to make the pans too long and the movement too slow."

Sniffles' squeaky voice was provided by Bernice Hansen, a veteran voice artist best known for her animal characters. Jones derived Sniffles' name from the fact that he always had "a code in da nose." *Directed by Chuck Jones. Technicolor. A Warner Brothers release.*

Voices:
Sniffles: Bernice Hansen

Merrie Melodies
1939: *Naughty But Mice* (Jones/May 30), *Little Brother Rat* (Jones/Sept. 2) and *Sniffles The Bookworm* (Jones/Dec. 2).

1940: *Sniffles Takes A Trip* (Jones/May 22), *The Egg Collector* (Jones/July 20) and *Bedtime For Sniffles* (Jones/Nov. 23).

1941: *Sniffles Bells The Cat* (Jones/Feb. 1), *Toy Trouble* (Jones/Apr. 12) and *Brave Little Bat* (Jones/Sept. 27).

1943: *The Unbearable Bear* (Jones/Apr. 17).

1944: *Lost And Foundling* (Jones/Aug. 30).

Looney Tunes
1946: *Hush My Mouse* (Jones/May 4).

SPEEDY GONZALES

Possessing the speed of the Road Runner and the quick–wittedness of Tweety bird, Speedy Gonzales was the mischievous Mexican mouse, jaunty in his chic sombero, who boasted a spitfire running speed of 100 miles per hour. He was often paired with Sylvester the Cat and Daffy Duck in adventures reminiscent of MGM's Tom and Jerry cartoons.

The idea for Speedy's character originated in a Robert McKimson cartoon of 1953 called, *Cat–Tails For Two*. The story was about an idiotic cat–and–dog team who sneak into a Mexican strip in search of mice but discover that the rodents are too fast to be caught. The head mouse is unnamed in the film and bears little resemblance to the Speedy movie audiences grew up with.

Friz Freleng remembered McKimson's mouse character two years later and redesigned him with animator Hawley Pratt into "the fastest mouse in all of Mexico." Speedy's first cartoon was the 1955 entry, *Speedy Gonzales*. The film was accorded the film industry's highest honor, an Academy Award, for best cartoon of the year.

In upcoming adventures, Speedy was given a comic side-kick, Slowpoke Rodriquez, whose lethargic personality never caught on. He was limited to occasional guest appearances. *Directors were Robert McKimson, Friz Freleng, Hawley Pratt, Rudy Larriva and Alex Lovy. Technicolor. A Warner Brothers release.*

Voices:
Speedy Gonzales: Mel Blanc

Merrie Melodies
1953: *Cat–Tails For Two* (McKimson/Aug. 29).

1955: *Speedy Gonzales* (with Sylvester the Cat/Freleng/Sept. 17/A.A. winner).

1957: *Tabasco Road* (with Sylvester the Cat/McKimson/July 20/A.A. nominee).

1960: *West of The Pesos* (with Sylvester the Cat/McKimson/Jan. 23).

" SPEEDY GONZALES "

© WARNER BROS. PICTURES INC.

Boasting a spitfire running speed, Friz Freleng's Speedy Gonzales kept far ahead of his pursuers in assorted Warner Brothers misadventures. © Warner Brothers, Inc.

1963: *Mexican Cat Dance* (Freleng/Apr. 20) and *Chili Weather* (with Sylvester/Freleng/Aug. 17).

DePatie–Freleng Enterprises Releases
1964: *Road to Andaly* (with Sylvester the Cat/Freleng, Pratt/Dec. 26).

1965: *Cats And Bruises* (with Sylvester the Cat/Freleng/Jan. 30), *The Wild Chase* (Freleng/Feb. 27), *Suppressed Duck* (with Daffy Duck/McKimson/May 22) and *Go Go Amigo* (with Daffy Duck/McKimson/Nov. 20).

1966: *Muchos Locos* (McKimson/Feb. 5), *Mexican Mouse-piece* (with Daffy Duck/McKimson/Feb. 26), *Snow Excuse* (with Daffy Duck/McKimson/May 21), *Feather Finger* (with Daffy Duck/McKimson/Aug. 20), *Chili Corn Corny* (with Daffy Duck/McKimson/Oct. 23) and *A Taste of Catnip* (with Daffy Duck/McKimson/Dec. 3).

Warner Brothers Releases
1967: *Daffy's Diner* (with Daffy Duck/McKimson/Jan. 21), *The Music Mice–Tro* (with Daffy Duck/Larriva/May 27), *Speedy Ghost To Town* (with Miguel/Lovy/July 29) and *Go Away Stowaway* (with Daffy Duck/Lovy/Sept. 30).

1968: *Skyscraper Caper* (with Daffy Duck/Lovy/Mar.9).

Looney Tunes
1957: *Gonzales' Tamales* (with Sylvester the Cat/Freleng/Nov. 30).

1958: *Tortilla Flaps* (McKimson/Jan. 18).

1959: *Mexicali Shmoes* (with Slowpoke Rodriguez/Freleng/July 4) and *Here Today, Gone Tamale* (Freleng/Aug. 29).

1961: *Cannery Woe* (McKimson/Jan. 7), *The Pied Piper of Guadalupe* (with Sylvester, Slowpoke Rodriguez/Freleng, Pratt/Aug. 19/A.A. nominee).

1962: *Mexican Borders* (with Sylvester the Cat, Slowpoke Rodriguez/Freleng, Pratt/May 12).

DePatie–Freleng Enterprises Releases
1964: *A Message To Gracias* (with Sylvester the Cat/McKimson/Feb. 8), *Nuts And Volts* (with Sylvester the Cat/Freleng/Apr. 25) and *Pancho's Hideaway* (Freleng, Pratt/Oct. 24).

1965: *It's Nice To Have Mouse Around The House* (with Sylvester the Cat/Freleng, Pratt/Jan. 16) and *Tease For Two* (with Goofy Gophers/McKimson/Aug. 28).

1966: *The Astroduck* (with Daffy Duck/McKimson/Jan. 1), *Daffy Rents* (with Daffy Duck/McKimson/Mar. 26), *A–Haunting We Will Go* (with Daffy Duck, Witch Hazel/McKimson/Apr. 16), *A Squeak In The Deep* (with Daffy Duck/McKimson/July 19), *Swing Ding Amigo* (with Daffy Duck/McKimson/Sept. 6) and *A Taste Of Catnip* (with Daffy Duck/McKimson/Dec. 3).

Warner Brothers Releases
1967: *Quacker Tracker* (with Daffy Duck/Larriva/Apr. 29), *The Spy Swatter* (with Daffy Duck/Larriva/June 24), *Rodent To Stardom* (with Daffy Duck/Lovy/Sept. 23) and *Fiesta Fiasco* (with Daffy Duck/Lovy/Dec. 9).

1968: *See Ya Later, Gladiator* (with Daffy Duck/Lovy/June 29).

SPIKE

Originally developed as a supporting character in MGM's *Droopy* series, Tex Avery featured this gentle bulldog in traditional chaotic cartoon situations in a starring series of his own. Bill Thompson, also the voice of Droopy, played Spike in the series. *Directed by Tex Avery. Technicolor. A Metro–Goldwyn–Mayer release.*

Voices:
Spike: Bill Thompson

1949: *Counterfeit Cat* (Dec. 24).

1950: *Ventriloquist Cat* (May 27) and *Garden Gopher* (Sept. 30/originally *Sting Time In The Rockies*).

1951: *Cock A Doodle Dog* (Feb. 10).

1952: *Rock–A–Bye Bear* (July 12).

SPIKE AND CHESTER

Spike, a tough street–wise dog, and his admiring pal, Chester, were short–lived screen stars who appeared in several Warner Brothers cartoons. The tandem began their screen careers in 1952's *Tree For Two*, co–starring Sylvester the Cat, of "Tweety and Sylvester" fame. *Directed by Friz Freleng. Technicolor. A Warner Brothers Release.*

Voices:
Spike: Mel Blanc, **Chester:** Stan Freberg

Merrie Melodies
1952: *Tree For Two* (with Sylvester the Cat/Oct. 4).

Looney Tunes
1954: *Dr. Jerkyl's Hide* (May 8).

SPIKE AND TYKE

William Hanna and Joseph Barbera created this father–and–son dog team—Spike, the gruff father, and Tyke, the impish son—as supporting players in MGM's *Tom and Jerry* series. The characters first appeared as Tom and Jerry in 1942's *Dog Trouble*. Hanna and Barbera later modified and cast the pair in their own series in the late 1950s. The series had a brief existence, primarily because it never captured the imagination of their original appearances.

Spike and Tyke later served as the basis for Hanna and Barbera's popular television characters, Augie Doggy and Doggy Daddy. *Directed by William Hanna and Joseph Barbera. Technicolor. CinemaScope. A Metro–Goldwyn–Mayer release.*

Voices:
Spike: Bill Thompson, Daws Butler

1942: *Dog Trouble* (with Tom and Jerry/Apr. 18).

1944: *The Bodyguard* (with Tom and Jerry/July 22) and *Puttin' On The Dog* (with Tom and Jerry/Oct. 28).

1945: *Quiet Please* (with Tom and Jerry/ Dec. 22/A.A. winner).

1946: *Cat Fishin'* (with Tom and Jerry/Mar. 15) and *Solid Serenade* (with Tom and Jerry/Aug. 31).

1947: *The Invisible Mouse* (with Tom and Jerry/Sept. 27).

1948: *The Truce Hurts* (with Tom and Jerry/July 17).

1949: *Heavenly Puss* (with Tom and Jerry/July 9) and *Love That Pup* (with Tom and Jerry/Oct. 1).

1950: *The Framed Cat* (with Tom and Jerry/Oct. 21).

1951: *Slicked–Up Pup* (with Tom and Jerry/Sept. 8).

1952: *Fit To Be Tied* (with Tom and Jerry/July 26) and *The Doghouse* (with Tom and Jerry/Nov. 29).

1953: *That's My Pup* (with Tom and Jerry/Apr. 25).

1954: *Hic–Cup Pup* (with Tom and Jerry/Apr. 17) and *Pet Peeve* (with Tom and Jerry/Nov. 20/CinemaScope).

1955: *Pup On A Picnic* (with Tom and Jerry/Apr. 30/ CinemaScope).

1956: *Barbecue Brawl* (with Tom and Jerry/Dec. 14).

1957: *Give And Tyke* (Mar. 29/first Spike and Tyke/ CinemaScope), *Scat Cats* (July 26/CinemaScope) and *Tom's Photo Finish* (with Tom and Jerry/Nov. 1/CinemaScope).

SPUNKY

Spunky, one of several minor *Noveltoons* characters, appeared on the screen for the first time in 1944's *Yankee Doodle Donkey.* The character did not star again in another cartoon until 14 years after his screen debut. *Directed by Isadore Sparber. Technicolor. A Famous Studios Production released through Paramount Pictures.*

1944: *Yankee Doodle Donkey* (Nov. 27).

1958: *Okey Dokey Donkey* (Sparber/May 16).

STONE AGE CARTOONS

Following the success of *Gulliver's Travels* (1939), Max Fleischer unveiled two cartoon series, the first featuring the comic exploits of stone age life. The series pre–dated TV's "The Flintstones" by 20 years, but, unlike the television classic, this novel series died a quick death. No central characters starred in the films, which may have been one reason for the series' failure. *Technicolor. No voice credits. A Fleischer Studios Production released through Paramount Pictures.*

1940: *Granite Hotel* (Apr. 26), *The Foul Ball Player* (May 24), *The Ugly Dino* (June 14), *Wedding Belts* (July 5), *Way Back When A Razberry Was A Fruit* (July 26), *The Fulla Bluff Man* (Aug. 9), *Springtime In The Rock Age* (Aug. 30), *Pedagogical Institution (College To You)* (Sept. 13) and *Way Back When Women Had Their Weigh* (Sept. 26).

SUGARFOOT

Originally a character in a Woody Woodpecker cartoon, Walter Lantz attempted to cast the lame horse, Sugarfoot, in a cartoon series of his own. The series did not produce much interest, however, as only two films were produced. *Directed by Paul J. Smith. Technicolor. A Walter Lantz Production released through Univeral Pictures.*

1954: *A Horse's Tale* (Feb. 15) and *Hay Rube* (June 7).

SUPERMAN

First conceived by Jerry Siegel and Joe Schuster for "Action Comics," this legendary man of steel was adapted to the screen in 1941, based on the comic book novelizations.

As in the comics, the city of Metropolis was the newspaper beat for mild–mannered reporter Clark Kent of the *Daily Planet.* Beneath his meek exterior was a Herculean superhero able to leap tall buildings in a single bound, more powerful than a locomotive and faster than a speeding bullet.

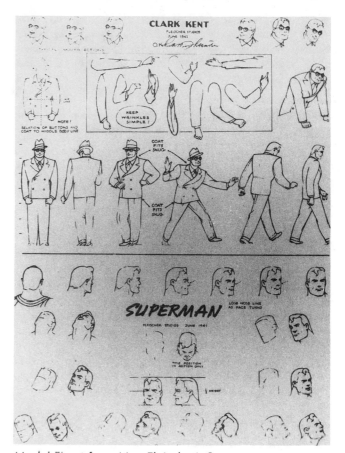

Model Sheet from Max Fleischer's Superman cartoon series.

The supporting cast of characters was also intact: pretty newspaper gal Lois Lane, cub–reporter Jimmy Olsen, and blustering editor–in–chief Perry White.

Both Fleischer Studios and Famous Studios produced the series. *The Japoteurs* was the first Famous cartoon. The original Fleischer cartoons used Rotoscoping to give animation a semi–realistic look and attention to detail never to be matched in later television versions of the series. Action and special effects were key elements of the series, which was backed by a tremendous promotional campaign when it was introduced.

Director Dave Fleischer contracted two actors from the radio version, Bud Collyer and Joan Alexander, to voice Clark Kent/Superman and Lois Lane. *Directors were Dave Fleischer, Seymour Kneitel, Isadore Sparber and Dan Gordon. Technicolor. A Fleischer Studios and Famous Studios Production released through Paramount Pictures.*

Voices:

Clark Kent/Superman: Clayton "Bud" Collyer, **Lois Lane:** Joan Alexander

Fleischer Studios Releases

1941: *Superman* (Fleischer/Sept. 26/originally *The Mad Scientist*/A.A. nominee) and *The Mechanical Monsters* (Kneitel/Nov. 21).

1942: *Billion Dollar Limited* (Fleischer/Jan. 9), *The Arctic Giant* (Fleischer/Feb. 27), *The Bulleteers* (Fleischer/Mar. 26), *The Magnetic Telescope* (Fleischer/Apr. 24), *Electric Earthquake* (Fleischer/May 15), *Volcano* (Fleischer/July 10) and *Terror On The Midway* (Fleischer/Aug. 28).

Famous Studios Releases
1942: *Japoteurs* (Kneitel/Sept. 18), *Showdown* (Sparber/ Oct. 16), *Eleventh Hour* (Gordon/Nov. 20) and *Destruction, Inc* (Sparber/Dec. 25).

1943: *The Mummy Strikes* (Sparber/Feb. 19), *Jungle Drums* (Gordon/Mar. 26), *Underground World* (Kneitel/June 18) and *Secret Agent* (Kneitel/July 30).

SWIFTY AND SHORTY

A fast–talking con man, Swifty, and his pudgy friend, Shorty, appeared in this series of misadventures patterned after comedy greats, Abbott and Costello. Formerly "Jeepers and Creepers," the characters under their new identities were re–cast in several cartoon shorts—*Noveltoon* and *Modern Madcap* releases—before being given their own star–billed series in 1964. Comedian Eddie Lawrence, who voiced the *Jeepers and Creepers* series, supplied the voices for this series as well. *Directed by Seymour Kneitel and Howard Post. Technicolor. A Famous Studios Production released through Paramount Pictures.*

Voices:
Swifty: Eddie Lawrence, **Shorty:** Eddie Lawrence

1962: *Without Time Or Reason* (Kneitel/Jan./*Noveltoon*), *Hi–Fi Jinx* (Kneitel/Mar./*Modern Madcap*) and *T.V. Or Not T.V.* (Kneitel/Mar./*Noveltoon*).

1964: *Panhandling On Madison Avenue* (Kneitel/Apr.), *Fizzicle Fizzle* (Kneitel/Apr.), *Sailing Zero* (Kneitel/Apr.), *Fix That Clock* (Kneitel/May), *A Friend In Tweed* (Kneitel/May), *The Once–Over* (Kneitel/June), *Call Me A Taxi* (Kneitel/July), *Highway Snobbery* (Kneitel/July), *Hip Hip Ole* (Kneitel/Sept.), *Accidents Will Happen* (Kneitel/Sept.) and *The Bus Way To Travel* (Kneitel/Oct.).

1965: *Interior Decorator* (Post/June), *Ocean Bruise* (Post/ Sept.), *Getting Ahead* (Post) and *Les Boys* (Post/Dec.).

SWING SYMPHONIES

Popular jazz tunes of the 1940s were the basis of this series produced and created by Walter Lantz. Episodes featured no running characters and early versions concentrated on boogie–woogie type music evidenced by such series titles as *Yankee Doodle Swing Shift* and *Cow Cow Boogie.*

Lantz paid a hefty price to produce these ambitious musical oddities, from $9,500 to $12,000 per one–reeler. As he told biographer Joe Adamson: "I loved to make musicals, but you can't cheat on musicals. You've got to animate to the beat."

In 1944, the series ran its course and two years later, Lantz replaced it with another musical series entitled, *Musical Miniatures. Directed by Walter Lantz, Alex Lovy, Ben Hardaway, Emery Hawkins, James "Shamus" Culhane and Dick*

Popular songs like "Cow Cow Boogie" were adapted into one-reel cartoons for Walter Lantz's Swing Symphonies series. © Walter Lantz Productions

Lundy. Black–and–white. Technicolor. A Walter Lantz Production released through Universal Pictures.

1941: *$21,000 A Day Once A Month* (Lantz/Dec. 1).

1942: *Juke Box Jamboree* (Lovy/July 27), *Yankee Doodle Swing Shift* (Lovy/Sept. 21) and *Boogie Woogie Sioux* (Lovy/ Nov. 30).

1943: *Cow Cow Boogie* (Lovy/Jan. 5), *Egg Cracker Suite* (with Oswald the Rabbit/Hardaway, Hawkins/Mar. 22), *Swing Your Partner* (with Homer Pigeon/Lovy), *Pass The Biscuits Mirandy* (Culhane/Aug. 23) and *Boogie Woogie Man* (Culhane/Sept. 27).

1944: *Jungle Jive* (Culhane/May 15) and *Abou Ben Boogie* (Culhane/Sept. 18).

1945: *The Pied Piper of Basin Street* (Culhane/Jan. 15) and *The Sliphorn King of Polaroo* (Lundy/Mar. 19).

SYLVESTER THE CAT

Often co–starring opposite the resourceful canary Tweety, Sylvester the Cat enjoyed an accomplished solo career before teaming up with the slippery yellow canary. The lisping cat, whose voice was similar to Daffy Duck's, was first used in Friz Freleng's 1945, *Life With Feathers,* ironically appearing with a lovelorn lovebird. It was in this film debut he uttered his now famous line of "Sufferin' succotash."

Sylvester next appeared in Freleng's *Peck Up Your Troubles* (1945), this time opposite a woodpecker, and as a ringleader of a quartet of cats in Bob Clampett's *Kitty Kornered* (1946), before Freleng paired the exasperated cat with Tweety the bird in 1947's *Tweety Pie.* (Clampett did the preliminary story for the film, but Freleng assumed the property after Clampett left the studio that same year.)

While the cartoon became the first starring role for Sylvester, it also became the first Warner cartoon to win an Oscar for Best Short Subject of the year. (In the film, he is referred to as Thomas, not Sylvester.) Sylvester was given a series of his own in 1953, appearing in cartoons opposite his ever-energetic son, Sylvester Jr., and Hippety Hopper, the hopping kangaroo, who Sylvester constantly mistakes for an oversized "mouse." The sly pussycat made intermittent appearances with Elmer J. Fudd and Porky Pig in other cartoon shenanigans. *Directed by Friz Freleng, Charles M. Jones, Bob Clampett, Robert McKimson, Hawley Pratt and Gerry Chiniquy. Technicolor. A Warner Brothers release.*

Voices:

Sylvester the Cat: Mel Blanc, **Sylvester Jr.:** Mel Blanc, **Tweety:** Mel Blanc

Merrie Melodies

1945: *Life With Feathers* (Freleng/Mar. 24/A.A. nominee) and *Peck Up Your Troubles* (Freleng/Oct. 20).

1947: *Doggone Cats* (Davis/Oct. 25).

1948: *Back Alley Oproar* (with Elmer Fudd/Freleng/Mar. 27) and *Scaredy Cat* (with Porky Pig/Jones/Dec. 21).

1949: *Mouse Mazurka* (Freleng/June 11), *Swallow The Leader* (McKimson/Oct. 14) and *Hippety Hopper* (with Hippety Hopper/McKimson/Nov. 19).

1952: *Little Red Rodent Hood* (Freleng/May 3) and *Tree For Two* (Freleng/Oct. 4).

1953: *A Mouse Divided* (Freleng/Jan. 31), *A Peck O' Trouble* (McKimson/Mar. 28) and *Cats–A–Weigh* (with Sylvester Jr., Hippety Hopper/McKimson/Nov. 28).

1954: *Bell Hoppy* (with Hippety Hopper/McKimson/Apr. 17) and *Claws For Alarm* (with Porky Pig/Jones/May 22).

1955: *Lighthouse Mouse* (with Hippety Hopper/McKimson/Mar. 12), *A Kiddie's Kitty* (Freleng/Aug. 20), *Speedy Gonzales* (with Speedy Gonzales/Freleng/Sept. 17/A.A. winner) and *Pappy's Puppy* (Freleng/Dec. 17).

1956: *The Unexpected Guest* (McKimson/June 2), *The Slap–Hoppy Mouse* (with Hippety Hopper/McKimson/Sept. 1) and *Yankee Dood It* (with Elmer Fudd/Freleng/Oct. 13).

1957: *Mouse–Taken Identity* (with Hippety Hopper, Junior/McKimson/Nov. 16).

1960: *West Of Pesos* (with Speedy/Freleng/Jan. 23) and *Trip For Tat* (with Tweety/Freleng/Oct. 19).

1961: *D'Fightin' Ones* (Freleng/Apr. 22).

1963: *Chili Weather* (with Speedy Gonzales/Freleng/Aug. 17) and *Claws In The Lease* (with Sylvester Jr./McKimson/ Nov. 9).

DePatie–Freleng Enterprises Releases
1965: *Cats and Bruises* (with Speedy Gonzales/Freleng, Pratt/Jan. 30).

Looney Tunes
1946: *Kitty Kornered* (with Porky Pig/Clampett/June 8).

1948: *Hop Look And Listen* (with Hippety Hopper/McKimson/Apr. 17) and *Kit For Cat* (with Elmer Fudd/Freleng/ Nov. 6).

1950: *The Scarlet Pumpernickel* (with Daffy Duck, Porky Pig, Elmer Fudd and Momma Bear/Jones/Mar. 4) and *Pop 'Em Pop!* (with Hippety Hopper, Junior/McKimson/Nov. 6).

1951: *Canned Feud* (Freleng/Feb. 3).

1952: *Who's Kitten Who* (with Hippety Hopper, Junior/McKimson/Jan. 5) and *Hoppy Go Lucky* (with Hippety Hopper/McKimson/Aug. 9).

1954: *Dr. Jerkyl's Hide* (with Spike and Chester/Freleng/ May 8) and *By Word Of Mouse* (Freleng/Oct. 2).

1955: *Jumpin' Jupiter* (with Porky Pig/Jones/Aug. 6).

1956: *Too Hop To Handle* (with Hippety Hopper, Junior/McKimson/Jan. 28) and *Heir–Conditioned* (with Elmer Fudd/ Freleng/Nov. 26).

1959: *Cat's Paw* (with Junior/McKimson/Aug. 15).

1960: *Goldimouse And The Three Cats* (Freleng/Mar. 16) and *Mouse Garden* (with Junior, Sam/Freleng/July 16).

1961: *Hoppy Daze* (with Hippety Hopper/McKimson/Feb. 11) and *Birds Of A Feather* (McKimson/Apr. 1).

1962: *Fish And Slips* (with Junior/McKimson/Mar. 10).

DePatie–Freleng Enterprises Releases
1964: *Freudy Cat* (with Hippety Hopper/McKimson/Mar. 14).

TALKARTOONS

Billed as "actual talking pictures" in theater ads, this series represented the Fleischer Studios' initial entrance into the sound cartoon arena. Films starred a host of subsequently famous characters, including Betty Boop, Bimbo and Koko the Clown.

Early entries featured post–synched dialogue and music added after completion of the productions, with dialogue being kept to a minimum and peppy musical scores carrying the films. In the beginning, having no accomplished musical director to create songs, the Fleischers purchased the rights of popular songs to use as soundtracks. The series' first star was Bimbo, resurrected by the Fleischers from the *Out of the Inkwell* series.

While the series celebrated Bimbo's return to the screen, the series' sixth cartoon release of 1930, *Dizzy Dishes,* introduced another character in her formative stages, Betty Boop, invented and drawn by animator Grim Natwick. In 1931, Koko The Clown was brought back as a supporting player in the series, after a brief retirement from the screen. *Directed by Dave Fleischer. Black–and–white. A Fleischer Studios Production released through Paramount Pictures.*

1929: (Copyright dates are marked by a ©) *Noah's Lark* (© Oct. 25) and *Accordion Joe* (© Dec. 12).

1930: *Marriage Wows* (© Jan. 8), *Radio Riot* (Feb. 13), *Fire Bugs* (May 9), *Wise Flies* (July 18), *Dizzy Dishes* (with Betty Boop/Aug. 9), *Barnacle Bill* (Aug. 31), *Swing, You Sinner* (Sept. 24), *The Grand Uproar* (Oct. 3), *Sky Scraping* (Nov. 1), *Up To Mars* (Nov. 20) and *Mysterious Mouse* (Dec. 26).

1931: *The Ace Of Spades* (Jan. 16), *Tree Saps* (Feb. 3), *Teacher's Pest* (Feb. 7), *The Cow's Husband* (Mar. 13), *The Bum Bandit* (Apr. 3), *The Male Man* (Apr. 24), *Silly Scandals* (with Betty Boop), *Twenty Legs Under The Sea* (June 6), *The Herring Murder Case* (June 26), *Bimbo's Imitation* (with Betty Boop/July 24), *Bimbo's Express* (with Betty Boop/Aug. 22), *Minding The Baby* (with Betty Boop/Sept. 26), *In The Shade Of The Old Apple Sauce* (Oct. 16), *Mask–A–Raid* (with Betty Boop/Nov. 7), *Jack And The Beanstalk* (with Betty Boop/Nov. 21) and *Dizzy Red Riding Hood* (with Betty Boop/Dec. 12).

1932: *Any Rags* (with Betty Boop/Jan. 2), *Boop–Oop–A–Doop* (with Betty Boop/Jan. 16), *The Robot* (Feb. 5), *Minnie The Moocher* (with Betty Boop, Cab Calloway and His Orchestra/Feb. 26), *Swim Or Sink* (with Betty Boop/Mar. 11), *Crazy Town* (with Betty Boop/Mar. 25), *The Dancing Fool* (Apr. 8), *A Hunting We Will Go* (with Betty Boop/Apr. 29), *Chess–Nuts* (May 13), *Hide And Seek* (May 26), *Admission Free* (with Betty Boop/June 10) and *The Betty Boop Limited* (with Betty Boop/July 1).

TASMANIAN DEVIL

One Warner Brothers star who was very popular on screen in a handful of cartoon misadventures was that whirling dervish, the Tasmanian Devil, who buzz–sawed his way through everything in his path. Robert McKimson originated the character and Mel Blanc, Warner's resident voice artist, supplied the voice. Blanc, who described the voice as "growl slobbering, indecipherable gibberish," supposedly told McKimson while voicing the first cartoon, "I defy you or anybody else to tell me he doesn't sound like a Tasmanian Devil."

In all, the Tasmanian Devil appeared in five cartoons, most of them opposite Bugs Bunny. *Directed by Robert McKimson. Technicolor. A Warner Brothers release.*

Voices:
Tasmanian Devil: Mel Blanc

Looney Tunes
1954: *Devil May Hare* (with Bugs Bunny/McKimson/June 19).

Merrie Melodies
1957: *Bedeviled Rabbit* (with Bugs Bunny/McKimson/Apr. 13) and *Ducking The Devil* (with Daffy Duck/McKimson/Aug. 17).

1962: *Bill Of Hare* (with Bugs Bunny/McKimson/June 9).

1964: *Dr. Devil And Mr. Hare* (With Bugs Bunny/McKimson/Mar. 28).

TERRY BEARS

Originally Terrytoons' studio mascots, these rascally twin bears starred in their own cartoon series for the studio. *Directors were Connie Rasinski, Ed Donnelly and Mannie Davis. Technicolor. A Terrytoons Production released through 20th Century–Fox.*

Voices:
Terry Bears: Roy Halee, Phillip A. Scheib, Doug Moye

1951: *Tall Timber Tale* (Rasinski/July) and *Little Problems* (Donnelly/Sept.).

1952: *Papa's Little Helpers* (Davis/Jan.), *Papa's Day Of Rest* (Davis/Mar.), *Little Anglers* (Rasinski/July), *Nice Doggy* (Donnelly/Oct.) and *Picnic With Papa* (Davis/Dec.).

1953: *Thrifty Cubs* (Davis/Jan.), *Snappy Snap Shots* (Donnelly/Mar.), *Plumber's Helpers* (Rasinski/May), *Open House* (Donnelly/Aug.), *The Reluctant Pup* (Davis/Oct.) and *Growing Pains* (Donnelly/Dec.).

1954: *Pet Problems* (Donnelly/Apr.) and *Howling Success* (Rasinski/July).

1956: *Baffling Business* (Rasinski/Apr.).

TERRYTOONS

Featuring assembly–line animation and repetitive story formulas, *Terrytoons* was, remarkably, one of the longest, continuous series in cartoon history. The series never achieved the critical success or cult status of Disney, Warner and MGM cartoons, yet endured despite the fact most films starred incidental characters.

Paul Terry created the series after forming his own studio in 1929, with partner Frank Moser. Audio–Cinema Studios agreed to finance the cartoons and provided working space for the animators at the old Edison studio in the Bronx. Under the agreement, Terry and Moser worked without pay until Audio Cinema recouped its costs for these animated adventures.

Educational Pictures distributed the first cartoons, released with a synchronized soundtrack and based on popular music of the day. In 1934, Terry broke ground and built his Terrytoons studio in New Rochelle, New York, where the vast majority of these films were produced until the studio closed down in 1968.

Despite the addition of sound, Terry relied mostly on ragtime musical soundtracks and loads of action, featuring little dialogue between characters in these episodes. Except for some films produced in the 1950s, most cartoons had no main character.

Terry was one of the last to change over to color, filming the series in black–and–white. In 1938, he finally gave in to industry pressures and produced his first color *Terrytoons, String Bean Jack*. However, Terry remained unconvinced about producing more color cartoons because of the great expense; black–and–white animation was considerably less expensive. He therefore used color sparingly until 1943 when he completely converted over to the process since black–and–white had faded in popularity altogether.

For additional *Terrytoons* entries, see *Mighty Mouse, Heckle and Jeckle, Farmer Al Falfa, Foofle, Kiko the Kangaroo, Puddy the Pup, Dinky Duck, Dimwit, Gandy Goose, Good Deal Daily, Little Roquefort, The Terry Bears, Hector Heathcote, Sidney the Elephant, James Hound, Astronut, Luno, Hashimoto, Sad Cat, Phoney Baloney, Possible Possum, Deputy Dawg, Clint Clobber, Gaston Le Crayon, Willie Walrus and John Doormat. Directors were Paul Terry, Frank Moser, Mannie Davis, George Gordon, Jack Zander, Dan Gordon, John Foster, Connie Rasinski, Volney White, Ed Donnelly, Bob Kuwahara, Dave Tendlar, Al Kouzel and Martin B. Taras. Black–and–white. Technicolor. CinemaScope. A Terrytoons Production released through Educational Pictures and 20th Century–Fox.*

Educational Pictures Releases

1930: *Caviar* (Terry, Moser/Feb. 23), *Pretzels* (Terry, Moser/ Mar. 9), *Spanish Onions* (Terry, Moser/Mar. 23), *Indian Pudding* (Terry, Moser/Apr. 6), *Roman Punch* (Terry, Moser/ Apr. 20), *Hot Turkey* (Terry, Moser/May 4), *Hawaiian Pineapple* (Terry, Moser/May 4), *Swiss Cheese* (Terry, Moser/June 1), *Codfish Balls* (Terry, Moser/June 1), *Hungarian Goulash* (Terry, Moser/June 15), *Bully Beef* (Terry, Moser/July 13), *Kangaroo Steak* (Terry, Moser/July 27), *Monkey Meat* (Terry, Moser/Aug. 10), *Chop Suey* (Terry, Moser/Aug. 24), *French Fried* (Terry, Moser/Sept. 7), *Dutch Treat* (Terry, Moser/Sept. 21), *Irish Stew* (Terry, Moser/Oct. 5), *Fried Chicken* (Terry, Moser/Oct. 19), *Jumping Beans* (Terry, Moser/Nov. 2), *Scotch Highball* (Terry, Moser/Nov. 16), *Salt Water Taffy* (Terry, Moser/Nov. 30), *Golf Nuts* (Terry, Moser/Dec. 14) and *Pigskin Capers* (Terry, Moser/Dec. 28).

1931: *Popcorn* (Terry, Moser/Jan. 11), *Go West, Big Boy* (Terry, Moser/Feb. 22), *Quack Quack* (Terry, Moser/Mar. 8), *Sing Sing Prison* (Terry, Moser/Apr. 19), *The Fireman's Bride* (Terry, Moser/May 3), *A Day To Live* (Terry, Moser/May 31), *2000 B.C.* (Terry, Moser/June 14), *Blues* (Terry, Moser/June 28), *By The Sea* (Terry, Moser/July 12), *Her First Egg* (Terry, Moser/July 26), *Jazz Mad* (Terry, Moser/Aug. 9), *Canadian Capers* (Terry, Moser/Aug. 23), *Jesse And James* (Terry, Moser/ Sept. 6), *Around The World* (Terry, Moser/Oct. 4), *Jingle Bells* (Terry, Moser/Oct. 18), *The Black Spider* (Terry, Moser/ Nov. 1), *China* (Terry, Moser/Nov. 15), *The Lorelei* (Terry, Moser/Nov. 29), *Summertime* (Terry, Moser/Dec. 13) and *Aladdin's Lamp* (Terry, Moser/Dec. 27).

1932: *The Villain's Curse* (Terry, Moser/Jan 10), *Noah's Outing, The Spider Talks* (Terry, Moser/Feb. 7), *Peg Leg Pete* (Terry, Moser/Feb. 21), *Bull–Ero* (Terry, Moser/Apr. 3), *Ra-*

dio Girl (Terry, Moser/Apr. 17), *Romance* (Terry, Moser/May 15), *Bluebeard's Brother* (Terry, Moser/May 29), *The Mad King* (Terry, Moser/June 26), *Cocky Cockroach* (Terry, Moser/ July 10), *Sherman Was Right* (Terry, Moser/Aug. 21), *Burlesque* (Terry, Moser/Sept. 4), *Southern Rhythm* (Terry, Moser/ Sept. 18), *College Spirit* (Terry, Moser/Oct. 16), *Hook Ladder Number One* (Terry, Moser/Oct. 30), *The Forty Thieves* (Terry, Moser/Nov. 13), *Toyland* (Terry, Moser/Nov. 27), *Hollywood Diet* (Terry, Moser/Dec. 11) and *Ireland Or Bust* (Terry, Moser/Dec. 25).

1933: *Jealous Lover* (Terry, Moser/Jan. 8), *Robin Hood* (Terry, Moser/Jan 22), *Hansel And Gretel* (Terry, Moser/Feb. 5), *Tale Of A Shirt* (Terry, Moser/Feb. 19), *Down On The Levee* (Terry, Moser/Mar. 5), *Who Killed Cock Robbin?* (Terry, Moser/Mar. 19), *Oh Susanna* (Terry, Moser/Apr. 2), *Romeo And Juliet* (Terry, Moser/Apr. 16), *Pirate Ship* (Terry, Moser/ Apr. 30), *Cinderella* (Terry, Moser/May 28), *King Zilch* (Terry, Moser/June 11), *The Banker's Daughter* (with Fanny Zilch, Oil Can Harry/Terry, Moser/June 11), *The Oil Can Mystery* (with Fanny Zilch, Oil Can Harry, Strongheart/Terry, Moser/ June 25), *Fanny In The Lion's Den* (with Fanny Zilch, Oil Can Harry, Strongheart/Terry, Moser/July 23), *Hypnotic Eyes* (with Fanny Zilch, Oil Can Harry, Strongheart/Terry, Moser/ Aug. 11), *Grand Uproar* (Terry, Moser/Aug. 25), *Fanny's Wedding Day* (with Fanny Zilch, Strongheart/Terry, Moser/ Oct. 6), *A Gypsy Fiddler* (Terry, Moser/Oct. 6), *Beanstalk Jack* (Terry, Moser/Oct. 20), *Robinson Crusoe* (Terry, Moser/ Nov. 17/© as *Shipwrecked Brothers*), *Little Boy Blue* (Terry, Moser/Nov. 30), *In Venice* (Terry, Moser/Dec. 15) and *The Sunny South* (Terry, Moser/Dec. 29).

1934: *Holland Days* (Terry, Moser/Jan. 12), *The Three Bears* (Davis/Jan. 26), *Rip Van Winkle* (Terry, Moser/Feb. 9), *The Last Straw* (Terry, Moser/Feb. 23), *A Mad House* (Terry, Moser/Mar. 23), *Joe's Lunch Wagon* (Terry, Moser/Apr. 6), *Just A Clown* (Terry, Moser/Apr. 20), *The King's Daughter* (Terry, Moser/May 4), *The Lion's Friend* (Terry, Moser/May 18), *Pandora* (Terry, Moser/June 1), *Slow But Sure* (Terry, Moser/June 15), *See The World* (Terry, Moser/June 29), *My Lady's Garden* (Terry, Moser/July 13), *Irish Sweepstakes* (Terry, Moser/July 27), *Busted Blossoms* (Terry, Moser/Aug. 10), *Mice In Council* (Terry, Moser/Aug. 24), *Jail Birds* (Terry, Moser/Sept. 21), *The Black Sheep* (Terry, Moser/Oct. 5), *The Magic Fish* (Terry, Moser/Oct. 17), *Hot Sands* (Terry, Moser/ Nov. 2), *Tom, Tom The Piper's Son* (Terry, Moser/Nov. 16), *Jack's Snack* (Terry, Moser/Nov. 30), *South Pole Or Bust* (Terry, Moser/Dec. 14) and *The Dog Show* (Terry, Moser/ Dec. 28).

1935: *The First Show* (Terry, Moser/Jan. 11), *The Bullfight* (Terry, Moser/Feb. 8), *Fireman Save My Child* (Terry, Moser/ Feb. 22), *The Moth And The Spider* (Terry, Moser/Mar. 8), *Peg Leg Pete, The Pirate* (Terry, Moser/Apr. 19), *A Modern Red Riding Hood* (Terry, Moser/May 3), *Five Puppets* (Terry, Moser/May 17), *Opera* (Terry, Moser/May 31), *King Looney XIV* (Terry, Moser/June 14), *Amateur Night* (Terry, Moser/ July 12), *The Foxy–Fox* (Terry, Moser/July 26), *Chain Letters* (Terry, Moser/Aug. 9), *Birdland* (Terry, Moser/Aug. 23), *Circus Days* (Terry, Moser/Sept. 6), *Hey Diddle Diddle* (Terry,

Moser/Sept 20), *Foiled Again* (with Fanny Zilch, Oil Can Harry, Strongheart/Terry, Moser/Oct. 14), *Football* (Terry, Moser/Oct. 18), *Aladdin's Lamp* (Terry, Moser/Nov. 15), *Southern Horse–Pitality* (Terry, Moser/Nov. 29), *Ye Olde Toy Shop* (Terry, Moser/Dec. 13) and *The Mayflower* (Terry, Moser/Dec. 27).

1936: *The Feud* (Terry, Moser/Jan. 10), *Off To China* (Terry, Moser/Mar. 20), *A Wolf In Cheap Clothing* (Terry, Moser/Apr. 17), *The Busy Bee* (May 29), *The Sailor's Home* (June 12), *A Tough Egg* (Terry, Moser/June 26) and *Robin Hood In An Arrow Escape* (Terry, Davis. G. Gordon/Nov. 13).

1937: *Salty McGuire* (Davis, G. Gordon/Jan. 8), *Bug Carnival* (Davis, G. Gordon/Apr. 16), *Schoolbirds* (Davis, G. Gordon/Apr. 30), *The Paper Hangers* (Davis/July 30), *The Villain Still Pursued Her* (with Oil Can Harry/Sept. 3), *A Bully Frog* (Terry, Davis, G. Gordon/Sept. 18), *The Saw Mill Mystery* (with Oil Can Harry/Rasinski/Oct. 29), *The Timid Rabbit* (Davis/Nov. 26), *The Billy Goat Whiskers* (Foster/Dec. 10) and *The Barnyard Boss* (Rasinski/Dec. 24).

1938: *The Lion Hunt* (Davis/Jan. 7), *Bugs Beetle And His Orchestra* (Foster/Jan. 21), *Just Ask Jupiter* (Davis/Feb. 18), *A Mountain Romance* (Davis/Apr. 1), *Robinson Crusoe's Broadcast* (Foster/Apr. 15), *Maid In China* (Rasinski/Apr. 29), *The Big Top* (Terry, Davis/May 12), *Here's To Good Old Jail* (Donnelly/June 10), *The Last Indian* (Rasinski/June 24), *Milk For Baby* (Davis/July 8), *Mrs. O'Leary's Cow* (Donnelly/July 22) and *Eliza Runs Again* (Rasinski/July 29/last *Educational Pictures* release).

20th Century–Fox Releases
1938: *Chris Columbo* (Donnelly/Aug. 12), *String Bean Jack* (Foster/Aug. 26/first in Technicolor), *Wolf's Side Of The Story* (Rasinski/Sept. 23), *The Glass Slipper* (Davis/Oct. 7), *The Newcomer* (with Panda Bear/Davis/Oct. 21), *The Stranger Rides Again* (Davis/Nov. 4), *Housewife Herman* (Donnelly/Nov. 18) and *Village Blacksmith* (Davis/Dec. 2).

1939: *The Owl And The Pussycat* (Donnelly/Jan. 13/Technicolor), *One Gun Gary In The Nick Of Time* (with One Gun Gary/Donnelly/Jan. 27), *The Three Bears* (Davis/Feb. 10/Technicolor), *Frozen Feet* (Rasinski/Feb. 24), *The Nutty Network* (Davis/Mar. 24/Technicolor), *The Cuckoo Bird* (Davis/Apr. 7), *Their Last Bean* (Donnelly/Apr. 21), *Barnyard Eggcitement* (Davis/May 5/Technicolor), *Nick's Coffee Pot* (Rasinski/May 19), *The Price Guest* (Davis/June 2), *Africa Squawks* (Rasinski/June 30), *Old Fire Horse* (Donnelly/July 28), *Two Headed Giant* (Rasinski/Aug. 11), *The Golden West* (Davis/Aug. 25), *Sheep In The Meadow* (Davis/Sept. 22), *The Watchdog* (Donnelly/Oct. 20), *One Mouse In A Million* (Rasinski/Nov. 3), *A Wicky–Wacky Romance* (Davis/Nov. 17/Technicolor), *The Ice Pond* (Davis/Dec. 15) and *The First Robin* (Rasinski/Dec. 29).

1940: *A Dog In A Mansion* (Donnelly/Jan. 12), *Edgar Runs Again* (Davis/Jan. 26), *Harvest Time* (Rasinski/Feb. 9/Technicolor), *The Hare And The Hounds* (Donnelly/Feb. 23), *All's Well That Ends Well* (Davis/Mar. 8), *Just A Little Bull* (Donnelly/Apr. 19/Technicolor), *Wot's All Th' Shootin' Fer* (White/

May 3), *Swiss Ski Yodelers* (Donnelly/May 17), *Catnip Capers* (Davis/May 31), *Professor Offkeyski* (Rasinski/June 14), *Dover's Rescue* (White/June 28), *Rupert The Runt* (Davis/July 12), *Love In A Cottage* (White/July 28), *Billy Mouse's Akwakade* (Donnelly/Aug. 9/Technicolor), *Club Life In Stone Age* (Davis/Aug. 23), *Touchdown Demons* (White/Sept. 20), *How Wet Was My Ocean* (Donnelly/Oct. 4/Technicolor), *Happy Haunting Grounds* (Davis/Oct. 18), *Landing Of The Pilgrims* (Rasinski/Nov. 1/Technicolor), *Plane Goofy* (Donnelly/Nov. 29), *Snowman* (Davis/Dec. 3) and *Temperamental Lion* (Rasinski/Dec. 27/Technicolor).

1941: *What A Little Sneeze Will Do* (Donnelly/Jan 10), *Hairless Hector* (White/Jan. 24), *Mississippi Swing* (Rasinski/Feb. 7/Technicolor), *When Knights Were Bold* (White/Mar. 21), *The Baby Seal* (Rasinski/Apr. 10), *Uncle Joey* (Davis/Apr. 18/Technicolor), *The Dog's Dream* (Donnelly/May 2), *The Magic Shell* (Davis/May 16), *What Happens At Night* (Rasinski/May 30/Technicolor), *Horse Fly Opera* (Donnelly/June 13), *Good Old Irish Tunes* (Rasinski/June 27), *Bringing Home The Bacon* (Davis/July 11/*Aesop's Fable*), *Twelve O'Clock And All Ain't Well* (Donnelly/July 25), *Ice Carnival* (Donnelly/Aug. 22), *Uncle Joey Comes To Town* (Davis/Sept. 19), *The Frozen North* (Rasinski/Oct. 17), *Back To The Soil* (Donnelly/Nov. 14), *The Bird Tower* (Davis/Nov. 28/Technicolor) and *A Yarn About Yarn* (Rasinski/Dec. 12/Technicolor).

1942: *The Torrid Toreador* (Donnelly/Jan. 9/Technicolor), *Happy Circus Days* (Rasinski/Jan. 23/Technicolor), *Funny Bunny Business* (Donnelly/Feb. 6), *Cat Meets Mouse* (Davis/Feb. 20/Technicolor), *Eat Me Kitty, Eight To A Bar* (Davis/Mar. 6), *Oh Gentle Spring* (Rasinski/Apr. 3), *Neck And Neck* (Davis/May 15/Technicolor), *The Stork's Mistake* (Donnelly/May 29), *All About Dogs* (Rasinski/June 12/Technicolor), *Wilful Willie* (Rasinski/June 26), *All Out for 'V'* (Aug. 7/Technicolor/A.A. nominee), *School Daze* (with Nancy/Sept. 18/Technicolor), *Doing Their Bit* (with Nancy/Oct. 30/Technicolor/aka *Nancy's Little Theatre*), *Ickle Meets Pickle* (Rasinski/Nov. 13), *Barnyard Waac* (Donnelly/Dec. 11/Technicolor) and *Somewhere In The Pacific* (Davis/Dec. 25/Technicolor).

1943: (All in Technicolor from this point on.) *Barnyard Blackout* (Davis/Mar. 5), *Shipyard Symphony* (Donnelly/Mar. 19), *Patriotic Pooches* (Rasinski/Apr. 9), *The Last Round–Up* (Davis/May 15), *Mopping Up* (Donnelly/June 25), *Keep 'Em Growing* (Davis/May 28), *Yokel Duck Makes Good* (Donnelly/Nov. 26) and *The Hopeful Donkey* (Davis/Dec. 17).

1944: *The Butcher of Seville* (Donnelly/Jan. 7), *The Helicopter* (Donnelly/Jan. 21), *A Day In June* (Mar. 3), *My Boy Johnny* (May 12/ A.A. nominee), *Carmen Veranda* (Davis/July 28), *The Cat Came Back* (Rasinski/Aug. 18), *A Wolf's Tale* (Rasinski/Oct. 27) and *Dear Old Switzerland* (Donnelly/Dec. 22).

1945: *Ants In Your Pantry* (Davis/Feb. 16), *Smoky Joe* (Rasinski/May 25), *The Fox And The Duck* (Davis/Aug. 24), *Swooning The Swooners* (Rasinski/Sept. 14) and *The Watch Dog* (Donnelly/Sept. 28).

1946: *The Tortoise Wins Again* (Rasinski/Aug. 9), *The Snow Man* (Rasinski/Oct. 11), *The Housing Problem* (Davis/Oct. 25) and *Beanstalk Jack* (Donnelly/Dec. 20).

1947: *One Note Tony* (Rasinski/© Oct. 22) and *The Wolf's Pardon* (Donnelly/Dec. 5).

1948: *Felix The Fox* (Davis/Jan.), *Hounding The Hares* (Donnelly/Apr.), *Mystery In The Moonlight* (Donnelly/May), *Seeing Ghosts* (Davis/June) and *The Hard Boiled Egg* (Rasinski/Oct.).

1949: *The Wooden Indian* (Rasinski/Jan.), *The Lyin' Lion* (Rasinski/Aug.), *Mrs. Jones Rest Farm* (Donnelly/Aug.), *A Truckload Of Trouble* (Rasinski/Oct. 25), *Flying Cops And Saucers* (Rasinski/Nov.) and *Paint Pot Symphony* (Rasinski/Dec.).

1950: *Better Late Than Never* (with Victor the Volunteer/Donnelly/Mar. 17), *Aesop's Fable: Foiling The Fox* (Rasinski/Apr.), *The Red Headed Monkey* (Davis/July 7), *All This And Rabbit Stew* (with Dingbat/Rasinski/July), *The Dog Show* (Donnelly/Aug.), *If Cats Could Sing* (Donnelly/Oct.) and *Sour Grapes* (with Dingbat/Davis/Dec.).

1951: *Squirrel Crazy* (with Nutsy/Davis/Jan.), *Woodman Spare That Tree* (Donnelly/Feb.), *Stage Struck* (with Half Pint/Davis/Feb.), *The Elephant Mouse* (with Half Pint/Davis/May), *Aesop's Fable: Golden Egg Goosie* (Donnelly/Aug.) and *The Helpful Genie* (Rasinski/Oct.).

1952: *Mechanical Bird* (Donnelly/Feb.), *Time Gallops On* (Davis/Apr.), *The Happy Cobblers* (Davis/May), *Flipper Frolics* (Rasinski/July), *Mysterious Cowboy* (Davis/Sept.) and *Happy Valley* (Donnelly/Sept. 1/Aesop's Fable).

1953: *Sparky The Firefly* (Rasinski/Sept./Aesop's Fable).

1954: *Nonsense Newsreel* (Davis/Mar.) and *Pride Of The Yard* (with Percival Sleuthound/Donnelly/Aug.).

1955: *A Yokohama Yankee* (Rasinski/Jan.), *The First Flying Fish* (Rasinski/Feb./Aesop's Fable), *Bird Symphony* (Rasinski/Apr./CinemaScope), *Phoney News Flashes* (Rasinski/May), *Foxed By A Fox* (Rasinski/May), *Last Moust Of Hamlin* (Rasinski/June) and *Little Red Hen* (Rasinski/July/CinemaScope).

1956: *Clockmakers Dog* (Rasinski/Jan.), *Park Avenue Pussycat* (Rasinski/Jan./CinemaScope), *Uranium Blues* (Rasinski/Mar./CinemaScope), *Hep Mother Hubbard* (Rasinski/Mar.), *Oceans Of Love* (Rasinski/May/CinemaScope), *Lucky Dog* (Rasinski/May/CinemaScope), *Police Dogged* (with Clancy the Bull/Rasinski/July/CinemaScope) and *The Brave Little Brave.* (Davis/July).

1957: *Gag Buster* (with Spoofy/Rasinski/Feb./CinemaScope), *A Hare Breadth Finish* (Rasinski/Feb.), *A Bum Steer* (with Beefy/Davis/Mar./CinemaScope), *The Bone Ranger* (with Sniffer/Rasinski/Apr./CinemaScope), *Love Is Blind* (Davis/May) and *Flebus* (Pintoff/Aug./CinemaScope).

1958: (All in CinemaScope from this point on.) *The Juggler Of Our Lady* (Kouzel/Apr.).

1959: *A Tale Of A Dog* (Tendlar/Feb.), *The Fabulous Firework Family* (Kouzel/Aug.) and *The Leaky Faucet* (Taras/Dec.).

1960: *The Misunderstood Giant* (Rasinski/Feb.), *Aesop's Fable: The Tiger King* (Rasinski/Mar.), *Hearts And Glowers* (Taras/June) and *Tin Pan Alley Cat* (Tendlar/Oct.).

1964: *The Red Tractor* (with Duckwood/Tendlar/Feb.), *Search For Misery* (with Pitiful Penelope/Kuwahara), *Short-Term Sheriff* (with Donkey Otie, Duckwood/Tendlar) and *Oil Thru The Day* (with Duckwood/Tendlar).

1966: *Champion Chump* (with Martian Moochers/Kuwahara/Apr.) and *The Cowardly Watchdog* (with Martian Moochers/Kuwahara/Aug.).

TEX AVERY CARTOONS

The former Warner Brothers director, who joined MGM in 1942, supervised various spoofs and comedy-musical cartoons with the basic Avery humor of hyperbole and character gyrations intact. His cartoons featured fast-paced, violent, zany moments, punctuated with outrageous takes by his cartoon stars. When a character does a take in an Avery cartoon, his eyes literally pop out, his jaw drops to the floor like porch steps and his tongue gyrates vigorously as he screams. Avery's cartoons were based on the "survival-of-the-fittest" theme, obviously to some extreme.

Avery produced practically every other major non-Hanna and Barbera MGM cartoon from 1942 to 1955, starting with *Blitz Wolf,* which won an Academy Award for Best Short Subject. Like his other MGM series—*Droopy, George and Junior,* and *Screwy Squirrel*—these cartoon specialties delved into the unusual only as Tex Avery could, from lampooning detective mysteries in *Who Killed Who?* (1943) to discovering the formula to create a giant-sized canary in *King-Sized Canary* (1947).

Avery also took a subject that was taboo—sex—to another level of lunacy, directing his own "updated" versions of nursery tales: *Red Hot Riding Hood* (1943), *Swing Shift Cinderella* (1945) and *Uncle Tom's Cabana* (1947), all starring a lustful Wolf who at the sight of a curvacious female co-star turns into a human pretzel of delirious sexual desire.

In 1954, Avery left MGM to join Walter Lantz Studios, where he directed the *Chilly Willy* series.

See Droopy, George and Junior, Screwy Squirrel and Spike for additional entries. *Directed by Tex Avery. Technicolor. A Metro-Goldwyn-Mayer release.*

1942: *The Blitz Wolf* (Aug. 22/A.A. winner) and *The Early Bird Dood It* (Aug. 29).

1943: *Red Hot Riding Hood* (May 8), *Who Killed Who?* (June 5), *One Ham's Family* (Aug. 14) and *What's Buzzin' Buzzard* (Nov. 27).

1944: *Batty Baseball* (Apr. 22).

1945: *Jerky Turkey* (Apr. 7) and *Swing Shift Cinderella* (Aug 25/originally *Wolf, Swingshift Cindy, Red Hot Cinderella* and *The Glass Slipper*).

1946: *The Hick Chick* (June 15).

1947: *Uncle Tom's Cabana* (July 19), *Slap Happy Lion* (Sept. 20/re: May 28, 1955) and *King–Size Canary* (Dec. 6/re: Oct. 21, 1955).

1948: *What's Price Fleadom* (Mar. 20/re: Dec. 2, 1955), *Little Tinker* (May 15/re: May 14, 1955), *Half–Pint Pygmy* (Aug. 17), *Lucky Ducky* (Oct. 9/re: Jan. 6, 1956) and *The Cat That Hated People* (Nov. 12/re: Jan. 20, 1956).

1949: *Bad Luck Blackie* (Jan. 22/re: Nov. 9, 1956/originally *Two Black Cats*), *House Of Tomorrow* (June 11/re: Mar. 16, 1956), *Doggone Tired* (July 30/re: Apr. 6, 1956) and *Little Rural Red Riding Hood* (Sept. 17/re: Dec. 28, 1956).

1950: *The Cuckoo Clock* (June 10/re: Jan. 19, 1957), *Ventriloquist Cat* (May 27) and *The Peachy Cobbler* (Dec. 9/re: May 24, 1957).

1951: *Symphony In Slang* (June 6/re: June 13, 1958) and *Car Of Tomorrow* (Sept. 22).

1952: *Magical Maestro* (Feb. 9), *One Cab's Family* (May 15) and *Rock–A–Bye Bear* (July 12).

1953: *Little Johnny Jet* (Apr. 18/A.A. nominee) and *T.V. Of Tomorrow* (June 6).

1954: *Billy Boy* (May 8), *Farm Of Tomorrow* (Sept. 18) and *The Flea Circus* (Nov. 6).

1955: *Field And Scream* (Apr. 30), *The Fird Bad Man* (Sept. 30) and *Cellbound* (Nov. 25).

1957: *The Cat's Meow* (Jan. 25/remake of *Ventriloquist Cat*).

THE THREE BEARS

Warner animator Chuck Jones originated this series depicting domestic life of an American family, with bears playing the roles of Papa, Mamma and Junior. The trio first appeared in the 1944 *Bugs Bunny And The Three Bears,* reenacting the Goldilocks fable with a comical twist. Jones brought the characters back to the screen in four more cartoon adventures, each one offering a humorous view of the trials and tribulations of this abnormal family. *Directed by Chuck Jones. Technicolor. A Warner Brothers release.*

Voices:
Papa Bear: Billy Bletcher, **Mama Bear:** Bea Benadaret, **Junior Bear:** Stan Freberg

Merrie Melodies
1944: *Bugs Bunny And The Three Bears* (Feb. 26).

1949: *The Bee–Deviled Bruin* (May 14).

1951: *A Bear For Punishment* (Oct. 20).

Looney Tunes
1948: *What's Bruin, Bruin?* (Feb. 28).

1949: *Bear Feat* (Dec. 10).

Poncho (right) shows skinny apprentice toad, Toro, the way in The Tijuana Toads. *© DePatie–Freleng Enterprises*

THE TIJUANA TOADS

This late 1960s series followed the humorous exploits of a bossy Spanish–accented toad, Poncho, who demonstrates for his inexperienced, skinny apprentice, Toro, how to catch flies and cope with basic necessities of life as a toad in inventively funny situations. The toads were later renamed "The Texas Toads" (the characters also changed their names to Fatso and Banjo) when segmented on TV's "The Pink Panther Laff and a Half Hour and a Half Show." *Directors were Friz Freleng, Hawley Pratt, Robert McKimson, Sid Marcus, Gerry Chiniquy, Art Leonardi, Art Davis and Dave Detiege. Technicolor. A DePatie–Freleng/Mirisch Films Production released through United Artists.*

1969: *The Tijuana Toads* (Aug. 6), *A Pair of Greenbacks* (Dec. 16) and *Go For Croak* (Dec. 25).

1970: *The Froggy, Froggy Duo* (Mar. 15), *Hop And Chop* (June 17), *Never On Thirsty* (Aug. 5) and *A Dopey Hacienda* (Dec. 6).

1971: *Snake In The Gracias* (Jan. 24), *Two Jumps And A Chump* (Mar. 28), *Mud Squad* (Apr. 28), *The Egg Of Ay–Yi–Yi* (June 6), *A Leap In The Deep* (June 20), *The Fastest Tongue In The West* (June 20), *Croakus Pocus* and *Serape Happy* (Dec. 26).

1972: *Frog Jog* (Apr. 23) and *Flight To The Finish* (Apr. 30).

TITO

The adventures of a small, portly Mexican boy named Tito and his burro companion, Burrito, comprised this short–lived series for Columbia Pictures. The characters, who were created by Dave Fleischer, later found new life in "Real Screen" and "Fox and the Crow" comics. *Directed by Bob Wickersham and Howard Swift. Produced by Dave Fleischer and later Ray Katz. Voice credits unknown. Technicolor. A Columbia Pictures release.*

1942: *Tito's Guitar* (Wickersham/Oct. 30/*Color Rhapsody*).

1945: *Fiesta Time* (Wickersham/Apr. 4/*Color Rhapsody*).

1947: *Loco Lobo* (Swift/Jan. 9/*Color Rhapsody*).

TOBY THE PUP

Columbia producer Charles Mintz, who produced several major cartoon series for the studio, hired two of Max Fleischer's best animators, Dick Huemer and Sid Marcus, to head a new animation unit in California to expand his cartoon operations and sell a separate series to RKO–Radio Pictures. It was Marcus who devised the character for that series, Toby the Pup, a malicious, frisky pup who headlined in only 12 films. *Directed by Dick Huemer and Sid Marcus. Black–and–white. Voice credits unknown. A RKO–Van Beuren release.*

1930: *The Museum* (Aug. 19), *Toby The Fiddler* (Sept. 1), *Toby The Miner* (Oct. 1), *Toby The Showman* (Nov. 22) and *The Bug House* (Dec. 7).

1931: *Circus Time* (Jan. 25), *Toby The Milkman* (Feb. 25), *Brown Derby* (Mar. 22), *Down South* (Apr. 15), *Halloween* (May 1), *Toby The Bull Thrower* (June 7) and *Aces Up.*

TODDLE TALES

This series was Burt Gillett's first following his defection from Walt Disney Studios to direct new cartoons for Van Beuren. Only three films were made in the series, which blended live–action sequences of two children with animated animal characters in each adventure. The filmed openings led into each story which might involve why dogs wag their tails or how ducks evolved, based on discussions with these animals. *Directors were Burt Gillett, Steve Muffati, Jim Tyer and Tom Palmer. Black–and–white. Cinecolor. Voice credits unknown. A RKO–Van Beuren release.*

1934: *Granfather's Clock* (Gillett, Tyer/June 29), *Along Came A Duck* (Gillett, Muffati/Aug. 10) and *A Little Bird Told Me* (Gillett, Tyer/Sept. 7).

TOM AND JERRY (MGM)

MGM's madcap adventures of the feuding alley cat, Tom, and his mischief–making nemesis, Jerry the mouse, won seven Academy Awards during their heyday.

The idea for this pairing came from veteran animators William Hanna and Joseph Barbera, who later created the likes of Yogi Bear, Ruffy and Reddy and countless other characters after opening their own studio in the late 1950s. "We asked ourselves what would be a normal conflict between characters provoking comedy while retaining a basic situation from which we could continue to generate plots and stories," Hanna once recalled. "We almost decided on a dog and a fox before we hit on the idea of using a cat and a mouse."

Hanna and Barbera named the characters based on hundreds of suggestions submitted by studio employees in a contest staged at the MGM lot. (In their screen debut Tom was

Tom and Jerry from their first screen appearance, Puss Gets The Boot (1940). The characters were created by William Hanna and Joseph Barbera. © Turner Entertainment

actually called "Jasper.") The first Tom and Jerry cartoon, *Puss Gets The Boot,* was produced and released in 1940, despite producer Fred Quimby's reservations about the characters. ("What can you do with a cat and a mouse that would be different?")

The first cartoon quickly established the entire tone of the series: Tom, the mischievous house cat, trying to outfox the equally clever mouse, Jerry. The formula remained the same throughout the history of the series, though the characters underwent gradual changes in their appearance. (In earlier films they looked homey before being given more distinctive personalities of their own.)

Besides starring in cartoon shorts, Tom and Jerry also appeared as animated characters in live–action sequences of two classic MGM musicals: Gene Kelly's *Anchor's Aweigh* (1944) (Jerry only) and Esther Williams' *Dangerous When Wet* (1953) featuring both characters swimming with Williams in complete synchronization.

Quimby produced the series until his retirement in 1955; from then through 1958 Hanna and Barbera performed dual roles as the series' producers and directors.

The popular screen tandem lost some of their comedy flair after Hanna and Barbera left MGM to launch their own production company, Hanna–Barbera Productions. From 1961 to 1962, Gene Deitch, a Czech cartoon director, tried animating new Tom and Jerry adventures which were unmemorable at best.

In 1963, former Warner Brothers animator/director Chuck Jones and producer Les Golden, who formed Sib–Tower 12 Productions (later renamed MGM Animation/Visual Arts), convinced MGM to allow them to produce a third series of films. But even under the watchful eye of Jones the films failed to generate much excitement. As one anonymous MGM executive remarked after a board of directors screening: "Those are god awful!"

Even Jones has admitted making the cartoons was a mistake: "They were not my characters and I didn't really understand them as well as, let's say, the Road Runner and Coyote. The

Tom and Jerrys I did look like the Road Runner and Coyote in cat and mouse drag!" *Other series directors included Ben Washam, Abe Levitow, Tom Ray and Jim Pabian. Technicolor. CinemaScope. A Metro–Goldwyn–Mayer release.*

1940:   *Puss Gets The Boot* (with Mammy/Hanna, Barbera/ Feb. 10).

1941:   *The Midnight Snack* (with Mammy/Hanna, Barbera/ July 19/re: Feb. 27, 1948) and *The Night Before Christmas* (Hanna, Barbera/Dec. 6/A.A. nominee).

1942:   *Fraidy Cat* (Hanna, Barbera/Jan. 17), *Dog Trouble* (with Spike and Mammy/Hanna, Barbera/Apr. 18), *Puss 'N' Toots* (Hanna, Barbera/May 30), *The Bowling Alley Cat* (Hanna, Barbera/July 18) and *Fine Feathered Friend* (Hanna, Barbera/ Oct. 10/re: Jan. 1, 1949).

1943:   *Sufferin' Cats* (with Meathead/Hanna, Barbera/Jan. 16/re: June 4, 1949), *Lonesome Mouse* (with Mammy/Hanna, Barbera/May 22/re: Nov. 26, 1949), *Yankee Doodle Mouse* (Hanna, Barbera/June 26/A.A. winner) and *Baby Puss* (with Meathead/Hanna, Barbera/Dec. 25).

1944:   *Zoot Cat* (with Toots/Hanna, Barbera/Feb. 26), *Million Dollar Cat* (Hanna, Barbera/May 6/re: May 6, 1954), *The Bodyguard* (with Spike/Hanna, Barbera/July 22), *Puttin' On The Dog* (with Spike/Hanna, Barbera/Oct. 28/re: Oct. 20, 1951) and *Mouse Trouble* (Hanna, Barbera/Nov. 23/re: Dec. 12, 1951/A.A. winner/originally *Cat Nipped* and *Kitty Foiled*).

1945:   *The Mouse That Comes To Dinner* (with Toots, Mammy/Hanna, Barbera/May 5/re: Jan. 19, 1952/originally *Mouse To Dinner*), *Mouse In Manhattan* (Hanna, Barbera/July 7/ originally *Manhattan Serenade*), *Tee For Two* (Hanna, Barbera/July 21), *Flirty Birdy* (Hanna, Barbera/Sept. 22/re: July 4, 1953/originally *Love Boids*) and *Quiet Please* (Hanna, Barbera/Dec. 22/A.A. winner).

1946:   *Springtime For Thomas* (with Toots/Hanna, Barbera/ Mar. 30), *The Milky Waif* (with Nibbles/Hanna, Barbera/May 18), *Trap Happy* (with Meathead/Hanna, Barbera/June 29/re: Mar. 6, 1954) and *Solid Serenade* (with Spike, Toots, Meathead/Hanna, Barbera/Aug. 31).

1947:   *Cat Fishin'* (with Spike/Hanna, Barbera/Feb. 22/re: Oct. 30, 1954), *Part–Time Pal* (with Mammy/Hanna, Barbera/ Mar. 15/originally *Fair Weathered Friend*), *The Cat Concerto* (Hanna, Barbera/Apr. 26/A.A. winner), *Dr. Jekyll And Mr. Mouse* (Hanna, Barbera/June 14/A.A. nominee), *Salt Water Tabby* (with Toots/Hanna, Barbera/July 12), *A Mouse In The House* (with Mammy/Hanna, Barbera/Aug. 30) and *The Invisible Mouse* (Hanna, Barbera/Sept. 27).

1948:   *Kitty Foiled* (Hanna, Barbera/May 1), *The Truce Hurts* (with Spike/Hanna, Barbera/July 17), *Old Rockin' Chair Tom* (Hanna, Barbera/Sept. 18), *Professor Tom* (Hanna, Barbera/ Oct. 30) and *Mouse Cleaning* (with Mammy/Hanna, Barbera/ Dec. 11/A.A. winner).

1949:   *Polka Dot Puss* (Hanna, Barbera/Feb. 26/re: Sept. 28, 1956), *The Little Orphan* (with Nibbles/Hanna, Barbera/Apr. 30/A.A. winner), *Hatch Up Your Troubles* (Hanna, Barbera/ May 14/A.A. nominee/remade as *The Egg and Jerry*), *Heavenly*

Puss (Hanna, Barbera/July 9/re: Oct. 26, 1956), *Cat and Mermouse* (Hanna, Barbera/Sept. 3), *Love That Pup* (with Spike and Tyke/Hanna, Barbera/Oct. 1), *Jerry's Diary* (Hanna, Barbera/Oct. 22) and *Tennis Chumps* (Hanna, Barbera/Dec. 10).

1950:   *Little Quacker* (Hanna, Barbera/Jan. 7), *Saturday Evening Puss* (Hanna, Barbera/Jan. 14/originally *Party Cat*), *Texas Tom* (with Toots/Hanna, Barbera/Mar. 11), *Jerry And The Lion* (Hanna, Barbera/Apr. 8/originally *Hold That Lion*), *Safety Second* (Hanna, Barbera/July 1/originally *F'r Safety Sake*), *Tom And Jerry In The Hollywood Bowl* (Hanna, Barbera/Sept. 16), *The Framed Cat* (Hanna, Barbera/Oct. 21) and *Cueball Cat* (Hanna, Barbera/Nov. 25).

1951:   *Casanova Cat* (Hanna, Barbera/Jan. 6), *Jerry And The Goldfish* (Hanna, Barbera/Mar. 3), *Jerry's Cousin* (Hanna, Barbera/Apr. 7/originally *City Cousin* and *Muscles Mouse*), *Sleepy Time Tom* (Hanna, Barbera/May 26), *His Mouse Friday* (Hanna, Barbera/July 7), *Slicked Up Pup* (with Spike and Tyke/ Hanna, Barbera/Sept. 8), *Nit Witty Kitty* (Hanna, Barbera/Oct. 6) and *Cat Napping* (Hanna, Barbera/Dec. 8).

1952:   *Flying Cat* (Hanna, Barbera/Jan. 12), *Duck Doctor* (Hanna, Barbera/Feb. 16), *Two Mouseketeers* (Hanna, Barbera/ Mar. 15/A.A. winner), *Smitten Kitten* (Hanna, Barbera/Apr. 12), *Triplet Trouble* (Hanna, Barbera/Apr. 19), *Little Runaway* (Hanna, Barbera/June 14), *Fit To Be Tied* (Hanna, Barbera/July 26), *Push–Button Kitty* (Hanna, Barbera/Sept. 6), *Cruise Cat* (Hanna, Barbera/Oct. 18) and *The Dog House* (Hanna, Barbera/Nov. 29).

1953:   *The Missing Mouse* (Hanna, Barbera/Jan. 10), *Jerry And Jumbo* (Hanna, Barbera/Feb. 21), *Johann Mouse* (Hanna, Barbera/Mar. 21/A.A. winner/narration by Hans Conried), *That's My Pup* (with Spike and Tyke/Hanna, Barbera/May 28), *Just Ducky* (Hanna, Barbera/Sept. 5), *Two Little Indians* (Hanna, Barbera/Oct. 17) and *Life With Tom* (Hanna, Barbera/Nov. 21).

1954:   *Puppy Tale* (Hanna, Barbera/Jan. 23), *Posse Cat* (Hanna, Barbera/Jan. 30), *Hic–Cup Pup* (with Spike and Tyke/ Hanna, Barbera/Apr. 17/originally *Tyke Takes A Nap*), *Little School Mouse* (Hanna, Barbera/May 29), *Baby Butch* (Hanna, Barbera/Aug. 14), *Mice Follies* (Hanna, Barbera/Sept. 4), *Neopolitan Mouse* (Hanna, Barbera/Oct. 21), *Downhearted Duckling* (Hanna, Barbera/Nov. 13), *Pet Peeve* (Hanna, Barbera/Nov. 20/CinemaScope) and *Touche Pussy Cat* (with Toots/ Hanna, Barbera/Dec. 18/re: May 21, 1955/CinemaScope).

1955:   *Southbound Duckling* (Hanna, Barbera/Mar. 12/re: June 25, 1955/CinemaScope), *Pup On A Picnic* (with Spike and Tyke/Hanna, Barbera/Apr. 30/CinemaScope), *Mouse For Sale* (Hanna, Barbera/May 21/CinemaScope), *Designs On Jerry* (Hanna, Barbera/Sept. 2/CinemaScope), *Tom and Cherie* (Hanna, Barbera/Sept. 9/CinemaScope), *Smarty Cat* (Hanna, Barbera/ Oct. 14/CinemaScope), *Pecos Pest* (Hanna, Barbera/Nov. 11) and *That's My Mommy* (Hanna, Barbera/Nov. 19/CinemaScope).

1956:   (All in CinemaScope from this point on.) *The Flying Sorceress* (Hanna, Barbera/Jan. 27), *The Egg and Jerry* (Hanna, Barbera/Mar. 23/remake of *Hatch Up Your Troubles*), *Busy*

Buddies (Hanna, Barbera/May 4), *Muscle Beach Tom* (Hanna, Barbera/Sept. 7), *Down Beat Bear* (Hanna, Barbera/Oct. 21), *Blue Cat Blues* (Hanna, Barbera/Nov. 6) and *Barbecue Brawl* (Hanna, Barbera/Dec. 14).

1957: *Tops With Pops* (Hanna, Barbera/Feb. 22/remake of *Love That Pup*), *Timid Tabby* (Hanna, Barbera/Apr. 19), *Feedin' The Kiddie* (Hanna, Barbera/June 7/remake of *The Little Orphan*), *Mucho Mouse* (Hanna, Barbera/Sept. 6) and *Tom's Photo Finish* (Hanna, Barbera/Nov. 1).

1958: *Happy Go Ducky* (Hanna, Barbera/Jan. 3/originally *One Quack Mind*), *Royal Cat Nap* (Hanna, Barbera/Mar. 7), *Vanishing Duck* (Hanna, Barbera/May 2), *Robin Hoodwinked* (Hanna, Barbera/June 6) and *Tot Watchers* (Hanna, Barbera/Aug. 1).

Rembrandt Releases

1961: *Switchin' Kitten* (Deitch/Sept. 7), *Down And Outing* (Deitch/Oct. 26) and *It's Greek To Me—Ow* (Deitch/Dec. 7).

1962: *High Steaks* (Deitch/Jan.), *Mouse Into Space* (Deitch/Feb.), *Landing Stripling* (Deitch/Apr.), *Calypso Cat* (Deitch/June), *Dikie Moe* (Deitch/July), *The Tom And Jerry Cartoon Kit* (Deitch/Aug.), *Tall In The Trap* (Deitch/Sept.), *Sorry Safari* (Deitch/Oct.), *Buddies Thicker Than Water* (Deitch/Nov.) and *Carmen Get It* (Deitch/Dec.).

Sih—Tower 12 Productions Releases

1963: *Penthouse Mouse* (Jones).

1964: *The Cat Above, The Mouse Below* (Jones), *Is There A Doctor In The Mouse?* (Jones) and *Unshrinkable Jerry Mouse* (Jones).

1965: *Tom—Ic Energy* (Jones), *Ah—Sweet Mouse Story Of Life* (Jones), *The Brothers Carry—Mouse—Off* (Fabian), *Bad Day At Cat Rock* (Jones), *Haunted Mouse* (Jones), *I'm Just Wild About Jerry* (Jones), *Of Feline Bondage* (Jones), *Tom Thumb* (Jones), *The Year Of The Mouse* (Jones), *The Cat's Me—Ouch* (Jones) and *Jerry—Go—Round* (Levitow).

1966: *Duel Personality* (Jones), *Jerry Jerry Quite Contrary* (Jones), *Love Me, Love My Mouse* (Washam), *Puss 'N' Boats* (Levitow), *Filet Meow* (Levitow), *Matinee Mouse* (Ray), *A—Tominable Snowman* (Levitow) and *Catty Cornered* (Levitow).

1967: *Cat And Duplicat* (Jones), *O Solar Meow* (Levitow), *Guide Mouse—Ille* (Levitow), *Rock 'N' Rodent* (Levitow), *Cannery Rodent* (Jones), *The Mouse From H.U.N.G.E.R.* (Jones), *Surf Bored Cat* (Levitow), *Shutter Bugged Cat* (Ray), *Advance And Be Mechanized* (Washam) and *Purr Chance To Dream* (Washam).

TOM AND JERRY (VAN BEUREN)

This was not MGM's famous cat—and—mouse team but rather an earlier duo of rawboned leader Tom and his dumpy cohort Jerry in primitively animated stories combining action and ragtime music with little onscreen dialogue. The series, produced by Van Beuren, was developed by John Foster and studio newcomers George Stallings and George Rufle, both veteran animators of the New York animation circuit. Following the series' first entry, *Wot A Night* (1931), the studio produced 26 cartoons over the next three years before the characters were retired. *Directors were John Foster, George Stallings, Frank Tashlin, George Rufle, Frank Sherman and Harry Bailey. Black—and—white. Voice credits unknown. A RKO—Van Beuren release.*

1931: *Wot A Night* (Foster, Stallings/Aug. 1), *Polar Pals* (Foster, Rufle/Sept. 5), *Trouble* (Foster, Stallings/Oct. 10), *Jungle Jam* (Foster, Rufle/Nov. 14) and *A Swiss Trick* (Foster, Stallings/Dec. 19).

1932: *Rocketeers* (Foster, Rufle/Jan. 30), *Rabid Hunters* (Foster, Stallings/Feb. 27), *In The Bag* (Foster, Rufle/Mar. 26), *Joint Wipers* (Foster, Stallings/Apr. 23), *Pet and Pans* (May 14), *The Tuba Tooter* (Foster, Stallings/June 4), *Plane Dumb* (Foster, Rufle/June 25), *Redskin Blues* (Foster, Stallings/July 23), *Jolly Fish* (Foster, Stallings/Aug. 19), *Barnyard Bunk* (Foster, Rufle/Sept. 6), *A Spanish Twist* (Foster, Stallings/Oct. 7), *Piano Tooners* (Foster, Rufle/Nov. 11) and *Pencil Mania* (Foster, Stallings/Dec. 9).

1933: (Copyright dates are marked by a ©.) *Tight Rope Tricks* (Foster, Rufle/Jan. 6), *The Magic Mummy* (Foster, Stallings/Feb. 7), *Panicky Pup* (Foster, Bailey/Feb. 24/*Aesop's Fable*), *Puzzled Pals* (Stallings, Sherman/© Mar. 31), *Happy Hoboes* (Stallings, Rufle/Mar. 31), *Hook And Ladder Hokum* (Stallings, Tashlin/Apr. 28), *In The Park* (Sherman, Rufle/© May 26) and *The Phantom Rocket* (Sherman, Rufle/July 31).

TOMMY TORTOISE AND MOE HARE

Loosely based on the concept of the timeless children's fable, "Tortoise and the Hare," this series concerned the humorous exploits of a smart rabbit, Moe, and a dumb tortoise, Tommy, who somehow manages to outsmart the super—intelligent hare in outlandish situations. The films were produced for Paramount's *Noveltoons* series. *Directed by Isadore Sparber and Dave Tendlar. Technicolor. A Famous Studios Production released through Paramount Pictures.*

1953: *Winner By A Hare* (Sparber/Apr. 17).

1955: *Rabbit Punch* (Tendlar/Sept. 30).

1956: *Sleuth But Sure* (Tendlar/Mar. 23).

1957: *Mr. Money Gags* (Sparber/June 7).

TOONERVILLE TROLLEY

Fontaine Fox's popular comic strip inspired this abbreviated sound cartoon series, featuring the Skipper, the Powerful Katrinka and the Terrible—tempered Mr. Bang, which was released under the RKO—Van Beuren *Rainbow Parade* series. Director Burt Gillett purchased the rights to make the films in hopes of insuring greater box office success for the fledgling Van Beuren cartoon studio. *Directed by Burt Gillett and Tom Palmer. Black—and—white. A RKO—Van Beuren release.*

1936: *Toonerville Trolley* (Gillett, Palmer/Jan. 17), *Trolley Ahoy* (Gillett/July 3) and *Toonerville Picnic* (Gillett/Oct. 2).

Tweety unknowingly walks into the mouth of a cat who plans on making him his next meal in Bob Clampett's 1944 cartoon, Birdy And The Beast. It was the second Tweety cartoon ever made. © Warner Brothers, Inc. (Courtesy: Bob Clampett Animation Art)

TWEETY AND SYLVESTER

The bird–hungry cat Sylvester plotted fruitlessly against the clever canary, Tweety, whose immortal battle cry for 15 years upon Sylvester's entrance was "I tawt I taw a puddy tat. I did, I did see a puddy tat!"

Both characters made separate film debuts before becoming a team. They shared top billing in 39 cartoons between 1947 and 1964, garnering two Academy Awards—for *Tweetie Pie* (1947) and *Birds Anonymous* (1957)—and three Oscar nominations. The films alternately featured another series regular, sweet, bespectacled Granny, Tweety's owner, who was far from sweet when Sylvester was around, pounding on him whenever he attempted to lay his hands on her baby–faced, baby–voiced pet bird.

Mel Blanc voiced both characters. His voice for Sylvester was similar to Daffy Duck's, featuring the same sputtering delivery and slurred voice. The only difference was his recorded dialogue was sped up in the sound studio. As for the voice of Tweety, Bob Clampett developed the idea of what the small bird should sound like. Top layout artist Michael Sasanoff and animator/director Robert McKimson both recalled that Clampett used to talk in the "baby talk voice" later used for Tweety while just kidding around at the studio.

Clampett created Tweety, basing the baby bird's wide–eyed stare on a childhood picture of himself. Tweety's famous catchphrase, "I Tawt I Taw A Putty Tat," was actually derived from a phrase Clampett had used years earlier in a letter to a friend next to a drawing of a little bird. (The catchphrase became so popular that in 1950 Warner Brothers story man Warren Foster composed a song using the phrase as its title. The record sold more than two million copies and became a novelty in England.)

Clampett directed the first three cartoons in the series, beginning with 1942's *A Tale Of Two Kitties*, which co-starred Babbit and Catstello, a pair of cats resembling famed comedians, Abbott and Costello. Friz Freleng took over the series after Clampett left the studio in 1946. Freleng directed the bulk of the series, with additional titles produced under the direction of Hawley Pratt and Gerry Chiniquy. *Technicolor. A Warner Brothers release.*

Voices:
Tweety: Mel Blanc, **Sylvester the Cat:** Mel Blanc, **Granny:** Bea Bendaret, June Foray

1942: *A Tale Of Two Kitties* (with Babbit and Catstello/Clampett/Nov. 21/first Tweety cartoon).

1944: *Birdy And the Beast* (Clampett/Aug. 19).

1945: *A Grusome Twosome* (Clampett/June 9).

1947: *Tweetie Pie* (Freleng/May 3/A.A. winner).

1948: *I Taw A Putty Tat* ((Freleng/Apr. 2).

1949: *Bad Ol' Putty Tat* (Freleng/July 23).

1950: *Home Tweet Home* (Freleng/Jan. 14).

1951: *Room And Bird* (Freleng/June 2) and *Tweety's S.O.S.* (with Granny/Freleng/Sept. 22).

1953: *Fowl Weather* (Freleng/Apr. 4), *Tom Tom Tomcat* (Freleng/June 27) and *Catty Cornered* (Freleng/Oct. 31).

1954: *Muzzle Tough* (Freleng/June 26).

1955: *Tweety's Circus* (Freleng/June 4).

1956: *Tree Cornered Tweety* (Freleng/May 19) and *Tugboat Granny* (with Granny/Freleng/June 13).

1957: *Tweet Zoo* (Freleng/Jan. 12), *Tweety And The Beanstalk* (Freleng/May 16) and *Birds Anonymous* (Freleng/Aug. 10/A.A. winner).

1958: *A Bird In A Bonnet* (Freleng/Sept. 27).

1959: *Trick Or Tweet* (Freleng/Mar. 21), *Tweet And Lovely* (Freleng/July 18) and *Tweet Dreams* (Freleng/Dec. 5).

1960: *Hyde And Go Tweet* (Freleng/May 14) and *Trip For Tat* (Freleng/Oct. 29).

1961: *The Last Hungry Cat* (Freleng/Dec. 2).

DePatie–Freleng Enterprises Releases
1964: *Hawaiian Aye Aye* (Chiniquy/June 27).

Looney Tunes
1950: *All A–Bir–r–d* (Freleng/June 24) and *Canary Row* (Freleng/Oct. 7).

1951: *Puddy Tat Twouble* (Freleng/Feb. 24) and *Tweet Tweet Tweety* (Freleng/Dec. 15).

1952: *Gift Wrapped* (Freleng/Feb. 16), *Ain't She Tweet* (Freleng/June 21) and *Bird In A Guilty Cage* (Freleng/Aug. 30).

1953: *Snow Business* (Freleng/Jan. 17) and *A Streetcar Named Sylvester* (Freleng/Sept. 5).

1954: *Dog Pounded* (Freleng/Jan. 2).

1955: *Sandy Claws* (Freleng/Apr. 2/A.A. nominee) and *Red Riding Hoodwinked* (Freleng/Oct. 29).

1956: *Tweet and Sour* (Freleng/Mar. 24).

1957: *Greedy For Tweety* (Freleng/Sept. 28).

1958: *A Pizza Tweety Pie* (Freleng/Feb. 22).

1961: *Rebel Without Claws* (Freleng/July 15).

1962: *The Jet Cage* (Freleng/Sept. 22).

UPA CARTOON SPECIALS

This series featured previous characters like Gerald McBoing Boing and other cartoon stars in cartoon specials produced by United Productions of America (UPA), which later produced television strips based on Dick Tracy and Mr. Magoo.

One cartoon in the series, *The Tell–Tale Heart* (1953), was adapted from a story by Edgar Allen Poe. Only one film was nominated for an Academy Award, the series' last entry, *The Jaywalker* (1956). *Directors were Bill Hurtz, Art Babbitt, Theodore Tee Hee, Ted Parmelee, Bob Cannon, Abe Liss, Paul Julian and Osmond Evans. Technicolor. A UPA Production released through Columbia Pictures*

1953: *A Unicorn In The Garden* (Hurtz/Sept. 24) and *The Tell–Tale Heart* (Parmelee/Dec. 27/narrated by actor James Mason).

1954: *Bringing Up Father* (Hurtz/Jan. 14), *Ballet–Oops* (Cannon/Feb. 11), *The Man On The Flying Trapeze* (Parmelee/Apr. 8), *Fudget's Budget* (Cannon/June 17), *Kangaroo Courting* (Burness/July 22) and *How Now Boing Boing* (with Gerald McBoing Boing/Cannon/Sept. 9).

1955: *Spare The Child* (Liss/Jan. 27), *Four Wheels And No Brake* (with Pete Hothead/Parmelee/Mar. 24), *Baby Boogie* (Julian/May 19), *Christopher Crumpet's Playmate* (Cannon/Sept. 8) and *Rise Of Duton Lang* (Evans/Dec. 1).

1956: *The Jaywalker* (Cannon/May 31/A.A. nominee).

WALT DISNEY SPECIALS

When *Silly Symphonies* faded into screen history, Walt Disney produced new cartoon specials to replace the old animated favorites. This long–running series proved equally successful for the studio, reaping eight Academy Award nominations and three Oscar statuettes for Best Short–Subject of the Year.

Over the years, several well–known Disney characters appeared in the series, including Scrooge McDuck, Winnie the Pooh and Roger Rabbit. *Directors were Dick Rickard, Norm Ferguson, Eric Larson, Bob Cormack, Gerry Geronimi, Bill Roberts, Ham Luske, Jack Kinney, Charles Nichols, Jack Hannah, Wilfred Jackson, Ward Kimball, Bill Justice, Woolie Reitherman, Les Clark, John Lounsbery, Don Bluth, Tim Burton, Darrell Van Citters, Rick Reinert, Michael Cedeno*

and Rob Minkoff. Technicolor. A Walt Disney Production released through RKO Radio Pictures and later Buena Vista.

RKO Radio Pictures Releases
1938: *Ferdinand The Bull* (Rickard/Nov. 25/A.A. winner).

1939: *The Practical Pig* (Rickard/Feb. 24).

1943: *Education For Death* (Geronimi/Jan. 15), *Reason And Emotion* (Roberts/Aug. 27/A.A. nominee) and *Chicken Little* (Geronimi/Dec. 17).

1944: *The Pelican And The Snipe* (Luske/Jan. 7).

1950: *The Brave Engineer* (Kinney/Mar. 3) and *Morris The Midget Moose* (Hannah/Nov. 24).

1952: *Lambert, The Sheepish Lion* (Hannah/Feb. 8/A.A. nominee), *Susie The Little Blue Coupe* (Geronimi/June 6) and *The Little House* (Jackson/Aug. 8).

1953: *Melody* (Nichols, Kimball/May 28/aka: *Adventures In Music*/Disney's first 3–D cartoon), *Football Now And Then* (Kinney/Oct. 2) *Toot, Whistle, Plunk And Boom* (Nichols, Kimball/Nov. 10/A.A. winner/Disney's first CinemaScope cartoon/a Buena Vista release) and *Ben And Me* (Luske/Nov. 10/A.A. nominee/a Buena Vista release).

1954: *Two For The Record* (Kinney/Apr. 23/from *Make Mine Music*), *Pigs Is Pigs* (Kinney/May 21/A.A. nominee), *Johnny Fedora And Alice Bluebonnet* (Kinney/May 21/from *Make Mine Music*), *Casey Bats Again* (Kinney/June 18), *The Martins And The Coys* (Kinney/June 18/from *Make Mine Music*), *Casey At The Bat* (Geronimi/July 16/from *Make Mine Music*), *Little Toot* (Geronimi/Aug. 13/from *Melody Time*), *Willie The Operatic Whale* (Geronimi, Luske, Cormack/Aug. 17/from *Make Mine Music*/a Buena Vista release), *Once Upon A Wintertime* (Luske/Sept. 17/from *Melody Time*) and *Social Lion* (Kinney/Oct. 15)

1955: *Contrasts In Rhythm* (Kinney, Luske/Mar. 11/from *Melody Time*), *Pedro* (Luske/May 13/from *Saludos Amigos*), *Aquarela Do Brasil* (Jackson/June 24/from *Saludos Amigos*), *The Flying Gauchito* (Ferguson, Larson/July 15/from *The Three Caballeros*), *Peter And The Wolf* (Geronimi/Sept. 14/from *Make Mine Music*/a Buena Vista release) and *Johnny Appleseed* (Jackson/Dec. 25/from *Melody Time*/a Buena Vista release).

Buena Vista Releases
1956: *Hooked Bear* (Hannah/Apr. 27/CinemaScope), *Jack And Old Mac* (Justice/July 18), *Man In Space* (Kimball/July 18), *In The Bag* (Hannah/July 27/CinemaScope) and *A Cowboy Needs A Horse* (Justice/Nov. 6).

1957: *The Story of Anyburg U.S.A.* (Geronimi/June 19), *The Truth About Mother Goose* (Reitherman, Justice/Aug. 28/A.A. nominee) and *Mars And Beyond* (Kimball/Dec. 26).

1958: *Paul Bunyan* (Clark/Aug. 1), *Our Friend The Atom* (Luske/Aug.) and *The Legend of Sleepy Hollow* (Kinney, Geronimi/Nov. 26/from *The Adventures Of Ichabod And Mr. Toad*).

1959: *Noah's Ark* (Justice/Nov. 10/A.A. nominee).

1960: *Goliath II* (Reitherman/Jan. 21/A.A. nominee).

1961: *The Sage Of Windwagon Smith* (Nichols/Mar. 16).

1962: *A Symposium On Popular Songs* (Justice/Dec. 19/A.A. nominee).

1966: *Winnie The Pooh And The Honey Tree* (Reitherman/Feb. 4).

1967: *Scrooge McDuck And Money* (Luske/Mar. 23).

1968: *Winnie The Pooh And The Blustery Day* (Reitherman/Dec. 20/A.A. winner).

1969: *It's Tough To Be A Bird* (Kimball/Dec. 10/A.A. winner).

1970: *Dad, Can I Borrow The Car* (Kimball/Sept. 30).

1971: *Bongo* (Kinney/Jan. 20/from *Fun And Fancy Free*).

1974: *Winnie The Pooh And Tigger Too* (Lounsbery/Dec. 20/A.A. nominee).

1975: *The Madcap Adventures Of Mr. Toad* (Kinney/Dec. 25/from *The Adventures Of Ichabod And Mr. Toad*).

1978: *The Small One* (Bluth/Dec. 16).

1980: *Mickey Mouse Disco* (June 25/compilation cartoon).

1981: *Once Upon A Mouse* (July 10/compilation cartoon).

1982: *Vincent* (Burton/Oct. 1) and *Fun With Mr. Future* (Van Citters/Oct. 27).

1983: *Winnie The Pooh And A Day For Eeyore* (Reinert/Mar. 11).

1987: *Oilspot And Lipstick* (Cedeno/July 28).

1989: *Tummy Trouble* (with Roger Rabbit, Baby Herman/animation directed by Rob Minkoff; live–action by Frank Marshall/July 23).

WALTER LANTZ CARTUNE SPECIALS

Walter Lantz, creator of Woody Woodpecker, Andy Panda and others, lived out his love for music by initiating this series of musical cartoon novelties in 1934, produced in the same form as Disney's *Silly Symphonies* and Warner's early *Merrie Melodies*. No main characters were prominent in these animated efforts, which were based on hit songs of the day. Early titles were filmed in two–strip Cinecolor and then later three–strip Technicolor. *Directors were Walter Lantz, Lester Kline, Alex Lovy, Burt Gillett, Ben Hardaway, Emery Hawkins, James "Shamus" Culhane, Dick Lundy, Elmer Perkins, Paul J. Smith, Tex Avery, Pat Lenihan, Don Patterson and Jack Hannah. Cinecolor. Technicolor. A Walter Lantz Production released through Universal Pictures and United Artists.*

1934: *Jolly Little Elves* (Oct. 1/A.A. nominee) and *Toyland Premiere* (Dec. 7).

1935: *Candy Land* (Apr. 12), *Springtime Serenade* (May 27), *Three Lazy Mice* (July 15) and *The Fox And The Rabbit* (Sept. 30).

1938: *Nellie, The Sewing Machine Girl* (Apr. 11), *Tail End* (Apr. 25), *Movie Phoney News* (May 30), *Nellie, The Indian Chief's Daughter* (June 26), *Voodoo In Harlem* (July 18), *Ghost Town Frolics* (Kline/Sept. 5), *Hollywood Bowl* (Perkins/Oct. 5), *Baby Kittens* (Lovy/Dec. 19), and *Little Blue Blackbirds* (Lenihan/Dec. 26).

1939: *Soup To Mutts* (Kline/Jan. 9), *I'm Just A Jitterbug* (Lovy/Jan. 23), *Magic Beans* (Kline/Feb. 3/*Nertsery Rhyme*), *Birth Of A Toothpick* (Gillett/Feb. 27), *Little Tough Mice* (Lovy/Mar. 13), *One–Armed Bandit* (Lovy/Mar. 27), *Crackpot Cruise* (Lovy/Apr. 10), *Charlie Cuckoo* (Perkins/Apr. 24), *Nellie Of The Circus* (Lovy/May 8), *Bolo Mola Land* (Lovy/May 28), *The Bird On Nellie's Hat* (Lovy/June 19), *Arabs With Dirty Fezzes* (Lovy/July 31), *Snuffy Skunk's Party* (Perkins/Aug. 7), *Slap Happy Valley* (Lovy/Aug. 31/*Crackpot Cruise* cartoon), *A–Haunting We Will Go* (Gillett/Sept. 4/first cartoon in three–strip Technicolor; previous cartoons filmed in two–strip Cinecolor), *Scrambled Eggs* (Lovy/Nov. 20) and *The Sleeping Princess* (Gillett/Dec. 4/Technicolor/*Nertsery Rhyme* cartoon).

1940: *Recruiting Daze* (Lovy/Oct. 28) and *Syncopated Sioux* (Lantz/Dec. 30).

1941: *Fair Today* (Lantz/Feb. 24), *Hysterical High Spots Of American History* (Lantz/Mar. 31), *Scrub Me Mama With A Boogie Beat* (Lantz/Mar. 28), *Salt Water Daffy* (Lantz/June 9), *The Boogie Woogie Bugle Boy of Company B* (Lantz/Sept. 1/A.A. nominee) and *Man's Best Friend* (Lantz/Oct. 20).

1942: *Mother Goose On The Loose* (Lantz/Apr. 13) and *Air Radio Warden* (Lovy/Dec. 21).

1943: *Canine Commandos* (Lovy/June 28).

United Artists Releases
1948: *Kiddie Koncert* (Lundy/Apr. 23).

Universal Pictures Releases
1953: *The Dog That Cried Wolf* (Smith/Mar. 23).

1954: *Dig That Dog* (Patterson/Apr. 12) and *Broadway Bow Wows* (Patterson/Aug. 2).

1955: *Crazy Mixed–Up Pup* (Avery/Feb. 14/A.A. nominee), *Sh–h–h–h!!* (Avery/June 6) and *Flea For Two* (Patterson/July 20).

1957: *The Plumber of Seville* (Lovy/Mar. 11), *Goofy Gardner* (Lovy/Aug. 26) and *The Bongo Punch* (with Pepito Chickeeto/Lovy/Dec. 30).

1960: *Freeloading Feline* (Hannah/Sept. 7) and *Hunger Strife* (Hannah/Oct. 5).

1961: *Eggnaper* (Hannah/Feb.), *Papoose On The Loose* (Smith/Apr. 11), *Bears And The Bees* (Hannah/May) and *Tin Can Concert* (Hannah/Oct. 31).

WILLIE THE WALRUS

As an experiment, Terrytoons cast a walrus in arctic misadventures in an effort to possibly develop new cartoon star material. This series, like several other attempts, was short lived. *Directed by Mannie Davis, Connie Rasinski. Technicolor. A Terrytoons Production released through 20th Century–Fox.*

1954: *Arctic Rivals* (Davis/June).

1955: *An Igloo For Two* (Rasinski/Mar.).

WILLIE WHOPPER

When animator Ub Iwerks ceased production of his *Flip the Frog* series, he created this screen replacement, an imaginative liar named Willie Whopper whose tall tales were the foundation for unusual stories and situations. Adventures opened with Willie standing in front of a *Looney Tunes*–type oval, bragging to viewers, "Say, did I ever tell you this one?" The roly–poly freckle–faced boy never matched the popularity of Iwerks' Flip the Frog, however, and was soon abandoned. *Produced and directed by Ub Iwerks. Black–and–white. Cinecolor. A Celebrity Pictures Production released through Metro–Goldwyn–Mayer.*

1933: *Play Ball* (Sept. 6), *Spite Flight* (Oct. 14), *Stratos–Fear* (Nov. 11) and *Davy Jones* (Dec. 9/Cinecolor).

1934: (Copyright dates are marked by a ©.) *Hell's Fire* (Jan. 6/Cinecolor), *Robin Hood Jr* (Feb. 3), *Insultin' The Sultan* (Apr. 14), *Reducing Creme* (May 19), *Rasslin' Round* (© June 1), *The Cave Man* (July 6), *Jungle Jitters* (July 24), *Good Scout* (© Sept. 1) and *Viva Willie* (© Sept. 20).

WILLOUGHBY WREN

This abbreviated Columbia Pictures cartoon series starred a canary–like bird who acquires tremendous strength each time he dons a magical cap containing particles of hair from Samson, the legendary strongman. Without the hat, he loses his power and becomes meek and helpless. The cartoons were released under the *Phantasy* and *Color Rhapsody* cartoon banners. *Directors were Bob Wickersham and Howard Swift. Technicolor. Voices credits unknown. A Columbia Pictures release.*

1943: *Willoughby's Magic Hat* (Wickersham/Apr. 20/*Phantasy* cartoon).

1944: *Magic Strength* (Wickersham/Feb. 4/*Phantasy* cartoon).

1945: *Carnival Courage* (Swift/Sept. 6/*Color Rhapsody*).

WINDY

Featured in various misadventures, this dumbfounded country bear starred briefly in his own series for creator Walter Lantz. Veteran voice artist Daws Butler provided the vocal characterization for the bumpkin bear. *Directed by Paul J. Smith. Technicolor. A Walter Lantz Production released through Universal Pictures.*

Voices:
Windy: Daws Butler

1958: *Salmon Yeggs* (Smith/Mar. 24) and *Three–Ring Fling* (Lovy/Oct. 6).

1959: *Truant Student* (with Breezy/Smith/Jan. 5) and *Bee Bopped* (with Breezy/Smith/June 15).

WINNIE THE POOH

Children's author A. A. Milne's honey–loving Winnie the Pooh was adapted for the screen in a series of delightfully animated cartoon shorts produced by Walt Disney under the studio's *Walt Disney Specials* banner. Joined by Eeyore, Piglet, Rabbit, Tigger and Christopher Robin, Pooh first appeared on movie screens in 1966's *Winnie The Pooh And The Honey Tree,* directed by Woolie Reitherman. The series received two Academy Award nominations, winning an Oscar for 1968's *Winnie the Pooh And The Blustery Day.* All short–subjects in the series were later rebroadcast as prime–time network specials. In 1977, Pooh starred in his first full–length feature, "The Many Adventures of Winnie the Pooh." *Directed by Woolie Reitherman, John Lounsbery and Rick Reinert. Technicolor. A Walt Disney Production released through Buena Vista.*

Voices:
Winnie the Pooh: Sterling Holloway, Hal Smith, **Eeyore:** Ralph Wright, **Owl:** Hal Smith, **Piglet:** John Fiedler, **Christopher Robin:** Bruce Reitherman, John Walmsley, Kim Christianson, **Kanga:** Barbara Luddy, Julie McWhirter Dees, **Roo:** Clint Howard, Dori Whitaker, Dick Billingsley, **Rabbit:** Junius Matthews, Will Ryan, **Tigger:** Paul Winchell, **Gopher:** Howard Morris

1966: *Winnie The Pooh And The Honey Tree* (Reitherman/Feb. 4).

1968: *Winnie The Pooh And The Blustery Day* (Reitherman/Dec. 20/A.A. winner).

1974: *Winnie The Pooh And Tigger Too* (Lounsbery/Dec. 20/A.A. nominee).

1983: *Winnie The Pooh And A Day For Eeyore* (Reinert/Mar. 11).

WOODY WOODPECKER

This hammering woodpecker with the "Ha–hah–ha–hah" laugh was Walter Lantz's prized creation. Screwball by nature, the redheaded menace was first introduced as the perfect foil in Andy Panda's 1940 cartoon, *Knock Knock,* bearing a strong resemblance to the nutty characterizations of Warner's early Daffy Duck and Bugs Bunny.

Legend long had it that Lantz invented Woody after honeymooning with his wife, former Broadway/screen actress Grace Stafford, with a pesky woodpecker who pounded the roof of their honeymoon cottage as inspiration. Unfortunately, the story was a Hollywood press agent's fabrication since Lantz's honeymoon actually occurred one year after Woody's first cartoon appearance.

"My wife suggested that since I had animated animals like mice, rabbits and so forth that maybe I should invent some kind of woodpecker character. I thought it was a good idea so I created Woody," Lantz later recalled.

In 1941, Lantz officially launched Woody in his own series, casting the malicious woodpecker in a cartoon using his name in the title. Veteran actor Mel Blanc supplied the voice of Woody in the first four or five cartoons. Ben "Bugs" Hardaway, who left Warner to become a storyman for Lantz, lent his vocal talents to the character after Blanc's departure and continued to develop new stories for the series at the same time.

Hardaway did not handle the dual responsibility for long. In 1948, Lantz decided a change was needed and auditioned 50 actors for the "new" voice of Woody. Lantz was not present at the auditions, but he was responsible for making the final choice. Of those who auditioned on tape, he picked the talent who sounded the best. His selection: Grace, his wife, who had "tried out" without informing her husband.

Stafford was first employed in the 1948 Woody Woodpecker release, *Banquet Busters* and remained the voice of Woody until the series ended 24 years later in 1972. By her request, she did not receive voice credit until 1952; she was afraid children would be "disillusioned if they knew a woman" had voiced the famed woodpecker.

Lantz later packaged the early Woody cartoons in a half-hour television series, "The Woody Woodpecker Show," which was first broadcast in 1957 on ABC and was sponsored by Kellogg for nine consecutive seasons. The films are still syndicated today throughout most U.S. television markets and abroad. *Directors were Walter Lantz, Don Patterson, Paul J. Smith, Alex Lovy, Jack Hannah, Sid Marcus, Emery Hawkins, Milt Schaffer, James "Shamus" Culhane, Dick Lundy, Ben Hardaway and Cal Dalton. Technicolor. A Walter Lantz Production released through Universal Pictures and United Artists.*

Voices:

Woody Woodpecker: Mel Blanc, Ben Hardaway, Grace Stafford

1940: *Knock Knock* (with Andy Panda/Lantz/Nov. 25).

1941: *Woody Woodpecker* (Lantz/July 7/originally *Cracked Nut*), *The Screwdriver* (Lantz/Aug. 11) and *What's Cookin'?* (Lantz/Nov. 24/originally *Pantry Panic*).

1942: *Hollywood Matador* (Lantz/Feb. 9), *Ace In The Hole* (Lovy/June 22) and *The Loan Stranger* (Lovy/Oct. 19).

1943: *The Screwball* (Lovy/Feb. 25), *The Dizzy Acrobat* (May 31/A.A. nominee) and *Ration Bored* (Hawkins, Schaffer/July 26).

1944: *Barber of Seville* (Culhane/Apr. 10), *The Beach Nut* (Culhane/Oct. 16) and *Ski For Two* (Culhane/Nov. 13).

1945: *Chew–Chew Baby* (Culhane/Feb. 5), *Woody Dines Out* (Culhane/May 4), *Dippy Diplomat* (Culhane/Aug. 27) and *Loose Nut* (Culhane/Dec. 17).

1946: *Who's Cooking Who?* (Culhane/June 24), *Bathing Buddies* (Lundy/July 1), *The Reckless Driver* (Culhane/Aug. 26) and *Fair Weather Friends* (Culhane/Nov. 18).

United Artists Releases

1947 *Musical Moments From Chopin* (with Andy Panda/Lundy/Feb. 24/A.A. nominee/*Musical Miniature*), *Smoked Hams (Lundy/Apr. 28), Coo–Coo Bird* (Lundy/June 9), *Well Oiled* (Lundy/June 30), *Solid Ivory* (Lundy/Aug. 25) and *Woody, The Giant Killer* (Lundy/Dec. 15).

1948: *The Mad Hatter* (Lundy/Feb.), *Banquet Busters* (with Andy Panda/Lundy Mar. 12), *Wacky–Bye Baby* (Lundy/May), *Wet Blanket Policy* (Lundy/Aug. 27) and *Wild And Woody* (Lundy/Dec. 31).

Universal Pictures Releases

1949: *Drooler's Delight* (Lundy/Mar. 25).

1951: (Copyright dates are marked by a ©.) *Puny Express* (Lundy/Jan. 22), *Sleep Happy* (Lantz/Mar. 26), *Wicket Wacky* (Lantz/© May 28), *Sling Shot 6–7/8* (Lantz/July 23), *Redwood Sap* (Lantz/Oct. 1), *Woody Woodpecker Polka* (Lantz/Oct. 29) and *Destination Meatball* (Lantz/Dec. 24).

1952: *Born To Peck* (Lantz/Feb. 25), *Stage Hoax* (Lantz/Apr. 21), *Woodpecker In The Rough* (Lantz/June 16), *Scalp Treatment* (Lantz/Sept. 18), *The Great Who Dood It* (Lantz/Oct. 20) and *Termites From Mars* (Patterson/Dec. 8).

1953: *What's Sweepin?* (Patterson/Jan. 5), *Bucaneer Woodpecker* (Patterson/Apr. 20), *Operation Sawdust* (Patterson/June 15), *Wrestling Wrecks* (Patterson/July 20), *Hypnotic*

Walter Lantz's Woody Woodpecker experienced many physical changes during his years as a screen star.
© Walter Lantz Productions

Hick (Patterson/Sept. 26/in 3–D), *Belle Boys* (Patterson/Sept. 14) and *Hot Noon* (Smith/Oct. 12).

1954: *Socko In Morocco* (Patterson/Jan. 18), *Alley To Bali* (Patterson/Mar. 15), *Under The Counter Spy* (Patterson/May 10), *Hot Rod Huckster* (Patterson/July 5), *Real Gone Woody* (Smith/Sept. 20), *Fine Feathered Frenzy* (Patterson/Oct. 25) and *Convict Concerto* (Patterson/Nov. 20).

1955: *Helter Shelter* (Smith/Jan. 17), *Witch Crafty* (Smith/Mar. 14), *Private Eye Pooch* (Smith/May 19), *Bedtime Bedlam* (Smith/July 4), *Square Shooting Square* (Smith/Sept. 26), *Bunco Busters* (Smith/Nov. 21) and *The Tree Medic* (Lovy/Dec. 19).

1956: *After The Ball* (Smith/Feb. 13), *Get Lost* (Smith/Mar. 12), *Chief Charlie Horse* (Smith/May 7), *Woodpecker From Mars* (Smith/July 2), *Calling All Cuckoos* (Smith/ Sept. 24), *Niagra Fools* (Smith/Oct. 22), *Arts And Flowers* (Smith/Nov. 19) and *Woody Meets Davy Crewcut* (Lovy/Dec. 17).

1957: *Red Riding Hoodlum* (Smith/Feb. 11) *Box Car Bandit* (Smith/Apr. 8), *Unbearable Salesman* (Smith/June 3), *International Woodpecker* (Smith/July 1), *To Catch A Woodpecker* (Lovy/July 29), *Round Trip To Mars* (Smith/Sept. 23), *Fodder and Son* (Smith/Nov. 4) and *Dopey Dick And The Pink Whale* (Smith/Nov. 15).

1958: *Misguided Missile* (Smith/Jan. 27), *Watch The Birdie* (Lovy/Feb. 24), *Half–Empty Saddles* (Smith/Apr. 21), *His Better Elf* (Smith/July 14), *Everglade Raid* (Smith/Aug. 11), *Tree's A Crowd* (Smith/Sept. 8) and *Jittery Jester* (Smith/Nov. 3).

1959: *Tom Cat Combat* (Smith/Mar. 2), *Log Jammed* (Smith/Apr. 20), *Panhandle Scandal* (Lovy/May 18), *Woodpecker In The Moon* (Lovy/July 13), *The Tee Bird* (Smith/July 13), *Romp In A Swamp* (Smith/Aug. 7) and *Kiddie League* (Smith/Nov. 3).

1960: *Billion-Dollar Boner* (Lovy/Jan. 5), *Pistol–Packin' Woodpecker* (Smith/Mar. 2), *Heap Big Hepcat* (Smith/Mar. 30), *Ballyhooey* (Lovy/Apr. 20), *How To Stuff A Woodpecker* (Smith/May 18), *Bats In The Belfry* (Smith/June 16), *Ozark Lark* (Smith/July 13), *Southern Fried Hospitality* (with Gabby Gator/Hannah/Nov. 28) and *Fowled–Up Falcon* (Smith/Dec. 20).

1961: *Poop Deck Pirate* (Hannah/Jan. 10), *The Bird Who Came To Dinner* (Smith/Mar. 7), *Gabby's Diner* (with Gabby Gator/Hannah Apr.), *Sufferin' Cats* (Smith/June), *Frankenstymied* (Hannah/July 4), *Busman's Holiday* (Smith/Aug.), *Phantom Of The Horse Opera* (Smith/Oct.) and *Woody's Kook–Out* (Hannah/Nov.).

1962: *Rock–A–Bye Gator* (with Gabby Gator/Hannah/Jan. 9), *Home Sweet Homewrecker* (Smith/Jan. 30), *Room And Bored* (Smith/Mar. 6), *Rocket Racket* (with Gabby Gator/Hannah/Apr. 24), *Careless Caretaker* (Smith/May 29), *Tragic Magic* (Smith/July 3), *Voodoo Boo–Hoo* (Hannah/Aug. 14), *Growin' Pains* (Smith/Sept.) and *Little Woody Riding Hood* (with Gabby Gator/Smith/Oct.).

1963: *Greedy Gabby Gator* (with Gabby Gator/Marcus/ Jan.), *Robin Hood Woody* (Smith/Mar.), *Stowaway Woody* (Marcus/May), *Shutter Bug* (Smith/June), *Coy Decoy* (Marcus/

July 9), *The Tenants' Racket* (Marcus/Aug. 30), *Short In The Saddle* (Smith/Sept. 30), *Teepee For Two* (Marcus/Oct. 29), *Science Friction* (Marcus/Nov.) and *Calling Dr. Woodpecker* (Smith/Dec. 24).

1964: *Dumb Like A Fox* (Marcus/Jan. 7), *Saddle–Sore Woody* (Smith/Apr. 7), *Woody's Clip Joint* (Marcus/May), *Skinfolks* (Marcus/July 7), *Get Lost! Little Doggy* (Marcus/Sept.), *Freeway Fracus* (Smith/Sept.) and *Roamin' Roman* (Smith/Dec.).

1965: *Three Little Woodpeckers* (Marcus/Jan. 1), *Woodpecker Wanted* (Smith/Feb. 1), *Birds Of A Feather* (Marcus/ Mar. 1), *Canned Dog Feud* (Smith/Apr. 1), *Janie Get Your Gun* (Smith/May 1), *Sioux Me* (Marcus/June) and *What's Peckin?* (Smith/July 1).

1966: *Rough Riding Hood* (Marcus/Jan. 1), *Lonesome Ranger* (Smith/Feb. 1), *Woody And The Beanstalk* (Smith/ Mar. 1), *Hassle In A Castle* (Smith/Apr.), *The Big Bite* (Smith/ Apr. 1), *Astronut Woody* (Smith/May), *Monster Of Ceremonies* (Smith/May) and *Practical Yolk* (Smith/May 1).

1967: *Sissy Sheriff* (Smith/Jan. 1), *Have Gun—Can't Travel* (Smith/Feb. 1), *The Nautical Nut* (Smith/Mar. 1), *Hot Diggity Dog* (Smith/Mar. 1), *Horse Play* (Smith/Apr. 1) and *Secret Agent Woody* (Smith/May 1).

1968: *Lotsa Luck* (Smith), *Fat In The Saddle* (Smith/June 1), *Feudin', Fightin' 'N' Fussin'* (Smith/June 1), *A Peck Of Trouble* (Smith/July 1), *A Lad In Bagdad* (Smith/Aug. 1), *One Horse Town* (Smith/Oct. 1) and *Woody The Freeloader* (Smith).

1969: *Hook Line And Stinker* (Smith), *Little Skeeter* (Smith), *Woody's Knightmare* (Smith/May 1), *Tumbleweed Greed* (Smith/June 1), *Ship Ahoy, Woody* (Smith/Aug. 1), *Prehistoric Super Salesman* (Smith/Sept. 1) and *Phony Pony* (Smith/ Nov. 1).

1970: *Seal On The Loose* (Smith/May 1), *Wild Bill Hiccup* (Smith/June 1), *Coo Coo Nuts* (Smith/July 1), *Hi–Rise Wise Guys* (Smith/Aug. 1), *Buster's Last Stand* (Smith/Oct. 1) and *All Hams On Deck* (Smith/Nov. 9).

1971: *Flim Flam Fountain* (Smith/Jan. 5), *Sleep Time Chimes* (Smith/Feb. 1), *Reluctant Recruit* (Smith), *How To Trap A Woodpecker* (Smith), *Woody's Magic Touch* (Smith), *Kitty From The City* (Smith), *Snoozin' Bruin Woody* (Smith) and *Shanghai Woody* (Smith).

1972: *Indian Corn* (Smith), *Gold Diggin' Woodpecker* (Smith), *Pecking Holes In Poles* (Smith), *Chili Con Corny* (Smith), *Show Biz Eagle* (Smith), *For The Love Of Pizza* (Smith), *The Genie With The Light Touch* (Smith) and *Bye Bye Blackboard* (Smith).

YOSEMITE SAM

A primary cartoon foil for Bugs Bunny, this pint–sized, short–tempered cowboy, who called himself "the roughest, toughest hombre" in the West, came out guns ablazing in his screen debut opposite the carrot–eating rabbit in 1945's *Hare Trigger*.

Friz Freleng, who directed the film, was responsible for creating Yosemite. "I was looking for a character strong enough to work against Bugs Bunny . . . So I thought to use the smallest guy I could think of along with the biggest voice I could get," Freleng told Warner Brothers historian Steven Schneider.

Freleng used a similar character in his 1944 *Stage Door Cartoon,* who looked and sounded like Yosemite and had only a walk–on part in the film. According to writer Michael Maltese, Freleng drew from several personas—himself included—in developing the loud–mouthed Yosemite. His primary influences were Red Skelton's Sheriff Deadeye, a bone–headed cowboy short on "smarts," and Bob Clampett's gun–slinger character based on Deadeye and comic–strip star Red Ryder in his 1944 *Buckaroo Bugs.*

Yosemite's appearances were limited to supporting roles throughout his career; he never starred in his own series. Today, the character is still seen daily in television reruns of the studio's *Merrie Melodies* and *Looney Tunes* package and in frequent prime–time animated specials. *Directors were Friz Freleng, Ken Harris, Hawley Pratt and Gerry Chiniquy. Technicolor. A Warner Brothers Release.*

Voices:
Yosemite Sam: Mel Blanc

Looney Tunes
1948: *Bucaneer Bunny* (with Bugs Bunny/Freleng/May 8).

1950: *Mutiny On The Bunny* (with Bugs Bunny/Freleng/Feb. 11) and *Big House Bunny* (with Bugs Bunny/Freleng/Apr. 22).

1951: *Rabbit Every Monday* (with Bugs Bunny/Freleng/Feb. 10) and *The Fair Haired Hare* (with Bugs Bunny/Freleng/Apr. 14).

1952: *14 Carrot Rabbit* (with Bugs Bunny/Freleng/Feb. 16) and *Hare Lift* (with Bugs Bunny/Freleng/Dec. 20).

1954: *Captain Hareblower* (with Bugs Bunny/Freleng/Feb. 16).

1955: *Sahara Hare* (with Bugs Bunny/Freleng/Mar. 26) and *Roman Legion Hare* (with Bugs Bunny/Freleng/Nov. 12).

1956: *Rabbitson Crusoe* (with Bugs Bunny/Freleng/Apr. 28).

1957: *Piker's Peak* (with Bugs Bunny/Freleng/May 25).

1958: *Knighty–Knight Bugs* (with Bugs Bunny/Freleng/Aug. 23/A.A. winner).

1959: *Wild And Wooly Hare* (with Bugs Bunny/Freleng/Aug. 1).

1960: *Horse Hare* (with Bugs Bunny/Freleng/Feb. 13).

1961: *Prince Violent* (with Bugs Bunny/Freleng, Pratt/Sept. 2).

1962: *Shishkabugs* (with Bugs Bunny/Freleng/Dec. 8).

DePatie–Freleng Enterprises Releases
1964: *Dumb Patrol* (with Bugs Bunny, Porky Pig/Chiniquy/Jan. 18).

Merrie Melodies
1945: *Hare Trigger* (with Bugs Bunny/Freleng/May 5).

1948: *Bugs Bunny Rides Again* (with Bugs Bunny/Freleng/June 12).

1950: *Bunker Hill Bunny* (with Bugs Bunny/Freleng/Sept. 23).

1951: *Ballot Box Bunny* (with Bugs Bunny/Freleng/Oct. 6).

1953: *Southern Fried Rabbit* (with Bugs Bunny/Freleng/May 2) and *Hare Trimmed* (with Bugs Bunny/Freleng/June 20).

1958: *Hare–Abian Nights* (with Bugs Bunny/Harris/Feb. 28).

1960: *Lighter Than Hare* (with Bugs Bunny/Freleng/Dec. 17).

1961: *Honey's Money* (Freleng/Sept. 1).

1963: *Devil's Feud Cake* (with Bugs Bunny/Freleng/Feb. 9).

FULL–LENGTH ANIMATED FEATURES

The following section is a complete listing of full–length animated features which received wide theatrical distribution in the United States only. Excluded from this section are those features which incorporate small percentages of animation in combination with live action.

Films displaying minor animated sequences which are not mentioned in this section include: *King of Jazz* (1930), which features a four–minute animated opening by Walter Lantz (the first animation to be done in two–color Technicolor); *Hollywood Party* (MGM, 1934), in which an animated Mickey Mouse appears; *She Married A Cop* (1939), featuring Paddy the Pig in a cartoon segment, also seen in the film's remake *Sioux City Sue* (1947) starring Gene Autry; *Victory Through Air Power* (Disney, 1943); *So Dear To Heart* (Disney, 1945); *Anchors Aweigh* (MGM, 1944), featuring Gene Kelly and Jerry Mouse in a popular dance sequence; *Dangerous When Wet* (MGM, 1953), which teams Tom and Jerry with Esther Williams in an underwater sequence; *My Dream Is Yours* (Warner, 1949), the Doris Day–Jack Carson film highlighted by animated appearances of Bugs Bunny and Tweety bird (Bugs appeared one year earlier in another Jack Carson film, *Two Guys From Texas*); *Destination Moon* (1950), featuring Woody Woodpecker in a brief bit of animated business; *Mary Poppins* (1965), in which Julie Andrews and Dick Van Dyke dance in perfect synchronization with several animated penguins; and *Bedknobs And Broomsticks* (1971).

In instances where animated characters play a major part in the story structure of live–action/animated films (i.e., *The Incredible Mr. Limpet*, *Pete's Dragon* and *Roger Rabbit*), those productions have been included.

Technical credits appear with each listing, being limited to the production staff (producer, director, animators, etc.) and voice artists. Production sidelights and other items of interest have been entered under production notes (abbreviated as "PN") whenever appropriate.

The following key translates abbreviations for technical staff listed under each film:

anim:	key animators
anim design:	animated design
anim dir:	animation directors
asst anim dir:	assistant animation directors
asst dir:	assistant director
cart sc:	cartoon score
cart st:	cartoon story
d:	director
l/a dir:	live action director
m:	music
m/a:	music associates
md:	musical direction
m/l:	music and lyrics
m/s:	music and songs
m/sc:	musical score
m/superv:	musical supervision
p:	producer
prod dir:	production director
prod superv:	production supervisor
scr:	screenplay
scr st:	screen story
seq dir:	sequence directors
st:	story
st ad:	story adaptation
st dev:	story development
st dir:	story direction
superv anim:	supervising animators
superv dir:	supervising directors
w:	writer

THE ADVENTURES OF ICHABOD AND MR. TOAD (1949)

A Walt Disney Production released by RKO Radio Pictures. p: Walt Disney; prod superv: Ben Sharpsteen; d: Jack Kinney, Clyde Geronimi, James Algar; dir anim: Frank Thomas, Ollie Johnston, Wolfgang Reitherman, Milt Kahl, John Lounsbery,

Ward Kimball; st: Erdman Penner, Winston Hibler, Joe Rinaldi, Ted Sears, Homer Brightman, Harry Reeves; md: Oliver Wallace; anim: Fred Moore, John Sibley, Marc Davis, Hal Ambro, Harvey Toombs, Hal King, Hugh Fraser, Don Lusk. Songs: "Ichabod," "Katrina," "The Headless Horseman" and "Merrily on Our Way." Running time: 68 minutes.

Voices:

Mr. Toad: Eric Blore, **Cyril:** J. Pat O'Malley, **Rat:** Claude Allister, **John Ployard:** John McLeish, **Mole:** Colin Campbell, **Angus MacBadger:** Campbell Grant, **Winky:** Alec Harford. "Ichabod" narrated by Bing Crosby. "Willows" narrated by Basil Rathbone.

This somewhat forgotten Disney feature combines two half–hour adaptations: Washington Irving's *Legend of Sleepy Hollow,* the story of schoolmaster Ichabod Crane's encounter with the famed horseman and his jack–o–lantern head, and Kenneth Grahame's *Wind in the Willows,* featuring the misadventures of Mr. Toad Hall, a whimsical toad who is wrongly accused of car thievery and tries proving his innocence. Bing Crosby ("Ichabod") and Basil Rathbone ("Willows") provided narration for the films.

PN: The film's original title was *Two Fabulous Characters,* but was changed prior to its release.

THE ADVENTURES OF THE AMERICAN RABBIT (1986)

A Toei Animation Production released by Clubhouse Pictures. p: Masaharu Etoh, Masahisa Saeki, John G. Marshall; d: Fred Wolf, Nobutaka Nishizawa; w: Norm Lenzer (based on the characters created by Stewart Moskowitz); m/l: Mark Volman, Howard Kayland, John Hoier; anim: Shingo Araki, Kenji Yokoyama, Yukiyoshi Hane, Yoshitaka Yashima, Shigeo Matoba, Hirohide Shikishima, Ikuo Fudanuki, Katsuyoshi Nakatsuru, Takashi Nashizawa. Running time: 85 minutes.

Voices:

Theo: Bob Arbogast, **Tini Meeny:** Pat Freley, **Rob/American Rabbit:** Barry Gordon, **Rodney:** Bob Holt, **Dip/Various Characters:** Lew Horn **Bruno:** Norm Lenzer, **Vultor/Buzzard:** Ken Mars, **Too Loose:** John Mayer, **Lady Pig:** Maitzi Morgan, **Ping Pong:** Lorenzo Music, **Bunny O'Hare:** Lauri O'Brien, **Mentor:** Hal Smith, **Mother:** Russi Taylor, **Fred Red:** Fred Wolf.

Loosely based along the lines of Superman, mild–mannered, bespectacled Rob Rabbit obtains supernatural powers following a bizarre encounter with a mystical rabbit wizard, enabling him to restore peace and order as a super–rabbit.

ALAKAZAM THE GREAT (1961)

A Toei Animation Production released by American International Pictures. p: Lou Rusoff (U.S.), Hiroshi Okawa (Japan); d: Lee Kresel (U.S.), Teiji Yabushita, Osamu Tezuka, Daisaku Shirakawa (Japan); scr: Lou Rusoff, Lee Kresel (U.S.), Keinosuke Uekusa (Japan), m: Les Baxter; anim: Koichi Mori, Yasuo

Otsuka, Masao Kumagawa, Akira, Daikubara, Hideo Furusawa. Songs: "Ali The Great," "Bluebird in the Cherry Tree," "Under the Waterfall" and "Aliki–Aliko–Alakazam." Running time: 84 minutes.

Voices:

Alakazam: Frankie Avalon, **De De:** Dodie Stevens, **Sir Quigley Broken Bottom:** Jonathan Winters, **Lulipopo:** Arnold Stang, **Narrator:** Sterling Holloway.

Alakazam, a shy and modest monkey, is chosen by his peers to be the monarch of all animals on earth. When the power goes to his head, King Amo, ruler of Majutsoland, the celestial island where all retired magicians reside, imprisons Alakazam in a cave to teach him a lesson. He is later released from confinement with the stipulation that he go about the countryside performing good deeds.

PN: Released in Japan in 1960 in ToeiScope as *Saiyu–ki,* the film was re–edited and re–titled for American release, running four minutes shorter than the original production.

ALICE IN WONDERLAND (1951)

A Walt Disney Production released by RKO Radio Pictures. p: Walt Disney; prod. superv: Ben Sharpsteen; d: Clyde Geronimi, Hamilton Luske, Wilfred Jackson; anim dir: Milt Kahl, Ward Kimball, Frank Thomas, Eric Larson, John Lounsbery, Ollie Johnston, Wolfgang Reitherman, Marc Davis, Les Clark, Norman Ferguson; st: Winston Hibler, Bill Peet, Joe Rinaldi, Bill Cottrell, Joe Grant, Del Connell, Ted Sears, Erdman Penner, Milt Banta, Dick Kelsey, Dick Huemer, Tom Oreb, John Walbridge; m/sc: Oliver Wallace; anim: Hal King, Judge Whitaker, Hal Ambro, Bill Justice, Phil Duncan, Bob Carlson, Don Lusk, Cliff Nordberg, Harvey Toombs, Fred Moore, Marvin Woodward, Hugh Fraser, Charles Nichols. Songs: "Very Good Advice," "In a World of My Own," "All in a Golden Afternoon," "Alice in Wonderland," "The Walrus and the Carpenter," "The Caucus Race," "I'm Late," "Painting the Roses Red," "March of the Cards," "Twas Brillig," "The Unbirthday Song," "We'll Smoke the Blighter Out," "Old Father William and "A E I O U." Running time: 75 minutes.

Voices:

Alice: Kathryn Beaumont, **Mad Hatter:** Ed Wynn, **Caterpillar:** Richard Haydn, **Cheshire Cat:** Sterling Holloway, **March Hare:** Jerry Colonna, **Queen of Hearts:** Verna Felton, **Walrus, Carpenter, Tweedledee and Tweedledum:** J. Pat O'Malley, **White Rabbit, Dodo:** Bill Thompson, **Alice's Sister:** Heather Angel, **Door Knob:** Joseph Kearns, **Bill Card Painter:** Larry Grey, **Nesting Mother Bird:** Queenie Leonard, **King of Hearts:** Dink Trout, **The Rose:** Doris Lloyd, **Dormouse:** James Macdonald, **Card Painters:** The Mello Men, **Flamingoes:** Pinto Colvig, **Card Painter:** Ken Beaumont.

Based on Lewis Carroll's two books, *Alice in Wonderland* and *Through the Looking Glass,* this classic Disney feature traces young Alice's dream of falling through space and time into a magical land of make–believe where she meets everything from the disappearing Cheshire Cat to the White Rabbit ("I'm late, I'm late for a very important date!").

ALL DOGS GO TO HEAVEN (1989)

A Sullivan Bluth Studios Ireland Ltd. Production in association with Goldcrest Films released by United Artists. p: Don Bluth, Gary Goldman, John Pomeroy; d: Don Bluth; scr: Davis Weiss; st: Don Bluth, Ken Cromar, Gary Goldman, Larry Leker, Linda Miller, Monica Parker, John Pomeroy, Guy Schulman, David Steinberg, David N. Weiss; m: Ralph Burns; anim dir: John Pomeroy, Linda Miller, Ralph Zondag, Dick Zondag, Lorna Pomeroy–Cook, Jeff Etter, Ken Duncan; anim: Jeffrey J. Varab, Jean Morel, Cathy Jones, Anne–Marie Bardwell, Silvia Hoefnagels, John Hill, Gary Perkovac, Fernando Moro, Ralf Palmer, Tom Roth, Charlie Bonifacio, Paul Newberry, Alain Costa, David G. Simmons, Michel Gagne, John Power, T. Daniel Hofstedt, Enis Tahsin Ozgur. Songs: "You Can't Keep a Good Dog Down," "Let Me Be Surprised," "What's Mine Is Yours," "Let's Make Music Together," "Soon You'll Come Home" and "Hallelujah." Running time: 84 minutes.

Voices:

Itchy: Dom DeLuise, **Charlie:** Burt Reynolds, **Dog Caster:** Daryl Gilley, **Vera:** Candy Devine, **Killer:** Charles Nelson Reilly, **Carface:** Vic Tayback, **Whippet Angel:** Melba Moore, **Anne–Marie:** Judith Barsi, **Harold:** Rob Fuller, **Kate:** Earleen Carey, **Stella Dallas:** Anna Manahan, **Sir Reginald:** Nigel Pegram, **Flo:** Loni Anderson, **King Gator:** Ken Page, **Terrier:** Godfrey Quigley, **Mastiff:** Jay Stevens, **Puppy:** Cyndi Cozzo, **Gambler Dog:** Thomas Durkin, **Puppy:** Kelly Briley, **Fat Pup:** Dana Rifkin, **The Don Bluth Players:** John Carr, John Edding, Jeff Etter, Dan Hofstedt, Dan Kuenster, Dan Molina, Mark Swan, Taylor Swanson, David Weiss, Dick Zondag.

Set in the canine world of New Orleans, circa 1939, this fun–filled, heart–warming story traces the exploits of Charlie B. Barkin, a German shepherd with a con man's charm, who gets a reprieve (he is sent back from heaven to perform some acts of goodness before he will be allowed in) and befriends a little orphan girl, Anne–Marie, kidnapped by his scurvy old gang.

PN: Production of *All Dogs Go to Heaven*—estimated at $13 million—took 19 months to complete, including six months of research, character development and pre–production. More than 1.5 million individual drawings were needed to produce this animated adventure. The film features a musical score by Academy Award–winning composer Ralph Burns (*Cabaret, All That Jazz*) and original songs by Charles Strouse (*Annie*). The film marked the first production for the Sullivan Bluth Studios, relocated from Hollywood to Dublin, Ireland.

ALLEGRO NON TROPPO (1976)

A Bruno Bozetto Film Production release. p & d: Bruno Bozetto; scr: Guido Manuli, Maurizo Nichetti, Bruno Bozetto; m: Debussy, Dvorak, Ravel, Sibelius, Vivaldi, Stravinsky; anim: Guiseppe Lagana, Walter Cavazzuti, Giovanni Ferrari, Giancarlo Cereda, Giorgio Valentini, Guido Manuli, Paolo Albicocco, Giorgio Forlani. Running time: 80 minutes.

Cast:

(live action) Maurizo Nichetti, Nestor Garay, Maurizio Micheli, Maria Luisa Giovannini

A parody of Walt Disney's famed *Fantasia* featuring six different animated stories fitted to classical music conducted by such noted artists as Herbert von Karajan, Hans Stadlmair and Lorin Maazel. The film intersperses live action between each of the symphonic pieces which feature English subtitles and animation. Musical selections are: "Afternoon of a Faun" by Debussy, "Slavonic Dance No. 7" by Dvorak, "Bolero" by Ravel, "Valse Triste" by Sibelius, "Concerto in C Minor" by Vivaldi and "The Firebird" by Stravinsky.

THE AMERICAN TAIL (1986)

An Amblin Entertainment Production released by Universal Pictures. p: Don Bluth, John Pomeroy, Gary Goldman; d: Don Bluth; w: Judy Freudberg, Tony Geiss (based on the story by David Kirschner, Judy Freudberg, Tony Geiss); m: James Horner; anim dir: John Pomeroy, Dan Kuenster, Linda Miller; anim: Lorna Pomeroy, Gary Perkovac, Jeff Etter, Ralph Zondag, Skip Jones, Kevin Wurzer, Dave Spafford, Dick Zondag, Dave Molina, Heidi Guedel, Ann Marie Bardwell, Jesse Cosio, Ralph Palmer, T. Daniel Hofstedt. Songs: "There Are No Cats in America," "Never Say Never," "Somewhere Out There," "A Duo" and "Stars and Stripes Forever." Running time: 80 minutes.

Voices:

Mama Mousekewitz: Eric Yohn, **Papa Mousekewitz:** Nehemiah Persoff, **Tanya Mousekewitz:** Amy Green, **Fievel Mousekewitz:** Phillip Glasser, **Henri:** Christopher Plummer, **Warren T. Rat:** John Finnegan, **Digit:** Will Ryan, **Moe:** Hal Smith, **Tony Toponi:** Pat Musick, **Bridget:** Cathianne Blore, **Honest John:** Neil Ross, **Gussie Mausheimer:** Madeline Kahn, **Tiger:** Dom DeLuise

Charlie (voiced by Burt Reynolds) leads an all–canine conga line in "All Dogs Go To Heaven" (1989), a tale of rascals, puppies and true love. © Goldcrest & Sullivan Bluth Ltd.

When a clan of Jewish mice are forced to emigrate, little Fievel Mousekewitz is separated from his family, which is enroute to New York. The cherubic mouse makes it to the New Land via a glass bottle and he encounters many adventures—including his share of cats—until he is successfully reunited with his family.

PN: The song, "Somewhere Out There," received a 1986 Oscar nomination for "Best Song."

THE ARISTOCATS (1970)

A Walt Disney Production released by Buena Vista. p: Wolfgang Reitherman, Winston Hibler; d: Wolfgang Reitherman; st: Larry Clemmons, Vance Gerry, Frank Thomas, Julius Svendsen, Ken Anderson, Eric Cleworth, Ralph Wright (based on a story by Tom McGowan and Tom Rowe); m: George Bruns; dir anim: Milt Kahl, Frank Thomas, Ollie Johnston, John Lounsbery; anim: Hal King, Eric Larson, Eric Cleworth, Julius Svendsen, Fred Hellmich, Walt Stanchfield, Dave Michener. Songs: "The Aristocats," "Scales and Arpeggios," "She Never Felt Alone" and "Thomas O'Malley Cat." Running time: 78 minutes.

Voices:

Thomas O'Malley: Phil Harris, **Duchess:** Eva Gabor, **Roquefort:** Sterling Holloway, **Scat Cat:** Scatman Crothers, **Chinese Cat:** Paul Winchell, **English Cat:** Lord Tim Hudson, **Italian Cat:** Vito Scotti, **Russian Cat:** Thurl Ravenscroft, **Berlioz:** Dean Clark, **Marie:** Liz English, **Toulouse:** Gary Dubin, **Frou–Frou:** Nancy Kulp, **Georges Hautecourt:** Charles Lane, **Madame Adelaide Bonfamille:** Hermione Baddeley, **Edgar:** Roddy Maude–Roxby, **Uncle Waldo:** Bill Thompson, **Lafayette:** George Lindsey, **Napoleon:** Pat Buttram, **Abigail Gabble:** Monica Evans, **Amelia Gabble:** Carole Shelley, **French Milkman:** Pete Renoudet.

Duchess, a cat, and her three well–bred kittens, Berlioz, Toulouse and Marie, try finding their way back to Paris after a jealous butler (Edgar) angrily abandons them in the countryside.

PN: This was the first animated feature to be produced without Walt Disney, who died four years prior to this production. It was billed in advertisements as a "jazz musical." Original budget: $4 million. Re–released in 1980.

BABAR: THE MOVIE (1989)

A Nelvana Production released by New Line Cinema. p: Patrick Loubert, Michael Hirsh, Clive A. Smith; d: Alan Bunce; scr; Peter Sauder, J. D. Smith, John De Klein, Raymond Jaffelice, Alan Bunce (adapted from a story by Sauder, Loubert and Hirsh based on characters created by Jean and Laurent de Brunhoff); m/s: Milan Kymlicka; anim dir: John Laurence Collins; anim: Roberto Curilli, Marc Eoche–Duval, Pierre Fassel, Bruno Gaumetou, Catherine Poulain, Pascal Ropars, Thierry Schiel. Songs: "Elephantland March," "The Best We Both Can Be," "Monkey Business," "Committee Song" and "Rataxes Song." Running time: 70 minutes.

Voices:

King Babar, the Elder; Gordon Pinsent, **Queen Celeste/**

The boyhood days of King Babar (left) and his ensuing struggles against a tyrannical cult are recalled in Babar: The Movie (1989), based on the popular children's book series by Jean and Laurent de Brunhoff. (Courtesy: Nelvana Limited)

Old Lady: Elizabeth Hanna, **Isabelle:** Lisa Yamanaka, **Flora:** Marsha Moreau, **Pom:** Bobby Becken, **Alexander:** Amos Crawley, **Boy Babar:** Gavin Magrath, **Young Celeste:** Sarah Polley, **Pompadour:** Stephen Ouimette, **Cornelius:** Chris Wiggins, **Zephir:** John Stocker, **Rataxes:** Charles Kerr, **Old Tusk:** Stuart Stone, **Celeste's Mom:** Angela Fusco

In the form of a bedtime story, King Babar recalls for his children his first day as boy king of Elephantland and his ensuing battle to save the nearby village—the home of his sweetheart, Celeste—from decimation by a tyrannical cult of elephant enslaving rhinos.

BAMBI (1942)

A Walt Disney Production released by RKO Radio Pictures. p: Walt Disney; superv dir: David D. Hand; st dir: Perce Pearce; st ad: Larry Morey; st dev: George Stallings, Melvin Shaw, Carl Fallberg, Chuck Couch, Ralph Wright (based on the book by Felix Salten); m: Frank Churchill, Edward H. Plumb; seq dir: James Algar, Bill Roberts, Norman Wright, Sam Armstrong, Paul Satterfield, Graham Heid; superv anim: Franklin Thomas, Milt Kahl, Eric Larson, Oliver M. Johnston Jr.; anim: Fraser Davis, Bill Justice, Bernard Garbutt, Don Lusk, Retta Scott, Kenneth Hultgren, Kenneth O'Brien, Louis Schmitt, John Bradbury, Joshua Meador, Phil Duncan, George Rowley, Art Palmer, Art Elliot. Songs: "Love Is a Song," "Let's Sing a Gay Little Spring Song," "Little April Shower" and "Looking for Romance (I Bring You a Song)." Running time: 69–1/2 minutes.

Voices:

Bambi: Bobby Stewart, **Bambi:** Donnie Dunagan, **Bambi:** Hardy Albright, **Bambi:** John Sutherland, **Bambi's mother:** Paula Winslowe, **Faline:** Cammie King, **Faline:** Ann Gillis, **Aunt Ena, Mrs. Possum:** Mary Lansing, **Prince of the Forest:** Fred Shields, **Friend Owl;** Bill Wright, **Flower:** Stanley

Alexander, **Flower:** Sterling Holloway, **Thumper:** Peter Behn, **Thumper, Flower:** Tim Davis, **Mrs. Quail:** Thelma Boardman, **Mrs. Rabbit:** Marjorie Lee

Additional Voices:

Marion Darlington, Thelma Hubbard, Otis Harlan, Jeanne Christy, Janet Chapman, Bobette Audrey, Jack Horner, Francesca Santoro, Babs Nelson, Sandra Lee Richards, Dolyn Bramston Cook and Elouise Woodward

A newborn prince of the forest (Bambi) learns about love, friendship and survival—with the help of fellow forest dwellers including Flower the skunk and Thumper the rabbit—as he conquers both men and nature to take his rightful place as king of the forest.

THE BLACK CAULDRON (1985)

A Walt Disney Production in association with Silver Screen Partners II released through Buena Vista. p: Joe Hale; d: Ted Berman, Richard Rich; st: David Jonas, Vance Gerry, Al Winson, Roy Morita, Ted Berman, Peter Young, Richard Rich, Art Stevens, Joe Hale (based on Lloyd Alexander's five *Chronicles of Prydain* books); m: Elmer Bernstein; anim: Andreas Deja, Phil Nibbelink, Hendel Butoy, Steven Gordon, Dale Baer, Doug Krohn, Ron Husband, Shawn Keller, Jay Jackson, Mike Gabriel, Barry Temple, Phillip Young, Tim Ferriter, Jesse Cosio, Ruben Aquino, Ruben Procopio, Cyndee Whitney, Vicki Anderson, George Scribner, David Block, Mark Henn, Charlie Downs, Terry Harrison, Sandra Borgmeyer, David Pacheco. Running time: 80 minutes.

Voices:

Taran: Grant Bardsley, **Eilonwy:** Susan Sheridan, **Dallben:** Freddie Jones, **Fflewddur Fflam:** Nigel Hawthorne, **King Eidilleg:** Arthur Malet, **Gurgi, Doli:** John Byner, **Orddu:** Eda Reiss Merin, **Orwen:** Adele Malia–Morey, **Orgoch:** Billie Hayes, **The Horned King:** John Hurt, **Creeper, Henchman:** Phil Fondacaro, **Narrator:** John Huston, **Fairfolk:** Lindsday Ric, Brandon Call, Gregory Levinson, **Henchmen:** Peter Renaday, James Almanzar, Wayne Allwine, Steve Hale, Phil Nibbelink, Jack Laing

Taran, a young man who dreams of becoming a warrior, is put to the test as he battles the evil Horned King, who is determined to gain possession of the "black cauldron," a source of supernatural power, to use to further his misdeeds. Taran is joined by a cast of characters in his quest, including Princess Eilonwy, Hen Wen, a psychic pig and Gurgi, a sycophantic creature.

PN: More than 2.5 million drawings were used in creating this $25 million feature, which took 10 years to complete. The film was shot in 70–millimeter, only the second to ever be done in that wide–screen format (the first was *Sleeping Beauty* in 1959). The movie was also the first Disney cartoon feature to merit a "PG" rating.

BON VOYAGE, CHARLIE BROWN (AND DON'T COME BACK) (1980)

A Lee Mendelson– Bill Melendez Production released through Paramount Pictures. p & d: Lee Mendelson, Bill Melendez; w: Charles M. Schulz (based on the "Peanuts" characters); m: Ed Bogas, Judy Munsen; anim: Sam Jaimes, Hank Smith, Al Pabian, Joe Roman, Ed Newmann, Bill Littlejohn, Bob Carlson, Dale Baer, Spencer Peel, Larry Leichliter, Sergio Bertolli. Running time: 75 minutes.

Voices:

Charlie Brown: Arrin Skelley, **Peppermint Patty:** Laura Planting, **Marcie:** Casey Carlson, **Linus:** Daniel Anderson, **Sally Brown:** Annalisa Bartolin, **Snoopy:** Bill Melendez, **Waiter/ Baron/Driver/Tennis Announcer/English Voice/American Male:** Scott Beads

As exchange students, Charlie Brown and the gang visit both England, where Snoopy competes at Wimbledon, and France, where they find themselves the guests of a mysterious benefactor in a historic chateau.

A BOY NAMED CHARLIE BROWN (1969)

A Lee Mendelson–Bill Melendez Production released by New General Pictures. p: Lee Mendelson, Bill Melendez; d: Bill Melendez; w: Charles M. Schulz; m: Vince Guaraldi; m/s: Rod McKuen; anim: Ed Levitt, Bernard Gruver, Ruth Kissane, Dean Spille, Eleanor Warren, Frank Smith, Faith Kovaleski, Rudy Zamora, Bill Littlejohn, Philip Roman, Richard Thompson, Frank Braxton, Everett Brown, Bob Matz, Ken O'Brien, Alan Shear. Songs: "Piano Sonata Opus 13 (Pathetique)," "Failure Face," "Champion Charlie Brown," "Cloud Dreams," "Charlie Brown and His All Stars," "We Lost Again," "Blue Charlie Brown," "Time to Go to School," "I Only Dread One Day at a Day," "By Golly I'll Show 'Em," "Class Champion," "School Spelling Bee," "Start Boning Up on Your Spelling, Charlie Brown," "You'll Either Be a Hero . . . Or a Goat," "Bus Station," "Do Piano Players Make a Lot of Money?," "I've Got to Get My Blanket Back," "Big City," "Found Blanket," "National Spelling Bee," "B–E–A–G–L–E," "Homecoming," "I'm Never Going to School Again," "Welcome Home, Charlie Brown" and "I Before E." Running time: 86 minutes.

Voices:

Charlie Brown: Peter Robbins, **Lucy:** Pamelyn Ferdin, **Linus:** Glenn Gilger, **Sally:** Erin Sullivan, **Patty:** Sally Dryer Barker, **Violet:** Ann Altieri, **Pigpen:** Christopher Defaria, **Schroeder:** Andy Pforsich, **Frieda:** Linda Mendelson, **Singers:** Betty Allan, Loulie Norman, Gloria Wood, **Boys:** David Carey, Guy Pforsich, **Snoopy:** Bill Melendez

Charlie Brown, who never seems able to do anything right, surprises himself and his friends by being chosen for the national spelling bee in New York. True to form, he loses, on national television no less, but is nevertheless given a hero's welcome when he returns home.

BRAVESTARR, THE MOVIE (1988)

A Filmation Production released by Taurus Entertainment. p: Lou Scheimer; d: Tom Tataranowicz; scr: Bob Forward, Steve Hayes; m: Frank W. Becker; superv anim: Brett Hisey. Running time: 91 minutes.

Voices:

Charlie Adler, Susan Blu, Pat Fraley, Ed Gilbert, Alan Oppenheimer, Erik Gunden, Erika Scheimer

Bravestarr, who comes from a place steeped in Indian culture to futuristic New Texas, meets his nemesis, Tex-Hex, for the first time.

PN: In movie theater ads, this film was billed as *Bravestarr, The Movie,* even though initially prints of the film reflected the original title, *Bravestarr, The Legend.*

BUGS BUNNY, SUPERSTAR (1975)

A Hair Raising Films Inc. release through Warner Brothers. p & d: Larry Jackson; anim dir: Chuck Jones, Bob Clampett, Tex Avery, Friz Freleng, Robert McKimson. Running time: 91 minutes.

Voices:

Mel Blanc: **Narrator:** Orson Welles

Famed Warner Brothers animators Friz Freleng, Tex Avery and Bob Clampett appear in this documentary film on Warner Brothers cartoons of the forties. Interspersed between interview segments are complete cartoon versions of *What's Cooking Doc?, A Wild Hare, I Taw a Putty Tat, Rhapsody Rabbit, Corny Concerto, Walky Talky Hawky, The Old Grey Hare, My Favorite Duck* and *Hair Raising Hare.*

THE BUGS BUNNY/ROAD RUNNER MOVIE (1979)

A Warner Brothers release. p & d: Chuck Jones; w: Michael Maltese, Chuck Jones; m: Carl Stalling, Milt Franklyn; anim: Phil Monroe, Ben Washam, Ken Harris, Abe Levitow, Dick Thompson, Lloyd Vaughan, Virgil Ross, Manny Perez, Irv Anderson. Running time: 92 minutes.

Voices:

Mel Blanc

Bugs Bunny looks back on his past triumphs in this entertaining compilation which bridges 20 minutes of new animation with old Warner cartoons, in full or part. (New footage has Bugs giving audiences a tour of his Beverly Hills estate as he fondly recalls the highlights of his 40–year career.) The four complete cartoons featured are *Hare-Way to the Stars, Duck Amuck, Bully For Bugs* and *Rabbit Fire* plus excerpts from eight others, along with an 11–minute Road Runner tribute consisting of 31 gags culled from 16 cartoons.

PN: Warner Brothers had a difficult time deciding what to call this feature. The original titles that were bantered about included *The Great Bugs Bunny/Road Runner Chase* and *The Great American Bugs Bunny/Road Runner Chase.*

BUGS BUNNY'S THIRD MOVIE— 1001 RABBIT TAKES (1982)

A Warner Brothers release. p: Friz Freleng; seq dir: Dave Detiege, Friz Freleng; m: Rob Walsh, Bill Lava, Milt Franklyn, Carl Stalling; anim: Warren Batchelor, Bob Bransford, Marcis Fertig, Terrence Lennon, Bob Matz, Norm McCabe, Tom Ray, Virgil Ross. Running time: 76 minutes.

Voices:

Mel Blanc, Shep Menken, Lennie Weinrib.

As rival book salesman for "Rambling House Publishers," Bugs Bunny and Daffy Duck travel the world to find new areas to market their wares, including the Arabian desert. Other characters featured include Yosemite Sam, Tweety and Sylvester. New animated wraparounds introduce several complete cartoons, previously released to theaters: *Ali Baba Bunny, Apes Of Wrath, Betwitched Bunny, Cracked Quack, Goldimouse And The Three Cats, Mexican Boarders, One Froggy Evening, Pied Piper of Guadalupe* and others.

PN: The sequel to this third Bugs Bunny compilation is 1983's *Daffy Duck's Movie: Fantastic Island.*

THE CARE BEARS ADVENTURE IN WONDERLAND (1987)

A Nelvana Production released by Cineplex Odeon Films. p: Michael Hirsh, Patrick Loubert, Clive A. Smith; d: Raymond Jafelice; w: Susan Snooks, John De Klein (based on a story by Peter Sauder); m: Trish Cullen; m/l: John Sebastian, Maribeth Solomon; anim: John Laurence Collins. Running time: 75 minutes.

Voices:

Grumpy Bear: Bob Dermer, **Swift Heart Rabbit,** Eva Almos, **Brave Heart Lion/Dum:** Dan Hennessey, **Tenderheart Bear:** Jim Henshaw, **Good Luck Bear:** Marla Lukofsky, **Lots–a– Heart Elephant:** Luba Goy, **White Rabbit:** Keith Knight, **Alice:** Tracey Moore, **Wizard:** Colin Fox, **Dim/Cheshire Cat:** John Stocker, **Caterpillar:** Don McManus, **Queen of Wonderland:** Elizabeth Hanna, **Flamingo:** Alan Fawcett, **Mad Hatter/Jabberwocky:** Keith Hampshire, **Princess:** Alyson Court

Combining the flavor of Lewis Carroll's *Alice in Wonderland* and Frank Baum's *Wizard of Oz,* this third Care Bears feature casts the cuddly characters in Wonderland where they search for Alice, who has been abducted by the evil–doing wizard who has designs on ruling the great land. Along the way, they meet up with all sorts of interesting characters— The Mad Hatter, Tweedledee and Tweedledum, Cheshire Cat and others—who appeared in the Disney classic, *Alice in Wonderland.*

Noble Heart Horse (left) and True Heart Bear (second from left), the co–founders of the Care Bear Family, and Care Bears Cubs Secret Cub (second from right) and Tenderheart (right) look on as Care Cousin Cub Lil' Bright Heart Raccoon slides down a rainbow in Care Bears Movie II: A New Generation (1986). (Courtesy: Nelvana Limited)

THE CARE BEARS MOVIE (1985)

A Nelvana Production released by Samuel Goldwyn. p Michael Hirsch, Patrick Loubert, Clive Smith; d: Arna Selznick; w: Peter Sauder; m: John Sebastian, Walt Woodward, Trish Cullen; m/l: John Sebastian, title song; anim: Lillian Andre, John De Klein, Ian Freedman, Michelle Houston, Pat Knight, Paul Riley, Lynn Yamazaki, Rejean Bourdages, Chris Delaney, Scott Glynn, Bob Jaques, Beverly Newberg–Lehman, Gian Celestri, Mike Fallows, John Hooper, Trevor Keen, Mark Pudeleiner, Cynthia Swift, Ralf Zonda. Running time: 75 minutes.

Voices:

Mr. Cherrywood: Mickey Rooney, **Love–a–Lot Bear:** Georgie Engel, **Brave Heart Lion:** Harry Dean Stanton

In the land of Care–a–Lot two orphaned siblings, Kim and Jason, develop friendships with the cuddly animals and experience the warm, good feelings of these creatures. Such feelings are temporarily dashed by the Evil Spirit, who casts a third child, Nicholas, under his power. Nicholas is to help the Evil Spirit by creating spells that remove all the care and feeling from the world.

CARE BEARS MOVIE II: A NEW GENERATION (1986)

A Nelvana Production released by Columbia Pictures. p: Michael Hirsh, Patrick Loubert, Clive A. Smith; d: Dale Schott; scr; Peter Sauder; m: Patricia Cullen; anim dir: Charles Bonifacio. Songs: "Our Beginning," "Flying My Colors," "I Care for You," "Growing Up," "Care Bears Cheer Song" and "Forever Young." Running time: 77 minutes.

Voices:

True Heart Bear: Maxine Miller, **Noble Heart Horse:** Pam Hyatt, **Dark Heart/The Boy:** Hadley Kay, **Christy:** Cree Summer Francks, **Dawn:** Alyson Court, **John:** Michael Fantini

True Heart Bear and Noble Heart Horse venture from their home base at the Great Wishing Star on a mission to a summer camp to teach a couple of self–centered youngsters the virtues of sharing and caring.

CAT CITY (1987)

A Pannonia Film/Sefel Pictures release. d: Bela Ternovsky; w: Jozsef Nepp; m: Tamas Deak; anim: Jozsef Gemes, Zoltan Maros. Running time: 93 minutes.

The entire mice population may soon be extinct thanks to a secret weapon developed by a group of nasty cats, who are slowly taking over the world. Intermaus, an international mouse intelligence agency, enlists the services of its top agent, Grabowski, to find the blueprints to the weapon and restore order.

PN: This film was produced by Budapest's top animation studio, Pannonia, and was initially released in the United States at the Los Angeles Animation Celebration. Features English subtitles.

CHARLOTTE'S WEB (1973)

A Hanna–Barbera Production released by Paramount Pictures. p: William Hanna, Joseph Barbera; d: Charles A. Nichols, Iwao Takamoto; w: Earl Hamner Jr. (based on the book by E. B. White); m: Richard M. Sherman, Robert M. Sherman; anim: Hal Ambro, Ed Barge, Lars Galonius, Dick Lundy, Irv Spence, Ed Aardal, Lee Dyer, Bob Gow, George Kreisl, Don Patterson, Carlo Vinci, O. E. Callahan, Hugh Fraser, Volus Jones, Ed Parks, Ray Patterson, Xenia. Songs: "Charlotte's Web," "A Veritable Smorgasbord," "There Must Be Something More," "I Can Talk," "Mother Earth and Father Time," "We've Got Lots in Common," "Deep in the Dark" and "Zuckerman's Famous Pig." Running time: 94 minutes.

Voices:

Charlotte: Debbie Reynolds, **Templeton:** Paul Lynde, **Wilbur:** Henry Gibson, **Narrator:** Rex Allen, **Mrs. Arable:** Martha Scott, **Old Sheep:** Dave Madden, **Avery:** Danny Bonaduce, **Geoffrey:** Don Messick, **Lurvy:** Herb Vigran, **The Goose:** Agnes Moorehead, **Fern Arable:** Pam Ferdin, **Mrs. Zuckerman, Mrs. Fussy:** Joan Gerber, **Homer Zuckerman:** Robert Holt, **Arable:** John Stephenson, **Henry Fussy:** William B. White

Wilbur, a runt pig who has been a pet of a New England farmer, is sold to a neighbor where he is told by a sheep that he is ticketed for the slaughter house. His life changes upon meeting a spider named Charlotte, who devotes all her energies to saving Wilbur from a pig's fate.

Alvin, Theodore and Simon travel the world to several faraway places in their first full—length feature, The Chipmunk Adventure (1987). (Courtesy: Bagdasarian Productions)

THE CHIPMUNK ADVENTURE (1987)

A Bagdasarian Production released by Samuel Goldwyn. p: Ross Bagdasarian Jr.; d: Janice Karman; w: Janice Karman, Ross Bagdasarian Jr.; m: Randy Edelman; anim: Skip Jones, Don Spencer, Andrew Gaskill, Mitch Rochon, Becky Bristow. Songs: "Witch Doctor," "Come On—a My House," "Diamond Dolls," "The Girls of Rock and Roll," "Wooly Bully," "I, Yi, Yi, Yi, Yi/ Cuanto Le Gusta," "My Mother" and "Getting Lucky." Running time: 76 minutes.

Voices:

Alvin/Simon/Dave Seville: Ross Bagdasarian Jr.; **Theodore/ Brittany/Jeanette/Eleanor:** Janice Karman; **Miss Miller:** Dody Goodman; **Claudia Furschtien:** Susan Tyrell; **Klaus Furschtien:** Anthony DeLongis; **Sophie:** Frank Welker; Nancy Cartwright; Ken Samson; Charles Adler; Philip Clark; George Poulos; Pat Pinney

Dave Seville goes off to Europe, leaving the unhappy Chipmunks home with their babysitter, Miss Miller. Alvin dreams of world travel and convinces Simon and Theodore to enter a hot air balloon race around the world against the Chipettes, Brittany, Jeanette and Eleanor. During their globe—trotting, the Chipmunks and Chipettes unwittingly assist a pair of international diamond smugglers, hiding illegal gems in toy dolls at stops in Greece, Africa, Egypt, Rio and several other faraway places.

PN: Thirty years after his father created The Chipmunks, Ross Bagdasarian Jr. produced this feature following a television revival of his father's famous characters. Feature was released on home video by Warner Brothers Home Video.

CINDERELLA (1950)

A Walt Disney Production released by RKO Radio Pictures. p: Walt Disney; prod superv: Ben Sharpsteen; d: Wilfred Jackson, Hamilton Luske, Clyde Geronimi; dir anim: Eric Larson, Ward Kimball, Norman Ferguson, Marc Davis, John Lounsbery, Milt Kahl, Wolfgang Reitherman, Les Clark, Ollie Johnston, Frank Thomas; st: Kenneth Anderson, Ted Sears, Homer Brightman, Joe Rinaldi, William Peet, Harry Reeves, Winston Hibler, Erdman Penner (based on the traditional story as told by Charles Perrault); md: Oliver Wallace, Paul J. Smith; anim: Marvin Woodward, Hal Ambro, George Nicholas, Hal King, Judge Whitaker, Fred Moore, High Fraser, Phil Duncan, Cliff Nordberg, Ken O'Brien, Harvey Toombs, Don Lusk. Songs: "Bibbidi—Bobbidi—Boo," "So This Is Love," "A Dream Is a Wish Your Heart Makes," "Cinderella," "The Work Song" and "Oh Sing, Sweet Nightingale." Running time: 74 minutes.

Voices:

Cinderella: Ilene Woods, **Prince Charming:** William Phipps, **Stepmother:** Eleanor Audley, **Stepsisters:** Rhoda Williams, Lucille Bliss, **Fairy Godmother:** Verna Felton, **King, Grand Duke:** Luis Van Rooten, **Jaq, Gus, Bruno:** James Macdonald

Poor orphaned Cinderella is a slave to her stepmother and two stepsisters in an environment endured only through her friendship with animals. Her fairy godmother transforms her rags into a beautiful gown, and she is given only until midnight to attend the King's ball where his son (Prince Charming) yearns to find the girl of his dreams.

The glass slipper appears to be a perfect fit for poor orphaned Cinderella in a scene from Walt Disney's full—length cartoon release, Cinderella (1950). © Walt Disney Productions (Courtesy: The Museum of Modern Art/Film Stills Archive)

COONSKIN (1975)

An Albert S. Ruddy Production released by Bryanston Pictures. p: Albert S. Ruddy; d & w: Ralph Bakshi; m: Chico Hamilton;

seq anim: Irven Spence, Charlie Downs, Ambrozi Palinoda, John E. Walker Sr.; anim: Thomas A. Ray, Edward J. Barge, Fred Hellmich, Bob Carlson, John Sparey, Lars Calonius, Raymond Patterson. Running time: 82 minutes.

Voices:

Samson/Brother Bear: Barry White, **Preacher/Brother Fox:** Charles Grodone, **Pappy/Old Man Bone:** Scatman Crothers, **Randy/Brother Rabbit:** Phillip Thomas

Three rural black men seek new direction in their lives to escape the ghetto life of crime and other vices.

PN: Combining live–action and animation, *Coonskin* was originally meant for Paramount Pictures but the studio giant passed on distributing the film due to the strong racial overtones of the feature. Upon its initial release, the film provoked objections to its depictions of blacks from the Congress of Racial Equality (CORE). Consequently, after a brief run in 1975, the film was quickly shelved. To calm racial tension, the film was later released on video under a new title: *Streetfight.* Film's working titles were *Bustin' Out, Coon Skin* and *Coonskin No More.*

DAFFY DUCK'S QUACKBUSTERS (1988)

A Warner Brothers release. p: Steven S. Greene, Kathleen Helppie Shipley; d & w: Greg Ford, Terry Lennon; m: Carl Stalling, Milt Franklyn, Bill Lava; anim: Brenda Banks, Norm McCabe, Rebecca Rees, Mark Kausler, Nancy Beiman, Daniel Haskett, Darryl Van Citters, Frans Vischer. Running time: 72 minutes.

Voices:

Mel Blanc, Roy Firestone, B. J. Ward

After inheriting a million dollars, Daffy starts a ghost–busting business with Bugs Bunny and Porky Pig for the sole purpose of destroying the ghost of J. B. Cubish, his benefactor. Cartoons featured: *Prize Pest, Water Water Ever Hare, Hyde And Go Tweet, Claws For Alarm, The Abominable Snow Rabbit, Transylvania 6–500, Punch Trunk* and *Jumpin' Jupiter.* The film also contained the first new cartoon short produced by the studio in several decades, *The Duxorcist.*

DAFFY DUCK'S MOVIE: FANTASTIC ISLAND (1983)

A Warner Brothers release. p & d: Friz Freleng; scr: John Dunn, David Detiege, Friz Freleng; seq dir: David Detiege, Friz Freleng, Phil Monroe; anim: Brenda Banks, Warren Batchelor, Bob Bransford, Brad Case, Terrence Lennon, Bob Matz, Norm McCabe, Sam Nicholson, Jerry Ray, Richard Thompson. Running time: 78 minutes.

Voices:

Mel Blanc, June Foray, Les Tremayne

In this spoof of TV's "Fantasy Island," Daffy Duck and Speedy Gonzales become shipwrecked on a desert island. Finding a treasure map belonging to Yosemite Sam, they begin digging for buried treasure and instead discover a wishing well that—in answer to a wish—magically changes the island into a fantasy paradise. This new footage introduces several complete cartoons: *Bucaneer Bunny, Stupor Duck, Greedy Tweety, Banty Raids, Louvre Come Back,* and others. Other Warner Brothers characters featured are Tweety, Sylvester the Cat, Tasmanian Devil and Pepe Le Pew.

DICK DEADEYE—OR DUTY DONE (1975)

A Bill Melendez Production, London, released by International Releasing Corporation. p: Steven C. Melendez; d: Bill Melendez; st: Robin Miller and Leo Rost; m: Jimmy Horowitz (with additional lyrics by Robin Miller); anim dir: Dick Horn. Running time: 80 minutes.

Voices:

Dick Deadeye: Victor Spinetti, **Yum Yum:** Linda Lewis, **Sorcerer, Captain of the Pinafore:** Peter Reeves, **Pirate King:** George A. Cooper, **Little Buttercup:** Miriam Karlin, **Nanki, Poo:** John Newton, **Rose Maybud:** Julia McKenzie, **Monarch of the Sea, Major General:** Francis Ghent, **Judge:** Barry Cryer, **Princess Zara, Queen Elizabeth:** Beth Porter, singing voice of **Monarch of the Sea, Major General:** John Baldry, singing voice of **Nanki, Poo:** Casey Kelley, singing voice of **Rose Maybud:** Lisa Strike, singing voice of **Pirate King:** Ian Samwell

Dick Deadeye, that scurrilous villain of Gilbert and Sullivan's most popular operetta, *H.M.S. Pinafore,* is transformed into the most unlikely hero in this cartoon parody, featuring rock versions of 26 classic Gilbert and Sullivan tunes from five operettas: *H.M.S. Pinafore, The Mikado, The Pirates of Penzance, The Sorcerer* and *Trial By Jury.* The plotline involves Deadeye's attempts to rescue the Ultimate Secret from the Sorcerer and the Pirate King, commissioned to do so by no other than the Queen herself.

PN: Bill Melendez, best known as the creator of countless "Peanuts" television specials, directed this cartoon feature, which was produced in England and released theatrically in the United Kingdom and America.

DIRTY DUCK (1977)

A Murakami–Wolf Production released by New World Pictures. p: Jerry Good; d, w & anim: Charles Swenson; m: Mark Volman and Howard Kaylan—Flo and Eddie. Running time: 75 minutes.

Voices:

Mark Volman, Robery Ridgeley, Walker Edmiston, Cynthia Adler, Janet Lee, Lurene Tuttle, Jerry Good, Howard Kaylan

Willard Eisenbaum, a shy, lonely, inept, sexually frustrated insurance company employee, is thrown by fate into the company of a large, sailor–suited duck who is convinced that some good sex will straighten Willard out.

PN: Like Ralph Bakshi's *Fritz the Cat,* this film was X–rated.

DUCKTALES: THE MOVIE, TREASURE OF THE LOST LAMP (1990)

A Walt Disney Animation (France) S.A. Production released by Buena Vista. p & d: Bob Hathcock; scr: Alan Burnett; m: David Newman; seq dir: Paul Brizzi, Gaetan Brizzi, Clive Pallant, Mattias Marcos Rodric, Vincent Woodcock; anim: Gary Andrews, James Baker, Javier Gutierrez Blas, Eric Bouillette, Moran Caouissin, Caron Creed, Caroline Cruikshank, Roberto Curilli, Sylvain DeBoissy, Joe Ekers, Mark Eoche-Duval, Pierre Fassal, Al Gaivoto, Manolo Galiana, Bruno Gaumetou, Dina Gellert-Nielsen, Arnold Gransac, Teddy Hall, Peter Hausner, Francisco Alaminos Hodar, Daniel Jeannette, Nicholas Marlet, Bob McKnight, Ramon Modiano, Sean Newton, Brent Odell, Catherine Poulain, Jean-Christopher Roger, Pascal Ropars, Stephane Sainte-Foi, Alberto Conejo Sanz, Anna Saunders, Ventura R. Vallejo, Jan Van Buyten, Duncan Varley, Simon Ward-Horner, and Johnny Zeuten. Songs: "DuckTales Theme." Running time: 74 minutes.

Voices:

Scrooge McDuck: Alan Young, **Launchpad:** Terence McGovern, **Huey, Duey, Louie, Webby:** Russi Taylor, **Dijon:** Richard Libertini, **Merlock:** Christopher Lloyd, **Mrs. Featherby:** June Foray, **Duckworth:** Chuck McCann, **Mrs. Beakley:** Joan Gerber, **Genie:** Rip Taylor; Other voices: Charlie Adler, Jack Angel, Steve Bulen, Sherry Lynn, Mickie T. McGowan, Patrick Pinney, Frank Welker

Scrooge McDuck travels to the far ends of the earth in search of the elusive buried treasure of legendary thief Collie Baba. With his companions Huey, Dewey and Louie, Webby and Launchpad McQuack, Scrooge discovers not only the treasure but also that there's a mysterious madman named Merlock who's out to stop him.

DUMBO (1941)

A Walt Disney Production released by RKO Radio Pictures. p: Walt Disney; superv dir: Ben Sharpsteen; scr st: Joe Grant, Dick Huemer (based on a story by Helen Aberson and Harold Pearl); st dev: Bill Peet, Aurie Battaglia, Joe Rinaldi, George Stallings, Webb Smith; m: Oliver Wallace, Frank Churchill, Ned Washington; seq dir: Norman Ferguson, Wilfred Jackson, Bill Roberts, Jack Kinney, Sam Armstrong; anim dir: Vladimir Tytla, Fred Moore, Ward Kimball, John Lounsbery, Arthur Babbitt, Wolfgang Reitherman; anim: Hugh Fraser, Howard Swift, Harvey Toombs, Don Towsley, Milt Neil, Les Clark, Hicks Lokey, Claude Smith, Berny Wolf, Ray Patterson, Jack Campbell, Grant Simmons, Walt Kelly, Joshua Meador, Don Patterson, Cy Young, Bill Shull, Art Palmer. Songs: "Look Out for Mr. Stork," "Baby Mine," "Pink Elephants on Parade," "Casey Junior," "Song of the Roustabouts" and "When I See an Elephant Fly." Running time: 63½ minutes.

Baby elephant Dumbo takes his first flight in a scene from the classic Walt Disney feature, Dumbo (1941).
© Walt Disney Productions (Courtesy: The Museum of Modern Art/Film Stills Archive)

Voices:

Narrator: John McLeish, **Timothy Mouse:** Ed Brophy, **Ringmaster:** Herman Bing, **Casey Jr.:** Margaret Wright, **Messenger Stork:** Sterling Holloway, **Elephant:** Verna Felton **Elephant:** Sarah Selby, **Elephant:** Dorothy Scott, **Elephant:** Noreen Gamill, **Joe, Clown:** Billy Sheets, **Clown:** Billy Bletcher, **Skinny:** Malcolm Hutton, **Crows:** Cliff Edwards, **Crows:** Jim Carmichael, **Crows:** Johnson Choir, **Clown:** Eddie Holden, **Roustabouts:** The King's Men, **Boy:** Harold Manley, **Boy:** Tony Neil, **Boy:** Charles Stubbs

Mrs. Jumbo, a circus elephant, patiently awaits the stork's delivery of her own baby elephant. The young elephant is like no other—with ears as large as sails, he is affectionately dubbed "Dumbo." Dumbo's imperfection becomes an asset. He is billed as a top circus attraction, experiencing triumphs and failures of circus life.

FANTASIA (1940)

A Walt Disney Production released by RKO Radio Pictures. p: Walt Disney; prod superv: Ben Sharpsteen; st dir: Joe Grant, Dick Huemer; "Toccata and Fugue in D Minor" by Johann Sebastian Bach: d: Samuel Armstrong; st: Lee Blair, Elmer Plummer, Phil Dike; anim: Cy Young, Art Palmer, Daniel MacManus, George Rowley, Edwin Aardal, Joshua Meador, Cornett Wood; "The Nutcracker Suite" by Peter Ilich Tchaikovsky: d: Samuel Armstrong; st: Sylvia Moberly–Holland, Norman Wright, Albert Heath, Bianca Majolie, Graham Heid; anim: Arthur Babbitt, Les Clark, Don Lusk, Cy Young, Robert Stokes; "The Sorcerer's Apprentice" by Paul Dukas: d, James Algar; st: Perce Pearce, Carl Fallberg; superv anim: Fred Moore, Vladimir Tytla; anim: Les Clark, Riley Thomson, Marvin Woodward, Preston Blair, Edward Love, Ugo D'Orsi, George Rowley, Cornett Wood; "The Rite of Spring" by Igor Stravinsky: d: Bill Roberts, Paul Satterfield; st: William Martin, Leo Thiele, Robert

Mickey Mouse hypnotizes the brooms to do his water chores in "The Sorcerer's Apprentice" scene from Walt Disney's Fantasia (1940). © Walt Disney Productions (Courtesy: The Museum of Modern Art/Film Stills Archive)

Sterner, John Fraser McLeish; superv anim: Wolfgang Reitherman, Joshua Meador; anim: Philip Duncan, John McManus, Paul Busch, Art Palmer, Don Tobin, Edwin Aardal, Paul B. Kossoff, "Pastoral Symphony" by Ludwig van Beethoven, d: Hamilton Luske, Jim Handley, Ford Beebe; st: Otto Englander, Webb Smith, Erdman Penner, Joseph Sabo, Bill Peet, George Stallings; superv anim: Fred Moore, Ward Kimball, Eric Larson, Arthur Babbitt, Oliver M. Johnston Jr., Don Towsley; anim: Berny Wolf, Jack Campbell, Jack Bradbury, James Moore, Milt Neil, Bill Justice, John Elliotte, Walt Kelly, Don Lusk, Lynn Karp, Murray McLennan, Robert W. Youngquist, Harry Hamsel; "Dance of the House" by Amilcare Ponchielli: d: T. Hee, Norman Ferguson; superv anim: Norman Ferguson; anim: John Lounsbery, Howard Swift, Preston Blair, Hugh Fraser, Harvey Toombs, Norman Tate, Hicks Lokey, Art Elliott, Grant Simmons, Ray Patterson, Frank Grundeen; "Night on Bald Mountain" by Modest Mussorgsky and "Ave Maria" by Franz Schubert: d: Wilfred Jackson; st: Campbell Grant, Arthur Heinemann, Phil Dike; superv anim: Vladimir Tytla; anim: John McManus, William N. Shull, Robert W. Carlson Jr., Lester Novros and Don Patterson. Running time: 120 minutes.

Cast:

Deems Taylor: Himself, **Leopold Stokowski and the Philadelphia Symphony Orchestra:** Themselves, **Mickey Mouse:** Sorcerer's Apprentice.

Walt Disney set new standards for animation with this film, featuring eight different pieces of classical music—Tchaikovsky's "The Nutcracker Suite," Bach's "Toccata and Fugue in D Minor," and others—visually interpreted by the Disney artists. Most memorable moment of the film is Mickey Mouse's performance in "The Sorcerer's Apprentice," where he tries to perform his master's spells.

PN: Among Walt Disney's plans for this animated, symphony—laden classic was to shoot the film in wide screen and stereophonic sound, film some scenes in 3—D and perfume theaters with floral scent during the "Nutcracker Suite" flower ballet. Tight money stymied Disney's plans but he did embellish the film with an innovative fully—directional sound system he called "Fantasound."

FANTASTIC PLANET (1973)

A Les Films Armorial/Service De Recherche Ortif Production released by New World Pictures. p: Simon Damiani, Andre Valio—Cavaglione; d: Rene Laloux; w: Rene Laloux, Roland Topor (based on the novel *Ems En Serie* by Stefen Wul); m: Alain Gorogeur; anim: Joseph Kabrt, Josef Vana, Jindrick Barta, Zdena Bartova, Bohumil Sedja, Zdenek Sob, Karel Strebl, Jiri Vokoum. Running time: 71 minutes.

Voices:

Barry Bostwick, Marvin Miller, Olan Soule, Cynthia Adler, Nora Heflin, Hal Smith, Mark Gruner, Monika Ramirez, Janet Waldo

This avant—garde tale of social injustice, relates the story of the Draggs, 39—foot—tall inhabitants of the planet Yagam, who keep the Oms—who have evolved from humans—as pets. Terr, one of the Oms, is accidentally educated by the Draggs and, after uniting with his people, helps them achieve equality with the Draggs once and for all.

PN: This French—Czech full—length animated fantasy was winner of a Grand Prix award at the 1973 Cannes Film Festival.

FIRE AND ICE (1984)

A Ralph Bakshi/Frank Frazetta Production released by 20th Century Fox/Producers Sales Organization. p: Ralph Bakshi, Frank Frazetta; d: Ralph Bakshi; w: Roy Thomas, Gerry Conway (based on a story and characters by Ralph Bakshi); m: William Kraft; anim: Brenda Banks, Carl A. Bell, Bryan Berry, Lillian Evans, Steve Gordon, Debbie Hayes, David Hoover, Charles Howell, Adam Kuhlman, Mauro Maressa, Russell Mooney, Jack Ozark, William Recinos, Mitch Rochnon, Tom Tataranowicz, Bruce Woodside. Running time: 81 minutes.

Voices:

Larn: Randy Norton, **Teegra:** Cynthia Leake, **Darkwolf:** Steve Sandor, **Nekron:** Sean Hannon, **Jarol:** Leo Gordon, **Taro:** William Ostrander, **Juliana:** Eileen O'Neill, **Roleil:** Elizabeth Lloyd Shaw, **Otwa:** Micky Morton, **Tutor:** Tamara Park, **Monga:** Big Yank, **Pako:** Greg Elam, **Subhuman Priestess:** Holly Frazetta, **Envoy:** Alan Koss, **Defender Captain:** Hans Howes, **Subhumans:** James Bridges, Shane Callan, Archie Hamilton, Michael Kellogg, Dale Park, Douglas Payton

Teegra, the beautiful young daughter of the evil Ice Lord, is taken hostage by the Subhumans, considered extinct after the glacial destruction of the city Fire Keep. The Subhumans prove to be no match for the Ice Lord and his powerful Dragonhawks, but a mysterious hero, Darkwolf, prevails in destroying the sorcerer once and for all.

PN: Working title: *Sword and the Sorcery.*

THE FOX AND THE HOUND (1981)

A Walt Disney Production released through Buena Vista. p: Wolfgang Reitherman, Art Stevens; d: Art Stevens, Ted Berman, Richard Rich; st: Larry Clemmons, Ted Berman, Peter Young, Steve Hulett, David Michener, Burny Mattinson, Earl Kress, Vance Gerry (based on the book by Daniel P. Mannix); superv anim: Randy Cartwright, Cliff Nordberg, Frank Thomas, Glen Keane, Ron Clements, Ollie Johnston; anim: Ed Gombert, Dale Oliver, Ron Husband, David Block, Chris Buck, Hendel S. Butoy, Darrell Van Citters, Phillip Young, John Musker, Jerry Rees, Chuck Harvey, Phil Nibbelink, Dick N. Lucas, Jeffrey J. Varab, Michael Cedeno. Running time: 83 minutes.

Voices:

Tod: Mickey Rooney, **Copper:** Kurt Russell, **Big Mama:** Pearl Bailey, **Amos Slade:** Jack Albertson, **Vixey:** Sandy Duncan, **Widow Tweed:** Jeanette Nolan, **Chief:** Pat Buttram, **Porcupine:** John Fiedler, **Badger:** John McIntire, **Dinky:** Dick Bakalyan, **Boomer:** Paul Winchell, **Young Tod:** Keith Mitchell, **Young Copper:** Corey Feldman

A young fox and puppy dog become the best of friends one summer but are separated when the dog's owner, a hunter, takes the dog away for the winter. Returning the following spring, the dog (now a fully trained hunting dog) and the fox learn what it is like to be enemies.

PN: The film displayed the talents of a new crop of artists that were developed during a 10–year program at the studio, supervised by veteran Disney animators Wolfgang Reitherman, Eric Larson and Art Stevens. Working title: *The Fox and the Hound.*

FRITZ THE CAT (1972)

A Steve Krantz Production released by Cinemation Industries. p: Steve Krantz; d & w: Ralph Bakshi (based on characters created by Robert Crumb); m: Ed Bogas, Ray Shanklin; anim: Virgil Ross, Manuel Perez, John Sparey. Running time: 78 minutes.

Voices:

Fritz the Cat: Skip Hinnant; Rosetta LeNoire; John McCurry; Judy Engles

Recreating the pop culture and social agonies of the '60s, this political, racial and sexual satire traces the sexual and political exploits of Fritz the Cat, a college–age cat who dabbles in drugs, radical politics and hedonism. By film's end, following his many encounters, he rejects violence and cruelty but still embraces sex.

PN: Directed by Ralph Bakshi, a former Terrytoons animator, the film was the first to ever receive an X–rating, mostly for vulgar overtones. The film was originally announced on July 15, 1971 by Steve Krantz as the first project of his new firm. The Fritz feature was to become the first of three planned features by Krantz. The others: *Arrivederci, Rudy!,* based on the life of Valentino, and *Dick Tracy, Frozen, Fried and Buried Alive,* tracing the career of Chester Gould's detective through the '30s and '40s. Unlike Fritz, the films were never produced.

FRIZ FRELENG'S LOONEY LOONEY BUGS BUNNY MOVIE (1981)

A Warner Brothers release. p & d: Friz Freleng; scr; John Dunn, David Detiege, Friz Freleng, Phil Monroe, Gerry Chiniquy; m: Rob Walsh, Don McGinnis, Milt Franklyn, Bill Lava, Shorty Rogers, Carl Stalling; anim: Warren Batchelor, Charles Downs, Marcia Fertig, Bob Matz, Manuel Perez, Virgil Ross, Lloyd Vaughan. Running time: 80 minutes.

Voices:

Mel Blanc, June Foray, Frank Nelson, Frank Welker, Stan Freberg, Ralph James.

Veteran Warner Brothers director Friz Freleng was given his hand at producing and directing this compilation feature following the success of Chuck Jones' *The Bugs Bunny/Road Runner Movie.* Freleng combined new animation with previously exhibited cartoons, broken into three acts: Yosemite Sam, playing the devil (shaped around 1963's *Devil's Feud Cake*); Bugs outsmarting a dopey gangster duo, Rocky and Mugsy, who are holding Tweety hostage; and Bugs serving as master of ceremonies for a humorous spoof of Hollywood awards programs. Cartoons featured during the film are: *Knighty Knight Bugs, Sahara Hare, Roman Legion Hare, High Diving Hare, Hare Trimmed, Wild and Wooly Hare, Catty Cornered, Golden Yeggs, The Unmentionables, Three Little Bops* and *Show Biz Bugs,* the latter an Academy Award–winner.

FUN AND FANCY FREE (1947)

A Walt Disney Production released by RKO Radio Pictures. p: Walt Disney; prod superv: Ben Sharpsteen; l/a dir: William Morgan; anim dir: Jack Kinney, Bill Roberts, Hamilton Luske; st: Homer Brightman, Harry Reeves, Ted Sears, Lance Nolley, Eldon Dedini, Tom Oreb, with "Bongo" based on an original story by Sinclair Lewis; md: Charles Wolcott; m/sc: Paul J. Smith, Oliver Wallace, Eliot Daniel; anim dir: Ward Kimball, Les Clark, John Lounsbery, Fred Moore, Wolfgang Reitherman; anim: Hugh Fraser, Phil Duncan, Judge Whitaker, Arthur Babbitt, John Sibley, Marc Davis, Harvey Toombs, Hal King, Ken O'Brien, Jack Campbell. Songs: "Fun and Fancy Free," "Lazy Countryside," "Too Good to Be True," "Say It with a Slap," "Fee Fi Fo Fum," "My Favorite Dream," "I'm a Happy Go–Lucky Fellow," "Beanero" and "My, What a Happy Day." Running time: 73 minutes.

Cast:

Edgar Bergen, Luana Patten, Charlie McCarthy, Mortimer Snerd.

Voices:

Narrator/Bongo: Dinah Shore, **The Singing Harp:** Anita Gordon, **Jiminy Cricket:** Cliff Edwards, **Willie The Giant:** Billy Gilbert, **Donald Duck:** Clarence Nash; The King's Men, The Dinning Sisters, and the Starlighters

Radio stars Edgar Bergen and Charlie McCarthy and cartoon star Jiminy Cricket appear in this Walt Disney feature comprising two animated stories threaded together by live action and animated wraparounds. Cartoon sequences include: *Bongo,*

Mewsette, a naive country girl cat (voiced by Judy Garland), is the object of boyfriend Jaune–Tom's love in Gay Purr–ee (1962). © Warner Brothers, Inc.

the Wonder Bear, about a circus bear who escapes from the circus and finds the companionship of Lulubelle, a cute female bear, and *Mickey and the Beanstalk,* a clever retelling of the famed "Jack and the Beanstalk" tale featuring Mickey, Donald, Goofy, and, of course, the Giant (Willie).

GAY PURR–EE (1962)

A UPA (United Pictures of America) Production released by Warner Brothers. p: Henry G. Saperstein; d: Abe Levitow; w: Dorothy and Chuck Jones, Ralph Wright; anim: Fred Madison, Art David, Ken Harris, Ben Washam, Phil Duncan, Hal Ambro, Ray Patterson, Grant Simmons, Irv Spence, Don Lusk, Volus Jones, Harvey Toombs, Hank Smith. Songs: "Mewsette," "Roses Red Violets Blue," "Take My Hand, Paree," "The Money Cat," "Little Drops of Rain," "Rubbles," "Paris Is a Lonely Town" and "The Horses Won't Talk." Running time: 85 minutes.

Voices:

Mewsette: Judy Garland; **Jaune–Tom:** Robert Goulet; **Robespierre:** Red Buttons; **Mme. Rubens–Chatte:** Hermione Gingold; **Meowrice:** Paul Frees; Morey Amsterdam; Mel Blanc; Julie Bennett; Joan Gardiner

Mewsette, a naive country girl cat, becomes tired of peasant–type cats and leaves the farm on the next train to Paris to explore new adventures. She is followed on foot by her boyfriend, Jaune–Tom, and his tiny companion, Robespierre, who set out to rescue her from Meowrice, a suave city cat who plans to marry her.

GOBOTS: BATTLE OF THE ROCK LORDS (1986)

A Hanna–Barbera/Tonka Toys Production released by Clubhouse Pictures/Atlantic Releasing. p: Kay Wright; d: Ray Patterson; w: Jay Segal; md: Hoyt Curtin; anim dir: Paul Sebella; superv anim: Janine Dawson. Running time: 75 minutes.

Voices:

Solitaire: Margot Kidder, **Nuggit:** Roddy McDowall, **Boulder:** Michael Nouri, **Magmar:** Telly Savalas, **Turbo/Cop–Tur/Talc:** Arthur Burghardt, **Nick:** Ike Eisenmann, **Cy–Kill:** Bernard Erhard, **Crasher:** Marilyn Lightstone, **Matt:** Morgan Paull, **Leader–1:** Lou Richards, **A. J.:** Leslie Speights, **Scooter/Zeemon/Rest–Q/Pulver–Eye/Sticks/Narliphant:** Frank Welker, **Slime/Stone/Granite/Narligator:** Michael Bell, **Stone Heart/Fossil Lord:** Foster Brooks, **Vanguard:** Ken Campbell, **Herr Friend/Crack–Pot/Tork:** Philip Lewis Clarke, **Pincher/Tombstone/Stone:** Peter Cullen, **Brimstone/Klaws/Rock Narlie:** Dick Gautier, **Marbles/Hornet:** Darryl Hickman, **Small Foot:** B. J. Ward, **Fitor:** Kelly Ward, **Heat Seeker:** Kirby Ward

On Quartex, a planet peopled by various species of living rock, the evil Rock Lord Magmar is bent on seizing control of the entire planet. This spurs the noble Guardian GoBots into action, using a variety of devices to thwart the enemy Renegade GoBots to prevent the Rock Lords from taking control.

THE GREAT MOUSE DETECTIVE (1986)

A Walt Disney/Silver Screen Partners II Production released by Buena Vista. p: Burny Mattinson; d: John Musker, Ron Clements, Dave Michener, Burny Mattinson; st ad: Pete Young, Vance Gerry, Steve Hulett, Ron Clements, John Musker, Bruce M. Morris, Matthew O'Callaghan, Burny Mattinson, Dave Michener, Melvin Shaw (based on the book *Basil of Baker Street* by Eve Titus); m: Henry Mancini; superv anim: Mark Henn, Glen Keane, Robert Minkoff, Hendel Butoy; anim: Matthew O'Callaghan, Mike Gabriel, Ruben A. Aquino, Jay Jackson, Kathy Zielinski, Doug Krohn, Phil Nibbelink, Andreas Deja, Phil Young, Shawn Keller, Ron Husband, Joseph Lanzisero, Rick Farmiloe, David Pruiksma, Sandra Borgmeyer, Cyndee Whitney, Barry Temple, David Block, Ed Gombert, Steven E. Gordon. Songs: "The World's Greatest Criminal Mind," "Goodbye, So Soon," and "Let Me Be Good to You." Running time: 74 minutes.

Voices:

Professor Ratigan: Vincent Price, **Basil/Bartholomew:** Barrie Ingham, **Dawson:** Val Bettin, **Olivia:** Susanne Pollatschek, **Fidget:** Candy Candido, **Mrs. Judson:** Diana Chesney, **The Mouse Queen:** Eve Brenner, **Flaversham:** Alan Young, **Sherlock Holmes:** Basil Rathbone, **Watson:** Laurie Main, **Lady Mouse:** Shani Wallis, **Bar Maid:** Ellen Fitzhugh, **Citizen/Thug Guard:** Walker Edmiston, **Thug Guards:** Wayne Allwine, Val Bettin, Tony Anselmo

Ratigan, an evil rat, wants to control the mouse world and kidnaps a brilliant mouse toymaker to build a mechanical rodent robot to begin his quest. His initial plans are to dethrone the mouse queen but he never counted on two factors getting in his way: Basil and Dr. Dawson, two Holmesian mice hired by the toymaker's daughter to track down her father. The pair not only find the toymaker but successfully thwart Ratigan's plans.

PN: Unlike *The Black Cauldron*, which cost $36 million to make, *The Great Mouse Detective* was produced for only $13 million and recovered its cost in three weeks.

GULLIVER'S TRAVELS (1939)

A Fleischer Studios Production released by Paramount Pictures. p: Max Fleischer; d: Dave Fleischer; w: Dan Gordon, Ted Pierce, Izzy Sparber, Edmond Seward (based on a story by Seward from the novel by Jonathan Swift); m: Victor Young; anim dir: Seymour Kneitel, Willard Bowsky, Tom Palmer, Grim Natwick, William Hanning, Rolland Crandall, Tom Johnson, Robert Leffingwell, Frank Kelling, Winfield Hoskins, Orestes Calpini; anim: Graham Place, Arnold Gillespie, Otto Feuer, David Tendlar, George Germanetti, James Culhane, Nicholas Tafuri, Al Eugster, Joseph D'Igalo, Nelson Demorset, Reuben Grossman, Abner Kneitel, Frank Endres, Joseph Oriolo, Stan Quackenbush, Harold Walker, Lod Rossner, Joe Miller, Lou Zukor, Frank Smith, Ben Clopton, James David, Bill Noland, Edwin Rehberg, Stephen Muffati, Irving Spector, Sam Stimson, Ted Dubois, Edward Smith, Tony Pabian, George Moreno, Thurston Harper, William Sturm and Robert Bentley. Songs: "It's a Hap–Hap–Happy Day," "Bluebirds in the Moonlight," "All's Well," "We're All Together Again," "Forever," "Faithful" and "Faithful Forever." Running time: 75 minutes.

Voices:

Singing voice of the **Prince**: Lanny Ross, singing voice of the **Princess**: Jessica Dragonette

With the success of Walt Disney's *Snow White and the Seven Dwarfs*, animators Max and Dave Fleischer tried their own hand at a full–length animated feature shaped around the popular romance of Jonathan Swift. The film centers on the adventures of shipwrecked Lemuel Gulliver on an island inhabited by tiny people in the kingdom of Lilliput and his attempts to escape the island and return to his homeland.

In an effort to rival Disney's feature–length cartoons, Max Fleischer countered with his own full–length film, Gulliver's Travels (1939). (Courtesy: Republic Pictures)

GULLIVER'S TRAVELS BEYOND THE MOON (1966)

A Toei films Production released through Continental Distributing. p: Hiroshi Okawa; d: Yoshio Kuroda; w: Shinichi Sekizawa (based on the character in the novel by Jonathan Swift); m/s: Milton and Anne Delugg; anim dir: Hideo Furusawa. Songs: "The Earth Songs," "I Wanna Be Like Gulliver," "That's the Way It Goes" and "Keep Your Hopes High." Running time: 85 minutes.

Hit by a car and knocked unconscious, a young boy dreams he is with Dr. Gulliver, a toy–soldier colonel, a crow, and a dog on a trip to the planet Hope. There they discover a princess who tells them the planet is being run by robots who have gone out–of–control. The boy and Dr. Gulliver destroy the robots—who melt when hit by water—and free the planet from captivity.

PN: Produced in Japan, this full–length animated feature was retitled for American release. It was formerly titled: *Gulliver No Uchu Ryoko.*

HAPPILY EVER AFTER (1990)

A Filmation/First National Film Production released by Kel-Air Entertainment. p: Lou Scheimer; d: John Howley; scr: Robby London, Martha Moran; m: Frank W. Becker; seq dir: Gian Celestri, Ka Moon Song, Lawrence White. Running time: 74 minutes.

Voices:

Snow White: Irene Cara, **Scowl:** Edward Asner, **Muddy:** Carol Channing, **Looking Glass:** Dom DeLuise, **Mother Nature:** Phyllis Diller, **Blossom:** Zsa Zsa Gabor, **Critterina, Marina:** Linda Gary, **Sunflower:** Jonathan Harris, **Prince:** Michael Horton, **Sunburn:** Sally Kellerman, **Lord Maliss:** Malcolm McDowell, **Moonbeam, Thunderella:** Tracey Ullman, **Batso:** Frank Welker

The evil queen's brother, Lord Maliss, seeks to avenge his sister's death by evening the score with Snow White, who is rescued by the Prince.

PN: This unauthorized sequel to the Walt Disney classic *Snow White And The Seven Dwarfs* began production in 1986 simultaneously with another unauthorized sequel to a Disney masterpiece, *Pinocchio And The Emperor Of The Night,* which was released in 1987.

HEATHCLIFF: THE MOVIE (1986)

A DIC–Audiovisual–LBS Communications–McNaught Syndicate Production released by Atlantic Releasing and Clubhouse Pictures. p: Jean Chalopin; d: Bruno Bianchi; w: Alan Swayze (based on the comic strip "Heathcliff" by George Gately); anim: Junko Ace, Kenichi Arani, Ildo Fudamoki, Kichi Ilkino, Kiroshi Ishiddori, Toshteru Kosayashi, Ky Ota, Seiji Okada,

Masie Otake, Kazulo Shirata, Keiko Shirai, Tasuchido Tamamoto, Tanzo Tamazaki. Running time: 73 minutes.

Voices:
Heathcliff: Mel Blanc

Featuring new introductory footage, the film incorporates numerous adventures from the television series with the famed comic strip feline becoming involved in all kinds of escapades.

HEAVY METAL (1981)

An Ivan Reitman/Leonard Mogel Production released by Columbia Pictures. p: Ivan Reitman; d: Gerald Potterton; w: Dan Goldberg and Len Blum (based on work and stories by Richard Corben, Angus McKie, Dan O'Bannon, Thomas Warkentin, Berni Wrightson); m: Elmer Bernstein; anim design: Warkentin McKie, Dan O'Bannon, Richard Corben, Juan Gimenez, Lee Mishkin. Running time: 91 minutes.

Voices:
Roger Bumpass, Jackie Burroughs, John Candy, Joe Flaherty, Don Francks, Martin Lavut, Eugene Levy, Marlyn Lightstone, Alice Playten, Harold Ramis, Susan Roman, Richard Romanos, August Schellenberg, John Vernon, Zal Yanovsky

Seven segments backed by original rock music comprise this adult cartoon fantasy based on stories from *Heavy Metal* magazine.

HEAVY TRAFFIC (1973)

A Steve Krantz Production released by American International Pictures. p: Steve Krantz; d & scr: Ralph Bakshi, m: Ray Shanklin, Ed Bogas; anim: Bob Bransford, Ed De Mattia, Milt Gray, Volus Jones, Bob Maxfield, Manny Perez, Tom Ray, Lloyd Vaughan, Carlo Vinci, J. E. Walker Sr., Bob Bemiller, Irv Spence, Manny Gould, Barney Posner, Fred Hellmich, Nick Tafuri, Martin Tarab, Dave Tendlar, Alex Ignatiev with "fantasy animation" by Mark Kausler. Running time: 78 minutes.

Voices:
Joseph Kaufman, Beverly Hope Atkinson, Frank De Kova, Terri Haven, Mary Dean Lauria, Jacqueline Mills, Lillian Adams, Jim Bates, Jamie Farr, Robert Easton, Charles Grodone, Michael Brandon, Morton Lewis, Bill Striglos, Jay Lawrence, Lee Weaver

Young cartoonist Michael, the virginal offspring of a Mafia member, leaves home after violently quarreling with his Jewish mother and takes a black girl, Rosa, as his mistress.
PN: Like *Fritz the Cat,* the film received an X rating, even though the content was not as visually and aurally explicit as Bakshi's first effort. It was originally to be based on Hubert Selby's *Last Exit to Brooklyn* but a deal between Selby and Bakshi fell through.

HERE COME THE LITTLES (1983)

A DIC Enterprises Production released by Atlantic Releasing. p: Jean Chalopin, Andy Heward, Tetsuo Katayama; d: Bernard Deyries; w: Woody Kling; m: Haim Saban, Shuky Levy; anim dir: Tsukasa Tannai, Yoshinobu Michihata; anim: Yoshinobu Michihata, Masako Shinohara, Koichi Maruyama, Atsuko Tanaka, Keiko Hara, Chie Uratani, Yoko Sakaurai, Yayoi Kobayashi, Masanori Ono, Masaki Endo, Makiko Tutaki. Running time: 77 minutes.

Voices:
Henry Bigg: Jimmy E. Keegan, **Lucy Little:** Bettina Bush, **Tom Little:** Donovan Freberg, **Uncle Augustus:** Hal Smith, **William Little:** Gregg Berger, **Helen Little:** Patricia Parris, **Grandpa Little:** Alvy Moore, **Dinky Little:** Robert David Hall, **Mrs. Evans:** Mona Marshall

When Henry Bigg's parents are lost in Africa, the boy is sent to live with his mean Uncle Augustus, who wants to be Henry's guardian so he can tear down Henry's house and build a shopping center. The Littles, Tom and Lucy, who accidentally wind up in Henry's suitcase, reveal themselves to Henry, who is astonished to learn of their existence but pledges to help them escape.

HEY, GOOD LOOKIN' (1982)

A Ralph Bakshi Production released through Warner Brothers. p, d & w: Ralph Bakshi; m: John Madara, Ric Sandler; anim: Brenda Banks, Carl Bell, Bob Carlson, John Gentilella, Steve Gordon, Manny Perez, Virgil Ross, John Sparey, Irven Spence, Tom Tataranwicz, Robert Taylor, and John E. Walker, Sr. Running time: 76 minutes.

Voices:
Vinnie: Richard Romanus, **Crazy Shapiro:** David Proval, **Roz:** Tina Bowman, **Eva:** Jesse Welles, **Solly:** Angelo Grisanti, **Stompers:** Danny Wells, Bennie Massa, Gelsa Palao, Paul Roman, Larry Bishop, Tabi Cooper, **Waitress:** Juno Dawson, **Chaplain:** Shirley Jo Finney, **Yonkel:** Martin Garner, **Alice:** Terry Haven, **Max:** Allen Joseph, **Chaplain:** Phillip M. Thomas, **Old Vinnie:** Frank de Kova, **Sal:** Candy Candido, **Italian Man:** Ed Peck, **Italian Women:** Lillian Adams, Mary Dean Lauria, Gelsa: Donna Ponterotto, **The Lockers Staging and Choreography:** Toni Basil

Vinnie, a slicked hair '50s type (resembling John Travolta), is the head of a white youth street gang, The Stompers, whose rivals are a black group known as The Chaplains in this 1950s genre spoof.
PN: Ralph Bakshi completed principal work on this animated feature in 1975, but it was shelved by Warner Brothers for seven years before it was actually released.

HEY THERE, IT'S YOGI BEAR (1964)

A Hanna–Barbera Production released by Columbia Pictures. p&d: William Hanna, Joseph Barbera; w: William Hanna, Joseph Barbera, Warren Foster; m: Marty Paich; anim dir: Charles A. Nichols, anim: Don Lusk, Irv Spence, George Kreisl, Ray Patterson, Jerry Hathcock, Grant Simmons, Fred Wolf, Don

Peterson, Ken Harris, Gerry Chiniquy, George Goepper, Edwin Aardal, Ed Parks, Kenneth Muse, and Harry Holt. Songs: "Hey There, It's Yogi Bear," "Ven–E, Ven–O, Ven–A," "Like I Like You," "Wet Whistle," "St. Louie" and "Ash Can Parade." Running time: 89 minutes.

Voices:
Yogi Bear: Daws Butler; **Boo Boo, Ranger Smith:** Don Messick; **Cindy Bear:** Julie Bennett; **Grifter:** Mel Blanc; **Corn Pone:** Hal Smith; **Snively:** J. Pat O'Malley; James Darren; Jean VanderPyl

Yogi Bear, the self–proclaimed king of Jellystone Park, and pal Boo Boo travel cross–country in search of Yogi's girlfriend, Cindy, who has been captured by a circus. The adventure winds up in New York, where Ranger Smith comes to the rescue of all three.

PN: The film was Yogi's first full–length animated feature and the first cartoon feature ever for Hanna–Barbera Productions.

HUGO THE HIPPO (1976)

A Brut/Hungarofilm Pannonia Filmstudio Production released by 20th Century–Fox. p: Robert Halmi; d: Bill Feigenbaum; scr: Thomas Baum; m: Bert Keyes; anim dir: Joszef Gemes; anim: Kati Banki, Zsuka Dekany, Edit Hernadi, Ivan Jenkovszky, Mikloa Kaim, Edit Szalai, Andras Szemenyei, Csaba Szorady, Sarolta Toth. Songs: "It's Really True," "I Always Wanted to Make a Garden," "Somewhere You Can Call Home," "H–I–P–P–O–P–O–T–A–M–U–S," "You Said a Mouthful," "Best Day Ever Made," "Mr. M'Bow–Wow," "Wherever you Go, Hugo," "Harbor Chant" and "Zing Zang." Running time: 76 minutes.

Voices:
Narrator: Burl Ives, **The Sultan:** Robert Morley, **Aban Khan:** Paul Lynde, **Jorma:** Ronnie Cox, **Jorma's Father:** Percy Rod-

A forlorn baby hippo struggles to survive against hippo–haters of the world in the Hungarian–produced feature, Hugo The Hippo (1976). © 20th Century–Fox

riguez, **Royal Magician:** Jesse Emmette, **Judge:** Len Maxwell, **Grown Ups and Children:** Tom Scott, Don Marshall, H. B. Barnum III, Marc Copage, Charles Walken, Lee Weaver, Richard Williams, Frank Welker, Ron Pinkard, Michael Rye, Marc Wright, Ellsworth Wright, Vincent Esposito, Court Benson, Peter Benson, Mona Tera, Bobby Eilbacher, Len Maxwell, Peter Fernandez, Allen Swift, Derek Power, Frederick O'Neal, Al Fann, Thomas Anderson, Jerome Ward, Shawn Campbell, Lisa Huggins, John McCoy, Alicia Fleer, Lisa Kohane, Bobby Dorn, Pat Bright, Robert Lawrence, **Special Voice Effects:** Frank Welker, Nancy Wible, Jerry Hausner, **Vocalist:** Marie Osmond, **Vocalist:** Jimmy Osmond

A forlorn baby hippo struggles to survive against hippo–haters of the world, led by Aban Khan (voiced by Paul Lynde), and seeks the companionship of others to feel needed and loved.

PN: The first feature film for both producer Robert Halmi and director Bill Feigenbaum, this inventively designed film was made in Hungary and released in the United States.

THE INCREDIBLE MR. LIMPET (1962)

A Warner Brothers release. p: John C. Rose; d: Arthur Lubin; scr: James Brewer and John C. Rose; m: Frank Perkins; anim dir: Vladimir Tytla, Gerry Chiniquy, Hawley Pratt; seq dir: Robert McKimson. Running time: 99 minutes.

Cast:
Henry Limpet: Don Knotts, **Bessie Limpet:** Carole Cook, **George Stickle:** Jack Weston, **Commander Harlock:** Andrew Duggan, **Admiral Spewter:** Larry Keating, **Admiral Fivestar:** Charles Meredith, **Admiral Doemitz:** Oscar Beregi

Voices:
Limpet: Don Knotts, **Ladyfish:** Elizabeth MacRae, **Crusty:** Paul Frees

In this live–action/animated feature, Don Knotts plays a retiring Walter Mitty–type bookkeeper who, depressed by his inability to join the navy (he's classified as 4–F because of his eyesight), accidentally falls into the ocean and is suddenly transformed into a fish. In his new role, he makes friends, finds a sweetheart and aides the U. S. war effort by helping convoys cross the ocean to knock off enemy U–Boats.

PN: Film's original working titles were *Henry Limpet, Mister Limpet* and *Be Careful How You Wish.* Arthur Lubin, the film's director, was best known for directing several of Abbott and Costello's most successful feature–length comedies at Universal.

JETSONS: THE MOVIE (1990)

A Hanna-Barbera Production released by Universal Pictures. p & d: William Hanna and Joseph Barbera; w: Dennis Marks; m: John Debney (with original songs by Tiffany); anim dir: David Michener; anim: Frank Adriana, Oliver "Lefty" Callahan,

David Feiss, Don MacKinnon, and Irv Spence. Songs: "Jetsons Main Title," "Gotcha," "Maybe Love, Maybe Not," "Staying Together," "I Always Thought I'd See You Again," "First Time In Love," "You And Me," "Home," "We're The Jetsons" (Jetsons' rap) and "With You All The Way." Running Time: 82 minutes.

Voices:

George Jetson: George O'Hanlon, **Mr. Spacely:** Mel Blanc, **Jane Jetson:** Penny Singleton, **Judy Jetson:** Tiffany, **Elroy Jetson:** Patric Zimmerman, **Astro:** Don Messick, **Rosie the Robot:** Jean Vander Pyl, **Rudy 2:** Ronnie Schell, **Lucy 2:** Patti Deutsch, **Teddy 2:** Dana Hill, **Fergie Furbelow:** Russi Taylor, **Apollo Blue:** Paul Kreppel, **Rocket Rick:** Rick Dees; Michael Bell, Jeff Bergman, Brian Cummings, Brad Garrett, Rob Paulsen, Susan Silo, Janet Waldo, B. J. Ward, Jim Ward, Frank Welker

This film version of the classic cartoon show finds the fun-loving foursome, accompanied by their faithful companion/dog, Astro, moving to outer space when George receives a promotion. While their family adjusts to their new home in the Intergalactical Garden estates, George heads for his new job as vice president of the Spacely Sprocket factory. Trouble looms, however, with the discovery that someone is sabotaging the factory and its machinery.

PN: Based on the popular '60s TV show, this full-length feature grossed $5 million during the first weekend of its release. One unpopular move was the ousting of actress Janet Waldo, the original voice of Judy Jetson, who recorded all her dialogue and was then dumped for the youthful pop singer Tiffany. The film's settings and vehicles were designed using advanced computer animated techniques created by deGraf/Wahrman and Kroyer Films.

JOURNEY BACK TO OZ (1974)

A Filmation Associates Production released by EBA. p: Norm Prescott, Lou Scheimer; w: Fred Ladd, Norm Prescott d: Hal Sutherland; m/l: Sammy Cahn, James Van Heusen; anim superv: Amby Paliwoda. Running time: 90 minutes.

Voices:

Dorothy: Liza Minelli; **Scarecrow:** Mickey Rooney; **Tin-Man:** Danny Thomas; **Cowardly Lion:** Milton Berle; **Aunt Em:** Margaret Hamilton; **Mombi, the Bad Witch:** Ethel Merman; **Glinda, the Good Witch:** Rise Stevens; **Pumpkinhead:** Paul Lynde; **Woodenhead:** Herschel Bernardi; **The Signpost:** Jack E. Leonard; Paul Ford; Mel Blanc; Dallas McKennon; Larry Storch

Ever since the MGM/Judy Garland classic, filmmakers have wanted to return to the land of Oz, which is the focal point of this animated sequel featuring the same well-known characters—Dorothy, Tin Man, Scarecrow and the Cowardly Lion—in all-new adventures in the "land over the rainbow."

PN: This animated feature was originally produced in 1964, but was not released until nearly 10 years later.

THE JUNGLE BOOK (1967)

A Walt Disney Production released by Buena Vista. p: Walt Disney; d: Wolfgang Reitherman; dir anim; Milt Kahl, Frank Thomas, Ollie Johnston Jr., John Lounsbery; st: Larry Clemmons, Ralph Wright, Ken Anderson, Vance Gerry (based on Rudyard Kipling's *The Jungle Book* stories); m: George Bruns; anim: Hal King, Eric Larson, Walt Stanchfield, Eric Cleworth, Fred Hellmich, John Ewing, Dick Lucas. Songs: "I Wanna Be Like You," "Trust in Me," "My Own Home," "That's What Friends Are For," "Colonel Hathi's March" and "The Bare Necessities." Running time: 78 minutes.

Voices:

Baloo the Bear: Phil Harris, **Bagheera the Panther:** Sebastian Cabot, **King Louise of the Apes:** Louis Prima, **Shere Khan, the tiger:** George Sanders, **Kaa, the snake:** Sterling Holloway, **Colonel Hathi, the elephant:** J. Pat O'Malley, **Mowgli, the man-cub:** Bruce Reitherman, **Elephants:** Verna Felton, Clint Howard, **Vultures:** Chad Stuart, Lord Tim Hudson, J. Pat O'Malley, Digby Wolfe, **Wolves:** John Abbott, Ben Wright, **Girl:** Darleen Carr

This animated adaptation of Rudyard Kipling's classic story deals with Mowgli, an Indian boy abandoned at birth, who is raised as a wolf cub, and 10 years later is returned to his people by Bagheera, the panther who protected him as a child. In his jungle setting, Mowgli makes friends with Baloo, a happy-go-lucky bear, and lives life anew in the jungle, but not without a few close encounters with King Louie, Colonel Hathi and Shere Khan.

PN: The last animated film to bear the creative stamp of Walt Disney, who died in 1966.

LADY AND THE TRAMP (1955)

A Walt Disney Production released by Buena Vista. p: Walt Disney; d: Hamilton Luske, Clyde Geronimi, Wilfred Jackson; dir anim: Milt Kahl, Frank Thomas, Ollie Johnston, John Lounsbery, Wolfgang Reitherman, Eric Larson, Hal King, Les Clark; st: Erdman Penner, Joe Rinaldi, Ralph Wright, Donald Da Gradi (based on an original story by Ward Greene); m/sc: Oliver Wallace; anim: George Nicholas, Hal Ambro, Ken O'Brien, Jerry Hathcock, Eric Cleworth, Marvin Woodward, Ed Aardal, John Sibley, Harvey Toombs, Cliff Nordberg, Don Lusk, George Kreisl, Hugh Fraser, John Freeman, Jack Campbell, Bob Carlson. Songs: "He's a Tramp," "La La Lu," "Siamese Cat Song," "Peace on Earth" and "Bella Notte." Running time: 76 minutes.

Voices:

Darling, Si, Am, Peg: Peggy Lee, **Lady:** Barbara Luddy, **Tramp:** Larry Roberts, **Trusty:** Bill Baucom, **Aunt Sarah:** Verna Felton, **Tony:** George Givot, **Jim Dear, Dog Catcher:** Lee Millar, **Bull, Dachsie, Jock, Joe:** Bill Thompson, **Beaver, Pet-Store Clerk:** Stan Freberg, **Boris:** Alan Reed, **Toughby, Professor, Pedro:** Dallas McKennon, **Dogs in Pound:** The Mello Men

Lady, a pretty female cocker spaniel, falls in love with Tramp, a stray who values his liberty above all else. The heart of the story deals with the unusual bonding of the two characters—the more refined Lady and the outcast Tramp—embattled with two neighborhood mutts, Jock and Caesar, who yearn for Lady's love.

THE LAND BEFORE TIME (1988)

A Sullivan Bluth Studios Production released by MGM/United Artists. p: Don Bluth, Gary Goldman, John Pomeroy; d: Don Bluth; scr: Stu Krieger; st: Judy Freudberg, Tony Geiss; m: James Horner; anim dir: John Pomeroy, Linda Miller, Ralph Zondag, Dan Kuenster, Lorna Pomeroy, Dick Zondag; anim: Anne Marie Bardwell, Victoria Brewster, Colm Duggan, Ken Duncan, Jeff Etter, Mark Fisher, Michael Gagne, Raul Garcia, Patrick Gleeson, Ken Hammerstorm, T. Daniel Hofstedt, Jon Hooper, Skip Jones, Jean Morel, Paul Newberry, Ralf Palmer, Gary Perkovac, John Power. Running time: 63 minutes.

Voices:

Narrator/Rooter: Pat Hingle, **Littlefoot's Mother:** Helen Shaver, **Littlefoot:** Gabriel Damon, **Grandfather:** Bill Erwin, **Cera:** Candy Hutson, **Daddy Topps:** Burke Barnes, **Ducky:** Judith Barsi, **Petrie:** Will Ryan

A young brontosaurus named Littlefoot is orphaned when a tyrannosaurus attacks and separates his flock. He sets off in search of the Great Valley, a legendary land of lush vegetation where dinosaurs can live and thrive in peace. Along the way he meets four other youngsters, each a member of a different dinosaur family. Together they encounter incredible obstacles while learning unforgettable lessons about life.

THE LAST UNICORN (1982)

A Rankin–Bass Production released by ITC. p & d: Arthur Rankin Jr., Jules Bass; w: Peter S. Beagle (based on the novel by Peter S. Beagle); m: Jimmy Webb; anim: Yoshiko Sasaki,

Ducky the Anatosaurus meets up with Littlefoot in Don Bluth's fantasy–adventure, The Land Before Time (1988).
© Universal City Studios

Masahiro Yoshida, Kayoko Sakano, Fukuo Suzuki, Ioru Hala, Guy Kubo. Running time: 88 minutes.

Voices:

Schmendrick the Magician: Alan Arkin, **Prince Lir:** Jeff Bridges, **The Last Unicorn/Lady Amalthea:** Mia Farrow, **Molly Grue:** Tammy Grimes, **The Butterfly:** Robert Klein, **Mommy Fortuna:** Angela Lansbury, **King Haggard:** Christopher Lee, **Capt. Cully:** Keenan Wynn, **The Talking Cat:** Paul Frees, **The Speaking Skull:** Rene Auberjonois

A young unicorn accompanied by a magician journeys to release the rest of her breed from the tyranny of an evil king.

THE LITTLE MERMAID (1989)

A Walt Disney Pictures presentation in association with Silver Screen Partners IV released by Buena Vista. p: Howard Ashman, John Musker; d: Ron Clements, John Musker; scr: Ron Clements, John Musker; m: Alan Menken; anim dir: Mark Henn, Glen Keane, Duncan Marjoribanks, Ruben Aquino, Andreas Deja, Matthew O'Callaghan; anim: Michael Cedeno, Rick Farmiloe, Shawn E. Keller, David Pruiksma, Dan Jeup, Phil Young, Anthony DeRosa, David Cutler, Nik Ranieri, Dave Spafford, Jay Jackson, Barry Temple, James Baxter, Kathy Zielinski, Jorgen Klubien, Chris Bailey, Tony Fucile, Chris Wahl, Chuck Harvey, Tom Sito, Will Finn, Doug Krohn, Leon Joosen, Russ Edmonds, David P. Stephen, Ellen Woodbury, Ron Husband, David A. Pacheco, Tony Anselmo, Rob Minkoff. Songs: "Under the Sea," "Part of Your World," "Poor Souls," "Les Poissons," "Fathoms Below" and "Daughters of Triton." Running time: 82 minutes.

Voices:

Louis: Rene Auberjonois, **Eric:** Christopher Daniel Barnes, **Ariel:** Jodi Benson, **Ursula:** Pat Carroll, **Scuttle:** Buddy Hackett, **Flounder:** Jason Marin, **Triton:** Kenneth Mars, **Grimsby:** Ben Wright, **Sebastian:** Samuel E. Wright

Against her father's wishes, young mermaid princess Ariel travels beyond her world to the one above the sea where she falls in love with a human prince in this cartoon adaptation of the Hans Christian Andersen tale.

LORD OF THE RINGS (1978)

A Fantasy Films/Saul Zaentz Production released by United Artists. p: Saul Zaentz; d: Ralph Bakshi; w: Chris Conkling, Peter S. Beagle (based on the stories by J. R. R. Tolkien); m: Leonard Roseman; anim: Craig Armstrong, Dale Baer, Brenda Banks, Carl Bell, Jesus Cortes, Lillian Evans, Frank Gonzales, Steven Gordon, Sean Joyce, Lenord Robinson, Chrystal Russell, Paul Smith, Irven Spence, Hank Tucker, Edward Wexler, Bruce Woodside, James A. Davis. Running time: 131 minutes.

Voices:

Frodo: Christopher Guard, **Gandalf:** William Squire, **Sam:** Michael Scholes, **Aragon:** John Hurt, **Merry:** Simon Chandler, **Pippin:** Dominic Guard, **Bilbo:** Norman Bird, **Boromir:** Michael Graham–Fox, **Legolas:** Anthony Daniels, **Gimli:** David Buck, **Gollum:** Peter Wood Thorpe, **Saruman:** Fraser Kerr, **Theoden:** Phillip Stone, **Wormtongue:** Michael Deacon, **El-**

rond: Andre Murell, **Innkeeper:** Alan Tilvern, **Galadriel:** Annette Crosbie, **Treebeard:** John Westbrook

The Dark Lord Sauron possesses rings of great evil with which he can control Middle Earth, but that all changes when one of the rings falls into the hands of Hobbit Bilbo Baggins, who passes the ring and its inherent power onto his nephew, Frodo, to take up the battle.

PN: The film employs Bakshi's rotoscope technique of animating live–action characters to create a lifelike effect.

MAD MONSTER PARTY (1967)

A Rankin–Bass Production released by Videocraft International. p: Arthur Rankin Jr.; d: Jules Bass; w: Len Korobkin, Harvey Kirtzman, Forrest J. Ackerman (based on a story by Rankin); m/l: Maury Laws, Jules Bass. Filmed in Animagic. Running time: 94 minutes.

Voices:

Baron Boris von Frankenstein: Boris Karloff; **Frankenstein's Wife:** Phyllis Diller; Ethel Ennis; Gale Garnett; Allen Swift

Using three–dimensional figures in a process called Animagic, this stop–action animated film lampoons the horror film genre, featuring all the monsters—The Werewolf, Dracula, the Creature from the Black Lagoon, King Kong, Dr. Jekyll and Mr. Hyde, The Mummy and others—as attendees at a convention for the Worldwide Organization of Monsters. Their purpose: to select a new leader for the soon–to–be retired Baron Boris von Frankenstein.

THE MAGIC PONY (1979)

A Soyuzmult Film Studios Production released by Action Entertainment. p: C. B. Wismar; d: Ivan Ivanov–Vano; scr: George Malko (based on the Russian folktale by Peter Yershow); m: Tom Ed Williams; anim: Lev Milchin. Songs: "Ride a Magic Pony," "Lonely Child," "A Whale of a Day" and "On This Beautiful Day." Running time: 80 minutes.

Voices:

King: Jim Backus; **Red Haired Groom:** Hans Conreid; **Zip the Pony:** Erin Moran; **Ivan:** Johnny Whitaker; Diane Alton; Robb Cigne; John Craig; Wayne Heffley; Jason Wingreen; Sandra Wirth

Ivan and his three brothers are sent to watch over the fields, in hope of catching the culprit responsible for the destruction of the wheat crop. Ivan catches the person—a Magic Pony, who leads him on a fascinating adventure where he encounters a range of characters, from an emperor to a terrifying whale.

MAKE MINE MUSIC (1946)

A Walt Disney Production released by RKO Radio Pictures. p: Walt Disney; prod superv: Joe Grant; d: Jack Kinney, Clyde Geronimi, Hamilton Luske, Robert Cormack, Joshua Meador; st: Homer Brightman, Dick Huemer, Dick Kinney, John Walbridge, Tom Oreb, Dick Shaw, Eric Gurney, Silvia Holland, T. Hee, Dick Kelsey, Jesse Marsh, Roy Williams, Ed Penner, James Bodero, Cap Palmer, Erwin Graham; md: Charles Wolcott; m/a: Ken Darby, Oliver Wallace, Edward H. Plumb; anim: Les Clark, Ward Kimball, Milt Kahl, John Sibley, Hal King, Eric Larson, John Lounsbery, Oliver M. Johnston Jr., Fred Moore, Hugh Fraser, Judge Whitaker, Harvey Toombs, Tom Massey, Phil Duncan, Hal Ambro, Jack Campbell, Cliff Nordberg, Bill Justice, Al Bertino, John McManus, Ken O'Brien. Songs: "Johnny Fedora and Alice Bluebonnet," "All the Cats Join In," "Without You," "Two Silhouettes," "Casey, the Pride of Them All," "The Martins and the Coys," "Blue Bayou," "After You've Gone" and "Make Mine Music." Running time: 75 minutes.

Voices:

Nelson Eddy, Dinah Shore, Benny Goodman and Orchestra, The Andrew Sisters, Jerry Colonna, Andy Russell, Sterling Holloway, The Pied Pipers, The King's Men, The Ken Darby Chorus, and featuring Tania Riabouchinska and David Lichine

Like *Fantasia,* this Disney production adapted popular music to the screen, featuring a collection of those melodies in animated sequences, including "The Martins and the Coys," a cartoon version of an age–old hillbilly feud; "A Tone Poem," a mood piece based on Ken Darby's chorus of "Blue Bayou"; "A Jazz Interlude," with Benny Goodman and his orchestra leading a vignette drawn version of "All the Cats Join In."

THE MAN CALLED FLINTSTONE (1966)

A Hanna–Barbera Production released by Columbia Pictures. p & d: William Hanna, Joseph Barbera; w: Harvey Bullock, R. S. Allen (based on a story by Harvey Bullock and R. S. Allen, and story material by Joseph Barbera, William Hanna, Warren Foster, Alex Lovy); m: Marty Paich, Ted Nichols; anim dir: Charles A. Nichols; anim: Irv Spence, George Goepper, George Nicholas, Edward Barge, Edwin Aardal, Jerry Hathcock, Don Lusk, Kenneth Muse, Richard Lundy, Bill Keil, Ed Parks, John Sparey, Allen Wilzbach, George Kreisl, George Germanetti, Carlo Vinci, Hugh Fraser, Hicks Lokey. Songs: "Pensate Amore," "Team Mates," "Spy Type Guy," "The Happy Sounds of Paree," "The Man Called Flintstone," "When I'm Grown Up" and "Tickle Toddle." Running time: 90 minutes.

Voices:

Fred Flintstone: Alan Reed Sr.; **Barney Rubble:** Mel Blanc; **Wilma Flintstone:** Jean VanderPyl; **Betty Rubble:** Gerry Johnson; Don Messick; Janet Waldo; Paul Frees; Harvey Korman; John Stephenson; June Foray

Resembling American spy, Rock Slag, wounded while chasing international spy, Green Goose and his girlfriend, Tanya, Fred Flintstone is asked to take Rock's place and fly to Rome (with his family, of course) to help corral Green Goose once and for all. The whole thing turns out to be a trap and the real Slag, now fully recovered, comes to Fred's rescue.

PN: The film's working title was *That Man Flintstone.*

THE MAN FROM BUTTON WILLOW (1965)

An Eagle Film Production released by United Screen Artists. p: Phyllis Bounds Detiege; d & w: Dave Detiege; m: George Stoll, Robert Van Eps; anim: Ken Hultgren, Don Towsley, Don Lusk, George Rowley. Running time: 81 minutes.

Voices:

Justin Eagle: Dale Robertson; **Sorry:** Edgar Buchanan; **Stormy:** Barbara Jean Wong; Howard Keel; Herschel Bernardi; Ross Martin; Verna Felton; Shep Menken; Pinto Colvig; Cliff Edwards; Thurl Ravenscroft; John Hiestand; Clarence Hash; Edward Platt; Buck Buchanan

Intrigue and espionage are key elements of this action–packed adventure about the first United States government undercover agent, Justin Eagle, who recovers a kidnapped government official and thwarts plans to sabotage a state railroad.

THE MANY ADVENTURES OF WINNIE THE POOH (1977)

A Walt Disney Production released through Buena Vista. p: Wolfgang Reitherman; d: Wolfgang Reitherman, John Lounsbery; st: Larry Clemmons, Vance Gerry, Ken Anderson, Ted Berman, Ralph Wright, Xavier Atencio, Julius Svendsen, Eric Cleworth; m/l: Richard Sherman, Robert B. Sherman; anim: Hal King, Milt Kahl, Ollie Johnston, Art Stevens, Cliff Nordberg, Eric Larson, Gary Goldman, Burny Mattinson, John Pomeroy, Chuck Williams, Richard Sebast, John Lounsbery, Frank Thomas, Eric Cleworth, John Sibley, Don Bluth, Walt Stanchfield, Hal Ambro, Dale Baer, Fred Hellmich, Bill Keil, Andrew Gaskill. Running time: 74 minutes

Voices:

Narrator: Sebastian Cabot, **Winnie the Pooh:** Sterling Holloway, **Tigger:** Paul Winchell, **Roo:** Clint Howard, **Roo:** Dori Whitaker, **Christopher Robin:** Timothy Turner, **Christopher Robin:** Bruce Reitherman, **Christopher Robin:** Jon Walmsley, **Kanga:** Barbara Luddy, **Eeyore:** Ralph Wright, **Rabbit:** Junius Matthews, **Gopher:** Howard Morris, **Piglet:** John Fiedler, **Owl:** Hal Smith

A. A. Milne's beloved children's stories come alive in this collection of Winnie the Pooh cartoon shorts (*Winnie The Pooh And The Honey Tree, Winnie The Pooh And The Blustery Day* and *Winnie The Pooh And Tigger Too*) combined with new animation and released as a full–length feature.

MELODY TIME (1948)

A Walt Disney Production released by RKO Radio Pictures. p: Walt Disney; prod superv: Ben Sharpsteen; anim dir: Clyde Geronimi, Wilfred Jackson, Hamilton Luske, Jack Kinney; st: Winston Hibler, Harry Reeves, Ken Anderson, Erdman Penner, Homer Brightman, Ted Sears, Joe Rinaldi, Art Scott, Bob Moore, Bill Cottrell, Jesse Marsh, John Walbridge. "Little Toot" by Hardie Gramatky; md: Eliot Daniel, Ken Darby; dir anim: Eric Larson, Ward Kimball, Milt Kahl, Oliver M. Johnston Jr., John Lounsbery, Les Clark; anim: Harvey Toombs, Ed Aardal, Cliff Nordberg, John Sibley, Ken O'Brien, Judge Whitaker, Marvin Woodward, Hal King, Don Lusk, Rudy Larriva, Bob Cannon, and Hal Ambro. Songs: "Melody Time," "Little Toot," "The Lord Is Good to Me," "The Pioneer Song," "Once Upon a Wintertime," "Blame It on the Samba," "Blue Shadows on the Trail," "Pecos Bill," "Trees" and "The Flight of the Bumblebee." Running time: 75 minutes.

Cast:

Roy Rogers, Luana Patten, Bobby Driscoll, Ethel Smith, Bob Nolan, the Sons of the Pioneers

Voices/Musicians:

Master of Ceremonies: Buddy Clark; The Andrews Sisters; Fred Waring and his Pennsylvanians; Frances Langford; Dennis Day; **Aracaun Bird:** Pinto Colvig; with Freddy Martin and his Orchestra featuring Jack Fina

The last of Disney's musical fantasies, this musical melange features live action and animated episodes based on popular songs of the day. Several key animated sequences make up the film, among them: "Blame It on the Samba," with Donald Duck and *Saludos Amigos* co–star Jose Carioca in this animated samba backed by Ethel Smith and the Dinning Sisters; "Johnny Appleseed," featuring the voice of actor/singer Dennis Day as narrator; and "Little Toot," the story of a young tugboat's determination to be successful, sung by The Andrews Sisters.

METAMORPHOSES (1978)

A Sanrio Films release. p: Terry Ogisu, Hiro Tsugawa, Takashi; d & w: Takashi (based on Ovid's "Metamorphoses"); seq dir: Jerry Eisenberg, Richard Huebner, Sadao Miyamato, Amby Paliwoda, Ray Patterson, Manny Perez, George Singer, Stan Walsh; anim: Edwin Aardal, John Ahern, Mikiharu Akabori, Robert Carlson, Brad Case, Marija Dail, Edward DeMattia, Joan Drake, Edgar Friedman, Edwardo Fuentes, Morris Gollub, Fred Grable, Masami Hata, Fred Hellmich, Ernesto Lopez, Daniel Noonan, Ken O'Brian, Jack Ozark, William Pratt, Thomas Ray, Virgil Ross, Glenn Schmitz, Martha Swanson, Reuben Timmins, James Walker, John Walker, Shigeru Yamamoto, Rudolfo Zamora. Running time: 89 minutes.

Five of the most familiar Greek and Roman myths—creation, the hunter Actaeon turned into a stag by the goddess Diana, Orpheus and Eurydice, Mercy and the House of Envy, Perseus and Medusa and Phaeton and the sun chariot—are integrated into this cartoon adaptation of five tales of classic mythology by Ovid.

PN: Three years in the making, *Metamorphoses* was first screened in the fall of 1977 but pulled back from general release for some additional post–production work.

MISTER BUG GOES TO TOWN (1940)

A Fleischer Studios Production released by Paramount Pictures. p: Max Fleischer; d: Dave Fleischer; w: Dave Fleischer, Dan Gordon, Ted Pierce, Isadore Sparber, William Turner, Mike Meyer, Graham Place, Bob Wickersham, Cal Howard; md: Leigh Harline; m/l: Hoagy Carmichael, Frank Loesser, Herman Timberg, Four Marshals and Royal Guards. Songs: "We're the Couple in the Castle," "Boy, Oh Boy," "Katy–Did, Katy–Didn't," "Bee My Little Baby Bumble Bee" and "I'll Dance at Your Wedding." Running time: 78 minutes.

Voices:

Kenny Gardner, Gwen Williams, Jack Mercer, Ted Pierce, Mike Meyer, Stan Freed, Pauline Loth

Bug life on Broadway sets the stage for this second feature by animators Max and Dave Fleischer chronicling an insect colony's never–ending battle against the human race. The film's central characters are Honey Bee and grasshopper Hoppity, the love interests of the story, and the nasty C. Bagley Beetle and his hoodlum henchmen, Swat the Fly and Smack the Mosquito, who make life miserable in bug town.

PN: This was the last cartoon feature for the Fleischer brothers, who parted company after making the film. Unlike *Gulliver's Travels*, this film was not a financial success.

THE MOUSE AND HIS CHILD (1977)

A deFaria–Lockhart–Murakami–Wolf/Sanrio release. p: Walt deFaria; d: Fred Wolf, Chuck Swenson; w: Carol Mon Pere (based on the novel by Russell Hoban); m: Roger Kellaway; anim: Fred Wolf, Chuck Swenson, Dave Brain, Vince Davis, Gary Mooney, Mike Sanger, Lu Guarnier, Willie Lye, Bob Zamboni, Brad Base, Irv Anderson, Duane Crowther. Running time: 83 minutes.

Voices:

Manny: Peter Ustinov, **Eutrepe:** Cloris Leachman, **Seal:** Sally Kellerman, **Frog:** Andy Devine, **Mouse:** Alan Barzman, **Mouse Child:** Marcy Swenson, **Iggy:** Neville Brand, **Clock/Hawk:** Regis Cordic, **Elephant:** Joan Gerber, **Muskrat:** Bob Holt, **Startling/Teller:** Maitzi Morgan, **Crow:** Frank Nelson, **Crow:** Cliff Norton, **Serpentina:** Cliff Osmond, **Paper People:** Iris Rainer, **Jack in the Box:** Bob Ridgeley, **Bluejay/The Paper People:** Charles Woolf, and Mel Leven

Based on Russell Hoban's novel, the film centers around the story of a mechanical mouse and his son who have one wish: to be self–winding.

MY LITTLE PONY: THE MOVIE (1986)

A Sunbow/Marvel Production in association with Hasbro Inc. released by DeLaurentis Films. p: Joe Bacal, Tom Griffin, Michael Joens; (no director listed); w: George Arthur Bloom; m: Rob Walsh (theme song "My Little Pony" by Spencer

Michilin and Ford Kinder); superv anim: Pierre DeCelles, Michael Fallows, Ray Lee; anim dir: Brad Case, Joan Case, Gerry Chiniquy, Charlie Downs, Bill Exter, Milton Gray, Song-pil Kim, Heungsun Kim, Margaret Nichols, Karen Peterson, Tom Ray, Bob Shellhorn, Bob Treat, Gregg Vanzo, Gwen Wetller, Jaeho Hong, Nak Jong Kim, Michihiro Kanayama, Akinori Matsubara. Running time: 90 minutes.

Voices:

Grundle King: Danny DeVito, **Droggle:** Madeline Kahn, **Hydia:** Cloris Leachman, **Reeka:** Rhea Perlman, **The Moonchick:** Tony Randall, **Megan:** Tammy Amerson, **The Smooze:** Jon Bauman, **Baby Lickety Split/Bushwoolie #1:** Alice Playten, **Spike/Woodland Creature:** Charlie Adler, **Grundle:** Michael Bell, **Buttons/Woodland Creature/Bushwoolie:** Sheryl Bernstein, **Lofty/Grundle/Bushwoolie:** Susan Blu, **North Star:** Cathy Cavadini, **Gusty/Bushwoolie #4:** Nancy Cartwright, **Grundle/Ahgg:** Peter Cullen, **Sundance/Bushwoolie #2:** Laura Dean, **Magic Star:** Ellen Gerstell, **Molly:** Keri Houlihan, **Fizzy/Baby Sunshine:** Katie Leigh, **Danny:** Scott Menville, **Sweet Stuff:** Laurel Page, **Wind Whistler:** Sarah Partridge, **Morning Glory/Rosedust/Bushwoolie/Skunk:** Russi Taylor, **Shady/Baby Lofty:** Jill Wayne, **Bushwoolie #3/Grundle:** Frank Welker

In Ponyland, the Little Ponies' annual Spring Festival is about to begin. While enjoying their festive spring party, the evil witch Hydia is plotting to turn Ponyland into a wasteland. When her attempt fails, she decides to cover Ponyland with a purple ooze called the "Smooze."

THE NINE LIVES OF FRITZ THE CAT (1974)

A Steve Krantz Production released by American International Pictures. p: Steve Krantz; d: Robert Taylor; scr: Fred Halliday, Eric Monte, Robert Taylor; m: Tom Scott, L.A. Express; anim: Robert Taylor, Don Williams, Paul Sommer, Manny Perez, Manny Gould, Bob Bachman, Art Vitello, Milt Gray, Marty Taras, Frank Andrina, Bob Bemiller, Jim Davis, Jack Foster, Herb Johnson, Volus Jones, Bob Maxfield, Cosmo Anzilotti, John Gentilella, John Freeman, Fred Hellmich, Bob Bransford, John Bruno. Running time: 76 minutes.

Voices:

Fritz: Skip Hinnant; Reva Rose; Bob Holt

Married and tired of his nagging wife, Fritz gets high on marijuana and experiences some of the better times in his life—seducing his kid sister, acting as Hitler's orderly and blasting off to Mars among others—in this sequel to the 1972 original.

NUTCRACKER FANTASY (1979)

A Sanrio Films release. p: Walt deFaria, Mark L. Rosen, Arthur Tomioka; d: Takeo Nakamura; w: Thomas Joachim, Eugene Fornier (based on *The Nutcracker and the Mouse King* by E. T. A. Hoffman, adaptation by Shintaro Tsuji); m: Peter Illych

Tchaikovsky (adapted and arranged by Akihito Wakatsuki, Kentaro Haneda). Running time: 82 minutes.

Voices:
Narrator: Michele Lee, **Clara:** Melissa Gilbert, **Aunt Gerda,** Lurene Tuttle, **Uncle Drosselmeyer/Street Singer/Puppeteer/Watchmaker:** Christopher Lee, **Queen Morphia:** Jo Anne Worley, **Chamberlain/Poet/Wiseman:** Ken Sansom, **King Goodwin:** Dick Van Patten, **Franz Fritz:** Roddy McDowall, **Indian Wiseman/Viking Wiseman:** Mitchel Gardner, **Chinese Wiseman/Executioner:** Jack Angel, **Otto Von Atra/French Wiseman/Clovis:** Gene Moss, **Queen of Time:** Eva Gabor, **Mice Voices:** Joan Gerber, Maxine Fisher, **Princess Mary:** Robin Haffner

A young girl dreams of romance and adventure in a world inhabited by a king whose daughter has been turned into a sleeping mouse and can only be transformed and reawakened by a heroic prince.

PN: This Japanese production, filmed and dubbed in English for American release, featured puppet animation.

THE NUTCRACKER PRINCE (1990)

A Lacewood Production released by Warner Brothers. p: Kevin Gillis; d: Paul Schibli; scr: Patricia Watson (based on "The Nutcracker And The Mouseking" by E.T.A. Hoffman); m: Peter Ilich Tchaikovsky (arranged by Victor Davies and performed by the London Symphony Orchestra under the direction of Boris Brott). Running time: 72½ minutes.

Voices:
Nutcracker Prince: Kiefer Sutherland, **Clara:** Megan Follows, **Mouseking:** Mike MacDonald, **Uncle Drosselmeier:** Peter Boretski, **Mousequeen:** Phyllis Diller, **Pantaloon:** Peter O'Toole

Young Clara Stahlbaum discovers a wooden nutcracker in the shape of a toy soldier under her Christmas tree. Her eccentric Uncle Drosselmeier tells her the story of the nutcracker, a young man named Hans, who was put under a spell by a wicked, vengeful Mousequeen. Clara dismisses the story, but that night everything her uncle told her unfolds before her eyes.

OF STARS AND MEN (1961)

A John and Faith Hubley Film. p: John and Faith Hubley; d: John Hubley; w: John and Faith Hubley, Harlow Shapley (based on the book *Of Stars and Men* by Shapley); anim dir: William Littlejohn, Gary Mooney; anim: John Hubley, Patricia Byron, Faith Hubley, Nina Di Gangi. Running time: 53 minutes.

Voices:
Dr. Harlow Shapley, Mark Hubley, Hamp Hubley

Man's scientic world is interpreted in this film by animation husband–and–wife team John and Faith Hubley. The film's central character, Man, reveals his place in the universe—in space, time, matter and energy—and the meaning of life.

OLIVER AND COMPANY (1988)

A Walt Disney/Silver Screen Partners III Production released by Buena Vista. d: George Scribner; st: Vance Gerry, Mike Gabriel, Joe Ranft, Jim Mitchell, Chris Bailey, Kirk Wise, Dave Michener, Roger Allers, Gary Trousdale, Kevin Lima, Michael Cedeno, Pete Young, Leon Joosen (based on Charles Dickens' *Oliver Twist*); anim scr: Jim Cox, Timothy J. Disney, James Mangold; m/superv: Carole Childs (original score by J. A. C. Redford); superv anim: Mike Gabriel, Glen Keane, Ruben A. Aquino, Hendel Butoy, Mark Hehn, Doug Krohn; anim: Phil Young, Leon Joosen, Russ Edmonds, Will Finn, Barry Temple, Ron Husband, Rick Farmiloe, Dave Pruiksma, Chris Bailey, Viki Anderson, Keven Lima, Shawn Keller, Tony Fucile, Anthony DeRosa, Jay Jackson, Kathy Zielinski, Kevin Wurzer, Jorgen Klubien, David P. Stephen, Dan Jeup, David Cutler, Jeffrey Lynch. Running time: 72 minutes.

Voices:
Oliver: Joey Lawrence, **Dodger:** Billy Joel, **Tito:** Cheech Marin, **Einstein:** Richard Mulligan, **Francis:** Roscoe Lee Browne, **Rita:** Sheryl Lee Ralph, **Fagin:** Dom DeLuise, **Roscoe:** Taurean Blacque, **Desoto:** Carl Weintraub, **Sykes:** Robert Loggia, **Jenny:** Natalie Gregory, **Winston:** William Glover, **Georgette:** Bette Midler

A rollicking take–off of Dickens' masterpiece with little orphan Oliver, a homeless kitten, taken in and cared for and taught "street smarts" by a pack of lovable hip dogs led by a human Fagin.

OLIVER TWIST (1974)

A Filmation Studios production released by Warner Brothers. p: Lou Scheimer, Norman Prescott; d: Hal Sutherland; m: George Blais. Running time: 75 minutes.

Voices:
Oliver Twist: Josh Albee; **Fagin:** Les Tremayne; Phil Clark; Cathleen Cordell; Michael Evans; Lola Fischer; Robert Holt; Davy Jones; Larry D. Mann; Dallas McKennon; Billy Simpson; Larry Storch; Jane Webb; Helene Winston

In mid-19th century London, an orphan boy finds that he is really the heir to a large fortune in this musical version of Charles Dickens' timeless novel.

PN: Originally released as a full–length feature, the film was re–edited and broadcast as a prime–time special on NBC in 1981.

ONE HUNDRED AND ONE DALMATIONS (1961)

A Walt Disney Production released by Buena Vista. p: Walt Disney; d: Wolfgang Reitherman, Hamilton Luske, Clyde Geronimi; st: Bill Peet (based on *The Hundred and One Dal-*

mations by Dodie Smith); m: George Bruns; dir anim: Milt Kahl, Frank Thomas, Marc Davis, John Lounsbery, Ollie Johnston, Eric Larson; anim: Hal King, Les Clark, Cliff Nordberg, Blaine Gibson, Eric Cleworth, John Sibley, Art Stevens, Julius Svedsen, Hal Ambro, Ted Berman, Bill Keil, Don Lusk, Dick Lucas, Amby Paliwoda. Songs: "Cruella De Vil," "Dalmation Plantation" and "Kanine Krunchie Commercial." Running time: 79 minutes.

Voices:

Pongo: Rod Taylor, **Perdita:** Lisa Daniels, **Perdita:** Cate Bauer, **Roger Radcliff:** Ben Wright, **Anita Radcliff:** Lisa Davis, **Nanny, Queenie, Lucy:** Martha Wentworth, **The Colonel, Jasper Badun, etc.:** J. Pat O'Malley, **Horace Badun, Inspector Craven:** Fred Worlock, **Cruella De Vil, Miss Birdwell:** Betty Lou Gerson, **Towser:** Tudor Owen, **Quizmaster, Collie:** Tom Conway, **Danny:** George Pelling, **The Captain:** Thurl Ravenscroft, **Sergeant Tibs:** Dave Frankham, **Television Announcer, Labrador:** Ramsay Hill, **Princess:** Queenie Leonard, **Duchess:** Marjorie Bennett, **Rolly:** Barbara Beaird, **Patch:** Mickey Maga, **Penny:** Sandra Abbott, **Lucky:** Mimi Gibson, **Rover:** Barbara Luddy, **Dirty Dawson:** Paul Frees, **Singer of TV Commercial:** Lucille Bliss

Additional voices:

Bob Stevens, Max Smith, Sylvia Marriott, Dallas McKennon, Rickie Sorensen, Basil Ruysdael

The spotted dogs owned by the British couple, Roger and Anita, grow in multitude when their prized pets Pongo and Perdita produce 15 beautiful dalmation puppies. The newborns fall prey to a rich and cunning woman, Cruella De Vil, a self–professed fur–lover. Aided by henchmen Jasper and Horace, she steals the poor pups and makes plans to turn them into fur coats!

PN: Costing approximately $4 million to produce, this Disney classic featured the use of Xerography, whereby Disney animators made multiple copies of drawings thus eliminating the necessity to draw 101 separate dogs for the mass character scenes. In one scene, the puppies are shown watching a clip from Disney's Academy Award–winning short, *Flowers and Trees,* on the TV set (their favorite show features canine TV star Thunderbolt).

PETER PAN (1953)

A Walt Disney Production released by RKO Radio Pictures. p: Walt Disney; d: Hamilton Luske, Clyde Geronimi, Wilfred Jackson; dir anim: Milt Kahl, Frank Thomas, Wolfgang Reitherman, Ward Kimball, Eric Larson, Ollie Johnston, Marc Davis, John Lounsbery, Les Clark, Norman Ferguson; st: Ted Sears, Bill Peet, Joe Rinaldi, Erdman Penner, Winston Hibler, Milt Banta, Ralph Wright, Bill Cottrell (adapted from the play and books by Sir James M. Barrie); m/sc: Oliver Wallace; anim: Hal King, Cliff Nordberg, Hal Ambro, Don Lusk, Ken O'Brien, Marvin Woodward, Art Stevens, Eric Cleworth, Fred Moore, Bob Carlson, Harvey Toombs, Judge Whitaker, Bill Justice, Hugh Fraser, Jerry Hathcock, Clair Weeks. Songs: "The Elegant Captain Hook," "The Second Star to the Right," "What Makes the Red Man Red?", "You Can Fly, You Can Fly," "Your Mother and Mine," "A Pirate's Life," "March of the Lost Boys (Tee Dum Tee Dee)" and "Never Smile at a Crocodile." Running time: 76–½ minutes.

Voices:

Peter Pan: Bobby Driscoll, **Wendy:** Kathryn Beaumont, **Captain Hook, Mr. Darling:** Hans Conried, **Mr. Smee and other pirates:** Bill Thompson, **Mrs. Darling:** Heather Angel, **John Darling:** Paul Collins, **Michael:** Tommy Luske, **Indian Chief:** Candy Candido, **Narrator:** Tom Conway

Left in the care of a nursemaid, Wendy, Michael and John, the children of Mr. and Mrs. Darling of Bloomsbury, London, are swept away to fascinating adventures with fairy–tale hero Peter Pan, who, along the way, saves the children from long–time nemesis Captain Hook.

PETE'S DRAGON (1977)

A Walt Disney Production released by Buena Vista. p: Ron Miller, Jerome Courtland; d: Don Chaffey; anim dir: Don Bluth; w: Malcolm Marmorstein (based on a story by Seton I. Miller and S. S. Field); m: Irwin Kostal; anim: John Pomeroy, Ron Clements, Gary Goldman, Bill Hajec, Chuck Harvey, Randy Cartwright, Cliff Nordberg, Glen Keane. Songs: "Candle on the Water," "I Saw a Dragon," "It's Not Easy," "Every Little Piece," "The Happiest Home in These Hills," "Brazzle Dazzle Day," "Boo Boo Bopbopbop (I Love You Too)," "There's Room for Everyone," "Passamashloddy" and "Bill of Sale." Running time: 134 minutes.

Cast:

Nora: Helen Reddy, **Dr. Terminus:** Jim Dale, **Lampie:** Mickey Rooney, **Hoagy:** Red Buttons, **Lena Gogan:** Shelley Winters, **Pete:** Sean Marshall, **Miss Taylor:** Jean Kean, **The Mayor:** Jim Backus, **Merle:** Charles Tyner, **Grover:** Gary Morgan, **Willie:** Jeff Conway, **Paul:** Cal Bartlett, **Captain:** Walter Barnes, **Store Proprietor:** Robert Easton, **Man with Visor:** Roger Price, **Old Sea Captain:** Robert Foulk, **Egg Man:** Ben Wrigley, **Cement Man:** Joe Ross, **Fishermen:** Al Checco, Henry Slate, Jack Collins

Voices:

Elliott the Dragon: Charlie Callas

Pete, an orphaned little boy, runs away from his foster family and makes friends with an animated dragon named Elliott, who becomes the child's new companion.

PN: Elliott was the film's only animated star, appearing in live–action scenes with characters throughout the film. The film was cut by 30 minutes for its 1984 re–release.

THE PHANTOM TOLL BOOTH (1970)

A Chuck Jones Production released by Metro–Goldwyn–Mayer. p: Chuck Jones, Abe Levitow, Les Goldman; d: Chuck Jones, Abe Levitow, David Monahan; w: Chuck Jones, Sam

Rosen (based on the book by Norton Juster); m: Dean Elliott; anim dir: Ben Washam, Hal Ambro, George Nicholas, anim: Irv Spence, Bill Littlejohn, Richard Thompson, Tom Ray, Philip Roman, Alan Zaslove, Edwin Aardal, Ed DeMattia, Xenia, Lloyd Vaughan, Carl Bell. Songs: "Milo's Song," "Time Is a Gift," "Word Market," "Numbers Are the Only Things That Count," "Rhyme and Reason Reign," "Don't Say There's Nothing to Do in the Doldrums" and "Noise, Noise, Beautiful Noise." Running time: 90 minutes.

Cast:
Milo: Butch Patrick

Voices:
Mel Blanc, Daws Butler, Candy Candido, Hans Conried, June Foray, Patti Gilbert, Shep Menken, Cliff Norton, Larry Thos, Les Tremayne

Milo, a young lad bored with life, is taken to the Kingdom of wisdom where he embarks on a magical journey with new friends, Tock and Humburg, to rescue the Princesses of Rhyme and Reason. He returns home through the toll booth in his room from which he came. The film opens and closes with live–action sequences of Milo, played by "Munsters" star Butch Patrick, who is transformed into an animated character once he is transported into this land of make–believe.

PN: Chuck Jones directed this film, the first full–length feature of his career.

PINOCCHIO (1940)
A Walt Disney Production released by RKO Radio Pictures. p: Walt Disney; superv dir: Ben Sharpsteen, Hamilton Luske; seq dir: Bill Roberts, Norman Ferguson, Jack Kinney, Wilfred Jackson, T. Hee; anim dir: Fred Moore, Franklin Thomas, Milton Kahl, Vladimir Tytla, Ward Kimball, Arthur Babbitt, Eric Larson, Wolfgang Reitherman; st (adaptation): Ted Sears, Otto Englander, Webb Smith, William Cottrell, Joseph Sabo, Erdman Penner, Aurelius Battaglia (based on the story by Collodi aka: Carlo Lorenzini); m/l: Leigh Harline, Ned Washington, Paul J. Smith; anim: Jack Campbell, Berny Wolf, Don Towsley, Oliver M. Johnston Jr., Don Lusk, John Lounsbery, Norman Tate, John Bradbury, Lynn Karp, Charles Nichols, Art Palmer, Joshua Meador, Don Tobin, Robert Martsch, George Rowley, John McManus, Don Patterson, Preston Blair, Les Clark, Marvin Woodward, Hugh Fraser and John Elliotte. Songs: "When You Wish Upon a Star," "Little Woodenhead," "Hi Diddle Dee Dee (An Actor's Life for Me)," "I've Got No Strings" and "Give A Little Whistle." Running time: 88 minutes.

Voices:
Pinocchio: Dickie Jones, **Geppetto:** Christian Rub, **Jiminy Cricket:** Cliff Edwards, **The Blue Fairy:** Evelyn Venable, **J. Worthington Foulfellow:** Walter Catlett, **Gideon:** Mel Blanc, **Lampwick:** Frankie Darro, **Stromboli and The Coachman:** Charles Judels, **Barker:** Don Brodie

The story of toymaker Geppetto and his wooden puppet creation, Pinocchio, became Walt Disney's second feature–length attempt in three years. Given life by the Blue Fairy, Pinocchio is joined by Jiminy Cricket, appointed as "his

conscience," to lead him through real–life adventures of boyhood.

PINOCCHIO AND THE EMPEROR OF THE NIGHT (1987)
A Filmation Associates Production released by New World Pictures. p: Lou Scheimer; d: Hal Sutherland; w: Robby London, Barry O'Brien, Dennis O'Flaherty (based on a story by Dennis O'Flaherty from *The Adventures of Pinocchio* by Carlo Collodi); m: Anthony Marinelli, Brian Banks; m/l: Will Jennings, Barry Mann, Steve Tyrell, Anthony Marinelli; superv anim: John Celestri, Chuck Harvey, Kamoon Song; anim: Robert Alvarez, Carl Bell, Bob Carlson, Yi–Cheh Chen, Doug Crane, James Davis, Zeon Davush, Edward DeMattia, Will Finn, Fernanado Gonzalez, Steve Gordon, Fred Grable, Laurie K. Graves, Daniel Haskett, Ruth Kissene, Clarke Logerstrom, Jung Woo Lee, Ernesto Lopex, Marcea Manta, Mauro Maressa, Costy Mustatea, Enory Myrick, Bill Nines, Eduardo Olivares, Jack Ozark, Kevin Petrilak, Young Kyu Rhim, Lenord Robinson, Joe Roman, Mike Sanger, Louis Scarborough, Thomas Sito, Bruce W. Smith, Jason So, Ken Southworth, Leo Sullivan, Bob Tyler, Larry White, Allen Wilzback, and Bruce Woodside. Songs: "Love Is the Light Inside Your Heart," "You're a Star," "Do What Makes You Happy" and "Neon Cabaret." Running time: 88 minutes.

Voices:
Scalawag: Edward Asner, **Geppetto:** Tom Bosley, **Twinkle:** Lana Beeson, **Emperor of the Night:** James Earl Jones, **Fairy Godmother:** Rickie Lee Jones, **Gee Willikers:** Don Knotts, **Pinocchio:** Scott Grimes, **Bee–Atrice:** Linda Gary, **Lt. Grumblebee:** Jonathan Harris, **Puppetino:** William Windom, **Igor:** Frank Welker

Woodcarver mentor Geppetto assigns former puppet creation Pinocchio to deliver a jewel box to the mayor. Despite a friendly warning from Gee Willikers, a toy glowbug brought to life by the Blue Fairy, Pinocchio becomes sidetracked along the way. He encounters a shifty racoon and monkey assistant who con him out of the jewel box. Ashamed, he joins the traveling circus, and continues his search for the missing jewel box.

PINOCCHIO IN OUTER SPACE (1965)
A Swallow/Belvision Production released by Universal Pictures. p: Norm Prescott, Fred Ladd; d: Ray Goossens; w: Fred Laderman (based on an idea by Prescott from the story by Carlo Collodi); m: F. Leonard, H. Dobelaere, E. Schurmann; m/l: Robert Sharp, Arthur Korb. Running time: 71 minutes.

Voices:
Nurtle the Turtle: Arnold Stang; **Pinocchio:** Peter Lazer; Conrad Jameson; Cliff Owens; Mavis Mims; Kevin Kennedy; Minerva Pious; Jess Cain; Norman Rose

Turned back into a puppet by Geppetto, Pinocchio becomes friends with an outer–space creature, Nurtle the Turtle, whose

Pinocchio receives advice from his creator/mentor Geppetto in a scene from Pinocchio In Outer Space (1965).
© *Universal Pictures*

spaceship has accidentally landed on Earth. Pinocchio helps Nurtle get back on course and joins him on a trip to Mars where they encounter the menacing Astro the Flying Whale, who plans to invade Earth.

PN: Film was titled *Pinocchio Dans l'Espace* for its Belgian release. Working title: *Pinocchio's Adventure in Outer Space*

THE PLAGUE DOGS (1984)

A Nepenthe Productions released by United International Pictures. p, d & w: Martin Rosen; m: Patrick Gleason; anim dir: Ton Guy, Colin White. Running time: 103 minutes.

Voices:

John Hurt, Christopher Benjamin, James Bolam, Nigel Hawthorne, Warren Mitchell, Bernard Hepton, Brian Stirner, Penelope Lee, Geoffrey Mathews, Barbara Leigh–Hunt, John Bennet, John Franklyn–Robbins, Bill Maynard, Malcolm Terris, Judy Geeson, Phillip Locke, Brian Spink, Tony Church, Anthony Valentine, William Lucas, Dandy Nichols, Rosemary Leach, Patrick Stewart

Two dogs escape from a government research establishment in England's Lake District, one of them already the victim of experimental brain surgery. Their mission is to find a kind master, an island where they may be safe from pursuit and their own dread.

PN: Filmmaker Martin Rosen, of *Watership Down* fame, produced this film, which was originally previewed in London two years before its American release.

POGO FOR PRESIDENT—I GO POGO (1984)

A Stowar Enterprises/Possum Productions release. p, d & w: Marc Paul Chinoy; m: Gary Baker, Thom Flora; anim dir: Stephen Chodo; anim: Diedre A. Knowlton, Stephen Oakes,

Kim Blanchette, R. Kent Burton, Louise Campbell, Justin Kohn, Ruth Schwartz. Running time: 82 minutes.

Voices:

Pogo: Skip Hinnant; Jonathan Winters; Vincent Price; Ruth Buzzi; Stan Freberg; Jimmy Breslin; Arnold Stang; Bob McFadden; Len Maxwell; Bob Kaliban; Marcia Savella; Mike Schultz. Special guest appearance by Jimmy Breslin.

Election year fever sweeps the Okenfenokee Swamp as everyone's favorite possum suddenly finds himself recruited for the nation's highest office by all of his friends, including Albert, Howland and Porky Pine. Produced in stop–motion animation, the film is based on Walt Kelly's unforgettable "Pogo" cartoon strip.

PORKY PIG IN HOLLYWOOD (1986)

A Films Incorporated Production released by Warner Brothers. d: Tex Avery, Friz Freleng, Bob Clampett, Frank Tashlin, Chuck Jones; w: Rich Hogan, Tubby Millar, Ben Hardaway, Frank Tashlin, Dave Monahan, Ernest Gee; m: Carl Stalling; anim: Rob Scribner, Chuck Jones, Vive Rosto, Robert McKimson, Robert Cannon, Norman McCabe, Virgil Ross, John Carey, I. Ellis. Compiled by George Feltenstein. Running time: 102 minutes.

Voices:

Mel Blanc

This limited release compilation was a tribute to Warner Brothers' famed stuttering pig. It featured a collection of classic cartoons: *You Oughta Be In Pictures* (1940), *Wholly Smoke* (1938), *Porky's Romance* (1937), *Porky's Preview* (1941), *Daffy Doc* (1938) and *Porky's Movie Mystery* (1938).

POUND PUPPIES AND THE LEGEND OF BIG PAW (1988)

A Family Home Entertainment and Tonka Corp. presentation of an Atlantic/Kushner–Locke Production in association with the Maltese Companies released by Tri–Star. p: Donald Kushner, Peter Locke; d: Pierre DeCelles; scr: Jim Carlson, Terrence McDonnell; m: Steve Tyrell. Running time: 76 minutes.

Voices:

McNasty: George Rose, **Whopper:** B. J. Ward, **Nose Marie:** Ruth Buzzi, **Cooler:** Brennan Howard, **Collette:** Cathy Cadavini, **Bright Eyes:** Nancy Cartwright

The Pound Puppies foil the efforts of a nasty old man with an evil laugh (McNasty) whose goal is to take over the world by recovering the Bone of Scone, a mystical relic possessing great magical powers.

THE PUPPETOON MOVIE (1987)

An Expanded Entertainment release. p & w: Arnold Leibovit; m: Buddy Baker; anim: Peter Kleinow. Running time: 80 minutes.

A long–overdue tribute to the work of filmmaker George Pal, whose stop–action technique influenced creators of similar characters from Gumby to the Pillsbury Doughboy. Nine films from the '30s and '40s are contained in the feature. They are: *Hoola Boola, John Henry And The Inky Poo, Tubby The Tuba, Tulips Shall Grow, Jasper In A Jam, Philips Broadcast of 1938, Philip's Calvacade, Sleeping Beauty, South Sea Sweetheart* and *Together In The Weather*.

RACE FOR YOUR LIFE, CHARLIE BROWN (1977)

A Bill Melendez Production released by Paramount Pictures. p: Lee Mendelson, Bill Melendez; d: Bill Melendez, Phil Roman; w: Charles M. Schulz (based on the "Peanuts" characters by Schulz); m: Ed Bogas; anim: Don Lusk, Bob Matz, Hank Smith, Rod Scribner, Ken O'Brien, Al Pabian, Joe Roman, Jeff Hall, Sam Jaimes, Bob Bachman, George Singer, Bill Littlejohn, Bob Carlson, Patricia Joy, Terry Lennon, Larry Leichliter. Songs: "Race for Your Life, Charlie Brown," "The Greatest Leader," "Charmine" and "She'll Be Comin' Round the Mountain." Running time: 75 minutes.

Voices:

Charlie Brown: Duncan Watson; **Schroeder:** Gregory Felton; **Peppermint Patty:** Stuart Brotman; **Sally:** Gail Davis; **Linus:** Liam Martin; **Lucy:** Melanie Kohn; **Marci:** Jimmie Ahrens; **Bully:** Kirk Jue; **Another Bully:** Jordan Warren; **Another Bully:** Tom Muller; **Singers:** Ed Bogas, Larry Finlayson, Judith Munsen, David Riordan, Roberta Vandervort; Bill Melendez; Fred Van Amburg

The Peanuts gang is off to camp for a summer of misadventures, including building a raft for the "big race" only to be outdone by the competing team who "buy" their raft. Aside from the race, Snoopy has an altercation with a nasty feline and Lucy leads the other girls in an anti–boy campaign.

RAGGEDY ANN AND ANDY (1977)

A Lester Osterman Production released by 20th Century–Fox. p: Richard Horner; d: Richard Williams; scr: Patricia Thackray and Max Wilk (based on the stories and characters created by Johnny Gruelle); m: Joe Raposo; seq dir: Gerald Potterton; anim: Richard Williams, Grim Natwick, Art Babitt, Emory Hawkins, Tissa David, Gerald Potterton, Gerry Chiniquy, Hal Ambro, John Bruni, Charlie Downs, John Kimball and Spencer Peel. Songs: "I Look and What Do I See!", "No Girl's Toy," "Rag Dolly," "Poor Babette," "A Miracle," "Ho–Yo," "Candy Hearts," "Blue," "The Mirage," "I Never Get Enough," "I Love You," "Loony Anthem," "It's Not Easy Being King," "Hooray for Me," "You're My Friend" and "Home." Running time: 84 minutes.

Cast:

Marcella: Claire Williams

Voices:

Raggedy Ann: Didi Conn, **Raggedy Andy:** Mark Baker, **The Camel with the Wrinkled Knees:** Fred Struthman, **Babette:**

Niki Flacks, **Captain Contagious:** George S. Irving, **Queasy:** Arnold Stang, **The Greedy:** Joe Silver, **The Loony Knight:** Alan Sues, **King Koo–Koo:** Marty Brill, **Gazooks:** Paul Dooley, **Grandpa:** Mason Adams, **Maxi–Fixit:** Allen Swift, **Susie Pincushion:** Hetty Galen, **Barney Beanbag/Socko:** Sheldon Harnick, **Topsy:** Ardyth Kaiser, **The Twin Pennies:** Margery Gray, Lynne Stuart

A search ensues for Babette, a French doll, who is kidnapped by another doll, Captain Contagious, in the toy–filled playroom of a young girl named Marcella, seen in live–action in this animated feature. Doll mates Raggedy Ann and Andy embark on a magical journey to rescue Babette, successfully navigating through a forbidding forest, a tossing sea, a looney kingdom and other dangers along the way.

PN: The two–year production, which cost approximately $4 million to make, was financed by International Telephone and Telegraph and Bobbs–Merrill, their literary subsidiary. Originally the project was designed as a Hallmark Hall of Fame television special with Liza Minelli and Goldie Hawn being considered for Raggedy Ann's role. Actress Claire Williams, who played Marcella, is the daughter of the film's head animator, Richard Williams.

RAINBOW BRITE AND THE STAR STEALER (1985)

A DIC Enterprises Production released by Warner Brothers. p: Jean Chalopin, Andy Heyward, Tetsuo Katayama; d: Bernard Deyries, Kimio Yabuki; w: Howard R. Cohen (based on a story by Chalopin, Howard R. Cohen, and characters developed by Hallmark Properties); m: Haim Saban, Shuki Levy; anim: Kaoru Hirata, Satoe Nishiyama, Fukuo Yamamoto, Mitsuru Aoyama, Masaki Kajishima, Nobuyuki Haga, Yasunopri Miyazawa, Kazuhiko Miyake, Yasushi Tanizawa, Kinichiroi Suzuki, Masami Shimada, Shinichi Imakuma, Yasuyuki Tada, Makoto Shinjou, Junzo Ono, Toshio Kaneko, Tado Katsu Yoshida, Michio Ikeda, Hitomi Kakubari, Atsumi Hashimoto, Kiyomi Masuda, Katsuo Takasaki, Yoshio Mukainakano, Hiroshi Oikawa, Shigetaka Kiyoyama, Katsuko Kanazawa, Takashi Hyodo, Akinobia Takahashi, Takennori Mihara. Songs: "Brand New Day" and "Rainbow Brite and Me." Running time: 97 minutes.

Voices:

Rainbow Brite: Bettina; **Lurky, On–X, Buddy Blue, Dog Guard, Spectran, Slurthie, Glitterbot:** Patrick Fraley; **Murky, Castle Monster, Glitterbot, Guard, Skydancer, Slurthie:** Peter Cullen; **Twin, Shy Violet, Indigo, La La Orange, Spectran, Sprites:** Robbie Lee; **Starlite, Wizard, Spectran:** Andre Stojka; **Krys:** David Mendenhall; **The Princess, The Creature:** Rhonda Aldrich; **Orin, Bombo, TV Announcer:** Les Tremayne; **Red Butler, Witch, Castle Creature, Spectran, Patty O'Green, Canary Yellow:** Mona Marshall; **Count Blogg:** Jonathan Harris; **Stormy:** Marissa Mendenhall; **Brian:** Scott Menville; **Popo:** Charles Adler; **Sergeant Zombo:** David Workman

A spoiled princess steals the planet Spectra for her "jewel collection." Little Rainbow, riding her flying horse Starlite, saves the planet, accompanied by a young boy, Krys, on his mechanical horse, On–X.

PN: The film was part of a trend of toy– and merchandise–inspired animated features, the others being based on such children's favorites as The Smurfs, He–Man and the Masters of the Universe, GoBots, and G.I. Joe.

THE RELUCTANT DRAGON
(1941)

A Walt Disney Production released by RKO Radio Pictures. p: Walt Disney; 1/a dir: Alfred L. Werker; anim dir: Hamilton Luske; asst anim dir: Jim Handley, Ford Beebe, Erwin Verity; asst dir: Jasper Blystone; scr: Ted Sears, Al Perkins, Larry Clemmons, Bill Cottrell, Harry Clark; anim: Ward Kimball, Fred Moore, Milt Neil, Wolfgang Reitherman, Bud Swift, Walt Kelly, Jack Campbell, Claude Smith and Harvey Toombs. Songs: "Oh Fleecy Cloud," "To an Upside Down Cake," "Radish So Red," " 'Tis Evening" and "The Reluctant Dragon." Running time: 72 minutes.

Cast:

Robert Benchley: (Himself), **Studio artist:** Frances Gifford, **Mrs. Benchley:** Nana Bryant, **Studio guide:** Buddy Pepper, **Florence Gill and Clarence Nash:** Themselves; Alan Ladd, John Dehner, Truman Woodworth, Hamilton McFadden, Maurice Murphy, Jeffy Corey, **Studio cop:** Henry Hall, **Orchestra leader:** Frank Faylen, **Slim:** Lester Dorr, **Guard:** Gerald Mohr, and members of the staff including Walt Disney, Ward Kimball, Norman Ferguson.

Voices:

The Dragon: Barnett Parker, **Sir Giles:** Claud Allister, **The Boy:** Billy Lee, **Donald Duck:** The Rhythmaires, Clarence Nash, **Goofy:** Pinto Colvig, **Baby Weems' narrator:** Gerald Mohr, **Baby Weems:** Leone LeDoux, **Baby Weems:** Raymond Severn, **John Weems:** Ernie Alexander, **Mrs. John Weems:** Linda Marwood, **FDR:** Art Gilmore, **Walter Winchell:** Edward Marr, **How to Ride a Horse narrator:** John McLeish, **Reluctant Dragon narrator:** J. Donald Wilson.

Part live–action and animation, this film delves into the behind–the–scenes making of cartoons, with comedian Robert Benchley, in live action, being pursuaded by his onscreen wife (Nana Bryant) to approach Walt Disney about producing a cartoon based on *The Reluctant Dragon,* a delightful children's book by Kenneth Grahame. The film traces Benchley's visit to the Disney studio and the ultimate production of this tale about a dragon who loathes terrorizing people. Goofy appears in the film showing animator Ward Kimball's making of his latest cartoon, *How to Ride a Horse.*

THE RESCUERS (1977)

A Walt Disney Production released by Buena Vista. p: Wolfgang Reitherman; d: Wolfgang Reitherman, John Lounsbery, Art Stevens; st: Larry Clemmons, Ken Anderson, Vance Gerry, David Michener, Burny Mattinson, Frank Thomas, Fred Lucky, Ted Berman, Dick Sebast (from *The Rescuers* and *Miss Bianca*

by Margery Sharp); m: Artie Butler (songs by Carol Connors, Ayn Robbins, Sammy Fain, and Robert Crawford); anim dir: Ollie Johnston, Frank Thomas, Milt Kahl, Don Bluth; anim: John Pomeroy, Andy Gaskill, Art Stevens, Chuck Harvey, Bob McCrea, Cliff Nordberg, Gary Goldman, Dale Baer, Ron Clements, Bill Hajee, Glen Keane. Songs: "The Journey," "Rescue Aid Society," "Tomorrow Is Another Day," "Someone's Waiting for You" and "The U.S. Air Force Song." Running time: 77 minutes.

Voices:

Bernard: Bob Newhart, **Miss Bianca:** Eva Gabor, **Mme. Medusa:** Geraldine Page, **Mr. Snoops:** Joe Flynn, **Ellie Mae:** Jeanette Nolan, **Luke:** Pat Buttram, **Orville:** Jim Jordan, **Rufus:** John McIntire, **Penny:** Michelle Stacy, **Chairman:** Bernard Fox, **Gramps:** Larry Clemmons, **Evinrude:** James Macdonald, **Deadeye:** George Lindsey, **TV Announcer:** Bill McMillan, **Digger:** Dub Taylor, **Deacon:** John Fiedler

Two mice, Bernard and Miss Bianca, set out to rescue a girl, Penny, held captive in a swamp by the evil Mme. Medusa.

PN: This beautifully animated feature took four years to make at a cost of nearly $8 million.

THE RESCUERS DOWN UNDER
(1990)

A Walt Disney Picture in association with Silver Screen Partners IV released by Buena Vista. p: Thomas Schumacher; d: Hendel Butoy and Mike Gabriel; scr: Jim Cox, Karey Kirkpatrick, Byron Simpson, Joe Ranft; m: Bruce Broughton; superv anim: Glen Keane, Mark Henn, Russ Edmonds, David Cutler, Ruben A. Aquino, Nik Ranieri, Ed Gombert, Anthony De Rosa, Kathy Zielinski, Duncan Marjoribanks; anim: James Baxter, Ron Husband, Will Finn, David Burgess, Alexander S. Kupershmidt, Chris Bailey, Mike Cedeno, Rick Farmiloe, Jacques Muller, Dave Pruiksma, Rejean Bourdages, Roger Chiasson, Ken Duncan, Joe Haidar, Ellen Woodbury, Jorgen Klubien, Gee Fwee Border, Barry Temple, David P. Stephan, Chris Wahl, Larry White, Brigitte Hartley, Doug Krohn, Phil Young, Tom Roth, and Leon Joosen. Songs: "Black Slacks" and "Waltzing Matilda." Running time: 74 minutes.

Voices:

Bernard: Bob Newhart, **Miss Bianca:** Eva Gabor, **Wilbur:** John Candy, **Jake:** Tristan Rogers, **Cody:** Adam Ryen, **McLeach:** George C. Scott, **Frank:** Wayne Robson, **Krebbs:** Douglas Seale, **Joanna,** Special Vocal Effects: Frank Welker, **Chairmouse, Doctor:** Bernard Fox, **Red:** Peter Firth, **Baitmouse:** Billy Barty, **Francois:** Ed Gilbert, **Faloo, Mother:** Carla Meyer, **Nurse Mouse:** Russi Taylor

In Australia, young Cody discovers that evil McLeach has captured the magnificent eagle, Marahute. He manages to set her free only to be kidnapped himself, and later to see her recaptured.

PN: This sequel to Disney's *The Rescuers* was released simultaneously with a brand new Mickey Mouse short, *The Prince And The Pauper,* co-starring pals Goofy, Donald Duck and Pluto.

ROBIN HOOD (1973)

A Walt Disney Production released by Buena Vista. p: Wolfgang Reitherman; d: Wolfgang Reitherman; st: Larry Clemmons (based on character and story conceptions by Ken Anderson) m: (songs by) Roger Miller, Floyd Huddleston, George Bruns, Johnny Mercer; dir anim: Milt Kahl, Frank Thomas, Ollie Johnston, John Lounsbery; anim: Hal King, Art Stevens, Cliff Nordberg, Burny Mattinson, Eric Larson, Don Bluth, Dale Baer, Fred Hellmich. Songs: "Not in Nottingham," "Whistle Stop," "Love" and "The Phoney King of England." Running time: 83 minutes.

Voices:

Allan–a–Dale: Roger Miller, **Prince John, King Richard:** Peter Ustinov, **Sir Hiss:** Terry Thomas, **Robin Hood:** Brian Bedford, **Maid Marian:** Monica Evans, **Little John:** Phil Harris, **Friar Tuck:** Andy Devine, **Lady Kluck:** Carole Shelley, **Sheriff of Nottingham:** Pat Buttram, **Trigger:** George Lindsay, **Nutsy:** Ken Curtis, **Skippy:** Billy Whitaker, **Sis:** Dana Laurita, **Tagalong:** Dora Whitker, **Toby Turtle:** Richie Sanders, **Otto:** J. Pat O'Malley, **Crocodile:** Candy Candido, **Mother Rabbit:** Barbara Luddy, **Church Mouse:** John Fiedler

All the familiar characters appear in this animated version of the classic story, instead featuring cartoon animals in the title roles—Robin Hood and Maid Marian are foxes, Little John is a bear and the ever–villainous Prince John is a mangy lion—in this return to Sherwood Forest and Robin's battles with the Sheriff of Nottingham.

ROCK AND RULE (1984)

A Nelvana Limited Production released by Metro–Goldwyn–Mayer/United Artists. p: Patrick Loubert, Michael Hirsh; d: Clive A. Smith; scr: Peter Sauder, John Halfpenny; st: Patrick Loubert, Peter Sauder; m: Patrick Cullen; anim: Anne Marie Bardwell, Dave Brewster, Charles Bonifacio, Robin Budd, Chuck Gammage, Frank Nissen, Bill Speers, Tom Sito, Gian–Franco Celestri, Roger Allers, Wendy Perdue, John Collins, Devenand Ramsaran, Elaine Despins, Louis Scarborough, Terry Godfrey, Dale Schott, Larry Jacobs, Ken Stephenson, Ralph Palmer. Songs: "Angel's Song," "Invocation Song," "Send Love Through," "Pain and Suffering," "My Name Is Mok," "Born to Raise Hell," "I'm the Man," "Ohm Sweet Ohm," "Dance, Dance, Dance" and "Hot Dogs and Sushi." Running time: 79 minutes.

Voices:

Mok: Don Francks, **Omar:** Paul Le Mat, **Angel:** Susan Roman, **Mok's Computer:** Sam Langevin, **Dizzy:** Dan Hennessey, **Stretch/Zip:** Greg Duffell, **Toad:** Chris Wiggins, **Sleazy:** Brent Titcomb, **Quadhole/1st Radio Announcer:** Donny Burns, **Mylar/2nd Radio Announcer:** Martin Lavut, **Cindy:** Catherine Gallant, **Other Computers:** Keith Hampshire, **Carnegie Hall Groupie:** Melleny Brown, **Edna:** Anna Bourque, **Borderguard:** Nick Nichols, **Uncle Mikey:** John Halfpenny, **Sailor:** Maurice LaMarche, **Aunt Edith:** Catherine O'Hara

The war is over. The only survivors are street animals—dogs, cats and rats. From them, a new race of mutants evolve.

When the only survivors of a war are street animals, a new race of mutants evolve in the fantasy–adventure, Rock And Rule (1984). The film was the first feature–length production by Nelvana Limited in Canada. (Courtesy: Nelvana Limited)

In this new world, Mok, an aging superstar, tries to find the last element in a diabolical plan to raise a demon that will give him immense power. The missing element is a voice, and he finds that voice in Angel, a female singer who plays with a local band in the small town of Ohmtown. He steals her away to post–apocalypse Nuke York to launch his plan into action.

PN: *Rock and Rule* was the first full–length feature film produced by the Canadian–based animation company, Nelvana Limited, which has since delivered several box–office feature–length hits based on the adventures of *The Care Bears*. The film features an original soundtrack by rock artists Cheap Trick, Debbie Harry, Lou Reed, Iggy Pop and a special performance by Earth, Wind and Fire.

SALUDOS AMIGOS (1943)

A Walt Disney Production released by RKO Radio Pictures. p: Walt Disney; st: Homer Brightman, Ralph Wright, Roy Williams, Harry Reeves, Dick Huemer, Joe Grant; md: Charles Wolcott; m: Ed Plumb, Paul Smith; seq dir: Bill Roberts, Jack Kinney, Hamilton Luske, Wilfred Jackson; anim: Fred Moore, Ward Kimball, Milt Kahl, Milt Neil, Wolfgang Reitherman, Les Clark, Bill Justice, Vladimir Tytla, John Sibley, Hugh Fraser, Paul Allen, John McManus, Andrew Engman, Dan MacManus and Joshua Meador. Songs: "Saludos Amigos," "Brazil" and "Tico Tico." Running time: 43 minutes.

Voices:

Donald Duck: Charles Nash, **Jose Carioca:** Jose Oliveira, **Goofy:** Pinto Colvig

This animated production, though far short of feature film length, was released by Disney as an animated feature. Travelogue footage—filmed on location in South America—is incorporated into the film, which features four cartoon shorts strung together to portray the Latin–American influence on the United States.

Sequences include Donald Duck as a naive tourist who runs into trouble while sightseeing; the adventures of Pedro the airplane, who grows up to be an airmail plane just like his dad; "El Gaucho Goofy," the misadventures of Goofy playing out the life of a gaucho—with little success; and, finally, tropical bird Jose (or Joe) Carioca, who takes Donald on a tour of South America, teaching him the samba along the way.

SANTA AND THE THREE BEARS
(1970)

A R and S Film Enterprises Production released by Ellman Enterprises. p,w&d: Tony Benedict; m: Doug Goodwin, Tony Benedict, Joe Leahy; anim: Bill Hutton, Tony Love, Volus Jones. Running time: 63 minutes.

Cast:
Grandfather: Hal Smith, **Beth:** Beth Goldfarb, **Brian:** Brian Hobbs

Voices:
Ranger/Santa Claus: Hal Smith, **Nana:** Jean VanderPyl, **Nikomi:** Annette Ferra, **Chinook:** Bobby Riaj

Two cute wide—eyed bear cubs (Nikomi and Chinook) put off hibernating in Yellowstone National Park to wait for the arrival of Santa Claus. So the cubs are not disappointed, the park's cheery, grandfatherly forest ranger agrees to impersonate Santa Claus at the mother bear's request. The film opens, in live—action, with a kindly old grandfather (played by Hal Smith) relating the tale to his grandchildren.

THE SECRET OF NIMH (1982)

A Don Bluth Production released through MGM/UA. p: Don Bluth, Gary Goldman, John Pomeroy; d: Don Bluth; anim dir: John Pomeroy, Gary Goldman; st: Don Bluth, John Pomeroy, Gary Goldman, Will Finn (based on the novel, *Mrs. Frisby and the Rats of NIMH*, by Robert C. O'Brien; m: Jerry Goldsmith; anim: Lorna Pomeroy, Skip Jones, Dave Spafford, Will Finn, Linda Miller, Dan Kuenster, Heidi Guedel, David Molna, Emily Jiulano, Kevin M. Murzer. Running time: 82 minutes.

Voices:
Elizabeth Hartman, Dom DeLuise, Hermione Baddeley, Arthur Malet, Peter Strauss, Paul Shenar, Derek Jacobi, John Carradine, Shannen Doherty, Will Wheaton, Jodi Hicks, Ian Fried, Tom Hatten, Lucille Bliss, Aldo Ray

A recently widowed mother mouse (Mrs. Bisby) desperately tries finding a new home for her brood before the old one is destroyed by spring plowing. Her task gets complicated by the severe illness of her son, who is too sick to move.

PN: Co—creators of the film were Don Bluth, Gary Goldman, and John Pomeroy, both former Disney animators who walked out of the studio in a dispute over standards and struck out on their own. Working title: *Mrs. Frisby and the Rats of NIMH.*

Justin (center) tries to fend off dastardly Jenner, while Mrs. Brisby looks on in a scene from The Secret Of NIMH *(1982). © United Artists*

THE SECRET OF THE SWORD
(1985)

A Filmation Associates Production released by Atlantic Releasing. p: Arthur Nadel; d: Ed Friedman, Lou Kachivas, Marsh Lamore, Bill Reed, Gwen Wetzler; scr: Larry Ditillo, Robert Forward. Running time: 87 minutes.

Voices:
He-Man: John Erwin, **She-Ra:** Melendy Britt, **Hordak:** George DiCenzo; Linda Gary, Erika Scheimer, Erik Gunden, Alan Oppenheimer

He-Man discovers he has a twin sister, She-Ra, who was kidnapped shortly after her birth by the evil Hordak. She has been raised by Hordak to combat He-Man. He-Man sets about to reunite her with their family.

PN: the film was originally called "Princess of Power" prior to its release.

SHINBONE ALLEY (1971)

A Fine Arts Film released by Allied Artists. p: Preston M. Fleet; d: John David Wilson; w: Joe Darion (based on the book for the musical play by Darion, Mel Brooks, from the "Archy and Mehitabel" stories by Don Marquis); m: George Kleinsinger; anim: Frank Andrina, John Sparey, Amby Paliwoda, Gil Rugg, George Waiss, Bob Bransford, Jim Hiltz, Fred Grable, Brad Chase, Frank Gonzales, Barrie Nelson, Ken Southworth, Russ Von Neida, Frank Onaitis, Bob Bemiller, Rudy Cataldi, Spencer Peel, Selby Daley. Songs: "I Am Only a Poor Humble Cockroach," "Blow Wind Out of the North," "Cheerio My Deario (Toujours Gai)," "Ah, the Theater, the Theater," "What Do We Care If We're Down and Out?," "The Moth Song," "Lullaby for Mehitabel's Kittens," "The Shinbone Alley Song," "The Lightning Bug Song," "Here Pretty Pretty Pussy," "Ladybugs of the Evening," "Archy's Philosophies," "They Don't Have it

Here," "Romeo and Juliet" and "Come to Meeoww." Running time: 83 minutes.

Voices:
Mehitabel: Carol Channing, **Archy:** Eddie Bracken, **Big Bill Sr.:** Alan Reed, **Tyrone T. Tattersall:** John Carradine, Jackie Ward Singers; Ken Sansom; Hal Smith; Joan Gerber; Sal Delano.

A poet is transmigrated into the body of a cockroach named Archy, whose back alley adventures and love for a sexy street cat (Mehitabel) make up the plotline of this surrealistic tale.

PN: Based on the long—running comic strip of the same name, the film was animated in the style of The Beatles' *Yellow Submarine,* mixing visuals in a montage—like fashion. Carol Channing and Eddie Bracken recreated roles originally played by Eartha Kitt and Bracken on Broadway.

SLEEPING BEAUTY (1959)

A Walt Disney Production released through Buena Vista. p: Walt Disney; d: Hamilton Luske, Clyde Geronimi, Wilfred Jackson; st: Erdmann Penner, Joe Rinaldi, Ralph Wright, Donald Da Gradi (based on an original story by Ward Greene); m: Oliver Wallace; dir anim: Milt Kahl, Frank Thomas, Marc Davis, Ollie Johnston Jr., John Lounsbery; seq dir: Eric Larson, Wolfgang Reitherman, Les Clark. Songs: "Once Upon A Dream," "Hail The Princess Aurora," "I Wonder," "The Skumps" and "Sleeping Beauty Song." Running time: 75 minutes.

Voices:
Princess Aurora, Briar Rose: Mary Costa, **Maleficent:** Eleanor Audley, **Merryweather:** Barbara Luddy, **King Stefan:** Taylor Holmes, **Prince Phillip:** Bill Shirley, **Flora:** Verna Felton, **Fauna:** Barbara Jo Allen, **King Hubert:** Bill Thompson, **Maleficent's Goons:** Candy Candido, Pinto Colvig, Bob Amsberry, **Owl:** Dallas McKennon, **Narrator:** Marvin Miller

Aurora, the daughter of good king Stephen and his wife, is given beauty, goodness and charm by three good fairies only to become victimized by a bad fairy, who casts a spell on her that she will prick her finger on a spindle when she is 16 and die. Fortunately, one of the good fairies intervenes and changes the spell so that Aurora's fate is deep sleep rather than death. She will only awaken with a loving kiss.

THE SMURFS AND THE MAGIC FLUTE (1984)

A First Performance Pictures/Studios Belvision coproduction in association with Stuart R. Ross released by Atlantic Releasing Corporation. p: Jose Dutillieu; d & w: John Rust; m: Michel Legrand; superv anim: Eddie Lateste; anim: Nic Broca, Marcel Colbrant, Louis—Michel Carpentier, Borge Ring, Bjorn Frank Jensen, Per Ulvar Lygum, Birgitta Jannson, Christiane Segers, Jean—Pol Chapelle, John Vander Linden, Christine Schotte, Jean—Claude De Ridder, Godelieve Zeghers. Running time: 74 minutes.

Voices:
Cam Clarke, Grant Gottschall, Patty Foley, Mike Reynolds, Ted Lehman, Bill Capizzi, Ron Gans, X. Phifer, Dudly Knight, John

Rust, Richard Miller, David Page, Durga McBroom, Michael Sorich, Robert Axelrod

Somehow a magic flute—which has the power to make people dance uncontrollably when it is played—has gotten out of Smurfland and into the hands of young practical joker Peewit and good knight Johan. But when Peewit loses the flute to the sinister bandit Oilycreep, the Smurfs make plans to retrieve the magical instrument.

PN: Film was called *V'la Les Schtroumpfs* for its Belgian release.

SNOOPY COMES HOME (1972)

A Lee Mendelson—Bill Melendez Production released by National General Pictures. p: Lee Mendelson, Bill Melendez; d: Bill Melendez; scr: Charles Schultz; m: Donald Ralke; m/l: Richard M. Sherman, Robert B. Sherman; anim: Ed Levitt, Bernard Gruver, Evert Brown, Frank Smith, Dean Spille, Ellie Bogardus, Al Shean, Sam Jaimes, Jacques Vausseu, Rod Scribner, Hank Smith, Ruth Kissane, Emery Hawkins, Carole Barnes, Beverly Robbins, Eleanor Warren, Faith Kovaleski, Manon Washburn, Don Lusk, Rudy Zamora, Bob Carlson, Bill Littlejohn, Phil Roman, Jim Pabian, Al Pabian, Adele Lenart, Joice Lee Marshall, Dawn Smith, Lou Robards, Joanne Lansing, Debbie Zamora, Gwenn Dotzler, Chandra Poweris, Celine Miles. Songs: "Snoopy, Come Home," "Lila's Tune," "Fun on the Beach," "Best of Buddies," "Changes," "Partners," "Getting It Together" and "No Dogs Allowed." Running time: 80 minutes.

Voices:
Charlie Brown: Chad Webber, **Lucy Van Pelt:** Robin Kohn, **Linus Van Pelt:** Stephen Shea, **Schroeder:** David Carey, **Lila:** Johanna Baer, **Sally:** Hilary Momberger, **Peppermint Patty:** Chris DeFaria, **Clara:** Linda Ercoli, **Frieda:** Linda Mendelson, **Snoopy:** Bill Melendez

Snoopy feels like an outcast after being confronted by "No Dogs Allowed" signs no matter where he goes—the beach, the library, the bus, the hospital—to the point that he decides to settle affairs, drafting a "Last Will and Testament," before ending it all.

SNOW WHITE AND THE SEVEN DWARFS (1937)

A Walt Disney Production released by RKO Radio Pictures. p: Walt Disney; superv dir: David Hand; seq dir: Perce Pearce, Larry Morey, William Cottrell, Wilfred Jackson, Ben Sharpsteen; w: Ted Sears, Otto Englander, Earl Hurd, Dorothy Ann Black, Richard Creedon, Dick Richard, Merrill De Maris, Webb Smith (based on the fairy tale "Sneewittchen" in collection of *Kinderund Hausmarchen* by Jacob Grimm, Wilhelm Grimm); m: Frank Churchill, Leigh Harline, Paul Smith, Morey; superv anim: Hamilton Luske, Vladimir Tytla, Fred Moore, Norman Ferguson; anim: Frank Thomas, Dick Lundy, Arthur Babbitt, Eric Larson, Milton Kahl, Robert Stokes, James Algar, Al Eugster, Cy Young, Joshua Meador, Ugo D'Orsi, George Rowley, Les Clark, Fred Spencer, Bill Roberts, Bernard Garbutt, Grim Natwick, Jack Campbell, Marvin Woodward, James Culhane,

Walt Disney's Snow White And The Seven Dwarfs *(1937) was the first full–length animated feature in cartoon history. The film remains one of the top grossing cartoon features of all time. © Walt Disney Productions (Courtesy: The Museum of Modern Art/Film Stills Archive)*

Stan Quackenbush, Ward Kimball, Wolfgang Reitherman, Robert Martsch. Songs: "I'm Wishing," "One Song," "With a Smile and a Song," "Whistle While You Work," "Heigh Ho," "Bluddle–Uddle–Um–Dum," "The Dwarfs' Yodel Song" and "Some Day My Prince Will Come." Running time: 83 minutes.

Voices:
Snow White: Adriana Caselotti, **The Prince:** Harry Stockwell, **The Queen:** Lucille LaVerne, **Bashful:** Scotty Mattraw, **Doc:** Roy Atwell, **Grumpy:** Pinto Colvig, **Happy:** Otis Harlan, **Sleepy:** Pinto Colvig, **Sneezy:** Billy Gilbert, **The Magic Mirror:** Moroni Olsen, **Humbert, The Queen's Huntsman:** Stuart Buchanan

Classic good versus evil tale of ever-sweet orphan princess Snow White, who although she is forced to work as a household servant to the Queen—a vain woman who will have no rival—becomes the most beautiful in the land. In retaliation, the Queen casts a spell on Snow White—brought on by the bite of a poisonous apple—which can only be broken by a kiss from the Prince to bring her back to life.

PN: The first full–length animated feature of any kind, this film is still considered a milestone in animated cartoon history. The picture took four years to complete and went over budget. (Originally set at $250,000, the film cost $1,488,000 to produce.) It grossed $8.5 million during its first release (then the highest grossing first release film of all time). Subsequent reissues in 1944, 1952, 1958, 1967, 1975, 1983 and 1987 have proven even more worthwhile. The 1987 release alone grossed over $50 million.

Pinto Colvig, listed as the voice of Sleepy and Grumpy, was a veteran Disney voice artist who was also the voice of Goofy. Billy Gilbert, who played Sneezy, won the role after auditioning for Walt Disney by performing his famous "sneezing" routine. Gilbert was best known for numerous supporting roles in Laurel and Hardy comedies.

One sequence involving Snow White's mother dying in childbirth was cut from the story during production, even though stills from the scene were published in *Look* magazine's preview of the film, as well as authorized book versions, comic strips and comic books based on the film.

An animated pencil test from a scene cut from the film, the "soup eating sequence," was broadcast in 1956 on Disney's "Disneyland" TV show (the episode was called "The Plausible Impossible"), the sketches for the deleted "bed–building" sequence were shown on a special celebrating *Snow White*'s 50th anniversary.

The film sparked one controversial spoof: Bob Clampett's Warner Brothers cartoon, *Coal Black and de Sebben Dwarfs* (1938), featuring an all–black version of this popular tale. (It is not shown on local television stations due to its obvious racial overtones.)

SONG OF THE SOUTH (1946)
A Walt Disney Production released by RKO Radio Pictures. p: Walt Disney; anim dir: Wilfred Jackson; scr: Dalton Reymond, Morton Grant, Maurice Rapf; st: Dalton Reymond (based on the *Tales of Uncle Remus* by Joel Chandler Harris); cart st: William Peet, Ralph Wright, George Stallings; md: Charles Wolcott; cart sc: Paul J. Smith; dir anim: Milt Kahl, Eric Larson, Oliver M. Johnston Jr., Les Clark, Marc Davis, John Lounsbery; anim: Don Lusk, Tom Massey, Murray McClellan, Jack Campbell, Hal King, Harvey Toombs, Ken O'Brien, Al Coe, Hal Ambro, Cliff Nordberg, Rudy Larriva. Songs: "How Do You Do?," "Song of the South," "That's What Uncle Remus Said," "Sooner or Later," "Everybody's Got a Laughing Place," "Zip–A–Dee–Doo–Dah," "Let the Rain Pour Down" and "Who Wants to Live Like That?" Running time: 94 minutes.

Cast:
Sally: Ruth Warrick, **Uncle Remus:** James Basket, **Johnny:** Bobby Driscoll, **Ginny:** Luana Patten, **Grandmother:** Lucile Watson, **Aunt Tempy:** Hattie McDaniel, **Toby:** Glenn Leedy, **The Faver Boys:** George Nokes, Gene Holland, **John:** Erik Rolf, **Mrs. Favers:** Mary Field, **Maid:** Anita Brown

Voices:
Brer Fox: James Baskett, **Brer Bear:** Nicodemus Stewart, **Brer Rabbit:** Johnny Lee

In Tom Sawyer–like fashion, Uncle Remus recalls the simple truths of the Old South, instilling good morals in the mind of Johnny, a youngster who comes to rely on Remus as his main companion. The two are joined by a friendly little girl, Ginny, and along the way many of Remus' old tales come to life via animated sequences featuring the likes of Brer Rabbit, Brer Fox and Brer Bear.

STARCHASER: THE LEGEND OF ORIN (1985)
A Steven Hahn Production released by Atlantic Releasing. p: Steven Hahn; d: Steven Hahn, John Sparey; w: Jeffrey Scott; m: Andrew Belling; anim dir: Mitch Rochon, Jang–Gil Kim; anim: Yoon Young Sang, Jung Yul Song, Bill Kroyer. Running time: 101 minutes.

Voices:
Orin: Joe Colligan, **Dagg:** Carmen Argenziano, **Elan Aviana:** Noelle North, **Zygon:** Anthony Delongis, **Arthur:** Les Tremayne, **Silica:** Tyke Caravelli, **Magreb:** Ken Samson, **Auctioneer/Z. Gork:** John Moschita Jr, **Minemaster:** Mickey Morton, **Pung/Hopps:** Herb Vigran, **Shooter:** Dennis Alwood, **Kallie:** Mona Marshall, **Aunt Bella:** Tina Romanus, Ryan MacDonald; John Garwood; Joseph Dellasorte; Philip Clarke; Mike Winslow; Thomas H. Watkins; Daryl T. Bartley; Barbera Harris and Company.

A young robot/human retrieves a magic sword and overtakes a piratical captain of a spaceship to free other humans in the underground world.

PN: The film's screenwriter, Jeffrey Scott, is the grandson of Moe Howard of Three Stooges fame and the son of Three Stooges producer Norman Maurer. Produced in 3–D.

THE SWORD IN THE STONE (1963)

A Walt Disney Production released by Buena Vista. p: Walt Disney; d: Wolfgang Reitherman; dir anim: Frank Thomas, Milt Kahl, Ollie Johnston, John Lounsberry; st: Bill Peet (based on the book by T. H. White); m: George Bruns; anim: Hal King, Eric Cleworth, Eric Larson, Cliff Nordberg, John Sibley, Hal Ambro, Dick Lucas. Songs: "A Most Befuddling Thing," "Blue Oak Tree," "Mad Madame Mim," "That's What Makes the World Go Round," "Higitus Figitus" and "The Legend of the Sword in the Stone." Running time: 79 minutes.

Voices:
Wart: Ricky Sorenson, **Sir Ector, Narrator:** Sebastian Cabot, **Merlin:** Karl Swenson, **Archimedes:** Junius Matthews, **Sir Pelinore:** Alan Napier, **Sir Kay:** Norman Alden, **Madame Mim, Granny Squirrel:** Martha Wentworth, **Girl Squirrel:** Ginny Tyler, **Scullery Maid:** Barbara Jo Allen, **Wart:** Richard and Robert Reitherman

As the title implies, the sword imbedded in stone is central to this story featuring Wart, a foster–son of Sir Ector who undertakes lessons in life from Merlin the Magician. Setting off for a jousting tournament in London with Ector and his son Sir Kay, Wart returns to retrieve Kay's forgotten sword. To save time, he pulls a sword from the legendary stone unaware that the man who does so becomes the rightful king of all of England.

THE THREE CABALLEROS (1945)

A Walt Disney Production released by RKO Radio Pictures. p: Walt Disney; prod superv/dir: Norman Ferguson; seq dir: Clyde Geronimi, Jack Kinney, Bill Roberts; d: Harold Young (Patzcuaro, Veracruz, Acapulco); st: Homer Brightman, Ernest Terrazzas, Ted Sears, Bill Peet, Ralph Wright, Elmer Plummer, Roy Williams, William Cottrell, Del Connell, James Bodrero; md: Charles Wolcott, Paul J. Smith, Edward H. Plumb; anim: Ward Kimball, Eric Larson, Fred Moore, John Lounsbery, Les Clark, Milt Kahl, Hal King, Franklin Thomas, Harvey Toombs,

Bob Carlson, John Sibley, Bill Justice, Oliver M. Johnston Jr., Milt Neil, Marvin Woodward and Don Patterson. Songs: "The Three Caballeros," "Os Quindins De Yaya," "You Belong to My Heart," "Mexico," "Have You Ever Been to Baia?", "Pandeiro & Flute," "Pregoes Carioca" and "Lilongo." Running time: 71 minutes.

Cast:
Aurora Miranda, Carmen Molina, Dora Luz, Nestor Amaral, Almirante, Trio Calaveras, Ascencio del Rio Trio and Padua Hill Players.

Voices:
Donald Duck: Clarence Nash, **Jose Carioca:** Jose Oliveira, **Panchito:** Joaquin Garay, **Narrator:** Fred Shields, **Narrator:** Frank Graham, **Narrator:** Sterling Holloway, "Mexico" sung by Carlos Ramirez

The Latin–American setting of Brazil serves as a background for this musical combining live–action personalities and cartoon figures on the same screen. Donald Duck is the central cartoon character in the animated storyline of his journey to the native lands of Baia where he falls in love with a beautiful saleslady and sees the city aboard a magic flying serape. Donald is paired in the film with old pal Jose Carioca, a tropical bird friend who appeared with Donald in 1943's *Saludos Amigos*, and new addition, Panchito, a Mexican charro rooster.

THE TRANSFORMERS: THE MOVIE (1986)

A Sunbow–Marvel Entertainment Production released by DEG. p: Joe Bacal, Tom Griffin; d: Nelson Shin, Kozo Morishita; w: Ron Friedman, Flint Dille (based on the Hasbro toy, "The Transformers"); m: Vince DiCola; anim: Toei Animation Company. Running time: 86 minutes.

Voices:
Planet Unicron: Orson Welles, **Ultra Magnus:** Robert Stack, **Galvatron:** Leonard Nimoy, **Wreck Gar:** Eric Idle, **Hot Rod/ Rodimus Prime:** Judd Nelson, **Kup:** Lionel Stander, **Blurr:** John Moschitta, **Kranix:** Norm Alden, **Astrotrain:** Jack Angel, **Prowl/Scrapper/Swoop/Junkion:** Michael Bell, **Grimlock:** Gregg Berger, **Arcee:** Susan Blu, **Devastator:** Arthur Burghardt, **Spike/Brown/Shockwave:** Cory Burton, **Cyclonus/ Quintesson Leader:** Roger C. Carmel, **Quintesson Judge:** Rege Cordic, **Prime/Ironhide:** Peter Cullen, **Jazz:** Scatman Crothers, **Dirge:** Bud Davis, **Inferno:** Walker Edmiston, **Perceptor:** Paul Eiding, **Blitzwing:** Ed Gilbert, **Bumblebee:** Dan Gilvean, **Blaster:** Buster Jones, **Scourge:** Stan Jones, **Cliffjumper:** Casey Kasem, **Starscream:** Chris Latta, **Daniel:** David Mendenhall, **Gears:** Don Messick, **Shrapnel:** Hal Rayle, **Kickback:** Clive Revill, **Bonecrusher/Hook/Springer/Slag:** Neil Ross, **Soundwave/Megatron/Rumble/Frenzy/Wheelie/Junkion:** Frank Welker

Set in the year 2005, the Transformers and their arch–enemies, the Deceptions, are at war with each other when an Earthly group, the Autobots, enter the picture and help send the Deceptions into outer space. The Deceptions return rejuvenated after Unicron, a powerful planetary force, intercedes and refits the group's leader with a new body and new name (he's now called Galvatron) so they can renew the war with Autobots once again.

PN: *Citizen Kane* director Orson Welles was the voice of Unicron.

TREASURE ISLAND (1972)

A Filmation Studios production released by Warner Brothers. p: Lou Scheimer, Norman Prescott; d: Hal Sutherland; m: George Blais. Songs: "Fifteen Men on a Dead Man's Chest," "Find the Boy/Find the Mouse and We Find the Map" and "Proper Punishment." Running time: 75 minutes.

Voices:

Long John Silver: Richard Dawson, **Captain Flint:** Larry Storch, **Jim Hawkins:** Davy Jones, **Squire Trelawney:** Larry D. Mann, **Mother:** Jane Webb, **Parrot:** Dal McKennon

Young Jim Hawkins and his newfound friend Hiccup the Mouse take to the high seas in search of buried treasure in this musical version of Robert Louis Stevenson's classic children's tale.

PN: In 1980, NBC aired this feature–length movie as a prime–time special, edited for broadcast.

TWICE UPON A TIME (1983)

A Korty Films and Lucasfilm Ltd. Production released by the Ladd Company through Warner Brothers. p: Bill Couturie; d: John Korty, Charles Swenson; scr: John Korty, Charles Swenson, Suella Kennedy, Bill Couturie; m: Dawn Atkinson, Ken Melville; seq dir: Brian Narelle, Carl Willat, Henry Selick; anim: Will Noble, David Pettigrew, Deborah Short, George Evelyn, John Armstrong, Peter Crosman, Kris Moser, Peggy Okeya, Kai Pindal. Songs: "Twice Upon a Time," "Life Is But a Dream," "Out on My Own," "Heartbreak Town" and "Champagne Time." Running time: 75 minutes.

Voices:

Ralph, the All–Purpose Animal: Lorenzo Music, **The Fairy Godmother:** Judith Kahan Kampmann, **Synonamess Botch:** Marshall Efron, **Rod Rescueman/Scuzzbopper:** James Crana, **Flora Fauna:** Julie Payne, **Greensleeves:** Hamilton Camp, **Narrator/Chief of State/Judges and Bailliff:** Paul Frees **Mum:** as himself

Action–adventure–fantasy–comedy about two oddballs, Ralph, the All–Purpose Animal, and Mum, his prankster sidekick, who are so eager to be heroes that they do something very wrong in trying to do something very right.

PN: Film was the first to utilize a revolutionary new animation process, Lumage animation, developed by Korty Films, which previously produced six years of animated episodes for TV's "Sesame Street" and "The Electric Company," as well as the CBS special, "A Christmas Without Snow." The technique enables depth, translucent color and textural effects usually impossible to achieve in standard cel animation.

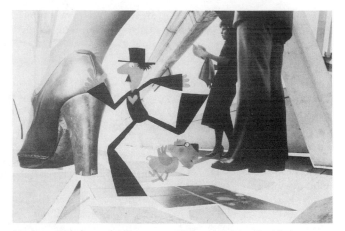

Heroes Ralph and Mum search for the Magic Mainspring among the strange Rushers of Din in a scene from the animated comedy–fantasy, Twice Upon A Time (1983). © Warner Brothers, Inc.

VAMPIRES IN HAVANA (1987)

An Insituto del Arte and Industria Cinematograficos–Television Espanola–Drunoik Production release. p: Paco Prats; d & w: Juan Padron; m: Rembert Eques; anim: Mario Garcia–Montes, Jose Reyes, Noel Lima. Running time: 80 minutes.

A group of Chicago–based vampires, who head up a local Mafioso, are after a secret formula developed by a Cuban scientist. The potent serum will enable vampires to survive in the sunlight.

PN: First screened in its native Cuba in 1985 as *Vampiros En La Habana*, this full–length animated feature was retitled and released in America two years later.

THE WACKY WORLD OF MOTHER GOOSE (1967)

A Rankin–Bass Production released by Videocraft International. p: Arthur Rankin Jr.; d: Jules Bass; w: Romeo Muller (based on characters created by Charles Perrault in the book *Mother Goose Tales*); m/l: George Wilkins, Jules Bass. Running time: 81 minutes.

Voices:

Mother Goose: Margaret Rutherford

Fabled storybook character Mother Goose gets mixed up with secret agents and other well–known storybook characters, Sleeping Beauty, Tom Thumb and others, in this fantasy adventure.

THE WATER BABIES (1979)

A Productions Associates and Adridne Films Production released by Pethurst International. p: Peter Shaw; d: Lionel Jeffries; scr: Michael Robson (based on Charles Kingsley's novel); s: Phil Coulter, Bill Martin; anim: Mirsolaw Kijowiez (Film Polski), J. Stokes, Cuthbert Cartoons. Running time: 93 minutes.

Cast:
Grimes: James Mason, **Mrs. Doasyouwouldbedoneby:** Billie Whitelaw, **Masterman:** Bernard Cribbins, **Lady Harriet:** Joan Greenwood, **Sir John:** David Tomlinson, **Sladd:** Paul Luty, **Tom:** Tommy Pender, **Ellie:** Samantha Gates

A young chimney sweep's apprentice and his dog accidentally fall into a pond and are transformed into "water babies" who inhabit an eternal underwater playground.

PN: Based on Charles Kingsley's children's novel, the film combines live–action and animation. Budget: $2 million.

WATERSHIP DOWN (1978)
A Nepenthe Production released by Avco Embassy Pictures. p, d & w: Martin Rosen (based on the novel by Richard Adams); m: Angela Morley, Malcolm Williamson; superv anim: Philip Duncan; anim dir: Tony Guy; superv anim: Philip Duncan. Running time: 92 minutes.

Voices:
Hazel: John Hurt, **Fiver:** Richard Briers, **Bigwig:** Michael Graham-Cox, **Capt. Holly:** John Bennett, **Blackberry:** Simon Cadell, **Pipkin:** Roy Kinnear, **Dandelion:** Richard O'Callaghan, **Silver:** Terence Rigby, **Chief Rabbit:** Sir Ralph Richardson, **Cowslip:** Denholm Elliott, **Kehaar:** Zero Mostel, **Clover:** Mary Maddox, **Hyzenthlay:** Hannah Gordon, **Cat:** Lyn Farleigh, **Gen. Woundwort:** Harry Andrews, **Campion:** Nigel Hawthorne, **Blackavar:** Clifton Jones, **Black Rabbit:** Joss Ackland, **Narrator:** Michael Hordern

A colony of rabbits, threatened by the destruction of their warren, run off to find a new home safe from the menace of human rule.

A scene from Watership Down (1978), based on Richard Adams' celebrated best seller about a colony of rabbits who flock to escape the menace of human rule. © Avco Embassy Pictures

PN: First U.S. showing was at the World Science Fiction and Fantasy Convention in Phoenix, Arizona. World premiere: London. Producer Martin Rosen spent three years supervising this product at a cost of $4.8 million. Rosen, who co–produced *Women in Love,* had never before worked in animation. Singer/songwriter Art Garfunkel sings two songs in the film.

WHO FRAMED ROGER RABBIT? (1988)
An Amblin Entertainment/Touchstone Pictures Production released by Buena Vista. d: Richard Zemeckis; scr: Jeffrey Price, Peter Seaman (based on novel, *Who Censored Roger Rabbit?* by Gary K. Wolf); m: Alan Silvestri; anim dir: Richard Williams; superv anim: Andreas Beja, Russell Hall, Phil Nibbelink, Simon Wells; anim: Tom Sito, Roger Chiasson, David Byers–Brown, Alvaro Gaivato, Nik Ranieri, Rob Stevenhagen, Alyson Hamilton, James Baxter, Jacques Muller, Joe Haidar, Alan Simpson, Caron Creed, Alain Costa, Raul Garcia, Brigitte Hartley, Greg Manwaring, Colin White, Marc Gordon–Bates, Brent Odell, Mike Swindall, Chuck Gammage, Peter Western, Gary Mudd, Dave Spafford. Running times

Cast:
Eddie Valiant: Bob Hoskins, **Judge Doom:** Christohper Lloyd, **Dolores:** Joanna Cassidy, **Marvin Acme:** Stubby Kaye, **R. K. Maroon:** Alan Tilvern, **Lt. Santino:** Richard Le Parmentier

Voices:
Roger Rabbit, Benny the Cab: Charles Fleischer, **Jessica Rabbit:** Kathleen Turner, **Baby Herman:** Lou Hirsch, **Betty Boop:** Mae Questel, **Daffy Duck, Porky Pig, Tweety Bird, Sylvester the Cat, Bugs Bunny:** Mel Blanc, **Hippo:** Mary T. Radford, **Yosemite Sam:** Joe Alaskey, **Droopy:** Richard Williams, **Lena Hyena:** June Foray, **Mickey Mouse:** Wayne Allwine, **Bullet #1:** Pat Buttram, **Bullet #2:** Jim Cummings, **Bullet #3:** Jim Gallant, **Singing Sword:** Frank Sinatra, **Minnie Mouse:** Russi Taylor, **Goofy, Wolf:** Tony Pope, **Woody Woodpecker:** Cherry Davis

Famed cartoon star Roger Rabbit is sabotaging his screen career by worrying over his wife's carrying on with another "toon." The studio assigns a detective to follow the wife and spy on her in this live action/animated romp.

WIZARDS (1977)
A Bakshi Production released by 20th Century–Fox. w, p & d: Ralph Bakshi; m: Andrew Belling; seq anim: Irv Spence; anim: Brenda Banks, Irv Spence, Martin B. Taras, Robert Taylor, Arthur Vitello. Running time: 80 minutes.

Voices:
Avatar: Bob Holt, **Elinore:** Jesse Wells, **Weehawk:** Richard Romanus, **Peace:** David Proval, **President:** James Connell, **Blackwolf:** Steve Gravers, **Fairy:** Barbara Sloane, **Frog:** Angelo Grisant, **Priest:** Hyman Wien, **Deewhittle:** Christopher Tayback, **Sean:** Mark Hamil, **General:** Peter Hobbs, **Prostitute:** Tina Bowman

An evil twin brother/wizard named Blackwolf seeks to extend the evil sphere of his domain in the land of Scortch. He battles for supremacy against his brother Avatar, wizard of Montagar, who is totally the opposite of Blackwolf in personality and beliefs.

YELLOW SUBMARINE (1968)

An Apple Films/King Features Production released by United Artists. p: Al Brodax; d: George Dunning; st: Lee Minoff (based on a song by John Lennon and Paul McCartney); scr: Lee Minoff, Al Brodax, Jack Mendelsohn, Erich Segal; md: George Martin; anim dir: Jack Stokes, Bob Balser. Running time: 89 minutes.

Voices:

Paul McCartney, Ringo Starr, John Lennon, George Harrison, Dick Emery, Paul Angelus, Lance Percival

Inspired by its title song, this musical fantasy (billed as a "modyssey") finds the legendary lads from Liverpool fighting to save the undersea kingdom of Pepperland from a horde of anti–music monsters, the Blue Meanies. The fearless four meet a multitude of strange and original characters throughout their voyage: the U.S. Calvary, King Kong, Paul's Clean Old Grandad and Lucy in the Sky with Diamonds.

PN: First previewed at the Pavillion in London in July 1968. Film began its exclusive Los Angeles engagement Nov. 13 at the Village Theatre, Westwood, following its gala premier the

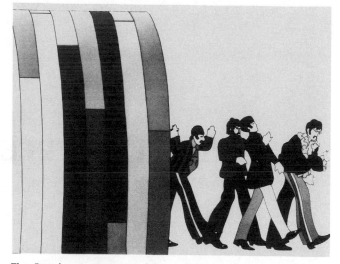

The Beatles, in animated form, fight to save the undersea kingdom of Pepperland from a horde of anti–music monsters in Yellow Submarine *(1968). (Courtesy: King Features Productions)*

previous evening at the Bing Theatre of the Los Angeles County Museum of Art. Lance Percival, one of the film's vocal talents, earlier voiced the characters of Paul and Ringo in the 1960's animated television series, which, coincidentally, was produced by Al Brodax, also producer of the Fab Four's animated feature.

ANIMATED TELEVISION SPECIALS

THE ADVENTURES OF ENERGY

One in a series of syndicated specials under the title of "LBS Children's Theatre," this half–hour special chronicled the ways in which man harnessed energy throughout the ages. *A DIC Audiovisual Production. Color. Half–hour. Premiered: 1983–1984. Syndicated.*

THE ADVENTURES OF HUCKLEBERRY FINN

Mark Twain's classic adventure was faithfully retold, from rafting down the Mississippi to Huck's friendship with the runaway slave Jim, in this animated special sponsored by Kenner Toys. A "Kenner Family Classics" special. *A John Erichsen Production in association with Triple Seven Concepts. Color. Half–hour. Premiered on CBS: November 23, 1984.*

THE ADVENTURES OF SINBAD

Sinbad volunteers to recover Baghdad's magic lantern and its genie from the wicked Old Man of the Sea, but is met by danger at every turn facing dragons, cyclops and other formidable foes in this half–hour special produced for CBS. The program was one of 15 such specials produced by Australia's Air Programs International under the series banner of "Famous Classic Tales." *An Air Program International Production. Color. Half–hour. Premiered on CBS: November 27, 1980.*

Voices:
Peter Corbett, Barbara Frawley, Ron Haddrick, Phillip Hinton, Bevan Wilson

THE ADVENTURES OF THE GET ALONG GANG

Six friendly animals—Montgomery, Dotty, Bingo, Zipper, Portia and Woolma—find their values of honesty and friendship tested as they participate in a big scavenger hunt, which is undermined by slime–ball Catchum Crocodile and Leland Lizard. Produced as a TV pilot for the weekly Saturday–morning series, the special aired on CBS the same year the weekly series debuted. (The series was later syndicated as part of the 90–minute weekend series, "Kideo TV," in 1986.) *A Scholastic Production in association with Those Characters From Cleveland and Nelvana Limited. Color. Half–hour. Premiered: 1984.*

Voices:
Montgomery Moose: Charles Haid, **Dotty Dog:** Mara Hobel, **Zipper Cat:** Jim Henshaw, **Bingo Beaver:** Maria Lufofsky, **Portia Porcupine:** Gloria Figura, **Woolma Lamb:** Julie Cohen, **Catchum Crocodile:** Dan Hennessey, **Leland Lizard:** Dave Thomas, **Officer Growler:** Mark Gordon, **Mr. Hoffnagel:** Wayne Robson, **The Announcer:** Bruce Pirrie

THE ADVENTURES OF THE SCRABBLE PEOPLE IN "A PUMPKIN NONSENSE"

This first–run syndicated special recounts the tale of a magical pumpkin patch where a small boy (Tad) and a girl (Terry), accompanied by Mr. Scrabble, are transported to a town called Nonsense, where they learn of the unhappiness of the Scrabble People and try to help spread goodness among the townspeople. *An Arce Production with James Diaz Studios. Color. Half–hour. Premiered: October 31, 1985.*

Voices:
Tad/Terry: Brianne Sidall, **Sir Scrabble:** Kevin Slattery, **Rot:** Bob Singer, **Muddler:** George Atkins, **Lexa:** Melissa Freeman, **Rotunda:** Kathy Hart Freeman

AESOP'S FABLES

Comedian Bill Cosby, appearing in live–action wraparounds, hosts two animated "Aesop's Fables"—the tortoise and the hare; and the tale of two children (Joey and Marta), in live–action/animation, who are lost in an enchanted forest—in this half–hour special produced jointly by Lorimar Productions and Filmation. Cosby's appeal with children was the principal reason for his hosting the special, as his Filmation–produced "Fat Albert and the Cosby Kids" was a popular Saturday morning installment on CBS, which also aired the special. *A Filmation Production in association with Lorimar Productions. Color. Half–hour. Premiered on CBS: October 31, 1971. Rebroadcast on CBS: December 23, 1974.*

Cast:

Aesop: Bill Cobsy, **Joey:** Keith Hamilton, **Marta:** Jerelyn Fields

Voices:

Tortoise: John Byner, **Hare:** Larry Storch, **Eagle:** Roger C. Carmel, **Lady Eagle:** Jane Webb, **Donkey:** John Erwin, **Owl:** Dal McKennon

ALICE IN WONDERLAND (1966)

Unlike the Walt Disney full–length feature adaptation, this half–hour special was a musical spoof of the Lewis Carroll classic, following the adventures of Alice and her dog Fluff in Wonderland where they meet an amusing assortment of characters including several new creations: Hedda Hatter, a female counterpart of the Mad Hatter; Humphrey Dumpty, whose voice was patterned after Humphrey Bogart; and the White Knight, voiced by Bill Dana in his Jose Jimenez character. The full title of the program was "Alice in Wonderland (or "What's A Nice Kid Like You Doing In A Place Like This?")." *A Hanna–Barbera Production. Color. Half–hour. Premiered on ABC: March 30, 1966. Rebroadcast on ABC: November 19, 1967.*

Voices:

Alice: Janet Waldo, Doris Drew (singing), **Cheshire Cat:** Sammy Davis Jr., **White Knight:** Bill Dana, **Queen of Hearts:** Zsa Zsa Gabor, **White Rabbit:** Howard Morris, **Hedda Hatter:** Hedda Hopper, **Mad Hatter:** Harvey Korman, **Alice's Father/ Humphrey Dumpty:** Allan Melvin, **King of Hearts/March Hare:** Daws Butler, **Dormouse/Fluff, Alice's dog:** Don Messick, **Caterpillar:** Alan Reed, Mel Blanc

ALICE IN WONDERLAND (1973)

Arthur Rankin Jr. and Jules Bass, who created such classic specials as "Rudolph, the Red–Nosed Reindeer" and "Frosty the Snowman," produced this second animated version of the children's fairy tale, with Alice making that familiar visit to Wonderland where she encounters a host of strange and unusual characters—Mad Hatter, March Hare, Cheshire Cat and others—in this wonderfully entertaining syndicated special. The program was broadcast under the umbrella title of "Festival of Family Classics." *A Rankin–Bass Production in association with Mushi Studios. Color. Half-hour. Premiered: February 11, 1973. Syndicated.*

Voices:

Carl Banas, Len Birman, Bernard Cowan, Peg Dixon, Keith Hampshire, Peggi Loder, Donna Miller, Frank Perry, Henry Ramer, Billie Mae Richards, Alfie Scopp, Paul Soles

ALICE'S ADVENTURES IN WONDERLAND

Slipping into dreamland, Alice becomes caught up in the whimsical world of Wonderland. She is met by the March Hare, who, noticeably upset, is running late. She follows the frantic hare and joins a tea party with the Mad Hatter, which is where the rest of her madcap adventure unfolds. *A Greatest Tales Production. Color. Half–hour. Premiered: 1983–1984. Syndicated.*

Voices:

Billie Lou Watt, Peter Fernandez, Gilbert Mack, Ray Owens

ALL ABOUT ME

A young boy falls asleep in class and dreams of taking a tour of his own body in this musical fantasy that explores the functions of various organs and other biological wonders. The program aired on NBC as part of the "NBC Children's Theatre." *An Animated Cartoon Production. Color. Half–hour. Premiered on NBC: January 13, 1973.*

AN ALL–NEW ADVENTURE OF DISNEY'S SPORT GOOFY

Popular Disney canine Goofy is the star of this prime–time special which included scenes from various cartoon shorts (narrated by Stan Freberg) previously released to theaters and combined new footage, narrated by Los Angeles Lakers sports announcer Chick Hearn, who calls the "play–by–play," leading up to a new 20–minute short, "Sport Goofy in Soccermania." *A Happy Feets Production for Walt Disney Television. Color. One hour. Premiered on NBC: May 27, 1987.*

Voices:

Goofy (old): Pinto Colvig, **Goofy (new):** Tony Pope, **Scrooge McDuck:** Will Ryan, **Beagle Boys/Gryo/Gearless:** Will Ryan, **Museum Curator:** Phil Proctor, **Narrator:** Stan Freberg, **Sportscaster:** Chick Hearn

THE AMAZING BUNJEE VENTURE

Accidentally sent back to the year 100 million B.C. after tampering with their father's newest invention, Karen and Andy Winsborrow encounter prehistoric animals and make a new friend, Bunjee, an elephant–like creature who can fly. Returning home, the Winsborrows adopt the strange animal and embark on modern–day adventures together. The two-part program was broadcast as part of the "ABC Weekend Specials." *A Hanna–Barbera Production. Color. Half–hour. Premiered on ABC: March 24 and March 31, 1984. Rebroadcast on ABC: September 15 and 22, 1984; January 18 and 25, 1986; September 12 and 19, 1987; December 10 and 17, 1988.*

Voices:

Bunjee: Frank Welker, **Karen Winsborrow:** Nancy Cartwright, **Andy Winsborrow:** Robbie Lee, **Mr. Winsborrow:**

Michael Rye, **Mrs. Winsborrow:** Linda Gary, **Baby #1:** Linda Gary, **Baby #2:** Nancy Cartwright, **Waxer/Drasto:** John Stephenson, **Willy/Pterodactyl/Tyrannosaur:** Frank Welker

ANIMALYMPICS: WINTER GAMES

Olympic–style sports competition takes on a new meaning as animals compete in events of the first Animalia Winter Games, covered by four reporters—Henry Hummel, Rugs Turkel, Keen Hacksaw and Barbara Warbles—for the Z.O.O. network in this cartoon spoof built around songs and vignettes. *A Lisberger Production. Color. Half–hour. Premiered on NBC: February 1, 1980. Rebroadcast on NBC: July 4, 1982.*

Voices:

Henry Hummel: Michael Fremer, **Rugs Turkel:** Billy Crystal, **Keen Hacksaw:** Harry Shearer, **Barbara Warbles:** Gilda Radner, **Brenda Springer:** Gilda Radner

THE ARABIAN KNIGHTS

A courageous young teenager, Pindar, tries to win the hand of his love, Fatha, from her uncle Omar, the Thief of Baghdad, by taking on the impossible mission of capturing the treasure guarded by the great and powerful Genie of the lamp and the magic slippers of the Cruel Caliph in this half–hour syndicated "Festival of Family Classics" special. *A Rankin–Bass Production in association with Mushi Studios. Color. Half–hour. Premiered: February 4, 1973. Syndicated.*

Voices:

Carl Banas, Len Birman, Bernard Cowan, Peg Dixon, Keith Hampshire, Peggi Loder, Donna Miller, Frank Perry, Henry Ramer, Billie Mae Richards, Alfie Scopp, Paul Soles

ARCHIE AND HIS NEW FRIENDS

The familiar comic–book characters of Archie, Jughead, Betty and Veronica are joined by a new character, Sabrina the Teenage Witch, in this prime–time special that tells the story of Sabrina's attempt to conceal her magical powers and fit in with the rest of the Riverdale High School crowd. Sabrina was formally introduced to television audiences one day earlier with the debut of CBS's "The Archie Comedy Hour." *A Filmation Production. Color. Half–hour. Premiered on CBS: September 14, 1969.*

Voices:

Archie Andrews: Dal McKennon, **Jughead Jones:** Howard Morris, **Veronica Lodge:** Jane Webb, **Betty Cooper:** Jane Webb, **Sabrina:** Jane Webb, **Reggie Mantle/Moose:** John Erwin

THE ARCHIE, SUGAR SUGAR, JINGLE JANGLE SHOW

Selected scenes from the Saturday morning series "The Archies" were featured in this half–hour special which pre-

sented four popular songs (performed by the rock group, "The Archies") from the earlier series and comic vignettes introducing each segment. Songs included on the show were "Sugar Sugar," the Archies number–one hit record in 1969; "Jingle Jangle," "Who's My Baby" and "You've Got to Have an Image." *A Filmation Production. Color. Half–hour. Premiered on CBS: March 22, 1970.*

Voices:

Archie Andrews: Dal McKennon, **Jughead Jones:** Howard Morris, **Betty Cooper:** Jane Webb, **Veronica Lodge:** Jane Webb, **Sabrina:** Jane Webb, **Reggie Mantle/Moose:** John Erwin

AROUND THE WORLD IN 80 DAYS

The familiar Jules Verne voyage of Phineas Fogg, who tries to win a wager by making a trip around the globe in approximately 80 days, is the premise of this two–part animated recreation produced for first–run syndication. A "Festival of Family Classics" special. *A Rankin–Bass Production in association with Mushi Studios. Color. Half–hour. Premiered: November 12 and 19, 1972. Syndicated.*

Voices:

Carl Banas, Len Birman, Bernard Cowan, Peg Dixon, Keith Hampshire, Peggi Loder, Donna Miller, Frank Perry, Henry Raymer, Billie Mae Richards, Alfie Scopp, Paul Soles

B. C.: A SPECIAL CHRISTMAS

John Hart's daily comic strip inspired this yuletide special, featuring the voices of radio's Bob and Ray (Bob Elliott and Ray Goulding). In the film, Peter and Wiley make plans to cash in on the Christmas season by selling trees and gift rocks that are supposedly from a mythical gift-giver they have created named "Santa Claus" (the scheme backfires when the real Santa Claus shows up unexpectedly). B. C., who had the only nonspeaking role next to Santa Claus, appeared briefly in this half-hour program. *A Cinera Production in association with Hardlake Animated Pictures and Field Enterprises. Color. Half-hour. Premiered: 1971. Syndicated.*

Voices:

Peter: Bob Elliott, **Wiley:** Ray Goulding, **Fat Broad:** Barbara Hamilton, **Cute Chick:** Melleny Brown, **Thor:** Henry Ramer, **Clumsy:** Keith Hampshire, **Curls:** John Stocker

B. C.: THE FIRST THANKSGIVING

The cavemen (Peter, Wiley, Thor and Curls) discover fire and Fat Broad decides to heat up a vat of rock soup she is preparing for dinner. Since "there's only one way to flavor rock soup and that's with a dead turkey," she sends them all out on a cross–country chase for the bird, complicated by the fact that nobody knows what a turkey is. B. C. did not talk in the special, which is based on Johnny Hart's popular strip of the

Fat Broad prepares to catch a turkey for Thanksgiving, unaware her subject is closer than she thinks in a scene from "B. C.: The First Thanksgiving." (Courtesy: MG/ Perin Inc.)

same name. Sponsor: General Mills. *A Levitow–Hanson Films Production in association with Field Enterprises. Color. Half–hour. Premiered on NBC: November 19, 1972.*

Voices:

Peter: Don Messick, **Wiley:** Bob Holt, **Thor:** Don Messick, **Clumsy:** Daws Butler, **Grog:** Bob Holt, **Turkey:** Don Messick, **Fat Broad/Cute Chick:** Joanie Sommers

BABAR AND FATHER CHRISTMAS

Christmas comes to the people of Celesteville in Elephant Land in the form of Father Christmas, who spreads his good cheer and toys to the little elephants of the land. His arrival is not without its share of delays, however. Retaxes the Rhinocerous stops at nothing to foil Father Christmas' effort, until, of course, King Babar intervenes and successfully spoils the rhino's plans. *An Atkinson Film–Arts/MTR Ottawa Production in association with the CBC. Color. Half–hour. Premiered on HBO: December 5, 1986. Rebroadcast on HBO: December 9–24, 1986.*

Voices:

Babar: Jim Bradford, **Celeste:** Louise Villeneuve, **Arthur:** Kemp Edwards, **Zephir:** Rick Jones, **Retaxes:** Les Lye, **Father Christmas:** Les Lye, **Lazzaro/Podular:** Rick Jones, **Pom:** Amie Charlebois, **Flora:** Courtney Caroll, **Alexander:** Kai Engstcad, **Professor:** Noel Council, **Secretary/Elf #1:** Bridgitte Robinson, **Elderberry/Elf #2/Boatman:** Derek Diorio, **Gendarme:** Roch Lafortune, **Mice:** Rick Jones

BABAR COMES TO AMERICA

In this second animated special based on the Babar tales of French writer–artist Jean de Brunoff, King Babar receives a telegram inviting him and his wife, Queen Celeste, to visit America and make a movie in Hollywood. They board a hot air balloon to embark on their journey, but encounter a terrible storm and crash on an island, where they're rescued by a whale who just happens to be traveling to New York.

Upon arriving in the Big Apple, they decide to sightsee—driving first to Washington, D.C. and having dinner at the White House and then going on to New Orleans where they travel up the Mississippi on a riverboat—before resuming their journey to Los Angeles to begin work on the movie. Peter Ustinov narrated and provided all the character voices for the program, which was based on two of the Barbar books—*Travels of Babar* by Jean de Brunoff and *Babar in America* by his son, Laurent de Brunoff, who also penned the script. Sponsors: Health–Tex and Burger Chef. *A Lee Mendelson–Bill Melendez Production in association with Laurent de Brunhoff and with the cooperation of Random House. Color. Half–hour. Premiered on NBC: September 7, 1971. Rebroadcast on NBC: February 27, 1972.*

Voices:

Babar, King of Elephant Land: Peter Ustinov, **Celeste, his queen:** Peter Ustinov, **Arthur, Babar's cousin:** Peter Ustinov, **Cornelius, the elder elephant:** Peter Ustinov, **Narrator:** Peter Ustinov

BABAR, THE LITTLE ELEPHANT

The first of two prime–time animated specials adapted from the popular French children's book series, tracing the story of the elephant who would be king and based on the first three books from the series. The program was originally entitled, "The Story of Babar, the Little Elephant." Sponsor: Viking Carpets. *A Lee Mendelson–Bill Melendez Production in association with Laurent de Brunoff and the cooperation of Random House. Color. Half–hour. Premiered on NBC: October 21, 1968. Rebroadcast on NBC: April 21, 1969.*

Voices:

Narrator: Peter Ustinov

BAD CAT

Based upon two children's books about one cat's struggle for acceptance, this half–hour adaptation tells the story of Bad Cat, the undisputed "King Cat" of Fulton Street, who, despite his reputation for being a troublemaker, is really a good cat. After moving to a new neighborhood, he tries to re–establish himself but first must overcome the animosity of a new group of cats, led by bully cat Riff, who challenges him to a mouse catching contest. An "ABC Weekend Special." *A Ruby–Spears Production. Color. Half–hour. Premiered on ABC: April 14, 1984. Rebroadcast on ABC: September 29, 1984; October 28, 1985; November 12, 1988.*

Voices:

Bad Cat: Bart Braverman, **Gordon:** Hal Smith, **Neddy:** Tress MacNeille, **Vernon Turner:** Bobby Ellerbee, **Jim Harrison:** Alan Young, **Steve Harrison:** Steve Spears, **Pam Harrison:** Amy Tunik, **Champ:** Frank Welker, **Diedra:** Judy Strangis,

Dimples: Didi Conn, **Riff:** Jon Bauman, **Mouser:** Marvin Kaplan

THE BALLAD OF PAUL BUNYAN

The life and times of children's favorite Paul Bunyan, a giant lumberjack who wields a magic axe, is recreated, beginning with his early struggles as a child (he is found afloat in his crib and raised by two lumberjacks, Crosscut Kelly and Stump Watson) to his legendary feats of skill and strength as the most respected axeman around. The program climaxes with Bunyan challenging the hated Panhandle Pete, a ruthless lumber boss, in three logger's trials—log–rolling, arm–wrestling and hole–digging. Bunyan wins by digging a hole so big it becomes Niagara Falls. A "Festival of Family Classics" special. *A Rankin–Bass Production in association with Mushi Studios. Color. Half–hour. Premiered: January 7, 1973. Syndicated.*

Voices:

Carl Banas, Len Birman, Bernard Cowan, Peg Dixon, Keith Hampshire, Peggi Loder, Donna Miller, Frank Perry, Henry Ramer, Billie Mae Richards, Alfie Scopp, Paul Soles

THE BALLAD OF SMOKEY THE BEAR

Movie tough guy Jimmy Cagney, as Smokey the Bear's big brother, Big Bear, narrates this charming half–hour special that recalls the trials and tribulations of the U.S. Forest Service fire–prevention campaign spokesperson, from his early challenges as a tiny cub to his courageous acts on behalf of those in trouble as a wise adult. Songs featured on the program included "Ballad of Smokey the Bear" (sung by Cagney and a chorus), "Tell It To A Turtle," "Delilah," "Don't Wait," "All Together," "Curiosity" and "Anyone Can Move A Mountain." The special was produced using the spectacular life–like stop–motion animated puppet process called Animagic. Sponsor: General Electric. *A Rankin–Bass Production in association with Videocraft International. Color. Half–hour. Premiered on NBC: November 24, 1966. Rebroadcast on NBC: May 5, 1968; May 4, 1969.*

Voices:

Big Bear: James Cagney, **Smokey:** Barry Pearl, **Smokey's friends: Turtle:** William Marine, **Beaver:** Herbert Duncan, **Mrs. Beaver:** Rose Marie Jun, **Fox:** George Petrie, **Mama:** Bryna Raeburn

BANANA SPLITS IN HOCUS POCUS PARK

Costumed live–action animals Fleegle (the dog), Drooper (the lion), Bingo (the gorilla) and Snorky (the elephant) stars of TV's "The Banana Splits Adventure Hour," appear in this live–action/animated fantasy in which they meet a magician with special powers. The one–hour special premiered on "The ABC Saturday Superstar Movie" series. *A Hanna–Barbera Production. Color. One hour. Premiered on ABC: November 25, 1972 (on "The ABC Saturday Superstar Movie").*

Voices:

Snorky: (no voice), **Drooper:** Allan Melvin, **Bingo/Frog/Octopus:** Daws Butler, **Fleegle/Tree:** Paul Winchell, **Witch:** Joan Gerber, **Hocus/Pocus:** Howard Morris

BANJO, THE WOODPILE CAT

Banjo, an adventurous young cat, runs away to the big city where he becomes lost. Together with his newfound friend, Crazy Legs (voiced by Scatman Crothers), he searches for a truck, from which he came, to take him back home. Program preceded the network premiere of "Stanley, the Ugly Duckling." *A Banjo Production in association with Don Bluth Productions. Color. Half–hour. Premiered on ABC: May 1, 1982. Rebroadcast on ABC: August 7, 1983.*

Voices:

Banjo, the Woodpile Cat: Sparky Marcus, **Crazy Legs:** Scatman Crothers, **Zazu:** Beah Richards, **Papa Cat/Freeman:** Jerry Harper, **Mama Cat/Cleo:** Georgette Rampone, **Jean:** Ann E. Beesley, **Emily:** Robin Muir, **Farmer/Warehouseman:** Ken Samson, **Announcer:** Mark Elliott, **Vocalists:** Jackie Ward, Sally Stevens, Sue Allen

BARBIE AND THE ROCKERS

Barbie and the Rockers overwhelm with their music, which develops a common bond between the nations of the world. As her concert tour comes to a close, Barbie is named First Goodwill Ambassador for World Peace. With the tour over, the group feels a little blue until Barbie reveals the greatest tour ever—a concert in space. The half–hour syndicated special was based on the popular Mattel Toys doll. *A DIC Enterprises Production in association with Mattel. Color. Half–hour. Premiered: Fall 1987. Syndicated.*

Voices:

Barbie: Sharon Lewis

Additional Voices:

John Stocker, Veena Sood, Debbie Lick, Nikkie Sharp, Lynn Johnson, Michael Benyaer, John Payne, Doc Harris, Viktoria Langton, Gary Chalk, Catherine Mead, Doug Parker

THE BEAR WHO SLEPT THROUGH CHRISTMAS

Ted E. Bear, who has never seen Christmas because he's always snoozing through winter, decides to fight hibernation to stay awake to witness the glorious event for the first time in his life. Sponsor: Florists Telegraphic Delivery Service (FTD). *A Sed–bar Production in association with DePatie–Freleng Enterprises. Color. Half–hour. Premiered on NBC: December 17, 1973. Rebroadcast on NBC: December 16, 1974; December 25, 1977; December 19, 1978; December 23, 1980; CBS: December 15, 1979.*

Voices:

Ted E. Bear: Tom Smothers, **Patti Bear:** Barbara Feldon, **Professor Werner Von Bear:** Arte Johnson, **Santa Claus:**

Robert Holt, **Weather Bear:** Kelly Lange, **Honey Bear:** Michael Bell

Additional Voices:

Casey Kasem and Caryn Paperny

BEAUTY AND THE BEAST

Of five children who live in a plush mansion, only one is kind and good and full of love. Her name is Beauty. While the others are selfish and greedy, especially sisters Jacqueline and Erwina, Beauty makes the best of everything in life, even when her father falls on hard times and they are forced to move from their mansion to a tiny cottage and lead a meager lifestyle. Moreover, she comes through where her sisters fail by taking up with the Beast, who promises not to kill her father if he sacrifices her beauty to him. Based on the Madame Leprince de Beaumont children's story. A "Kenner Family Classics" daytime special. *A Ruby–Spears Production in association with TCG Products. Color. Half–hour. Premiered on CBS: November 25, 1983. Rebroadcast on CBS: November 22, 1984.*

Voices:

Beauty/Jacqueline: Janet Waldo, **Queen/Old Crone:** Janet Waldo, **Beast/Prince:** Robert Ridgely, **Erwina/Statcly Lady:** Linda Gary, **Messenger Boy:** Linda Gary, **Merchant/Sailor/Male Voice:** Stacy Keach Jr., **Rene/Cockatoo:** Alan Young, **Gerard:** Paul Kirby

BE MY VALENTINE, CHARLIE BROWN

It's Valentine's Day and cupid is already busy at work, especially at Birchwood School, where Linus displays his affection for his homeroom teacher by buying her a huge box of candy. Unfortunately, Sally thinks the candy is for her and reciprocates with a homemade card for Linus. Meanwhile, Lucy continues her quest to win Schroeder's affection, while poor hopeless heart Charlie Brown continues to wait for his cards to arrive in the mail. Sponsors: Kellogg's, Dolly Madison, Peter Paul Cadbury and Nabisco. *A Lee Mendelson–Bill Melendez Production in cooperation with United Feature Syndicate. Color. Half–hour. Premiered on CBS: January 28, 1975. Rebroadcast on CBS: February 10, 1976; February 14, 1977; February 9, 1979; February 11, 1983; February 11, 1984; February 14, 1987.*

Voices:

Charlie Brown: Duncan Watson, **Linus Van Pelt:** Stephen Shea, **Lucy Van Pelt:** Melanie Kohn, **Sally Brown:** Lynn Mortensen, **Schroeder:** Greg Felton, **Violet/Frieda:** Linda Ercoli

THE BERENSTAIN BEARS' CHRISTMAS TREE

Papa Bear goes against the advice of Mama Bear not to get a Christmas tree, and sets out to find the perfect tree himself in the woods of Bear Valley. During his journey, he encounters the animals of the forest and realizes that by taking a tree he could jeopardize the homes of other creatures less fortunate. *A Cates Brothers Company Production in association with Perpetual Motion Pictures. Color. Half–hour. Premiered on NBC: December 3, 1979. Rebroadcast on NBC: December 15, 1980.*

Voices:

Papa Bear: Ron McLarty, **Mama Bear:** Pat Lysinger, **Brother Bear:** Jonathan Lewis, **Sister Bear:** Gabriela Glatzer, **Narrator:** Ron McLarty

THE BERENSTAIN BEARS' EASTER SURPRISE

It's that time of year again—Easter. Only this year the weather seems uncooperative as Bear Valley is blanketed with snow. With no sign of spring in sight, Papa Bear takes it upon himself to find the Easter Hare, Boss Bunny, and see why Easter hasn't arrived on time. *A Joseph Cates Production in association with Perpetual Motion Pictures. Color. Half–hour. Premiered on NBC: April 14, 1981. Rebroadcast on NBC: April 6, 1982; April 20, 1984.*

Voices:

Papa Bear: Ron McLarty, **Mama Bear:** Pat Lysinger, **Brother Bear:** Knowl Johnson, **Sister Bear:** Gabriela Glatzer, **Boss Bunny:** Bob McFadden, **Narrator:** Ron McLarty

THE BERENSTAIN BEARS' LITTLEST LEAGUER

The moral of this children's special is that parents should never heap their expectations upon their children. Papa Bear finds that out for himself, in a big way, when he tries making his son—and later his daughter—into successful Little League ballplayers with the dream of them someday turning pro. *A Joseph Cates Production in association with Buzzco Productions. Color. Half–hour. Premiered on NBC: May 6, 1983. Rebroadcast: May 20, 1984 (as "The Berenstain Bears Play Ball").*

Voices:

Papa Bear: Ron McLarty, **Mama Bear:** Pat Lysinger, **Brother Bear:** Knowl Johnson, **Sister Bear:** Gabriela Glatzer, **Narrator:** Ron McLarty

THE BERENSTAIN BEARS MEET BIG PAW

The legend of Big Paw—a monster who eats bears at Thanksgiving to punish them because they're "insufficiently grateful" for nature's bounty—is the premise of this holiday prime–time special. *A Joseph Cates Production in association with Perpetual Motion Pictures. Color. Half–hour. Premiered on NBC: November 20, 1980. Rebroadcast on NBC: November 24, 1981.*

Voices:

Papa Bear: Ron McLarty, **Mama Bear:** Pat Lysinger, **Brother Bear:** Jonathan Lewis, **Sister Bear:** Gabriela Glatzer, **Big Paw/Announcer:** Bob Kaliban, **Narrator:** Ron McLarty

THE BERENSTAIN BEARS' VALENTINE SPECIAL

Cupid's arrows get the best of Brother Bear and Sister Bear as both critters become preoccupied with the idea of loving someone. Brother Bear, who is a star ice–hockey player, encounters the most difficulty as he prepares for the upcoming Valentine's Day Hockey Game. *A Joseph Cates Production in association with Perpetual Motion Pictures. Color. Half–hour. Premiered on NBC: February 13, 1982. Rebroadcast on NBC: February 12, 1983.*

Voices:

Papa Bear: Ron McLarty, **Mama Bear:** Pat Lysinger, **Brother Bear:** Knowl Johnson, **Sister Bear:** Gabriela Glatzer, **Bearcaster/Others:** Jerry Sroka, **Narrator:** Ron McLarty

THE BLACK ARROW

Adapted from the Robert Louis Stevenson story, this half–hour special recreates the adventures of a young heir, orphaned at birth, who joins the band of forest outlaws known as the Brotherhood of the Black Arrow. A "Famous Classic Tales" special. *An Air Programs International Production. Color. Half–hour. Premiered on CBS: December 2, 1973. Rebroadcast on CBS: September 22, 1974.*

Voices:

Alistair Duncan, Jeannie Drynan, Tim Elliott, Barbara Frawley, Ron Haddrick, John Lliewellyn, Owen Weingott

BLACK BEAUTY

Born and raised in the lush English countryside, sweet–tempered Black Beauty is taught by his mother to be a friend to man. In true testimony to his mother, Beauty's faith in the goodness of man is put to the test again and again in this touching and heartwarming story based on Anna Sewell's children's novel, first published in 1877. A "Famous Classic Tales" special. *A Hanna–Barbera Production. Color. Half–hour. Premiered on CBS: October 28, 1978. Rebroadcast on CBS: November 11, 1979; November 6, 1983 (as "Kenner Family Classics").*

Voices:

Narrator: Alan Young

Additional Voices:

Robert Comfort, Cathleen Cordell, Alan Dinehart, Mike Evans, David Gregory, Colin Hamilton, Laurie Main, Patricia Sigris, Barbara Stevens, Alan Young, Cam Young.

THE BLINKINS

Blink, Sparkle, Flicker, Flashy and Shady are selected to perform in the annual Flower of Spring Ceremony to bring the first ray of Spring sunshine to Blinkin Land. Slime, a swamp monster, has different plans. Along with Grog the Frog, he captures the Blinkins to prevent sunshine and the new season from making its way. *A MCA Television Production in association with TMS Entertainment. Color. Half–hour. Premiered: Spring 1986. Syndicated.*

Voices:

Mr. Benjamin the Owl: Burgess Meredith, **Grog the Frog:** Paul Williams, **Blink:** Missy Gold, **Shady:** Tracey Gold, **Baby Twinkle:** Brandy Gold, **Flashy:** Sagan Lewis, **Sparkle:** Carrie Swenson, **Flicker/Pettiford:** Louise Chamis, **Slime:** Chris Latta, **Announcer:** Henry Gibson

THE BLINKINS AND THE BEAR

New challenges await the spunky Blinkins as they follow Mr. Benjamin Owl's advice by gathering food for the winter— they stock up on nuts, berries and other delights—but their precious supply is endangered by bad guys, Grog the Frog and Sneed the Bear, who disrupt the proceedings. *A MCA Television Production in association with TMS Entertainment. Color. Half–hour. Premiered: September, 1986. Syndicated.*

Voices:

Blink: Noelle North, **Flashy:** Daryl Wood, **Sparkle:** Carrie Swenson, **Flicker/Baby Twinkle:** Louise Chamis, **Shady:** Jennifer Darling, **Mr. Benjamin the Owl:** Burgess Meredith, **Sneed the Bear:** Chris Latta, **Grog the Frog:** Hamilton Camp, **Announcer:** Alan Young

THE BLINKINS AND THE BLIZZARD

The Blinkins come to the aid of a poor little girl who is lost in the woods after she loses her precious doll. Lighting up the forest, they guide her to a cave to avoid an oncoming snowstorm. Villainous Grog the Frog and Sneed the Bear decide to make life miserable for the Blinkins and the young girl, but, fortunately, the clever fireflies get out of trouble and are able to lead the girl home safely through a serious snow blizzard. *A MCA Television Production in association with TMS. Color. Half–hour. Premiered: December, 1986. Syndicated.*

Voices:

Blink: Noelle North, **Flashy:** Daryl Wood, **Sparkle:** Carrie Swenson, **Flicker/Baby Twinkle:** Louise Chamis, **Shady:** Jennifer Darling, **Mr. Benjamin the Owl:** Burgess Meredith, **Sneed the Bear:** Chris Latta, **Grog the Frog:** Hamilton Camp, **Announcer:** Alan Young

BLONDIE AND DAGWOOD

The world's favorite comic–strip couple trades places when Blondie gets a job after Dagwood Bumstead gets fired. Dagwood's boss, J. C. Dithers, usually relents and rehires Dagwood after firing him, but this time J. C. insists he won't take Dagwood back—ever. That leaves Blondie forced to cope with two big problems: having no weekly paycheck and having Dagwood home every day. Loni Anderson provides the voice of Blondie. Based on the comic strip "Blondie" by Dean Young and Stan Drake. *A Marvel Animation Production with King Features Entertainment in association with Toei Animation. Color. Half—hour. Premiered on CBS: May 15, 1987. Rebroadcast on CBS: October 12, 1988.*

Voices:

Blondie Bumstead: Loni Anderson, **Dagwood Bumstead:** Frank Welker, **Alexander Bumstead:** Ike Eisenmann, **Cookie Bumstead:** Ellen Gerstell, **Daisy, the Bumstead's dog:** Pat Fraley, **Julius Dithers:** Alan Oppenheimer, **Cora Dithers/ Mrs. Hannon:** Russi Taylor, **Tootsie Woodley:** Laurel Page, **Mr. Beasley/Herb Woodley:** Jack Angel

BLONDIE AND DAGWOOD: "SECOND WEDDING WORKOUT"

In their second prime—time special, the Bumsteads' 20th wedding anniversary falls on the same day as the deadline for a building project Dagwood must complete in order to receive a bonus to pay for Blondie's new ring—which he loses. *A King Features Entertainment Production in association with*

An All New, Full Color, Animated, Half-Hour Special

The world's favorite comic—strip couple trades places when Blondie gets a job after Dagwood Bumstead gets fired in the one—hour prime—time special, "Blondie And Dagwood." © King Features Entertainment

King Services, Inc. Color. Half—hour. Premiered on CBS: November 1, 1989.

Voices:

Blondie Bumstead: Loni Anderson, **Dagwood Bumstead:** Frank Welker, **Alexander Bumstead:** Ike Eisenmann, **Cookie Bumstead:** Ellen Gerstell, **Daisy, the Bumsteads' dog:** Pat Fraley, **Julius Dithers:** Alan Oppenheimer, **Cora Dithers:** Russi Taylor

THE BOLLO CAPER

On the verge of extinction, two leopards—Bollo and Nefertiti—try to save their species from a band of trappers who are capturing and killing their kind to sell the skins to their boss, a famed New York furrier. An "ABC Weekend Special." *A Rick Reinert Production. Color. Half—hour. Premiered on ABC: February 2, 1985. Rebroadcast on ABC: November 16, 1985; August 16, 1986; November 29, 1986; July 11, 1987.*

Voices:

Bollo: Michael Bell, **Nefertiti/Lulu La Looche:** Ilene Latter, **Clamper Carstair:** Hal Smith, **Snag Carstair:** Will Ryan, **Lion/ Iceberg/Emperor:** Hal Smith, **Chestnut/Monkey #1:** Will Ryan, **Felix the Furrier:** Pete Renaday, **President/Monkey #2:** Pete Renaday

THE BRADY KIDS ON MYSTERIOUS ISLAND

Teenagers Greg, Peter, Bobby, Marcia, Jan and Cindy of television's "The Brady Bunch" perform as rock musicians and encounter a few spooks on a strange island in this one—hour animated adventure which officially launched the first season for "The ABC Saturday Superstar Movie." The production preceded the weekly Saturday morning series, "The Brady Kids." The movie's working title was, "Jungle Bungle." *A Filmation Production for Paramount Television. Color. One hour. Premiered on ABC: September 9, 1972.*

Voices:

Greg Brady: Barry Williams, **Peter Brady:** Christopher Knight, **Bobby Brady:** Michael Lookinland, **Marcia Brady:** Maureen McCormick, **Jan Brady:** Eve Plumb, **Cindy Brady:** Susan Olsen, **Marlon:** Larry Storch

BUGS BUNNY: ALL—AMERICAN HERO

The carrot—eating rabbit recalls past events in America's glorious history in this half—hour special which combines full versions and clips from several old Warner cartoons re—edited to tell a complete story. The program was primarily shaped around the 1954 Bugs Bunny cartoon, "Yankee Doodle Bugs." Other cartoons, in whole or in part, included: "Bunker Hill Bunny," "Dumb Patrol," "Rebel Without Claws" and "Ballot Box Bunny." *A Warner Brothers Television Production. Color. Half—hour. Premiered on CBS: May 4, 1981. Rebroadcast on CBS: March 10, 1982; April 16, 1983; May 26, 1984; May 10, 1985; January 7, 1986; June 18, 1987; September 20, 1988.*

Voices:
Mel Blanc, June Foray

THE BUGS BUNNY EASTER SPECIAL

When the Easter Bunny becomes ill, Granny turns to Bugs to help her find the right recruit who can fulfill the job of delivering baskets of eggs to children throughout the world. Offered the job himself, Bugs demurs but stages an audition for others to apply for the position. (One persistent applicant is Daffy Duck, who doesn't understand why he isn't taken seriously for the job.) Program includes complete versions of theatrical cartoon favorites, such as "For Scenti—mental Reasons," "Knighty Knight Bugs," "Robin Hood Daffy," "Sahara Hare," "Birds Anonymous," plus clips from five other cartoons. *A DePatie—Freleng Production for Warner Brothers Television. Color. Half—hour. Premiered on CBS: April 7, 1987. Rebroadcast on CBS: March 18, 1978; April 13, 1979; April 2, 1980; April 14, 1984; March 30, 1985; March 25, 1989.*

Voices:
Mel Blanc, June Foray

BUGS BUNNY IN SPACE

Following the box—office sensation of *Star Wars,* CBS aired this half—hour collection of the best moments from science—fiction oriented Warner Brothers cartoons strewn together to represent a common theme. The special contained several cartoons featuring Bugs Bunny, as well as the classic "Duck Dodgers In The 24—1/2th Century." *A Warner Brothers Television Production. Color. Half—hour. Premiered on CBS: September 6, 1977. Rebroadcast on CBS: April 18, 1978.*

Voices:
Mel Blanc

BUGS BUNNY/LOONEY TUNES ALL—STAR 50TH ANNIVERSARY SPECIAL

In honor of Warner Brothers' golden cartoon anniversary, several well—known stars—David Bowie, Steve Martin, Bill Murray, Kirk Douglas, Cher, George Burns and others—are featured in this tribute in the form of interviews recalling their favorite memories of Bugs Bunny and the other Warner Brothers cartoon characters. Cartoon footage and rare pencil tests round out the program, plus interviews with Mel Blanc, Friz Freleng and Chuck Jones. Other guest stars: Eve Arden, Candice Bergen, Jeff Goldblum, Jeremy Irons, Quincy Jones, Penny Marshall, Mike Nichols, Geraldine Page, Molly Ringwald, Danny Thomas, Billy Dee Williams and Chuck Yeager. *A Broadway Video Production in association with Warner Brothers Television. Color. One hour. Premiered on CBS: January 14, 1986. Rebroadcast on CBS: July 24, 1987 (as "The Bugs Bunny/Looney Tunes Jubilee").*

Voices:
Mel Blanc

THE BUGS BUNNY MOTHER'S DAY SPECIAL

When Bugs and Granny encounter a blundering stork, their discussion turns to Mother's Day, which acts as a bridge to various sequences culled from Warner Brothers cartoons, including "Stork Naked," "Apes Of Wrath" and "Goo Goo Goliath." *A Warner Brothers Television Production. Color. Half—hour. Premiered on CBS: May 12, 1979. Rebroadcast on CBS: May 12, 1984; May 10, 1985; May 8, 1987.*

Voices:
Mel Blanc, June Foray

THE BUGS BUNNY MYSTERY SPECIAL

In a spoof of Alfred Hitchcock, Porky Pig hosts this compilation of crime cartoons, both complete cartoons and excerpts, which entail a string of "whodunit" plots starring a melange of Warner characters. *A Warner Brothers Television Production. Color. Half—hour. Premiered on CBS: October 15, 1980. Rebroadcast on CBS: December 5, 1981; March 8, 1983; March 10, 1984; September 14, 1984; June 5, 1987.*

Voices:
Mel Blanc

BUGS BUNNY'S BUSTIN' OUT ALL OVER

Three new cartoons, created by Chuck Jones, are presented in this half—hour special: Bugs recalling his childhood and first encounter with an infant Elmer Fudd; his capture by Marvin Martian; and Wile E. Coyote's near—completion of a 30—year chase to catch the Roadrunner. *A Chuck Jones Enterprises Production in association with Warner Brothers Television. Color. Half—hour. Premiered on CBS: May 21, 1980. Rebroadcast on CBS: March 20, 1981; May 5, 1984; April 6, 1985; June 5, 1987; April 19, 1988; April 19, 1989.*

Voices:
Mel Blanc

BUGS BUNNY'S HOWL—OWEEN SPECIAL

Monstrous events occur in this compendium of old Warner Brothers cartoons as Tweety, Daffy Duck, Porky Pig, Sylvester the Cat and, of course, Bugs Bunny experience strange encounters of the Halloween—kind. Cartoons featured are "Bedeviled Rabbit," "Rabbit Every Monday" and clips from eight additional one—reelers, including "Beep Beep," "Canned Feud" and "Trip For Tat." *A Warner Brothers Television Production. Color. Half—hour. Premiered on CBS: October 26, 1977. Rebroadcast on CBS: October 25, 1978; October 31, 1979; October 29, 1980; October 27, 1981; October 25, 1989.*

Voices:
Mel Blanc, June Foray

BUGS BUNNY'S LOONEY CHRISTMAS TALES

Warner cartoon directors Friz Freleng and Chuck Jones animated three all–new cartoons, each with a Christmas theme, for this half–hour special that spotlights the traditional values of the yuletide season using an assortment of Warner characters. The titles of the three cartoons were "Bugs Bunny's Christmas Carol," a spoof of the Charles Dickens' classic; "Freeze Frame"; and "Fright Before Christmas." *A DePatie–Freleng Enterprises Production with Chuck Jones Enterprises and Warner Brothers Television. Color. Half–hour. Premiered on CBS: November 27, 1979. Rebroadcast on CBS: December 13, 1980; November 27, 1981; December 6, 1982; December 4, 1984; December 24, 1987; December 17, 1988.*

Voices:
Mel Blanc, June Foray

BUGS BUNNY'S MAD WORLD OF TELEVISION

In new footage, Bugs Bunny is the new head of entertainment for the QTTV Network. His first task is to bolster the station's sagging ratings with new, original programming. He explores a number of options, most of which are represented in footage from previously exhibited cartoons made for theaters. *A Warner Brothers Television Production. Color. Half–hour. Premiered on CBS: January 11, 1982. Rebroadcast on CBS: April 2, 1983; September 14, 1983; July 28, 1984; September 6, 1985.*

Voices:
Mel Blanc

BUGS BUNNY'S THANKSGIVING DIET

Bugs Bunny, playing a diet doctor, counsels his patients—Porky Pig, Sylvester the Cat and others—against holiday overeating, prescribing his favorite cure: a series of cartoons to reduce the urge. Features full versions of "Bedeviled Rabbit," "Rabbit Every Monday" and clips from eight others. *A Warner Brothers Television Production. Color. Half–hour. Premiered on CBS: November 15, 1979. Rebroadcast on CBS: November 10, 1981; November 12, 1983; November 20, 1984; November 26, 1985; November 26, 1987; November 23, 1988; November 22, 1989.*

Voices:
Mel Blanc, June Foray

BUGS BUNNY'S VALENTINE

In the unusual role of "cupid," Elmer Fudd strikes love into the heart of Bugs Bunny, who experiences the fresh bloom of romance through a series of classic Warner cartoons, complete and edited, strung together in one common theme. *A Warner Brothers Television Production. Color. Half–hour. Premiered on CBS: February 14, 1979. Rebroadcast on CBS: February 13, 1980; February 4, 1981; February 2, 1982; February 11, 1984; February 11, 1986; February 4, 1988.*

Voices:
Mel Blanc

BUGS BUNNY'S WILD WORLD OF SPORTS

The "Sportsman of the Year Award" is announced in ceremonies at the Arthur Q. Bryan Pavillion, utilizing many clips of sporting activities from previous Warner Brothers cartoons, including "Raw Raw Rooster," "Sports Chumpions," "To Duck Or Not To Duck," and others. Oh, yes, the winner is Foghorn Leghorn, of all characters. *A Warner Brothers Television Production. Color. Half–hour. Premiered on CBS: February 15, 1989.*

Voices:
Mel Blanc

BUGS VS. DAFFY: BATTLE OF THE MUSIC VIDEO STARS

As cross–town rival disc jockeys, Bugs Bunny, of music channel W.A.B.B.I.T., and Daffy Duck, of radio station K.P.U.T., try topping each other as they introduce various song sequences from old Warner cartoons. Naturally, Bugs gets the higher ratings. *A Warner Brothers Television Production. Color. Half–hour. Premiered on CBS: October 21, 1988.*

Voices:
Mel Blanc

BUNNICULA, THE VAMPIRE RABBIT

This spooky but comical tale tells the story of a supernatural rabbit and his loving friendship amongst a small–town family and its pets as told by the family's dog, Harold, an easy–going, intelligent mutt, in this adaptation of Deborah and James Howe's popular children's book, *Bunnicula, A Rabbit–Tale of Mystery.* An "ABC Weekend Special." *A Ruby–Spears Production. Color. Half–hour. Premiered on ABC: January 9, 1982. Rebroadcast on ABC: April 17, 1982; October 9, 1982; October 29, 1983.*

Voices:
Harold/Roy: Jack Carter, **Chester/Stockboy/Hank:** Howard Morris, **Toby Monroe:** Pat Peterson, **Mr. Monroe/Storekeeper:** Alan Young, **Mrs. Monroe/Gertie/Alice:** Janet Waldo, **Boss/Andy:** Alan Dinehart

THE CABBAGE PATCH KIDS' FIRST CHRISTMAS

When the Cabbage Patch Kids help a disabled girl and one of their own get adopted, they discover the true meaning of Christmas spirit and the importance of self–worth in this Ruby–Spears animated holiday special. *A Ruby–Spears Pro-*

Harold, a down–to–earth dog, and Chester, an imaginative cat, realize their worst fear: their pet rabbit is really a vampire in a scene from the Ruby–Spears special, "Bunnicula, The Vampire Rabbit." © Ruby–Spears Enterprises

duction in association with Heywood Kling Productions. Color. Half–hour. Premiered on ABC: December 7, 1984. Rebroadcast on ABC: December 13, 1985.

Voices:

Otis Lee: Scott Menville, **Dawson Glenn:** Josh Rodine, **Cannon Lee:** David Mendenhall, **Sybil Sadie:** Phenina Segal, **Rachel "Ramie" Marie:** Ebony Smith, **Tyler Bo:** Vaughn Jelks, **Paula Louise:** Ann Marie McEvoy, **Jenny:** Gini Holtzman, **Colonel Casey:** Hal Smith, **Xavier Roberts:** Sparky Marcus, **Lavender Bertha:** Tress MacNeille, **Cabbage Jack/Gus:** Arthur Burghardt, **Beau Weasel/Fingers:** Neil Ross

THE CANTERVILLE GHOST

When the Otis family moves into their new house in Canterville, they get more than they bargained for when a 300–year–old ghost attempts to scare them from the house in this delightful adaptation of the Oscar Wilde story. This half–hour special was produced for CBS–owned and –operated stations in Los Angeles, Chicago, New York and Philadelphia, and was syndicated to other stations nationwide. *A CBS Television Production in association with Orkin–Flaum Productions and Calabash Productions. Color. Half–hour. Premiered: Fall 1988. Syndicated.*

Voices:

The Ghost: Dick Orkin, **General:** Brian Cummings, **Father:** Louis Arquette, **Mother:** Janet Waldo, **Virginia Otis,** their daughter: Susan Blu, **Washington:** Michael Sheehan, **Ned and Ted,** the twins: Nancy Cartwright, Mona Marshall, **Mrs. Umney,** the maid: Kathleen Freeman

CAP'N O. G. READMORE MEETS DR. JEKYLL AND MR. HYDE

While holding their Friday Night Book Club meeting, Cap'n O. G. and his friends, Kitty Literature, Ol' Tome Cat, Wordsy and Lickety Page, turn to reading the Robert Louis Stevenson classic, *The Strange Case Of Dr. Jekyll and Mr. Hyde.* The story becomes so enthralling that Wordsy is sucked into the story—literally—and Cap'n O. G. follows to save him. Of all people, Robert Louis Stevenson gets them out of the mess by writing them out of the story. An "ABC Weekend Special." *An ABC Entertainment Production in association with Rick Reinert Productions. Color. Half–hour. Premiered on ABC: September 13, 1986. Rebroadcast on ABC: August 8, 1987; May 3, 1989; November 4, 1989.*

Voices:

Cap'n O. G. Readmore: Neil Ross, **Wordsy/Ol' Tome Cat/Poole:** Stanley Jones, **Vendor/Master of Ceremonies:** Neil Ross, **Robert Louis Stevenson:** Stanley Jones, **Kitty Literature/Olivia:** Ilene Latter, **Heathpote:** Ilene Latter, **Lickety Page/Calypso LaRose:** Lucille Bliss, **Edward Hyde/Newcommon:** Hal Smith

CAP'N O. G. READMORE MEETS LITTLE RED RIDING HOOD

To teach him a lesson for hating villains, Cap'n O. G. is turned into the Big Bad Wolf from the classic children's tale, "Little

The scare tactics of a 300–year–old ghost fail to impress the daughter of the new owners of the Canterville mansion in a scene from "The Canterville Ghost," a syndicated special based on a popular Oscar Wilde story. © Orkin–Flaum Productions.

Red Riding Hood," so he can understand what being a villain is really like. *An ABC Entertainment Production in association with Rick Reinert Productions. Color. One hour. Premiered on ABC: October 1, 1988. Rebroadcast on ABC: January 13, 1990; April 14, 1990.*

Voices:

Cap'n O. G. Readmore: Neil Ross, **Lickety Page:** Lucille Bliss, **Ol' Tome Cat:** Stanley Ross, **Wordsy:** Will Ryan, **Kitty Literature:** Ilene Latter

Additional Voices:

Hal Smith, Lana Janell Beeson

CAP'N O. G. READMORE'S JACK AND THE BEANSTALK

In an effort to promote reading, this Saturday afternoon special takes a unique approach, featuring a bright, articulate cat, Cap'n O. G. Readmore and his friends, Kitty Literature, Ol' Tome Cat, Wordsy, Lickety Page and Dog–Eared, as vehicles to encourage a love of literature among young people. As members of the Friday Night Book Club, they meet to discuss classic literature. This time their discussion of favorite fairy tales takes them back to "Jack and the Beanstalk," revealed to them when the bookshelves in the room suddenly open and they are transported to this land of make-believe. An "ABC Weekend Special." *An ABC Entertainment Production in association with Rick Reinert Productions. Color. Half–hour. Premiered on ABC: October 12, 1985. Rebroadcast on ABC: October 4, 1986; January 7, 1989.*

Voices:

Cap'n O. G. Readmore: Neil Ross, **Kitty Literature:** Ilene Latter, **Ol' Tome Cat:** Stanley Jones, **Wordsy:** Will Ryan, **Lickety Page:** Lucille Bliss, **Jack:** Stanley Jones, **Jack's Mother:** Lucille Bliss, **Giant:** Hal Smith, **Giant's Wife:** Ilene Latter, **Harp:** Ilene Latter, **Humpty Dumpty:** Will Ryan, **Little Old Man:** Hal Smith, **Hen:** Lucille Bliss

CAP'N O. G. READMORE'S PUSS IN BOOTS

Cap'n O. G., the literate feline, and his friends, Lickety Page, Ol' Tome Cat and Kitty Literature, experience first–hand the story of "Puss In Boots" in this "ABC Weekend Special." *An ABC Entertainment Production in association with Rick Reinert Productions. Color. One hour. Premiered on ABC: September 10, 1988. Rebroadcast on ABC: January 13, 1990.*

Voices:

Cap'n O. G. Readmore: Neil Ross, **Lickety Page:** Lucille Bliss, **Ol' Tome Cat:** Stanley Jones, **Kitty Literature:** Ilene Latter **Wordsy:** Will Ryan

THE CARE BEARS BATTLE THE FREEZE MACHINE

The diabolical Professor Coldheart plans to use his greatest invention, called the Freeze Machine, to no good by freezing all the children in town. The Care Bears (with new characters, Hugs and Tugs) come down to Earth from Care–A–Lot to prevent this fiendish plot from being carried out. *A MAD Production in association with Those Characters From Cleveland and Atkinson Film–Arts. Color. Half–hour. Premiered: April, 1984. Syndicated.*

Voices:

Dominic Bradford, Bob Dermer, Abby Hagyard, Rick Jones, Les Lye, Anna MacCormack, Brodie Osome, Noreen Young

THE CARE BEARS IN THE LAND WITHOUT FEELINGS

The 10 original members of the Care Bears, popular greeting card characters, bring friendship, love and caring to a young boy named Kevin, a runaway, who becomes ensnared by the evil Professor Coldheart. The program was the first special based on this wholesome gang, who were created in 1981 by Those Characters From Cleveland, a subsidiary of American Greetings card company. *A MAD Production in association with Those Characters From Cleveland and Atkinson Film–Arts. Color. Half–hour. Premiered: April, 1983.*

Voices:

Andrea Blake, Justin Cammy, Abby Hagyard, Rick Jones, Les Lye, Anna MacCormack, Kathy MacLennan

CARLTON YOUR DOORMAN

A misfit of society who was heard but not seen on the television sitcom, "Rhoda," Carlton the Doorman was transformed into a full figure character whose adventures were unusual at best in this prime–time special based on the character created by James L. Brooks, Allan Burns, David David and Lorenzo Music (the voice of the character in the sitcom and the special). The program was awarded an Emmy Award as Outstanding Animated Program in 1979. *A MTM Production in association with Murakami–Wolf–Swenson. Color. Half–hour. Premiered on CBS: May 21, 1980.*

Voices:

Carlton: Lorenzo Music, **Charles Shaftman:** Jack Somack, **Mrs. Shaftman:** Lucille Meredith, **Carlton's Mother:** Lurene Tuttle, **Darlene:** Kay Cole, **Mr. Gleason/Fat Man:** Paul Lichtman, **Dog Catcher:** Alan Barzman, **Parrot:** Bob Arbogast, **Pop:** Charles Woolf, **D. J.:** Roy West

CARNIVAL OF ANIMALS

Chuck Jones wrote, produced and animated this half–hour special based on the music of Camille Saint–Saens and the poetry of Ogden Nash, starring a variety of animals—lions, roosters, elephants and others—and Warner cartoon stars Bugs Bunny, Daffy Duck and Porky Pig. One major highlight: Bugs and Daffy, resplendent in black ties and tails, playing twin concert pianos along with a live orchestra conducted by Michael Tilson Thomas. *A Chuck Jones Enterprises Production in association with Warner Brothers Television. Color.*

Half–hour. Premiered on CBS: November 22, 1976. Rebroadcast on CBS: July 12, 1979.

Voices:
Bugs Bunny/Daffy Duck/Porky Pig: Mel Blanc

CARTOON ALL–STARS TO THE RESCUE

More than 20 animated characters from Saturday–morning cartoon shows band together to help a 14–year–old (Michael) lick his addiction to drugs in this half–hour special shown on all three networks, some 200 independent stations, and numerous cable services. The characters come to his rescue after his sister (Corey) discovers that he has stolen her piggy bank to support his habit. George C. Scott is the voice of an evil spirit, Smoke, who continually tempts the teenager into using drugs. The all–star cartoon cast included the Chipmunks; Bugs Bunny; Daffy Duck; Garfield; Winnie the Pooh; Huey, Dewey and Louie; Baby Kermit; Baby Piggy; Slimer; Brainy Smurf; Papa Smurf; and others.

Roy E. Disney served as the program's executive producer, with Buzz Potamkin producing. The special was produced in cooperation with the license holders of the program's cartoon stars: Alien Productions, Bagdasarian Productions, Columbia Pictures Television, DIC Enterprises, Film Roman, Hanna–Barbera Productions, Henson Associates, Marvel Productions, Murakami–Wolf–Swenson Films, Southern Star Productions, The Walt Disney Company and Warner Brothers.

The anti–drug special produced a record–high 22.0 rating (more than 30 million viewers), the highest rating ever for a Saturday–morning children's program. The program's theme song: "Wonderful Ways to 'Say No.'" *An Academy of Television Arts and Sciences Foundation Production. Color. Half–hour. Premiered: April 21, 1990.*

Voices:
Michael: Jason Marsden, **Corey:** Lindsey Parker, **Mom:** Laurie O'Brien, **Dad:** Townsend Coleman, **Alf:** Paul Fusco, **Bugs Bunny:** Jeff Bergman, **Daffy Duck:** Jeff Bergman, **The Chipmunks: Alvin:** Ross Bagdasarian, **Theodore:** Janice Karman, **Simon:** Ross Bagdasarian, **Papa Smurf:** Don Messick, **Brainy Smurf:** Danny Goldman, **Smurfette:** Julie Dees, **Garfield:** Lorenzo Music, **Huey:** Russi Taylor, **Dewey:** Russi Taylor, **Louie:** Russie Taylor, **Winnie the Pooh:** Jim Cummings, **Tigger:** Jim Cummings, **Slimer:** Frank Welker, **Michaelangelo:** Townsend Coleman, **Baby Kermit:** Frank Welker, **Baby Piggy:** Laurie O'Brien, **Baby Gonzo:** Russi Taylor, **Smoke:** George C. Scott

Additional Voices:
Wayne Collins, Joey Dedio, George Irene, Aaron Lohr

CASPER'S FIRST CHRISTMAS

Casper and his big wacky ghost friend, Hairy Scary, face their last winter in a battered old house. Hairy becomes upset when a joyful group of characters—Yogi Bear, Boo Boo, Snagglepuss and others—get lost and decide to make Christmas Eve merry by visiting Casper. Hairy tries to scare their Christmas spirits

away until a touching gesture changes his heart. *A Hanna–Barbera Production. Color. Half–hour. Premiered on NBC: December 18, 1979. Rebroadcast on NBC: December 5, 1980; December 14, 1981; Disney Channel: December 12, 1990.*

Voices:
Casper: Julie McWhirter, **Hairy Scary:** John Stephenson, **Augie Doggie/Doggie Daddy:** John Stephenson, **Huckleberry Hound:** John Stephenson, **Snagglepuss/Quick Draw McGraw:** John Stephenson, **Yogi Bear:** John Stephenson, **Boo Boo:** Don Messick, **Santa Claus:** Hal Smith

CASPER'S HALLOWEEN SPECIAL

It's Halloween night and Casper, the friendly ghost, decides to dress up and go out trick–or–treating like the rest of the children. Hairy Scary tries spoiling the fun by playing a few pranks and goes beyond the limits of good fun when he disappoints a group of orphan children. The special's story title was "He Ain't Scary, He's Our Brother." *A Hanna–Barbera Production. Color. Half–hour. Premiered on NBC: October 30, 1979. Rebroadcast on NBC: November 1, 1981.*

Voices:
Casper: Julie McWhirter, **Hairy Scary:** John Stephenson, **Mr. Duncan/Skull:** Hal Smith, **J. R.:** Diane McCannon, **Winifred the Witch:** Marilyn Schreffler, **Black Cat:** Frank Welker, **Butler/Rural Man:** John Stephenson, **Nice Man/Dog:** Frank Welker, **Lovella:** Ginny Tyler, **Bejewelled Dowager/Rural Lady:** Ginny Tyler, **Gervais/Carmelita/Nice Lady:** Lucille Bliss, **Screech:** Michael Sheehan, **Dirk:** Greg Alter

CASTLE

This public–television special, based on the book by David Macaulay (also one of the principal voice artists), follows the construction of a 13th–century Welsh Castle while examining life in medieval England, combining live–action and animation. *A Unicorn Projects Production. Color. One hour. Premiered on PBS: October 5, 1983.*

Voices:
Sarah Bullen, David Macaulay

CATHY

Comic–strip heroine Cathy Andrews searches for happiness in this half–hour animated special based on creator Cathy Guisewite's nationally syndicated strip. The story comically plays the upswing in Cathy's career (a nomination for her company's "Employee of the Year") against the downswing in her personal life (her long-time boyfriend is seeing another woman). Seeing red, Cathy reluctantly renews her quest for Mr. Right, prodded by her chum Andrea. *A Lee Mendelson–Bill Melendez Production in association with Universal Press Syndicate and Bill Melendez Productions. Color. Half–hour. Premiered on CBS: May 15, 1987. Rebroadcast on CBS: January 5, 1988.*

Voices:
Cathy: Kathleen Wilhoite, **Irving:** Robert F. Paulsen, **Andrea:** Allison Argo, **Anne,** Cathy's mother: Shirley Mitchell, **Bill,** Cathy's father: William L. Guisewite, **Charlene:** Emily Levine, **Mr. Pinkley:** Gregg Berger, **Brenda:** Desiree Goyette, **M. C.:** Robert Towers

CATHY'S LAST RESORT

Career woman Cathy finds herself on a romantic island vacation with Charlene, the receptionist, and hoards of yuppie parents with babies in tow. Managing to meet a nice single guy, she must contend with the sudden appearance of her ever–undependable, workaholic boyfriend, Irving, who, at the last minute, had backed out of the trip. Program was written and illustrated by "Cathy" creator/cartoonist Cathy Guisewite. *A Lee Mendelson–Bill Melendez Production in association with Universal Press Syndicate. Color. Half–hour. Premiered on CBS: November 11, 1988.*

Voices:
Cathy: Kathleen Wilhoite, **Irving:** Robert F. Paulsen, **Anne,** Cathy's mother: Shirley Mitchell, **Bill,** Cathy's father: William L. Guisewite, **Andrea:** Allison Argo, **Mr. Pinkley:** Gregg Berger, **Charlene:** Emily Levine

Additional Voices:
Frank Welker, Heather Kerr, Jamie Neal

CATHY'S VALENTINE

Comic–strip heroine Cathy and her boyfriend Irving try rekindling their romance before Valentine's Day, with Cathy going all out to impress her beau by getting a makeover and buying a new dress even though her mother believes "romance has nothing to do with what you wear, it's what you have in your cupboard." *A Lee Mendelson–Bill Melendez Production in association with Universal Press Synicate. Color. Half-hour. Premiered on CBS: February 10, 1989.*

Voices:
Cathy: Kathleen Wilhoite, **Irving:** Robert F. Paulsen, **Anne,** Cathy's mother: Shirley Mitchell, **Bill,** Cathy's father: William L. Guisewite, **Andrea:** Allison Argo, **Mr. Pinkley:** Gregg Berger, **Charlene:** Emily Levine

Additional Voices:
Jerry Houser, Loren Dunsworth, Susan Silo, Sheryl Bernstein, Jamie Smith

A CHARLIE BROWN CELEBRATION

This one–hour animated special consists of several different stories of various lengths derived from the best comic strips ever done by "Peanuts" creator/cartoonist Charles Schulz. Segments include Charlie Brown's ill–fated attempt at kite flying, Peppermint Patty going to Dog Obedience School, and Lucy and Schroeder at the piano discussing marriage. Charles Schulz hosts the program, which was originally to be called "The Best of Charlie Brown." *A Lee Mendelson–Bill Melendez Production in association with Charles M. Schulz Creative Associates and United Features Syndicate. Color. Half–hour. Premiered on CBS: May 24, 1982. Rebroadcast on CBS: February 18, 1984.*

Voices:
Charlie Brown: Michael Mandy, **Lucy Van Pelt:** Kristen Fullerton, **Linus Van Pelt:** Earl "Rocky" Reilly, **Sally Brown:** Cindi Reilly, **Schroeder:** Christopher Donohoe, **Peppermint Patty:** Brent Hauer, **Polly/Truffles:** Casey Carlson, **Marcie:** Shannon Cohn, **Snoopy:** Bill Melendez, **Announcer:** John Hiestand

A CHARLIE BROWN CHRISTMAS

It may be Christmas but Charlie Brown is depressed. Acting as his psychiatrist, Lucy suggests that he get involved with the holiday festivities by directing their Christmas play. To set the proper mood, he is sent out to find the "perfect" Christmas tree to decorate the stage. In the process, he searches through hundreds of shiny aluminum trees, tinsel and blinking lights for the "real" unornamented meaning of yuletide. According to executive producer Lee Mendelson, the show, which was the first of the "Peanuts" specials, was the first half–hour prime–time cartoon without a laugh track and the first to have kids—not adults—do the voices. The program was bestowed both Emmy and Peabody awards for program excellence *A Lee Mendelson–Bill Melendez Production in association with Charles M. Schulz Creative Associates and United Feature Syndicate. Color. Half–hour. Premiered on CBS: December 9, 1965. Rebroadcast on CBS: December 11, 1966; December 10, 1967; December 8, 1968; December 7, 1969; December 5, 1970; December 7, 1971; December 12, 1972; December 6, 1973; December 17, 1974; December 15, 1975; December 18, 1976; December 12, 1977; December 18, 1978; December 10, 1979; December 9, 1980; December 10, 1981; December 16, 1982; December 12, 1983; December 5, 1984; December 4, 1985; December 12, 1986; December 11, 1987; December 14, 1988; December 22, 1989.*

Voices:
Charlie Brown: Peter Robbins, **Lucy Van Pelt:** Tracy Stratford, **Linus Van Pelt:** Christopher Shea, **Schroeder:** Chris Doran, **Peppermint Patty:** Karen Mendelson, **Sally Brown:** Cathy Steinberg, **Freida:** Ann Altieri, **Pigpen/Shermy:** Chris Doran, **Violet:** Sally Dryer–Barker

CHARLIE BROWN'S ALL STARS

His team having just lost their 999th game in a row, Charlie Brown reaches new depths of depression until a glimmer of hope arrives. He gets an offer to have his team sponsored—to be in a real league with real uniforms. Unfortunately, he later learns that his sandlot crew can't play in the real league because his players include a dog and several girls. *A Lee Mendelson–Bill Melendez Production in association with Charles M. Schulz Creative Associates and United Feature Syndicate. Color. Half–hour. Premiered on CBS: June 6, 1966.*

Charlie Brown takes a header in more ways than one as he leads the "Peanuts" gang to their 999th straight loss in "Charlie Brown's All–Stars," a half–hour special based on Charles Schulz's beloved comic strip. © United Feature Syndicate (Courtesy: CBS)

Rebroadcast on CBS: April 10, 1967; April 6, 1968; April 13, 1969; April 12, 1970; April 3, 1982.

Voices:

Charlie Brown: Peter Robbins, **Linus Van Pelt:** Christopher Shea, **Lucy Van Pelt:** Sally Dryer-Barker, **Schroeder:** Glenn Mendelson, **Sally Brown:** Cathy Steinberg, **Peppermint Patty:** Lynn Vanderlip, **Frieda:** Ann Altieri, **Pigpen:** Jeff Ornstein, **Violet:** Karen Mendelson, **Shermy/Umpire:** Kip DeFaria

A CHARLIE BROWN THANKSGIVING

Before going to his grandmother's condominium for a traditional turkey dinner, Charlie Brown celebrates America's oldest holiday in a rather unorthodox fashion with the rest of the "Peanuts" gang. With his little stand–by, Linus, and the slightly questionable help of Snoopy and Woodstock, Charlie devises the most unusual Thanksgiving menu (potato chips, popcorn, jelly beans, buttered toast and ice cream) since 1621, served, traditionally enough, around a ping–pong table in Charlie's backyard. *A Lee Mendelson–Bill Melendez Production in association with Charles M. Schulz Creative Associates and United Feature Syndicate. Color. Half–hour. Premiered on CBS: November 20, 1973. Rebroadcast on CBS: November 21, 1974; November 22, 1975; November 22, 1976; November 21, 1977; November 15, 1978; November 19, 1979; November 25, 1980; November 23, 1981; November 20, 1984; November 26, 1985; November 25, 1986; November 24, 1987; November 23, 1989.*

Voices:

Charlie Brown: Todd Barbee, **Linus Van Pelt:** Stephen Shea, **Lucy Van Pelt:** Robin Kohn, **Peppermint Patty:** Kip DeFaria, **Sally Brown:** Hilary Momberger, **Marcie:** Jimmy Ahrens, **Franklin:** Robin Reed, **Snoopy:** Bill Melendez

THE CHARMKINS

The Charmkins find themselves in the throes of danger when their friend Lady Slipper, a talented dancer, is abducted by Dragonweed and his band of henchmen, Briar Patch, Thorny, Skunkweed and the Bramble Brothers. Dragonweed captures the pretty creature after he becomes enamored of her dancing. (He wants her to dance for him and nobody else.) The Charmkins develop a rescue plan and return Lady Slipper back to Charm World unharmed. *A Sunbow Productions in association with Marvel Productions. Color. Half–hour. Premiered: June, 1983. Syndicated.*

Voices:

Dragonweed: Ben Vereen, **Brown–Eyed Susan:** Aileen Quinn, **Poison Ivy:** Sally Struthers, **Skunkweed:** Ivy Austin, **Willie Winkle:** Martin Biersbach, **Lady Slipper:** Lynne Lambert, **Bramble Brother #1:** Chris Murney, **Bramble Brother #2:** Bob Kaliban, **Briarpatch/Crocus:** Chris Murney, **Thorny:** Gary Yudman, **Popcorn:** Peter Waldren, **Blossom:** Freddi Webber, **Announcer:** Patience Jarvis, Tina Capland, **Vocalists:** Helen Leonhart, Jamie Murphy, Helen Miles

A CHIPMUNK CHRISTMAS

The Chipmunks (Alvin, Theodore and Simon) show their Christmas spirit by giving a gravely ill boy (Tommy Waterford) Alvin's prized harmonica to perform at Carnegie Hall on Christmas Eve. *A Bagdasarian Production. Color. Half–hour. Premiered on NBC: December 14, 1981. Rebroadcast on NBC: December 13, 1982; December 9, 1983; December 5, 1986; December 16, 1988.*

Voices:

Alvin/Simon/David Seville: Ross Bagdasarian Jr., **Theodore:** Janice Karman

A CHIPMUNK REUNION

After discovering that they were adopted at birth, Alvin, Theodore and Simon embark on their personal journey to uncover their real mother. David Seville and the Chipettes— Brittany, Jeanette and Elenore—form a search party and go after the Chipmunks to resolve the situation before it gets too far out of hand. *A Bagdasarian Production in association with Ruby–Spears Productions. Color. Half–hour. Premiered on NBC: April 13, 1985. Rebroadcast on NBC: December 22, 1985.*

Voices:

Alvin/Simon/David: Ross Bagdasarian Jr., **Theodore/Brittany/Jeanette/Elenore:** Janice Karman, **Vinnie:** June Foray

A CHRISTMAS CAROL (1970)

The spirit of Christmas is explored in this hour–long adaptation of Charles Dickens' classic tale of the money–grubbing businessman Ebenezer Scrooge, who is visited by several ghostly beings that make him understand the importance of giving. Program aired opposite ABC's premiere of the Rankin–

Bass special, "Santa Claus Is Coming To Town." A "Famous Classic Tales" special. *An Air Programs International Production. Color. One hour. Premiered on CBS: December 13, 1970. Rebroadcast on CBS: December 12, 1971; December 10, 1972; December 8, 1973; December 14, 1974; December 13, 1975; December 18, 1976; December 10, 1977; November 26, 1978; November 25, 1979; November 28, 1980; December 6, 1981; November 28, 1982; December 4, 1983.*

Voices:
C. Duncan, Ron Haddrick, John Llewellyn, T. Mangan, Bruce Montague, Brenda Senders, T. Kaff (vocalist), C. Bowden (vocalist)

A CHRISTMAS CAROL (1971)

Actor Alistair Sim, who portrayed the character of Scrooge in a 1951 live–action feature, recreates the role in this half–hour special that tells the story of one man's greed versus the true meaning of Christmas. *A Richard Williams Production. Color. Half–hour. Premiered on ABC: December 21, 1971. Rebroadcast on ABC: December 15, 1972; December 14, 1973; December 7, 1974.*

Voices:
Ebenezer Scrooge: Alistair Sim, **Bob Cratchit:** Melvin Hayes, **Mrs. Cratchit:** Joan Sims, **Tiny Tim:** Alexander Williams, **Marley's Ghost:** Sir Michael Hordern, **Ragpicker/Fezziwig:** Paul Whitsun–Jones, **Scrooge's nephew/Charity Man:** David Tate, **Ghost of Christmas Past:** Diana Quick, **Ghost of Christmas Present:** Felix Felton, **Ghost of Christmas Yet to Come:** Annie West, **Mrs. Dilber:** Mary Ellen Ray, **Narrator:** Sir Michael Redgrave

A CHRISTMAS CAROL (1984)

Unlike previous versions, this syndicated special, based on the Charles Dickens story, was 90 minutes in length, faithfully recreating the famed children's classic for another generation of television viewers. *A Burbank Films Production. Color. One hour and a half. Premiered: November, 1984. Syndicated.*

Voices:
Ron Haddrick, Philip Hinton, Sean Hinton, Barbara Frawley, Robin Stewart, Liz Horne, Bill Conn, Derani Scarr, Anne Hardy

CHRISTMAS COMES TO PAC–LAND

While making his familiar trek across the skies on Christmas Eve, Santa Claus develops sleigh trouble and crash lands in Pac–Land. The Pac family comes across Santa and, along with policemen Morris and O'Pac, they pool their resources to repair the sleigh and get Santa and his reindeer back on course. *A Hanna–Barbera Production. Color. Half–hour. Premiered on ABC: December 16, 1982. Rebroadcast on ABC: December 8, 1983.*

Voices:
Pac–Man: Marty Ingels, **Mrs. Pac:** Barbara Minkus, **Pac–Baby:** Russi Taylor, **Chomp Chomp:** Frank Welker, **Sour Puss/Santa:** Peter Cullen, **Morris/Reindeer:** Frank Welker, **O'Pac:** Chuck McCann, **Blinky and Pinky Monsters:** Chuck McCann, **Sue Monster:** Susan Silo, **Clyde Monster:** Neilson Ross, **Inky Monster:** Barry Gordon

CHRISTMAS EVERY DAY

Based on a short story by William Dean Howells, this first–run special tells the story of a young girl (Lucy) who wishes that Christmas lasted forever. Her father relates a story, told in flashback, of another girl who made the same wish but lived to regret it. This half–hour special was produced for CBS–owned and –operated stations in Chicago, New York, Los Angeles and Philadelphia and syndicated to stations throughout the country. *A CBS Television Production in association with Orkin–Flaum Productions and Calabash Productions. Color. Half–hour. Premiered: December 20, 1986. Syndicated.*

Voices:
Tilly/Cissy: Stacy Q. Michaels, **Ned/Butcher/Policemen:** Brian Cummings, **Helen/Franny/Will:** Miriam Flynn, **Christmas Fairy:** Edie McClurg, **Grace/Lucy:** Marla Frumkin, **George/Pete:** Dick Orkin

CHRISTMAS IS

The religious meaning of Christmas is witnessed through the eyes of a young boy (Benji) and his shaggy dog (Waldo) who are sent back to the scene of the Nativity, where Christ is born. The characters appeared in three additional specials, each with a religious theme, which were underwritten by the International Lutheran Layman's League. *A Screen Images Production for Lutheran Television. Color. Half–hour. Premiered: November 7, 1970. Syndicated.*

Voices:
Benji: Richard Susceno, **Innkeeper:** Hans Conried, **Waldo/Joseph:** Don Messick, **Mary:** Colleen Collins

Additional Voices:
June Foray, Jerry Hausner, Vic Perrin

CHRISTMAS LOST AND FOUND

Young Davey Hanson, star of the stop–motion animation series "Davey and Goliath," conveys the Christian meaning of the yuletide season in this holiday special—one of six specials sponsored by the Lutheran Church of America—as he helps a discouraged young boy find happiness by letting him play the part of a king, a role originally intended for Davey, in an upcoming Christmas pageant. "Gumby" creator Art Clokey produced the special. *A Clokey Production for the Lutheran Church of America. Color. Half–hour. Premiered: 1965. Syndicated.*

Voices:
Davey Hanson/Sally Hanson/Mary Hanson: Norma Mc-
Millan, Nancy Wible, **Goliath/John Hanson:** Hal Smith

THE CHRISTMAS MESSENGER

The true message of Christmas is realized when a young boy
joins a group of Christmas carollers, encouraged by a friendly
stranger whose real identity is revealed only to enhance their
appreciation of the holiday season. Richard Chamberlain narrated the special. *A Shostak and Schwartz/Gerald Potterton
Production in association with Reader's Digest. Color. Half-
hour. Premiered: 1975. Syndicated.*

Voices:
Narrator: Richard Chamberlain

THE CHRISTMAS RACCOONS

It is two days before Christmas and Cyril Sneer, in his desire
to harvest all the trees in the Evergreen Forest, cuts down
the "Raccoondominium" of Ralph, Melissa and Bert. With the
help of Schaeffer, the Raccoons set out to thwart Cyril's plans
and save the forest. Based on the characters of the Canadian-
produced series, "The Raccoons." *A Gillis–Wiseman Production in association with Atkinson Film–Arts. Color. Half-
hour. Premiered: December, 1980. Syndicated.*

Voices:
Dan: Rupert Holmes, **Julie:** Tammy Bourne, **Tommy:** Hadley
Kay, **Schaeffer:** Carl Banas, **Ralph:** Bobby Dermer, **Melissa:**
Rita Coolidge, **Bert:** Len Carlson, **Cyril Sneer:** Michael Magee,
Cedric Sneer: Fred Little, **Narrator:** Rich Little, **Vocalists:**
Rita Coolidge, Rupert Holmes

A CHRISTMAS STORY

With the arrival of Christmas not too far away, Timmy, a
bright little boy, decides to make a special request of Santa
this year. He sits down and writes his idea in the form of a
letter, which he believes has been mailed but instead gets
misplaced. Pals Goober the dog and Gumdrop the mouse
discover the letter and set out to deliver it to Santa so Timmy's
wish comes true at Christmas. *A Hanna–Barbera Production.
Color. Half–hour. Premiered: December, 1972. Syndicated.*

Voices:
Mother/Girl: Janet Waldo, **Timmy/Boy:** Walter Tetley, **Dad/
Squirrel:** Don Messick, **Goober/Sleezer/Runto:** Paul Win-
chell, **Gumdrop/Second Dog:** Daws Butler, **Santa/Fatcat:**
Hal Smith, **Polecat/Postman/First Dog:** John Stephenson,
Vocalists: Paul DeKorte, Randy Kemner, Stephen McAndrew,
Susie McCune, Judi Richards

A CHRISTMAS TREE

Charles Dickens himself, in animated form, takes two children,
Peter and Mary, on the adventure of their lives as they relive
tales of the Christmases of his youth, including the story of a

magical Christmas tree that grows as high as the sky. The
program was adapted from six Christmas–themed stories by
Dickens and was produced as part of the syndicated "Festival
of Family Classics" series. *A Rankin–Bass Production in
association with Mushi Studios. Color. Half–hour. Premiered: December 17, 1972. Syndicated.*

Voices:

Carl Banas, Len Birman, Bernard Cowan, Peg Dixon, Keith
Hampshire, Peggi Loder, Donna Miller, Frank Perry, Henry
Raymer, Billie Mae Richards, Alfi Scopp, Paul Soles

THE CHRISTMAS TREE TRAIN

Buttons, a young cub bear, and Rusty, a young fox, are
accidentally transported by train, known as "The Christmas
Tree Train," along with evergreens cut by lumberjacks to the
big city. Buttons' and Rusty's parents, Rosey and George Fox,
and Bridget and Abner Bear seek help from "Jonesy," the
Ranger of the forest, in finding them. The half–hour program
was one in a series of "Buttons and Rusty" specials for first–
run syndication. *An Encore Enterprises Production. Color.
Half–hour. Premiered: December, 1983. Syndicated.*

Voices:
Rusty/Rosie: Kathy Ritter, **Buttons:** Barbara Goodson, **Ranger
Jones:** Billy Boyett, **Abner/Santa Claus:** Alvy Moore, **George:**
Billy Ratner, **Bridgett:** Morgan Lofting

A CHUCKLEWOOD EASTER

As Easter approaches, Buttons and Rusty are busy practicing
their egg–decorating skills, using eggs innocently borrowed
from various nests in the park without their owners' knowledge. Panic breaks out when several animals discover the eggs
missing, and, in the meantime, Rusty and Buttons are put on
trial for invading the secret home of the Easter Bunny. *An
Encore Enterprises Production. Color. Half–hour. Premiered:
April, 1987. Syndicated.*

Voices:
Rusty/Bluebell: Mona Marshall, **Buttons:** Barbara Goodson,
Abner: Alvy Moore, **George/Easter Bunny:** Robert Axelrod,
Bridgett: Oceana Mars, **Skipper:** Dan Roth, **Ranger Jones:**
Bill Boyett

CINDERELLA

This clever spoof of the classic children's tale tells the story
of misfit Cinderella, transformed into a radiant beauty by her
fairy godmother, but something is amiss as the characters are
not as perfect as they seem. Cinderella's fairy godmother is
absent–minded and Prince Charming is a bumbling fool, yet
somehow everything comes out right as Cinderella and Prince
Charming get married after all in this first–run special for
television. A "Festival of Family Classics" special. *A Rankin–
Bass Production. Color. Half–hour. Premiered: September
17, 1972. Syndicated.*

Cinderella dances with handsome Prince Charming in a scene from the Rankin–Bass special, "Cinderella." Rankin–Bass Productions (Courtesy: Viacom International)

Voices:
Carl Banas, Len Birman, Bernard Coward, Peg Dixon, Keith Hampshire, Peggi Loder, Donna Miller, Frank Perry, Henry Raymer, Billie Mae Richards, Alfie Scopp, Paul Soles

A CITY THAT FORGOT ABOUT CHRISTMAS

Following his impatience over the long wait for Christmas, Benji's grandfather relates to him, his friend Martin and Benji's dog, Waldo, the story of a visitor (Matthew) who changed the lives of the townspeople in preparation for the coming of Jesus on Christmas Eve. *A Screen Images Production for Lutheran Television. Color. Half–hour. Premiered: December, 1974. Syndicated.*

Voices:
Benji's grandfather: Sebastian Cabot, **Benji:** David Kelly, **Matthew,** the wood carver: Sebastian Cabot, **Wicked Mayor:** Charles Nelson Reilly, **Henchman:** Louis Nye, **Waldo,** Benji's dog: Don Messick

Additional Voices:
June Foray, Vic Perrin

A CLAYMATION CHRISTMAS CELEBRATION

The California Raisins join a host of other animated clay figures in song–and–dance renditions of traditional Christmas carols. Included are a trio of shuffling camels in "We Three Kings" and a "claymated" Quasimodo conducting "Carol of the Bells." *A Will Vinton Production. Color. Half–hour. Premiered on*

CBS: December 21, 1987. Rebroadcast on CBS: December 23, 1988; December 21, 1989.

CLEROW WILSON AND THE MIRACLE OF P. S. 14

Recreating characters introduced on his NBC series, "The Flip Wilson Show," comedian Flip Wilson, as the voice of his nine–year–old self Clerow Wilson (his rightful name), recalls the struggle of his early childhood at the New Jersey school he attended, combining warmth and humor, in this prime–time network special, one of two based on Wilson's childhood adventures. *A DePatie–Freleng Enterprises Production in association with Clerow Productions and NBC. Color. Half–hour. Premiered on NBC: November 12, 1972. Rebroadcast on NBC: November 19, 1973.*

Voices:
Clerow/Geraldine Jones/Herbie/Reverend LeRoy/The Devil: Flip Wilson, **Freddie:** Richard Wyatt Jr., **Miss Davis:** Vivian Bonnett, **Li'l David:** Kenney Ball, **Robert Jackson:** Phillip Brown, **Dickie Porter:** Larry Oliver

CLEROW WILSON'S GREAT ESCAPE

Comedian Flip Wilson plays many of his favorite characters—Geraldine Jones, Freddie the playboy, Ralph the invisible dog, Li'l David, Reverend Leroy and others—in this animated story, adapted from his own personal experiences as a small boy who is adopted into a mean family and attempts to escape. *A DePatie–Freleng Enterprises Production in association with Clerow Productions and NBC. Color. Half–hour. Premiered on NBC: April 3, 1974. Rebroadcast on NBC: December 16, 1974.*

Voices:
Clerow Wilson/Geraldine Jones/Ralph/Reverend LeRoy/Herbie/The Devil: Flip Wilson

COMPUTERS ARE PEOPLE, TOO!

The technology of computer animation is demonstrated through a variety of film clips, showing the marvels of computer–generated images, told by talking computers and hosted by Elaine Joyce, who takes viewers through this world of visual entertainment. *A Walt Disney Television Production. Color. One hour. Premiered: May 22, 1982. Syndicated.*

Voices:
Billy Bowles, Joe Campanella, Nancy Kulp

THE CONEHEADS

That unusual alien family from the planet Remulak, first seen in a series of comedy sketches on NBC's "Saturday Night Live," continue their mission to rebuild their space fleet, using humans as their slaves. Based on characters created by Dan

Aykroyd, Tom Davis and Lorne Michaels. *A Rankin–Bass Production in association with Broadway Video. Color. Half–hour. Premiered on NBC: October 14, 1983.*

Voices:
Beldar: Dan Aykroyd, **Prymaat:** Jane Curtin, **Connie:** Laraine Newman

Additional Voices:
Cynthia Adler, Tom Davis, Robert McFadden

A CONNECTICUT RABBIT IN KING ARTHUR'S COURT

Bugs Bunny plays a wise–guy Connecticut wabbit as Daffy Duck (King Arthur), Porky Pig (a varlat), Elmer Fudd (Sir Elmer Fudd) and Yosemite Sam join the fun in this loosely based adaptation of the Mark Twain classic, "plagiarized" by Chuck Jones, who produced this all–new special for CBS. The program was later retitled, "Bugs Bunny in King Arthur's Court." *A Chuck Jones Enterprises Production for Warner Brothers Television. Color. Half–hour. Premiered on CBS: February 23, 1978. Rebroadcast on CBS: November 22, 1978; (as "Bugs Bunny in King Arthur's Court") November 17, 1979; August 19, 1981; March 10, 1982.*

Voices:
Mel Blanc

A CONNECTICUT YANKEE IN KING ARTHUR'S COURT

Through clever thinking and the use of modern inventions, the inventive Connecticut Yankee encounters the likes of Merlin the Magician and King Arthur's knights in a series of medieval battles in this made–for–television daytime special under the "Famous Classic Tales" banner. *An Air Programs International Production. Color. Half–hour. Premiered on CBS: November 26, 1970. Rebroadcast on CBS: November 25, 1971; November 23, 1972 (in New York on WPIX).*

Voices:
Connecticut Yankee: Orson Bean

Additional Voices:
Ron Haddrick, Barbara Llewellyn, John Llewellyn, L. Ostrich, Brenda Senders

A COSMIC CHRISTMAS

Three creatures from outer space and their pet mascot journey to Earth on their mission to discover the bright star, the Star of Bethlehem, and find the true meaning of Christmas. *A Nelvana Limited Production in association with the CBC. Color. Half–hour. Premiered: December 6, 1977. Syndicated.*

Voices:
Peter: Joey Davidson, **Dad/Plutox/Santa Joe:** Martin Lavut, **Lexicon:** Richard Davidson, **Amalthor:** Duncan Regehr, **Mom:** Patricia Moffat, **Grandma:** Jane Mallett, **Police Chief Snerk:**

Marvin Goldhar, **Marvin:** Greg Rogers, **The Mayor:** Chris Wiggins, **Townies:** Nick Nichols, Marion Waldman

THE COUNT OF MONTE CRISTO

Edmond Dantes, a young sailor, escapes from prison 15 years after his imprisonment and, after assuming the identity of his dead companion, sets sail to the Isle of Monte Cristo where he uncovers fabulous treasure and acquires a new persona, the Count of Monte Cristo, and wages war on his enemies. *A Hanna–Barbera Production. Color. One hour. Premiered on CBS: September 23, 1973. Rebroadcast on CBS: December 7, 1974.*

Voices:
Elizabeth Crosby, Tim Elliott, Barbara Frawley, Ron Haddrick, Richard Meike

THE CRICKET IN TIMES SQUARE

Adapted from the 1960 book by George Selden, a liverwurst–loving cricket named Chester C. Cricket is transported in a picnic basket from a field in Connecticut to the Times Square subway. There, the genteel Chester is befriended by Tucker Mouse, Harry the Cat and Mario the Newsboy, whose parents' newsstand is suffering from severe lack of sales. When Tucker and Harry discover that Chester has the uncanny gift of being able to reproduce any music he hears, they convince him to perform during rush hour to attract business to the newsstand. The special was the recipient of the Parent's Choice Award for excellence in television programming. *A Chuck Jones Enterprises Projection. Color. Half–hour. Premiered on ABC: April 24, 1973. Rebroadcast on ABC: January 30, 1974; November 9, 1974.*

Voices:
Chester C. Cricket: Les Tremayne, **Harry the Cat:** Les Tremayne, **Tucker the Mouse:** Mel Blanc, **Mario Bellini:** Kerry MacLane, **Mario's Father:** Les Tremayne, **Mario's Mother:** June Foray, **Music Teacher:** Les Tremayne

THE CRICKET ON THE HEARTH

Cricket Crockett is no ordinary cricket. He has a heart and soul and becomes the saving grace of poor toymaker Caleb Plummer and his troubled daughter, Bertha, who make him a permanent member of their family at Christmas, in this musical adaptation of the Charles Dickens fantasy. The one–hour special starred Danny Thomas and was broadcast during his weekly network series, "The Danny Thomas Hour." Daughter Marlo Thomas co–starred and joined Thomas in several musical numbers, their first such feat on film together. *A Rankin–Bass Production in association with Videocraft International. Color. One hour. Premiered on NBC: December 18, 1967 (on "The Danny Thomas Hour"). Rebroadcast on NBC: November 25, 1971.*

Voices:
Cricket Crockett: Roddy McDowell, **Caleb Plummer:** Danny Thomas, **Bertha:** Marlo Thomas, **Edward:** Ed Ames, **Tackle-**

ton: Hans Conried, **Moll:** Abbe Lane, **Uriah/Sea Captain:** Paul Frees

CURIOUS GEORGE

Named for his natural inquisitiveness, this little monkey and his big city friend, the Man in the Yellow Hat, encounter numerous misadventures in this half–hour special comprised of several four–minute cartoons from the "Curious George" cartoon series broadcast on Canadian television. *A Lafferty, Harwood and Partners Production in association with Milktrain Productions. Color. Half–hour. Premiered: 1983. Syndicated.*

Voices:
Narrator: Jack Duffy

CYRANO

French folk-hero Cyrano de Bergerac conquers injustice in his quest to help his beautiful friend, Roxanne, in this adaptation of Edmond Rostand's romantic play. The special was first broadcast as an "ABC Afterschool Special." *A Hanna–Barbera Production. Color. Half–hour. Premiered on ABC: March 6, 1974. Rebroadcast on ABC: April 9, 1975.*

Voices:
Cyrano de Bergerac: Jose Ferrer, **Roxanne:** Joan Van Ark, **Ragueneau:** Kurt Kasznar, **Comte de Guiche:** Martyn Green, **Christian de Neuvillette:** Victor Gerber, **Duenna:** Jane Connell, **First Cadet/de Brigny:** Alan Oppenheimer, **Richelieu:** John Stephenson

DAFFY DUCK AND PORKY PIG MEET THE GROOVIE GOOLIES

Warner Brothers cartoon stars Daffy Duck and Porky Pig join forces with Horrible Hall's The Groovie Goolies in this comic tale of Phantom's efforts to sabotage the movie studio. The made–for–television cartoon premiered on "The ABC Saturday Superstar Movie." *A Filmation Studios Production in cooperation with Warner Brothers. Color. One hour. Premiered on ABC: December 16, 1972 (on "ABC Saturday Superstar Movie"). Rebroadcast on ABC: December 29, 1973.*

Voices:
Daffy Duck/Porky Pig: Mel Blanc, **The Groovie Goolies (Count Dracula/Hagatha/Frankie/Bella La Ghostly/Sabrina/Wolfie/Bonapart/Mummy/Dr. Jekyll–Hyde/Ghouliland/Hauntleroy/Ratso and Batso):** Jane Webb, Howard Morris, Larry Storch, Larry D. Mann

DAFFY DUCK'S EASTER SHOW

The malevolent mallard stars in three new cartoon adventures related to Easter—"Yolks On You," "The Chocolate Chase" and "Daffy Goes North"—in his first–ever prime–time special, which preceded NBC's Saturday–morning series "The Daffy and Speedy Show," which was introduced in the fall of 1981. *A DePatie–Freleng Enterprises Production for Warner Broth-*

ers Television. Color. Half–hour. Premiered on NBC: April 1, 1980. Rebroadcast on NBC: April 14, 1981; April 6, 1982; CBS: April 16, 1984; April 6, 1985.

Voices:
Mel Blanc

DAFFY DUCK'S THANKS–FOR–GIVING SPECIAL

In trying to convince the studio to buy his idea for a sequel to his classic film "Duck Dodgers In The 24½th Century," Daffy Duck shows the producer all of his great films of the past (interspersed with clips from his former theatrical film accomplishments). After the producer finally relents, the show concludes with a screening of "The Return Of Duck Dodgers In The 24½th Century," a 1977 cartoon Chuck Jones produced as a companion piece for the science–fiction thriller, *Star Wars. A Chuck Jones Enterprises Production for Warner Brothers Television. Color. Half–hour. Premiered on NBC: November 20, 1980. Rebroadcast on NBC: November 24, 1981; CBS: November 12, 1983; November 26, 1987.*

Voices: Mel Blanc

DANIEL BOONE

Daniel Boone tells his true life story, separating fact from fable, as he reflects upon his life and accomplishments for a writer eager to portray the real story in this daytime children's special produced under CBS' "Famous Classic Tales" program banner. *A Hanna–Barbera Production. Color. Half–hour. Premiered on CBS: November 27, 1981. Rebroadcast on CBS: November 25, 1982.*

Voices:
Daniel Boone: Richard Crenna, **Rebecca:** Janet Waldo, **Daniel Boone, age 14:** Bill Callaway, **Henry Miller:** Mike Bell, **Running Fox:** Bill Callaway, **First Settler/Mr. Harding:** Mike Bell, **Stearns/Assemblyman/Squire Boone:** John Stephenson, **Sarah/James/Quiet Dove:** Joan Gerber, **Washington/Col. Morgan/Second Settler:** Joe Baker, **White Top/Painter/Floor Leader:** Vic Perrin, **Blackfish/Business Man/Indian Dragging Canoe:** Barney Phillips, **Girty/Oconostata/Finley:** Michael Rye

DAVID COPPERFIELD

The story of David Copperfield, one of Charles Dickens' most beloved creations, is revealed in this 90–minute cable–television special that takes viewers through every stage of his life—his birth, his youth and his adulthood—and the many struggles he encounters along the way. *A Burbank Films Production. Color. One hour and a half. Premiered on HBO: October 2, 1984.*

Voices:
Ross Higgins, Phillip Hinton, Robyn Moore, Judy Nunn, Moya O'Sullivan, Robin Steward, John Stone

DAVY CROCKETT ON THE MISSISSIPPI

American frontiersman Davy Crockett and his talking pet bear, Honeysuckle, are joined by an orphaned boy, Matt Henry, as they journey to meet the Indians on behalf of the United States' president as part of a peace–keeping mission. *A Hanna–Barbera Production. Color. One hour. Premiered on CBS: November 20, 1976. Rebroadcast on CBS: October 22, 1977; November 2, 1980; November 26, 1982.*

Voices:

Davy Crockett: Ned Wilson, **Matt Henry:** Randy Gray, **Honeysuckle/Pete/The Settler:** Mike Bell, **Mike Fink/Flatboat Sailor:** Ron Feinberg, **Running Wolf/Jake:** Kip Niven, **Settler's Wife/Amanda/Susie:** Pat Parris, **Sloan/Andrew Jackson/Blacksmith:** John Stephenson

DECK THE HALLS WITH WACKY WALLS

Six Wallwalkers (Wacky, Big Blue, Springette, Stickum, Crazylegs and Bouncing Baby Boo) are sent to Earth from their distant planet to find what Christmas is all about in this half–hour animated special based on the Wacky Wallwalker toys. *A NBC Entertainment Production in association with Buzzco Productions. Color. Half–hour. Premiered on NBC: December 11, 1983.*

Voices:

Wacky: Daws Butler, **Big Blue:** Peter Cullen, **Spingette:** Tress MacNeille, **Stickum:** Marvin Kaplan, **Crazylegs:** Howard Morris, **Bouncing Baby Boo:** Frank Welker, **Darryl:** Scott Menville

Additional Voices:

Sharman Di Vono, Cheri Eichen, Bill Scott

DENNIS THE MENACE: MAYDAY FOR MOTHER

In his first prime–time special, neighborhood terror Dennis the Menace encounters a variety of problems to create a special gift for his mother, Alice Mitchell, for Mother's Day. As usual, he annoys everyone in the process, including next–door–neighbor Mr. Wilson. The special was based on an original story by creator Hank Ketcham. *A DePatie–Freleng Enterprises Production in association with Mirisch Films. Color. Half–hour. Premiered on NBC: May 8, 1981. Rebroadcast on NBC: May 6, 1983.*

Voices:

Dennis Mitchell: Joey Nagy, **Alice Mitchell:** Kathy Garver, **Henry Mitchell:** Bob Holt, **George Wilson:** Larry D. Mann, **Martha Wilson:** Elizabeth Kerr, **Margaret:** Nicole Eggert

Additional Voices:

James Hackett, Herbert Rudley, Seth Wagerman, Nancy Wible

THE DEVIL AND DANIEL MOUSE

Jan and Daniel Mouse, recently unemployed folk–singers, try making a fresh start of their careers, only for Jan to sign a contract with B. L. Zebub, the devil in disguise, to sell her soul to become a rock star legend. After hearing the news, Daniel makes a valiant attempt to save her from further temptation. *A Nelvana Limited Production in association with the CBC. Color. Half–hour. Premiered: October 22, 1978. Syndicated.*

Voices:

Daniel Mouse: Jim Henshaw, John Sebastian (singing), **Jan:** Annabelle Kershaw, Laurel Runn (singing), **B. L. Zebub, the devil:** Chris Wiggins, **Weez Weasel/Pawnbroker:** Martin Lavut, **Rock Emcee:** John Sebastian, **Interviewer:** Dianne Lawrence

DIG

Explaining the wonders of Earth, Adam and his dog Bones explore the geological structure of the planet during a fascinating journey in which they meet strange characters and encounter various phenomena. The special aired in place of CBS' "The Monkees," which was in re–runs on Saturday mornings. *A Hubley Studio Production. Color. Half–hour. Premiered on CBS: April 8, 1972. Rebroadcast on CBS: May 5, 1973.*

Voices:

Adam: Ray Hubley, **Mother:** Maureen Stapleton, **Rocco:** Jack Warden, **Fossil Pillar:** Morris Carnovsky, **First Rock:** Phil Leeds, **Vocalists:** Harry "Sweets" Edison, Don Elliott, Ruth Price

A DISNEY CHRISTMAS GIFT

Favorite scenes from Walt Disney Studios' classic animated features, including *Peter Pan, Bambi, Ichabod and Mr. Toad* and several memorable cartoon shorts, were tied–in with Christmas for this prime–time holiday special. *A Walt Disney Television Production. Color. One hour. Premiered on CBS: December 20, 1983.*

Voices:

Peter Pan: Bobby Driscoll, **Fairy Godmother:** Verna Felton, **Cinderella:** Ilene Woods

DISNEY'S ALL–STAR MOTHER'S DAY ALBUM

The subject of motherhood is celebrated in this compilation special featuring clips from assorted Disney cartoons. Film clips were drawn from memorable features and cartoon short–subjects, among them, *Dumbo, The Jungle Book,* and others. *A Walt Disney Television Production. Color. One hour. Premiered on CBS: May 9, 1984.*

Voices:

Fairy Godmother: Verna Felton, **Cinderella:** Ilene Woods

DISNEY'S ALL–STAR VALENTINE PARTY

Popular Los Angeles radio disc–jockey Rick Dees narrates this collection of scenes from classic Disney cartoons that depict love and friendship. Scenes were culled from *Mickey's Rival* (1936), *The Brave Tin Soldier* (1938), *Pluto's Heart Throb* (1949) and others. *A Walt Disney Television Production. Color. One hour. Premiered on CBS: February 14, 1984.*

Voices:
Narrator: Rick Dees

DISNEY'S DTV "DOGGONE" HITS

Animated sequences set to rock music culled from classic Disney cartoons highlights this salute to man's best friend, with musical segments featuring Kenny Rogers, Huey Lewis and Deniece Williams. *A Walt Disney Television Production. Color. One hour. Premiered on NBC: February 19, 1988.*

DISNEY'S DTV "DOGGONE" VALENTINE

Hosted by Mickey Mouse, Minnie Mouse, Professor Ludwig von Drake and others, this one–hour special salutes man's best friend with a series of entertaining clips of favorite dog scenes and characters culled from Disney full–length features and cartoon shorts. *An Andrew Solt Production in association Walt Disney Television. Color. One Hour. Premiered on NBC: February 13, 1987.*

Voices:
Mickey Mouse: Wayne Allwine, **Minnie Mouse/Dalamation Puppy:** Russi Taylor, **Professor Ludwig von Drake:** Albert Ash, **Jiminy Cricket:** Eddie Carroll, **Goofy:** Bill Farmer, **Pongo:** Will Ryan, **Dalmation Puppies:** Lisa St. James, **Radio Announcer:** Maurice La Marche, **Announcer:** J. J. Jackson

DISNEY'S DTV VALENTINE

Clips from Disney cartoons timed to rock and roll music highlight this Valentine's Day special, hosted by Mickey Mouse, Donald Duck, Jiminy Cricket and Professor Ludwig von Drake. *An Andrew Solt Production in association with Walt Disney Television. Color. One hour. Premiered on NBC: February 14, 1986. Rebroadcast on NBC: September 7, 1986 (as "Disney's DTV Romancin").*

Voices:
Mickey Mouse: Les Perkins, **Donald Duck:** Tony Anselmo, **Jiminy Cricket:** Eddie Carroll, **Professor Ludwig von Drake:** Paul Frees, **Gruffi, the Gummi Bear:** Corey Burton, **Goofy/Pongo:** Will Ryan, **Chip/Dale/Female Voice:** Judith Searle, **Dalemation Puppies #1, #2:** Lisa St. James, **Princess Aura:** Mary Costa, **Prince Phillip:** Bill Shirley, **Announcer:** Paul Frees

DISNEY'S FLUPPY DOGS

Off course from their real destination, several out–of–this–universe dogs (Stanley, Ozzie, Tippi, Bink and Dink), who possess magical powers, arrive on Earth where they are forced to act like normal dogs when their real presence sends panic into local citizens. Unfortunately, being normal has its drawbacks as they are captured and locked up in the city pound, where their teenage friends, Jaimie and Claire, aid their escape in order for them to return home through the interdimensional doorway from which they came. *A Walt Disney Television Production in association with TMS Entertainment. Color. One hour. Premiered on ABC: November 27, 1986. Rebroadcast on ABC: August 30, 1987 (as "The Sunday Disney Movie").*

Voices:
Jaimie Bingham: Carl Stevens, **Bink/Tippi:** Susan Blu, **Stanley:** Marshall Efron, **Mrs. Bingham:** Cloyce Morrow, **Ozzie:** Lorenzo Music, **Claire:** Jessica Pennington, **Wagstaff:** Michael Rye, **Haimish/Attendant/Dink:** Hal Smith

DISNEY'S HALLOWEEN TREAT

Halloween is the theme of this Disney prime–time special, featuring witches, goblins and ghouls and classic Disney characters in a collection of excerpts from favorite screen moments of the past. *A Walt Disney Television Production. Color. One hour. Premiered on CBS: October 30, 1982. Rebroadcast on CBS: October 29, 1983.*

Voices:
Peter Pan: Bobby Driscoll, **Si/Am** ("Lady and the Tramp"): Peggy Lee

DONALD DUCK'S 50TH BIRTHDAY

Comedian Dick Van Dyke hosts this hour–long golden anniversary retrospective of Hollywood's favorite duck, utilizing clips from films throughout his career introduced by special guests. Guests included Ed Asner, Bruce Jenner, Cloris Leachman, John Ritter, Kenny Rogers, Donna Summer, Andy Warhol, Henry Winkler, and *Star Wars* characters C–3PO and R2D2. *An Andrew Solt Production in association with Walt Disney Television. Color. One hour. Premiered on CBS: November 13, 1984. Rebroadcast on CBS: October 29, 1985.*

Voices:
Donald Duck: Clarence Nash, **C–3PO:** Anthony Daniels, **R2D2:** (electronic)

A DOONESBURY SPECIAL

Zonker Harris, the lead character in Garry Trudeau's popular "Doonesbury" strip, reflects on social and political issues of the past—flower children, college campus bombings and other cynical observations—in this nostalgic half–hour special, which was released to theaters as well and received an Academy Award nomination for Best Animated Film. *A John and Faith*

Mike reflects on social and political issues of the past in "A Doonesbury Special," based on Garry Trudeau's popular syndicated strip. © Universal Press Syndicate (Courtesy: The Hubley Studio)

Hubley Films Production in association with Universal Press Syndicate. Color. Half—hour. Premiered on NBC: November 27, 1977.

Voices:
Zonker Harris: Richard Cox, **Joanie Caucus:** Barbara Harris, **Mike:** David Grant, **Mark Slackmeyer/Ralphie:** Charles Levin, **B.D.:** Richard Bruno, **Boopsie:** Rebecca Nelson, **Rev. Scott Sloan:** Rev. William Sloane Coffin Jr., **Referee:** Jack Gilford, **Kirby:** Mark Baker, **Frank:** Eric Elice, **Calvin:** Ben Haley Jr., **Sportscaster:** Will Jordan, **Ellie:** Linda Baer, **Howie:** Eric Jaffe, **Jeannie:** Michelle Browne, **Rufus:** Thomas Baxton, **Magus:** Lenny Jackson, **Virgin Mary:** Patrice Leftwich, **Jimmy Thudpacker:** Jimmy Thudpacker

DOWN AND OUT WITH DONALD DUCK

The up—and—down life of Donald Duck is chronicled in this "60 Minutes"—style "duckumentary" that combines clips from more than 30 hours of previously exhibited Donald Duck cartoons to give audiences a different perspective of the famed duck, including his inability to keep his temper in check. *A Garen—Albrecht Production in association with Walt Disney Television. Color. One hour. Premiered on NBC: March 25, 1987. Rebroadcast on NBC: April 29, 1988.*

Voices:
Donald Duck/Daisy Duck: Tony Anselmo, **Huey/Dewey/Louie:** Tony Anselmo, **Professor Ludwig von Drake:** Albert Ash, **Mickey Mouse:** Les Perkins, **Goofy/Peg—Leg Pete:** Will Ryan, **Narrator:** Stan Freberg, **Announcer:** Harry Shearer

DR. SEUSS' HALLOWEEN IS GRINCH NIGHT

The people of Whoville are plagued by a "sour—sweet wind," suggesting only one thing—the nasty Grinch, who dwells atop dreadful Mt. Crumpit, cannot be far away. This time, he carries out his plan of provoking the townspeople but encounters a young lad, Ukariah, who bravely faces the evil Grinch in order to save his people. Joining the Grinch in his acts of evil—doing: his dog, Max. Hans Conreid, effective in earlier specials, returns as the program's narrator. *A Dr. Seuss and A. S. Giesel Production in association with DePatie—Freleng Enterprises. Color. Premiered on ABC: October 29, 1977. Rebroadcast on ABC: October 26, 1978; October 28, 1979; October 30, 1980.*

Voices:
Grinch: Hans Conreid, **Grandpa Joseph:** Hal Smith, **Grandma Mariah:** Irene Tedrow, **Ukariah:** Gary Shapiro

Additional Voices:
Jack DeLeon, Henry Gibson

DR. SEUSS' HORTON HEARS A WHO!

Hearing a small voice—"as if some tiny person were calling for help"—Horton the Elephant discovers microscopic creatures floating aboard a speck of dust, headed by the miniscule Dr. Whoovy, who is trying to convince his followers there is another world outside theirs. For "pretending" to talk to his unseen dust friends, Horton is finally seized by his jungle companions, but all comes to a happy ending as Whoovy in turn hears a voice from an even smaller fleck of dust. Based on the Dr. Seuss children's fable of the same name, the program played up the theme: "A person's a person no matter how small." *A Chuck Jones Enterprises Production in association with The Cat In The Hat Productions and MGM—TV. Color. Half—hour. Premiered on CBS: March 19, 1970. Rebroadcast on CBS: September 19, 1971; July 31, 1972; April 20, 1973; February 4, 1974; March 24, 1975; March 19, 1976; May 13, 1977; August 4, 1978.*

Voices:
Narrator: Hans Conreid

Additional Voices:
June Foray, Chuck Jones

DR. SEUSS' HOW THE GRINCH STOLE CHRISTMAS

Perennial favorite based on the popular Dr. Seuss fable about old meanie Grinch almost ruining Christmas for the townspeople of the little village of Whoville because either "his heart was two sizes small or he wore tight shoes." The heartless Grinch succeeds at removing all the gifts and decorations from the town, but, after finding fault with his misdeed, he later returns all the gifts to the townspeople as if nothing had happened. CBS is said to have spent $350,000 for this animated special, originally sponsored by the Foundation for Commercial Banks. The program pre—empted the network's "Lassie" series, airing in its time slot. *A Chuck Jones Enterprises Production in association with The Cat in the Hat Productions and MGM—TV. Color. Half—hour. Premiered on CBS: December 18, 1966. Rebroadcast on CBS: December*

17, 1967; December 22, 1968; December 21, 1969; December 2, 1970; December 7, 1971; December 4, 1972; December 10, 1973; December 13, 1974; December 12, 1975; December 18, 1976; December 10, 1977; December 16, 1978; December 19, 1979; November 28, 1980; December 16, 1981; December 18, 1982; December 12, 1983; December 5, 1984; December 7, 1985; December 17, 1986; December 11, 1987.

Voices:
Grinch: Thurl Ravenscroft (singing), **Cindy Lou:** June Foray, **Narrator:** Boris Karloff

DR. SEUSS ON THE LOOSE

Dr. Seuss returns in this animated trilogy based on three of his classic fables—*The Sneetches,* featuring ostrich–like creatures who learn to treat each other as equals; *Green Eggs and Ham,* showing the silliness of prejudice; and *The Zax,* dealing with the subject of stubborness—which Seuss (Ted Geisel) co–produced. *A DePatie–Freleng Enterprises Production in association with CBS. Color. Half–hour. Premiered on CBS: October 15, 1973. Rebroadcast on CBS: October 28, 1974; November 21, 1975; March 9, 1976; July 12, 1979.*

Voices:
The Cat in the Hat (host): Allan Sherman, **Zax** (narrator): Hans Conried, **Joey/Sam–I–Am:** Paul Winchell, **Zax/Sylvester McMonkey McBeam:** Bob Holt

DR. SEUSS' PONTOFFEL POCK, WHERE ARE YOU?

Misfit Pontoffel Pock has blown his opportunity at the pickle factory and gets a second chance when some good fairies provide him with a push–button piano that has the power to transport him anywhere. After a false start, he lands in Casbahmopolis, where, in a short time, he becomes taken with an eyeball dancer—and vice versa—and they return, via the magical piano, for a second chance at success at the pickle factory. *A Dr. Seuss and A. S. Geisel Production in association with DePatie–Freleng Enterprises. Color. Half–hour. Premiered on ABC: May 2, 1980. Rebroadcast on ABC: July 31, 1981.*

Voices:
Pontoffel Pock: Wayne Morton, **Neepha Pheepha:** Sue Allen, **McGillicuddy:** Hal Smith

Additional Voices:
Ken Lundie, Don Messick, Joe Raposo

DR. SEUSS' THE BUTTER BATTLE BOOK

In the first new Dr. Seuss special in seven years, the Yooks square off against the Zooks, separated by a Great Wall and a philosophical disagreement over which side to butter their bread on, in this musical adaptation of Dr. Seuss' parable about the arms race. The half–hour special was produced exclusively for Ted Turner's nostalgia movie channel, TNT. *A*

Pontoffel Pock, a young character who flops as a pickle–packer, finds new horizons when the good fairies heed his pleas and provide him with a push–button piano that transports him through time and space in the ABC television special "Dr. Seuss' Pontoffel Pock, Where Are You?" Dr. Seuss and A. S. Geisel Productions/DePatie–Freleng Enterprises (Courtesy: ABC)

Bakshi Production in association with Ted S. Geisel. Color. Half–hour. Premiered on TNT: November 13, 1989.

Voices:
Narrator: Charles Durning

Additional Voices
Christopher Collins, Miriam Flynn, Clive Revill, Joseph Cousins

DR. SEUSS' THE CAT IN THE HAT

Two children who are bored by the prospects of staying home all day because of the rain are greeted by a surprise visitor, the Cat in the Hat, who turns the house upside down looking for his moss–covered three–handled gradunza. He virtually destroys the home in the process, but he magically restores the structure to its former state before the kids' mother returns. *A DePatie–Freleng Enterprises Production. Color. Half–hour. Premiered on CBS: March 10, 1971. Rebroadcast on CBS: April 11, 1972; February 20, 1973; January 4, 1974; January 31, 1975; March 30, 1976; August 20, 1979; September 20, 1980; May 15, 1987; January 5, 1988.*

Voices:
Cat in the Hat: Allan Sherman, **Karlos K. Krinklebein:** Daws Butler, **Boy:** Tony Frazier, **Girl:** Pamelyn Ferdin, **Mother:** Gloria Camacho, **Thing 1:** Thurl Ravenscroft, **Thing 2:** Lewis Morford

DR. SEUSS' THE GRINCH GRINCHES THE CAT IN THE HAT

Grouchy Grinch follows through on his plans to get even with the Cat in the Hat after he drives in his path during a countryside jaunt. The Grinch employs a variety of self–made contraptions to get even but instead is taught manners by the amiable Cat in the Hat. *A Dr. Seuss and A. S. Geisel Production in association with Marvel Productions. Color. Half–hour. Premiered on ABC: May 20, 1982. Rebroadcast on ABC: August 7, 1983.*

Voices:

Mason Adams, Joe Eich, Bob Holt, Marilyn Jackson, Melissa Mackay, Frank Welker, Richard B. Williams.

DR. SEUSS' THE HOOBER– BLOOB HIGHWAY

Young humans are sent down an imaginary ribbon of light— known as the Hoober–Bloob Highway—to Earth by the chief dispatcher, Hoober–Bloob, who beforehand briefs those about to depart for the world below on the pros and cons of Earthbound living. Dr. Seuss (Ted Geisel) wrote the special, making his bow writing specifically for television. *A DePatie– Freleng Enterprises Production. Color. Half–hour. Premiered on CBS: February 19, 1975. Rebroadcast on CBS: March 23, 1976; November 15, 1977; September 9, 1981.*

Voices:

Bob Holt, Hal Smith

DR. SEUSS' THE LORAX

The Lorax, a spokesman for saving trees from the woodsman's axe, sets out to stop the evil Once–ler from destroying all the trees in the forest to help local industrialists prosper. Program originally aired in the time slot usually reserved for CBS' "Gunsmoke." *A DePatie–Freleng Enterprises Production. Color. Half–hour. Premiered on CBS: February 14, 1972. Rebroadcast on CBS: March 28, 1973; March 25, 1974; July 19, 1977; August 4, 1978.*

Voices:

Lorax/Once–ler: Bob Holt, **Boy:** Harlen Carraher, **Other Voices:** Athena Lorde, **Narrator:** Eddie Albert

EARTHDAY BIRTHDAY

Two star–touched baby dinosaurs join forces and recruit other creatures to save the planet. Led by the magical dinosaur fairy, It Zwibble, the Zwibble Dibbles, a group of adorable, socially responsible baby dinosaurs, pledge to care for the Earth and give it a birthday party, where children from all over the world take the Zwibble Dibble Pledge and learn how they can make a difference in this half–hour that tied–in with the international celebration of Earth Day, April 22, 1990. The program was produced and directed by Academy Award nominee Michael Sporn ("Lyle, Lyle Crocodile"). *A Michael Sporn Animation Production. Color. Half–hour. Premiered on HBO: April 22, 1990.*

Voices:

Christopher Reeve, Lainie Kazan, Fred Gwynne, Gregory Per- ler, Jonathan Goch, Jonathan Gold, Meghan Andrews, Gina Marle Huaman, Larry White, John Cannemaker

THE EASTER BUNNY IS COMIN' TO TOWN

Through the wonders of Animagic, Fred Astaire, as old friend/ mailman S. D. Kluger from "Santa Claus Is Comin' To Town," relates how the traditions of Easter—the Easter bunny, dec- orating eggs and chocolate bunnies—first came about in the town of Kidville, a city reserved for children and the excite- ment brought by the holiday. Astaire sings the title song and "Can Do" out of six original songs written for the program. *A Rankin–Bass Production. Color. One hour. Premiered on ABC: April 6, 1977. Rebroadcast on ABC: March 20, 1978; April 14, 1978; April 5, 1980.*

Voices:

S. D. Kluger (narrator): Fred Astaire, **Sunny, the Easter Bunny:** Skip Hinnant, **Chugs:** Robert McFadden, **Hallelujah Jones:** Ron Marshall, **King Bruce:** James Spies, **Lilly Long- tooth:** Meg Sargent

Additional Voices:

Gia Andersen, George Brennan, Stacey Carey, Jill Choder, Karen Dahle, Laura Dean, Michael McGovern, Ray Owens, Allen Swift

EASTER FEVER

The Easter Bunny, alias Jack the Rabbit, is the subject of a celebrity–type roast in honor of his retirement from the Easter egg business. Several show–biz stars, Don Rattles and Steed Martin (animal characterizations of comedians Don Rickles and Steve Martin), head the all–star salute. Just when he thinks his career is over, however, Jack is convinced by a pleading aardvark to change his mind and play the Easter Bunny once more. *A Nelvana Limited Production in associ- ation with the CBC. Color. Half–hour. Premiered: March 30, 1980. Syndicated.*

Voices:

Jack, the Easter Bunny: Garrett Morris, **Don Rattles/Steed Martin:** Maurice LaMarche, **Santa Claus/Baker:** Chris Wig- gins, **Madame Malegg:** Jeri Craden, **Aardvark:** Jim Henshaw, **Scarlett O'Hare:** Catherine O'Hara, **Scrawny Chicken:** Mel- leny Brown, **Ratso Rat:** Larry Mollin, **Announcer:** Don Fer- guson

EASTER IS

Benji is confronted with the prospects of losing his pet dog, Waldo, if he doesn't pay the dog's captor ransom money in the amount of five dollars. Waldo manages to escape after chewing through the rope to which he was tied, making his return home even more dramatic by coming back to his master on the morning of Easter. *A Screen Images Production for Lutheran Television. Color. Half–hour. Premiered: March, 1974. Syndicated.*

Voices:

Benji: David Kelly, **Schoolteacher:** Leslie Uggams, **Martin:** Phillip Morris

Additional Voices:

Joan Gardner, Shelley Hines, Darla Hood, Dina Lynn, Bob Norris, Gary Shapiro, Dru Stevens, Les Tremayne

THE EMPEROR'S NEW CLOTHES

Danny Kaye lends his voice to this animated version of the Hans Christian Andersen classic about the vain Emperor Klockenlocher, who is duped into paying one million dollars for a suit made from "invisible cloth," in this live–action/animation special, featuring the stop–motion process of Animagic, which utilizes the life–like qualities of three–dimensional figures and the magical fantasy of animation. Portions of the special were shot on–location in Andersen's native Denmark. Kaye was most familiar with the famed storyteller as he played the title role in a 1952 movie about Andersen's life. *A Rankin–Bass Production. Color. One hour. Premiered on ABC: February 21, 1972 (as "The Enchanted World of Danny Kaye: The Emperor's New Clothes").*

Voices:

Marmaduke (narrator): Danny Kaye, **Emperor Klockenlocher:** Cyril Ritchard, **Princess Klockenlocher:** Imogene Coca, **Mufti:** Allen Swift, **Jasper:** Robert McFadden

EVERYBODY RIDES THE CAROUSEL

Based on the works of psychiatrist Erik H. Erikson, this unusual 90–minute prime–time special deals with the eight stages of human life—from infancy to old age—presented in fable–like form, skillfully animated by John and Faith Hubley.* *A Hubley Studio Production. Color. One hour and a half. Premiered on CBS: September 10, 1976.*

Voices:

Mother: Judith Coburn, **Baby #1/Maura #2/Adolescent:** Georgia Hubley, **Baby #2:** Ray Hubley, **Baby (cries)/Emily/Adolescent #5:** Emily Hubley, **Babies' Relative #1/Cafeteria Woman:** Jane Hoffman, **Babies' Relative #2:** Lou Jacobi, **Babies' Relative #3:** Lane Smith, **Babies' Relative #4:** Eleanor Wilson, **Maura #1:** Maura Washburn, **Maura's Mother:** Linda Washburn, **Maura's Father:** Mike Washburn, **Bruce/Student #2:** Bruce E. Smith, **Bruce's Mother:** Jane E. Smith, **Bruce's Father:** Mortimer Shapiro, **Student #1:** John Infantanza, **Boy:** Leeds Atkinson, **Girl:** Jenny Lumet, **Oracle:** Jo Carrol Stoneham, **Adolescent #1:** Alvin Mack, **Adolescent #2:** Michael Hirst, **Adolescent #3:** Barbara Gittleman, **Lovers:** Charles Levin, Meryl Streep, **Dinah:** Dinah Manoff, **Dinah's Father:** John Randolph, **Dinah's Mother:** Sarah Cunningham, **Tulane:** Tulane Bridgewater, **Tulane's Mother:** DeeDee Bridgewater, **Librarian:** William Watts, **Couple in Bed:** Lawrence (David) Pressman, Lanna Saunders, **Cafeteria Man:** Jack Gilford, **Halloween Woman:** Juanita Moore, **Halloween Man:** Harry Edison

*Ciccly Tyson hosted the special and actress Meryl Streep contributed her voice to the production.

THE FABULOUS SHORTS

Lee Mendelson, co–producer of television's "Peanuts" specials, produced this collection of Academy Award–winning cartoons, which included domestic and foreign winners. Clips were featured from nearly 20 films, including Mickey Mouse's *Steamboat Willie* (1928), Bugs Bunny's *Knighty Knight Bugs* (1958) and two Mr. Magoo shorts, *When Magoo Flew* (1954) and *Mr. Magoo's Puddle Jumper* (1956). The special was hosted by actor Jim Backus, also the voice of Mr. Magoo. *A Lee Mendelson Production. Color. Half–hour. Premiered on NBC: October 17, 1968.*

FAERIES

Oisin, a middle–aged hunter, who is magically transformed into a 15–year–old, offers his help to the Trows to save the faerie world from the evil shadow of the Faerie King, who is threatening their very existence. *A MHV and Friends Production in association with Tomorrow Entertainment. Color. Half–hour. Premiered on CBS: February 25, 1981. Rebroadcast on CBS: July 31, 1982; August 13, 1983.*

Voices:

Faerie King/Shadow: Hans Conried, **Oisin:** Craig Schaefer, **Princess Niamh:** Morgan Brittany, **Puck/Fir Darrig:** Frank Welker, **Kobold:** Bob Arbogast, **Hags:** June Foray, Linda Gary, **Trows/Hunters:** Mel Wells, Frank Welker, Bob Arbogast

A FAMILY CIRCUS CHRISTMAS

Daddy, Mommy, Billy, P.J., Dolly and Jeffy are preparing for Christmas when Jeffy gives Santa a near–impossible request: bring his deceased grandfather back to visit the family for the holidays. Through a miracle, grandpop appears and it's a merry, merry Christmas indeed. *A Cullen–Kasden Production in association with the Register and Tribune Syndicate. Color. Half–hour. Premiered on NBC: December 18, 1979. Rebroadcast on NBC: December 5, 1980; December 20, 1981.*

Voices:

Mommy: Anne Costello, **Daddy:** Bob Kaliban, **Billy:** Mark McDermott, **Dolly:** Missy Hope, **Jeffy/P.J.:** Nathan Berg, **Santa Claus:** Allen Swift, **Vocalist:** Sarah Vaughan

A FAMILY CIRCUS EASTER

Billy, Dolly, and Jeffy succeed in trapping the Easter Bunny to find out why it hides the eggs in this prime–time holiday special which premiered on NBC. *A Cullen–Kasden Productions in association with the Register and Tribune Syndicate. Color. Half–hour. Premiered on NBC: April 8, 1982. Rebroadcast on NBC: April 1, 1983.*

Voices:

Mommy: Anne Costello, **Daddy:** Bob Kaliban, **Billy:** Mark McDermott, **Dolly:** Missy Hope, **Jeffy/P.J.:** Nathan Berg, **Easter Bunny:** Dizzy Gillespie

THE FAMILY DOG

The story of a suburban middle–class family and their pet pooch is told from the dog's perspective in three related stories that showcase the animal's true feelings about its owners in humorous fashion. The program was billed as "A Special Animated Adventure" of Steven Spielberg's short–lived NBC series, "Amazing Stories." *A Hyperion–Kushner–Locke Production in association with Amblin Entertainment and Universal Television. Color. Half–hour. Premiered on NBC: February 16, 1987 (on "Amazing Stories"). Rebroadcast on NBC: September 11, 1987.*

Voices:
Father: Stan Freberg, **Mother:** Mercedes McCambridge, **Billy:** Scott Menville, **Baby Sister:** Annie Potts

Additional Voices:

Jack Angel, Brooke Ashley, Brad Bird, Marshall Efron, Stanley Ralph Ross

THE FAT ALBERT CHRISTMAS SPECIAL

The true meaning of Christmas—to love one another—is portrayed in this third Fat Albert special in which Tyrone, the owner of the junkyard where Fat Albert's clubhouse sits, threatens to demolish the shack as an act of nastiness while the Cosby Kids, busy working up a Christmas pageant, help a little boy, Marshall Franklin, whose father and pregnant mother are stranded outside in their car. *A Filmation Production in association with Bill Cosby Productions. Color. Half–hour. Premiered on CBS: December 18, 1977. Rebroadcast on CBS: November 27, 1978; November 27, 1979; December 24, 1980.*

Voices:
Fat Albert: Bill Cosby, **Mushmouth/Bill:** Bill Cosby, **Russell:** Jan Crawford, **Weird Harold:** Gerald Edwards, **Rudy:** Eric Suter

Additional Voices:

Erika Carroll, Eric Greene, Kim Hamilton, Julius Harris, Ty Henderson

THE FAT ALBERT EASTER SPECIAL

The spirit of Easter is conveyed as Fat Albert and the gang observe the joy of the holiday season by spreading good cheer to others. *A Filmation Production in association with Bill Cosby Productions. Color. Half–hour. Premiered on CBS: April 3, 1982. Rebroadcast on CBS: March 10, 1983.*

Voices:
Fat Albert: Bill Cosby, **Mushmouth/Mudfoot/Bill:** Bill Cosby, **Russell:** Jan Crawford, **Weird Harold:** Gerald Edwards, **Rudy:** Eric Suter

Fat Albert, dressed as Santa Claus, helps out little Marshall Franklin, whose family is stranded in the snow, in "The Fat Albert Christmas Special." © Bill Cosby/Filmation (Courtesy: CBS)

THE FAT ALBERT HALLOWEEN SPECIAL

Fat Albert and the Cosby Kids are treated to an old–fashioned Halloween, with a trip to the cemetery where a witch jumps out, a visit to that ol' bum Mudfeet where they learn about how to get tricked out of their treats and an encounter with a frightening widow who lives in a house on the hill. *A Filmation Production in association with Bill Cosby Productions. Color. Half–hour. Premiered on CBS: October 24, 1977. Rebroadcast on CBS: October 24, 1978; October 22, 1979; October 22, 1980; October 27, 1981.*

Voices:
Fat Albert: Bill Cosby, **Mushmouth/Bill:** Bill Cosby, **Russell:** Jan Crawford, **Weird Harold:** Gerald Edwards, **Rudy:** Eric Suter, **Other Voices:** Erika Carroll

THE FIRST CHRISTMAS

A nun cares for a young boy (Lukas) who is blinded by a lightning bolt in a small Abbey in the south of France in this heartwarming holiday special. *A Rankin–Bass Production.*

Color. Half-hour. Premiered on NBC: December 19, 1975. Rebroadcast on NBC: December 18, 1976; December 15, 1979.

Voices:

Sister Theresa (narrator): Angela Lansbury, **Father Thomas:** Cyril Ritchard, **Lukas:** David Kelly, **Sister Catherine:** Iris Rainer, **Sister Jean:** Joan Gardiner, **Louisa:** Dina Lynn

Additional Voices:

Sean Manning, Don Messick, Hilary Momberger, Dru Stevens, Greg Thomas

THE FIRST EASTER RABBIT

Folksy Burl Ives sings and tells the story of the first Easter rabbit, whose special assignment from the good fairy is to deliver painted Easter eggs to children. His mission is not without its obstacles, however, as three comedic con bunnies try to stop him. Adapted from the best-selling book *The Velveteen Rabbit*, Ives sings four songs, including Irving Berlin's famous melody "Easter Parade." *A Rankin-Bass Production. Color. Half-hour. Premiered on NBC: April 9, 1976. Rebroadcast on NBC: March 19, 1978; April 7, 1979; April 9, 1981.*

Voices:

Great Easter Bunny (narrator): Burl Ives, **Stuffy:** Robert Morse, **Flops:** Stan Freberg, **Zero/Spats:** Paul Frees, **Mother:** Joan Gardner, **Whiskers:** Don Messick, **Glinda:** Dina Lynn, **Vocalists:** Burl Ives, Robert Morse, Christine Winter

FIVE WEEKS IN A BALLOON

Inspired by the Jules Verne story, three adventurers travel across the wilds of Africa via a hot-air balloon, led by famed explorer Dr. Samuel Ferguson, to reclaim for Queen Victoria a priceless diamond that is thought to be located on Devil's Peak. *A Hanna-Barbera Production. Color. One hour. Premiered on CBS: November 24, 1977. Rebroadcast on CBS: September 30, 1978; November 23, 1981.*

Voices:

Narrator: John Stephenson, **Dr. Samuel Ferguson:** Laurie Main, **Duke of Salisbury:** Laurie Main, **Oliver:** Loren Lester, **Queen Victoria:** Cathleen Cordell, **Irumu/King Umtali:** Brooker Bradshaw, **Le Griffe/1st & 2nd Poacher:** Johnny Hayner, **Native:** Gene Whittington

FLASH GORDON: THE GREATEST ADVENTURE

This full-length made-for-television fantasy tells the complete story of space-age hero, Flash Gordon, who, as a State Department employee in Warsaw, takes it upon himself to prevent the powerful Ming the Merciless from bringing his wave of destruction to the planet Earth. *A Filmation Production. Color. Two hours. Premiered on NBC: August 21, 1982. Rebroadcast on NBC: September 5, 1982; September 26, 1982.*

Voices:

Flash Gordon: Robert Ridgely, **Dale Arden:** Diane Pershing, **Dr. Zarkov:** David Opatoshu, **Ming the Merciless:** Bob Holt, **Vultan:** Vic Perrin, **Princess Aura:** Melendy Britt, **Prince Barin:** Robert Douglas, **Thun:** Ted Cassidy

THE FLIGHT OF DRAGONS

The good wizards select a young Boston writer, Peter Dickenson, to stop the menacing Red Wizards and reclaim a magic crown belonging to their race in this two-hour stop-motion (Animagic) special, produced by Arthur Rankin and Jules Bass, creators of perennial television favorites "Rudolph the Red-Nosed Reindeer" and "Frosty the Snowman," among others. *A Rankin-Bass Production. Color. Two hours. Premiered on ABC: August 3, 1986.*

Voices:

Peter Dickenson: John Ritter, **Carolinus:** Harry Morgan, **Ommadon:** James Earl Jones, **Smrgol:** James Gregory, **Gorbash:** Cosie Costa, **Arak:** Victor Buono, **Danielle:** Nellie Bellflower, **Princess Melisande:** Alexandra Stoddart, **Pawnbroker:** Larry Storch, **Vocalist:** Don McLean

Additional Voices:

Jack Lester, Robert McFadden, Don Messick, Ed Peck

A FLINTSTONE CHRISTMAS

Fred's holiday job as a part-time Santa at a Bedrock department store lands him in the real Santa's shoes on Christmas Eve in this half-hour holiday special, which was sub-titled, "How the Flintstones Saved Christmas." *A Hanna-Barbera Production. Color. Half-hour. Premiered on NBC: December 7, 1977. Rebroadcast on NBC: December 11, 1978.*

Voices:

Fred Flintstone: Henry Corden, **Barney Rubble:** Mel Blanc, **Betty Rubble:** Gay Hartwig, **Wilma Flintstone:** Jean VanderPyl, **Pebbles Flintstone:** Gay Hartwig, **Bamm-Bamm Rubble:** Lucille Bliss, **Mrs. Santa:** Virginia Gregg, **Real Santa:** Hal Smith, **Ed the Foreman/Otis:** Don Messick, **George Slate,** Fred's boss: John Stephenson

THE FLINTSTONE KIDS' "JUST SAY NO" SPECIAL

Fred, Wilma, Barney and Betty, in their pre-teen years, convey the importance of saying "no" to drugs in this half-hour prime-time special tied-in with former First Lady Nancy Reagan's national campaign to fight drug addiction. A cartoon take-off of rock singer Michael Jackson (called "Michael Jackstone") appears on the program. The program was first broadcast in prime-time and then rebroadcast as an "ABC Weekend Special." *A Hanna-Barbera Production. Color. Half-hour. Premiered on ABC: September 15, 1988. Rebroadcast on ABC: September 24, 1988 (on "ABC Weekend Special").*

Voices:
Wilma: Elizabeth Fraser, **Freddy:** Scott Menville, **Barney:** Hamilton Camp, **Betty:** B. J. Ward, **Philo:** Bumper Robinson, **Stoney:** Dana Hill, **Dottie:** Shuko Akune, **Joey:** David Markus, **Clyde:** Scott Menville, **Mr. Slaghoople:** Michael Rye, **Mrs. Slaghoople:** Jean VanderPyl, **Dino/Fang:** Frank Welker, **Officer Quartz:** Rene Levant, **Edna Flinstone:** Henry Corden, **Fluffy Woman:** Jean VanderPyl, **Crusher:** Frank Welker, **Irate Man:** Michael Rye, **Angry Adult:** Jean VanderPyl, **Mrs. Gravelson/Female Announcer:** B. J. Ward, **Michael Jackstone:** Kip Lennon

THE FLINTSTONES: FRED'S FINAL FLING

With just 24 hours to live (or so he believes), Fred takes a final fling until his eyes close . . . from exhaustion. He awakens to discover the predictions of his demise were premature, but the lesson he learned will last a lifetime. *A Hanna–Barbera Production. Color. Half–hour. Premiered on NBC: October 18, 1981. Rebroadcast on NBC: August 1, 1982.*

Voices:
Fred Flintstone: Henry Corden, **Barney Rubble:** Mel Blanc, **Betty Rubble:** Gay Autterson, **Wilma Flintstone:** Jean VanderPyl, **Pebbles Flinstone:** Jean VanderPyl, **Dino:** Mel Blanc, **Frank Frankenstone:** John Stephenson, **Monkey #2/Turtle #2:** Henry Corden, **Elephant:** Jean VanderPyl, **Monkey #3:** Mel Blanc, **Nurse/Turtle #1:** Gay Autterson, **Dinosaur/Monkey #1:** John Stephenson, **Doctor/Fish #1 & 2/Parrot/Pigasaurus:** Don Messick

THE FLINTSTONES: JOGGING FEVER

Fred gets it from all sides about his bulging waistline, including from his boss, Mr. Slate, who tells him to shape up. Fred decides it's time to do something, so he takes up jogging and really finds out how badly out of shape he is. *A Hanna–Barbera Production. Color. Half–hour. Premiered on NBC: October 11, 1981. Rebroadcast on NBC: July 25, 1982.*

Voices:
Fred Flintstone: Henry Corden, **Barney Rubble:** Mel Blanc, **Wilma Flintstone:** Jean VanderPyl, **Betty Rubble:** Gay Autterson, **Pebbles Flintstone:** Jean VanderPyl, **Dino:** Mel Blanc, **Frank Frankenstone:** John Stephenson, **George Slate,** Fred's boss: John Stephenson, **Nurse #1:** Jean VanderPyl, **Nurse #2:** Gay Autterson, **Workman #2:** Henry Corden, **Turtle:** Mel Blanc, **Dinosaur/Pterodactyl/Bird/Snake:** John Stephenson, **Creeply/Announcer:** Frank Welker, **Control Tower Operator/Workman #1/Hipposaurus:** Wayne Norton

THE FLINTSTONES: LITTLE BIG LEAGUE

Fred and Barney go to bat as coaches of opposing Little League teams and find their friendship crumbles as the big playoff game approaches in the hour–long special for prime–time

television. *A Hanna–Barbera Production. Color. One hour. Premiered on NBC: April 6, 1976. Rebroadcast on NBC: October 10, 1980.*

Voices:
Fred Flinstone: Henry Corden, **Barney Rubble:** Mel Blanc, **Wilma Flintstone:** Jean VanderPyl, **Betty Rubble:** Gay Hartwig, **Pebbles Flintstone:** Pamela Anderson, **Bamm–Bamm Rubble:** Frank Welker, **Dino:** Mel Blanc, **Officer:** Ted Cassidy, **Judge:** Herb Vigran, **Dusty:** Lucille Bliss, **Lefty:** Randy Gray

Additional Voices:
Don Messick, John Stephenson

THE FLINTSTONES MEET ROCKULA AND FRANKENSTONE

The Flintstones and the Rubbles don crazy costumes to compete on the "Make a Deal Or Don't" game show and win a romantic trip to Count Rockula's castle in Rocksylvania. *A Hanna–Barbera Production. Color. One hour. Premiered on NBC: October 3, 1980.*

Voices:
Fred Flintstone: Henry Corden, **Barney Rubble:** Mel Blanc, **Wilma Flintstone:** Jean VanderPyl, **Betty Rubble:** Gay Autterson, **Count Rockula:** John Stephenson, **Frankenstone:** Ted Cassidy, **Frau G.:** Jean VanderPyl, **Monty Marble:** Casey Kasem, **Igor/Wolf:** Don Messick, **Silica/Bat:** Lennie Weinrib

THE FLINTSTONES' NEW NEIGHBORS

Fred and Wilma are reluctant to greet their new neighbors, the Frankenstones, whose house is furnished with the weirdest creature comforts. *A Hanna–Barbera Production. Color. Half–hour. Premiered on NBC: September 26, 1980.*

Voices:
Fred Flintstone: Henry Corden, **Barney Rubble:** Mel Blanc, **Wilma Flintstone:** Jean VanderPyl, **Betty Rubble:** Gay Autterson, **Pebbles Flintstone:** Jean VanderPyl, **Bamm–Bamm Rubble:** Don Messick, **Dino:** Mel Blanc, **Frank Frankenstone:** John Stephenson, **Oblivia Frankenstein:** Pat Parris, **Stubby Frankenstone:** Jim McGeorge, **Hidea Frankenstone:** Julie McWhirter, **Creeply/Mother Pterodactyl:** Frank Welker, **Scorpion:** Henry Corden, **Vulture:** Don Messick, **Pterodactyl Chicks:** Don Messick, Mel Blanc, Frank Welker

THE FLINTSTONES' 25TH ANNIVERSARY CELEBRATION

Using clips from past "Flintstones" episodes, along with all–new animation created especially for this program, Tim Conway, Harvey Korman and Vanna White host this nostalgic special, tracing the unique history of television's first prime–time animated program. *A Hanna–Barbera Production. Color. One hour. Premiered on CBS: May 20, 1986.*

Wilma discovers she has a fastball that's worth a thousand clams to the Bedrock Dodgers team in a scene from "The Flintstones: Wind–Up Wilma" special. © Hanna–Barbera Productions

Voices:

Fred Flintstone: Alan Reed, Henry Corden, **Wilma Flintstone:** Jean VanderPyl, **Barney Rubble:** Mel Blanc, **Betty Rubble:** Bea Benadaret, **Yogi Bear/Huckleberry Hound:** Daws Butler, **Quick Draw McGraw:** Daws Butler, **Scooby–Doo/Scrappy–Doo:** Don Messick

THE FLINTSTONES: WIND–UP WILMA

Wilma's mean wind-up in the supermarket, where she throws a melon and knocks two thieves unconscious for trying to steal her grocery money, turns her into an instant local celebrity. She is offered a baseball contract to pitch for the local Bedrock Dodger team, whose attendance is lagging and which could use her talent to boost interest. *A Hanna–Barbera Production. Color. Half–hour. Premiered on NBC: October 4, 1981. Rebroadcast on NBC: March 7, 1982.*

Voices:

Fred Flintstone: Henry Corden, **Barney Rubble:** Mel Blanc, **Wilma Flintstone:** Jean VanderPyl, **Betty Rubble:** Gay Autterson, **Pebbles Flintstone:** Jean VanderPyl, **Dino:** Mel Blanc, **Frank Frankenstone:** Julie McWhirter, **Turtle #2/Elephant:** Henry Corden, **Clothespin Bird:** Jean VanderPyl, **Female Cop/Cuckoo Bird:** Gay Autterson, **Animal/La Shale/Rocky:** Julie McWhirter, **Announcer/Bird #1/Turtle #1:** Don Messick, **Mean/Checker/Chick #1:** Joe Baker, **Stub/Cop:** Jim McGeorge, **Sheep/Rooster/Umpire/Reporter #1/Thief/1st Man/Voice:** Paul Winchell, **Creeply/Bird #2/Finrock:** Frank Welker

FOR BETTER OR FOR WORSE: THE BESTEST PRESENT

Originally made for Canadian television audiences, this special deals with the nightmarish adventures of a normal, everyday family during Christmas. The program was based on cartoonist Lynn Johnston's syndicated comic strip, "For Better or For Worse." *An Atkinson Film–Arts Production in association with Telefilm, Canada. Color. Half–hour. Premiere (U. S.) on HBO: December, 1986.*

Voices:

Michael Patterson: Aaron Johnston, **Elizabeth "Lizzy" Patterson:** Katherine Johnston, **Elly Patterson:** Abby Hagyard, **John Paterson:** William H. Stevens Jr., **Walter Lederhaus:** Billy Van, **Connie:** Anna MacCormick, **Lawrence:** Dominic Bradford, **Vocalist:** Scott Binkley

THE FOURTH KING

Spotting a "strange new light in the sky"—the star of Bethlehem—the animals of the land decide to send an emissary of their own—a lion, sparrow, rabbit, beaver and turtle—to be represented too, along with the three traveling kings at the manger where the Christ child is to be born. *A RAI Television Production in association with NBC. Color. Half–hour. Premiered on NBC: December 23, 1977.*

Voices:

Lion: Ted Ross, **Sparrow:** Laurie Beechman, **Turtle:** Arnold Stang, **Beaver:** Bob McFadden, **Rabbit:** Ed Klein

FREEDOM IS

In his dreams, Benji and his pet dog Waldo are transported back in time to the Revolutionary War, where they learn all about freedom with the help of new friend Jeremiah Goodheart. *A Screen Images Production for Lutheran Television. Color. Half–hour. Premiered: Summer, 1976. Syndicated.*

Voices:

Benji: David Kelly, **Jeremiah Goodheart:** Jonathan Winters, **Samuel:** Richard Roundtree, **Ben Franklin:** Joseph Cotton, **John Adams:** Edward Asner, **Thomas Jefferson:** Dan Dailey, **Jason:** Philip Morris

FROM THE EARTH TO THE MOON

The early triumphs of an adventurous group, the Gun Club, who attempt to reach the moon by launching a manned vessel, is related in this half–hour syndicated special produced overseas. *An Air Programs International Production. Color. Half–hour. Premiered: 1976. Syndicated.*

Voices:

Alistair Duncan, Ron Haddrick, Phillip Hinton, Shane Porteous.

FROSTY'S WINTER WONDERLAND

In this sequel to 1969's "Frosty the Snowman," Frosty's moppet friends create a wife for the usually joyful snowman who they find is really lonely. Jack Frost, jealous of the snowman's newfound happiness, makes every effort to make life miserable for him once again. Andy Griffith narrates and sings in this imaginatively wrought special. Songs featured include "Frosty" and "Winter Wonderland." *A Rankin–Bass Production. Color. Half–Hour. Premiered on ABC: December 2, 1976. Rebroadcast on ABC: December 3, 1977; December 13, 1978; November 25, 1979; December 23, 1981; December 1, 1982.*

Voices:
Frosty the Snowman: Jackie Vernon, **Crystal the Snowgirl:** Shelley Winters, **Parson:** Dennis Day, **Jack Frost:** Paul Frees, **Children:** Shelley Hines, Eric Stern, **Others:** Manfred Olea, Barbara Jo Ewing, **Narrator:** Andy Griffith, **Vocalists:** The Wee Winter Singers

FROSTY THE SNOWMAN

Based on a song of the same name by Jack Rollins and Steve Nelson, this perennial favorite traces the origin of America's best-known snowman—brought to life by a magic hat on Christmas Eve—and his struggle to get to the North Pole before spring arrives. Like its forerunner "Rudolph the Red–Nosed Reindeer," the program was produced in Animagic, a then–revolutionary stop–motion animation process using doll–like puppets. *A Rankin–Bass Production. Color. Half–hour. Premiered on CBS: December 7, 1969. Rebroadcast on CBS: December 5, 1970; December 5, 1971; December 4, 1972; December 10, 1973; December 8, 1974; December 12, 1975; December 17, 1976; December 10, 1977; November 30, 1978;*

America's favorite snowman, Frosty, consoles his friend Karen in the perennial Christmas special, "Frosty The Snowman." © Rankin–Bass Productions (Courtesy: Family Home Entertainment)

December 8, 1979; November 28, 1980; November 27, 1981; December 21, 1982; December 14, 1983; December 11, 1984; December 7, 1985; December 12, 1986; December 9, 1987; November 28, 1988; December 22, 1989.

Voices:
Frosty the Snowman: Jackie Vernon, **Professor Hinkle:** Billy DeWolfe, **Karen,** Frosty's friend: June Foray, **Santa Claus:** Paul Frees, **Narrator:** Jimmy Durante

A GARFIELD CHRISTMAS SPECIAL

Jon goes home to the farm for the holidays. While Odie works on a mystery gift, Garfield plans to surprise Grandma. An Emmy Award nominee. *A Film Roman Production in association with United Media and Paws. Color. Half–hour. Premiered on CBS: December 21, 1987. Rebroadcast on CBS: December 23, 1988; December 21, 1989.*

Voices:
Garfield: Lorenzo Music, **Jon Arbuckle:** Thom Huge, **Odie:** Gregg Berger, **Mom:** Julie Payne, **Dad:** Pat Harrington, **Doc Boy:** David Lander, **Grandma:** Pat Carroll

GARFIELD GOES HOLLYWOOD

When the TV show "Pet Search" announces a pet talent contest, Jon devises an act for himself, Garfield and Odie: Jonny Bop and the Two Steps. They win the local event and head to Hollywood for the finals, where Garfield and Odie cut Jon out of the act and become The Dancing Armandos. An Emmy Award nominee. *A Film Roman Production in association with United Media and Paws. Color. Half–hour. Premiered on CBS: May 8, 1987. Rebroadcast on CBS: March 16, 1988.*

Voices:
Garfield: Lorenzo Music, **Jon Arbuckle:** Thom Huge, **Odie/ Bob/Grandma Fogerty/Announcer:** Gregg Berger, **Herbie:** Nino Tempo, **National TV Host:** Frank Welker

GARFIELD: HIS NINE LIVES

Garfield hosts a look at his nine lives. At the end, he is luckily given an additional nine. The segments that make up the special: "In the Beginning," where the "Creator" decides to design a cat; "Cave Cat," showing the prehistoric origins of cats; "King Cat," revealing Garfield's royal heritage; "In the Garden," the story of Garfield's sharing joy in a whimsical world of fantasy with a young girl (Cloey); "Court Musician," with Garfield as the inventor of jazz; "Stunt Rat," featuring Garfield working in silent films; "Diana's Piano," a touching tale about the cycle of life and death; "Lab Animal," offering a strange tale of an experiment that goes awry; "Garfield," the origin of the famed comic–strip character; and "Space Cat," his travels in the distant future and a distant galaxy. *A Film Roman Productions in association with United Media and Paws. Color. One hour. Premiered on CBS: November 22, 1988.*

Voices:

Garfield: Lorenzo Music, **Odie:** Gregg Berger, **The Creator:** Lindsay Workman, **Narrator** ("Cave Cat"): Gregg Berger, **Junior:** Thom Huge, **Black Bart:** Nino Tempo, **Announcer** ("In the Garden"): Desiree Goyette, **Jester** ("Court Musician"): Gregg Berger, **Director** ("Stunt Kat"): Jim Davis, **Sara** ("Diana's Piano"): Desiree Goyette, **Jon Arbuckle** ("Garfield"): Thom Huge, **Garfield's Mom** ("Garfield"): Desiree Goyette, **Captain Mendelson** ("Space Cat"): Frank Welker

GARFIELD IN PARADISE

Garfield, Odie and Jon vacation in the tropics at a cheap resort. When they go exploring, they meet a lost tribe that worships 1950s automobiles and is preparing a human and cat sacrifice for the volcano god. An Emmy Award nominee. *A Film Roman Production in association with United Media and Paws. Color. Half–hour. Premiered on CBS: May 27, 1986. Rebroadcast on CBS: January 16, 1987; November 23, 1988; April 24, 1989.*

Voices:

Garfield: Lorenzo Music, **Jon Arbuckle:** Thom Huge, **High Rama Lama:** Wolfman Jack, **Hotel Clerk/Salesman:** Frank Nelson, **Odie Pigeon:** Gregg Berger, **Owooda:** Desiree Goyette, **Mai Tai/Stewardess:** Julie Payne, **Monkey:** Nino Tempo, **Woman/Cat:** Carolyn Davis, **B. G. Voices:** Hal Smith, **Vocalists:** Desiree Goyette, Thom Huge, Lorenzo Music, Lou Rawls

GARFIELD IN THE ROUGH

When Jon announces they are going on vacation, Garfield's enthusiasm wanes when he discovers Jon plans a camping trip. Life in the wild gets dangerous when an escaped panther enters the campgrounds. An Emmy Award winner. *A Film Roman Production in association with United Media and Paws. Color. Half–hour. Premiered on CBS: October 26, 1984. Rebroadcast on CBS: March 23, 1985; August 21, 1987.*

Voices:

Garfield: Lorenzo Music, **Jon Arbuckle:** Thom Huge, **Odie/ Ranger #1/Announcer:** Gregg Berger, **Ranger #2:** George Wendt, **Dicky Beaver:** Hal Smith, **Billy Rabbit:** Orson Bean, **Girl Cats/Arlene:** Desiree Goyette, **Vocalists:** Desiree Goyette, Thom Huge, Lou Rawls

GARFIELD ON THE TOWN

On the way to the vet's, Garfield slips out of the car and attempts to make it as a street cat. While in the inner city, he discovers his birthplace and family. An Emmy Award winner. *A Lee Mendelson–Bill Melendez Production in association with United Media Productions. Color. Half–hour. Premiered on CBS: October 28, 1983. Rebroadcast on CBS: March 10, 1984; December 28, 1985.*

Voices:

Garfield: Lorenzo Music, **Jon Arbuckle:** Thom Huge, **Raoul:** George Wendt, **Ali Cat:** Gregg Berger, **Mom,** Garfield's mother: Sandi Huge, **Liz:** Julie Payne, **Grandfather:** Lindsay Workman,

Garfield's unenthusiastic arrival at a flea–bitten resort is further punctuated by the discovery of Odie, who has stowed away in a suitcase, in the prime–time special, "Garfield In Paradise." © United Feature Syndicate Inc. (Courtesy: CBS)

Girl Cat #2 and #3: Allyce Beasley, **Girl Cat #1:** Desiree Goyette, **Vocalists:** Desiree Goyette, Lou Rawls

GARFIELD'S BABES AND BULLETS

In this satire of detective films of the 1940s, Garfield fantasizes (in black and white) on a rainy day about being Sam Spayed, a Private Investigator handling a case involving a mysterious woman. An Emmy Award winner. *A Film Roman Production in association with United Media and Paws. Color. Half–hour. Premiered on CBS: May 23, 1989.*

Voices:

Garfield: Lorenzo Music, **Jon Arbuckle:** Thom Huge, **Odie:** Gregg Berger, **Burt Fleebish:** Gregg Berger, **Thug:** Thom Huge, **Kitty:** Julie Payne, **Tanya:** Desiree Goyette, **Professor O'Felix:** Lindsay Workman, **Lt. Washington:** Nino Tempo

GARFIELD'S HALLOWEEN ADVENTURE

Garfield and Odie get dressed up as pirates to go trick or treating. When they attempt to cross the river in a rowboat, they accidentally end up at a haunted house where ghostly pirates are expected any minute. An Emmy Award winner. *A Film Roman Production in association with United Media Productions. Color. Half–hour. Premiered on CBS: October 30, 1985. Rebroadcast on CBS: October 24, 1986; October 23, 1987; October 28, 1988; October 30, 1989.*

Voices:

Garfield: Lorenzo Music, **Jon Arbuckle:** Thom Huge, **Odie:** Gregg Berger, **Old Man:** Lindsay Workman, **TV Announcer:** Gregg Berger, **Woman:** Desiree Goyette, **Vocalists:** Lorenzo Music, Lou Rawls

GARFIELD'S THANKSGIVING SPECIAL

The day before Thanksgiving, Garfield is put on a diet and Liz, the veternarian, agrees to have Thanksgiving dinner with Jon. However, when Jon's cooking manages to destroy the meal, Grandma arrives in time to save the day and Garfield is given a reprieve from fasting. An Emmy Award winner. *A Film Roman Production in association with United Media and Paws. Color. Half—hour. Premiered on CBS: November 22, 1989.*

Voices:
Garfield: Lorenzo Music, **Jon Arbuckle:** Thom Huge, **Odie:** Gregg Berger, **Liz/Scale:** Julie Payne, **Grandma:** Pat Carroll, **Vocalists:** Lou Rawls, Desiree Goyette

GIDGET MAKES THE WRONG CONNECTION

In this animated spin—off of the "Gidget" television series, Frances "Gidget" Lawrence recounts her own and her surfer friends' attempt to expose a ring of gold smugglers in this one—hour movie originally broadcast on the "The ABC Saturday Superstar Movie" series. *A Hanna—Barbera Production. Color. One hour. Premiered on ABC: November 18, 1972 (on "The ABC Saturday Superstar Movie"). Rebroadcast on ABC: October 6, 1973; March 16, 1974. Syndicated.*

Voices:
Gidget: Kathy Gori, **Rink/Steve:** Denny Evans, **Killer/Gorgeous Cat/Capt. Parker:** Don Messick, **Ralph Hightower/R. C. Man:** Mike Road, **Radio (Voice):** Don Messick, **Bull/Capt. Shad:** Bob Hastings, **Barbara Hightower:** Virginia Gregg, **Jud:** David Lander

THE GLO FRIENDS SAVE CHRISTMAS

When the Wicked Witch of the North Pole unveils her fiendish plans to prevent Santa Claus from delivering toys to the creatures of Gloland, the Glo Friends unhatch their own counterattack on the mean witch so Santa can spread his good cheer to everyone. *A Sunbow Production in association with Marvel Productions. Color. Half—hour. Premiered: November, 1985. Syndicated.*

Voices:
Santa Claus: Carroll O'Connor, **Blanche,** Wicked Witch of North Pole: Sally Struthers

Additional Voices:
Charlie Adler, Jill Choder, Townsend Coleman, Laura Dean, Pat Fraley, Ellen Gerstell, Renae Jacobs, Mona Marshall, Michael Mich, Lorenzo Music, Laurie O'Brien, Patti Paris, Susan Silo, Frank Welker

GNOMES

Revenge is the order of the day when Tor, a young gnome, is set to marry Lisa from the city but the arch—rival trolls, angry because the gnomes keep releasing their prey before they can eat it, decide to grab the unsuspecting gnomes when they're assembled for the nuptial ceremony. *A Zanders Animation Parlor Production in association with Tomorrow Entertainment. Color. One hour. Premiered on CBS: November 11, 1980. Rebroadcast on CBS: August 28, 1982; August 27, 1983.*

Voices:
Arthur Anderson, Rex Everhart, Anne Francine, Hetty Galen, Gordon Halliday, Bob McFadden, Corrinne Orr, Joe Silver

GOLDILOCKS

The familiar children's tale of "Goldilocks and the Three Bears" is recreated in this live—action/animation version, which features the voices of the Crosby family (Bing, Kathryn, Mary Frances and Nathaniel). *A DePatie—Freleng Enterprises Production in association with NBC. Color. Half—hour. Premiered on NBC: March 31, 1970. Rebroadcast on NBC: October 24, 1970.*

Voices:
Goldilocks: Mary Frances Crosby, **Papa Bear:** Bing Crosby, **Mama Bear:** Kathryn Crosby, **Baby Bear:** Nathaniel Crosby, **Bobcat:** Paul Winchell, **Other Voices:** Avery Schreiber

THE GOOD, THE BAD AND HUCKLEBERRY HOUND

Set in the Old West town of Two Bit, Huckleberry Hound has a plan: to cash in a gold nugget, buy a quaint country farm and raise goats and pigs. But fate has other plans. Dinky, Pinky and Finky Dalton, the notorious Dalton gang, steal Huck's gold nugget. Huckleberry decides it's time someone cleans up the town so he becomes the new sheriff. This two-hour special was the first in a series of feature—length cartoons made for first—run syndication for "Hanna—Barbera's Superstars 10" package. *A Hanna—Barbera Production. Color. Two hours. Premiered: 1988. Syndicated.*

Voices:
Huckleberry Hound: Daws Butler, **Baba Looey/Peter Potamus/Yogi Bear/Hokey Wolf/Snagglepuss/Quick Draw McGraw:** Daws Butler, **Boo Boo/Narrator:** Don Messick, **Finky/Fat Boy Kid/Rooster/Baby/Little Boy:** Pat Fraley, **Magilla Gorilla/Dinky/Announcer:** Alan Melvin, **Pinky/News Anchorman/Pig:** Charlie Adler, **Stinky/Steer/Station Announcer/Bailiff/Laughing Donkey:** Michael Bell, **Dentist/Governor/Mr. Peebles/Photographer/Chuckling Chipmunk:** Howie Morris, **Judge Flopner/Horse/Chef/Race Track Announcer/Mission Control:** Frank Welker, **Rusty/Desert Flower/Wife/Little Old Lady/Fat Girl:** B. J. Ward, **Red Eye:** Pat Buttram

THE GREAT BEAR SCARE

In the small forest community of Bearbank, the resident bear population is menaced by a group of monsters. Ted E. Bear, voiced by Tommy Smothers, is selected to quell the dastardly bunch, becoming a local hero to the populace and his special friend, Patti Bear, anchorbear for the local TV station's "Bear Witness News." *A DimenMark Films Production. Color. Half–hour. Premiered: October, 1982. Syndicated.*

Voices:
Ted E. Bear: Tom Smothers, **Patti Bear:** Sue Raney, **Professor Werner Von Bear:** Hans Conried, **Dracula:** Louis Nye, **C. Emory Bear:** Hal Smith, **Miss Witch:** Lucille Bliss

THE GREAT CHRISTMAS RACE

The Lollipop Dragon and his friends must defeat Baron Bad Blood to save the children from having to eat liver lollipops on Christmas morning. *A Blair Entertainment Production in association with Pannonia Film. Color. Half–hour. Premiered: November, 1986. Syndicated.*

Voices:
Lollipop Dragon: Gary Wilmot, **Princess Gwendolyn:** Jill Lidstone, **Prince Hubert:** Pat Starr, **Blue Eyes:** Karen Fernald, **Glider/Queen:** Eva Hadden, **Baron Bad Blood:** Stephen Thorne, **Cosmo the Cunning/King:** Dennis Greashan

THE GREAT EXPECTATIONS

Overcoming early misfortunes as a child, Phillip Pirrip—called "Pip"—inherits a sizable fortune and learns many valuable lessons in a series of adventures that follow. *A Burbank Films Production. Color. Half–hour. Premiered: Fall 1984. Syndicated.*

Voices:
Barbara Frawley, Marcus Hale, Philip Hinton, Simon Hinton, Liz Horne, Bill Kerr, Moya O'Sullivan, Robin Stewart

THE GREAT HEEP

In this hour–long fantasy/adventure, *Star Wars* droids R2–D2 and C–3PO arrive on the planet Biitu to meet their new master and are shocked to find that a gigantic evil droid, the Great Heep, has turned the planet into a wasteland and captured their master, Mungo Baobab, a merchant/explorer. The famed movie serial droids devise a daring scheme to free Mungo, defeat the forces of the Empire and liberate Biitu from the Great Heep forever. Adapted from George Lucas' *Star Wars* film series. *A Nelvana Limited Production in association with Hanho Heung–Up and Mi-Hahn Productions for Lucasfilm. Color. One hour. Premiered on ABC: June 7, 1986.*

Voices:
C–3PO: Anthony Daniels, **R2–D2:** (electronic), **Mungo Baobab:** Winston Rekert, **Admiral Screed:** Graeme Campbell, **Fridge:** Noam Zylberman, **Captain Cag/Announcer:** Dan Hennessey, **Gulper:** Dan Hennessey, **KT–10:** Melleny Brown, **Darva:** Melleny Brown, **The Great Heep:** Long John Baldry

GULLIVER'S TRAVELS

The adventure–seeking Gulliver learns the true meaning of friendship as he assists the Lilliputians in this colorful adap-

tation of the Jonathan Swift classic. A "CBS Famous Classic Tales" special. *A Hanna–Barbera Production. Color. One hour. Premiered on CBS: November 18, 1979. Rebroadcast on CBS: November 9, 1980.*

Voices:
Gulliver: Ross Martin, **Filmnap/Jester Pirate:** Hal Smith, **Bolgolam/Lilliputian King/Brobdingnag King:** John Stephenson, **Lilliputian/Mob Member #1:** Ross Martin, **Reldresal/Old Fisherman/Blefuscu King:** Don Messick, **Farmer/Brobdingnag Minister/Mob Member#2:** Regis Cordic, **Lilliputian Queen/Brogdingnag Queen:** Julie Bennett, **Farmer's Wife/Glumdalclitch:** Janet Waldo

HAGAR THE HORRIBLE: "HAGAR KNOWS BEST"

Hagar the Horrible, the most famous Viking of all, is on his way home from a two–year business trip ravaging foreign lands. As his ship nears the port, visions of a "Father Knows Best" family life dance in his helmeted head. But once he is home his expectations don't match up. *A Hanna–Barbera Production in association with King Entertainment. Color. Half–hour. Premiered on CBS: November 1, 1989.*

Voices:
Hagar: Peter Cullen, **Honi:** Lydia Cornell, **Helga:** Lainie Kazan, **Hamlet:** Josh Rodine, **Lucky Eddie:** Jeff Doucett, **Olaf:** Hank Saroyan, **Lute/Instructor:** Donny Most, **Doorman:** Hank Saroyan, **Kid:** Josh Rodine, **Principal:** Frank Welker, **Joe:** Jeff Doucette, **Al:** Frank Welker, **Snert/Kvaak:** Frank Welker, **Teacher:** Jack Tice, **Narrator:** Frank Welker

HALLOWEEN WHO–DUN–IT?

Davey Hanson and his dog Goliath, stars of the popular religious stop–motion animation series "Davey and Goliath," return in this first–run special providing a new lesson on Christian living tied in with Halloween. *A Clokey Production for the Lutheran Church of America. Color. Half–hour. Premiered: 1977. Syndicated.*

Voices:
Davey Hanson/Sally Hanson/Mary Hanson: Norma McMillan, Nancy Wible, **Goliath/John Hanson:** Hal Smith

HANNA–BARBERA'S 50TH: A YABBA DABBA DOO CELEBRATION

Hosts Tony Danza and Annie Potts lead a madcap cast of live and animated guests in this festive two–hour special celebrating 50 years of animated magic by Oscar–winning animators William Hanna and Joseph Barbera. Highlighting the special is comedian Whoopi Goldberg singing the Flintstones theme song and Victor Borge conducting an animated symphony orchestra. Other special guests included Sammy Davis Jr., Phyllis Diller, Betty White, Jonathan Winters, Valerie Harper and even Los Angeles Dodgers manager Tommy Lasorda. Interspersed throughout the special were clips from assorted

Hanna–Barbera cartoons, plus new animated segments. *A Hanna Barbera Production. Color. Two hours. Premiered on TNT: July 17, 1989.*

Voices:
Greg Berg, Mel Blanc, Henry Corden, Casey Kasem, Don Messick, Penny Singleton, John Stephenson, Jean VanderPyl

HAPPILY EVER AFTER

Troubled by the news of her parents' divorce, Molly Conway, who like most children dreams of living happily ever after, forms a group with her offbeat friends ("The Skywalkers") to try to prevent her parents from breaking up. *A JZM–Bill Melendez Production in association with Wonderworks and Bill Melendez Productions, London, England. Color. One Hour. Premiered on PBS: October 21, 1985 (on PBS's "Wonderworks" anthology series).*

Voices:
Narrator: Carol Burnett, **Molly Conway:** Cassandra Coblentz, **Alice Conway:** Carrie Fisher, **Carl Conway:** Henry Winkler, **Tommy Johnson:** Danny Colby, **George Johnson:** Danny DeVito, **Rose Johnson:** Rhea Perlman, **Joey Fabrizio:** Jeremy Schoenberg, **Dom Fabrizio:** Dana Ferguson, **Mary O'Connell:** Gini Holtzman, **Darlene Kashitani:** Karrie Ullman, **Woody Coleman:** Carl Stevens, **Molly's Daughter:** Keri Houlihan, **What's His Name:** Brett Johnson

HAPPY ANNIVERSARY, CHARLIE BROWN

Twenty–five years of the "Peanuts" comic strip is celebrated in this retrospective special, containing clips from 14 Charlie Brown television specials. The special is hosted by Carl Reiner and features wraparound interview segments with "Peanuts" creator Charles Schulz. *A Lee Mendelson Production in association with Charles M. Schulz Creative Associates and United Feature Syndicate. Color. One hour. Premiered on CBS: January 9, 1976.*

Voices:
Charlie Brown: Duncan Winston, **Schroeder:** Greg Felton, **Sally Brown:** Gail M. Davis, **Lucy Van Pelt:** Lynn Mortensen, **Linus Van Pelt:** Liam Martin, **Peppermint Patty:** Stuart Brotman

HAPPY BIRTHDAY BUGS: 50 LOONEY YEARS

Bugs Bunny, the Oscar–winning rabbit of Warner Brothers fame, turns 50 and his golden anniversary is celebrated in grand style in this freewheeling one–hour special. The program includes a musical salute by Little Richard; an "Entertainment Tonight" portrait by Mary Hart; "A Current Affair" spoof with Maury Povich and Milton Berle, who plays an actor claiming to be the real Bugs; a tribute by Bill Cosby and Whoopie Goldberg to the late Mel Blanc, who created the voice of Bugs Bunny; and recurrent reports by Joe Garagiola on anti–Bugs protests being mounted by Daffy Duck, who's

upset because he wasn't feted two years early for his own 50th anniversary in show business. Clips from various Warner cartoons are interspersed throughout the program, starring Elmer Fudd, Porky Pig, Road Runner and Wile E. Coyote. *A Warner Brothers Television Production. Color. One hour. Premiered on CBS: May 9, 1990.*

Voices:
Mel Blanc

HAPPY BIRTHDAY, CHARLIE BROWN

In honor of this 30th year as a comic strip and 15th year on television, CBS' Phyllis George hosts this hour–long salute to Charlie Brown combining clips from past specials and a special guest appearance by creator Charles Schulz. *A Lee Mendelson Production in association with Charles M. Schulz Creative Associations and Bill Melendez Productions. Color. One Hour. Premiered on CBS: January 5, 1979.*

Voices:
Charlie Brown: Arrin Skelley, Peter Robbins, **Linus Van Pelt:** Daniel Anderson, **Sally Brown:** Annalisa Bortolin, **Marcie:** Casey Carlson, **Lucy Van Pelt:** Sally Dryer–Barker, Michelle Muller, **Dolores:** Leticia Ortiz, **Peppermint Patty:** Laura Planting, **Franklin:** Ronald Hendrix, **Vocalists:** Don Potter, Becky Reardon, Larry Finlayson

HAPPY BIRTHDAY, DONALD DUCK

Expanding on the story of the 1949 cartoon, *Donald's Happy Birthday,* Huey, Dewey and Louie, Donald's mischievous nephews, make plans for a special birthday party for their famed but temperamental uncle. Donald surprises his nephews with his own plans for his birthday—watching footage of his old cartoons. The special was retitled and rebroadcast in two other versions on NBC after its initial premiere on rival network ABC. *A Walt Disney Television Production. Color. One Hour. Premiered on ABC: November 21, 1956 (as "At Home With Donald Duck" on the program, "Disneyland"). Rebroadcast on ABC: May 8, 1957; NBC: November 7, 1976 (on "The Wonderful World Of Disney"); April 4, 1979 (as "Happy Birthday, Donald Duck").*

Voices:
Donald Duck: Clarence Nash

HAPPY EASTER

The lesson of Easter is delivered as Davey attends the Easter pageant and is overtaken by emotion after watching a rehearsal of the Passion Play. *A Clokey Production for the Lutheran Church of America. Color. Half–hour. Premiered: 1967. Syndicated.*

Voices:
Davey Hanson/Sally Hanson/Mary Hanson: Norma McMillan, Nancy Wible, **Goliath/John Hanson:** Hal Smith

HAPPY NEW YEAR, CHARLIE BROWN

The "Peanuts" gang rings in 1986 with Marcie and Peppermint Patty throwing a big New Year's Eve bash which Charlie Brown at first decides not to attend. He instead plans to curl up with a big book, Tolstoy's *War and Peace,* which he has to read over the holidays as a school assignment. That doesn't stop him from lugging the tome to Lucy's pre–party dance class, however, and taking a break to attend Marcie's and Peppermint Patty's party with Tolstoy, of course, in tow. *A Lee Mendelson–Bill Melendez Production in association with Charles M. Schulz Creative Associates and United Feature Syndicate. Color. Half–hour. Premiered on CBS: January 1, 1986. Rebroadcast on CBS: January 1, 1987; December 28, 1988.*

Voices:

Charlie Brown: Chad Allen, **Charlie Brown** (singing): Sean Collins, **Peppermint Patty:** Kristi Baker, **Lucy Van Pelt:** Melissa Guzzi, **Lucy Van Pelt** (singing): Tiffany Billings, **Linus Van Pelt:** Jeremy Miller, **Sally Brown:** Elizabeth Lyn Fraser, **Schroeder:** Aron Mandelbaum, **Marcie:** Jason Muller, **Off–Camera Singer:** Desiree Goyette

THE HAPPY PRINCE

The story of a royal statue which makes friends with a small swallow is told in this bittersweet tale based on the Oscar Wilde story. *A Gerald Potterton Production in association with Reader's Digest. Color. Half–hour. Premiered: 1975. Syndicated.*

Voices:

Statue: Christopher Plummer, **Swallow:** Glynis Johns

THE HARLEM GLOBETROTTERS MEET SNOW WHITE

The wizards of the basketball court play gargoyles working for a wicked witch—really a vain queen—who has cast a spell on Snow White. *A Hanna–Barbera Production. Color. One hour and a half. Premiered on NBC: September 27, October 4, October 11 and October 18, 1980 (as a four–part serial on "Fred and Barney Meet the Shmoo"). Syndicated.*

Voices:

Curly Neal: Stu Gilliam, **Geese:** John Williams, **Marques:** Robert DoQui, **Li'l John:** Buster Jones, **Dunbar:** Adam Wade, **Nate:** Scatman Crothers, **Baby Face Paige:** Mork Davitt, **Snow White:** Russi Taylor, **Prince:** Michael Bell, **Marva:** Diane McCannon, **Queen of Grimmania:** Gay Autterson, **Count Revolta:** John Stephenson

HE–MAN AND SHE–RA—A CHRISTMAS SPECIAL

The villainous Skeletor, arch–rival of He–Man and She–Ra, tries to stop the spread of Christmas joy on Earth, but his diabolical plan is squelched when Prince Adam (He–Man) and Princess Adora (She–Ra) launch their own counterattack. *A Filmation Production. Color. One hour. Premiered: November, 1985. Syndicated.*

Voices:

Adam/He–Man: John Erwin, **Adora/She–Ra:** Melendy Britt, **Skeletor:** Alan Oppenheimer, **Madam Razz/Shadow Weaver:** Linda Gary, **Hordak/Bow:** George DiCenzo, **Orko:** Eric Gunden

Additional Voices:

Lana Beeson, Erika Scheimer, R. D. Robb

HERE COMES GARFIELD

In his first prime–time animated special, Garfield the cat lives up to his reputation as being "both thorny and funny" when he and his pint–sized playmate, Odie the mutt, play havoc with a nasty neighbor. Unfortunately, their friskiness lands Odie in the city pound and it is up to rueful Garfield, even fatter and sassier from his midnight snacking, to break into the pound and get Odie out. An Emmy Award nominee. *A Lee Mendelson–Bill Melendez Production in association with United Feature Syndicate. Color. Half–hour. Premiered on CBS: October 25, 1982. Rebroadcast on CBS: November 26, 1983; May 17, 1985; October 12, 1988.*

Voices:

Garfield: Lorenzo Music, **Jon Arbuckle:** Sandy Kenyon, **Odie:** Gregg Berger, **Hubert:** Henry Corden, **Reba/Skinny:** Hal Smith, **Fast Eddie/Fluffy:** Hank Garrett, **Salesman:** Gregg Berger, **Little Girl:** Angela Lee, **Vocalists:** Lou Rawls, Desiree Goyette

HERE COMES PETER COTTONTAIL

Danny Kaye hosts and narrates this whimsical hour–long Animagic special—using stop–motion puppet animation—recounting the delightful tale of Peter Cottontail and his efforts to deliver more eggs than Irontail, an evil rabbit, who is interested in dethroning him as "the Easter Rabbit." Based on the popular children's book *The Easter That Overslept,* the program was conceived by the same team that produced earlier seasonal favorites, including "Rudolph the Red–Nosed Reindeer" and "Little Drummer Boy." *A Rankin–Bass Production in association with Videocraft International. Color. One hour. Premiered on ABC: April 4, 1971. Rebroadcast on ABC: March 30, 1972; CBS: April 13, 1976; April 8, 1977; March 24, 1978; April 10, 1979; March 28, 1980; April 10, 1981.*

Voices:

Seymour S. Sassafrass: Danny Kaye, **Peter Cottontail:** Casey Kasem, **Irontail:** Vincent Prince, **Donna:** Iris Rainer, **Antoine/Wellington B. Bunny:** Danny Kaye, **Bonnie:** Joan Gardner

Additional Voices:

Paul Frees, Greg Thomas, Jeffrey A. Thomas.

HE'S YOUR DOG, CHARLIE BROWN

Snoopy's sudden attack of bad manners makes him so unpopular with the "Peanuts" clan that Charlie Brown decides to ·send him back to the Daisy Hill Puppy Farm for a refresher course in obedience training. The program marked Snoopy's first starring role for prime–time. *A Lee Mendelson–Bill Melendez Production in association with Charles M. Schulz Creative Associates and United Feature Syndicate. Color. Half–hour. Premiered on CBS: February 14, 1968. Rebroadcast on CBS: February 20, 1969; February 15, 1970; February 13, 1971, February 14, 1972; June 5, 1973.*

Voices:

Charlie Brown: Peter Robbins, **Linus Van Pelt:** Chris Shea, **Lucy Van Pelt:** Sally Dryer–Barker, **Peppermint Patty:** Gail DeFaria, **Frieda/Patty:** Anne Altieri, **Violet:** Linda Mendelson

HEY, HEY, HEY, IT'S FAT ALBERT

The first cartoon adaptation of comedian Bill Cosby's fictional childhood characters, this half–hour special combined sketchy–styled animated drawings superimposed over live–action footage to tell the story of Cosby's boyhood chums from North Philadelphia who are preparing for a big football match against rival street–gang members, the Green Street Terrors. *A Filmation Production in association with Bill Cosby Production. Color. Half–hour. Premiered on NBC: November 12, 1969. Rebroadcast on NBC: April 17, 1970; September 12, 1971.*

Voices:

Fat Albert: Bill Cosby, **Mushmouth/Mudfoot/Dumb Donald:** Bill Cosby, **Russell:** Stephen Cheatham, **Weird Harold:** Gerald Edwards, **Bucky:** Jan Crawford, **Rudy:** Eric Suter

Concept drawing of the Fat Albert character from his first prime–time special, "Hey, Hey, Hey, It's Fat Albert."
© Bill Cosby/Filmation

Additional Voices:

Ernestine Wade, Solomon Young, Alvin Hillard, Gary Moore, Ben Anderson

HIAWATHA

Legendary brave Hiawatha encounters his greatest test of courage when his tribe is put under the spell of Pearl Feather, an evil medicine man, who seeks revenge by starving his tribe. Based on the Henry Wadsworth Longfellow poem, this program was broadcast in syndication as part of the "Festival of Family Classics." *A Rankin–Bass Production in association with Mushi Studios. Color. Half–hour. Premiered: September 24, 1972. Syndicated.*

Voices:

Carl Banas, Len Birman, Bernard Cowan, Peg Dixon, Keith Hampshire, Peggi Loder, Donna Miller, Frank Perry, Henry Raymer, Billie Mae Richards, Alfie Scopp, Paul Soles

THE HOBBIT

Self–doubting hobbit Bilbo Baggins leads a quest through Middle Earth to recover stolen treasure from the terrifying dragon, Smaug, and finds a magical ring in this 90–minute special based on the J. R. R. Tolkein literary classic. Glen Yarbrough sang the special's theme song, "The Greatest Adventure." *A Rankin–Bass Production. Color. One hour and a half. Premiered on NBC: November 27, 1977. Rebroadcast on CBS: May 19, 1979.*

Voices:

Bilbo Baggins: Orson Bean, **Gandalf the wizard:** John Huston, **Thorin Oakenshield,** king dwarf: Hans Conried, **Dragon Smaug:** Richard Boone, **Gollum:** Theodore, **Elvenking:** Otto Preminger, **Elrond:** Cyril Ritchard

Additional Voices:

Paul Frees, John Stephenson, Don Messick, Jack DeLeon

HOORAY FOR THE THREE WISEMEN

In the year 2000, three wisemen are sent to Earth in a spacecraft to deliver gifts to the newborn Christ child in this Italian–produced special made in six episodes. *A Cineteam Realizzazioni Production in association with Radiotelevisione Italiana. Color. Premiered: 1987. Syndicated.*

Voices:

Gaspar: Albert Eddy, **Balthasar:** Leroy Villanueva, **Melchor:** Tony McShear, **Kid:** Dennis Khalili–Borna, **Joseph:** Michael Connor, **Mary:** Eric Rose, **Herod:** Michael McComohie (singing), **Shepherd:** Simon Prescott

Additional Voices:

Janus Blythe, Susan Sacker, Samuel J. Salerno

THE HORSE THAT PLAYED CENTERFIELD

The New York Goats, a professional baseball team, are perennial losers. They hold every "worst record" in baseball. Their luck turns when a baseball–playing horse, Oscar, joins the team. The "ABC Weekend Special" was aired in two parts. *A Ruby–Spears Enterprises Production for ABC. Color. Half–hour. Premiered on ABC: February 24 and March 3, 1979. Rebroadcast on ABC: September 29 and October 6, 1969; July 5 and 12, 1980; June 13 and 20, 1981; June 5 and 12, 1982; May 28 and June 4, 1983; June 15 and 22, 1985; March 4 and 11, 1989; September 16 and 23, 1989.*

Voices:

John Erwin, Joan Gardner, Allan Melvin, Don Messick, Howard Morris, Alan Oppenheimer, Brad Sanders

HOW BUGS BUNNY WON THE WEST

Actor Denver Pyle, well–known for various roles in movie westerns, tells how Bugs Bunny and Daffy Duck were true pioneers of the West in this half–hour special which features excerpts from previously released Warner cartoons. *A Warner Brothers Television Production. Color. Half–hour. Premiered on CBS: November 15, 1978. Rebroadcast on CBS: September 10, 1979; September 18, 1980; March 8, 1983; January 13, 1984; May 30, 1984; January 18, 1985; September 20, 1985; August 21, 1987.*

Voices:

Mel Blanc

I LOVE CHIPMUNKS, VALENTINE SPECIAL

Valentine's Day to the Chipmunks marks the long–awaited social event of the year—the Valentine's Day dance and a chance to win the prestigious Valentine's couple award. Alvin and Chipette Brittany learn a lesson in honesty and love as they become the model Valentine's couple. *A Ruby–Spears Enterprises Production in association with Ross Bagdasarian Productions. Color. Half–hour. Premiered on NBC: February 12, 1984. Rebroadcast on NBC: February 13, 1985.*

Voices:

Alvin: Ross Bagdasarian Jr., **Simon:** Ross Bagdasarian Jr., **Theodore:** Janice Karman, **Simon:** Ross Bagdasarian Jr., **David Seville:** Ross Bagdasarian Jr., **The Chipettes** (Brittany/ Jeanette/Elenore): Janice Karman

Additional Voices:

Julie McWhirter Dees, Frank Welker

THE INCREDIBLE BOOK ESCAPE

Actress Quinn Cummings, as a young boy named P. J. (in live action), gets accidentally locked in the children's reading room of the local public library, only to become acquainted with the characters from several picture books who come to life in a blend of live–action/animation. A "CBS Library Special." *A Bosustow Entertainment Production. Color. One hour. Premiered on CBS: June 3, 1980. Rebroadcast on CBS: November 28, 1980.*

Voices:

Mrs. Page: Ruth Buzzi, **Myra:** Penelope Sundrow, **Ghost–in–the–Shed:** George Gobel, **Princess:** Tammy Grimes, **Lord Garp/Prince:** Arte Johnson, **Professor Mickimecki:** Hans Conried, **Melvin Spitznagle:** Sparky Marcus, **Mrs. Spitznagle:** June Foray, **Mr. Spitznagle:** Jack Angel

THE INCREDIBLE DETECTIVES

On a visit to a local museum, Davey Morrison is kidnapped by two guards, with few clues left behind for the police to track his whereabouts. Davey's three talented pets—Madame Cheng, a slightly vain Siamese cat; Hennesy, a gabby black crow; and Reggie, a sophisticated but stuffy bulldog—set out on their own to investigate and find Davey's kidnappers. *A Ruby–Spears Enterprises Production. Color. Half–hour. Premiered on ABC: November 17, 1979. Rebroadcast on ABC: March 20, 1980; September 27, 1980.*

Voices:

Madame Cheng: Mariene Aragon, **Reggie:** Laurie Main, **Hennesy:** Frank Welker, **Davey Morrison:** Albert Eisenmann

Additional Voices

Stan Freberg, Michael Rye, John Stephenson

THE INCREDIBLE, INDELIBLE, MAGICAL, PHYSICAL MYSTERY TRIP

This educational and entertaining fantasy tracks the journey of two young children, Joey and Missy, through the mistreated body of their Uncle Carl, who has done little in his life to maintain his health. The kids make their trip after being miniaturized by their cartoon companion, Timer, in this "ABC Afterschool Special" that combines live–action and animation. *A DePatie–Freleng Enterprises Production in association with ABC. Color. Half–hour. Premiered on ABC: February 7, 1973. Rebroadcast on ABC: October 24, 1973; March 4, 1978 (on "ABC Weekend Specials").*

Voices:

Timer: Len Maxwell, **Joey:** Peter Broderick, **Missy:** Kathy Buch

INTERGALACTIC THANKSGIVING

Two families, who are disimilar in nature (one is hard–working and dedicated; the other is self–centered and all–consuming), travel in space to parts unknown in search of a new planet where they can settle. Produced in Canada, the special first aired in that country before it was broadcast in the United States. *A Nelvana Limited Production in associ-*

ation with the CBC. Color. Half–hour. Premiered: October, 1979. Syndicated.

Voices:

King Goochie: Sid Caesar, **Ma Spademinder:** Catherine O'Hara, **Pa Spademinder:** Chris Wiggins, **Victoria Spademinder:** Jean Walker, **Magic Mirror:** Martin Lavut, **Notfunnyenuf:** Derek McGrath, **The Bug:** Al Waxman, **Bug Kid:** Toby Waxman

IS THIS GOODBYE, CHARLIE BROWN?

In this funny yet poignant treatment of the trauma friends suffer when they must separate, Lucy and Linus are moving away from their pint–sized community when their father is transferred to a new job in another city, a situation so appalling to Charlie Brown that he's left speechless . . . well, almost. Before the goodbyes can be said, however, certain matters must be cleared up first, like Lucy selling her psychiatry practice (a bearded Snoopy quickly buys it and then raises the fee from five to 50 cents) and the question of a goodbye party, which is resolved when Snoopy offers the services of his Joe Cool's Catering to prepare the event. *A Lee Mendelson–Bill Melendez Production in association with Charles M. Schulz Creative Associates and United Media Syndicate. Color. Half–hour. Premiered on CBS: February 21, 1983. Rebroadcast on CBS: February 13, 1984.*

Voices:

Charlie Brown: Brad Kesten, **Linus Van Pelt:** Jeremy Schoenberg, **Lucy Van Pelt:** Angela Lee, **Marcie:** Michael Dockery, **Sally Brown:** Stacy Heather Tolkin, **Peppermint Patty:** Victoria Vargas, **Schroeder/Franklin:** Kevin Brando, **Snoopy:** Jose C. Melendez

IT'S A BRAND NEW WORLD

Four children experience the wonders of the Bible in stories about Noah and Samson told in music and song. The program was one of six specials which aired on NBC under the heading of "NBC Special Treat." *An Elias Production in association with D & R Productions. Color. One Hour. Premiered on NBC: March 8, 1977. Rebroadcast on NBC: April 9, 1977; December 5, 1977.*

Voices:

Teacher/Noah: Joe Silver, **Elijah/Samson:** Malcolm Dodd, **Aaron:** Dennis Cooley, **Jezebel:** Boni Enten, **Barnabas:** George Hirsch, **Samson's Brother:** Charmaine Harma, **Vocalists:** Sylvester Fields, Hilda Harris, Maeretha Stewart

IT'S A MYSTERY, CHARLIE BROWN

Sally needs something to bring to show and tell at school and takes Woodstock's nest as an example of a prehistoric bird nest. Meanwhile, Snoopy, thinking he's Sherlock Holmes, tries to find the thief of his little friend's nest. *A Lee Mendelson–Bill Melendez Production in association with Charles M.*

Schulz Creative Associates and United Feature Syndicate. Color. Half–hour. Premiered on CBS: February 1, 1974. Rebroadcast on CBS: February 17, 1975.

Voices:

Charlie Brown: Todd Barbee, **Lucy Van Pelt:** Melanie Kohn, **Linus Van Pelt:** Stephen Shea, **Peppermint Patty:** Donna Forman, **Marcie:** Jimmie Ahrens, **Sally Brown:** Lynn Mortensen, **Pigpen:** Thomas A. Muller

IT'S AN ADVENTURE, CHARLIE BROWN

This one–hour animated special was one of a series of programs featuring different stories based on the best comic strips by "Peanuts" cartoonist Charles M. Schulz. Segments include Lucy's plot to get rid of Linus' security blanket and Peppermint Patty's and Marcie's stint as caddies at a golf course. Host: Charles M. Schulz. *A Lee Mendelson–Bill Melendez Production in association with Charles M. Schulz Creative Associates and United Feature Syndicate. Color. Half–hour. Premiered on CBS: May 16, 1983. Rebroadcast on CBS: November 5, 1983; September 19, 1987.*

Voices:

Charlie Brown: Michael Catalano, **Lucy Van Pelt:** Angela Lee, **Linus Van Pelt:** Earl "Rocky" Reilly, **Sally Brown:** Cindi Reilly, **Peppermint Patty:** Brent Hauer, **Schroeder:** Brad Schachter, **Marcie:** Michael Dockery, **Ruby:** Jenny Lewis, **Austin:** Johnny Graves, **Leland:** Joel Graves, **Milo:** Jason Muller, **Caddymaster:** Gerard Goyette Jr., **Camp Kids:** Brandon Crane, Brian Jackson, Kevin Brando, **Snoopy:** Jose Melendez, **Announcer:** John Hiestand

IT'S ARBOR DAY, CHARLIE BROWN

Sally's lack of knowledge of the significance of Arbor Day inspires some members of the "Peanuts" gang to set things right by embarking on a seed planting spree, using the baseball field as their garden plot. Meanwhile, unsuspecting Charlie Brown is busy preparing strategy for the opening game of the baseball season, unaware that the baseball diamond has been turned into a jungle without his consent. *A Lee Mendelson–Bill Melendez Production in association with Charles M. Schulz Creative Associates and United Feature Syndicate. Color. Half–hour. Premiered on CBS: March 16, 1976. Rebroadcast on CBS: March 14, 1977; April 10, 1978; March 24, 1980.*

IT'S FLASHBEAGLE, CHARLIE BROWN

Snoopy plays a John Travolta–type character in this animated musical parody of such films as *Flashdance* and *Staying Alive,* featuring various musical vignettes that center around a hoe–down, aerobic exercise, a game of "Lucy Says" and, of course, Snoopy on the disco dance floor. *A Lee Mendelson–Bill Melendez Production in association with Charles M. Schulz*

Creative Associates and United Feature Syndicate. Color. Half–hour. Premiered on CBS: April 16, 1984. Rebroadcast on CBS: January 1, 1985; May 27, 1986; April 19, 1988.

Voices:

Charlie Brown: Brett Johnson, Brad Kesten, **Charlie Brown** (singing): Kevin Brando, **Sally Brown:** Stacy Ferguson, **Peppermint Patty:** Gini Holtzman, **Marcie:** Keri Houlihan, **Shroeder:** Gary Goren, Kevin Brando, **Linus Van Pelt:** Jeremy Schoenberg, **Linus** (singing): David Wagner, **Lucy Van Pelt:** Heather Stoneman, **Lucy** (singing): Jessie Lee Smith, **Snoopy:** Jose Melendez, **Tommy,** the kid: Gary Goren, **Vocalists:** Joseph Chemay, Joey Harrison Scarbury, Desiree Goyette

---

IT'S MAGIC, CHARLIE BROWN

Snoopy checks out a book on magic from the library and begins practicing magic tricks before putting on a show for Charlie Brown and the other kids. For his first trick, he succeeds at making Charlie Brown invisible, but encounters trouble in making him reappear. While Snoopy figures out how to make him reappear, Charlie plays his own tricks on members of the "Peanuts" gang. *A Lee Mendelson–Bill Melendez Production in association with Charles M. Schulz Creative Associates and United Feature Syndicate. Color. Half–hour. Premiered on CBS: April 28, 1981. Rebroadcast on CBS: March 22, 1982; March 23, 1985; May 24, 1988.*

Voices:

Charlie Brown: Michael Mandy, **Snoopy:** Jose Melendez, **Linus:** Earl "Rocky" Reilly, **Sally:** Cindi Reilly, **Marcie:** Shannon Cohn, **Peppermint Patty:** Brent Hauer, **Lucy:** Sydney Penny, **Schroeder/Kid/Franklin:** Christopher Donohoe

---

IT'S THE EASTER BEAGLE, CHARLIE BROWN

Linus insists that an Easter beagle will magically appear to hand out candy on Easter morning. But, with fresh memories of their futile vigil for the Great Pumpkin, the "Peanuts" gang make their own novel preparations, including boiling eggs without the shells. *A Lee Mendelson–Bill Melendez Production in association with Charles M. Schulz and United Feature Syndicate. Color. Half–hour. Premiered on CBS: April 9, 1974. Rebroadcast on CBS: March 26, 1975; April 12, 1976; April 4, 1977; March 19, 1978; April 9, 1979; March 26, 1986.*

Voices:

Charlie Brown/Schroeder: Todd Barbee, **Lucy Van Pelt:** Melanie Kohn, **Linus Van Pelt:** Stephen Shea, **Peppermint Patty:** Linda Ercoli, **Sally Brown:** Lynn Mortensen, **Violet/Frieda:** Lynn Mortensen, **Marcie:** James Ahrens

---

IT'S THE GIRL IN THE RED TRUCK, CHARLIE BROWN

Live–action and animation combine in this tale of puppy love in the desert as Snoopy's brother Spike relates in a letter to Charlie Brown and Snoopy that he has found a special someone who brings new meaning to his quiet, carefree days of cooking flapjacks and listening to French–language tapes. She is Jenny (played by Jill Schulz, the daughter of "Peanuts" creator Charles M. Schulz), a perky aerobics instructor who drives a clunky red pickup truck. But Spike's happiness does not last: Jenny has a boyfriend, Jeff, who lures her from the idyllic desert life she has come to love. *A Lee Mendelson–Bill Melendez Production in association with Charles M. Schulz Creative Associates and United Feature Syndicate. Color. One hour. Premiered on CBS: September 27, 1988.*

Voices:

Charlie Brown: Jason Riffle, **The French Instructor:** Steve Stoliar

Cast (Live Action):

Jenny: Jill Schulz, **Jeff:** Greg Deason, **Mollie:** Mollie Boice

---

IT'S THE GREAT PUMPKIN, CHARLIE BROWN

The Halloween season means happiness for Charlie Brown, who has finally been invited to a party. As for the true spirit of this festive holiday, Linus convinces Charlie and his pals from the Charles Schulz "Peanuts" comic strip that the arrival of the Great Pumpkin "with his bag of toys for all the good children" is near. The show featured the first appearance of Snoopy's Red Baron character. Because of Charlie Brown's complaint that all he got for Halloween was a "rock," gifts poured in to CBS and Charles Schulz's office after the special first aired. *A Lee Mendelson–Bill Melendez Production in association with Charles M. Schulz Creative Associates and United Features Syndicate. Color. Half–hour. Premiered on CBS: October 27, 1966. Rebroadcast on CBS: October 26,*

Linus and Lucy take up a vigil in a pumpkin patch awaiting the arrival of the legendary Great Pumpkin, who brings gifts to good little boys and girls, in "It's The Great Pumpkin, Charlie Brown." © United Feature Syndicate Inc. (Courtesy: Bill Melendez Productions)

1967; October 24, 1968; October 26, 1969; October 24, 1970; October 23, 1971; October 28, 1974; October 23, 1976; October 30, 1978; October 22, 1979; October 24, 1980; October 30, 1981; October 25, 1982; October 28, 1983; October 26, 1984; October 30, 1985; October 24, 1986; October 23, 1987; October 25, 1989.

Voices:

Charlie Brown: Peter Robbins, **Linus Van Pelt:** Chris Shea, **Lucy Van Pelt:** Sally Dryer–Barker, **Sally Brown:** Cathy Steinberg, **Frieda/Violet:** Anne Altieri, **Peppermint Patty:** Kip DeFaria, **Pigpen:** Gai Defaria, **Patty:** Lisa DeFaria, **Schroeder** (off camera)/**Shermy:** Glenn Mendelson

IT'S YOUR FIRST KISS, CHARLIE BROWN

Unlikely hero Charlie Brown is faced with two horrendous challenges in this half–hour animated special: He is the kicker for the local football team at the annual homecoming football game and he has been chosen to escort Heather, the homecoming queen, to the celebration dance and give her the "traditional kiss." As if that were not enough, he is left trying to dazzle the little red–haired queen during the game with Lucy, that ghoulgirl of the gridiron, as his ballholder. *A Lee Mendelson–Bill Melendez Production in association with Charles M. Schulz Creative Associates and United Feature Syndicate. Color. Half–hour. Premiered on CBS: October 24, 1977. Rebroadcast on CBS: January 8, 1979; January 14, 1980; January 30, 1981; November 24, 1987.*

Voices:

Charlie Brown/Roy/Kid: Arrin Skelley, **Peppermint Patty:** Laura Planting, **Linus/Schroeder:** Daniel Anderson, **Lucy/Heather:** Michelle Muller, **Franklin/Shermy/Pigpen:** Ronald Hendrix

IT'S YOUR 20TH TELEVISION ANNIVERSARY, CHARLIE BROWN

"Peanuts" creator Charles M. Schulz hosts a toast to his characters' 20th television anniversary, with most of the hour being dedicated to clips from 26 "Peanuts" specials which have aired in prime–time since 1965. Among the highlights are scenes from "What Have We Learned, Charlie Brown?," a moving visit to the D–day site in France; the adventures of Snoopy as the Masked Marvel, North Pole sled dog, magician extraordinaire and the dancing "Flashbeagle"; and vignettes of bossy Lucy, blanket–cuddling Linus, Snoopy's fine feathered friend, Woodstock, independent Peppermint Patty and, on the pitcher's mound, good old Charlie Brown. *A Lee Mendelson–Bill Melendez Production in association with Charles M. Schulz Creative Associates and United Feature Syndicate. Color. One Hour. Premiered on CBS: May 14, 1985. Rebroadcast on CBS: February 10, 1987.*

IT WAS A SHORT SUMMER, CHARLIE BROWN

Assigned to write a 500–word theme on his summer vacation, Charlie Brown agonizes over the rememberance of things past, including summer camp and his tent mates' competing against the girls in baseball, swimming and canoeing, all spelling defeat and disaster. His last hope of beating the girls is the Masked Marvel (Snoopy), who enters a wrist wrestling match against Lucy. *A Lee Mendelson–Bill Melendez Production in association with Charles M. Schulz Creative Associates and United Feature Syndicate. Color. Half–hour. Premiered on CBS: September 27, 1969. Rebroadcast on CBS: September 16, 1970; September 29, 1971; September 7, 1972; June 27, 1983.*

Voices:

Charlie Brown: Peter Robbins, **Lucy Van Pelt:** Pamelyn Ferdin, **Linus Van Pelt:** Glenn Gilger, **Sally Brown:** Hilary Momberger, **Peppermint Patty:** Kip DeFaria, **Frieda:** Ann Altieri, **Sophie/Shirley/Clara:** Sally Dryer-Barker, **Shermy:** David Carey, **Pigpen:** Gai DeFaria, **Violet:** Linda Mendelson, **Schroeder:** John Daschback, **Roy/Kid/Boy:** Matthew Liftin, **Snoopy:** Bill Melendez

IVANHOE

Twelfth–century knight Ivanhoe, aided by Robin Hood and his Merry Men, rescue Lady Rebecca, held captive by Prince John, in this loosely based adaptation of Sir Walter Scott's romantic fantasy adventure. *An Air Programs International Production. Color. Half–hour. Premiered on CBS: November 27, 1975. Syndicated.*

Voices:

Alistair Duncan, Barbara Frawley, Chris Haywood, Mark Kelly, John Llewellyn, Helen Morse, Bevan Wilson

JACK AND THE BEANSTALK

Gene Kelly heads the cast of live actors and animated characters in this live–action/animation musical based on the popular children's fable. The original story remains intact as Jack (played by Bobby Riha) is conned by street peddler Jeremy Keen (Gene Kelly) into exchanging the family cow for a handful of magic beans that will sprout a giant beanstalk and take him to the giant's skyward castle where treasures of every kind abound. The special reunited Kelly with producers, Joe Barbera and William Hanna, who animated Kelly's spectacular dance sequence with Jerry Mouse (of "Tom and Jerry" fame) in the 1945 MGM musical *Anchors Aweigh. A Hanna–Barbera Production. Color. One hour. Premiered on NBC: February 26, 1967. Rebroadcast on NBC: January 16, 1968; CBS: January 15, 1971. Syndicated.*

Cast:

Jeremy Keen: Gene Kelly, **Jack:** Bobby Riha, **Mother:** Marian McKnight

Voices:
Around the Mouse: Chris Allen, **Monster Cat:** Dick Beals, **Princess Serena:** Janet Waldo, Marni Nixon (singing), **Giant:** Ted Cassidy, **Woggle Bird:** Cliff Norton, **Announcer:** Art Gilmore

JACK FROST

After falling in love with a beautiful blonde, Elisa, of January Junction—a village terrorized by Kubla Kraus, an ogre who lives in a castle—Jack Frost is granted his wish to become human but is foiled in his pursuit of the girl when she falls for a handsome knight instead. *A Rankin–Bass Production. Color. One Hour. Premiered on NBC: December 13, 1979. Rebroadcast on NBC: December 5, 1980. Syndicated.*

Voices:
Pardon–Me–Pete, the groundhog: Buddy Hackett, **Jack Frost:** Robert Morse, **Elisa:** Debra Clinger, **Elisa's Father:** Larry Storch, **Elisa's Mother:** Dee Stratton, **Kubla Kraus/Father Winter:** Paul Frees, **Danny,** the ventriloquist dummy: Larry Storch, **Snip the Snowflake Maker:** Don Messick, **Holly:** Diana Lynn, **TV Announcer:** Dave Garroway, **Other Voices:** Sonny Melendrez

JACK O'LANTERN

In an unusual plotline, Jack O'Lantern, a staple of Halloween, encounters trouble in the form of an evil witch, Zelda, who is fervent in her attempt to snatch Jack's magic pot of gold, and her doting warlock husband, Sir Archibald. The strange tale is recalled, in flashback, by the grandfather of two children, Michael and Colleen, whose interest in the story serves as a sub–plot. A "Festival of Family Classics" special. *A Rankin–Bass Production in association with Mushi Studios. Color. Half–hour. Premiered: October 29, 1972. Syndicated.*

Voices:
Carl Banas, Len Birman, Bernard Cowan, Peg Dixon, Keith Hampshire, Peggi Loder, Donna Miller, Frank Perry, Henry Raymer, Billie Mae Richards, Alfie Scopp, Paul Soles

THE JACKIE BISON SHOW

Animation and live action were blended in this unsold comedy pilot, which aired as a prime–time special about a buffalo (billed as "America's beast of buffoonery") who is the host of his own TV show. The program was inspired by "The Jack Benny Show." *A Stein & Illes Production in association with Brillstein/Grey Productions, Akom Productions and Broadcast TV Arts. Color. Half–hour. Premiered on NBC: July 2, 1990.*

Voices:
Jackie Bison: Stan Freberg, **Larry J. Lizard,** his announcer: Richard Karron, **Jill St. Fawn,** his girlfriend: Jane Singer, **Mrs. St. Fawn,** Jill's mother: Jayne Meadows

Additional Voices:
Rose Marie, Pat Paulsen, Gabriel Damon, Harry Shearer

THE JEAN MARSH CARTOON SPECIAL

Jean Marsh and Grover Monster, one of the original Muppets, host this collection of animated cartoons for children, including films by animators Chuck Jones, John Hubley and others. Program is also known as "The Grover Monster Cartoon Special." *A KQED–TV Production for PBS. Color. One hour. Premiered on PBS: March 10, 1975.*

THE JETSONS MEET THE FLINTSTONES

The distant past and the far future collide when a time machine catapults the Jetsons (George, Jane, Judy and Elroy) back in time to come face–to–face with Stone Age citizens Fred and Wilma Flintstone and their best friends, Betty and Barney Rubble, in this two–hour special, the third in a series of original animated movies for first–run syndication distributed as part of "Hanna–Barbera's Superstars 10" package. *A Hanna–Barbera Production. Color. Two hours. Premiered: 1987. Syndicated.*

Voices:
Fred Flintstone: Henry Corden, **Wilma Flintstone:** Jean VanderPyl, **Barney Rubble:** Mel Blanc, **Betty Rubble:** Julie Dees, **Mr. Spacely:** Mel Blanc, **Dino:** Mel Blanc, **George Jetson:** George O'Hanlon, **Jane Jetson:** Penny Singleton, **Judy Jetson:** Janet Waldo, **Elroy Jetson:** Daws Butler, **Astro/Rudi:** Don Messick, **Rosie:** Jean VanderPyl, **Didi:** Brenda Vaccaro, **Mr. Slate:** John Stephenson, **Cogswell/Henry:** Daws Butler, **Mac/Announcer:** Don Messick, **Female Computer:** Janet Waldo, **Turk Tarpit:** Hamilton Camp, **Iggy:** Jon Bauman, **Dan Rathmoon/Johnny:** Frank Welker, **Jet Rivers/Investor:** Julie Dees, **Mr. Goldbrick:** Frank Welker, **Mrs. Spacely:** Jean VanderPyl, **Moderator/Investor:** John Stephenson, **Knight:** Henry Corden, **Store Manager/Robot:** Don Messick, **Poker Player:** John Stephenson, **Panelist/Harem Girl:** Julie Dees

JIM HENSON'S MUPPET BABIES

Stars of their own successful Saturday–morning cartoon show, the Muppet Babies made their first appearance in cartoon form in this prime–time special for CBS. The premise has the characters acting like show–biz stars in situations taped before a video camera, including a movie take–off *(Star Wars)* and a rock music video. The story title for the program was "Gonzo's Video Show." *A Henson Associates Production in association with Marvel Productions. Color. Half–hour. Premiered on CBS: December 18, 1984.*

Voices:
Kermit/Beaker: Frank Welker, **Piggie:** Laurie O'Brien, **Fozzie/Scooter:** Greg Berg, **Rowlf:** Katie Lee, **Skeeter/Animal:** Howie Mandel, **Gonzo:** Russi Taylor, **Nanny:** Barbara Billingsley

JOHNNY APPLESEED

Folk hero Johnny Appleseed goes up against a quack doctor who claims his bottled medicine cures more ills than Johnny's own apple medicine. A "Family Festival of Classics" special. *A Rankin–Bass Production in association with Mushi Studios. Color. Half–hour. Premiered: November 5, 1972. Syndicated.*

Voices:
Carl Banas, Len Birman, Bernard Cowan, Peg Dixon, Keith Hampshire, Peggi Loder, Donna Miller, Frank Perry, Henry Raymer, Billie Mae Richards, Alfie Scopp, Paul Soles

JOURNEY BACK TO OZ

Dorothy and her friends, the Scarecrow, Tin–Man and the Cowardly Lion, return to save Oz from the Mombi, the Bad Witch in this sequel to the 1939 MGM classic, featuring the voices of Mickey Rooney, Danny Thomas, Milton Berle, Ethel Merman and one original *Wizard of Oz* cast member, Margaret Hamilton (The Wicked Witch of the West), in the role of Aunt Em. Originally released theatrically, the film was repackaged as a holiday special; with additional live–action sequences of Bill Cosby as the program's Host Wizard. The feature was rebroadcast in syndication in 1978 under the "SFM Holiday Network" banner. *A Filmation Production. Color. Two hours. Premiered on ABC: December 5, 1976. Syndicated.*

Voices:
Dorothy: Liza Minnelli, **Scarecrow:** Mickey Rooney, **Tin–Man:** Danny Thomas, **Cowardly Lion:** Milton Berle, **Aunt Em:** Margaret Hamilton, **Mombi,** the Bad Witch: Ethel Merman, **Glinda,** the Good Witch: Rise Stevens, **Pumpkinhead:** Paul Lynde, **Woodenhead:** Herschel Bernardi, **The Signpost:** Jack E. Leonard

Additional Voices:
Mel Blanc, Dallas McKennon, Larry Storch

JOURNEY TO THE CENTER OF THE EARTH

Professor Linderbrook, his friend Alex and guide Hans take the journey of their lifetime as they head out on a mission to explore the Earth's core in this animated adaptation of the Jules Verne science fiction novel. A "Famous Classic Tales" special. *An Air Programs International Production. Color. One hour. Premiered on CBS: November 13, 1977. Rebroadcast on CBS: November 23, 1978. Syndicated.*

Voices:
Lynette Curran, Alistair Duncan, Barbara Frawley, Ron Haddrick, Bevan Wilson.

KIDNAPPED

David Balfour, the rightful heir of the Master of the House of Shaws, gets kidnapped so that his uncle can control his inheritance and remove him from the picture altogether. Program was adapted from the Robert Louis Stevenson novel.

A "Famous Classic Tales" special. *An Air Programs International Production. Color. One hour. Premiered on CBS: October 22, 1973. Syndicated.*

THE KING KONG SHOW

The great ape, whose colossal strength and great size enable him to conquer all others, was featured in two episodes shown back–to–back in this one–hour preview of the Saturday–morning series that premiered on ABC. *A Rankin–Bass Production. Color. One–hour. Premiered on ABC: September 6, 1966.*

THE KINGDOM CHUMS: LITTLE DAVID'S ADVENTURE

Based on the Biblical story of David and Goliath, this holiday special, which opens with live–action footage, details the adventures of Little David, Christopher and Magical Mose, who welcome three children—transformed into cartoon form—to the world of the Kingdom Chums, where the world's greatest stories unfold, all leading up to David's man–to–man challenge with Goliath. *An ABC Production in association with DIC Enterprises and Diana Kerew Productions. Color. One Hour. Premiered on ABC: November 28, 1986.*

Cast:
Mary Ann: Jenna Van Oy, **Peter:** Christopher Fitzgerald, **Sauli:** Andrew Cassese

Voices:
Little David: Scott Menville, Sandi Patti (singing), **Magical Mose:** John Franklin, **Christopher/Cat Soldier:** Billy Bowles, **Goliath/Fox Soldier #3:** Jim Cummings, **Eliab/Fox Soldier #2:** Townsend Coleman, **King Saul:** Paul Winchell, **Frog Servant/Fox Soldier #1/Rat Soldier #1:** Phil Proctor, **Vocalists:** John Franklin, Sandi Patti, Mitchell Winfield

KING OF THE BEASTS

The animal cast from "Noah's Ark" returns in this half–hour sequel about a lion who assumes the role of "king of the beasts," only to drive one of his rivals, Croc the crocodile, into setting up his own solitary kingdom atop a mount. Songs and story were written by executive producer Charles G. Mortimer Jr., director Shamus Culhane and John Culhane. *A Shamus Culhane Production in association with Westfall Productions. Color. Half–hour. Premiered on NBC: April 9, 1977. Rebroadcast on NBC: April 19, 1978. Syndicated.*

Voices:
Noah: Henry Ramer, **Crocodile:** Paul Soles, **Lion:** Carl Banas, **Male Elephant** Murray Westgate, **Female Elephant:** Bonnie Brooks, **Male Giraffe/Camel:** Jay Nelson, **Polar Bear:** Don Mason, **Ostrich/Female Penguin:** Ruth Springford, **Walrus:** Jack Mather, **Female Baby Croc:** Judy Sinclair, **Male Baby Croc/Mouse:** Cardie Mortimer

KISSYFUR: BEAR ROOTS

Gus and Kissyfur, a father–and–son team of performing circus bears, escape from the big–top to join the community of Paddlecab County, but are not easily welcomed by the other resident animals until they rescue the community from the jaws of two hungry alligators, Jolene and Floyd. The program was based on characters created by Phil Melendez, characters that also inspired their own Saturday–morning series. *An NBC Production in association with DIC Enterprises. Color. Half–hour. Premiered on NBC: December 22, 1985.*

Voices:

Kissyfur: R. J. Williams, **Gus:** Edmund Gilbert, **Jolene:** Terence McGovern, **Floyd/Stuckey:** Stu Rosen, **Duane:** Neil Ross, **Beehonie/Miss Emmy/Toot:** Russi Taylor, **Lennie:** Lennie Weinrib, **Uncle Shelby:** Frank Welker

KISSYFUR: THE BIRDS AND THE BEARS

In their attempt to impress Miss Emmy Lou's smarter–than–average niece Donna, Kissyfur and his swamp friends build a raft and recklessly travel upstream, only to get caught in a strong undertow and become the target of swamp 'gators, Jolene and Floyd, returning characters from the first Kissyfur special, "Bear Roots." *A NBC Production in association with DIC Enterprises. Color. Half–hour. Premiered on NBC: March 30, 1986.*

Voices:

Kissyfur: R. J. Williams, **Gus:** Edmund Gilbert, **Jolene:** Terence McGovern, **Floyd/Stuckey:** Stu Rosen, **Duane:** Neil Ross, **Beehonie/Miss Emmy/Toot:** Russi Taylor, **Lennie:** Lennie Weinrib, **Uncle Shelby:** Frank Welker

KISSYFUR: THE LADY IS A CHUMP

When the search goes out for a new babysitter for Kissyfur, Gus hires a sweet nanny who turns out to be Floyd the alligator—bent on a good meal—in disguise. *A NBC Production in association with DIC Enterprises. Color. Half–hour. Premiered on NBC: June 1, 1986.*

Voices:

Kissyfur: R. J. Williams, **Gus:** Edmund Gilbert, **Jolene:** Terence McGovern, **Floyd/Stuckey:** Stu Rosen, **Duane:** Neil Ross, **Beehonie/Miss Emmy/Toot:** Russi Taylor, **Lennie:** Lennie Weinrib, **Uncle Shelby:** Frank Welker

KISSYFUR: WE ARE THE SWAMP

Old buzzard Flo and his snake Reggie lure Kissyfur and his swamp buddies up to a magical tree where anything is possible—even swimming in a water–filled hole—with the plans of making the critters into their main dish for dinner. *A NBC Production in association with DIC Enterprises. Color. Half–hour. Premiered on NBC: July 6, 1986.*

Voices:

Kissyfur: R. J. Williams, **Gus:** Edmund Gilbert, **Jolene:** Terence McGovern, **Floyd/Stuckey:** Stu Rosen, **Duane:** Neil Ross, **Beehonie/Miss Emmy/Toot:** Russi Taylor, **Lennie:** Lennie Weinrib, **Uncle Shelby:** Frank Welker, **Flo:** Marilyn Lightstone

LASSIE AND THE SPIRIT OF THUNDER MOUNTAIN

Television's most famous collie appeared in cartoon form for the first time in this one–hour feature–length story which was later rebroadcast as two episodes on Saturday morning's "Lassie Rescue Rangers" series. *A Filmation Production with Lassie Television. Color. One hour. Premiered on ABC: November 11, 1972 (on "The ABC Saturday Superstar Movie").*

Voices:

Ben Turner: Ted Knight, **Laura Turner,** his wife: Jane Webb, **Susan Turner:** Lane Scheimer, **Jackie Turner:** Keith Sutherland **Ben Turner/Gene Fox:** Hal Harvey, **Lassie:** Lassie, **Narrator:** Ted Knight

THE LAST OF THE CURLEWS

Native to the Arctic shoreland, the curlews, tall, striped birds, are on the verge of extinction. All that remain are two survivors, a male and a female, who search endlessly for a mate to keep their species alive. In the course of their tion, they encounter two hunters who have little concern about their species' survival in this "ABC Afterschool Special." An Emmy Award winner. *A Hanna–Barbera Production. Color. One Hour. Premiered on ABC: October 4, 1972. Rebroadcast on ABC: March 7, 1973.*

Voices:

Stan: Ross Martin, **Mark:** Vinnie Van Patten, **Bird Calls:** Ginny Tyler, **Narrator:** Lee Vines

THE LAST OF THE MOHICANS

During the French and Indian War, Cora, the daughter of French Commander Allan Munro, is abducted by the traitorous Magua Indians. Scout Hawkeye and the last two Mohicans, Chingachook and his son Uncas, work to free the girl from her captors and aid the French in the capture of the Magua tribe. Based on a novel by James Fenimore Cooper. A "Famous Classic Tales" special. *A Hanna–Barbera Production. Color. One hour. Premiered on CBS: November 27, 1975. Rebroadcast on CBS: November 25, 1981. Syndicated.*

Voices:

Hawkeye: Mike Road, **Uncas:** Casey Kasem, **Chingachook:** John Doucette, **Cora Munro:** Joan Van Ark, **Alice Munro:** Kristina Holland, **Duncan Heyward:** Paul Hecht, **Magua/Soldier:** Frank Welker, **Colonel Allen Munro/Delaware Chief:** John Stephenson

THE LAST OF THE RED–HOT DRAGONS

Once a powerful force, an old flying dragon, who has lost his fire–breathing ability, regains his skills in time to save Noah's ark–bound animals, who are left stranded at the North Pole, by melting a block of ice, which traps the creatures in a dark cave. *A Shamus Culhane Production in association with Erredia Productions and Westfall Productions. Color. One hour and a half. Premiered on NBC: April 1, 1980. Syndicated.*

Voices:
Dragon: John Culhane, **King Lion:** Carl Banas, **Crocodile:** Paul Soles, **Elephant:** Murray Westgate, **Penguin:** Ruth Springford, **Polar Bear:** Don Mason, **Baby Girl Crocodile:** Judy Sinclair, **Baby Boy Crocodile:** Cardie Mortimer

THE LEGEND OF HIAWATHA

Great Indian legend Hiawatha, who is half man and half god, teaches his people how to meet the challenges of everyday life in this adaptation of the famed Henry Wadsworth Longfellow poem. A "Kenner Family Classics" special. *An Atkinson Film–Arts Production in association with Triple Seven Concepts. Color. One hour. Premiered on CBS: November 24, 1983. Rebroadcast on NBC: December 4, 1984 (as "NBC Special Treat"). Syndicated.*

Voices:
Tim Atkinson, Barry Edward Blake, Gary Chalk, Arline Van Dine, Les Lye, Anna MacCormick, Michael Voss

THE LEGEND OF ROBIN HOOD

The classic tale of Robin Hood and his Merry Men, who rob from the rich to give to the poor, is colorfully retold in this hour–long adaptation that traces Robin's crusade to rid England of the underhanded Prince John. A "Famous Classic Tales" special. *An Air Programs International Production. Color. One hour. Premiered on CBS: November 14, 1971. Rebroadcast on CBS: November 11, 1972; September 30, 1973. Syndicated.*

Voices:
Tim Elliott, Peter Guest, Ron Haddrick, John Kingley, John Llewellyn, Helen Morse, Brender Senders

THE LEPRECHAUNS' CHRISTMAS GOLD

Art Carney, as the oldest of the Killakilarney clan, narrates and sings this story of a young cabin boy lost on an uncharted island who unwittingly frees a caterwauling Banshee who tries to steal the leprechauns' pot of gold. *A Rankin–Bass Production. Color. Half–hour. Premiered on ABC: December 23, 1981. Rebroadcast on ABC: December 20, 1983. Syndicated.*

Voices:
Barney Killakilarney (narrator): Art Carney, **Faye Killakilarney:** Peggy Cass, **Dinty Doyle:** Ken Jennings, **Old Mag:** Christine Mitchell, **Child/Others:** Glynnis Bieg, Michael Moronosk

LIBERTY AND THE LITTLES

On their way to New York City for the Fourth of July, a storm forces the Littles (Dinky, Grandpa, William, Helen, Tom and Lucy) to crash near the Statue of Liberty. There they make friends with two children, Michelle and Pierre, and help them escape from a tiny 19th–century community contained inside the structure. Michelle and Pierre learn the meaning of liberty in a free land. Based on John Peterson's popular children's book series, the special aired in three parts as an "ABC Weekend Special." The characters appeared in their own successful Saturday–morning series, "The Littles," also broadcast on ABC. *An ABC Entertainment Production in association with DIC Enterprises. Color. Half–hour. Premiered on ABC: October 18, October 25 and November 1, 1986. Rebroadcast on ABC: August 18, August 25 and September 1, 1989.*

Voices:
Tom Little: David Wagner, **Lucy Little:** Bettina Rush, **Grandpa Little:** Alvy Moore, **Dinky Little:** Robert David Hall, **Helen Little:** Patti Parris, **William Little:** Gregg Berger, **Michelle/ Pierre:** Katie Lee, **Pere Egalitaire:** Jim Morgan, **General/ Massey:** Earl Boen

THE LIFE AND ADVENTURES OF SANTA CLAUS

The origin of jolly old St. Nick, alias Santa Claus, is recounted in this Animagic stop–motion animation special that traces the life of this merry old soul, from his early childhood to his rise as the world's foremost agent of goodwill, in this hour–long holiday special adaptation of the 1902 story by *Wizard of Oz* author L. Frank Baum. *A Rankin–Bass Production. Color. One hour. Premiered on CBS: December 17, 1985. Rebroadcast on CBS: December 2, 1986; December 3, 1987; December 24, 1988.*

Voices:
Great Ak: Alfred Drake, **Old Santa,** Earl Hammond, **Young Santa:** J. D. Roth, **Tingler:** Robert McFadden, **Necile:** Lesley Miller, **King Awgwa:** Earle Hyman, **Wind Demon:** Larry Kenney, **Weekum:** Joey Grasso, **Children:** Amy Anzelowitz, Josh Blake, Ari Gold, **Others:** Jamie Lisa Murphy, Lynne Lipton, Peter Newman, **Vocalists:** Al Dana, Margaret Dorn, Arlene Mitchell, Marty Nelson, David Ragaini, Robert Ragaini, Annette Sanders

LIFE IS A CIRCUS, CHARLIE BROWN

Snoopy falls in love, leaves home and becomes a big–top star in a traveling circus. That's some change for a small–town beagle, who is smitten by a fancily preened French poodle named Fifi, a performer in the circus who wins Snoopy's affection. After clowning around in Fifi's act, Snoopy joins the circus for real—as "Hugo the Great"—and steals center stage, performing antics on a unicycle, the high wire and, ultimately, the trapeze. Meanwhile, Charlie Brown is understandably distraught over his lost pet, receiving little comfort from Linus, who philosophizes "It's difficult not to be enticed by romance and excitement, Charlie Brown. There's more to life than a plastic supper dish." *A Lee Mendelson–Bill Melendez Production in association with Charles M. Schulz Creative Associates and United Feature Syndicate. Color. Half–hour. Premiered on CBS: October 24, 1980. Rebroadcast on CBS: January 11, 1982; January 17, 1983.*

Voices:

Charlie Brown: Michael Mandy, **Snoopy:** Bill Melendez, **Schroeder/Kids:** Christopher Donohoe, **Linus Van Pelt:** Earl "Rocky" Reilly, **Lucy Van Pelt:** Kristen Fullerton, **Peppermint Patty:** Brent Hauer, **Marcie:** Shannon Cohn, **Polly:** Casey Carlson

THE LION, THE WITCH AND THE WARDROBE

Based on the children's book of the same name, four children are magically transported, via a giant wardrobe, into the wonderful land of Narnia, where they help a kingly lion vanquish a wicked queen who holds the land in the grip of winter. The program was broadcast in two parts. *A Children's Television Workshop Production in association with Bill Melendez Productions, the Episcopal Radio–TV Foundation, T. V. Cartoons and Pegbar Productions. Color. One hour. Premiered on CBS: April 1 and April 2, 1979. Rebroadcast on CBS: April 22 and April 23, 1980.*

Voices:

Lucy: Rachel Warren, **Susan:** Susan Sokol, **Peter:** Reg Williams, **Edmund:** Simon Adams, **Mr. Tumnus:** Victor Spinetti, **Professor:** Dick Vosburgh, **Mr. Beaver:** Don Parker, **Mrs. Beaver:** Liz Proud, **Asian:** Stephen Thorne, **White Witch:** Beth Porter

THE LITTLE BROWN BURRO

A dejected little burro, who finds he has no place in society, is reassured when he is bought by Joseph and travels to Bethlehem, carrying Mary to the site of baby Jesus' birth. *A Titlecraft/Atkinson Film–Arts Production in association with D. W. Reid Films. Color. Half–hour. Premiered (U. S.): December, 1978. Syndicated.*

Voices:

Little Brown Burro: Bonnie Brooks, **Omar:** Paul Soles, **Narrator:** Lorne Greene

Additional Voices:

Carl Banas, Nick Nichols, Henry Ramer

Aaron, a six–year–old orphan, conveys his happiness by beating his drum in a scene from the perennial Christmas favorite, "Little Drummer Boy." © Rankin–Bass Productions (Courtesy: Family Home Entertainment)

LITTLE DRUMMER BOY

An exceptional tale set in ancient times about Aaron, a six–year–old orphaned drummer boy, who, along with his drum and three animal friends—a lamb, a camel and a donkey—learns the lesson of love and the true meaning of the holy season by journeying with the Three Wise Men to Bethlehem to witness the birth of Christ. *The Teachers Guide to Television* listed the special as "a specially selected program of education value" prior to its network premiere. Animation for the program was by Animagic, a stop–motion process using puppets and making their movements appear life–like. The program was backed by the Vienna Boys Choir. *A Videocraft International Production in association with NBC. Color. Half–hour. Premiered on NBC: December 19, 1968. Rebroadcast on NBC: December 18, 1969; December 16, 1970; December 14, 1971; December 10, 1972; December 9, 1973; December 14, 1974; December 14, 1975; December 23, 1977; December 23, 1980.*

Voices:

Aaron: Teddy Eccles, **Haramed:** Jose Ferrer, **Ali/Other voices:** Paul Frees, **Narrator:** Greer Garson

LITTLE DRUMMER BOY, BOOK II

In this sequel to 1968's "The Little Drummer Boy," Aaron returns to undertake an incredible journey with one of the wise men, Melchoir—to find a man named Simeon who has constructed a set of Silver Bells to be rung to herald the birth of Christ—in this Animagic special, produced by Arthur Rankin and Jules Bass, who created such perennial holiday special favorites as "Santa Claus Is Comin' to Town" and "Frosty the Snowman." Greer Garson, who narrated the first special, served as the program's story teller. *A Rankin–Bass Production. Color. Half–hour. Premiered on NBC: December 13, 1976. Rebroadcast on NBC: December 23, 1977; December 21, 1978; December 23, 1980.*

Voices:
Aaron: David Jay, **Melchoir:** Allen Swift, **Brutus:** Zero Mostel, **Simeon:** Ray Owens, **Plato:** Robert McFadden, **Narrator:** Greer Garson

LITTLE GOLDEN BOOKLAND

Little Golden Bookland is in danger. Storms have broken a hole in the breakwater, and a new storm is on the way. If the hole isn't repaired, Harbortown could be flooded and Beamer, the venerable old lighthouse, could be washed away. Scuffy the Tugboat volunteers to save the day, along with his friends Tootle the Train, Katy Caboose, Pokey Little Puppy and Shy Little Kitten, in this animated version of the well–known children's book characters. *A DIC Enterprises Production in association with Western Publishing Company. Color, Half–hour. Premiered: 1989.*

Voices:
Tootle the Train: Dillan Bouey, **Pokey Little Puppy:** Chiara Zanni, **Shy Little Kitten:** Tony Balshaw, **Katy Caboose:** Emily Perkins, **Scuffy the Tugboat:** Tony Ail, **Tawny Scrawny Lion:** Graham Andrews, **Saggy Raggy Elephant:** Lelani Marrell, **Baby Brown Bear:** Tony Dakota, **Beamer:** Imbert Orchard

THE LITTLE MERMAID

Once comfortable with her lifestyle under the sea, a beautiful mermaid princess experiences a change of heart when she is saved by a young prince in this philosophical adaptation of the popular Hans Christian Andersen tale. The program preceded a rebroadcast of "Dr. Seuss' Horton Hears a Who" in its original broadcast on CBS. *A Gerald Potterton Production in association with Reader's Digest. Color. Half–hour. Premiered on CBS: February 4, 1974. Rebroadcast on CBS: January 31, 1975. Syndicated.*

Voices:
Narrator: Richard Chamberlain

THE LITTLE RASCALS CHRISTMAS SPECIAL

Filmdom's *The Little Rascals,* who cavorted in more than 100 live–action comedy shorts for Hal Roach in the 1920s and 1930s, return in a prime–time animated special revolving around Spanky and his younger brother Porky who mistakenly think they're getting an electric train for Christmas. Former *Rascals* Darla Hood Granson (playing Spanky's mother) and Matthew "Stymie" Beard (the town butcher), both since deceased, lent their voices to the program. *A King World Presentation in association with Muller–Rosen Productions and Murakami–Wolf–Swenson Films. Color. Half–hour. Premiered on NBC: December 3, 1979. Rebroadcast on NBC: December 15, 1980; December 20, 1981.*

Voices:
Alfalfa: Jimmy Gatherum, **Spanky:** Phillip Tanzini, **Darla:** Randi Kiger, **Stymie:** Al Jocko Fann, **Porky:** Robby Kiger, **Mom:** Darla Hood Granson, **Sidewalk Santa:** Jack Somack, **Butcher:** Matthew "Stymie" Beard, **Man:** Cliff Norton, **Sales Clerk:** Frank Nelson, **Delivery Man:** Melville A. Levin, **Uncle Hominy:** Hal Smith, **Sales Lady:** Naomi Lewis, **Tough Kid:** Ike Eisenmann

THE LITTLE TROLL PRINCE

Set among the rustic fjords and snow–covered villages of scenic Norway, this delightful parable tells the story of Bu, the crown prince of the trolls, who learns the true meaning of Christmas in this first–run syndicated special produced in conjunction with the International Lutheran Laymen's League. *A Hanna-Barbera Production in association with Wang Film Productions, Inc. and Cuckoo Nest Studios. Color. Half–hour. Premiered: 1987. Syndicated.*

Voices:
Bu: Danny Cooksey, **Borch,** his two-headed brother: Rob Paulsen and Laurie Faso, **Prag,** his two-headed brother: Neilson Ross and Frank Welker, **King Ulvik Head # 1:** Vincent Price, **King Ulvik Head # 2:** Jonathan Price, **Queen Sirena:** Cloris Leachman, **Professor Nidaros:** Don Knotts, **Stav:** Charlie Adler, **Ribo/Krill/Father:** Michael Bell, **Kristi:** Ami Foster, **Sonja:** Christina Lange, **Bjorn:** William Christopher, **Witch/Mrs. Bjorn:** B.J. Ward, **Spectator # 1:** Rob Paulsen, **Spectator #2:** Laurie Faso, **Spectator #3:** Neilson Ross, **Troll:** Frank Welker

LOST IN SPACE

Hopping aboard their space shuttle, Jupiter II, Craig Robinson and his crew embark on a peace–saving mission to help the peaceful Throgs ward off the Tyranos, metallic creatures who have declared war on their planet, in this animated version of television's popular science fiction series "Lost in Space." The hour–long movie, which featured several new characters, premiered on "The ABC Saturday Superstar Movie" series. *A Hanna–Barbera Production. Color. One hour. Premiered on ABC: September 8, 1973 (on "The ABC Saturday Superstar Movie"). Rebroadcast on ABC: January 5, 1974. Syndicated.*

Voices:
Craig Robinson: Mike Bell, **Deana Carmichael:** Sherry Alberoni, **Linc Robinson:** Vince Van Patten, **Dr. Smith:** Jonathan Harris, **Robot:** Don Messick, **Lar:** Sidney Miller, **Kal:** Ralph James, **Brack** (child): Don Messick, **Tyrano Twin One:** Sidney Miller, **Tyrano Twin Two:** Ralph James, **Tyrano Guard:** Mike Bell, **Announcer/Narrator:** Don Messick

LOVE AMERICAN STYLE: "LOVE AND THE OLD–FASHIONED FATHER"

Tom Bosley plays the father of a teenager who wants to go on a water skiing weekend with her hippie boyfriend in an "All in the Family"–styled cartoon based on a script by R. S. Allen and Harvey Bullock, executive producers of the live–action "Love American Style" series. The program was one of two pilots that aired in the series' late–night time–slot. (Its predecessor was an episode called "Love and the Private Eye.") *A Hanna–Barbera Production for Paramount Television. Color. Half–hour. Premiered on ABC: February 11, 1972.*

Voices:

Father: Tom Bosley, **Mother:** Joan Gerber, **Alice:** Tina Holland

Additional Voices:

David Hayward, David Lander, Ernestine Wade, Sidney Miller, Mitzi McCall

LOVE AMERICAN STYLE: "LOVE AND THE PRIVATE EYE"

Private eye Melvin Danger, a master of disguises who believes he is irresistible to women, delivers a large payroll to an industrial tycoon but loses both payroll and tycoon in the process in this half–hour pilot produced and directed by William Hanna and Joseph Barbera. Originally entitled "Melvin Danger Plus Two," the story was written by R. S. Allen and Harvey Bullock. Voice artist Lennie Weinrib is credited with having done six character voices for the show. *A Hanna–Barbera Production for Paramount Television. Color. Half–hour. Premiered on ABC: January 28, 1972.*

Voices:

Melvin Danger: Richard Dawson

Additional Voices:

Cynthia Adler, Robert Holt, Mitzi McCall, Lennie Weinrib, John Stephenson, Loren Farber (Vocalist), Paul DeKorte (Vocalist), Jean Merlino (Vocalist)

LUCKY LUKE

This made–for–television movie returns viewers to the wild and woolly days of the Old West, with all the ingredients of a classic sagebrush saga, the strong, silent hero (Lucky Luke), his gallant horse (Jolly), the loyal dog (Bushwack) and the gang of hardened desperadoes (the Dalton Boys), in an affectionate spoof of the western. *A Hanna–Barbera Production in association with Gaumont Productions and Dargaud Editeur. Color. Two hours. Premiered: 1985. Syndicated.*

Voices:

Lucky Luke: Bill Callaway, **Jolly Jumper:** Bob Ridgely, **Averell:** Bob Holt, **Ma Dalton:** Mitzi McCall, **Jack:** Rick Dees, **Bushwhack:** Paul Reubens, **William:** Fred Travalena, **Joe:** Frank Welker

LYLE, LYLE CROCODILE: THE MUSICAL: "THE HOUSE ON EAST 88TH ST."

This music–filled family special tells the enchanting tale about a family who moves into a new home to find it's already inhabited by a talented reptile named Lyle the Crocodile. The charming green character wins their hearts, and his new family is wonderfully happy—until Lyle's rightful owner returns to claim him in this animated version of Bernard Waber's popular tale, *The House on East 88th St.* The delightfully animated program features the voice of Tony Randall and music by three–time Tony Award–winner Charles Strouse. Animator Michael Sporn produced and directed this program, which was first released as a theatrical cartoon short and won a 1985 Academy Award nomination for "Best Animated Short." *A Michael Sporn Animation Production. Color. Half–hour. Premiered on HBO: November 18, 1987. Rebroadcast on HBO: November 23, 1987; November 26, 1987; November 29, 1987; December 4, 1987; December 8, 1987.*

Voices:

Lyle the Crocodile: Tony Randall

Additional Voices:

Liz Callaway, Devon Michaels, Charles Strouse, Heidi Stallings, Arnold Stang, Rick Parks, Lainie Zera

MADELINE

In an old vine–covered house in Paris live 12 little girls. The smallest and bravest of them all is Madeline. The young girl experiences many adventures with her housemates and their loving guardian, Miss Clavel, in this musical tale based on the classic 1930s' children's book about the importance of love, sharing and friendship. *A DIC Enterprise Production. Color. One hour and a half. Premiered on HBO: November 7, 1988.*

Madeline, the smallest and bravest of 12 girls, experiences many new adventures shaped around the importance of love, sharing and friendship in the HBO special, "Madeline." © DIC Enterprises, Inc.

Voices:

Madeline: Marsha Moreau, **Miss Clavel:** Judith Orban, **Vendor:** John Stocker, **Madeline's friends:** Loretta Jafelice, Linda Kash, Wendy Lands, Daccia Bloomfield, Tara Charendoff

THE MAD, MAD, MAD COMEDIANS

The comedy routines of several well–known comedians, culled from excerpts of radio programs and television sketches, are brought to life in this simplistic animated special. *A Bruce Stark Production in association with ABC. Color. Half–hour. Premiered on ABC: April 7, 1970.*

Voices:

Jack Benny: Jack Benny, **George Burns:** George Burns, **The Marx Brothers:** Groucho Marx, Chico Marx, Harpo Marx, **Smothers Brothers:** Tom Smothers, Dick Smothers, **Christopher Columbus:** Flip Wilson, **George Jessel:** George Jessel, **Phyllis Diller:** Phyllis Diller, **Jack E. Leonard:** Jack E. Leonard, **Henny Youngman:** Henny Youngman, **W. C. Fields:** Paul Frees

MAD, MAD, MAD MONSTERS

Baron von Frankenstein invites his old friends—Count Dracula, the Wolfman, the Mummy, the Invisible Man and his wife, and his own assistant Igor—to the ballroom of the Transylvania–Astoria to witness his marriage to the "perfect bride" he has created for himself in this hour–long program, which was first broadcast as part of the "ABC Saturday Superstar Movie" series. The production was later broadcast on its own as a children's special in reruns on the network and then in syndication. *A Rankin–Bass Production. Color. One hour. Premiered on ABC: September 23, 1972 (on "ABC Saturday Superstar Movie"). Syndicated.*

Voices:

Allen Swift, Bradley Bolke, Rhoda Mann, Bob McFadden

THE MAGICAL MYSTERY TRIP THROUGH LITTLE RED'S HEAD

Live–action and animation are combined in this story of Little Red, a young girl, who is used in an experiment by two youngsters (Carol and Larry) who, reduced in size, explore the girl's mind and learn how people express and deal with their feelings from the inside. An "ABC Afterschool Special." *A DePatie–Freleng Enterprises Production. Color. One hour. Premiered on ABC: May 15, 1974. Rebroadcast on ABC: December 11, 1974; April 29, 1978 (as "ABC Weekend Specials").*

Voices:

Timer: Lennie Weinrib, **Carol:** Diane Murphy, **Larry:** Ike Eisenmann, **Little Red:** Sarah Kennedy, **Mother/Adeline/Diane:** Joan Gerber

THE MAGIC LOLLIPOP ADVENTURE

In his animated debut, Lollipop Dragon, named for his love of lollipops, appears doomed when Baron Bad Blood, bent on undermining the success of the lollipop industry in the land of Tumtum, steals the magic wand that gives the lollipops their flavor. *A Blair Entertainment Production in association with Pannonia Film. Color. Half–hour. Syndicated. Premiere: 1986.*

Voices:

Lollipop Dragon: Gary Wilmot, **Cosmo the Cunning/King/Herald:** Dennis Greashan, **Baron Bad Blood:** Stephen Thorne, **Hairy Troll:** Gary Wilmot, **Blue Eyes:** Karen Fernald, **Magic Mirror/Prince Hubert:** Pat Starr, **Princess Gwendolyn:** Jill Lidstone, **Glider/Queen/Lady of the Forest:** Eva Hadden

THE MAGIC OF DR. SNUGGLES

Kindly Dr. Snuggles enters the great balloon race in hope of winning prize money to help Granny Toots build a new cat hospital. However, a couple of treacherous hoodlums have their own plan to win the race—at any cost. This hour–long special was based on the popular television series, "Dr. Snuggles." *An American Way Production in association with DePatie–Freleng Enterprises. Color. One hour. Premiered: 1985. Syndicated.*

Voices:

Danielle Romeo, Lacoya Newsome, Cindy Kozacik, Tony Roscia, Pearl Terry, David Scott

MARCO POLO

Aided by his servant Ton–Ton, famed adventurer Marco Polo is thrust in the middle of a war between Kubla Khan and the city of Siang–yan Fu in China in the year 1260 A.D., and wins the respect of the Khan as he saves the Province of Yunnan from destruction and returns Khan's captured daughter to safety. *An Air Programs International Production. Color. One hour. Premiered: 1972. Syndicated.*

Voices:

Alistair Duncan, Tim Eliott, Ron Haddrick, Mark Kelly, John Llewellyn, Helen Morse.

MARVIN: BABY OF THE YEAR

Tom Armstrong's witty, precocious, be–diapered comic–strip character is entered into a "baby of the year" contest by his grandparents in the first prime–time special based on Armstrong's beloved creation. *A Southern Star Production. Color. Half–hour. Premiered on CBS: March 10, 1989.*

Voices:

Marvin: Dana Hill, **Chrissy's Mother:** Ruth Buzzi, **Grandma:** Erin Donica, **Meagan:** Patti Dworkin, **Mom:** Kathy Garver, **Dad:** Dave Madden, **Vince:** Jerry Sroka, **Grandpa:** John Stephenson, **Announcer:** Frank Welker

MARVIN—FIRST FLIGHT

Appearing to be "Mr. Average," Marvin is no ordinary Joe. He builds robots in his underground laboratory, and his mechanical marvels do some rather remarkable things. His newest creation, Maxwell, can change shape, from robot to rocket to automobile, and accommodate Marvin with whatever form of transportation he requires. The half–hour special aired on "Special Delivery" on Nickelodeon several years after its United Kingdom television debut. All character voices were performed by voice–artist Chris Harris. *A Link Licensing Limited Production. Color. Half–hour. Premiered on Nickelodeon: August 1, 1987.*

Voices:

Chris Harris

MARVIN—LONDON CALLING

Sid and Stan are a couple of naughty but likable villains who have invented a "Blitzer"—a gun that stuns people briefly, enabling them to steal lots of money from shops and banks. With help from his robots Buffer, Maxwell and Micron, Marvin puts the culprits behind bars where they belong. *A Link Licensing Limited Production. Color. Half–hour. Premiered on Nickelodeon: 1989.*

Voices:

Chris Harris

MASTER OF THE WORLD

Captain Robur, the mad inventor of a fantastic flying machine who bills himself as "Master of the World," sets out to destroy Washington D. C., with Inspector Strock of the Federal Police fresh on his heels. A "Famous Classic Tales" special. *An Air Programs International Production. Color. One hour. Premiered on CBS: October 23, 1976. Syndicated.*

Voices:

Tim Elliott, John Ewart, Ron Haddrick, Judy Morris, Matthew O'Sullivan

MEET JULIE

This is the story of nine–year–old Carol McAlister, her father, David, and a very special doll named Julie. David is the owner of a small firm that provides security services for companies. When he lands an assignment guarding a jeweled collar to be worn by a rare Snow Leopard at an exhibit at the Louvre, David sees the opportunity for international acclaim that can bolster the image of his struggling company. The Snow Leopard, Samantha, is Carol's favorite animal at the Bronx Zoo so David decides to surprise his daughter by taking her along with him on the job to Paris. As an added surprise, he gives his daughter a special computerized doll, Julie, to take with her on the trip. *A DIC Enterprises Production. Color. Half–hour. Premiered: Fall 1987. Syndicated.*

Voices:

Julie: Nicole Lyn, **Carol:** Karen Burthwright

Additional Voices:

Blaine Fairman, Dan Hennessey, Peggy Mahon, Mike Meyers, Greg Morton, John Stocker

MEET THE RAISINS: THE STORY OF THE CALIFORNIA RAISINS

The California Raisins return in their second prime–time special, this time given recognizable personalities and names (A. C., Red, Stretch and Beebop), in a clever rock documentary parody highlighted by home movies, stills, clips and interviews tracing the Raisins' rise to stardom from their early days in a band called the Vine–yls. *A Will Vinton Production. Color. Half–hour. Premiered on CBS: November 4, 1988.*

A MERRY MIRTHTOWN CHRISTMAS

Bert Worm, a new resident of Wormingham, is banned from the town's annual holiday pageant after he bungles preparations for the event. The clumsy worm is given a second chance when he proves he can sing. *A Perennial Pictures Production. Color. Half–hour., Premiered on Showtime: November–December, 1984. Syndicated.*

Voices:

Bert Worm: Jerry Reynolds, **Crystal Crawler:** Rachel Rutledge, **Teddy Toddlers:** Jerry Reynolds, **Wilbur Diggs:** Jerry Reynolds, **Baggs:** Jerry Reynolds, **Wormaline Wiggler:** Miki Mathioudakis, **Eulalia Inch/Agnes/Dribble:** Peggy Nicholson, **Mayor Filmor Q. Pettiworm:** Russ Harris, **Eudora Vanderworm:** Russ Harris

MICKEY'S CHRISTMAS CAROL

Walt Disney's beloved cartoon creations—Mickey Mouse, Donald Duck, Goofy and others—are cast in this updated version of the Charles Dickens Christmas classic, which features new animation and three previously exhibited adventures—"The Art of Skiing" (1941), "Donald's Snow Fight" (1942) and "Pluto's Christmas Tree" (1952)—in this one–hour holiday special, first released as a brand–new theatrical short in 1983. *A Walt Disney Television Production. Color. One hour. Premiered on NBC: December 10, 1984. Rebroadcast on NBC: December 22, 1985; December 15, 1986; December 4, 1987.*

Voices:

Mickey Mouse (Bob Cratchit): Wayne Allwine, **Uncle Scrooge McDuck** (Ebenezer Scrooge): Alan Young, **Donald Duck** (Fred): Clarence Nash, **Goofy** (Ghost of Jacob Marley): Hal Smith, **Jiminy Cricket** (Ghost of Christmas Past): Eddie Carroll, **Willie the Giant** (Ghost of Christmas Present): Will Ryan, **Black Pete** (Ghost of Christmas Future): Will Ryan, **Morty** (Tiny Tim): Susan Sheridan, **Daisy Duck** (Isabel): Pat Parris

MICKEY'S HAPPY VALENTINE

Mickey, Minnie, Donald Duck and Daisy Duck wrestle with romance in a series of animated sequences accompanied by rock music in this hour–long prime–time special. Included is the 1938 cartoon, "Brave Little Tailor," in which Mickey saves mouse–in–distress Minnie from a giant. *A Walt Disney Television Production. Color. One hour. Premiered on NBC: February 12, 1989 (on "The Magical World of Disney").*

Voices:

Mickey Mouse: Walt Disney, **Minnie Mouse:** Marcellite Garner, **Donald Duck:** Clarence Nash

MICKEY'S 60TH BIRTHDAY

Mickey Mouse suddenly disappears during the taping of his birthday special and it is up to live and animated stars to deal with the crisis. The show features the casts of "Family Ties" and "Cheers" and other NBC stars. Jill Eikenberry and John Ritter play news anchor people who keep America informed on the search for the missing Mickey Mouse. *A Walt Disney Television Production. Color. One hour. Premiered on NBC: November 3, 1988 (on "The Magical World of Disney").*

THE MINI–MUNSTERS

Herman, Grandpa and the rest of TV's "The Munsters" clan, in animated form, discover that their hearse–dragster runs on music instead of gas in this made–for–television feature which aired on "The ABC Saturday Superstar Movie." *A Universal Television Production. Color. One hour. Premiered on ABC: October 27, 1973. Rebroadcast on ABC: January 12, 1974.*

Voices:

Herman Munster: Richard Long, **Grandpa:** Al Lewis

A MIRTHWORM MASQUERADE

The Mirthworms are all excited. It's time for the annual Masquerade Ball in Wormingham. But leave it to the evil Miss Wormaline Wiggler to spoil the fun when she tries to have herself crowned Queen of the Masquerade ball by tampering with the voting process, even though Bert Worm's honey, Crystal Crawler, has the most votes. *A Perennial Pictures Production. Color. Half–hour. Premiered: April 11, 1987. Syndicated.*

Voices:

Bert Worm: Jerry Reynolds, **Crystal Crawler:** Rachel Rutledge, **Wormaline Wiggler:** Miki Mathioudakis, **Teddy Toddlers/Wilbur Diggs:** Jeff Reynolds, **Prince Pringle:** Jerry Reynolds, **Homer/Armbruster:** Jerry Reynolds, **Agnes/Dribble/Eulalia Inch:** Peggy Nicholson, **Eudora Vanderworm:** Russ Harris, **Mayor Filmore Q. Pettiworm:** Russ Harris, **Brooks:** Michael N. Ruggiero, **Chester/Arnold:** Adam Dykstra

MISS SWITCH TO THE RESCUE

In this two–part special based on the characters created by Barbara Brooks Wallace, Miss Switch, a good witch in the

Miss Switch (right), a good witch who hides her true identity as a substitute schoolteacher, comes to the aid of a kidnapped youngster in the ABC Weekend Special, "Miss Switch To The Rescue." © Ruby–Spears Enterprises

form of a substitute teacher, comes to the aid of young Rupert when a bad warlock he unwittingly lets out of the bottle kidnaps the boy's friend, Amelia, in this "ABC Weekend Special." *A Ruby–Spears Enterprises Production. Color. Half–hour. Premiered on ABC: January 16 and 23, 1982. Rebroadcast on ABC: April 24 and May 1, 1982; June 18 and 25, 1983; February 9 and 16, 1985; July 5 and 12, 1986; April 4 and 11, 1987; February 11 and 18, 1989.*

Voices:

Miss Switch/Guinevere: Janet Waldo, **Rupert P. Brown III/Peatmouse:** Eric Taslitz, **Amelia Matilda Daley:** Nancy McKeon, **Mordo:** Hans Conreid, **Smirch:** Hal Smith, **Banana/Conrad:** Phillip Tanzini, **Bathsheba/Saturna** (Crone): June Foray, **Witch's Book/Old Salt/Mayor:** Walker Edmiston, **Teacher/Barmaid:** Anne Lockhart, **Hector:** Alan Dinehart

MISUNDERSTOOD MONSTERS

Three terrific monster tales—*Beauty and the Beast, Creole* and *The Reluctant Dragon*—are featured in this live–action/animation afternoon children's special that combines filmed scenes of host Meeno Peluce, star of TV's "The Voyagers" and "The Bad News Bears." *A Bosustow Entertainment Production. Color. One hour. Premiered on CBS: April 7, 1981. Rebroadcast on CBS: January 1, 1982. Syndicated.*

Voices:

Mouth: Avery Schreiber, **Creole:** Mickey Rooney, **Bird:** Georgia Engel, **Alligator:** Arte Johnson, **Reluctant Dragon:** Alan Sues, **St. George:** Louis Nye, **Boy:** Sparky Marcus, **Beauty:** Claire Bloom, **Beast:** Michael York, **Narrators:** John Carradine, James Earl Jones, Mickey Rooney

MOBY DICK

Herman Melville's tragic story of the great white whale, Moby Dick, relentlessly pursued by Captain Ahab and his crew, is retold in this first–run hour–long animated special. *An Air Programs International Production. Color. One Hour. Premiered: 1975. Syndicated.*

Voices:

Alistair Duncan, Tim Elliott, Ron Haddrick, Mark Kelly, John Llewellyn

MONSTER BED

Trapped in a world of monsters, a young boy tries to go home in this "ABC Weekend Special." *A Marvel Production. Color. One hour. Premiered on ABC: September 9, 1989 (on "ABC Weekend Special").*

Voices:

Charlie Adler, Brandon Crane, Peter Cullen, Katie Leigh, Laurie O'Brien, Hank Saroyan

MOUSE OF THE MAYFLOWER

In this animated re–telling of the first Thanksgiving, William Mouse (voiced by Tennessee Ernie Ford) accompanies the Pilgrims to America and aids these valiant pioneers in their struggle for freedom in a new world. *A Rankin–Bass Production. Color. Half–hour. Premiered on NBC: November 23, 1968. Rebroadcast on NBC: November 25, 1971. Syndicated.*

Voices:

William Mouse (narrator): Tennessee Ernie Ford, **Pricilla Mullens:** Joanie Sommers, **John Alden:** John Gary, **Miles Standish:** Eddie Albert, **William Bradford/Quizzler/Others:** Paul Frees, **Indian Mouse/Scurv/Others:** June Foray

MOWGLI'S BROTHERS

Roddy McDowall narrates the story of a small boy raised by wolves and taught about love, justice and the jungle code of loyalty in this final installment based on Rudyard Kipling's *The Jungle Book*, adapted for television by Chuck Jones. *A Chuck Jones Enterprises Production. Color. Half–hour. Premiered on CBS: February 11, 1976. Rebroadcast on CBS: May 6, 1977; April 4, 1978; June 16, 1979; August 19, 1981. Syndicated.*

Voices:

Mowgli/Shere Khan/Akela/Tabaqui/Babheera/Baloo: Roddy McDowall, **Mother Wolf:** June Foray

MY LITTLE PONY

Thirteen–year–old Megan and her pony friends, who live in magical Dream Valley, find their perfect life ruined when the villainous half–horse Tirac arranges for the Stratadons to kidnap several of the ponies to whisk them away to his dingy Midnight Castle. He underestimates the power of Megan's

winged–pony, Firefly, and Moochick the magician, in a fantasy adventure that features several cute musical numbers. *A Sunbow Production in association with Marvel Productions. Color. Half–hour. Premiered: April, 1984. Syndicated.*

Voices:

Firefly: Sandy Duncan, **Moochick:** Tony Randall

Additional Voices:

Charlie Adler, Tammy Amerson, Fran Brill, Victor Caroli, Laura Dean, Carol Goodheart, Lani Groves, Yolanda Erica, Lee Lewis, Lynne Lipton, Ullanda McCullough, Gerrianne Raphael, Ron Taylor

MR. MAGOO'S CHRISTMAS CAROL

Lovable bumbler Mr. Magoo is cast as the skinflint Ebenezer Scrooge in this first made–for–TV animated special presented as a play within a play with Magoo headlining a Broadway production based on the Charles Dickens classic. Sponsor: U. S. Time Corporation. *A UPA Production. Color. One hour. Premiered on NBC: December 18, 1962. Rebroadcast on NBC: December 13, 1963; December 18, 1964; December 17, 1965; December 17, 1966; December 17, 1967. Syndicated.*

Voices:

Ebenezer Scrooge (Mr. Magoo): Jim Backus, **Bob Cratchit:** Jack Cassidy, **Mrs. Cratchit/Children:** Laura Olsher, **Tiny Tim/Christmas Past:** Joan Gardner, **Belle Fezzlwig,** Scrooge's first love, Jane Kean, **Marley's Ghost:** Royal Dano, **Brady/James:** Morey Amsterdam, **Christmas Present:** Les Tremayne, **Old Fezzlwig/Undertaker/Men:** Paul Frees, **Young Scrooge:** Marie Matthews, **Stage Manager/Billings/Milkman:** John Hart

MR. MAGOO'S STORYBOOK SNOW WHITE

The fairy tale version of "Snow White and the Seven Dwarfs" is updated in this prime–time special, featuring Mr. Magoo (George) as the elder member of the dwarfs (each the spitting image of him) who protect Snow White from danger. Unlike Walt Disney's feature–length treatment, the dwarfs have names dissimilar to those of the original characters: Axelrod (the leader), Bartholomew (a wizard), Cornelius (a magician), Dexter (a legal expert), George (a daydreamer), Eustes and Ferdinand, who possess no special abilities whatsoever.

Originally broadcast as a two–part episode on NBC's weekly series "The Famous Adventures of Mr. Magoo," the program was rebroadcast in syndication as "Mr. Magoo's Storybook" in an hour–long format encompassing three fanciful fables starring Mr. Magoo (the others: "Don Quixote" and "A Midsummer Night's Dream"). *A UPA Productions of America Production. Color. Half–hour. Premiered on NBC: 1964 (as part of "The Famous Adventures of Mr. Magoo"). Syndicated.*

Voices:

George (Mr. Magoo): Jim Backus, **Axelrod/Bartholomew/Cornelius/Dexter/Eustes/Ferdinand:** Jim Backus, **Snow**

White: Julie Bennett, **Queen/Bertha the Peddler/Zelda the Gypsy/Old Crone:** Joan Gardner, **Prince Valor:** Howard Morris, **Demon/Hunter:** Marvin Miller

MR. MAGOO'S TREASURE ISLAND

The proprietor of a seaside inn holds a map leading to buried treasure and is found out by a pack of cutthroat pirates (Blind Pew, Black Dog and Others), who set out to find the treasure, led by the seafaring Long John Silver (played by Mr. Magoo) and his crew. The program was originally produced as an episode of NBC's "The Famous Adventures of Mr. Magoo" and later rebroadcast as a syndicated special. *A UPA Productions of America Production. Color. Half–hour. Premiered on NBC: 1964–1965 (as part of "The Famous Adventures of Mr. Magoo"). Syndicated.*

Voices:

Long John Silver (Mr. Magoo): Jim Backus, **Jim Hawkins:** Dennis King, **Jarvis:** Marvin Miller

Additional Voices:

Paul Frees, Joan Gardner, Dallas McKennon

MY LITTLE PONY: ESCAPE FROM CATRINA

Following a costume ball in her honor, Megan must save the baby ponies of Dream Valley from the evil cat–like creature Catrina, in this second first–run special based on the popular greeting card characters. *A Sunbow Production in association with Marvel Productions and Toei Animation. Color. Half–hour. Premiered: April, 1985. Syndicated.*

Voices:

Rep: Paul Williams, **Catrina:** Tammy Grimes

Additional Voices:

Charlie Adler, Tammy Amerson, Ivy Austin, Laura Dean, Denny Dillon, Patience Jarvis, Lynne Lambert, Ullanda McCullough, Alice Playten

MY SMURFY VALENTINE

Smurfette learns an important lesson about love as the Smurfs save the world from the spell of the evil sorceress Chlorhydris, who plans to unleash her villainy after causing a total eclipse of the sun, while the equally villainous wizard Gargamel meets the perfect mate in this charming half–hour Valentine's special based on the characters created by Belgian artist Pierre "Peyo" Culliford. Comedian Joe Besser, a former member of the Three Stooges comedy team, is the voice of cupid. *A Hanna–Barbera Production in association with SEPP International. Color. Half–hour. Premiered on NBC: February 13, 1983.*

Voices:

Papa Smurf/Azrael/Vulture: Don Messick, **Harmony/Greedy/Ogre:** Hamilton Camp, **Handy/Lazy/Grouchy:** Michael Bell,

Vanity: Alan Oppenheimer, **Brainy/Serpent/Ogre:** Danny Goldman, **Clumsy/Bear/Serpent #1:** Bill Callaway, **Smurfette:** Lucille Bliss, **Gargamel:** Paul Winchell, **Jokey/Smurfberry Bird:** June Foray, **Poet/Hefty/Cat:** Frank Welker, **Cupid:** Joe Besser, **Chlorhydris:** Amanda McBroom

THE MYSTERIOUS ISLAND

Five Confederate prisoners (Gideon, Herbert, Neb, Captain Harding and Captain Jack) escape during the Civil War in a hot–air balloon, only to crash–land on a remote island in the Pacific where they encounter danger and destruction in this adaptation of the Jules Verne novel. A "Famous Classic Tales" special. *An Air International Production. Color. One hour. Premiered on CBS: November 15, 1975. Rebroadcast on CBS: November 25, 1976; April 14, 1990. Syndicated.*

Voices:

Alistair Duncan, Tim Elliott, Ron Haddrick, Mark Kelly, John Llewellyn

NANNY AND THE PROFESSOR

The story of Phoebe Figalilly, the enchanting housekeeper of Professor Harold Everett who possesses the ability to spread love and joy, is caricatured in this hour–long animated story based on the popular 1970s television show of the same name. The program premiered on "The ABC Saturday Superstar Movie" series during the 1972 season. The following season, a sequel was made entitled "Nanny and the Professor and the Phantom of the Circus." *A Fred Calvert Production. Color. One hour. Premiered on ABC: September 30, 1972. Rebroadcast on ABC: December 8, 1973. Syndicated.*

Voices:

Nanny (Phoebe Figalilly): Juliet Mills, **Professor Everett:** Richard Long, **Hal Everett:** David Doremus, **Prudence Everett:** Kim Richards, **Butch Everett:** Trent Lehman, **Aunt Henrietta:** Joan Gerber

NANNY AND THE PROFESSOR AND THE PHANTOM OF THE CIRCUS

When Aunt Henrietta reports the mysterious disappearance of several performers from her traveling circus, Nanny, Professor Everett and company try locating the source of the problem in this sequel to 1972's animated version of television's "Nanny and the Professor" series. Like the previous cartoon, the one–hour program featured the voices of several actors from the original series and was originally broadcast on "The ABC Saturday Superstar Movie" series for Saturday–morning television. *A Fred Calvert Production. Color. One hour. Premiered on ABC: November 17, 1973 (on "The ABC Saturday Superstar Movie"). Syndicated.*

Voices:

Nanny (Phoebe Figalilly): Juliet Mills, **Professor Everett:** Richard Long, **Hal Everett:** David Doremus, **Prudence Everett:** Kim Richards, **Butch Everett:** Trent Lehman, **Aunt**

Henrietta: Joan Gerber, **Waldo:** Thurl Ravenscroft, **Zambini:** Walker Edmiston, **Lazlo:** Paul Shively, **Arturo:** Dave Ketchum

NESTOR, THE LONG–EARED CHRISTMAS DONKEY

Nestor, a young, ridiculous looking donkey, is chosen above all others to guide Mary and Joseph to Bethlehem in this animated variation of "The Ugly Duckling" based on a song by Gene Autry. Singer/songwriter Roger Miller narrates the Animagic production, featuring additional music and lyrics by Maury Laws and Jules Bass. *A Rankin–Bass Production. Color. Half–hour. Premiered on ABC: December 3, 1977. Rebroadcast on ABC: December 13, 1978; December 7, 1979. Syndicated.*

Voices:

Nestor, the long–eared donkey: Eric Stern, **Nestor's Mother:** Linda Gary, **Tillie,** the cherub: Brenda Vaccaro, **Olaf:** Paul Frees, **Girl Donkey #1:** Iris Raincr, **Girl Donkey #2:** Shirley Hines, **Roman Soldier:** Don Messick, **Narrator:** Roger Miller

THE NEW MISADVENTURES OF ICHABOD CRANE

Based on the Washington Irving novel, cowardly schoolteacher Ichabod Crane rescues the tiny village of Sleepy Hollow from the supernatural forces of the Headless Horseman and the evil witch, Velma Van Dam, who has cast a spell upon the quiet little town, in this syndicated special originally produced for Canadian television. *A Titlecraft–Lou Reda Production in association with Atkinson Film–Arts Productions. Color. Half–hour. Premiere (U.S.): October, 1979.*

Voices:

Ichabod Crane: The Amazing Kreskin, **Washington:** Pat Buttram, **Wolf:** George Lindsay, **Velma Van Dam:** Hazel Shermet, **Rip Van Winkle:** Larry Mann, **Mayor:** Monty Morgan, **Vocalist:** Bobby Van

NEW YEAR PROMISE

Young Davey Hanson resolves that he won't yell at his little sister Sally any more and decides the only way he can keep his promise is not to talk to her at all, which causes his sister to run away in this religious special produced in conjunction with the Lutheran Church of America. Art Clokey, creator of "Gumby," produced the special, featuring puppets brought to life by stop–motion animation. *A Clokey Production for the Luthern Church of America. Color. Half–hour. Premiered: January, 1967. Syndicated.*

Voices:

Davey Hanson/Sally Hanson/Mary Hanson: Norma McMillan, Nancy Wible, **Goliath/John Hanson:** Hal Smith

NICHOLAS NICKLEBY

Nicholas Nickleby, a young energetic lad, learns some valuable lessons about life through a series of misadventures involving the kidnapping of his sister, the death of his long–time friend, Smike, and the suicide of his uncle Ralph Nickleby in this colorfully produced adaptation of Charles Dickens' classic novel. *A Burbank Films Production. Color. Half–hour. Premiered: Fall 1984. Syndicated.*

THE NIGHT BEFORE CHRISTMAS

Television star Art Linkletter hosts this yuletide special about Clement Clark Moore, a professor who writes a special story, "A Visit from St. Nicholas," for his ailing daughter, Charity, who becomes seriously ill with pneumonia. The special was backed by the music of the Norman Luboff Choir. *An ELBA Production in association with Playhouse Pictures. Color. Half–hour. Premiered: December, 1968. Syndicated.*

Voices:

Douglas Crowther, Barbara Eiler, Virginia Gregg, Hal Smith, Olan Soule, Laura Turnbull, Shari Turnbull

THE NIGHT THE ANIMALS TALKED

Animals in the place of humans reenact the scene of the Nativity where the Christ child is born, with a new wrinkle— the animals accept the "visitor" and spread the message of love to all mankind. *A Gamma Films Production. Color. Half–hour. Premiered on ABC: December 9, 1970. Rebroadcast on ABC: December 17, 1971; December 15, 1972; December 15, 1973; December 24, 1977. Syndicated.*

Voices:

Donkey: Frank Porella, **Ox:** Joe Silver, **Cow:** Pat Bright, **Goat:** Bob Kaliban

NOAH'S ANIMALS

The Biblical story of Noah's Ark undergoes a new treatment through the help of animation, this time personifying animals who set off after the storm to find land, led by a raven who Noah has trusted to bring all the animals aboard for the 40–day voyage. *A Shamus Culhane Production in association with Westfall Productions. Color. Half–hour. Premiered on ABC: April 5, 1976. Rebroadcast on ABC: December 25, 1977. Syndicated.*

Voices:

Noah: Henry Ramer, **Crocodile:** John Soles, **Female Elephant:** Bonnie Brooks, **Male Giraffe/Camel:** Jay Nelson, **Ostrich:** Ruth Springford, **Polar Bear:** Don Mason, **Lion:** Carl Banas, **Walrus:** Jack Mather, **Male Elephant:** Murray Westgate, **Female Baby Crocodile:** Judy Sinclair, **Male Baby Crocodile:** Cardie Mortimer, **Others:** Wendy Thatcher

NO MAN'S VALLEY

In this Thanksgiving special, a construction company threatens the sanctuary of a band of condors, which sends out a scout, Elliot, in search of a fabled animal refuge for endangered species known as No Man's Valley. One of its inhabitants, Pat

A small group of animals celebrate the victory of a band of condors against a local construction company in the CBS network special, "No Man's Valley." Lee Melendez–Phil Howort Productions (Courtesy: Bill Melendez Productions)

the Passenger Pigeon, returns with Elliot to guide the other condors back so they will be safe from extinction. *A Lee Mendelson–Phil Howort Production in association with Frank Fehmers Productions and Bill Melendez Productions. Color. Half–hour. Premiered on CBS: November 23, 1981. Rebroadcast on CBS: September 12, 1982. Syndicated.*

Voices:
Chief: Henry Corden, **Elliot:** Frank Buxton, **Abe:** Art Metrano, **George:** Hal Smith, **Nipponia:** Chanin Hale, **Fred Firmwing:** Arnold Stang, **Pere David:** Barney Phillips, **Daniel:** Joe E. Ross, **Pat:** Desiree Goyette, **Nobody Panda:** Richard Deacon, **Herman:** John Stephenson

THE NOTORIOUS JUMPING FROG OF CALAVERAS COUNTY

Dan'l Webster and Reverend Leonidas W. "Jim" Smiley, two members of a small mining community, wager $40 with a stranger in a contest over which frog can jump the farthest in this humorous half–hour special based on Mark Twain's famous short story. *A Severo Perez Production. Color. Half–hour. Premiere: 1983–1984. Syndicated.*

THE NUTCRACKER

After playing with their set of wooden soldiers, the children of a well–to–do European family are forgetful in putting away their toys, leaving them unwrapped under the Christmas tree. As the housemaid is cleaning up, she discovers one wooden soldier—known as a nutcracker—left out of the bunch. Holding him close to her, she begins to dream what it would be like to have the brave soldier go into battle. *A Soyuzmultfilm Studios Production. Color. Half–hour. Premiered on CBS: November 25, 1978. Rebroadcast on CBS: November 27, 1980. Syndicated.*

OFF ON A COMET

Led by French Captain Hector Servadac, a band of people of all races and ethnic origins become stranded on a comet racing through space and learn to live in their new environment, only to find their existence threatened when they realize the comet is on a crash–course with Earth in this hour–long special based on the Jules Verne novel, *Hector Servadac: Travels and Adventures Through the Solar System. An Air Programs International Production. Color. One hour. Premiered: 1976. Syndicated.*

Voices:
Barbara Frawley, Ron Haddrick, Philip Hinton, Shane Porteous, Bevan Wilson

THE OLD CURIOSITY SHOP

The tragic tale of one granddaughter's love for her poor grandfather is the basis of this 90–minute special in which the young girl (Little Nell) takes to the road to raise money to lift her grandfather out of debt. The program was based on the Charles Dickens novel. *A Burbank Films Production. Color. One hour and a half. Premiered: 1984. Syndicated.*

Voices:
John Benton, Jason Blackwell, Wallas Eaton, Penne Hackforth–Jones, Brian Harrison, Doreen Harrop, Ross Higgins, Sophie Horton, Jennifer Mellett

OLIVER AND THE ARTFUL DODGER

When it is revealed that Oliver is an heir to the estate of the wealthy Mr. Brownlow, his wicked nephew, Snipe, sets out to find the will and destroy it. Snipes is unsuccessful thanks to some help from Oliver's special friend, The Artful Dodger, in this animated recreation of Charles Dickens' popular novel *Oliver Twist.* The program was first broadcast as a two–part episode of "The ABC Saturday Superstar Movie" series on Saturday mornings before it was rebroadcast as a daytime special on both ABC and in syndication. *A Hanna–Barbera Production. Color. One hour. Premiered on ABC: October 21 and 28, 1972 (on "The ABC Saturday Superstar Movie"). Rebroadcast on ABC: December 15 and 22, 1973. Syndicated.*

Voices:
Oliver: Gary Marsh, **The Dodger/Fishmonger:** Mike Bell, **Flip/Boy:** John Walmsley, **Deacon/Happy Harry/Twig:** Darryl Pollack, **Louisa/Lilibit:** Pamelyn Ferdin, **Snipe/Furniture Man:** Dick Dawson, **Mrs. Puddy/Rose/Tess/Old Hag:** Joan Gerber, **Mr. Bumble/Coachman:** Ronald Long, **Mrs. Grunch/Mistress Dreadly/Farmer's Wife/The Old Crone:** Anna Lee, **Mr. Grunch/Goodfriend/Butcher/Mr. Brownlow/Mr. Highbottle:** John Stephenson, **The Doctor/Farmer/Constable/Master Dreadly:** Bernard Fox, **Pastry Cook/House Agent/Midget Workman/Hero** (Dog): Don Messick, **Narrator:** Michael Evans

OLIVER TWIST (1981)

Charles Dickens' classic novel inspired this hour–long pro-gram, which was first released as a full–length feature and then reedited for television. This time, Oliver is paired with a new friend, Squeaker the Cricket, who helps him search for his inheritance while matching their wits with several colorful villains along the way (Fagin, Mr. Bumble, The Artful Dodger and Bill Sikes). *A Filmation Production in association with Warner Brothers Television. Color. One hour. Premiered on NBC: April 14, 1981 (as "NBC Special Treat").*

Voices:
Oliver Twist: Josh Albee, **Fagin:** Les Tremayne

Additional Voices:

Phil Clark, Cathleen Cordell, Michael Evans, Lola Fischer, Robert Holt, Davy Jones, Larry D. Mann, Dallas McKennon, Billy Simpson, Larry Storch, Jane Webb, Helene Winston

OLIVER TWIST (1984)

The story of impoverished orphan Oliver Twist, who struggles to find his inheritance, is captured in this 90–minute special for first–run syndication. *A Burbank Films Production. Color. One hour and a half. Premiered: 1984. Syndicated.*

Voices:

Faye Anderson, Bill Conn, Wallas Eaton, Barbara Frawley, Ross Higgins, Sean Hinton, Robin Ramsey, Derani Scarr, Robin Stewart

ON VACATION WITH MICKEY MOUSE AND FRIENDS

Jiminy Cricket hosts this wacky look at the most memorable vacations of several of Walt Disney's most beloved characters in this collection of previously released theatrical cartoons—*Canine Caddy* (1941), *Bubble Bee* (1949), *Goofy and Wilbur* (1939), *Dude Duck* (1951), *Mickey's Trailer* (1951) and *Hawaiian Holiday* (1937)—which was first broadcast as an episode of ABC's prime–time series, "Disneyland," in 1956. The program was later retitled and rebroadcast on both NBC and ABC as an hour–long special. *A Walt Disney Television Production. Color. One hour. Premiered on ABC: March 7, 1956 (on "Disneyland"). Rebroadcast on NBC: April 11, 1979 (as "On Vacation With Mickey Mouse and Friends"); ABC: June 29, 1986 (on "The Disney Sunday Movie").*

Voices:
Jiminy Cricket (host): Cliff Edwards, **Mickey Mouse:** Wayne Allwine, **Donald Duck:** Clarence Nash

PAC–MAN HALLOWEEN SPECIAL

Baby Pac experiences Halloween for the first time, but Mez-maron and his chomping Ghost Monsters threaten to disrupt the seasonal fun in this half–hour prime–time special based on the popular Atari video game characters. Entitled "Trick or Chomp," the program was actually an episode originally broadcast on the characters' popular Saturday–morning series. *A Hanna–Barbera Production. Color. Half–hour. Premiered on ABC: October 30, 1982.*

Voices:
Pac–Man: Marty Ingels, **Ms. Pac:** Barbara Minkus, **Baby Pac:** Russi Taylor, **Chomp Chomp:** Frank Welker, **Sour Puss:** Peter Cullen, **Mezmaron:** Alan Lurie, **Sue Monster:** Susan Silo, **Inky Monster:** Barry Gordon, **Blinky Monster/Pinky Monster:** Chuck McCann, **Clyde Monster:** Neilson Ross

PETER AND THE MAGIC EGG

Peter Paas the rabbit helps Mama and Papa Doppler, who raised him from birth, save their farm from greedy Tobias Tinwhiskers in this Easter tale, which is told by Uncle Amos Egg, an egg farmer, whose mortgage is about to be foreclosed by the same evil Tinwhiskers. Peter is helped in his quest by several other animal friends, among them, Feathers the duck, Lollychops the lamb and Terrence the turtle. *A RLR Associates in association with Murakami–Wolf–Swenson Films. Color. Half–hour. Premiered: March, 1983. Syndicated.*

Voices:
Uncle Amos Egg: Ray Bolger, **Tobias Tinwhiskers/Cotton:** Bob Ridgely, **Peter Paas:** Al Eisenmann, **Terrence:** Charles Woolf, **Feathers:** Joan Gerber, **Lollychops:** Russi Taylor, **Papa Doppler/Kookybird:** Bob Holt

THE PICKWICK PAPERS

The humorous escapades of Samuel Pickwick and the mem-bers of his literary group, the Pickwick Club, are the premise for this 90–minute adaptation of the Charles Dickens novel. *A Burbank Films Production. Color. One hour and a half. Premiered: 1985.*

PINK PANTHER IN "A PINK CHRISTMAS"

The Pink Panther, in his first prime–time animated special, appears alone, cold and hungry in New York's Central Park in the 1890s, trying desperately to get himself a Christmas dinner, even if it entails getting arrested, in this heartwarming animated holiday special. As in his theatrical cartoon series, the non–speaking panther relies considerably on visual hu-mor, this time neatly tied into a Christmas–themed setting. Sponsor: Parker Brothers. *A DePatie–Freleng Enterprises pro-duction in association with Mirisch–Geoffrey Productions. Color. Half–hour. Premiered on ABC: December 7, 1978. Rebroadcast on ABC: December 16, 1979. Syndicated.*

PINK PANTHER IN "OLYMPINKS"

Timed to coincide with the 1980 Winter Olympics, the Pink Panther finds the odds stacked against him in this cartoon version of the Olympics—called "Olympinks"—in which he tries to win at any cost but often pays the price for his effort.

The lonely Pink Panther, who is smitten by the vision of a lovely lady panther, gets into all sorts of wild and wonderful misadventures when he is hired by a very special delivery service in "Pink At First Sight," an ABC prime-time Valentine's Day special. © DePatie–Freleng Enterprises (Courtesy: ABC)

The special aired during the final quarter of the Lake Placid Winter Olympics, broadcast on the same network, ABC. *A DePatie–Freleng Enterprises Production in association with Mirisch–Geoffrey Productions. Color. Half–hour. Premiered on ABC: February 22, 1980. Syndicated.*

PINK PANTHER IN "PINK AT FIRST SIGHT"

In this Valentine's Day special, the Pink Panther longs for a lady panther and fantasizes about every female he meets. He is ready to give up until a pretty panther comes along in the local park and wins not only his attention but his love. *A Marvel Production in association with Mirisch–Geoffrey Productions and DePatie–Freleng Enterprises. Color. Half–hour. Premiered on ABC: May 10, 1981. Rebroadcast on ABC: May 29, 1982. Syndicated.*

Voices:

Weaver Copeland, Brian Cummings, Marilyn Schreffler, Hal Smith, Frank Welker

PINOCCHIO'S CHRISTMAS

The little wooden boy Pinocchio is back in an all–new Christmas adventure that finds him falling in love with a little girl marionette, Julietta, while working as an added attraction for Maestro Fire–Eater. Along the way he meets up with a sly old fox and money–hungry cat and, of course, Papa Geppetto in this Animagic adventure. *A Rankin–Bass Production. Color. One hour. Premiered on ABC: December 3, 1980. Rebroadcast on ABC: December 24, 1982. Syndicated.*

Voices:

Pinocchio: Todd Porter, **Geppetto:** George S. Irving, **Maestro Fire–Eater:** Alan King, **The Cat:** Pat Bright, **Julietta/Lady Azura:** Diane Leslie, **Dr. Cricket:** Robert McFadden, **Children:** Tiffany Blake, Carl Tramon, Alice Gayle

Additional Voices:

Gerry Matthews, Robert McFadden, Ray Owens, Allen Swift

PLAY IT AGAIN, CHARLIE BROWN

For years Lucy has tried to get Schroeder's attention. She makes yet another attempt after Peppermint Patty tells her that she has an opening in the PTA program at school for Schroeder to play the piano. Lucy thus offers Schroeder his first "big break," for which he is most appreciative, but her only reward is a "thank you" in return. *A Lee Mendelson–Bill Melendez Production in association with Charles M. Schulz Creative Associates and United Feature Syndicate. Color. Half–hour. Premiered on CBS: March 28, 1971. Rebroadcast on CBS: April 11, 1972; February 11, 1973.*

Voices:

Charlie Brown: Chris Inglis, **Lucy Van Pelt:** Pamelyn Ferdin, **Linus Van Pelt:** Stephen Shea, **Sally Brown:** Hilary Momberger, **Schroeder:** Danny Hjeim, **Frieda:** Linda Mendelson, **Peppermint Patty:** Kip DeFaria

THE POGO SPECIAL BIRTHDAY SPECIAL

Walt Kelly's charming comic strip character, known for his wit and pointed satire, comes to life in this television special based on classic Pogo stories. Kelly, who coproduced the special with animator Chuck Jones, is credited with writing the program and providing voices for three of the characters. Sponsor: Procter and Gamble. *A Chuck Jones Enterprises Production in association with MGM–TV. Color. Half–hour. Premiered on NBC: May 18, 1969. Rebroadcast on NBC: February 22, 1970; February 20, 1971.*

Voices:

Pogo Possum: June Foray, **Mam'selle Hepzibah:** June Foray, **Porky Pine/Bunny Rabbit/Basil the Butterfly:** Chuck Jones, **P. T. Bridgeport the Bear/Albert the Alligator/Dr. Howland Owl:** Walt Kelly, **Churchy–la–Femme/Beauregard Bugleboy:** Les Tremayne

THE POINT

Oblio, a young lad, searches for acceptance after he is banished from his homeland because his head is not pointed like the rest of the locals and because not having a "point" is against the law. Originally narrated by Academy Award–winning actor Dustin Hoffman, this 90–minute special was produced for ABC's "Movie of the Week," and beamed at an earlier hour than usual to grab the child audience as well as adults. Harry Nilsson, who wrote the original story, also composed seven songs for the program.

Oblio, a young lad, searches for acceptance in "The Point." © Nilsson House Music, Inc./Murakami–Wolf Productions (Courtesy: Murakami–Wolf–Swenson Films)

In later rebroadcasts of the program, Hoffman was replaced by Alan Barzman (1974) as the father/narrator, while Ringo Starr succeeded Barzman by performing the same task for the videocassette version released in 1986. *A Nilsson House Music Production in association with Murakami–Wolf–Swensons Films. Color. One hour and a half. Premiered on ABC: February 2, 1971. Rebroadcast on ABC: December 7, 1974.*

Voices:
Father (narrator): Dustin Hoffman, Alan Barzman, Ringo Starr, **Son/Oblio:** Michael Lookinland, **The King/Leafman/Oblio's Father:** Paul Frees, **The Count:** Lennie Weinrib, **Rockman:** Bill Martin, **Oblio's Mother:** Joan Gerber, **Count's Son:** Buddy Foster

POOCHIE

Poochie, a lovable pink pup, goes on an exciting journey to Egypt with her computer robot, Hermes, to help a young boy, Danny Evans, find his father who has disappeared inside a pyramid. Poochie learns of the boy's troubles while answering mail in the absence of her owner, E. G. Prince, a millionaire publisher who is off doing important things. *A DIC Enterprises Production in association with Mattel. Color. Half–hour. Premiered: June, 1984. Syndicated.*

Voices:
Poochie: Ellen Gerstell, **Hermes:** Neil Ross, **Zipcode:** Fred Travalena, **Koom:** Jennifer Darling, **Danny Evans:** Katie Leigh

POPEYE MEETS THE MAN WHO HATED LAUGHTER

Seafaring sailor Popeye and a bumper crop of comic–strip favorites (Blondie and Dagwood, the Katzenjammer Kids, the Little King, Steve Canyon, Flash Gordon, the Phantom, Tim Tyler, Beetle Bailey, and Jiggs and Maggie), who appear in animation for the first time, meet their match when an evil man tries to prevent the spread of laughter in the world in this "ABC Saturday Superstar Movie." The made–for–television feature was directed by cartoon veterans Jack Zander and Hal Seeger and written by Lou Silverton. Original music was scored by Elliott Schiprut. *A King Features Production. Color. One hour. Premiered on ABC: October 7, 1972 (on "The ABC Saturday Superstar Movie"). Rebroadcast on ABC: February 9, 1974. Syndicated.*

Voices:
Popeye: Jack Mercer

THE POPEYE SHOW

Aired in prime–time, this half–hour special was comprised of four excerpts from the Saturday–morning series, "The All–New Popeye Hour," in which the spinach–gulping sailor, his stringbean girlfriend Olive, and world–class bully Bluto are subjected to a series of misadventures. *A Hanna–Barbera Production in association with King Features Entertainment. Color. Half–hour. Premiered on CBS: September 13, 1978.*

Voices:
Popeye: Jack Mercer, **Olive Oyl:** Marilyn Schreffler, **Bluto:** Allan Melvin, **Wimpy:** Daws Butler

THE POPEYE VALENTINE SPECIAL

Olive Oyl sets sail on a Valentine's Day Sweetheart Cruise, captained by hamburger–eating Wimpy, in search of "Mr. Right." She discovers in the end that the best man for her is Popeye. The story title of the program was "Sweethearts at Sea." *A Hanna–Barbera Production in association with King Features Entertainment. Color. Half–hour. Premiered on CBS: February 14, 1979. Rebroadcast on CBS: February 13, 1980; January 30, 1981; February 2, 1982.*

Voices:
Popeye: Jack Mercer, **Olive Oyl/Sea Hag/Bathing Beauty #1:** Marilyn Schreffler, **Bluto:** Allan Melvin, **Wimpy:** Daws Butler, **King Neptune/Man–In–The–Moon:** Barney Phillips, **Jeep/Princess/Bathing Beauty #2:** Ginny McSwain

POUND PUPPIES

Thrilling adventures, heartwarming moments and irresistible characters abound in this two–hour animated escape comedy in the vein of wartime feature *Stalag 17* and television's "Hogan Heroes," except here the breakouts are masterminded by mutts. Led by the raffish, charming Cooler, the Pound Puppies, a band of merry doggies, operate the Pound Puppy Mission Control Center, located in the dank depths of the City Pound. Their mission is to find homes for hapless puppies that get caught in the net of Dabney Nabbit, the diligent if sloppy dogcatcher. This first–run movie inspired production of the Saturday–morning series, "Pound Puppies," which was broadcast on ABC. *A Hanna–Barbera Production. Color. Two hours. Premiered: October, 1985. Syndicated.*

Voices:

Cooler: Dan Gilvezan, **Violet/TV Newscaster:** Gail Matthius, **Scrounger:** Ron Palillo, **Bright Eyes/Mom:** Adrienne Alexander, **Howler/Fat Cat:** Frank Welker, **Barkerville/Dad:** Alan Oppenheimer, **Mayor Fisk:** Sorrell Brooke, **Chief Williams:** Garrett Morris, **Bigelow:** Jonathan Winters, **Tubbs/Pound Puppy #4:** Avery Schreiber, **Nabbitt/Pound Puppy #3:** Henry Gibson, **The Nose:** Jo Anne Worley, **Flack/Nathan/ Pound Puppy #1:** Charles Adler, **Itchy/Snitchy/Louie:** Don Messick, **Fist/Pound Puppy #2:** Ed Begley Jr., **Mother Superior/Old Lady:** June Foray, **Doc West/Chelsea:** Victoria Carroll, **Sarah:** Laura Duff

PUFF AND THE INCREDIBLE MR. NOBODY

An insecure young boy (Terry) creates his own imaginary friend, Mr. Nobody. He soon believes his abilities to make up songs, jokes, games and paint pictures originate from the mythical character. Puff teaches the young lad that his creativity comes from within and not from his friend. *A Yarrow–Muller/Murakami–Wolf–Swenson Films Production for the My Company. Color. Half–hour. Premiered on CBS: May 17, 1982. Rebroadcast on CBS: August 30, 1985. Syndicated.*

Voices:

Puff: Burgess Meredith, **Terry:** David Mendenhall, **Mr. Nobody:** Robert Ridgely, **Girl:** Diana Dumpis, **Boy:** Billy Jacoby, **Mom:** Joan Gerber, **Dad:** Bob Holt, **Professor K:** Hal Smith

PUFF THE MAGIC DRAGON

Puff comes to the aid of a small boy, afraid to face life, and he helps solve the boy's problems by taking the boy on a trip to his homeland, teaching the boy to be brave and see things as they really are. Based on the Peter, Paul and Mary song of the same name. Writer Peter Yarrow added new lyrics to go with the story. *A Yarrow–Muller/Murakami–Wolf–Swenson Films Production for the My Company. Color. Half–hour. Premiered on CBS: October 30, 1978. Rebroadcast on CBS: September 10, 1979; April 28, 1981. Syndicated.*

Voices:

Puff: Burgess Meredith, **Jackie Draper:** Phillip Tanzini, **Pirate/Pieman/Sneeze:** Bob Ridgely, **Mother/Star:** Maitzi Morgan, **Father:** Peter Yarrow, **Bold Doctor:** Regis Cordic, **Tall Doctor:** Frank Nelson, **Short Doctor:** Charles Woolf

PUFF THE MAGIC DRAGON IN THE LAND OF THE LIVING LIES

The irresistible Puff deals with a young girl, who lies to make herself feel better after her parents' divorce, by taking her to the Land of the Living Lies so she can recognize that her lying fools nobody and only hurts herself. *A Yarrow–Muller/Murakami–Wolf–Swenson Film Production for the My Company. Color. Half–hour. Premiered on CBS: November 17, 1979. Rebroadcast on CBS: October 22, 1980. Syndicated.*

Voices:

Puff: Burgess Meredith, **Sandy:** Mischa Lenore Bond, **Talking Tree:** Alan Barzman, **Kid Umpire/Boy Who Cried Wolf/Boy With Huge Ears:** Ike Eisenmann, **Mother/Talking Pumpkin/ Little Girl:** Joan Gerber, **Judge/Bailiff/Zealot:** Gene Moss, **Baron Munchausen/Snake/Attorney/Basketball Player:** Robert Ridgely, **Father:** Peter Yarrow

THE PUPPY'S AMAZING RESCUE

While celebrating Tommy's birthday in his parents' mountaintop cabin, Petey the puppy and Dolly, Tommy's sister, get separated during a massive snowslide, after which Petey heads up a search party to find her. An "ABC Weekend Special." *A Ruby–Spears Enterprises Production. Color. Half–hour. Premiered on ABC: January 26, 1980. Rebroadcast on ABC: May 3, 1980; September 6, 1980; March 26, 1983.*

Voices:

Petey: Bryan Scott, **Tommy:** John Joseph Thomas, **Dolly:** Nancy McKeon

Additional Voices:

Hettie Lynn Hurtes, John Stephenson, Janet Waldo, Frank Welker

THE PUPPY SAVES THE CIRCUS

In his fourth afternoon children's special, Petey, the frisky pup, suffers a serious bout of amnesia after he is accidentally struck by a car driven by George Goodbee and his granddaughter, Gloria, of the "Goodbee Giant Traveling Circus." With no memory of his past, he winds up performing in the circus (as "Rags II, the Funny Wonder Puppy"), where, unfortunately, his life is put in great danger. The program marked the fifth season debut of the "ABC Weekend Specials." *A Ruby–Spears Enterprises Production. Color. Half–hour. Premiered on ABC: September 12, 1981. Rebroadcast on ABC: March 6, 1982; October 23, 1982; March 3, 1984.*

Voices:

Petey: Sparky Marcus, **Dolly:** Nancy McKeon, **Tommy:** Tony O'Dell, **George Goodbee/Sligh:** Alan Young, **Gloria Goodbee:** Janet Waldo, **Emily:** Linda Gary, **Dad/Abdullah:** John Stephenson, **Kiki/Vet:** Alan Dinehart, **Tiger/Lead Pony/Clown:** Frank Welker

THE PUPPY'S GREAT ADVENTURE

Petey the puppy's happiness turns to bitter sorrow when his master, Tommy, is adopted out of the Public Home for Boys by a wealthy jeweler and his wife who refuse to take Petey, too; sequel to "The Puppy Who Wanted A Boy." An "ABC Weekend Special." *A Ruby–Spears Enterprises Production. Color. Half–hour. Premiered on ABC: February 3, 1979. Rebroadcast on ABC: May 12, 1979; September 2, 1979.*

Voices:

Petey: Bryan Scott, **Tommy:** John Joseph Thomas, **Dolly:** Nancy McKeon

Scatman Crothers, Joan Gerber, Allan Melvin, John Stephenson, Frank Welker

THE PUPPY WHO WANTED A BOY

The natural bond between a dog and a boy is the core of this half–hour special, adapted from Catherine Woolley's sentimental children's story, in which Sonny, a lonely puppy, seeks the companionship of a 12–year–old orphan (Tommy) to fulfill his search for an owner to call his own. An "ABC Weekend Special." *A Ruby–Spears Enterprises Production. Color. Half–hour. Premiered on ABC: May 6, 1978. Rebroadcast on ABC: September 23, 1978; January 21, 1979; October 27, 1979.*

Voices

Sonny/Petey: Todd Turquand, **Tommy:** John Joseph Thomas

Additional Voices:

Mike Bell, Joan Gerber, Bob Holt, Larry Mann, Hazel Shermet, Frank Welker

PUSS–IN–BOOTS

Wearing boots that possess magical powers, Orlando the cat is given the ability to speak and uses his newfound talent to elevate his master (Jacques) in the community, thus enabling him to pursue his first and only love—the king's daughter. *A Rankin–Bass Production in association with Mushi Studios. Color. Half–hour. Premiered: December 9, 1972. Syndicated.*

Voices:

Carl Banas, Len Birman, Bernard Cowan, Peg Dixon, Keith Hampshire, Peggi Loder, Donna Miller, Frank Perry, Henry Raymer, Billie Mae Richards, Alfie Scopp, Paul Soles

THE RACCOONS AND THE LOST STAR

The evil Cyril Sneer, a dastardly aardvark, plots to conquer Earth from his hollowed fortress on a far–away planet, but must first recover a special "gold star," which powers his technological wizardry to complete his mission. But, as usual, Bert Raccoon and his friends thwart his evildoing and restore peace among the planets through determination, courage and friendship. Produced in Canada, the program was the third special based on the popular Canadian cartoon series, "Raccoons." *A Gillis–Wiseman Production in association with Atkinson Film–Arts Productions. Color. Half–hour. Premiered (U. S.): December, 1983. Syndicated.*

Voices:

Bert Raccoon/Pig General: Len Carlson, **Ralph Raccoon:** Bobby Dermer, **Melissa Raccoon:** Dottie West, **Julie:** Tammy Bourne, **Tommy:** Hadley Kay, **Dan the Ranger:** John Schneider, **Schaeffer,** Julie and Tommy's dog. Carl Banas, **Cyril Sneer/Snag:** Michael Magee, **Cedric Sneer/Pig General:** Fred

RACCOONS ON ICE

The Raccoons and their friends wage a courageous effort to save and preserve the Evergreen Lake, climaxing with an exciting game of ice–hockey against sinister Cyril Sneer's ferocious team of "Bears"; this half–hour syndicated cartoon coincided with the opening of the 1982 National Hockey League Stanley Cup playoffs. *A Gillis–Wiseman Production in association with Atkinson Film–Arts Productions. Color. Half–hour. Premiered: December 20, 1981. Syndicated.*

Voices:

Bert Raccoon: Len Carlson, **Ralph Raccoon:** Bobby Dermer, **Melissa Raccoon:** Rita Coolidge, **Schaeffer:** Carl Banas, **Cyril Sneer/Snag:** Michael Magee, **Cedric Sneer:** Fred Little, **Sophia Tu Tu:** Sharon Lewis, **Julie:** Tammy Bourne, **Tommy:** Hadley Kay, **Ferlin:** Danny Gallivan, **Narrator:** Rich Little, **Vocalist:** Leo Sayer

RAGGEDY ANN AND ANDY IN THE GREAT SANTA CLAUS CAPER

Alexander Graham Wolf, the inventor of "Gloopstick," plans to use the breakable plastic cube to sabotage Christmas for children all over the world. His sinister scheme is ruined when Comet, one of Santa's reindeer gets wind of Wolf's plans and enlists Raggedy Ann and Raggedy Andy to help. *A Chuck Jones Enterprises Production in association with Bobbs–Merrill Company. Color. Half–hour. Premiered on CBS: November 30, 1978. Rebroadcast on CBS: December 10, 1979; December 9, 1980. Syndicated.*

Voices:

Raggedy Ann/Comet: June Foray, **Raggedy Andy:** Daws Butler, **Alexander Graham Wolf/Santa:** Les Tremayne

RAGGEDY ANN AND ANDY IN THE PUMPKIN WHO COULDN'T SMILE

Raggedy Ann and Raggedy Andy bring together a lonely boy and lonely pumpkin—the only one left in the patch on Halloween night—to make Halloween special in this touching tale about giving for giving's sake, based on the famous rag doll characters created by Johnny Gruelle. *A Chuck Jones Enterprises Production in association with Bobbs–Merrill Company. Color. Half–hour. Premiered on CBS: October, 31, 1979. Rebroadcast on CBS: October 29, 1980. Syndicated.*

Voices:

Raggedy Ann/Aunt Agatha: June Foray, **Raggedy Andy:** Daws Butler, **The Pumpkin:** Les Tremayne, **Ralph:** Steven Rosenberg

Little, **Sophia Tu Tu/Broo:** Sharon Lewis, **Narrator:** Rich Little

RAINBOW BRITE: PERIL IN THE PITS

Arch–villain Murky Dismal and his henchman, Lurky, try to drain the Earth of its color and remove all the happiness from the world, but are foiled by Rainbow Brite, her flying horse, Starlite, and their special friends of Rainbowland, the Color Kids (Buddy Blue, Shy Violet, Indigo, La La Orange, Tickled Pink, Patty O'Green, Red Butler and Canary Yellow) in this animated special based on the popular greeting card characters. *A Hallmark Properties Production in association with DIC Enterprises Productions. Color. Half–hour. Premiered: June, 1984. Syndicated.*

Voices:

Rainbow Brite: Bettina Rush, **Starlite/Spectran:** Andre Stojka, **Brian:** Scott Menville, **Murky Dismal:** Peter Cullen, **Lurky/ Buddy Blue/Puppy Brite:** Patrick Fraley, **Twink/Shy Violet/ Indigo/La La Orange:** Robbie Lee, **Krys:** David Mendenhall, **Count Blogg:** Jonathan Harris, **Stormy:** Marissa Mendenhall, **Princess/Moonglow/Tickled Pink:** Ronda Aldrich, **Patty O'Green/Red Butler/Canary Yellow/Castle Creature:** Mona Marshall

RAINBOW BRITE: THE BEGINNING OF RAINBOWLAND

Rainbow Brite goes back to her roots to see how her world began, while relating the beginning of her own magical power and friendship with her friends, including the Color Kids, in this two–part special based on the Hallmark greeting card characters, broadcast in half–hour timeslots over two consecutive days. *A Hallmark Properties Production in association with DIC Enterprises Productions. Color. Half–hour. Premiered: April, 1985. Syndicated.*

Voices:

Rainbow Brite: Bettina Rush, **Starlite/Spectran:** Andre Stojka, **Brian:** Scott Menville, **Murky Dismal:** Peter Cullen, **Lurky/ Buddy Blue/Puppy Brite:** Patrick Fraley, **Twink/Shy Violet/ Indigo/La La Orange:** Robbie Lee, **Krys:** David Mendenhall, **Count Blogg:** Jonathan Harris, **Stormy:** Marissa Mendenhall, **Princess/Moonglow/Tickled Pink:** Ronda Aldrich, **Patty O'Green/Red Butler/Canary Yellow/Castle Creature:** Mona Marshall

RAINBOW BRITE: THE MIGHTY MONSTROMURK MENACE

Terror strikes the happy inhabitants of Rainbowland when Monstromurk, a powerful monster held captive in a bottle for 700 years, is let loose by that good–for–nothing aardvark, Murky Dismal, who wants to make the people of this happy–go–lucky world as miserable as he is. *A Hallmark Properties Production in association with DIC Enterprises Productions. Color. Half–hour. Premiered: December, 1984. Syndicated.*

Voices:

Rainbow Brite: Bettina Rush, **Starlite/Spectran:** Andra Stojka, **Brian:** Scott Menville, **Murky Dismal:** Peter Cullen, **Lurky/**

Rainbow Brite and her flying horse, Starlite, begin their mission in a scene from "Rainbow Brite: Peril In The Pits." © Hallmark Cards Inc. All rights reserved. (Courtesy: DIC Enterprises)

Buddy Blue/Puppy Brite: Patrick Fraley, **Twink/Shy Violet/ Indigo/La La Orange:** Robbie Lee, **Krys:** David Mendenhall, **Count Blogg:** Jonathan Harris, **Stormy:** Marissa Mendenhall, **Princess/Moonglow/Tickled Pink:** Ronda Aldrich, **Patty O'Green/Red Butler/Canary Yellow/Castle Creature:** Mona Marshall

THE RAISINS: SOLD OUT!

In this fanciful Claymation rockumentary, slick manager Leonard Limabean pressures the California Raisins to accept a new member into the group, hotshot performer Lick Broccoli, in this stop–motion animated special. Songs included "I Heard It Through the Grapevine," "Respect," "Mr. Pitiful" and "Demolition Rock." *A Will Vinton Production. Color. Half–hour. Premiered on CBS: May 2, 1990.*

THE REAL GHOSTBUSTERS: "LIVE! FROM AL CAPONE'S TOMB!"

The Ghostbusters swoop into action to prevent the fanatical invention of an anti–Halloween machine from destroying the holiday and its traditions in their first-ever prime–time special. The half–hour program was originally produced as an episode of the popular Saturday–morning series. *A DIC Enterprises Production. Color. Half–hour. Premiered on ABC: October 29, 1989.*

Voices:

Slimer: Frank Welker, **Peter Venkman:** Dave Coulier, **Winston Zeddmore:** Edward L. Jones, **Egon Spengler:** Maurice LaMarche, **Janine Melintz:** Kathi E. Soucie, **Ray Stantz:** Frank Welker

REALLY ROSIE

Singer–composer Carole King takes on the role of Rosie, who, dressed up like a film star, persuades her friends, the Nutshell Kids, into making musical film tests for a picture she wants to make, "What Happened to Chicken Soup?" This half–hour animated musical special was based on characters from Maurice Sendak's *Nutshell Library. A Sherriss Productions in association with D & R Productions. Color. Half–hour. Premiered on CBS: February 19, 1975. Rebroadcast on CBS: June 8, 1976 (as "Maurice Sendak's Really Rosie").*

Voices:

Rosie: Carole King

Additional Voices:

Baille Gerstein, Mark Hampton, Alice Playten, Dale Soules

THE RED BARON

When the princess of Pretzelheim is kidnapped by the evil cat, Putzi, legendary flying ace, the Red Baron (played by a schnauzer), comes out of retirement to lead a new squadron of flyers to reclaim the princess and defeat the mastermind behind this sinister plan, Catahari. The program originally aired as an episode of "The ABC Saturday Superstar Movie" and was rebroadcast as a half–hour children's special. *A Rankin–Bass Production. Color. Half–hour. Premiered on ABC: December 9, 1972 (on "The ABC Saturday Superstar Movie"). Rebroadcast on ABC: January 26, 1974. Syndicated.*

Voices:

Bradley Bolke, Robert McFadden, Rhoda Mann, Allen Swift

THE REMARKABLE ROCKET

An incredible firework rocket (Remarkable Rocket), who displays the attitudes and emotions of humans, is the subject of this charming adaptation of the Oscar Wilde story about the experiences of a group of fireworks who prepare to be set off during a royal wedding celebration. *A Potterton Production in association with Reader's Digest. Color. Half–hour. Premiered: 1974. Syndicated.*

Voices:

Narrator: David Niven, **Other Voices:** Graham Stark

THE RETURN OF THE BUNJEE

Bunjee, the elephant–like prehistoric creature, and his two young friends, Karen and Andy, wind up in the Middle Ages when their father's time–traveling machine is accidentally switched on in this sequel to "The Amazing Bunjee Venture," adapted from the popular children's book, *The Bunjee Venture,* by Stan McMurty. *A Hanna–Barbera Productions. Color. Half–hour. Premiered on ABC: April 6 and 12, 1985. Rebroadcast on ABC: September 21 and 28, 1985; April 21 and 28, 1990.*

Voices:

Bunjee: Frank Welker, **Karen Winsborrow:** Nancy Cartwright, **Andy Winsborrow:** Robbie Lee, **Mr. Winsborrow:**

Michael Rye, **Mrs. Winsborrow:** Linda Gary, **Others:** Peter Cullen, Pat Musick, **Narrator:** Michael Rye

THE RETURN OF THE KING

Continuing J. R. R. Tolkein's saga of the Hobbits, Frodo—kin to the aged Bilbo—sets off to destroy the now evil Ring in the fires of Mount Doom, thereby making it possible for the noble Aragon to return to his kingdom victorious over the hideous realm of Sauron. *A Rankin–Bass Production in association with Toei Animation. Color. Two hours. Premiered on ABC: May 11, 1980. Rebroadcast on ABC: July 21, 1983. Syndicated.*

Voices:

Frodo: Orson Bean, **Samwise:** Roddy McDowall, **Gandalf:** John Huston, **Aragorn:** Theodore Bikel, **Denethor:** William Conrad, **Gollum:** Theodore Bikel, **Minstrel:** Glenn Yarbrough

Additional Voices:

Nellie Bellflower, Paul Frees, Casey Kasem, Sonny Mclendrez, Don Messick, John Stephenson

RETURN TO OZ

L. Frank Baum's classic children's tale was given an animated treatment in this General Electric Fantasy Hour production, in which Dorothy returns to the Land of Oz in order to help her former cronies—Socrates (Strawman), Rusy (Tinman) and Dandy Lion (Cowardly Lion)—who have lost their brains, heart and courage respectively. The program marked the first special produced by filmmakers Arthur Rankin and Jules Bass, creators of numerous holiday specials and Saturday–morning cartoon series. They previously produced an animated series on Oz, "Tales of the Wizard of Oz," distributed to television stations worldwide in 1961. *A Rankin–Bass Production in association with Videocraft International and Crawley Films. Color. One Hour. Premiered on NBC: February 9, 1964. Rebroadcast on NBC: February 21, 1965. Syndicated.*

Voices:

Dorothy: Susan Conway, **Dandy Lion/Wizard:** Carl Banas, **Socrates** (Strawman): Alfie Scopp, **Rusy** (Tinman): Larry Mann, **Munchkins:** Susan Morse, **Glinda/Wicked Witch:** Pegi Loder

RIKKI–TIKKI–TAVI

Adopted by a British family in India, Rikki–Tikki–Tavi, a brave mongoose, fights to protect the people who've been so kind to him, saving them from two dreaded cobras, in this wonderful cartoon adaptation of Rudyard Kipling's *The Jungle Book.* Orson Welles narrates the program. Sponsor: Nestle. *A Chuck Jones Enterprises Production. Color. Half–hour. Premiered on CBS: January 9, 1975. Rebroadcast on CBS: April 12, 1976; April 4, 1977; January 23, 1978, February 9, 1979. Syndicated.*

Voices:

Rikki–Tikki–Tavi: Orson Welles, **Nag/Chuchundra:** Shepard Menken, **Teddy:** Michael LeClaire, **Nagaina/Dazee's**

Wife/Mother: June Foray, **Father:** Les Tremayne, **Darzee:** Lennie Weinrib, **Narrator:** Orson Welles

ROBIN HOOD

The Sheriff of Nottingham finally gets his men—Robin Hood and his Merry Men—by capturing the Sherwood Forest outlaws with a plan that tugs at their heartstrings involving a woodcutter, his son and the boy's sheepdog in this new version of the popular tale. A "Festival of Family Classics" special. *A Rankin–Bass Production. Color. Half–hour. Premiered: November 26, 1973. Syndicated.*

Voices:

Carl Banas, Len Birman, Bernard Cowan, Peg Dixon, Keith Hampshire, Peggi Loder, Donna Miller, Frank Perry, Henry Raymer, Billie Mae Richards, Alfie Scopp, Paul Soles

ROBIN HOODNIK

Animals are cast in human roles in this colorful rendition of the classic fantasy tale. Robin and his pack of happy critters are prime targets of the Sherrif of Nottingham, who has already attempted to capture the canine Robin and his friends—at last count—239 times and failed every time. Aided by his faithful deputy, Oxx, the Sheriff tries again, this time to stop Robin from marrying the lovely Maid Marian by unhatching a secret potion. The hour–long program first aired on "The ABC Saturday Superstar Movie" series (the working title of the production was "Cartoon Adventures of Robin Hound"). *A Hanna–Barbera Production. Color. One Hour. Premiered on ABC: November 4, 1972 (on "The ABC Saturday Superstar Movie"). Syndicated.*

Voices:

Robin Hood: Lennie Weinrib, **Alan Airedale/Whirlin' Merlin/Lord Scurvy/Friar Pork/Little John:** Lennie Weinrib, **Sheriff of Nottingham/Carbuncle:** John Stephenson, **Oxx:** Joe E. Ross, **Donkey/Town Crier/Buzzard:** Hal Smith, **Scrounger/Richard the Iron–Hearted:** Daws Butler, **Maid Marian/Widow Weed:** Cynthia Adler

ROBINSON CRUSOE (1972)

The resourceful Robinson Crusoe is shipwrecked on a tropical island and must find new means of survival until the day he will be rescued in this animated retelling of Daniel Defoe's beloved adventure novel. A "Famous Classic Tales" special. *An Air Programs International. Color. One hour. Premiered on CBS: November 23, 1972. Rebroadcast on CBS: October 8, 1973. Syndicated.*

Voices:

Alistair Duncan, Ron Haddrick, Mark Kelly, John Llewellyn, Owen Weingott

ROBINSON CRUSOE (1973)

After saving a man (Friday) from island cannibals, Robinson Crusoe and his talking parrot, Poll, save the captain of a ship from his mutinous crew and find their ticket to freedom from the island on which they have been stranded in this "Festival of Family Classics" special for first–run syndication. *A Rankin–Bass Production in association with Mushi Studios. Color. Half–hour. Premiered: February 18, 1973. Syndicated.*

Voices:

Carl Banas, Len Birman, Bernard Cowan, Peg Dixon, Keith Hampshire, Peggi Loder, Donna Miller, Frank Perry, Henry Raymer, Billie Mae Richards, Alfie Scopp, Paul Soles

ROBOTMAN AND FRIENDS

An evil robot (Roberon) makes a series of attempts to convert three friendly robots (Robotman, Stellar and Oops) into hating people instead of loving them, but fails on all counts thanks to the robot's Earthbound friends, Michael and his Uncle Thomas. The special was based on the Kenner toy product which was also turned into a daily comic strip for United Feature Syndicate in 1985. *A DIC Enterprises Production in association with United Media. Color. One hour and a half. Premiered: October, 1985. Syndicated.*

Voices:

Robotman: Greg Berg, **Roberon/Sound–Off:** Frank Welker, **Stellar:** Katie Leigh, **Uncle Thomas Cooper:** Phil Proctor, **Michael/Oops:** Adam Carl

ROCKIN' WITH JUDY JETSON

When intergalactic rock star Sky Rocker announces a surprise concert at the Cosmic Coliseum, the news sends George and Jane Jetson's teenage daughter, Judy, into orbit inspiring her to write a song for her music idol in this two–hour movie based on the beloved television fantasy/comedy series, "The Jetsons." *A Hanna–Barbera Production. Color. Two hours. Premiered: 1988. Syndicated.*

Voices:

Judy Jetson: Janet Waldo, **Jane Jetson,** her mother: Penny Singleton, **George Jetson,** her father: George O'Hanlon, **Elroy Jetson,** her brother: Daws Butler, **Rosie,** the Jetson's maid: Jean VanderPyl, **Astro,** the Jetson's dog: Don Messick, **Mr. Microchips:** Hamilton Camp, **Nicky:** Eric Suter, **Ramm:** Beau Weaver, **Iona:** Cindy McGee, **Starr:** Pat Musick, **Felonia:** Ruth Buzzi, **Quark:** Charlie Adler, **Gruff:** Peter Cullen, **Commander Comsat:** Peter Cullen, **Sky Rocker:** Rob Paulsen, **Manny:** Hamilton Camp, **Dee–Jay:** Beau Weaver, **Rhoda Starlet:** Selette Cole, **Fan Club President:** Pat Musick, **Bouncer:** Peter Cullen, **Zany:** Rob Paulsen, **Zowie:** Pat Musick, **High Loopy Zoomy:** P. L. Brown, **Zippy:** B. J. Ward, **Zappy:** Charlie Adler, **Zilchy:** Pat Fraley, **Mr. Spacely:** Mel Blanc

THE ROMANCE OF BETTY BOOP

It's 1939 and Betty's working two jobs to keep body and soul together: selling shoes by day and headlining at her Uncle Mischa's club at night. While dreaming of millionaire, Waldo, she is pursued by humble iceman, Freddie, and gangster, Johnny Throat, Uncle Mischa's ruthless creditor. Desiree Goyette, who displayed her singing prowess in several Charlie Brown television specials, is the voice of Betty. *A King Features Entertainment Production in association with Lee Mendelson–Bill Melendez Productions. Color. Half–hour. Premiered on CBS: March 20, 1985. Rebroadcast on CBS: December 31, 1987.*

Voices:

Betty Boop: Desiree Goyette, **Freddie:** Sean Allen, **Waldo Van Lavish:** Derek McGrath, **Johnny Throat/Punchie:** George R. Wendt, **Beverly:** Marsha Meyers, **Mischa Bubbles:** Sandy Kenyon, **Parrot:** Frank W. Buxton, **Chuckles:** Robert Towers, **Ethnic Voices:** Ron Friedman, **Announcer:** John Stephenson, **Vocalists:** Desiree Goyette, Sean Allen

ROMIE–0 AND JULIE–8

Fresh off the assembly line, two robots, Romie–0 and Julie–8, fall in love even though they are kept apart by the two companies who manufactured them in this innovative rendition of the classic love story. *A Nelvana Limited Production in association with CBC. Color. Half–hour. Premiered (U.S.): April 1979. Syndicated.*

Voices:

Romie–0: Greg Swanson, **Julie–8:** Donann Cavin, **Mr. Thunderbottom:** Max Ferguson, **Ms. Passbinder:** Marie Aloma, **Gizmo:** Nick Nichols, **Junk Monster:** Bill Osler, **Vocalists:** John Sebastian, Rory Block, Richard Manuel

ROSE–PETAL PLACE

Singer/actress Marie Osmond is the voice of Rose–Petal, a magical flower whose beauty and kindness triumphs over evil in an enchanting garden world known as Rose–Petal Place in this live–action/animation special. *A Ruby–Spears Enterprises Production. Color. Half–hour. Premiered: May, 1984. Syndicated.*

Two robots, kept apart by the companies who manufactured them, hopelessly fall in love in the Romeo and Juliet–inspired, "Romie–O and Julie–8." © Nelvana Limited

Cast:

Little Girl in the Garden: Nicole Eggert

Voices:

Rose–Petal: Marie Osmond, **Nastina:** Marilyn Schreffler, **Sunny Sunflower/Daffodil:** Susan Blu, **Orchid/Little Girl/Lily Fair:** Renae Jacobs, **Iris:** Candy Ann Brown, **P. D. Centipede/Seymour J. Snailsworth/Tumbles/Elmer/Horace Fly:** Frank Welker

ROSE–PETAL PLACE II: REAL FRIENDS

In this sequel to "Rose–Petal Place," Rose–Petal, the magical flower fairy, returns to help her garden friends learn an important lesson about friendship and trust. *A Ruby–Spears Enterprises Production in association with David Kirschner Productions and Hallmark Properties. Color. Half–hour. Premiered: April, 1985. Syndicated.*

Cast:

Little Girl in the Garden: Nicole Eggert

Voices:

Rose Petal: Maria Osmond, **Sunny Sunflower/Canterbury Belle/Fuschia:** Susan Blu, **Elmer/Horace Fly/Seymour J. Snailsworth/P. D. Centipede/Tumbles:** Frank Welker, **Nastina/Lily Fair/Marigold:** Marilyn Schreffler, **Sweet Violet/Cherry Blossom:** René Jacobs, **Ladybug:** Stacy McLaughlin

RUDOLPH AND FROSTY'S CHRISTMAS IN JULY

Frosty the Snowman and Rudolph the Red–Nosed Reindeer leave the cozy confines of the North Pole and Santa's company to help an ailing circus down south in July, but find trouble lurking in the form of the villainous Winterbolt. *A Rankin–Bass Production. Color. Half–hour. Premiered on ABC: November 25, 1979. Rebroadcast on ABC: December 20, 1981.*

Voices:

Santa Claus (narrator): Mickey Rooney, **Rudolph:** Billy Richards, **Frosty:** Jackie Vernon, **Crystal,** Frosty's wife: Shelley Winters, **Mrs. Santa Claus:** Darlene Conley, **Winterbolt:** Paul Frees, **Milton,** the ice cream salesman: Red Buttons, **Scratcher,** the jealous reindeer: Alan Sues, **Lilly,** the circus owner: Ethel Merman, **Lanie,** Lilly's daughter: Shelby Flint, **Big Ben:** Harold Peary

RUDOLPH'S SHINY NEW YEAR

Happy, the Baby New Year, has run away from Father Time and unless he's found there will be no new year and the calendar will remain locked on December 31st forever. Rudolph the Red–Nosed Reindeer saves the day by embarking on a special mission with Santa to bring Happy back in time for the calendar to change over to the new year. Program features an original score by Johnny Marks, including his original hit song, "Rudolph the Red–Nosed Reindeer." *A Rankin–Bass Production. Color. One hour. Premiered on*

ABC: December 10, 1976. Rebroadcast on ABC: December 11, 1977; December 9, 1978; December 16, 1979; December 14, 1980; December 10, 1981; December 6, 1982. Syndicated.

Voices:
Father Time (narrator): Red Skelton, **Rudolph:** Billie Richards, **Sir Tentworthree/Camel:** Frank Gorshin, **One Million B. C.:** Morey Amsterdam, **Santa Claus/Aeon:** Paul Frees, **Big Ben:** Hal Peary

RUDOLPH, THE RED–NOSED REINDEER

Inspired by Johnny Marks' best–selling song, this gaily colored Animagic special tells the story of Rudolph, the reindeer with the illuminating red nose, who saves Christmas by safely guiding Santa through a terrible storm on Christmas Eve. Burl Ives, appearing as Sam the Snowman, narrates the program, which was first broadcast on NBC in 1964 under the title of "General Electric's Fantasy Hour." *A Videocraft International Production. Color. Half–hour. Premiered on NBC: December 6, 1964 (on "General Electric Fantasy Hour"). Rebroadcast on NBC: December 5, 1965; December 4, 1966; December 8, 1967; December 6, 1968; December 5, 1969; December 4, 1970; December 6, 1971. Rebroadcast on CBS: December 8, 1972; December 7, 1973; December 13, 1974; December 3, 1975; December 1, 1976; November 30, 1977; December 6,*

Hermy the Elf sings joyfully as friend Rudolph looks on in the perennial prime–time Christmas special, "Rudolph, The Red–Nosed Reindeer." © Rankin–Bass Productions (Courtesy: Family Home Entertainment)

1978; December 6, 1979; December 3, 1980; December 14, 1981; December 1, 1982; December 3, 1983; December 1, 1984; December 3, 1985; December 9, 1986; December 15, 1987; December 5, 1988; December 15, 1989.

Voices:
Sam the Snowman (narrator): Burl Ives, **Rudolph:** Billie Richards, **Hermy the Elf:** Paul Soles, **Yukon Cornelius:** Larry D. Mann, **Santa Claus:** Stan Francis, **Clarice:** Janet Orenstein

Additional Voices:
Corinne Connely, Peg Dixon, Paul Kligman, Alfie Scopp

RUMPELSTILTSKIN

Actor Christopher Plummer narrates the tale of a maiden forced to spin straw into gold to save her father in this animated rendition of the Grimm Brothers' fairy tale which debuted on Canadian television and was syndicated in the United States. *An Atkinson Film–Arts Production in association with Telefilm Canada and CTV. Color. Half–hour. Premiered (U. S.): December, 1985. Syndicated.*

Voices:
Rumpelstiltskin: Robert Bockstael, **Miller:** Les Lye, **Miller's Daughter/Queen:** Charity Brown, **King:** Al Baldwin, **Narrator:** Christopher Plummer

SANTA AND THE THREE BEARS

Two bear cubs, Nikomi and Chinook, experience the joy and magic of Christmas for the very first time in this hour–long musical that was originally released theatrically in 1970 and rebroadcast via syndication as a holiday special. Live–action sequences of a kindly old grandfather relating the tale to his grandchildren introduce the animated story. *A Tony Benedict Production in association with Key Industries. Color. One Hour. Premiered: 1970. Syndicated.*

Cast:
Grandfather: Hal Smith, **Beth:** Beth Goldfarb, **Brian:** Brian Hobbs

Voices:
Ranger: Hal Smith, **Nana:** Jean VanderPyl, **Nikomi:** Annette Ferra, **Chinook:** Bobby Riha

SANTABEAR'S FIRST CHRISTMAS

A young bear carries out a good deed for the woodcutter and his granddaughter who have given him a home after he is separated from his family at the North Pole. Santa Claus recognizes the bear's giving nature and appoints him as his helper to deliver toys to the animals of the forest. Thus, he becomes known as Santabear. *A Rabbit Ears Production. Color. Half–hour. Premiered on ABC: November 22, 1986.*

Voices:
Narrator: Kelly McGillis

Fred Astaire, as mailman S. D. Kluger, hosts and narrates the Animagic network special, "Santa Claus Is Coming To Town." © Rankin–Bass Productions (Courtesy: Family Home Entertainment)

SANTA CLAUS IS COMING TO TOWN

The life and times of Santa Claus—his abandonment as a child, his christening as Kris Kringle and eventual marriage to Jessica the schoolmarm—is the essence of this holiday favorite produced in Animagic and narrated by actor/singer Fred Astaire, who likewise appears, in puppet form, as the town's mailman, S. D. Kluger. *A Rankin–Bass Production. Color. Half–hour. Premiered on ABC: December 14, 1970. Rebroadcast on ABC: December 3, 1971; December 1, 1972; November 30; 1973; December 5, 1974; December 9, 1975; December 12, 1976; December 1, 1977; December 10, 1978; December 2, 1979; December 8, 1980; December 19, 1981. Syndicated.*

Voices:

S. D. Kluger (narrator): Fred Astaire, **Kris Kringle**: Mickey Rooney, **Jessica**: Robie Lester, **Winter Warlock**: Keenan Wynn, **Tanta Kringle**: Joan Gardner, **Burgermeister**: Paul Frees, **Children**: Diana Lynn, Greg Thomas

SCHOOL . . . WHO NEEDS IT?

School bells are ringing but Davey (of TV's "Davey and Goliath") and his friends in the Jickets clubhouse decide to protest going back to school. On opening day, they march around campus carrying signs with slogans—"Down With School," "I Hate School" and "School—Who Needs It?"—to illustrate their point. The boys finally come around when their teacher extends an understanding hand and initiates the beginning of a special friendship. *A Clokey Production for the Lutheran Church of America. Color. Half–hour. Premiered: August–September, 1971. Syndicated.*

Voices:

Davey Hanson/Sally Hanson/Teacher: Norma McMillan, Nancy Wible, **Goliath**: Hal Smith

SCOOBY AND THE GHOUL SCHOOL

Scooby–Doo, Shaggy and Scrappy–Doo find themselves mixed up in a mess of monsters when they accept jobs as gym teachers at a girls' finishing school in this two–hour made–for–television movie. The film was produced as part of "Hanna–Barbera's Superstars 10" movie package for first–run syndication. *A Hanna–Barbera Production. Color. Two hours. Premiered: 1988. Syndicated.*

Voices:

Scooby–Doo/Scrappy–Doo: Don Messick, **Shaggy**: Casey Kasem, **Miss Grimwood**: Glynis Johns, **Elsa Frankensteen**: Pat Musick, **Winnie Werewolf**: Marilyn Schreffler, **Sibella Dracula**: Susan Blu, **Tannis the Mummy**: Patty Maloney, **Phantasma the Phantom**: Russi Taylor, **Matches**: Frank Welker, **Colonel Calloway**: Ronnie Schell, **Daddy Dracula/Frankenstein Senior**: Zale Kessler, **Phantom Father**: Hamilton Camp, **Papa Werewolf**: Frank Welker, **Mummy Daddy**: Andre Stojka, **Revolta**: Ruta Lee, **The Grim Creeper**: Andre Stojka, **Baxter**: Remy Auberjonois, **Tug**: Scott Menville, **Miguel**: Aaron Lohr, **Jamaal**: Bumper Robinson, **Grunt**: Jeff B. Cohen

SCOOBY AND THE RELUCTANT WEREWOLF

Cowardly canine Scooby–Doo and his best pal, Shaggy, are funny–car drivers who get into monstrous trouble when Dracula discovers that once every several hundred years (this according to the "Grimness Book of Records"), when conditions are right, a new werewolf can be created. The two–hour special was produced for "Hanna–Barbera's Superstar 10" movie package for first–run syndication. *A Hanna–Barbera Production. Color. Two hours. Premiered: 1988. Syndicated.*

Voices:

Scooby–Doo/Scrappy–Doo: Don Messick, **Shaggy**: Casey Kasem, **Googie**: B. J. Ward, **Vana Pira**: Pat Musick, **Dracula**: Hamilton Camp, **Dreadonia**: Joan Gerber, **Repulsa**: B. J. Ward, **Bonejangles**: Brian Mitchell, **Frankenstein**: Jim Cummings, **Mummy**: Alan Oppenheimer, **Skull Head**: Jim Cummings, **Brunch**: Rob Paulsen, **Crunch**: Frank Welker, **Screamer**: Mimi Seton, **Dr. Jeckyll/Mr. Hyde**: Ed Gilbert

SCOOBY–DOO MEETS THE BOO BROTHERS

Ghostly peril, hairbreadth escapes and a search for lost treasure turn Scooby–Doo, Scrappy–Doo and Shaggy's visit to a Southern plantation into spine–tingling adventure in this two–hour animated feature produced as part of "Hanna–Barbera's Superstar 10" syndicated movie package. *A Hanna–Barbera Production. Color. Two hours. Premiered: 1987. Syndicated.*

Voices:

Scooby–Doo/Scrappy–Doo: Don Messick, **Shaggy:** Casey Kasem, **Sheriff:** Sorrell Booke, **Farguard:** Arte Johnson, **Freako:** Ronnie Schell, **Shreako:** Rob Paulsen, **Meako:** Jerry Houser, **Sadie Mae:** Victoria Carroll, **Billy Bob:** Bill Callaway, **Confederate Ghost:** Bill Callaway, **Skull Ghost/Skeleton:** Arte Johnson, **Mayor:** Michael Rye, **Uncle Beauregard/Ape:** Bill Callaway, **Demonstrator Ghost:** Ronnie Schell, **Hound:** Don Messick

Scruffy, an orphaned puppy, shares the friendship of her canine companions in a scene from the ABC Weekend Special, "Scruffy." © Ruby–Spears Enterprises

SCOOBY GOES HOLLYWOOD

Scooby–Doo, the clumsy but lovable canine, romps through delightful capers in order to hit the big time in Hollywood by landing his own prime–time television show. *A Hanna–Barbera Production. Color. One hour. Premiered on ABC: December 23, 1979. Rebroadcast on ABC: January 25, 1981.*

Voices:

Scooby–Doo: Don Messick, **Shaggy:** Casey Kasem, **Fred:** Frank Welker, **Velma:** Pat Stevens, **Daphne:** Heather North Kenney, **Baby Scooby–Doo:** Frank Welker, **C. J.:** Rip Taylor, **Director/First V. P./Terrier:** Stan Jones, **Jesse Rotten/V. P./Jackie Carlson;** Michael Bell, **Cherie/Sis/Receptionist:** Marilyn Schreffler, **Lavonne/Second Woman/Waitress:** Joan Gerber, **Kerry/Girl Fan/Executive Secretary:** Ginny McSwain, **Brother/Guard/Announcer's Voice:** Patrick Fraley, **Bulldog/Second Man:** Don Messick, **First Man/Pilot's Voice:** Casey Kasem, **Afghan/The Groove:** Frank Welker, **First Woman/Lucy Lane:** Pat Stevens, **Treena/Mailgirl:** Heather North Kenney

SCRUFFY

In this three–part adventure, Scruffy, an orphaned puppy, searches for a new home and to find true love in her life for the first time. Cold and hungry, she becomes friends with a Shakespearean street actor, Joe Tibbles, who teaches her some new tricks which they use to make money in order to live. Their special relationship ends suddenly when Tibbles dies following one of their performances. Downcast, Scruffy finds a new friend in another stray dog, Butch, but only after he saves her from almost drowning after she falls off a bridge. Along with Butch, she joins a pack of other strays who look out for each other. An "ABC Weekend Special." *A Ruby–Spears Enterprises Production. Color. Half–hour. Premiered on ABC: October 4, 11 and 18, 1980. Rebroadcast on ABC: February 7, 14 and 21, 1981; February 13, 20 and 27, 1982; February 26, March 5 and March 12, 1983.*

Voices:

Scruffy: Nancy McKeon **Tibbles:** Hans Conried, **Butch:** Michael Bell, **Dutchess:** June Foray, **Narrator:** Alan Young

Additional Voices:

Alan Dinehart, Walker Edmiston, Linda Gary, Michael Rye, Janet Waldo, Frank Welker

THE SECRET WORLD OF OG

Living every kid's greatest fantasy, five brothers and sisters—Penny, Pamela, Patsy, Peter and their baby brother, Pollywog—are taken to a world of games and make–believe in a strange underground world called OG, inhabited by small green creatures who live in mushroom–shaped buildings and play games based on the characters found in comic books they've stolen from the children's rooms. *A Hanna–Barbera Production. Color. Half–hour. Premiered on ABC: April 30, May 7 and May 14, 1983. Rebroadcast on ABC: December 3, 10 and 17, 1983; October 27, November 10 and November 17, 1984; March 15, 22 and 29, 1986; February 21, February 28 and March 7, 1987.*

Voices:

OG: Fred Travalena, **Penny:** Noelle North, **Pamela:** Marissa Mendenhall, **Patsy:** Brittany Wilson, **Peter:** Josh Rodine, **Pollywood/Green Lady/Woman's Voice:** Julie McWhirter Dees, **Mother/Old Lady:** Janet Waldo, **Old Man/Glub Villager:** Fred Travalena, **Yukon "Yukie" Pete,** family dog: Peter Cullen, **Earless,** Pollywog's cat: Peter Cullen, **Long John Silver:** Peter Cullen, **Flub/Blib/Little Green Man #2/Floog/Little OG's Boy:** Dick Beals, **Sheriff/Little Green Man #1/Butcher/Villager/Mushroom Harvester:** Hamilton Camp, **Teacher:** Beth Clopton, **Pirate #1/Mayor/Man's Voice:** Dick Erdman, **Worker/Cowboy #1/Green Deputy:** Michael Rye, **Victim #2/Green Man:** Joe Medalis, **Victim #1/Elder OG/OG Father:** Andre Stojka, **Narrator:** Michael Rye

THE SELFISH GIANT

Faithfully adhering to Oscar Wilde's short story of the same name, this animated half–hour special deals with the efforts of Snow, Frost, North Wind and Hail—to keep the Giant's walled garden in a perpetual state of winter because he has forbidden children to play in it. Seeing his selfish ways, the Giant makes an effort to reform himself, opening up his heart to a stray child, who later repays the favor in this appealing Christian parable. Originally produced as a theatrical short–subject, the film was nominated for an Academy Award as Best Animated Short Subject in 1972. The program was first broadcast in Canada the year before. David Niven narrated the original version of the production, later replaced by Paul Hecht. *A Gerald Potterton Production in association with Reader's Digest. Color. Half–hour. Premiered on CBS: March 28, 1973. Rebroadcast on CBS: March 25, 1974; April 6, 1976. Syndicated.*

Voices:
Narrator: David Niven, Paul Hecht

SHE'S A GOOD SKATE, CHARLIE BROWN

Peppermint Patty enters her first major ice skating competition. With her coach, Snoopy, and faithful companion, Marcie, at her side, she runs into the usual Charlie Brown–like problems en route to the skating competition where a real disaster strikes. Woodstock saves the day. *A Lee Mendelson–Bill Melendez Production in association with Charles M. Schulz Creative Associates and United Feature Syndicate. Color. Half–hour. Premiered on CBS: February 25, 1980. Rebroadcast on CBS: February 25, 1981; February 10, 1982; February 23, 1988.*

Voices:
Charlie Brown: Arrin Skelley, **Marcie:** Casey Carlson, **Peppermint Patty:** Patricia Patts, **Coach/Announcer:** Scott Beach, **Teacher:** Debbie Muller, **Bully:** Tim Hall, **Snoopy:** Jose Melendez, **Woodstock** (singing): Jason Serinus, **Singer:** Rebecca Reardon

SILENT NIGHT

The heartwarming tale of Austrian pastor Joseph Mohr, who wrote the famed Christmas carol, is the premise of this animated production about the origin of the popular yuletide song, including the first time it was ever performed on Christmas Eve in 1818. *A National Telefilm Associates Presentation. Color. Half–hour. Premiered: December, 1977. Syndicated.*

SILVERHAWKS

This hour–long special marked the debut of the first–run syndicated series, containing the first two episodes, which follow the fate of the universe in the year 2839, with a volunteer android team—who are part metal and part human—sent by Earth to keep law and order in the galaxy. The program was based on the popular line of action toys produced by Kenner Products. *A Rankin–Bass Production in association with Pacific Animation. Color. One hour. Premiered: January, 1986. Syndicated.*

Voices:
Quicksilver: Peter Newman, **Melodia/Steelheart:** Maggie Jackson, **Windhammer:** Doug Preis, **Mon*Star/Stargazer:** Earl Hammond, **Poker–Face/BlueGrass/Time–Stopper:** Larry Kenney, **HardWare/Steelwill/Yes–Man/Mo–Lec–U–Lar:** Robert McFadden, **Hotwing:** Adolf Caesar, Doug Preis

SIMPLE GIFTS

The spirit of holiday gift–giving in its simplest form is the running theme of this one–hour collection of cartoon segments—"The Christmas Boy," "December 25, 1941," "The Great Frost," "Lost and Found," "A Memory of Christmas," "My Christmas" and "No Room at the Inn"—each adapted from well–known stories and produced by some of America's most noted animators and artists. *A R. O. Blechman Production for PBS. Color. One hour. Premiered on PBS: December 16, 1978.*

Voices:
Narrators: Jose Ferrer ("A Memory of Christmas"), Hermione Gingold ("The Great Frost")

THE SIMPSONS CHRISTMAS SPECIAL

The animated family from "The Tracy Ullman Show" prepares for the holidays, but it's rough sledding for household–head Homer, who is forced to resort to desperate measures when his Christmas bonus is canceled and Marge's family money goes to erase the tatoo son Bart thought would be the perfect gift. Entitled "Simpsons Roasting Over An Open Fire" the show was originally produced as part of the first season of

The Simpsons get into the spirit of Christmas in the Fox Network special, "The Simpsons Christmas Special."
© Fox Network

"The Simpsons" television show, which turned into a ratings sensation for Fox Network. *A Klasky/Csupo Production. Color. Half–hour. Premiered on Fox Network: December 17, 1989.*

Voices:
Homer J. Simpson: Dan Castellaneta, **Marge Simpson:** Julie Kavner, **Bart Simpson:** Nancy Cartwright, **Lisa Simpson:** Yeardley Smith, **Maggie Simpson:** (no voice), **Other Voices:** Harry Shearer

SLEEPING BEAUTY

Adding several new characters and sub–plots, the story of the beautiful young princess who is cast under a spell by the wicked old witch is re–told, but this time with a new twist. The princess and her subjects throughout the entire kingdom remain in perpetual sleep during her curse. None of them, including the princess, can be awakened until the handsome, bravehearted Prince Daring puckers up and arouses the sleeping beauty from her sleep with a kiss. A "Festival of Family Classics" special. *A Rankin–Bass Production in association with Mushi Studios. Color. Half–hour. Premiered: January 21, 1973. Syndicated.*

Voices:
Carl Banas, Len Birman, Bernard Cowan, Peg Dixon, Keith Hampshire, Peggi Loder, Donna Miller, Frank Perry, Henry Raymer, Billie Mae Richards, Alfie Scopp, Paul Soles

THE SMURFIC GAMES

The Smurfs discover the spirit of friendly competition when they hold their first Olympic–styled "Smurfic Games," which divide the village into two teams—East versus West. Meanwhile, Gargamel tries to activate a special medallion with deadly powers to use against the Smurfs. The special was nominated for an Emmy. *A Hanna–Barbera Production in association with SEPP International. Color. Half–hour. Premiered on NBC: May 20, 1984. Rebroadcast on NBC: May 11, 1985.*

Voices:
Papa Smurf/Azrael: Don Messick, **Baby Smurf:** Julie Mc-Whirter Dees, **Smurfette:** Lucille Bliss, **Clumsy/Painter/Dragon:** Bill Callaway, **Grouchy/Handy/Lazy/Argus:** Michael Bell, **Greedy/Harmony:** Hamilton Camp, **Jokey:** June Foray, **Hefty/Frog/Bird/Poet:** Frank Welker, **Tailor:** Kip King, **Gargamel:** Paul Winchell, **Bigmouth:** Lennie Weinrib, **Vanity:** Alan Oppenheimer

SMURFILY EVER AFTER

As the Smurfs celebrate the wedding of their beloved Laconia, the mute wood elf, Smurfette hopes to find her "Mr. Right." Unfortunately, her dreams are frustrated by her failure to accept someone's imperfections until she sees imperfections in herself. The special was closed–captioned for the hearing impaired. *A Hanna–Barbera Production in association with SEPP International. Color. Half–hour. Premiered on NBC: February 13, 1985. Rebroadcast on NBC: March 30, 1986.*

Voices:
Papa Smurf/Azrael: Don Messick, **Smurfette:** Lucille Bliss, **Hefty/Monster:** Frank Welker, **Handy/Lazy/Grouchy:** Michael Bell, **Jokey:** June Foray, **Gargamel:** Paul Winchell, **Clumsy:** Bill Callaway, **Vanity:** Alan Oppenheimer, **Brainy:** Danny Goldman, **Greedy/Woody:** Hamilton Camp, **Tailor:** Kip King, **Farmer:** Alan Young, **Elderberry:** Peggy Webber, **Bramble:** Robbie Lee, **Pansy:** Susan Blu, **Lilac:** Janet Waldo, **Holly:** Alexandria Stoddart, **Acorn:** Patti Parris

THE SMURFS

Two months after its successful debut on Saturday morning, this colony of little blue people was featured in their first prime–time special, featuring three episodes from their weekly series: "Supersmurf," "The Smurfette" and "The Baby Smurf." *A Hanna–Barbera Production in association with SEPP International. Color. One hour. Premiered on NBC: November 29, 1981.*

Voices:
Papa Smurf/Azrael: Don Messick, **Gargamel:** Paul Winchell, **Brainy:** Danny Goldman, **Clumsy:** Bill Callaway, **Hefty:** Frank Welker, **Jokey:** June Foray, **Smurfette:** Lucille Bliss, **Vanity:** Alan Oppenheimer, **Greedy/Harmony:** Hamilton Camp, **Lazy/Handy/Grouchy:** Michael Bell

THE SMURFS' CHRISTMAS SPECIAL

The Smurfs must use every little ounce of goodness and love they can muster to battle an even greater evil than Gargamel in this half–hour holiday special filled with colorful animation and music. *A Hanna–Barbera Production in association with SEPP International. Color. Half–hour. Premiered on NBC: December 13, 1982. Rebroadcast on NBC: December 9, 1983; December 22, 1984; December 5, 1986.*

Voices:
Papa Smurf/Azrael/Horse: Don Messick, **Harmony/Greedy/Bailiff:** Hamilton Camp, **Jokey/Squirrel:** June Foray, **Gargamel:** Paul Winchell, **Smurfette:** Lucille Bliss, **Grouchy/Lazy/Handy:** Michael Bell, **Grandfather/Vanity/Servant:** Alan Oppenheimer, **Stranger:** Rene Auberjonois, **William:** David Mendenhall, **Gwenevere:** Alexandra Stoddart, **Brainy:** Danny Goldman, **Clumsy/Painter/Wolf #1:** Henry Polic, **Hefty:** Frank Welker

THE SMURFS SPRINGTIME SPECIAL

The Smurfs prepare for their big Easter festival, while Gargamel, the Smurfs' archenemy, conspires with his wizardly godfather, Balthazar, to ruin the festivities. An Emmy Award winner. *A Hanna–Barbera Production in association with SEPP International. Color. Half–hour. Premiered on NBC: April 8, 1982. Rebroadcast on NBC: April 1, 1983; April 20, 1984.*

Voices:

Gargamel: Paul Winchell, **Papa Smurf/Azrael:** Don Messick, **Smurfette:** Lucille Bliss, **Mother Nature/Jokey:** June Foray, **Handy/Grouchy/Lazy:** Michael Bell, **Clumsy:** Bill Callaway, **Harmony:** Hamilton Camp, **Balthazar:** Keene Curtis, **Brainy/Tailor:** Danny Goldman, **Vanity:** Alan Oppenheimer, **Hefty/Poet/Duckling:** Frank Welker

SNOOPY'S GETTING MARRIED, CHARLIE BROWN

Good grief! Snoopy's getting married because he's flipped for a worldly French poodle who, like him, "thinks *Citizen Kane* is the best movie ever." For the big event, Snoopy rents a tux, has his doghouse done up for the reception, and asks his brother Spike, who later flirts with the bride–to–be, to be his "best beagle." However, a real twist occurs when the girl—er, dog—of Snoopy's dreams runs off with a golden retriever and leaves Snoopy behind. *A Lee Mendelson–Bill Melendez Production in association with Charles M. Schulz Creative Associates and United Feature Syndicate. Color. Half–hour. Premiered on CBS: March 20, 1985. Rebroadcast on CBS: January 16, 1987; March 16, 1988.*

Voices:

Charlie Brown: Brett Johnson, **Lucy Van Pelt:** Heather Stoneman, **Linus Van Pelt:** Jeremy Schoenberg, **Schroeder:** Danny Colby, **Peppermint Patty:** Gini Holtzman, **Sally Brown:** Stacy Ferguson, **Sally** (singing): Dawn S. Leary, **Marcie:** Keri Houlihan, **Pigpen/Franklin:** Carl Steven, **Snoopy:** Jose Melendez

SNOOPY: THE MUSICAL

Based on the popular 1974 play, this one–hour animated special is composed of a series of tuneful vignettes, with Snoopy headlining this cartoon adaptation. Musical sequences include "Edgar Allen Poe," a clever melody about the jitters experienced when being called on in school; "Poor Sweet Baby," a lighthearted ballad pairing hapless Charlie Brown and lovelorn Peppermint Patty; and "The Vigil," a song about Linus' woeful watch for the Great Pumpkin. Music and lyrics were written by Larry Grossman and Hal Hackady. *A Lee Mendelson–Bill Melendez Production in association with Charles M. Schulz Creative Associates and United Feature Syndicate. Color. One hour. Premiered on CBS: January 29, 1988.*

Voices:

Snoopy: Cameron Clarke, **Charlie Brown:** Sean Collins, **Lucy:** Tiffany Billings, **Peppermint Patty:** Kristi Baker, **Linus:** Jeremy Miller, **Sally:** Ami Foster

THE SNOWMAN

Based on the book by Raymond Briggs, the art of mime and music are combined to tell the story of a young boy who builds a snowman which comes to life during a dream on Christmas Eve. The program, which premiered on HBO, was rebroadcast on PBS, with David Bowie serving as its host. *A Snowman Enterprises Production in association with T. V. Cartoons. Color. Half–hour. Premiered on HBO: December 26, 1983. Rebroadcast on PBS: December 2, 1985; December 25, 1986.*

THE SNOW QUEEN

Two small children, Gerta and Kay, embark on a dangerous journey to rescue Gerta's brother who has been kidnapped by the evil Snow Queen in this charming adaptation of the Hans Christian Andersen classic. Originally produced overseas, the program was reedited and redubbed for American broadcast. *A Greatest Tales Production. Color. Half–hour. Premiered: 1977. Syndicated.*

Voices:

Gerta: Donna Ellio, **Kay:** Peter Nissen

Additional Voices:

Ray Owens, Billie Lou Watt, Gilbert Mack, Peter Hernandez

SNOW WHITE

Ruled by her cruel stepmother, the Queen, the enslaved Snow White escapes to the forest where she receives shelter and protection from the Seven Dwarfs, only to be hunted down by the Queen, disguised as a wicked old witch, who sells her a poisoned apple. A "Festival of Family Classics" special. *A Rankin–Bass Production in association with Mushi Studios. Color. Half–hour. Premiered: March 4, 1973. Syndicated.*

Voices:

Carl Banas, Len Birman, Bernard Cowan, Peg Dixon, Keith Hampshire, Peggi Loder, Donna Miller, Frank Perry, Henry Raymer, Alfie Scopp, Paul Soles

A SNOW WHITE CHRISTMAS

Adapted from the Grimm Brothers' fairy tale, the story of Snow White is given a new twist and new characters, as she teams up with seven giants (not dwarfs)—Thinker, Finicky, Corney, Brawny, Tiny, Hicker and Weeper—to stop the evil Queen from ruining Christmas. *A Filmation Production. Color. One hour. Premiered on CBS: November 19, 1980. Rebroadcast on CBS: December 7, 1983.*

Voices:

Snow White: Ericka Scheimer, **Finnicky/Corney/Tiny/Brawny/Hicker/Weeper/Villager:** Arte Johnson, **Wicked Queen/Hag:** Melendy Britt, **Queen:** Diane Pershing, **Grunyon:** Charlie Bell, **Mirror:** Larry D. Mann, **Thinker:** Clinton Sundberg

THE SOLDIER'S TALE

In this post–World War I story, a young soldier sells his soul—represented by his violin—to the Devil only to have second thoughts about the idea in this animated version of the classic Russian children's fable written by Igor Stravinsky.

A R. O. Blechman Production for PBS. Color. One hour. Premiered on PBS: March 19, 1981. Rebroadcast on PBS: October 30, 1981.

Voices:

Devil: Max Von Sydow, **Princess:** Galina Panova, **Narrator:** André Gregory

SOMEDAY YOU'LL FIND HER, CHARLIE BROWN

Charlie Brown experiences another romantic adventure, this time after watching a local football game on television. He falls in love with a little girl (Mary Jo) he sees in a beauty shot on television and, after the game ends, he sets out to find her with the help of co–detective Linus. *A Lee Mendelson–Bill Melendez Production in association with Charles M. Schulz Creative Associates and United Feature Syndicate. Color. Half–hour. Premiered on CBS: October 30, 1981. Rebroadcast on CBS: March 21, 1983.*

Voices:

Charlie Brown: Grant Wehr, **Linus Van Pelt:** Earl Reilly, **Little Girl** (Mary Joe): Jennifer Gaffin, **Snoopy:** Jose Melendez, **Loretta:** Nicole Eggert, **Teenager:** Melissa Strawmeyer, **Singer:** Rebecca Reardon

THE SORCERER'S APPRENTICE

When a poor young boy (Hans) sets out to seek his fortune, he accepts a job as the Sorcerer's apprentice only to learn that the Sorcerer uses his magical powers for the purposes of evil in this adaptation of the Jacob Grimm fairy tale classic. *A Gary Moscowitz Production in association with Astral Bellevue Pathe'. Color. Half–hour. Premiered: October, 1984. Syndicated.*

Voices:

Narrator: Vincent Price

THE SPECIAL MAGIC OF HERSELF THE ELF

Nasty King Thorn and his daughter, Creeping Ivy, steal Herself the Elf's magical wand in order to take nature into their own evil hands in this half–hour syndicated special featuring music composed and performed by Judy Collins. *A Scholastic Production in association with Those Characters From Cleveland and Nelvana Limited. Color. Half–hour. Premiered: April, 1983. Syndicated.*

Voices:

Herself the Elf: Priscilla Lopez, **Creeping Ivy:** Ellen Greene, **King Thorn:** Jerry Orbach, **Willow Song:** Georgia Engel, **Meadow Morn:** Denny Dillon, **Snow Drop:** Terri Hawkes, **Wilfie:** Jim Henshaw, **Wood Pink:** Susan Roman, **Vocalist:** Judy Collins

Herself the Elf shows off the powers of her magical wand in "The Special Magic Of Herself The Elf." © Scholastic Productions

A SPECIAL VALENTINE WITH THE FAMILY CIRCUS

In this television debut of Bill Keane's "Family Circus" characters, P. J., Dolly, Billy and Jeffy do everything possible to outdo each other in impressing their parents with "love" for Valentine's Day. Special features the Sammy Fain–E. Y. Harburg tune, "If Every Day Were Valentine's Day." *A Cullen–Kasden Production in association with the Register and Tribune Syndicate. Color. Half–hour. Premiered on NBC: February 10, 1978. Rebroadcast on NBC: February 8, 1980; February 13, 1983.*

Voices:

Mommy: Anne Costello, **Daddy:** Bob Kaliban, **Billy:** Mark McDermott, **Dolly:** Missy Hope, **Jeffy:** Nathan Berg, **P. J./ Teacher:** Suzanne Airey, **Bus Driver:** Sammy Fain

THE SPIRIT OF '76

Historical events related to the birth of the United States are presented through live action, animation and song in this overture of five–minute stories. *A MG Films Productions. Color. Half–hour. Premiered: July, 1984. Syndicated.*

Voices:

Narrator: Oscar Brand

SPORT GOOFY (1983)

Athletic competition and sporting events comprise this first in a series of cartoon specials starring lovable dope Goofy in a collection of theatrical shorts from the 1940s, including *How to Play Baseball* (1942), *How To Swim* (1942) and *Tennis Racquet* (1949). *A Walt Disney Television Production. Color. Half–hour. Premiered: May 21–June 12, 1983. Syndicated.*

Voices:

Goofy: Pinto Colvig, George Johnson

SPORT GOOFY (1983)

Goofy returns in this second syndicated special starring the daffy canine in a series of sports—oriented cartoons: *How to Play Football* (1944), *Goofy's Glider* (1940) and *Get Rich Quick* (1951). *A Walt Disney Television Production. Color. Half—hour. Premiered: August 21—September 24, 1983. Syndicated.*

Voices:

Goofy: Pinto Colvig, George Johnson

SPORT GOOFY (1983)

In his third sports spoof special, Goofy is featured in three memorable cartoons originally released to theaters: *Hockey Homicide* (1945), *Double Dribble* (1946) and *The Art Of Skiing* (1941). *A Walt Disney Television Production. Color. Half—hour. Premiered: November 6—December 19, 1983. Syndicated.*

Voices:

Goofy: Pinto Colvig, George Johnson

STANLEY, THE UGLY DUCKLING

Stanley, a klutzy young duck, tried to be anything but a duck, by striking out on his own with a loner fox named Nathan, who takes him under his wing and tried to help him become somebody. Through a series of misadventures, Stanley learns the vital lesson of liking himself for what he is, faults and all. This special followed the network premiere of another half—hour animated special, "Banjo the Woodpile Cat." An "ABC Weekend Special." *A Fine Arts Production in association with I Like Myself Productions. Color. Half—hour. Premiered on ABC: May 1, 1982. Rebroadcast on ABC: February 4, 1984; Nickelodeon: July 20, 1986.*

Voices:

Stanley: Susan Blue, **Nathan the Fox:** Jack DeLeon, **Eagle One:** Wolfman Jack

Additional Voices:

Brian Cummings, Lee Thomas, Rick Dees, Julie McWhirter

STAR FAIRIES

Created from stars, this tiny band of creatures (Spice, Nightsong, Jazz, True Love and Whisper) embarks on a very special mission—to grant the wishes of every child in the world, led by the energetic and intelligent Princess Sparkle from the Land of Wishecometrue. The half—hour special was actually broadcast as part of a two—hour package which included Pound Puppies" and "The Harlem Globetrotters Meet Snow White." *A Hanna—Barbera Production. Color. Two hours. Premiered: October, 1985. Syndicated.*

Voices:

Spice: Didi Conn, **True Love:** Jean Kasem, **Jazz:** Susan Blu, **Nightsong:** Ta Tanisha, **Whisper:** Marianne Chinn, **Sparkle/ Michelle/Mother:** B. J. Ward, **Troll:** Billy Barty, **Giant:** Michael Nouri, **Dragon Head #1:** Howard Morris, **Dragon Head #2:** Arte Johnson, **Harvey:** Shavar Ross, **Benjamin:** Matthew Gotlieb, **Jennifer:** Holly Berger, **Puppy/Lavandar/ Vanity:** Frank Welker, **Freddie/Frump/Spectre:** Michael Bell, **Giggleby:** Jerry Houser, **Blunderpuff/Elf:** Don Messick, **Wishing Well:** Herschel Bernardi, **Winthrop the Wizard:** Jonathan Winters, **Hillary:** Drew Barrymore

A STAR FOR JEREMY

Wondering about the meaning of the Christmas star atop his family's tree one Christmas Eve, young Jeremy learns the truth in a dream which transports him to the place where God assigns stars to their place in the universe. *A TPC Communications Production. Color. Half—hour. Premiered: December, 1984. Syndicated.*

Voices:

Leif Ancker, James Gleason, Charlotte Jarvis, Larry Kenny, Stacy Melodia, Christopher Potter, Tia Relbling

THE STINGIEST MAN IN TOWN

Charles Dickens' classic "A Christmas Carol" is revisited, this time set in 1840s London with Scrooge supplying his standard penny—pinching nastiness before the phantoms, known as Christmas Past and Present, pay him a visit to change his self—centered ways. Narration is provided by Tom Bosley as an insect called B. A. H. Humbug. *A Rankin—Bass Production. Color. One hour. Premiered on NBC: December 23, 1978. Rebroadcast on NBC: December 22, 1979. Syndicated.*

Voices:

B. A. H. Humbug (narrator): Tom Bosley, **Ebenezer Scrooge:** Walter Matthau, **Young Scrooge:** Robert Morse, **Ghost of Marley:** Theodore Bikel, **Fred:** Dennis Day, **Tiny Tim:** Robert Rolofson, **Mrs. Crachit:** Darlene Conley, **Ghost of Christmas Past:** Paul Frees, **Martha:** Debra Clinger, **Belinda:** Steffanie Calli, **Peter:** Eric Hines, **Boy:** Charles Matthau, **Scrooge's fiancee:** Diana Lee

Additional Voices:

Sonny Melendrez, Dee Stratton, Shelby Flint

STRAWBERRY SHORTCAKE AND THE BABY WITHOUT A NAME

In Strawberry Land, Strawberry Shortcake is joined by friends Plum Puddin', Peach Blush and Baby Without A Name for her annual summer camp—out. At night, while telling scary stories around the campfire, Baby Without A Name disappears into the forest to become friends with a lovable, big—footed monster. Meanwhile, Strawberry Shortcake and the others are kidnapped by the evil Peculiar Purple Pieman and Sour Grapes. The special was one of six programs based on the American Greetings card characters. *A MAD Production in association* with *Those Characters From Cleveland and Nelvana Limited. Color. Half–hour. Premiered: March, 1984. Syndicated.*

Voices:

Sun (narrator): Chris Wiggins, **Strawberry Shortcake:** Russi Taylor, **Peculiar Purple Pieman:** Bob Ridgely, **Sour Grapes/ Fig–Boot:** Jeri Craden, **Plum Puddin':** Laurie Waller, **Lemon Meringue/Lime Chiffon:** Melleny Brown, **Peach Blush/ Orange Blossom:** Susan Roman, **Lullaberry Pie:** Monica Parker, **Orange Blossom:** Cree Summer Francks

STRAWBERRY SHORTCAKE IN BIG APPLE CITY

Strawberry Shortcake ventures to Big Apple City to compete in a bake–off against the nasty Peculiar Purple Pieman, who does everything possible to prevent her from baking her specialty—a strawberry shortcake—so he can win the contest. *A RLR Associates Production in association with Those Characters From Cleveland and Perpetual Motion Pictures. Color. Half–hour. Premiered: April, 1981. Syndicated.*

Voices:

Sun (narrator): Romeo Muller, **Strawberry Shortcake:** Russi Taylor, **Peculiar Purple Pieman:** Bob Ridgely, **Coco Network:** Bob Holt, **Orange Blossom:** Diane McCannon, **Blueberry Muffin/Apple Dumplin'/Apricot:** Joan Gerber, **Vocalists:** Flo and Eddie

STRAWBERRY SHORTCAKE MEETS THE BERRYKIDS

This time around, the Peculiar Purple Pieman and Sour Grapes are foiled in their plan to make exotic perfume out of little Berrykins, tiny fairies who give scent and flavor to fruit, thanks to Strawberry Shortcake and her friends. *A MAD Production in association with Those Characters From Cleveland and Nelvana Limited. Color. Half–hour. Premiered: Spring, 1985. Syndicated.*

Voices:

Sun (narrator): Chris Wiggins, **Strawberry Shortcake:** Russi Taylor, **Peculiar Purple Pieman:** Bob Ridgely, **Sour Grapes:** Jeri Craden, **Banana Twirl/Banana Berrykin:** Melleny Brown, **Berry Princess/Peach Blush/Peach Berrykin:** Susan Roman, **Plum Puddin'/Plum Berrykin/Orange Blossom:** Laurie Waller, **Raspberry Tart/Blueberry Muffin:** Susan Snooks, **VO:** Patrick Black, **Vocalists:** Nadia Medusa, Ben Sebastian, John Sebastian, Russi Taylor, Nicole Wills

STRAWBERRY SHORTCAKE: PETS ON PARADE

Strawberry Shortcake must guard the new tricycle that will be awarded to the winner of the "Second Annual Grand Old Petable Pet Show and Pet Parade" in Strawberry Land from— who else?—the villainous Peculiar Purple Pieman and his cohort Sour Grapes, who, as usual, try to ruin all of the fun. *A Muller–Rosen Production in association with Those Char-*

acters *From Cleveland and Murakami–Wolf–Swenson Films and Toei Doga Productions. Color. Half–hour. Premiered: April, 1982. Syndicated.*

Voices:

Sun (narrator): Romeo Muller, **Strawberry Shortcake:** Russi Taylor, **Peculiar Purple Pieman:** Bob Ridgely, **Blueberry Muffin/Apple Dumplin':** Joan Gerber, **Huckleberry Pie:** Julie McWhirter, **Vocalists:** Flo and Eddie

STRAWBERRY SHORTCAKE'S HOUSEWARMING SURPRISE

After she moves into a big new house, Strawberry Shortcake's friends decide to give her a surprise housewarming party, but receive two uninvited guests—Peculiar Purple Pieman and Sour Grapes—who unleash a devilish plot to eat everything in sight and steal Strawberry Shortcake's famous recipes to publish as a cookbook. *A MAD Production in association with Those Characters From Cleveland and Nelvana Limited. Color. Half–hour. Premiered: April, 1983. Syndicated.*

Voices:

Sun (narrator): Chris Wiggins, **Strawberry Shortcake:** Russi Taylor, **Peculiar Purple Pieman:** Bob Ridgely, **Sour Grapes:** Jeri Craden, **Captain Cackle/VO:** Jack Blum, **Lime Chiffon:** Melleny Brown, **Huckleberry/Parfait/Lem:** Jeanine Elias, **Blueberry/Crepe Suzette/Ada:** Susan Roman, **Vocalists:** Phil Glaston, Bill Keith, Sharon McQueen, Ben Sebastian, John Sebastian

SUPER DUCKTALES

Scrooge McDuck, Huey, Dewey and Louie fight the Beagle Boys' attempts to steal the McDuck fortune in this prime–time special based on the popular weekday series, "Duck–Tales." The special premiered on NBC's "The Magical World of Disney." *A Walt Disney Television Production. Color. One hour. Premiered on NBC: March 26, 1989 (on "The Magical World of Disney").*

Voices:

Scrooge McDuck: Alan Young, **Huey:** Russi Taylor, **Dewey:** Russi Taylor, **Louie:** Russi Taylor

THE SWISS FAMILY ROBINSON (1973)

Fritz and Franz, the sons of the shipwrecked Robinson family, are rescued five years after they and their parents are shipwrecked, returning to civilization with a young girl they discover on the island. A "Family of Festival Classics" special. *A Rankin–Bass Production in association with Mushi Studios. Color. Half–hour. Premiered: January 13, 1973. Syndicated.*

Voices:

Carl Banas, Len Birman, Bernard Cowan, Peg Dixon, Keith Hampshire, Peggi Loder, Donna Miller, Frank Perry, Henry Raymer, Billie Mae Richards, Alfie Scopp, Paul Soles

THE SWISS FAMILY ROBINSON (1973)

Survival is the name of the game for a family of travelers who become shipwrecked on a deserted island in this one–hour special based on Johann Wyss's popular adventure story. *An Air Programs International Production. Color. One hour. Premiered on CBS: October 28, 1973. Rebroadcast on CBS: November 28, 1974. Syndicated.*

Voices:

Jeannie Drynan, Alistair Duncan, Barbara Frawley, Ron Haddrick, Brender Senders

TABITHA AND ADAM AND THE CLOWN FAMILY

Tabitha and Adam Stephens, the off–spring from television's "Bewitched," are teenaged witch and warlock in a circus setting in this hour–long animated spin–off of the popular weekly sitcom. *A Hanna–Barbera Production. Color. One hour. Premiered on ABC: December 2, 1972 (on "The ABC Saturday Superstar Movie"). Syndicated.*

Voices:

Tabitha Stephens: Cindy Eilbacher, **Adam Stephens:** Michael Morgan, **Max:** John Stephenson, **Julie:** Shawn Shepps, **Ernie:** Gene Andrusco, **Mike:** Frank Welker, **Ronk/Mr. McGurk/Haji/Ducks:** Paul Winchell, **Muscles/Boris/Third Cyclone:** Hal Smith, **Big Louie/Count Krumley/Mr. McGuffin:** Lennie Weinrib, **Second Cyclone/Trumpet/Voice:** Don Messick, **Marybell/Georgia:** Janet Waldo, **Hi–Rise/First Cyclone:** Pat Harrington, **Glenn/Yancy:** John Stephenson, **Scooter:** Michael Morgan, **Railroad Conductor:** Paul Winchell

TAKE ME UP TO THE BALLGAME

Baseball is given a wider field of play as a sandlot baseball team consisting of animals is pitted against the Outer–Space All–Stars, a team who has never lost a game, in an intergalactic playoff to determine the best team in the universe. Earth's team is recruited for the match–up by an interplanetary promoter named Irwin, voiced by comedian Phil Silvers. The half–hour fantasy special aired in Canada and in the United States. *A Nelvana Limited Production in association with CBC. Color. Half–hour. Premiered (U. S.). September, 1980. Syndicated.*

Voices:

Irwin: Phil Silvers, **Beaver:** Bobby Dermer, **Eagle:** Derek McGrath, **Commissioner:** Don Ferguson, **Announcer:** Paul Soles, **Edna:** Anna Bourque, **Jake:** Maurice LaMarche, **Mole:** Melleny Brown, **Vocalist:** Rick Danko

A TALE OF TWO CITIES

This 90–minute special recalls the French Revolution story of Sidney Carton, a dispirited English barrister, who saves French aristocrat Charles Darnay from execution at the guillotine, in this vivid adaptation of Charles Dickens' well–known story. *A Burbank Films Production. Color. One hour and a half. Premiered: 1984. Syndicated.*

Voices:

John Benton, John Everson, Phillip Hinton, Liz Horne, Moya O'Sullivan, Robin Stewart, John Stone, Henry Szeps, Ken Wayne

A TALE OF TWO WISHES

In this live–action/animated special about wish–making, Jane, a girl whose wishes never seem to come true, becomes friends with Skeeter, a wise but gentle storyteller, who, as hosts, introduce a series of animated tales that help Jane understand how to turn her dreams into reality. *A Bosustow Entertainment Production. Color. One hour. Premiered on CBS: November 8, 1981. Rebroadcast on CBS: July 6, 1982. Syndicated.*

Cast:

Jane: Tracey Gold, **Skeeter:** Rick Nelson, **Grandmother:** Bibi Osterwald, **Mother:** Judy Farrell, **Father:** Bob Ross, **Margaret:** Seeley Ann Thumann, **Daniel:** Chad Krentzman

TALES OF WASHINGTON IRVING

Author Washington Irving's two most popular folktales, "The Legend of Sleepy Hollow" and "Rip Van Winkle," are featured in this one–hour special produced as part of CBS's "Famous Classic Tales" package of animated children's specials. *An Air Programs International Production. Color. One hour. Premiered on CBS: November 1, 1970. Rebroadcast on CBS: October 24, 1971. Syndicated.*

Voices:

Mel Blanc, George Firth, Joan Gerber, Byron Kane, Julie McWhirter, Don Messick, Ken Samson, Lennie Weinrib, Brian Zax, Larraine Zax.

THE TALKING PARCEL

Penelope, a 12–year–old girl, discovers a parcel along the seashore that "talks." It turns out the voice is actually that of Parrot, a real talking parrot, who escaped from the land of Mythologia where its ruler, Wizard H. H. Junketury, has been imprisoned by the fire–breathing Cockatrices. The pair sets out on a remarkable journey to return Mythologia to its rightful leader. *A Cosgrove–Hall Production. Color. Half–hour. Premiered: 1983–1984. Syndicated.*

Voices:

Penelope: Lisa Norris, **Parrot:** Freddie Jones, **Hortense,** the Flying Train: Mollie Sugden, **Ethelred:** Roy Kinnear, **H. H. Junketbury:** Edward Kelsey, **Chief Cockatrice:** Windsor Davies, **Oswald,** the Sea Serpent: Sir Michael Hordern, **Werewolf:** Peter Woodthorpe, **Duke Wensleydale:** Harvey Ashby, **Others:** Raymond Mason, Daphne Oxenford

TATTERTOWN

In a town where everything comes to life—misfit toys, broken machines and musical instruments—Debbie, a young girl, tries to prevent her stuffed doll, Muffett, who suddenly comes to life, from taking over the mystical town with the help of a compatriot, the evil Sidney Spider, in a storyline that ties into the meaning of Christmas. The half—hour Christmas special was actually the pilot to what was announced as the first prime—time animated series for the all—kids' network, Nickelodeon. Ralph Bakshi based the idea on a concept he originated 30 years earlier called "Junk Town." *A Bakshi Animation Production. Color. Half—hour. Premiered on Nickelodeon: December, 1988.*

THANKSGIVING IN THE LAND OF OZ

Dorothy returns to Oz and joins forces with her friends Jack Pumpkinhead (The Scarecrow), the Hungry Tiger (The Cowardly Lion) and Tic—Toc (The Tin Man) to undermine the efforts of Tyrone the Terrible Toy Maker, who is trying to gain control of Winkle Country, a community in Oz. The program was later retitled and rebroadcast as "Dorothy In The Land Of Oz." *A Muller—Rosen Production in association with Murakami—Wolf—Swenson Films. Color. Half—hour. Premiered on CBS: November 25, 1980. Rebroadcast on CBS: December 10, 1981 (as "Dorothy In The Land Of Oz"); Showtime: November, 1985; November, 1986. Syndicated.*

Voices:

Wizard of Oz (narrator): Sid Caesar, **Dorothy:** Mischa Bond, **Jack Pumpkinhead:** Robert Ridgely, **Tic—Toc:** Joan Gerber, **Hungry Tiger:** Frank Nelson, **Aunt Em:** Lurene Tuttle, **Tyrone,** the Terrible Toy Tinker: Robert Ridgely, **Ozma,** Queen of Oz: Joan Gerber, **Uncle Henry:** Charles Woolf

THE THANKSGIVING THAT ALMOST WASN'T

Johnny Cooke, a young Pilgrim boy, and Little Bear, son of an Indian, are both discovered missing. Jeremy Squirrel hears of his friends' plight and goes to find them in the woods. He puts himself at great risk during their rescue, having to ward off a hungry timberwolf. The story ends happily as the Pilgrims and the Indians invite Johnny as their guest of honor for Thanksgiving. *A Hanna—Barbera Production. Color. Half—hour. Premiered: November, 1972. Syndicated.*

Voices:

Johnny Cooke: Bobby Riha, **Little Bear:** Kevin Cooper, **Janie/Mom/Mary Cooke:** Marilyn Mayne, **Jimmy/Son Squirrel/Mom Squirrel:** June Foray, **Jeremy Squirrel/Dad:** Hal Smith, **Dad Squirrel/Francis Cooke/Indian** (Massasoit): Vic Perrin, **Wolf/Rabbit/Sparrow #1:** Don Messick, **Sparrow #2:** John Stephenson

THAT GIRL IN WONDERLAND

Marlo Thomas, in the role of Ann Marie from her popular prime—time series "That Girl," reprises her character in this animated spin—off in which she portrays a childrens book editor who daydreams and imagines herself as the heroine of various fairy tales ("The Wizard of Oz," "Snow White," "Sleeping Beauty," "Cinderella" and "Goldilocks"). The program was originally broadcast as part of "The ABC Saturday Superstar Movie." *A Rankin—Bass Production. Color. One hour. Premiered on ABC: January 13, 1974 (on "The ABC Saturday Superstar Movie"). Rebroadcast on ABC: March 2, 1974. Syndicated.*

Voices:

Ann Marie: Marlo Thomas

Additional Voices:

Patricia Bright, Dick Hehmeyer, Rhoda Mann, Ted Schwartz

THERE'S NO TIME FOR LOVE, CHARLIE BROWN

Charlie Brown and his gang go on a school field trip to what is supposed to be a museum. Unfortunately, they mistake the local super market as the museum and do their report on that instead. When they discover their mistake, they all fear that they'll get failing grade on their reports. *A Lee Mendelson—Bill Melendez Production in association with Charles M. Schulz Creative Associates and United Feature Syndicate. Color. Half—hour. Premiered on CBS: March 11, 1973. Rebroadcast on CBS: March 17, 1974.*

Voices:

Charlie Brown: Chad Webber, **Linus Van Pelt:** Stephen Shea, **Lucy Van Pelt:** Robin Kohn, **Sally Brown:** Hillary Momberger, **Peppermint Patty:** Kip DeFaria, **Schroeder:** Jeffrey Bailly, **Franklin:** Todd Barbee, **Marcie:** Jimmie Ahrens

THIS IS AMERICA, CHARLIE BROWN—THE BIRTH OF THE CONSTITUTION

It's spring 1787, on the steps of Constitution Hall, where Charlie Brown and company are witnessing history in the making: the signing of America's most important document, the Constitution. *A Lee Mendelson—Bill Melendez Production in association with Charles M. Schulz Creative Associates and United Feature Syndicate. Color. Half—hour. Premiered on CBS: October 28, 1988.*

Voices:

Charlie Brown: Erin Chase, Jason Rifle, **Lucy Van Pelt:** Ami Foster, **Linus Van Pelt:** Jeremy Miller, Brandon Stewart, **Sally Brown:** Christina Lange, **Peppermint Patty:** Jason Mendelson, **Marcie:** Keri Houlihan, **Mr. Madison/Mr. Randolf:** Bud Davis, **Mr. Jerry/Mr. Rutledge/Mr. Pinkey:** Shepard Menken, **Mr. Sherman/Mr. Ellsworth:** Chuck Olsen, **Ben Franklin/George Washington:** Hal Smith, **Mr. Morris/Mr. Wilson/Delegates:** Frank Welker

THIS IS AMERICA, CHARLIE BROWN—THE BUILDING OF THE TRANSCONTINENTAL RAILROAD

Charlie Brown tells the story of the building of the Transcontinental Railroad, completed in 1869 at Promontory, Utah with Snoopy driving the final golden spike in this animated version. *A Lee Mendelson–Bill Melendez Production in association with Charles M. Schulz Creative Associates and United Feature Syndicate. Color. Half-hour. Premiered on CBS: February 10, 1989.*

Voices:

Charlie Brown: Erin Chase, **Peppermint Patty:** Jason Mendelson, **Linus Van Pelt:** Brandon Stewart, **Sally Brown:** Brittany Thorton, **Marcie:** Marie Lynne Wise, **Mr. Watson:** Gregg Berger, **Thomas Edison/Alexander Bell:** Frank Welker, **Marion Edison:** Alissa King, **Housekeeper:** Julie Payne

THIS IS AMERICA, CHARLIE BROWN—THE GREAT INVENTORS

As part of a school project, Sally, with questionable support from Snoopy, reports on the array of products and services developed after the Civil War. This leads into stories about such early American industrialists/pioneers as Alexander Graham Bell, Thomas Edison and Henry Ford. *A Lee Mendelson–Bill Melendez Production in association with Charles M. Schulz Creative Associates and United Feature Syndicate. Color. Half-hour. Premiered on CBS: March 10, 1989. Rebroadcast on CBS: July 11, 1990.*

Voices:

Charlie Brown: Erin Chase, **Lucy Van Pelt:** Erica Gayle, **Peppermint Patty:** Jason Mendelson, **Sally Brown:** Brittany Thorton, **Franklin:** Hakeem Abdul Samad, **Marcie:** Marie Lynn Wise, **Schroeder:** Curtis Anderson, **Group Singers:** Kristi Baker, Tiffany Billings, Sean Collins, Ami Jane Foster, **Vocalists:** Nichole Buda, Cameron Clarke, Desiree Goyette, Lou Rawls

THIS IS AMERICA, CHARLIE BROWN—THE MAYFLOWER VOYAGE

The first of eight prime-time specials recalling great events in American history, Charlie Brown and the gang sail with the Pilgrims from England to America in 1620. After 65 days of coping with rough seas and the cracking of the ship's main beam, the voyagers finally arrive on America's shores where they witness the signing of the Mayflower Compact and celebrate the first Thanksgiving feast with the Pilgrims and the Indians. *A Lee Mendelson–Bill Melendez Production in association with Charles M. Schulz Creative Associates and United Feature Syndicate. Color. Half-hour. Premiered on CBS: February 10, 1989.*

Voices:

Charlie Brown: Erin Chase, **Lucy Van Pelt:** Erica Gayle, **Linus Van Pelt:** Brandon Stewart, **Peppermint Patty:** Jason Mendelson, **Sally Brown:** Brittany Thorton, **Marcie:** Tani Taylor Powers, **Miles Standish/Man #2:** Gregg Berger, **Samoset/Crewman #1:** Christopher Collins, **Pilgrim Child:** Sean Mendelson, **Squanto/Man #1:** Frank Welker

THIS IS AMERICA, CHARLIE BROWN—THE MUSIC AND HEROES OF AMERICA

Just as Schroeder is about to give a concert on American music, Lucy suggests that her report on American heroes, with props, will dress up his act. Over Schroeder's objections, the teacher thinks that Lucy has a good idea. So, with musical accompaniment from Snoopy, Charlie Brown, Pigpen and Linus, Schroeder recreates the accomplishments of such musical greats as John Phillip Sousa, George M. Cohan and Irving Berlin, and covers the evolution of blues, jazz and ragtime music. *A Lee Mendelson–Bill Melendez Production in association with Charles M. Schulz Creative Associates and United Feature Syndicate. Color. Half-hour. Premiered on CBS: February 10, 1989.*

Voices:

Charlie Brown: Erin Chase, **Linus Van Pelt:** Brandon Stewart, **Schroeder:** Curtis Anderson, **Telegraph Operator:** Gregg Berger, **Vocalists:** Carvin Winans, Marvin Winans, Michael Winans, Ronald Winans

THIS IS AMERICA, CHARLIE BROWN—THE NASA SPACE STATION

In a dream, Linus finds himself on board a space station. Lucy is the spacecraft's bossy commander and Snoopy is the operator. The crew, which also includes Peppermint Patty, Charlie Brown, Sally, Pigpen and Franklin, are part of a mission to test human survival in outer space for 90 days. *A Lee Mendelson–Bill Melendez Production in association with Charles M. Schulz Creative Associates and United Feature Syndicate. Color. Half-hour. Premiered on CBS: November 11, 1988. Rebroadcast on CBS: June 27, 1990.*

Voices:

Charlie Brown: Erin Chase, **Linus Van Pelt:** Brandon Stewart, **Lucy Van Pelt:** Erica Gayle, **Peppermint Patty:** Jason Mendelson, **Sally Brown:** Brittany Thorton, **Franklin:** Grant Gelt, **Houston Control:** Gregg Berger, **Reporter:** Frank Welker

THIS IS AMERICA, CHARLIE BROWN—THE SMITHSONIAN AND THE PRESIDENCY

In historic Washington, D. C., Charlie Brown and his friends visit the Smithsonian Institute and the Presidency Exhibit at the Museum of American History where, through flashbacks, they relive many great Presidential moments—from President

Lincoln's famed Gettysburg address to Franklin Delano Roosevelt's memorable "fireside" chats. The Peanuts gang concludes that the presidency is a tough job and requires the talents of a special kind of person. *A Lee Mendelson–Bill Melendez Production in association with Charles M. Schulz Creative Associates and United Feature Syndicate. Color. Half–hour. Premiered on CBS: April 19, 1989. Rebroadcast on CBS: July 18, 1990.*

Voices:

Charlie Brown: Erin Chase, **Lucy Van Pelt:** Erica Gayle, **Linus Van Pelt:** Brandon Stewart, **Peppermint Patty:** Jason Mendelson, **Sally Brown:** Brittany Thorton, **Marcie/Girl:** Marie Lynn Wise, **Franklin:** Hakeen Abdul Samad, **Samuel:** Gregg Berger, **John Muir:** Hal Smith, **Abe Lincoln/Teddy Roosevelt:** Frank Welker

THIS IS AMERICA, CHARLIE BROWN—THE WRIGHT BROTHERS AT KITTY HAWK

It is December 16, 1903: Charlie Brown accompanies Linus to visit his cousin Dolly in Kitty Hawk, North Carolina where, on the following day, the Wright Brothers will risk their lives in their attempt to fly. Meanwhile, Woodstock demonstrates his own principles of flight to Snoopy. *A Lee Mendelson–Bill Melendez Production in association with Charles M. Schulz Creative Associates and United Feature Syndicate. Color. Premiered on CBS: November 4, 1988. Rebroadcast on CBS: June 20, 1990.*

Voices:

Charlie Brown: Erin Chase, **Linus Van Pelt:** Brandon Stewart, **Peppermint Patty:** Jason Mendelson, **Marcie:** Tani Taylor Powers, **Dolly:** Brandon Horne, **Orville Wright:** Gregg Berger, **Wilbur Wright:** Frank Welker

THIS IS YOUR LIFE, DONALD DUCK

Spoofing Ralph Edwards' "This Is Your Life" series, host Jiminy Cricket recounts the life of honored guest, Donald Duck, in a series of cartoon flashbacks derived from several classic Disney cartoons—*Donald's Better Self* (1938), *Donald's Lucky Day* (1938), *Donald Gets Drafted* (1942), *Sky Trooper* (1942), *Working For Peanuts* (1953), *Mickey's Amateurs* (1937), *Bee at the Beach* (1950) and *Donald's Diary* (1954)—in this hour–long special which first aired on ABC in 1960. The program was later rebroadcast in prime–time on NBC as an episode of "The Wonderful World of Disney" and then in 1980 as a NBC special. *A Walt Disney Television Production. Color. One hour. Premiered on ABC: March 11, 1960 (as "Walt Disney Presents"). Rebroadcast on NBC: February 13, 1977 (on "The Wonderful World of Disney"); February 22, 1980 (as "NBC Special").*

Voices:

Jiminy Cricket: Cliff Edwards, **Donald Duck:** Clarence Nash

THE THREE MUSKETEERS

Swashbuckling heroes Athos, Porthos and Aramis foil the plan of the ruthless Cardinal de Richelieu conspiring against the honorable King Louis XIII in this colorful rendition of Alexandria Dumas' famed historical novel. *A Hanna–Barbera Production. Color. One hour. Premiered on CBS: November 23, 1973. Rebroadcast on CBS: November 28, 1974; November 22, 1979. Syndicated.*

Voices:

James Condon, Neil Fitzpatrick, Barbara Frawley, Ron Haddrick, Jane Harders, John Martin, Richard Meikle

THUNDERCATS

Years into the future, when mankind is extinct, a group of noble, moralistic humanoids (Jaga, Tygra, Cheetara, Wilykat, Wilykit, Panthro and Snarf) from the distant planet of Thun–DERa depart for the Third Earth to instill the laws and ideals of their own doomed planet and ward off evil, represented by the ageless devil–priest Mumma–Ra and his hideous Mutants. Based on characters created by Ted Wolf, this one–hour special preceded the premiere of the first–run syndicated series. *A Rankin–Bass Production in association with Pacific Animation. Color. One hour. Premiered: January–February, 1985. Syndicated.*

Voices:

Lion–O/Jackalman: Larry Kenney, **Snarf/S–S–Slithe:** Robert McFadden, **Cheetara/Wilykit:** Lynne Lipton, **Panthro:** Earle Hyman, **Wilykat/Monkian/Tygra:** Peter Newman, **Mumma–Ra/Vultureman/Jaga:** Eart Hammond

THUNDERCATS HO!

In this two–hour made–for–television movie, the Thundercats square off again with their archenemy Mumma–Ra, who assigns the evil Ma–Mut to search out and destroy the heroic gladiators of outer space. The program officially marked the debut of the second season of the "Thundercats" series. The feature–length special was later edited into a five–part half–hour mini–series for broadcast. *A Rankin–Bass Production in association with Pacific Animation. Color. Two hours. Premiered: October, 1986. Syndicated.*

Voices:

Lion–O/Jackalman: Larry Kenney, **Lynx–O/Snarf/S–S–Slithe:** Robert McFadden, **Cheetara/Wilykit:** Lynne Lipton, **Panthro:** Earle Hyman, **Wilykat/Monkian/Ben–Gali/Tygra:** Peter Newman, **Mumma–Ra/Vultureman/Jaga:** Earl Hammond, **Pumyra:** Gerrianne Raphael

THE TIN SOLDIER

The one–legged Tin Soldier of the famed Hans Christian Andersen tale comes to life in this entertaining and heart-warming adaptation, featuring two new characters, a pair of mice named Fred and Sam, who befriend the Tin Soldier. The program was produced for Canadian television and also broadcast in the United States. *An Atkinson Film—Arts Production in association with Telefilm Canada and CTV. Half—hour. Premiered (U. S.): December, 1986. Syndicated.*

Voices:

Fred: Terrence Scammell, **Sam:** Pier Kohl, **Boy:** Adam Hodgins, **Lefty/Rat #1/Rat #3:** Rick Jones, **King Rat/Rat #2/Rat #4:** Robert Bockstael, **Narrator:** Christopher Plummer

THE TINY TREE

A young crippled girl and several small meadow animals become friends with a tiny whispering tree which is transformed into a glowing Christmas tree for the lonely youngster who is wheelchair—bound. Johnny Marks provides music and lyrics for the songs, with narrator Buddy Ebsen singing one of the melodies in this half—hour Christmas special produced under the "Bell System Family Theatre" banner. Sponsor: AT&T. *A DePatie—Freleng Enterprises Production. Color. Half—hour. Premiered on NBC: December 14, 1975 (on "Bell System Family Theatre"). Rebroadcast on NBC: December 12, 1976; ABC: December 18, 1977; CBS: December 16, 1978; December 19, 1979. Syndicated.*

Voices:

Squire Badger (narrator): Buddy Ebsen, **Hawk:** Allan Melvin, **Turtle:** Paul Winchell, **Lady Bird/Little Girl:** Janet Waldo, **Boy Bunny/Girl Raccoon:** Stephen Manley, **Groundhog/Father/Beaver/Mole:** Frank Welker, **Vocalist:** Roberta Flack

'TIS THE SEASON TO BE SMURFY

Wild Smurf celebrates Christmas during his first winter in Smurf Village and the other Smurfs learn a lesson about the true meaning of the holiday when they help bring some holiday cheer to the lives of an old toy seller and his gravely ill wife. *A Hanna—Barbera Production in association with SEPP International. Color. Half—hour. Premiered on NBC: December 13, 1987.*

Voices:

Papa Smurf/Azrael: Don Messick, **Smurfette:** Lucille Bliss, **Hefty/Monster:** Frank Welker, **Handy/Lazy/Grouchy:** Michael Bell, **Jokey:** June Foray, **Gargamel:** Paul Winchell, **Clumsy:** Bill Callaway, **Vanity:** Alan Oppenheimer, **Brainy:** Danny Goldman, **Greedy/Woody:** Hamilton Camp, **Tailor:** Kip King, **Farmer:** Alan Young, **Timber:** Bernard Erhard, **Snappy:** Pat Musick, **Slouchy,** Noelle North **Nat:** Charlie Adler, **Poet:** Frank Welker, **Baby Smurf/Sassette:** Julie Dees, **Grandpa:** Jonathan Winters, **Puppy:** Frank Welker, **Chitter:** Don Messick, **Thief:** Charlie Adler, **Gustav:** Les Tremayne, **Rich Man:** Bill Callaway, **Hans:** Justin Gocke, **Willem:** William Schallert, **Anna:** Pat Musick, **Doctor:** Alan Oppenheimer, **Elise:** Peggy Weber, **Sheriff:** Jess Douchette

TO THE RESCUE

Davey and his dog Goliath join a group of youngsters at the Roaring River Camp during summer vacation and form an emergency rescue squad to rescue a man and his daughter from the wreckage of a disabled light airplane. *A Clokey Production for the Lutheran Church of America. Color. Half—hour. Premiered: 1975. Syndicated.*

Voices:

Davey Hanson/Sally Hanson/Mary Hanson: Norma Mc-Millan, Nancy Wible, **Goliath/John Hanson:** Hal Smith

TOM SAWYER

Mark Twain, in animated form, narrates this popular folktale set along the Mississippi River in the pre—Civil War days, the story primarily focuses on the adventures of Tom Sawyer and Becky Sharpe who get lost during a cave exploration and are thought to be dead by the townspeople back home. During their journey, they discover famed desperado Injun Joe and his hidden treasure of gold coins. A "Festival of Family Classics" special. *A Rankin—Bass Production in association with Mushi Studios. Color. Half—hour. Premiered: February 25, 1973. Syndicated.*

Voices:

Carl Banas, Len Birman, Bernard Cowan, Peg Dixon, Keith Hampshire, Peggi Loder, Donna Miller, Frank Perry, Henry Raymer, Billie Mae Richards, Alfie Scopp, Paul Soles

TOP CAT AND THE BEVERLY HILLS CATS

Top Cat and his buddies, Benny the Ball, Brain, Spook, Fancy and Choo Choo, are up to their old tricks scamming money from unwary citizens by posing as "Alley Scouts." Their plan is to do good deeds, whether they're needed or not, and then hit their "victims" for a reward. This tactic doesn't meet with much success. Their fortunes change when Benny inherits the Beverly Hills estate of an eccentric old lady who he once helped without asking for a reward. This two—hour special was produced as part of "Hanna—Barbera's Superstars 10" package of first—run animated features for television. *A Hanna—Barbera Production. Color. Two hours. Premiered: 1988. Syndicated.*

Voices:

Top Cat: Arnold Stang, **Benny the Ball:** Avery Schreiber, **Choo Choo:** Marvin Kaplan, **Spook/Brain:** Leo de Lyon, **Fancy—Fancy/Officer Dibble:** John Stephenson, **Mrs. Vandergelt:** Linda Gary, **Snerdly:** Henry Polic II, **Rasputin:** Frank Welker, **Kitty Glitter:** Teresa Ganzel, **Sid Buckman:** Dick Erdman, **Lester Pester:** Rob Paulson, **Warden:** Kenneth Mars, **Manager:** Dick Erdman

TREASURE ISLAND (1971)

In the high-seas journey of a lifetime, young Jim Hawkins, the first to discover Captain Flint's treasure map, joins Long John Silver and his crew of buccaneers in search of buried treasure in this hour—long special based on Robert Louis Stevenson's classic adventure tale. A "Famous Classic Tales" special. *An*

Air Programs International Production. Color. One hour. Premiered: November 28, 1971. Syndicated.

Voices:
Ron Haddrick, John Kingley, John Llewellyn, Bruce Montague, Brenda Senders, Colin Tilley

TREASURE ISLAND (1980)

Young Jim Hawkins' quest to uncover buried treasure and save his life at the same time is recounted in this musical version based on Robert Louis Stevenson's popular adventure story. This time, several new faces were added to the standard cast of characters. They included Hiccup the mouse, Jim's special friend, who keeps him safe when trouble lurks around every corner. The program was originally released in 1972 as a full–length feature and reedited for broadcast. Melissa Sue Anderson hosted the program. *A Filmation Production in association with Warner Brothers Television. Color. One hour. Premiered on NBC: April 29, 1980. Rebroadcast on NBC: January 31, 1981. Syndicated.*

Voices:
Long John Silver: Richard Dawson, **Captain Flint:** Larry Storch, **Jim Hawkins:** Davy Jones, **Squire Trelawney:** Larry D. Mann, **Mother:** Jane Webb, **Parrot:** Dal McKennon

TREASURE ISLAND REVISITED

Long John Silver, Jim Hawkins and the rest of the cast are depicted as animals in this rendition of the familiar adventure tale. Made for Japanese television, the program was later dubbed into English and released in the United States. *An American International Television Production in association with Toei Animation and Titan Productions. Color. One hour. Premiered: February, 1972. Syndicated.*

THE TROLLS AND THE CHRISTMAS EXPRESS

Christmas is almost ruined when six dastardly Trolls dress up as elves to undermine Santa's village and prevent the delivery of toys on Christmas day. *A Titlecraft Production in association with Atkinson Film–Arts. Color. Half–hour. Premiered on HBO: December 9, 1981.*

Voices:
Trogio: Hans Conreid, **Narrator:** Roger Miller

Additional Voices:
Carl Banas, Len Carlson, Paul Soles, Billie Mae Richards

THE TROUBLE WITH MISS SWITCH

Miss Switch, a good witch disguised as a school teacher, faces banishment since her witchcraft is out of date. She enlists two students, Rupert and Amelia, to help her carry out a special plan to foil the bad witch, Saturna, and become a witch of good standing again in this two–part fantasy/adventure. An

"ABC Weekend Special." *A Ruby–Spears Enterprises Production. Color. Half–hour. Premiered on ABC: February 16 and 23, 1980. Rebroadcast on ABC: May 31 and June 7, 1980; September 13 and 20, 1980; April 18 and 25, 1981; July 3 and 10, 1982; January 22 and 29, 1983; May 25 and June 1, 1985; October 14 and 21, 1989.*

Voices:
Miss Switch: Janet Waldo, **Rupert P. Brown III** ("Rupe"): Eric Taslitz, **Amelia Matilda Daley:** Nancy McKeon, **Bathsheba/Saturna:** June Foray

Additional Voices:
Alan Dinehart, Phillip Tanzini, Frank Welker

TUKIKI AND HIS SEARCH FOR A MERRY CHRISTMAS

A young Eskimo boy travels around the world and experiences the meaning of Christmas through a variety of celebrations. *A Titlecraft Production in association with Atkinson Film–Arts. Color. Half–hour. Premiered (U. S.): December, 1979. Syndicated.*

Voices:
Tukiki: Adam Rich, **Northwind:** Sterling Holloway, **Vocalist:** Stephanie Taylor

Additional Voices:
Sharon Burke, Bob Dermer, Fred Little, Bill Luxton, Bernard McManus, Richard Perigrine, Lee St. Louis, Noreen Young

THE TURKEY CAPER

In this third Rusty and Buttons special, Ranger Jones reads the story about the first Thanksgiving to the bear cub, Buttons, and his young fox friend, Rusty. The story has special meaning for the pair when they encounter two young turkeys, Priscilla and Marty, who ask for their help in rescuing the wild turkeys of the forest who have been captured. *An Encore Enterprises Production. Color. Half–hour. Premiered: November, 1985. Syndicated.*

Voices:
Rusty/Rosie: Kathy Ritter, **Buttons:** Barbara Goodson, **Ranger Jones:** Bill Boyett, **Abner:** Alvy Moore, **George:** Bill Ratner, **Bridgett:** Morgan Lofting

'TWAS THE NIGHT BEFORE CHRISTMAS

The hearts of every child in Junctionville are broken when their letters to Santa Claus are returned marked, "Not Accepted by Addressee!," indicating Santa's decision to cancel his annual visit to the tiny town. Father Mouse sets out to find the culprit responsible so his children and others are not disappointed in this holiday special loosely based on Clement Moore's Christmas poem. *A Rankin–Bass Production. Color. Half–hour. Premiered on CBS: December 8, 1974. Rebroadcast on CBS: December 9, 1975; December 17, 1976; Decem-*

A mouse family anxiously watches as Santa Claus descends the chimney in the animated musical special, " 'Twas The Night Before Christmas." © Rankin–Bass Productions (Courtesy: CBS)

ber 12, 1977; December 18, 1978; December 8, 1979; December 13, 1980; December 16, 1981; December 18, 1982; December 14, 1983; December 11, 1984; December 4, 1985; December 17, 1986; December 9, 1987.

Voices:
Joshua Trundel, the Clockmaker (narrator): Joey Grey, **Albert Mouse:** Tammy Grimes, **Mayor of Junctionville:** John McGiver, **Father Mouse:** George Gobel, **Vocalists:** The Wee Winter Singers

Additional Voices:
Patricia Bright, Scott Firestone, Robert McFadden, Allen Swift, Christine Winter

---

20,000 LEAGUES UNDER THE SEA (1972)

Scientific journalist Pierre Aronnax, his 16–year–old assistant, Conrad, and famed harpooner, Ned Land, join Captain Nemo for a fantastic underseas journey to the fabled lost continent of Atlantis in this two–part special based on Jules Verne's classic novel. A "Festival of Family Classics" special. *A Rankin–Bass Production in association with Mushi Studios. Color. One hour. Premiered: October, 1972. Syndicated.*

Voices:
Carl Banas, Len Birman, Bernard Cowan, Peg Dixon, Keith Hampshire, Peggi Loder, Donna Miller, Frank Perry, Henry Raymer, Billie Mae Richards, Alfie Scopp, Paul Soles

---

20,000 LEAGUES UNDER THE SEA (1973)

Captain Nemo dispels the rumor about a giant sea monster by bringing his mystical ship "Nautilus" to the surface and making believers out of marine research scientist, Pierre Aronnax and Ned Land, who try to harpoon the ship thinking it is the mammoth sea monster. A "Famous Classic Tales" special. *A Hanna–Barbera Production. Color. Half–hour. Premiered on CBS: November 22, 1973. Rebroadcast on CBS: November 16, 1974. Syndicated.*

Voices:
Tim Elliott, Ron Haddrick, Don Pascoe, John Stephenson

THE 2000 YEAR OLD MAN

Carl Reiner and Mel Brooks created this half–hour animated special, geared at adults more than children, featuring an interviewer (Reiner) talking about life with a 2000–year–old man who has lived a full life. ("When I say 'the old days' I don't mean the George M. Cohan days!") Consequently, the Old Man relates his observations on a range of topics, among them: the discovery of women, the first song ("Fear caused singing and songs came out of it!"), historical and legendary people and his first job (manufacturing Stars of David). Dialogue for the special was recorded before a live studio audience. *A Crossbow/Acre Enterprises Production in association with Leo Salkin Films. Color. Half–hour. Premiered on CBS: January 11, 1975. Rebroadcast on CBS: April 11, 1975. Syndicated.*

Voices:
Interviewer: Carl Reiner, **Old Man:** Mel Brooks

UNCLE SAM MAGOO

Myopic Mr. Magoo wanders through the full spectrum of American history and encounters the likes of George Washington, Ben Franklin, Davy Crockett, Mark Twain and Paul Bunyan in this well–written animated special combining a lively musical score by award–winning composer Walter Scharf. Popular songs recalling America's historic past include "The Yellow Rose of Texas," "I'm a Yankee Doodle Dandy" and "Jimmy Crack Corn." Sponsor: Maxwell House. *A UPA Production. Color. One hour. Premiered on NBC: February 15, 1970. Syndicated.*

Voices:
Mr. Magoo: Jim Backus, **Uncle Sam/John Alden/Miles Standish/Paul Revere:** Lennie Weinrib, **Davy Crockett/James Marshall/Johnny Appleseed:** Lennie Weinrib, **Captain John Parker/Robert E. Lee/Daniel Webster/John F. Kennedy:** Lennie Weinrib, **Mark Twain/John Sutter/President/Daniel Boone:** Barney Phillips, **Patrick Henry/U. S. Grant/Martin Luther King/Abraham Lincoln:** Barney Phillips, **Indian Chief** (American)/**Indian Chief** (Tropical)/**John Smith:** Bob Holt, **Powhattan/Massasoit/Francis Scott Key:** Bob Holt, **Kit Carson/Paul Bunyan/Franklin D. Roosevelt:** Bob Holt, **Harry Truman/Wendell Willkie:** Bob Holt, **Leif Ericson/**

Mr. Magoo retraces moments in American history in a scene from the NBC network special "Uncle Sam Magoo." © UPA Productions

Columbus/Elder Brewster/Tom Paine: Dave Shelley, **Thomas Jefferson/Woodrow Wilson:** Dave Shelley, **Priscilla/Betsy Ross/Tom Sawyer/Amelia Earhart:** Patti Gilbert, **Eleanor Roosevelt/Susan B. Anthony:** Patti Gilbert, **George Washington/Walt Whitman/Oliver Wendell Holmes:** John Himes, **Dwight D. Eisenhower/Herbert Hoover/Carl Sandburg:** Bill Clayton, **Benjamin Franklin/Thomas Wolfe/George Washington Carver:** Sid Grossfield, **Others:** Sam Rosen

THE VELVETEEN RABBIT (1985)

Academy Award—winning actress Meryl Streep narrates the story of a velveteen toy rabbit, given to a small boy at Christmas, which is made real by the child's love. *A Rabbit Ears Production in association with Random House Home Video. Color. Half—hour. Premiered on PBS: March 9–24, 1985.*

Voices:
Narrator: Meryl Streep

THE VELVETEEN RABBIT (1985)

Margery Williams' classic tale of a stuffed toy rabbit who comes to life is set to music in this half—hour animated special narrated by actor Christopher Plummer. *An Atkinson Film—Arts Production in association with Telefilm Canada and CTV. Color. Half—hour. Premiered (U. S.): April, 1985. Syndicated.*

Voices:
Jones; Don Westwood, **Tin Soldier:** Jim Bradford, **Rabbit #1/Rabbit #2:** Rick Jones, **Skin Horse:** Bernard McManus, **Doctor:** Eddie Nunn, **Fairy Queen:** Charity Brown, **Narrator:** Christopher Plummer

THE VELVETEEN RABBIT (1985)

Of all the gifts he receives for Christmas, young Robert's favorite is a velveteen toy rabbit. Soon Velvee, as he is called, becomes his favorite plaything, but the special friendship they share becomes threatened when Robert turns seriously ill and Velvee is on the verge of being destroyed. *A Hanna–Barbera Production. Color. Half–hour. Premiered on ABC: April 20, 1985. Rebroadcast on ABC: October 19, 1985; December 20, 1986.*

Voices:
Velvee: Chub Bailey, **Robert:** Josh Rodine, **Skin Horse/Nana:** Marilyn Lightstone, **Father:** Peter Cullen, **Tug:** Bill Scott, **Scungilli:** Barry Dennen, **Spinner:** Hal Smith, **Mouse:** Frank Welker, **Brenda:** Jodi Carlisle, **Harry:** Brian Cummings, **Mother/Nursery Fairy:** Beth Clopton

A VERY MERRY CRICKET

Chester C. Cricket returns in this sequel to 1973's "The Cricket in Times Square," this time with pals Tucker R. Mouse and Harry the Cat. Tired of the cacophony and commercialism of Manhattan yuletide, Chester sets off from Connecticut to return to the Big Apple and use his musical attributes to bring the real meaning back to Christmas. *A Chuck Jones Enterprises Production. Color. Half–hour. Premiered on ABC: December 14, 1973. Rebroadcast on ABC: November 28, 1974; December 5, 1978. Syndicated.*

Voices:
Chester C. Cricket/Harry the Cat: Les Tremayne, **Tucker the Mouse/Alley Cat:** Mel Blanc

WALT DISNEY PRESENTS MICKEY, DONALD AND SPORT GOOFY SHOW (1984)

Mickey Mouse, Donald Duck and Goofy star in a collection of old cartoon shorts comprising this holiday season compilation entitled, "Happy Holidays." The show features *Pluto's Christmas Tree* (1952), *The Clock Watcher* (1945) and *How To Ride A Horse* from *The Reluctant Dragon* (1941), full–length feature. *A Walt Disney Television Production. Color. Half–hour. Premiered: December 1–23, 1984. Syndicated.*

Voices:
Mickey Mouse: Jim MacDonald, **Donald Duck:** Clarence Nash, **Goofy:** Pinto Colvig

WALT DISNEY PRESENTS MICKEY, DONALD AND SPORT GOOFY SHOW (1984)

Subtitled "Snowtime," various Disney characters appear in this first–run special presenting a collection of previously released cartoons, including *Lend A Paw* (1941), *Chip 'N' Dale* (1947) and *How To Fish* (1942). *A Walt Disney Television Production. Color. Half–hour. Premiered: November 17–December 23, 1984.*

Voices:
Mickey Mouse: Jim MacDonald, **Donald Duck:** Clarence Nash, **Goofy:** Pinto Colvig

WALT DISNEY PRESENTS SPORT GOOFY'S OLYMPIC GAMES SPECIAL

Like the previously syndicated "Sports Goofy" specials, this version features a selection of memorable Goofy sports cartoons, among them, *Olympic Champ* (1942), *Goofy Gymnastics* (1949), *Hot To Swim* (1942) and *Art of Self—Defense* (1941). *A Walt Disney Television Production. Color. Half—hour. Premiered: June 2—17, 1984. Syndicated.*

Voices:
Goofy: Pinto Colvig, George Johnson

WALT DISNEY'S MICKEY, DONALD AND SPORT GOOFY SHOW

Entitled "Getting Wet," this half—hour syndicated special is comprised of water—themed cartoon shorts featuring a variety of Disney characters. Cartoons featured include *The Simple Things* (1953), *Chips Ahoy* (1956) and *Aquamania* (1961). *A Walt Disney Television Production. Color. Half—hour. Premiered: September 7—23, 1984. Syndicated.*

Voices:
Mickey Mouse: Jim MacDonald, **Donald Duck:** Clarence Nash, **Goofy:** Pinto Colvig

WEEP NO MORE, MY LADY

In the Mississippi backwoods, Skeeter, a 13—year—old boy, discovers a stray dog who he adopts and names My Lady. After training her into a good bird—dog, he accepts a challenge from the nastiest character around, Alligator Ike, to see whose dog is the best. Ike later seeks revenge when My Lady wins. An "ABC Weekend Special." *A Ruby—Spears Enterprises Production. Color. Half—hour. Premiered on ABC: February 10, 1979. Rebroadcast on ABC: May 19, 1979; September 8, 1979; July 19, 1980; May 30, 1981; September 5, 1981; April 9, 1983; June 2, 1984; May 30, 1981; September 5, 1981; April 9, 1983; June 2, 1984.*

Voices:
Skeeter: Jeremy Lawrence, **Uncle Jess:** Alan Oppenheimer, **Alligator Ike:** Larry D. Mann, **Mr. Rackman:** Michael Rye

WEIRD HAROLD

While Weird Harold's bizarre pranks are not approved by his neighborhood chums, Fat Albert is relying on him to participate with the group in the Great Go—Cart Race. Unfortunately, the race turns out differently than they expected when Fat Albert, Weird Harold and Young Bill (Bill Cosby) careen recklessly down a dangerous hill, crash their soap—box derbies and are arrested. This program was the second Fat Albert special following "Hey, Hey, Hey, It's Fat Albert," which premiered in 1969. *A Filmation Production in association with Bill Cosby Productions. Color. Half—hour. Premiered on NBC: May 4, 1973. Rebroadcast on NBC: September 7, 1973.*

Voices:
Fat Albert/Mushmouth/Young Bill/Father: Bill Cosby, **Weird Harold:** Gerald Edwards, **Judge:** Henry Silva

WHAT A NIGHTMARE, CHARLIE BROWN

After devouring too much pizza, Snoopy has a nightmare that he is suddenly at the North Pole as part of a husky dog sled team. From here the plot to this half—hour animated special unfolds, centering around Snoopy's attempt at adapting to being a "real dog" in the adventures that follow. *A Lee Mendelson—Bill Melendez Production in association with Charles M. Schulz Creative Associates and United Feature Syndicate. Color. Half—hour. Premiered on CBS: February 23, 1978. Rebroadcast on CBS: April 13, 1987.*

Voices:
Charlie Brown: Liam Martin, **Snoopy:** Bill Melendez

WHAT HAVE WE LEARNED, CHARLIE BROWN?

In this mostly serious and reflective Memorial Day salute, Charlie Brown reminisces about the "Peanuts" group's adventures while taking part in a student—exchange program in France. Their countryside journey leads them to a beach, Omaha Beach to be exact, where Allied forces began their invasion of Europe on June 6, 1944, triggering a retelling of the D—day attack rendered in animation and newsreel footage. A later visit to the World War I battlefield of Ypres in Belgium sparks historical views on the "war to end all wars," with Linus movingly reciting John McCrae's famous poem, "In Flanders Field." "Peanuts" creator Charles Schulz hosted the program. *A Lee Mendelson—Bill Melendez Production in association with Charles M. Schulz Creative Associates and United Feature Syndicate. Color. Half—hour. Premiered on CBS: May 30, 1983. Rebroadcast on CBS: May 26, 1984; May 29, 1989.*

Voices:
Charlie Brown: Brad Kesten, **Sally Brown:** Stacey Heather Tolkin, **Linus Van Pelt:** Jeremy Schoenberg, **Marcie/Shermy:** Michael Dockery, **Peppermint Patty:** Victoria Vargas, **French Madam:** Monica Parker, **Snoopy:** Bill Melendez

WHICH WITCH IS WITCH?

Buttons and Rusty, the stars of several first—run specials, experience their first Halloween together. Dressed up in costumes, they make several new friends and overcome trouble at a Halloween party thrown by Ranger Jones. *An Encore Enterprises Production. Color. Half—hour. Premiered: October, 1984. Syndicated.*

Voices:
Rusty/Rosie: Kathy Ritter, **Buttons/Christie:** Barbara Goodson, **Abner:** Alvy Moore, **George:** Bill Ratner, **Bridgett:** Morgan Lofting, **Ranger Jones:** Bill Boyett

THE WHITE SEAL

In the second of two "Jungle Book" animated specials ordered for the 1974–1975 season by CBS, Roddy McDowall narrates the story of Kotick the white seal, who grows up from playful sprout to become leader of his group, taking them to a spectacular island safe from the savage seal hunters. *A Chuck Jones Enterprises Production. Color. Half–hour. Premiered on CBS: March 24, 1975. Rebroadcast on CBS: October 17, 1975; May 13, 1977; September 9, 1981. Syndicated.*

Voices:

Kotick/Sea Catch/Sea Cow/Killer Whale/Walrus: Roddy McDowall, **Matkah:** June Foray, **Narrator:** Roddy McDowall

WHY, CHARLIE BROWN, WHY?

Janice, a new "Peanuts" character, is a school friend of Linus' and Charlie Brown's who develops leukemia. The story traces her treatment—and eventual recovery—and how it must be dealt with by Linus, Charlie Brown and the rest of the gang, as well as by her own siblings and even a schoolyard bully. The program was produced in cooperation with the American Cancer Society. *A Lee Mendelson–Bill Melendez Production in association with Charles M. Schulz Creative Associates and United Feature Syndicate. Color. Half–hour. Premiered on CBS: March 16, 1990.*

Voices:

Charlie Brown: Kaleb Henley, **Janice Emmons:** Olivia Burnette, **Linus Van Pelt:** Brandon Stewart, **Sally Brown:** Andrienne Stiefel, **Little Sister:** Brittany Thorton, **Big Sister:** Lindsay Sloane, **The Bully:** Dion Zamora

WILLIE MAYS AND THE SAY–HEY KID

Baseball great Willie Mays, playing himself, recounts the tale of the near–impossible catch he makes to clinch the National League pennant, thanks to a special wish he is granted by an eccentric angel. The story gets deeper, however, as he cares for a poor orphan girl (Veronica) who turns out to be his godchild in this one–hour special which originally aired as part of "The ABC Saturday Superstar Movie" series. *A Rankin–Bass Production. Color. One hour. Premiered on ABC: October 14, 1972 (on "The ABC Saturday Superstar Movie"). Rebroadcast on ABC: September 22, 1973; February 16, 1974. Syndicated.*

Voices:

Willie Mays: Willie Mays, **Veronica:** Tina Andrews, **Iguana:** Paul Frees, **Veronica's Aunt:** Ernestine Wade

THE WIND IN THE WILLOWS

Ratty, Badger and Mole struggle to keep boastful Mr. Toad from danger and try to save Toad Hall from destruction by evil weasels in this two–hour made–for–television movie based on Kenneth Grahame's popular children's classic. The program was supposed to be a faithful version of the original story, unlike previous versions such as Walt Disney's "The Adventures of Ichabod and Mr. Toad" (1949). *A Rankin–Bass Production in association with Cuckoos Nest Animation. Color. Two hours. Premiered on ABC: July 5, 1987. Rebroadcast on ABC: September 12, 1987.*

Voices:

Mr. Toad: Charles Nelson Reilly, **Ratty:** Roddy McDowall, **Badger:** José Ferrer, **Moley:** Eddie Bracken, **Wayfarer:** Paul Frees, **Magistrate:** Robert McFadden, **Vocalist:** Judy Collins

Additional Voices:

Jeryl Jagoda, Ron Marshall, Gerry Matthews, Ray Owens, Alice Tweedle

WINNIE THE POOH AND A DAY FOR EEYORE

Based on a story by A. A. Milne, creator of this children's classic, Winnie the Pooh and his friends—Rabbit, Piglet and Roo—learn that everyone has forgotten Eeyore's birthday. With Christopher Robin's help, they throw a surprise party for the sorrowful looking donkey. The special was the first production starring the characters since "Winnie the Pooh and Tigger Too," produced 12 years earlier. *A Walt Disney Television Production. Color. Half–hour. Premiered on Disney Channel: May 6, 1986.*

Voices:

Winnie the Pooh: Hal Smith, **Eeyore:** Ralph Wright, **Piglet:** John Fiedler, **Rabbit:** Will Ryan, **Christopher Robin:** Kim Christianson, **Roo:** Dick Billingsley, **Kanga:** Julie McWhirter Dees, **Tigger:** Paul Winchell

WINNIE THE POOH AND THE BLUSTERY DAY

Broadcast as a prime–time special, this Academy Award–winning short–subject relates Pooh's and Piglet's frightening encounter with a giant windstorm that blows them skyward, crashing into and destroying the Owl's treehouse. Making up for the damage, Christopher Robin and the animals build Owl a new home. *A Walt Disney Television Production. Color. Half–hour. Premiered on NBC: November 30, 1970. Rebroadcast on NBC: December 1, 1971; November 29, 1972; November 28, 1973; November 26, 1974; December 1, 1978.*

Voices:

Winnie the Pooh: Sterling Holloway, **Eeyore:** Ralph Wright, **Owl:** Hal Smith, **Christopher Robin:** Jon Walmsley, **Kanga:** Barbara Luddy, **Roo:** Clint Howard, **Rabbit:** Junius Matthews, **Gopher:** Howard Morris, **Tigger:** Paul Winchell, **Piglet:** John Fiedler, **Narrator:** Sebastian Cabot

WINNIE THE POOH AND THE HONEY TREE

Winnie the Pooh's love for honey gets the best of him as he becomes overweight from over–consumption of the sweet stuff in this theatrical short–subject broadcast as a prime–

time special. *A Walt Disney Television Production. Color. Half–hour. Premiered on NBC: March 10, 1970. Rebroadcast on NBC: March 22, 1971; March 14, 1972; April 4, 1973; March 26, 1974; November 25, 1977; January 21, 1990 (on "Magical World of Disney").*

Voices:

Winnie the Pooh: Sterling Holloway, **Eeyore:** Ralph Wright, **Owl:** Hal Smith, **Christopher Robin:** Bruce Reitherman, **Kanga:** Barbara Luddy, **Roo:** Clint Howard, **Rabbit:** Junius Matthews, **Gopher:** Howard Morris, **Narrator:** Sebastian Cabot

WINNIE THE POO AND TIGGER TOO

Consumed with joy, Tigger is in a bouncing mood so much so that his friends Pooh, Rabbit and Piglet look for solutions to "unbounce" him in this animated special originally produced as a theatrical cartoon short. *A Walt Disney Television Production. Color. Half–hour. Premiered on NBC: November 28, 1975 (as "NBC Holiday Special"). Rebroadcast on ABC: November 25, 1976; CBS: December 11, 1982; August 30, 1983.*

Voices:

Winnie the Pooh: Sterling Holloway, **Tigger:** Paul Winchell, **Rabbit:** Junius Matthews, **Piglet:** John Fiedler, **Kanga:** Barbara Luddy, **Roo:** Dori Whitaker, **Christopher Robin:** Timothy Turner, **Narrator:** Sebastian Cabot

WITCH'S NIGHT OUT

Gilda Radner provides the voice of a washed–up witch who turns two small children into the monsters of their choice only to fulfill the fantasies of the town's entire adult population as well in this prime–time Halloween special. *A Leach–Rankin Production in association with Rankin–Bass Productions. Color. Half–hour. Premiered on NBC: October 27, 1978. Rebroadcast on NBC: October 30, 1979. Syndicated.*

Voices:

Witch ("The Godmother"): Gilda Radner, **Rotten:** Bob Church, **Goody:** John Leach, **Tender:** Naomi Leach, **Small:** Tony Molesworth, **Malicious:** Catherine O'Hara, **Mincely:** Fiona Reid, **Bazooey:** Gerry Salsberg

THE WORLD OF SECRET SQUIRREL AND ATOM ANT

The first cartoon preview aired in prime time, this hour–long special gave viewers a glimpse of the characters from the Saturday–morning series, "The Atom Ant/Secret Squirrel Show" in two back–to–back episodes. The series officially debuted on October 2, 1965. *A Hanna–Barbera Production. Color. One hour. Premiered on NBC: September 12, 1965.*

Voices:

Secret Squirrel: Mel Blanc, **Morocco Mole:** Paul Frees, **Atom Ant:** Howard Morris, **Mr. Moto/Others:** Don Messick

THE WORLD OF STRAWBERRY SHORTCAKE

This first special based on the popular greeting card characters introduced Strawberry Shortcake, a cute little girl who wears a frilly white apron, and her friends of the fantasy world called Strawberry Land. Joined by Huckleberry Pie, Blueberry Muffin, Apple Dumplin' and Raspberry Tart, Strawberry Shortcake enjoys the goodness of the land, but their happiness is intruded upon from time to time by the diabolical Peculiar Purple Pieman who is always out to spoil their fun. The program aired as an Easter special and was the first of six "Strawberry Shortcake" specials produced for first–run syndication. *A RLR Associates Production in association with Those Characters From Cleveland and Murakami–Wolf–Swenson Films. Color. Half–hour. Premiered: March–April, 1980. Syndicated.*

Voices:

Sun (narrator): Romeo Muller, **Strawberry Shortcake:** Russi Taylor, **Peculiar Purple Pieman:** Bob Ridgely, **Huckleberry Pie:** Julie McWhirter, **Blueberry Muffin/Apple Dumplin':** Joan Gerber, **Raspberry Tart:** Pamela Anderson, **Ben Bean/Escargot:** Bob Holt, **Vocalists:** Flo and Eddy

YABBA DABBA 2

Host Bill Bixby salutes the prolific careers of animators William Hanna and Joseph Barbera in this compilation special of clips from their cartoon success, from both their MGM days and as the heads of their own studio, Hanna–Barbera Productions. The show featured clips of Tom and Jerry, Scooby–Doo, Ruff and Reddy, the Flintstones and others. *A Hanna–Barbera Production in association with Robert Guenette Productions. Color. One hour. Premiered on CBS: October 12, 1979. Rebroadcast on CBS: June 1, 1982.*

YANKEE DOODLE

The spirit of the Revolutionary War, including Paul Revere's historic midnight ride to warn the Colonials, is witnessed by Danny, a 12–year–old boy, and his Midnight Militia friends, Freddy and Timmy, in this special about freedom and independence. A "Festival of Family Classics" special. *A Rankin–Bass Production in association with Mushi Studios. Color. Half–hour. Premiered: 1972–1973. Syndicated.*

Voices:

Carl Banas, Len Birman, Bernard Cowan, Peg Dixon, Keith Hampshire, Peggi Loder, Donna Miller, Frank Perry, Henry Raymer, Billie Mae Richards, Alfie Scopp, Paul Soles

YANKEE DOODLE CRICKET

Chester C. Cricket, star of "The Cricket in Times Square" and "A Very Merry Cricket," stars in this fanciful view of American history as recreated by the ancestors of Chester, Harry the Cat and Tucker R. Mouse. *A Chuck Jones Enterprises Production. Color. Half–hour. Premiered on ABC: January 16, 1975. Rebroadcast on ABC: June 28, 1976. Syndicated.*

Voices:
Chester C. Cricket/Harry the Cat: Les Tremayne, **Tucker R. Mouse:** Mel Blanc, **Other Voices:** June Foray

YEAR WITHOUT A SANTA CLAUS

This stop–motion Animagic special features the voices of Mickey Rooney, again picking up Santa's reins—as he did in the 1970 "Santa Claus Is Coming to Town"—only this time feeling the world has lost the Christmas spirit and that he is "much too tired for Christmas capers." Mrs. Claus sends Jingle and Jangle Bells off to find samples of seasonal cheer to bolster Santa. Unaccustomed as they are to the ways of the world, however, they fall into trouble with the miserable Snowmiser and Heatmiser. His reindeer returned to him safely, and Santa recovers from his disenchantment with the holiday season to make his traditional sleigh ride on Christmas Eve to distribute toys to the children of the world. Adapted from Pulitzer Prize–winner Phyllis McGinley's book, the special features the hit songs "Blue Christmas" and "Here Comes Santa Claus." *A Rankin–Bass Production. Color. One hour. Premiered on ABC: December 10, 1974. Rebroadcast on ABC: December 10, 1975; December 14, 1976; December 9, 1977; December 10, 1978; December 9, 1979; December 21, 1980. Syndicated.*

Voices:
Mrs. Santa Claus (narrator): Shirley Booth, **Santa Claus:** Mickey Rooney, **Snowmiser:** Dick Shawn, **Heatmiser:** George S. Irving, **Jingle Bells:** Robert McFadden, **Jangle Bells:** Bradley Bolke, **Mother Nature:** Rhoda Mann, **Mr. Thistlewhite:** Ron Marshall, **Ignatius Thistlewhite:** Colin Duffy, **Blue Christmas Girl:** Christine Winter, **Vocalists:** Christine Winter

YES, VIRGINIA, THERE IS A SANTA CLAUS

Animated retelling of eight–year–old Virginia O'Hanlon's letter to a *New York Sun* editor in 1897 asking if Santa Claus really exists. Program was co–produced by Bill Melendez, who was also associated with Charles M. Schulz's "Peanuts" specials—cornerstones of prime–time animation. *A Burt Rosen Company Production in association with Wolper Productions and Bill Melendez Production. Color. Half–hour. Premiered on ABC: December 6, 1974. Rebroadcast on ABC: December 5, 1975. Syndicated.*

Voices:
Virginia O'Hanlon: Courtney Lemmon, **Miss Taylor:** Susan Silo, **Billie:** Billie Green, **Specs:** Sean Manning, **Mary Lou:** Tracy Belland, **Arthur:** Christopher Wong, **Amy:** Vickey Ricketts, **Peewee:** Jennifer Green, **Officer Riley:** Herb Armstrong, **Sergeant Muldoon:** Arnold Ross, **Vocalist:** Jimmy Osmond, **Narrator:** Jim Backus

YOGI AND THE INVASION OF THE SPACE BEARS

Yogi Bear is on a rampage—and no picnic basket is safe in Jellystone Park. He swears to turn over a new leaf but before he does he and Boo Boo are kidnapped by aliens who plan to clone them by the thousands. This syndicated two–hour special was produced as part of "Hanna–Barbera's Superstar 10" movie package. *A Hanna–Barbera Production. Color. Two hours. Premiered: 1988. Syndicated.*

Voices:
Yogie Bear: Daws Butler, **Boo Boo:** Don Messick, **Cindy Bear:** Julie Bennett, **Ranger Smith:** Don Messick, **Ranger Jones:** Michael Rye, **Ranger Brown:** Patric Zimmerman, **Ranger Roubidoux:** Peter Cullen, **Boy:** Rob Paulson, **Little Girl:** Maggie Roswell, **Man:** Townsend Coleman, **Wife:** Rob Paulson, **Dax Nova:** Frank Welker, **Zor One:** Townsend Coleman, **Zor Two:** Rob Paulson, **Mountain Bear:** Sorrell Booke, **Guy:** Michael Rye, **Girl:** Victoria Carroll, **Ranger One:** Sorrell Booke, **Boy:** Townsend Coleman, **Owner:** Peter Cullen, **Ranger Two:** Patric Zimmerman, **Worker Kid:** Frank Welker

YOGI AND THE MAGICAL FLIGHT OF THE SPRUCE GOOSE

Everyone's favorite bear leads a gang of his friends to Long Beach, California for a tour of the Spruce Goose, the largest cargo plane ever built. While there, they are somehow locked inside the huge plane after closing time. To their amazement, the plane takes off following the path of a stardust stairway, taking them on the voyage of a lifetime. This two–hour made–for–television movie was syndicated as part of "Hanna–Barbera's Superstar 10" movie package. *A Hanna–Barbera Production. Color. Two hours. Premiered: 1987. Syndicated.*

Voices:
Yogi Bear: Daws Butler, **Boo Boo:** Don Messick, **Quick Draw McGraw:** Daws Butler, **Snagglepuss:** Daws Butler, **Huckleberry Hound:** Daws Butler, **Augie Doggie:** Daws Butler, **Doggie Daddy:** John Stephenson, **Mumbley:** Don Messick, **Dread Baron:** Paul Winchell, **Merkin:** Frank Welker, **Firkin:** Dave Coulier, **Pelican:** John Stephenson, **Bernice:** Marilyn Schreffler

YOGI BEAR'S ALL–STAR COMEDY CHRISTMAS CAPER

Yogi Bear and Boo Boo sneak off into the city and make Christmas merry for a lonely little rich girl, Judy Jones, with some help from their old friends in this all–star Hanna–Barbera holiday special. *A Hanna–Barbera Production. Color. Half–hour. Premiered on CBS: December 21, 1982. Rebroadcast on CBS: December 18, 1984; Disney Channel: December 12, 1990.*

Voices:
Yogi Bear: Daws Butler, **Boo Boo:** Don Messick, **Quick Draw McGraw/Huckleberry Hound/Snagglepuss/Hokey Wolf:** Daws Butler, **Snooper/Blabber/Augie Doggie/Mr. Jinks/Dixie/Wally Gator:** Daws Butler, **Ranger Smith/Pixie:** Don Messick, **Judy Jones:** Georgi Irene, **Doggie Daddy/Butler/Announcer:** John Stephenson, **Mr. Jones/Zookeeper #1/Sergeant:** Hal Smith, **Mrs. Jones/P. A. Voice/Lady in the Street:** Janet Waldo, **Yakky Doodle/Zookeeper #2:** Jimmy Weldon, **Magilla Gorilla/Chief Blake/Murray:** Allan Melvin,

Fred Flintstone/Policeman/Security Guard #1: Henry Corden, **Barney Rubble/Bulldog/Security Guard #2:** Mel Blanc

YOGI'S ARK LARK

The Biblical tale of "Noah's Ark" is given a different twist in this animated rendering featuring Yogi Bear, Boo Boo and a host of Hanna–Barbera cartoon favorites. The feature–length story, which originally aired on "The ABC Saturday Superstar Movie," served as the successful pilot for the Saturday–morning series, "Yogi's Gang," in which the program was rebroadcast in two parts. *A Hanna–Barbera Production. Color. One hour. Premiered on ABC: September 16, 1972 (on "The ABC Saturday Superstar Movie"). Syndicated.*

Voices:

Yogi Bear: Daws Butler, **Baba Looey/Wally Gator/Huckleberry Hound/Lambsy/Quick Draw McGraw/Snagglepuss:** Daws Butler, **Top Cat:** Daws Butler, **Boo Boo/Atom Ant/So So/Moby Dick/Touche' Turtle:** Don Messick, **Paw Rugg/1st Truck Driver:** Henry Corden, **Magilla Gorilla/2nd Truck Driver:** Allan Melvin, **Maw Rugg/Floral Rugg/Woman:** Jean VanderPyl, **Squiddly/Hokey Wolf/Yakky Doodle:** Walker Edmiston, **Cap'n Noah:** Lennie Weinrib, **Benny/Doggie Daddy/Hardy:** John Stephenson

YOGI'S FIRST CHRISTMAS

Huckleberry Hound, Snagglepuss, Augie Doggie and Doggie Daddy all arrive at Jellystone Lodge for their annual Christmas celebration with cartoon pals, Yogi Bear and Boo Boo. Their festivities gain added meaning when they discover that the owner, Mrs. Throckmorton, plans to sell the lodge to make way for a freeway in this two–hour made–for–television movie. *A Hanna–Barbera Production. Color. Half–hour. Premiered: November 22, 1980. Syndicated.*

Yogi Bear heads a cast of characters in some yuletide fun in the two–hour made–for–television movie "Yogi's First Christmas." © Hanna–Barbera Productions

Voices:

Yogi Bear: Daws Butler, **Boo Boo:** Don Messick, **Huckleberry Hound/Augie Doggie/Snagglepuss:** Daws Butler, **Ranger Smith/Herman the Hermit:** Don Messick, **Doggie Daddy/Mr. Dingwell:** John Stephenson, **Cindy Bear/Mrs. Throckmorton:** Janet Waldo, **Otto the Chef/Santa Claus:** Hal Smith, **Snively:** Marilyn Schreffler

YOGI'S GREAT ESCAPE

Ranger Smith receives a distressing phone call from the Park Commissioner. Because of financial crisis, Jellystone Park will be closed and Yogi Bear and all the other bears must move to a zoo. To avoid incarceration, Yogi and his diminutive sidekick, Boo Boo, lead Ranger Smith on a cross–country chase in this two–hour made–for–television movie, broadcast as part of "Hanna–Barbera's Superstar 10" series of first–run animated films for television. *A Hanna–Barbera Production. Color. Two hours. Premiered: 1987. Syndicated.*

Voices:

Yogi Bear: Daws Butler, **Boo Boo:** Don Messick, **Ranger Smith:** Don Messick, **Quick Draw McGraw:** Daws Butler, **Wally Gator:** Daws Butler, **Snagglepuss:** Daws Butler, **Buzzy:** Susan Blu, **Bopper:** Frank Welker, **Bitsy:** Edan Gross, **Skinny Kid:** Josh Rodine, **Chubby Kid:** Dustin Diamond, **Leader Kid:** Scott Menville, **Trapper:** Bill Callaway, **Yapper:** Frank Welker, **Bandit Bear:** Allan Melvin, **Li'l Brother Bear:** Hamilton Camp, **Little Cowgirl:** Susan Blu, **Reporter:** Patrick Fraley, **Swamp Fox Boy:** Tress MacNeille, **Swamp Fox Girl:** Susan Blu, **Dad:** Bill Callaway, **Real Ghost:** Frank Welker, **Cowboy Kid #1:** Patrick Fraley, **Cowboy Kid #2/Mom/Boy:** Tress MacNeille, **Swamp Fox Kid:** Patrick Fraley, **Girl/Swamp Fox Kid #2:** Susan Blu

YOU DON'T LOOK 40, CHARLIE BROWN

Television star Michele Lee hosts this hour–long retrospective covering 40 years in the life of cartoonist Charles Schulz and his blockheaded alter ago, Charlie Brown. The tribute features highlights from, appropriately, 40 television specials, including the first, "A Charlie Brown Christmas." Special guests were B. B. King, David Benoit, Joe Williams, Desiree Goyette, Joey Scarbury, Bill Melendez, and Cathy Guisewite. *A Lee Mendelson–Bill Melendez Production in association with Charles M. Schulz Creative Associates and United Feature Syndicate. Color. One hour. Premiered on CBS: February 2, 1990.*

YOU'RE A GOOD MAN, CHARLIE BROWN

This hour–long cartoon adaptation of the 1967 off–Broadway musical featuring the "Peanuts" characters charts the ups and downs of hapless Charlie Brown, for whom life is a constant source of frustration. First, it is a bothersome homework assignment. Then, at the baseball team's big game, his popularity is put on the line—and disaster strikes on the mound. Lucy, meanwhile, learns a valuable lesson about her piano-playing heartthrob, Schroeder: "Never try to discuss marriage with a musician." The program marked Snoopy's speaking debut, with his voice supplied by Robert Towers, a member of the 1967 Los Angeles stage cast. *A Lee Mendelson–Bill Melendez Production in association with Charles M. Schulz Creative Associates and United Feature Syndicate. Color. Half–hour. Premiered on CBS: November 6, 1985.*

Voices:

Charlie Brown: Brad Keston, **Charlie Brown** (singing): Kevin Brando, **Linus Van Pelt:** David Wagner, **Lucy Van Pelt:** Jessie Lee Smith, **Schroeder:** Jeremy Reinbolt, **Marcie:** Michael Dockery, **Sally Brown:** Tiffany Reinbolt, **Snoopy:** Robert Towers

YOU'RE A GOOD SPORT, CHARLIE BROWN

Charlie Brown enters a motocross race, but not until Lucy pulls the ol' placekick trick on him. To win the race, Charlie finds himself up against some pretty stiff competition: Peppermint Patty and the Masked Marvel (Snoopy). In a separate subplot, Snoopy gets a "tennis lesson" from his pal Woodstock. *A Lee Mendelson–Bill Melendez Production in association with Charles M. Schulz Creative Associates and United Feature Syndicate. Color. Half–hour. Premiered on CBS: October 28, 1975. Rebroadcast on CBS: January 23, 1978.*

Voices:

Charlie Brown: Duncan Watson, **Linus Van Pelt:** Liam Martin, **Lucy Van Pelt:** Melanie Kohn, **Peppermint Patty:** Stuart Brotman, **Marcie:** Jimmie Ahrens, **Sally Brown:** Gail M. Davis, **Schroeder:** Liam Martin, **Loretta:** Melanie Kohn, **Franklin/ Kid:** Duncan Winston

YOU'RE IN LOVE, CHARLIE BROWN

For the first time, Charlie Brown is in love! The object of his affection is a little girl in his class who is unaware of Charlie's feelings towards her. Unable to work up to the courage to speak to her, he instead writes a note to break the ice. Gravel–voiced, tomboy Peppermint Patty makes her debut in the program, first trying to solve "Chuck's" baseball problems and then getting between what she thinks is "an affair d'amour" between Charlie and Lucy. *A Lee Mendelson–Bill Melendez production in association with Charles M. Schulz Creative Associates and United Feature Syndicate. Color. Half–hour. Premiered on CBS: June 12, 1967. Rebroadcast on CBS: June 10, 1968; June 11, 1969; June 10, 1970; June 7, 1971; June 3, 1972.*

Voices:

Charlie Brown: Peter Robbins, **Linus Van Pelt:** Christopher Shea, **Sally Brown:** Cathy Steinberg, **Lucy Van Pelt:** Sally Dryer Barker, **Peppermint Patty:** Gail DeFaria, **Violet:** Anne Altieri

YOU'RE NOT ELECTED, CHARLIE BROWN

After taking a private poll, Lucy determines that Charlie Brown is not suited to run for student body president at school but instead finds that her insecure brother, Linus, is the perfect candidate. Just as it looks like Linus has the election in the bag, however, he throws it all away during a debate with his opponent by mentioning "The Great Pumpkin" whereupon he is laughed out of the election. *A Lee Mendelson–Bill Melendez production in association with Charles M. Schulz Creative Associates and United Feature Syndicate. Color. Half–hour. Premiered on CBS: October 29, 1972. Rebroadcast on CBS: October 15, 1973; September 23, 1976.*

Voices:

Charlie Brown: Chad Webber, **Lucy Van Pelt:** Robin Kohn, **Linus Van Pelt:** Stephen Shea, **Sally Brown:** Hilary Momberger, **Russell:** Todd Barbee, **Violet:** Linda Ercoli, **Schroeder:** Brian Kazanjian, **Loud Child in Audience:** Brent McKay

Additional Voices:

Jay Robertson, Danny Lettner, David Zuckerman, Joshua McGowan

YOU'RE THE GREATEST, CHARLIE BROWN

With his school hosting their local Junior Olympics, Charlie Brown enters the decathalon event in hopes of helping his school win the meet. Everyone has faith in him except the "Peanuts" gang. Afraid that he'll blow it, they include Marcie as his backup. Coming down to the last event, all Charlie has to do is win the 1500–meter race to put his school on top. Unfortunately, he doesn't watch where he is running and runs off the track, losing the race and the olympics for his school. *A Lee Mendelson–Bill Melendez Production in association with Charles M. Schulz Creative Associates and United Feature Syndicate. Color. Half–hour. Premiered on CBS: March 19, 1979. Rebroadcast on CBS: March 5, 1980; March 20, 1981.*

Voices:

Charlie Brown: Arrin Skelley, **Lucy Van Pelt/Girl:** Michelle Muller, **Marcie/Crowd:** Casey Carlson, **Linus Van Pelt/Crowd:** Daniel Anderson, **Fred Fabulous:** Tim Hall, **Peppermint Patty:** Patricia Patts, **Announcer:** Scott Beach, **Snoopy:** Bill Melendez

ZIGGY'S GIFT

Veteran cartoon strip character Ziggy brings his proverbial heart of gold to television in his first prime–time special as a recruited street Santa Claus who becomes mixed up with the leader of a band of fraudulent Santas wanted by the police. During such escapades, the non–speaking Ziggy still manages to perform several good deeds, such as saving a Christmas tree from being cut down, rescuing a stray cat and liberating dozens of turkeys awaiting the chopping block. Ziggy creator Tom Wilson wrote the story. *A Welcome Productions in association with Universal Press Syndicate. Color. Half-hour. Premiered on CBS: December 1, 1982. Rebroadcast on CBS: December 8, 1983.*

Voices:

Crooked Santa: Richard Williams, **Officer O'Connor:** Tom McGreevey, **Butcher:** Tony Giorgio, **Announcer:** John Gibbons, **Vocalist:** Harry Nilsson

Additional Voices:

David Arias, Perry Botkin, Katrina Fried, Natasha Fried, Jack Hanrahan, Linda Harmon, Anna Ostblom, Latoya Prescod, Gloria Gale Prosper, Andy Raub, Terry Stillwell–Harriton, Lena Tabori, Holly Williams, Tim Williams, Tom Wilson, Tom Wilson Jr.

TELEVISION CARTOON SERIES

THE ABC SATURDAY SUPERSTAR MOVIE

The concept of feature–length cartoons for television was born with this popular Saturday morning series. Famous television and cartoon figures were adapted into hour–long stories, along with new concepts made for television. In all, 16 films were made during the first season, each costing approximately $300,000 to produce. Hanna–Barbera Productions produced most of the entries. Additional cartoons were produced by Rankin–Bass Productions, Fred Calvert Productions and King Features Productions (details for each production, except for "Luvcast U. S. A.," are available in the Animated Television Specials section). For its second and final season, the series was retitled, "The New Saturday Superstar Movie." *A Hanna–Barbera/Rankin–Bass/Fred Calvert/Filmation/ Warner Brothers/King Features Production. Color. One hour. Premiered on ABC: September 9, 1972–August 31, 1974.*

Episodes:
1972–73 "The Brady Kids on Mysterious Island" (working title: "Jungle Bungle"), "Yogi's Ark Lark," "Mad, Mad, Mad Monsters," "Nanny And The Professor," "Popeye Meets The Man Who Hated Laughter," "Willie Mays And The Say–Hey Kid," "Oliver Twist And The Artful Dodger" (two parts), "Robin Hoodnik" (working title: "Cartoon Adventures Of Robin Hound"), "Lassie And The Spirit of Thunder Mountain," "Gidget Makes The Wrong Connection," "The Banana Splits In Hocus Pocus Park" (live–action/animated), "Tabitha And Adam And The Clown Family," "The Red Baron," "Daffy Duck And Porky Pig Meet The Groovie Goolies," "Luvcast U. S. A." and "That Girl In Wonderland."
1973–1974 "Lost In Space," "Nanny And The Professor And The Phantom Circus" and "The Mini–Munsters."

ABBOTT AND COSTELLO

The antics of Hollywood's memorable comedy team, Bud Abbott and Lou Costello, are recreated in this series of animated misadventures. Bud Abbott, the fast–talking straightman, was at the time in dire financial straits and actually voiced his own character. (The cartoons were his primary source of income and barely paid for his medical bills. He passed away in 1974.) His gullible partner, roly–poly Lou Costello, who succumbed to a heart attack in 1959, was played by actor Stan Irwin in the series. *A Hanna–Barbera Production for RKO–Jomar Productions. Color. Half–hour. Premiered: Fall 1967. Syndicated.*

Voices:
Bud Abbott: Himself, **Lou Costello:** Stan Irwin

Additional Voices:
Mel Blanc, Hal Smith, John Stephenson, Don Messick, Janet Waldo

Movie comedy greats Abbott and Costello were re–teamed in a series of new cartoon adventures for television. Only Abbott was able to provide his own voice. © Hanna–Barbera Productions

Episodes:
"Go Go Goliath," "Dog Gone Dog," "In The Soup," "Cops And Saucers," "There Auto Be A Law," "Tiny Terror," "The Cloud Monster," "The Gravity Grabber," "Big Bird Break Out," "The Vikings," "Sahara You?," "Going Buggy," "Eskimo Pie–Eyed," "The Forty Thieves," "Lube–A–Tuba," "Down In The Dumps," "Wizardland," "Frail Whale," "Tooth Or Consequences," "Sitting Pity," "The Mark Of El Zap," "Catman On A Hot Tin Roof," "Elephantasy," "Shutter Bugged Sea Serpent," "Super Lou," "Stand–In–Stand–Off," "Mouse Route," "Kooks And Spooks," "Dinosaur Dilemma," "The Indestructible Space Suit," "Frigid Fugitive," "The Astro–Nuttys," "Mighty Midget Mustang," "The Bouncing Rubber Man," "Galoots In Armour Suits," "The Purple Baron," "The Two Musketeers," "Abbott And Costello In Blunderland," "Skyscraper–Napper," "Going To Pot," "A Creep In The Deep," "Crying High," "Germ Squirm," "Weird Neighbors," "Pigskin Pickle," "Two On The Isle," "The Moleman Mine," "Lashed But Leashed," "Space Toy Tyrants," "The Little Fay Boy Cried Wolf," "Wacky Wax Work," "Werewolf Whim–Wham," "Monsterkeet," "Invader Raider," "A Goose Misuse," "Who Needs Arrest?," "Paddle Boat Pirate," "Going, Going–Gun!," "Road Race Ruckus," "Gone–Ghosts," "Baby Buggy," "Hey, Abbott!," "Drumsticks Along The Mohawk," "A Car Is Born," "Teenie Weenie Genie," "Lumbering Lummoxes," "Professor Uncles' Ants," "High Wire Lion," "Fish–Hooked," "Magic Monster," "Planet Plant," "Space Beard," "Marauding Mummy," "Baby Shoo," "The Long, Long Camper," "Puppet Enemy Number One," "Phantom Of The Hoss Opera," "Fumbled Fable," "Rabbit Grabbers," "The Vacuum Villain," "The Big Cannon Monster," "Glass Reunion," "A Guest In The Nest," "Gone Like The Wind," "Gadzooka," "Merry Misfits," "Broom Gloom," "The Hound Hounders," "Rescue Miscue," "Fighting The Clock," "Sinister Professor Sinister," "Ship Ahooey," "Pigs In A Picnic," "Mounty–Bounty," "Super Terror Strikes Again," "No Place Like Rome," "Texas Jack," "Follow The Bouncing Blob," "Not So Sweet Sioux," "The Queen Of Diamonds," "Picture Frame–Up," "Luma Tricks," "Pearl Diving Perils," "Bounty Booty," "G. I. Jokers," "Tasmanian Terror," "Dangerous Buck," "The Gadget King," "The Fiendish Farmer," "The Ice–Tronauts," "Gator Baiter," "Rabbit Rouser," "Save a Cave," "Wild Man, Wild," "Which Witch Is Which?," "Super Knight," "Son Of Konk," "Shooting The Works," "Doggies By The Dozen," "Rhino Riot," "Bully For Lou," "Cherokee Choo-Choo," "Hotel Suite And Sour," "Shoo Shoes," "Teensy Vs. Weensys," "Tragic Magic," "Carnival Of Menace," "Hullaba-Lou," "Get 'Im Tiger," "Mountain Mischief," "The Drastic Driller," "Turkish Daffy," "Yankee Doodle Dudes," "Gorilla Thriller," "The Eighth Dwarf," "Super Car," "Run Of De Mille Pictures," "Rodeo Rumpus," "The Sinister Stinger," "Magic Mix–Up," "Bad Day At High Noon," "Shock Treatment," "Tom All–Thumbs," "Starlight Starfright," "Private General Nuisance," "Trigger Tracks" and "Pinocchio's Double Trouble."

THE ADDAMS FAMILY
Popular TV ghouls Gomez Addams, wife Morticia, bald Uncle Fester and zombie butler Lurch travel across the country with the rest of the family, telling hair–raising stories in a haunted wagon, complete with moat. *A Hanna–Barbera Production.*

Characters' copyrights owned by Charles Addams. Color. Half–hour. Premiered on NBC: September 8, 1973–August 30, 1975.

Voices:
Gomez Addams: Lennie Weinrib, **Morticia:** Janet Waldo, **Uncle Fester:** Jackie Coogan, **Lurch:** Ted Cassidy, **Wednesday:** Cindy Henderson, **Pugsley:** Pat Harrington Jr., **Grandmama:** Janet Waldo

Additional Voices:
Bob Holt, John Stephenson, Don Messick, Herb Vigran, Howard Caine, Lennie Weinrib

Episodes:
"Addams Family In New York," "Follow That Loaf Of Bread," "Left In The Lurch," "Boola Boola," "The Fastest Creepy Camper In The West," "The Mardi Gras Story," "Aloha Hoolamagoola," "The Reluctant Astronauts—Trip To The Moon," "The Great Balloon Race," "The Circus Story," "Ghost Town," "The Addams Family At Sea," "The Voodoo Story," "The Roller Derby Story," "Addams Go West" and "The Addams Family At The Kentucky Derby."

THE ADVENTURES OF BATMAN
In Gotham City, millionaire playboy Bruce Wayne and his youthful ward, Dick Grayson, in the guise of the famed caped crusader Batman and boy wonder Robin, battle the nefarious schemes of the Joker, the Penguin, the Riddler, the Catwoman, Mr. Freeze, Mad Hatter and Simon the Pieman in this half–hour action series that was originally part of 1968's "The Batman/Superman Hour" (see entry for information). The dynamic duo was joined in several episodes by Batgirl. *A Filmation Production in association with Ducovny Productions. Color. Half–hour. Premiered on CBS: September 13, 1969–September 6, 1970.*

Voices:
Bruce Wayne/Batman: Olan Soule, **Dick Grayson/Robin:** Casey Kasem, **Barbara Gordon/Batgirl:** Jane Webb, **Alfred Pennyworth,** Wayne's butler: Olan Soule

Episodes:
"Batman Feature" (one 12–minute episode per show).
"My Crime Is Your Crime," "The Cool Cruel Mr. Freeze," "How Many Herrings In A Wheel Barrow," "The Nine Lives Of Batman," "Bubi, Bubi, Who's Got The Ruby," "Big Birthday Caper," "Partners In Peril," "Hizzoner The Joker (Joker For Mayor)," "The Crime Computer," "A Game Of Cat And Mouse," "Will The Real Robin Please Stand," "Simon The Pieman," "From Catwoman With Love," "A Perfidious Pieman Is Simon," "The Fiendish Frigid Fraud," "The Jigsaw Jeopardy" and "It Takes Two To Make A Team."
"Batman and Robin" (one part per show).
"Bird Out Of Hand," "The Joke's On Robin," "In Again Out Again Penguin," "Long John Joker," "1001 Faces Of The Riddler," "Two Penguins Too Many," "The Underworld Underground Caper," "Mr. Freeze's Frozen Vikings," "The Great Scarecrow Scare," "Beware of Livin' Dolls," "He Who Swipes The Ice Goes To The Cooler," "A Mad Mad Tea Party,"

"Perilous Playthings," "The Cool Cruel Christmas Caper," "Enter The Judge" and "Wrath of The Riddler."

THE ADVENTURES OF GULLIVER

The tiny folks of Lilliput hold captive the giant, Gulliver, who saves the city and people from destruction, gaining his terrified six—inch tall hosts' trust and respect. The citizens of Lilliput help Gulliver find his missing father and buried treasure, and overcome the foul deeds of the evil Captain Leech. *A Hanna—Barbera Production. Color. Half—hour. Premiered on ABC: September 14, 1968—September 5, 1970.*

Voices:

Gary Gulliver: Jerry Dexter, **Thomas Gulliver:** John Stephenson, **Captain Leech:** John Stephenson, **King Pomp:** John Stephenson, **Flirtacia:** Jenny Tyler, **Eger:** Don Messick, **Glum:** Don Messick, **Tagg:** Herb Vigran, **Bunko:** Allan Melvin

Episodes:

"Dangerous Journey," "The Capture," "The Valley Of Time," "The Forbidden Pool," "The Perils Of Lilliputs," "Hurricane Island," "Exit Leech," "The Tiny Island," "Mysterious Forest," "Little Man Of The Year," "The Rescue," "The Dark Sleep," "The Runaway," "The Masquerade," "The Missing Crown," "Gulliver's Challenge" and "The Hero."

THE ADVENTURES OF HOPPITY HOOPER

The comic escapades of a trio of talking animals—naive, lovable frog, Hoppity Hooper; and associates, Professor Waldo Wigglesworth, a fast—thinking fox; and Fillmore, a dim—witted but good—natured bear—who travel across the country in a medicine—show wagon to explore various get—rich schemes. One such ploy involved selling "Indian Guide Elixir," a hair growing tonic, to some nearby townspeople, who grew tipsy instead of hair.

Two episodes of four—part cliff—hangers were shown each week, plus episodes of three other components: "Fractured Fairytales" (repeated from "Rocky and His Friends"), which spoofed beloved fairy tales; "Mr. Know—It—All," with none other than Bullwinkle Moose offering solutions to common everyday problems (first seen on "The Bullwinkle Show"); and "Commander McBragg," a boastful, bushy—browed retired naval commander who tells tall tales about his career, which premiered on "Tennessee Tuxedo and His Tales" (see individual series for episodic information). The program later contained reruns of "Peabody's Improbable History," hosted by intelligent beagle Peabody and his brainy adopted son, Sherman, who transport themselves back in time to visit historical events through the power of their WABAC machine.

In the fall of 1965, after the first 26 episodes aired on ABC, they were reedited and repackaged for syndication under the title of "Uncle Waldo." With the network series still on the air, the syndicated version featured only two other recurring segments besides the Hoppity Hooper reruns: "Fractured Fairytales" and "Peabody's Improbable History," the latter repeated from "Rocky and His Friends" (see series for voice credits and episode title information).

Jay Ward, the father of such cartoon favorites as Rocky and Bullwinkle, Dudley Do—Right and Crusader Rabbit, created the series. *A Hooper Production in association with Jay Ward Productions. Color. Half—hour. Premiered on ABC: September 26, 1964—September 2, 1967. Syndicated.*

Voices:

Hoppity Hooper: Chris Allen, **Professor Waldo Wigglesworth:** Hans Conreid, **Fillmore,** the Bear: Bill Scott, **Narrator, "Fractured Fairytales":** Edward Everett Horton, **Commander McBragg:** Kenny Delmar, **Bullwinkle Moose:** Bill Scott

Episodes:

"Hoppity Hooper" (two episodes per show).
"Ring—A—Ding Spring" (1–4), "Rock 'N' Roll Star" (5–8), "Diamond Mine" (9–12), "Costra Nostra" (13–16), "Giant of Hootin' Holler" (17–20), "Detective Agency" (21–24), "Olympic Star" (25–28), "Ghost" (29–32), "Masked Martian" (33–36), "Jumping Frog Contest" (37–40), "Traffic Zone" (41–44), "Wottabango Corn Elixer" (45–48), "Frog Prince of Monomania" (49–52), "Colonel Clabber—Limberger Cheese Statue" (53–56), "The Giant Cork" (57–60), "Ferkle To Hawaii" (61–64), "Halloween" (65–68), "Christmas" (69–72), "Horse Race Follies" (73–76), "Jack And The Beanstalk" (77–80), "Granny's Gang" (81–84), "Golf Tournament" (85–88), "The Dragon Of Eubetcha" (89–92), "Rare Butterfly Hunt" (93–96), "Oil's Well At Oasis Gardens" (97–100) and "Wonder Water" (101–104).

THE ADVENTURES OF JONNY QUEST

One of the most nostalgically popular animated television series of the 1960s, "The Adventures of Jonny Quest" was developed by artist Doug Wildey for Hanna—Barbera Productions. The series recounted the adventures of 11—year—old Jonny and his brilliant scientist father, Dr. Benton Quest. Accompanied by bodyguard—tutor Roger "Race" Bannon, a mysterious Indian boy named Hadji and fearless bulldog Bandit, they embark on a global expedition that becomes more fantastic with each stop. They encounter living gargoyles, dragons, invisible monsters and unravel various mysteries along the way. Episodes from the original network series were later broadcast as part of "The Godzilla Power Hour" and "Godzilla Super 90."

In 1987, Hanna—Barbera revived this animated classic and produced all—new episodes which were seen in syndication as part of "The Funtastic World Of Hanna—Barbera," expanded to two hours in length. Of the original main cast, only Don Messick returned to voice Dr. Bendit Quest and Bandit. Jonny Quest's voice was provided by Scott Menville, Hadji's voice by Rob Paulsen and "Race" Bannon by Sonny Granville Van Duesen. For other supporting characters, voice work was done by several well—known performers, such as Roger Carmel, Les Tremayne, Dick Gautier, Rene Auberjonois, Keye Luke, George Takei and Ed Begley Jr. *A Hanna—Barbera Production. Color. Half—hour. Premiered on ABC: September 18, 1964—September 9, 1965. Rebroadcast on CBS: September 9,*

Race Bannon, Jonny Quest and his dog Bandit ward off attacking scuba divers in a scene from "The Adventures Of Jonny Quest." © Hanna–Barbera Productions

1967–September 5, 1970; NBC: September 11, 1971–September 2, 1972; September, 1979–September 6, 1981. Premiere (new series): September, 1987. Syndicated.

Voices:

Dr. Benton Quest: John Stephenson, Don Messick, **Jonny Quest:** Tim Matthieson, Scott Menville, **Roger "Race" Bannon:** Mike Road, Sonny Granville Van Dusen, **Hadji,** Indian companion: Danny Gravo, Rob Paulsen, **Bandit,** their dog: Don Messick

Episodes:

1964–1965 (Network) "Double Danger," "The Curse Of Anubis," "The Mystery Of The Lizardmen," "Riddle Of The Gold," "Arctic Splash Down," "Calcutta Adventure," "Pursuit Of The Po–Ho," "Shadow Of The Condor," "Treasure Of The Temple," "Dr. Zin's Robot Spy," "Dreadful Doll," "Skull And Double–Crossbone," "A Small Matter Of Pygmies," "Dragons Of Ashida," "Turu The Terrible," "Attack Of The Tree People," "The Fraudulent Volcano," "The Werewolf Of The Timberland," "The Invisible Monster," "Pirates From Below," "The Devil's Tower," "The House of Seven Gargoyles," "Terror Island," "Monster In The Monastery," "The Sea Haunt" and "The Quetong Missile Mystery."

1987–1988 (Syndication). "Peril Of Reptillian," "Nightmares Of Steel," "Aliens Among Us," "Deadly Junket," "Forty Fathoms Into Yesterday," "Vikong Lives," "The Monolith Man," "Secret Of The Clay Warriors," "Warlord Of The Sky," "The Scourge Of Skybord," "Temple of Gloom," "The Creeping Unknown" and "Skullduggery."

THE ADVENTURES OF LARIAT SAM

A preschooler series written especially for "The Captain Kangaroo Show," casting honest but friendly cowboy, Lariat Sam, and his poetry–reading horse Tippytoes (known as the "Wonder Horse") in offbeat stories about the Old West. Sam's recurring nemesis: Badlands Meeney. Stories were presented in three parts and the series was created by Robert Keeshan's company, Robert Keeshan Associates. Keeshan, incidentally, was better known to viewers as Captain Kangaroo. The cartoons were later packaged for syndication. A CBS Terrytoons Productions. Black–and–white. Color. Five minutes. Half hour. Premiered on CBS: September 10, 1962–August 27, 1965.

Voices:

Lariat Sam: Dayton Allen, **Tippytoes,** his horse: Dayton Allen

Episodes:

"Horse Opera Hoax," "Arts And Craftiness," "Cowhide 'N' Seek," "Mark Of Zero," "Badlands Cannonball," "Rock–A–Bye Badlands," "Ding–A–Ling Circus Saga," "Bushwack In Toyland," "Below The Water Lion," "Water Color Witchcraft," "Great Race For Office Space," "Weatherman Mish Mosh" and "People Catcher."

Lariat Sam, a strong, friendly cowboy, and his poetry–reading horse Tippytoes starred in Old West misadventures written especially for "The Captain Kangaroo Show." (Courtesy: Viacom International)

THE ADVENTURES OF POW POW

The stories of a young Indian boy were recounted in this limited animated series first telecast on "Captain Kangaroo" in 1957. Twenty–six episodes were produced with stories based on Indian folklore and related fables. In 1958, the program was syndicated to local stations throughout the country. A Sam Singer Production. Black–and–white. Five *minutes. Half–hour. Premiered on CBS: 1957. Syndicated: 1958.*

THE ADVENTURES OF RAGGEDY ANN AND ANDY

Secretly coming to life in Marcella's playroom, Raggedy Ann and brother Andy and their raggedy friends—Raggedy Cat, Raggedy Dog, Grouchy Bear, the Camel with the Wrinkled Knees and others—are hurled into whimsical adventures. Anything and everything is possible in the world of Raggedys, a world populated by dragons, perriwonks, fairies and—yes—even the presence of evil. *A CBS Animation Production. Color. Half–hour. Premiered on CBS: September 17, 1988–December 24, 1988.*

Voices:

Raggedy Ann: Christina Lange, **Raggedy Andy:** Josh Rodine, **Marcella:** Tracy Rowe, **Grouchy Bear:** Charlie Adler, **Raggedy Cat:** Kath Soucie, **Raggedy Dog:** Dana Hill, **Camel:** Ken Mars, **Sunny Bunny:** Katie Leigh

Episodes:

"Perriwonk Adventure," "Pirate Adventure," "Mabbit Adventure," "Beastly Ghost Adventure," "Pixling Adventure," "Ransom Of Sunny Bunny," "Megamite Adventure," "Boogeyman Adventure," "Raggedy's Christmas Adventure," "Sacred Cat Adventure," "Little Chicken Adventure," "Warrior Star" and "Magic Wings Adventure."

THE ADVENTURES OF TEDDY RUXPIN

Flying in a wonderous airship, Teddy Ruxpin, Newton Gimmick (an eccentric genius inventor) and Grubby (a valiant octopede) set forth in their quest to uncover the true purpose of a series of long lost ancient crystals recently discovered by the trio. Their daily adventures bring them face to face with the forces of the evil overlords, M.A.V.O. (Monsters and Villains Organization), whose sole purpose is to enslave the furry, feathered and scaled populace of the vast Land of Grundo. *A DIC Enterprises Production. Color. Half–hour. Premiered: September, 1987. Syndicated.*

Voices:

Teddy Ruxpin: Phil Barron, **Gimmick:** John Stocker, **Grubby:** Will Ryan, **Tweeg:** John Koensgen, **L. B. Prince Arin:** Robert Bauxthall, **Leota:** Holly Larocque, **Aruzia:** Abby Hagyard, **Wooly What's It:** Pierre Paquette

Episodes:

"The Treasure Of Grundo," "Beware Of The Mudblups," "Guest Of The Grunges," "In The Fortress Of The Wizard," "Escape From The Treacherous Mountains," "Take A Good Look," "Grubby's Romance," "Tweeg's Mom," "The Surf Grunges," "The New M.A.V.O. Member," "The Faded Fobs," "The Medicine Wagon," "Tweeg Gets The Tweezles," "The Lemonade Stand," "The Rainbow Mine," "The Wooly What's–It," "Sign Of A Friend," "One More Spot," "Elves And Woodsprites," "Grundo Graduation," "Double Grubby," "King Nogburt's Cas-

tle," "The Day Teddy Met Grubby," "Secret Of The Illiops," "Through Tweeg's Fingers," "Uncle Grubby," "The Crystal Book," "Teddy And The Mudblups," "Win One For The Twipper," "Tweeg Joins M.A.V.O.," "The Mushroom Forest," "Anything In The Soup," "Capture," "To The Rescue," "Escape From Mavo," "Leekee Lake," "The Third Crystal," "Up For Air," "The Black Box," "The Hard To Find City," "Grubby's Story," "Tweeg The Vegetable," "Wizardland," "The Ying Zoo," "The Big Escape," "Teddy Ruxpin's Birthday," "Wizardweek," "Air And Water Races," "The Great Grundo Ground Race," "A Race To The Finish," "Autumn Adventure," "Gizmos And Gadgets," "Harvest Feast," "Wooly And The Giant Snowzos," "Winter Adventure," "Teddy's Quest," "Thin Ice," "Fugitives," "Musical Oppressors," "The Mavo Costume Ball," "Father's Day," "The Journey Home," "On The Beaches," "L. B.'s Wedding" and "The Mystery Unravels."

THE ADVENTURES OF THE GALAXY RANGERS

In 2086, two peaceful alien Ambassadors come to the World Federation of Earth. They are Waldo Zeptic from the planet Andor and Zozo from the planet Kirin. They seek help against an interstellar syndicate of alien outlaws, space pirates and outer space criminals that are terrorizing their planets. In order to deal effectively with the developing problems of alien affairs, the World Federation forms an organization called BETA, the Bureau of Extra–Terrestrial Affairs. The commander of BETA is Joseph Walsh, who launches this special team of crime-fighters—Zachary Fox, Doc Hartford, Niko, and Goose—to protect mankind from alien enemies in outer space. *A Gaylord Production in association with Transcom Media and ITF Enterprises. Color. Half–hour. Premiered: September 15, 1986. Syndicated.*

Voices:

The Galaxy Rangers: Zachary Fox: Jerry Orbach, **Doc Hartford:** Hubert Kelly, **Niko:** Laura Dean, **Goose:** Doug Preis, **Others: Command Joseph Walsh:** Earl Hammond, **Lazarus Slade/Captain Kidd/Wildfire Cody/King Spartos:** Earl Hammond, **Buzzwang:** Sandy Marshall, **Mogel the Space Sorcerer/The General/Nimrod/Jackie Subtract/Bubblehead the Memory Bird:** Doug Preis, **Queen of the Crown/The Kiwi Kids:** Corinne Orr, **Zozo/Squeegie/GV/Little Zach Foxx/Brappo:** Bob Bottone, **Waldo/Geezi the Pedulont/Q–Ball/Larry/Scarecrow/Kilbane/Crown Agent:** Henry Mandell, **Maya/Annie Oh/Mistwalker:** Maia Danzinger, **Macross:** Ray Owen, **Aliza Foxx/Jessica Foxx:** Laura Dean

Episodes:

"Phoenix," "New Frontier," "Tortuna," "Chained," "Smuggler's Gauntlet," "Mist Walker," "Wildfire," "Ghost Station," "One Million Emotions," "Traasah," "Mindnet," "Tune Up," "Space Sorcerer," "Progress," "Queen's Lair," "Ax," "Shaky," "Space Moby," "Scarecrow," "The Power Within," "Games," "Showtime," "Psychocrypt," "Renegade Rangers," "Edge Of Darkness," "Magnificent Kiwi," "Armada," "Birds Of A Feather," "Stargate," "Buzzwang's Folly," "Heart Of Tarkon," "Murder On The Andorian Express," "Lady Of The Light," "Moth-moose," "Natural Balance," "Ariel," "In Sheep's Clothing," "Marshmellow Trees," "Shoot out," "Bronto Bear," "Invasion," "Rogue Arm," "Aces And Apes," "Badge Of Power," " Boomtown," "Supertroopers," "Galaxy Stranger," "Lords Of The Sands," "Changeling," "Promised Land," "Westride," "Rainmaker," "Battle Of The Bandits," "Rusty And The Boys," "Trouble At Texton," "Horsepower," "Ariel," "Don Quixote Cody," "Tortuna Rock," "Fire And Iron," "Tower Of Combat," "Gift Of Life," "Sundancer" and "Heartbeat."

ADVENTURES OF THE LITTLE KOALA

Roobear, a boy koala bear, experiences various adventures through which he learns the importance of life, parents, friends and the world around him. Also featured are Roobear's parents, Mama and Papa, his younger sister, Laura, as well as penguins, rabbits, kangaroos and other animals in lively and heartwarming stories. *A Cinar Films Production. Color. Half-hour. Premiered on Nickelodeon: June 1, 1987.*

Voices:

Roobear: Steven Bednarski, **Laura, his sister:** Morgan Hallett, **Papa,** Roobear's father: Walter Masscy, **Mama,** Roobear's mother: Jane Woods, **Miss Lewis:** Bronwen Mantel, **Floppy:** Tim Webber, **Mimi:** Barbara Poggemiller, **Betty:** Cleo Paskal

Episodes:

(two per show) "A Whale Of A Ride," "Laura Finds An Egg," "The Mysterious Moa Bird," "Love That Baby Moa!," "A Eucalyptus Rocket," "Penguins Don't Fly," "Mommy Can Fly," "The Secret Of The McGillicuddy Vase," "The Amazing Boomerang," "The Runaway Hat," "Conquering Mount Breadknife," "Save The Eucalyptus," "Heavenly Fireworks," "Save That Junk," "Monster Scoop," "Biggest Jigsaw Puzzle In The World," "Who Will Be The Flower Queen?," "Circus Day," "Roobear The Babysitter," "Papa Makes Pie," "The Moon Goodess," "The Flying Doctor," "The Dinosaur Egg," "Treasure Hunt," "Nurse Pamie," "Any Mail Today?," "The Winner," "A Hundred Year Old Camera," "Papa On Stilts," "Detective Roobear," "Save The Butterflies," "A Broken Umbrella," "Is Weather A Frog?," "Lost In A Race," "The King Of The Castle," "Hang Gliding With Roobear," "Snow White And The Seven Koalas," "Roobear's Invention," "Pamie Falls In Love," "The Koala Bear Gang," "Back To Nature," "Roobear Saves The Day," "Editor-In-Chief Roobear," "The Ghost Ship," "Balloon Pamie," "Old Clock Tower," " Mingle Takes A Dive," "The Writing On The Wall," "A Ride In A Space Ship," "Is Mingle A Nuisance?" and "Allowance Problems."

THE ADVENTURES OF THE LITTLE PRINCE

Based on the tiny plant of B–612, the Little Prince, an extraordinary small boy, travels to Earth and other planets where he makes new friends and helps solve their problems, shedding light on what is really important in life—faith, courage, friendship and caring.

First syndicated in 1982, the program captured high ratings in most major markets. (On WABC–TV in New York, it topped its competition, which included "NBC Children's Theater," "Bullwinkle," "The Pink Panther" and "Captain Kangaroo"; it was also number–one in its time slot on KABC–TV in Los Angeles.) In 1985, the program began its second run on cable–television's Nickelodeon. The series was highly recommended by the National Education Association for children's viewing. Jameson Brewer, best known for his scripting of the Walt Disney classic *Fantasia,* wrote and produced the series. *A Jambre/Gallerie International Films Production. Color. Half–hour. Premiered: September 1982. Syndicated.*

Voices:

The Little Prince: Julie McWhirter Dees, **Swifty,** the space bird: Hal Smith, **Others:** Janet Waldo, Pamela Ziolkowski

Episodes:

"Higher Than Eagles Fly!," "Shipwreck!," "On Wings Of Love," "Rob The Rainbow," "A Small Alien," "Somewhere In Space," "Visit To Another Planet," "The Perfect Planet," "The Wolf Pack," "The Star Gazer," "Last Voyage Of The Rose," "The Chimney Sweep," "The Greatest Gift," "Too Big For This World!," "The Winning Ride," "To Be A Man," "The Magic Case," "Always Listen To a Fox," "Hitch Onto Halley's Comet," "A Light In The Storm," "What Makes Mitzi Mean?," "The Wishing Stone," "A Different World," "Erase All Beauty" and "Play It Again, Sean!"

ALF

That wonderful, wise–cracking alien, Alf, relives his pre–Earth days on the planet Melmac—the wild and wacky adventures in the Orbit Guard, at home with his family and hanging out at the local diner—in this half–hour animated series based on the hit NBC comedy series of the same name. *An Alien Production in association with DIC Enterprises and Saban Productions. Color. Half–hour. Premiered on NBC: September 12, 1987–September 2, 1989.*

Voices:

Alf: Paul Fusco, **Sgt. Staff/Cantfayl:** Len Carlson, **Flo:** Peggy Mahon, **Augie/Rhoda:** Pauline Gillis, **Stella:** Ellen–Ray Hennessey, **Skip:** Rob Cowan, **Larson Petty/Bob:** Thick Wilson, **Curtis:** Michael Fantini, **Harry:** Stephen McMulkin, **Sloop:** Dan Hennessey

Episodes:

1987–1988 "The Phantom Pilot," "Hair Today, Bald Tomorrow," "Two For The Brig," "Home Away From Home," "Gordon Ships Out," "Pismo And The Orbit Gyro," "The Birdman of Melmac," "20,000 Years In Driving School," "The Pride Of The Shumways," "Captain Bobaroo," "Neep At The Races," "Salad Wars" and "Tough Shrimps Don't Dance."
1988–1989 "Clams Never Sang For My Father," "Flodust Memories," "Family Feud," "The Spy From East Velcro," "A Mid–Goomer Night's Dream," "The Bone Losers," "Thank Gordon For Little Girls," "Looking For Love In All The Wrong Places," "Hooray For Mellywood," "Housesitting For Pokispi," "He Ain't Seafood, He's My Brother," "The Slugs of Wrath" and "Skipper's Got A Brand New Dad."

ALF TALES

Alf and friends star in irreverent versions of classic children's fairy tales. *An Alien Production in association with DIC Enterprises. Color. Half–hour. Premiered on NBC: September 10, 1988–September 1990.*

Voices:
Alf: Paul Fusco, **Flo:** Peggy Mahon, **Augie/Rhoda:** Paulina Gillis, **Stella:** Ellen–Ray Hennessey, **Skip:** Rob Cowan, **Larson Petty/Bob:** Thick Wilson, **Sloop:** Dan Hennessey

Additional Voices:
Noam Zylberman, Michael Lamport, Maria Lukofsky, Stephen Ouimette, Harvey Atkin, Jayne Eastwood, John Stocker, Don Francks, Debra Theaker, Greg Morton, Nick Nichols, Greg Swanson, Len Carlson, Ray Kahnert, Eva Almos, Linda Sorenson

Episodes:
"Robin Hood," "Sleeping Beauty," "Cinderella," "The Legend Of Sleepy Hollow," "Jack And The Beanstalk," "The Aladdin Brothers And Their Lamp," "Rapunzel," "Rumplestiltskin," "The Princess And The Pea," "Alice In Wonderland," "John Henry," "The Three Little Pigs," "Peter Pan," "Hansel And Gretel," "The Wizard Of Oz," "Little Red Riding Hood," "The Emperor's New Clothes," "The Elves And The Shoemaker," "Goldilocks And The Three Bears," "King Midas" and "Snow White."

THE ALL–NEW EWOKS

The fuzzy little creatures of *Star Wars* fame return in all–new adventures on the distant forest moon of Endor, led by young scout Wicket, in this spin–off of "The Ewoks Star Wars Droids Adventure Hour," which aired on ABC. *A Lucasfilm Production in association with Nelvana Limited, Hanho Heung–Up and Mi–Hahn Productions. Color. Half–hour. Premiered on ABC: November 8, 1986–September 5, 1987.*

Voices:
Wicket: Denny Delk, **Teebo:** Jim Cranna, **Princess Kneesa:** Jeanne Reynolds, **Latara:** Sue Murphy, **Shodu:** Esther Scott, **Logray:** Rick Cimino

Additional Voices:
Michael Pritchard, Bob Sarlatte, Morgan Upton, Lucille Bliss, Richard Nelson, Dan St. Paul, Richard Devon

Episodes:
"The Crystal Cloak," "The Wish Plant," "A Gift For Shodu," "Home Is Where The Shrieks Are," "Princess Latara," "The Raich," "The Totem Master," "Gone With The Mimphs," "The First Apprentice," "The Season Scepter," "A Warrior And A Lurdo," "Hard Sell," "Night Of The Stranger," "Prow Beaten," "Baga's Rival," "Horville's Hut Of Horrors," "The Tragic Flute," "Just My Luck," "Bringing Up Norky," "Battle For The Sunstar," "Party Ewok" and "Malani The Warrior."

THE ALL–NEW GUMBY

The famous green man returns in all–new, first–run syndicated episodes produced by the character's creator, Art Clokey.

Famous green man Gumby and pal Pokey from a promotional still for "The All–New Gumby" series. © Premavision

The program intermixed episodes from the original cult series with new original stories.

Dallas McKennon, the original voice of Gumby, trained several actors through his company, Dalmac Productions, to alternate as the character's voice in this series revival. Creator Art Clokey reprised the role of Pokey (he also voiced Prickle), while wife Gloria lent her vocal talent to the character, Goo.

Initially, the series premiered in 80 television markets nationwide. It has since received airplay on stations in Australia and Europe. *A Clokey Production in association with Premavision. Color. Half–hour. Premiered: September, 1988. Syndicated.*

Voices:
Gumby: Dalmac Productions, **Pokey/Prickle:** Art Clokey, **Professor Cap:** Dalmac Productions, **Goo:** Gloria Clokey

Episodes:
1988–1989 (three episodes per show) "Richochet Pete," "King For A Day," "Train Trouble," "Motor Mania," "Rain Spirits," "The Groobee," "Foxy Boxy," "Tricky Train," "The Kachines," "Tree Trouble," "Puppy Talk," "Mystic Magic," "Goo For Pokey," "The Magic Flute," "Eager Beavers," "The Zoops," "Pokey Express," "Trapped On The Moon," "Mason Hornet," "Tail Tale," "Yard Work Made Easy," "Lawn Party," "The Rodeo King and Pokey," "Do It Yourself Gumby," "Lost And Found," "The Racing Game," "The Big Eye," "Hair Raising Adventure," "Fantastic Farmer," "Gopher Trouble," "The Missle Bird," "This Little Piggy," "Little Lost Pony," "The Blockheads," "Dragon Daffy," "Stuck On Books," "Chicken Feed," "Pilgrims On The Rocks," "Pigfon In A Plum Tree," "Clay Trix," "Outcast Marbles," "Gold Rush Gumby," "Bully For Gumby," "Hot Ice," "Gumby's Fire Department," "Hot Rod Granny," "School For Squares," "Gumby Concerto," "Too Loo," "Treasure For Honey," "Space Ball," "In A Fix," "Witty Witch," "Turnip Trap," "Gumby Business," "Dragon Witch," "Northland Follies," "The Blue Goo," "Moon Trip," "Good Knight Story," "Hidden Valley," "The Glob," "How Not To Trap Lions," "Moon Madness," "Black Knight," "The Magic

Show," "Seige Of Boonesborough," "Shady Lemonade," "Eggs And Trixy," "Mirrorland," "Sad King Ott's Daughter," "Baby Gumby," "Toy Fun," "Lion Drive," "Prickles Turn Artist," "Wishful Thinking," "Mysterious Fires," "Toy Capers," "Grub Grabber Gumby," "Odd Balls," "El Toro," "Egg Trouble," "Who's What," "Sticky Pokey," "Toy Crazy," "Candidate For President," "All Broken Up," "Bone For Nopey," "Scrooge Loose," "Gabby Aunty," "Indian Challenge," "The Moon Boggles," "Toy Joy," "Lovely Bunch Of Coconuts," "Super Spray," "Behind The Puff Ball," "Robot Rumpus," "Gumby League," "Gumby Racer," "Making Squares," "Baker's Tour," "The Golden Iguana," "Prickle's Problem," "The Golden Gosling," "Even Steven," "The Mocking Monkey," "Point Of Honor," "Reluctant Gargoyle," "Tricky Ball," "Pokey Minds The Baby," "The Magic Wand," "Toying Around," "In The Dough," "A Groobe Fight," "Dog Catcher," "Piano Rolling Blues," "Son Of Liberty," "Pokey's Price," "Gumby Crossing," "The Delaware," "Ferris Wheel Mystery," "Rain For Roo," "Haunted Hot Dog," "Gumby On The Moon," "Santa Witch," "Lion Around," "Small Planets" and "Of Clay And Critters."

1989–1990 "A Gumby Day," "Strange Circus Animals," "A Cottage For Granny," "The Music Ball," "Shrink–A–Dink," "Hatching Out," "Mirror–Aculus Recovery," "As The Worm Turns," "Wild Girls," "Lost Treasure," "The Beetle And The Caterpillar," "A Smashing Hit," "Gumbot," "Guitar Magic," "Gumbitty Doo Dah," "A Miner Affair," "All Cooped Up," "Gumby's Circus," "The Elephant And The Dragon," "Denali's House," "Ostrich Feathers," "B. D. Party In Middle Ages," "The Big City," "Of Note," "Humbug," "Fun Day," "Denali Blues," "The Fliver 500," "Minga Sitting," "Real Seal," "Melon Felons," "Merry Go Pumpkin," "Time Kapp–sule," "The Search," "Educational TV," "Band Contest," "The Big Squirt," "Little Lost Girl," "Command Performance," "Witch Way," "Children For Sale," "Sleepytime Robbers," "The Wind Bag," "Lotta Hot Air," "Wild Horse," "The Plant," "Naughty Boy," "Young Granny," "Balloonacy," "Picnic," "Gumbastic," "Funtasia," "Rip Van Prickle," "Great Mastadon Robbery," "Wild Train Ride," "Artic Antics," "Runaway Camel," "Abominable Doughman," "Astrobots," "Blocks In The Head," "A Dolly For Minga," "Lost Arrow," "My–O–Maya," "Geese Grief," "Fox Hunt," "Goo's Pies," "Moving Experiences," "Gumby's Close Encounters," "Flying Carpets," "Minga's Follies," "High As A Kite," "Proxy Gumby," "Prickle's Baby Brudder," "Goo And The Queen" (Part 1), "Goo And The Queen" (Part 2), "Little Denali Lost," "Clay Play," "Knightmare," "Lost In Chinatown," "Joker's Wild," "Pokey Ala Mode," "Robot Farm," "Forbidden Mine" (Part 1), "Forbidden Mine" (Part 2), "Skate Board Rally," "Goo's M. V.," "Best In The Block," "Lost Birthday," "Just Train Crazy," "Wickiups And Bullrushes," "Kangaroo Express," "Kid Brother Kids," "Clayfully Yours," "Gumby Music Video" and "Time Out."

THE ALL–NEW PINK PANTHER SHOW

The never–discouraged feline returned to star in this series of new cartoons made for television, highlighted by the addition of a new supporting character in cartoons of his own: Crazylegs Crane, a mixture of Red Skeleton's Klem Kadiddle-

hopper and Edgar Bergen's Mortimer Snerd. *A DePatie–Freleng Enterprises Production. Color. Half–hour. Premiered on ABC: September 9, 1978–September 1, 1979.*

Voices:

Crazylegs Crane: Larry D. Mann, **Crane Jr.:** Frank Welker, **Dragonfly:** Frank Welker

Episodes:

"Pink Panther" (two per show).
"Pink Quacker," "Pink Lightning," "The Pinkologist," "A Pink In The Drink," "Sprinkle Me Pink," "Pink S.W.A.T.," "String Along In Pink," "Pink And Shovel," "Pink U.F.O.," "Cat And The Pinkstalk," "Pink Bananas," "Pink Breakfast," "Toro Pink," "Pink In The Woods," "Pinktails For Two," "Pink Pull," "Spark Plug Pink," "Pink Lemonade," "Super Market Pink," "Pink Daddy," "Pink Pictures," "Pink Z.Z.Z.," "Pink Suds," "Doctor Pink," "Dietetic Pink," "Pink Trumpet," "Yankee Doodle Pink," "The Pink Press," "Pet Pink Pebbles," "Star Pink" and "The Pink Of Bagdad."
"Crazylegs Crane" (one per show).
"Life With Feather," "Crane Brained," "King Of The Swamp," "Sonic Broom," "Winter Blunderland," "Storky And Hatch," "Fly–By–Knight" "Sneaker Snack," "Barnacle Bird," "Animal Crackups," "Jet Feathers," "Nest Quest," "Bug Off," "Beach Bummer," "Flower Power" and "Trail Of The Lonesome Mine."

THE ALL–NEW POPEYE HOUR

In this third series featuring the spinach–gulping sailor, Popeye picks up where he left off, defending his love for his girlfriend, Olive Oyl, by battling the bullying, girl–stealing Bluto, in adventures which were less violent than the theatrical sound cartoons originally produced by Max Fleischer.

Jack Mercer, the veteran salty voice of Popeye, wrote many of the cartoon scripts for the show, which featured several other familiar characters: hamburger–munching Wimpy; Pappy, Popeye's father; and Popeye's four nephews.

The program contained three segments in the 1978–1979 season: "The Adventures of Popeye," following the continuing exploits of Popeye and Bluto; "Dinky Dog," the misadventures of the world's largest dog; and "Popeye's Treasure Hunt," tracing Popeye and Olive Oyl's search for buried treasure, foiled by the everscheming Bluto. For the 1979–1980 season, a fourth segment was added to the show: "Popeye's Sports Parade," featuring Popeye in various sports competitions. Thirty–second spots known as "Popeye Health and Safety Tips" were featured on the show during each season. *A Hanna–Barbera Production in association with King Features Syndicate. Color. One hour. Premiered on CBS: September 9, 1978–September 5, 1981.*

Voices:

Popeye: Popeye: Jack Mercer, **Olive Oyl,** his girlfriend: Marilyn Schreffler, **Bluto,** Popeye's nemesis: Allan Melvin, **Wimpy,** Popeye's friend: Daws Butler, **The Evil Sea Hag:** Marilyn Schreffler, **Dinky Dog: Dinky:** Frank Welker, **Uncle Dudley,** Dinky's owner: Frank Nelson, **Sandy,** his niece: Jackie Joseph, **Monica, his niece:** Julie Bennett

Episodes:
"The Adventures of Popeye" (three per show).
1978–1979 "Popeye Goes Sailing," "Popeye And The Bean-stalk," "Popeye The Carpenter," "Popeye And The Pest," "Pop-eye Out West," "A Day At Muscle Beach," "Olive's Shining Hour," "The Big Wheel," "A Bad Knight For Popeye," "Popeye The Sleepwalker," "A Seal With Appeal," "A Whale Of A Tale," "Popeye And Bigfoot," "Heir–Brained Popeye," "The Ski's The Limit," "Here Stew You," "The Crunch For Lunch Bunch," "Popeye The Plumber," "Close Encounters Of The Third Spinach," "Wilder Than Usual Blue Yonder," "Popeye Snags The Seahag," "Spinach Fever," "Popeye's Finest Hour," "Pop-eye Meets The Blutostein Monster," "Popeye Goes Holly-wood," "Popeye And The Pirates," "Popeye's Engine Com-pany," "The Three Ring Ding–A–Ling," "The Decathalon Dilemma," "Popeye Goes Sightseeing," "Chips Off The Old Ice Block," "Shark Treatment," "Getting Popeye's Goat," "Ship Ahoy," "A Day At The Rodeo," "Bluto's Bike Bullies," "Popeye Of The Klondike," "Mother Goose Is On The Loose," "Popeye Versus Machine," "Steeple Chase At Ups And Downs," "A Camping We Will Go," "Popeye The Robot," "Ballet–Hooey," "Take Me Out To The Brawl Game," "Bully Dozer," "Yukon County Mountie," "The Spinach Bowl" and "Popeye's Roots."
1979–1980 "Popeye The Lone Legionnaire," "The Loneliness Of The Long Distance Popeye," "Roller Rink–A–Dink," "Wotsa Matterhorn?," "Free Hauling Brawl," "Popeye's High School Daze," "Popeye Gets Scooped," "Olive's Bugged House Blues," "Polly Wants Some Spinach," "Building Blockheads," "Old McPopeye Had A Farm," "Bad Day At The Bakery," "Westward Ho! Ho!," "Queen of The Load," "Love On The Rocks," "Pop-eye The Painter," "Swee' Pea Plagues A Parade," "Pedal–Powered Popeye," "On Mule–Itary Detail," "Paddle Wheel Popeye," "Take It Or Lump It," "Popeye's Aqua Circus," "Boo Who," "Popeye's Poodle Problem" and "The Game."
"Dinky Dog" (one per show).
1978–1979 "Dinky, Ahoy!," "To Boo Or Not To Boo," "Dinky At The Circus," "Dinky's Nose For News," "Camp's Kookie-haha," "Foggy Doggy," "Dinky The Movie Star," "Attic Antics," "Heap Cheap Hotel," "Bark In The Park," "Flabby Arms Farm," "The Bow–Wow Blues Band," "Easel Does It," "Dinky At The Bat," "Phi Beta Dinky" and "Abominable Dinky."
1979–1980 "Like It Or Lamp It," "Castaway Canine," "Gon-dola, But Not Forgotten," "Loch Ness Mess," "There's No Place Like Nome," "Rockhead Hound," "Buckingham Bow Wow" and "Trees A Crowd."
"Popeye's Treasure Hunt" (one per show).
1978–1979 "I Wants Me Mummy," "The Terrifyink Tran-sylvanian Treasure Trek," "The Sword Of Fitzwilly," "Play It Again, Popeye," "Captain Meno's Sunken Treasure," "The Del-monica Diamond," "The Treasure Of Howe's Bayou," "Cold-finger," "Spring Daze In Paris," "A Horse Of A Flying Color," "The Mask Of Gorgonzola," "I Left My Spinach In San Fran-cisco," "A Trio In Rio," "Popeye At The Center Of The Earth," "Boola Boola Hula" and "The Treasure Of Werner Schnitzel."
1979–1980 "Popeye In Wonderland," "Plunder Down Under" and "The Reel Hollywood Treasure Hunt."
"Popeye's Sports Parade" (one per show).
1979–1980 "King Of The Rodeo," "Fantastic Gymnastics,"

"Water Ya Doin?," "The Great Decathalon Championship" and "Sky High Fly Try."
"Popeye Health and Safety Tips" (30–second spots).
1978–1979 "Junk Food," "Smoking," "Drugs," "Exercise," "Prescription Medicine," "Importance Of Breakfast," "Immu-nization," "Skateboard," "Alcohol," "Toothache," "Sleep," "Bi-cycle," "Balanced Meals," "Don't Overeat," "Household Cleaners," "Sharp Utensils," "Home Safety Toys," "Bathroom Safety," "Electricity," "Don't Accept Rides From Strangers," "Don't Play With Matches," "Crossing The Street," "Don't Open Doors To Strangers" and "Clean Hands."
1979–1980 "Sunburn," "Don't Smoke," "Don't Eat House Plants," "Roller Skating," "A Friendly Attitude," "Seat Belts," "Sportsmanship," "Buying Safe Toys," "Sled Safety," "Off Road Mini–Bike Safety," "Ski Safety," "City Sled Safety," "Boating Safety," "Roller Skates II," "Swimming I," "School Bus," "Play Ground I," "Swimming Pools," "Hiking," "Aerosol Sprays," "Indoor Insecticides," "Hazards—Bike Safety III," "Signaling—Bike Safety IV," and "Control—Bike Safety V."
1980–1981 "Bike Wheels," "Tricycle Safety," "Bike Tires," "Bike Gears And Seat," "Extinguishing Campfires," "Mopeds," "Oiling Your Bike," "Bike Accessories," "Toe Clips," "Check-ing Your Bike," "Being Seen At Night," "Swings," "Bike Safety—Loose Parts," "Campfires," "Bike Breaks," "Kites," "Clothing Fires," "Sports Clothing," "Construction Sites," "Paint Poison-ing," "Waterfront Safety," "Vacant Houses And Dumps," "Rail-road Trestles," "Refrigerators," "House Fires," "Ice Skating," "Toys," "Unsafe Substitutes," "Safe Use Of Ladder," "Parked Cars," "Leaving A Parked Car" and "Amusement Park Safety."

ALL–NEW POUND PUPPIES
In the fall of 1987, following the success of 1986's "Pound Puppies" on Saturday mornings, ABC returned with new epi-sodes of this children's favorite about adorable puppies who live in a pound waiting to be adopted by children. The program usually featured two 11–minute episodes per show, but some weeks ran one 22–minute episode during the half–hour broadcast. *A Hanna–Barbera Production. Color. Half-hour. Premiered on ABC: September 26, 1987–September 3, 1988.*

Voices:
Nose Marie: Ruth Buzzi, **Cooler:** Dan Gilvezan, **Holly:** Ami Foster, **Katrina Stoneheart:** Pat Carroll, **Brattina Stone-heart:** Adrienne Alexander, **Cat Gut:** Frank Welker, **Bright Eyes:** Nancy Cartwright, **Whopper:** B. J. Ward, **Howler:** Bobby Morse

Episodes:
(11–minute episodes) "Tail Of The Pup," "Whopper Gets The Point," "The Bird Dog," "Where Do Puppies Come From?," "Pups On The Loose," "The Invisible Friend," "King Whop-per," "Casey Come Home," "Kid In The Doghouse," "Tuffy Gets Fluffy," "Little Big Dog," "Good Night Sweet Pups," "The Bright Eyes Mob," "The Rescue," "Nose Marie Day," "Snow Puppies," "Where's The Fire," "Bright Lights, Bright Eyes," "The Wonderful World Of Whopper" and "Dog And Caterpil-lar."

(22–minute episodes) "Garbage Night, The Musical," "Peter Pup" and "Cooler, Come Back."

THE ALL–NEW SCOOBY AND SCRAPPY–DOO SHOW

Cowardly Great Dane Scooby–Doo and his feisty pint–sized nephew, Scrappy–Doo, brave ghosts, goblins and ghouls to crack a series of mysteries in all–new comedy adventures. The series, which featured two 11–minute episodes per show, was broadcast in combination with "The Puppy's Further Adventures" (see entry for information), produced by Ruby–Spears Productions. *A Hanna–Barbera Production. Color. Half–hour. Premiered on ABC: September 10, 1983–September 1, 1984.*

Voices:

Scooby–Doo: Don Messick, **Scrappy–Doo:** Don Messick, **Shaggy:** Casey Kasem, **Daphne:** Heather North

Episodes:

(two per show) "Scoobygeist," "The Dinosaur Deception," "The Quagmire Quake Caper," "Scoobsie," "The Hound Of The Scoobyvilles," "No Sharking Zone," "Wizards And Warlocks," "Who's Minding The Monster?," "Scooby Ala Mode," "Carnival Caper," "Scooby And The Barbarian," "The Mark Of Scooby," "Scooby Doo And Cyclops, Too," "Scooby Of The Jungle," "Scooby Roo," "The Creature From The Chem Lab," "No Thanks, Masked Manx," "The Scooby Coupe," "The Fall Dog," "Scooby And The Minotaur," "Scooby Pinch Hits," "Scooby's Gold Medal Exhibit," "Where Is Scooby Doo?" (Part 1), "Where Is Scooby Doo?" (Part 2), "Wedding Bell Boos" (Part 1) and "Wedding Bell Boos" (Part 2).

THE ALL–NEW SUPER FRIENDS HOUR

Even though Hanna–Barbera's first superheroes cartoon series failed, the amazing popularity of TV's "Wonder Woman" and "The Six Million Dollar Man" spurred network interest in reviving the old "Super Friends" program.

When it was again unveiled in 1977, more young children and teenagers than before tuned in, making "The All–New Super Friends Hour" a huge ratings success. The network renewed the series for the following season. Four additional comic book characters joined the League of Justice in these adventures. *A Hanna–Barbera Production. Color. One hour. Premiered on ABC: September 10, 1977–September 2, 1978.*

Voices:

Narrators: Bill Woodson, Bob Lloyd, **Wonder Woman:** Shannon Farnon, **Superman:** Danny Dark, **Aquaman:** Norman Alden, **Batman:** Olan Soule, **Robin:** Casey Kasem, **Zan:** Mike Bell, **Jayna:** Liberty Williams

Episodes:

"League of Justice" (one per show).
"The Invasion Of The Earthers," "City In A Bottle," "Will The World Collide," "Day Of The Planet Creatures," "The Super Friends Versus The Super Friends," "The Voyage Of The Mysterious Time Creatures," "The Planet Of The Neanderthals," "The Mind Maidens," "The Water Beast," "The Coming Of The Arthopods," "Exploration Earth," "The Lion Men," "The Tiny World Of Terror," "The Mummy Of Nazca" and "The Ghost."
"Super Friends" (three per program).
"Joy Ride," "The Whirlpool," "Brain Machine," "Hitchhike," "Space Emergency," "Invasion Of The Hydronoids," "Game Of Chicken," "Volcano," "Secret Four," "Drag Race," "Fire," "Doctor Fright," "Vandals," "The Energy Mass," "The Monster Of Dr. Droid," "Tiger On The Loose," "Antidote," "Attack Of The Giant Squid," "The Shark," "Flood Of Diamonds," "The Enforcer," "Cheating," "Attack Of The Killer Bees," "The Fifty–Foot Woman," "Handicap," "Alaska Peril," "The Collector," "Initiation," "River Of Doom," "The Invisible Menace," "Pressure Point," "The Day Of The Rats," "Forbidden Power," "Prejudice," "The Tibetan Raiders," "The Man Beats Of Xra," "Dangerous Prank," "Cable Car Rescue," "Frozen Peril," "The Runaways," "Time Rescue," "The Marsh Monster," "Stowaways," "Rampage" and "The Protector."

ALVIN AND THE CHIPMUNKS

This series revival featured the same cast of characters—Alvin, Theodore, Simon and manager David Seville—in all–new adventures produced by Ross Bagdasarian's son, Ross Jr., who took over the family business in 1977 and created new and inventive material with his wife, Janice Karman. Adventures dealt with more contemporary and modern issues and introduced the Chipmunks' female companions, the Chipettes (Jeanette, Brittany and Eleanor). The series was changed to simply "The Chipmunks" during the 1988 season. *A Bagdasarian Production in association with DIC Enterprises. Color. Half–hour. Premiered on NBC: September 17, 1983–September 1, 1990.*

Voices:

David Seville: Ross Bagdasarian Jr., **Alvin:** Ross Bagdasarian Jr., **Simon:** Ross Bagdasarian Jr., **Theodore:** Janice Karman, **Jeanette:** Janice Karman, **Brittany:** Janice Karman, **Eleanor:** Janice Karman, **Miss Miller:** Dodie Goodman

Additional Voices:

Thom Watkins, Frank Welker, Julie McWhirter, Alan Young, Tress MacNeille, Ken Sansom, Phillip Clarke, Derek Barton

Episodes:

1983–1984 "The T. V. Stars," "The Cruise," "Uncle Harry," "Urban Chipmunk," "Unidentified Flying Chipmunk," "The Chipettes," "From Here To Fraternity," "Alvin . . . And The Chipmunk," "Swiss Family Chipmunks," "Mr. Fabulous," "Rock 'N' Robot," "Mother's Day," "Grandma And Grandpa Seville," "The Incredible Shrinking Dave," "The 'C' Team," "The Chipmunk Story" (Part 1), "The Chipmunk Story" (Part 2), "Bully Ballet," "The Chip–Punks," "The Trouble With Nanny," "Angelic Alvin," "Baseball Heroes," "May The Best Chipmunk Win," "A Dog's Best Friend Is His Chipmunk," "Santa Harry," and "The Curse Of Lontiki."

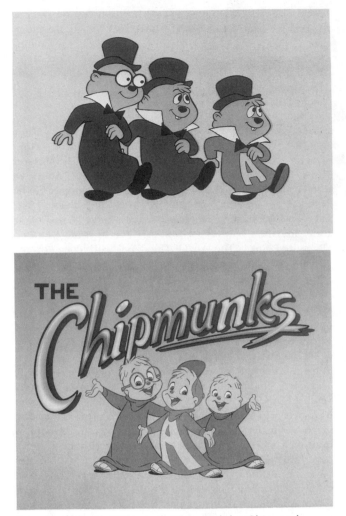

Popular record album stars Alvin and the Chipmunks, from the original 1960s series (top) and the 1980s series revival (bottom) for Saturday morning television. © Bagdasarian Productions/ Ruby–Spears Enterprises

1984–1985 "A Horse, Of Course," "Don't Be A Videot," "The Chipmunk Who Bugged Me," "Lights, Camera, Alvin," "Rich And Infamous," "The Camp Calomine Caper," "Guardian Chipmunks," "The Picture Of Health," "My Fair Chipette," "The Victrola Awards," "Royally Received," "Gone Fishin'," "Some Entrancing Evening," "Match Play," "Setting The Record Straight," "The Gang's All Here," "Father's Day Muffins," "Alvin On Ice," "Operation Theodore," "The Greatest Show–Offs On Earth," "New And Improved Simon," "Maids In Japan," "Snow Job," "Snow Wrong," "Hat Today, Gone Tomorrow" and "Carsick."
1985–1986 "Court Action," "A Chip Off The Old Tooth," "The Chipmunks Go To Washington," "Romancing Miss Stone," "Three Alarm Alvin," "Soccer To Me," "The Secret Life Of David Seville," "Film Flam," "Good Old Simon," "Sisters," "Who Ghost There?," "The Chipette Story," "A Little Worm In The Big Apple," "Every Chipmunk Tells A Story," "Staying Afloat," "The Prize Isn't Right," "The Gold Of My Dreams," "Mind Over Matterhorn" and "Alvin's Oldest Fan."

1986–1987 "A Rash Of Babies," "Help Wanted: Mommy" (Parts 1 and 2), "Miss Miller's Big Gamble," "Cinderella? Cinderella!" (Parts 1 and 2), "T. V. Or Not T. V.," "Experiment in Error," "Hooping It Up," "Whatever Happened To Dave Seville?," "Middle–Aged Davey," "Chipmunk Vice," "Sweet Smell Of Success," "Simon Seville Superstar," "How You Gonna Keep 'Em Down On The Farm?" and "I Love L.A."
1987–1988 "Back To Dave's Future," "Alvin, Alvin, Alvin!," "Sincerely, Theodore," "Simon Says," "My Pharaoh Lady," "When The Chips Are Down," "Dave's Dream Cabin," "Tell It To The Judge," "Ask Alvin," "Old Friends," "Just One Of The Girls," "Mystery Of Seville Manor," "Theodore Lucks Out," "Big Dreams," "Going Down To Dixie" and "Island Fever."
1988–1989 "The Brunch Club," "Chipmunkmania," "Dreamlighting," "Food For Thought," "Elementary, My Dear Simon," "Alvin In Analysis," "Wings Over Siesta Grande," "Treasure Island," "Grounded Chipmunk," "Cadet's Revenge," "Alvey's Angels," "Dave's Getting Married" (first cartoon under new series title, "The Chipmunks"), "Quarterback In Curlers," "Going For Broke," "Amazing Chipmunks," "No Chipmunk Is An Island," "Babysitter Fright Night," "Special Kind Of Champion," "The Wall," "Queen Of The High School Ballroom," "The Phantom," "Psychic Alvin," "Dave's Wonderful Life," "Uncle Adventure," "Once Upon A Crime," "Alvin's Not So Super Hero," "Mad About Alvin," "Alvin's Obsession," "Theodore And Juliet," "Theodore's Life As A Dog," "Luck O' The Chipmunks" and "Vinny's Visit."
1989–1990 "Cookie Chomper III," "Merry Christmas, Mr. Carrol," "Nightmare On Seville Street," "A Day In The Life," "All Worked Up," "Unfair Science," "Shaking The Family Tree," "Hearts And Mr. Flowers," "The Maltese Chipmunk," "Inner Dave," "Thinking Cap Trap," "Dr. Simon And Mr. Heartthrob," "Phantom Of The Rock Opera," "Like Father, Like Son," "Bye, George," "Too Hip To Be Dave," "Three Chipmunks And A Puppy," "The Return Of Uncle Adventure," "Dear Diary," "The Legend Of Sleeping Brittany," "Home, Sweet Home," "Princess And The Pig" and "Alvin In Neverland."

THE ALVIN SHOW

Popular recording stars, the Chipmunks (Alvin, Theodore and Simon) and their writer–manager, David Seville, starred in this weekly half–hour cartoon series. Following ABC's introduction of two prime–time cartoon programs in 1960, "Bugs Bunny" and "The Flintstones," CBS followed suit in 1961 with the Chipmunks.

The series combined three Chipmunk episodes every week, two of which were sing–a–long segments built around their songs, and another sequence featuring "The Adventures of Clyde Crashcup," a wacky inventor who took credit for inventing everything, accompanied by his whispering, bald–domed assistant, Leonardo.

Although the series performed poorly in prime time (it was opposite "Wagon Train"), interest in these lovable characters reached a fever pitch. Dolls, hand puppets, bubble bath and other merchandise soon appeared in stores, as well as several Chipmunk record albums which went gold and platinum.

Songwriter Ross Bagdasarian, who adopted the pseudonym of David Seville in real life, created and supplied the voice of all four characters: Alvin, the egotistical, girl–loving leader; Theodore, the faithful, giggling follower; Simon, the intelligent, bespectacled bookworm always dragged into trouble by his brothers; and David Seville, the Chipmunks' peacemaking manager whose temper was easily drawn out by Alvin's excessive mischief ("Aaaalllviiinn!").

In 1958, after Bagdasarian first employed a recording technique of "speeding up" the voices (voices recorded at a slow speed then played back twice as fast) to record his first hit record, "Witch Doctor," the Chipmunks were born. Using this technique, he introduced the squirrely foursome that same year with their first record, "The Chipmunk Song," which sold more than five million copies seven weeks after its release.

Bagdasarian deserves no credit for giving the group its name, however. His children, Carol, Ross, Jr. and Adam, are the ones responsible for naming the characters. After hearing sound recordings, they told their father the voices sounded like chipmunks to them (until then, he had planned to make the characters rabbits or butterflies).

As for the characters' individual names, Bagdasarian reportedly named them after Liberty Records executives Al (Alvin) Bennett and Si (Simon) Warnoker and recording engineer Ted (Theodore) Keep. Liberty was the exclusive recording label for the Chipmunks songs.

CBS moved the series to Saturday mornings after its first season before it was cancelled. The series remained on television in syndication through the end of the summer of 1966, even though only one season of cartoons was made. NBC brought back the series in 1979 when the characters experienced a resurgence in popularity, appealing to a whole new generation of children. *A Format Films/Bagdasarian Film Corp. Production. Color. Half–hour. Premiered on CBS: October 14, 1961–September 12, 1962. Rebroadcast on NBC: February 17, 1979–September 1, 1979.*

Voices:

David Seville: Ross Bagdasarian, **The Chipmunks:** Ross Bagdasarian, **Clyde Crashcup:** Shepard Menken

Additional Voices:

June Foray, Lee Patrick, Bill Lee, William Sanford, Reg Dennis, Joe Besser

Episodes:

"Alvin And The Chipmunks" (two per show).
"Good Neighbor," "Ostrich," "Squares," "Sam Valiant: Private Nose," "Overworked Alvin," "Alvin's Curse," "Alvin's Alter Ego," "Stanley The Eagle," "Fancy," "Sam Valiant: Real Estate," "Dude Ranch," "Camping Trip," "Bentley Van Rolls," "The Whistler," "Love Sick Dave," "Jungle Rhythm," "Theodore's Dog," "Hillbilly Son," "Little League," "Eagle In Love," "Alvin's Studio," "Haunted House," "Sir Alvin," "Good Manners," "Eagle Music" and "Disc Jockey."
"Chipmunk Musical Segments."
"Buffalo Gals," "America The Beautiful," "Mexico: The Brave Chipmunks," "Yankee Doodle," "Italy—Oh Gondaliero," "I Wish I Could Speak French," "August Dear," "Working On The Railroad," "When Johnny Comes Marching Home," "Swanee River," "Old MacDonald Cha–Cha–Cha," "Switzerland: The Magic Mountain," "Japanese Banana," "The Pidgin English

Hula," "Stuck In Arabia," "I Wish I Had A Horse," "Chipmunk Fun," "Good Morning Song," "Alvin For President," "Home On The Range," "Witch Doctor," "Lilly Of Laguna," "Spain," "Row Your Boat," "Swing Low, Sweet Chariot," "Comin' Thru' The Rye," "Coming Around The Mountain," "Pop Goes The Weasel," "If You Love Me," "Maria From Madrid," "Alvin's Orchestra," "The Little Dog," "The Chipmunk Song," "Alvin's Harmonica," "Three Blind–Folded Mice," "Twinkle, Twinkle Little Star," "Clementine," "Sing A Goofy Song," "Daisy," "On Top Of Old Smokey," "Whistle While Your Work," "Ragtime Cowboy Joe," "My Wild Irish Rose," "The Band Played On," "Jeanie With The Light Brown Hair," "Funiculi–Funicula," "Git Along Little Doggies," "The Man On The Flying Trapeze," "Polly Wolly Doodle," "Down In The Valley," "The Alvin Twist" and "Strolling In The Park."
"The Adventures of Clyde Crashcup" (one per show).
"Clyde Crashcup Invents Jokes," "Self Preservation," "Clyde Crashcup Invents Glass," "Clyde Crashcup Invents The Chair," "Clyde Crashcup Invents The West," "Clyde Crashcup Invents Baseball," "Clyde Crashcup Invents The Bathtub," "Clyde Crashcup Invents The Wife," "Clyde Crashcup Invests Flight," "Clyde Crashcup Invents The Baby," "Clyde Crashcup Invents The Stove," "Clyde Crashcup Invents Music," "Clyde Crashcup Invents First Aid," "Clyde Crashcup Invents Electricity," "Clyde Crashcup Invents Egypt," "Clyde Crashcup Invents The Bed," "Clyde Crashcup Invents The Telephone," "Clyde Crashcup Invents Do–It–Yourself," "The Time Machine," "Clyde Crashcup Invents The Shoe," "Physical Fitness," "Clyde Crashcup Invents The Ship," "This Is Your Life, Clyde Crashcup," "The Birthday Party," "Clyde Crashcup Invents Self Defense" and "Clyde Crashcup Invents Craschcupland."

THE AMAZING CHAN AND THE CHAN CLAN

Fictional Chinese detective Charlie Chan, aided by his 10 children, combine comedy and adventure in crime investigations. Chan was voiced by actor Keye Luke, who portrayed the wise–monk, Master Po, on TV's "Kung Fu." *A Hanna–Barbera Production in association with Leisure Concepts Incorporated. Color. Half–hour. Premiered on CBS: September 9, 1972–September 22, 1974.*

Voices:

Charlie Chan: Keye Luke, **Henry:** Bob Ito, **Stanley:** Stephen Wong, Lennie Weinrib, **Suzie:** Virginia Ann Lee, Cherylene Lee, **Alan:** Brian Tochi, **Anne:** Leslie Kumamota, Jody Foster, **Tom:** Michael Takamoto, John Gunn, **Flip:** Jay Jay Jue, Gene Andrusco, **Nancy:** Beverly Kushida, **Mimi:** Leslie Juwai, Cherylene Lee, **Scooter:** Robin Toma, Michael Morgan, **Chu–Chu, the dog:** Don Messick

Additional Voices:

Lisa Gerritsen, Hazel Shermit, Janet Waldo, Len Wood

Episodes:

"The Crown Jewel Caper," "Eye Of The Idol," "Will The Real Charlie Chan Please Stand Up!," "The Phantom Sea Thief," "To Catch A Pitcher," "The Fat Lady Caper," "Captain Kidd's Doubloons," "Double Trouble," "The Great Illusion Caper,"

"The Bronze Idol," "The Mummy's Tomb," "The Mardi Gras Caper," "The Gypsie Caper," "The Greek Caper," "White Elephant" and "Scotland Yard."

THE AMAZING THREE

First released in Japan as "W 3"—meaning "Wonder Three"— this Japanese–made series was edited and dubbed by Joe Oriolo Productions for syndication in America. The plotline involved three outer space aliens sent to Earth by the Galactic Congress to determine whether the "warlike planet" should be destroyed for the purpose of preserving universal peace. In disguise, the trio—Bonnie (a rabbit), Ronnie (a horse) and Zero (a duck with a Beatle haircut)—make their intentions known to a young Earthling, Kenny Carter, who befriends them and helps them in their fight against evil. Japanese cartoon legend Osamu Tezuka, best remembered for inventing "Astro Boy," created and produced the series. *A Mushi Productions. Color. Half–hour. Syndicated: September, 1967. Voice credits unknown. Episode titles unknown.*

AMIGO AND FRIENDS

A friend from across the border, Spanish–speaking Amigo takes children on educational and entertaining adventures involving a variety of themes, from the pyramids to Shakespeare to electricity to life on the moon. Hanna–Barbera Productions created this refreshingly innovative, 52–episode series which was syndicated and distributed in the United States. The series was also dubbed into Spanish, French, German, Mandarin and Hebrew and exported to other countries, including Spain, Hungary, Czechoslovakia and Mexico. *A Televisa, S. A. Production in association with Hanna–Barbera Productions. Color. Half–hour. Premiered: 1980. Syndicated.*

Voices:
Amigo: Don Messick, **Narrator:** John Stephenson

Episodes:
1980–1981 (four episodes per show) "The Constellations," "Alexander Graham Bell," "Little Amigo Meets King Tut," "Soccer," "Little Amigo Meets Don Quixote," "Little Amigo Meets Pablo Picasso," "Little Amigo Meets Statue Of Liberty," "Tennis," "Little Amigo Meets Daniel Boone," "Little Amigo Meets Henry Ford," "Canals Of Venice," "Baseball" and "Simon Bolivar."
1981–1982 "The Pyramids," "The Milky Way," "The Nile," "The Great Wall Of China," "The International Dateline," "Mt. Everest," "The State Of Vatican City," "The Tower Of London," "The Planets," "Notre Dame," "The Eiffel Tower," "The Parthenon," "The Sun," "Lost City Of Atlantis," "The Amazon," "The Colosseum," "Yosmite," "Atomic Energy," "Grand Canyon," "The Wailing Wall," "The Universe," "Safety Tips," "Father Junipero Serra," "Captain Cook," "James Watt," "Eli Whitney And The Cotton Gin," "Julius Caesar," "Lewis And Clark," "Michelangelo," "Mont Saint Michel," "George Washington Carver," "Madame Curie," "The Game Of Rugby," "Amerigo Vespucci," "Rembrandt," "Genghis Kahn," "The Golf Story," "Yellowstone Park" and "Luther Burbank."

ANIMATOONS

Well–known fairy tales and original children's stories were brought to life in this educational and entertaining series designed to encourage development of verbal skills, vocabulary and creative expression in children. The series was distributed with teacher's guides recapping each story or moral and was highly endorsed by parents and teachers throughout the country. *An Animatoons Production in association with Language Arts Films/Radio and Television Packagers. Color. Half–hour. Syndicated: 1967.*

Voices:
Narrator: Nancy Berg

Episodes:
"Mario And The Marvelous Gift," "The Rivals," "The Lost Sun," "Peter And The Wolf," "Goldilocks And The Three Bears," "The Sheperd's Hat," "The Haunted Mill," "Alexander And The Sleep People," "The Enchanted Cranes," "The Good Little Gremlin," "High Hill," "The Useless Jug," "The Great Detective," "The Adventures of Candy The Squirrel," "Ali Baba And The Forty Thieves," "The Dragon," "The Four Coins," "The First Violin," "The Fearless Hunter," "The Shivering King," "The King's Secret," "Fox And Thrush," "The Apple," "The Magic Stick," "Bear Cub And River Inhabitant," "Mrs. Smith And Mrs. Jones," "Two Tails," "The Little Stork," "Orange Neck" and "The Little Bear On The Road."

AQUAMAN

Born in Atlantis, Aquaman, who rules the Seven Seas and water creatures through telepathic brain waves, protects his kingdom from intruders and possible destruction. This half–hour series repeated episodes which first appeared on "The Superman/Aquaman Hour," containing two of his adventures and one with guest superheroes, among them, Teen Titans, Flash, Hawkman, Green Lantern and Atom. *A Filmation Production. Color. Half–hour. Premiered on CBS: September 14, 1968–September 7, 1969.*

Voices:
Aquaman: Ted Knight, **Aqualad:** Jerry Dexter, **Mera:** Diana Maddox

Additional Voices:
Marvin Miller

Episodes:
"Aquaman" (two 7–minute episodes per show) "Menace Of The Black Manta," "Rampaging Reptile Men," "Return Of Nepto," "Fiery Invaders," "Sca Raiders," "War Of The Water Worlds," "Volcanic Monster," "Crimson Monster From Pink Pool," "Ice Dragon," "Deadly Drillers," "Vassa— Queen Of Mermen," "Microscopic Monster," "Onslaught Of The Octomen," "Treacherous Is The Torpedoman," "Satanic Saturnians," "Brain—Brave And Bold," "Where Lurks The Fisherman," "Mephistos Marine Marauders," "The Trio Of Terror," "The Torp, The Magneto, And The Claw," "Goliaths Of The Deep–Sea Gorge," "Sinister Sea Scamp," "Devil Fish," "The

Sea Scavengers," "In Captain 'Cuda's Clutches," "The Mirror–Man From Planet Imago," "The Sea Sorcerer," "The Sea Snares Of Captain Sly," "The Undersea Trojan Horse," "The Vicious Villainy Of Vassa," "Programmed For Destruction," "The War Of The Quatix And Bimphabs," "The Stickman Of Stygia," "Three Wishes To Trouble," "The Silver Sphere" and "The Old Man Of The Sea (To Catch A Fisherman)"

"Guest Superheroes" (one 7–minute episode per show).

"Between Two Armies" (Justice League of America), "Target Earth" (Justice League of America), "Bad Day On Black Mountain" (Justice League of America), "Invasion Of The Beetle People" (Atom), "The Planet Machine" (Atom), "House Of Doom" (Atom), "The Monster Machine" (Teen Titans), "Monster Roundup" (Teen Titans), "Operation Rescue" (Teen Titans), "The Chemo Creature" (Flash), "Take A Giant Step" (Flash), "To Catch A Blue Bolt" (Flash), "Peril From Pluto" (Hawkman), "A Visit To Venus" (Hawkman), "The Twenty–Third Dimension" (Hawkman), "Evil Is As Evil Does" (Green Lantern), "The Vanishing World" (Green Lantern) and "Sirena—Empress Of Evil" (Green Lantern).

THE ARCHIE COMEDY HOUR

In response to first season ratings success of "The Archie Show," CBS brought back creator Bob Montana's "Archie" comic book characters in an hour–long series featuring musical numbers and further adventures of the gang. Another series component was Sabrina, the Teenage Witch, whose popularity later spawned a spin–off series of her own. *A Filmation Production. Color. One hour. Premiered on CBS: September 13, 1969–September 5, 1970.*

Voices:

Archie Andrews: Dallas McKennon, **Jughead Jones:** Howard Morris, **Betty Cooper:** Jane Webb, **Veronica Lodge:** Jane Webb, **Reggie Mantle:** John Erwin, **Sabrina, the Teenage Witch:** Jane Webb, **Big Moose:** Howard Morris, **Big Ethel:** Jane Webb, **Carlos:** Jose Flores

ARCHIE'S BANG–SHANG LALAPALOOZA SHOW

Archie and his regular cohorts, Jughead, Betty, Veronica and Reggie, share the blame as they encounter new situations in the city of Riverdale in this shortened and retitled version of "The New Archie/Sabrina Hour." The program also featured the adventures of Sabrina, the Teenage Witch, who inspired her own Saturday–morning cartoon shows. *A Filmation Production. Color. Half–hour. Premiered on NBC: November 26, 1977–January 28, 1978.*

Voices:

Archie Andrews: Dallas McKennon, **Jughead Jones:** Howard Morris, **Betty Cooper:** Jane Webb, **Veronica Lodge:** Jane Webb, **Reggie Mantle:** John Erwin, **Big Moose:** Howard Morris, **Big Ethel:** Jane Webb, **Carlos:** Jose Flores, **Mr. Weatherbee:** Dallas McKennon, **Miss Grundy:** Jane Webb, **Sabrina, the Teenage Witch:** Jane Webb

ARCHIE'S FUNHOUSE

Assisted by a Giant Juke Box, Archie and the gang play favorite dance numbers and perform sketches in a music–comedy–variety show format that mixed live footage of a studio audience comprised of children responding to the skits, jokes and other comedy vignettes which made up the show. The series aired on Sunday mornings during the final season of its network run. *A Filmation Production. Color. Half–hour. Premiered on CBS: September 12, 1970–September 2, 1973.*

Voices:

Archie Andrews: Dallas McKennon, **Jughead Jones:** Howard Morris, **Betty Cooper:** Jane Webb, **Veronica Lodge:** Jane Webb, **Reggie Mantle:** John Erwin, **Big Moose:** Howard Morris, **Big Ethel:** Jane Webb, **Carlos:** Jose Flores, **Mr. Weatherbee:** Dallas McKennon, **Miss Grundy:** Jane Webb

THE ARCHIE SHOW

Perennial students Archie, Jughead, Betty, Reggie, Veronica and Sabrina cause scholastic havoc in the classrooms of Riverdale High School. Based on the "Archie" comic book by Bob Montana, the show comprised two 10–minute skits and a dance–of–the–week selection. *A Filmation Production. Color. Half–hour. Premiered on CBS: September 14, 1968–September 6, 1969.*

Voices:

Archie Andrews: Dallas McKennon, **Jughead Jones:** Howard Morris, **Betty Cooper:** Jane Webb, **Veronica Lodge:** Jane Webb, **Reggie Mantle:** John Erwin, **Sabrina, the Teenage Witch:** Jane Webb, **Big Moose:** Howard Morris, **Big Ethel:** Jane Webb, **Dilton:** Howard Morris, **Mr. Weatherbee:** Dallas McKennon, **Miss Grundy:** Jane Webb, **Carlos:** Jose Flores

Episodes:

(two per show) "The Added Distraction," "Who Is Afraid Of Reggie Wolf," "A Hard Day's Knight," "Chimp Off The Old

The Archies perform a dance–of–the–week selection on "The Archie Show." © The Archie Company. Permission granted for reprint by Filmation Studios

Block," "Beauty Is Only Fur Deep," "The Disappearing Act," "The Prize Winner," "The Circus," "Hot Rod Drag," "Jughead's Double," "The Great Marathon," "Field Trip," "Snow Business," "Anchor's Away," "Way–Out Like West," "Flying Saucers," "The Computer," "Jughead Simpson Jones," "Kids Day," "Par One," "PFC Hot Dog," "Groovy Ghosts," "Rocket Rock," "The Old Sea Dog," "Jughead's Girl," "Dilton's Folly," "Private Eye Jughead," "Strike Three," "Reggie's Cousin," "Cat Next Door," "The Jones Farm" and "Veronica's Veil."

ARCHIE'S TV FUNNIES

Following "Archie's Funhouse," CBS added this half–hour series to its 1971 fall Saturday–morning cartoon show lineup. This time around, Archie and his gang produce their own weekly television show featuring their favorite comic–strip stars, in addition to their own madcap adventures.

Nine popular comic strips were adapted into supporting segments of their own: "Dick Tracy," "Moon Mullins," "Smokey Stover," "Emmy Lou," "The Katzenjammer Kids," "Alley Oop," "Nancy Sluggo," "Here Come the Dropouts" and "Broom Hilda." The new episodes of Archie were later repeated with new opening and ending segments in 1973's "Everything's Archie" series. Meanwhile, "The Captain and the Kids," "Alley Ooop," "Nancy and Sluggo" and "Broom Hilda" were resurrected on NBC's "Fabulous Funnies." (No studio records exist of the episode titles or complete voice credits for these segments.) *A Filmation Production. Color. Half–hour. Premiered on CBS: September 11, 1971–September 1, 1973.*

Voices:
Archie Andrews: Dallas McKennon, **Jughead Jones:** Howard Morris, **Betty Cooper:** Jane Webb, **Veronica Lodge:** Jane Webb, **Reggie Mantle:** John Erwin, **Big Moose:** Howard Morris, **Big Ethel:** Jane Webb, **Carlos:** Jose Flores, **Mr. Weatherbee:** Dallas McKennon, **Miss Grundy:** Jane Webb, **Broom Hilda/Sluggo/Oola:** June Foray, **Hans Katzenjammer:** June Foray, **Fritz Katzenjammer:** June Foray, **Captain Katzenjammer/King Guzzle:** Alan Oppenheimer, **Alley Oop:** Bob Holt, **Nancy:** Jayne Hami

Episodes:
"Archie" (one per show).
"Escaped Hippo," "Flying Saucer," "Bank Robbery," "Wacky Races—Archie Style," "Air Circus," "The Ghost Of Swedlow Swamp," "Riverdale Talent Tournament," "Rodney Rinkydink," "Mount Riverdale," "Riverdale Super Store," "Edge Of The Night," "Riverdale Woods," "The Reggie Game," "Mom's Chicken Sickle Stand," "Our Town, Riverdale" and "Outside Interference."

AROUND THE WORLD IN 80 DAYS

Based on Jules Vernes' novel, the show is set in merry old England in 1872. Millionaire Phileas Fogg has just asked Lord Maze for the hand of his niece, Belinda, in marriage. Her uncle objects, unless Phileas first proves himself worthy of Belinda.

And so the great race is on. Maze presumptuously bets 20,000 pounds against Fogg's chances of traveling around the world in 80 days, but not without a double–cross. The evil Mister Fix is contracted by Maze to spoil Fogg's trip in the allotted time. *An Air Programs International Production. Color. Half–hour. Premiered on NBC: September 9, 1972– September 1, 1973. Syndicated.*

Voices:
Phileas Fogg: Alistair Duncan, **Jean Passepartout:** Ross Higgins, **Mister Fix:** Max Obinstein

ARTHUR AND THE SQUARE KNIGHTS OF THE ROUND TABLE

In Camelot, King Arthur's legendary square knights "protect" the royal crown of England. *An Air Programs International Production. Color. Half–hour. Premiered: 1968. Syndicated.*

ASTRO BOY

Based on one of Japan's most popular comic–strip and cartoon characters—known as Tetsuwam–Atom (The Mighty Atom)—this pint–sized android was brought to America by NBC Films, which syndicated the English–dubbed series in 1963. Like the original series, Astro Boy—his Americanized name—was a modern–looking crime fighter created by Dr. Boynton (Dr. Tenma in the Japanese version) of the Institute of Science, who sells the mechanical boy to a circus as a side–show attraction. Rescued by kindly Dr. Elefun (formerly Dr. Ochanomizu), Astro Boy uses his remarkable powers to defend justice and fight the galaxy's most fiendish villains: Phoenix Bird, Sphinx, Long Joan Floater, Crooked Fink, the Mist Men and Zero, the invisible.

In October, 1964, the popularity of Astroboy reached its zenith in America. Ratings for the action–packed series surpassed all three national network stations and all independent stations in New York. Astroboy received higher ratings than "Maverick," "Cheyenne," "Trails West" and "Superman." More people in New York watched Astroboy than watched the

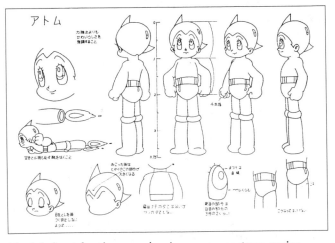

Model sheet for the popular Japanese cartoon series, "Astro Boy."

network news. In all, 104 episodes were broadcast in the United States (the episodic listing features only 103 known titles, translated in English). *A Mushi Productions. Black–and–white. Color. Half–hour. Premiered: September 7, 1963. Syndicated.*

Voices:

Astro Boy/Astro Girl: Billie Lou Watt, **Dr. Elefun:** Ray Owens

Episodes:

"The Birth of Astro Boy," "Colosso," "Expedition To Mars," "The Sphinx," "Cross Island," "Grass Boy," "Zero, The Invisible Robot," "Silver Comet," "Hullabaloo Land," "The Spirit Machine," "Strange Voyage," "The Artificial Sun," "The Deep Freeze," "One Million Mammoth Snails," "Gangor, The Monster," "Secret Agent 3–Z," "The Haunted Ship," "Time Machine," "The Cosmic Giant," "Toxor, The Mist Man," "Satellite R–45," "Sea Serpent Isle," "The Deadly Flies," "Kingdom Of The Sea," "The Strange Birthday Presents," "Don Tay's Infernal Machine," "Pearl People," "The Wacky Machine," "Memory Day," "The Super Duper Robot," "Mysterious Cosmic Rays," "The Moon Monsters," "The Three Magicians," "The Beast From 20 Fathoms," "Planet X," "The Elixir Of Life," "Astroboy Goes To School," "The Asteroid Menace," "The Mysterious Cat," "The Abominable Snowman," "Deadline To Danger," "The Island Of Mystery," "Ditto," "Cleopatra's Heart," "The Return Of Cleopatra," "Phantom Space Ship," "The Gigantic Space Crab," "The Great Space Horse," "3D Tee Vee," "Westward, Ha!," "Jimbo, The Great," "Snow Lion," "Dogma Palace," "The Man–Made Iceberg," "Vampire Vale," "The Terrible Tidal Wave," "Vikings," "The Devil Doll," "Dinosaur Dilemma," "The Clock Tower Mystery," "The Flower Monster," "Attack From Space," "Shipwreck In Space," "Big Titan," "Mission To The Middle Of The World," "Inca Gold Fever," "The Monster Machine," "The Holligan Whodunit," "Funnel To The Future," "Super Brain," "A Mighty Minute," "The Dream Machine," "The Robot Olympics," "Dunder, Bird Of Doom," "Dolphins In Distress," "The Mad Beltway," "The Terrible Time Gun," "Space Princess," "Mighty Microbe Army," "Horrible King Horrid," "Mystery Of Amless Dam," "Galon From Galaxy," "The Three Robotiers," "Brother Jetto," "Angel Of The Alps," "Magic Punch Card," "The Great Rocket Robbery," "Contest In Space," "Gift Of Zero," "A Deep, Deep Secret," "The Wonderful Christmas Present," "Uncharted World," "Jungle Mystery," "The Terrible Spaceman," "The Mighty Mite From URSA Minor," "General Astro," "Mystery Of Metalman," "Super Human Beings," "Phoenix Bird," "Menace From Mercury," "Dangerous Mission," "Planet 13" and "Prisoners In Space."

THE ASTRONUT SHOW

First seen in an episode of "Deputy Dawg" and in several theatrical cartoons from 1964–1965, this tiny, friendly alien from outer space was featured in his own half–hour series for syndication. In the late 1960s, the program contained the following components: "Hashimoto," "Sidney" and "Luno, the Flying Horse," each stars of their own theatrical film series. In the 1970s, Viacom, the program's distributor, reprogrammed the series with supporting episodes from other

Terrytoons' favorites: "Sad Cat," "Possible Possum" and "James Hound." *A Terrytoons Production. Color. Half–hour. Premiered: August 23, 1965. Syndicated.*

Voices:

Astronut: Dayton Allen, Lionel Wilson, Bob McFadden, **Oscar Mild,** his friend: Bob McFadden, **Hashimoto:** John Myhers, **Hanako,** his wife: John Myhers, **Yuriko:** John Myhers, **Saburo:** John Myhers, **Sidney,** the Elephant: Lionel Wilson, Dayton Allen, **Stanley,** the Lion: Dayton Allen, **Cleo,** the Giraffe: Dayton Allen, **Sad Cat:** Bob McFadden, **Gadmouse:** Bob McFadden, **Impressario:** Bob McFadden, **Letimore:** Bob McFadden, **Fenimore:** Bob McFadden, **Possible Possum:** Lionel Wilson, **Billy Bear:** Lionel Wilson, **Owlawishus Owl:** Lionel Wilson, **Macon Mouse:** Lionel Wilson, **James Hound:** Dayton Allen

Episodes:

"Astronut" (one per show).

"Brother From Outer Space," "Oscar's Moving Day," "The Kisser Plant," "Oscar's Birthday Present," "Outer Space Gazette," "Molecular Mixup," "Hokey Home Movies," "Twinkle, Twinkle, Little Telestar," "Weather Magic," "The Sky's The Limit," "Gems From Gemini," "Robots In Toyland," "Martian Moochers," "Oscar's Thinking Cap," "Jolly Jupiter," "The Invisibeam," "The Proton Pulsator," "Space Jet," "Scientific Sideshow," "No Space Like Home," "Haunted Housecleaning," "Movie Magic," "Balloon Snatcher," "Space Cowboy," "Martian Recipe" and "Going Ape."

"Hashimoto" (one per show).

"Hashimoto–San," "House Of Hashimoto," "So Sorry, Pussycat," "Night Life In Tokyo," "Honorable Cat Story," "Son Of Hashimoto," "Strange Companion," "Honorable House Cat," "Honorable Family Problem," "Loyal Royalty," "Honorable Paint In The Neck," "Pearl Crazy," "Tea House Mouse," "Cherry Blossom Festival," "Spooky–Yaki," "The Potter's Wheel Heel" and "Doll Festival."

"Sidney" (one per show).

"Sick, Sick Sidney," "Sidney's Family Tree," "Hide And Go Seek," "Tusk, Tusk," "The Littlest Bully," "Two–Ton Baby Sitter," "Banana Binge," "Meat, Drink, And Be Merry," "Really Big Act," "Clown Jewels," "Tree Spree," "Send Your Elephant To Camp," "Peanut Battle," "Fleet's Out," "To Be Or Not To Be," "Home Life," "Sidney's White Elephant," "Driven To Extraction" and "Split–Level Treehouse."

"Luno" (one per show).

"The Missing Genie," "Trouble In Baghdad," "Roc–A–Bye Sinbad," "King Rounder," "Who's Dragon," "The Gold Dust Bandit," "Melvin The Magnificent," "Adventure By The Sea," "The Poor Pirate," "The Square Planet," "The Flying Chariot," "Jungle Jack," "Mixed Up Matador," "Island Of The Giants," "King Neptune's Castle" and "The Prehysteric Inventor."

"Sad Cat" (one per show).

"The Apprentice Good Fairy," "Don't Spill The Beans," "The Third Musketeer," "Dress Reversal," "Scuba Duba Doo," "Dribble Drabble," "Judo Kudos," "Grand Prix Winner," "All Teed Off," "Big Game Fishing," "Commander Great Guy," "The Abominable Mountaineers," and "Loops And Swoops."

"Possible Possum" (one per show).

"Freight Fright," "Darn Barn," "The Pickle Pirate," "Kooky

Cucumbers," "Black And Blue Jay," "Hobo Hassle," "Southern Super Market," "Don't Burro Trouble," "Happy Hollow Hay Ride," "Watch Me Butterfly," "Findin' The Phantom," "The Bold Eagle," "Surface Surf Aces," "Trestle Hassle," "Happy Hollow Turkey Shoot," "Swamp Water Taffy," "Rootin' Tootin' Pumpkin Lootin'," "The Red Swamp Fox," "Popcorn Pachers," "Snowboat Showoff," "Git That Guitar," "Slinky Mink," "The Toothless Beaver," "Big Bad Bobcat," "Berry Funny," "Friendship," "Big Mo," "The Chestnut Nut," "Sleep Slip Up," "The General's Little Helpers," "The Rock Hound," "Mount Piney," "Pirate Plunder Blunder," "Surprisin' Exercisin'," "Swamp Snapper," "Harm Sweet Home" and "The Steel Stealer."
"James Hound" (one per show).
"Give Me Liberty," "Dr. Ha Ha," "Dream Napping," "Rain Drain," "Fancy Plants," "Mr. Winlucky," "The Monster Maker," "The Phantom Skyscraper," "A Voodoo Spell," "The Heat's Off," "Bugged By A Bug," "Dr. Rhinestone's Theory," "Baron Von Go–Go," "Which Is Witch?," "Frozen Sprarklers," "It's For The Birds" and "Traffic Trouble."

THE ATOM ANT/SECRET SQUIRREL SHOW

Essentially two half–hour programs combined, "The Atom Ant/Secret Squirrel Show" was a one–hour block of cartoons comprised of two main stars and their supporting regulars. Atom Ant, a superhero ant, starred in his action episodes, followed by "The Hillbilly Bears," the rustic adventures of an idiotic backwoods family, and "Precious Pup," a troublesome, snickering hound who fools his kindly millionairess owner (Granny Sweet) into thinking he's faithful, obedient and "precious."

Trench–coated Secret Squirrel, a parody of Ian Fleming's James Bond, was the series' other main star. Along with his partner Morocco Mole (who sounded like Peter Lorre), the ever–clever squirrel encountered danger in assignments throughout the world. The cartoon components for this half of the show were "Squiddly Diddly," a star–struck squid who hopes to break into show business, and "Winsome Witch," a good–natured witch who uses her evil sorcery to perform good deeds.

To promote the new Saturday–morning series, NBC broadcast a special hour–long preview on September 12, 1965, entitled, "The World of Secret Squirrel and Atom Ant." In January, 1967, the network separated the two half–hour entities and programmed them independently. (See "The Atom Ant Show" and "The Secret Squirrel Show.") The two series were again merged under the old title and format in the fall of that year. *A Hanna–Barbera Production. Color. One hour. Premiered on NBC: October 2, 1965–January, 1967. Rebroadcast on NBC: September 9, 1967–September 7, 1968.*

Voices:

Atom Ant: Howard Morris, Don Messick, **Secret Squirrel:** Mel Blanc, **Morocco Mole:** Paul Frees, **The Hillbilly Bears: Paw Rugg:** Henry Corden, **Maw Rugg/Floral Rugg:** Jean VanderPyl, **Shag Rugg:** Don Messick, **Precious Pup: Precious Pup:** Don Messick, **Granny Sweet:** Janet Waldo, **Squiddly Diddly: Squiddly Diddly:** Paul Frees, **Chief Winchley:** John Stephenson, **Winsome Witch:** Jean VanderPyl

Episodes:

"Atom Ant" (two per show).
1965–1966 "Up And Atom," "Crankenshaft's Monster," "Gem–A–Go–Go," "Ferocious Flea," "Rambling Robot," "Nobody's Fool," "Atom Ant Meets Karate Ant," "Fastest Ant In The West," "Mistaken Identity," "How Now Bow Wow," "Dragon Master," "The Big Gimmick," "Super Blooper," "Wild, Wild Ants," "Dina–Sore," "Amusement Park Amazement," "Bully For Atom Ant," "Termighty Mean," "Nine Strikes You're Out" and "Go West, Young Ant."
1966–1967 "Pteraducktyl Soup," "Up In The Air Squares," "Mouse–Rouser," "Knight–Fight," "Killer Diller Gorilla" and "Rock–A–Bye Boo Boo."
"Hillbilly Bears" (one per show).
1965–1966 "Woodpecked," "Goldilocks And The Four Bears," "Detour For Sure," "Stranger Than Friction," "Anglers Aweigh," "Going, Going Gone Gopher," "Courtin' Disaster," "Picnic Panicked," "Judo Kudos," "Just Plane Around," "War Games," "Bricker Brats," "Slap Happy Grandpappy," "Do The Bear," "Pooped Pops," "Leaky Creek," "My Fair Hillbilly," "Rickety–Rockety–Raccoon," "Modern Inconvenience" and "Rabbit Rumble."
1966–1967 "Speckled Heckler," "Whirly Bear," "Saucy Saucers," "Chipper Chirper," "Gettin' Paw's Goat" and "Buzzin' Cuzzins."
"Precious Pup" (one per show).
1965–1966 "Precious Jewels," "Doggone Dognapper," "Bites And Gripes," "Queen Of The Road," "Crook Out Cook Out," "Next Of Kin," "Bowling Pinned," "Poodle Pandemonium," "Dog Tracks," "Sub–Marooned," "Lady Bugged," "Test In The West," "Bones And Groans," "Girl Whirl," "Butterfly Net," "Precious' Bone," "The Bird Watcher," "Dog Trained," "Oliver Twisted" and "Pup Skip And Jump."
1966–1967 "A Grapple For The Teacher," "Pot–Time Work," "A Fiend In Need," "Ski Sickness," "Mascot Massacre" and "A. M. Mayhem."
"Secret Squirrel" (two per show).
1965–1966 "Yellow Pinkie," "Wolf In Cheap Cheap Clothing," "Scotland Yard Caper," "Sub Swiper," "Royal Run Around," "Masked Granny," "Robin Hood And His Merry Muggs," "Five Is A Crowd," "It Stopped Training," "Wacky Secret Weapon," "Cuckoo Clock Cuckoo," "Catty Cornered," "Leave Wheel Enough Alone," "Jester Minute," "Not So Idle Idol," "Gold Rushed," "Double Ex–Double Cross," "Captain Kidd's Not Kidding," "Tusk–Tusk" and "Bold Rush."
1966–1967 "Robot Rush," "Hi Spy," "The Pink Sky Mobile," "Scuba–Duba Duba," "Spy In The Sky" and "Ship Of Spies."
"Squiddly Diddly" (one per show).
1965–1966 "Way Out Squiddly," "Show Biz Squid," "The Canvas Back Squid," "Nervous Service," "Westward Ha," "Sea Grunt," "Chief Cook And Bottle Washer," "Squid On The Skids," "Double Trouble," "Squid Kid," "Booty And The Beast," "Clowning Around," "Surprise Prize," "Baby Squidder," "Naughty Astronaut," "The Ghost Is Clear," "Lucky Ducky," "Foxy Seal," "Squiddly Double Diddly" and "Hollywood Folly."
1966–1967 "One Black Knight," "Yo Ho Ho," "Phoney Fish," "Gnatman," "Robot Squid" and "Jewel Finger."
"Winsome Witch" (one per show).
1965–1966 "Have Broom Will Travel," "Prince Of A Pup," "Operation Broom Switch," "The Hansel And Gretel Case,"

"The Little Big League," "Schoolteacher Winnie," "Good Red Riding Hood," "Winnie's Baby," "How Now Cinderella," "Have Broom Will Zoom," "Winnie The Sheriff," "Welcome Wagging," "Shoo Spy," "Hollywood Or Busted," "Wolfcraft Vs. Witchcraft," "Tallyho The Hunter," "Witch Witch," "Ugly Duckling Trouble" and "Witch Witch Is Witch."
1966–1967 "Potluck," "Pussycat–Man," "Sheriff Winnie," "Wee Winnie Witch," "Sea–Dogged" and "Wild Wild Witch."

THE ATOM ANT SHOW

Atomized glasses transform a peek–eyed ant into the world's mightiest insect superhero in this Hanna–Barbera favorite. Other cartoons featured were "Precious Pupp" and "Hillbilly Bears." The series was first broadcast in combination with the adventures of Secret Squirrel as "The Atom Ant/Secret Squirrel Show." In January 1967, the two were separated and given their own shows, only to be rejoined again in the original format in September of that year. The series continued in this manner until it completed its network broadcast. (See "The Atom Ant/Secret Squirrel Show" for voice credits and episode listings.) *A Hanna–Barbera Production. Color. Half–hour. Premiered on NBC: January 1967–September 7, 1968.*

BABAR

That playful pachyderm who has delighted generations of young readers stars in this half–hour series which was broadcast on HBO following its original debut on Canada's CBC–TV. Flashbacks depict the mythical world of Babar, recounting his personal conflicts that arise when as a little boy he tries to juggle growing up along with handling the grown–up responsibilities of being a king. Each episode cost approximately $400,000 to animate. Laurent de Brunhoff, the son of Babar's creator, Jean de Brunhoff, authorized the series—the first weekly attempt at animating Babar—which was produced by the same studio responsible for 1989's *Babar: The Movie.* The series was the recipient of the cable industry's 1989 Ace Award for outstanding programming achievement. *A Nelvana Production in association with The Clifford Ross Company and the CBC. Color. Half–hour. Premiered on HBO: April 9, 1989.*

Voices:
Adult Babar: Gordon Pinsent, **Young Babar:** Gavin Magrath, **Celeste:** Tara Charendoff

Additional Voices: Stephen Ouimette, Chris Wiggins, John Stocker

Episodes:
"The Gift," "School Days," "Between Friends," "King Tuttle's Voice," "Peer Pressure," "Tour De Celesteville," "The Rhino War," "The Intruder," "Monkey Business," "Double The Guards," "The Elephant Express," "Conga The Terrible," "Remember When," "Special Delivery," "The Celesteville Enquirer," "To Tell Or Not To Tell," "Witch's Potion," "Fathers And Sons," "Uncle Arthur And The Pirates," "My Dinner With Rataxes," "The Coin," "A Charmed Life," "A Tale Of Two Siblings," "The Unsalted Sea Serpent," "Ghost For A Day" and "Boys Will Be Boys."

BAGGY PANTS AND NITWITS

Comedians Arte Johnson and Ruth Buzzi provide the voices for animated versions of their popular "Laugh–In" television characters, Tyrone and Gladys. Tyrone, a gray–haired, feeble man, is a crime–fighting superhero whose strength comes from his faithful cane, Elmo. Gladys, his female companion, guides Tyrone's efforts. Baggy Pants, a cat in Charlie Chaplin dress is featured in silent comedy routines. *A DePatie–Freleng Enterprises Production. Color. Half–hour. Premiered on NBC: September 11, 1977–September 2, 1978.*

Voices:
Tyrone: Arte Johnson, **Gladys,** his wife: Ruth Buzzi

Additional Voices:
Joan Gerber, Joe Besser, Frank Nelson

Episodes:
"Baggy Pants" (one per show).
"Construction Caper," "Lost Dog," "Hobo And Forgetful Freddy," "The Movie Man," "Circus Circus," "The Painter's Helper," "Electric Girlfriend," "A Pressing Job," "A Haunting Experience," "Horse Laff," "The Magician's Assistant," "The Frog" and "Beach Fun."
"The Nitwits" (one per show).
"Earthquake McBash," "The Dynamic Energy Robber," "Splish Splash," "The Hopeless Diamond Caper," "The Evil Father Nature," "Mercury Mike And His Jet Bike," "Rustle Hustle," "False Face Filbert," "Genie Meanie," "Chicken Lady," "Simple Simon And The Mad Pieman," "The Hole Thing!" and "Ratman!"

BAILEY'S COMETS

Comet members Barnaby, Bunny, Wheelie, Sarge and Pudge skate against 17 roller derby teams in a continuing race around the world in search of hidden treasure. Other teams included: The Black Hats, The Broomer Girls, The Cosmic Rays, The Doctor Jekyll/Hydes, The Duster Busters, The Gargantuan Giants, The Gusta Pastas, The Hairy Madden Red Eyes, The Mystery Mob, The Ramblin' Rivets, The Rock 'n' Rollers, The Roller Bears, The Roller Coasters, The Stone Rollers, The Texas Flycats and The Yo Ho Hos. Created by Joe Ruby and Ken Spears, the series lasted four months into the first Saturday morning season before it was shifted to Sunday mornings for the completion of its network run. *A DePatie–Freleng Enterprises Production. Color. Half–hour. Premiered on CBS: September 9, 1973–August 31, 1975.*

Voices:
Barnaby Bailey: Carl Esser, **Pudge:** Frank Welker, **Wheelie:** Jim Begg, **Candy:** Karen Smith, **Bunny:** Sarah Kennedy, **Sarge:** Kathi Gori, **Dude:** Robert Holt, **Dooter Roo:** Daws Butler, **Gabby:** Don Messick

Episodes:
(two per show) "Skateroo To The Carlsbad Clue!," "To Win Or Toulouse," "Rahja And Out," "Ghost Of A Clue," "Heading Home," "Roman Race Ruin," "Transylvania Mad Transit," "Phillipine Flip Flop," "Space Race," "Slow 'N' Go To Tokyo," "Lochness Mess," "Deep Blue Clue," "South American Slip

Up," "Goldfever Goof Up," "A Kooky Clue And A Mummy Too," "Kenya Catch That Clue," "An Abominable Clue," "Madagascar Mix–Up," "Bear Blunder Down Under," "Trans Turkey Fowl Up," "Amazon Jungle Bungle," "Swiss Swap Switch," "Hawaii Five Uh Oh," "Heidelberg Robot Hang Up," "Netherland Bouble Trouble," "Too Strong For Hong Kong," "A Doggone Danish Clue," "Hungarian Cluelosh," "Gobi Desert Goof Up," "Sargasso Sea You Later," "Fast Lap In Lapland" and "What's Buzzin' Canadian Cousin?"

THE BANANA SPLITS ADVENTURE HOUR

Live actors in animal suits—known as the Banana Splits (Fleegle, Drooper, Bingo and Snorky)—hosted this hour–long format comprised of their own misadventures, a live–action adventure series, "Danger Island," and four cartoon segments: "The Three Musketeers," "The Arabian Knights," "Hillbilly Bears" and "The Micro Venture." The program marked Hanna–Barbera's first live–action/animation show for television. For voice credits to the "Hillbilly Bears," see "The Atom Ant/Secret Squirrel Show." *A Hanna–Barbera Production. Color. One hour. Premiered on NBC: September 7, 1968–September 5, 1970.*

Voices:

Fleegle, the dog: Paul Winchell, **Drooper,** the lion: Allan Melvin, **Bingo,** the gorilla: Daws Butler, **Snorky,** the elephant: Don Messick, **The Three Musketeers: D'Artagan:** Bruce Watson, **Porthos:** Barney Phillips, **Aramis:** Don Messick, **Athos:** Jonathan Harris, **Toulie:** Teddy Eccles, **The Queen:** Julie Bennett, **Lady Constance:** Julie Bennett, **The Arabian Knights: Bez:** Henry Corden, **Evil Vangore:** Paul Frees, **Raseem:** Frank Gerstle, **Princess Nida:** Shari Lewis, **Prince Turhan:** Jay North, **Fariik:** John Stephenson, **The Micro Venture: Professor Carter:** Don Messick, **Jill Carter:** Patsy Garrett, **Mike Carter:** Tommy Cook, **Danger Island: Professor Irwin Hayden:** Frank Aletter, **Leslie Hayden:** Ronnie Troup, **Link Simmons:** Michael Vincent, **Morgan,** the castaway: Rockne Tarkington, **Chongo:** Kahana, **Mu–Tan:** Victor Eberg, **Chu:** Rodrigo Arrendondo

Episodes:

(The character Toulie was misspelled as "Tooly" in episode titles of this series.)

"The Arabian Knights" (one per show).

"The Ransom," "The Joining Of The Knights," "A Trap For Turham," "The Great Gold Robbery," "Isle Of Treachery," "The Wizard Of Ramnizar," "Sky Raiders Of The Desert," "The Sultan's Plot," "The Reluctant Empress," "The Challenge," "The Great Brass Beast," "The Coronation Of Bakaar," "The Desert Pirates," "The Royal Visitor," "The Spy," "The Fabulous Fair," "The Jewels Of Joowar" and "The Prisoner."

"The Micro Venture."

"Exploring An Ant Colony," "The Dangerous Desert," "The Backyard Jungle" and "The Tiny Sea."

"The Three Musketeers" (one per show).

"A Letter Of Peril," "The Red Duke," "The Littlest Musketeer," "The Moorish Galley," "The Jewel Of India," "The Ring," "The

Plot Of The Puppetmaster," "The Evil Falconer," "The Pirate Adventure," "The True King," "Tooly's Dream," "The Mysterious Message," "The Challenge Of The Crown," "The Outlaw Archer," "A Fair Day For Tooly," "The Haunted Castle," "Tooly's Surprise" and "Tooly's Treasure Hunt."

BARBAPAPA

Reminiscent of "The Smurfs," this Dutch import was originally marketed in the late 1970s by LBS (Lexington Broadcasting System). The program received exposure in this country following the success of LBS's other Dutch–produced series, "Dr. Snuggles." *A LBS Communications Presentation. Color. Half–hour. Premiere: 1981. Syndicated.*

BARKER BILL'S CARTOON SHOW

This first network weekday cartoon series served as a daily showcase for the vintage black–and–white films from the Terrytoons library. Sponsored by Post Sugar Jets, the 15–minute cartoon show was seen twice a week, with only the picture of the program's host seen on camera with an off–camera announcer providing the introductions of the animated films. Terrytoons characters featured on the show included Farmer Al Falfa, Kiko the Kangaroo, Puddy the Pup and others. In 1956, "Barker Bill's Cartoon Show" ended and was replaced by a syndicated program, "Terry Toons Club" (later retitled "Terry Toons Circus"), hosted by Claude Kirchner on WWOR–TV, New York.

That same year, creator Paul Terry sold his 1,400 *Terrytoons* to CBS for an estimated $3.5 million. Terrytoons continued as a division of CBS Films, distributing new cartoon releases to theaters and producing new programs for the network. *A Terrytoons Production. Black–and–White. Fifteen minutes. Premiered on CBS: November 18, 1953–November 25, 1956.*

THE BARKLEY'S

An outspoken, opinionated canine bus driver, Arnie Barkley (copied after TV's Archie Bunker), clashes with his progressive family over timeworn socially related topics. *A DePatie–Freleng Enterprises Production. Color. Half–hour. Premiered on NBC: September 9, 1972–September 1, 1973.*

Voices:

Arnie Barkley: Henry Corden, **Agnes,** his wife: Joan Gerber, **Terri,** Barkley's daughter: Julie McWhirter, **Chester,** the eldest son: Steve Lewis, **Roger,** the youngest son: Gene Andrusco

Additional Voices:

Frank Welker, Bob Hall, Don Messick, Bob Frank, Michael Bell

Episodes:

"The Match Breaker," "Finders Weepers," "Lib And Let Lib," "Half–Pint Hero," "No Place For A Lady," "For The Love Of Money," "Keeping Up With The Beagles," "Play No Favorites," "Law And Misorder," "The Great Disc Jockey," "Barkley Beware," "Arnie Come Clean" and "The Talent Agency Caper."

BATFINK

Called into action on a private hotline by the Chief of Police, this pointy–eared crime–fighter with wings of steel and Super Sonic Sonar foils ruthless criminals, mobsters and all–around bad guys, with the help of his Japanese assistant, Karate, in this animated parody of comic–book superhero, Batman. The series was created by former Fleischer animator Hal Seeger, who originated T.V.'s "Milton the Monster." *A Hal Seeger Production. Color. Half–hour. Premiered: Fall 1967. Syndicated.*

Voices:
Batfink: Frank Buxton, **Karate:** Len Maxwell

Episodes:
(five per show) "The Atom Boom," "The Backward Box," "The Baffling Bluffs Hugo–A–Go–Go," "Bat Patrol," "Batfink On The Rocks," "Batfink, This Is Your Life," "Beanstalk Jack," "The Beep–Booper," "Big Ears Ernie," "Blankenstein," "The Bomber Bird," "Bouncey Bouncey Batfink," "Bowl Brummel," "Brain Washday," "Bride And Doom," "Brother Goose," "Buster The Ruster," "The Chocolate Covered Diamond," "Cinderobber," "The Copycat Bat," "Crime College," "Crimes In Rhymes," "Curly The Cannonball," "Daniel Boom," "The Devilish Device," "Dig That Crazy Mountain," "The Dirty Sinker," "Double Double Crossers," "Ebenezer The Freezer," "Ego A–Go–Go," "Father Time Bombed," "Fatman Strikes Again," "Fleiderfink," "Gloves On The Go Go," "Gluey Louie," "Go Fly A Bat," "Goldstinger," "Goldyunlocks And The Three Bears," "Goo Goo A–Go–Go," "Greasy Gus," "The Great Escape," "Gypsy James," "Hugo For Mayor," "Hugo Here, Hugo There," "Hugo's Joke," "The Human Pretzel," "The Indian Taker," "Jerkules," "Judy Jitsu," "Jumping Jewelry," "The Kangaroobot," "The Kooky Chameleon," "The Living Doll," "The Mad Movie Maker," "Magneto The Magnificent," "Manhole Manny," "Mark Of Zero," "The Mean Green Midget," "Mike The Mimic," "MPFTBRM," "Mryon The Magician," "Napoleon Blown Apart," "Nuts Of The Round Table," "Old King Cruel," "Out Out Darn Spot," "Party Marty," "Pink Pearl Of Persia," "Presto–Change–O–Hugo," "Queenie Bee," "Ringading Brothers," "Robber Hood," "The Rotten Rainmaker," "Roz, The Schnozz," "Sandman Sam," "The Shady Shadow," "The Short Circuit Case," "Skinny Minnie," "Slow Down, Speed Up!," "The Sonic Boomer," "Spin The Batfink," "Sporty Morty," "Stupidman," "The Super Trap," "Swami Salami," "The Thief From Baghdad," "The Time Stopper," "Topsy Turvy," "Tough MacDuff," "The Trojan Horse Thief," "Unhappy Birthday," "Victor The Predictor," "Watch My Smoke," "Whip Van Winkle," "The Wishbone Boner," "Yo Yo A–Go–Go" and "The Zap Sap."

BATMAN AND THE SUPER 7

NBC broadcast this hour–long compendium of previous episodes of Filmation's "Batman and Robin," "Web Woman," "The Freedom Force," "Superstretch" and "Manta and Moray, Monarch of the Deep" cartoons, which originally aired as part of CBS' "Tarzan and the Super 7" series (See "Tarzan and the Super 7" for voice and episodic information.) *A Filmation Production. Color. One hour. Premiered on NBC: September 27, 1980–September 5, 1981.*

THE BATMAN/SUPERMAN HOUR

Well–known comic–book heroes, Superman and Batman, appear in separate segments of this Saturday–morning series. No stranger to television, the Man of Steel was previously featured on "The New Adventures of Superman" (1966–1967) and "The Superman/Aquaman Hour Of Adventure" (1967–1968). Episodes of Superman were repeated from the first series, while the Batman and Robin adventures were newly produced for television. (Episodes of the latter were rebroadcast as part of "The Adventures of Batman.") *A Filmation Production. Color. One hour. Premiered on CBS: September 14, 1968–September 6, 1969.*

Voices:
Clark Kent/Superman: Bud Collyer, **Lois Lane:** Joan Alexander, **Narrator:** Jackson Beck, **Bruce Wayne/Batman:** Olan Soule, **Dick Grayson/Robin:** Casey Kasem, **Alfred Pennyworth:** Olan Soule

Episodes:
"Superman" (three per show).
"The Chimp Who Made It Big," "The Saboteurs," "The Imp–Practical Joker," "Luthor Strikes Again," "Superman Meets Braniac," "The Deadly Fish," "The Prankster," "Menace Of The Lava Men," "The Iron Eater," "War Of The Bee Battalion," "The Return of Braniac," "The Wicked Warlock," "The Image Maker," "Two Faces Of Superman," "Merlin's Magic Marbles," "Invisible Raiders," "Malevolent Mummy," "Threat Of The Thrutans," "Three–Man Of Arbora," "Mission Of Planet Peril," "Mermen Of Emor," "The Lethal Lightening Bug," "Wisp Of Wickedness," "The Prehistoric Pterodactyls," "The Abominable Iceman," "Seed Of Disaster," "Neolithic Nightmare," "Superman Meets His Match—Almost," "The Deadly Icebergs," "The Pernicious Parasite," "The Toys Of Doom," "The Robot Of Riga," "Return Of The Warlock," "Ape Army Of The Amazon," "The Atomic Superman," "The Deadly Super–Doll," "The Fearful Force Phantom," "The Electro–Magnetic Monster," "The Insect Raiders," "The Warlock's Revenge," "The Men From A.P.E.," "The Frightful Fire Phantom," "The Halyah Of The Himalayas," "A.P.E. Strikes Again," "The Bird–Men From Lost Valley," "The Toyman's Super Toy," "Superman's Double Trouble," "Luthor's Loco Looking Glass," "The Night Of The Octopod," "The Cage Of Glass," "Braniac's Blue Bubbles" and "Luthor's Fatal Fireworks."
"Batman and Robin" (one per show).
"My Crime Is Your Crime," "The Cool Cruel Mr. Freeze," "How Many Herrings In A Wheel Barrow," "The Nine Lives Of Batman," "Bubi, Bubi, Who's got The Ruby," "Big Birthday Caper," "Partners In Peril," "Hizzoner The Joker (Joker For Mayor)," "The Crime Computer," "A Game Of Cat And Mouse," "Will The Real Robin Please Stand," "Simon The Pieman," "From Catwoman With Love," "A Perilous Pieman Is Simon," "The Fiendish Frigid Fraud," "The Jigsaw Jeopardy" and "It Takes Two To Make A Team."

THE BATMAN/TARZAN ADVENTURE HOUR

This hour–long fantasy/action series combined new adventures of famed caped crusaders, Batman and Robin, from 1977's "The New Adventures of Batman and Robin," and eight new episodes of Tarzan, mixed with reruns from his half–hour series, "Tarzan, Lord of the Jungle." *A Filmation Production. Color. One hour. Premiered on CBS: September 10, 1977–September 2, 1978.*

Voices:

Tarzan: Robert Ridgely, **Batman:** Adam West, **Robin:** Burt Ward, **Bat–Mite:** Lennie Weinrib

Episodes:

"Batman and Robin" (one per show).
"The Pest," "The Moonman," "Trouble Identity," "A Sweet Joke On Gotham City," "The Bermuda Rectangle," "Bite–Sized," "Reading, Writing and Wronging," "The Chameleon," "He Who Laughs last," "The Deep Freeze," "Dead Ringers," "Curses! Oiled Again!," "Birds Of A Feather Fool Around Together," "Have An Evil Day" (two parts) and "This Looks Like A Job For Bat–Mite!"
"Tarzan, Lord of the Jungle" (one per show).
"Tarzan And The Sunken City Of Atlantis," "Tarzan And The Bird People," "Tarzan And The Colossus Of Zome," "Tarzan And The Beast In The Iron Mask," "Tarzan And The Amazon Princess" and "Tarzan And The Conquistadors"

BATTLE OF THE PLANETS

G–Force, a superhuman watchdog squad—Jason, Tiny, Princess and Keyop—commanded by their daring leader Mark Venture, defend the Earth's galaxy from the ever–villainous Zoltar, the ruler of the dying planet Spectra, who has designs on overtaking the galaxy in this space–age adventure series. The first major Japanese import hit since "Speed Racer," the program was produced by Tasunko Productions, which also produced the latter. First televised in Japan from 1972–1974 under the title "Gatchaman," the program was retitled and dubbed by producer Sandy Frank who acquired the property for syndication in the United States. Since its American premiere, the series was repackaged by Ted Turner's Turner Entertainment Systems as "G–Force" and broadcast briefly on WTBS. *A Tasunko Productions. Color. Half–hour. Syndicated: October, 1978.*

Voices:

7–Zark–7/Keyop: Alan Young, **Zoltar:** Keye Luke, **Mark Venture,** Casey Kasem, **Princess:** Janet Waldo, **Jason:** Ronnie Schell, **Tiny/Dr. Anderson:** Alan Dinehart

Episodes:

"Attack Of The Space Terrapin," "Rescue Of The Astronauts," "The Space Mummy," "The Space Serpent," "Ghost Ship Of Planet Mir," "Big Robot Gold Grab," "Ace From Outer Space," "Fearful Sea Amenone," "The Jupiter Moon Menace," "A Swarm Of Robot Ants," "Space Rocket Escort," "Beast With A Sweet Tooth," "Perilous Pleasure Cruise," "The Thing With 1,000 Eyes," "Microfilm Mystery," "The Alien Beetles," "A Whale Joins G–Force," "Mad New Ruler Of Spectra," "The Sea Dragon," "Magnetic Attraction," "The Musical Mummy," "The Fiery Lava Giant," "The Bat–Ray Bombers," "Race Against Disaster," "The Ghostly Grasshopper," "The Galaxy Girls," "Curse Of The Cuttlefish" (Part 1), "Curse Of The Cuttlefish" (Part 2), "Demons Of The Desert," "Siege Of The Squids," "Orion, Wonderdog Of Space," "The Fierce Flowers" (Part 1), "The Fierce Flowers" (Part 2), "The Space Rock Concert," "Prisoners In Space," "Victims Of The Hawk," "Raid Of Riga," "Seals Of Sytron," "Giant Gila Monster," "The Capture Of The Galazy Code," "Raid On A Nearby Planet," "Keyop Does It All," "Peaks Of Planet Odin," "The Sky Is Falling!" (Part 1), "The Sky Is Falling!" (Part 2), "Raid Of The Red Scorpion," "Mammoth Shark Menace," "Fastest Gun In The Galaxy," "Giant From Planet Zyr," "Secret Island," "Giant Space Bat," "Attack Of The Alien Wasp," "Decoys Of Doom," "Zoltar Strikes Out," "The Great Brain Robbery," "Raid Of The Space Octopus," "Silent City," "Peril In The Pyramids," "Rage Of Robotoids," "The Alien Bigfoot," "Invasion Of The Locusts," "Space Safari," "Museum Of Mystery," "Peril Of The Preying Mantis," "The Awesome Ray Force," "The Duplicate King," "Defector To Spectra," "Panic Of The Peacock," "Mission To Inner Space," "Spectra Space Spider," "Super Space Spies," "Cupid Does It To Keyop," "Tentacles From Space," "Island Of Fear," "The Awesome Armadillo," "Invasion Of Space Center" (Part 1), "Invasion Of Space Center" (Part 2), "Save The Space Colony," "Charioteers Of Changu," "Vacation On Venus," "Rockets Out Of Control," "G–Force Defector," "Strike At Spectra," "G–Force In The Future" and "The Conway Tape Tap."

THE BEAGLES

This canine rock and roll duo, Stringer and Tubby (called "The Beagles"), croon their way in and out of trouble in this timely cartoon parody of Liverpool's Fab Four, The Beatles, who were riding the crest of their popularity when this series was produced. Featuring five–minute serialized adventures, the program was produced by the creators of TV's "Underdog" and "Tennessee Tuxedo." *A Total Television Production. Color. Half–hour. Premiered on CBS: September 10, 1966– September 2, 1967; ABC: September 9, 1967–September 7, 1968 (reruns). Voices unknown.*

Episodes:

"Ghosts, Ghouls And Fools" (1–2), "Dizzy Dishwashers" (3–6), "Drip, Drip, Drips" (7–10), "Tubby Troubles" (11–14), "I'm Gonna Capture You" (15–18), "Foreign Legion Flops" (19–22), "The Braves" (23–26), "Man In The Moon" (27–30), "Captain Of The Ship" (31–34) and "I Feel Like Humpty Dumpty" (35–36).

BEANY AND CECIL (1962)

Created by Bob Clampett, formerly an animator for Warner Brothers, the high–seas adventures of Cecil (the sea–sick serpent) and his friends Beany Boy and Captain Huffenpuff (Beany's uncle) evolved from a daily 15–minute puppet show

The cast of characters from Bob Clampett's original "Beany And Cecil" series. © Bob Clampett Productions

which was first broadcast in 1949 on Los Angeles television station, KTLA Channel 5. The show became so popular locally that Paramount Television picked up the series and offered it nationwide in 1950.

The show, which originated from Paramount Studios, was more than an ordinary puppet show; it was a continuing serial utilizing broad slapstick gags, and imaginative stories and characters unseen in the medium before. During its run, the show won three Emmy Awards and in 1962 the characters were transformed into a weekly animated series. (Many cartoons were actually produced three years earlier and released theatrically by United Artists to foreign countries only, including Canada and Australia.)

Sponsored by Mattel Toy Company, the show was first billed as "Matty's Funnies with Beany and Cecil." (After three months the program's title was appropriately shortened to "Beany and Cecil.") Each week, sailing on the "Leakin' Lena," Beany and company encountered a host of unusual characters along the way, such as Homer the Baseball Playing Octupuss, Careless the Mexican Hareless, Tear–a–Long the Dotted Lion, the Terrible Three–Headed Threep and the most dastardly, Dishonest John ("Nya–hah–hah!"), a series regular.

The cartoons became a particular favorite of many adults during its long run, including such surprising notables as Lionel Barrymore, Jimmy Stewart, Albert Einstein and Joan Crawford. (Groucho Marx, who was a fan of the puppet version, once told Clampett that 'Time for Beany' "is the only kid's show adult enough for my daughter Melinda to watch.")

Clampett admittedly drew from various influences to create each character. Captain Huffenpuff was based on a Baron Munchausen–type teller of tall tales. (Originally Clampett considered naming him Captain Hornblower.) Cecil was inspired by a 1920's silent feature Clampett remembered as a child, called "Lost World," featuring pre–historic dinosaurs. Beany was reminiscent of the precocious Charlie McCarthy, one of Clampett's personal favorites. And Dishonest John was patterned, in part, after one of Clampett's previous bosses at Warner Brothers, who he and his fellow animators affectionately called "Dirty Dalton."

Jim McGeorge lent his voice for Beany and Captain Huffenpuff, while Irv Shoemaker spoke for Cecil and Dishonest John. (Stan Freberg and Daws Butler did the voices during the first few years of the puppet show.)

Like many cartoons from this era, "Beany and Cecil" ran into censorship problems with the network. "It was rather ridiculous what the network would censor," Clampett once recalled. "They'd see a cartoon like 'Beanyland' and they'd say, 'Oh, you can't have that caricature of Walt Disney in there say, 'I'll make this my Dismal Land.' I'd say, 'Where's Disney in there? The character is Dishonest John and everybody knows who he is.' In another cartoon, it was the same thing. I had Dishonest John packaging the moon as cheese and bringing it back to Earth to sell it. On the package, I had the word 'Krafty' and ABC was afraid the Kraft Cheese Company would sue them."

One element of the series Clampett and his peers initially underestimated was the popularity of the trademark propellor cap worn by Beany. As Clampett once recalled in an interview prior to his death in 1984: "The funny thing about that is, when I first put the propellor on Beany's cap nearly everyone I showed the sketches to said, 'That would be funny for a one time use, but it will never wear well.' Their feelings were so unanimous that, for a short time, I switched to another type of cap before using my own intuition and going back to the propellor cap."

Following its prime–time run on ABC, the series remained on the network until 1968. The cartoons were then syndicated the following year by ABC Films. In the fall of 1989, the series was resyndicated in the United States, where it had been absent from the airwaves for more than a decade. (The series continued to be shown overseas, where it still plays in many markets.) In markets where the show premiered—Baltimore, Chicago, Houston, Dallas, Tampa, San Francisco and Boston— the program scored high ratings and refueled interest in the series nationwide. *A Bob Clampett Production. Color. Half–hour. Premiered on ABC: January 1962–December 1968. Syndicated: 1968–1976; 1989– .*

Voices:
Captain Huffenpuff: Jim McGeorge, **Beany Boy:** Jim McGeorge, **Cecil, the Sea-Sick Serpent:** Irv Shoemaker, **Dishonest John:** Irv Shoemaker

Episodes:
(four per show) "Beany And Cecil Meet Billy The Squid," "Beany's Buffalo Hunt," "The Phantom Horse Of The Opera," "Little Ace From Outer Space," "Beany Meets The Birds," "Super–Cecil," "Yo Ho And A Bubble Of Gum," "20,000 Little Leaguers Under The Sea," "The Dirty Birdy," "The Spots Off A Leopard," "The Vil Vast Vasteland," "The Greatest Schmoe On Earth," "Thunderbolt The Wondercolt," "Davey Crickett," "Invasion Of Earth By Robots," "Beany And Jackstalk," "Custard's Last Stand," "The Wildman Of Wildsville," "Beanyland," "The Illegal Eagle Egg," "A Trip To Schmoon," "The Indiscreet Squeet," "The Capture Of Ping Pong," "The Attack Of The Man Eater Skeeters," "Tommy Hawk," "The Warring 20s," "Sleeping Beauty And The Beast," "Cecil Meets The Singing Dinosaur," "The Capture Of Tear–A–Long The Dotted Lion," "Here Comes The Schmoeboat," "Ben Hare," "The Humbug," "The Seventh Voyage Of Singood," "Cecil Meets Cecilia," "Thumb Fun," "Dirty Pool," "The Rat Race For Space," "Madd Isle Of Madhattan," "Rin–Tin–Can," "Strange Objects," "Beany And Cecil Meet The Invisible Man," "Beany Flips His Lid," "The Fleastone Kop Kaper," "Beany Blows His Top," "The Dreaded Three–Headed Threep," "A Hero By Trade," "Buffalo Billy," "The Invisibile Man Has Butterfingers," "Grime Doesn't Pay," "Never Eat Quackers In Bed," "Cecil Gets Careless," "Dishonest John Meets Cowboy Starr," "Ain't I A Little Stinger?," "Hare Today, Gone Tomorrow," "Beany's Beany–Cap Copter," "Cecil Always Saves The Day," "Davey Crickett's Leading Lady–Bug," "Malice In Blunderland," "Ain't That A Cork In The Snorkle?," "A Living Doll," "'Taint Crickett, Crickett," "Ten Foot Tall And Wet," "Wot The Heck," "Cecil's Comical Strip," "Cheery Cheery Beany," "Hare–Cules And The Golden Fleecing," "D. J. The Dee Jay," "Dragon Train," "Makes A Sea Serpent Sore," "Beany's Resid-Jewels," "The Hammy Awards," "Cecil's Scrape-Book," "The Singin' Swingin' Sea Serpent," "Nye Ha Ha!," "There Goes A Good Squid," and "There's No Such Thing As A Sea Serpent."

BEANY AND CECIL (1988)

In the fall of 1988, Bob Clampett's "Beany and Cecil" characters were featured in this short–lived series revival, this time poking fun at the 1980's culture and themes. Broadcast in a 7:00 A.M. time slot by ABC, the program was cancelled after only five episodes aired. *A Bob Clampett Production in association with DIC Enterprises. Color. Half–hour. Premiered on ABC: September 10, 1988–October 8, 1988.*

Voices:
Beany Boy: Mark Hildreth, **Cecil,** the Sea–Sick Serpent: Billy West, **Captain Huffenpuff:** Jim McGeorge, **Dishonest John:** Maurice La Marche

Episodes:
(two episodes per show except pilot) "Framed Freep" (pilot), "Radio With A Bite," "Brotherhood Of Blech," "Bad Guy Flu," "D. J.'s Disappearing Act," "Cecil Meets Clambo," "The Golden Menu," "Monsterous Monster" (episode from original series) and "Courtship Of Cecelia."

THE BEATLES

Throughout the 1960s, these mop–headed musicians (better known as John, Paul, George and Ringo) dominated the musical scene like no other group. Their music landed them atop national record charts and on several major television shows, including "The Ed Sullivan Show," wowing teenagers throughout America in the process. The group's success also inspired a weekly animated cartoon series.

Produced in 1965, the series came about through the efforts of producer Al Brodax at King Features after he was approached by an ABC executive with the idea of producing "a Beatles cartoon." Famous toymaker A. C. Gilmer, who envisioned a merchandising goldmine, financed the series.

Premiering on ABC on Saturday, September 25, 1965, at 10:30 A.M., the show was an instant ratings hit. It racked up a 13 score (or 52 share), then unheard of in daytime television. Each half–hour show consisted of two sing–a–longs, emceed by the Beatles. (Lyrics were flashed on the screen so viewers could join in.) The first episodes aired were "I Want to Hold Your Hand" and "A Hard Day's Night."

Besides two weekly cartoons, the Beatles cartoon show was famous for its clever bridges between episodes and commercials. These included dry, comic vignettes, such as Ringo buying a newspaper from a street vendor and getting hit by a car, only to complain afterwards, "There's not a word in here (in the paper) about me accident!"

The voices of the Beatles' cartoon lookalikes were supplied by two voice actors, Paul Frees (John and George) and Lance Percival (Paul and Ringo). Animation was sent overseas (TVC of London, which produced the Beatles cult feature, *The Yellow Submarine,* and Astransa, an Australian company, did the bulk of the animation) and scripts were turned out rather easily since episodes were based on popular Beatles songs.

"It took about four weeks to animate each film and I enjoyed it immensely," recalled Chris Cuddington, a series animator. "The characters were easy to draw, and the stories were simple and uncomplicated."

Following the first season's success, Brodax considered producing four Beatles prime–time animated specials. But plans to produce them and several other musical–based cartoon series—animated versions of Herman's Hermits and Freddie and the Dreamers—never fully materialized.

The Beatles remained on ABC for three more years, the final two seasons being reruns of original cartoons. The series lost ground during its second season after it was slated opposite CBS' "Space Ghost," part of a powerful Saturday morning lineup which included "Frankenstein Jr. and the Impossibles," "Mighty Mouse" and "The Mighty Heroes." ("Space Ghost" won the time slot with a 9.6, 44 share, while the Beatles slid into second with 7.6, 36 share.)

In the fall of 1968, the series was moved to Sunday mornings where it remained until its final broadcast in 1969. *A King Features Production. Color. Half–hour. Premiered on ABC: September 25, 1965–September 7, 1969. Syndicated.*

Voices:

John Lennon: Paul Frees, **Ringo Starr:** Lance Percival, **George Harrison:** Paul Frees, **Paul McCartney:** Lance Percival

Episodes:

(two per show) "A Hard Day's Night," "I Want To Hold Your Hand," "Do You Want To Know A Secret," "If I Fell," "Please, Mr. Postman," "Devil In Her Heart," "Not A Second Time,"

Paul, George and John enjoy Ringo's appearance on television in "The Beatles" cartoon series, featuring actual recordings of the famed Liverpool musicians. © King Features Entertainment

"Slow Down," "Baby's In Black," "Misery," "You've Really Got A Hold On Me," "Chains," "I'll Get You," "Honey, Don't," "Any Time At All," "Twist And Shout," "Little Child," "I'll Be Back," "Long Tall Sally," "I'll Cry Instead," "I'll Follow The Sun," "When I Get Home," "Everybody's Trying To Be My Baby," "I Should Have Known Better," "I Wanna Be Your Man," "I'm A Loser," "Don't Bother Me," "No Reply," "I'm Happy Just To Dance With You," "Mr. Moonlight," "Can't Buy Me Love," "It Won't Be Long," "Anna," "I Don't Wanna Spoil The Party," "Matchbox," "Thank You Girl," "From Me To You," "Boys," "Dizzy Miss Lizzy," "I Saw Her Standing There," "What You're Doing," "Money," "Komm Gib Mir Deine Hand," "She Loves You," "Bad Boy," "Tell Me Why," "I Feel Fine," "Hold Me Tight," "Please Please Me," "There's A Place," "Roll Over, Beethoven," "Rock And Roll Music," "Eight Days A Week," "I'm Looking Thru You," "Help," "We Can Work It Out," "I'm Down," "Run For Your Life," "Drive My Car," "Tell Me What You See," "I Call Your Name," "The Word," "All My Loving," "Day Tripper," "Nowhere Man," "Paperback Writer," "Penny Lane," "Strawberry Fields," "And Your Bird Can Sing," "Got To Get You Into My Life," "Good Day Sunshine," "Ticket To Ride," "Taxman," "Eleanor Rigby," "Tomorrow Never Knows," "I've Just Seen A Face," "Wait" and "I'm Only Sleeping."

BEETLEJUICE

Based on the characters from director Tim Burton's hit movie of the same name, this weekly animated series tells the story of an eccentric con–artist and his relationship with a 12–year–old Earth girl (Lydia Deetz) that centers around the surrealistic adventures in the Neitherworld, the place where Beetlejuice resides. *A Warner Brothers/Nelvana Production in association with The Geffen Film Company and Tim Burton Inc. Color. Half–hour. Premiered on ABC: September 9, 1989–September 1, 1990.*

Voices:
Beetlejuice: Stephen Ouimette, **Lydia Deetz:** Alyson Court, **Charles,** Lydia's father: Roger Dunn, **Delia,** Lydia's mother: Elizabeth Hanna

Episodes:
1989–1990:
(20-minute stories)
"Critter Sitters" (pilot episode), "Laugh Of The Party," "Pest Of The West," "Worm Welcome," "Quit While You're A Head," "Prince Of Neitherworld" and "Cousin B.J."
(10-minute stories)
"The Big Face Off," "Skeletons In Your Closet," "It's The Pits!," "A Dandy Handyman," "Bad Neighbor Beetlejuice," "Out Of My Mind," "A Bizarre Bazaar," "Poopsie," "Stage Fright," "Spooky Tree," "Campfire Ghouls" and "Pat On The Back."

BELLE AND SEBASTIAN

Produced in Japan, this 30-minute series tells the story of a young boy (Sebastian), who is abandoned at birth by his mother and raised by the master of the cabin (Old Seasal) in which he was born. He makes a companion of nature in a mountaintop village where children unceasingly tease him for being "a parentless child." One day, his life changes when he makes friends with a big white dog, Belle, who is lonely and does not believe in human beings anymore. The two experience high adventure and the special bonds of friendship in this touching adaptation of the successful children's book series by author Cecile Aubrey. *A MK Company and Visual 80 Production in association with Toho Company Ltd. Color. Half-hour. Premiered on Nickelodeon: June, 1984.*

Episodes:
"Belle Meets Sebastian," "The Hunt For Belle," "A Night In The Mountains," "The Journey Begins," "Escaping Smugglers," "A Visit To Jail," "Meeting Sara," "A Promise To Sara," "Farewell To Sara," "The Case Of The Missing Sheep," "Puppy Love," "Operation Substitute," "The Runaway Car," "An Act Of Bravery," "Billy, The Kid Bank Robber," "The Old Man By The Sea," "Phantoms On A Ship," "Smuggled On Board," "The Secret Of The Castle Ghost," "The Ghost's Revenge," "Kidnapped," "Chased By Desperados," "Mistaken Identities," "Doublecrossed," "Meeting At The Mountain," "Isabel's Scarf," "The Three Sisters," "Building A New Home," "Belle And Sebastian Are Separated," "It's A Boy," "Reunited At Last," "When Johnny Comes Marching Home," "Sebastian Loses His Best Friend," "Come Back To Me," "One Mistake After Another," "Poisoned," "The Big Sleep," "Mom Didn't Forget Me," "Don't Drink The Water," "Belle Is Captured," "Help, Save Belle," "Make New Friends And Keep The Old," "On A Train Bound For Battle," "Traveling On The Underground Railroad," "The Kind Heart Of Inspector Garcia," "Climbing A Wall Of Stone," "A Storm Brews," "A Snowy Reunion," "The Devil's Corridor," "Belle Risks Her Life," "Mom Makes Up Her Mind" and "A Happy Ending."

THE BERENSTAIN BEARS

Beartown, a tiny hamlet whose economy is based solely on honey, is home to the Bear Family: Papa Q. Bear; Mama;

Brother and Sister Bear; Grizzly and Gran, the grandparents; and the hilarious incompetent group of ne'er-do-wells, chief among them Raffish Ralph and Weasel McGreed, whose antics always seem to throw a monkey wrench into the Bear Family's best-laid plans in this Saturday-morning series adaptation of the beloved children's book characters created by Stan and Jan Berenstain. *A Southern Star Production. Color. Half-hour. Premiered on CBS: September 14, 1985–September 5, 1987.*

Voices:
Ruth Buzzi, Brian Cummings, Christine Lange, Marissa Mendenhall, David Mendenhall, Frank Welker, John Rodine

Episodes:
1985–1986 (two per show) "Berenstain Bears Go Fly A Kite," "Berenstain Bears And The Trojan Pumpkin," "Berenstain Bears And The Spooky Old Mansion," "Berenstain Bears And The Fly-Away Pizza," "Berenstain Bears And The Giant Bat Cave," "Berenstain Bears And The Wild Wild Honey," "Berenstain Bears And The Neighborly Skunk," "Berenstain Bears And The Missing Pumpkin," "Berenstain Bears And Too Much Birthday," "Berenstain Bears To The Rescue," "Berenstain Bears And The Soccer Star," "Berenstain Bears Shoot The Rapids," "Berenstain Bears And Knight To Remember," "Berenstain Bears And The Superduper Bowl," "Berenstain Bears And The Not-So-Buried Treasure," "Berenstain Bears And Condemned Backscratcher," "Berenstain Bears And Kong For A Day," "Berenstain Bears Blaze A Trail," "Berenstain Bears And No Girls Allowed," "Berenstain Bears And The Missing Dinosaur Bone," "Berenstain Bears And The Spookiest Pumpkin," "Berenstain Bears And Dancing Bees," "Berenstain Bears Learn About Strangers," "Berenstain Bears And The Disappearing Honey," "Berenstain Bears In The Dark" and "Berenstain Bears Ring The Bell."
1986–1987 "Berenstain Bears And Messy Room," "Berenstain Bears And The Terrible Termite," "Berenstain Bears Forget Their Manners," "Berenstain Bears And The Wicked Weasel Spell," "Berenstain Bears And The Truth," "Berenstain Bears Save The Bees," "Berenstain Bears Get In A Fight," "Berenstain Bears And The Bigpaw Problem," "Berenstain Bears Get Stage Fright," "Berenstain Bears Go Bonkers Over Honkers," "Berenstain Bears And The Great Honey Pipeline," "Berenstain Bears And The Great Grizzly Comet," "Berenstain Bears And The Sure-Fire Bait," "Berenstain Bears And The Cat's Meow," "Berenstain Bears And The Trouble With Friends," "Berenstain Bears And The Coughing Catfish," "Berenstain Bears And The Substitute Teacher," "Berenstain Bears And The Mansion Mystery," "Berenstain Bears Bust A Ghost," "Berenstain Bears And The Ice Monster," "Berenstain Bears And The Crystal Ball Caper," "Berenstain Bears And The Raid On Fort Grizzly," "Berenstain Bears And The Forbidden Cave," "Berenstain Bears And The Hot Air Election," "Berenstain Bears And Life With Papa" and "Berenstain Bears Save The Farm."

THE BEST OF SCOOBY–DOO

Classic episodes of the cowardly canine detective Scooby-Doo and his companions, Fred, Shaggy, Daphne and Velma, were rebroadcast in this "best of" format for Saturday morning

Characters from Stan and Jan Berenstain's beloved children's books were adapted for television in Hanna–Barbera's "The Berenstain Bears." © Southern Star Productions

television. The show combined previously broadcast episodes from past Scooby–Doo programs. *A Hanna–Barbera Production. Color. Half–hour. Premiered on ABC: September 10, 1983–September 1, 1984.*

Voices:
Scooby–Doo: Don Messick, **Fred:** Frank Welker, **Shaggy:** Casey Kasem, **Daphne:** Heather North, **Velma:** Nicole Jaffe, Pat Stevens, Maria Frumkin

THE BETTY BOOP SHOW

National Television Associates (NTA), who had earlier acquired the rights to Betty Boop, tried to rekindle interest in the "Boop–Boop–A–Doop" girl by distributing color–painted prints of Max Fleischer's original theatrical cartoons in half–hour packages. (The master negatives were sent overseas to Korea where they were meticulously hand–colored.) *A Max Fleischer Production distributed by NTA. Color. Half–hour. Premiered: Fall 1971. Syndicated.*

Voices:
Betty Boop: Mae Questel

Episodes:
(four per show) "Admission Free," "Any Rags," "Baby Be Good," "Be Human," "Be Up To Date," "Betty Boop And Grampy," "Betty Boop And Little Jimmy," "Betty Boop And The Little King," "Betty Boop For President," "Betty Boop In Blunderland," "The Betty Boop Limited," "Betty Boop, M.D.," "Betty Boop's Bamboo Isle," "Betty Boop's Big Boss," "Betty Boop's Birthday," "Betty Boop's Bizzy Bee," "Betty Boop's Crazy Inventions," "Betty Boop's Halloween Party," "Betty Boop's Kerchoo," "Betty Boop's Lifeguard," "Betty Boop's May Party," "Betty Boop's Museum," "Betty Boop's Penthouse," "Betty Boop's Prize Show," "Betty Boop's Rise To Fame," "Betty Boop's Trial," "Betty Boop's Ups And Downs," "Bimbo's Express," "Boop Oop–A–Doop," "Candid Candidate," "Crazy Town," "The Dancing Fool," "Ding Dong Doggie," "Dizzy Red Riding Hood," "The Foxy Hunter," "Grampy's Indoor Outing," "Ha! Ha! Ha!," "Happy You And Merry Me," "Henry, The Funniest Living American," "The Hot Air Salesman," "Housecleaning Blues," "A–Haunting We Will Go," "I Heard," "I'll Be Glad When You're Dead, You Rascal You," "The Impractical Joker," "Is My Palm Red?," "Jack And The Beanstalk," "Judge For A Day," "Keep In Style," "A Language Of All My

Own," "Let Me Call You Sweetheart," "Little Nobody," "A Little Soap And Water," "Making Friends," "Making Stars," "Mask–A–Raid," "Minding The Baby," "Minnie The Moocher," "More Pep," "Morning, Noon And Night," "Mother Goose Land," "Musical Mountaineers," "My Friend The Monkey," "The New Deal Show," "No, No A Thousand Times No!," "Not Now," "The Old Man Of The Mountain," "One With The New," "Parade Of The Wooden Soldiers," "Pudgy In Thrills And Chills," "Pudgy Takes A Bow–Wow," "Pudgy the Watchman," "Red Hot Mama," "Rhythm On The Reservation," "Riding The Rails," "Romantic Melodies," "Sally Swing," "The Scared Crows," "Service With A Smile," "She Wronged Him Right," "Silly Scandals," "Snow White," "So Does An Automobile," "A Song For A Day," "Stop That Noise," "Stopping The Show," "Swat That Fly," "Swim Or Sink," "The Swing School," "Taking The Blame," "There's Something About A Soldier," "Training Pigeons," "Valle Melodies," "We Did It," "When My Ship Comes In," "Whoops I'm A Cowboy," "You're Not Built That Way" and "Zula Hula."

BEVERLY HILLS TEENS

This series centers around the lives, loves and longings of a group of typical, fun–loving American teenagers, who just happen to be fabulously wealthy, set against a backdrop of comically exaggerated examples of their wealth—Jacuzzis in gym class, waiters serving milkshakes from silver trays and elegant, carpeted classrooms where each student has his own Louis XIV desk, complete with antique phone. *A DIC Enterprises Production. Color. Half–hour. Premiered: September, 1987. Syndicated.*

Voices:

Buck/Wilshire: Michael Beattie, **Pierce Thorndyke:** Stephen McMulkin, **Shanelle Spencer:** Michelle St. John, **Tara/Jett:** Karen Bernstein, **Jillian/Bianca/Blaise:** Tracy Moore, **Switchboard:** Joanna Schellenberg, **Fifi:** Linda Sorensen, **Nikki Darling:** Corrine Koslo, **Gig/Dad:** Mark Saunders, **Larke/Dog:** Mary Long, **Troy:** Jonathan Potts, **Radley/Guitar:** Hadley Kay

Episodes:

"Double–Surfing Double–Cross," "The Dog Ate My Homework," "The Make Over," "My Fair Wilshire," "Robot Romance," "Casting Call," "Down And Out In The Teenclub," "Chase Of A Lifetime," "Downhill Racer," "Radley Wipes Out," "Shipwrecked," "Halloween In The Hills," "Visit From A Prince," "Camp Camping," "Dream Date," "The Perfect Gift," "A Time To Remember," "Chester The Matchmaker," "Who Wears The Pants?," "Open For Business," "Operation: Soap Opera," "Teenclub Carnival," "Potions Of Love," "The Teen Cup," "Ghost Story," "Fairy Tale Flake Out," "Nothing But The Gossip," "Now We're Cooking!," "Old At Heart," "Death Valley 500," "Star Split," "Double Your Trouble," "Take My Hostage, Please!," "Trouble Times Three," "Bianca's Dream," "Pierce's Hundred Dollars," "Look Deep Into My Eyes," "The Commercial," "Hold The Anchovies!," "From Rad To Worse," "Scene Stealer," "A Splitting Image," "Diet, Please," "Jillian's Lesson," "What The Hex Happening?," "Don't Judge A Book By Its Cover–Girl," "Private Club—Ghosts Only," "Poll Climbers,"

"Rampage," "That Winning Smile," "Eye Of The Tigress," "Take Me Out To The Ballgame," "The Slumber Party," "Roughing It," "The Buck Stops Here," "The Kindest Cut Of All," "Bianca's Diary," "Go With The Flu," "Nikki's Big Break," "McTech, P.I.," "The Tortoise And The Dare," "Greens With Envy," "Troy Triathlon," "Miracle At The Teenclub" (Part 1) and "Miracle At The Teenclub" (Part 2).

THE BIG WORLD OF LITTLE ADAM

The fantastic future of space exploration where man will face the greatest challenges of his existence is seen through the eyes of Little Adam and his big brother Wilbur in this series of action–packed episodes. Fred Ladd, the producer of TV's "Speed Racer" and others, produced the series. John Megna, the voice of Little Adam, is actress Connie Stevens' brother. *A Little Adam Production Incorporated. Color. Half–hour. Premiered: 1965. Syndicated.*

Voices:

Little Adam: John Megna, **Wilbur,** his brother: Craig Seckler

Episodes:

"Man On The Moon," "Plane That Flies Into Space," "Rescue In Space," "Man Learns To Fly," "The Space Tug," "Escape From Earth," "Flight To Mars," "Steps To The Moon," "Island In Space," "Rescue By Air," "The Aerospace Plane," "Our Place In Space," "How Not To Fly To Venus," "Pitch Yaw And Roll," "From Rocks To Rockets," "Discovery Of Space," "Platforms In Space," "Our Wandering Planet," "Blue Print For Outer Space," "From Earth To Pluto," "The War Of The Satellites," "The Man In Space Ship Five," "So End The Bends," "Voices From The Moon," "Weightless In Space," "The Force Of Gravity," "The Worst Pilot In The Sky," "Breathing In Space," "The Key To Space," "Bubble Trouble," "What's Really Moving," "The Man Moons Of Earth," "Eyes In The Sky," "The Star That Talks," "Seeing Is Deceiving," "The Noise Barrier," "Braving The Jetstream," "The Middle Ear," "Target Venus," "Life On Other Planets," "A Magnet Called Earth," "Man In A Spacesuit," "The Dust Storm," "Flying The Blizzard," "Stormy Weather," "The Highest Wind," "What Makes The Winter," "Man With A Heart," "What Scares You," "Kitty Hawk To Mars," "Scuba Divers Of Space," "The Big Boom," "The First Rocket," "OAO Telescope In Space," "The Perfect Launch," "Symbols For Space," "Thinking Machines," "Stop That Rocket," "Missiles From Space," "The Human Camera," "Design For Tomorrow," "Orbits Through Space," "Battle In Outer Space," "Flying Under Pressure," "The Automatic Astronaut," "The Flying Spaceport," "The Plot To Kill Gravity," "The Path Of The Planets," "To Space And Back," "Why Planets Stay Up," "Secrets Of Space," "To Tame The Moon," "Traffic Jam In Space," "Can Man Make It," "Sybil Sees The Future," "The World Of Tomorrow," "Pictures From Space," "The Star Gazers," "The Amazing Masesr," "Zero Plus Five," "Robots In Command," "Ruby Red Beam," "Track Of The Capsule," "A Far Away Cry," "The Time Machine," "So You Want To Fly," "My Pop The Pilot," "Signals In Smoke," "The Missing Spaceman," "Flight Commands," "The Flaming Re–Entry," "Return

A look into the fantastic future of space adventure is vividly told through the eyes of two boys in the action—packed series, "The Big World Of Little Adam." © Little Adam Productions Inc. (Courtesy: Fred Ladd)

To Earth," "Gemini: The Space Twins," "Rendezvous In Space," "Docking In Orbit," "Echo In Space," "Mercury: Man In Space," "Mercury In Orbit," "Around The World In 90 Minutes," "Recovery At Sea," "Weatherman In Space," "Aim For The Sun" and "Closer To The Stars."

BIONIC SIX

The Bennett family, endowed by a beneficient scientist with bionic capabilities, employs their special talents to combat evil and advance the cause of justice and universal peace. Their main adversary: the evil Dr. Scarab and his minions of destruction, whose goal is to use science for their own selfish motives. *A TMS Production in association with MCA/Universal. Color. Half—hour. Premiered: April 19, 1987—November 16, 1987. Syndicated.*

Voices:

J. D. Bennett: Norman Bernard, **Helen Bennett:** Carol Bilger, **Meg Bennett:** Bobbi Block, **Jack Bennett:** John Stephenson, **Eric Bennett:** Hal Rayle, **Bunji Bennett:** Brian Tochi, **Madam O:** Jennifer Darling, **Dr. Scarab:** Jim MacGeorge, **F.L.U.F.F.I.:** Neil Ross, **Klunk:** John Stephenson, **Glove:** Frank Welker, **Mechanic:** Frank Welker, **Chopper:** Frank Welker

Additional Voices:

Shuko Akune, Bever—Leigh Banfield, Susan Blu, Arthur Burghardt, Michael Mish, Howard Morris, Michael Sheehan

Episodes:

"Valley Of Shadows," "Enter The Bunji," "Eric Bats A Thousand," "Klunk In Love," "Radio Scarab," "Family Affair," "Back To The Past" (Part 1), "Back To The Past" (Part 2), "Happy Birthday, Amadeus," "Brain Food," "Just A Little Handicap," "Bionics On! The First Adventure," "Fugitive F.L.U.F.F.I.," "Nick Of Time," "Youth Or Consequence," "Extra Innings," "Return Of The Bunji," "Crown Of The Scarab King," "1001 Bionic Nights," "The Perceptor File," "Masterpiece," "House Rules," "Holidaze," "Nightmare At Cypress Cove," "Music Power," "The Hive," "Mindlink," "I Compute, Therefor I Am," "Pass/ Fail," "Born To Be Bad," "A Clean Slate" (Part 1), "A Clean Slate" (Part 2), "Spin Out," "The Man In The Moon," "The Case Of The Baker Street Bionics," "Now You See Me . . .," "The Glitch," "Crystal Clear," "You've Come A Long Way, Baby!," "Up And Atom," "Home Movies," "Scarabscam," "Kleidoscope," "Once Upon A Crime," "Bone Of Contention," "Mrs. Scarab," "The Secret Life Of Wellington Forsby," "The Fungus Among Us," "Bottom Of The Ninth Planet," "Triple Cross," "I, Scarab" (Part 1), "I, Scarab" (Part 2), "Scabracadabra," "A Matter Of Gravity," "Call Of The Bunji," "A Super Bunch Of Guys," "The Monkey Has Landed," "The Elemental," "I Am The Viper," "Junk Heap," "Shadow Boxer," "Ready, Aim, Fired," "Love Note," "The Return Of Mrs. Scarab" and "That's All, Folks."

BIRDMAN AND THE GALAXY TRIO

Three winged superheroes—Birdman, assistant Birdboy and eagle companion, Avenger—encounter world forces under the command of Falcon 7. The other half of the superhero talent, billed on the same show, was the Galaxy Trio. Stories depict nemeses of the spaceship Condor 1 and its principal pilots, Vapor Man, Galaxy Girl and Meteor Man, who all possess superhuman strength. *A Hanna—Barbera Production. Color. Half—hour. Premiered on NBC: September 9, 1967—September 14, 1968.*

Voices:

The Birdman: Ray Randall/Birdman: Keith Andes, **Birdboy:** Dick Beals, **Falcon 7:** Don Messick, **The Galaxy Trio: Vapor Man:** Don Messick, **Galaxy Girl:** Virginia Eiler, **Meteor Man:** Ted Cassidy

Episodes:

"The Birdman" (two per show).
"The Menace Of Dr. Millenium," "X, The Eliminator," "The Ruthless Ringmaster," "Morto, The Marauder," "Birdman Versus Cumulus, The Storm King," "Nitron, The Human Bomb," "Birdman Versus The Mummer," "The Quake Threat," "Avenger For Ransom The Brain Thief," "Birdman Versus The Constructor," "The Bird Girl," "Birdman Meets Reducto," "Serpents Of The Deep," "Hannibal The Hunter," "The Purple Moss," "The Incredible Magnatroid," "Vulturo, The Mind Taker," "The Wings Of Fear," "Birdman Versus Dr. Freezoids," "Train Trek," "Number One," "The Deadly Duplicator," "The Deadly Trio," "Professor Nightshade," "The Chameleon," "The Empress Of Evil," "Birdman Meets Birdboy," "Birdman Meets Moray Of The Deep," "Birdman And The Monster Of The Mountains," "The Return Of Vulturo," "Birdman In The Revenge Of Dr. Millenium," "The Wild Weird West," "The Ant Ape," "Morto Rides Again" and "Skon Of Space."
"The Galaxy Trio" (one per show).
"Revolt Of The Robots," "The Battle Of The Aquatrons," "Galaxy Trio Versus The Moltens Of Meteorus," "Galaxy Trio Versus Growliath," "Galaxy Trio And The Sleeping Planet," "Galaxy Trio And The Cave Men Of Primevia," "Titan, The

Titanium Man," "Computron Lives," "Space Fugitives," "The Eye Of Time," "The Duplitrons," "The Demon Raiders," "The Rock Men," "Return To Aqueous," "Space Slaves," "Invasion Of The Sporoids," "Gralik Of Gravitas" and "Plastus The Pirate Planet."

THE BISKITTS

A group of pint–sized pups—only a doggie–biscuit tall—are named caretakers of the royal treasure following the death of Biskitt Island's good wise king. They constantly thwart the ongoing pilfering plots of King Max, despot of the rundown kingdom of Lower Suburbia, who is determined to steal the treasure along with mangy dogs, Fang and Snarl, and his inept jester, Shecky. *A Hanna–Barbera Production. Color. Half–hour. Premiered on CBS: September 17, 1983–September 1, 1984.*

Voices

Waggs: Darryl Hickman, **Lady:** B. J. Ward, **Scat:** Dick Beals, **Sweets:** Kathleen Helppie, **Spinner/Bump/Flip:** Bob Holt, **Shecky:** Kip King, **Shiner:** Jerry Houser, **Scatch/Fang/Dog Foot:** Peter Cullen, **King Max/Fetch/Snarl:** Ken Mars, **Wiggle:** Jennifer Darling, **Downer:** Henry Gibson, **Mooch:** Marshall Efron

Episodes:

(two per show) "As The Worm Turns," "Trouble In The Tunnel," "The Moonpond," "Fly Me To The Goon," "Up To His Old Tricks," "Spinner's Surprise," "Dogfoot," "Turnaround Hound," "A Dark And Stormy Knight," "Rogue Biskitt," "Two Leagues Under The Pond," "A Biskitt Halloween," "The Biskitt Who Cried Woof," "Around The Swamp In A Daze," "Moving Day," "The Bone In The Stone," "The Trojan Biskitt," "Snatched From Scratch," "The Golden Biskitt," "Belling The Wildcat," "King Max's War," "Raiders Of The Lost Bark," "The Princess And The Plea," "Shecky's Last Laugh," "The Swamp Monster" and "May The Best Biskitt Win."

BLACKSTAR

John Blackstar, an intergalactic soldier of fortune, is drawn through a black hole into an alternate universe where, through the use of a mystical Power Star, he undertakes fantastic adventures fraught with peril, magic and mystery. *A Filmation Production. Half–hour. Color. Premiered on CBS: September 12, 1981–August 20, 1983.*

Voices:

John Blackstar: George DiCenzo

Additional Voices:

Linda Gary, Alan Oppenheimer, Pat Pinney

Episodes:

"City Of The Ancient Ones," "Search For The Starsword," "The Lord Of Time," "The Mermaid Of Serpent Sea," "The Quest," "Space Wrecked," "Lightning City Of The Clouds," "Kingdom Of Neptul," "Tree Of Evil," "The Air Whales Of Anchar," "Overlord's Big Spell," "Crown Of The Sorceress" and "The Zombie Monster."

BOZO THE CLOWN

Frizzy redhaired clown Bozo, former comic strip favorite and Capitol Records star, found new avenues via syndicated television when Larry Harmon produced new cartoons featuring Bozo and his circus pal Butchy Boy. The series has remained in continuous syndication since its premiere in 1959. *A Larry Harmon Picture Corporation Production. Color. Half–hour. Syndicated: 1959.*

Voices:

Bozo the Clown: Larry Harmon, **Butchy Boy:** Larry Harmon

Episodes:

"Bozo Meets The Creepy Gleep," "Six Gun Fun," "Horse Fly In The Sky," "Bozo Meets The Missing Link," "A Slick Trick On Mopy Dick," "Dinky Toots His Own Horn," "The Space Ace Saves Face," "Bird Brain Bozo," "Bozo Meets King Glum," "Bozo's First Prize Surprise," "Back To Back With Ack Ack Flack," "Three Cheers For The Rocketeers," "Charley Horse Of Another Color," "Sailing The Sea With South Sea McGee," "Doggone Dog," "Bye Bye Fly Guy," "Sea Serpent Seance," "Flying Carpet Capers," "Bozo's Bozomobile," "Yoo Hoo Kangaroo," "Eager Beaver Bozo," "Bozo The Lion Hearted," "Bully For Bozo," "Slippery Bly International Spy," "The Beast With The Least," "Big Deal On A Small Wheel," "Whammy Bammy Al Kazami," "Doubloon Goons," "The Tin Can Man," "Go-Gho Ghosts," "Hot Rod Bozo," "Bear Hunter Bozo," "Bozo The Moon Goon," "Hark Hark The Shark," "Hollywood Holdup," "Funny Face Ace," "Creepy Teepee," "The Missing Sphinx Of King Jinx," "Please Please Hercules," "Nightmare Scare," "Big Man In Tin Can," "Deep Freeze Squeeze," "Flying Shoes Blues," "Shanghai Shenanigans," "Million Dollar Mutt," "Spy Guy Surprise," "Ill Will Chills," "Sir Bozo And The Fire Breathing Dragon," "Copter Cap Capers," "Bozo Meets Mister Monster," "Bean Stalk Bozo," "Red Riding Hood Hoodwinks," "Chills And Thrills With Boothill McGill," "Admiral Bozo Beats The Fleet," "Oodles Ducks Dille Ma," "Injun Fun," "Trouble Shooter Scooter," "Injuneer Bozo," "Goldilocks Yocks," "Mish Mash Magic," "Okey Dokey Smoky," "Cony Island Capers," "Ozark Lark," "Horse Thief Grief," "Ship Shape Ape," "Missing Missile Fizzle," "Tally Ho Bozo," "Dragon Lagoon," "Broken Bones Jones," "Bozo's Ape Escape," "Pint Size Surprise," "Kitt Kat Spat," "Monster Madness," "Stormy Knight Fright," "Baby Sitters Jitters," "Sheep Thief Grief," "Chicken Hearted Bozo," "Good Deed Indeed," "Bulldog Bully," "Yoo–Hoo Uranium," "Space Gun Fun," "Knight Fight Fright," "Go Go Go Bozo," "Wild Hare Scare," "Bowler Bozo," "Bozo And The Corny Crow," "Super Salesman Bozo," "Good Luck Duck," "Bo Peeps Sheep," "Termite Fight Fright," "Rootin' Tootin' Six Gun Shootin' ", "Gag Bag Bozo," "Bozo In 3–Bear Scare," "Mail Man Mixup," "Bozo's Spunky Monkey," "Paleface Chase," "Killer Diller Miller," "Ship Shape Ship Mates," "Bozo And The Space Pirates," "Creepy Crenshaw Bungling Burglar," "Space Ace Elvis," "Texas Stranger Danger," "Super Duper Trouble Shooter," "Go–Go–Pogo–Pogo," "Big Lab Confab," "Square Shootin' Square," "Car Thief Keith," "Broad Sword Discord," "Big Boo–Boo On A Fast Choo–Choo," "Food Pest Jest," "Bad News Cruise," "Whipper Snapper Snipper," "Tip Top Bell Hop," "Fish Tanks Pranks," "Real Gone Leprechaun," "Lake Resort Sport," "Eagle's Nest Pest," "Rickety Rackety Rocketeer," "Little Naggin' Dragon," "Big Dealer On A Stern Wheeler," "Hop–Chest Quest," "Mill Pond Thrill Chill," "Piggy Bank Prank," "Charter–Service Nerbous," "Sidewalk Peddler's Meddler," "Razzle Dazzle Castle Hassle," "Four Flusher Gusher," "The Big Cake Bake," "Show Biz Whiz," "Papoose On The Loose," "Hurricane Belinda," "Ski Lodge Hodge Podge," "Chicken Burgler Bungler," "Manhunt Stunts," "Big Tree Spree," "Teeny Weeny Meany," "Rockey's Snack Attack," "Fast Pace Sky Chase," "A Glutton For Mutton," "South Of The Border Disorder," "Okey Dokey Hokey Pokey," "Big Flop Train Hop," "Pie In The Eye Guy," "Big Clown Shake–Down," "Flim–Flam For Ali Kablam," "All Mind Gold Mine," "Ball Park Lark," "Bozo's Icy Escapade," "High Fly Rug Spy," "Freeloader Railroader," "Gate Crasher Smasher," "Happy–Gas Gasser" and "Dance Of The Ants."

THE BRADY KIDS

Recreating their roles from TV's "The Brady Bunch," Greg, Peter, Bobby, Marcia, Janice and Cindy were featured in this animated spin–off focusing on the kids' problems as independent–minded young adults. Joining the wholesome youngsters were Ping and Pong, Chinese–speaking twin Pandas, and Marlon, a magical black myna bird. The Brady characters were voiced by the original television series cast. *A Filmation Production. Color. Half–hour. Premiered on ABC: September 16, 1972–August 31, 1974.*

Voices:

Marcia Brady: Maureen McCormick, **Greg Brady:** Barry Williams, **Janice Brady:** Eve Plumb, **Peter Brady:** Christopher Knight, **Cindy Brady:** Susan Olsen, **Bobby Brady:** Michael Lookinland, **Marlon:** Larry Storch

Episodes:

1972–1973 "Jungle Bungle" (two parts), "Double Trouble," "Lone Gone Silver," "Cindy's Super Friend," "Pop Goes The Mynah," "Who Was That Dog?," "It Ain't Necessarily Snow," "A Funny Thing Happened On The Way To The Football Field," "That Was No Worthy Opponent, That Was My Sister," "You Took The Words Right Out Of My Tape," "Give Me A Home Where The Panda Bears Roam," "It's All Greek To Me," "The Big Time," "The Birthday Party," "The Richest Man In The World" and "Wings."
1973–1974 (new episodes combined with reruns) "Frankincense," "Teacher's Pet," "Marcia's Lab," "Ceiling Zero" and "Who Believes In Ghosts?"

BRAVESTARR

Combining the best of the Old West and the space–age future, this western fantasy/adventure takes place on the distant planet of New Texas where lawman Bravestarr and his friends J. B., a woman, Fuzzy and his sidekick, Thirty–Thirty, fight for the cause of justice wherever evil lurks. *A Filmation Production. Color. Half–hour. Syndicated: September, 1987.*

Voices:

Charlie Adler, Susan Blu, Pat Fraley, Ed Gilbert, Alan Oppenheimer, Erika Scheimer

Episodes:

"Call To Arms," "The Bounty Hunter," "Buddy," "The Day The Town Was Taken," "Bravestarr And The Three Suns," "Bravestarr And The Medallion," "The Witnesses," "Handlebar And Rampage," "Legend Of A Pretty Lady," "Sunrise, Sunset," "Wildboy," "Tex But No Hex," "Space Zoo," "Claim Jumpers," "Scuzz And Fuzz," "To Talk A Mile," "Big 30 And Little Wimble," "Kerium Fever," "Memories," "Hail, Hail The Gang's All Here," "Eyewitnesses," "The Vigilantes," "Eye Of The Beholder," "The Wrong Hands," "An Older Hand," "Tex's Terrible Night," "Trouble Wears A Badge," "Who Am I?," "Hostage," "The Good, The Bad, And The Clumbsy," "Tunnel Of Terror," "Balance Of Power," "Runaway Planet," "Call Of The Wild," "Disappearance Of Thirty–Thirty," "The Taking Of Thistledown 123," "A Day In The Life Of A New Texas Judge," "Rampage," "Lost Mountain," "Thirty–Thirty Goes Camping," "Running Wild," "Ship Of No Return," "The Little Lie That Grew," "Brothers In Crime," "Sherlock Holmes In The 25th Century" (Part 1), "Sherlock Holmes In The 25th Century" (Part 2), "New Texas Blues," "Jerimiah And The Prairie People," "Ballad Of Sara Jane," "Brother's Keeper," "Bravestarr And The Empress," "Nomad Is An Island," "The Blockade," "Shake Hands With Long Arm John," "Strength Of The Bear," "Thirty–Thirty Goes Camping" and "No Drums, No Trumpets."

BUCKY AND PEPITO

This early animated series dealt with the adventures of Bucky, a young boy with a wild imagination and the spirit of an explorer, and his best friend, Pepito, the inventor. *A Sam Singer Production. Half–hour. Black–and–white. Premiered: 1958. Syndicated.*

Voices:
Bucky: Dallas McKennon

BUFORD AND THE GALLOPING GHOST

This half–hour mystery series was comprised of two weekly cartoon segments—"The Buford Files," following the exploits of Buford the bloodhound and two teenagers solving crimes; and "The Galloping Ghost," the misadventures of Nugget Nose, a ghost of an Old West prospector who haunts a dude ranch—which originally aired as part of ABC's 90–minute series, "Yogi's Space Race," in 1978. *A Hanna–Barbera Production. Color. Half–hour. Premiered on NBC: February 3, 1979–September 1, 1979.*

Voices:

Buford the Bloodhound: Frank Welker, **Cindy Mae,** his aide: Pat Harris, **Woody,** his aide: David Landsberg, **Sheriff Dupres:** Henry Corden, **Deputy Goofer:** Roger Peltz, **Nugget Nose,** the ghost: Frank Welker, **Fenwick Fuddy,** the ranch owner: Hal Peary, **Wendy,** his assistant: Marilyn Schreffler, **Rita,** his assistant: Pat Harris

Episodes:

"Buford Files." (one per show) "The Demon Of Ur," "The Vanishing Stallion," "The Swamp Hermit," "The Man With The

Orange Hair," "The Missing Bank," "Swamp Saucer" "Scare In The Air," "Buford And The Beauty," "Peril In The Park," "The Magic Whammy," "The Haunting Of Swamp Manor," "The Case Of The Missing Gator" and "Don't Monkey With Buford." "The Galloping Ghost." (one per show) "The Phantom Of The Horse Opera," "Too Many Crooks," "Sage Brush Sargeant," "The Bad News Bear," "Robot Round–Up," "Pest In The West," "Rock Star Nuggie," "Frontier Fortune Teller," "I Want My Mummy," "The Eclipse Of Mr. Sunshines," "Klondike Kate," "A Ghost Of A Chance" and "Elmo The Great."

THE BUGS BUNNY AND TWEETY SHOW

Bugs Bunny, Tweety and Sylvester return in this program containing classic Warner Brothers cartoons in which they star. *A Warner Brothers Production. Color. Half–hour. Premiered on ABC: September 13, 1986–*

Voices:
Mel Blanc

THE BUGS BUNNY/LOONEY TUNES COMEDY HOUR

Hour–long anthology of cartoon adventures featuring Bugs Bunny, the Road Runner, Daffy Duck, Foghorn Leghorn, Sylvester the Cat and Pepe Le Pew. The series debut on ABC marked the end of the rascally rabbit's long association with CBS, where "The Bugs Bunny/Road Runner Show" had remained a staple of Saturday morning television since its premiere in 1968. *A Warner Brothers Production. Color. One–hour. Premiered on ABC: September 7, 1985–September 6, 1986.*

Voices:
Mel Blanc

THE BUGS BUNNY/ROAD RUNNER HOUR

Bugs Bunny and the Road Runner and Coyote combined to become one of the most popular Saturday morning vehicles when reruns of their old cartoons were broadcast for the first time on CBS in September 1968. The pairing of these two Warner Brothers superstars resulted in consistently high ratings for its time period throughout its 17–year run on CBS. The format was changed only once in its history. In April 1976, the program was simultaneously aired on Tuesday nights in prime–time under the title of "The Bugs Bunny/ Road Runner Show." By November, 1977, the series was expanded to 90 minutes, remaining in this mode through the beginning of the 1981–1982 season. That fall the series returned to one-hour and continued in this vein until ending its run on CBS in September, 1985. *A Warner Brothers Production. Color. One hour. One hour and a half. Premiered on CBS: September 14, 1968–September 4, 1971. Rebroadcast on CBS: September 6, 1975–November, 1977 (as "The Bugs Bunny/Road Runner Hour"); April, 1972–June, 1976 (as "The Bugs Bunny/Road Runner Show"); November, 1977–*

September, 1981 (as "The Bugs Bunny/Road Runner Show"); September 12, 1981–September 7, 1985.

THE BUGS BUNNY SHOW

Like its rival CBS, who brought "The Flintstones" to prime–time, ABC premiered this package of Warner Brothers cartoons, starring "the screwy rabbit" and his friends (Elmer Fudd, Yosemite Sam, Tweety and Sylvester the Cat, and the Road Runner), in prime time; it contained significant amounts of new animated material specially made for television. The program remained in prime–time for two seasons, before it was moved to Saturday mornings, where it dominated kiddie show ratings in its time slot for more than 20 years. *A Warner Brothers Production. Color. Half–hour. Premiered on ABC: October 11, 1960–September 25, 1962. Rebroadcast on ABC: April 1962–September, 1968; Rebroadcast on CBS: September 11, 1971–September 1, 1973; Rebroadcast on ABC: September 8, 1973–August 30, 1975.*

Voices:
Mel Blanc

THE BULLWINKLE SHOW

With new components added, this program was basically a retitled version of the "Rocky and His Friends" series, previously broadcast on ABC from 1959 to 1961. Again, Rocky, the flying squirrel, and Bullwinkle, the moose, tangle with the nefarious Mr. Big, a midget with grandiose ideas, and his two Russian agents, Boris Badenov and Natasha Fataly, in two cliff–hanging episodes.

Other holdovers from the former series were "Aesop and Son," "Fractured Fairy Tales" (which alternated each week with "Aesop and Son"), "Peabody's Improbable History" (which rotated every week with "Dudley Do–Right of the Mounties") and "Mr. Know–It–All" (for episode titles of each see "Rocky And His Friends"). Two new segments were added to the show: "Dudley Do–Right of the Mounties," repackaged later as "The Dudley Do–Right Show," and "Bullwinkle's Corner," short, nonsensical poetry readings by the famed cartoon moose.

In 1981, after eight years off network television, the series returned for a brief run on NBC. *A Jay Ward Production in association with Producers Associates for Television. Color. Half–hour. Premiered on NBC: September 24, 1961–September 15, 1963. Rebroadcast on NBC: September 21, 1963–September 5, 1964; Rebroadcast on ABC: September 20, 1964–September 2, 1973; Rebroadcast on NBC: September 12, 1981–July 24, 1982.*

Voices:
Bullwinkle: Bill Scott, **Rocky:** June Foray, **Boris Badenov:** Paul Frees, **Natasha Fataly:** June Foray, **Aesop:** Charles Ruggles, **Peabody:** Bill Scott, **Sherman:** Walter Tetley, **Dudley Do–Right:** Bill Scott, **Inspector Fenwick:** Paul Frees, **Nell,** Dudley's girlfriend: June Foray, **Snidely Whiplash:** Hans Conreid, **Narrators:** William Conrad ("Bullwinkle"), Edward Everett Horton ("Fractured Fairy Tales") Charles Ruggles ("Aesop and Son")

Additional Voices:

Skip Craig, Barbara Baldwin, Adrienne Diamond

Episodes:

"Rocky and Bullwinkle" (two per show).

"Jet Formula" (1–40), "Box Top Robbery" (41–52), "Upsidasium" (53–88), "Metal Munching Mice" (89–104), "Greenprint Oogle" (105–116), "Rue Brittania" (117–124), "Buried Treasure" (125–138), "Last Angry Moose" (139–142), "Wailing Whale" (143–156), "Three Mooseketeers" (157–164), "Lazy Jay Ranch" (165–182), "Missouri Mish Mash" (183–208), "Topsy Turvy World" (209–222), "Painting Theft" (223–228), "Guns Of Abalone" (229–232), "Treasure Of Mote Zoom" (233–240), "Goof Gas Attack" (241–248), "Banana Formula" (259–260), (break in production), "Bumbling Brothers Circus" (301–310), "Mucho Loma" (originally "Much Mud" 311–316), "Pottsylvania Creeper" (317–322), "Moosylvania" (323–326), "Ruby Yacht" (327–332), "Bulls Testimonial Dinner" (333–338), "The Weather Lady" (339–344), "Louse On 92nd Street" (345–350), "Wassmotto U" (351–362) and "Moosylvania Saved" (363–366).

"Aesop and Son" (one episode every other week).

"The Lion And The Mouse," "The Mice In Council," "The Fox And The Stork," "The Wolf In Sheep's Clothing," "The Hare And The Tortoise," "The Hare And The Hound," "The Hares And The Frog," "The Frogs And The Beaver," "The Lion And The Aardvark," "The Jackrabbits And The Mule," "The Dog And The Shadow," "The Cat And The Fifteen Mice," "The Goldfish And The Bear," "The Vain Cow," "The Canary And The Musical Hares," "The Fox And The Minks," "The Owl And The Wolf," "The Centipede And The Snail," "The Fox And The Owl," "The Hound And The Wolf," "The Fox And The Winking Horse," "The Sick Lion," "The Porcupine And The Tigers," "Son Of The Masked Clock," "The Hen And The Cat," "The Five Hens," "The Three Bears," "The Robin, The Pelican, And The Angleworm," "The Eagle And The Beetle," "The Fox And The Hound," "The Bears And The Dragon," "The Fox And The Woodman," "The Country Frog And The City Frog," "The Fox And The Rabbit," "The Hare And The Tortoise," "The French Poodle And The Alley Cat" and "The Fox And The Three Weasels."

"Fractured Fairy Tales" (one episode every other week).

"Goldilocks," "Fee Fi Fo Fum," "Rapunzel," "Puss And Boots #1," "Enchanted Fish," "Beauty And The Beast," "Brave Little Tailor," "Rumpelstiltskin," "Princess And The Pea," "Sweet Little Beat," "Dick Whittington's Cat," "Cinderella," "Elves And The Shoemaker," "Tom Thumb," "Sir Galahad," "Snow White," "Sleeping Beauty," "Pinocchio," "Little Red Riding Hood," "Androcles And The Lion," "King Midas," "Riding Hoods Anonymous," "Ugly Duckling," "Hansel And Gretel," "Dancing Cinderella," "Goose That Laid The Golden Egg," "Three Little Pigs #1," "Slipping Beauty," "Snow White, Inc.," "Rumpestiltskin Returns," "Leaping Beauty," "Puss And Boots #2," "Jack And The Beanstalk," "Tom Thumb #2," "Aladdin," "The Three Bears," "Enchanted Frog," "Pied Piper #2," "Beauty And The Beast," "The Magical Fish," "Prince Darling," "Son Of Beauty Of The Beast," "The Frog Prince," "The Golden Goose," "Son Of Rumpelstiltskin," "Elves And The Shoemaker," "Speeding Beauty," "Fisherman And His Wife," "The Princess And The Goblins," "Snow White Meets Rapunzel," "The Little Princess," "Thom Tum," "Slow White And Nose Red," "Prince Hyacinth And Dear Princess," "The Giant And The Beanstalk," "The Enchanted Fly," "Felicia And The Pot Of Pinks," "Hans Clinker," "The Witches' Broom," "Son Of King Midas," "The Magic Chicken," "Aladdin And His Lamp," "The Enchanted Goat," "The Thirteen Helmets," "The Prince And The Popper," "Booty And The Beast," "Little Red Riding Hood," "Goldilocks And The Three Bears," "The Ugly Almond Duckling," "John's Orge Wife," "The Absent–Minded King," "The Mysterious Castle," "The Little Tinker," "Sweeping Beauty," "The Teeth Of Baghdad," "The Little Men In The Boat," "Red White," "Cutie And The Bird," "The Tale Of A King," "Peter And The Three Pennies," "The Wishing Hat," "Son Of Snow White," "Jack B. Nimble," "Potter's Luck," "The Magic Lichee Nuts," "The King And The Witch," "The Seven Chickens" and "Sweeping Beauty #2."

"The Improbable History of Mr. Peabody" (one episode every other week).

"Show Opening," "Napoleon," "Lord Nelson," "Wyatt Earp," "King Arthur," "Franz Schubert," "Lucretia Borgia," "Sir Walter Raleigh," "Robert Fulton," "Annie Oakley," "The Wright Brothers," "George Armstrong Custer," "Alfred Nobel," "Marco Polo," "Richard The Lion Hearted," "Don Juan," "William Tecumseh Sherman," "First Kentucky Derby," "P. T. Barnum," "Stanley And Livingstone," "Louis Pasteur," "Robin Hood," "Robinson Crusoe," "Ponce de Leon," "John L. Sullivan," "Leonardo Da Vinci," "Paul Revere," "Confucius," "Nero," "Francis Scott Key," "Captain Matthew Clift," "Balboa," "Peter Cooper," "The Battle Of Bunker Hill," "The Pony Express," "Stephen Decatur," "Alexander Graham Bell," "Commander Peary," "Pancho Villa," "Lord Francis Douglas," "Sitting Bull," "Christopher Columbus," "The French Foreign Legion," "Guglielmo Marconi," "Scotland Yard," "John Holland," "Louis XVI," "Francisco Pizarro," "Daniel Boone," "Jesse James," "Shakespeare," "Zebulon Pike," "The First Golf Match," "William Tell," "James Whistler," "Ferdinand Magellan," "Sir Issac Newton," "Kit Carson," "The First Caveman," "Johann Gutenberg," "Buffalo Bill," "Hans Christian Oersted," "Leif Ericson," "John Sutter," "Ludwig Van Beethoven," "Calamity Jane," "The Surrender Of Cornwallis," "The First Prince Charlie," "Reuter," "Geronimo," "The Great Wall Of China," "The Marquis Of Queensbury," "Jim Bowie," "Edgar Allan Poe," "Charge Of The Light Great Pyramid," "James Audubon," "Mata Hari," "Galileo," "Wellington At Waterloo," "Florence Nightingale," "Henry The Eighth," "First Indianapolis Auto Race," "Captain Kidd," "The Texas Rangers" and "Cleopatra."

"Mr. Know–It–All" (one episode per show).

"How To Train A Doggy," "How To Tame Lions," "How To Cook A Turkey's Goose," "How To Have A Swimming Pool," "How To Sell Vacuum Cleaners," "How To Cure The Hiccups," "How To Open A Jar Of Pickles," "How To Get Into The Movies," "How To Catch A Bee," "How To Be A Cow Puncher," "How To Escape From Devil's Island," "How To Shoot Par Golf," "How To Be A Magician," "A Monstrous Success," "How To Remove A Moustache," "How To Fall Asleep," "Unwanted Guest," "How To Be A Star Reporter," "How To Do Stunts In The Movies," "How To Run A 4–Minute Mile," "How To Be A Big Game Hunter," "How To Be A Barber," "How To Water

Ski," "How To Be An Indian," "How To Own A Hi–Fi," "How To Be A Human Fly," "How To Be A Hitch–Hiker," "How To Be A Hobo," "How To Disarm A Live TNT Bomb," "How To Be A Beatnik," "How To Conquer Your Fear Of Height," "How To Fix A Flat," "How To Avoid Tipping The Waiter," "Rocky And Bullwinkle Fan Club #1," "How To Buy A Used Car," "How To Be An Archeologist," "How To Travel Through The West," "Rocky And Bullwinkle Fan Club #2," "How To Sell An Encyclopedia," "Rocky And Bullwinkle Fan Club #3," "How To Wash Windows," "Rocky And Bullwinkle Fan Club #4," "Rocky And Bullwinkle Fan Club #5," "Rocky And Bullwinkle Fan Club #6," "Boris' Fan Club," "Rocky And Bullwinkle Fan Club #7," "How To Win Friends," "How To Be A Good Umpire," "How To Interview A Scientist," "Rocky And Bullwinkle Fan Club #8," "Rocky And Bullwinkle Fan Club #9," "Member Of The Peace Corps," "Money Back," "Temperamental Movie Star," "How To Have A Hit Record," "How To Make The Neighbors Quiet," "Tennis Game," "How To Sell Soap," "Top Flight Stock Salesman" and "Bully At The Beach."

"Dudley Do–Right of the Mounties" (one episode every other week).

"The Disloyal Canadians," "Finding Gold," "Mortgagin' The Mountie Post," "Trap Bait," "Masked Ginny Lynne," "The Centaur," "Railroad Tracks," "Foreclosing Mortgages," "Snidely Mounted Police," "Mother Love," "Mountie Bear," "Inspector Dudley Do–Right," "Recruiting Campaign," "Out Of Uniform," "Lure Of The Footlights," "Bullet Proof Suit," "Miracle Drug," "Elevenworth Prision," "Saw Mill," "Mountie Without A Horse," "Mother Whiplash's Log Jam," "Stolen Art Masterpiece," "Mechanical Dudley," "Flicker Rock," "Faithful Dog," "Coming–Out Party," "Robbing Banks," "Skagway Dogsled–Pulling Contest," "Canadian Railway's Bridge," "Niagra Falls," "Snidely's Vic Whiplash Gym," "Marigolds," "Trading Places," "Top Secret," "The Locket," "The Inspector's Nephew," "Matinee Idol" and "Snidely Arrested."

"Bullwinkle's Corner" (one per show).

"The Swing," "Little Miss Muffet," "The Horn," "Where Go The Boats," "My Shadow," "I Love Little Pussy," "Taffy," "Wee Willie Winkle," "Little Jack Horner," "Queen Of Hearts," "Tom Tom The Piper's Son," "Barbara Frietchie," "Rockybye Baby," "The Village Blacksmith," "The Children's Hour," "The Barefoot Boy," "The Raven," "Woodman Spare That Tree," "Excelsior," "Simple Simon," "Hickory Dickory Dock," "Little Bo Beep," "The Daffodils," "The Bee," "Peter Piper," "Pat A Cake," "Thanksgiving Day," "Sing A Song Of Sixpence," "How To Be Happy," "The Wind," "I Shot An Arrow," "Jack Be Nimble," "Merrie Had A Little Lamb," "See A Pin," "Ole Mother Hubbard," "The Cherry Tree," "Tommy Tucker," "Grandfather's Clock" and "A Wet Sheet And A Flowing Sea."

BUTCH AND BILLY AND THEIR BANG BANG WESTERN MOVIES

Billy Bang Bang and his brother, Butch, provide commentary for this series of cliff–hanging adventures featuring Bronco Bill, an Old West lawman. The program was comprised of back–to–back five–minute episodes. *Color. Half–hour. Premiered: 1961. Syndicated.*

Voices:
Bronco Bill: Bob Cust, **Billy Bang Bang:** Steve Krieger, **Butch Bang Bang:** Danny Krieger

BUTCH CASSIDY AND THE SUN DANCE KIDS

United States government agents work undercover as the rock group, "Butch Cassidy and the Sun Dance Kids," which consists of teenagers Butch, Merilee, Harvey and Stephanie. Stories depicted the World Wide Talent agency team and its dog, Elvis, engaged in dangerous global spy adventures. *A Hanna–Barbera Production. Color. Half–hour. Premiered on NBC: September 8, 1973–August 31, 1974.*

Voices:
Butch: Chip Hand, **Merilee:** Judi Strangis, **Harvey:** Micky Dolenz, **Stephanie** (Steffy): Tina Holland, **Elvis:** Frank Welker, **Mr. Socrates:** John Stephenson

Episodes:
"The Scientist," "One Of Our Ships Is Missing," "The Counterfeiters," "Double Trouble," "The Pearl Caper," "The Gold Caper," "Road Racers," "Hong Kong Story," "Operation G–Minus," "Orient Express," "Parrot Caper," "The Super Sub" and "The Haunted Castle."

CALIFORNIA RAISINS

Will Vinton's "Claymation" stars, noted for their Motown–style singing in a series of popular commercials for California raisin growers, take viewers on a "Magical Mystery Tour" from a penthouse above their recording studio, accompanied by their hapless show–biz manager, in this Saturday–morning series spin–off, which premiered on CBS. *A Murakami–Wolf–Swenson Films Production. Color. Half–hour. Premiered on CBS: September 16, 1989–September 8, 1990.*

Voices:
Cam Clark, Dorian Harewood, Jim Cummings, Brian Mitchell, Cree Summers, Rebecca Summers, Gailee Heideman, Michelle Marianna, Todd Tolces, Brian Cummings.

Episodes:
"The Apple, Raisin Style," "There's No Business Like Shoe Business," "School Is Cool," "A Royal Mess," "Lights, Camera Disaster," "The Good, The Bad And The Broccoli," "Abracadabra Beebop," "The Grape Outdoors," "Rocket N' Rollin' Raisins," "Hold That Jungle," "Olvera Street," "Picture Perfect Shirelle" and "Family Reunion."

CALVIN AND THE COLONEL

Loosely patterned after their long–running radio series "Amos 'n' Andy," Freeman Gosden and Charles Correll created this animated series featuring the comedy mishaps of two Southern backwoods animals—the shrewd fox, Colonel Montgomery J. Klaxon and his dim–witted, cigar–smoking bear friend, Calvin Burnside. *A Kayro Production. Black–and–white. Half–hour.*

"Amos 'n' Andy" stars Freeman Gosden and Charles Correll created and voiced this animated spin—off of their popular radio characters, "Calvin And The Colonel."

Premiered on ABC: October 3, 1961—September 22, 1962. Syndicated.

Voices:

Colonel Montgomery J. Klaxon: Freeman Gosden, **Maggie Belle Klaxon,** his wife: Virginia Gregg, **Calvin Burnside:** Charles Correll, **Sister Sue:** Beatrice Kay, **Gladys:** Gloria Blondell, **Oliver Wendell Clutch,** lawyer: Paul Frees

Additional Voices:

Frank Gerstle, Barney Phillips

Episodes:

"Back To Nashville," "Calvin Gets Psychoanalyzed," "Calvin's Glamour Girl," "Calvin's Tax Problem," "The Carnappers," "Cloakroom," "Colonel Outfoxes Himself," "Colonel Traps A Thief," "The Colonel's Old Flame," "The Costume Ball," "Jealousy," "Jim Dandy Cleaners," "Magazine Romance," "Money In The Closet," "Nephew Newton's Fortune," "The Polka Dot Bandit," "The Ring Reward," "Sister Sue And The Police Captain," "Sycamore Lodge," "TV Job," "Thanksgiving Dinner," "Wheeling And Dealing," "The Winning Number," "Woman's Picnic" and "The Wrecking Crew."

CAMP CANDY

A group of smart—mouthed kids spend summer under the supervision of their camp director, John Candy, the head counselor, head cook and head handyman of Camp Candy, where roasting marshmallows over a campfire, listening to favorite ghost stories or scaring girl campers with frogs and lizards help make camp life a special experience for everyone. *A DIC Enterprises Production. Color. Half—hour. Premiered on NBC: September 2, 1989—September 1, 1990.*

Voices:

John Candy: Himself, **Binky:** Tony Ail, **Rex:** Lewis Arquette, **Nurse Molly:** Valri Bromfield, **Iggy:** Tom Davidson: **Robin:** Danielle Fernandes, **Vanessa:** Willow Johnson, **Chester:** Danny Mann, **Rick:** Andrew Seebaran, **Alex:** Chiara Zanni

Episodes:

"The Forest's Prime Evil," "Small Foot—Big Trouble," "Katchatori Creature," "Tough As Nayles," "Getting The Bird," "Best Behavior," "Fools Gold," "Slight Of Hand," "Thanks, But No Pranks," "Mind Over Matter," "The Brat Pact," "May The Best Parents Win," "Not So Brave Brave," "Opposites Attract," "Indian Love Call," "Rick Gets The Picture," "Spoiled Sports," "Poor Little Rich Girl" and "Christmas In July."

CAPTAIN CAVEMAN AND THE TEEN ANGELS

The idea of three luscious nubile sleuths named "Charlie's Angels" in teasing one—hour TV dramas uncorked several parodies and late—night variety—show spoofs. Predictably, animated cartoons picked up on the idea as well, featuring a primitive super—sleuth caveman and his three Teen Angels in tame but clever half—hour mysteries. Episodes originally aired as part of "Scooby's All—Star Laff—A—Lympics" and "Scooby's All—Stars," and were repeated when the characters were given their own half—hour timeslot. The series replaced another

Camp director John Candy supervises a group of smart—mouthed kids in the Saturday morning series, "Camp Candy." © DIC Animation City Inc. and Saban Productions

half–hour animated program on ABC, "Spider–Woman." During the 1980–1981 season, Captain Caveman returned in new adventures on "The Flintstones Comedy Show," which was broadcast on NBC. *A Hanna–Barbera Production. Color. Half–hour. Premiered on ABC: March 8, 1980–June 21, 1980.*

Voices:
Captain Caveman: Mel Blanc, **Dee Dee:** Vernee Watson, **Brenda:** Marilyn Schreffler, **Taffy:** Laurel Page

Episodes:
(two per show) "The Kooky Case Of The Cryptic Keys," "The Mixed Up Mystery Of Deadman's Reef," "What A Flight For A Fright," "The Case Of The Creaky Charter Boat," "Big Scare In The Big Top," "Double Dribble Riddle," "The Crazy Case Of The Tell–Tale Tape," "The Creepy Claw Caper," "Cavey And The Kabuta Clue," "Cavey And The Weirdo Wolfman," "The Disappearing Elephant Mystery," "The Fur Freight Fright," "Ride 'Em Caveman," "The Strange Case Of The Creature From Space," "The Mystery Mansion Magic Mix–Up," "Playing Footsie With Bigfoot," "The Scarifying Seaweed Secret," "The Dummy," "Cavey And The Volcanic Villain," "Prehistoric Panic," "Cavey And The Baffling Buffalo Men," "Dragonhead," "Cavey And The Murky Mississippi Mystery," "Old Cavey In New York," "Cavey And The Albino Rhino," "Kentucky Cavey," "Cavey Goes To College," "The Haunting Of Hog's Hollow," "The Legend Of Devil's Run," "The Mystery Of The Meandering Mummy," "The Old Caveman And The Sea" and "Lights, Camera . . . Cavey."

CAPTAIN FATHOM

Filmed in Superanivision, this 1965 animated series follows the adventures of a submarine captain and his battle against evil in this underwater counterpart of Cambria Studios' "Clutch Cargo" and "Space Angel" series, produced in the same illustrative art style. Adventures were introduced by Capt'n Sailor Bird, a parrot. Episodes had no story titles, but instead were numbered in the order of production. *A Cambria Studios Production. Black–and–White. Color. Half–hour. Syndicated: 1965.*

Voices:
Captain Fathom: Warren Tufts

Additional Voices:
Margaret Kerry, Hal Smith, Tom Brown, Ned LeFebver

CAPTAIN HARLOCK AND THE QUEEN OF 1,000 YEARS

The aging queen and members of a nomadic planet, Millenia, plan to invade Earth and claim it as their new homeland. Earth's only hope against this alien threat is Captain Harlock, head of an interstellar space galleon, who protects and defends his home planet. *A Harmony Gold Production. Color. Half–Hour. Premiered: September, 1985. Syndicated.*

Episodes:
"Genesis," "The Inferno," "Mystery Of The Observatory," "Simple Diversions," "Origins," "Deadly Games," "Clash Of

Will," "The Knockout Punch," "The Hidden Land," "Life Sentence," "Zero Hour," "Revelations," "Boot Camp," "Battle Stations," "Survival Time," "Under Sea Encounter," "Desert Sands," "Healing Ways," "The Abduction," "World of Ransoms," "Journey Into Darkness," "Hot Seat," "Knights Without Honor," "Firing Line," "Royal Treatment," "Lone Justice," "Passion Play," "Cat And Mouse," "The Last Laugh," "The Raiding Party," "The Dark Dimension," "Fire And Brimstone," "The White Ship," "Command Performance," "Glory Days," "The Price Of Failure," "The Days Of My Youth," "Chain Game," "The Master Builder," "Return Engagement," "To Catch A Captain," "Double Jeopardy," "Danger Below," "The Deadly Duel," "Lightning Strikes Twice," "Queen's Gambit," "Mutual Destruction," "The Shocking Truth," "The Set Up," "The Sound Of Laughter," "Treason Is In The Eye Of The Beholder," "Date With Destiny," "Balance Of Power," "The Gauntlet," "Ray Of Hope," "Phoenix Rising," "Manifest Destiny," "Friend Or Foe," "Walking Wounded," "White Water," "Coast Guard," "Vengeance," "Anchors Away" and "A New Beginning."

CAPTAIN INVENTORY

Various network–run series from Hanna–Barbera's cartoon library were redistributed to television via syndication for local programming. The program rotated adventures from the following: "Birdman and The Galaxy Trio," "The Fantastic Four," "Frankenstein Jr. and The Impossibles," "Herculoids," "Moby Dick and the Mighty Mightor," "Shazzan!" and "The Space Ghost and Dino Boy." (See individual series for voice and episodic information.) *A Hanna–Barbera Production. Color. Half–hour. Premiered: 1973. Syndicated.*

CAPTAIN N: THE GAME MASTER

Keven Keene, a young Nintendo gamestar, is "sucked" into his TV set and becomes Captain N, the ultimate hero who saves Videoland from the evil machinations of Mother Brain and her host of video villains, including King Hippo and the Eggplant Wizard. Along with his loyal dog, Duke, Kevin pulls together the disorganized heroes of Videoland—Simon Belmont, Mega Man and Kid Icarus—to become the N–Team, charged with keeping Princess Lana in power and holding the forces of evil at bay. Series was based on the phenomenally successful Nintendo games. *A DIC Enterprises Production in association with Nintendo Of America Inc. Color. Half–hour. Premiered on NBC: September 9, 1989–September 1990.*

Voices:
Kevin Keene/Captain N: Matt Hill, **King Hippo:** Gary Chalk, **Dr. Wiley:** Ian James Corlett, **Eggplant Wizard:** Mike Donovan, **Kid Icarus:** Alessandro Juliani, **Simon Belmont:** Andrew Kavadas, **Megaman:** Doug Parker, **Princess Lana:** Venus Terzo, **Duke:** Tomm Wright, **Mother Brain:** Levi Stubbs Jr., **Narrator:** Matt Hill

Episodes:
"Kevin In Videoland," "Mr. & Mrs. Mother Brain," "How's Bayou," "Videolympics," "Mega Trouble For Megaland," "Nightmare On Mother Brain's Street," "Three Men And A

Kevin Keene, a young Nintendo gamestar, fights the evil machinations of Mother Brain and her host of video villains in "Captain N: The Game Master." © DIC Animation City Inc. and Nintendo of America Inc.

Dragon," "Simon The Ape–Man," "Wishful Thinking," "The Most Dangerous Game Master," "Metroid Sweet Metroid," "In Search Of The King" and "Happy Birthday, Mega Man."

THE CARE BEARS (1985)

The lovable bears of Care–A–Lot come down to earth in their cloud mobiles to help children with their problems. Along with the Care Bear Cousins, who live in the Forest of Feelings, the Care Bears make the world a happier place with their motto of caring and sharing. First series to be based on the popular children's book characters. *A DIC Enterprises Production. Color. Half–hour. Premiered: September, 1985. Syndicated.*

Voices:

Tenderheart Bear: Billie Mae Richards, **Friend Bear:** Eva Almos, **Grumpy Bear:** Bobby Dermer, **Birthday Bear:** Melleny Brown, **Bedtime Bear:** Laurie Waller Benson, **Love A Lot Bear:** Linda Sorenson, **Wish Bear:** Janet Lane Green, **Good Luck Bear:** Dan Hennessey, **Share Bear:** Patrice Black, **Champ Bear:** Terry Sears, **Care Bear Cousins: Brave Heart Lion:** Dan Hennessey, **Gentle Heart Lamb:** Louba Goy, **Swift Heart Rabbit:** Eva Almos, **Bright Heart Raccoon:** Jim Henshaw **Lotsa Heart Elephant:** Louba Goy, **Playful Heart Monkey:** Marla Lukovsky, **Proud Heart Cat:** Louise Valance, **Cozy Heart Penguin:** Pauline Penny, **Treat Heart Pig:** Pauline Penny, **Loyal Heart Dog:** Dan Hennessey

Episodes:

"The Birthday," "Camp," "Braces," "Split Decision," "The Lucky Charm," "Soap Box Derby," "The Last Laugh," "The Show Must Go On," "The Forest Of Misfortune," "The Magic Mirror," "Daydreams," "Runaway," "Mayor For A Day," "The Night The Stars Went Out," "The Magic Shop," "Concrete Rain," "Dry Spell," "Drab City," "Wedding Bells," "The Old Man And The Lighthouse," "The Cloud Worm" and "The Girl Who Cried Wolf."

CARE BEARS (1988)

Tenderheart, Grumpy, Cheer, Champ, Grams Bear, Hugs and Tugs are but a few of the cuddly characters of Care–A–lot, a place where feelings of caring are expressed by symbols on the tummies of the bears. *A Nelvana Limited Production. Half–hour. Color. Premiered: September, 1988. Syndicated.*

Voices:

Melleny Brown, Bob Dermer, Luba Goy, Dan Hennessey, Tracey Moore, Pauline Rennie, Billie Mae Richards, Susan Roman, John Stocker, Chris Wiggins

Episodes:

(two episodes per show) "The Thing That Came To Stay," "Lotsa Heart's Wish," "Tugs The Brave," "The Turnabout," "The Space Bubbles," "Desert Gold," "Coconut Crazy," "Camp," "Cheer Of The Jungle," "Oroder On The Court," "The Wrath Of Shreeky," "Under The Bigtop," "Birthday," "The Sleeping Giant," "The Show Must Go On," "Day Dreams," "Magic Mirror," "The Gift Of Caring," "The Dry Spell," "The Land Without Feelings," "The Mystery Of The Phantom," "The Night The Stars Went Out," "Care–A–Lot's Birthday," "The Two Princesses," "Braces," "The Care Bears Town Parade," "Care Bears Battle The Freeze Machine," "No Business Like Show Business," "The Care–A–Lot Games," "Runaway," "The Great Race," "Songfellow Strum And His Magic Train," "The Care Bears Exercise Show," "The Camp Out," "Soap Box Derby," "The Lost Gift," "The Fountain Of Youth," "Treat Heart Baba And The Two Thieves," "Concrete Rain," "The Cloud Worm," "One Million C.B.," "The Girl Who Cried Wolf," "Home Sweet Homeless," "Hearts At Sea," "Ski Trouble," "Perils Of The Pyramid," "The Care Bear Book Of Food Facts And Fables," "The Magic Shop," "The Show Down," "The Fabulous Care Bears Safety Game," "Mayor For A Day," "Grin And Bear It," "Grams Cooking Corner," "King Of The Moon," "Bad Luck Friday," "On Duty," "It's Raining, It's Pouring," "I, Robot Heart," "Wedding Bells," "The Factory Of Uncaring," "A Hungry Little Guy," "The Best Way To Make Friends," "Food Frolics," "The Old Man And The Lighthouse," "Cheer Bear's Chance," "Beautiful Dreamer," "The Most Ancient Gift," "The Frozen Forest," "The Big Star Round–Up," "The Secret Of The Box," "Doctor Brightenstein's Monster," "Music Video," "Drab City," "The Long Lost Care Bears," "Bedtime For Care–A–Lot," "Forest Of Misfortune," "The Purple Chariot," "The Caring Crystals," "Birthday Blues," "Caring For Spring," "Grams Bear's Thanksgiving," "Split Decision," "The Care Fair Scare," "The Cloud Of Uncaring," "Grumpy's Little Friend," "The Last Laugh," "Home Safety Video," "The Cloud Monster," "Grumpy's Three Wishes," "Bravest Of The Brave," "Grams Cooking Corner," "The Care Bear Exercise Show," "Grin And Bear It," "The Perils Of The Pyramid" and "Ski Trouble."

THE CARE BEARS FAMILY

Based on the hit motion picture, each of the bears, from the founding fathers to the little cubs, represent an individual human emotion in this Canadian–produced Saturday morning series which aired on ABC. *A Nelvana Production. Color. Half–hour. Premiered on ABC: September 13, 1986–September 5, 1987. Rebroadcast on ABC: September 26, 1987–January 23, 1988*

Voices:

Melleny Brown, Bob Dermer, Luba Goy, Dan Hennessey, Tracey Moore, Pauline Rennie, Billie Mae Richards, Susan Roman, John Stocker, Chris Wiggins

Episodes:
1986–1987:
"Care–A–Lot's Birthday," "Sharing," "The Great Race," "Caring," "Grumpy's Three Wishes," "Letter," "Home Sweet Homeless," "Stage Fright," "Lost At Sea," "The Sleeping Giant," "Grumpy Dad," "The Camp Out," "I, Robot Heart," "Winning," "The Big Star Roundup," "Sharing," "The Bravest Little Brave," "Caring," "All Powerful Mr. Beastly," "Order On The Court," "Litter," "Long Lost Care Bears," "Stage Fright," "Grams Bears Thanksgiving," "Grumpy Dad," "Cloud Of Uncaring" and "Grumpy Dad."
1987–1988: (new episodes combined with reruns) "The Wrath Of Shreeky," "The Magic Lamp," "Desert Gold," "The Gift Of Caring," "The Two Princesses," "The Cloud Monster," "The Purple Chariot," "Grumpy The Clumsy," "The Best Way To Make Friends" and "The Caring Crystals."

CARTOON CLASSICS

A collection of serialized animated features grouped and sold to more than 100 world–wide television markets in the 1960s. The package included science fiction thrillers and fairy tale classics segmented into cliff–hanging episodes. The first package of cartoons went on the air in 1958, with additional fully animated stories syndicated in 1960 and 1965. Boxing promoter Bill Cayton, who originally entered television with his "Greatest Fights of the Century" series, produced the "Cartoon Classics" series. (Cayton later served as boxing manager for heavyweight champion Mike Tyson.) *A Radio and Television Packagers Production. Color. Half–hour. Syndicated: 1958*

Episodes:
"The Space Explorers" (26 episodes), "The Frog Princess" (19 episodes), "Beauty And The Beast" (16 episodes), "The Magic Antelope" (13 episodes), "The Strange Circus" (6 episodes), "The Fisherman And The Fish" (11 episodes), "The Enchanted Princes" (13 episodes), "New Adventures Of The Space Explorers" (34 episodes), "Gunnar The Sailor" (10 episodes), "The Tiny Oxen" (10 episodes), "Omar And The Ogres" (8 episodes), "The Woodcutter's Wish" (10 episodes), "The Amazing Gift" (10 episodes), "The Fire Bird" (20 episodes), "The Valiant Knight" (10 episodes), "Journey To The Beginning Of Time" (28 episodes), "The Underseas Explorers" (27 episodes), "Wanda And The Wicked Princess" (19 episodes), "Tale Of The Northern Lights" (17 episodes), "The Brave Duckling" (6 episodes), "The Ice Witch" (7 episodes),

"Mr. E From Tau Ceti" (20 episodes) and Hans Christian Andersen's "The Wild Swans" (20 episodes).

CARTOON FUN

In the fall of 1965, ABC added this short–lived series to its Saturday–morning lineup. The half–hour program featured a collection of Jay Ward and Total Television characters seen in repeat episodes, among them, Hoppity Hooper, Dudley Do–Right, Commander McBragg and Aesop and Son. (See these individual cartoons for voice and episodic information.) *A Producers Associates for Television Production. Color. Half–hour. Premiered on ABC: September 26, 1965–December 19, 1965.*

CARTOONIES

Ventriloquist Paul Winchell and his famed wooden sidekicks, Jerry Mahoney and Knucklehead Smith, hosted this half–hour program of theatrical cartoon shorts, featuring films originally produced for Paramount's *Modern Madcaps* and *Noveltoons* series. Characters featured were Goodie the Gremlin, the Cat and Jeepers and Creepers. Initially, the program was titled "Cartoonsville." *A Paramount Cartoon Studios Production. Color. Half–hour. Premiered on ABC: April 6, 1963–September 28, 1963.*

CASPER AND THE ANGELS

The year is 2179, and Casper the friendly ghost is assigned to help a pair of Space Patrol Officers, Minnie and Maxi, maintain law and order in Space City, tangling with cosmic criminals and solving space emergencies in the process. A new character featured in the series was the ghostly Hairy Scary, who provided comic relief. Casper is a character owned and copyrighted by Harvey Cartoons. Originally he was co–created by Paramount animator Joe Oriolo, producer of TV's "Felix the Cat" and "Mighty Hercules" series. (Oriolo collaborated with Sy Reit on the character's conception.) *A Hanna–Barbera Production. Color. Half–hour. Premiered on NBC: September 22, 1979–May 3, 1980.*

Voices:
Casper: Julie McWhirter, **Hairy Scary,** his assistant: John Stephenson, **Officer Mini:** Laurel Page, **Officer Maxi:** Dian McCannon, **Commander:** John Stephenson

Episodes:
(two 11–minute episodes per show) "Casper's Golden Chance," "Space Circus," "Casper's Camp–Out," "Casper Ghosts West," "Strike Four," "The Space Pirate," "The Cat Burglar," "Shipwrecked," "The Smiling Lisa," "Something Fishy," "A Pocket Full O' Schemes," "A Tale Of Two Trashmen," "T.V. Or Not T.V.," "Fatula," "Gone To The Dogs," "Private Eyeball To Eyeball," "Champ For A Day," "The Ghost Robbers," "Aunt Mary Scarey," "The Ice Heist," "The Impossible Scream," "A Shoplifting Experience," "The Commander Is Missing," "Prehistoric Hi–Jinx," "Love At First Fright" and "Savin' Grace In Outer Space."

CASPER THE FRIENDLY GHOST AND COMPANY

Repackaged version of previously exhibited Paramount Pictures cartoons—retitled "Harveytoons" in the early 1960s—starring Casper the Friendly Ghost, Baby Huey, Little Audrey and Herman and Katnip. *A Paramount Cartoon Studios Production for Harvey Films. Color. Half–hour. Premiered: 1974. Syndicated.*

THE CATTANOOGA CATS

Like "The Banana Splits Adventure Hour," this second live–action animation series from Hanna–Barbera featured costumed actors as a feline rock group (Cheesie, Kitty Jo, Scoots, Groove and Country), who not only starred in segments of their own but also hosted the cartoon–filled show.

Cartoon segments were: "It's the Wolf," the madcap adventures of an overzealous wolf (Mildew) whose meal plans are based on snatching one elusive lamb named Lambsy; "Around the World in 79 Days," the globe–trotting adventures of Phineas Fogg Jr., who travels around the world with two teenage friends (Jenny and Happy) in 79 days instead of 80; and "Autocat and Motormouse," a cat and mouse who beat each other at a different game: race car competitions.

Following the first season, the program was reduced to a half–hour. *A Hanna–Barbera Production. Color. One hour. Half–hour. Premiered on ABC: September 6, 1969–September 5, 1970. Rebroadcast on ABC: September 13, 1970–September 4, 1971 (half hour).*

Voices:

Cheesie: Julie Bennett, **Kitty Jo:** Julie Bennett, **Scoots:** Jim Begg, **Groove:** Casey Kasem **Country:** Bill Callaway, **Mildew, the wolf:** Paul Lynde, **Lambsy:** Daws Butler, **Bristle Hound, Lamby's protector:** Allan Melvin, **Phineas Fogg Jr.:** Bruce Watson, **Jenny Trent:** Janet Waldo, **Happy:** Don Messick, **Smerky:** Don Messick, **Crumdon:** Daws Butler, **Bumbler:** Allan Melvin, **Autocat:** Marty Ingels, **Motormouse:** Dick Curtis

Episodes:

"It's the Wolf." (one per show) "It's The Wolf," "When My Sheep Comes In," "High Hopes," "A Sheep In The Deep," "Lambsy Divey In Winter Blunder Land," "Merry–Go–Roundup," "Super Scientific Sheep Sitting Service," "Any Sport In A Storm," "Magic Wanderer," "Runaway–Home," "Smart Dummy," "Channel–Chasers," "Mask Me No Questions," "Freeway–Frenzy," "Slumber Jacks," "Pow–Wow Wolf," "Ghost Of A Chance," "Lambscout Cookout Or Mildew," "Wolf In Sheep's Clothing," "To Beach His Own," "Sheep–Scene Stealer," "How To Cook A Lamb" (working title: "Kookie Cook Book Cook"), "Trained Tripped," "Spring Lamb" and "I Never Met A Lamb I Didn't Like."

"Around the World in 79 Days" (one per show).

"The Race Is On," "Swiss Mis–Adventure," "Arabian Daze," "Madrid Or Busted," "Mr. Bom Bom," "India Or Bust," "Snow Slappy," "Finney, Finney, Fun, Fun," "The Argentiney Meany," "The Tree Man," "Saucy Aussie," "Crumden's Last Stand,"

"Egyptian Jinx," "Border Disorder," "Troubles In Dutch," "The Fiji Weegees" and "Hawaiian Hangup."

"Autocat and Motormouse" (one per show).

"Wheelin' And Dealin'," "Party Crasher," "Water Sports," "What's The Motor With You?," "Mini Messenger," "Wild Wheelin' Wheels," "Soggy To Me," "Crash Course," "Fueling Around," "Buzzin' Cousin," "Snow–Go," "Hard Days Day," "Tally Ha Ha," "Hocus Focus," "Kitty Kitty Bang Bang," "King Size Kaddy," "Catch As Cat Can," "Catnapping Mouse," "Paint That Ain't," "I've Been Framed," "Match Making Mouse," "Electronic Brainstorm," "Brute Farce," "Bouncing Buddies," "Ramblin' Wreck From Texas," "Two Car Mirage," "Alacazap!," "Genie And The Meany," "Choo Choo Cheetah," "The Fastest Mouse In The West," "Cat Skill School," "The Cool Cat Contest," "Lights! Action! Catastrophe!" and "Follow That Cat."

C.B. BEARS

Three bruin investigators (Hustle, Bump and Boogie), travel a rigged up garbage truck (equipped with C.B. and closed circuit TV), to solve mysteries and strange encounters. The three clumsy bears were lead–ins to five other cartoon regulars: "Shake, Rattle and Roll," the misadventures of three ghostly innkeepers in need of a rest; "Undercover Elephant," starring a bumbling secret agent in "Mission Impossible"–type situations; "Heyyy, It's the King," an animalized parody of Henry Winkler's "Fonzie" (now a smart–alecky lion) from TV's "Happy Days"; "Blast Off Buzzard," a Road Runner and Coyote re–creation casting a non–speaking buzzard (Blast–Off) and snake (Crazylegs) in the title roles; and "Posse Impossible," the mishaps of three clumsy cowboys in the Old West. *A Hanna–Barbera Production. Color. One hour. Premiered on NBC: September 10, 1977–June 17, 1978.*

Voices:

C.B. Bears: Hustle: Daws Butler, **Bump:** Henry Corden, **Boogie:** Chuck McCann, **Charlie:** Susan Davis, **Shake, Rattle & Roll: Shake:** Paul Winchell, **Rattle:** Lennie Weinrib, **Roll:** Joe E. Ross, **Sidney Merciless:** Alan Oppenheimer, **Undercover Elephant: Undercover Elephant:** Daws Butler, **Loud Mouse:** Bob Hastings, **Chief:** Michael Bell, **Heyy, It's the King: The King:** Lennie Weinrib, **Skids:** Marvin Kaplan, **Yukayuka:** Lennie Weinrib, **Big H:** Sheldon Allman, **Clyde:** Don Messick, **Sheena:** Ginny McSwain, **Clyde the Ape:** Don Messick, **Posse Impossible: Sheriff:** Bill Woodson, **Stick:** Daws Butler, **Blubber:** Chuck McCann, **Duke:** Daws Butler

Episodes:

"C.B. Bears" (one per show).

"The Missing Mansion Mystery," "The Doomsday Mine," "Follow That Mountain," "The Valley Of No Return," "The Fright Farm," "Drackenstein's Revenge," "Water, Water Nowhere," "Wild, Wild Wilderness," "Island Of Terror," "Go North, Young Bears," "The Invasion Of The Blobs," "Disaster From The Skies" and "The Disappearing Satellites."

"Heyyy, It's the King" (one per show).

"The Blue Kangaroo," "The First King On Mars," "The Riverbed 5000," "Surf's Up," "The King And His Jokers," "Hot Gold Fever," "The Carnival Caper," "The Unhappy Heavy

Hippo," "The King For Prez," "Snowbound Safari," "The Great Billionaire Chase Case," "Boat Fever" and "Go For It, King." "Posse Impossible" (one per show).

"Big Duke And Li'l Lil," "Trouble At Ghostarado," "The Not So Great Train Robbery," "The Alabama Brahma Bull," "The Crunch Bunch Crash Out," "One Of Our Rivers Is Missing," "Sneakiest Rustler In The West," "Bad Medicine," "Busting Boomerino," "Roger The Dodger," "Riverboat Sam, The Gambling Man," "The Invisible Kid" and "Calamity John." "Undercover Elephant" (one per show).

"The Sneaky Sheik," "Baron Von Rip 'Em Off," "The Moanin' Lisa," "Pain In The Brain," "The Great Hospital Hassle," "Latin Losers," "Dr. Doom's Gloom," "Chicken Flickin' Capon Caper," "Undercover Around The World," "Irate Pirates," "Perilous Pigskin," "Swami Whammy" and "The Disappearing Duchess."

"Shake, Rattle, and Roll" (one per show).

"Guess What's Coming To Dinner," "The Ghostly Goul Is A Ghastly Ghost," "There's No Pest Like A Singing Guest," "Shake The Lion Hearted," "The Real Cool Ghoul," "Spooking Is Hazardous To Your Health," "Spooking The Spook," "From Scream To Screen," "Gloom And Doom De–Doom," "Polt R. Geist," "Too Many Kooks," "A Scary Face From Outer Space" and "Health Spa Spooks."

"Blast Off Buzzard" (one per show).

"Buzzard, You're A Turkey," "Hard Headed Hard Hat," "Hearts And Flowers, Buzzards And Snakes," "The Egg And Aye, Aye, Aye," "Testing, One, Two, Three," "Ho, Ho, Ho, It's The Birthday Buzzard," "Wheelin' And Reelin'," "Buzzard, Clean Up Your Act," "Backyard Buzzard," "Spy In The Sky," "First Class Buzzard," "Freezin' And Sneezin'" and "Cousin Snakey Is A Groove."

CBS CARTOON THEATER

Comedian Dick Van Dyke hosted this half–hour collection of Terrytoons cartoons, which originated from WCBS, New York. Four cartoons were shown on each program, including the madcap adventures of "Heckle and Jeckle," "Little Roquefort" and "Dinky Duck." The program was the first network prime–time series featuring animation. *A CBS Terrytoons Production. Black–and–white. Half–hour. Premiered on CBS: June 13, 1956–September 5, 1956.*

Voices:
Gandy Goose: Arthur Kay, **Heckle:** Dayton Allen, Roy Halee, **Jeckle:** Dayton Allen, Roy Halee, **Little Roquefort:** Tom Morrison, **Percy the Cat:** Tom Morrison

CBS STORYBREAK

Bob Keeshan, of "Captain Kangaroo" fame, hosts this weekly series of animated films based on favorite children's books. *A CBS Television Production. Color. Half–hour. Premiered on CBS: March 30, 1985–September 8, 1990.*

Episodes:
"Arnold Of The Ducks," "Chocolate Fever," "C.L.U.T.Z.," "The Double Disappearance Of Watler Fozbek," "Dragon's Blood,"

"The Gammage Cup," "The Great Ringtail Garbage Caper," "Grinny," "Hank The Cowdog," "Harry, The Fat Bear Spy," "How To Eat Fried Worms," "Hugh Pine," "Jeffrey's Ghost And The Leftover Baseball Team," "Mama Don't Allow," "Max And Me And The Time Machine," "The Monster's Ring," "The Pig Plantagenet," "Raggedy Ann And Andy And The Camel With The Wrinkled Knees," "Ratha's Creature," "Robbut: A Tale Of Tailes," "The Roquefort Gang," "The Shy Stegosaurus Of Cricket Creek," "What Happened In Hamelin," "Witch–Cat," "Yeh–Shen: A Cinderella Story From China" and "Zucchini."

THE CENTURIONS

Computer Scientist Crystal Kane and her top secret team of computer–operated warriors, called Centurions, try saving the world from destruction at the hands of Doctor Terror's Doom Drones in this first–run action/adventure series. *A Ruby–Spears Enterprises Production. Color. Half–hour. Premiered: 1985. Syndicated.*

Voices:
Ace McCloud: Neil Ross, **Jake Rockwell:** Vince Edwards, **Max Ray/Dr. Wu:** Pat Fraley, **Crystal Kane:** Diane Pershing, **Rex Charger:** Bob Ridgely, **John Thunder:** Michael Bell, **Doc Terror:** Ron Feinberg, **Hacker:** Edmund Gilbert, **Amber:** Jennifer Darling

Episodes:
"The Sky Is On Fire," "Battle Beneath The Sea," "Denver Is Down," "Micro Menace," "Tornado Of Terror," "Found: One Lost World," "Operation Starfall," "Sand Doom," "Cold Calculations," "Novice," "Double Agent," "You Only Love Twice," "Firebird," "Traitor's Three," "Terror On Ice," "Counterclock Crisis," "An Alien Affair," "Zombie Master," "Malfunction," "Child's Play," "Monsters From Below," "Broken Beams," "The Warrior," "Attack Of The Plant–Borgs," "Let The Games Begin," "Hole In The Ocean—Part 1," "Hole In The Ocean—Part 2," "The Mummy's Curse," "Battle Beneath The Ice," "Hacker Must Be Destroyed," "Incredible Shrinking . . .," "The Chameleon's Sting," "Return Of Captain Steele," "Max Ray . . . Traitor," "Whalesong," "Showdown At Skystalk," "Three Strikes . . .," "Road Devils," "Crack In The World," "Atlantis Adventure—Part 1," "Atlantis Adventure—Part 2," "Live At Five," "Night On Terror Mountain," "The Better Half—Part 1," "The Better Half—Part 2," "That Old Black Magic," "Film At Eleven," "Return Of Cassandra," "Revenge," "To Dare Dominion—Part 1," "To Dare Dominion—Part 2," "Firecracker," "Ghost Warrior," "Zone Danger," "Let The Lighting Fall," "Breakout," "Sungrazer," "Day Of The Animals," "The Cyborg Centurion" and "Man Or Machine" (Five parts).

CHALLENGE OF THE GOBOTS

Earth becomes the battleground in a titanic interplanetary struggle between good and evil when a distant, scientifically advanced world erupts in war. On the high–tech planet GoBotron, the noble Guardian GoBots—a race of robots able to transform into vehicles—pursue the evil Renegade GoBots who scheme to enslave Earth and exploit its resources to conquer GoBotron and the Galaxy in this first–run series based on the famed action–figure toys. *A Hanna Barbera Production in association with the Tonka Corporation. Color. Half-hour. Premiered: 1984. Syndicated.*

Voices:

Leader-1: Lou Richards, **Turbo:** Arthur Burghardt, **Scooter:** Frank Welker, **Cy-Kill:** Bernard Erhard, **Cop–Tur:** Bob Holt **Crasher:** Marilyn Lightstone, **Matt Hunter:** Morgan Paull, **A. J. Foster:** Leslie Speights, **Nick Burns:** Sparky Marcus, **Dr. Braxis:** Rene Auberjonois

Episodes:

1984–85 "Battle For GoBotron," "Target Earth," "Conquest On Earth," "Earth Bound" and "The Final Conflict."
1985–1986 "Time Wars," "Forced Alliance," "Invasion From The 21st Level" (Part 1), "Cy–Kill's Cataclysmic Trap," "Sentinel," "Genius And Son," "Invasion From The 21st Level" (Part 2), "Renegade Alliance," "Dawn World," "Speed Is Of The Essence," "Trident's Triple Threat," "Renegade Rampage" (Part 1), "It's The Thought That Counts," "Nova Beam," "Cold Spell," "The Quest For Roguestar," "Cy–Kill's Shrinking Ray," "Doppleganger," "Gameworld," "Crime Wave," "Scooter Enhanced," "Wolf In The Fold," "The GoBot Who Cried Renegade," "Cy–Kill's Escape" (Part 1—GoBotron Saga), "Renegade Rampage" (Part 2), "Lost On GoBotron," "Steamer's Defection," "Ultra Zod," "Whiz Kid," "In Search Of Ancient GoBonauts," "Fitor To The Finish," "Depth Charge," "Auto Madic," "Quest For The Creator" (Part 2—GoBotron Saga), "The Seer," "Pacific Overtures," "Transfer Point," "Tarnished Image," "The Ring Of Fire," "The Third Column," "The Fall Of Gobotron," "Renegade Carnival," "Clutch Of Doom," "A New Suit For Leader," "Escape From Elba," "Flight To Earth," "The Gift," "The Last Magic Man," "Element Of Danger," "Destroy All Guardians," "Braxis Gone Bonkers," "The Final Victory," "The Secret Of Halley's Comet," "Et Tu Cy–Kill," "The Gobots That Time Forgot," "Terror In Atlantis," "Inside Job," "Mission Gobotron," "Quest For A New Earth" and "Guardian Academy."

CHALLENGE OF THE SUPER FRIENDS

Evil forces unite to annihilate the guardians of humanity— Superman, Batman and Robin, Wonder Woman, Aquaman and other comic book superheroes of the Hall of Justice—who are forced to use all their supernatural powers to combat the wicked Legion of Doom. *A Hanna–Barbera Production. Color. Half–hour. Premiered on ABC: September 8, 1978–September 15, 1979.*

Voices:

Narrator: Bill Woodson, **Super Friends: Superman:** Danny Dark, **Batman:** Olan Soule, **Robin:** Casey Kasem, **Wonder Woman:** Shannon Farnon, **Aquaman:** Bill Callaway, **Zan/ Gleek:** Mike Bell, **Jayna:** Liberty Williams, **Computer:** Casey Kasem, **Black Vulcan:** Buster Jones, **Samurai/Flash/Hawkman:** Jack Angel, **Apache Chief/Green Lantern:** Mike Rye,

Flash/Hawkman: Jack Angel, **Legion of Doom: Luthor:** Stanley Jones, **Brainiac/Black Manta:** Ted Cassidy, **Toyman:** Frank Welker, **Giganta:** Ruth Forman, **Cheeta:** Marlene Aragon, **Riddler:** Mike Bell, **Captain Cold:** Dick Ryal, **Sinestro:** Vic Perrin, **Scarecrow:** Don Messick, **Bizarro:** Bill Callaway, **Solomon Grundy:** Jimmy Weldon, **Grodd the Gorilla:** Stanley Ross

Episodes:

"Wanted: The Superfriends," "Invasion Of The Fearians," "The World's Deadliest Game," "The Time Trap," "Trial Of The Superfriends," "The Monolith Of Evil," "The Giants Of Doom," "Secret Origins Of The Superfriends," "Revenge On Gorilla City," "Swamp Of The Living Dead," "Conquerors Of The Future," "The Final Challenge," "Fairy Tale Of Doom," "Doomsday," "Superfriends: Rest In Peace" and "History Of Doom."

THE CHARLIE BROWN AND SNOOPY SHOW

Charles Schulz's beloved comic strip characters come to life in animated vignettes focusing on school, sports and, of Snoopy in this half–hour series consisting of three separate stories based on Schulz's popular comic strip. *A Lee Mendelson–Bill Melendez Production in association with Charles M. Schulz Creative Associates and United Feature Syndicate. Color. Half–hour. Premiered on CBS: September 17, 1983– August 16, 1986.*

Voices:

Charlie Brown: Brad Kesten, Brett Johnson, **Linus:** Jeremy Schoenberg, **Lucy:** Angela Lee, Heather Stoneman, **Schroeder:** Kevin Brando, Danny Colby, **Peppermint Patty:** Victoria Hodges, Gini Holtzman, **Marcie:** Michael Dockery, Keri Holtzman, **Rerun:** Jason Muller (Mendelson), **Frieda:** Mary Tunnell, **Little Girl:** Dana Ferguson, **Franklin:** Carl Steven, **Singer** (theme song): Desiree Goyette, **Singer:** Joseph Chemay, **Singer:** Joey Harrison Scarbury

Episodes:

1983–1984 #1: "Shaking," "Spaghetti," "Football," "Baseball," "Toast," "Snow Sculpture," "Sit," "School," "Kite," "The Blanket," "Sally"; #2: "Snoopy And Woodstock," "Sally," "Piano," "Baseball," "Sunset," "Football," "Security Blanket," "Kite," "Woodstock," "Clinging Snoopy"; #3: "Woodstock," "Baseball," "Sally," "Piano," "Blanket"; #4: "Sally And Snoopy," "Football," "Beads," "Love," "Snowballs," "Kite Flying," "Linus And Lucy," "Baseball"; #5: "Kiss," "Peppermint Patty," "Charlie Brown Lost," "Snoopy"; #6: "Crawl," "Marcie," "Truffles," "The Lost Ballfield"; #7: "Shoveling," "Rerun," "Lost Blanket," "The Manager"; #8: "Kite–Eating Tree," "Sally," "Camp," "Lucy Loves Schroeder," "Scared Snoopy"; #9: "Charlie Brown And Lucy," "Kite," "The Dance," "Thiebault"; #10: "Straws," "Lucy Baseball," "Peppermint Patty," "Daisy Hill Puppy Cup," "Linus And Lucy"; #11: "Gold Stars," "Blanket," "Piano," "Teaching"; #12: "Sally At School," "Football," "School Patrol," "Blanket," "The Team"; and #13: "Vulture," "Blanket," "Peppermint Patty," "Rerun" and "Rainy Day."
1984–1985 (new episodes combined with reruns) #1: "Snoo-

py's Foot," "Giant," "Rerun"; #2: "The Pelican," "Great Pumpkin," "Spike"; and #3: "Snoopy's Robot," "Linus And The Blanket," "Friends."

CHIP 'N DALE RESCUE RANGERS

Following the enormous success of its number–one rated daily animated series "DuckTales," Walt Disney introduced this first–run syndicated animated companion featuring chipmunk favorites Chip and Dale in cliff–hanger stories filled with mystery and intrigue, Indiana Jones–style. The fast-talking, ever-squabbling pair are heads of a small eccentric group of animal characters who solve cases which lead to bigger crimes with far–reaching consequences. Chip and Dale's team of investigators: Monterey Jack, a raucous, back–slapping musclemouse who is Dale's right–hand; Zipper the fly; Gadget, a consummate inventor who doubles as Chip and Dale's romantic interest; and Sewer Al, a six–and–a–half foot cajun alligator who acts as the enforcer. *A Walt Disney Production. Color. Half–hour. Syndicated: September 1989.*

Voices:
Corey Burton, Peter Cullen, Jim Cummings, Tress MacNeille

Episodes:
"Catteries Not Included," "Three Men And A Booby," "The Carpetsnaggers," "Piratsy Under The Sea," "Adventures In Squirrelsitting," "Flash The Wonder Dog," "The Pound Of The Baskervilles," "Parental Discretion Retired," "Riskey Beesness," "Bearing Up Baby," "Out To Launch," "Dale Beside Himself," "Kiwis Big Adventure," "A Lad In The Lamp," "Battle Of The Bulge," "My Science Project," "Ghost Of A Chance," "An Elephant Never Suspects," "A Case Of Stageblight," "The Luck Stops Here," "Fake Me To Your Leader," "Last Train To Cashville," "The Case Of The Cola Cult," "Throw Mummy From The Train," "A Wolf In Cheap Clothing," "Prehysterical Pet," "Robocat," "Does Pavlov Ring A Bell?", "A Creep In The Deep," "Seer No Evil," "Chocolate Chips," "Chipwrecked Shipmunks," "The Last Leprechaun," "Doubl 'O' Chipmunks," "Song Of The Night 'N Dale," "Love Is A Many Splintered Thing," "Weather Or Not," "Out Of Scale," "Gadget Goes Hawaiian," "To The Rescue Special" (Part 1), "To The Rescue Special" (Part 2), "To The Rescue Special" (Part 3), "To The Rescue Special" (Part 4), "To The Rescue Special" (Part 5), "Good Times, Bat Times," "Short Order Cooks," "When Mice Were Men," "It's A Bird, It's Insane, It's Dale," "One–Upman–Chip," "Zipper Come Home," "Shell Shocked," "Puffed Rangers," "A Fly In The Ointment," "Dirty Rotten Diapers," "Mind Your Own Cheese & Q's," "Pie In The Sky," "A Chorus Crime," "Le Purrfect Crime," "When You Fish Upon A Star," "A Lean On The Property," "Rest Home Rangers," "The Pied Piper Power Play" and "Gorilla My Dreams."

CHUCK NORRIS' KARATE KOMMANDOS

Action film star Chuck Norris supplied his own voice in this short–lived syndicated series, in which the former karate champ encounters worldly villains, including Super Ninja and an evil empire known as Vulture. *A Ruby Spears Enterprises*

Action film star Chuck Norris, in animated form, from the short–lived syndicated series, "Chuck Norris' Karate Kommandos." © Ruby–Spears Enterprises

Production. Color. Half–hour. Premiered: September, 1986. Syndicated.

Voices:
Chuck Norris: Himself, **Tabe,** Ninga Henchman: Robert Ito, **Too Much:** Mona Marshall, **Kimo:** Keye Luke, **Reed:** Sam Fontana, **Pepper:** Kathy Garver, **The Claw:** Bill Martin, **Super Ninja:** Keone Young, **President:** Alan Oppenheimer

Episodes:
"Deadly Dolphin," "Target: Chuck Norris," "Terror Train," "Menace From Space" and "Island Of The Walking Dead."

CLUE CLUB

The adventures of four professional teenage detectives—Pepper, Larry, Dotty and D. D.—who collect clues to unsolvable crimes in the same manner as celebrated London sleuth Sherlock Holmes. The foursome is assisted in their search for clues by two cowardly dogs, Woofer and Wimper. *A Hanna–Barbera Production. Color. Half–hour. Premiered on CBS: August 14, 1976–September 3, 1977. Rebroadcast on CBS: September 10, 1978–September 2, 1979.*

Voices:
Larry: David Jolliffe, **D. D.:** Bob Hastings, **Pepper:** Patricia Stich, **Dotty:** Tara Talboy, **Woofer:** Paul Winchell, **Wimper:** Jim McGeorge, **Sheriff Bagley:** John Stephenson

Episodes:

"The Paper Shaper Caper," "The Case Of The Lighthouse Mouse," "Who's To Blame For Empty Frame," "The Real Gone Gondola," "The Weird Seaweed Creature Caper," "The Green Thumb Caper," "The Disappearing Airport Caper," "The Walking House Caper," "The Solar Energy Caper," "The Vanishing Train Caper," "The Dissolving Statue Caper," "The Missing Pig Caper," "One Of Our Elephants Is Missing," "The Amazing Heist," "The Pre–Historic Monster Caper" and "The Circus Caper."

CLUTCH CARGO

Established author Clutch Cargo travels the globe in search of adventure with his constant companions Swampy, Spinner and dog Paddlefoot. Piloting his plane anywhere a friend needs help, Clutch uses only his wits to defeat the villains. Created by one–time cartoonist Clark Haas, these five–minute serialized adventures combined limited animation and a live–action process called Synchro-Vox, invented by Ed Gillette and first used for "talking animal" commercials in the 1950s. This economical but unsophisticated method superimposed the human lips of voice actors over the mouths of their animated counterparts, the only parts of the characters that moved. Twenty–six half hour shows, each consisting of five five–minute episodes, were produced for the low–budget series between 1957 and 1960. In 1990, the series was shown for the first time in nearly three decades on The Comedy Channel. *A Cambria Productions. Color. Half–hour. Premiered: March, 1959. Syndicated.*

Voices:

Clutch Cargo: Richard Cotting, **Swampy:** Hal Smith, **Spinner/Paddlefoot:** Margaret Kerry

Action was the name of the game for globe–trotting adventurer Clutch Cargo in five–minute episodes produced for syndication.

Episodes:

(known titles) "Clutch Cargo And The Friendly Headhunters," "Arctic Bird Giant," "Pearl Pirate," "Race Car Mystery," "The North Woods Mystery," "Clutch Cargo And Twaddle In Africa," "Clutch Cargo And The Lost Plateau," "Clutch Cargo And The Ghost Ship," "Clutch Cargo And The Rustlers," "Clutch Cargo And The Missing Train," "The Devil Bird," "Clutch Cargo And Pipeline To Danger," "Clutch Cargo And The Air Race," "The Sky Circus," "The Cropdusters," "Clutch Cargo And The Dinky Incas," "Kangaroo Express," "Clutch Cargo And The Shipwreckers," "Clutch Cargo And The Counterfeiters," "Dynamite Fury," "Alaskan Adventure," "Swiss Mystery," "Pirate Isle," "Clutch Cargo And The Smog Smuggler," "Test Flight," "Deadend Gultch," "The Flying Bus," "Road Race," "Feather Fuddle," "Water Wizards," "Terrible Tiger," "The Circus," "Rush Pilots," "Cheddar Cheater," "The Blunder Bird," "The Case Of Ripcord Van Winkle," "Cookie Caper" and "The Big 'X'."

COLONEL BLEEP

A universe light years away is the setting for action and adventure in which Colonel Bleep and his Space Deputies, Scratch the Caveman and Squeak the Puppet, battle Doctor Destructo, master criminal of the universe. Four six–minute episodes were shown per half hour. *A Soundac Color Production. Color. Half–hour. Premiered: 1957. Syndicated.*

THE COMIC STRIP

Produced in the manner of "Funtastic World of Hanna–Barbera" and "Super Sunday," this two–hour series was a marathon of first–run cartoons featuring several stars in their own episodic adventures: "Karate Kat," a klutzy karate expert who heads a detective agency (obviously inspired by the popularity of the *The Karate Kid* feature film series); "The Street Frogs," streetwise frogs who encounter comedy and adventure; "The Mini–Monsters," the antics of two brat youngsters and their summer camp monster pals, Dracky, Franklyn, Mumm–O, Blank–O and Wolfie; and "Tigersharks," an intrepid group of explorers and their underwater adventures. *A Rankin–Bass Production. Color. Two hours. Syndicated: September, 1987.*

Voices:

Karate Kat: Robert McFadden, Earl Hammond, Maggie Jakobson, Gerrianne Raphael, Larry Kenney, **Mini–Monsters:** Robert McFadden, Jim Meskimen, Maggie Jakobson, Seth Green, Jim Brownold, Josh Blake, Danielle DuClos, Peter Newman, **Street Frogs:** Gordy Owens, Gary V. Brown, Tanya Willoughby, Carmen De Lavallade, Ron Taylor, Daniel Wooten, Donald Acree, Robert McFadden, **Tigersharks:** Robert McFadden, Earl Hammond, Larry Kenney, Peter Newman, Jim Meskimen, Jim Brownold, Camille Banora

Episodes:

"Karate Kat" (one per show).
"The Katzenheimer Kaper," "The Sardine Turnover Kaper," "The Mousemobile Kaper," "The Crow Key Kaper," "The Kata Hari Kaper," "The Picat–So Kaper," "Ticktocking Along," "The

Koffee Kup Kaper," "Kat Tracks," "The Bank Heist," "The Tabby Tire Tracker," "The Pink Sphinx," "Cats Ahoy," "The Cousin Kaper," "The Bathtub Bandits," "Pretty Kitty Kaper," "The Kattensniffer Kaper," "The Cats 'N Bats Caper," "The Tabby Telemann Kaper," "Cat Goes Ape," "The Ghost Of Legs Larue," "Kat's Paw," "The Twin Brother Kaper," "The Amnesia Kaper" and "The Lonely Hearts Kaper,"

"Mini–Monsters" (one per show).

"Camp Mini–Mon–The First Day," "The Belly Ache," "Alien," "Practical Joke Day," "Parent's Day," "Melissa's Magic Painting," "They're Not Monsters," "The Big Fight," "The Swim Meet," "Cawfield Blows His Cool," "The Magic Feather," "The Switch," "Wolfie's Bet," "La Goon In Love," "Mini–Mon's Horse," "Dr. Jeckyl And Mr. Claws," "Ghosts In The Night," "House For Sale," "Campy Goody Twoshoe," "Franklyn Builds A Friend," "Mumm–O's Birthday," "Home Movies," "The Inspection," "A Visit From Ooze," "Phantom Of The Mess Hall" and "Dracky's Bat."

"Street Frogs" (one per show).

"The Hop Line," "The Crate," "Typhoon Takes Off," "The Drop Out," "Loretta Goes To Hollywood," "Rapperman," "Fiddling Around," "The Super," "The Babysitters," "Frog T.V.," "Surprise Fights," "Take Out," "Moose's Ride," "The Car Show," "Bye Bye Toad," "High Fashion Frogs," "Fleet Frogs," "The Derby," "The Night Job," "The Hairdo," "Misty Marvelous," "The Street Fair," "Wilfred Returns," "When I Grow Up" and "The Phone Call."

"Tigersharks" (one per show).

"The Fish Tank," "Sark To The Rescue," "Save The Sark," "The Deep Fryer," "Bowfin," "Pappagallo's Present," "The Lighthouse," "Go With The Flow," "Termagant," "The Terror Of Dragonstein," "The Search For Redfin," "The Kraken," "Stowaway," "Iced," "The Volcano," "A Question Of Age," "Eye Of The Storm," "Departure," "Murky Waters," "The Spellbinder," "The Waterscope," "The Point Of No Return," "The Scavenger Hunt," "Paradise Island," "The Treasure Map" and "Redfin Returns."

COMMONWEALTH CARTOON PACKAGE

Cartoon favorites "Flip the Frog," "Willie Whopper," Paul Terry's "Aesop's Fables," and others comprised this series of vintage cartoons offered for local programming. Several early Walt Disney cartoon shorts were also included in this syndicated package. *Black–and–white. Half–hour. Premiered: 1951. Syndicated.*

THE COMPLETELY MENTAL MISADVENTURES OF ED GRIMLEY

Comedian Martin Short teamed up with Hanna–Barbera Productions to produce this half–hour Saturday–morning show based on his famed "Saturday Night Live" character, Ed Grimley, a sweetly nerdy guy who lives in a funky Victorian apartment with a goldfish named Moby and a clever rat named Sheldon. Plotlines include his encounters with the ever–

cranky Mr. Freebus, Ed's landlord, who wants more than anything to evict him; Miss Malone, his gorgeous down–the–hall neighbor for whom Ed shyly expresses "extreme liking"; the Truly Remarkable Gustav Brothers, identical twins who look nothing alike and interrupt the show to explain the scientific phenomena involved in Ed's peril of the moment; and Ed's favorite television program, Count Floyd and his "Really Scaaary Stories Show," which he watches religiously. (Trouble is, the Count's tales never scare anybody.) *A Hanna–Barbera Production. Color. Half–hour. Premiered on NBC: September 10, 1988–September 2, 1989.*

Voices:

Ed Grimley: Martin Short, **Count Floyd:** Joe Flaherty, **Sheldon:** Frank Welker, **Miss Malone:** Katherine O'Hara, **Mr. Freebus:** Jonathan Winters, **Mrs. Freebus:** Andrea Martin, **The Gustav Brothers: Roger:** Jonathan Winters, **Wendell:** Danny Cooksey

Episodes:

"Tall, Dark and Hansom," "E. G., Go Home," "Ed's In Hot Water," "Ed's Debut," "Good Neighbor Ed," "Grimley, P.F.C.," "Moby Is Lost," "Crate Expectations," "Driver Ed," "Blowin' In The Wind," "Eyewitness Ed," "Eddy, We Hardly Knew Ye" and "The Irving Who Came To Dinner."

COOL McCOOL

Bumbling detective McCool was created by cartoonist Bob Kane, the co–creator of "Batman," in the vein of Maxwell Smart, agent 86, who stumbled his way to the solution of crimes. The show also contained one Keystone Kop–like adventure of Harry McCool, Cool's father, who chases down thieves and other no–goods with the help of two klutzy policemen, Tom and Dick. *A King Features Production. Color. Half–hour. Premiered on NBC: September 10, 1966–August 30, 1969.*

Voices:

Cool McCool: Bob McFadden, **Number One,** his boss: Chuck McCann, **Friday,** Number One's secretary: Carol Corbett, **Riggs,** a scientific genius: Chuck McCann

Episodes:

"Cool McCool" (two per show).

"Big Blowout," "Fine Feathered Friends," "If That Hat Fits," "House That Jack Built," "The Odd Boxes Caper," "Garden Of Evil," "Rocket Racket," "Queen's Ransom," "Big Brainwash," "Shrinking The Slinker," "The Box Fox," "Bagging The Windbag," "Will The Real Coolmobile Please Stand Up?," "Owl On The Prowl," "Sniffin', Snoozen', Sneezin'," "How No Fowl Owl," "Caps And Robbers," "Romantic Rattler," "Jack In The Boxer," "Love Is A Gas," "Who Stole My 32 Secret Agents?," "500–Pound Canary," "Fun And Games," "Mother Greta's Wrinkle Remover," "Two Fats And A Fink," "Rock–A–Bye For Rattler," "Hi Jacker Jack," "The Wind Goddess," "Hot McHott," "A Growing Problem," "Oh, Say Can You Send," "What Goes Up Must Come Down," "Birds Of A Feather," "The Box Popper," "Owl's Well That Ends Well," "A Tree Is A Tree," "Whistler's Mommy Case" and "College Of Crooks."

"Harry McCool" (one per show).

Bumbling detective Cool McCool stumbled his way into solving crimes in Saturday morning's "Cool McCool" series. © King Features Entertainment

"Phantom Of The Opera House," "Horsehide And Go Seek," "Vanishing Shoehorns," "Pie In Your Eye," "Woodchopper," "Gym Dandy," "Big Top Cops," "The New Car," "Three Men On A House," "Fowl Play," "The Jet Set Yet," "McCool Jazz," "Dog Tired," "High Jokers," "Time Out," "Monkey Dizziness," "Green Dragon," "Lots Of Balloony," "Goat Chasers," and "In The Dough."

C.O.P.S.

Former F.B.I. special agent Baldwin P. ("Bulletproof") Vess tries eradicating organized crime in Empire City with the help of his C.O.P.S. crime-fighting force, each member a master of a special skill and dedicated to the cause of justice. *A DIC*

Enterprises Production. Color. Half-hour. Premiered: September, 1988. Syndicated.

Voices:

Baldwin P. ("Bulletproof") Vess: Ken Ryan, **Longram:** John Stocker, **The Big Boss/Mace:** Len Carlson, **Badvibes:** Ron Rubin, **Buttons McBoom Boom/Bowzer:** Nick Nichols, **Berserko:** Paul De La Rosa, **Rock Krusher:** Brent Titcomb, **Squeeky:** Marvin Goldhar, **Turbo Tu-Tone:** Dan Hennessey, **Nightshade:** Jane Schoettle, **Bullseye:** Peter Keleghan, **Highway/Barricade:** Ray James, **Hardtop:** Darren Baker, **Mainframe:** Mary Long, **Whitney Morgan:** Jeri Craden, **Mirage:** Liz Hanna, **Ms. Demeanor** Paulina Gillis

Episodes:

"The Case Of The Stuck-Up Blimp," "The Case Of The Crime Circus," "The Case Of The Baffling Bugman," "The Case Of Berserko's Big Surprise," "The Case Of The Bogus Justice Machines," "The Case Of The Prison Break-In," "The Case Of The Pardner In Crime," "The Case Of C.O.P.S. File #1" (Parts 1 and 2), "The Case Of The Blur Bandits," "The Case Of The Bulletproof Waldo," "The Case Of The Blitz Attack," "The Case Of The Baby Badguy," "The Case Of The Thieving Robots," "The Case Of The Highway Robbery," "The Case Of The Crime Convention," "The Case Of The Crook With 1000 Faces," "The Case Of The Super Shakedown," "The Case Of The Criminal Mall," "The Case Of The Big Bad Boxoids," "The Case Of The Half-Pint Hero," "The Case Of The Brilliant Berserko," "The Case Of The Big Frame-Up," "The Case Of The Sinister Spa," "The Case Of The Cool Caveman," "The Case Of The Wayward Whiz Kid," "The Case Of The Stashed Cash," "The Big Boss's Master Plan" (Parts 1 and 2), "The Case Of The Criminal Games," "The Case Of The Iceberg Pirates," "The Case Of The Giveaway Gold," "The Case Of The Big Little Green Men," "The Case Of The Crook With A Conscience," "The Case Of Mace's Romance," "The Case Of The Crime Nobody Heard," "The Case Of The Bogus Bride," "The Case Of The Visiting Mother," "The Case Of The Ghost Crooks," "The Case Of The Lying Lie Detector," "The Case Of The Disappearing Dough," "The Case Of Mukluk's Luck," "The Case Of The Baby Badguy's Return," "The Case Of The Rock And Roll Robbers," "The Case Of The Boy Who Cried Sea Monster," "The Case Of The Runaway Buzzbomb," "The Case Of The Missing Masterpiece," "The Case Of The Lesser Of Two Weevils," "The Case Of The Big Boss's Bye-Bye," "The Case Of The Iron C.O.P. And Wooden Crooks," "The Case Of The Midas Touch," "The Case Of The Ready Room Mutiny," "The Case Of The High Iron Hoods," "The Case Of The Kangaroo Caper," "The Case Of The Missing Memory," "The Case Of The Lowest Crime," "The Case Of The Crooked Contest," "The Case Of The Ransomed Rascal," "The Case Of The Spotless Kingpin," "The Case Of The Lawless Lady," "The Case Of The Lost Boss," "The Case Of The Bad Luck Burglar," "The Case Of The Big Boss's Big Switch," "The Case Of The Red-Hot Hoodlum" and "The Case Of The Invisible Crime."

COUNT DUCKULA

Unlike most vampires whose thirst for blood knows no earthly limits, Count Duckula is a reluctant vampire with a hankering for show business who, instead of blood, sucks on broccoli sandwiches. His Castle Duckula and its occupants—Igor, Nanny and Dr. Von Goosewing—are transported anywhere in the world on command, where they experience many madcap adventures. *A Cosgrove–Hall Production. Color. Half–hour. Premiered on Nickelodeon: February 6, 1988.*

Voices:
Count Duckula: David Jason, **Igor:** Jack May, **Nanny:** Brian Trueman, **Von Goosewing:** Jimmy Hibbert, **Other Voices:** Ruby Wax, **Narrator:** Barry Clayton

Episodes:
"No Sax Please—We're Egyptian," "Vampire Vacation," "One Stormy Night," "Transylvania Homesick Blues," "Mutinous Penguins," "Dr. Von Goosewing's Invisible Ray," "Down Under Duckula," "All In A Fog," "Open To The Public," "The Ghost Of McCastle McDuckula," "Igor's Busy Day," "Auto Duck," "The Vampire Strikes Back," "Hard Luck Hotel," "Hunchbudgie Of Notre Dame," "Dear Diary," "Rent–A–Butler," "Jungle Duck," "Mobile Home," "Fright At The Opera," "Dr. Goosewing And Mr. Duck," "Town Hall Terrors," "Sawdust Ring," "Duckula And The Broccoli Stalk," "The Family Reunion," "Ghostly Gold," "Ducknapped," "The Lost Valley," "Incredible Shrinking Duck," "Hi–Duck," "Prime Time Duck," "Blood Sucking Fruit Bats Of The Lower Amazon," "The Count And The Pauper," "Artic Circle," "Transylvanian Takeaway," "Whodonit?," "No Yaks Please—We're Tibetian," "Beau Duckula," "Mississippi Duck," "Amnesiac Duck," "Wax Museum," "Return Of The Curse," "Lost City Of Atlantis," "Bad Luck Duck," "Private Beak," "Astro Duck," "Unreal Estate," "Bombay Duck," "They Were Werewolves," "Duck Ahoy" and "The Great Ducktective."

THE COUNT OF MONTE CRISTO

Those who pervert justice for their own ends are the targets of the Count of Monte Cristo and his two friends, Rico and

A scene from the animated version of the classic Alexander Dumas adventure, "The Count Of Monte Cristo."
© Halas & Batchelor Productions

Jacopo. Cristo has one consuming passion—to see injustice of any sort uncovered and denounced. Halas and Batchelor, once the largest animation film production studio in Europe, produced this cartoon import in 1974. *A Halas and Batchelor/R.A.I. Production. Color. Half–hour. Premiered: 1974. Syndicated.*

Voices:
George Roubicek, Jeremy Wilkin, Bernard Spear, Peter Hawkins, Miriam Margoyles, Jean England, David de Keyser

Episodes:
"Skullduggery," "The Mad Marquis," "The Curse Of Magdapur," "The Fortress Of Invention," "Island Under Siege," "Fortune Hunters," "Cristo Disgraced," "Caverns Of Slavery," "Legend Of Hermandez," "Downfall Of Dumklott," "Bridge Bomber," "Dastardly D'Arcy," "The Black Orchid," "Rogues Gallery," "Music Hath Charms," "Search For Power" and "Destroy The Tower."

COURAGEOUS CAT AND MINUTE MOUSE

Comic-book artist Bob Kane, who created TV's "Cool McCool," parodied his own creation of caped crusaders Batman and Robin in this first–run series which featured a crimefighting cat and mouse who fight for truth, justice and self–protection in Empire City (a takeoff of Gotham City in the Batman series). Relying on a multi–purpose Catgun and Catmobile, Courageous Cat and Minute encounter such villains as the Frog (his real name is "Chauncey" and he is patterned after movie tough guy Edward G. Robinson), his assistant Harry the Gorilla, Rodney Rodent, Black Cat, Professor Noodle Stroodle and Professor Shaggy Dog. *A Trans–Artist Production. Color. Half–hour. Premiered: September, 1960. Syndicated.*

Voices:
Courageous Cat/Minute Mouse: Bob McFadden

Episodes:
"The Case Of Cousin Outrageous," "The Case Of The Abandoned Movie Sets," "The Case Of The Auto Tycoons," "The Case Of The Backward Clock," "The Case Of The Bank Robbery," "The Case Of The Big Ball Game," "The Case Of The Big Movie Star," "The Case Of The Big Party," "The Case Of The Big Pipe Line," "The Case Of The Big Race," "The Case Of The Big Squeeze," "The Case Of The Monster Vine," "The Case Of The Robot," "The Case Of The Draggy Dragster," "The Case Of The Fortune Teller," "The Case Of The TV Mystery," "The Case Of The Crime Kits," "The Case Of The King–Size Caper," "The Case Of The Big Trial," "The Case Of The Blinking Planet," "The Case Of The Boxing Champ," "The Case Of The Carnival Capers," "The Case Of The Cat Cave Treasure," "The Case Of The Construction Caper," "The Case Of The Counterfeiters," "The Case Of The Creatures From Down Under," "The Case Of The Crime Lab," "The Case Of The Diamond Smugglers," "The Case Of The Embassy Stake Out," "The Case Of The Fabulous Diamond," "The Case Of The Flying Eye," "The Case Of The Flying Saucer," "The Case Of The Frogmen," "The Case Of The Fugitive At Large," "The

Case Of The Gasoline War," "The Case Of The Golden Statue," "The Case Of The Great Circus Mystery," "The Case Of The Gun Mixup," "The Case Of The Haunted House," "The Case Of The Hermit Of Creepy Hollow," "The Case Of The Invisible Robbers," "The Case Of The Iron Shark," "The Case Of The Mad Cowboys," "The Case Of The Mad Painter," "The Case Of The Mad Scientist," "The Case Of The Magic Wand," "The Case Of The Mail Train Robbery," "The Case Of The Masked Raiders," "The Case Of The Minced Spies," "The Case Of The Mind Reader," "The Case Of The Missing Masterpiece," "The Case Of The Missing Partner," "The Case Of The Mysterious Submarine," "The Case Of The Mysterious Weather," "The Case Of The Nine Lives," "The Case Of The Northwoods Caper," "The Case Of The Opera Singer," "The Case Of The Peace Pipe," "The Case Of The Perfect Alibi," "The Case Of The Professor's Machine," "The Case Of The Rescue Squad," "The Case Of The Robber Rabbit," "The Case Of The Saggin' Dragon," "The Case Of The Scheming Cleaners," "The Case Of The Secret Weapon," "The Case Of The Shoo Shoo Fly," "The Case Of The Sniffer Machine," "The Case Of The Spies' Return," "The Case Of The Stolen Cheese," "The Case Of The Stolen Pyramid," "The Case Of The TV Director," "The Case Of The Thinking Cap," "The Case Of The Trampoline Performers," "The Case Of The Undercover Agents," "The Case Of The Unmentionables," "The Case Of The Unthinkables," "The Case Of The Visiting Patient," "The Case Of The Waterfront Caper," "The Case Of The Museum," "Disguise The Limit," "Monster From Outer Space" and "The Return Of The Shoo Shoo Fly."

CRUSADER RABBIT

"Rocky and Bullwinkle" creator Jay Ward and Alexander Anderson, the nephew of cartoon producer Paul Terry, originated the long–eared rabbit, Crusader, and pal Ragland ("Rags") T. Tiger in 1948, one year before they were "test marketed" as what historians call the "first cartoon serial" and "first limited animation series" made for television. Ward and Alexander first spotted the characters in a film presentation called, "The Comic Strips of Television," along with two other features, "Hamhock Jones" and "Dudley Do–Right."

For many years it was commonly believed the show was syndicated in 1949. Research has concluded that the series was actually test marketed the year before it aired nationally. (Unlike syndication, it was sold on a city–to–city basis, premiering in different cities on different dates due to the method of distribution.) The first Los Angeles air date was Tuesday, August 1, 1950.

Jerry Fairbanks, a contract film supplier, was executive producer of the 1949–1951 series, which the networks turned down. The program aired during the 1950–1951 season on NBC–owned and –operated stations in several markets. Initially, 130 five–minute cliff–hanging episodes were produced.

In 1957, television producer Shull Bonsall, owner of TV Spots, produced a new color series that was similar in nature to the original program. This time, the series syndicated and appeared on several NBC affiliate stations. *A Jerry Fairbanks Production/Creston Studios Production. Black–and–white. Color. Premiere: Fall, 1949 (original series) and Fall, 1957 (new series). Syndicated.*

Crusader Rabbit and his friend Raglands T. Tiger were test marketed in 1948 on local television stations before their series aired nationwide.

Voices:

Crusader Rabbit: Lucille Bliss, Ge Ge Pearson, **Ragland T. Tiger:** Vern Louden, **Dudley Nightshade:** Russ Coughlan, **Narrator:** Roy Whaley

Episodes:

(four–minute black–and–white) "Crusader Vs. The State Of Texas" (1–15), "Crusader Vs. The Pirates" (16–35), "Crusader And The Rajah Of Rinsewater" (36–55), "Crusader And The Schmohawk Indians" (56–70), "Crusader And The Great Horse Mystery" (71–90), "Crusader And The Circus" (91–100), "Crusader In The Tenth Century" (101–130), "Crusader And The Mad Hollywood Scientist" (131–145), "Crusader And The Leprechauns" (146–170) and "Crusader And The Showboat" (171–195).

(four–minute color) "The Great Uranium Hunt" (1–20), "The Yukon Adventure" (21–40), "Tales Of Schmerwood Forest" (41–60), "West We Forget" (61–80), "Sahara You" (81–100), "Gullibles Travels" (101–120), "Should Auld Acquaintance Be For Cotton" (121–140), "Nothing Atoll" (141–160), "Scars And Stripes" (161–180), "Apes Of Rath" (181–200), "Caesar's Salad" (201–220), "The Great Baseball Mystery" (221–240) and "The Search For The Missing Links"

CYBORG BIG "X"

Akira, a young refugee, is changed into a cyborg by Nazi renegade scientists who place his brain in the body of a powerful robot. As Cyborg Big "X," he uses a special magnetic pen as his sole weapon to do battle with those who could use science for nefarious ends. Created by Osamu Tezuka, the originator of "Astro Boy," the half–hour science fiction series was adapted from Tezuka's comic strip, "Bix X." The series was first telecast in Japan in 1964 before it was broadcast in the United States three years later. *A Global Production. Color. Half–hour. Premiered: Fall, 1967. Syndicated.*

THE DAFFY DUCK SHOW

For years the wacky, malicious Daffy Duck pleaded with Bugs Bunny for his own TV show. His ardent efforts were finally rewarded when NBC and the Warner Brothers cartoon department packaged a series starring the slurred–talking duck and a host of other Warner characters—Pepe Le Pew, Speedy Gonzales and Foghorn Leghorn—from old theatrical one-reelers. The show consisted of vintage Warner Brothers and DePatie–Freleng cartoons produced during the 1950s and 1960s. *A Warner Brothers Production. Color. Half–hour. Premiered on NBC: November 4, 1978–September, 1981.*

Voices:

Daffy Duck: Mel Blanc, **Pepe Le Pew:** Mel Blanc, **Speedy Gonzales:** Mel Blanc, **Foghorn Leghorn:** Mel Blanc

DANGER MOUSE

The British Secret Service's most dashing rodent safeguards the lives of everyone who values justice and liberty, waging war against the forces of evil—usually in the form of Baron Silas Greenback—in this British import from the makers of the hit series, "Count Duckula," who first appeared in several episodes of this program before he was given his own series. Each program varied, containing either one complete story or two episodes (the latter varied in length) per half–hour broadcast. On September 28, 1981, the series premiered on the United Kingdom's ITV Network. It wasn't syndicated in this country until three years later on Nickelodeon. *A Cosgrove Hall Production. Color. Half–hour. Premiered on Nickelodeon: June 4, 1984. Syndicated.*

Voices:

Danger Mouse: David Jason, **Penfold,** his faithful assistant: Terry Scott, **Baron Silas Greenback:** Edward Kelsey, **Stiletto,** Greenback's henchman: Brian Trueman, **Colonel K/ Nero:** David Jason, **Narrator:** David Jason

Episodes:

"The Hickory Dickory Dock Dilemma," "Penfold B.F.," "One Hundred And Fifty Million Years Lost," "Who Stole The Bagpipes?," "Long Lost Crown Affair," "Bandits, Beans And Ballyhoo," "Alping Is Snow Easy Matter," "Trouble With Ghosts," "Project Moon," "Custard," "Public Enemy Number One," "Gremlin Alert," "One Of Our Stately Homes Is Missing," "Statues," "Journey To The Earth's Cor!," "The Dream Machine," "By George, It's A Dragon," "Tut Tut It's Not Pharoah," "Cor! What A Picture," "Demons Aren't Dull," "Aaargh! Spiders!," "The Clock Strikes Back," "The Day Of The Suds," "The Great Bone Idol," "Rogue Robots," "The Next Ice Age," "Four Heads Are Better Than One," "Plague Pyramids," "The Aliens Are Coming," "Die Laughing," "Remote Controlled Chaos," "The Strange Case Of The Ghost Blues," "Viva Danger Mouse," "The Chicken Run," "Tiptoe Through The Penfolds," "Bad Luck Eye Of The Little Yellow God," "The Good The Bad And The Motionless," "Once Upon A Timeslip," "It's All White, White Wonder," "Play It Again, Wufgang," "The Planet Of The Cats," "Quark Quark!," "Beware Of Mexicans Delivering Milk," "The Four Tasks Of Danger Mouse," "The Duel," "The Return Of Count Duckula," "Mechanised Mayhem," "Multiplication Fable," "Ee Tea," "Lost Found And Spellbound," "Close Encounters Of The Absurd Kind," "The Invasion Of Colonel K," "The Tower Of Terror," "The Oddball Run Around," "Have You Fled From Any Good Books Lately," "What A 3–Point Turn–Up For The Book," "Ice Station Camel," "Hear Hear," "Trip To America," "The Man From Gadget," "Cat–Astrophe," "Afternoon Off—With The Fangboner," "The Martian Misfit," "The Spy Who Came In The From The Cold," "Lord Of The Bungle," "Nero Power," "The World Of Machines," "Tampering With Time Tickles," "Danger Mouse Saves The World," "The Wild Wild Goose Chase," "Danger Mouse On The Orient Express," "The Ultra Secret Secret," "Duckula Meets Frankenstoat," "Where There's A Well There's A Way," "All Fall Down" and "Turn Of The Tide."

DASTARDLY AND MUTTLEY AND THEIR FLYING MACHINES

Villainous Dick Dastardly, his fumbling henchdog Muttley, and an entourage of World War I flying aces pursue American courier Yankee Doodle Pigeon (who was voiceless) to intercept top–secret information in this offbeat show with bad guys as the series' title characters. The series theme song, "Stop That Pigeon," was written by Bill Hanna and Hoyt Curtin. *A Hanna–Barbera Production. Color. Half–hour. Premiered on CBS: September 13, 1969–September 3, 1971.*

Voices:

Dick Dastardly: Paul Winchell, **Muttley:** Don Messick, **Klunk:** Don Messick, **Zilly:** Don Messick, **The General:** Paul Winchell

Episodes:

"Dastardly and Muttley" (two per show).

"Stop That Pigeon," "Follow That Feather," "Operation Anvil," "Fur Out Furlough," "Sky Hi–IQ," "Sappy Birthday," "A Plain Shortage Of Planes," "Barnstormers," "Shape Up Or Ship Out," "Zilly's A Dilly," "The Cuckoo Patrol," "The Swiss Yelps," "Pest Pilots," "Eagle–Beagle," "Fly By Knights," "There's No Fool Like A Re–Fuel," "Lens A Hand," "Movies Are Badder Than Ever," "Home Sweet Homing Pigeon," "Vacation Trip Trap," "Stop Watch Pigeon?," "Ceiling Zero–Zero," "Who's Who," "Operation Birdbrain," "Medal Muddle," "Go South Young Pigeon," "Too Many Kooks," "Ice See You," "Balmy Swami," "Camouflage Hop–Aroo," "Have Plane Will Travel,"

"Windy Windmill," "Plane Talk" and "Happy Bird Day."
"Magnificent Muttleys" (one per show).
"Mutiny On The Bounty," "What New Old Bean?," "The Marvelous Mutt–Dini," "The Bad Actor," "Big Top," "The Masked Muttley," "Daniel Boone," "Wild Mutt Muttley," "Movie Stuntman," "The Aquanuts," "The Astromutt," "Leonardo De Muttley," "Start Your Engines," "Channel Swimmer," "Professor Muttley," "Admiral Bird Dog" and "Super Muttley."
"Dick Dastardly Blackouts" (four per show).
"Barber," "Hot Soup," "Barn Dance," "Empty Hangar," "Prop Wash," "Grease Job," "Carpet," "The New Mascot," "Arnold," "Pineapple Sundae," "Obedience School," "The Elevator," "Automatic Door," "Robot," "Airmail," "Boxing," "Hare Grower," "Horseshoe," "Bowling Pin," "Echo," "Fast Freight," "Home Run," "Shrink Job," "Wall Tile," "Strange Equipment," "Runaway Stripe," "Deep Reading," "Shell Game," "Spring Time," "Parachute," "Snap Job," "Slightly Loaded," "Dog's Life," "Real Snapper," "The Ice Cream Tree," "Gathering Firewood," "Runaway Rug," "Muscle Builder," "Fishing," "Rainmaker," "Six Cylinder Sonata," "A Little Punchy," "Left Hanging," "Big Turnover," "Mop Up," "Beach Blast," "Simply Smashing," "Giant Jaws," "The Window Washer," "Black Magic," "Hay There," "Taking A Belting," "Lead Ashtray" and "Left Burning."

Davey Hanson and his talking dog Goliath are flanked by Davey's father in a scene from the long–running religious series, "Davey And Goliath."

DAVEY AND GOLIATH

Long–running 15–minute religious series conceived by Art Clokey, creator of Gumby and Pokey, tracing the saga of young Davey Hanson and his talking dog, Goliath, who solve everyday problems while relating the word of God in an entertaining and less preachy fashion. Like "Gumby," the series was filmed in pixillation, a stop–motion photography process used limitedly for television.

Funded by the Lutheran Council of Churches, the series was first syndicated in 1960. (Initial experimental efforts were conducted the year before.) The series was not only a huge success in the United States but was subsequently dubbed in Spanish, Portuguese and Spanish. Six 30–minute specials were also produced featuring the same cast of characters ("To The Rescue," "Happy Easter," "School . . . Who Needs It?," "Halloween Who–Dun–It," "Christmas Lost And Found" and "New Year Promise"). Production of the series ended when funding from the church foundation ran out. The program is still seen in many television markets today, though minus five of the series' original episodes which were removed from circulation for various reasons ("On the Line," "Polka Dot Tie," "Ten Little Indians," "Man of the House" and "The Gang"). *A Clokey Production. Color. Half–hour. Syndicated: 1960–1965.*

Voices:
Davey: Norma McMillan, **Goliath:** Hal Smith

Additional Voices:
Richard Belsh, Nancy Wible

Episodes:
"Lost In A Cave," "Stranded On An Island," "The Wild Goat," "The Winner," "The New Skates," "Cousin Barney," "The Kite," "The Mechanical Man," "The Time Machine," "On The Line," "The Polka Dot Tie," "All Alone," "Pilgrim Boy," "The

Silver Mine," "Ten Little Indians," "Boy Lost," "A Sudden Storm," "The Bell Ringer," "Not For Sale," "The Shoemaker," "The Runaway," "Officer Bob," "The Parade," "The Dog Show," "The Waterfall," "Happy Landing," "Editor–In–Chief," "Man Of The House," "Bully Up A Tree," "Big Apple," "The Bridge," "The Gang," "The Lemonade Stand," "Hocus Pocus," "Good Neighbor," "A Dime, A Dollar," "Rags And Buttons," "Jeep In The Deep," "The Stopped Clock," "Who Me?," "If At First You Don't Succeed," "Finders Keepers," "Kokkaburra," "The Caretakers," "The Hard Way," "Rickey–Rackety," "Help!," "Boy In Trouble," "The Greatest," "Blind Man's Bluff," "Who's George?," "Six–Seven–Six–Three," "Zillion Dollar Combo," "Upside Down And Backwards," "Louder, Please," "Ready Or Not," "Kum Ba Yah," "What's His Name," "Pieces Of Eight," "Chicken," "The Doghouse Dream House," "The Good Bad Luck," "The Watchdogs" and "Come, Come To The Fair."

DEFENDERS OF THE EARTH

The year is A.D. 2015. The human race is about to fall under the evil control of Ming the Merciless, famous intergalactic villain from the planet Mongo. Who can stop him? A team of the most adventurous, powerful, cunning and daring super heroes in the universe—Flash Gordon, The Phantom, Mandrake the Magician and Lothar—who join forces for the battle of their careers as "Defenders of the Earth," overtaking Ming with the help of their descendents: Rick Gordon, Flash's scientific genius son; Jedda Walker, the Phantom's mysterioius daughter; L. J. (Lothar Junior), the street–wise son of Lothar; Kshin, a 10–year–old orphaned Oriental boy; and Zuffy, a cute and cuddly ball of alien fur.

Originaly produced in 1985, the series was not broadcast until the following season. *A Marvel Production in associa-*

tion with King Features Entertainment. Color. Half–hour. Premiered: September, 1986. Syndicated.

Voices:

William Callaway, Adam Carl, Ron Feinberg, Buster Jones, Loren Lester, Sarah Partridge, Diane Pershing, Peter Renaday, Lou Richards, Peter Mark Richman, Dion Williams

Episodes:

"Escape From Mongo," "The Creation Of Monitor," "A Demon In His Pocket," "A House Divided," "Bits And Chips," "The Root Of Evil," "Cold War," "The Sleeper Awakers," "The Revenge Of Astra," "The Hall Of Wisdom," "The Mind Warrior," "The Lost Jewels Of Tibet," "The Mind Warriors" (Part II), "The Evil Of Dr. Dark," "Diamonds Are Ming's Best Friends," "The Men Of Frost," "Battleground," "The Panther Peril," "Fury Of The Deep," "Family Reunion," "The Defense Never Rests," "Like Father, Like Daughter," "The Would Be Defender," "Doorways Into Darkness," "Deal With The Devil," "Terror In Time," "Ming's Household Help," "The Starboy," "The Gods Awake," "The Ghost Walks Again," "The Book Of Mysteries," "The Future Comes But Once," "Kshin And The Ghost Ship," "The Carnival Of Dr. Kalihari," "The Mystery Of The Book," "Flash Times Four," "The Frozen Heart," "Rick Gordon, One Man Army," "The Rites Of Zesnan," "Audie The Tweak," "Return Of The Sky Band," "Dracula's Potion," "One Of The Guys," "100 Proof Highway," "The Time Freezer," "The Prince Makes His Move," "Prince Triumphant," "The Prince Weds," "The Prince's Royal Hunt," "The Prince's Dethroned," "Lothar's Homecoming," "Suspended Sabotage," "The Call Of The Eternals," "The Return Of Dr. Dark," "The Deadliest Battle," "The Necklace Of Oros," "Torn Space," "Ming Winter," "The Golden Queen" (Part 1), "The Golden Queen" (Part 2), "Flesh And Blood," "Drowning World," "The Adoption of Kshin," "Street Smarts" and "Ming's Thunder Lizards."

DENNIS THE MENACE

Comic–strip artist Hank Ketcham's popular newspaper strip inspired this first-run animated series starring the All–American handful, Dennis, whose zest for life gets him into scrape after scrape and situations beyond his control. With his shaggy dog, Ruff, by his side, Dennis keeps the neighborhood in an uproar as his good–hearted intentions, misdirected helpfulness and insatiable curiosity spell trouble, much to the chagrin of his baffled Midwestern parents and neighbor, Mr. Wilson. *A DIC Enterprises Production. Color. Half–hour. Premiered: September, 1986. Syndicated. Premiered on CBS: September 12, 1987–September 3, 1988.*

Voices:

Dennis Mitchell: Brennan Thicke, **Alice,** his mother: Marilyn Lightstone, **Henry,** his father: Maurice LaMarche, **Mr. Wilson:** Maurice LaMarche, **Martha Wilson:** Marilyn Lightstone, **Joey,** Dennis' friend: Jeannie Elias, **Margaret,** Dennis' friend: Jeannie Elias, **Dick/Jim:** Hark Sound

Episodes:

(Network) "Young At Heart," "Gorilla Warfare," "It's Magic Time," "The Incredible Shrinking Dennis," "Swiss Family

Comic–strip artist Hank Ketcham's All–American handful, Dennis the Menace, brought his own brand of mischief to television in the animated "Dennis The Menace" series. © Mithras XCVIII, XCIX, CIX and CX Limited Partnerships. Dennis the Menace and all related characters © Hank Ketcham Enterprises Inc. (Courtesy: DIC Enterprises Inc.)

Mitchell," "The Great Pie Swap," "Instant Replay," "Thor–Sicle," "Seal Of Approval," "A Word From Our Sponsor," "Loch Ness Mess," "A Froggy Day," "Kooked Goose," "Pell Mell Hotel," "Shared Interest," "Wilson's Night Out," "Super Duper Dennis," "Dennis Of The Jungle," "Tunnel Vision," "Hassle In The Castle," "Frankenstymied," "Snow Wars," "Menaced Marriage," "Crummy Mummy," "The Moroccan Pigeon," "Little Beauty Shop Of Horrors," "Box Office Smash," "Underwater Wonderworld," "Water On The Brain," "A Fox Tale," "Dennis Of The Yukon," "The Wright Stuff," "Safe At Home," "Dennis In Wonderland," "The Old Ball Game," "Pie In The Eye," "Climb Of The Century," "Ice Show Snow–Off," "It Came From Planet Dennis," "Menace Of The Mine Shaft," "A Step Ahead," "The Boss Gets Scalped," "Journey To The Center Of Uncle Charlie's Farm," "Home Destruction," "Dennis The Businessman," "3–D and Me," "Dennis' Yard Sale," "Lean, Green, Jumping Machine," "Gold Strike," "Disaster On The Green," "Camp Over Here/Over There," "Space Menace," "Baseball's Best Ballplayer," "10–4 Dennis," "The Love Rowboat," "Ruff To The Rescue," "Hullabaloo In Harmony Homes," "Dennis Conquers The Navy," "Dennis And The Gypsy Woman," "Margaret's Birthday Party," "Come Fly With Me" and "A Visitor From Outer Space."

(Syndication) "Building A Better Dog House," "Train That Boy," "So Long Old Paint," "Hic!," "Wet 'N Wild," "All The President's Menace," "Double Dennis," "Professor Myron Mentalapse," "Cheer Up," "Lights, Camera, Mud!," "Give Me Liberty, Or Give Me Dennis," "The Defective Detector," "Help Not Wanted," "Dennis And The Dragon," "Nothin' To Be Afraid Of," "Racetrack Menace," "Ruff Come Home," "Dennis Predicts," "Dangerous Detour," "Soccer It To Me, Dennis," "Animalympics," "Dennis Race 2000," "Trembly Assembly," "Genie Madness," "Wilson The Menace," "Whale Of A Tale," "Private I," "It's A Ruff Life," "The Wizzer Of Odd," "The

Magic Flute," "G. I. George," "Going Ape," "Strong Medicine," "Time Bomb," "Future Fortune," "Fishing For Trouble," "A Hair–Raising Tale," "Jungle Bungle," "Shark Treatment," "Funhouse Grouch," "Ghost Blusters," "Spa Blahs," "Here, Kitty," "Tenting Tonight," "The Monster Of Mudville Flats," "Dennis Takes The Cake," "Wild West Showdown," "The Pride Of Stardom," "Snowman Madness," "No Bones About It," "Barber Shop Disharmony," "Attack Of The Giant Tomatoes," "Going To The Dogs," "Ruff's Hat Trick," "Second Honeymoon," "The Abominable Snow Menace," "Heroes Unwelcome," "Lemon–Aid," "Circus Berserkus," "Clip–Joint Capers," "A Better Mousetrap," "The Cloneheads," "Chitty Chitty Moon Walk," "Canine Car Wash," "Dr. Dennistein," "A Couple Of Coo-Coos," "Nothing But The Tooth," "The Invisible Kid," "Bowling For Dennis," "Ancient Olympics," "Boy Ahoy," "Having A Marble–Ous Time," "The Longest Half–Yard," "Shock Therapy," "Sounds In The Night," "Young Sherlock Dennis," "A Moving Experience," "Invasion Of The Blob," "Ruff's Masterpiece," "Wheeling And Double–Dealing," "Life In The Fast Lane," "Vampire Scare," "Phantom Of The Wax Museum," "Up, Up, And Oh Boy!," "My Fair Dennis," "A Good Knight's Work," "Quiet Riot," "A Feeling For Stealing," "Dennis Does Hollywood," "Big Baby," "Mummy's Little Boy," "Beaver-Mania," "Medieval Evil," "After Hours," "Charmed I'm Sure," "Stop That Car," "Say Uncle," "K–9 Kollege," "So Sorry," "Give A Little Whistle," "Wilson For Mayor," "Part–Time Helper," "Lights, Camera, Auction," "Dennis In Venice," "Strike Up The Band," "Door To Door Bore," "Yo Ho Ho!," "Hail To The Chief," "Wanted: Scarface Wilson," "Fool For Gold," "Tale Of A Tux," "Marky The Menace," "The Magic Pen," "Ride 'Em Cowboy," "A Nightmare At The Opera," "The Company Picnic," "Dennis The Pirate," "The Life You Save," "Tanks For The Memory," "Dennis At The Movies," "Aw Nuts," "Mayan Mayhem," "The Big Power Trip," "The Big Bicycle Thief," "The Big Candied Apple," "Laundry Business," "Dennis And The Deep," "Mr. Wilson's Diet," "Up, Up And Away," "Meatball Mess," "The Prodigy," "Dennis Springs Into Action," "The Chimp," "A Royal Pain," "Henry The Menace," "The Supermarket," "Horsing Around," "The Hen Party," "Camping Out," "Dennis The Genius," "The Backyard Band," "Hopping Mad," "Dennis The Kangaroo Cavalry," "Dennis Destroys Dallas," "Dennis Plasters Pamplona," "Bicycle Mania," "High Steel," "Million Dollar Menace," "Black And Blue Hawaii," "Yard Wars," "Oil's Well That Ends Well," "Dennis The Barnstormer," "Little Dogs Lost," "Housepests," "Dinosaur Doozle," "Yankee Doodle Dennis," "Houschusband Henry," "The Martians Are Coming," "Handy Dandy Dennis," "Pool Haul," "Dennis In Mircochipland," "Trial And Error," "Back To The Drawing Board," "Timber Wolves," "Faulty Alarm," "Surf's Up," "Queen Of Chinatown," "Fashionable Menace," "Dennis Rocks Out," "Deserted With Dennis" and "The Karate Kiddie."

DENVER, THE LAST DINOSAUR

The adventures of fun–loving dinosaur, Denver, and his group of ingenious young friends, Wally, Jeremy, Shades and Mario, who bring him into the mainstream of the 20th century in contemporary situations. Following its debut, the program captured the number one spot for viewers aged two–11,

A group of ingenious teenagers bring a fun–loving dinosaur into the mainstream of 20th-century life in "Denver, The Last Dinosaur." © World Events/Calico Productions

beating all other kids' shows, including "DuckTales," "Teenage Mutant Ninja Turtles," and "The Jetsons," and was recommended for viewing by the National Education Association. *A World Events/Calico Productions presentation. Half–hour. Color. Premiered on KTTV–Ch. 11, Los Angeles, April 29, 1988. Syndicated.*

Voices:

Wally: Adam Carl, **Jeremy:** Adam Carl, **Mario:** Cam Clark, **Shades:** Cam Clark, **Morton Fizzback:** Brian Cummings, **Professor Funt:** Brian Cummings, **Denver The Last Dinosaur:** Pat Fraley, **Chet:** Rob Paulsen, **Motley:** Rob Paulsen, **Heather:** Kath Soucie, **Casey:** Kath Soucie

Additional Voices: Jack Angel, Tress MacNeille, Frank Welker

Episodes:

"Denver, The Last Dinosaur," "In The Chips," "Videooh," "The Monster Of Lost Lake," "Denver Makes The Grade," "Big Top Denver," "The Misunderstanding," "Lions, Tigers And Dinos," "Change Of Heart," "Bronco–Saurus," "Denver, Dino–Star," "Dinoland," "Winning," "Enter The Dino," "Radio Denver," "The Phantom Of The Movie Theatre," "Missing Links," "Dog Gone Denver," "Party Time," "Aunt Shadies Ghost Town," "Movie–Starus," "Denver At Sea," "Ski Denver," "Beach Blanket Dino," "History Repeats Itself," "Battle Of The Bands," "The Comic Book Caper," "Carnival," "Pen Pal," "Chinatown,"

"Denver, The Lost Dinosaur," "Denver And The Cornstalk," "Tea Time For Denver," "Camp–Out," "Birthday Party From Outerspace," "Art Show," "Food Wars," "Dino–Cise," "Denver, The Last Dragon," "High Flying Denver," "Denver At The Digs," "Chef Denver," "Fizzback's Follies," "Dinos Are My Life," "Bayou Blues," "Canatta," "Pluto Needs People," "Arabian Adventure," "Venice Beach Blast," "Big News Denv," "Viva Denver!" and "There's No Business, Like Snow Business."

DEPUTY DAWG

A not so bright Southern lawman, Deputy Dawg, fumbles his way to maintaining law and order in Mississippi, hounded by a pack of pranksters. His best friends and worst enemies are other animals from the South: Vincent "Vince" Van Gopher, Ty Coon the Raccoon, Muskie the Muskrat and Pig Newton. In October, 1960, the pot–bellied sheriff debuted in over 47 television markets, sponsored by W. H. Lay Potato Chips. The success of the character inspired Terrytoons to release several of the made–for–television cartoons theatrically in 1962. Seven years later, Deputy Dawg premiered on NBC in a new vehicle, "The Deputy Dawg Show." The series repeated episodes from the original series and featured two additional segments comprised of previously released theatrical cartoons: "Gandy Goose" and "Terrytoon Classics." *A Terrytoons Production. Color. Half–hour. Syndicated: October, 1960 ("Deputy Dawg"). Premiered on NBC: September 11, 1971– September 2, 1972 ("The Deputy Dawg Show").*

Voices:

Deputy Dawg: Dayton Allen, **Vincent Van Gopher:** Dayton Allen, **Ty Coon:** Dayton Allen, **The Sheriff:** Dayton Allen

Episodes:

"Deputy Dawg." "The Yoke's On You," "Space Varmit," "Shotgun Shambles," "Seize You Later, Alligator," "Li'l Whooper," "Welcome Mischa Mouse," "Cotton–Pickin' Picnic," "Henhouse Hassle," "Law And Disorder," "Rabid Rebel," "Friend Fox," "Deputy Dawg's Nephew," "Dog-Gone Catfish," "National Spoof Day," "Aig Plant," "Penguin Panic," "People's Choice," "Kin Folk," "Lynx Th' Jinx," "The Bird Burglar," "Watermelon Watcher," "Dragon My Foot," "Star For A Day," "Th' Two Inch Inchworm," "Nobody's Ghoul," "Honey Tree," "Where There's Smoke," "Oil Tycoons," "Rebel Trouble," "Big Chief No Treaty," "Beaver Battle," "Ship Aha Ha," "The Fragant Vagrant," "Noise Annoys," "Tennessee Walkin' Horse," "Peanut Pilferer," "Mr. Moose," "National Lazy Day," "Little Red Fool House," "Astronaut," "Echo Park," "Physical Fatness," "Corn Cribber," "Herman The Hermit," "Heat Wave," "Long Island Duckling," "Tents Moments," "Dagnabit Rabbit," "Tourist Tirade," "Orbit A Little Bit," "Dry Spell," "Terrific Traffic," "Safe An' Insane 4th," "Low Man Lawman," "Open Wide," "Th' Catfish Poachin' Pelican" "The Milkweed From Space," "Bad Luck Day," "Royal Southern Dismounted Police," "Stuck Duck," "Go Go Gor–rilla," "Grandpa Law," "Champion Whooper Teller," "Daddy Frog Legs," "Science Friction," On The Lam With Ham," "Just Ghost To Show You," "Mama Magnolia's Pecan Pies," "Lawman To The Rescue," "Peach Pluckin' Kan-

garoo," "The Never Glades," "Feud For Thought," "The Poster Caper," "Diamonds In The Rough," "Double–Barreled Boom Boom," "Spare That Tree," "The Pig Rustler," "Chicken Bull," "Hex Marks The Spot," "Something To Crow About," "Catfish Crisis," "How Bix Whiz," "Save Ol' Piney," "Pinch Hittin' For A Pigeon," "Mountain Melvin Meets Hairy Harry," "Protestin' Pilot," "Mule–Itary Maneuvers," "Millionaire Deputy," "All Tuckered Out," "The Hungry Astronaut," "Museum Of Th' South," "Scare Cure," "The Great Train Robbery," "Corn Pone Limited," "Space Invitation," "You're Fired An' I'm Fired," "The Pink Flamingo," "Imperfect Crime," "Obnoxious Obie," "Elusive Louie" and "The Governor's Guide."

THE DICK TRACY SHOW

Originally titled "The Adventures of Dick Tracy," the famed comic–strip hero battles the world's most ruthless criminals (Flattop, B. B. Eyes, Pruneface, Mumbles, the Brow, Oodles, the Mole, Sketch Paree, Cheater Gunsmoke, Itchy and Stooge Viller) with the questionable help of his diminutive–brained team of law enforcers—Hemlock Holmes, Jo Jitsu, Heap O'Calory, Go Go Gomez and The Retouchables—in this series of five–minute episodes first syndicated in 1961. Four episodes were shown on the program, each telling a complete story.

Chester Gould, Dick Tracy's creator, developed the series format and supervised the initial episode. In an interview, he later admitted he disliked the series. "We were catering to very small fry and I think we would have been smarter to have taken a more serious view of the thing and played it more or less straight," he said. *A UPA Production. Color. Half–hour. Premiered: September, 1961. Syndicated.*

Voices:

Dick Tracy: Everett Sloane

Episodes:

"Two Heels On Wheels" (with Hemlock Holmes), "Pearl Thief Grief" (with Jo Jitsu), "Surprised Package" (with Heap O'Calory), "Red Hot Riding Hoods" (with Hemlock Holmes), "Champ Chumps" (with Jo Jitsu, Stooge Viller, Mumbles), "A Boodle Of Loot" (with Hemlock Holmes, Stooge Viller, Mumbles), "Scrambled Yeggs" (with Jo Jitsu, Flattop), "Jewel Fool" (with Jo Jitsu, Flattop), "Gruesome Twosome" (with Heap O'Calory, Pruneface, Itchy), "The Onion Ring" (with Hemlock Holmes, Stooge Viller, Mumbles), "The Oyster Caper" (with Jo Jitsu), "Tanks A Heap" (with Heap O'Calory, Stooge Viller, Mumbles), "The Stockyard Caper" (with Hemlock Holmes, Brow, Oodles), "Racer Chaser" (with Jo Jitsu, Stooge Viller, Mumbles), "Rogue's Gallery" (with Heap O'Calory, Mole, Sketch Paree), "Snow Monster" (with Jo Jitsu, Flattop), "The Penny Ant Caper" (with Heap O'Calory, Pruneface, Itchy), "Lab Grab" (with Jo Jitsu, Brow, Oodles), "The Catnip Caper" (with Hemlock Holmes, Stooge Viller, Mumbers), "Brian Game" (with Jo Jitsu, Brow, Oodles), "Big Bank Bungle" (with Heap O'Calory, Pruneface, Itchy), "Funny Money" (with Hemlock Holmes, Stooge Viller, Mumbles), "Tick Tock Shock" (with Heap O'Calory, Brow, Oodles), "The Purple Boy" (with Hemlock Holmes, Pruneface, Itchy), "Cooked Crooks" (with Jo Jitsu, Stooge Viller, Mumbles), "Flea Ring Circus" (with Hem-

THE MOST FAMOUS

IN THE

UPA's popular TV version of America's number–one comic strip, "Dick Tracy." © UPA Productions

lock Holmes), "Mummy's The Word (with Jo Jitsu), "Escape From Sing Song" (with Hemlock Holmes, Brow, Oodles), "Cheater Gunsmoke" (with Hemlock Holmes, Cheater Gunsmoke), "Hooked Crooks" (with Hemlock Holmes, Pruneface, Itchy), "The Parrot Caper" (with Jo Jitsu, B. B. Eyes, Flattop), "The Banana Peel Deal" (with Hemlock Holmes, Brow, Oodles), "The Boomerang Ring" (with Jo Jitsu, Pruneface, Itchy), "Wheeling And Stealing" (with Hemlock Holmes, Sketch Paree, Mole), "Phoney Pharmer" (with Hemlock Holmes, B. B. Eyes, Flattop), "The Elephant Caper" (with Jo Jitsu, Sketch Paree, Mole), "Baggage Car Bandits" (with Hemlock Holmes, B. B. Eyes, Flattop), "The Platter–Puss Plot" (with Hemlock Holmes, Pruneface, Itchy), "The Vile In Case" (with Jo Jitsu, Brow, Oodles), "The Nickle Nabbers" (with Hemlock Holmes, Pruneface, Itchy), "The Newspaper Caper" (with Jo Jitsu, Pruneface, Itchy), "The Bearskin Game" (with Hemlock Holmes, Stooge Viller, Mumbles), "Grandma Jitsu" (with Jo Jitsu, Sketch Paree, Mole), "Tobacco Load" (with Hemlock Holmes, Cheater Gunsmoke), "Gym Jam" (with Jo Jitsu, Flattop), "Tacos Tangle" (with Go Go Gomez, Jo Jitsu, B. B. Eyes), "Rock–A–Bye Guys" (with Hemlock Holmes, Stooge Viller, Mumbles), "Bowling Ball Bandits" (with Hemlock Holmes, B. B. Eyes, Flattop), "Snow Job" (with Go Go Gomez, Pruneface, Itchy), "Bomb's Away" (with Hemlock Holmes, Stooge Viller, Mumbles), "The Retouchables" (with Hemlock Holmes, Stooge Viller, Mumbles), "The Ruby Of Hamistan" (with Jo Jitsu, Sketch Paree, Mole), "Stamp Scamp" (with Hemlock Holmes, B. B. Eyes), "The Elevator Lift" (with Jo Jitsu, B. B. Eyes, Flattop), "Rocket Racket" (with Hemlock Holmes, Sketch Paree, Mole), "Horse Race Chase" (with Go Go Gomez, Brow, Oodles), "Better Come Clean" (with Hemlock Holmes, B. B. Eyes, Flattop), "The Flower Pot" (with Jo Jitsu, Sketch Paree, Mole), "Alligator Baggers" (with Hemlock Holmes, Brow,

Oodles), "The Log Book Case" (with Jo Jitsu), "Lochness Monster" (with Go Go Gomez, Brow, Oodles), "The Cold Cash Caper" (with Hemlock Holmes, Stooge Viller, Mumbles), "Smashing The Ring Ring" (with Jo Jitsu, Pruneface, Itchy), "The Fish Flickers" (with Hemlock Holmes, Brow, Oodles), "Hotel Havoc" (with Go Go Gomez, Stooge Viller, Mumbles), "The Big Blowup" (with Go Go Gomez, B. B. Eyes, Flattop), "The Cabash Express" (with Jo Jitsu, Sketch Paree, Mole), "The Cop and Saucer" (with Jo Jitsu, Brow, Oodles), "The Copped Copper Caper" (with Go Go Gomez, B. B. Eyes, Flattop), "The Windmill Caper" (with Go Go Gomez, Brow, Oodles), "The Copy Cat Caper" (with Go Go Gomez, Sketch Paree, Mole), "The Two–Way Stretch" (with Jo Jitsu, Brow, Oodles), "Hot On The Trail" (with Go Go Gomez, Pruneface, Itchy), "Fowl Play" (with Go Go Gomez, Sketch Paree), "Small Time Crooks" (with Jo Jitsu, Brow, Oodles), "The Lighthouse Creepers" (with Go Go Gomez, Brow, Oodles), "The Skyscraper Caper" (with Go Go Gomez, Brow, Oodles), "The Gold Grabbers" (with Go Go Gomez, Pruneface, Itchy), "Down In The Drain" (with Jo Jitsu, Sketch Paree, Mole), "The Old Mummy Case (with Go Go Gomez, Brow, Oodles), "Evil Eye Guy" (with Hemlock Holmes, Sketch Paree), "Gangtown" (with Go Go Gomez, B. B. Eyes, Flattop), "The Camera Caper" (with Go Go Gomez, Stooge Viller, Mumbles), "Mole In The Hole" (with Hemlock Holmes), "The Old Suit Case" (with Go Go Gomez, B. B. Eyes), "The Big Punch" (with Go Go Gomez, Sketch Paree, Mole), "Rocket 'N' Roll" (with Jo Jitsu, Stooge Viller, Mumbles), "The Venetian Blind" (with Jo Jitsu, Sketch Paree, Mole), "The Manor Monster" (with Go Go Gomez, Pruneface), "Trick Or Treat" (with Jo Jitsu, Sketch Paree, Mole), "Steamboat Steal" (with Go Go Gomez, Sketch Paree, Mole), "Feathered Frenzy" (with Go Go Gomez, Stooge Viller, Mumbles), "Oil's Well" (with Go Go Gomez, Sketch Paree, Mole), "The Pigeon Coup" (with Jo Jitsu, Stooge Viller, Mumbles), "Mardi Gras Grab" (with Jo Jitsu, Pruneface, Itchy), "The Medicine Showcase" (with Go Go Gomez, Sketch Paree, Mole), "Crookter's Last Stand" (with Go Go Gomez, Stooge Viller, Mumbles), "The Monkey Tale" (with Hemlock Holmes, Sketch Paree, Mole), "Two Goons In The Fountain" (with Jo Jitsu, Pruneface, Itchy) "The Tower Of Pizza" (with Hemlock Holmes, Brow, Oodles), "The Film Can Caper" (with Go Go Gomez, Stooge Viller, Mumbles), "Lumber Scamps" (with Hemlock Holmes, Brow, Oodles), "The Castle Caper" (with Go Go Gomez, Pruneface, Itchy), "A Case For Alarm" (with Go Go Gomez, B. B. Eyes, Flattop), "Football Brawl" (with Jo Jitsu, Pruneface, Itchy), "Court Jester" (with Go Go Gomez, Stooge, Mumbles), "The Great Whodunit" (with Go Go Gomez, B. B. Eyes, Flattop), "The Ivory Rustlers" (with Go Go Gomez, Stooge Viller, Mumbles), "The Island Racket" (with Go Go Gomez, Pruneface, Itchy), "Ham On The Lam" (with Hemlock Holmes, Brow, Oodles), "Crime Flies," "The Big Steal" (with Hemlock Holmes, B. B. Eyes, Flattop), "Air Freight Fright" (with Jo Jitsu, Pruneface, Itchy), "The Chinese Cookie Caper" (with Hemlock Holmes, Stooge Viller, Mumbles), "The Van Vandals" (with Jo Jitsu, Brow, Oodles), "Hawaiin Guy" (with Jo Jitsu, Stooge Viller, Mumbles), "Kidnap Trap" (with Hemlock Holmes, Brow, Oodles), "Trickery At Sea" (with Jo Jitsu, Stooge Viller, Mumbles), "The Fixed Stare Case" (with Go Go Gomez, Sketch Paree, Mumbles), "The Hot Ice Bag" (with

Hemlock Holmes, Stooge Viller, Mumbles), "Ghostward Hot!" (with Hemlock Holmes, Stooge Viller, Mumbles), "The Bird Brain Pickers" (with Hemlock Holmes, Sketch Paree, Itchy), "The Big Wig" (with Go Go Gomez, Stooge Viller, Mumbles), "The Bank Prank" (with Jo Jitsu, B. B. Eyes, Flattop), "The Last Blast" (with Hemlock Holmes, Stooge Viller, Mumbles), "The Lie Detector" (with Hemlock Holmes, Stooge Viller, Mumbles), "Quick Cure Quacks" (with Jo Jitsu, Pruneface, Itchy), "The Sweepstakes Caper" (with Jo Jitsu, Stooge Viller, Mumbles), "Choo Choo Boo Boo" (with Hemlock Holmes, B. B. Eyes, Flattop) and "The Stuffed Pillowcase" (with Go Go Gomez, Stooge Viller, Mumbles).

DINK, THE LITTLE DINOSAUR

The Earth is a new, raw place of wonder and awe, scorched by volcanoes, showered by meteor storms and shaken by giant earthquakes, where survival is an everyday adventure. It is also the world of one small, adventuresome little brontosauraus, Dink, a self-assured, sometimes scheming dinosaur who rallies his group of friends around him in a never-ending quest for fun, adventure and discovery. *A Ruby-Spears Enterprises Production. Color. Half-Hour. Premiered on CBS: September 2, 1989-September 1, 1990.*

Voices:

Dink: R. J. Williams, **Amber,** the lively corythosaurs: Anndi McAfee, **Shyler,** the bashful edaphosaurus: Ben Granger, **Flapper,** the boastful pterodon: S. Scott Bullock, **Scar,** the nervous compsognathus: Frank Welker, **Crusty,** an old sea turtle: Frank Welker

Episodes:

(two per show) "Shell Game," "Dink, Come Home," "Shyler's Friend," "Phantom Of The Cave," "White Beauty," "Uncle Longbeak," "Crusty's Baby," "Badge Of Courage," "Dry River," "Tricera-Scat," "Search," "The Gentle Hunter," "A New Home For Crusty," "Old Timers," "Amber's Crusade," "Mystery Of The Broken Claw," "Surprise," "Wish Mountain," "The Hollow Tree," "Small Stuff," "Lights Out," "Encounter At Flatrock," "Land Of No Return," "Sea Rescue," "Raiders Of The Lost Nest" and "The Sky Is Falling At Green Meadow."

DINOSAUCERS

Searching for ways to save the quake-racked planet Reptilon from destruction, the Dinosaucers, the planet's only inhabitants, come to Earth where they enlist the help of four youngsters, the Secret Scouts, to find the secret that will save their own world and keep them safe from the depredation of their brutal enemies, the Tryannos, in this futuristic action-adventure series. *A DIC Enterprises Production in association with Michael Maliani Productions. Color. Half-hour. Premiered: September, 1987. Syndicated.*

Voices:

Bonehead/Bronto-Thunder: Marvin Goldhar, **Genghis 'Rex'/Plesio:** Dan Hennessey, **Quackpot/Allo:** Len Carlson, **Steggy:** Ray Kahnert, **Brachio:** Don McManus, **Tricero:** Rob Cowan, **Ichthyo:** Thick Wilson, **Terrible Dactyl/Ankylo:**

John Stocker, **Dimetro:** Chris Wiggins, **Styraco:** Gordon Masten, **Sara:** Barbara Redpath, **Paul:** Richard Yearwood, **Ryan:** Simon Reynolds, **David:** Leslie Toth

Episodes:

"Rockin' Reptiles," "Dinosaur Valley," "Be Prepared," "A Real Super Hero," "Divide And Conquer," "That Shrinking Feeling," "The Detective Defector," "Trick Or Treat," "A Man's Best Friend In His Dogasaurus," "The First Show," "Take Us Out To The Ball Game," "Sleeping Booty," "Hooray For Hollywood," "Burgers Up!," "Happy Egg Day To You!," "For The Love Of Teryx," "Chariots Of The Dinosaucers," "Mommy Dino-Dearest," "Teacher's Pest," "Trouble In Paradise," "The Prehistoric Purge," "Dino-Chips," "Attack Of The Fur Balls," "Seeing Purple," "War Of The Worlds . . . II," "The Dinolympics," "The Friend," "Fine-Feathered Friend," "Those Reptilon Nights," "I Got Those Ol' Reptilon Blues Again, Mommasaur," "The Babysitter," "The Trojan Horsesaurus," "Scents Of Wonder," "Beauty And The Bonehead," "Hook, Line And Stinker," "Carnivore In Rio," "The Truth About Dragons," "Frozen Fur Balls," "Eggs Marks The Spot," "Inquiring Minds," "The Whale's Song," "Karatesaurus Wrecks," "Beachblanket Bonehead," "Cindersaurus," "The Bone Ranger And Bronto," "Monday Night Clawball," "The Quackup Of Quackpot," "The Heart And Sole Of Big Foot," "The Age Of Aquariums," "There's No Such Think As Stego Claws," "Lochs And Bay Gulls," "The Scales Of Justice," "Camp Tyranno," "Reduced For Clarence," "Toy-Ranno Store Wars," "Saber-Tooth Or Consequences," "The Museum Of Natural Humans," "It's An Archaeopteryx—It's A Plane—It's Thunder Lizard!," "Dinosaur Dundy," "Allo And Cos-stego Meet The Abominable Snowman," "Sarah Had A Little Lambeosaurus," "Applesaucers," "The T-Bones' Stakes," "I Was A Teenage Human" and "We're Off To See The Lizard."

DISNEY'S ADVENTURES OF THE GUMMI BEARS

Zummi, Gruffi, Grammi, Cubbi, Sunni and Tummi Gummi find themselves in enchanting escapades as they face new foes and find new friends in the mythical forests of Gummi Glen. From encounters with menacing giants and ogres, to the excitement of discovering lost treasure, the Gummies join together for a captivating series of intriguing and whimsical adventure in this Saturday-morning series produced by Walt Disney Television Animation. NBC broadcast the first four seasons beginning in September, 1985. The show moved to ABC in September, 1989, when it merged with "The New Adventures of Winnie the Pooh" for its fifth season. Thg program combined half-hour and 15-minute episodes. *A Walt Disney Production. Color. Half-hour. Premiered on NBC: September 14, 1985-September 2, 1989. Rebroadcast on ABC: September 9, 1989-September 1, 1990 (As "Disney's Gummi Bears/Winnie the Pooh Hour").*

Voices:

Cavin: Christian Jacobs, Brett Johnson, **Chummi:** Jim Cummings, **Sunni Gummi:** Katie Leigh, **Tummi Gummi:** Lorenzo Music, **Augustus "Gusto" Gummi:** Rob Paulsen, **Zummi Gummi:** Paul Winchell, **Gruff Gummi:** Bill Scott, Corey Burton, **Cubbi Gummi:** Noelle North, **Toadie:** Bill Scott,

Corey Burton, **Sir Tuxford:** Bill Scott, Roger C. Carmel, Chuck McCann, **Angelo Davini:** Bill Scott, **Ogre:** Bill Scott, **Zorlock:** Lennie Weinrib, **Ditto the Boggle:** Frank Welker, **Chillbeard Jr.:** Frank Welker, **Slumber Sprite:** Paul Winchell, **Clutch:** Paul Winchell, **Tuck:** Paul Winchell, **Giggalin:** Paul Winchell, **King Gregor:** Michael Rye, **Duke Igthorn:** Michael Rye, **Sir Gowan:** Michael Rye, **Stir Ponch:** Howard Morris, **Sir Thornberry:** Walker Edmiston, **Princess Calla:** Noelle North, **Malsinger,** the wizard: Michael Rye, **Troll,** the horse: Michael Rye, **Unwin of Dunwyn:** Will Ryan, **Gad/Zook/Ogres:** Will Ryan, **The Carpie King/Knight:** Will Ryan, **Trina,** the sheperdess: Pat Parris, **Aquarianne,** the mermaid: Pat Parris, **Mobile Tree:** June Foray, Noelle North, Katie Leigh, **Giant,** with the Wishing Stone: Bob Holt, **Dom Gordo of Ghent:** Bob Holt, **Tadpole:** Chuck McCann, **The Bubble Dragon:** Lorenzo Music, **The Most Peaceful Dragon in the World:** June Foray, **Marsipan:** Tress MacNeille, **Great Oak/Mother/Lady Bane:** Tress MacNeille

Episodes:
1985–1986 (11–minute episodes) "The Sinister Sculptor," "Zummi Makes It Hot," "Someday My Prints Will Come," "The Oracle," "When You Wish Upon A Stone," "Loopy, Go Home," "A–Hunting We Will Go," "The Fence Sitter," "Night Of The Gargoyle," "Sweet and Sour Gruffi," "Duel Of The Wizards," "What You See Is Me," "Toadie's Wild Ride," "Bubble Trouble," "Gummi In A Strange Land" and "Light Makes Right."
(22–minute episodes) "A New Beginning," "A Gummi In A Gilded Cage," "A Gummi By Any Other Name" and "The Secret Of The Juice."
1986–1987 (11–minute episodes) "Faster Than A Speeding Tummi," "For A Few Sovereigns More," "Over The River And Through The Trolls," "You Snooze, You Lose," "A Hard Dazed Knight," "Do Unto Ogres" and "Little Bears Lost,"
(22–minute episodes) "Up, Up And Away," "The Crimson Avenger," "For Whom The Spell Holds," and "My Gummi Lies Over The Ocean."
1987–1988 (11–minute spisodes) "Too Many Cooks," "Just A Tad Smarter," "If I Were You," "Eye Of The Beholder," "Presto Gummo," "A Tree Grows In Dunwyn," "Water Way To Go," "Boggling The Bears," "Close Encounters Of The Gummi Kind," "Snows Your Old Man," "Mirthy Me" and "Gummi Dearest."
(22–minute episodes) "Day Of The Beevilweevils" and "The Knights Of The Gummadoon."
1988–1989 (11–minute episodes) "Music Hath Charms," "Dress For Success," "A Knight To Remember," "Gummies Just Want to Have Fun," "There's No Place Like Home," "Color Me Gummi," "Tummi's Last Stand," "Ogre Baby Boom," "The Crimson Avenger Strikes Again," "The White Knight," "Good Neighbor Gummi" and "Girl's Knight Out."
(22–minute episodes) "The Magnificent Seven Gummies," "He Who Laughs Last," "Top Gum" and "Gummies At Sea."

DISNEY'S GUMMI BEARS/ WINNIE THE POOH HOUR

In 1989, Disney's Gummi Bears, which ran for four successful seasons on NBC, moved to rival network ABC and merged

with "The New Adventures of Winnie the Pooh" in all–new episodes in this fantasy/adventure hour for Saturday–morning television. *A Walt Disney Television Production. Color. One hour. Premiered on ABC: September 8, 1989–September 1, 1990.*

Voices:
Cavin: R. J. Williams, **Zummi Gummi:** Jim Cummings, **Gruffi Gummi:** Corey Burton, Bill Scott, **Grammi Gummi:** June Foray, **Cubbi Gummi:** Noelle North, **Sunni Gummi:** Katie Leigh, **Tummi Gummi:** Lorenzo Music, **Augustus "Gusto" Gummi:** Rob Paulsen, **Sir Tuxford/Arte Deco:** Brian Cummings, **Toadie:** Corey Burton, Bill Scott, **Princess Calla:** Noelle North, **Gad/Zook/Orgres/Unwin:** Will Ryan, **King Gregor/Duke Igthorn:** Michael Rye, **Winnie the Pooh:** Jim Cummings, **Christopher Robin:** Tim Hoskins, **Tigger:** Paul Winchell, Jim Cummings, **Eeyore:** Peter Cullen, **Piglet:** John Fiedler, **Gopher:** Michael Gough, **Roo:** Nicholas Melody, **Mom/Kanga:** Patty Parris, **Rabbit:** Ken Samson, **Owl:** Hal Smith

Episodes:
Gummi Bears.
1989–1990 (11–minute episodes) "Let Sleeping Giants Lie," "A Gummi A Day Keeps The Doctor Away," "Bridge On The River Gummie," "The Life Of The Party," "My Kingdom For A Pie," "The World According To Gusto," "Princess Problems," "A Gummi Is A Gummi's Best Friend" and "Never Give A Gummie An Even Break."
(22–minute episodes) "The Road To Ursalia," "Ogre For A Day," "Beg, Burrow and Steal" and "Return To Ursalia."
"Winnie the Pooh"
1989–1990 (11–minute episodes) "Where, Oh Where Has My Piglet Gone?," "Up, Up And Awry," "Fast Friends," "Prize Piglet," "Caws And Effect," "Pooh Moon," "Oh Bottle," "What's The Score, Pooh?," "Eeyi Eeyi Eeyore," "Owl In The Family," "Rock–A–Bye Pooh Bear," "Rabbit Takes A Holiday," "Sham Pooh" and "Tigger's Houseguest."
(five–minute episodes) "The Monster Frankenpooh" and "Three Little Piglets."
(17–minute episodes) "No Rabbit's A Fortress" and "Eeyore's Tail Tale."
(22–minute cpisode) "Un–Valentine's Day."

DO DO—THE KID FROM OUTER SPACE

This British–made series imitated popular Japanese imports, featuring the adventures of Do Do and his pet company, aliens from the atomic planet Hydro, who come to Earth to help a noted scientist, Professor Fingers, perform research on many scientific mysteries left unresolved. *A Halas and Batchelor Production. Color. Half–hour. Premiered: August 23, 1965. Syndicated. Voice credits and episodes unknown.*

DRAGON'S LAIR

In King Ethelred's kingdom, one knight outshines them all— Dirk the Daring. He performs great deeds and protects the kingdom and his beautiful Princess Daphne from creepy vil-

Dirk the Daring looks straight into the mouth of the ferocious dragon, Cinge, to prove to his love, Princess Daphne, that he is the bravest man in the world in the animated, "Dragon's Lair." © Ruby–Spears Enterprises

lains and a fiery dragon. *A Ruby Spears Enterprise Production. Color. Half–hour. Premiered on ABC: September 8, 1984–April 20, 1985.*

Voices:
Dirk the Daring: Bob Sarlatte, **Princess Daphne:** Ellen Gerstell, **King Ethelred:** Fred Travalena, **Timothy:** Michael Mish, **Cinge:** Arthur Burghardt, **Bertram:** Peter Cullen, **Storyteller:** Clive Revill

Episodes:
"The Tale Of The Enchanted Gift," "Sir Timothy's Quest," "The Tournament Of The Phantom," "The Smithee's Haunted Armor," "The Pool Of Youth," "The Story Of Old Alf," "The Song Of The Wind Chimes," "The Girl From Crow's Wood," "Mirror, Mirror," "The Snow Witch," "The Tale Of Dirk's New Sword," "The Legend Of The Giant's Name" and "The Mist Of Wishes."

DRAK PACK

Drak, Frankie and Howler, teenage descendants of the famed monsters, Dracula, Frankenstein and the Werewolf, atone for the sins of their great ancestors by using their special powers for the good of mankind. Their main adversary is the world's worst villain, Dr. Dred, and his O.G.R.E. group, the Organization Of Generally Rotten Endeavors. *A Hanna–Barbera Production. Color. Half–hour. Premiered on CBS: September 6, 1980–September 12, 1982.*

Voices:
Drak Jr.: Jerry Dexter, **Frankie:** Bill Callaway, **Howler:** Bill Callaway, **Big D, Dracula:** Alan Oppenheimer, **Dr. Dred:**

Hans Conreid, **Vampira:** Julie McWhirter, **Mummy Man:** Chuck McCann, **Toad:** Don Messick, **Fly:** Don Messick

Episodes:
"Night Of The Terbites," "Mind Your Manners, Dr. Dred," "A Dire Day At Dredfulland," "Dred Goes Hollywood," "Dreadful Weather We're Having," "The Grimmest Book Of Records," "Dr. Dred Is a Shrinker," "Time Out For Dr. Dred," "International Graffiti," "The Hideout Hotel," "Dred's Photo Finish," "Color Me Dredful," "Happy Birthday Dr. Dred," "Plunder Of Pirate's Park," "Package Deal" and "It's In The Bag Dr. Dred."

DRAWING POWER

In this live–action/animated series, Pop, a white–haired chief animator, and his assistants, Lenny and Kari, dream up educational cartoon messages in a small animation studio, leading into one of several cartoon segments featured each week. Recurring cartoon segments were "The Book Report," "Bus Stop," "Pet Peeves," "Professor Rutabaga," "Superperson U." and "What Do You Do Dad, (Mom)?" The half–hour program was by the producers of the award–winning children's series, "Schoolhouse Rock." *A Newhall–Yohe Production. Color. Half–hour. Premiered on NBC: October 11, 1980–May 16, 1981.*

Cast:
Pop: Bob Kaliban, **Lenny:** Lenny Schultz, **Kari:** Kari Page

DR. SNUGGLES

Peter Ustinov is the voice of Dr. Snuggles, a good–natured veterinarian who travels anywhere to care for animals via his pogo stick. Ustinov supplied the voice of several other characters in the series as well. *A KidPix Production. Color. Half–hour. Premiered: September 12, 1981. Syndicated.*

Voices:
Dr. Snuggles: Peter Ustinov

DUCKTALES

The first daily animated television series from Walt Disney Studios, "DuckTales" was the studio's answer to *Raiders of the Lost Ark* and *Romancing the Stone*, focusing on the daring exploits of that cantankerous canard, Donald Duck's uncle, Scrooge McDuck, the world's richest tightwad. Scrooge is joined by a collection of familiar friends and relatives, including Donald's nephews, Huey, Dewey and Louie, in adventures mixed with fowl play and risky undertakings on the far side of the world. New characters introduced on the show included Launchpad McQuack, a soldier of outrageous fortune; Mrs. Beakley, the governess to Scrooge's grandnephews; Webbigail Vanderduck, Mrs. Beakley's pesky granddaughter; Doofus, Launchpad's greatest fan and biggest hinderance; and a quartet of masked heavies called the Beagle Boys. Fred Wolf of Murakami–Wolf–Swenson acted as supervising producer for 65 episodes. *A Walt Disney Production. Color. Half–hour. Premiered: September 21, 1987. Syndicated.*

Voices:

Scrooge McDuck: Alan Young, **Launchpad McQuack:** Terence McGovern, **Huey:** Russi Taylor, **Dewey:** Russi Taylor, **Louie:** Russi Taylor, **Webbigail Vanderduck:** Russi Taylor, **Doofus:** Brian Cummings, **Gyro Gearloose:** Hal Smith, **Flintheart Glomgold:** Hal Smith, **Magica de Spell:** June Foray

Episodes:

"Back To The Klondike," "Earth Quack," "Sweet Duck Of Youth," "Micro–Ducks From Outer Space," "Scrooge's Pet," "Dinosaur Ducks," "The Money Vanishes," "Lost Crown Of Genghis Khan," "The Pearl Of Wisdom," "Masters Of Djinni," "The Mirror Quacked/Take Me Out Of the Ball Game," "Maid Of The Myth," "Hero For Hire," "Armstrong," "Sit Gyro De Gearloose," "Merit Time Adventure," "Bermuda Triangle Tangle," "Horse Scents," "Curse Of Castle McDuck," "Send In The Clones," "Superdoo," "Hotel Strangeduck," "Launchpad's Civil War," "Don't Give Up The Ship," "Wrongway to Ronguay," "Three Ducks Of The Condor," "Duckman Of Aquatraz," "Home Sweet Homer," "Cold Duck," "Too Much Of A Gold Thing," "Much Ado About Scrooge," "Top Duck," "Where No Duck Has Gone," "Robot Robbers," "Magica's Shadow War," "A Drain On The Economy," "Ducks Of The West," "A Whale Of A Bad Time," "Sphinx For The Memories," "Aquaducks," "Time Teasers," "Back Out In The Outback," "Working For Scales," "Raiders Of The Lost Harp," "Luck Of The Duck," "The Golden Fleecing," "Down And Out In Duckburg," "The Right Duck," "Scroogerello," "Double–O–Duck," "Jungle Duck," "Back To The Future," "Duckworth's Revolt," "Spies In Their Eyes," "Launchpad's Last Crash," "Uncrashable Hindentanic," "Dime Enough For Luck," "Duck In The Iron Mask," "Status Seekers," "Nothing To Fear," "Dr. Jeckle And Mr Hyde," "Once Upon A Dime," "All Ducks On Deck," "Ducky Horror Picture Show," "Till Nephews Do Us Part," "Marking Time," "The Duck Who Would Be King," "Bubba Trubba," "Gone With The Bin," "Ali Bubba's Cave," "Liquid Assets," "Frozen Assets," "Full Metal Duck," "Billionare Beagle Boys Club," "Money To Burn," "The Land Of Trala La," "My Mother The Psychic," "Allowance Day," "Bubbeo And Juliet," "The Good Muddah's," "Yuppy Ducks," "Blue Collar Scrooge," "Metal Attraction," "Bubba's Big Brainstorm," "Dough Ray Me," "Beaglemania," "The Big Flub," "A Case Of Mistaken Secret Identity," "The Bride Wore Stripes," "The Unbreakable Bin," "Attack Of The Fifty–Foot Webby," "Ducky Mountain High," "The Masked Mallard," "The Duck Who Knew Too Much," "Scrooge's Last Adventure," "Duck Valentine," "Attack Of The Metal Mites," "New Gizmo Kids On The Block," "The Golden Goose, Part 1," and "The Golden Goose, Part 2."

DUDLEY DO–RIGHT AND HIS FRIENDS

"(See "The Dudley Do–Right Show.")

THE DUDLEY DO–RIGHT SHOW

First introduced on 1961's "The Bullwinkle Show," inept Royal Canadian Mountie Dudley Do–Right returned along

Bumbling mountie Dudley Do–Right rescues his long–time sweetheart, Nell, in a scene from Jay Ward's "The Dudley Do–Right Show." © Jay Ward Productions

with girlfriend Nell, Inspector Fenwick and Snidely Whiplash for more madcap fun in this weekly half–hour series for Saturday–morning television. The program repeated adventures previously seen on "The Bullwinkle Show" (see "The Bullwinkle Show" for episodic information), in addition to previous segments that debuted on "Rocky and His Friends." They were: "Aesop and Son," "Fractured Fairy Tales" and "Peabody's Improbable History." (For voice credits and episode titles see "Rocky and His Friends" and "The Bullwinkle Show.") The series was later retitled and syndicated as "Dudley Do–Right and His Friends." *A Jay Ward Production with Producers Associates for Television. Color. Half–hour. Premiered on ABC: April 27, 1969–September 6, 1970.*

Voices:

Dudley Do–Right: Bill Scott, **Nell Fenwick:** June Foray, **Inspector Ray K. Fenwick:** Paul Frees, **Snidely Whiplash:** Hans Conreid, **Narrator:** Paul Frees

THE DUKES

The hilarious folks of Hazard County compete in an around–the–world race in this action–adventure series based on the tremendously successful prime–time series, "The Dukes of Hazard." This time greedy little Boss Hogg and dopey Sheriff Rosco scheme to foreclose the mortgage on the Dukes. This causes Bo, Luke and Daisy to race the trusty General Lee, the hottest supercharged car ever, to raise money for the poor folks in Hazard County and rescue the mortgage. The animated program features the voices of the stars of the live–action network series.

During the 1982–83 season, the series aired as a mid–season replacement. The following year, the program entered its second season on CBS' fall roster. It only lasted on the network one month before it was cancelled and replaced with Ruby–Spears Enterprises' "Plasticman." *A Hanna–Barbera Production. Color. Half–hour. Premiered on CBS: February 5, 1983–October 29, 1983.*

Voices:

Boss Hogg; Sorrell Booke, **Daisy Duke:** Catherine Bach, **Vance Duke:** Christopher Mayer, **Bo Duke, Daisy's cousin:** John Schneider, **Luke Duke, Daisy's cousin:** Tom Wopat, **Uncle Jesse:** Denver Pyle, **Sheriff Rosco Coltrane:** James Best, **Flash/Smokey/General Lee:** Frank Welker

Episodes:

1982–1983 "Jungle Jitters," "The Dukes Of Venice," "Put Up Your Dukes," "Morocco Bound," "The Secret Satellite," "The Dukes Of London," "Greece Fleece," "The Dukes In India," "The Dukes In Urbekistan," "A Hogg In Hong Kong," "The Dukes Of Scotland," "The Dukes Do Paris" and "The Dukes In Switzerland."
1983–1984 "Boss O'Hogg And Little People," "Tales Of The Vienna," "The Kid From Madrid," "A Dickens Of A Christmas," "The Canadian Caper," "The Dukes In Hollywood" and "A Hogg In The Foggy Bogg ."

DUNGEONS AND DRAGONS

Based on the popular fantasy game, this series traces the adventures of six children (Sheila, Hank, Eric, Diana, Presto and Bobby), who pile into an amusement park ride, only to find themselves on the most mysterious and terrifying ride of all—a trip through time into the realm of dungeons and dragons. In crossing the barrier from reality to fantasy, each youngster takes on the role of a different character in the game to help the group escape ever–present dangers in the quest to return home.

Willie Aames and Adam Rich, stars of TV's "Eight Is Enough," play the characters of the Range Hank and the Wizard Pesto, respectively. Donny Most of "Happy Days" fame is the Cavalier Eric. *A Marvel Production in association with Dungeons & Dragons Entertainment Group, a division of TSR Incorporated. Color. Half–hour. Premiered on CBS: September 17, 1983–September 5, 1987.*

Voices:

Hank: Willie Aames, **Eric:** Donny Most, **Sheila:** Katie Leigh, **Diana:** Toni Gayle Smith, **Presto:** Adam Rich, **Bobby:** Ted Field III, **Dungeon Master:** Sidney Miller, **Venger:** Peter Cullen

Episodes:

1983–1984 "The Night Of No Tomorrow," "The Eyes Of The Beholder," "The Hall Of Bones," "Valley Of The Unicorns," "In Search Of The Dungeon Master," "Beauty And The Bog-beast," "The Prison Without Walls," "Servant Of Evil," "Quest Of The Skeleton Warrior," "The Garden Of Zinn," "The Box," "The Lost Children" and "P–r–e–s–t–o Spells Disaster."
1984–1985 "The Girl Who Dreamed Tomorrow," "The Trea-sure Of Tardos," "City At The Edge Of Midnight," "The Traitor," "Day Of The Dungeon Master," "The Last Illusion," "The Dragon's Graveyard" and "Child Of The Stargazer."
1985–1986 "The Dungeon At The Heart Of Dawn," "Citadel Of Shadow," "The Timelost," "Odyssey Of The 12th Talisman," "The Winds of Darkness" and "Cave Of The Fairie Dragons."

DYNOMUTT, DOG WONDER

In the summer of 1978, ABC repeated the adventures of this cape–crusading bionic dog and his faithful leader, the Blue Falcon, who were both introduced on "The Scooby Doo/ Dynomutt Hour" in 1976. Created by Joe Ruby and Ken Spears, who formed their own animation studio, Ruby–Spears Enterprises, Dynomutt's voice and mannerisms were pat-terned after Ed Norton (Art Carney) of "The Honeymooners."

Before being given its own half–hour time slot that summer, Dynomutt reappeared earlier that season in four two–part broadcasts as part of "Scooby's All–Star Laff–A–Lympics." (The cartoons were retitled, "The Blue Falcon and Dyno-mutt.") In the fall of 1980, Dynomutt surfaced again briefly as co–star of "The Godzilla/Dynomutt Hour With The Funky Phantom" on NBC. *A Hanna–Barbera Production. Color. Half–hour. Premiered on ABC: June 3, 1978–September 2, 1978.*

Voices:

Dynomutt, Dog Wonder: Frank Welker, **The Blue Falcon:** Gary Owens, **Focus 1:** Ron Feinberg, **Mayor:** Larry Mc-Cormick, **Narrator:** Ron Feinberg

Episodes:

"The Great Brain . . . Train Robbery," "The Day And Night Crawler," "The Harbor Robber," "Everybody Hyde," "What Now, Lowbrow," "Sinister Symphony," "Don't But Super-mugg," "Factory Recall," "The Queen Hornet," "The Wizard Of Ooze," "Tin Kong," "The Awful Ordeal With The Head Of Steel," "The Blue Falcon Versus The Red Vulture," "The Injustice League Of America," "The Lighter Than Air Raid" and "The Prophet Profits."

THE EIGHTH MAN

Comic–strip adaptation of Japanese bionic crimefighter re-born from the body of a murdered police detective found by Professor Genius, who transforms him into super robot, To-bor, The Eighth Man. Resuming the chase for his own killers, Tobor's true identity is known only to Chief Fumblethumbs of the Metropolitan International Police, for whom he helps fight crime in the city. Along the way, he encounters such notorious villains as The Armored Man, Dr. Demon and The Light That Burned, as well as the criminal organization, Inter-crime. First telecast on Japanese television, the series was dubbed in English by Joe Oriolo Productions, producers of TV's "Felix the Cat." *A TCJ Animation Center Production. Color. Half–hour. Premiered: September 7, 1965. Syndicated.*

EMERGENCY PLUS FOUR

In this cartoon spin–off from the live–action adventure show "Emergency," four youngsters (Sally, Matt, Jason and Randy) help Los Angeles County paramedics rescue endangered citi-zens from burning buildings and other perils. The youngsters are taught basic rescue techniques required in the face of danger.

According to producer Janis Diamond, "The children really responded well to the show. It was an educational venture for them. Fire departments across the country requested prints of the show so they could be shown at fire prevention and safety seminars for children."

Kevin Tighe and Randolph Mantooth, stars of the original "Emergency," voiced the animated version of their characters. *A Fred Calvert Production. Color. Half–hour. Premiered on NBC: September 8, 1973–September 4, 1976.*

Voices:

Roy DeSoto: Kevin Tighe, **John Gage:** Randolph Mantooth, **Sally:** Sarah Kennedy, **Matt:** David Joliffe, **Jason:** Donald Fullilove, **Randy:** Peter Haas

Additional Voices:

Richard Paul, Jack DeLeon

Episodes:

1973–1974 "Desert Storm," "Danger At Fantasy Park," "The Circus Story," "Sunken Plane, "River Of Peril," "Fire At Sea," "Tsumi," "Brush Fire," "Oil's Well," "Winter Nightmare" and "Cry Wolf."
1974–1975 "Bicycle Thieves," "S.O.S. Help Us," "King Of The Mountain," "Stuntman," "Odyssey" (two parts), "Out Of The Blue," "After Burner," "Wheels Of Fire," "Ghost Of Billy Silver," "The Old Crox" and "Blast Off."

EVERYTHING'S ARCHIE

The fourth in a series of "Archie" comic strip series, this entry featured repeat episodes of the previous network shows ("The Archie Show," "The Archie Comedy Hour," "Archie's Funhouse" and "Archie's TV Funnies") combined with new animated wraparounds of the cast. *A Filmation Production. Color. Half-hour. Premiered on CBS: September 8, 1973–January 26, 1974.*

Voices:

Archie Andrews: Dallas McKennon, **Jughead Jones:** Howard Morris, **Betty Cooper:** Jane Webb, **Veronica Lodge:** Jane Webb, **Reggie Mantle:** John Erwin, **Sabrina:** Jane Webb, **Big Ethel:** Jane Webb, **Big Moose:** Howard Morris, **Carlos:** Jose Flores

THE EWOKS AND STAR WARS DROIDS ADVENTURE HOUR

The enchantment of George Lucas' box–office sensation *Star Wars* was spun–off into this Saturday–morning series, featuring brand–new adventures of those lovable droids R2–D2 and C3PO, as well as those cuddly creatures, the Ewoks, in this hour–long science–fiction fantasy series. Two half–hour episodes made up the program.

In "Ewoks," the furry tribe of peace–loving characters, now the Endorian equivalents of teenagers, enjoy new encounters on the distant forest moon of Endor with friends Princess Kneesa and the mischevious Latara. Young Ewoks scout Wicket leads the pack as they journey through their fantastic world in episodes dealing with life, death, love and friendship.

The second half, "Droids: The Adventure of R2–D2 and C3PO," recounts the years between the rise of the Empire and the beginning of the Star Wars in animated stories told with a liberal comic touch and always from the droids' point of view. Each episode was a self–contained story—no cliff–hanger endings—with only elements of each story resolved in a climactic third or fourth episode.

The program ran only for one season on ABC, but in 1986 the network aired a new series of Ewoks cartoons entitled, "The All New Ewoks." Both series were produced by George Lucas' production company Lucasfilm in association with Canada's leading animation house, Nelvana Limited. *A Lucasfilm Production in association with Nelvana Limited, Hanho Heung–Up and Mi–Hahn Productions. Color. One hour. Premiered on ABC: September 7, 1985–November 30, 1985.*

Voices:

The Ewoks: Wicket: Jim Henshaw, **Widdle,** Wicket's brother: John Stocker, **Weechee,** Wicket's oldest brother: Greg Swanson, **Teebo:** Eric Peterson, **Paploo:** Paul Chato, **Deej:** Richard Donat, **Shodu:** Nonnie Griffin, **Winda:** Leanne Coppen, **Princess Kneesaa:** Cree Summer Francks, **Latara:** Taborah Johnson, **Logray,** the medicine man: Doug Chamberlain, **Chief Chirpa:** George Buza, **Aunt Bozzie:** Pam Hyatt, **Malani:** Alyson Court, **Aunt Zephee:** Pam Hyatt, **Baby Wiley:** Michael Fantini, **Baby Nippet:** Leanne Coppen, **Lumat:** George Buza, **Ashma:** Paulina Gillis, **Chukah–Trok:** Don McManus, **Erphram Warrick:** Antony Parr, **Kaink:** Pauline Rennie, **Mring-Mring** (Gupin): Ron James, **Ubel:** Hadley Kay, **Punt:** Rob Cowan, **Morag:** Jackie Burroughs, **Singing Maiden:** Glori Gage, **Bondo:** Don McManus, **Trebla:** Alan Fawcett, **Jinda Boy:** Greg Swanson, **Rock Wizard:** Desmond Ellis, **Mooth:** John Stocker, **Zut:** Joe Matheson, **Dobah:** Diane Polley, **Nahkee:** George Buza, **Hoom:** John Stocker, **Hoona:** Myra Fried, **King Corneesh:** Dan Hennessey, **Urgah:** Melleny Brown, **Dulok Shaman:** Don Francks, **Dulok Scout:** John Stocker, **Shaman's Nephew:** Hadley Kay, **Murgoob:** Eric Peterson, **Trome #1:** Dan Hennessey, **Trome #2:** Marvin Goldhar, **Trome #3:** Peter Blais, **Droids: R2–D2:** (electronic), **C3PO:** Anthony Daniels, **C3PO** (guide track): Graham Haley, **"The Trigon One"** (episodes 1–4) **Thall Joben:** Andrew Sabiston, **Jord Dusat:** Dan Hennessey, **Kea Moll:** Lesleh Donaldson, Terri Hawkes, **Tig Fromm:** Maurice Godin, **Sisc Fromm:** Michael Kirby, **Vlix:** Marvin Goldhar, **Demma Moll:** Toby Tarnow, **Boba Fett:** George Buza, Ken Pogue, **BL–17:** Graham Haley, **Proto 1:** Long John Baldry, **Zebulon Dak:** Donny Burns, **Clones:** Marvin Goldhar, **Sleazy Guard:** Marvin Goldhar, **Mercenary Droid:** Dan Hennessey, **"Mon Julpa"** (episodes 5–8, 13) **Jann Tosh:** Milah Cheylov, **Jessica Meade:** Taborah Johnson, **Uncle Bundy:** Dan Hennessey, **Kleb Zellock:** Donny Burns, **Mon Julpa/Kez–Iban:** Michael Lefebvre, **Kybo Ren:** Don Francks, **Jyn Obah:** Don McManus, **Sollag:** John Stocker, **Zatec–Cha:** John Stocker, **Vinga:** Dan Hennessey, **Yorpo:** Dan Hennessey, **IG–88:** Don McManus, **Doodnik:** George Buza, **Auctioneer:** Don McManus, **Miner:** Don McManus, **Miner:** John Stocker, **Lord Toda:** Graeme Campbell, **Princess Gerin:** Cree Summer Francks, **Coby Toda:** Jamie Dick, Christopher Young, **Greej:** John Stocker, **Captain**

Stroon: Chris Wiggins, **Mr. Slarm:** J. Gordon Masten, **"The Adventures of Mungo Baobab"** (episodes 9–12) **Mungo Baobab:** Winston Reckert, Barry Greene, **Admiral Screed:** Graeme Campbell, **Governor Koong:** Don Francks, **Gaff:** Rob Cowan, **Auren Yomm:** Jan Austin, **Nilz Yomm/Noop:** Peter MacNeill, **Old Ogger:** Eric Peterson, **Lin–D:** John Stocker, **Bun–Dingo:** Michael Kirby, **Announcer at the Games:** Michael Kirby, **Bola Yomm:** Pam Hyatt, **Galley Master:** John Stocker, **Krox:** Rob Cowan

Episodes:
"The Ewoks" (one per show).
"Cries Of The Trees," "The Haunted Village," "Rampage Of The Phlogs," "To Save Deej," "The Travelling Jindas," "The Tree Of Light," "The Curse Of The Jindas," "Land Of The Gupins," "Sun Star Vs. Shadow Stone," "Wicket's Wagon," "The Three Lessons" and "Blue Harvest."
"Droids: The Adventures of R2–D2 and C3PO" (one per show).
"The Trigon One: The White Witch," "The Trigon One: Escape Into Terror," "The Trigon One: The Trigon Unleashed," "The Trigon One: A Race To The Finish," "Mon Julpa: The Lost Prince," "Mon Julpa: The New King," "Mon Julpa: The Pirates of Tarnooga," "Mon Julpa: The Revenge Of The Kybo Ren," "The Adventures Of Mungo Baobab: Coby The Starhunters," "The Adventures Of Mungo Baobab: Tail Of The Roon Comets," "The Adventures Of Mungo Baobab: The Roon Games," "The Adventures Of Mungo Baobab: Across The Roon Sea" and "Mon Julpa: The Frozen Citadel."

THE FABULOUS FUNNIES

Animated vignettes starring comic strip characters such as Nancy and Sluggo, Broom Hilda, Alley Oop and the Katzenjammer Kids. According to *Los Angeles Times* television critic Lee Marguilies, the show's premiere was "heavy–handed in its effort to present children with prosocial messages." The series featured all–new episodes combined with repeat adventures first shown on "Archie's TV Funnies." *A Filmation Production. Color. Half–hour. Premiered on NBC: September 9, 1978–September 1, 1979.*

Voices:
Broom Hilda/Sluggo/Oola/Hans and Fritz Katzenjammer: June Foray, **Nancy:** Jayne Hamil, **Captain Katzenjammer/King Guzzle:** Alan Oppenheimer, **Alley Oop:** Bob Holt

Episodes:
"Animal Crack–Ups," "School Daze," "Comic–ition," "Bods And Clods," "Save Our World," "But, Would You Want Your Sister To Marry An Artist," "Money Madness," "Fear," "Different Jokes For Different Folks," "Death," "Safety Second," "Drinking" and "Shot In The Light."

FAMILY CLASSICS THEATRE

Thirteen hour–long animated specials based on popular juvenile novels, comprised this series of literary masterpieces converted to animation. Telecast as holiday specials, the films were produced by two animation studios, Australia's Air Programs International and Hanna–Barbera Productions. (See Animated Television Specials for details on each production.) The final season repeated specials which had been previously shown. *An Air Programs International/Hanna–Barbera Production. Color. One hour. Premiered on CBS: November 14, 1971.*

Episodes:
1970–1971 "Tales Of Washington Irving," "A Connecticut Yankee In King Arthur's Court," and "A Christmas Carol."
1971–1972 "The Legend Of Robin Hood" and "Treasure Island."
1972–1973 "Robinson Crusoe" and "The Prince And The Pauper,"
1973–1974 "The Count of Monte Cristo," "Kidnapped," "The Swiss Family Robinson," "20,000 Leagues Under The Sea," "The Three Musketeers" and "The Black Arrow."

FAMILY CLASSIC TALES

Following the success of "Family Classics Theatre," CBS commissioned this series of new animated features for children, packaged as fall holiday specials (see Animated Television Specials for details on each production) under a new title, "Family Classic Tales." *An Air Programs International/Hanna–Barbera Production. Color. One hour. Premiered on CBS: November 15, 1975.*

Episodes:
1975–1976 "Mysterious Island," "Ivanhoe" and "The Last Of The Mohicans."
1976–1977 "Master Of The World," "Davy Crockett On The Mississippi," "Journey To The Center Of The Earth" and "Five Weeks In A Balloon."
1978–1979 "Black Beauty."
1979–1980 "Gulliver's Travels" and "The Adventures Of Sinbad."
1981–1982 "Daniel Boone."

THE FAMOUS ADVENTURES OF MR. MAGOO

The myopic Mr. Magoo portrays various literary and historical characters—William Tell, Long John Silver, Don Quixote and others—in this hour–long series which sometimes combined two half–hour stories in one program. The show marked Magoo's first entry into prime–time as a regular weekly series. *A UPA Production. Color. One hour. Premiered on NBC: October 10, 1964–August 21, 1965.*

Voices:
Mr. Magoo: Jim Backus

Additional Voices:
Marvin Miller, Dick Kleiner, Julie Bennett, Everett Sloane, Dallas McKennon, Dick Nelson, Dennis King Jr., Shepard Menken, Laura Olsher, Johnny Coons, Joan Gardner, Howard Morris, Robbie Lester, Judy Lescher, Joan Crosby, Paul Frees, Virginia Eller, Nancy Wible

Episodes:
"The Three Musketeers #1," "The Three Musketeers #2," "Robin Hood" (four parts), "Snow White" (two parts), "Treasure Island" (two parts), "Cyrano," "King Arthur," "The Count Of Monte Cristo," "William Tell," "Don Quixote" (two parts), "Rip Van Winkle," "Noah's Ark," "Captain Kidd," "Moby Dick," "Paul Revere," "Gunga Din," "Midsummer Night's Dream," "Sherlock Holmes," "Dr. Frankenstein" and "Dick Tracy."

FANGFACE

Producers Joe Ruby and Ken Spears, formerly top cartoon show creators for Hanna–Barbera, opened shop and animated for ABC their first Saturday–morning kid series under the production company, Ruby–Spears. The program dealt with the misadventures of four teenagers—Biff, Kim, Puggsy and Fangs (the latter two reminiscent of Leo Gorcey and Huntz Hall of "Bowery Boys" fame)—who fight the forces of evil with the help of Fangs (actually Sherman Fangsworth), who turns into a werewolf. The series only lasted one full season, but Fangface returned with a new partner, Fangpuss, in new adventures as part of "The Plastic Man Comedy–Adventure Show" during the 1979–1980 season. *A Ruby–Spears Enterprises Production. Color. Half–hour. Premiered on ABC: September 9, 1978–September 8, 1979.*

Voices:
Fangface: Jerry Dexter, **Biff:** Frank Welker, **Puggsy:** Bart Braverman, **Kim:** Susan Blu

Episodes:
"A Heap Of Trouble," "A Creep From The Deep," "The Shocking Creature Feature," "Eastward Ho To The UFO," "The Great Ape Escape," "Dinosaur Daze," "Don't Abra When Yoyu Cadabra," "Space Monster Mishap," "The Invisible Menace Mix–Up," "The Cuckoo Carnival Calamity," "Begone, You Amazon" and "Snow Job Jitters."

FANTASTIC FOUR

Superheroes Mr. Fantastic, the Invisible Girl, the Human Torch and the Thing take on the city's most ruthless criminals and sinister evildoers. The team of the Fantastics is composed of scientist Reed Richards (Mr. Fantastic), who can stretch his body into various contortions; his wife, Sue (The Invisible Girl); Ben Grim, alias the Thing, who, once transformed, has the power of a thousand horses; and Johnny Storm, the Human Torch. *A Hanna–Barbera Production in association with Marvel Comics Group. Color. Half–hour. Premiered on ABC: September 9, 1967–March 15, 1970.*

Voices:
Reed Richards: Gerald Mohr, **Sue Richards:** Jo Ann Pflug, **Johnny Storm:** Jack Flounders, **Ben Grimm:** Paul Frees

Episodes:
"Klaus," "Menace Of The Mole Men," "Diablo," "The Red Ghost," "Invasion Of The Super Skulls," "Three Predictions Of Dr. Doom," "The Way It All Began," "Behold A Distant Star," "Prisoners Of Planet X," "The Mysterious Molecule

The Invisible Girl, the Human Torch, Mr. Fantastic and the Thing prepare for trouble in Saturday morning's "The Fantastic Four." © Marvel Comics Group (Courtesy: Hanna–Barbera Productions)

Man," "Danger In The Depths," "Demon Of The Deep," "Return Of The Moleman," "It Started On Yancy Street," "Galactus," "The Micro World Of Dr. Doom," "Blast Starr, The Living Bomb Burst," "The Terrible Tribunal," "Rama–Tut" and "The Deadly Director."

FANTASTIC MAX

Part of "The Funtastic World of Hanna–Barbera," this half–hour adventure series follows the earthly and outer–space encounters of a precocious 16–month–old toddler who returns from an unscheduled trip aboard a rocket (on a trip to Cape Canaveral he crawls on board a spacecraft and blasts off into space), only with a few surprises: an alien friend and a robot babysitter, who make life for Max and his family anything but dull. *A Hanna–Barbera Production. Color. Half–hour. Premiered: September, 1988. Syndicated.*

Voices:
Max: Ben Ryan Ganger, **FX,** his pea–green alien friend: Nancy Cartwright, **A. B. Sitter,** his babysitter: Gregg Berger, **Mom,** Max's mother: Gail Matthius, **Dad,** Max's father: Paul Eiding, **Zoe,** his six–year–old sister: Elisabeth Harnois, **Ben,** his five–year–old neighbor: Benji Gregory

Episodes:
1988–1989 "The Loon In The Moon," "Toys Will Be Toys," "All In A Babe's Work," "The Big Sleep," "Attack Of The Cubic Rubes," "Monkey Bee, Monkey Do," "Cooking Mother Goose," "Journey To The Center Of My Sister," "Carrot Encounters Of The Third Kind," "The Baby Who Fell To Earth," "Beach Blanket Baby," "Stitches In Time" and "From Here To Twinkle–Twinkle."
1989–1990 "Boo Who?," "Ben And The Black Mailer," "Cowboy Max," "Straight Flush," "Rats Like Us," "Grab Bag Rag," "Movie Star Max," "To Tell The Tooth," "Dr. Max And Baby

Hyde," "Guess Who's Coming To Dinner?," "A. B. Phone Home," "Puzzle, Puzzle Toil And Trouble" and "Blarney Fife."

FARMER AL FALFA

The prestigious straw–hatted, overall–clad farmer was the principal star of this film package made up of old Terrytoon cartoons and brand new segments. *A Terrytoons Production. Black–and–White. Color. Half–hour. Premiered: 1956. Syndicated.*

FAT ALBERT AND THE COSBY KIDS

One of the staples of comedian Bill Cosby's standup act in the early 1960s was his childhood recollections of Fat Albert and the gang from North Philadelphia. Real life situations were cleverly adapted to amusing and educational cartoons by Filmation in this long–running half–hour series which earned an Emmy Award nomination in 1974. Topics covered drug addiction, family life and other social problems of everyday life.

"There were other educational programs before 'Fat Albert,'" said Filmation president Lou Scheimer in an interview. "But, by and large, the two ingredients had never had a balance and a blending before as did 'Fat Albert.' And no program had ever been undertaken with such distinguished educators taking an active part in the actual productions of scripts and visuals."

Bill Cosby voiced several characters in the series besides serving as its host in live–action wraparounds that opened and closed the program and introduced the animated segments. Before the original series aired on Saturday mornings, NBC broadcast four years earlier a prime–time special, "Hey, Hey, Hey, It's Fat Albert," which was well–received by critics and viewers alike. For the 1979–1980 season, the series changed its name to "The New Fat Albert Show."

In 1984, under the title of "Fat Albert and the Cosby Kids," Filmation produced a new crop of episodes combined with old episodes of the original series for syndication. (Records are unavailable for the titles of the new cartoons.) *A Filmation Production. Color. Half–hour. Premiered on CBS: September 9, 1972–September 1, 1979; September 8, 1979–August 25, 1984 (as "The New Fat Albert Show"). Syndicated.*

Voices:
Host: Bill Cosby, **Fat Albert:** Bill Cosby, **Mushmouth:** Bill Cosby, **Mudfoot:** Bill Cosby, **Dumb Donald:** Bill Cosby, **Brown Hornet:** Bill Cosby, **Russell:** Jan Crawford, **Bucky:** Jan Crawford, **Weird Harold:** Gerald Edwards, **Ruby:** Eric Suter, **Devery:** Eric Suter

Additional Voices:
Keith Allen, Pepe Brown, Erika Carroll, Lane Vaux

Episodes:
1972–1973 "Lying," "The Runt," "The Stranger," "Creativity," "Fish Out Of Water," "Moving," "Playing Hookey," "The Hospital," "Begging Benny," "The Hero," "The Prankster," "Four

Eyes," "The Tomboy," "Stagefright," "The Bully" and "Smart Kid."
1973–1974 (new episodes combined with reruns) "Mister Big Timer," "The Newcomer," "What Does Dad Do?," "Mom Or Pop," "How The West Was Lost" and "Sign Off."
1975–1976 (new episodes combined with reruns) "The Fuzz," "Ounce Of Prevention," "Fat Albert Meets Dan Cupid," "Take Two, They're Small," "The Animal Lover" and "Little Tough Guy."
1976–1977 (new episodes combined with reruns) "Smoke Gets In Your Hair," "What Say?," "Readin', Ritin', And Rudy," "Suede Simpson," "Little Business," "TV Or Not TV," "The Shuttered Window" and "Junk Food." (Cartoons from previous seasons were rebroadcast from 1977–1979)
1979–1980 (new episodes combined with reruns) "In My Merry Busmobile," "The Dancer," "Spare The Rod," "Sweet Sorrow," "Poll Time," "The Mainstream" and "Soft Core."

FELIX THE CAT

Producer Joe Oriolo, who took over production of the "Felix the Cat" comic strip, produced this series of new color episodes in which Felix sported a new sight gag—his magic bag of tricks. Stories depicted the scheming, bald–domed Professor and his bulldog assistant, Rock Bottom, endeavoring to steal Felix's magic bag to make him powerless. Such attempts failed miserably, with Felix always having the last laugh. Other scripts had Felix babysitting the Professor's nephew, Poindexter, an intellectual junior scientist. Other recurring characters included the Master Cylinder and Vavoom. Episodes were produced between 1958 and 1960 for broadcast. Five cliff–hanging episodes comprised a complete story. *A Felix the Cat Production for Trans–Lux Productions. Color. Half–hour. Premiered: January 4, 1960. Syndicated.*

Voices:
Felix the Cat: Jack Mercer, **The Professor:** Jack Mercer, **Poindexter:** Jack Mercer, **Rock Bottom:** Jack Mercer, **The Master Cylinder:** Jack Mercer, **Vavoom:** Jack Mercer

Episodes:
(five per show) "The Magic Bag," "Into Outer Space," "Abominable Snowman," "Felix Out West," "Felix The Cat Suit," "Electronic Brainwasher," "Do–It–Yourself Monster Book," "Blubberino The Whale," "Ghostly Concert," "Captain No–Kiddin'," "Egypt," "Detective Thinking Hat," "Balloon Blowee Machine," "Friday The 13th," "Stone Making Machine," "Penelope The Elephant," "Money Tree," "Oil And Indians Don't Mix," "The Glittering Jewels," "The Gold Car And County Fair," "Sheriff Felix Versus The Gas Cloud," "Felix's Gold Mine," "How To Steal A Gold Mine?," "Private Eye Felix And Pierre Moustache," "The Gold Fruit Tree," "The Flying Saucer," "Felix Baby–Sits," "Instant Money," "Master Cylinder—King Of The Moon," "The Invisible Professor," "Venus And The Master Cylinder," "The Termites Of 1960," "Moo Moo Island Oysters," "The Mouse And Felix," "King Neptune's S.O.S.," "Relax–A–Lawn Chair," "The African Diamond Affair," "Felix's Prize Garden," "Finally, The Magic Bag Is Mine!," "Felix And The Rhinoceros," "Felix Finder And The Ghost Town," "Snoopascope, A Magic Bag Of Tricks," "Stone Age

Felix," "The Gold Silkworms," "Felix And Vavoom," "The Jubilee Dime," "Movie Star Felix," "Youth Water," "Game Warden Felix," "Master Cylinder Captures Poindexter," "The Atomic Drive Explosion Of The Master Cylinder," "Super–Toy," "The Jewel Bird," "The Atomic Rocket Fuel," "The Hairy Berry Bush," "General Clang And The Secret Rocket Fuel," "The Rajah's Elephants," "The Exchanging Machine," "The Leprechaun," "The Master Cylinder's Spacegram," "The Leprechaun's Gold," "Felix And The Mid–Evil Ages," "The Capturing Of The Leprechaun King," "Martin The Martian Meets Felix The Cat," "The Professor's Committed No Crime!," "The Martian Rescue," "The Portable Closet, Rock Bottom," "Redbeard The Pirate," "A–Museum The Professor And Rock Bottom," "Redbeard The Pirate," "A–Museum The Professor And Rock Bottom," "The Professor's Instant Changer," "The Vacation Mirage," "Cat–Napped," "The Sea Monster And Felix," "The Diamond Tree," "King Of The Leprechauns," "The Magic Apples," "Oysters And Starfishes," "The Haunted House," "Gold Dipper Vavoom," "The Wizard And Sir Rock," "The Coal Diamonds," "Out West With Big Brownie," "Love–Sick Squirt Gun," "Mechanical Felix," "The Ski Jump," "Felix And The Beanstalk," "The Milky Way," "The Super Rocket Formula," "The Weather Maker," "The Giant Magnet," "The Instant Truck Melter," "The Pep Pill," "Leprechaun Gold From Rainbows," "The Magnetic Ray," "The Instant Grower," "The Professor's Ancester . . . The Wizard," "Luring The Magic Bag Of Tricks," "The Uranium Discovery," "Chief Standing Bull," "The Strongest Robot In The World," "Stairway To The Stars," "Cleaning House," "Vavoom Learns How To Fish," "The Golden Nugget," "The Genie," "Felix And Poindexter Out West," "The Bad Genie," "The Rajah's Zoo," "The Loan Business," "A Treasure Chest," "The Essence Of Money," "Mercury's Winged Sandals," "The $10,000 Vacation," "Brother Bottom Pebble," "The North Pole And A Walrus Hunt," "Cleopatra's Beauty Secrets," "The Trip Back From The North Pole," "The Golden Whale Babysitter," "North Pole Jail Hole," "Felix The Handyman" and "Public Enemies Number One And Two."

FESTIVAL OF FAMILY CLASSICS

Favorite literary classics for children were adapted into fully animated feature–length cartoons for this syndicated series of hour–long specials. (See Animated Television Specials for details on each title.) *A Rankin–Bass Production. Color. One hour. Premiered: 1972. Syndicated.*

Episodes:

"20,000 Leagues Under The Sea" (two parts), "Cinderella," "Hiawatha," "Puss–In–Boots," "Johnny Appleseed," "The Ballad of Paul Bunyan," "Jack O'Lantern," "Around The World In 80 Days," "Robin Hood," "Sleeping Beauty," "Alice In Wonderland," "A Christmas Tree," "Tom Sawyer," "Robinson Crusoe," "Yankee Doodle," "Swiss Family Robinson," "Arabian Nights" and "Snow White."

THE FLINTSTONE KIDS

The original members of "The Flintstones" cast are seen as 10–year–old children in this Saturday–morning show in which

Television's prehistoric favorites, Fred, Barney, Wilma, Betty and Dino, from their younger days, in "The Flintstone Kids." © Hanna–Barbera Productions

Fred, Barney, Wilma and Betty, together with their dinosaur "pup," Dino, get in and out of scrapes in the familiar surroundings of Bedrock. Complementing the characters is a rich assortment of supporting cast, including Rocky Ratrock, the neighborhood bully; Dreamchip Gemstone, the classic poor little rich girl; Philo Quartz, a budding private detective; and Nate Slate, who will grow up to be Bedrock's biggest businessman.

Three additional segments appeared on the program: "Captain Caveman and Son," exploits of the world's first superhero and his chip–off–the–old–block offspring, Cavey Jr.; "Dino's Dilemma's," demonstrating perils of prehistoric dogdom; and "Flintstone Funnies," a fantasy–adventure segment in which Fred and Barney, and Wilma and Betty let their imaginations lead them into exciting adventures. *A Hanna–Barbera Production. Color. One hour. Premiered on ABC: September 13, 1986–September 3, 1988.*

Voices:

Freddy: Lennie Weinrib, Scott Menville, **Barney:** Hamilton Camp, **Wilma:** Julie Dees, Elizabeth Lyn Fraser, **Betty:** B. J. Ward, **Dino:** Mel Blanc, **Ed Flintstone,** Fred's father: Henry Corden, **Edna Flintstone, Fred's mother:** Henry Corden, **Robert Rubble,** Barney's dad: Mel Blanc, **Rocky Ratrock:** Marilyn Schreffler, **Dreamchip Gemstone:** Susan Blu, **Phil Quartz:** Bumper Robinson, **Nate Slate:** Frank Welker, **Flab Slab:** Hamilton Camp, **Miss Rockbottom:** B. J. Ward, **Officer Quartz:** Rene Levant, **Fang:** Frank Welker, **Micky/Mica:** Julie Dees, **Granite Janet:** Susan Blu, **Tarpit Tommy:** Julie Dees, **Stalagbite:** Frank Welker, **Captain Caveman:** Mel Blanc, **Cavey Jr.:** Charles Adler, **Commissioner:** Lennie Weinrib, **Narrator:** Ken Mars

Episodes:

"The Flintstone Kids." (one per show)
1986–1987 "The Great Freddini," "Heroes For Hire," The Bad News Brontos," "Dusty Disappears," "Poor Little Rich Girl," "The Rock Concert That Rock Freddy" (Or "Born In The U.S. Cave"), Curse Of the Gemstone Diamond," "I Think

That I Shall Never See Barney Rubble As A Tree," "The Fugitives," "Freddy's Rocky Road To Karate," "Barney's Moving Experience," "The Little Visitor," "Grandpa For Loan" and "Freddy's First Crush."

1987–1988 (new episodes combined with reruns) "The Flintstone Fake Ache," "Better Buddy Blues," "Anything You Can Do, I Can Do Betty," "Camper Scamper," "A Tiny Egg," "Haircutastrophe," "Freddy The 13th," "Little Rubble, Big Trouble," "Philo's D–Feat" and "Rocky's Rocky Road."

"Captain Caveman and Son." (one per show)

1986–1987 "Freezy Does It," "Invasion Of The Mommy Snatchers," "The Ditto Master," "I Was A Teenage Grown–Up," "Grime And Punishment," "A Tale Of Too Silly," "To Baby Or Not To Baby," "Day Of The Villains," "Hero Today, Gone Tomorrow," "Curse Of The Reverse," "Captain Caveman's First Adventure," "Leave It To Mother" and "Greed It And Weep."

1987–1988 (new episodes combined with reruns) "Captain Knaveman," "Attack Of The Fifty Foot Teenage Lizard," "The Cream–Pier Strikes Back," "Captain Caveman's Super Cold," "The Big Bedrock Bully Bash" and "Captain Cavedog."

"Dino's Dilemmas." (one per show)

1986–1987 "Yard Wars," "Dreamchip's Cur Wash," "Dressed Up Dino," "Fred's Mechanical Dog," "The Butcher Shoppe," "Dressed Up Dino," "Fred's Mechanical Dog," "The Butcher Shoppe," "Dressed Up Dino," "The Vet," "The Dino Diet," "What Price Fleadom," "The Terror Within," "Revenge Of The Bullied," "The Chocolate Chip Catastrophe," "Watchdog Blues" and "Captain Cavepuppy,"

1987–1988 (new episodes combined with reruns) "Killer Kitty," "Who's Falutin Who?," "Bone Voyage," "World War Flea," "A Midnite Pet Peeve" and "The Birthday Shuffle," "Flintstone Funnies" (one per show).

1986–1987 "Bedrock P. I.'s," "Princess Wilma," "Frankenstone," "Rubble Without A Cause," "Indiana Flintstone," "Freddy In The Big House," "Sugar And Spies," "Monster From The Tar Pits," "Betty's Big Break," "Dino Goes Hollyrock," "Bedrock 'N Roll," "The Twilight Stone" and "Philo's Invention."

THE FLINTSTONES

The town of Bedrock spelled bedlam when the Flintstones and their neighbors, the Rubbles, got together, formulating what has been probably the most heralded situation–comedy cartoon series and the first "adult" cartoon show for television.

The familiar phrase "Yabba dabba do!" was made famous by blow–hard caveman and father, Fred Flintstone. Whenever he tangled with his next–door pal, half–witted practical joker Barney Rubble, normal modern stone–age situations always ran amuck.

The main characters, Fred, Barney and wives, Wilma and Betty, were adapted from "The Honeymooners" TV–show personalities. Both Fred and Barney bore more than a vague resemblance to Ralph Kramden (Jackie Gleason) and Ed Norton (Art Carney).

But the show's stars faced their share of physical problems which almost threatened the future of the series. For a full season after Mel Blanc's near fatal automobile accident in 1962, the show was taped in his bedroom where he lay in a cast from his neck to his toes. (Daws Butler filled in as the voice of Barney for at least two episodes.) As executive producer Joe Barbera explained, "The easy thing would have been to replace him, but we kept going and it worked. Sometimes we'd have as many as sixteen people crowded into his bedroom and we hung a mike in front of him."

Another season, Alan Reed (the voice of Fred Flintstone) had a cataract operation, but worked up to 20 minutes before his scheduled surgery. He returned to the job in four weeks.

Before Reed's operation, the studio taped his parts in advance and worked around him until he was healthy enough to work again. While he was suffering from cataracts, the scripts were typed in special one–inch letters so that Reed could read his lines.

When the show entered its fourth season, Barbera's other half, Bill Hanna, was quoted as saying, "He [Reed] tours the country in a leopard skin—he is Flintstone!" Reed died in 1977.

"The Flintstones," which premiered on ABC, was the first made–for–television cartoon series to air in prime time. (The first prime–time series were CBS' "Cartoon Theatre" and "Gerald McBoing–Boing.") The program aired on Friday nights at 7:30. Sponsors: Winston, Alka–Seltzer, One–A–Day Vitamins and Post Cereals. *A Hanna–Barbera Production. Color. Half–hour. Premiered on ABC: September 30, 1960–September 2, 1966. Rebroadcast: NBC: January 17, 1967–August 1969; September 6, 1967–September 5, 1970.*

Voices:

Fred Flintstone: Alan Reed, **Barney Rubble:** Mel Blanc, Daws Butler, **Wilma Flintstone:** Jean VanderPyl, **Betty Rubble:** Bea Benadaret, Gerry Johnson, **Pebbles:** Jean VanderPyl, **Dino,** the pet dinosaur: Chips Spam, **Bamm Bamm,** the Rubbles' son: Don Messick, **George Slate,** Fred's boss: John Stephenson

Episodes:

1960–61 "The Swimming Pool," "The Flintstone Flyer," "The Prowler," "The Baby Sitters," "The Engagement Ring," "No Help Wanted," "At The Races," "The Drive–In," "Hot Lips Hannigan," "The Split Personality," "The Snorkasaurus Hunter," "Hollyrock Here I Come," "The Girls' Night Out," "The Monster From The Tar Pits," "The Golf Champion," "The Sweepstakes Ticket," "The Hypnotist," "The Hot Piano," "The Big Bank Robbery," "Arthur Quarry's Dance Class," "Love Letters On The Rocks," "The Tycoon," "The Astronuts," "The Long Long Weekend," "In The Dough," "The Good Scout," "Rooms For Rent," "Fred Flintstone—Before Or After," "Droop Along Flintstone" and "Fred Flintstone Woos Again."

1961–1962 "The Hit Song Writer," "The Rock Quarry Story," "The Little White Lie," "The Soft Touchables," "Flintstone of Prinstone," "The Beauty Contest," "The Missing Bus," "Social Climbers," "The House Guest," "Alvin Brickrock Presents," "The Picnic," "The Masquerade Ball," "The X–Ray Story," "The Entertainer," "The Gambler," "Wilma's Vanishing Money," "A Star Is Almost Born," "Operation Barney," "Impractical Joker," "Feudin' And Fussin'," "The Happy Household," "This Is Your Lifesaver," "Fred Strikes Out," "The Rock Vegas Caper," "The Mailman Cometh," "Trouble–In–Law," "Divided We Sail," "Kleptomaniac Caper," "Latin Lover," "Take Me Out

Of The Ball Game," "Fred's New Boss" and "Dino Goes Hollyrock."

1962–1963 "The Twitch," "Barney The Invisible," "The Bowling Ballet," "Baby Barney," "The Buffalo Convention," "Here's Snow In Your Eyes," "The Little Stranger," "Ladies' Day," "Hawaiian Escapade," "Nothing But The Tooth," "High School Fred," "Dial 'S' For Suspicion," "Flashgun Freddie," "The Kissing Burglar," "The Birthday Party," "Wilma, The Maid," "The Hero," "Foxy Grandma," "The Surprise," "Mother–In–Law's Visit," "Fred's New Job," "The Blessed Event," "Carry On, Nurse Fred," "Ventriloquist Barney," "The Big Move," "Swedish Visitors" and "Divided We Sail."

1963–1964 "Dino Disappears," "Groom Gloom," "Fred's Monkeyshiners," "The Flintstone Canaries," "Glue For Two," "Big League Freddie," "Sleep On, Sweet Fred," "Old Lady Betty," "Kleptomaniac Pebbles," "Daddies Anonymous," "Daddy's Little Beauty," "Bedrock Hillbillies," "Little Bamm–Bamm," "Peek–A–Boo Camera," "Ann Margrock Presents," "Ten Little Flintstones," "Once Upon A Coward," "Fred El Terrifico," "Flintstone And The Lion," "Cave Scout Jamboree," "Ladies' Night At The Lodge," "Room For Two," "Reel Trouble," "Bachelor Daze," "Son of Rockzilla" and "Operation Switchover."

1964–1965 "Pebbles' Birthday Party," "Hop Happy," "Cinderellastone," "Monster Fred," "Itty Bitty Fred," "Bedrock Rodeo Round–Up," "A Haunted House Is Not A Home," "Dr. Sinister," "The Gruesomes," "Most Beautiful Baby In Bedrock," "Dino And Juliet," "King For A Night," "Indianrockolis 500," "Adobe Dick," "Fred's Flying Lesson," "Fred's Second Car," "Christmas Flintstone," "The Hatrocks And The Gruesomes," "Time Machine," "Moonlight Maintenance," "Sheriff For A Day," "Deep In The Heart Of Texarock," "Superstone," "The Rolls Rock Caper," "Fred Meets Hercurock," and "Surfin' Fred."

1965–1966 "House That Fred Built," "No Biz Like Show Biz," "Disorder In The Court," "Return Of Stoney Curtis," "The Great Gazoo," "Circus Business," "Rip Van Flintstone," "Samantha," "The Gravelberry Pie King," "The Stonefinger Caper," "Masquerade Party," "Shinrock A–Go–Go," "Royal Rubble," "Seeing Doubles," "How To Pick A Fight With Your Wife Without Really Trying," "Two Men On A Dinosaur," "Fred Goes Ape," "The Long, Long, Long, Weekend," "The Treasure of Sierra Madrock," "Curtain Call At Bedrock," "Boss For A Day," "Fred's Island," "Jealousy," "Dripper," "The Story Of Rocky's Raiders" and "My Fair Freddy."

THE FLINTSTONES COMEDY HOUR

Complete episodes of "The Flintstones" which had previously aired on the network in other formats reappeared in this hour–long Saturday morning series, which featured new episodes of "Pebbles and Bamm–Bamm," in combination with episodes which were originally broadcast on 1971's "Pebbles and Bamm–Bamm." (See program for episodic information.)

Other segments included brief vignettes, comedy gag and dance–of–the–week segments rotated in between the series' main cartoon components. (Unfortunately, episode titles could only be found for the new episodes of "Pebbles and Bamm–

Bamm," which are listed below.) The cartoons were repeated the following season under a new series title, "The Flintstones Show," plus as part of "Pebbles and Bamm–Bamm" and the syndicated "Fred Flintstone and Friends." *A Hanna–Barbera Production. Color. One hour. Premiered on CBS: September 9, 1972–September 1, 1973. Rebroadcast on CBS: September 8, 1973–January 26, 1974 (as "The Flintstones Show").*

Voices:

Fred Flintstone: Alan Reed, **Wilma Flintstone:** Jean VaderPyl, **Pebbles Flintstone:** Mickey Stevens, **Barney Rubble:** Mel Blanc, **Betty Rubble:** Gay Hartwig, **Bamm–Bamm Rubble:** Jay North, **Sylvester Slate,** Fred's boss: John Stephenson, **Penny:** Mitzi McCall, **Moonrock:** Lennie Weinrib, **Fabian:** Carl Esser, **Wiggy:** Gay Hartwig, **Bronto:** Lennie Weinrib, **Zonk:** Mel Blanc, **Noodles:** John Stephenson, **Stub:** Mel Blanc

Episodes:

Pebbles and Bamm–Bamm (one per show).
"Squawkie Talkies," "The Suitor Computer," "Bedlam In Bedrock" and "Beauty And The Beast."

THE FLINTSTONES COMEDY SHOW

The original cast of Fred, Barney, Wilma and Betty were featured in this new format of rollicking, fun–filled comedy set in the Stone Age town of Bedrock. The program contained six regular cartoon segments of various lengths every week: "The Flintstone Family Adventures," the further comic misadventures of the Flintstone and Rubble families; "Pebbles, Dino and Bamm–Bamm," with Pebbles, Bamm–Bamm, Dino and his friends at work solving various mysteries; and "Captain Caveman," the screwed–up prehistoric superhero who is aided by Wilma and Betty in warding off criminals.

In addition, the program included "The Bedrock Cops," the zany escapades of the Bedrock Police force, joined by part–time deputies Fred and Barney and their supernatural friend, Shmoo, in fighting crime: "Dino and the Cavemouse," in which the Flintstones' pet dinosaur, Dino, squares off with a wild house mouse in this frantic prehistoric version of "watchdog vs. mouse"; and "The Frankenstones," the misadventures of the Flintstones' new and "unusual" looking neighbors, plus a variety of musical and comedy blackouts featuring the series' prehistoric stars. *A Hanna–Barbera Production. Color. One hour and a half. Premiered on NBC: November 22, 1980–September 5, 1981.*

Voices:

Fred Flintstone: Henry Corden, **Wilma,** his wife: Jean VanderPyl, **Barney Rubble,** their neighbor: Mel Blanc, **Betty,** his wife: Gay Autterson, **Dino:** Mel Blanc, **Pebbles:** Russi Taylor, **Bamm–Bamm** Michael Sheehan, **George Slate,** Fred's boss: John Stephenson, **Penny:** Mitzi McCall, **Wiggy:** Gay Autterson, **Moonrock:** Lennie Weinrib, **Schleprock:** Don Messick, **Shmoo:** Frank Welker, **Sgt. Boulder:** Lennie Weinrib, **Cavemouse:** Russi Taylor, **The Frankenstones: Frank,** the hulking father: Charles Nelson Reilly, **Hidea,** his wife: Ruta Lee, **Atrocia,** their kooky daughter: Zelda Rubinstein, **Freaky,** their misfit son: Paul Ruebens, **Rockjaw:** Frank Welker

Episodes:
"The Flinstone Family Adventures." (one per show)
1980–1981 "R. V. Fever," "Sands Of Saharastone," "Gold Fever," "Bogged Down" "Be Patient, Fred," "Country Club Clods," "The Rockdale Diet," "Dino's Girl," "The Gourmet Dinner," "The Stand–In" and "Go Take A Hike."
1981–1982 "The Great Bedrock Air Race," "Fred's Last Resort," "The Not–Such–A–Pleasure Cruise," "Fred's Big Top Flop," "In A Stew," "Fred Vs. The Energy Crisis" and "Fred's Friend In Need."
"Pebbles, Dino and Bamm–Bamm." (one per show)
1980–1981 "Ghost Sitters," "The Secret Of Scary Valley," "The Witch Of The Wardrobe," "Monster Madness," "The Show Must Go On," "The Beast Of Muscle Rock Beach," "In Tune With Terror," "The Curse Of Tutrockamen," "The Hideous Hiss Of The Lizard Monster," "The Legend Of Haunted Forest" and "Double Trouble With Long John Silverock."
1981–1982 "A Night Of Fright," "The Dust Devil Of Palm Rock Springs," "Dino And The Zombies," "The Ghost Of The Neanderthal Giant," "Creature From The Rock Lagoon," "Dino And The Giant Spiders" and "The Ghastly Gatorsaurus."
"Captain Caveman. (one per show)
1980–1981 "Clownfoot," "The Masquerader," "The Animal Master," "The Mole," "Rollerman," "Vulcan," "Punk Rock," "Braino," "The Incredible Hunk," "The Ice Man" and The Mummy's Worse."
1981–1982 "Pinkbeard," "The Blimp," "Futuro," "Mister Big," "Stormfront And Weathergirl," "Crypto" and "Presto."
"The Bedrock Cops." (one per show)
1980–1981 "Fred Goes Ape," "Off The Beaten Track," "A Bad Case Of Rock Jaw," "Follow That Dogasaurus," "Mountain Frustration," "Bedlam On The Bedrock Express," "Hot Air To Spare," "Rockjaw Rides Again," "Pretty Kitty," "The Roller Robber" and "Put Up Your Duke."
1981–1982 "Undercover Shmoo," "On the Ball," "Shop Treatment," "Country Clubbed," "Barney And The Bandit," "Shore Thing" and "Rotten Actors."
"Dino And The Cavemouse." (one per show)
1980–1981 "Quiet Please," "Mouse Cleaning," "Camp Out Mouse," "Piece O' Cake," "Ghost Mouse," "Beach Party," "Disco Dino," "Going Ape," "Wet Paint," "Finger Lick'n Bad," "Rocko Socko," "Flying Mouse," "Arcade Antics," "Aloha Mouse," "Robin Mouse," "Dino Comes Home," "L'il Orphan Alphie," "A Fool For Pool," "The Bedrock 500," "Abra–Ca–Dino," "Pow Pow The Dyno–Mite" and "Double Trouble."
1981–1982 "Sleepy Time Trouble," "Goofed Up Golf," "S'No Place Like Home," "Super–Dupes," "Dinner For Two," "Invasion Of The Cheese Snatchers," "Handle With Scare," "The World's Strongest Mouse," "Trick Or Treat," "Bats All," "Do Or Diet," "Mouse For Sale," "The Invisible Mouse" and "Maltcheese Falcon."
"The Frankenstones." (one per show)
1980–1981 "Birthday Boy," "Potion Problems," "A Night On The Town," "Out Of Their League," "Clone For A Day," "A Stone Is Born," "A Rocks–Pox On You," "The Luck Stops Here," "The Monster Of Invention," "Rock And Rolling Frankenstone" and "Sand Doom."
1981–1982 "Pet Peeves," "The Charity Bizarre," "Getting The

Business," "Ugly Is Only Skin Deep," "Three Days Of The Mastadon," "First Family Fiasco" and "House Wars."

FONZ AND THE HAPPY DAYS GANG

Inspired by television's hit prime–time comedy series, Fonzie and the rest of the "Happy Days" gang (Richie, Ralph and Fonzie's cut–up dog, Mr. Cool) spread cool fun as they travel via a time machine to every time and place throughout Earth's history. Showing them the way is Cupcake, a young futuristic girl who pilots the craft, which they repaired for her following her unscheduled landing in Milwaukee in the year 1957.

Three original cast members of the popular television sit–com voiced their characters on the show. *A Hanna–Barbera Production. Color. Half–hour. Premiered on ABC: November 8, 1980–September 18, 1982.*

Voices:
Fonzie: Henry Winkler, **Richie:** Ron Howard, **Ralph:** Don Most, **Mr. Cool:** Frank Welker, **Cupcake:** DeeDee Conn

Episodes:
1980–1981 "King For A Day," "May The Farce Be With You," "Arabian Knights," "Bye Bye Blackbeard," "Westward Whoa," "Ming Fu To You, Too," "The Vampire Strikes Back," "You'll Never Get Witch," "The 20,000 Drachma Pyramid," "It's A Jungle Out There," "Gone With The Wand," "Science Friction" and "Greece Is The Word."
1981–1982 "The French Correction," "Time Schelp," "Kelp," "It's All Downhill From Here," "Double Jeopardy," "There's Fjord In Your Future," "There's No Place Like Rome," "Perilous Pauline," "Around The World In 80 Days," "All This And Timbuktu" and "Give Me A Hand—Something's Afoot."

FOO FOO

Somewhat forgotten British–made series about a transparent man in a pencil sketch world. Produced by England's most noted animation studio, Halas and Batchelor, the series was animated in the same modernistic style of UPA (United Productions of America), which changed the course of animation through limited animation fare like "Gerald McBoing Boing" and "Mr. Magoo." *A Halas Batchelor Production. Color. Half–hour. Syndicated: 1961.*

Episodes:
"The Gardener," "The Birthday Treat," "A Denture Adventure," "A Misguided Tour," "The Caddies," "Burglar Catcher," "The Art Lovers," "The Three Mountaineers," "Foo Foo's New Hat," "The Big Race," "The Treasure Hunt," "The Magician," "The Spy Train," "Insured For Life," "Automation Blues," "The Beggar's Uproar," "Sleeping Beauty," "The Reward," "The Dinner Date," "Beauty Treatment," "The Ski Resort," "Lucky Street," "The Stowaway," "A Hunting We Will Go," "The Pearl Divers," "Foo Foo's Sleepless Night," "The Salesman," "Art For Art's Sake," "The Dog Pound," "The Hypnotist," "Low Finance" and "The Scapegoat."

FOOFUR

A ragtag gang of canines chase adventures as they try to make it on their own, led by the lanky, good–natured blue hound dog, Foofur, who inherits an old house from his master that becomes home for his various friends and relatives. His household includes Fencer, a black alley cat who thinks he's the "baddest" critter on four paws; Rocki, Foofur's diminutive niece; Louis, a warm–hearted bulldog and his sheedog mate, Annabell; and dapper Fritz–Carlos and his mate, Hazel, the matriarch of the clan. *A Hanna–Barbera Production. Color. Half–hour. Premiered on NBC: September 13, 1986–September 3, 1988.*

Voices

Foofur: Frank Welker, **Rocki:** Christina Lange, **Annabell:** Susan Tolsky, **Hazel:** Pat Carroll, **Pepe:** Don Messick, **Chucky:** Allan Melvin, **Mel:** David Doyle, **Fencer:** Eugene Williams, **Louis:** Dick Gautier, **Fritz–Carlos:** Jonathan Schmock, **Mrs. Escrow:** Susan Silo, **Sam:** Chick Vennera, **Baby,** Peter Cullen, **Burt:** Bill Callaway, **Harvey:** Michael Bell

Episodes:

(two per show)
1986–1987 "A Clean Sweep," "A Little Off The Top," "Thicker Than Water," "The Last Resort," "Hot Over The Collar," "A Job Hunting We Will Go," "Nothing To Sneeze At," "Country Club Chaos," "You Dirty Rat," "A Royal Pain," "This Little Piggy's On T.V.," "Fencer's Freaky Friday," "Legal Beagles," "Bon Voyage Rocki," "Russian Through New York," "Fritz–Carlos Bombs Out," "A Moving Experience," "Dogstyles Of The Rich And Famous," "Foofur Falls In Love," "New Tricks" and "Mad Dogs And Englishmen."
1987–1988 "Pepe's Pet Peeve," "Clothes Make The Dog," "Boot Camp Blues," "My Pharoah Lady," "What Price Fleadom," "Winging It," "The Dog's Meow," "Friend Foofur's Foul–Up," "Alone At Last, Dahling," "Tooth Or Consequences," "Fencer Finds A Family," "The Nose Knows," "Just Bumming Around," "Annabell Goes Punk," "Just Like Magic," "Puppy Love," "Weekend In The Condo," "Bye, Bye Birdies," "Fencer Gets Soul," "Rocki's Big Fib," "You Bet Your Life," "Louis Sees The Light," "I Only Have Eyeglasses For You," "Scary Harry" and "Look Homeward, Foofur."

FRAGGLE ROCK

Jim Henson's successful muppet clan, the Fraggles, explore everyday adventures in the fun–loving Fraggle community. *A Jim Henson Production in association with Marvel Productions. Color. Half–hour. Premiered on NBC: September 12, 1987–September 3, 1988.*

Voices:

Wembley: Bob Bergen, **Gobo:** Townsend Coleman, **Architect:** Townsend Coleman, **Wrench:** Townsend Coleman, **Red:** Barbara Goodson, **Wingnut:** Barbara Goodson, **Mokey:** Mona Marshall, **Cotterpin:** Mona Marshall, **Ma Gorg:** Patti Parris, **Boober:** Rob Paulsen, **Sprocket:** Rob Paulsen, **Marjory:** Rob Paulsen, **Traveling Matt:** Pat Pinney, **Pa Gorg:** Pat Pinney,

Flange: Pat Pinney, **Doc:** John Stephenson, **Philo:** John Stephenson, **Gunge:** John Stephenson, **Storyteller:** Stu Rosen

Episodes:

"The Great Radish Round–Up," "Lucky Fargy," "A Growing Relationship," "Where No Fraggle Has Gone Before," "Necessity Is The Fraggle Of Invention," "Big Trouble For Little Fraggle," "No Fraggle Is An Island" (Part 1), "No Fraggle Is An Island" (Part 2), "Wembley And The Bemble," "A Fraggle For All Seasons," "The Best Of The Best," "Ambassador Gorg," "Gobo's Song," "Homebody Matt," "Laundry Never Lies," "What Boober's Nose Knows," "Mokey's Flood Of Creativity," "What The Doozers Did," "The Radish Fairy," "Fraggle Babble," "Wembley's Trip To Outer Space," "Fraggle Fool's Day," "The Funniest Joke In The Universe," "Red's Drippy Dilemma," "The Great Fraggle Freeze" (Part I) and "The Great Fraggle Freeze" (Part 2).

FRANKENSTEIN JR. AND THE IMPOSSIBLES

The awesomely strong, 30–foot tall Frankenstein Jr. protects the community and his boy owner, Buzz, from danger. Sharing billing with the mechanical monster were "The Impossibles," a trio of crime–fighting agents—Fluid Man, Multi–Man and Coil Man—posing as a rock and roll group. NBC later rebroadcast episodes of "Frankenstein Jr." as part of a mid–season replacement series called, "The Space Ghost/Frankenstein Jr." *A Hanna–Barbera Production. Color. Half–hour. Premiered on CBS: September 10, 1966–September 7, 1968.*

Voices:

Frankenstein Jr.: Ted Cassidy, **Buzz Conroy:** Dick Beals, **Dr. Conroy:** John Stephenson, **The Impossibles: Multi–Man:** Don Messick, **Fluid Man:** Paul Frees, **Coil Man:** Hal Smith

Episodes:

"Frankenstein Jr" (one per show).
"The Shocking Electrical Monster," "The Spyder Man," "The Menace From The Wax Museum," "The Alien Brain From Outer Space" (two parts), "UFO—Unidentified Fiendish Object," "The Unearthly Plant Creatures," "The Deadly Living Images," "The Colossal Junk Monster," "The Incredible Aqua–Monsters," "The Gigantic Ghastly Genie," "The Birdman," "The Invasion Of The Robot Creatures," "The Manchurian Menace," "The Mad Monster Maker," "The Monstermobile," "The Pilfering Putty Monster" and "The Spooktaculars."
"The Impossibles" (two per show).
"The Spinner," "The Perilous Paper Doll," "Beamatron," "The Bubbler," "The Burrower," "Timeatron," "Smogula," "The Sinister Speck," "Mother Gruesome," "Fero, The Fiendish Fiddler," "The Diabolical Dauber," "Televisatron," "The Wretched Professor Stretch," "Aquator," "The Devilish Dragster," "The Return Of The Spinner," "The Puzzler," "Satanic Surfer," "The Scurrilous Sculptor," "The Scheming Spraysol," "The Insidious Inflator," "The Artful Archer," "The Return Of The Perilous Paperman," "The Dastardly Diamond Dazzler," "Cronella Critch The Tricky Witch," "The Terrible Twister," "The Terrifying

Tapper," "Professor Stretch Bounces Back," "The Anxious Angler," "The Rascally Ringmaster," "Billy The Kidder," "The Fiendish Doctor Futuro," "The Infamous Mr. Instant," "The Crafty Clutcher," "The Not So Nice Mr. Ice" and "The Bizarre Battler."

FRED AND BARNEY MEET THE SHMOO

This 90–minute program was a collection of previously broadcast episodes of "The New Fred and Barney Show" and "The Thing" (originally combined as "Fred and Barney Meet the Thing"), plus repeat episodes from "The New Shmoo," only serialized into two parts. *A Hanna–Barbera Production. Color. One hour and a half. Premiered on NBC: December 8, 1979– November 15, 1980.*

Voices:

Fred and Barney: Fred Flintstone: Henry Corden, **Wilma Flintstone,** his wife: Jean VanderPyl, **Barney Rubble,** their friend: Mel Blanc, **Betty Rubble,** his wife: Gay Autterson, **Pebbles,** Fred's daughter: Jean VanderPyl, **Bamm–Bamm,** Barney's son: Don Messick, **Sylvester Slate,** Fred's boss; John Stephenson, **Dino,** Fred's pet dinosaur: Mel Blanc, **The Thing: Benjamin "Benjy" Grimm:** Wayne Morton, **The Thing:** Joe Baker, **Kelly,** Benjy's friend: Noelle North, **Betty,** Benjy's friend: Marilyn Schreffler, **Spike,** the bully: Art Metrano, **Ronald,** the rich kid: John Erwin, **Miss Twilly,** the teacher: Marilyn Schreffler, **Shmoo: Shmoo:** Frank Welker, **Nita:** Dolores Cantu–Primo, **Billy Joe:** Chuck McCann, **Mickey:** Bill Edelson

Episodes:

"Fred and Barney" (one per show).
"Sand–Witch," "Haunted Inheritance," "Roughin' It," "C. B. Buddies," "Bedrock Rocks," "Blood Brothers," "Barney's Chickens," "The Butler Did It . . . And Did It Better," "It's Not Their Bag," "Barney's Luck," "The Bad Luck Genie," "Fred And Barney Meet The Frankenstones," "Physical Fitness Fred," "Fred Goes To The Houndasaurs," "Moonlighters," "Dinosaur Country Safari" and "Stoneage Werewolf."
"The Thing" (one per show).
"The Picnic Panic," "Bigfoot Meets The Thing," "Junkyard Hijinks," "Gone Away Gulch," "Circus Stampede," "The Thing And The Queen," "Carnival Caper," "The Thing Blanks Out," "The Thing Meets The Clunk," "Beach Party Crashers," "Decepto The Great," "The Thing's The Play," "Double Trouble For The Thing," "To Thing Or Not To Thing," "The Big Bike Race," "The Thing And Treasure Hunt," "Out To Launch," "Day The Ring Didn't Do A Thing," "A Hot Air Affair At The Fair," "The Thing Goes To The Dogs," "The Thing Goes Camping," "Dude Ranch Rodeo," "Photo Finish," "Lights, Action, Thing," "The Thing and Captain's Ghost" and "The Thing And The Absent–Minded Inventor."
The Shmoo" (one per show).
"The Warlock Of Voodoo Island," "The Terror of The Trolls," "The Amazing Captain Mentor," "The Haunting Of Atlantis," "The Valley Where Time Stood Still," "The Return Of Dracula," "The Energy From Space," "The Ber–Shmoo–Da Triangle," "Swamp Of Evil" and "Monster Island."

FRED AND BARNEY MEET THE THING

Hanna–Barbera took prehistoric favorites, Fred Flintstone and Barney Rubble, and paired them with Marvel Comics' "The Thing," in this hour–long series comprised of new adventures of the Flintstone and Rubble families and separate stories revolving around the exploits of high school student, Benjamin Grimm, who changes himself into a orange hulk to fight crime. Episodes of both components were repeated on "Fred and Barney Meet The Shmoo, a 90–minute trilogy series. *A Hanna–Barbera Production. Color. One hour. Premiered on NBC: September 22, 1979–December 1, 1979.*

Voices:

Fred and Barney: Fred Flintstone: Henry Corden, **Wilma Flintstone,** his wife: Jean VanderPyl, **Barney Rubble,** their friend: Mel Blanc, **Betty Rubble,** his wife: Gay Autterson, **Pebbles,** Fred's daughter: Jean VanderPyl, **Bamm–Bamm,** Barney's son: Don Messick, **Sylvester Slate,** Fred's boss: John Stephenson, **Dino,** Fred's pet dinosaur: Mel Blanc, **The Thing: Benjy Grimm:** Wayne Norton, **The Thing:** Joe Baker, **Kelly,** Benjy's friend: Noelle North, **Betty,** Benjy's friend: Marilyn Schreffler, **Spike,** the bully: Art Metrano, **Ronald Redford,** the rich kid: John Erwin, **Miss Twilly,** the teacher: Marilyn Schreffler

Episodes:

"Fred and Barney" (one per show).
"Sand–Witch," "Haunted Inheritance," "Roughin' It," "C. B. Buddies," "Bedrock Rocks," "Blood Brothers," "Barney's Chickens," "The Butler Did It . . . And Did It Better," "It's Not Their Bag," "Barney's Luck," "The Bad Luck Genie," "Fred And Barney Meet The Frankenstones," "Physical Fitness Fred," "Fred Goes To The Houndasaurs," "Moonlighters," "Dinosaur Country Safari" and "Stone Age Werewolf."
"The Thing" (two per show).
"The Picnic Panic," "Bigfoot Meets The Thing," "Junkyard Hijinks," "Gone Away Gulch," "Circus Stampede," "The Thing And The Queen," "Carnival Caper," "The Thing Blanks Out," "The Thing Meets The Clunk," "Beach Party Crashers," "Decepto The Great," "The Thing's The Play," "Double Trouble For The Thing," "To Thing Or Not To Thing," "The Big Bike Race," "The Thing And The Treasure Hunt," "Out To Launch," "The Day The Ring Didn't Do A Thing," "A Hot Air Affair At the Fair," The Thing Goes To The Dogs," "The Thing Goes Camping," "Dude Ranch Rodeo," "Photo Finish," "Lights, Action, Thing," "The Thing And The Captain's Ghost" and "The Thing and The Absent–Minded Inventor."

FRED FLINTSTONE AND FRIENDS

In new animated wraparounds, Fred Flintstone (voiced by Henry Corden) hosted this series of Hanna–Barbera cartoons originally broadcast by various networks on Saturday mornings: "The Flintstones Comedy Hour," "Goober and the Ghost Chasers," "Jeannie," "Partridge Family: 2200 A.D..," "Pebbles and Bamm–Bamm" and "Yogi's Gang." *A Hanna–Barbera Production. Color. Half–hour. Premiered: September 1977. Syndicated.*

THE FUNKY PHANTOM

Three teenagers, Skip, Augie and April, and their dog, Elmo, release the ghost of Jonathan Wellington Muddlemore ("Musty" for short), a young patriot during the American Revolutionary War who has been trapped for two centuries inside the grandfather clock at Muddlemore Mansion where he had taken refuge from the Redcoats. Along with cat, Boo, Musty and his new friends travel the countryside to challenge injustice and uphold the ideals of the Declaration of Independence. Episodes of "The Funky Phantom" were later repackaged as part of "The Fun World of Hanna–Barbera" and "The Godzilla/ Dynomutt Show." *A Hanna–Barbera Production. Color. Half-hour. Premiered on ABC: September 11, 1971–September 1, 1972.*

Voices:

Jonathan (Musty) Muddlemore: Daws Butler, **April Stewart:** Tina Holland, **Skip:** Micky Dolenz, **Augie:** Tommy Cook

Additional Voices:

Jerry Dexter, Julie Bennett

Episodes:

"Don't Fool With A Phantom," "Heir Scare," "I'll Haunt You Later," "Who's Chicken?," "The Headless Horseman," "Spirit Spooked," "Ghost Town Ghost," "We Saw A Sea Serpent," "Haunt In Inn," "Mudsy Joins The Circus," "Pigskin Predicament," "The Liberty Bell Caper," "April's Foolish Day," "The Forest Prime Evil," "The Hairy Scarey Houndman," "Mudsy And The Muddlemore Mansion" and "Ghost Grabbers."

THE FUNNY COMPANY

As members of the Junior Achievement Club, an enterprising group of neighborhood children take on odd jobs to make money, with mixed results in this educational and entertaining series reminiscent of Hal Roach's "Our Gang" kids. Featured between each cartoon were two-minute educational wraparounds on various subjects, including physical science, hobbies, folklore and how-to themes. *A Funny Company Production. Color. Half-hour. Premiered: September, 1963. Syndicated.*

Voices:

Buzzer Bell/Shrinkin' Violette: Dick Beals, **Polly Plum:** Robie Lester, **Merry Twitter/Jasper N. Park:** Nancy Wible, **Terry Dactyl:** Ken Synder, **Dr. Todd Goodheart/ Belly Laguna/ Dr. Von Upp:** Hal Smith, **The Wisenheimer:** Bud Hiestand, **Broken Feather:** Tom Thomas

THE FUNTASTIC WORLD OF HANNA–BARBERA

In 1985, Hanna–Barbera Productions launched this syndicated cartoon block 90-minute broadcast on Sunday mornings. It was so successful that it was expanded to two hours of continuous cartoon fare. The package was first comprised of three newly animated half-hour series: "Yogi's Treasure Hunt," "The Paw Paws" and "Galtar and the Golden Lance."

In its two-hour form, new weekly adventures of "Johnny Quest" were added to the package.

The series' components changed in following years. In 1987, the producers added "Sky Commanders" and "The Snorks," retaining "Yogi's Treasure Hunt" and "Jonny Quest" as the other series regulars. The following season, the show consisted of "The Further Adventures of SuperTed," "Fantastic Max," "The Flintstone Kids" and "Richie Rich," with "Jonny Quest" and "Galtar and the Golden Lance" being the only returnees. The package was pared down in size for the 1989–1990 season. It featured "The Further Adventures of SuperTed," "Fantastic Max," "Paddington Bear" and "Richie Rich." (See individual series titles for voices and episode title information). *A Hanna–Barbera Production. Color. One hour and a half. Two hours. Premiered: September, 1985. Syndicated.*

FUN WORLD OF HANNA–BARBERA

Off-network series featuring episodes from past Hanna–Barbera shows: "Wacky Races," "Dastardly and Muttley," "Perils of Penelope Pitstop," "The Funky Phantom" and "Amazing Chan and the Chan Clan." (See individual series for information.) *A Hanna–Barbera Production. Color. Half-hour. Premiered: 1977. Syndicated.*

THE FURTHER ADVENTURES OF DR. DOLITTLE

In classic stories based on Hugh Lofting's novel, veterinarian Doctor Dolittle commands the animals of the world with his leadership abilities and conversational powers. With his 14-year-old assistant, Tommy Stubbins, and his animal friends, Dolittle attempts to thwart fiendish Sam Scurvy's efforts at world domination. *A DePatie–Freleng Enterprises Production. Color. Half-hour. Premiered on NBC: September 12, 1970–September 2, 1972. Syndicated.*

Voices:

Dr. Dolittle: Hal Smith, **Scurvy the pirate:** Lennie Weinrib, **Stubbins:** Don Messick, **Animals:** Robert Holt

Episodes:

"The Grasshoppers Are Coming, Hooray, Hooray!" "The Bird Who Was Afraid To Fly," "The Land Of The Tiger Moo," "The Great Turkey Race," "The Peanut Conspiracy," "The Bare Bear," "High Flying Hippo," "The Near-Sighted Bull," "The Silver Seals At The Circus," "A Girl For Grego Gorilla," "A Tale Of Two Snails," "A Fox Called . . . Sherlock?," "The Tomb Of The Phoenix Bird," "The Barnyard Rumble," "The Baffled Buffalo," "A Hatful Of Rabbit" and "Diamonds Are Not A Maharajah's Best Friend."

THE FURTHER ADVENTURES OF SUPERTED

A once-discarded teddy bear is brought to life by a spotted alien (Spottyman) from the planet Spot, who discovers the poor teddy and sprinkles him with cosmic dust that endows him with magical powers turning him into the cuddliest superhero in the universe. This half–hour fantasy/adventure series was broadcast on Sunday mornings as part of "The Funtastic World Of Hanna–Barbera." *A Hanna–Barbera Production. Color. Half–hour. Premiered: September, 1988.*

Voices:
SuperTed: Danny Cooksey, **Spottyman:** Patrick Fraley, **Texas Pete:** Victor Spinetti, **Skeleton:** Melvyn Hayes, **Bulk:** Marvin Kaplan

Episodes:
1988–1989 "Phantom Of The Grand Ol' Opry," "Dot's Entertainment," "Knox Knox Who's There," "I Want My Mummy," "Whale Of A Tale," "Texas Is Mine," "We Got Nutinkamun," "Sheepless Nights," "The Ruse Of The Raja," "Leave It To Space Beavers," "Farewell My Lovely . . . Spots," "Ben–Fur" and "Spotty Earns His Stripes."

THE GALAXY GOOF–UPS
When NBC shuffled its Saturday–morning cartoon lineup in November, 1978, "The Galaxy Goof–Ups" series, formerly segmented on "Yogi's Space Race," was given its own half–hour time slot. The cast of characters—Yogi Bear, Huckleberry Hound, Scarebear and Quack–Up—are intergalactic army officers under the astute command of Captain Snerdley, who find more time for disco dancing than protecting the universe. *A Hanna–Barbera Production. Color. Half–hour. Premiered on NBC: November 4, 1978–January 27, 1979.*

Voices:
Yogi Bear: Daws Butler, **Scarebear:** Joe Besser, **Huckleberry Hound:** Daws Butler, **Quack–Up:** Mel Blanc, **Captain Snerdley:** John Stephenson

Episodes:
"The Purloined Princess," "Defective Protectives," "Whose Zoo?," "The Space Pirates," "The Clone Ranger," "The Dopey Defenders," "Tacky Cat Strikes Again," "Space Station USA," "Hail, King Yogi!," "Dyno–Mite," "Vampire Of Space," "The Treasure Of Congo–Bongo" and "Captain Snerdley Goes Bananas."

GALAXY HIGH SCHOOL
These space–age adventures follow the exploits of Doyle Cleverlobe and Aimee Brightower, the first exchange students from Earth to attend an inter–stellar high school on the asteroid Flutor. Here the class bully is a slab of beef, the school gossip has five mouths, the blackboard sometimes erases the students, and vegetables mustn't eat in the school cafeteria—they're the sophomores. The series' provocative anti–drug episode, "Brain Blaster," was nominated for the prestigious Humanitas Award in 1987. *A TMS Entertainment Production. Color. Half–hour. Premiered on CBS: December 13, 1986–September 5, 1987. Rebroadcast on CBS: January 9, 1988–August 27, 1988.*

Voices:
Doyle Cleverlobe: Hal Rayle, **Aimee Brightower:** Susan Blu, **Rotten Roland:** Neil Ross, **Beef Bonk:** John Stephenson, **Biddy McBrain:** Pat Carroll, **Katrina:** Pat Carroll, **Gilda Gossip:** Nancy Cartwright, **Flat Freddy:** Nancy Cartwright, **Earl Ecch:** Guy Christopher, **Ollie Oilslick:** Gino Conforti, **Reggie Unicycle:** Gino Conforti, **Booey Bubblehead:** Jennifer Darling, **Wendy Garbo:** Jennifer Darling, **Coach Frogface:** Pat Fraley, **Sludge:** Pat Fraley, **Aimee's Locker:** Henry Gibson, **Doyle's Locker:** Henry Gibson, **Milo DeVenus:** David L. Lander, **The Creep:** Danny Mann, **Professor Icenstein:** Howard Morris, **Luigi LaBounci:** Howard Morris

Episodes:
"Welcome To Galaxy High," "Pizza's Honor," "The Beef Who Would Be King," "Where's Milo," "Those Lips, Those Eyes," "Doyle's New Friend," "Dollars And Sense," "Beach Blanket Blow–Up," "Brain Blaster," "Brat Pack," "Founder's Day," "Martian Mumps" and "It Came From Earth."

GALTAR AND THE GOLDEN LANCE
Astride his nobel steed Thork, the handsome and fearless warrior Galtar uses sword and sorcery to protect the lovely Princess Goleeta and rescue his planet from the scourge of the evil Tormack, whose minions killed Galtar's parents and destroyed his village, in this fantasy/adventure series, part of "The Funtastic World of Hanna–Barbera," which aired on Sunday Mornings. *A Hanna–Barbera Production. Color. Half–hour. Premiered: September, 1985.*

Voices:
Galtar: Lou Richards, **Goleeta:** Mary McDonald Lewis, **Tormack:** Brock Peters, **Ither:** Bob Arbogast, **Krimm:** Barry Dennen, **Otar:** George DiCenzo, **Pandat:** Don Messick, **Rak:** Bob Frank, **Zorn:** David Mendenhall, **Tuk/Thork/Koda:** Frank Welker

Episodes:
1985–1986 "Galtar And The Princess," "Skull Forest," "Mursa The Merciless," "Goleeta's Reunion," "Shadowhaunt," "Tormack's Trap," "Wicked Alliance," "Vikor's Raiders," "The Manta Marauders," "The Master Fighters," "The Maze Of Magus," "Falca—Priestess Of Prey," "Silver Sword," "Zorn Meets Marian," "Vikor's Revenge" and "Galtar's Challenge."
1986–1987 (new episodes combined with reruns) "Ither's Apprentice," "Antara The Terrible," "Tormack's Treachery," and "Love Of Evil."

GARFIELD AND FRIENDS
"Garfield" creator Jim Davis oversaw production of this Saturday–morning series featuring the further exploits of Garfield, Odie and Jon. Separate episodes in the series were based on Davis's other strip, "U. S. Acres," and revolved around the misadventures of Orson the Pig, Roy the Rooster and the rest of the gang. Also appearing on television for the first time was Nermal, the world's cutest kitten. Each episode was backed

by its own original music score. *A Film Roman Production in association with United Media and Paws Inc. Color. One hour. Premiered on CBS: October 15, 1988–*

Voices:

Garfield: Lorenzo Music, **Jon:** Thom Huge, **Binky:** Thom Huge, **Roy:** Thom Huge, **Odie:** Greg Berger, **Orson:** Greg Berger, **Nermal:** Desiree Goyette, **Sheldon:** Frank Welker, **Booker:** Frank Welker, **Bo:** Frank Welker, **Wade:** Howie Morris, **Liz:** Julie Payne, **Lanolin:** Julie Payne

Episodes:

"Garfield" (two episodes per show).

1988–1989 "Garfield's Moving Experience," "Good Mousekeeping," "Nighty–Nightmare," "Ode To Odie," "Fraidy Cat," "Nothing To Sneeze At," "Peace And Quiet," "Garfield Goes Hawaiian," "Box O' Fun," "School Daze," "Identity Crisis," "Up A Tree," "Weighty Problem," "Good Cat Bad Cat," "Cabin Fever," "Fair Exchange," "The Binky Show," "Don't Move," "Monday Misery," "Magic Mutt," "All About Odie," "Best Of Breed," "Green Thumbs Down," "Caped Avenger," "Forget me Not" and "Sales Resistance."

"Garfield Blackouts" (30–45 second segments).

"Crescent Roll, "Learn Something New Everyday," "Spider," "Screen Door," "Fetch," "Hot Dog Truck," "Bird Bath," "Plastic Flowers" and "Snow."

"Garfield Teaser" (one 30–45 segment per show).

"Dive Into A Glass Of Water," "Pet Door," "Jogging," "Doggy Coat," "Bees," "Someone In My Bed," "Howling," "Fire," "Party," "Camping," "Dogs," "Diving Board" and "Caped Avenger."

"U. S. Acres" (one episode per show).

"Wade You're Afraid" (Song: "Wade, You're Afraid"), "Banana Nose" (Song: "Banana Nose"), "Shell–Shocked Sheldon" (Song: "Come Out"), "Wanted: Wade" (Song: "What Harm Can It Do"), "Unidentified Flying Orson" (Song: "Read, Read"), "The Bad Sport" (Song: "Don't Be Afraid Of Something New"), "The Worm Turns" (Song: "The Worm"), "Return Of Power Pig" (Song: "Rumors"), "Keeping Cool" (Song: "Keep Cool"), "Short Story" (Song: "I'm Short"), "National Tapioca Pudding Day" (Song: "Giving a Gift"), "Shy Fly Guy" (Song: "I Should Fly") and "I Like Having You Around" (Song: "I Like Having You Around")

"U. A. Acres Blackouts" (30–45 second segments).

"Tractor," "Wade's Garden," "Tag," "A Bug," "The 20th Century," "More Straw," "Read Us A Book," "Yo-Yo," "Piggy Back," "Detective Pig" and "Kiss A Chicken."

"Garfield" (four episodes per show).

1989–1990 "Pest Of A Guest," "Fat And Furry," "Rip Van Kitty," "The Big Catnap," "The Great Getaway," "Hansel And Garfield," "Sludge Monster," "Heatwave Holiday," "One Good Fern Deserves Another," "Health Feud," "Legend Of The Lake," "The Black Book," "Binky Gets Canceled," "Cutie And The Beast," "The Lasagna Zone," "YoJumbo," "Pros And Cons," "Lights! Camera! Garfield!," "Polecat Flats," "Brain Boy," "Main Course," "Video Victim," "Robodie," "The Attack Of The Mutant Guppies," "The Curse Of Klopman," "Rainy Day Dreams," "Basket Brawl," "Cactus Jake Rides Again," "Mini–Mall Matters," "Binky Goes Bad," "Magic Mutt," "Monday Misery," "It Must Be True!," "Attention–Getting Garfield," "Cabin Fever,"

"Fair Exchange," "The Bear Facts," "Feeling Feline," "Arrivaderci, Odie!," "The Big Talker," "Cactus Makes Perfect," "Crime And Nourishment," "TV Of Tomorrow," "The Well Fed Feline," "Invasion Of The Big Robots," "First Class Feline," "Housebreak Hotel," "How To Be Funny!," "Mystic Manor," "The Legend Of Long Jon," "China Cat," "Beach Blanket Bonzo," "Lemon Aid," "Video Airlines," "The Mail Animal" and "Mummy Dearest."

"Garfield Blackouts." (two 30–45 second segments per show) "Muscles," "Asleep," "Wet Pets," "Water Wake–Up," "Soda Pop," "Little House," "On The Fence," "Dresser," "At The Zoo," "Hungry," "Snacking," "Twine," "Binky: Diamond," "Human Relic," "Quicksand," "Binky: Baseball," "Window Shades," "Big Date," "Bird Bath" (first season segment), "Dog Food," "Binky: Mountains," "Fetch" (first season segment), "Big Date," "Binky: Surgeons," "Dresser Fun," "Binky: Circus," "Stomach Asleep," "Driving Jon Crazy," "Binky: Building," "My Chair," "One For All," "Binky: Ballerina," "Knot In Cord," "Shower Surfing," "Cooking Jar," "Blamed," "Binky: Golf Pro," "Laundry," "The Bet," "Binky: Laryngitis" and "Banana Phone."

"Garfield Teasers" (30–45 second segments).

"Charades," "Birdhouse," "Food Fun," "Normal," "Country Club," "Apples," "Quicksand," "Slave To Passion," "Balloon," "Slave To Passion," "Daisy Waisy" and "Ready For Snow."

"U. S. Acres" (two episodes per show).

"Impractical Joker" (Song: "Can't Take A Joke"), "Grabbity," (Song: "Grabbity"), "Scrambled Eggs" (Song: "Rock Lullabye"), "Fortune Kooky" (Song: "Superstition"), "The Goodie-Go–Round" (Song: "Let's Get Together"), "Double–Oh Or son," "Show Stoppers," (Song: "Show Stoppers"), "Sleepytime Pig" (Song: "One, Two, Three, Snore"), "Rooster Revenge" (Song: "I Gotcha!"), "Hogcules" (Song: "Hogcules, Our Hero"), "First Aid Wade" (Song: "Doctors Are Your Friend"), "No Laughing Matter" (Song: "Laughter"), "Mud Sweet Mud" (Song: "My Waller"), "The Origin Of Power Pig" (Song: "Power Pig"), "Barn Of Fear," "Short Story" (first season segment), "Swine Trek" (Song: "Swine Trek"), "The Return Of Power Pig" (first season segment), "Gort Goes Good" (Song: "I Wanna Be Nice"), "Nothing To Be Afraid Of" (Song: "I'm Afraid"), "Hogcules II" (Song: "Hogcules"), "Little Red Riding Egg," "Hamelot" (Song: "Hamelot"), "Shelf–Esteem," "Flop Goes The Weasel" (Song: "I Am A Hero"), "Cock–A–Doodle Dandy" (Song: "Mr. Lips"), "Hog Noon" (Song: "Pig Without A Gun") and "Peanut–Brained Rooster" (Song: "Peanuts").

"U. S. Acres Blackouts" (30–45 second segments).

"Waller," "Teeter–Totter," "A Parade," "Popcorn," "Give Me A Home," "Imagination," "Morning Blast," "The Race," "Help," "Guppies," "Change Your Life," "Snow Fun," "Weather Report," "A Cold," "Let's Play," "I'm A Goner," "Bo Beep," "Let Go," "Dutch Door," "I'm A Goner" and "Tag Team."

THE GARY COLEMAN SHOW

"Different Strokes" star Gary Coleman is the voice of an apprentice guardian angel (Andy LeBeau) who, on probation in heaven, proves he is worthy of his wings by returning to Earth to solve people's problems. His heavenly superior, Angelica, rates his performance on her clipboard and suffers through his mistakes, while the evil character, Hornswoggle, tries to create problems for the little angel. The series was based on the character in the NBC–TV movie, "The Kid with the Broken Halo." *A Hanna–Barbera Production. Color. Half-hour. Premiered on NBC: September, 1982–September 10, 1983.*

Voices:
Andy LeBeau: Gary Coleman, **Angelica:** Jennifer Darling, **Hornswoggle:** Sidney Miller, **Spence:** Calvin Mason, **Tina:** La Shana Dendy, **Bartholomew:** Jerry Houser, **Chris:** Lauren Anders, **Lydia:** Julie McWhirter Dees, **Mack:** Steve Schatzberg, **Haggle:** Jeff Gordon

Episodes:
(two per show) "Going, Going, Gone," "Fouled Up Fossils," "You Oughta Be In Pictures," "Derby Daze," "Calamity Canine," "In The Swim," "Space Odd–Essey," "Hornswoggle's Hoax," "Cupid Andy," "Put Up Or Fix Up," "Haggle And Double Haggle," "Wuthering Kites," "Mansion Madness," "Keep On Movin' On," "Take My Tonsils, Please," "The Royal Visitor," "Dr. Livingston, I Presume," "Hornswoggle's New Leaf," "Haggle's Luck," "Mack's Snow Job," "Head In The Clouds," "The Future Tense," "The Prettiest Girl In Oakville," "Andy Sings The Blues," "Easy Money" and "Teacher's Pest."

GENTLE BEN

Television's favorite bear, who starred in the popular NBC adventure series returns as a super hero who embarks on many exciting but dangerous adventures throughout the world. *A Gentle Ben Animation Production. Color. Half-hour. Premiered: 1981. Syndicated.*

GEORGE OF THE JUNGLE

Jay Ward, creator of Rocky and Bullwinkle, produced this animated spoof of Edgar Rice Burrough's famed Tarzan character starring a dim–witted vine–swinging apeman named George, who protects the jungle and his wife, Ursula (Ward's version of Tarzan's wife, Jane), from the hazardous surroundings of the Imgwee Gwee Valley in Africa. George's main confidant and friend is a purplish gorilla, Ape (whose voice recalls actor Ronald Coleman's), who counsels him whenever he is in trouble. He also calls on his friendly elephant, Shep, who he thinks is a peanut–loving puppy.

Other cartoon segments featured were: "Super Chicken," the misadventures of simple minded Henry Cabot Henhouse III, who, after downing his famed Super Sauce, becomes a crimefighting super chicken; and "Tom Slick, Racer," a parody of race car competition following the exploits of American good ol' boy, Tom Slick, aided by his girlfriend, Marigold, and his grandmother, Gertie.

The series was the only Jay Way production ever to lose money (more than $100,000). *A Jay Ward Production. Color. Half-hour. Premiered on ABC: September 9, 1967–September 5, 1970.*

Voices:
George of the Jungle: Bill Scott, **Ursula,** his wife: June Foray, **Ape:** Paul Frees, **Super Chicken:** Bill Scott, **Fred the**

The vine–swinging exploits of Tarzan took on a different meaning in Jay Ward's comic spoof, "George Of The Jungle." © Jay Ward Productions

lion, his butler: Paul Frees, **Tom Slick:** Bill Scott, **Marigold,** Tom's girlfriend: June Foray, **Gertie,** Tom's grandmother: June Foray

Episodes:
"George of the Jungle" (one per show).
"The Sultan's Pearl," "Malady Lingers On," "The Gorilla God," "Oo–oo Bird," "Monkey Business," "Desperate Showers," "Little Siccors," "Next Time The Train," "The Trouble I Seed," "Big Flop At The Big Top," "Rescue In My Business," "Dr. Spritzer, I Presume," "Chi Chi Dog," "Treasure Of Sierra Madre," "Man Of All Hunting Seasons" and "Forest Prime Evil."
"Super Chicken" (one per show).
"The Zipper," "One Of Our States Is Missing," "The Oyster," "Wild Ralph Hiccup," "The Elephant Spreeder," "Rotten Hood," "Easter Bunny," "The Geezer," "The Noodle," "Rag Dolly," "Merlin Brando," "Fatman," "Briggs Bad Wolf," "The Laundry Man," "The Muscle" and "Dr. Gizmo."
"Tom Slick, Racer" (one per show).
"The Big Race," "Monster Rally," "Show What," "Send Me A Sub," "I Was Railroaded," "Cup–Cup Race," "Balloon Race," "Dranko The Dragster," "Overstocked," "Sneaky Sheik," "Indian–Apples 500," "Double Cross Country Race," "Cheap Skate Derby," "Irish Cheap Skate," "Bad Year Blimp" and "Swamp Buggy Race."

THE GERALD MCBOING BOING SHOW

This festival of UPA cartoons presented regular episodes and one–time features in a swiftly paced half–hour variety show format, hosted by Gerald McBoing Boing, one of UPA's most successful theatrical cartoon stars.

Recurring features on the show included "Meet the Artist," lighthearted stories based on the lives of famous artists; "Meet the Inventor," humorous and instructional stories of the trials and triumphs of the world's greatest inventors; "The Sleuth's

Apprentice," in which the self–confident Sleuth gets all the credit for the mysteries solved by his mild–mannered apprentice; and "Mr. Longview Looks Back," a comic version of Walter Cronkite's long–running "You Are There" series. In addition, the series showcased "The Twirlinger Twins," two energetic little girls with Buster Brown haircuts who sing songs, give recitations and take music lessons; "The Etiquette Series," starring the gentlemanly Mr. Charmley who is so intent upon learning proper techniques of etiquette that he frequently overlooks practicing them; and "Dusty of the Circus," the adventures of a young boy who enjoys a special relationship with the animals of his father's circus.

Rounding out the series were such one–time features as "Marvo the Magician," a pompous magician who is outdone by his little bearded assistant; "The Two Magicians," a tiny flutist and a huge tubist whose counterpoint includes outrageous practical jokes; "The Last Doubloon," in which a miserly pirate captain is sunk by one doubloon too many; and "The Matador and the Troubador," concerning the little brother of a famous matador who confuses bulls with a heel–tapping, flamenco style of fighting; and many others.

The program first aired on CBS in December, 1957, and was repeated in 1957. UPA syndicated the package in the late 1960s. Currently, the series is syndicated under the title of "The UPA Cartoon Show," shown on USA Network. *A UPA Production. Color. Half–hour. Premiered on CBS: December 16, 1956–March 10, 1957. Rebroadcast on CBS: May 30, 1958–October 3, 1958. Syndicated.*

Voices:

Commentator: Bill Goodwin, **Interpreter of Gerald's sound:** Bill Goodwin

Additional Voices: Marvin Miller
Episodes:
Meet the Artist.
"The Invisible Mustache Of Raoul Dufy," "The Merry Go Round In The Jungle" (artist Henri Rousseau), "The Day Of The Fox" and "The Performing Painter."
Meet the Inventor.
"Meet The Inventor—Samuel F. B. Morse," "Persistent Mr. Fulton" and "Meet The Inventor—Eli Whitney."
The Sleuth's Apprentice.
"The Lost Duchess" and "The Armored Car."
The Twirlinger Twins.
"Follow Me," "Ballet Lesson," "The Average Giraffe," "The Violin Recital" and "Alphabet Song."
Dusty Of The Circus.
"Turned Around Clown," "The Five Cent Nickel," "Lion On The Loose," "The Elephant Mystery," "The Sad Lion" and "The Bear Scare."
The Etiquette Series.
"Mr. Charmley Greets A Lady," "Mr. Charmley In The Jungle" and "Be Quiet, Kind And Gentle."
Music & Dance.
"The Matador And Troubador," "The Two Musicians," "Good Ole Country Music," "A Little Journey," "The 12 Days Of Christmas," "Blues Pattern," "Romeo Wherefore Art Thou," "Old Mac Donald," "Alouette," "The Little White Duck" and "The Magic Fiddle."

Adventure.
"The Little Boy Who Ran Aay," "The Last Doubloon," "Martians Come Back," "We Saw Sea Serpents," "The Genius Time Machine," "Trap Happy," "The Haunted Night" and "Colonel Puffington & Mr. Finch."
Animals and Birds.
"Peewee The Kiwi Bird," "The Lion Hunt," "Two By Two," "The 3 Horned Flink," "Mr. Buzzard," "I Had A Bird," "A Wounded Bird," "Prehistoric Eohippus," "A Horse Of Course" and "A Miserable Pack Of Wolves."
Westerns.
"The Outlaws," "The Trial Of Zelda Belle," "Has Bean With Don Coyote And Chico," "Quiet Town" and "The Quadrangle."
Fairy Tales.
"The Unenchanted Princess," "The 51st Dragon," "Just Believe In Make Believe," "Uncle Sneaky," "The Beanstalk Trial" and "The Last Knight."
Sports.
"Fight On For Old," "Der Team From Zwischendorf" and "Winter Sports."
Miscellaneous.
"The Freezee Yum Story," "Mr. Tingley's Tangle," "The Election," "Operation Heart Throb," "Aquarium," "The King And Joe," "Marvo The Magician," "Punch And Judy," "The Lost Duchess," "The Armored Car," "Nero Fiddles" and "Trojan Horse."

THE GET ALONG GANG

Traveling through the countryside in their Clubhouse Caboose, this lovable group of animal friends—Monty, the optimistic, leader moose; Dotty, the super–strong pooch; Woolma, a self–indulgent, cuddly lamb; and Zipper, the super–cool cat—lend a helping hand to those in need, demonstrating for children the value of honesty, friendship and cooperation. *A DIC Enterprises Production in association with Scholastic/*

Members of "The Get Along Gang" try lending a helping hand to their Clubhouse Caboose cohorts in a scene from the popular Saturday–morning series. © American Greetings Corp. (Courtesy: DIC Enterprises Inc.)

Lorimar Productions. Color. Half—hour. Premiered on CBS: September 15, 1984—September 7, 1985. Rebroadcast on CBS: September 14, 1985—August 30, 1986

Voices:

Bettina Bush, Donovan S. Freberg, Timothy Gibbs, Eva Marie Hesse, Georgi Irene, Nick Katt, Robbie Lee, Sherry Lynn, Sparky Marcus, Scott Menville, Don Messick, Chuck McCann, Frank Welker

Episodes:

"Zipper's Millions," "Half A Map Is Better Than None," "Caboose On The Loose," "Montgomery's Mechanical Marvel," "Head In The Clouds," "Hunt For The Beast," "Woolma's Birthday," "The Get Along Detectives," "The Get Along Gang Go Hollywood," "Them's The Brakes," "A Pinch Of This, A Dash Of That," "Bingo's Tale," "Engineer Roary," "The Pick Of The Litter," "Nose For News," "The Lighthouse," "The Wrong Stuff," "Uneasy Rider," "The Get Along Gang Minus One," "Camp Get Along," "Bingo's Pen Pal," "Follow The Leader," "School's Out," "The Bullies," "That's The Way The Cookie Crumbles" and "Snowbound Showdown."

G-FORCE

This short-lived cable series was a remake of syndicator Sandy Frank's "Battle of the Planets," featuring the same characters as before but with new names and identities. The crew members were now called Ace Goodheart (Mark), Dirk Daring (Jason), Agatha June (Princess), Hootie (Tiny) and Professor Brighthead (Anderson). Even the characters' famous tagline said when they changed into their battle outfits was changed from "Transmute!" to "Tranform!" Their outer space arch—nemesis was renamed Galactor (Spectera). Only six episodes aired on Turner's cable superstation, WTBS. *A Turner Entertainment Systems Production. Color. Half—hour. Premiered on WTBS.*

Voices:

Ace Goodheart, the leader: Sam Fontana, **Dirk Daring,** second in command; Cameron Clarke, **Professor Brighthead:** Jan Rabson, **Hootie:** Jan Rabson, **Agatha June:** Barbara Goodson, **Pee Wee:** Barbara Goodson, **Galactor:** Bill Capizzi

Episodes:

"The Robot Stegosaur," "The Blast At The Bottom Of The Sea," "The Strange White Shadow," "The Giant Centipoid," "The Phantom Fleet," "The Micro—Robots," "The Bad Blue Baron," "The Secret Of The Reef," "The Sting Of The Scorpion," "The Mighty Blue Hawk," "The Locustcid," "The Deadly Red Sand," "That Rainbow Ray," "The Giant Jellyfish Lens," "The Regenerating Robot," "The Beetle Booster," "The Whale Submarine," "The Racing Inferno," "The Mightiest Mole," "Race Of The Cyborgs," "The Mammoth Iron Ball," "The Neon Giant," "The Rock Robot," "The Secret Sting Ray," "The Anirobot," "Invisible Enemy," "The Project Called ROCK—E—X," "The Attack Of The Mantis," "The Sinister STAR—ONE," "The Giant Squid," "In The Tentacles' Grip," "Operation Aurora," "The Sun—Bird," "The Deadly Sea," "The Monster Plants," "Those Fatal Flowers," "Killer Music," "Swan Song Prison,"

"Human Robots," "The Shock Waves," "The Case Of The Kalanite," "The Deadly Valley," "The Super—Z—20," "The Camera Weapon," "The Mechanical Fang," "The Skeleton Curse," "Wheel Of Destruction," "The Secret Red Impulse," "The Van Allen Vector," "The Vengeance," "The Micro—Submarine," "The Bird Missile," "Battle At The North Pole," "The Super—Lazer," "Mystery Of The Haunted Island," "G—Force Agent 6," "Dream Of Danger," "The Snow Devil," "The Strange Strike—Out," "A Deadly Gift," "The Iron Beast," "When Fashion Was Fatal," "The Proto Monster," "Radioactive Island," "The Devil's Graveyard," "Mummy Mania," "The Abominable Snowman Cometh," "Plague Of Robots," "The Mammothodon," "Secret Of The Power," "The Crab Robot," "The Reverser Ray," "Shock Waves," "Battle On The Ocean Bottom," "Stolen Identity," "The Mind—Control Machine," "Force Of Mega—Robots," "The Flame Zone," "Web Of Danger," "The Secret of C—4" and "Galactor's Deadly Trap."

GHOSTBUSTERS

In an effort to capitalize on the Ghostbuster fever spawned by the blockbuster movie, this comedy—adventure series was not based on the Bill Murray—Dan Aykroyd comedy feature but rather a live—action comedy series starring former "F Troop" actors Forrest Tucker and Larry Storch entitled, "The Ghost Busters," which ran on CBS' Saturday morning schedule in 1975. The animated revival has the same themeline: three heroes—two human (Kong and Eddie) and a gorilla (Tracy)—who track down ghost, goblins and gremlins, only this time throughout the universe and back and forth in time. The show featured an all—new voice cast. *A Filmation/Tribune Broadcasting Company Production. Color. Half—hour. Premiered: September, 1986. Syndication.*

Voices:

Pat Fraley, Peter Cullen, Alan Oppenheimer, Susan Blu, Linda Gary, Erik Gunden, Erika Scheimer

Episodes:

"Witches Stew," "Mummy Dearest," "Wacky Wax Museum," "Statue Of Liberty," "The Ransom Of Eddie Spenser," "Eddie Takes Charge," "Tracy, Come Back," "A Friend In Need," "I'll Be A Son Of A Ghostbuster" (Part 1), "Frights Of The Round Table" (Part 2), "No Pharoah At All" (Part 3), "The Secret Of Mastodon Valley" (Part 4), "The Ones Who Save The Future" (Part 5), "No Snow," "Prime Evil's Good Deed," "The Haunting Of Gizmo," "The Headless Horseman Caper," "Banish The Banshee," "Rollerghoster," "He Went Brataway," "Looking Glass Warrior," "Laster And Future Rock," "Runaway Choo Choo," "Dynamite Dinosaur," "Ghostbunglers," "My Present To The Future," "Beastly Buggy," "Belfry Leads The Way," "Battle For Ghost Command," "Going Ape," "Cyman's Revenge," "Ghostnappers," "Inside Out," "The Sleeping Dragon," "The Phantom Of The Big Apple," "Shades Of Dracula," "Outlaw In-Laws," "Our Buddy Fuddy," "Train To Doom," "The Princess And The Troll," "Second Chance," "The Great Ghost Gorilla," "Doggone Werewolf," "That's No Alien," "Scareplane," "The Ghost Of Don Quixote," "The White Whale," "Whither Why," "Knight Of Terror," "The Girl Who Cried Vampire," "Little Big Bat," "Really Roughing It," "The Bad Old

Days," "The Curse Of The Diamond Of Gloom," "The Bind That Ties," "Like Father Like Son," "The Fourth Ghostbuster," "Country Goblin," "Cold Winter's Night," "Father Knows Beast," "Back To The Past," "Pretend Friends," "The Haunted Painting," "Maze Caves" and "The Way You Are."

GIGANTOR

Created by Dr. Sparks, this jet–propelled robot, designed for war but reprogrammed as an agent of peace, battles interplanetary evil with the help of 12–year–old Jimmy Sparks, the doctor's son, who takes over control of the robot after his father's death. In keeping the world free from destruction and despair, Gigantor comes face–to–face with such world–class villains as Dr. Katsmeow, Dangerous Dinosaurs, the Evil Robot Brain, invaders from the planet Magnapus and many others.

Shown on Japanese television from 1963 to 1967, the series rocketed to fame in the United States when the property was acquired and edited for American audiences by Trans–Lux, which distributed many other cartoon favorites, including "Felix the Cat" and "Mighty Mr. Titan." The program was produced by Fred Ladd (who produced "Astroboy" and "Speed Racer") and Al Singer. Theme music was by Lou Singer and Gene Raskin. *A TCJ Animation Center Production. Black–and–white. Half–hour. Premiered: January 5, 1966. Syndicated.*

Voices:

Billie Lou Watt, Peter Fernandez, Gilbert Mack, Cliff Owens

Episodes:

"Incredible Speed Machine," "Atomic Flame," "Treasure Mountain," "World In Danger," "The Grat Hunt," "Smoke Robot," "Giant Cobra," "The Robot Fire Bird," "The Magic Multiplier," "Submarine Base," "Space Submarine," "Monster From The Deep," "Target Jupiter," "Trap At 20 Fathoms," "Secret Formula Robbery," "Monster Magnet," "Evil Robot Brain," "Will The Real Gigantor Please Stand Up," "City Smashers," "Atomic Whale," "Badge Of Danger," "Dangerous Diamond," "Diamond Smugglers," "Battle Of Robot Giants," "Desert Fire," "Deadly Stingrays," "Robot Arsenal," "Devil's Gantry," "Dangerous Dinosaurs," "Robot Albatraus," "Magna Man Of Outerspace," "Mistery Missle," "The Freezer Ray," "The Plot To Lease Gigantor," "The Deadly Web," "Ransom At Point X," "Robot Olympics," "Return of Magna Man," "Vanishing Mountain," "Insect Monsters," "10,000 Gigantors," "Space Cats," "Gypsy Spaceship," "Gigantor Who?," "The Cross Bombs Caper," "Force Of Terror," "Struggle At The South Pole," "Battle At The Bottom Of The World," "Sting Of The Spider," "Return of The Spider," "Spider's Revenge" and "Secret Valley."

G. I. JOE (1985)

American television viewers first got a glimpse of the heroic escapades of famed comic book hero, G. I. Joe, in television's first animated mini–series, "G. I. Joe: A Real American Hero," broadcast in syndication for the 1983–1984 season. Both G. I. Joe and the mini–series format were so popular with viewers that a second five–part syndicated mini–series, "G. I.

Joe II" was produced for the 1984–1985 season. In the fall of 1985, "G. I. Joe" became a daily animated strip for television, featuring the further adventures of America's highly trained mission force who outwit and outmaneuver the forces of COBRA, a terrorist organization, led by villains Destro and the Baroness.

Because the G. I. Joe characters were so strongly defined as defenders of right against wrong, the series incorporated 30–second messages in each episode, with members of the G. I. Joe team showing young viewers "do's" and "don'ts" in such areas as safety, health and nutrition. *A Marvel Production in association with Sunbow Productions. Color. Half–hour. Premiered: September 23, 1985. Syndicated.*

Voices:

Charlie Adler, Jack Angel, Liz Aubrey, Jackson Beack, Michael Bell, Arthur Burghardt, Corey Burton, Bill Callaway, Peter Cullen, Brian Cummings, Pat Fraley, Hank Garret, Dick Gautier, Ed Gilbert, Dan Gilvezan, Dave Hall, Zack Hoffman, Kene Holiday, Jerry Houser, Chris Latta, Loren Lester, Mary McDonald Lewis, Chuck McCann, Michael McConnohie, Rob Paulsen, Pat Pinney, Lisa Raggio, Bill Ratner, Hal Rayle, Bob Remus, Neil Ross, Will Ryan, Ted Schwartz, John Stephenson, B. J. Ward, Lee Weaver, Frank Welker, Stan Wojno, Keoni Young

Episodes:

"Hi Freak," "Countdown For Zartan," "Cobra Sound Waves," "Cobra Stops The World," "Jungle Trap," "Haul Down The Heavens," "Battle For The Train Of Gold," "Operation Mind Menace," "Lights! Camera! Cobra!," "Cobra's Candidate," "Red Rocket's Glare," "Satellite Down," "Money To Burn," "The Phantom Brigade," "The Synthoid Conspiracy—Part 1," "The Synthoid Conspiracy—Part 2," "Spell Of The Siren," "Twenty Questions," "The Game's Master," "The Greenhouse Effect," "The Viper Is Coming," "The Funhouse," "Where The Reptiles Roam," "Lazers In The Night," "The Germs," "Worlds Without End—Part 1," "Captives Of Cobra—Part 1," "Bazooka Saw A Sea Serpent," "The Traitor—Part 1," "Cobra Quake," "Excalibur," "Cobra Claws Are Coming To Town," "Worlds Without End—Part 2," "Equ De Cobra," "Captives Of Cobra—Part 2," "Mini–Series (ep. #1)," "Rendezvous In The City Of The Dead" (Mini–Series ep. #2) "Three Cubes To Darkness" (Mini–Series ep. #3), "Chaos In The Sea Of Lost Souls" (Mini–Series ep. #4), "Mini–Series" (ep. #5), "An Eye for An Eye," "The Primordial Plot," "Flint's Vacation," "Hearts And Cannons," "The Traitor—Part 2," "The Gods Below," "Memories Of Mara," "The Wrong Stuff," "Last Hour To Doomsday," "Pit Of Vipers," "The Invaders," "Computer Complications," "Sink The Montana," "Cold Slither," "The Great Alaskan Land Rush," "Skeleton In Closet," "There Is No Place Like Springfield" (Part 1), "There Is No Place Like Springfield" (Part 2), "Let's Play Soldier," "Cobrathon," "Million Dollar Medic," "Rotten Egg," "Once Upon A Joe. . . . ," "Glamour Girls," "Iceberg Goes South," "The Spy Rooked Me," "Grey Hairs And Growing Pains," "My Brother's Keeper," "My Favorite Things," "Raise The Flagg," "G. I. Joe And The Golden Fleece," "Arise, Serpentor, Arise" (Five–Part Mini–Series), "The Most Dangerous Thing In The World," "Ninja Holiday," "Nightmare Assault," "Joe's Night Out," "Second Hand Emotions," "Not A Ghost Of

A Chance," "Sins Of Our Fathers," "In The Presence Of Mine Enemies" and "Into Your Tent I Will Silently Creep."

G. I. JOE (1989)

The overall goal of the COBRA special mission force is to master the power of Dragonfire, a natural energy like electricity—only infinitely more powerful—which is found in underground "lakes of fire" in a few locations around the world. Their mission is to tap the most powerful repository of all beneath Sorcerer's Mesa, an American Indian site in New Mexico, in this five–part mini–series which was based on the adventures of the popular syndicated series of the same name. *A DIC Enterprises Production. Color. Half–hour. Premiered: September, 1989. Syndicated.*

Voices:

Stalker: Lee Jeffery, **Lady Jaye:** Suzanne Errett, **Zarana:** Lisa Corps, **Rock & Roll:** Kevin Conway, **Mutt:** Dale Wilson, **Alley Viper:** Jim Byrnes, **Gnawgahyde:** Ian Corlett, **Scoop:** Michael Benyaer, **Copperhead:** Maurice LaMarche, **Lowlight:** Maurice LaMarche, **Serpentor:** Maurice LaMarche, **Spirit:** Maurice LaMarche, **Destro:** Maurice LaMauche, **Cobra Commander:** Chris Latta, **Baroness:** Morgan Lofting, **Sgt. Slaughter:** Himself

Episodes:

"Dragonfire—Day One," "Dragonfire—Day Two," "Dragonfire—Day Three," "Dragonfire—Day Four" and "Dragonfire—Day Five."

GILLIGAN'S PLANET

Most of the original cast of television's favorite castaways provided their voices for this updated version of the classic network sitcom in which the crew board a powerful rocketship built by the Professor that launches them off their island and maroons them on a remote planet in outer space. *A Filmation Production. Color. Half–hour. Premiered on CBS: September, 1982–September 10, 1983.*

Voices:

Gilligan, the first–mate: Bob Denver, **Jonas Grumby,** the skipper: Alan Hale Jr., **Thurston Howell III:** Jim Backus, **Lovey Howell,** his wife: Natalie Schafer, **Ginger Grant,** the movie star: Dawn Wells, **Mary Ann Summers,** the clerk, Dawn Wells, **Roy Hinkley,** the professor: Russell Johnson

Episodes:

"Amazing Colossal Gilligan," "Bumper To Bumper," "Gilligan's Army," "I Dream Of Genie," "Invaders Of The Lost Barque," "Journey To The Center Of . . . Planet," "Let Sleeping Minnows Lie," "Road To Boom," "Space Pirates," "Too Many Gilligans," "Turnabout Is Fair Play" and "Wings."

GLO FRIENDS

An influx of soft and cuddly characters entered the mainstream of animated cartoon fare following the success of "The Smurfs" and "Care Bears." This series was no exception, featuring

friendly, fearless creatures whose magical glow makes them extra appealing not only to children, but to the mean Moligans. *A Marvel Production in association with Sunbow Productions. Color. Half–hour. Premiered: September 16, 1986. Syndicated.*

Voices:

Charlie Alder, Michael Bell, Sue Blu, Bettina, Joey Camen, Roger C. Carmel, Nancy Cartwright, Townsend Coleman, Jeannie Elias, Pat Fraley, Ellen Gerstell, Skip Hinnant, Keri Houlihan, Katie Leigh, Sherry Lynn, Mona Marshall, Scott Menville, Sarah Partridge, Hal Rayle, Will Ryan, Susan Silo, Russi Taylor, B. J. Ward, Jill Wayne, Frank Welker

Episodes:

"Baby Gloworm Goes Bye–Bye," "Two Of A Kind," "Make No Mistake, It's Magic," "The Forest Brigade," "The Caverns Of Mystery," "The Front Page," "The Quest" (10 parts), "Beware Tales Of Gold That Lead To Thorny Trails," "The Masterpiece," "Bean Ball," "Glo Friends Meet The Glowees" (four parts), "Easy Money" (Two Parts) and "Wizard Of Rock."

GODZILLA AND THE SUPER 90

Formerly this series was called "The Godzilla Power Hour," but the half–hour adventures of "Jonny Quest" were added to boost the show's ratings and the title was therefore changed to reflect the program's newly expanded format.

Godzilla, the show's star, appeared in one segment as a friendly dragon joining forces with a scientist, Carl Rogers, to battle evil. Another segment, "Jana of the Jungle," focused on the adventures of a girl searching for her lost father in the rain forest where she lived as a child. *A Hanna–Barbera Production in association with Toho Co. Ltd. and Benedict Pictures Corporation. The character Godzilla © Toho Co. Ltd. and Benedict Pictures. All materials except the character Godzilla © Hanna–Barbera Productions. Color. One hour and a half. Premiered on NBC: November 4, 1978–September 1, 1978; September 9, 1978–October 28, 1978 (as "The Godzilla Power Hour").*

Voices:

Godzilla: Ted Cassidy, **Capt. Carl Rogers:** Jeff David, **Quinn,** Carl's aide: Brenda Thompson, **Pete,** Carl's aide: Al Eisenmann, **Brock,** Pete's friend: Hilly Hicks, **Godzooky,** Godzilla's sidekick: Don Messick, **Jana of the Jungle:** B. J. Ward, **Montaro:** Ted Cassidy, **Dr. Ben Cooper:** Michael Bell, **Natives:** Ross Martin, **Jonny Quest:** Tim Matthieson, **Dr. Benton Quest,** his father: John Stephenson, **Roger "Race" Bannon:** Mike Road, **Hadji,** Indian companion: Danny Bravo, **Bandit,** their dog: Don Messick

Episodes:

"Godzilla." (one per show) "The Firebird," "The Magavolt," "The Eartheater," "Attack Of The Stone Creatures," "The Seaweed Monster," "The Horror Of Forgotten Island," "The Energy Beast," "The Magnetic Terror," "The Colossus Of Atlantis," "Island Of Lost Ships," "The Breeder Beast," "The Sub–Zero Terror" and "The Time Dragons."
"Jana of the Jungle." (one per show) "The Golden Idol Of

The Gorgas," "Katuchi Danger," "Race For Life," "The Cordillera Volcano," "The Animal Snatchers," "The Renegade," "Rogue Elephant," "The Prisoner," "The Invaders," "Dangerous Cargo," "The Sting Of The Tarantula," "Countdown" and "Suspicion." "Jonny Quest." (one per show) (Studio records do not indicate which episodes were broadcast.)

THE GODZILLA SHOW

The favorite prehistoric monster comes alive again in new tales of adventure and suspense, saving the day for all mankind in times of natural or supernatural disaster. This was the third series try for Hanna–Barbera, featuring the 400–foot tall creature. Previously, the character starred in the short–lived "The Godzilla Power Hour," which was replaced after only two months by "Godzilla and the Super 90," an expanded version with the addition of classic "Jonny Quest" episodes to its roster.

In November, 1979, NBC combined "Godzilla" with reruns of "The Harlem Globetrotters" retitling the series, "The Godzilla/Globetrotters Adventure Hour." By September, 1980, "The Godzilla/Dynomutt Hour With Funky Phantom" replaced "The Godzilla/Globetrotters Adventure Hour." Like the former it featured reruns of previously broadcast Godzilla episodes and of network–run episodes of "Dynomutt, Dog Wonder" and "The Funky Phantom." Two months after its debut, the program was again changed. Dynomutt and the Funky Phantom were shelved in place of Hanna–Barbera's former network hit, "Hong Kong Phooey," which was paired with Godzilla under the title of "The Godzilla/Hong Kong Phooey Hour." (See individual series for voice credits and episodic information.) *A Hanna–Barbera Production. Color. Half–hour. Premiered on NBC: September 8, 1979–November 3, 1979; November 10, 1979–September 20, 1980 (as "The Godzilla/Globetrotters Adventure Hour); September 27, 1980–November 15, 1980 (as "The Godzilla/Dynomutt Hour With The Funky Phantom"); November 22, 1980–May 16, 1981 (as "The Godzilla/Hong Kong Phooey Hour"). Rebroadcast on NBC: May 23, 1981–September 5, 1981 (as "The Godzilla Show").*

Voices:
Godzilla: Ted Cassidy, **Godzooky,** his sidekick: Don Messick, **Captain Majors:** Jeff David, **Quinn:** Brenda Thompson, **Brock:** Hilly Hicks, **Pete:** Al Eisenman

Episodes:
"The City In The Clouds," "The Cyborg Whale," "Microgodzilla," "Pacific Peril," "The Beast Of Storm Island," "Moonlode," "The Golden Guardians," "Calico Clones," "Ghost Ship," "The Marco Beasts," "Valley Of The Giants," "Island Of Doom" and "The Deadly Asteroid.

GOLDIE GOLD AND ACTION JACK

A gorgeous 18–year–old with limitless wealth and charm, Goldie Gold, publisher of the *Gold Street Journal,* is a female James Bond who embarks on exciting adventures with her reporter/bodyguard Jack Travis, her editor Sam Gritt and her labrador Nugget to pursue stories and solve madcap capers with the aid of 007–type gadgetry. *A Ruby Spears Enterprises Production. Color. Half–hour. Premiered on ABC: September 12, 1981–September 18, 1982.*

Voices:
Goldie Gold: Judy Strangis, **Jack Travis,** her reporter: Sonny Melendrez, **Sam Gritt,** her editor: Booker Bradshaw

Additional Voices:
Henry Corden, Robert Ridgely

Episodes:
"Night Of The Crystal Skull," "Pirate Of The Airways," "Red Dust Of Doom," "Revenge Of The Ancient Astronaut," "Prophet Of Doom," Night Of The Walking Doom," "Island Of Terror," "Curse Of The Snake People," "Race Against Time," "Menace Of The Medallion," "Pursuit Into Peril," "The Return Of The Man Beast" and "The Goddess Of The Black Pearl."

GOOBER AND THE GHOST CHASERS

Using a similar format to "Scooby Doo, Where Are You?" Hanna–Barbera animated the adventures of reporters Tina, Ted, Gillie and Goober their pet dog, who investigate haunted houses and ghoulish mysteries for *Ghost Chasers* magazine.

Unlike the out–going Scooby, Goober is a meek character who actually becomes invisible when frightened by beasties or ghoulies. The series spotlighted guest stars throughout the season. The most regular were "The Partridge Family" in cartoon form. The program was later packaged as part of "Fred Flintstone and Friends" for syndication. *A Hanna–Barbera Production. Color. Half–hour. Premiered on ABC: September 8, 1973–August 31, 1975.*

Voices:
Goober: Paul Winchell, **Gillie:** Ronnie Schell, **Ted:** Jerry Dexter, **Tina:** Jo Anne Harris, **The Partridge Family: Laurie Partridge:** Susan Dey, **Chris Partridge:** Brian Forster, **Tracy Partridge:** Suzanne Crough, **Danny Partridge:** Danny Bonaduce

Additional Voices:
Alan Dinehart Jr., Alan Oppenheimer

Episodes:
"Assignment: The Ahaab Apparition," "Brush Up Your Shakespeare," "The Galloping Ghost" (with Wilt Chamberlain), "The Singing Ghost," "The Ghost Ship," "Aloha, Ghost," "Mummy Knows Best," "The Haunted Wax Museum," "The Wicked Witch Dog," "Venice Anyone?," "Is Sherlock Holme?," "A Hard Day's Knight," "Go West, Young Ghost, Go West," "That Snow Ghost," Inca Dinka Doo" and "Old MacDonald Had A Ghost EE–II–EEYOW."

GRIMM'S FAIRY TALES

Recalling those classic children's stories of the past, this beautifully animated half–hour series is a collection of the world–famous Grimm's Fairy Tales, presenting colorful re-tellings of such favorite tales as "Hansel and Gretel," "Snow White," "Puss N' Boots" and "Little Red Riding Hood." The series premiered on Nickelodeon, becoming a popular featured attraction on the station. Each episode ran close to 12 minutes. *A Nippon Animation Production. Color. Half–hour. Premiered on Nickelodeon: September, 1989.*

Episodes:
"Ali Baba And The Forty Thieves," "Cinderella," "Little Red Riding Hood," "Puss N' Boots," "Snow White," "The Little Mermaid," "The Three Little Pigs," "The Ugly Duckling," "The Wolf And The Seven Goats" and "The Boy And The Tigers."

THE GROOVIE GOOLIES

Humble Hall residents Count Dracula; Hagatha, his plump wife; Frankie, their son; Bella La Ghostly, the switchboard operator; Sabrina, the teenage witch; Wolfie, the werewolf; Bonapart, the accident–prone skeleton; Mummy, Bonapart's buddy; and others haunt trespassers with practical jokes and ghoulish mischief in this movie monster spoof produced for Saturday–morning television. The characters were originally introduced on 1970's "Sabrina and the Groovie Goolies" series on CBS, before they were resurrected by the network in their own weekly series. For its final two seasons, the series shifted to network rival ABC, where it was broadcast on Saturday and Sunday mornings in succession. *A Filmation Production. Color. Half–hour. Premiered on CBS: September, 1971–September 17, 1972.*

Voices:
Larry Storch, Don Messick, Howard Morris, Jane Webb, Dallas McKennon, John Erwin

GROOVIE GOOLIES AND FRIENDS

Like Hanna–Barbera, Filmation packaged for worldwide syndication their own collection of previous cartoon hits: "Groovie Goolies," "The Adventures of Waldo Kitty," "Lassie's Rescue Rangers," "The New Adventures of Gilligan," "My Favorite Martian" and 18 half–hour combinations of "M.U.S.H." "Fraidy Cat" and "Wacky and Packy." (See individual series for information.) *A Filmation Production. Color. Half–hour. Premeired: September, 1978. Syndicated.*

THE GUMBY SHOW

The adventures of this lovable green clay figure and his pet horse, Pokey, first appeared as a Saturday morning kids' show on NBC in 1957. The stop–action animated series was spun off from "Howdy Doody," on whose program Gumby was first introduced in 1956. Adventures were filmed via the process of pixillation—filming several frames at a time, moving the characters slightly, and then shooting more frames to achieve continuous motion.

Originally Bob Nicholson, best known for his portrayal of

Clarabell and Cornelius Cobb on "Howdy Doody," hosted the program, and later comedian Pinky Lee was host.

The six–minute, two–part and three–part adventures that made up the half–hour series were produced under the direction of superb stop–motion filmmaker Raymond Beck. The vintage series episodes are still in syndication today. (The program was also retitled, "The Adventures of Gumby.") *A Clokey Productions. Color. Half–hour. Premiered on NBC: March 16, 1957–November 16, 1957. Syndicated.*

Voices:
Gumby: Art Clokey, **Pokey:** Art Clokey

Episodes:
"Moon Trip," "Gumby On The Moon," "Trapped On The Moon," "Mirrorland," "Lost And Found," "Little Lost Pony," "The Blockheads," "The Fantastic Farmer," "Gopher Trouble," "The Black Knight," "Mysterious Fires," "Too Loo," "Gumby Concerto," "Robot Rumpus," "Yard Work Made Easy," "Toy Crazy," "Toy Joy," "Lion Around," "Lion Drive," "The Eggs and Trixie," "Egg Trouble," "Odd Balls," "Outcast Marbles," "Gumby Business," "Toy Run," "The Mocking Monkey," "How Not To Trap Lions," "The Magic Show," "The Magic Wand," "Pokey Express," "Indian Trouble," "The Racing Game," "Gumby Racer," "Rain Spirits," "The Kachinas," "Toying Around," "Toy Capers," "In The Dough," "Baker's Tour," "Tree Trouble," "Eager Beavers," "Train Trouble," "In A Fix," "The Zoops," "Even Steven," "The Glob," "Chicken Feed," "Hidden Valley," "The Groobee," "The Witty Witch," "Hot Rod Granny," "Ricochet Pete," "Northland Follies," "The Small Planets," "Sad King Ott's Daughter," "King For A Day," "Rain For Roo," "Santa Witch," "Scrooge Loose," "Pigeon In A Plum Tree," "Big Eye," "Dragon Witch," "Lawn Party," "Treasure For Henry" (without Gumby), "Who's What" (without Gumby), "Grub Grabber Gumby," "The Reluctant Gargoyles," "All Broken Up," "Wishful Thinking," "Turnip Trap," "The Rodeo King," "Dragon Daffy," "Gumby Baby Sits," "El Toro," "Dopey Nopey," "Tricky Ball," "Dog Catchers," "Bully For Gumby," "A Bone For Nopey," "Gabby Auntie," "Of Clay And Critters," "Foxy Box," "Siege Of Boonseborough," "Missile Bird," "Good Knight Story," "The Blue Goo," "Tail Tale," "A Hair Raising Adventure," "Motor Mania," "Sticky Pokey," "A Lovely Bunch of Coconuts," "Goo For Pokey," "Pokey Minds The Baby," "Candidate For President," "Gumby's Fire Department," "Making Squares," "The Golden Iguana," "School For Squares," "Super Spray," "The Magic Flute," "Point Of Honor," "Behind The Puff Ball," "The Ferris Wheel Mystery," "Mason Hornet," "Do It Yourself Gumby," "The Moon Boggles," "Prickle's Problem," "Haunted Hot Dog," "Hot Ice," "Piano Rolling Blues," "Pilgrim On The Rocks," "Pokey's Price," "Son Of Liberty" and "Gumby Crosses The Delaware."

THE HANNA–BARBERA NEW CARTOON SERIES

In the fall of 1962, following the success of its previous syndicated series, Hanna–Barbera introduced this trilogy of original cartoon programming featuring a new stable of stars: "Wally Gator," a "swinging gator from the swamp" who refuses to be confined to his home in the zoo; "Lippy the Lion," a blustering, bragging lion who gets into a multiplicity of messes with his buddy, a sorrowful hyena, Hardy Har Har; and "Touché Turtle," a well–meaning but inept swashbuckling turtle who goes on a series of avenging adventures with his dog, Dum Dum, to right the wrongs of the world.

Each series component contained 52 episodes and was produced for flexible programming, allowing stations to use each series together in longer time periods or scheduled separately in their own half–hour time slots. (For episodic titles see each individual series.) *A Hanna–Barbera Production. Color. Half–hour. Premiered: September, 1962. Syndicated.*

Voices:

Wally Gator: Daws Butler, **Mr. Twiddles:** Don Messick, **Lippy the Lion:** Daws Butler, **Hardy Har Har:** Mel Blanc, **Touché Turtle:** Bill Thompson, **Dum Dum:** Alan Reed

HANNA–BARBERA'S WORLD OF SUPER ADVENTURE

Syndicated package of super hero cartoons first produced for Saturday morning, including "The Fantastic Four," "Frankenstein Jr. and the Impossibles," "Space Ghost," "Herculoids," "Shazzan," "Moby Dick and the Mighty Mightor" and "Birdman and the Galaxy Trio." (See individual titles for information.) *A Hanna–Barbera Production. Color. Half–hour. Premiered: September, 1980. Syndicated.*

THE HARDY BOYS

Teenage sleuths Frank and Joe Hardy double as rock–and–roll musicians on a world tour as they solve crime and play some popular music (music was performed by a live band appropriately enough called "The Hardy Boys") in this updated version of Franklin W. Dixon's long–running series of children's detective novels. *A Filmation Production. Color. Half–hour. Premiered on ABC: September 6, 1969–September 4, 1971.*

Voices:

Frank Hardy: Byron Kane, **Joe Hardy:** Dallas McKennon, **Wanda Kay Breckenridge:** Jane Webb

THE HARLEM GLOBETROTTERS

Famed basketball illusionists Meadowlark Lemon, Curly, Gip, Bobby Joe and Geese perform benefits and defeat evil around the world with the help of their basketball finesse in this popular Saturday morning entry that was remarkably successful during its network run. In February, 1978, NBC repackaged the series and combined it with several other Hanna–Barbera favorites, including C. B. Bears, in a two hour series called "Go Go Globetrotters." All–new adventures of the internationally acclaimed "Wizards of the Court" were produced in 1979 under the new title of "The Super Globetrotters." (See latter series for complete information.) *A Hanna–Barbera Production. Color. Half–hour. Premiered on CBS: September 12, 1970–May 13, 1973. Rebroadcast on NBC: February 1978–September 2, 1978 (as "Go Go Globetrotters").*

Voices:

Meadowlark Lemon: Scatman Crothers, **Freddie "Curly" Neal:** Stu Gilliam, **Gip:** Richard Elkins, **Bobby Joe Mason:** Eddie "Rochester" Anderson, **Geese:** Johnny Williams, **Pablo:** Robert Do Qui, **Granny:** Nancy Wible, **Dribbles the dog:** (no voice)

Episodes:

1970–1971 "The Great Geese Goof–Up," "Football Zeros," "Hold That Hillbilly," "Bad News Cruise," "Rodeo Duds," "Double Dribble Double," "Heir Lions," "From Scoop To Nuts," "What A Day For A Birthday," "It's Snow Vacation," "The Great Ouch Doors," "Hooray For Hollywood," "Shook Up Sheriff," "The Wild Blue Yonder" and "Long Gone Gip."
1971–1972 (new shows combined with reruns) "A Pearl Of A Game," "Nothing To Moon About," "Pardon My Magic," "Granny's Royal Ruckus," "Soccer To Me" and "Jungle Jitters."

THE HEATHCLIFF AND DINGBAT SHOW

That tough, orange–striped cat of comic–strip fame co–stars in this Saturday morning series in which he typically takes great delight in annoying anyone he encounters. The program's second segment, "Dingbat and the Creeps," followed the misadventures of a vampire dog, a skeleton and a pumpkin who help people in trouble. *A Ruby–Spears Enterprises Production. Color. Half–hour. Premiered on ABC: October 4, 1980–September 5, 1981.*

Voices:

Heathcliff: Mel Blanc, **Mr. Schultz:** Mel Blanc, **Iggy:** Mel Blanc, **Spike/Muggsy:** Mel Blanc, **Milkman:** Mel Blanc, **Clem/Digby:** Henry Corden, **Dogsnatcher:** Henry Corden, **Crazy Shirley/Sonja:** June Foray, **Grandma/Marcy:** June Foray, **Dingbat and the Creeps: Dingbat:** Frank Welker, **Nobody, the pumpkin:** Don Messick, **Sparerib, the skeleton:** Don Messick

Episodes:

"Heathcliff" (six–minute episodes) "Kitty A La Carte," "Cake Flakes," "Cat In The Beanstalk," "Doggone Dog Catcher," "Angling Angler," "Feline Fugitive," "Red Hot Riding Hooded Heathcliff," "Rodeo Dough," "Mystery Loves Company," "Gold Digger Daze," "Lion Around The House," "Heathcliff And The Sleeping Beauty," "Robinson Cruise Ho," "The Watch Cat," "Star Trick," "Pinnochio Rides Again," "Milk Run Mayhem," "Pumping Iron" and "Mascot Rumble."
(four–minute episodes) "The Great Chase," "The Great Milk Factory Fracas," "Hives," "The Mouse Trapper," "The Big Fish Story," "The Great Cop 'N Cat Chase" and "Heathcliff Of Sherwood Forest."
"Dingbat and the Creeps." (six–minute episodes) "French Fried Fracas," "Window Washouts," "Health Nuts," "Treasure Haunt," "Showbiz Shenanigans," "Service Station Screwballs," "Bungling Babysitters," "Detective Ding–A–Lings," "Nautical Noodnicks," "Batty Boo–Ticians," "Retail Ruckus," "Creep Crop Crack–Ups," "No News Is Ghoul News," "Carnival Cut–Ups," "Nutty Knights," "High Flying Fools," "Heir Today, Gone

Tomorrow," "Football Flunkies," "It's a Snow Job For A Creep" and "Lumbering Loonies."

THE HEATHCLIFF AND MARMADUKE SHOW

In this series, the scruffy tomcat shared the spotlight with that imposing and lovable Great Dane, Marmaduke, who was featured in separate adventures, getting himself into all kinds of mischief without meaning to. Meanwhile, Heathcliff picks up where he left off by triumphing over his adversaries—Spike, the neighborhood bulldog; the garbage collector; the fish store owner; and the chef of the local restaurant. "Dingbat and the Creeps" also returned as an alternating segment in the series, and two 30-second teasers were added: "Marmaduke's Riddles" and "Marmaduke's Doggone Funnies." *A Ruby-Spears Enterprises Production. Color. Half-hour. Premiered on ABC: September 12, 1981–September 18, 1982.*

Voices:
Heathcliff: Mel Blanc, **Iggy:** Mel Blanc, **Mr. Schultz:** Mel Blanc, **Spike,** the bulldog: Mel Blanc, **Muggsy:** Mel Blanc, **Clem/Digby:** Henry Corden, **Dogsnatcher:** Henry Corden, **Crazy Shirley/Sonja:** June Foray, **Grandma/Marcy:** June Foray, **Dingbat and the Creeps: Dingbat:** Frank Welker, **Nobody,** the pumpkin: Don Messick, **Sparerib,** the skeleton: Don Messick, **Marmaduke: Marmaduke,** the Great Dane: Paul Winchell, **Phil Winslow,** his owner: Paul Winchell, **Dottie Winslow,** his wife: Russi Taylor, **Barbie Winslow,** their daughter: Russi Taylor, **Billy Winslow,** their son: Russi Taylor, **Missy:** Russi Taylor, **Mr. Snyder/Mr. Post:** Don Messick

Episodes:
"Heathcliff." (six-minute episodes) "Caught Cat Napping," "Dud Boat," "Clon'En Around," "Tabby And The Pirate," "Gator Go-Round" and "A Briefcase Of Cloak And Dagger." (four-minute episodes) "New Kit On The Block," "Cat Kit," "A Close Encounter," "Crazy Daze," "Mush, Heathcliff, Mush" and "Of Mice And Menace."
"Dingbat and the Creeps." (four-minute episodes) "Prized Pooch," "U.F. Oafs," "Safari Safs," "Door To Door Salescreeps," "Beach Blanket Bozos" and "Lemans-ter Rally."
"Marmaduke." (two five-minute episodes per show) "Fret Vet," "Suburban Cowboy," "Ghostly Goofup," "Kitty Sitter," "Babysitting Shenanigans," "Caper Cracker," "Wonder Mutt," "Marmaduke Of The Movies," "Misty Mystique," "Police Pooch," "Tricky Treat," "Wish Bones," "Bearly Camping," "Seagoing Watchdog," "Double Trouble Maker," "Bone To Pick With Marmaduke," "Beach Brawl," "Gold Fever Fracas," "Shuttle Off To Buffalo," "Barking For Dollars," "Leapin' Leprechaun," "Home Run Rover," "Playgrounded," "Gone With The Whim," "The Lemonade Kid" and "School Daze."
"Marmaduke Riddles." (30-second segments) "Dog Walk," "Canine Graduate," "Dog Duds," "Baseball Dog," "Cats And Dogs," "Neat Feline Moms," "Flea Circus," "Noisy Forest," "Puppy Shelter," "Clean Joke/Dirty Joke," "Tennis Shoes," "Timekeeper," "Railroad Dog" and "Monster Pooch."
"Marmaduke's Doggone Funnies." (30-second segments) "Hopping Hound," "Chicken Dog," "Cat Thief," "Chained

Pup," "Playful Poodle," "Performing Pooch," "The Small Car," "Puff Uses The Bathroom," "Chienne Goes To College," "Sausage Chewies," "Doll Clothes," "Buffy And The Sprinkler" and "Turntable."

HEATHCLIFF AND THE CATILLAC CATS

Self-confident, cunning, ruthless and mischievous, the crafty cat, Heathcliff, of comic-strip fame, terrorizes the neighborhood—any man, cat or dog, watch out!—with little regard for anyone but himself in this half-hour comedy series divided into two segments. The second half features the lively and imaginative escapades of the Catillac Cats (Hector, Wordsworth and Mungo), led by boss-cat Riff Raff, whose get-rich-quick schemes and search for the ultimate meal keep them embroiled in trouble in one episode after another. *A DIC Enterprises Production in association with LBS Communications and McNaught Syndicate. Color. Half-hour. Premiered: September, 1986. Syndicated.*

Voices:
Heathcliff: Mel Blanc, **Iggy:** Donna Christle, **Spike/Mugsy/Knuckles:** Derek McGrath, **Grandma:** Ted Ziegler, **Sonja:** Marilyn Lightstone, **Bush/Raul:** Danny Wells, **Milkman:** Stan Jones, **Fish Market Owner:** Danny Mann, **The Catillac Cats: Riff Raff/Wordsworth:** Stan Jones, **Mungo:** Ted Ziegler, **Hector:** Danny Mann, **Cleo:** Donna Christie, **Leroy,** the junkyard dog: Ted Ziegler

Episodes:
1986–1987 "Heathcliff." (one per show) "An Officer And An Alley Cat," "The Mad Dog Catcher," "Heathcliff And The King Of The Beasts," "The Gang's All Here," "Be Prepared," "Say Cheese," "A Piece Of The Rock," "The Super M.A.C. Menace," "Tally Ho, Heathcliff," "Spike's Slave," "Teed Off," "The Great Tuna Caper," "Trombone Terror," "Sealand Mania," "Meow Meow Island," "Pop's Parole," "Heathcliff Gets Canned," "Lard

Crafty cat Heathcliff sets his sights on the lovely Cleo in "Heathcliff And The Catillac Cats." © DIC Animation City, Inc./McNaught Syndicate, Inc./LBS Communication Inc. (Courtesy: DIC Enterprises)

Times," "The Big Break In," "Claws," "Baby Buggy Bad Guys," "Going Shopping," "Star Of Tomorrow," "The Siamese Twins," "Kitten Smitten," "Pumping Iron," "Family Tree," "Big Top Bungling," "Raiders Of The Lost Cat," "Snow Job," "Soap Box Derby," "The Great Pussini," "Sonja's Nephew," "Heathcliff's Double," "The Catfather," "Butter Up!," "Big Game Hunter," "Cat Food For Thought," "Service With A Smile," "Terrible Tammy," "Used Pets," "Brain Sprain," "Lion–Hearted Heathcliff," "Revenge Of The Kitty," "Cat Burglar Heathcliff," "Flying Heathcliff," "Heathcliff's Surprise," "Phantom Of The Garbage," "Heathcliff's Middle Name," "Rebel Without A Claws," "Spike's Cousin," "Gopher Broke," "Heathcliff Reforms," "Where There's An Ill There's A Way," "City Slicker Cat," "Blizzard," "Hospital Heathcliff," "Chauncey's Great Escape," "Copa Ca Heathcliff," "The Home Wreckers," "Heathcliff's Pet," "Smoke Gets In My Eyes," "Momma's Back In Town," "Bamboo Island," "Boom Boom Pussini," "Grandpa Vs. Grandpa," "Journey To The Center Of The Earth," "Junkyard Flood" and "May The Best Cat Win" (pilot).

"The Catillac Cats" (one per show).

"The Merry Pranksters," "For The Birds," "Carnival Capers," "Space Cat," "The Farming Life Ain't For Me," "Much Ado About Bedding," "The Babysitters," "Lucky," "Kitty Kat Kennels," "Leroy's In Love," "A Better Mousetrap," "Big Foot," "Prehysteric Riff Raff," "Whacked Out," "Cat Balloon," "Divide And Clobber," "Beach Blanket Mungo," "Going South," "Mungo Lays An Egg," "Yes, Sewer, That's My Baby," "Cat In The Hat," "Kitten Around," "Hector Spector," "A Camping We Will Go," "Mungo Gets No Respect," "Swamp Fever," "Crusin For a Bruisin," "Mungo's Dilemma," "Games Of Love," "Scardy Cats," "Cat Angles," "The Comedy Cat," "Hector's Takeover," "Condo Fever," "Cat Can Do," "In Search of Catlantis," "Jungle Vacation," "House Of The Future," "Circus Berserkus," "Soccer Anyone?," "Riff Raff The Gourmet," "Junkfood," "Dr. Mousetus," "Pecos' Treasure," "Who's Got The Chocolate?," "The Other Woman," "Harem Cat," "The Meow–Sic Goes Round And Round," "Monstro And Wolfhound," "Iron Cats," "Hector The Detector," "Super Hero Mungo," "Cleo Moves In," "The Mungo Mash," "Riff Raff's Mom," "Search For A Star," "Wishful Thinking," "Young Cat With A Horn," "The Big Swipe" and "Debutante Ball."

1987–1988 "Heathcliff" (one per show).

"The Whitecliffs Of Dover," "Nightmare In Beverly Hills," "The Shrink," "In The Beginning," "The Cat And The Pauper," "Rear Cat Window," "Spike's New Home," "Feline Good," "Dr. Heathcliff And Mr. Spike," "Heathcliff Gets Framed," "North Pole Cat," "It's A Terrible Life," "New York Sewer System," "Hair Of The Cat," "Heathcliff's Mom," "Spike's Coach," "Something Fishy," "Cat Day Afternoon," "Fortune Teller," "Missing In Action" and "Break An Egg."

"The Catillac Cats" (one per show).

"Hockey Pucks," "Brushing Up," "Catlympic Cat," "Time Warped," "Cat Days/Ninja Nights," "Mungo The Jungle," "Christmas Memories," "Life Saver," "The Cat In The Iron Mask," "A Letter To Granny," "Hector The Protector," "Mungo's Big Romance," "The Trojan Cadillac," "Bag Cat Sings The Blues," "Repo Cat," "Off Road Racer," "High Goon," "Leroy Gets Canned," "Tenting Tonight," "Cottontails, Chickens, And Colored Eggs" and "He Ain't Heavy, He's My Brother."

THE HECKLE AND JECKLE CARTOON SHOW

The two conniving, talking magpies of motion picture fame host a collection of other theatrically released Terrytoon cartoons and their own misadventures. Other cartoon segments featured studio stars Little Roquefort, Gandy Goose and Dinky Duck, plus miscellaneous cartoons under the segment title of "Terrytoon Classics," several of which starred the Terry Bears. (Titles for the latter segment were unavailable from the producer.) In 1977, Heckle and Jeckle were cast in a new series co–starring Mighty Mouse, entitled, "The New Adventures of Mighty Mouse and Heckle and Jeckle." *A CBS Terrytoons Production. Color. Half–hour. Premiered on CBS: October 14, 1956–September 1957. Rebroadcast on CBS: September 1965–September 3, 1966; Rebroadcast on NBC: September 6, 1969–September 7, 1971. Syndicated.*

Voices:

Heckle: Dayton Allen, Roy Halee, **Jeckle:** Dayton Allen, Roy Halee, **Little Roquefort/Percy the Cat:** Tom Morrison, **Gandy Goose/Sourpuss:** Arthur Kay, **Terry Bears:** Roy Halee, Philip A. Scheib, Doug Moye, **Dinky Duck:** (no voice)

Episodes:

"Heckle and Jeckle" (one per show).

"The Talking Magpies," "The Uninvited Pests," "McDougal's Rest Farm," "Happy Go Lucky," "Cat Trouble," "The Intruders," "Flying South," "Fishing By The Sea," "The Super Salesman," "The Hitch Hikers," "Taming The Cat," "A Sleepless Night," "Magpie Madness," "Free Entertainment," "Out Again, In Again," "Goony Golfers," "The Power Of Thought," "The Lion Hunt," "The Stowaways," "Happy Landing," "Hula Hula Land," "Dancing Shoes," "The Fox Hunt," "A Merry Chase," "King Tut's Tomb," "The Rival Romeos," "Bulldozing The Bull," "The Rainmaker," "Steeple Jacks," "Sno' Fun," "Movie Madness," "Off To the Opera," "Housebusters," "Moose On The Loose," "Hair Cut Ups," "Pill Peddlers," "Ten Pin Terrors," "Bargain Daze," "Log Rollers," "Blind Date," "Satisfied Customers," "Blue Plate Symphony," "Pirate's Gold," "Miami Maniacs," "Wild Life," "Thousand Mile Checkup," "Mint Men," "Trapeze Please," "Deep Sea Doodle," "Stunt Men," "Sappy New Year" and "Messed Up Movie Makers."

"Dinky Duck" (one per show).

"The Orphan Duck," "Much Ado About Nothing," "The Lucky Duck," "Welcome Little Stranger," "Life With Fido," "Dinky Finds A Home," "The Beauty Shop," "Flat Foot Fledgling," "The Foolish Duckling," "Sink Or Swim," "Wise Quacks," "Featherweight Champ," "The Orphan Egg," "The Timid Scarecrow" and "It's A Living."

"Little Roquefort" (one per show).

"Cat Happy," "Mouse and Garden," "Three Is A Crowd," "Musical Madness," "Seasick Sailors," "Pastry Panic," "The Haunted Cat," "City Slicker," "Hypnotized," "Good Mousekeeping," "Flop Secret," "Mouse Meets Bird," "Playful Puss," "Friday The 13th," "Mouse Menace," "Runaway Mouse," "Prescription For Percy," "The Cat's Revenge" and "No Sleep For Percy."

"Gandy Goose" (one per show).

"Gandy The Goose," "The Goose Flies High," "Doomsday,"

"G—Man Jitters," "Hook, Line And Sinker," "The Home Guard," "The One—Man Navy," "Slap Happy Hunters," "Sham Battle Shenanigans," "The Night," "Lights Out," "Tricky Business," "The Outpost," "Tire Trouble," "Night Life In The Army," "Camouflage," "Somewhere In Egypt," "Aladdin's Lamp," "The Frog And The Princess," "The Ghost Town," "Gandy's Dream Girl," "Post—War Inventions," "Fisherman's Luck," "Mother Goose Nightmare," "The Mosquito," "Who's Who In The Jungle," "The Exterminator," "Fortune Hunters," "It's All In The Stars," "The Golden Hen," "Peace—Time Football," "Mexican Baseball," "The Chipper Chipmunk," "Dingbat Land," "The Covered Pushcart," "Comic Book Land," "Dream Walking," "Wide Open Spaces," "Songs of Erin," "Spring Fever" and "Barnyard Actor."

THE HECTOR HEATHCOTE SHOW

A time machine enables a scientist (Hector Heathcote) to rewrite history by transporting him back to famous events that have shaped the world in this series of recycled cartoons that were originally distributed to theaters. The program's other cartoon components included, "Hashimoto" and "Sidney the Elephant." (See Theatrical Sound Cartoon Series for details.) *A CBS Terrytoons Production. Color. Half—hour. Premiered on NBC: October 5, 1963—September 25, 1965.*

Voices:

Hector Heathcote: John Myhers, **Hashimoto:** John Myhers, **Mrs. Hashimoto:** John Myhers, **Yuriko:** John Myhers, **Saburo:** John Myhers, **Sidney the Elephant:** Lionel Wilson, Dayton Allen, **Stanley the Lion:** Dayton Allen, **Cleo the Giraffe:** Dayton Allen,

Episodes:

"Hector Heathcote" (two per show).
"The Minute And A Half Man," "The Famous Ride," "Daniel Boone, Jr," "The Unsung Hero," "The First Fast Mail," "Crossing The Delaware," "Drum Roll," "Railroaded To Fame," "Klondike Strikes Out," "First Flight Up," "Riverboat Mission," "He—Man Seaman," "Tea Party," "A Bell For Philadelphia," "The Big Cleanup," "Flight To The Finish," "Peace Pipe," "The Hectormobile," "Belabor Thy Neighbor," "Har Har Harpoon," "Land Grab," "Train Terrain," "Hold The Fort," "Valley Forge Hector," "Lost And Foundations," "Wind Bag," "Hats Off To Hector," "Ice Cream For Help," "Expert Explorer," "Search For A Symbol," "Pig In A Poke," "Barrel Of Fun," "The First Telephone," "Messy Messenger" and "High Flyer."
"Hashimoto" (one per show).
"Hashimoto—San," "House of Hashimoto," "So Sorry, Pussycat," "Night Life In Tokyo," "Honorable Cat Story," "Son Of Hashimoto," "Strange Companion," "Honorable House Cat," "Honorable Family Problem," "Loyal Royalty," "Honorable Paint In The Neck," "Pearl Crazy," "Tea House Mouse," "Cherry Blossom Festival," "Spooky—Yaki," "The Potter's Wheel Heel" and "Doll Festival."
"Sidney the Elephant" (one per show).
"Sick, Sick Sidney," "Sidney's Family Tree," "Hide And Go Sidney," "Tusk, Tusk," "The Littlest Bully," "Two—Ton Baby Sitter," "Banana Binge," "Meat, Drink And Be Merry," "Really Big Act," "Clown Jewels," "Tree Spree," "Send Your Elephant

To Camp," "Peanut Battle," "Fleet's Out," "To Be Or Not To Be," "Home Life," "Sidney's White Elephant," "Driven To Extraction" and "Split—Level Treehouse."

HELLO KITTY'S FURRY TALE THEATER

Delightfully entertaining series of two weekly fairy tales, loosely adapted and contemporized, staged by this animal theater group—Hello Kitty (the star) and friends Tuxedo Sam, Chip and My Melody—who take different roles from story to story, match wits with series villains, Catnip and Grinder, and always end their stories with warmth and heart. *A DIC Enterprises Production in association with MGM/UA Television. Color. Half—hour. Premiered on CBS: September 19, 1984—September 3, 1988.*

Voices:

Hello Kitty: Tara Charendoff, **Tuxedo Sam:** Sean Roberge, **Chip:** Noam Zylberman, **My Melody:** Maron Bennett, **Grandpa Kitty:** Carl Banas, **Grandma Kitty:** Elizabeth Hanna, **Papa Kitty:** Len Carlson, **Mama Kitty:** Elizabeth Hanna, **Catnip:** Cree Summer Francks, **Grinder:** Greg Morton, **Fangora:** Denise Pidgeon

Episodes:

"Wizard of Paws," "Pinocchio Penguin," "Cinderkitty," "The Pawed Piper," "K.T.—The Kitty Terrestial," "Peter Penguin," "Kittylocks And The Three Bears," "Paws—The Greg White Dog—Shark," "Cat Wars," "Tar—Sam Of The Jungle," "Sleeping Kitty," "Kitty And The Kong," "Kitty And The Beast," "Little Red Bunny Hood," "Snow White Kitty And The One Dwarf," "Frankencat," "Catula," "Paws Of The Round Table," "Rumpeldogskin," "Robin Penguin," "Hello Mother Goose," "Crocodile Penguin," "Grinder Genie And The Magic Lamp," "The Ugly Duckling," "How Scrinchnip Stole Christmas" and "The Phantom Of The Theater."

HELP! IT'S THE HAIR BEAR BUNCH

Wonderland Zoo's three wild bear tenants—Hair, Square and Bubi—campaign for better living conditions in Cave Block #9. Following its network run, the series was syndicated under the title of "The Yo Yo Bears." *A Hanna—Barbera Production. Color. Half—hour. Premiered on CBS: September 11, 1971—September 2, 1972. Rebroadcast on CBS: September 1973—August 31, 1974. Syndicated.*

Voices:

Hair Bear: Daws Butler, **Bubi Bear:** Paul Winchell, **Square Bear:** Bill Callaway, **Mr. Peevly,** zoo curator: John Stephenson, **Botch,** Peevly's assistant: Joe E. Ross

Additional Voices:

Hal Smith, Jeannie Brown, Joan Gerber, Vic Perrin, Janet Webb, Lennie Weinrib

Episodes:

"Keep Your Keeper," "Raffle Ruckus," "Rare Bear Bungle," "Bridal Boo Boo," "No Space Like Home," "Love Bug Bungle,"

"Gobs of Gobaloons," "Ark Lark," "I'll Zoo You Later," "Panda Pandemonium," "Closed Circuit TV," "Goldilocks And The Three Bears," "The Bear Who Came To Dinner," "Unbearable Peevly," "The Diet Caper" and "Kling Klong Versus The Masked Marvel."

HE-MAN AND MASTERS OF THE UNIVERSE

Residing on the planet Eternia, He–Man (Prince Adam) and She–Ra (Princess Adora) clash with the forces of evil—namely the villainous Skeletor—in this action–adventure series based on the popular Mattel toy line. *A Filmation Production. Color. Half–hour. Premiered: September, 1985. Syndicated.*

Voices:

Prince Adam/He–Man: John Erwin, **Princess Adora/She–Ra:** Melendy Britt, **Skeletor:** Alan Oppenheimer

Additional Voices:

Linda Gary, George DiCenzo, Eric Gunden, Lana Beeson, Erika Scheimer, R. D. Bobb

THE HERCULOIDS

Futuristic animals Zok the laser dragon, Tundro the rhinoceros, Gloop and Gleep the friendly blobs, Igoo the rock–ape and Dorno, a young boy, strive to save Zandor, their benevolent king, and the primitive planet Amzot from alien invaders. Nine years after its network run, the series was given a new life as part of NBC's "Go Go Globetrotters/The Herculoids." *A Hanna–Barbera Production. Color. Half–hour. Premiered on CBS: September 9, 1967–September 6, 1969.*

Voices:

Zandor: Mike Road, **Tara:** Virginia Gregg, **Zok:** Mike Road, **Dorno:** Ted Eccles, **Gloop:** Don Messick, **Gleep:** Don Messick, **Igoo:** Mike Road

Episodes:

(two 10–minute episodes per show) "The Beaked People," "The Raiders," "The Ped Creatures," "Sarko, The Arkman," "The Mole Men," "The Pirates," "The Spider Man," "Mekkor," "The Lost Dorgyte," "Destroyer Ants," "Defeat Or Orgon," "The Android People," "Temple Of Trax," "The Swamp Monster," "Laser Lancers," "The Raiders Apes," "Tiny World Of Terror," "Prisoner Of The Bubblemen," "The Time Creatures," "The Gladiators Of Kyanite," "Mekkano, The Machine Master," "Invasion Of The Electrode Men," "Mission Of The Amatrons," "Queen Skorra," "Attack Of The Faceless People," "The Zorbots," "Return Of Sta–Lak," "Revenge Of The Pirates," "Ruler Of The Reptons," "The Island Of The Gravities," "Malak And The Metal Apes," "The Return Of Torrak," "The Antidote," "Attack From Space," "The Mutoids" and "The Crystalites."

HERE COMES THE GRUMP

Young American lad Terry and his dog, Bib, strive to save Princess Dawn from the evil Grump, who has put her under the Curse of Gloom in this animated fantasy. The Grump and his bumbling Jolly Green Dragon, use a decoy to keep Terry,

Bib and the princess from the exact location of the crystal key, hidden in the Whispering Orchids, which is the means of breaking the curse. *A DePatie–Freleng Enterprises Production. Color. Half–hour. Premiered on NBC: September 6, 1969–September 4, 1971.*

Voices:

Princess Dawn: Stefanianna Christopherson, **Terry,** the little boy: Jay North, **The Grump:** Rip Taylor

Episodes:

(two per show) "The Bloodywine Battle," "The Great Grump Crunch," "The Great Thorn Forest," "The Eenie Meenie Miner," "The Good Ghost Ship," "Grump Meets Peter Paintbrush," "The Lemonade Sea," "Beware of Giants," "Joltin' Jack In Boxia," "Visit To A Ghost Town," "A Mess For King Midix," "The Show Of Shoe–Cago," "Witch Is Witch?," "The Yuks of Gagville," "Toilin' Toolie Birds," "The Grand Slam Of Door City," "Under The Pea–Green Sea," "Sugar And Spite," "The Great Shampoo Of Snow White City," "The Grump Meets The Grouch–Grooch," "The Wily Wheelies," "The Blabbermouth Of Echo Island," "With Malice In Blunderland," "Apachoo Choo Choo," "A Hitch In Time," "The Shaky Shutter Bugs," "Sno Land Like Snow Land," "Good Grief, Mother Goose," "The Bailed–Up Bloonywoonies," "Cherub Land," "Meet The Blockheads," "Hoppy–Go–LuckyHippety Hoppies" and "Blunderland Flying Machine."

HONG KONG PHOOEY

The crime–fighting karate expert, Hong Kong Phooey, alias Penrod Pooch, a meek police station janitor, maintains justice through his martial–arts abilities (which he learned in a correspondence course) and kayos his opponents in the process. His means of transportation: the "Phooeymobile." After the series' initial run on ABC, the character later returned to the airwaves as a segment on "The Godzilla/Hong Kong Phooey Hour." (See that entry for details.) *A Hanna–Barbera Production. Color. Half–hour. Premiered on ABC: September 7, 1974–September 4, 1976. Rebroadcast on NBC: May 1981–September 5, 1981.*

Voices:

Penrod Pooch/Hong Kong Phooey: Scatman Crothers, **Sergeant Flint:** Joe E. Ross, **Rosemary,** the switchboard operator: Kathy Gori, **Spot,** Phooey's surly cat: Don Messick

Additional Voices:

Richard Dawson, Ron Feinberg, Casey Kasem, Jay Lawrence, Peter Leeds, Allan Melvin, Alan Oppenheimer, Bob Ridgely, Fran Ryan, Hal Smith, Lee Vines, Frank Welker, Janet Waldo, Paul Winchell, Lennie Weinrib

Episodes:

(two 10–minute episodes per show) "Car Thieves," "Zoo Story," "Cotton Pickin' Pocket Picker," "Iron Head, The Robot," "Grandma Goody," "Candle Power," "Penthouse Burglaries," "Batty Bank Mob," "The Voltage Villain," "The Giggler," "Professor Presto The Malevolent Magician," "TV Or Not TV," "Stop Horsing Around," "Mirror, Mirror On The Wall," "Great Movie Mystery," "Hong Kong Phooey Versus Hong Kong Phooey," "The Claw," "The Abominable Snowman," "Professor Crosshatch," "Green Thumb," "Goldfisher," "From Bad To Verse," "Kong And The Counterfeiters," "The Great Choo Choo Robbery," "Patty Cake, Patty Cake, Bakery Man," "Mr. Tornado," "The Little Crook Who Wasn't There," "Dr. Diguiso," "The Incredible Mr. Shrink" and "Comedy Cowboys" (20–minute episode).

HOT WHEELS

Created and produced by Ken Snyder, of TV's "Roger Ramjet" fame, this was the first series created by Anamorphic computer–animation. It starred Jack Wheeler, organizer of a young auto racers' club, who battles antagonists in racing competition. The series was the first cartoon show to offer safety tips and information tidbits on weather, the physical principles of flight and the hazards of smoking.

Stories depicted club members Janet Martin, Skip Frasier, Bud Stuart, Mickey Barnes, Ardeth Pratt and Kip Chogi explaining to children the dangers of auto racing while engaged in reckless race car competition. The show's theme song was written and performed by Mike Curb and the Curbstones. *A Pantomime Pictures/Ken Snyder Production. Color. Half–hour. Premiered on ABC: September 6, 1969–September 4, 1971.*

Voices:

Jack Wheeler/Doc Warren: Bob Arbogast, **Janet Martin:** Melinda Casey, **Mickey Barnes/Kip Chogi:** Albert Brooks, **Ardeth Pratt:** Susan Davis, **Tank Mallory/Dexter Carter:** Casey Kasem, **Mother O'Hare:** Nora Marlowe, **Mike Wheeler:** Michael Rye

Episodes:

(two per show) "Sky Sailor," "The Funny Money Caper," "Surf's Up," "The Winner," "The Hot Head," "Big Race," "The Family Car," "Fire Fighters," "The Jewel," "Fake Out—Stake Out," "The Buggy Ride," "Four Wheel Time Bomb," "Hit And Run," "It Takes A Team," "Ardeth The Demon" (formerly: "Ardeth The Highwayman"), "Like Father, Like Son," "Avalanche Country," "Danger Around The Clock," "Tough Cop," "Hotter Than The Devils," "Underground," "Rough Ride" (formerly: "The Test"), "Race To Space," "Monkey A–Okay," "Diamonds Are a Girl's Worst Friend," "Big Heart, Little Hearts," "Get Back On That Horse," "Hitchhike To Danger," "Dragon's Tooth Peak," "The Doc Warren Trophy Race," "Show–Off," "Drag Strip," "Mata Hari Ardeth" and "Slicker–Slicks."

THE HOUNDCATS

Government intelligence agents Dingdog, Puttypuss, Mussel Mutt, Stutz and Rhubarb undertake impossible missions in the Wild West. The comedy adventure series was a spoof of TV's "Mission Impossible" with cats and dogs as members of the task force. (Unlike in the long–running network series, these characters become hysterical when the recorded voice tells them the message will self–destruct in five seconds.) *A De-Patie–Freleng Enterprises Production. Color. Half–hour. Premiered on NBC: September 9, 1972–September 1, 1973.*

Voices:

Stutz, the group's leader: Daws Butler, **Mussel Mutt,** the ex—weightlifter dog: Aldo Ray, **Rhubarb,** the inventor: Arte Johnson, **Puttypuss,** cat of thousand faces: Joe Besser, **Dingdog,** the stuntman: Stu Gilliam

Additional Voices:

Joan Gerber, Michael Bell

Episodes:

"The Misbehavin' Raven Mission," "The Double Dealing Diamond Mission," "The Great Gold Train Mission," "The Over The Waves Mission," "There's No Biz Like Snow Biz Mission," "The Strangeless Than Fiction Mission," "The Ruckus On The Rails Mission," "The Who's Who That's Who Mission," "The Perilous, Possibly, Pilfered Plans Mission," "The French Collection Mission," "The Outta Sight Blight Mission," "Is There A Doctor In The Greenhouse Mission" and "The Call Me Madame X Mission."

THE HUCKLEBERRY HOUND SHOW

The noble–hearted, slow–talking, Southern–accented blood-hound, Huckleberry Hound, starred and hosted his own series, sponsored by Kellogg's Cereals and syndicated by Screen Gems, the television arm of Columbia Pictures. The program made its debut in 1958, and one year later, became the first animated cartoon to be awarded an Emmy by the Television Academy. By the fall of 1960, an estimated 16,000,000 Americans and foreign viewers were watching the droopy–eyed bloodhound.

The series' two companion cartoons on the show were "Pixie and Dixie," who are perpetually tormented by Mr. Jinks, a beatnik cat, and "Yogi Bear," who pilfers picnic baskets from vacationers at lovely Jellystone National Park. In 1960, "Hokey Wolf" was substituted for Yogi Bear, who starred in his own series the following season. Later, during the show's syndication run, "Yakky Doodle" was pulled from "The Yogi Bear Show" to replace Pixie and Dixie on the show. (For "Yakky Doodle" episodes see "The Yogi Bear Show.") Episodes of "Huckleberry Hound" were later recycled as part of 1967's "Yogi and His Friends." *A Hanna–Barbera Production. Color. Half–hour. Premiered: October 2, 1958. Syndicated.*

Voices:

Huckleberry Hound: Daws Butler, **Pixie:** Don Messick, **Dixie:** Daws Butler, **Mr. Jinks,** the cat: Daws Butler, **Yogi Bear:** Daws Butler, **Boo Boo,** his cub companion: Don Messick, **Ranger John Smith:** Don Messick, **Hokey Wolf:** Daws Butler, **Ding–a–Ling,** the fox: Doug Young

Episodes:

"Huckleberry Hound" (one per show).
1958–1959 "Sheriff Huckleberry," "Sir Huckleberry Hound," "Lion–Hearted Huck," "Rustler–Hustler Huck," "Huckleberry Hound Meets Wee Willy," "Hookey Daze," "Tricky Trapper," "Cock–A–Doodle Huck," "Two Corny Crows," "Freeway Patrol," "Dragon Slayer Huck," "Fireman Huck," "Sheep–Shape Sheepherder," "Skeeter Trouble," "Hokum Smokum," "Bird-

Huckleberry Hound (center) stands as master of ceremonies in "The Huckleberry Hound Show," featuring Jinx the cat, Pixie and Dixie (left), Boo Boo and Yogi Bear (right). © Hanna–Barbera Productions

house Blues," "Barbecue Hound," "Postman Panic," "Lion Tamer Huck," "Ski Champ Chump," "Little Red Riding Huck" and "The Touch Little Termite."

1959–1969 "Grim Pilgrim," "Ten Pin Alley," "Jolly Roger And Out," "Nottingham And Yeggs," "Somebody's Lion," "Cop And Saucer," "Pony Boy Huck," "A Bully Dog," "Huck The Giant Killer," "Pet Vet," "Picadilly Dilly," "Wiki Waki Huck" and "Huck's Huck."

1960–1961 "Spud Dud," "Legion Bound Hound," "Science Friction," "Nuts Over Mutts," "Knight School," "Huck's Hound Table," "Unmashed Avenger" (original working title: "Purple Pumpernickle"), "Hillbilly Luck," "Fast Gun Huck," "Asto–Nut Huck," "Huck And Ladder," "Lawman Huck" and "Cluck And Dagger."

1961–1962 "Caveman Huck," "Huck Of The Irish," "Jungle Bungle," "Bull–Fighter Huck," "Ben Huck," "Huck De Paree," "Bars And Stripes," "Scrubby Brush Man" and "Two For Tee Vee."

"Pixie and Dixie" (one per show).

1958–1959 "Pistol Packin' Pirate," "Judo Jack," "The Little Bird–Mouse," "Kit–Kat–Kit," "Scaredy Cat Dog," "Cousin Tex," "Jinks' Mice Device," "The Ghost With The Most," "Jiggers It's Jinks," "The Ace Of Space," "Jinks Junior," "Puppet Pals," "Jinks The Butler," "Mark Of The Mouse," "Hypnotize Surprise," "Jinks' Flying Carpet," "Dinky Jinks," "Nice Mice," "King–Size Surprise," "Cat–Nap Cat," "Mouse–Nappers" and "Boxing Buddy."

1959–1960 "Sour Puss," "Rapid Robot," "King Size Poodle," "Hi–Fido," "Batty Bat," "Mighty Mite," "Bird–Brained Cat," "Lend–Lease Meece," "A Good Good Fairy," "Heavens to Jinksy," "Goldfish Fever," "Pushy Cat" and "Puss In Boats."

1969–1961 "High Jinks," "Price For Mice," "Plutocrat Cat," "Pied Piper Pipe," "Woo For Two," "Party Peeper Jinks," "A Wise Quack," "Missilebound Cat," "Kind To Meeces Week," "Crewcat," "Jinksed Jinks," "Lightheaded Cat" and "Mouse For Rent."

1961–1962 "Jinks' Jinx," "Fresh Heir," "Mighty Mite," "Hercules," "Bombay Mouse," "Mouse Trapped," "Magician Jinks," "Meece Missiles" and "Homeless Jinks."

"Yogi Bear" (one per show).

1958–1959 "Yogi Bear's Big Break," "Slumber Party Smarty," "Pie Pirates," "Big Bad Bully," "Foxy Hound Dog," "Big Brave

Bear," "Tally Ho–Ho–Ho," "High–Fly–Guy," "Baffled Bear," "The Brave Little Brave," "The Stout Trout," "The Buzzin' Bear," "The Runaway Bear," "Be My Guest Pest," "Duck In Luck," "Bear On A Picnic," "Prize Fight Fright," "Brainy Bear," "Robin Hood Yogi," "Daffy Daddy," "Scooter Looter" and "Hide And Go Peek."

1959–1960 "Show Biz Bear," "Lullabye–Bye Bear," "Bare Face Bear," "Papa Yogi," "Stranger Ranger," "Rah Rah Bear," "Bear For Punishment," "Nowhere Bear," "Wound–Up Bear," "Be–Witched Bear," "Hoodwinked Bear," "Snow White Bear" and "Space Bear."

"Hokey Wolf" (one per show).

1960–1961 "Tricks And Treats," "Hokey Dokey," "Lamb–Hearted Wolf," "Which Witch Is Witch," "Pick A Chick," "Robot Pilot," "Boobs In The Woods," "Castle Hassle," "Booty On The Bounty," "Hokey In The Pokey," "Who's Zoo," "Dogged Sheep Dog," "Too Much To Bear," "Movies Are Bitter Than Ever," "Poached Yeggs," "Rushing Wolf Hound," "The Glass Sneaker," "Indian Giver," "Chock Full Chuck Wagon," "Bring 'Em Back a Live One," "A Star Is Bored," "West Of The Pesos," "Phoney–O And Juliet" and "Hokey's Missing Millions."

1961–1962 "Loot To Boot," "Guesting Games," "Sick Sense" and "Aladdin's Lamb Chops."

HULK HOGAN'S ROCK N' WRESTLING

One of wrestling's most outrageous stars inspired this animated sendup of the popular spectator sport, lending his name but not his voice to the series. Backed by a strong rock music soundtrack, the show featured stories about the wild and outrageous personalities of the high contact sport as well as battles between opponents on the wrestling mats. *A DIC Enterprise Production in association with Titan Sports. Color. One Hour. Premiered CBS: September 14, 1985–September 5, 1987.*

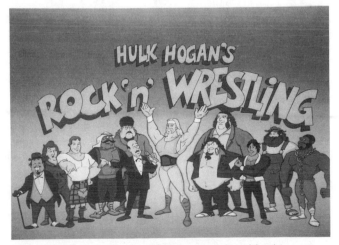

Famed body wrestler Hulk Hogan is joined by his unsavory looking cast in the CBS network series, "Hulk Hogan's Rock 'N' Wrestling." © Titan Sports Inc. and DIC Animation City Inc.

Voices:

Hulk Hogan: Brad Garret, **Capt. Lou Albano:** George R. DiCenzo, **Junkyard Dog:** James Avery, **Andre The Giant:** Ranald A. Feinberg, **Moolah/Richter:** Jodi Carlisle, **Volkoff:** Ronald Gans, **Roddy:** Charlie Adler, **Iron Shiek:** Aron Kincaid, **Big John Studd:** Chuck Licini, **Mr. Fuji:** Ernest Harada, **Tito Santana:** Joey Pento, **Superfly Snuka:** Lewis Arquette, **Mean Gene:** Neil Ross, **Hillbilly Jim:** Pat Fraley

Episodes:

"Cheaters Never Prosper," "The Four–Legged Pickpocket," "Andre's Giant Problem," "Clean Gene," "Gorilla My Dreams," "Driving Me Crazy," "Junkenstein," "Small But Mighty," "The Wrestler's New Clothes," "A Lesson In Scouting," "Rock 'N' Zombies," "The Duke Of Piperton," "Robin Hulk And His Merry Wrestlers," "The Last Resort," "Hog Society," "Wrestling Roommates," "Bucket," "Moolah's Ugly Salon," "Ballot Box Boneheads," "Ali Bano And The 40 Geeks," "Captain Lou's Crash Diet," "Muscle Madness," "Ten Little Wrestlers," "Big John's Car Lot," "Big Top Boobs," "The Foster Wrestler," "Ballet Buffoons," "Battle Of The Bands," "Amazons Just Wanna Have Fun," "The Art Of Wrestling," "The Blue Lagoons," "The Superfly Express," "Junkyard Dog's Junkyard Dog," "The Junkyard Dog," "Ghost Wrestlers," "My Fair Wrestler," "Rowdy Roddy Reforms," "The Wrong Stuff" and "Three Little Hulks."

I AM THE GREATEST: THE ADVENTURES OF MUHAMMAD ALI

Former heavyweight boxing champ Muhammad Ali supplied his own voice for this animated series which blended comedy, adventure and mystery in situations shaped around Ali's heroics. Joining him in his encounters are his niece and nephew, Nicky and Damon, and his public relations agent, Frank Bannister. Although Ali was a champion of the boxing ring, the series did not deliver a knockout blow in the ratings, and the

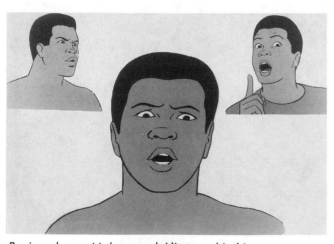

Boxing champ Muhammad Ali starred in his own cartoon series for NBC. The show received poor ratings and was pulled from the Saturday morning lineup midway into the season. © Farmhouse Films

series was cancelled at mid–season. *A Farmhouse Films Production. Color. Half–hour. Premiered on CBS: September 10, 1977–January 28, 1978.*

Voices:

Muhammad Ali: Himself, **Nicky,** his niece: Patrice Carmichael, **Damon,** his nephew: Casey Carmichael, **Frank Bannister:** Himself

Additional voices:

Bob Arbogast, Michael Baldwin, Jim Brik, Booker Bradshaw, Dianne Oyama Dixon, Joan Gerber, Peter Haas, Peter Kaskell, Stanley Jones, James Levon Johnson, Gene Moss, Wali Muhammad, Richard Paul, David Roberts, Paul Shively

Episodes:

"The Great Alligator," "The Air Fair Affair," "The Littlest Runner," "Ali's African Adventure," "Superstar," "The Haunted Park," "Caught In The Wild," "Volcano Island," "Oasis Of The Moon," "The Great Bluegrass Mountain Race," "The Werewolf Of Devil's Creek," "Sissy's Climb" and "Terror In The Deep."

INCH HIGH PRIVATE EYE

The Finkerton Detective Agency puts its best man on the case: the world's smallest private eye, Inch High, who is fashioned after Maxwell Smart, agent 86, of TV's "Get Smart." The thumbnail–sized detective relies on various weapons and disguises to capture criminals. His best friend in the world is his dog, Braveheart. *A Hanna–Barbera Production. Color. Half–hour. Premiered on NBC: September 8, 1973–August 31, 1974.*

Voices:

Inch High: Lennie Weinrib, **Lori,** his niece: Kathy Gori, **Gator,** his aide: Bob Lutell, **Mr. Finkerton,** his boss: John Stephenson, **Mrs. Finkerton:** Jean VanderPyl, **Braveheart,** Inch High's dog: Don Messick

Episodes:

"Diamonds Are A Crook's Best Friend," "You Oughta Be In Pictures," "The Smugglers," "Counterfeit Story," "The Doll Maker," "Mummy's Curse," "Music Maestro," "High Fashion," "Dude Cry," "The World's Greatest Animals," "The Cat Burglars," "Super Flea" and "The Return of Spumoni."

THE INCREDIBLE HULK

NBC added this series, featuring the hulking Marvel superhero, to its Saturday morning cartoon roster late in the 1984–1985 season. The program repeated episodes which first aired on the same network as part of "The Incredible Hulk/Amazing Spider–Man Hour." (See that series for episodic titles.) *A Marvel production. Color. Half–hour. Premiered on NBC: December 15, 1984–September 7, 1985.*

Voices:

Michael Bell, Susan Blu, Bill Callaway, Hamilton Camp, Victoria Carroll, Hans Conried, Robert Cruz, Jerry Dexter, George DiCenzo, Alan Dinehart, Walker Edmiston, Michael Evans, Al

Fann, Ron Feinberg, Elliott Field, June Foray, Pat Fraley, Kathy Garver, Dan Gilvezan, John Haymer, Bob Holt, Michael Horton, Stan Jones, Sally Julian, Stan Lee, Anne Lockhart, Keye Luke, Dennis Marks, Allan Melvin, Shepard Menken, Vic Perrin, Bob Ridgely, Neilson Ross, Stanley Ralph Ross, Michael Rye, Marilyn Schreffler, John Stephenson, Janet Waldo, B. J. Ward, Frank Welker, William Woodson, Alan Young

THE INCREDIBLE HULK/ AMAZING SPIDER–MAN HOUR

New episodes of the Incredible Hulk were added to this hour–long fantasy series which combined previously broadcast episodes of the popular Saturday–morning series, "Spider–Man and His Amazing Friends." *A Marvel Production. Color. One hour. Premiered on NBC: September 19, 1982–September 8, 1984.*

Voices:

Jack Angel, Michael Bell, Lee Briley, Bill Boyett, Cory Burton, Susan Blu, Wally Burr Bill Callaway, Hamilton Camp, Victoria Carroll, Phil Clarke, Hans Conreid, Rege Cordic, Henry Corden, Brad Crandall, Robert Cruz, Peter Cullen, Brian Cummings, Jeff David, Jack DeLeon, Jerry Dexter, George DiCenzo, Alan Dinehart, Walker Edmiston, Michael Evans, Al Fann, Ron Feinberg, Elliott Field, Ron Feinberg, June Foray, Pat Fraley, Brain Fuld, Kathy Garver, Linda Gary, Dan Gilvezan, John Haymer, Bob Holt, Michael Horton, Ralph James, Lynn Johnson, Stanley Jones, Sally Julian, Lee Lampson, Stan Lee, Anne Lockhart, Morgan Lofting, Keye Luke, Dennis Marks, Mona Marshall, John Mayer, Alan Melvin, Shepard Menken, Don Messick, Vic Perrin, Tony Pope, Richard Ramos, Bob Ridgely, Neilson Ross, Gene Ross, Stanley Ralph Ross, Michael Rye, Marilyn Schreffler, John Stephenson, Ted Schwartz, Gary Seger, Michael Sheehan, Andre Stojka, Janet Waldo, B. J. Ward, Frank Welker, Paul Winchell, William Woodson, Alan Young

Episodes:

"Incredible Hulk." (one episode per show) "Tomb Of The Unknown Hulk," "Prisoner Of The Monster," "Origins Of The Hulk," "When Monsters Meet," "The Cyclops Project," "Bruce Banner—Unmasked!," "The Creature And The Cavegirl," "It Lives! It Grows! It Destroys!," "The Incredible Shrinking Hulk," "Punks On Wheels," "Enter: The She–Hulk," "The Boy Who Saw Tomorrow" and "The Hulk Destroys Bruce Banner."
"Spider–Man." (two episodes per show) "Bubble, Bubble, Oil And Trouble," "Dr. Doom–Master Of The World," "Lizards, Lizards Everywhere," "Curiosity Killed The Spider–Man," "The Sandman Is Coming," "When Magneto Speaks . . . People Listen," "The Pied Piper Of New York Town," "The Doctor Prescribes Doom," "Carnival Of Crime," "Revenge Of The Green Goblin," "Triangle Of Evil," "The A–B–C's Of D–O–O–M," "The Sidewinder Strikes," "The Hunter And The Hunted," "The Incredible Shrinking Spider–Man," "The Unfathomable Professor Gizmo," "Canon Of Doom," "The Capture Of Captain America," "The Doom Report," "The Web Of Nephilia," "Countdown To Doom," "Arsenic And Aunt May," "The Vulture Has Landed," "Wrath Of The Sub–Mariner," "The Return Of Kingpin" and "Under The Wizard's Spell."

THE INHUMANOIDS

A group of ancient subhuman monsters from the center of the earth escape their fiery dwellings to wreck havoc and destruction. Only the Earth Corps, a team of brilliant human scientists, have the courage and scientific knowledge to combat the creatures. Two episodes originally aired as part of Marvel's "Super Saturday" and "Super Sunday" programs in January, 1986. *A Marvel Production in association with Sunbow Productions. Color. Half–hour. Premiered: September 21, 1986. Syndicated.*

Voices:

Michael Bell, William Callaway, Fred Collins, Brad Crandel, Dick Gautier, Ed Gilbert, Chris Latta, Neil Ross, Stanley Ralph Ross, Richard Sanders, Susan Silo, John Stephenson

Episodes:

"Cyphenoid," "The Surma Plan," "Cult Darkness," "Negative Polarity," "The Evil eye," "Primal Passions," "The Masterson Team" and "Auger For President."

INSPECTOR GADGET

Don Adams, formerly TV's Maxwell Smart, Agent 86, voiced this bumbling Inspector Clouseau–type, originally based in a small provincial town as a local police officer, who becomes the first gadgetized and bionic inspector working for Interpol. With the intelligent help of his young niece, Penny, and faithful, long–suffering dog, Brain, Gadget always manages to vanquish his enemies and come out victorious. *A DIC Enterprise Production in association with Field Communications Corp. and Lexington Broadcast. Color. Half–hour. Premiered on Nickelodeon: October 5, 1987. Syndicated.*

Voices:

Inspector Gadget: Don Adams, **Penny,** his niece: Cree Summer Francks, Holly Berger, **Brain,** his dog: Frank Welker, **Chief Quimby:** Maurice LaMarche, **Capeman:** Townsend Coleman, **Dr. Claw:** Frank Welker

Episodes:

1987–1988 "Monster Lake," "Down On The Farm," "Gadget At The Circus," "The Amazon," "Health Spa," "The Boat," "Haunted Castle," "Race To The Finish," "The Ruby," "A Star Is Lost," "All That Glitters," "Movie Set," "Amusement Park," "Art Heist," "Volcano Island," "The Invasion," "The Infiltration," "The Curse Of The Pharoah," "Mad Trap," "Basic Training," "Sleeping Gas," "Gadget's Replacement," "Greenfinger," "Gadget Goes West," "Lauch Time," "Photo Safari," "The Coo–Coo Clock Caper," "The Japanese Connection," "Arabian Nights," "A Clear Case," "Dutch Treat," "The Great Divide," "Eye Of The Dragon," "Doubled Agent," "Plantform Of The Opera," "Don't Hold Your Breath," "Gone Went The Wind," "King Wrong," "Pirate Island," "M.A.D. Academy," "No Flies On Us," "Luck Of The Irish," "Prince Of The Gypsies," "Old Man Of The Mountain," "The Emerald Duck," "Do Unto Udders," "Did You Myth Me?," "A Bad Altitude," "Funny Money," "Follow That Jet," "Dry Spell," "Smeldorado," "Quimby Exchange," "Weather In Tibet," "Unhenged," "Snakin' All Over," "In Seine,"

"Tree Guesses," "Birds Of A Feather," "So It Is Written," "Fang The Wonder Dog," "School For Pickpockets," "Quizz Master" and "Gadget In Winterland" (pilot).

1988–1989 "Magic Gadget," "The Great Wambini's Seance," "Wambini Predicts," "The Capeman Cometh," "Crashcourse In Crime," "Gadget's Gadgets," "Gadget In Minimadness," "The Incredible Shrinking Gadget," "Gadget Meets The Grappler," "Ghost Catchers," "Busy Signal," "Bad Dreams Are Made Of This," "Focus On Gadget," "Mad In The Moon," "N.S.F. Gadget," "Tryannosaurus Gadget," "Gadget's Roma," "Gadget's Clean Sweep," "Gadget Meets The Clan," "Gadget And Old Lace" and "Gadget And The Red Rose."

JABBERJAW

Capitalizing on the movie *Jaws,* Hanna–Barbera created the lovable but stupid white shark, Jabberjaw, who sounds like Curly Howard of The Three Stooges. He serves as mascot for four teenagers and their rock group living in an underwater civilization in A.D. 2021. The creators were Joe Ruby and Ken Spears. *A Hanna–Barbera Production. Color. Half–hour. Premiered on ABC: September 11, 1976–September 3, 1978.*

Voices:

Jabberjaw: Frank Welker, **Clam–Head:** Barry Gordon, **Bubbles:** Julie McWhirter, **Shelly:** Pat Paris, **Biff:** Tommy Cook

Great white shark Jabberjaw delivers a new beat with four teenagers and their rock group in the Saturday morning fantasy/adventure series "Jabberjaw."
© Hanna–Barbera Productions

Episodes:

"Dr. Lo Has Got To Go," "There's No Place Like Outer Space," "Run, Jabber, Run," "Atlantis Get Lost," "The Sourpuss Octopus," "Hang Onto Your Hat, Jabber," "The Great White Shark Switch," "Claim–Jumped Jabber," "Ali Jabber And The Secret Thieves," "Help, Help, It's The Phantom Kelp," "No Helpin' The Sculpin'," "The Bermuda Triangle Tangle," "Malice In Aqualand," "The Fast–Paced Chase Race," "There's No Heel Like El Eel" and "The Piranha Plot."

THE JACKSON 5IVE

Jackie, Marion, Jermaine, Tito and Michael, members of Motown's popular rock group, The Jackson 5ive, star in real–life situations that spotlight their comedic lifestyles, happenings and misadventures in cartoon form. *A Halas and Batchelor Production for Rankin–Bass Productions and Motown. Color. Half–hour. Premiered on ABC: September 11, 1971–September 1, 1973.*

Voices:

Jackie: Sigmund Jackson, **Tito:** Toriano Jackson, **Jermaine:** Jermaine Jackson, **David:** Marion Jackson, **Michael:** Michael Jackson

Additional Voices:

Paul Frees, Edmund Silvers, Joe Cooper

Episodes:

"It All Started With . . .," "Pinestock U. S. A.," "Drafted," "Mistaken Identity," "Bongo Baby Bongo," "Winner's Circle," "Cinderjackson," "The Tiny Five," "The Grovatron," "Ray And Charles: Superstars," "The Wizard Of Soul," "Jackson Island," "Farmer Jackson," "The Michael Look," "Jackson Street, U. S. A.," "Rasho Jackson," "The Rare Pearl," "Who's Hoozis," "Moe White," "Groove The Chief," "Michael In Wonderland," "Jackson And The Beanstalk" and "The Opening Act."

JAYCE AND THE WHEELED WARRIORS

Jayce, the son of a famous scientist, and his space–age crew, known as the Lightning League—Merc, a mercenary pilot; Gillian, a wise wizard; Flora, a half–plant/half–human girl; and Oon, a mechanical squire/slave—travel the universe in search of his father to reunite the root of a plant which can destroy Saw Boss and his evil plant followers, the Monster Minds, from taking over the universe. The series was based on the popular toy line. *A DIC Enterprise Production in association with WWP Productions. Color. Half–hour. Premiered: September, 1985. Syndicated.*

Voices:

Audric, Jayce's father: Dan Hennessey, **Jayce:** Darin Baker, **Flora:** Valerie Politis, **Oon:** Luba Goy, **Gillian:** Charles Joliffe, **Herc:** Len Carlson, **Saw Boss:** Giulio Kukurugya, **Monster Minds:** Dan Hennessey, Len Carlson, John Stocker, **Ko Kruiser:** Dan Hennessey, **Sawtrooper:** Dan Hennessey, **Terror Tank:** Len Carlson, **Gun Grinner:** John Stocker

The rash of rock group—inspired cartoon series included an animated version of famed Motown group "The Jackson 5ive." © Rankin—Bass Productions

Episodes:

"Escape From The Garden," "The Vase of Xiang," "Steel Against Shadow," "Silver Crusaders," "Ghostship," "Flora, Fauna And The Monster Minds," "Fire And Ice," "Space Outlaws," "Future Of The Future," "Underwater," "Frostworld," "Critical Mass," "The Purple Tome," "Hook, Line And Sinker," "Bloodstone," "The Slaves Of Adelbaren," "The Hunt," "Blockade Runners," "The Sleeping Princess," "Deadly Reunion," "Sky Kingdom," "Quest Into Shadow," "Unexpected Trouble," "Bounty Hunters," "Double Deception," "Gate World," "Space Thief," "Moon Magic," "Affair Of Honor," "Doom Flower," "The Stallions Of Sandeen," "Brain Trust," "Lighting Strikes Twice," "The Liberty Stone," "The Vines: The Liberty Stone, Part II," "The Spacefighter: The Liberty Stone, Part III," "Heart Of Paxtar: The Liberty Stone, Part IV," "Appointment At Forever: The Liberty Stone, Part V," "What's Going On?," "Dark Singer," "Swamp Witch," "Deadly Reflections," "Early Warning," "A Question Of Conscience," "Life Ship," "The Mirage Makers," "Do Not Disturb," "Dream World," "The Children Of Solarus II," "The Gardener," "Armada," "The Chimes Of Sharpis," "Galaxy Gamester," "Circus Planet," "Common Bond," "Mistress of Soul Tree," "The Life Eater," "Wasteland," "The Oracle," "Short Circuit, Long Wait," "Time And Time Again," "The Source," "The Raid," "The Squire Smith" and "Final Ride At Journey's End."

JEANNIE

In this cartoon spin—off of TV's "I Dream of Jeannie," Center City High School teenager Corry Anders discovers a magic lamp containing a lady genie and her bumbling apprentice, Babu. After he releases them from the bottle, the two become his grateful servants using their magical powers to help the young student out of trouble. The show was the top—rated cartoon series in its initial season. Actor Mark Hamill, of *Star Wars,* provided Corry's voice. *A Hanna—Barbera Production in association with Screen Gems. Color. Half—hour. Premiered on CBS: September 9, 1973—August 30, 1975.*

Voices:

Jeannie: Julie McWhirter, **Babu:** Joe Besser, **Corry:** Mark Hamill, **Henry Glopp, Corry's** friend: Bob Hastings, **Mrs. Anders,** Corry's mother: Janet Waldo

Additional Voices:

John Stephenson, Sherry Jackson, Michael Bell, Susan Silo, Tina Holland, Indira Dirks, Gay Hartwig, Vince Van Patten, Judy Strangis, Hal Smith, Julie Bennett, Vic Perrin

Episodes:

"Surf's Up," "The Decathalon," "The Great Ski Robbery," "Survival Course," "The Power Failure," "The Dognappers," "The Pigeon," "Helen Of Troy," "The Sailors," "The Kid Brother," "The Blind Date," "The Commercial," "Don Juan," "The Dog," "The Jinx" and "The Wish."

JEM

Jerrica Benton, a beautiful, ambitious and brilliant music executive and founder of a home for teenage runaways (named in part after her music company, Starlight Music), has a double identity: through a magical transformation, she becomes JEM, a glamorous rock star, who wages outrageous battles of the bands. The series was first introduced in 1985 as a segment within Marvel's "Super Sunday" show. The segment was met by such enormous viewer enthusiasm that after one season Marvel decided spin it off into a weekly, syndicated series. *A Marvel Production in association with Sunbow Production. Color. Half–hour. Premiered: August 3, 1986. Syndicated.*

Voices:

Charlie Adler, Tammy Amerson, Patricia Albrecht, Marlene Aragon, Allison Argo, Bobbi Block, Cathianne Blore, Sue Blue, Ellen Bernfield, Jan Britain, Anne Bryant, Wally Burr, Angela Cappelli, Kim Carlson, T. K. Carter, Cathy Cavadini, Linda Dangcil, Louise Dorsey, Walker Edmiston, Laurie Faso, Ed Gilbert, Dan Gilvezan, Diva Grey, Desiree Goyette, Lani Groves, Michael Horton, Ford Kinder, Jeff Kinder, Clyde Kusatu, Ulanda McCulloug, Kathi Marcuccio, Cindy McGee, Samantha Newark, Noelle North, Britta Phillips, Neil Ross, Jack Roth, Michael Sheehan, Hazel Shermet, Tony St. James, Terri Textor, Florence Warner, Valerie Wilson, Keone Young

Episodes:

1986–1987 "Falling Star," "Colliding Star," "Rising Star," "The World Hunger Shindig," "Adventures In China," "The Last Resorts," "In Stitches," "The Beginning," "The Betrayal," "Kimber's Rebellion," "Frame–Up," "The Battle Of The Bands," "The Music Awards" (Part 1), "The Music Awards" (Part 2), "The Rock Fashion Book," "Broadway Magic," "In Search Of The Stolen Album," "Hot Time In Hawaii," "The Princess And The Singer," "Island Of Deception," "Old Meets New," "Intrigue At the Indy 500," "The Jem Jam" (Part 1), "The Jem Jam" (Part 2), "Culture Clash" and "Glitter And Gold."
1987–1988 "Scandal," "Presidential Dilemma," "Talent Search" (Part 1), "Talent Search" (Part 2), "Treasure Hunt," "Trick Or Techrat," "The Bands Break Up," "Danse Time," "The Fan," "Journey To Shangra La," "One Jem Too Many," "Music Is Magic," "Father's Day," "The Jazz Player," "Rock 'N' Roll

Express," "The Middle Of Nowhere," "Roxy Rumbles," "Aztec Enchantment," "KJEM," "Video Wars," "Renaissance Woman," "Alone Again," "Marid Gras," "Homeland, Heartland," "Journey Through Time," "Beauty And The Rock Promoter," "Britrock," "Out Of The Past," "Hollywood Jem" (Part 1: "For Your Consideration"), "Hollywood Jem" (Part 2: "And The Winner Is . . ."), "The Stingers Hit Town" (Part 1), "The Stingers Hit Town" (Part 2), "Mid Summer Night's Madness," "The Day The Music Died," "That Old Houdini Magic," "Your 15 Minutes Are Up," "A Change Of Heart," "Riot's Hope" and "A Father Should Be . . ."

THE JETSONS

Hanna–Barbera's space–age answer to their prehistoric blockbuster, "The Flintstones," brought the Jetson family of the 21st century into living rooms in 1963. For a one-season show, the program remains immensely popular among viewers.

Stories depict the prospects of living in a futuristic society and showcase George Jetson, employee of Spacely Space Age Sprockets; his lovely, practical wife, Jane; his teeny–bopping daughter, Judy; and his inventive son, Elroy. They have the luxury of computer–operated housing facilities, a robot maid named Rosie and compact flying vehicles that fold into the size of a brief case.

In 1984, Hanna–Barbera produced a new series of half–hour episodes for first–run syndication, which were voiced by most of the original cast. *A Hanna–Barbera Production. Color. Half–hour. Premiered on ABC: September 23, 1962– September, 1964. Rebroadcast on CBS: September 4, 1965– September 5, 1966; Rebroadcast on NBC: September 10, 1966– September 7, 1967; Rebroadcast on CBS: September 13, 1969– September 5, 1970; Rebroadcast on NBC: September 11, 1971– August 31, 1975; February 3, 1979–September 5, 1981. Premiere (new series): September, 1984. Syndicated.*

Voices:

George Jetson: George O'Hanlon, **Jane Jetson:** Penny Singleton, **Judy Jetson:** Janet Waldo, **Elroy Jetson:** Daws Butler, **Cosmo C. Spacely,** George's boss: Mel Blanc, **Astro,** the family dog: Don Messick, **Rosie,** the robot maid: Jean VanderPyl, **Henry Orbit,** janitor: Howard Morris, **Cogswell,** owner of Cogswell Cog: Daws Butler, **Uniblab:** Don Messick

Additional Voices:

Shepard Menken

Episodes:

1962–1963 "A Date With Jet Screamer," "Rosie The Robot," "Jetson's Nite Out," "The Space Car," "The Coming Of Astro," "The Good Little Scouts," "Elroy's TV Show," "The Flying Suite," "Rosie's Boyfriend," "Uniblab," "Astro's Top Secret," "A Visit From Grandpa," "Las Venus," "Elroy's Pal," "Test Pilot," "Millionaire Astro," "The Little Man," "Jane's Driving Lesson," "G. I. Jetson," "Miss Solar System," "Private Property," "Dude Planet," "TV Or Not TV" and "Elroy's Mob."
1984–1985 (syndication) "The Vacation," "Space Bond," "Elroy Meets Orbitty," "Elroy In Wonderland," "Swiss Family Jetsons," "Winner Takes All," " High Moon," "Team Spirit,"

Space–age living always resulted in high comedy exploits in "The Jetsons." © Hanna–Barbera Productions

"Super George," "Little Bundle Of Trouble," "Dance Time," "Judy's Birthday Surprise," "High Tech Wreck," "Rip Off Rosie," "The Mirrormorph," "Mother's Day For Rosie," "Fugitive Fleas," "Far Out Father," "Astro's Big Moment," "The Cosmic Courtship Of . . . ," "Fantasy Planet," "Sno Relative," "One Strike You're Out," "Solar Snoops," "Rosie Come Home," "Family Fallout," "Instant Replay," "Haunted Halloween," "Future Tense," "The Wrong Stuff," "Judy Takes Off," "A Jetson Christmas Carol," "Dog Daze Afternoon," "Robots Revenge," "Jetson's Millions," "To Tell The Truth," "Judy's Elopement," "Grandpa And The Galactic . . . ," "Boy George" and "The Century's Best"

1987–1988 "Crime Games," "Astronomical I. Q.," "9 To 5 To 9," "Invisibly Yours, George," "Father/Daughter Dance," "Clean As A Hound's Tooth," "Wedding Bells For Rosie," "The Odd Pod," "Two Many Georges" and "Spacely For A Day."

JIM AND JUDY IN TELELAND

The various adventures of two children are related in this highly imaginative limited animated adventure show which was first produced in 1949–1950, combining cut–out animation and animation cels to create each story. The two characters, who began and closed each episode framed inside a television, encountered a host of unbelievable characters along the way—spies, pirates, giant insects and others—in this syndicated series which is believed to have been aired in weekly, five–minute time slots. Fifty–two episodes were produced in all. The program was later retitled "Bob and Betty in Adventureland." *A Television Screen/Film Flash Inc. Production. Black–and–white. Five minutes. Premiered: 1953. Syndicated.*

Voices:
Jim: Merrill Jolls, **Judy:** Honey McKenzie

JOHNNY CYPHER IN DIMENSION ZERO

Brilliant Earth scientist Johnny Cypher finds that he has superhuman powers enabling him to travel through the dimensions of inner–space and combat sinister forces. Each half–hour program featured four six–minute episodes. *A Seven Arts Production in association with Joe Oriolo Films. Color. Half–hour. Premiered: February, 1967. Syndicated.*

Voices:
Johnny Cypher: Paul Hecht, **Zeni**, his female assistant: Corinne Orr, **Rhom**, galactic being: Gene Allen

Episodes:
(four per show) "Rhom, Super Criminal," "Attack From Out Of Space," "The Menace Of Maroo," "The Eye Of Ramapoor," "The Deafening Sound Of Silence," "The Castle Of Mr. Mist," "The Butronic Troublemaker," "Menace Of The Flying Saucer," "The Shockman Of Shardu," "The Traiterous Dr. Flood," "Shoot–Out In Space," "Ten Top Diamond," "Invisible Fire Beam," "Liquefier Gun," "Seeds Of Chaos," "Barclay's Bullet," "Zomar The Merciless," "Johnny Cypher's Twin," "Ship Of Captain Krool," "Forget Ray Of Egghead," "The Deadly Beams," "The Giant Robot," "Johnny Versus Zena," "Wild Animal Hunter," "Invisible Enemy," "Everything Falls Up," "The Space Party," "Endless Zero," "The World Of Lost Men," "Johnny's Giant Friends," "The Doll Invaders," "The Interplanetary Olympiad," "The Crystal Cage," "The Runaway Rocket," "The

A brilliant Earth scientist travels through the dimensions of inner–space to combat sinister forces in "Johnny Cypher In Dimension Zero." © Seven Arts Productions/Joe Oriolo Films

Crooked Radar Beam," "The Rescue Of Robinson Cosmo," "Stolen Space Station," "The Mutant Monsters," "The Gravity Belt Mystery," "Snarl's Sinister Surprise," "Zero Hour For Glenn City," "The Robot," "Song Of Doom," "Zero Vs. Zero," "The 4-Armed Man," "Gorloch Against The Universe," "Return Of Frankenstein," "Mister Mist," "Mad Magic Of Eerin," "The Dyre Moth," "Mystery Of The Missing Pilots," "The Black Vapor," "8,000 Degrees Fahrenheit," "Multiplier Gun," "The Martian Plague," "The One-Inch Johnny Cypher," "The Lost Planet," "The Torchmen," "The Thing From Sea," "Gothan The Terrible," "Mission To Jandor," "Invasion Of The Shadowmen," "Billion Dollar Robbery," "Monster Of Mists," "The Evil Eye," "The Wandering World," "Race Against Time," "The Red Forest," "Tidal Wave Of Terror," "The Stolen Satellite," "Crisis On Volcos," "Rhom's Double," "The Mysterious Signal," "The Tower Of Majak," "Giganticus Serum," "The Abominable Snowman," "The Paper Perisher," "The Door To The Future," "Dangerous Games," "The Menace From Mercury," "Space Vacuums," "The Man Duplicator," "The Wild Blue Trap," "The Saturian Triclops," "The Incredible Sponge Man," "The Planet Of Little Men," "The Mothmen," "The Fear Of The Year," "Mission Miraculous," "The Pet Collectors," "Nero's Revenge," "The Circus Of Terror," "The Elusive Space Monster," "Time Marches Back," "Space Pirates," "The Deadly Blossom," "Magnetic Mayhem," "Rescue On The Moon," "Decent Into Peril," "The Time Warp," "Space Prospectors," "The Devil's Diamonds," "Electronic Monster," "Planet Of Gold," "Peril From The Past," "Farewell, Dr. Root," "Captain Nogo," "The Glass Giant," "Expedition To The Arctic," "20,000 Dangers Under The Sea," "The Trap," "An Element Of Danger," "Terror In The Toy Shop," "The Man With The Golden Hands," "The Hidden Peril," "Borgo's Beam," "Red Hot Planet," "The Coreman," "The Photo Spy," "The Gigantic Garble," "The Quick Quake Maker," "The Vularian," "Mission of Mercy," "Too Many Johnnies," "Strangest World Of All," "Operation Freeze," "The Haunted Planet," "Mysterious Meteorites," "Evil Mr. Esp" and "No More Dimension Zero."

JOKEBOOK

Twenty to 25 individually styled animated jokes selected from among a wide assortment of foreign and student films, award-winning cartoon shorts and original concepts highlight this colorful fantasy showcase of entertaining animation from throughout the world. Segments ranged from 20-seconds to three minutes each.

Marty Murphy, a cartoonist for various national magazines including *Playboy,* was a consultant on the series. Frank Ridgeway, syndicated cartoonist for hundreds of newspapers, and Jack Bonestell, cartoonist for national magazines, also contributed their unique styles to the show.

Some of the films shown included the Oscar-winning animated short subjects, "Crunch Bird" and "The Fly," which took "Best Animated Short Film" honors at the Academy Awards. The show's theme song was sung by comedian Scatman Crothers. *A Hanna-Barbera Production. Color. Half-hour. Premiered on ABC: April 23, 1982-May 7, 1982.*

Voices:

Henry Corden, Bob Hastings, Joan Gerber, Joyce Jameson, Don Messick, Sidney Miller, Robert Allen Ogle, Ronnie Schell, Marilyn Schreffler, Hal Smith, John Stephenson, Janet Waldo, Lennie Weinrib, Frank Welker

Episodes:

"Jokebook #1," "Jokebook #2," "Jokebook #3," "Jokebook #4," "Jokebook #5," "Jokebook #6" and "Jokebook #7."

JOSIE AND THE PUSSYCATS

Music promoter Alexander Cabot manages an all-girl rock group, the Pussycats, led by the ambitious Josie, whose desire to be the center of attention often results in a blow to her ego. The singing on the show was performed by Cathy Douglas, Patricia Holloway and Cherie Moore (short for Cheryl Ann Stopylmore), who is now better known as Cheryl Ladd. The character of Alexandra Cabot was voiced by Sherry Alberoni, a former Mouseketeer. *A Hanna-Barbera and Radio Comics Inc. Production. Color. Half-hour. Premiered on CBS: September 12, 1970-September 2, 1972.*

Voices:

Josie: Janet Waldo, **Melody,** the dim-witted blonde drummer: Jackie Joseph, **Valerie,** the guitarist: Barbara Pariot, **Alan:** Jerry Dexter, **Alexander Cabot III:** Casey Kasem, **Alexandra Cabot,** his sister: Sherry Alberoni, **Sebastian,** their pet cat: Don Messick

Episodes:

"The Nemo's A No No Affair," "A Greenthumb Is Not A Goldfinger," "The Secret Six Secret," "Chili Today and Hot Tamale," "The Midas Mix-Up," "Swap Plot Flop," "X Marks The Spot," "Never Mind A Master Mind," "Plateau Of The Apes Plot," "All Wrong In Hong Kong," "Strangemoon Over Miami," "The Great Pussycat Chase," "Melody Memory Mix-Up," "Spy School Spoof," "The Jumpin' Jupiter Affair" and "Don't Count On A Countess."

JOSIE AND THE PUSSYCATS IN OUTER SPACE

The Pussycats (Josie, Melody and Valerie) and company are accidentally launched into outer space when they become trapped in a NASA space capsule. Joined by their manager, Alexander; his sister, Alexandra; Alan; and a new member, Bleep the space mascot, the three teenage girls explore the vast regions of the universe. *A Hanna-Barbera and Radio Comics Inc. Production. Color. Half-hour. Premiered on CBS: September 9, 1972-January 26, 1974.*

Voices:

Josie: Janet Waldo, **Melody:** Jackie Joseph, **Valerie:** Barbara Pariot, **Alan:** Jerry Dexter, **Alexander Cabot III:** Casey Kasem, **Alexandra Cabot:** Sherry Alberoni, **Sebastian,** their cat: Don Messick, **Bleep,** the space mascot: Don Messick, **Group vocalists:** Cathy Douglas, Patricia Holloway, Cherie Moore

Episodes:

"Where's Josie?," "Make Way For The Multi–Men," "The Sleeping Planet," "Alien Alan," "The Water Planet," "The Sun Haters," "The Mini–Man Menace," "The Space Pirates," "Anything You Can Zoo," "Now You See Them, Now You Don't," "The Four–Eyed Dragon Of Cygnon," "The Forward Backward People Of Xarook," "The Hollow Planet," "All Hail Goddess Melody," "Outer Space Ark" and "Warrior Women Of Amazonia."

THE KARATE KID

The famed motion picture starring Ralph Macchio and Pat Morita inspired this animated adaptation about the continuing adventures of Daniel and Mr. Miyagi, stressing positive values. *A DIC Enterprises Production in association with Jerry Weintraub/Columbia Pictures Television Production. Color. Half–hour. Premiered on NBC: September 9, 1989–September 1, 1990. Syndicated.*

Voices:

Daniel: Joe Dedio, **Miyagi Yakuga:** Robert Ito, **Taki:** Janice Kawaye

Episodes:

"My Brother's Keeper," "The Greatest Victory," "The Homecoming," "The Tomorrow Man," "The Paper Hero," "All The World His Stage," "Over The Rainbow," "Walkabout," "East Meets West," "The Hunt," "The Gray Ghosts," "The Return Of The Shrine" and "A Little World Of His Own."

KIDD VIDEO

Zapped into the 4th dimension, four talented teenage rock musicians visit the wacky world of the Flip Side, a strange, bizarre place where the laws of nature don't exist and anything

Miyagi (center) demonstrates the fine art of self–defense for students Taki and Daniel in the animated adaptation of the famed motion picture "The Karate Kid." © Columbia Pictures Television Inc. All rights reserved. (Courtesy: DIC Enterprises Inc.)

is possible. It is a bright, airy, upbeat, non–threatening environment, except for the diabolical Master Blaster of Bad Vibes, who with the dubious help of The Copy Cats, tries stealing the famed musical group's sound. The live action/animated program was further highlighted by Top 40 hits, which were inventively animated. *A DIC Enterprise Production in association with Saban Productions. Color. Half–hour. Premiered on NBC: September 15, 1984–September 6, 1986.*

Voices:

Kidd, the group's leader: Bryan Scott, **Ash:** Steve Alterman, **Whiz:** Robbie Rist, **Carla:** Gabrielle Bennett, **Glitter,** Kidd Video's friend: Cathy Cavadini, **Master Blaster:** Peter Renaday, **The Copy Cats: Fat Cat:** Marshall Efron, **She Lion:** Susan Silo, **Cool Kitty:** Robert Towers

Episodes:

1984–1985 "To Beat The Band," "The Master Zapper," "Woofers And Tweeters," "Barnacolis," "The Pink Sphinx," "Cienega," "The Lost Note," "Music Sports," "Chameleons," "Euphonius, The Melodius Dragon," "Professor Maestro," "Grooveyard City" and "The Stone."

1985–1986 "Dream Machine," "Double Trouble," "No Place Like Home," "Having A Ball," "Old Time Rocks That Roll," "Starmaker," "Narra Takes A Powder," "Race To Popland," "Master Blaster Brat," "Twilight Double Header," "A Friend In Need," "Pirates And Puzzles" and "Who's In The Kitchen With Dinah?"

KIDEO TV

This 90–minute series packaged three formerly broadcast series for syndication, designed for weekend programming on independent television stations. Series components were "The Get–Along Gang," "Popples" and "Rainbow Brite" (the latter replaced a Japanese–made adventure cartoon, "Ulysses 31," which aired during the series' earliest months in syndication). *A DIC Enterprises Production in association with Mattel Toys. Color. One hour and a half. Premiered: September, 1986. Syndicated.*

KID KAPERS

One of the first cartoon shows on network weekend television, this 15–minute series consisted of early black–and–white cartoons made for the theaters. Though the content is not known, it is believed the films included Ub Iwerks' "Flip the Frog" and "Willie Whopper" or Paul Terry's silent "Aesop's Fables." *An ABC Television Presentation. Black–and–white. Fifteen minutes. Premiered on ABC: October 26, 1952–January 30, 1953.*

KID POWER

The Rainbow Club, a world–wide organization of kids from all cultural and ethnic backgrounds, struggles to save the environment and change the world in a positive manner through teamwork, friendship and sharing. *A Rankin–Bass*

Production. Color. Half–hour. Premiered on ABC: September 16, 1972–September 1, 1974.

Voices:

Wellington: Charles Kennedy Jr., **Oliver:** Jay Silverheels Jr., **Nipper:** John Gardiner, **Jerry:** Allan Melvin, **Connie:** Carey Wong, **Ralph:** Gary Shapiro, **Sybil:** Michele Johnson, **Diz:** Jeff Thomas, **Albert:** Greg Thomas

THE KID SUPER POWER HOUR WITH SHAZAM

Musical–live action segments of a funky rock group were used to introduce two weekly cartoon adventure series in this hour–long Saturday morning series: "Hero High," a training school for superheroes; and "Shazam," the exploits of three superheroes—Billy Batson (Shazam), Mary Freeman (Mary Marvel) and Freddy Freeman (Captain Marvel Jr.)—as they battle sinister forces of evil, among them, Sivana and Mr. Mind. *A Filmation Production. Color. One hour. Premiered on NBC: September 12, 1981–September 11, 1982.*

Voices:

Captain California: Christopher Hensel, **Glorious Gal:** Becky Perle, **Dirty Trixie:** Mayo McCaslin, **Misty Magic:** Jere Fields, **Rex Ruthless:** John Berwick, **Weatherman:** John Greenleaf, **Punk Rock:** John Venocour, **Mr. Sampson:** Alan Oppenheimer, **Miss Grim:** Erika Scheimer, **Billy Batson/Shazam:** Burr Middleton, **Mary Freeman/Mary Marvel:** Erika Scheimer, **Freddy Freeman/Captain Marvel Jr.:** Barry Gordon

Episodes:

Hero High. (two per show) "The Art Of Ballot," "What's News," "Rat Fink Rex," "Do The Computer Stomp," "Malt Shop Mayhem," "Boo Who," "Cover Twirl," "My Job Is Yours," "Girl Of His Dreams," "The Not So Great Outdoors," "Off Her Rocker," "Follow The Litter," "Jog–A–Long," "He Sinks Seaships," "Starfire Where Are You?," "The Captives," "High–Rise Hijinx," "Track Race," "A Clone Of His Own," "Game Of Chance," "The Umpire Strikes Back," "The Human Fly," "Big Bang Theory," "Law Of The Pack" and "A Fistfull Of Knuckles." Shazam. (episodes unavailable from producer)

KIMBA, THE WHITE LION

White lion cub Kimba and his friends patrol the jungle in order to keep peace in Africa 4,000 years ago. Some of Kimba's friends included Dan'l Baboon, Samson, Pauley Cracker and King Speckle Rex. Produced in Japan, the series was distributed by NBC's syndicated division. *A Mushi Studios Production. Color. Half–hour. Premiered: September 11, 1966. Syndicated.*

Voices:

Kimba, the White Lion: Billie Lou Watt

Episodes:

"Go White Lion," "Jungle Thief," "Dangerous Journey," "Great Caesar's Ghost," "Journey In Time," "Restaurant Trouble," "The Bad Baboon," "The Wind In The Desert," "The Insect

White lion cub Kimba shows she means business in the popular Japanese action–adventure series "Kimba The White Lion." (Courtesy: NBC)

Invasion," "Battle At Dead River," "Scrambled Eggs," "Chameleon Who Cried Wolf," "Gypsy's Purple Potion," "A Human Friend," "The Wild Wildcat," "City Of Gold," "The Last Poacher," "The Trappers," "The Hunting Ground," "Legend Of Hippo Valley," "The Magic Serpent," "The Volcanic Island," "The Flying Tiger," "Running Wild," "Destroyers From The Desert," "The Troublemaker," "The Gigantic Grasshopper," "The Mystery Of The Deserted Village," "Jungle Justice," "The Little Elephant," "The Nightmare Narcissus," "Adventure In The City," "Such Sweet Sorrow," "Diamonds In The Gruff," "The Runaway," "The Revolting Development," "Silvertail, The Renegade," "A Friend In Deed," "Two Hearts And Two Minds," "Soldier Of Fortune," "The Day The Sun Went Out," "The Red Menace," "Jungle Fun," "The Pretenders," "Monster Of The Mountain," "The Sun Tree," "The Cobweb Caper," "The Return Of Fancy Prancy" and "Catch 'Em If You Can."

KING FEATURES TRILOGY

Designed for flexible programming, this half–hour cartoon trilogy featured three comic–strip favorites adapted for television: "Beetle Bailey," a numbskull private whose mishaps at Camp Swampy unnerve his less–than–understanding superior, Sgt. Snorkel; "Krazy Kat," the further adventures of the lovable feline and friends Offisa Pup and Ignatz Mouse; and "Barney Google," the comic misadventures of the hayseed farmer and his friend Snuffy Smith, Louisa Smith (Snuffy's wife) and Jughaid Smith (Snuffy's nephew), who are constantly at odds with their feuding foe, Clem Cutplug. *A King Features Production. Color. Half–hour. Premiered: August 26, 1963, KTLA–TV, Ch. 5., Los Angeles. Syndicated.*

Voices:

Private Beetle Bailey: Howard Morris, **Sgt. Snorkel:** Allan Melvin, **Krazy Kat:** Penny Phillips, **Ignatz Mouse:** Paul Frees, **Barney Google:** Allan Melvin, **Snuffy Smith:** Howard Morris

Episodes:

"Beetle Bailey" (one per show).

"A Tree Is A Tree Is A Tree," "Hero's Reward," "Beetle's High Horps," "Psychological Testing," "Et Tu Otto," "Labot Shortage," "Home Sweet Swampy," "Don't Fiddle With The Brass," "The Sergeant's Master," "The Bull Of The Ball," "60 . . . Count 'Em . . . 60," "Grab Your Socks," "The Blue Ribbon," "Go Yeast Young Man," "We Love You," "Sgt. Snorkel," "Is This Trip Necessary?," "A Christmas Tale," "For Officers Only," "Bye Bye," "Young Lovers," "A Pass Is A Pass Is A Pass," "Leap No More," "My Lady," "Tattoo Tootsie Goodbye," "Welsh Rabbit," "Cosmo's Naught," "Camp Invisible," "V For Visitor," "Shutterbugged," "Little Pooch Lost," "Halftrack's Navy," "Don't Give Up The Swamp," "Hoss Laff," "The Red Carpet Treatment," "Lucky Beetle," "Sweet Sunday," "Operation Butler," "The Bridge On The River Y," "The Secret Weapon," "The Diet," "The Heir," "Breaking The Leash," "The Spy," "The Jinx," "The Courage Encourager," "Sgt. Snorkel's Longest Day," "Everything's Ducky," "The Play's The Thing," "Geronimo," "Son Of A Gun Of A Gun," "Zero's Dizzy Double Date" and "Dr. Jekyll And Beetle Bailey."

"Krazy Kat" (one per show).

"Keeping Up With The Krazy," "Mouse Blanche," "Housewarming," "The Quickest Brick In The West," "Sea Sore," "Sporting Chance," "Fizzical Fitness," "Monument To A Mouse," "Looney Park," "Network Nitwit," "Road To Ruin," "There Auto Be A Law," "Earthworm Turns," "Pilgrim's Regress," "Duel Personality." "The Purloined Persian," "Happy Daze," "Malicious Mousechicf," "An Arrow Escape," "The Desert Island," "Frozen Feud," "How To Win A Mouse," "Bungle In The Jungle," "Arty Smarty," "Stoned Thru The Ages," "Castle Hassle," "Krazy's Kristmas," "Carnival Capers," "Alp Wanted," "Big And Little," "Krazy And The Krooked Kaper," "A Kat's Tale," "Adman On The Loose," "Folly The Leader," "Serie-Ous Business," "No Such Luck," "Collector's Item," "Dreams Of Glory," "The Kat's Pajamas," "Monu–Mental Luff," "The World's Fair," "Tourist Attracktions," "Mountain Never–Rest," "A Star Is Born," "Odd For Art's Sake," "Don't Call Us, We'll Call You," "Potions Of Love," "Southern Hospital–ty," "My Fair Ignatz" and "Safari."

"Barney Google and Snuffy Smith" (one per show).

"Snuffy's Song," "The Method And Maw," "The Hat," "Snuffy's Turf Luck," "Take Me To Your Gen'rul," "Pie In The Sky," "The Berkley Squares," "The Shipwreckers," "The Master," "Barney Deals The Cars," "Snuffy Runs The Gamut," "The Tourist Trap," "Rip Van Snuffy," "Snuffy Goes To College," "Snuffy's Brush With Fame," "Give Me A Jail Break," "Glove Thy Neighbor," "Snuffy's Fair Lady," "Just Plain Kinfolk," "Off Their Rockers," "Snuffy Hits The Road," "My Kingdom For A Horse," "The Country Club Smiths," "Jughaid's Jumpin' Frog," "Turkey Shoot," "The Work Pill," "Jughaid For President," "Loweezy Makes A Match," "Fishin' Fools," "Little Red Jughaid," "Jughaid The Magician," "A Hoss Kin Dream," "It's Better To Give" (Christmas show)," "Spring Time And Sparkplug," "There's No Feud Like An Old Feud," "A Hauntin' Fer A Horse," "Feudin' And A–Fussin'," "Barney's Blarney," "Do Do That Judo," "Farm Of The Future," "Getting Snuffy's Goat," "Barney's Winter Carnival," "Keeping Up With The Joneses," "The Big Bear Hunt," "Ain't It The Tooth," "Bizzy Nappers,"

"The Buzz In Snuffy's Bonnet," "Settin' And–A–Frettin'," "Beauty And The Beast" and "Smoke Screams."

THE KING KONG SHOW

American scientist Professor Bond establishes a top research center in the remote island of Mondo in the Java Sea. His son Bobby becomes friends with the legendary 60–foot jungle beast, King Kong, who the professor feels may be helpful in his research. Instead, the professor, daughter Susan and Bobby battle the diabolical Dr. Who, an evil scientist who has more sinister designs on Kong.

Other cartoons included the adventures of a U.S. government agent, "Tom of T.H.U.M.B." (Tiny Humans Underground Military Bureau), and his Oriental assistant, Swinging Jack. The producer of the series has no record of voice credits or episodes. The program originally debuted in prime–time with a one–hour preview special featuring two half–hour episodes. (See Animated Television Specials for details.) *A Rankin–Bass Production with Videocraft International. Color. Half-hour. Premiered on ABC: September 10, 1966–August 31, 1969.*

KING LEONARDO AND HIS SHORT SUBJECTS

King Leonardo, the ruler of Bongo Congo, and his loyal, skunk companion, Odie Cologne (whose principal foes are Itchy Brother and Biggie Rat) headlined this popular Saturday morning entry, which also featured the adventures of "Tooter Turtle," a mild–mannered turtle who is transported back in time through feats of legerdemain performed by his friend, Mr. Wizard; and "The Hunter," a bumbling bloodhound detective who, under the command of Officer Flim Flanagan, is outwitted by a wily fast–back artist, the Fox. The series was

King Leonardo, the ruler of Bongo Congo, waits as loyal companion, Odie Cologne, adjusts the television antenna in the classic Saturday–morning series "King Leonardo And His Short Subjects." © Leonardo–TTV

later syndicated under the title of "King and Odie." *A Leonardo TV Production with Total TV Productions. Color. Half-hour. Premiered on NBC: October 15, 1960–September 28, 1963.*

Voices:

King Leonardo: Jackson Beck, **Odie Cologne:** Jackson Beck, **Biggie Rat:** Jackson Beck, **Itchy Brother:** Jackson Beck, **Mr. Tooter:** Allen Swift, **Mr. Wizard:** Frank Milano, **The Hunter:** Kenny Delmar, **The Fox:** Ben Stone

Episodes:

"King and Odie" (two per show).

"Riches To Rags," "Nose For The Noose," "Drumming Up The Bongos," "How High Is Up?," "Royal Amnesia," "Loon From The Moon," "Royal Bongo War Chant," "Showdown At Dybher Pass," "Duel To The Dearth," "Ringside Riot," "Bringing In Biggie," "Confound It Confusion," "Paris Pursuit," "The Awful Tower," "Beatnik Boom," "Call Out The Kids," "Trial Of The Traitors," "Battle Slip," "Heroes Are Made . . . With Salami," "The Big Freeze," "Fiesta Time," "The Carpenter," "Sticky Stuff," "Am I Glue," "Double Trouble," "Switcheroo Ruler," "Midnight Frolics," "Tito's Guitar," "No Bong Bongos," "The AD Game," "De–Based Ball," "Bats In The Ballpark," "Lost Lost Lennie," "Ghost Guests," "Fatal Fever," "Pulling The Mane Switch," "Dim Gem," "The Clanking Castle Caper," "The King And Me," "The Loves Of Lynetta Lion," "The Sport Of Kings," "Black Is White," "Cat–Nipped," "Dog, Cat And Canary," "Lead Foot Leonardo," "The Rat Race, "The Obey Ball," "Out Of The Depths," "The Loco Play," "Romeo And Joliet," "If At First You Don't Succeed, Try, Try Again," "Long Laugh Leonardo," "He Who Laughs Last," "East Side, West Side," "Coney Island Calamity," "An Ode In Code," "Two Beneath The Mast," "Hip Hip Hypnosis," "Odie Hit The Roadie," "Hunting A Hobby," "Teeing Off," "Smardi Gras," "Bayou Blues," "Stage Struck," "One Way Ticket To Venus," "Back To Nature," "My Vine Is Your Vine," "The Tourist Trade," "Bye Bye Bicycle," "Chicago Shenanigans," "Loop The Loop," "Uranium Cranium," "Mistaked Claim," "The Trail Of The Lonesome Mine," "The Treasure Of The Sierra Bongos," "Fortune Feller," "Wild And Wobbly," "Introducing Mr. Mad," "Falling Asleep," "Hup–Two–Three Hike," "Spring Along With Itch," "Left Alone Leonardo," "A Tour De Farce," "Get 'Em Up Scout," "The King Camps Out," "Offensive Defensive," "A Long, Long Trail A–Binding," "Treasure Train," "Hand Car Heroes," "Honey Business," (the following are in two parts) "Bye Bye Bees," "Royal Race," "Shifty Sail," "Asleep On The Deep," "An Ace For A King," "Odie Takes A Dive," "Go And Catch A Falling King," "Royal Rodeo," "Ride 'em Cowboy," (the following are in four parts), "S.O. Essex Calling," "The Big Falling Out," "Long Days Journey Into Fright" and "Making A Monkey Shine."

"Tooter Turtle" (one per show).

"Two–Fun Turtle (Fast On The Flaw)," "Failspin Tooter," "Sea Haunt (Follow The Fish)," "Highway Petrol–Man," "Knight Of The Square Table," "Mish–Mash–Mush (Painting For Gold)," "The Unteachables (Lawless Fears)," "Kink Of Swat (Babe Ruth)," "One Trillion B.C. (Dinosaur Dope)," "Olimping Champion (Weak Greek)," "Stuporman (Muscle Bounder),"

"Buffaloed Bill," "Moon Goon (Space Head)," "Robin Hood-wink," "Steamboat Stupe," "Souse Painter (Brush Boob)," "Railroad Engineer," "Quarterback Hack," "Overwhere," "Lumberjack," "Jerky Jockey," "Fired Fireman," "Sky Diver," "Tuesday Turtle," "Snafu Safari," "Anti–Arctic," "Master Builder," "Taxi Turtle," "Canned Camera," "Slowshoe Mountie," "Duck Haunted," "Bull Fright," "News Nuisance," "Foreign Fleegion," "Waggin' Train," "Anchors Away," "Vaudevillian," "Rod And Reeling" and "Man In The Blue Denim Suit."

"The Hunter" (one per show).

"The Brookloined Bridge," "Counterfeit Wants," "Haunted Hunter," "Fort Know Fox," "Stealing A March," "Horn Of Plenty," "Concrete Crook," "Subtracted Submarine," "Risky Ransom," "Unfaithful Old Faithful," "Armored Car Coup," "Telephone Poltergeist," "Sheepish Shamus," "Rustler Hustler," "Case Of The Missing Muenster," "Great Train Robbery," "Florida Fraud," "The Great Plane Robbery," "Girl Friday," "Stamp Sticky," "Statue Of Liberty Play," "The Frankfurter Fix," "Case Of The Missing Mower," "Fancy Fencing," "Racquet Racket," "Seeing Stars," "Elevator Escapade," "Hoola Hoop Havoc," "Counterfeit Newspaper Caper," "Diamond Dither," "Grand Canyon Caper," "Borrowed Beachland," "Peekaboo Pyramids," "Lincoln Tunnel Lark," "TV Set Terror," "Bye Bye Bell," "Time Marches Out," "Fox's Foul Play," "Bow Wow Blues," "Breaking In Big," "The Bank Dicks," "Eye On The Ball," "Breakout At Breakrock," "Getting The Business," "An Uncommon Cold," "The Pick–Pocket Pickle," "Goofy-Guarding," "The Big Birthday Blast," "Under The Spreading Treasure Tree," "School Days, Fool Days," "Fall Of The House Of The Hunter," "Using The Ole Bean," "The Case Of The Hunted Hunter," "The Purloined Piano Puzzle," "Record Rocket," "The Hunter's Magic Lamp," "Hi Ho Hollywood," "Two For The Turkey Trot," "Captain Horatio Hunter," "The Horn Of The Lone Hunter" and "Little Boy Blues."

KISSYFUR

Kissyfur, an eight–year–old bear cub, along with his circus bear father, Gus, escape from civilization to begin life anew deep in a swamp populated by other animals—some good, some bad— living simple lives untouched by human influence. *A NBC Production in association with DIC Enterprises. Color. Half–hour. Premiered on NBC: December 15, 1986–September 3, 1988.*

Voices:

Kissyfur: R. J. Williams, Max Mieir, **Gus,** Kissyfur's father: Edmund Gilbert, **Beehonie,** a rabbit: Russi Taylor, **Duane,** a persnickety pig: Neilson Ross, **Stuckey,** the porcupine: Stuart M. Rosen, **Toot,** a young beaver: Devon Feldman, Russi Taylor, **Floyd,** the alligator: Stuart M. Rosen, **Jolene,** the alligator: Terrence McGovern, **Miss Emmy Lou,** the schoolmarm: Russi Taylor, **Cackle Sister:** Russi Taylor, **Bessie:** Russie Taylor, **Lennie:** Lennie Weinrib, **Charles:** Lennie Weinrib, **Uncle Shelby:** Frank Welker, **Howie:** Frank Welker, **Claudette:** Frank Welker, **Ralph:** Susan Silo

Episodes:

1986–1987 "Home Sweat Home" "Here's The Beef," "Drop Me A Lion," "Pooped Pop," "The Duck Who Came To Dinner,"

"A Basket Case," "Gatoraid," "The Incredible Hunk," "Jam Wars," "The Bear Who Cried Wolf," "The Wishing Box," "To Tell The Tooth," "Whale Of A Tale," "Egg McGuffin," "Double Dare Bear," "Bearly A Bodyguard," "Kissyfur P.I.," "The Humans Must Be Crazy," "We Are The Swamp" and "The Birds And The Bears."

1987–1988 "Tooti's Treasure," "Cubs' Club," "Berried Alive," "Stuck With Stuckey," "Weight Not, Want Not," "Comrade Kissyfur," "You Ain't Nothin' But A Hound Dog," "Flipzilla," "The New Cub," "See You Later, Annie Gator," "Swarm Outside," "Evilfur," "Halo And Goodbye," "The Ballad Of Rebel Raccoon," "Got Those Baby Blues," "Home Sweet Swamp," "Three's A Crowd," "Just In Time," "The Shell Game," "The Great Swamp Swampi," "Like Father, Like Son," "G'Day Gator And G'Bye," "My Fair Lennie," "Fork–Tongued Frog," "The Great Swamp Taxi Race" and "Somethin' Cajun's Cookin.' "

THE KWICKY KOALA SHOW

Cartoon legend Tex Avery developed this series—his last animated production—starring a sweet and super speedy koala bear, reminiscent of his character, Droopy, who becomes entangled in numerous misadventures with the wily but hapless Wilford Wolf. The program featured three additional weekly cartoon segments: "Crazy Claws," a whirlwind wildcat whose snappy one–liners are his only defense against the schemes of Rawhide Clyde; "Dirty Dawg," the con–artist canine of the garbage dump, joined by alley–mate, and "The Bungle Brothers," two beagles (George and Joey) trying desperately to break into show business, seen in three one–minute segments per show. Avery, whose comedic visual gags created a new dimension in cartoons, worked the last two years of his life at Hanna–Barbera Productions until his death in 1980. *A Hanna–Barbera Production. Color. Half–hour. Premiered on CBS: September 21, 1981–September 11, 1982.*

Voices:

Kwicky Koala: Robert Allen Ogle, **Wilford Wolf:** John Stephenson, **Dirty Dawg:** Frank Welker, **Ratso:** Marshall Efron, **Crazy Claws:** Jim McGeorge, **Rawhide Clyde:** Robert Allen Ogle, **Bristletooth:** Peter Cullen, **Ranger Dangerfield:** Michael Bell, **George:** Michael Bell, **Joey:** Allan Melvin

Episodes:

"Kwicky Koala" (one per show).
"Sink Or Swim," "Robinson Caruso," "In A Pig's Eye," "Robin Hoodwink," "Kwicky Goes West," "Collector's Item," "The Incredible Lunk," "Race To Riches," "Kangaroo Kapers," "Double Trouble," "Around The World In 80 Seconds," "Kwicky's Karnival Kaper," "Scream Test," "Disguise The Limit," "Museum Mayhem" and "Cabin Crazy."
"Dirty Dawg" (one per show).
"Pigskin Pooch," "Dirty's Debut," "Dirty Dawg's Faux Paw," "Calling Dirty," "Lo–Cal Pals," "A Close Encounter Of The Canine Kind," "Pie–Eyed Pooch," "Dirty Money," "A Funny Thing Happened On The Way To The Zoo," "Urban Cowdawg," "Dirty–O And Juliet," "Sea Dawg Dirty," "Little White Lie," "The Great Dirtini," "Disco Dawg" and "Marathon Mutt."
"Crazy Claws" (one per show).
"Crazy It's Cold Outside," "The Claws Conspiracy," "Crazy Challenges," "Clyde's Birthday Surprise," "The Ice Rage," "Claws Encounters Of The Worst Kind," "Lookout Crazy," "Crazy Camping," "Gold Crazy," "See Saw Claws," "Choo Choo Crazy," "Bearly Asleep," "Old Blowhard," "Snow Biz," "Claws Ahoy" and "Battletrap Rawhide."
"The Bungle Brothers" (three per show).
"Hat Dance," "Dry Run," "Cheap Trick," "High Rollers," "Teeter Totter Act," "The Circus Cannon Act," "Trapeze Act," "Saw In Two," "Unicycle," "Big Pie Jump," "Honk If You Love Joey," "Sound Off," "Joey Juggling George," "The Toe Dancing Beagle Or What's Nureyev," "The Barrel Jump," "Karate Chop Act," "Tarzan Swing Act," "The Ventriloquist," "Rope Twirling Act," "High Wire Harness," "The Marionette Act," "Cream Pie," "Balloonatics," "Escape Artist," "Rock Band," "Circus Car," "Dueling Trombones," "Quiz Whiz Kid," "Stilts," "The Romeo And Juliet Act," "Animal Trainers," "Double Jump," "Pie Faced," "The Plumber's Helper," "Bungle Ballet," "Hang 20," "The Big Bang," "Flipped Out," "Bucking Bull," "Hamlet Lays An Egg," "The Magic Ring Act," "The Fly–Weight Weight Lifter," "Doop The Loop," "Heavy Ending," "Ice Follies," "Punchy Pirates," "Spring Is In The Air" and "Concert Pianist."

LADY LOVELYLOCKS

Set in the mystical Land of Lovelylocks, this action/adventure fairy tale centers on the life of a young ruler who learns the lessons of life and the ways of the world, while ruling her kingdom and struggling against the evil workings of Duchess Ravenwaves, who seeks to take over her kingdom. *A DIC Enterprises Production in association with Mattel. Color. Half–hour. Premiered: September, 1987. Syndicated.*

Voices:

Lady Lovelylocks: Tony St. Vincent, **Duchess Ravenwaves:** Louise Vallance, **Maiden Fairhair:** Jeannie Elias, **Maiden Curlycrown:** Louise Vallance, **Snags:** Jeannie Elias, **Comb Gnome,** the nasty gnome: Danny Mann, **Strongheart:** Danny Mann, **Prince** (as dog): Danny Mann, **Shining Glory:** Brian George, **Hairball:** Brian George, **Tanglet:** Brian George, **The Pixietails: Pixiesparkle:** Tony St. Vincent, **Pixiebeauty:** Jeannie Elias, **Pixieshine:** Brian George

Episodes:

"To Save My Kingdom," "Cruel Pretender," "Vanished," "The Wishing Bone," "The Discovery," "The Lake Of Reflections," "The Menace Of Mirror Lake," "Blue Moon," "The Bundle," "The Iceman Cometh," "The Power And The Glory," "Prince's Broken Heart," "The Noble Deed," "The Doubt," "The Dragon Tree," "The Capture," "The Keeper," "The Rallye," "Fire In The Sky" and "To Take A Castle."

LASSIE'S RESCUE RANGERS

Jack Wrather's famed TV collie roams the Rocky Mountains under the guidance of the Turner family who, along with Lassie and the forest animals, organize a "Forest Force" rescue team.

Stories depict Lassie (in animated form) and the group's attempts to save the already deteriorated environment. Two

Lassie and new owner, Ben Turner, hold a meeting of the Rescue Rangers, a task force composed of animals from the forest, in a scene from "Lassie's Rescue Rangers." © Rankin–Bass Productions in association with Jack Wrather Productions

of the series' principals were voiced by the son and daughter of director Hal Sutherland and producer Lou Scheimer. *A Filmation Production. Color. Half–hour. Premiered on ABC: September 8, 1973–August 30, 1975.*

Voices:

Narrator: Ted Knight, **Lassie:** Lassie, **Ben Turner:** Ted Knight, **Laura Turner:** Jane Webb, **Susan Turner:** Lane Scheimer, **Jackie Turner:** Keith Sutherland, **Ben Turner Jr.:** Hal Harvey, **Gene Fox:** Hal Harvey

Episodes:

"The Animals Are Missing," "Mystic Monster," "Lassie's Special Assignment," "The Imposters," "Deadly Cargo," "Grizzly," "Deep Sea Disaster," "Blackout," "Artic Adventure," "The Sunken Galleon," "Goldmine," "Rodeo," "Hullabaloo In Hollywood," "Tidal Wave" and "Lost."

LAUREL AND HARDY

Temperamental Oliver Hardy (the rotund one) always found himself in "another fine mess" when he and his whining, dim–witted friend, thin Stan Laurel, got together. This basic premise became the recurring theme of a cartoon version of the comic pair, co–produced by Larry Harmon, creator of "Bozo the Clown," and Hanna–Barbera Productions, which also produced a series of Abbott and Costello cartoons. With both comedians deceased, the voices of Stan and Ollie were recreated by Harmon and voice–artist Jim McGeorge. *A Hanna–Barbera Production for Wolper Productions and Larry Harmon Pictures. Color. Half–hour. Premiere: 1966. Syndicated.*

Voices:

Stan Laurel: Larry Harmon, **Oliver Hardy:** Jim McGeorge

Episodes:

(four per show). "Can't Keep A Secret Agent," "Mutt Tur," "How Green Was My Lawn Mower," "Prairie Panicked," "Mis-

sile Hassle," "No Moose Is A Good Moose," "The Bullnick," "High Fly Guys," "False Alarms," "Hillbilly Bully," "Ball Maul," "Handle With Care," "You And Your Big Mouse," "Sitting Roomers," "Babe's In Sea Land," "Rome Roamers," "Rocket Wreckers," "Hot Rod Hardy," "Knight Mare," "Defective Story," "Crash And Carry," "Desert Story," "Tale Of A Sale," "Fancy Trance," "Suspect In Custody," "Auto–Matic Panic," "Shiver Mr. Timbers," "Stand Out Stand In," "Big Bear Bungle," "Shrinking Shrieks," "Mounty Rout," "Bond Bombed," "What Fur," "Spook Loot," "Camera Bugged," "Plumber Pudding," "Robust Robot," "Vet Fleet," "Cooper Bopper," "Feud For Thought," "Love Me, Love My Puppy," "Wacky Quackers," "Truant Ruined," "Country Buzzin'," "Naps 'An Saps," "Bad Day In Baghdad," "The Missing Fink," "Always Leave 'Em Giggling," "Badge Budgers," "Two For The Crow," "Good Hoods," "Animal Shelter," "Tragic Magic," "Ring–A–Ding–King," "Ups And Downs," "Beanstalk Boobs," "Leaping Leprechaun," "Tourist Trouble," "The Genie Was Meanie," " Mars Little Helper," "Curfew For Kids," "Lion Around," "Shoot Down At Sundown," "Horse Detectives," "The Two Musketeers," "Ali Boo Boo," "Ghost Town Clowns," "Hurricane Hood," "Ride And Seek," "Tee Pee T.V.," " Shoe–Shoe Baby," "Train Strain," "Southern Hospitality," "Frog Frolic," " Shutter Bugged," "Circus Run Aways," "Witch Switch," "Pie In The Sky," " Slipper Slip–Up," "Sign Of The Times," "Two Many Cooks," "Flea's A Crowd," "Dingbats," "We Clothe At Five," "The Stone–Age Kid," "Quick Change," "Whing–Ding," "Termite Might," "To Bee Or Not To Bee," "Mistaken Identi–Tree," "Rodeo Doug," "Pet Shop Polly," "Laff Staff," "Try And Get It," "Riverboat Detectives," "Unhealthy Wealthy," "Honesty Always Pays," "Plant Rant," "Sky–High–Noon," "Jumpin' Judo," "Handy Dandy Diary," "Get Tough," "They Take The Cake," "Gold Storage," "Lots Of Bad Luck," " Kangaroo Kaper," "The Finks Robbery," "Strictly For The Birds," "Birds Of A Feather," "Bird Brains," "Switcheroony," "Mechanical Mess–Up," "Horsey Sense," "Bowling Boobs," "Dog Tired," "Wayout Campers," "Goofer Upper Golfers," "My Friend The Inventor," "Hard Days Work," "Sky–Scraper Scape," "Sleepy King," "Fair Play," "Fly–Foot Flatfeet," " Baboon Tycoon," "A Real Tycoon," "A Real Live Wife," "Wishy Washy Fishy Tale," "Stuporman," "Wheel And Deal Seal," "Wolf In Sheep's Clothing," "Lumber Jerks," "That's Show Biz," "A Clothes Call," "Boot Hill Bill," "Stop Action Faction," "Molecule Rule," "Peek–A–Boo Pachyderm," "Mummy Dummy," "Nitey Knight," "Fly Spy," "Franken–Stan," "Secret Agents O–O–O," "Flight Of The Bumble–Brains," "Salt Walter Daffy," "From Wrecks To Riches," "Truant Or Consequences" and "Flipped Van Winkles."

LAVERNE AND SHIRLEY IN THE ARMY

Prime–time's hit characters, Laverne DeFazio and Shirley Feeny, from the popular sitcom, "Laverne and Shirley," become privates in the Army and efforts to instill some military discipline into these two goof–ups fall short of completion. *A Hanna–Barbera Production in association with Paramount Pictures Corporation. Laverne and Shirley © 1981 Paramount Pictures Corporation. All material besides Laverne and Shirley*

© 1981 Hanna–Barbera Productions Inc. Color. Half–hour. Premiered on ABC: October 10, 1981–September 18, 1982.

Voices:

Laverne: Penny Marshall, **Shirley:** Cindy Williams, **Sgt. Turnbuckle:** Ken Mars, **Squeely,** his pet pig: Ron Palillo

Additional Voices:

Brad Crandall, Peter Cullen, Keene Curtis, Rick Dees, Dick Erdman, Joan Gerber, Bob Holt, Buster Jones, Zale Kessler, Henry Polic, Lou Richards, Bob Ridgley, John Stephenson, Russi Taylor, Frank Welker

Episodes:

"Invasion Of The Booby Hatchers," "Jungle Jumpers," "Naval Fluff," "April Fools In Paris," "I Only Have Ice For You," "When The Moon Comes Over The Werewolf," "Bigfoot," "Two Mini Cooks," "Super Wacs," "Meanie Genie," "Tokyo–Ho, Ho," "The Dark Knight" and "Super Duper Trooper."

LAVERNE AND SHIRLEY WITH THE FONZ

Laverne and Shirley's adventures in the Army continue, this time with the ever–cool Fonz (voiced by actor Henry Winkler, who played the character in the popular sitcom, "Happy Days"), now a chief mechanic for the Army's motorpool. Fonzie and his sidekick dog, Mr. Cool, add to the laughs and the messed–up missions in this half–hour comedy/adventure. The program repeated episodes from 1981's "Laverne and Shirley in the Army," in addition to featuring all–new episodes with the Fonz. *A Hanna–Barbera Production in association with Paramount Pictures Corporation. Color. Half–hour. Premiered on ABC: September 25, 1982–September 3, 1983.*

Voices:

Laverne: Penny Marshall, **Shirley:** Lynn Marie Stewart, **Sgt. Turnbuckle:** Ken Mars, **Squeely:** Ron Palillo, **Fonz:** Henry Winkler, **Mr. Cool,** his dog: Frank Welker

Episodes:

"Speed Demon Get Away," "Swamp Monster Speak With Forked Face," "Movie Madness," "One Million Laughs B.C.," "The Robot Recruit," "All The President's Girls," "Laverne And Shirley And The Beanstalk" and "Raider's Of The Lost Pork."

LAZER TAG ACADEMY

Thirteen–year–old Jamie Jaren returns to the present from the world of the future and, with the help of two young ancestors and the family's special powers, stops the villainous Sila Mayhem from changing the course of history. *A Ruby–Spears Enterprises Production. Color. Half–hour. Premiered on NBC: September 13, 1986–August 22, 1987.*

Voices:

Jamie Jaren: Moelle Harling, **Draxon Drear:** Booker Bradshaw, **Beth Jaren:** Christina MacGregor, **Tom Jaren:** Billy Jacoby, **Nicky Jaren:** R. J. Williams, **Andrew Jaren/Skugg:** Frank Welker, **Genna Jaren:** Tress MacNeille, **Professor Olanga:** Sid McCoy, **Charlie/Skugg:** Pat Fraley

A family blessed with special powers sets out to stop the villainous Sila Mayhem from changing the course of history in Ruby–Spears' "Lazer Tag Academy." © Ruby–Spears Enterprises and World of Wonder Inc.

Episodes:

"The Beginning," "Skugg Duggery," "Yamato's Curse," "Pay Dirt," "Charles' Science Project," "The Witch Switch," "The Olanga Story," "The Battle Hymn Of The Jarens," "Sir Tom Of Jaren," "Redbeard's Treasure," "Drear's Doll," "Starlyte On The Orient Express" and "Jamie And The Spitfires."

THE LEGEND OF ZELDA

Based on the celebrated Nintendo videogame, this fantasy/adventure series stars a 15–year–old adventurer (Nick) and a princess of the same age (Zelda), who fight monsters, ghosts and icky creatures while trying to save the kingdom of Hyrule from the dark depredations of the evil wizard, Ganon. *A DIC Enterprises Production in association with Nintendo of America Incorporated. Color. Half–hour. Premiered: September, 1989. Syndicated.*

Voices:

Zelda: Cyndy Preston, **Link:** Jonathan Potts, **Ganon,** the evil wizard: Len Carlson, **Harkinian:** Colin Fox, **Triforce of Wisdom:** Elizabeth Hanna, **Triforce of Power:** Allan Stewart Coates, **Moblin:** Len Carlson

Episodes:

"The Ringer," "Sing For The Unicorn," "Kiss 'N' Tell," "Doppelganger," "Fairies In The Spring," "The Missing Link," "Underworld Connections," "The Moblins Are Revolting," "The White Knight," "Cold Spells," "Stinging A Stinger," "A Hitch In The Works" and "That Sinking Feeling."

LEO THE LION

This sequel to NBC's "Kimba, the White Lion" was created by Kimba's originator, Osamu Tezuka. Unlike the first series, however, the character was not called Kimba—he was named Leo instead—and he was cast as an adult and the father of two cubs, who rule the jungle with him and his mate, Kitty. Little else is known about this production, which received some airplay on stations throughout the United States. Only 26 episodes were made in the series. *A Sonic International Production. Color. Half–hour. Premiered: 1966. Syndicated.*

Episodes:

(known titles) "The King Of The Jungle," "Rick The Lycon," "The Hide Of The Panja," "The Poachers," "Duel At Lubar Valley," "The Sabre Toothed Tiger," "The Marked Giraffe," "The Green Plague," "The Case Of The Moonlight Stones," "Secret Of The Moonlight Stones," "The Map Of Danger," "The Blue Lion," "The Last Hunt Of The Ahabi," "The First Adventure," "Dwimog The Mighty," "The Golden Bow," "The Falcons," "Lilly The Black Leopard," "Devil Falls," "The Steel Monster," "The House For Animals," "Agura The Terrible," "The Candle Rock," "The Silver Wolf" and "Adventure At Thunder Island."

LINUS THE LIONHEARTED

Four major stars—Jonathan Winters, Sterling Holloway, Carl Reiner and Sheldon Leonard—lent their voices to characters derived from the boxes of Post cereals and brought to life in this Saturday–morning series. The series revolved around the adventures of Linus the Lionhearted, the frail, docile ruler of the kingdom of animals in Africa, who first appeared on the boxes of Crispy Critters. His co–stars, Lovable Truly, the postman, and So–Hi, a small Chinese boy, were used to sell Alphabets and Sugar Crinkles. A third character, Sugar Bear, became famous on boxes of Post Cereals' Sugar Crisp.

Not everyone bowed to Linus' command, however. His not–so–loyal subjects—also the custodians of the Royal corn fields—were Rory Raccoon, Sascha Grouse, Dinny Kangaroo and Billie Bird. Linus, Sugar Bear, Lovable Truly, Rory Raccoon and So–Hi appeared weekly in their own adventures, with the entire cast spotlighted in episodes termed, "The Company." *An Ed Graham Production. Color. Half–hour. Premiered on CBS: September 26, 1964–September 3, 1966. Rebroadcast on ABC: September 25, 1966–September 7, 1969.*

Voices:

Linus: Sheldon Leonard, **Lovable Truly:** Sterling Holloway, **So–Hi:** Jonathan Winters, **Sugar Bear:** Sterling Holloway, **Billie Bird:** Ed Graham, **Sascha Grouse:** Carl Reiner, **Dinny Kangaroo:** Carl Reiner, **Rory Raccoon:** Carl Reiner, **The Japanese Giant:** Jonathan Winters

Episodes:

"Linus the Lionhearted." (one per show)
1964–1965 "Grouse," "Swami Bird," "Rocky Road To Riches," "Birds Gotta Swim," "Hiccups," "Hidden Talent," "Exercise," "A Gift For Linus," "Who Am I," "Help, Save The Mocking Bird," "Talking Rock," "The Reflection Pool," "Flying Lion–Pilot," "Linus' Coronation," "The Birds," "Remember The Birds," "Fishing For Relaxation," "Missing—One Throne," "Helping Hands," "Disney's Sydney Special," "Travel Is Broad-

ening," "Billy's Sydney Special," "Crocodile Tears," "The Sinking Island," "Surprise" and "That Winning Smile."
1965–1966 "Linus To The Rescue," "Shadow Thief," "No News Is Good News," "Surprise Attack," "Leaping Lizard," "Jungle Rot," "Nephew Norman," "The Census," "Booby Traps," "What's On Third," "Winner And Still King," "Around The World In 80 Gags" and "The Disappearing Act."
"Sugar Bear." (one per show)
1964–1965 "Room For One More," "Bad Apple," "Which Is Witch?," "Cry Wolf," "Water, Water, Everywhere," "Picture Me In Pictures," "Stop The Magic," "Granny's Broom" and "A Cake For Benjie."
1965–1966 "Mervyn Meets His Match," "Benjie, The Appprentice," "Rich Witch," "Singing Toad," "Mervyn's Museum," "Benjie's Revenge," "Mervyn's Genie," "Trick Banjo," "Head Over Heels," "Granny's Phone Booth," "Perilous Picnic," "Mervyn's Elevator," "Mervyn's Songbook," "Magic Rope Trick," "No Substitute For Sugar" and "Gotta Dance."
"The Company." (one per show)
1964–1965 "Mocking Bird," "Adrift On The Rapids," "Linus Plays, Linus Says," "Water Skiing," "Macy's Thanksgiving Day Balloon," "Sugar Bear, Linus Says," "Cheering Of The Grouse," "Joke Day," "Hide And Seek," "Suggestion Box," "Musical Chairs," "National Linus Admirers Day," "It's Rhyme Time," "Old Car," "Flying High," "The Picnic," "Mountain Climbing," "Treasure Hunt," "Cross Jungle Race," "The Voyage," "The Hand Grenade," "The Bicycle," "The Tank," "The Box," "Coconut Harvest" and "The Ski Race."
1966–1966 "Underwater," "Lost Kingdom," "Hand Car," "Skateboard," "Albino Gorilla," "Space Capsule," "Linus Submarine," "The Man Eating Plant," "Twin Gorillas," "The Peculiar Tree," "Ivory Tower," "Pre–Historic Perils" and "Cool Cousin."
"Lovable Truly." (one per show)
1964–1965 "Truly Chewy," "Beware Of The Dog Catcher," "Truly Scary," "It's A Dog Life," "Frank Pfaff Streetcleaner," "Wrong Dog," "Dog Gone," "Dog Pound," "One For The Book," "My Fuzzy Fugitive," "Toy Store," "Be Kind To Dogs Week," "One Way," "Making Movies," "Puncture Time," "Flop Flop," "Ups And Downs," "What's Up," "United We Stand," "A Visit To Dizzyland," "Keep Off The Grass," "It's A Bird Dog," "Double Trouble" and "The Flying Dog Catcher."
1965–1966 "Truly Heroic," "Truly Explosive," "The Counterfeiter," "The Spy," "Truly To The Rescue," "Carnival Cars," "Trestle Trouble," "Pony Express Postman," "Truly Monstrous," "Playing The Trains" and "The Flying Dog."
"Rory Raccoon." (one per show)
1964–1965 "Bye, Bye, Bad Bird," "Samples From Mars," "Faults Of The Toreador," "Winter Blunderland," "Circus Stars," "Rory Takes A Vacation," "Make Someone Happy," "Rory's Circus Act," "World's Worst Caddy," "Beautiful Baby Contest," "Vincent Van Crow, Artiste," "Big Chief Rain In The Face," "This Means Total War," "C. Claudius Dreams," "Some Total," "Rory Goes Skiing," "Numbskull And Crossbones," "The World's Greatest Hypnotist" and "Rest Cured."
"So–Hi." (one per show)
1964–1965 "So–Hi And The Bambo Stalk," "King Midas," "Sleeping Beauty," "The Night Before Christmas," "So–Hi And The Ugly Duckling," "When So–Hi Called Wolf," "Casey At

The Bat," "The Bear Who Danced Too Well," "Tortoise And The Hare," "Fisherman And His Wishes," "So–Hi And The Knight," "So–Hi And The Singing King," "The Princely Toad," "The Prince Who Wasn't Charming," "Little Red So–Hihood," "The Giant With Two Glass Jaws," "The Business–Like Witch," "The Wolf Who Changed His Spots," "CinderSo–Hi," "The Too–Particular Princess," "E.R. Jack Rumpelstiltskin," "The Jester Who Took Himself Seriously," "Huffy Miss Muffet," "The Walrus And The Carpenter," "The Poet Bandit" and "The Cat Who Looked At A Queen."

1965–1966 "Thieves Who Fell Out," "Magic Pig," "Genie Who Got His Wish," "King's Canary," "Twin Witches," "The Giant Who Liked People And Birds," "The Dragon Who Went Home To Mother," "The Scaredy Cat," "The Fast Sword," "Jolly Roger" and "The Princess Who Held On To Her Hand."

LIPPY THE LION

Hanna–Barbera, who created the likes of Huckleberry Hound and Yogi Bear, produced this series of outlandish jungle misadventures, pairing a con–artist lion (Lippy) with a sorrowful but pessimistic hyena (Hardy Har Har). The cartoons were offered to local stations as part of a trilogy, called "The Hanna–Barbera New Cartoon Series," featuring two other cartoon adventures, "Touche Turtle" and "Wally Gator." Although the films were sold to television stations as a package, the cartoons were often programmed independently of each other in their own half–hour time slots. *A Hanna–Barbera Production. Color. Half–hour. Premiered: September 3, 1962. Syndicated.*

Voices:
Lippy: Daws Butler, **Hardy Har Har:** Mel Blanc

Episodes:
(four per show) "Sea–Saw," "Watermelon Felon," "Scare To Spare," "Gulp And Saucer," "Map Happy," "Smile The Wild," "Charge Of The Fight Brigade," "Film Flam," "Gun Fighter Lippy," "Hick Hikers," "A Thousand And One Frights," "Double Trouble," "Laugh A Loaf," "Genie Is A Meany," "Bank For Everything," "Fiddle Faddled," "Kidnap Trap," "Witch Crafty," "Gas Again," "Horse And Waggin'," "Baby Bottled," "Hard Luck," "Show Use," "Injun Trouble," "Mouse In The House," "Crazy Cat Capers," "Phoney Pony," "Egg Experts," "Rabbit Romeo," "Bird In The Hand," "Legion Heirs," "Hoots And Saddles," "Monster Mix–Up," "Bye Bye, Fly Guy," "Wooden Nickels," "Two For The Road," "King's X," "Amusement Park Lark," "T For Two," "Tiny Troubles," "Flood For A Thought," "Hocus Pocus," "Shamrocked," "Ole Fuddy Duds," "Chow You Feelings," "Easy Doesn't It," "Drop Me A Line," "Map Sap," "Shark Shock," "No Spooking Allowed," "Me–My–Mine" and "Together Mess."

LITTLE CLOWNS OF HAPPYTOWN

The inhabitants of a small fantasy town (called Happytown, of course) are all born clowns and their goal in life is to spread the message that "happiness is good for you." Thirteen

episodes were produced and directed by Murakami–Wolf–Swenson Films for Marvel Productions. The program aired one week after ABC premiered most of its 1987–1988 Saturday morning schedule. *An ABC Entertainment Production in association with Marvel Productions and Murakami–Wolf–Swenson Films. Color. Half–hour. Premiered on ABC: September 26, 1987–September 2, 1988.*

Voices:
Charlie Adler, Sue Blu, Danny Cooksey, Pat Fraley, Ellen Gerstell, Howard Morris, Ron Palillo, Josh Rodine, Frank Welker

Episodes:
"Bebad's Pet Peeve," "Carnival Crashers," "Clowny Exchange," "Won't You Please Come Home . . . Blooper, Geek?," "Baby Blues," "Too Scared To Laugh," "City Clowns, Country Clowns," "Nobody's Useless," "To Mr. Pickleherring With Love," "Big Heart, Sweetheart," "To Be Or Not To Be . . . Me," "Lost And Not Found," "Only When I Laugh," "New Dad, No Dad," "I'm Just Like You," "The Chosen Clown," "Goodbye Grandma" and "Don't Tell Mom."

THE LITTLE RASCALS/RICHIE RICH SHOW

The classic fun and humor of the "Our Gang" short–subject series is recaptured in this animated comedy/mystery version, featuring Spanky, Buckwheat, Alfalfa, Darla, and their dog Pete. From their funky tree house, they plan new schemes and plots that send their adversaries into submission in hilarious fashion. The series was paired with all–new episodes of the world's richest youngster, Richie Rich, set in the town of Rich Hill. The character originally premiered in 1980's "The Richie Rich/Scooby–Doo Show." *A Hanna–Barbera Production in association with King Features Entertainment. Color. Half–hour. Premiered on ABC: September 19, 1982–September 1, 1984.*

Filmdom's lovable and mischievous kids of live–action comedy fame face adventure and fun in the comedy–mystery series, "The Little Rascals." © Hanna–Barbera Productions Inc. and King World Productions Inc.

Voices:
Spanky: Scott Menville, **Alfalfa:** Julie McWhirter Dees, **Darla:** Patty Maloney, **Buckwheat:** Shavar Ross, **Porky:** Julie McWhirter Dees, **Butch:** B. J. Ward, **Woim:** Julie McWhirter Dees, **Waldo:** B. J. Ward, **Pete,** the dog: Peter Cullen, **Police Officer Ed:** Peter Cullen, **Richie Rich:** Sparky Marcus, **George Rich,** his father: Stanley Jones, **Mrs. Rich,** his mother: Joan Gerber, **Dollar,** Richie's dog: Frank Welker, **Gloria,** Richie's girlfriend: Nancy Cartwright, **Freckles,** Richie's friend: Christian Hoff, **Irona,** the Rich's maid: Joan Gerber, **Cadbury,** the Rich's butler: Stanley Jones, **Professor Keenbean:** Bill Callaway, **Reggie Van Goh:** Dick Beals

Episodes:
"Little Rascals" (two 11–minute episodes per show).
1982–1983 "Rascal's Revenge," "Yachtsa Luck," "Just Desserts," "Grin And Bear It," "Beauty Queen For A Day," "Class Act," "Big Top Rascals," "Loot Fit To Print," "Tiny Terror," "Irate Pirates," "Science Fair And Foul," "Rock 'N' Roll Rascals," "Alfalfa's Athletes Feat," "Falling Heir," "Porky–O and Julie–Et," "Trash Can Treasure," "Alfalfa For President," "Flim Flam Film Fans," "Alfalfakazam," "Showdown Rascal Corral," "Poached Pooch," "King Of The Hobos," "Big City Rascals," "Cap'n Spanky's Showboat," "Darla's Dream Dance" and "Case Of the Puzzled Pals."
1983–1984 (new episodes combined with reruns) "Save Our Treehouse," "Wash And Werewolf," "Horse Sense," "After Hours," "A Not So Buenos Dias," "Fright Night," "The Big Sneeze," "The Zero Hero" and "Pete's Big Break."
"Little Rascal Vignettes" (30–second spots per show).
"He Who Runs Away," "Fish Fright," "Sea Song," "The Serenade," "Ice Escapades," "Go Cart Go," "Scoop Dupes," "A Swimming We Will Go," "The Surgeon," "No Hit Wit," "Out On A Limb," "Do Or Diet," "Fiscal Fitness" and "The Spare."
"Richie Rich."
1982–1983 (11–minute episodes) "The Youth Maker," "Genie With The Light Brown Hair," "The Collector," "The Giant Ape Caper," "The Haunting Of Castle Rich," "Richie Goes To Sirik," "Sky Hook" and "The Maltese Monkey."
(7–minute episodes) "Boy Of The Year," "Born Flea," "Everybody's Doing It," "The Pie–Eyed Piper," "Suavo," "Look–A–Like," "The Midas Touch" and "Mayda Money."
(three–minute episodes) "Busy Butler," "Dignified Doggy," "Shoe Biz," "Guard Dog," "Dollar's Exercise," "How Human" and "Hard To Study."
(30–second segments) "I Say You All," "Sugar Bowl," "Coin Flipper," "Ball Room," "Money Plant," "Giant Pearl," "Robot Bug Guards," "Snow Flopping," "Toy Dad," "Toy Plane," "Richie's Cube," "Spare Car," "Gold Frame" and "Chocolate Box."
1983–1984 (11–minute episodes) "The T.V. Phantom," "Richie Hood," "Rich No More," "A Whale Of A Tale," "Video World," "The Snowman Cometh," "The Ends Of The Earth," "The Irona Story" and "Mayday And The Monster."

THE LITTLES

These tiny, near–human creatures, who live behind the walls of people's houses, are discovered by a young boy who joins them in many of their adventures. Program was adapted from the popular Scholastic children's book series. *An ABC Enter-*

Tiny, near–human creatures are discovered by a young boy and experience the high road to adventure in the ABC network series, "The Littles." © American Broadcasting Companies Inc. (Courtesy: DIC Enterprises Inc.)

tainment and DIC Enterprises Production. Color. Half–hour. Premiered on ABC: September 10, 1983–September 6, 1986.

Voices:
Henry, the young boy: Jimmy E. Keegan, **Lucy:** Bettina Bush, **Tom:** Donavan Freberg, **Grandpa:** Alvy Moore, **Mrs. Bigg:** Laurel Page, **Mr. Bigg:** Robert David Hall, **Dinky:** Robert David Hall, **Ashley:** B. J. Ward, **Slick:** Patrick Fraley

Episodes:
1983–1984 "Beware Of The Hunter," "Lost City Of The Littles," "The Big Scare, "Lights, Cameras, Littles," "Spirits Of The Night," "The Little Winner," "A Big Cure For A Little Illness," "The Rats Are Coming! The Rats Are Coming!," "A Little Fairy Tale," "Prescription For Disaster," "The Little Scouts," "A Little Gold Alot Of Trouble" and "Dinky's Doomsday Pizza."
1984–1985 "A Little Rock And Roll," "Little Baby Sitters," "Forest Littles," "For The Birds," "Twins," "Looking For Grandpa," "Every Little Vote Counts" and "A Little's Halloween."
1985–1986 "Amazon Queen," "Tut, The Second," "When Irish Eyes Are Smiling," "The Wrong Stuff," "Deadly Jewels," "A Little Drunk," "Ben Dinky" and "The Little Girl Who Could."

LITTLE WIZARDS

A boy–prince seeks to regain his kingdom in this magical fantasy adventure. *A Marvel Production in association with Janson and Menville Productions. Color. Half–hour. Premiered on ABC: September 26, 1987–September 3, 1988.*

Voices:
Charlie Adler, Joey Camen, Peter Cullen, Katie Leigh, Danny Mann, Scott Menville, Amber Souza, Frank Welker

Episodes:
"The Singing Sword," "The Ugly Elfling," "Everything's Ducky," "Zapped From The Future," "I Remember Mama," "The Unicorn's Nada," "A Dragon Tale," "A Little Trouble," "Things

That Go Gump In The Night," "The Gump Who Would Be King," "Puff–Pod Blues," "Boo's Boyfriend" and "Big Gump's Don't Cry."

LONE RANGER

The noted avenger of evil and upholder of justice, also known as the Masked Man, and his faithful Indian companion, Tonto, battle villainous cowboys, cutthroats and ruthless land barons of the Old West. In 1980, Filmation produced a new series of cartoons as part of its "The Tarzan/Lone Ranger Adventure Hour." *A Lone Ranger Production in association with the Jack Wrather Corporation. Color. Half–hour. Premiered on CBS: September 10, 1966–September 6, 1969.*

Voices:
Lone Ranger: Michael Rye, **Tonto:** Shepard Menken, **Etcetera:** Marvin Miller, Hans Conried, **Warlock:** Marvin Miller, **Tiny Tom:** Richard Beals, **Black Widow:** Agnes Moorehead

Additional Voices:
Vic Perrin, Herbert C. Lytton, Glen Cochran, Nestor Paiva, Janet Waldo, Don Doolittle, Henry Corden, Frederic Villani, Paul Winchell, Howard Morris, Denver Pyle, Nancy Houch, Herb Vigran, Douglas Young, Jay North, Peter Leeds, Frank Gerstle, June Foray, Harold Peary

Episodes:
(three per show) 'Ghost Riders," "Wrather Of The Sun God," "Day Of The Dragon," "Bear Claw," "Hunter And The Hunted," "Mephisto," "Revenge Of The Mole," "Frog People," "Terror In Toyland," "Black Mask Of Revenge," "The Sacrifice," "Puppetmaster," "Valley Of The Dead" "Forest Of Death," "The Fly," "A Time To Die," "Ghost Tribe Of Commanche Flat," "Attack Of The Lilliputians," "Circus Of Death," "The Brave," "Cult Of The Black Widow," "El Conquistador," "Snow Creature," "The Prairie Pirate," "Man Of Silver," "Nightmare In Whispering Pine," "Sabotage," "Mastermind," "Lost Tribe Of Golden Giants," "Monster Of Scavenger Crossing," "The Black Panther," "Thomas The Great," "Island Of The Black Widow," "Paddle Wheeling Pirates," "Day At Death's Head Pass," "Mad, Mad, Mad, Mad Scientist," "The Kid," "Stone Hawk," "Sky Raiders," "The Man From Pinkerton," "Tonto And The Devil Spirit," "Deadly Glassman," "Black Knight," "Taka," "Fire Rain," "The Secret Warlock," "Wolfmaster," "Death Hunt," "The Secret Army Of General X," "The Cat People," "Night Of The Vampire," "Terrible Tiny Tom," "Fire Monster," "The Iron Giant," "Towntamers, Inc.," "Curse Of The Devil Doll," "It Came From Below," "The Trickster," "Crack Of Doom," "Mr. Midaas," "Black Arrow," "The Rainmaker," "Flight Of The Hawk," "The Avenger," "Battle At Barnaby's Bend," "Puppetmaster's Revenge," "Reign Of The Queen Bee," "Kingdom of Terror," "Quicksilver," "Legend Of Cherokee Smith," "The Day The West Stood Still," "Border Rats," "Lash And The Arrow" and "Spectre Of Death."

LOONEY TUNES

In 1955, in both New York (WABD–TV) and Los Angeles (KTLA–TV), Warner Brothers' library of pre–1948 "Looney Tunes," a calvacade of the studio's most memorable cartoon stars (Bosko, Buddy, Daffy Duck, Porky Pig and others), made their television premiere. (Initially the films were seen on weekdays with local personalities hosting the show.) At first, the studio released 190 cartoons under the series name to television. Prints of each film were black–and–white and it wasn't until 1969, when television stations across the country demanded color, that Warner Brothers struck color prints of those films which were originally produced in that form. In 1960, Warner added their post–1948 color "Looney Tunes" to the package for syndication. *A Warner Brothers Production. Black and white. Color. Half–hour. Premiered: April 11, 1955.*

MACRON I

It's A.D. 25245, a time of new galactic frontiers, astounding technology and terrifying evil. A teleportation experiment goes wrong and test pilot, David Jance, is rocketed through the center of the galaxy into another universe caught in a life–and–death struggle against the tyrannical armies of Grip, led by the villainous Dark Star. The good forces of both universes combine and form Macron 1 to defeat Dark Star's army in this action–packed adventure series, backed by the latest Top–40 rock tunes. Rock group Duran Duran performed the series' theme song, entitled, "Reflex." *A Saban Production. Color. Half–hour. Premiered: September, 1985. Syndicated.*

Voices:
Angeria Rigamonti, Bill Laver, Christopher Eric, Octavia Beaumont, Tamara Shawn, Rich Ellis, Susan Ling, Oliver Miller

THE MAGICAL PRINCESS GIGI

Light–hearted fantasy about the Princess from the Kingdom of Fairyland, who comes to earth as a 12–year–old mortal, but with the powers of a Fairy Princess, to do good deeds. The title of this Japanese import was originaly, "The Magical

Famous western star hero, the Lone Ranger, gallops off to brand–new animated adventures for television.
© Lone Ranger Productions

World Of Gigi." *A Harmony Gold Production. Color. Half-hour. Premiered: 1984. Syndicated.*

Voices:
Reva West, Lisa Paullette, Sal Russo, Abe Hurt, Betty Gustafson, Ryan O'Flannigan, Anita Pia, Sam Jones

THE MAGILLA GORILLA SHOW

The anxious, bewildered owner of Mr. Pebbles Pet Shop in Los Angeles, California makes futile bids to sell or even give away his permanent animal resident, an amiable and fun-loving gorilla named Magilla, who by nature stumbles into all sorts of fantastic and unbelievable incidents. His best friend is a little neighborhood girl called Ogee.

The gorilla made his entrance into syndicated television in January, 1964, as the star of this three–segment cartoon series. The two original components of the show were "Richochet Rabbit," a fast–paced rabbit sheriff who chases all dirty-deeders out of town with the aide of his deputy, Droop–a–Long Coyote; and "Breezly and Sneezly," the misadventures of a foolish polar bear (Breezly) and clear–minded arctic seal (Sneezly) who spend most of their time trying to infiltrate an Alaskan army base, Camp Frostbite, headed by camp commander, Colonel Fusby.

In the fall of 1964, "Breezly and Sneezly" were replaced by the adventures of "Punkin Puss and Mush Mouse," a pair of hillbilly cats who engage in a non–stop feud in the realm of "The Hatfields and the McCoys." With the exception of "Breezly and Sneezly," new episodes of each series regular were added to the program for each season during its original syndication and network run. Sponsor: Ideal Toys. *A Hanna–Barbera Production. Color. Half–hour. Premiered: January 14, 1964. Rebroadcast on ABC: January 1, 1966–September 2, 1967. Syndicated.*

Voices:
Magilla Gorilla: Allan Melvin, **Mr. Peebles:** Howard Morris, **Ogee:** Jean VanderPyl, **Breezly:** Howard Morris, **Sneezly:** Mel Blanc, **Colonel Fusby:** John Stephenson, **Punkin Puss:** Allan Melvin, **Mush Mouse:** Howard Morris, **Ricochet Rabbit:** Don Messick, **Droop–a–Long Coyote:** Mel Blanc

Episodes:
"Magilla Gorilla" (one per show).
1963–1964 "Big Game," "Gridiron Gorilla," "Private Magilla," "Bank Pranks," "Groovey Movie," "Airlift," "Come Blow Your Dough," "Mad Scientist," "Masquerade Party," "Come Back, Little Magilla," "Fairy Godmother," "Planet Zero," "Prince Charming," "Motorcycle Magilla" and "Is That Zoo?"
1964–1965 "Bird Brained," "Circus Ruckus," "Camp Scamps," "The Purple Mask," "Love At First Sight," "Pet Bet," "Makin' With The Magilla," "High Fly Guy" and "Deep Sea Doodle."
1965–1966 "That Was The Greek That Was," "Montana Magilla" and "Magilla Mix–Up."
1966–1967 (new episodes for network) "Wheelin' And Deal," "Mad Avenue Madness," "Beau Jest" and "Super–Blooper Heroes."
"Richochet Rabbit" (one per show).
1963–1964 "Atchison, Topeka, And San Jose," "Good Little

Bad Guy," "Cradle Robber," "West Pest," "TV Show," "Annie Hoaxley," "School Daze," "Sheepy Wolf," "Big Thinker" and "Two Too Many."
1964–1965 "Bad Guys Are Good Guys," "Itchy–Finger Gunslinger," "Clunko Bunko," "Slick Quick Gun," "Mostly Ghostly," "Will O' The Whip" and "Cactus Ruckus."
1965–1966 "Rapid Romance" and "El Loco, Loco, Loco, Loco Diablo."
1966–1967 (new episodes for network) "Big Town Show Down," "Space Sheriff," "Red Riding Richochet" and "Jail Break–In."
"Breezly and Sneezly" (one per show).
1964–1965 "No Place Like Home," "All Riot On The Northern Front," "Missle Fizzle," "Mass Masquerade," "Furry Furlough," "Bruin Ruin," "Freezing Fleas," "Stars and Gripes," "Armored Amour," "As The Snow Flies," "Snow Biz," "Unseen Trouble," "Nervous In The Service," "Birthday Bonanza" and "Wacky Waikiki."
1965–1966 "General Nuisance," "Rookie Wrecker," "Noodick Of The North," "The Fastest Bear In The North," "Snow Time Show Time" and "Goat–A–Go–Go."
1966–1967 (new episodes for network) "Spy In The Ointment" and "An Ill Wind."
"Punkin Puss And Mush Mouse" (one per show).
1963–1964 "Callin' All Kin," "Small Change," "Hornswoggled," "Gall Of The Wild," "Cat Nipped," "Amry–Nervy Game," "Seein' Is Believin'," "Courtin' Disaster," "A Tale Of Two Kitties," "Chomp Romp," "Catch As Cat Can Day," "Jump Bumps," "Nowhere–Bear," "Legend Of Bat Monsterson" and "Super Drooper."
1964–1965 "Pep Hep" and "Shot At And Missed."
1965–1966 "The Mouse from S.O.M.P." and "Hose Of A Ghost."
1966–1967 (new episodes for network) "Feudal Feud," "Heir Conditioning," "Hyde and Shriek" and "Misfortune Cookie."

MAPLETOWN

The Raccoon family and friends, based on Tonka's best-selling toy line, enjoy exciting adventures in this half-hour series for syndication. *A Saban/Maltese Companies Production in association with Toei Animation. Color. Half-hour. Premiered: Fall 1987. Syndicated.*

Voices:
Mrs. Maple: Janice Adams

Additional Voices:
Jeff Iwai, Wayne Kerr, Bebe Linet, Heidi Lenhart, Lou Pitt, Alice Smith, Jon Zahler, Tracey Alexander

Episodes:
"Welcome To Mapletown," "The Stolen Encklace," "The Pot That Wouldn't Hold Water," "The Greatest Treasure Of All," "A Baby Comes To Mapletown," "When Children Must Be Grownups," "The Case Of The Missing Candy," "Teacher Please Don't Go," "The House Made Of Love," "A Most Unlikely Heroine," "The Prettiest Dress In Mapletown," "The Children's Forest Patrol," "Medicine From Maple Mountain" and "The Ransom Of Maple Forest."

MARINE BOY

Campy series imported from Japan ("It's Marine Boy, brave and free, fighting evil beneath the sea . . .") about a daring aquaboy, the son of aquatic scientist Dr. Mariner, who dedicates himself to preserving the world for all mankind, most notably beneath the sea. Drawing oxygen from Oxygum, life–sustaining oxygen in gum form, he keeps the world safe as a member of the Ocean Patrol, an international defense organization headed by his father. With shipmates Bulton, Piper and pet dolphin Splasher (named "Whity" in the Japanese version), Marine Boy takes to the watery depths in their P–1 submarine to battle the Patrol's main foes—Captain Kidd, Count Shark and Dr. Slime—using special gear (a bullet–proof wet suit, propellor boots and an electric/sonic boomerang) to emerge victorious. The series was the second Japanese import to be produced in color (NBC's "Kimba the White Lion" was the first) and three of the series' 78 episodes (numbers 41, 55 and 57) never aired in the United States. Japanese series name: "Kaitai Shonen Marine." *A Japan Tele-cartoons Production. Color. Half–hour. Premiered: October, 1966. Syndicated.*

Voices:

Marine Boy/Neptina/Cli Cli: Corinne Orr, **Dr. Mariner:** Jack Curtis, **Bulton:** Peter Fernandez, **Piper:** Jack Grimes, **Splasher,** Marine Boy's dolphin: Jack Grimes, **Dr. Fumble:** Jack Grimes, **Commander:** Jack Grimes

Episodes:

"The Green Monster," "Danger 300 Fathoms," "Monsters Of The Deep," "Dangerous Starfish," "Amazing Shellfish" (only episode with Lint, Marine Boy's mother), "Mysterious Paradise" (first episode with Cli Cli), "Deepest Of The Deep," "Ghost Ship," "Monsterous Seaweed," "Super Mystery Boat," "Greatest Power," "Disaster On The High Seas," "Secret Of The Time Capsule," "Mystery Missing Vessel," "Menace Missing Bomb," "Danger In the Depths," "Gigantic Sea Farm," "Terror Of The Fire Ball," "Empire Of The Seal," "Operation Gold," "Terrifying Icebergs," "Whale Of Destruction," "Power Of Power," "5 Billion In Diamonds," "Cockscrew Straights," "Lighthouse Of Terror," "Invincible Force," "Vanishing Frogmen," "Panic Pacific," "24 Hours Til Doom," "Attack Of The Robot Spiders," "Great Bomb Robbery," "Operation Deep Deep," "Stolen Island," "Under Water Underworld," "Whale Rustlers," "Robot Raiders," "Robot Sharks," "Monster Search," "Well Hidden Plan," "Film Flam Of The High Seas," "Pirates Of The Deep," "Robot Brain," "Undersea Train Robbery," "Genius Dolphin" (features Splasher the talking dolphin), "Nuclear Patrolmen," "Undersea Lion," "Mini Micro Wave," "Ultra Freezer Freeze," "Tubsub Tanker Sub," "Tremendous Tremendo," "Spook Island," "Whale Who Blew Rainbows," "Showdown Of Sea," "Precious Robot," "Fight Of The Rocket," "Invincible Robots," "Island Of Treasure," "Thieves Of The Deep," "Wild Monster Man," "Vanishing Vessel," "Challenges Of The Pirates," "Land Of Strange Vikings," "Attack Of The Icebergs," "Deadly Tank," "Avenger Of The Sea," "Desperate Search," "Secret Of Gold Seaweed," "Fantastic Flash," "Stormy Brain Storm," "Gillman" and "Great Sea Escape."

MARVEL ACTION UNIVERSE

Spider–Man is among a cast of superhero characters featured in animated action/adventure stories adapted for television. Other components included "Dinoriders" and "RoboCop," the latter based on the hit motion picture. A cartoon version of the comic–book series, "X–Men," was originally planned as a regular segment of the series. One cartoon was produced, "Pryde of the X–Men," which aired during the series' syndicated run. *A Marvel Production. Color. One hour and a half. Premiered: October 2, 1988. Syndicated.*

Voices:

Charlie Adler, Michael Bell, Robert Bockstael, Earl Bowen, Barbara Budd, Wally Burr, Len Carlson, Andi Chapman, Cam Clarke, Joe Colligen, Peter Cullen, Shawn Donahue, Pat Fraley, Ronald Gans, Dan Gilvezan, Rex Hagon, Dan Hennessey, Ron James, Gordon Matson, Greg Morton, Noelle North, Allen Oppenheimer, Patrick Pinney, Susan Roman, Neil Ross, Susan Silo, Kath Soucie, John Stephenson, Alexander Stoddart, Alan Stewart–Coates, Chris Ward, Frank Welker

Episodes:

"Spider–Man" (one per show).
"Bubble, Bubble, Oil And Trouble," "Dr. Doom–Master Of The World," "Lizards, Lizards Everywhere," "Curiosity Killed The Spiderman," "The Sandman Is Coming," "When Magneto Speaks . . . People Listen," "The Pied Piper Of New York Town," "The Doctor Prescribes Doom," "Carnival Of Crime," "Revenge Of The Green Goblin," "Triangle Of Evil," "The A–B–C's Of D–O–O–M," "The Sidewinder Strikes," "The Hunter And The Hunted," "The Incredible Shrinking Spider–Man," "The Unfathomable Professor Gizmo," "Canon Of Doom," "The Capture Of Captain America," "The Doom Report," "The Web Of Nephilia," "Countdown To Doom," "Arsenic And Aunt May," "Wrath Of The Sub–Mariner!," "The Return Of Kingpin" and "Under The Wizard's Spell."
"Dinoriders" (one per show).
"The Rulon Stampede," "The Blue Skies Of Earth," "Toro, Toro, Torosaurus," "T–Rex," "Krulos," "Tagg, You're It!," "Thanksgiving," "To Lose The Path," "Enter The Commandos," "Battle For the Brontosaurus" and "One To Lead Us."
"Robocop" (one per show).
"Crime Wave," "The Scrambler," "Project Deathspore," "The Brotherhood," "The Man In The Iron Suit," "The Hot Seat," "No News Is Good News," "Night Of The Archer," "Rumble In Old Detroit," "A Robot's Revenge," "Into The Wilderness" and "Menace Of The Mind."

MARVEL SUPERHEROES

Five famous Marvel comic book characters—Incredible Hulk, Iron Man, Sub–Mariner, The Mighty Thor and Captain America—starred in this half–hour children's series based on the long–running comic book adventures. The films were animated in the style of comic book panels, with the characters appearing in a series of still poses (only their lips moved). The names of the actors who voiced the characters in the series remain unknown. *A Grantray–Lawrence Animation Production. Color. Half–hour. Syndicated: 1966–1968.*

Episodes:
(known titles listed only)
"Captain America."
"The Origin Of Captain America," "Wreckers Among Us," "Enter Red Skull," "The Girl From Cap's Past," "The Stage Is Set!," "30 Minutes To Live," "Midnight In Greymore Castle," "If This Be Treason," "When You Lie Down With Dogs," "Zemo And His Masters Of Evil," "Zemo Strikes," "The Fury Of Zemo," "The Sleeper Shall Awake," "Where Walks The Sleeper," "The Final Sleep," "The Sentinel And The Spy," "The Fantastic Origin Of The Red Skull" and "Lest Tyranny Triumph."
"Incredible Hulk."
"The Origin Of The Hulk," "Enter The Gorgon," "To Be A Man," "Micro Monsters," "The Lair Of The Leader," "To Live Again," "Brawn Against Brain," "Captured At Last" and "Enter . . . The Chameleon."
"Iron Man."
"Double Disaster," "Enter Happy Hogan," "Of Ice And Men," "The Moleman Strikes," "The Dragon Of Flames," "Decision Under The Earth," "The Death Of Tony Stark," "The Hands Of The Mandarin," "The Origin Of The Mandarin," "If I Die, Let It Be With Honor," "Fight On, For A World Is Watching," "What Price Victory?," "The Mandarin's Revenge," "The Mandarin's Death Ray" and "No One Escapes The Mandarin."
"Sub–Mariner."
"Doctor Doom's Day," "The Doomed Alligience," "Tug Of Death," "Atlantis Under Attack," "The Sands Of Terror," "The Iron Idol Of Infamy," "The Thing From Space," "No Escape For Namor," "A Prince Dies Fighting," "To Walk Amongst Men," "When Rises The Behemoth," "To The Death," "Not All My Power Can Save Me," "The Start Of The Quest," "When Fails The Quest," "The End Of The Quest," "Escape To No-where" and "A Prince There Was."
"The Mighty Thor."
"The Absorbing Man," "In My Hands, This Hammer," "Vengeance Of The Thunder God," "The Grey Gargoyle," "The Wrath Of Odin," "Triumph In Stone," "The Tomorrow Man," "Return Of Zarko," "Every Hand Against Him," "The Power Of The Thunder God," "The Power Of Odin," "Enter Hercules," "When Meet Immortals" and "Whom The Gods Would Destroy."

M.A.S.K.

Led by Matt Tracke, the Mobile Armored Strike Kommand (M.A.S.K.) is a secret organization that fights crime in an unusual fashion. By donning specially charged masks, they have extraordinary powers to undermine the villainous forces of VENOM, in their insidious plot for world control. The series was close–captioned for the hearing impaired. *A DIC Enterprises Production in association with Kenner Products, a division of Kenner Parker Toys Incorporated. Color. Half–hour. Premiered: September, 1985. Syndicated.*

Voices:
Matt Tracker: Doug Stone, **Alex Sector:** Brendon McKane **Floyd Malloy:** Brendon McKane, **Miles Mayhem:** Brendon McKane, **Jacques Lafleur:** Brendon McKane, **Nevada Rushmore:** Brendon McKane, **Brad:** Graem McKenna, **Calhoun**

Burns: Graem McKenna, **T–Bob:** Graem McKenna, **Buddy Hawkes:** Mark Halloran, **Ace Riker:** Mark Halloran, **Sly Rax:** Mark Halloran, **Gloria Baker:** Sharon Noble, **Vanessa Warfield:** Sharon Noble, **Scott:** Brennan Thicke, **Nash Gorey:** Doug Stone, **Dusty Hayes:** Doug Stone, **Bruno Shepard:** Doug Stone, **Boris Bushkin:** Doug Stone, **Max Mayhem:** Doug Stone, **Lester Sludge:** Brian George, **Jimmy Rashad:** Brian George

Episodes:
1986–1987 "The Deathstone," "The Star Chariot," "Book Of Power," "Highway To Terror," "Video Venom," "Dinosaur Boy," "The Ultimate Weapon," "The Roteks," "The Oz Effect," "Death From The Sky," "Magma Mole," "Solaria Park," "The Creeping Terror," "Assault On Liberty," "The Sceptre Of Rajim," "The Golden Goddess," "Mystery Of The Rings," "Bad Vibrations," "Ghost Bomb," "Cold Fever," "Mardi Gras Mystery," "The Secret Of Life," "Vanishing Point," "Counter–Clockwise Caper," "Plant Show," "Secret Of The Andes," "Panda Power," "Blackout," "A Matter Of Gravity," "The Lost Riches Of Rio," "Deadly Blue Slime," "The Currency Conspiracy," "Caesar's Sword," "Peril Under Paris," "In Dutch," "The Lippizaner Mystery," "The Sacred Rock," "Cured Of Soluma Gorge," "Green Nightmare," "Eyes Of The Skull," "Stop Motion," "The Artemis Enigma," "The Chinese Scorpion," "Riddle Of The Raven Master," "The Spectre Of Captain Kidd," "The Secret Of Stones," "The Lost Fleet," "Quest Of The Canyon," "Follow The Rainbow," "The Everglades Oddity," "Dragonfire," "The Royale Cape Caper," "Patchwork Puzzle," "Fog On Boulder Hill," "Plunder Of Glowworm Grotto," "Stone Trees," "Incident In Istanbul," "The Creeping Desert," "The Scarlet Empress," "Venice Menace," "Treasure Of The Nazca Plain," "Disappearing Act," "Gate Of Darkness," "The Manakara Giant" and "Raiders Of The Orient Express."
1987–1988 "Demoliltion Duel To The Death," "Where Eagles Dare," "Homeward Bound," "Battle Of The Giants," "Race Against Time," "Challenge Of The Masters," "For One Shining Moment . . .," "High Noon," "The Battle For Baja" and "Cliff Hanger."

MATTY'S FUNDAY FUNNIES

Mattel Toys sponsored this repackaged version of former Paramount Famous Studios cartoons—Casper the Friendly Ghost, Herman and Katnip, Little Audrey, Baby Huey and other minor characters from the studio's *Noveltoons* series (Buzzy the Crow, Owly the Owl, Finny the Goldfish, etc.)—which originally premiered on late Sunday afternoons on ABC. The films, renamed "Harveytoons" (after Harvey Publishing Company, which purchased the rights to the old cartoons), were presented by two weekly hosts, a young boy, Matty, and his Sisterbelle, who introduced each cartoon adventure.

Instantly successful with young audiences, the program was moved to prime–time in 1960, airing one hour before "The Flintstones." In 1962, the network overhauled the series by replacing the "Harveytoons" with the cartoon adventures of "Beany and Cecil," animated versions of Bob Clampett's syndicated puppet show, "Time for Beany." The show was initially retitled "Matty's Funnies with Beany and Cecil." In April,

1962, when ABC decided to drop the series' cartoon hosts, the program was simply named "Beany and Cecil." The riotous adventures of Beany, Cecil, Captain Huffenpuff and Dishonest John were given their own Saturday—morning time slot in January, 1963, after the "Matty's Funday Funnies" series concluded its network run. (See individual cartoon components for voice credit and episodic information.) *A Harvey Films and Bob Clampett Production for ABC. Black—and—white. Color. Premiered on ABC: October 11, 1959—December 29, 1962.*

MAXIE'S WORLD

One of the most popular students at Surfside High School, Maxie, a bright and pretty young girl, is the center of a series of adventures shaped around schoolmates, the loves of her life and her outside interests, including her own local weekly television show. *A DIC Enterprises Production. Color. Half-hour. Premiered: September, 1989. Syndicated.*

Voices:

Maxie: Loretta Jafelice, **Rob:** Simon Reynolds, **Carly:** Tara Charendoff, **Ashley:** Susan Roman, **Simone:** Suzanne Coy, **Jeri:** Nadine Rabinovitch, **Ferdie:** Yannick Bisson, **Mushroom:** Geoff Kahnert, **Mr. Garcia:** John Stocker

Episodes:

"Date Expectations," "Ride For Your Life," "Wheelie Bad Dudes," "The Not—So Great Outdoors," "Goodbye Ghoul World," "This Rap's For You," "To Be Or Not To Be Ferdie," "Misadentures In Babysitting," "Breaking Up Is Hard To Do," "Fat Chance," "The Maxie Horror Picture Show," "The Phantom Artists," "Two Guys For Every Girl," "Ashes to Ashley," "A Day In The Life Of Rob," "Surfside Over The Rainbow," "Very Superstitious," "I Was A Teenage Council Member," "Mushroom and Ferdie's Hysterical Historical Adventure," "Pirouettes and Forward Passes," "Friend Or UFO?," "Photo Opportunity," "Do Or Diary," "Beach Blanket Battle," "Teaching An Old Teacher New Tricks," "Hero Word—Ship," "Dear Hunk," "The Slumber Party," "A Dog's Tale," "The Five Finger Discount," "True Brit" and "Future Schlock."

MAX, THE 2000 YEAR OLD MOUSE

Producer Steve Krantz created Max, a lovable, little mouse, who takes viewers back through the most exciting world events of the past 2,000 years. The educational cartoon series combined film clips and still pictures to tell each story, hosted at the beginning and the end by the program's mouse historian. Memorable moments include Columbus discovering America, the *Mayflower* voyage, first Thanksgiving, Paul Revere's historic ride and the battle of New Orleans. For trivia buffs, the theme music for the program was later heard on Siskel and Ebert's movie—review series, "Sneak Previews," on PBS. *A Krantz Animation Production. Color. Half-hour. Syndicated: 1969. Voice credits unknown.*

Episodes:

"The Trojan War" (pilot), "The First Flight Of The Wright Brothers," "Sails Around The World With Magellan" "Hannibal

Lovable mouse Max takes viewers back 2,000 years to some of the most exciting scenes in America's history in "Max, The 2000 Year Old Mouse." (Courtesy: Westchester Films)

Crossing The Alps," "Tom Edison, The Wizard Of Menlo Park," "Paul Revere's Ride," "Cortez And Montezuma Of The Aztecs," "The Battle Of New Orleans," "Defeat Of The Spanish Armada," "The Battle Of Quebec," "Stanley And Livingston," "Sullivan Vs. Kilrain," "Louis Pasteur And The Battle Against Germs," "The Munity Aboard The Bounty," "Pickett's Charge And The Gettysburg Address," "The Buccaneers," "The Queen That Conquered Rome," "The Road To Conquest," "The Home Of The Braves," "Lawrence Of Arabia," "The Storming Of The Bastille," "From The Mayflower To The First Thanksgiving," "David And Goliath," "Simon Bolivar And The Battle Of New Granada," "How The Earl Of Huntingdon Became Robin Hood," "Lord Nelson At The Battle Of Trafalgar," "Mark Twain And The Jumping Frog," "A Voyage With Sinbad The Sailor," "The Genius General," "Things That Went Bang In The Sky" (Knights Of The Sky) "Black Jack Pershing," "The Girl That Conquered Kings (Joan Of Arc)," "The Master Of The World," "The San Francisco Earthquake," "Rides With Jesse James," "Farragut At Mobile Bay," "The Battle Of The Monitor And The Merrimack," "The Scourage Of Samarkand" (Temerlane), "Max Remembers The Alamo," "The Detectives Of Scotland Yard," "Henry Ford And The Tin Lizzie," "It's Magic," "Working On The Railroad," "Saladin—The Saracen Sword," "The Queen Who Kept Her Head" (Queen Elizabeth), "Warrior On Ice" (Alexander Nevski), "Lewis And Clark And The Bird Woman," "William The Conqueror At The Battle Of Hastings," "The Panama Canal And The Battle Against The Mosquito," "The Battle Of Agincourt," "Voyages With The Vikings," "Benedict Arnold," "John Peter Zenger," "The Trojan War," "Beauty And The Beast," "Aladdin And The Magic Lamp," "Daniel Boone," "Columbus," "Alexander The Great," "George Washington," "From Galley To Submarine," "Ben Franklin," "Moses," "Ali Baba And The Forty Thieves," "Joseph And His Brothers," "Noah," "Hero Of The Two Flags" (Lafayette), "Winner Of The West" (Buffalo Bill), "First Conqueror Of The World" (Marco Polo), "Thomas Jefferson," "Thunder—Lizard," "Andrew Jackson," "The Giant Of Kings," "The Planting Of James-town," "Makes An Aquarium," "Discovering Reptiles," "Good Knight" (Knighthood), "The Glory Of Rome," "Davy Crockett," "Johnny Appleseed," "Mike Fink," "Fighting Admiral" (John Paul Jones), "Genghis Kahn," "Catherine The Great," "Justinian And Belisarius", "Mohammed," "Galileo," "Charlemagne," "Leonardo de Vinci," "Attila The Hun," "Shackelton In Antartica," "Peary At The North Pole," "Michelangelo," "John Glenn," "Robert Goddard," "Richard Byrd," "Amelia Earhardt," "PT 109," "Lindbergh," "The Rebirth Of Art," "To The Moon," "Coldest Places On Earth," "With The World Conquerors," "Three Brave Presidents" and "The Best Shot."

MAYA THE-BEE

Maya, a friendly little bee, protects her other bug friends in stories that relate the importance of sharing, loving and friendship in this half–hour series based on Waldemar Bonsels' *The Adventures Of Maya the Bee. An Apollo Film Production for Saban International. Color. Half–hour. Premiered on Nickelodeon: January 1, 1990.*

Voices:

Maya: Pauline Little, **Willi:** Richard Dumont, **Flip:** R. J. Henderson, **Grimelda:** Anna MacCormack, **Cassandra:** Jane Woods

Episodes:

"Maya And The Ants," "Max The Earthworm," "Maya And The Frog," "The House Visit," "Grimelda's Web," "Something's Burning," "Grandma Locust," "Baby Cricket's First Symphony," "An Ant For A Day," "The Ant Hill," "The Jumping Contest," "Centipede," "The Littlest Hero," "A Plain Adventure," "Uninvited Guest," "Eggs, Eggs, Everywhere" (A Problem With Eggs), "Maya And The Firefly," "How Crickets Were Freed," "The Invisible Insect," "Alf The Elf," "That's What Friends Are For," "Emmet Goes On A Diet," "The Runaway Ant," "Maya Comes Home," "General Blusterby," "On The Run," "Flip N' Flap," "Maya To The Rescue," "Maya Survives Winter," "Spring Is Here," "Maya And Kurt's Rescue," "The Caterpillar Finds A Home," "Jack The Moth," "The Parasite Fly," "The Show–Off Cockroach," "Sailing The High Seas," "Captured," "The Reluctant Musician," "The Beauty Contest," "Flip's Greedy Relative," "Maya The Giantess," "Gus And Emma," "The Weight–Lifting Competition," "The Mysterious Cheese Thief," "Panic In The Meadow," "The Baby Bird," "Fleas In The Field," "Mouse In The Bottle," "City Slickers," "Willi Stands Guard," "Home Sweet Home," "The Guest From Outerspace," "The Marathon," "The Army Ants Are Coming" and "A Windy Adventure."

MEATBALLS AND SPAGHETTI

Rock musicians Meatballs and Spaghetti, his mod singer–wife, turned animated cartoon stars along with Clyde, Meatball's sidekick and Woofer, Spaghetti's loyal dog in a variety of misadventures featuring original songs performed by the famous rock group. *A Marvel Production in association with InterMedia Entertainment. Color. Half–hour. Premiered on CBS: September 18, 1982–September 10, 1985.*

Voices:

Jack Angel, Wally Burr, Phillip Clarke, Peter Cullen, Ronald Ganes, Barry Gordon, David Hall, Sally Julian, Morgan Lofting, Ron Masak, Bill Ratner, Ronnie Schell, Marilyn Schreffler, Hal Smith, Frank Welker, Paul Winchell

Episodes:

"Woofer The Wonder Dog," "Mixed Up Medical Reports," "Once Upon A Farm," "Spaghetti's Old Boyfriend," "Space Aliens," "Come Back Little Woofer," "Monkey Doodle Dandies," "Going To The Dogs," "Piracy On The High C's," "The Kid Sitters," "Foreign Legion Air–Heads," "Woofer Meets Tweeter," "A Christmas Tale," "Jazz Meets Jaws," "The Werewolf Story," "The Big Shrink," "Watch The Birdie," "Sunken Treasure Cruise," "Throwing The Bull," "The Caveman Story," "Robot Roadie," "Double Or Nothing," "Magical Moments," "Flying Carpet Caper" and "Beach Peaches."

MGM CARTOONS

First syndicated in 1960, this series offered for the first time Metro–Goldwyn–Mayer's pre–1948 animated films to television stations for local programming. The package included such studio cartoon favorites as "Tom and Jerry," "Barney Bear," "Screwy Squirrel," "George and Junior," "Bosko" (not the Warner Brothers' version), "Captain and the Kids" and "Happy Harmonies." (See individual series in Theatrical Sound Cartoon Series for details.) *A Metro–Goldwyn–Mayer Production. Black–and–White. Color. Premiered: September, 1960. Syndicated.*

Voices:

Barney Bear/Captain: Billy Bletcher, **Bosko:** Carmen Maxwell, **Little Cheezer:** Bernice Hansen, **George:** Frank Graham, **Junior:** Tex Avery

THE MIGHTY HERCULES

Mythological Greek hero Hercules, his beautiful maiden, Helena, and their half–human horse, Newton, traverse the plush Learien Valley of ancient Greece thwarting the machinations of the villainous Daedalius. The series' theme song, "The Mighty Hercules," was written by Johnny Nash. *An Adventure Cartoons Production in association with Trans–Lux. Color. Half–hour. Premiered: September, 1963. Syndicated.*

Voices:

Hercules: Jerry Bascome, **Newton/Tewt/Daedalius:** Jimmy Tapp, **Helena:** Helene Nickerson

Episodes:

(three per show) "Hercules Versus The Many–Headed Hydra," "Hercules Saves The Villagers," "Hercules And The Magic Arrows," "Hercules Battles The Krudes Beast," "The Chair Of Forgetfulness," "The Cave Of Death," "Medusa's Sceptre," "Search Of The Golden Apples," "The Bewitch Birds," "The Enchanted Pool," "The Endless Chasm," "The Thunderbolt Disc," "The Sun–Diamond Of Helios," "Hercules Protects Helena And Newton," "The Defiant Mask Of Vulcan," "The Golden Goblet," "The Lexas Lagoon," "Guarding Of The

Hercules captures long–time nemesis Daedalius in a scene from "The Mighty Hercules." © Joe Oriolo Productions

Olympic Torch," "Hercules Helps King Neptune," "Hercules Versus The Hideous Bird–Beast," "The Return Of The Mask," "Hercules Saves Helena," "The Magnetic Stone," "The Magic Rod," "The Minotaur," "Hercules And The Eternal Sleep," "The Clutching Clay Pool," "Princess Rhea," "The Valley Of Whirlwinds," "The Wild Boar," "The Magic Belt Of Hercules," "The Errand Of Mercy," "The Neamean Leion," "The Magician," "Dorian's Wreath," "The Unicorn," "Wilamene The Witch And The Magic Ring," "Diomedes' Evil Plot," "Hercules' Unwanted Powers," "The Enchanted Wolf," "Hercules Saves The Kingdom," "Hercules And His Two Rivals," "Hercules Saves The King," "The Thracian Army," "The Gems Of Venus," "The Golden Torch," "The Chameleon Creature," "Earthquake Valley," "Newton The Centaur," "Helena Kidnapped—Hercules To The Rescue," "Hercules And His Friends," "The Magic Sword," "Timon's Grandfather And Hercules," "Hercules Loses His Memory," "The Hall Of Justice," "The Cave Of Callisto," "The Powerless Hercules," "Omar, The Sultan's Champion," "Sandals Of Electra," "The Sea Witch," "The Giant," "Helena's Beauty," "The Island Of The Miros Monster," "Hercules And The Fireball," "Hercules Outwits The Magician," "The Evil Weapon," "The Giant Ruby," "The Owl Man," "The Chameleon Man," "Hercules Foils The Mask Of The Vulcan," "The Exploding Diamond," "Hercules And The Sea Witch," "The Magic Lamp," "The Owl–Man Of Panssus," "The Eruption Of The Mount Sirus," "The Deadly Gift," "The Thesian Thunderhorn," "The Dreaded Beast of Charon," "Hercules, Newton And The Evil Magician," "The Fiery Abyss," "The Giant Dragonfly," "Tewt's Magic Wand Trouble," "The Wings Of Mercury," "The Sea–Beast," "Prometheus In Dire Danger," "The Crafty Chameleon," "Kingdom Under The Glass Dome," "The Fantus Beast," "The Lyssidian Locusts," "Hercules Saves Calydon," "Helena's Jinx," "The Sinister Statue," "Friend Or Foe Of Centaur," "The Young Olympians," "The Feast Of Calydon," "The Lava Flow," "The Dreaded Draught," "Underwater Battle," "The Sidian Illusion Stone," "Timon To The Aid Of Hercules," "The Fiery Pits Of Pyros," "The Clovis Creature," "The Valley Of Storms," "The Centaur On Mischief Day," "The

Throne Of Calydon," "Battle Of The Magic Rings," "Diomedes And His Warriors" and "King For A Day."

THE MIGHTY HEROES

Terrytoons, creators of Mighty Mouse, produced this half–hour series for television featuring a strange quintet of crime–fighters—Diaper Man, Cuckoo Man, Rope Man, Strong Man and Tornado Man (each with a large "H" emblazoned on his costume)—who uses their wit and muscle to champion the likes of such arch–criminals as the Ghost Monster, Enlarger, Frog, Toy Man, Shocker, Shrinker and Scarecrow. Ralph Bakshi, of *Fritz the Cat* fame, created the series. *A Terrytoons Production. Color. Half–hour. Premiered on CBS: October 29, 1966–September 2, 1967.*

Voices:
The Mighty Heroes: Herschel Benardi, Lionel Wilson

Episodes:
"The Plastic Blaster," "The Frog," "The Junker," "The Shrinker," "The Ghost Monster," "The Stretcher," "The Monsterizer," "The Drifter," "The Shocker," "The Enlarger," "The Toy Man," "The Dusters," "The Big Freeze," "The Timekeeper," "The Scarecrow," "The Time Eraser," "The Return Of The Monsterizer," "The Paper Monster," "The Raven" and "The Bigger Digger."

THE MIGHTY MOUSE PLAYHOUSE

Brawny superhero Mighty Mouse, Terrytoons' most popular character, was the star of this pioneer cartoon show seen regularly on Saturday mornings beginning in 1955. The phenomenal success of the program paved the way for other cartoon studios to follow with their own fully animated series. (In 1957, Hanna–Barbera challenged Mighty Mouse with its long–running "Ruff and Reddy" series.) In addition to impacting the cartoon industry, the series revived the career of the super mouse. The program remained a staple of network television through 1966.

A year later, Viacom, which had purchased the Terrytoons library from CBS (the network had initially paid $3.5 million, short a king's ransom, for Paul Terry's entire library of films), packaged "The Mighty Mouse Show." In its original format, the series contained one or two Mighty Mouse adventures plus other "Terrytoons" featuring an assortment of Paul Terry's creations. Under the syndicated version, two series joined the package: "Luno," the time–traveling adventures of Tim and his flying white stallion; and "The Mighty Heroes," featuring a group of clumsy crime–fighting superheroes (Diaper Man, Cuckoo Man, Rope Man, Strong Man and Tornado Man). Episodes from both series received theatrical distribution as well.

Mighty Mouse later appeared in two series revivals, "The New Adventures of Mighty Mouse and Heckle and Jeckle," produced by Filmation, and "Mighty Mouse: The New Adventures." The latter was produced by animator Ralph Bakshi, who, incidentally, began his career working at Terrytoons. *A

CBS Terrytoons Production. Color. Half—hour. Premiered on CBS: December 10, 1955—October 2, 1966. Syndicated: 1967.

Voices:

Mighty Mouse: Tom Morrison, **The Mighty Heroes:** Lionel Wilson, Herschel Bernardi, **Luno,** the Wonder Horse: Bob McFadden, **Tim:** Bob McFadden

Episodes:

"Mighty Mouse." "The Mouse Of Tomorrow," "Frankenstein's Cat," "He Dood It Again," "Pandora's Box," "Down With Cats," "Super Mouse Rides Again," "The Wreck Of Hesperus," "The Champion Of Justice," "Mighty Mouse Meets Jekyll And Hyde Cat," "Wolf! Wolf!," "The Green Line," "The Two Barbers," "The Sultan's Birthday," "At The Circus," "Mighty Mouse And The Pirates," "The Port Of Missing Mice," "Raiding The Raiders," "Mighty Mouse And The Kilkenny Cats," "The Silver Streak," "Mighty Mouse And The Wolf," "Gypsy Life," "Bad Bill Bunion," "Mighty Mouse In Krakatoa," "Svengali's Cat," "The Wicked Wolf," "My Old Kentucky Home," "Throwing The Bull," "The Trojan Horse," "The Johnstown Flood," "Winning The West," "The Electronic Mouse Trap," "The Jail Break," "The Crackpot King," "The Hep Cat," "Crying Wolf," "The Dead End Cats," "Aladdin's Lamp," "The Sky Is Falling," "Mighty Mouse Meets Deadeye Dick," "A Date For Dinner," "The First Show," "A Fight To The Finish," "Swiss Cheese Family Robinson," "Lazy Little Beaver," "The Magician," "The Feudin' Hillbillies," "The Witch's Cat," "Love's Labor Won," "Mysterious Stranger," "Triple Trouble," "The Magic Slipper," "The Racket Buster," "A Cold Romance," "The Catnip Gang," "The Perils Of Pearl Pureheart," "Stop, Look, And Listen," "Anti—Cats," "Law And Order," "Beauty On The Beach," "Mother Goose's Birthday Party," "Sunny Italy," "Goons From The Moon," "Injun Trouble," "A Swiss Miss," "A Cat's Tale," "Prehistoric Perils," "Hansel And Gretel," "Happy Holland," "A Soapy Opera," "Hero For A Day," "Hot Rods," "When Mousehood Was In Flower," "Spare The Rod," "The Helpless Hippo," "The Reformed Wolf," "Outer Space Visitor," "The Mysterious Package" and "Cat Alarm."

"The Mighty Heroes" (one per show).

"The Plastic Blaster," "The Frog," "The Junker," "The Shrinker," "The Ghost Monster," "The Stretcher," "The Monsterizer," "The Drifter," "The Shocker," "The Enlarger," "The Toy Man," "The Duster," "The Big Freeze," "The Timekeeper," "The Scarecrow," "The Time Eraser," "The Return Of The Monsterizer," "The Paper Monster," "The Raven" and "The Bigger Digger."

"Luno" (one per show).

"The Missing Genie," "Trouble In Baghdad," "Roc—A—Bye Sinbad," "King Rounder," "Who's Dragon," "The Gold Dust Bandit," "Melvin The Magnificent," "Adventure By The Sea," "The Poor Pirate," "The Square Planet," "The Flying Chariot," "Jungle Jack," "Mixed Up Matador," "Island Of The Giants," "King Neptune's Castle" and "The Prehysteric Inventor."

MIGHTY MOUSE: THE NEW ADVENTURES

Tracing back to his origins as ordinary Mike the Mouse, the legendary Terrytoons star forges onward to his status as life—and—limb saving superhero in new cartoon adventures, including old characters Deputy Dawg and Oil Can Harry. *A Bakshi Animation Production. Color. Half—hour. Premiered on CBS: September 19, 1987—August 25, 1989.*

Voices:

Dana Hill, Beau Weaver, Patrick Pinney, Maggie Roswell

Episodes:

1987—1988 (two episodes per show) "Night On Bald Pate," "Mouse Of Another House," "Night Of Bat Rat," "Scrap—Happy," "Catastrophe Cat," "Scrappy's Field Day," "Me Yoww," "Witch Trick," "Bag Mouse," "First Deadly Cheese," "This Island Mouseville," "Mighty Musical Classics," "Littlest Tramp," "Puffy Goes Berserk," "League Of Super Rodents," "All You Need Is Glove," "It's Scrappy's Birthday," "Aqua—Guppy," "Animation Concerto," "Ice Goose Cometh," "Pirates With Dirty Faces," "Mighty's Benefit Plan," "See You In The Funny Papers," "Heroes And Zeros" and "Stress For Success."
1988—1989 "Bat With The Golden Tongue," "Mundane Voyage," "Day Of The Mice," "Still Oily After All These Years," "Mighty Mouse's Wedlock Whimsy," "Anatomy Of A Milquetoast," "Snow White And The Motor City Dwarfs," "Don't Touch That Dial," "Mouse And Super Mouse," "Bridge Of Mighty Mouse," "A Star Is Milked" and "Mighty's Tone Poem."

MIGHTY MR. TITAN

This super—robot who fights crime was issued to television by Trans—Lux, which distributed TV's "Felix the Cat" and others. Little is known about the program, but it appeared on the television scene out of the tremendous popularity of robotic cartoons, like "Gigantor," which were captivating youngsters in every city in America. *A Trans—Lux Presentation. Color. Half—hour. Syndicated: 1965.*

MIGHTY ORBOTS

In the 23rd century, robots have reached an advanced stage of sophistication. But five unique robots come together to form a single, incredible crime—fighting force, known throughout the galaxy as Mighty Orbots. *A TMS Entertainment and MGM/UA Entertainment Company/Intermedia Production. Color. Half—hour. Premiered on ABC: September 8, 1984—August 31, 1985.*

Voices:

Bo: Sherry Alberoni, **Boo:** Julie Bennett, **Dia:** Jennifer Darling, **Rob:** Barry Gordon, **Bort:** Jim MacGeorge, **Umbra:** Bill Martin, **Tor:** Bill Martin, **Rondu:** Don Messick, **Crunch:** Don Messick, **Ohno:** Noelle North, **(Returns):** Bob Ridgely, **Narrator:** Gary Owens

Episodes:

"Magnetic Menace," "The Wish World," "Trapped On The Prehistoric Planet," "The Dremlocks," "Devil's Asteroid," "Raid On The Stellar Queen," "The Jewel Of Targon," "The Phoenix Factor," "Leviathan," "Cosmic Circus," "A Tale Of Two Thieves," "Operation Eclipse" and "Invasion Of Shadow Star."

MILTON THE MONSTER

By mixing the ingredients of the hillbilly Gomer Pyle and the gothic Frankenstein, the Hal Seeger animators produced one lovable character, Milton the Monster. Milton resides with his golbin companions atop Horrible Hill in the city of Transylvania where they brew trouble for their visitors.

Milton shared the spotlight with several other cartoon characters, each featured in their own episodes. They included: "Fearless Fly," a tiny superhero insect who battles sinister bug villains; "Penny Penguin," a precocious child whose good deeds often backfire; "Muggy Doo," a sly, fast-talking fox who cons his way out of predicaments; "Stuffy Derma," a hobo who inherits a fortune but reverts back to living the simple pleasures of his former life–style; and "Flukey Luke," a private eye cowpoke who, aided by his faithful Irish–Indian companion, Two Feathers, thwarts the efforts of the evil Spider Webb. (Only episode titles for "Milton the Monster" and "Fearless Fly" were available from the producer.)

Jack Mercer, the voice of Popeye, co–wrote the production with Kin Platt. Cartoon veteran James "Shamus" Culhane directed the series. *A Hal Seeger Production. Color. Half–hour. Premiered on ABC: October 9, 1965–September 8, 1968. Syndicated.*

Voices:

Milton the Monster: Bob McFadden, **Fearless Fly/Stuffy Derma/Flukey Luke/Professor Weirdo:** Dayton Allen, **Muggy Doo/Two Feathers/ Count Kook:** Larry Best, **Penny Penguin:** Beverly Arnold

Episodes:

"Milton the Monster" (one per show).
"Hector The Protector," "Boys Meet Ghouls," "Abercrombie The Zombie," "The Pot Thickens," "Monster For Hire," "Monster Mutiny," "Medium Undone," "Horrorbaloo," "Goon Platoon," "Camp Gitchy Gloomy," "The Dummy Talks," "Kid Stuff," "Batnap," "Monster Vs. Mobster," "Doo To You," "V For Vampire," "The Hearse Thief," "Witch Crafty," "Scullgaria Forever," "Crumby Mummy," "Horror Scope," "Think Shrink," "The Flying Cup And Saucer," "Monster Sitter," "Dunkin' Treasure," "Fort Fangenstein," "Monstrous Monster" and "The Mummy's Thumb."
"Fearless Fly." (one per show) "A Monstrous Task," "Martians Meet Their Match," "Let's Phase It," "Under Waterloo," "The Spider Spiter," "Fearless Fly Meets The Monsters," "The Goofy Dr. Goo Fee," "Invincible Vs. Invisible," "Horse Shoo Fly," "Trick Of Treatment," "Fatty Karate," "Throne For A Loss," "The Sphinx Jinx," "The House Fly Guest," "Safari Harry," "Captain Flight," "Lady Deflylah," "Ferocious Fly," "Stage Fright," "Private Fly" and "Napoleon Bonefly."

MISSION MAGIC

By drawing a mystical circle on her blackboard, Miss Tickle, a school teacher, and a group of six high school students (Carol, Vinnie, Kim, Socks, Harvey and Franklin) travel back in time to lands of fantasy. Recording star Rick Springfield, who plays a trouble shooter, sang his own songs on each program. *A Filmation Production. Color. Half–hour. Premiered on ABC: September 1973–August 31, 1974.*

Voices:

Rick Springfield: Rick Springfield, **Miss Tickle,** teacher: Lola Fisher, **Kim,** student: Lane Scheimer, **Harvey,** student: Lola Fisher, **Franklin,** student: Lane Scheimer, **Socks,** student: Howard Morris

Episodes:

"The Land Of Backwards," "Modran," "Dissonia," "Land Of Hyde And Go Seek," "City Inside The Earth," "2600 A.D.," "Something Fishy," "Giant Steppes," "Statue Of Limitations," "Will The Real Rick Springfield Please Stand Up?," "Dr. Astro," "Dr. Daguerratype," "Nephren," "Modran Returns," "Horse Feathers" and "A Light Mystery."

MOBY DICK AND THE MIGHTY MIGHTOR

The show combines two cartoon segments, one featuring a protective white whale and shipwrecked youngsters, Tom and Tubb, in dangerous seafaring adventures; the other starring a young prehistoric boy, Tor, the Mighty Mightor, a superhuman jungle guardian. *A Hanna–Barbera Production. Color. Half–hour. Premiered on CBS: September 6, 1967–September 6, 1969.*

Voices:

Tom: Bobby Resnick, **Tubb:** Barry Balkin, **Scooby,** their pet seal: Don Messick, **Mightor:** Paul Stewart, **Tor:** Bobby Diamond, **Sheera:** Patsy Garrett, **Pondo:** John Stephenson, **Li'l Rok:** Norma McMillan, **Ork:** John Stephenson, **Tog:** John Stephenson

Episodes:

"Mighty Mightor" (two per show).
"The Monster Keeper," "The Tiger Men," "The Bird People," "The Serpent Queen," "Mightor Meets Tyrannor," "The Giant Hunters," "Return Of Korg," "Brutor, The Barbarian," "The Tusk People," "Kragel And The Caven Creatures," "The Snow Trapper," "The People Keepers," "The Tree Pygmies," "The Vulture Men," "Charr And The Fire People," "The Stone Men," "Vampire Island," "Cult Of the Cavebearers," "Attack Of The Ice Creatures," "Revenge Of The Serpent Queen," "Rok And His Gang," "The Scorpion Men," "The Sea Slavers," "A Big Day For Little Rok," "The Plant People," "Tribe Of The Witchmen," "The Return Of The Vulture Men," "Battle Of The Mountain Monsters," "Vengeance Of The Storm King," "The Mightiest Warrior," "Dinosaur Island," "Rok To The Rescue," "The Missing Village," "The Greatest Escape," "Rok And The Golden Rok" and "Battle Of The Mightors."
"Moby Dick" (one per show).
"The Sinister Sea Saucer," "The Electrifying Shoctopus," "The Crab Creatures," "The Sea Monster," "The Undersea World," "The Aqua–Bats," "The Iceberg Monster," "The Shark Men," "The Saucer Shells," "Moraya, The Eel Queen," "Toadus, Ruler Of The Dead Ships," "The Cereb Men," "The Vortex Trap," "The Sand Creature," "The Sea Ark," "The Shimmering Screen," "Soodak The Invader" and "The Iguana Men."

MONCHICHIS

In the tops of very tall trees, high above the clouds that cover the Earth's surface, lives a tribe of highly–developed monkey–like creatures known as the Monchichis. Looking out for the loving creatures is the wise Wizzar, who often conjures up powerful spells to save them from the evil grasp of the Grumplins, who live nearby in Grumplor. Fortunately, the Monchichis are smarter and more resourceful as they protect their treetop society in this colorful fantasy tale of good and evil. *A Hanna–Barbera Production. Color. Half–hour. Premiered on ABC: September 10, 1983–September 1, 1984.*

Voices:

Moncho: Bobby Morse, **Kyla:** Laurel Page, **Tootoo:** Ellen Gerstell, **Patchitt:** Frank Welker, **Thumkii:** Hank Saroyan, **Horrg:** Sidney Miller, **Wizzar:** Frank Nelson, **Snogs:** Bob Arbogast, **Shreeker/Snitchitt/Gonker:** Peter Cullen, **Yabbott/Fasit/Scumgor:** Laurie Faso

Episodes:

"Tickle Pickle," "Too Too Trouble," "Double Play," "Swamp Secret," "Dueling Wizzars," "Thumkii's Pet," "Misfit Grumplin," "Jingle Pods," "Cloud City," "Moncho's Gift," "Helpless Hero," "Grumpstaff Grief" and "The Charm Alarm."

MORK AND MINDY

Shazbot! The spaced–out spaceman from the planet Ork and friend, Mindy, played by Robin Williams and Pam Dawber in the hit prime–time television series, reprised their roles in these animated adventures in which Mork enrolls at Mt. Mount High, upon orders from his planet's superior, Orson, to learn more about the experiences of earthlings during adolescence. *A Hanna–Barbera Production in association with Ruby–Spears Enterprises. "Mork and Mindy" © 1982 Paramount Pictures Corporation. All material besides "Mork and Mindy" © 1982 Hanna–Barbera Productions. Color. Half–hour. Premiered on ABC: September 25, 1982–September 3, 1983.*

Voices:

Mork: Robin Williams, **Mindy:** Pam Dawber, **Doing,** Mork's pet: Frank Welker, **Fred McConnell,** Mindy's father: Conrad Janis, **Mr. Caruthers,** the principal: Stanley Jones, **Orson,** Mork's superior: Ralph James, **Eugene,** Mork's friend: Shavar Ross, **Hamilton,** Mork's friend: Mark Taylor

Additional Voices:

Dennis Alwood, Jack Angel, Dave Couwlier, Julie McWhirter Dees, Alan Dinehart, Walker Edmiston, Stan Freberg, Bob Holt, Katherine Leigh, Allan Melvin, Sidney Miller, Neilson Ross, Michael Rye, Steve Schatzberg, Marilyn Schreffler, Steve Spears, Larry Storch, Alan Young

Episodes:

"Who's Minding The Brat?," "The Greatest Shmo On Earth," "To Ork Or Not To Ork," "Orkan Without A Cause," " Mork Man Vs. Ork Man," "Which Witch Is The Witch?," "Every Doing Has His Day," "Beauty Or The Beast," "Morkel And Hyde," "The Wimp," "Ride 'Em Morkboy," "Meet Mork's Mom," "Muddle In A Huddle," "The Incredible Shrinking Mork," "On Your Mork, Get Set, Go," "The Invisible Mork," "The Fluke Spook," "Mayhem For The Mayor," "Coo–Coo Caveboy," "A Treasure Ain't No Pleasure," "The Mork With The Midas Touch," "Extra–Terrestial Toddler," "Time Slipper Slip–Up," "Super Mork," "Mork, P.I." and "Monkey On My Back–Pack."

THE MOST IMPORTANT PERSON

Originally seen daily on "Captain Kangaroo," this educational series aimed at preschoolers starred Mike, a baseball–capped boy, and Nicola, a pigtailed black girl, who present a variety of subjects relating the importance of physical and mental health. The films were subsequently syndicated. *A Sutherland Learning Associates Production. Color. Half–hour (syndication). Premiered on CBS: April 3, 1972–May 18, 1973 (on "Captain Kangaroo").*

MOTORMOUSE AND AUTOCAT

Sportscar maniac Autocat tries everything possible to beat his speedy arch–rival, Motormouse, in outlandish contests in this half–hour series for Saturday–morning television. The program repeated episodes of the former "It's the Wolf," both originally seen for the first time on "The Cattanooga Cats." (See entry for episodic information.) *A Hanna–Barbera Production. Color. Half–hour. Premiered on ABC: September 12, 1970–September 4, 1971.*

Voices:

Motormouse: Dick Curtis, **Autocat:** Marty Ingels, **Mildew Wolf:** Paul Lynde, **Lambsy:** Daws Butler, **Bristol Hound:** Allan Melvin

MR. MAGOO

The myopic, often irritable Mr. (Quincy) Magoo, played by actor Jim Backus, was given new life in this first–run series of misadventures featuring several of his relatives, including his beatnic nephew, Waldo, and his English nephew, Prezley. The Magoo adventures actually began on film as a theatrical cartoon series in 1949. Because of his renewed popularity, he was later featured in several prime–time specials ("Mr. Magoo's Christmas Carol" and "Uncle Sam Magoo") and his own prime–time show, "The Famous Adventures of Mr. Magoo," in which he portrayed different historical and literary characters in American history. His nearsighted persona was again revived by DePatie–Freleng's "What's New, Mr. Magoo" which debuted on CBS in 1977. *A UPA Production. Color. Half–hour. Premiered: November 7, 1960. Syndicated.*

Voices:

Mr. Magoo: Jim Backus, **Prezley:** Daws Butler, Paul Frees, Jerry Hausner, **Waldo:** Jerry Hausner, Daws Butler, **Millie,** Waldo's girlfriend: Julie Bennett, **Mother Magoo:** Jim Backus

Additional Voices:

Mel Blanc, John Hart, June Foray, Joan Gardner, Barney Phillips

Episodes:

"Military Magoo," "Magoo's Bear," "Mis–Guided Missile," "Magoo's Buggy," "Base On Bawls," "Magoo Gets His Man," "Thin Skinned Diver," "Martian Magoo," "Pet Sitters," "Robinson Crusoe Magoo," "Day At The Beach," "Fish 'N' Tricks," "Top The Music" (with Prezley and Waldo), "Masquerader Magoo" (with Waldo), "Beatnik Magoo," "Eagle Eye Magoo" (with Wheeler and Dealer), "Fox Pass" (with Prezley and Waldo), "The Billionaire," "Who's Lion?," "Mother's Cooking," "People Are A Scream," "Mother's Little Helper," "Double Trouble" (with Prezley and Waldo), "Top Pro Magoo," "Bring 'Em Back Waldo" (with Prezley and Waldo), "Three's A Crowd," "Beau Jest" (with Prezley and Waldo), "Shotgun Magoo," "This Is The Life," "The Real McGoys" (with Prezley and Waldo), "Night Club Magoo," "South Pacific Potluck" (with Prezley and Waldo), "Sing Sing Fling," "From Here To Fraternity," "Rassle Hassle" (with Prezley and Waldo), "High And Flighty," "The Vacuum Caper" (with Prezley and Waldo), "The Reunion," "Go West Magoo," "Saddle Battle" (with Prezley and Waldo), "Insomniac Magoo," "Requiem For A Bull" (with Prezley and Waldo), "Soft Shoe Magoo," "High Spy Magoo," "Hermit's Hideaway" (with Prezley and Waldo), "Cuckoo Magoo," "Fuel In The Sun" (with Prezley and Waldo), "Indoor Outing," "Life Can Be Miserable," "Lost Vegas" (with Prezley and Waldo), "Magoo's Ice Box," "The Lady In Black," "Foot Loose Moose," "Riding Hood Magoo," "The Record Breakers," "Teenage Magoo," "Robin Hood Magoo," "Green Thumb Magoo," "Lion Hearted Magoo," "Magoo Meets Frankenstein," "Magoo And The Beanstalk," "Magoo's Western Exposure," "First Aid Magoo," "Magoo's Gorilla Friend," "Bar–B–Q Magoo," "Magoo Meets McBoing Boing," "Buccaneer Magoo," "Magoo's Dutch Treat," "Decorator Magoo," "Cast Iron Magoo," "Marshal Magoo," "Foxy Magoo" (with Prezley and Waldo), "Maestro Magoo," "Tycoonland," "Night Fright," "Ten Strike Magoo," "Food Feud," "Angler Magoo," "Three Ring Magoo," "Magoo's Birthday Cake," "Marco Magoo," "Magoo's Pet," "Campaigner Magoo," "Magoo's Last Stand," "Fire Chief Magoo," "Danger Dan Magoo," "Hamlet On Rye," "Sno Ball Magoo," "Safety Magoo," "Choo, Choo, Magoo," "Slim Trim Magoo," "Magoo's Houseboy," "Magoo's Vacuum Cleaner," "Magoo's Dog," "Goo Goo Magoo," "Prince Charming Magoo," "Magoo's Goal Post," "Gasser Magoo," "Magoo's Caesar Solid," "Buffalo Magoo," "Cupid Magoo," "Hunter Magoo," "Goldilocks Magoo," "Magoo Hamster," "Gangbuster Magoo," "Magoo And Cholly," "Safari Tale," "Magoo's TV Set," "Magoo's GNU," "Tut Tut Magoo," "Perils Of Magoo," "Speedway Magoo," "Fix–It Magoo," "Hula Magoo," "Composer Magoo," "Short Order Magoo," "Magoo Goes Shopping," "Magoo At Blithering Heights," "Magoo's Surprise Party," "Piggy Bank Magoo," "Yachtsman Magoo," "Magoo's Roof Goof," "Cyrano Magoo," "Private Eye Magoo," "Who's Zoo Magoo?" and "Muscles Magoo."

MR. T

Tough guy Mr. T, of TV's "The A Team" fame, plays coach to a team of American teenage gymnasts who travel the world to competitions and wind up pursuing and capturing criminals in various locales. *A Ruby–Spears Enterprises Production.*

Television tough guy Mr. T fights crime with a team of teenage gymnasts in Saturday morning's "Mr. T." © Ruby–Spears Enterprises

Color. Half–hour. Premiered on NBC: September 17, 1983–September 6, 1986.

Voices:

Mr. T: Himself, **Robin:** Amy Linker, **Kim:** Siu Ming Carson, **Spike:** Teddy S. Field III, **Woody:** Phillip LaMarr, **Jeff:** Shawn Lieber, **Miss Bisby:** Takayo Fischer

Episodes:

1983–1984 "Mystery Of The Golden Medallions," "Mystery Of The Forbidden Monastery," "Mystery Of The Mind–Thieves," "Mystery On The Rocky Mountain Express," "The Hundred–Year–Old Mystery," "The Crossword Mystery," "The Ninja Mystery," "Dilemma Of The Double–Edged Dagger," "Secret Of The Special Sister," "Mystery Of The Silver Swan," "Case Of The Casino Caper," "Fade Out At 50,000 Feet" and "Riddle Of The Runaway Wheels."

1984–1985 "Mystery In Paradise," "Mystery Of The Black Box," "Mystery Of The Pantherman," "Mystery Of The Ghost Fleet," "Mystery Of The Ancient Ancestor," "Magical Mardi Gras Mystery," "Mystery Of The Disappearing Oasis," "Fortune Cookie Caper," "U.F.O. Mystery," "Mystery Of The Stranger" and "Cape Cod Caper."

1985–1986 "The Williamsburg Mystery," "Mission Of Mercy," "Mystery Of The Opened Crates," "The Playtown Mystery," "The Comeback Mystery" and "The Cape Kennedy Caper."

MUPPET BABIES

Animated versions of creator Jim Henson's familiar Muppet characters as small children who never actually leave their home, yet through their imaginations go anywhere, do anything and be anyone they choose. *A Marvel Production in association with Henson Associates. Color. Half–hour. One hour. One hour and a half. Premiered on CBS: September 15, 1984–September 7, 1985 (half–hour); September 14, 1985–September 6, 1986 (half–hour); September 13, 1986–Sep-*

tember 12, 1987 (one hour); September 19, 1987–September 3, 1988 (90 minutes); September 10, 1988–September 9, 1989 (one hour); September 16, 1989–September 8, 1990 (one hour).

Voices:
Fozzie: Greg Berg, **Scooter:** Greg Berg, **Animal:** Howie Mandel, Dave Coulier, **Bunsen:** Howie Mandel, Dave Coulier, **Rowlf:** Katie Leigh, **Piggy:** Laurie O'Brien, **Gonzo:** Russi Taylor, **Kermit:** Frank Welker, **Skeeter:** Howie Mandel, Frank Welker, **Beaker:** Frank Welker

Episodes:
1984–1985 "Noisy Neighbors," "Dental Hyjinks," "Who's Afraid Of The Big, Bad Dark?", "Raiders Of The Lost Muppet," "Scooter's Hidden Talent," "The Case Of The Missing Chicken," "What Do You Want To Be When You Grow Up", "Eight Take–Away One Equals Panic," "Close Encounters Of The Frog Kind," "Gonzo's Video Show," "Fun Park Fantasies," "From A Galaxy Far, Far Away . . ." and "Good Clean Fun."
1985–1986 "Piggy's Hyper–Activity Book," "Once Upon An Egg Timer," "The Great Cookie Robbery," "Out–Of–This–World History," "Snow White And The Seven Muppets," "I Want My Muppet T.V.," "Musical Muppets," "What's New At The Zoo?", "The Great Muppet Cartoon Show," "The Muppet Museum Of Art," "Fozzie's Last Laugh," "By The Book" and "When You Wish Upon A Muppet."
1986–1987 "Pigerella," "The Best Friend I Never Had," "The Weirdo Zone," "Muppets In Toyland," "The Muppet Broadcasting Company," "Kermit Goes To Washington," "Fozzie's Family Tree," "The Daily Muppet," "Scooter's Uncommon Cold," "Treasure Attic," "Around The Nursery In 80 Days," "Fine Feathered Enemies," "Muppet Goose," "Bad Luck Bear," "Of Mice and Muppets" and "Back To The Nursery."
1987–1988 "Muppetland," "Water Babies," "The Incredible Shrinking Weirdo," "Where No Muppet Has Gone Before," "Journey To The Center Of The Nursery," "This Little Piggy Went To Hollywood," "My Muppet Valentine," "Invasion Of The Muppet Snackers," "Twinkle Toe Muppets," "Weirdo For The Prosecution" (formerly: "Muppet Court"), "Muppet Island," "The Frog Who Knew Too Much," "Beach Blanket Babies" (formerly: "Poolside Pranksters"), "Old Mackermit Had A Farm," "Adventures In Muppet–Sitting," "The House That Muppets Built," "Masquerading Muppets" and "Nanny's Day Off."
1988–1989 "Muppets Not Included," "Beauty And The Schnoz," "The Pig Who Would Be Queen," "Is There A Muppet In The House?", "Slipping Beauty," "Muppet Baby Boom," "Scooter By Any Other Name," "He's A Wonderful Frog," "Elm Street Babies," "Plan 8 From Outer Space," "Junkyard Muppets," "The Air Conditioner At The End Of The Galaxy" and "Bug–Busting Babies."
1989–1990 "This Old Nursery," "And Now A Word From Our Muppets," "Six To Eight Weeks," "The Green Ranger," "Not Necessarily The Muppets," "Comic Capers," "Faster Than A Speeding Weirdo," "Skeeter And The Wolf," "Romancing The Weirdo," "The New Adventures Of Kermo Polo" and "Goosetown Babies."

MY FAVORITE MARTIANS

A Martian crash–lands in the vicinity of the Los Angeles freeway and is discovered by writer Tim O'Hara. Convincing O'Hara that revealing his true identity would cause worldwide panic, the alien assumes the identity of Tim's Uncle Martin and they become roommates. O'Hara must guard the well–being not only of Uncle Martin but also of his other space friend, Andromeda (or "Andy") in this cartoon spin–off of the TV hit, "My Favorite Martian," which starred Ray Walston and Bill Bixby. *A Filmation Production. Color. Half–hour. Premiered on CBS: September 8, 1973–August 30, 1975.*

Voices:
Martin O'Hara (Uncle Martin): Jonathan Harris, **Tim O'Hara:** Howard Morris, **Katy O'Hara,** Tim's niece: Jane Webb, **Lorelei Brown,** Tim's landlady: Jane Webb, **Bill Brennan,** security officer: Howard Morris, **Brad Brennan,** his son: Lane Scheimer, **Andromeda** (Andy), Martin's nephew: Howard Morris

Episodes:
"Check Up," "Life Style," "Home Schtick," "Wall To Wall Flower," "The Cleo Caper," "Robot Tailor," "Lonely Okie," "Triple Trouble," "The Incredible Shrinking Ship," "My Favorite Neighbor," "Allergy," "Truant Teacher," "Love Martian Style," "The Chump Who Cried Chimp," "The Credibility Gap" and "Garage Sail."

MY LITTLE PONY 'N' FRIENDS

Pastel colored, talking ponies who possess magical powers help three children—the only people on earth to know of the existence of the fairy tale region called Ponyland—overcome the villainy of the evil Stratadons in this first–run, fantasy adventure series. There were two 10–minute episodes each

Uncle Martin and his magazine friend, Tim O'Hara, of TV's "My Favorite Martian," experience all–new animated adventures joined by two new cast members, Andromeda, Martin's nephew (far left), and Katy O'Hara, Tim's niece (second from left). © Filmation

week along with one seven—minute segment of either "The Glo Friends," "Potato Head Kids" or "Moondreamers," which rotated as the series' third cartoon segment. *A Marvel Production in association with Sunbow Productions. Color. Half—hour. Premiered: September 15, 1986. Syndicated.*

Voices:

Charlie Adler, Michael Bell, Sue Blue, Bettina, Nancy Cartwright, Peter Cullen, Jeannie Elias, Ian Freid, Linda Gary, Susie Garbo, Ellen Gerstell, Melanie Gaffin, Scott Grimes, Skip Hinnant, Keri Houlihan, Christina Lang, Jody Lambert, Katie Leigh, Sherry Lynn, Kellie Martin, Ken Mars, Ann Marie McEvoy, David Mendenhall, Scott Menville, Brecken Meyer, Laura Mooney, Sarah Partridge, Andrew Potter, Russi Taylor, B. J. Ward, Jill Wayne, Frank Welker, Bunny Andrews, William Callaway, Adam Carl, Phillip Clarke, Danny Cooksey, Peter Cullen, Jennifer Darling, Marshall Efron, Pat Fraley, Elizabeth Frazer, Liz Georges, Robert Ito, Renae Jacobs, Robin Kaufman, Danny Mann, Tress MacNeille, Terry McGovern, Michael Mish, Clive Revill, Stu Rosen, Neil Ross, Ken Sanson, Rick Segal, Judy Strangis, Lennie Weinrib, Charlie Wolfe, Ted Zeigler

Episodes:

"My Little Pony" (two per show).
"The Ghost Of Paradise Estate" (five parts), "Fugitive Flowers" (two parts), "The Magic Coins" (four parts), "Revolt Of Paradise Estate" (two parts), "Crunch The Rockdog" (two parts), "Bright Lights" (four parts), "Return Of Tambelon" (four parts), "Baby, It's Cold Outside" (two parts), "Sweet Stuff And Treasure Hunt," "The Pony Puppy," ". . . Through The Door!" (two parts), "The Would—Be Dragonslayer," "The Glass Princess" (four parts), "Mish Mash Melee," "Woe Is Me" (two parts), "The Great Rainbow Caper," "The End Of Flutter Valley" (10 parts), "A Little Piece Of Magic," "Flight To Cloud Castle" (two parts), "Spike's Search," "Golden Horseshoes" (two parts), "Quest Of The Princess Ponies" (four parts), "Somnambula" "(two parts), "Ice Cream Wars," "The Prince And The Ponies," "My Little Pony" (two parts) and "Escape From Katrina" (two parts).
"Moondreamers" (one per show).
"Twinkle, Twinkle, Little Star Child" (Part 1), "Twinkle, Star Child" (Part 2), "The Dreamnapping," "Bucky's Comet," "Zodies On The Loose," "The Stars Of Stars," "Whimzee, Come Home," "The Night Mare" (Part 1), "The Night Mare" (Part 2), "Dreamland Express," "Stuck On Bucky," "The Dreamkin," "All In A Night's Sleep," "Igon The Terrable," "Minor Problems" and "The Poobah Of Pontoon."
"Potato Head Kids" (one per show).
"The Great Candy Caper," "The Trashcan Derby," "Small's Potatoes," "The Case Of The Fouled Up Pharoh," "Puff's New Job," "Potatolympics," "Pig Out," "Pot Of Gold," "Sam Spud, Private Eye," "Spike Spiked," "Robin Potato Head," "Surfin' Potatoes," "Potato Head Pirates," "The Curse Of The Silver Dragon," "Abbad'Un In A Bottle," "Poltergeist Potatoes," "One Potato, Zoo Potato," "A Side Order Of Soggy Spuds," "Horse Hide And Seek," "Left Foot Forward," "Follow The Chocolate Cake Road," "Romancing The Rock" and "The Grin—Ness Book Of Records."

"Glo Friends" (one per show).
"Baby Gloworm Goes Bye—Bye," "Two Of A Kind," "Make No Mistake, It's Magic," "The Forest Brigade," "The Caverns Of Mystery," "The Front Page," "The Quest" (10 parts), "Beware Tales Of Gold That Lead To Thorny Trails," "The Masterpiece," "Bean Ball," "Glo Friends Meet The Glowees" (four parts), "Easy Money" (two parts) and "Wizard Of Rook."

MY PET MONSTER

Whimsical tale of a young boy (Max) who longs for a best friend and finds one in the form of a furry stuffed animal who is transformed into a lovable six—foot monster. Program was produced by the creators of television's, "Care Bears." *A Nelvana Limited Production. Color. Half—hour. Premiered on ABC: September 12, 1987—September 3, 1988.*

Voices:

Max: Sunny Besen Thrasher, **Chuckie:** Stuart Stone, **Monster:** Jeff McGibbon, **Jill:** Alyson Court, **Beastur:** Dan Hennessey, **Mr. Hinkle:** Colin Fox, **Princess:** Tracey Moore, **Ame:** Tara Charandoff

Additional Voices:

Mary Long, Noam Zylberman, Simon Reynolds, Graham Haley, John Stocker, Maxine Miller, Robert Cait

Episodes:

"Goodbye Cuffs, Goodbye Monster!," "The Wolfmen Are Coming!," "Boogey Board Blues," "Rock-A-Bye Babysitters," "Monster Cookie Mix-Up!," "The Masked Muncher!," "Runaway Monster," "Escape From Monsterland!," "Finders Keepers," "My Poet Monster," "Little Bigfoot," "Monster Makes The Grade!," "Monster Movie Mayhem!," "Superhero For Hire!," "Gorill'A My Dreams" and "Rex Stalker—Monster Hunter!"

THE MYSTERIOUS CITIES OF GOLD

Led by young Esteban, the children of the Sun search for the cities of gold, crossing unchartered territory and discovering the unknown in this half—hour adventure series. All 39 episodes of the series were untitled, and voices are uncredited. *A MK Company Production. Color. Half—hour. Premiered on Nickelodeon: June 30, 1986.*

THE NBC COMICS

In 1950, NBC began broadcasting this series of newspaper strip adventures that featured strip—art panels filmed sequentially of strip characters in exciting three—minute adventures comprising this 15—minute program. Actually syndicated in 1949 as "Tele—Comics," the black—and—white series originally presented serialized adventures of "Joey and Jug," "Sa-Lih," "Brother Goose" and "Rick Rack, Special Agent."

When NBC picked up the series, four new characters were added appearing in stories of their own. They were: "Danny March," hired by the mayor as his personal detective to stop crime; "Kid Champion," a boxing story abut a youth (Eddie

Hale) who refuses to talk about his past; "Space Barton," who blasts off to Mars in a rocketship built by Professor Dinehart, an astronomer with his brother Jackie, a stowaway; and "Johnny and Mr. Do–Right," the exploits of a young boy and his dog.

Once the program finished its network run, it was again syndicated under the title of "Tele–Comics." The cartoons were never titled. *A Vallee Video Production. Black–and–white. Fifteen minutes. Syndicated: 1949. Premiered on NBC: September 18, 1950–March 30, 1951 (as "The NBC Comics").*

Voices:
Bob Bruce, Howard McNear, Pat McGeeham, Lurene Tuttle

THE NEW ADVENTURES OF BATMAN

The Caped Crusader and Boy Wonder face new dangers in these half–hour animated segments voiced by TV's original Batman and Robin, Adam West and Burt Ward. They are joined in their crime–fighting adventures by Batgirl and their prankish mascot, Bat–Mite. Episodes from the series were later repeated on "The Batman/Tarzan Adventure Hour," "Tarzan and the Super 7" and "Batman and the Super 7." (See individual series for information.) *A Filmation Production. Color. Half–hour. Premiered on CBS: February 10, 1977–September 10, 1977.*

Voices:
Batman: Adam West, **Robin:** Burt Ward, **Batgirl:** Melendy Britt, **Bat–Mite:** Lennie Weinrib

Episodes:
"The Pest," "The Moonman," "Trouble Identity," "A Sweet Joke On Gotham City," "The Bermuda Rectangle," "Bite–Sized," "Reading, Writing And Wronging," "The Chameleon," "He Who Laughs Last," "The Deep Freeze," "Dead Ringers," "Curses! Oiled Again!," "Birds Of A Father Fool Around Together," "Have An Evil Day" (two parts) and "This Looks Like A Job For Bat–Mite!"

Actors Adam West and Burt Ward reprised the roles of their famed cape crusading characters in "The New Adventures of Batman." Joining the cast: Bat–Mite (far left). © Filmation Associates—DC Comics Inc.

THE NEW ADVENTURES OF FLASH GORDON

Originally brought to the screen by actor Buster Crabbe as a favorite movie matinee serial, this animated re–creation of Alex Raymond's science–fiction epic follows the exploits of pilot Flash Gordon, Dale Arden and Dr. Zarkov as they brave the dangers of the planet Mongo, ruled by the evil dictator Ming the Merciless. *A Filmation Production in association with King Features. Color. Half–hour. Premiered on NBC: September 22, 1979–September 20, 1980.*

Voices:
Flash Gordon: Bob Ridgely, **Ming the Merciless:** Alan Oppenheimer, **Dr. Zarkov:** Alan Oppenheimer, **Aura:** Melendy Britt, **Dale:** Diane Pershing, **Thun:** Allan Melvin, **Voltan:** Allan Melvin

Episodes:
"A Plant In Peril," "The Monsters Of Mongo," "King Of The Hawkmen," "To Save Earth," "The Beast Men's Prey," "Into The Water World," "Adventure In Arboria," "The Frozen World," "Monster Of The Glacier," "Blue Magic," "King Flash," "Tournament Of Death," "Castaways In Tropica," "The Desert Hawk," "Revolt Of The Power Men" and "Ming's Last Battle."

THE NEW ADVENTURES OF GILLIGAN

The tales of the faithful charter ship *S. S. Minnow* and five dissimilar passengers who embark on a pleasure cruise and are shipwrecked on a deserted uncharted isle where they must learn survival techniques. Based on the popular TV series, this animated version starred original cast members, Alan Hale, Bob Denver, Jim Backus, Natalie Schafer, Jane Edwards and Russell Johnson. The animated series was broadcast three consecutive seasons, with the third and final season repeating adventures from the second season. (The second season combined new adventures with reruns from the first season.) *A Filmation Production. Color. Half–hour. Premiered on ABC: September 7, 1974–September 4, 1977. Syndicated.*

Voices:
Gilligan, bumbling first mate: Bob Denver, **Jonas Grumby,** the skipper: Alan Hale, **Ginger Grant,** movie actress: Jane Webb, **Thurston Howell III,** millionaire: Jim Backus, **Lovey Howell,** the millionaire's wife: Natalie Schafer, **Roy Hinkely,** the professor: Russell Johnson, **Mary Ann Summers:** Jane Edwards

Episodes:
1974–1975 "Off Limits," "Looney Moon," "Raven Mad," "Father Of His Island," "Wrong Way Robot (Yeah, Would You Want Your Sister To Marry One?)," "Opening Night," "Lollipop Casserole," "The Loners (Nobody's Island)," "The Go Trip (Kon–Tacky)," "The Olympiad," "In Their Own Image," "The Disappearing Act," "A Sinking Feeling," "The Reluctant Hero," "The Same Old Dream" and "Sputtering Eagle."
1975–1976 (new episodes combined with reruns) "Super

Gilligan," "Marooned Again," "Live And Let Live," "Wheels On Parade," "The Movie Makers," "Silence Is Leaden," "The Great Train Robbery" and "Moderation."

THE NEW ADVENTURES OF HUCK FINN

Mark Twain's immortal characters, Huck Finn, Tom Sawyer and Becky Thatcher, fleeing Injun Joe are engulfed in a whirling sea in this live–action/animated series with superimposed animated backgrounds. *A Hanna–Barbera Production. Color. Half–hour. Premiered on NBC: September 15, 1968–September 7, 1969.*

Cast:

Huck Finn: Michael Shea, **Tom Sawyer:** Kevin Schultz, **Becky Thatcher:** Lu Ann Haslam, **Injun Joe:** Ted Cassidy

Voices:

Hal Smith, Ted DeCorsia, Peggy Webber, Jack Krusacher, Paul Stewart, Mike Road, Vic Perrin, Charles Lane, Julie Bennett, Paul Frees, Marvin Miller

Episodes:

"The Eye Of Doorgah," "The Curse Of Thut," "The Little People," "Pirate Island," "The Castle Of Evil," "The Last Labor Of Hercules," "The Terrible Tempered Khaleef," "The Mission Of Captain Mordecai," "Huck Of La Mancha," "The Menace In The Ice," "Hunting The Hunter," "The Strange Experiment," "The Ancient Valley," "The Magic Shillelagh," "The Jungle Adventure," "The Gorgon's Head," "Prophecy Of Peril," "The Curse Of The Conquistador," "Son Of The Sun" and "All Whirlpools Lead To Atlantis."

THE NEW ADVENTURES OF MIGHTY MOUSE AND HECKLE AND JECKLE

Two of Terrytoons' most famous characters from the 1940s and 1950s returned in new animated adventures in this series revival, which was first broadcast on CBS in an hour–long format in 1979, then trimmed to a half–hour for its second and final season. In these updated stories, Heckle and Jeckle still find ways to get into trouble, while Mighty Mouse defends mice everywhere and protects his girlfriend Pearl Pureheart from the evil clutches of hs arch–enemy, Oilcan Harry, and his sidekick, Swifty. Two Mighty Mouse cartoons were featured on the show in serialized form. (He additionally appeared in brief environmental bulletins cautioning youngsters on wasting resources and littering.) Another series regular was "Quackula," the misadventures of a vampire mallard who terrorizes his landlord and others. (Episodes for the latter were not available from the producer.) *A Filmation Production. Color. One hour. Half–hour. Premiered on CBS: September 8, 1979–August 30, 1980. Rebroadcast on CBS: September 6, 1980–September 12, 1982.*

Voices:

Mighty Mouse: Alan Oppenheimer, **Pearl Pureheart,** his girlfriend: Diane Pershing, **Oilcan Harry,** the villain: Alan Oppenheimer, **Heckle:** Frank Welker, **Jeckle:** Frank Welker, **Quackula:** Frank Welker

Episodes:

"Mighty Mouse" (three per show).
"Mousetankamen," "Stop–Pay Troll," "The Treasure Of The Illo Armada," "The Exercist," "The Star Of Cucamonga," "Chapter One," "Chapter Two," "Chapter Three," "Chapter Four," "Chapter Five," "Chapter Six," "Chapter Seven," "Chapter Eight," "Chapter Nine," "Chapter Ten," "Chapter Eleven," "Chapter Twelve," "Gypsy Mice," "Loco Motivations," "Gangmous," "Wings," "Catula," "Mousrace," "No Time For Laughter," "Movie Mouse," "Mighty Mouse Meets Mick Jaguar," "Pheline Of The Rock Opera," "Cattan Nemo–Oh–Oh," "Snow Mouse," "Haunted House Mouse," "Cat Ness Monster," "Rugged Rodent," "Ding Dong," "Cattenstein," "Cat Of Baskervilles," "Chapter Thirteen," "Chapter Fourteen," "Chapter Fifteen," "Chapter Sixteen," "Pearl Of The Jungle," "Moby Whale," "Big Top Cat," "The Disorient Express," "The Maltese Mouse," "Beau Jest," "Curse Of The Cat," "Around The World in 80 Ways" and "Tugboat Pearl."
"Heckle and Jeckle" (two per show).
"Heckle and Jeckle Meet Goldfeather," "The Golden Egg," "The Heroes," "Cavebirds," "Show Business," "Spurs," "Birds Of Pardise," "The Open Road," "Robot Factory," "Farmer And The Crows," "Foreign Legion Birds," "Mail Birds," "The Malcon–Tents," "Bellhops," "Sphinx!," "Where There's A Will," "Identity Problem," "Time Warped," "Invisible Birds," "Marathon Birds," "Supermarket," "When Knighthood Was In Weeds," "Astrobirds," "Apartment Birds," "In The 25th Century," "Safari Birds," "In Wonderland" and "Arabian Nights And Days."

THE NEW ADVENTURES OF PINOCCHIO

Wooden boy Pinocchio and his creator/mentor Geppetto are featured in modernized, five–minute adventures based on Carlo Collodi's world–renown characters. The naive puppet is exposed to contemporary subjects, like beatniks and greedy movie producers. Filmed in Animagic, the series was produced by Arthur Rankin Jr. and Jules Bass, heads of Canada's Videocrafts International (later renamed Rankin–Bass Productions), who produced many perennial holiday specials, including "Rudolph the Red–Nosed Reindeer" and "Jack Frost." *A Videocrafts International Production. Color. Half–hour. Syndicated: 1961. Voice credits unknown.*

Episodes:

"It's No Joke Pinoc," "Ring–A–Ding–Ding," "Sprinkle Sprinkle Little Star," "10 Cents A Glance," "Pretty Pussycat–Nips," "Short Circuit," "It's Cool In The Cooler," "Back Stage Life," "All Down Hill," "Rocket To Fame," "Too Many Ghosts," "Horse Sense," "One Little Indian," "Cattle Rattle," "By Hook Or By Crook," "Not So Private Eye," "Cash And Carry Harry," "Dognet," "The Gold Brick Trick," "Simoro's Last Chance," "Romin' In The Glomin," "Flying Bagpipes," "Hide And Seek," "Stop Gap Sap," "Feud For All," "Glockenspiel," "Peanut Butter Battle," "Upside Down Town," "Robot Rhapsody," "Big Bomb

Bake," "Back–Track," "Hot Rod Hobo," "Duck Luck," "Danny The Boon," "Dynamite Bright," "O'Lafferty The Magnificent," "Lock–Stock And Crock," "Hup–Two–Three–Four," "No Banks Thanks," "The Crick Trick," "Grab Bag," "Pick–A–Pocket," "Kangaroo Capers," "Paunchy Pouch," "Kangaroo Caught," "Havin' A Ball," "A Choice Of Voice," "The Pale Inhale," "Down The Hatch," "Cricket High," "Detour For Sure," "Once Around Please," "The Vast Mast," "The Treasure Measure," "Not So Hot Knot," "The Big Top Stop," "Monkey See," "Big Shot," "A Ticklish Situation," "Clowning Around," "Stroll Around The Pole," "The Bear Facts," "Something's Fishy," "Fast Talk," "Snow Use," "The Highway Man," "To Track A Thief," "Sleep Watcher," "A Dog's Best Friend," "Thrown By The Throne," "The Cast–Offs," "Mutiny On The Clipper," "Floundering Around," "The Litterbugs," "Atlantis City," "Steed Stallion," "Chief Big Cheese," "The Water Boy," "The Little Train Robbery," "Simon Says," "Sky Spy," "Glockenspiel's Spiel," "The Gas Man Cometh," "The Impatient Patient," "The Astro–Nuts," "Special Delivery," "Go Fly A Kite," "Marooned," "The Foot Print," "Homeward Bound," "Wish, Wish And Away," "Lead On Leprechaun," "Westward Whoa," "TV Time," "Baby Big," "Stage West," "Draw Pardner," "The Race," "The Gold Bug," "Follow That Horse," "Away With The Wind," "The Hard Sell," "The Witch Switch," "Sky High," "Romeo Fibble," "Wanted," "Going Down," "Under Ground Found," "The Gold Bird," "The Big Heist," "Willy Wiggly," "Substitute," "Borschtville," "A Fair Trail," "The Rescue Rock," "Writers In The Sky," "The Zany Zombies," "Sleep Head," "The Boss Who Came To Dinner," "Witch Switch," "Witching You Well," "Candy Land," "Aw Fudge," "The Phoney Fairy," "The Fastest Wind," "Willy Nilly," "Hog Bellows," "An Ace In The Hole," "Rosco Romp" and "Lady Barber."

THE NEW ADVENTURES OF SUPERMAN

Mild–mannered *Daily Planet* reporter Clark Kent, alias Superman, whose only weakness is Kryptonite, frustrates criminal activities in Metropolis and elsewhere. The supporting cartoon segment was 'The Adventures of Superboy," chronicling Superman's youth in the town of Smallville, U. S. A. and featuring Krypto, Superboy's superdog. The series was one of six superhero cartoon programs scheduled back–to–back on Saturday mornings when it first premiered. Adventures later aired as part of "The Superman/Aquaman Hour" and "The Batman/Superman Hour." (See individual entries for information.) The series in its original format was repeated in its entirety during the 1969–1970 season. *A Filmation Production. Color. Half–hour. Premiered on CBS: September 16, 1966–September 2, 1967. Rebroadcast on CBS: September 1969–September 5, 1970.*

Voices:
Clark Kent/Superman: Bud Collyer, **Lois Lane:** Joan Alexander, **Superboy:** Bob Hastings, **Narrator:** Jackson Beck

Episodes:
"Superman" (two per show).
"The Chimp Who Made It Big," "The Saboteurs," "The Imp–Practical Joker," "Luthor Strikes Again," "Superman Meets Braniac," "The Deadly Fish," "The Prankster," "Menace Of

The Lava Man," "The Iron Eater," "War Of The Bee Battalion," "The Return of Braniac," "The Wicked Warlock," "The Image Maker," "Two Faces Of Superman," "Merlin's Magic Marbles," "Invisible Raiders," "Malevolent Mummy," "Threat Of The Thrutans," "Tree–Man Of Arbora," "Mission Of Planet Peril," "Mermen Of Emor," "The Lethal Lightening Bug," "Wisp Of Wickedness," "The Prehistoric Pterodactyls," "The Abominable Iceman," "Seed Of Disaster," "Neolithic Nightmare," "Superman Meets His Match—Almost," "The Deadly Icebergs," "The Pernicious Parasite," "The Toys Of Doom," "The Robot Of Riga," "Return Of The Warlock," "Ape Army Of The Amazon," "The Atomic Superman," "The Deadly Super–Doll," "The Fearful Force Phantom," "The Electro–Magnetic Monster," "The Insect Raiders," "The Warlock's Revenge," "The Men From A P E," "The Frightful Fire Phantom," "The Haylah Of The Himalayas," "A P E Strikes Again," "The Bird–Men From Lost Valley," "The Toyman's Super Toy," "Superman's Double Trouble," "Luthor's Loco Looking Glass," "The Night Of The Octopod," "The Cage Of Glass," "Braniac's Blue Bubbles" and "Luthor's Fatal Fireworks."
"Superboy" (one per show).
"The Man Who Knew Superboy's Secret," "Operation Counter Invasion," "The Terrible Trio," "Visitor From The Earth's Core," "The Super–Clown Of Smallville," "A Devil Of A Time," "Superboy's Super Dilemma," "Krypto, Super–Seeing Eye Dog," "Kyrpto's Calamitous Capers," "The Deep–Sea Dragon," "Superboy's Strangest Foe," "The Gorilla Gang," "The Spy From Outer Space" (two parts), "Krypto's Capricious Crony," "A Black Knight At Court," "The Beast That Went Berserk," "The Jinxed Circus," "Hurricane Fighters," "The Two Faced Beast," "The Great Space Chase," "The Chameleon Creature," "The Finger Of Doom," "The Revolt Of Robotville," "Krypto—K–9 Detective" and "The Neanderthal Cave Man Caper."

THE NEW ADVENTURES OF WINNIE THE POOH

A comedy/adventure series starring Winnie the Pooh and the other immortal characters from A. A. Milne's "Pooh" stories. The unforgettably charming characters of Milne's Hundred Acre Wood live in the imagination of young Christopher Robin, who joins them in a series of joyful escapades filled with laughter and whimsy. The program marked the first time that a classic Disney character was seen on Saturday–morning television. The series was in production for over a year before its network premiere, producing 25 half–hours for the first season (most Saturday morning shows get by with 13) which consisted of either two 11–minute episodes or one 22–minute story.

In the fall of 1989, the series was merged with "Disney's Adventures of the Gummi Bears" in all–new episodes in a new one–hour show called, "Disney's Gummi Bears/Winnie the Pooh Hour." (See series entry for information.) *A Walt Disney Television Production. Color. Half–hour. Premiered on ABC: September 10, 1988–September 2, 1989.*

Voices:
Winnie the Pooh: Jim Cummings, **Christopher Robin:** Tim Hoskins, **Tigger:** Paul Winchell, Jim Cummings, **Eeyore:** Peter Cullen, **Gopher:** Michael Gough, **Roo:** Nicholas Melody, **Mom/Kanga:** Patty Parris, **Owl:** Hal Smith

Episodes:
1988–1989 (11–minute episodes) "Friend, In Deed," "Donkey For A Day," "Balloonatics," "There's No Camp Like Home," "Stripes," "Trap As Trap Can," "Monkey See, Monkey Do Better," "Nothing But The Tooth," "Honey For A Bunny," "Gone With The Wind," "Me And My Shadow," "Rabbit Marks The Spot" (Song: "Pirates Is What We'll Be"), "Bubble Trouble," "Goodbye, Mr. Pooh," "To Catch A Hiccup," "Groundpiglet Day," "Fish Out Of Water," "Owl Feathers," "A Very, Very, Large Animal," "Lights Out," "Tigger, Private Ear," "Tigger's Shoes," "The 'New' Eeyore," "Party Poohper," "The Old Switcheroo" (Song: "The Bathtub Song"), "Things That Go Piglet," "The Masked Offender," "Luck Amok," "The Magic Earmuffs," "King Of The Beasties" (Song: "King Of The Beasties"), "The Rats Who Came To Dinner" and "My Hero" (Song: "Tigger's Waltz").
(22–minute episodes) "Pooh Oughta Be In Pictures," "Find Her, Keep Her," "The Piglet Who Would Be King," "Babysitter Blues," "Cleanliness Is Next To Impossible," "The Great Honey Pot Robbery," "Paw And Order," "How Much Is That Rabbit In The Window," "All's Well That Ends Well" and "The Wishing Bear."

THE NEW ARCHIES

The classic characters of Riverdale High—Archie, Jughead, Reggie, Betty and Veronica—meet new challenges with limitless imagination, dream big dreams and create havoc, this time as a group of nine–year–olds, with friendship always prevailing in spite of their efforts to outdo one another. *A DIC Enterprises Production in association with Saban Productions. Color. Half–hour. Premiered on NBC: September 12, 1987–September 3, 1988.*

Voices:
Archie: J. Michael Roncetti, **Eugene:** Colin Waterman, **Jughead** Michael Fantini, **Amani:** Karen Burthwright, **Reggie:** Sunny Bensen Thrasher, **Betty:** Lisa Coristine, **Veronica:** Allyson Court, **Big Ethel:** Jazzman Lausanne, **Coach:** Greg Swanson, **Miss Grundy:** Linda Sorensen, **Mr. Weatherbee:** Marvin Goldhar

Episodes:
"Ballot Box Blues," "The Visitor," "Thief! (Of Hearts)," "I Gotta Be Me . . . Or Is It You?," "The Last Laugh," "Sir Jughead Jones," "The Awful Truth," "Future Shock," "Stealing The Show," "Goodbye Ms. Grundy," "Jughead The Jinx," "Hamburger Helpers," "Telegraph, Telephone, Tell Reggie," "Jughead Predicts," "I Was A Twelve–Year–Old Werewolf," "The Prince Of Riverdale," "Loose Lips Stops Slips," "Wooden It Be Loverly," "Red To The Rescue," "Gunk For The Gold," "A Change Of Minds," "The Incredible Shrinking Archie," "Jughead's Millions," "Take My Butler, Please!," "The Making Of Mr. Right–Eous" and "Hooray For Hollywood."

THE NEW ARCHIE/SABRINA HOUR

Taking two of its most prized properties, Filmation produced this hour–long comedy series combining 13 previously broadcast episodes of Archie and the Riverdale High School gang from "The Archie Comedy Hour" and Sabrina, the teenage witch from 1971's "Sabrina, the Teenage Witch" series (unfortunately, studio records do not indicate which episodes were used), plus another animated segment called "Surprise Package."

In November, 1977, following poor ratings, NBC yanked the series off the air and put in its place a new, improved version, "Archie's Bang–Shang Lalapalooza Show." Unfortunately the show fared no better than the former series since it was opposite CBS's 90–minute version of "The Bugs Bunny/Road Runner Show," which dominated its time slot. *A Filmation Studios Production. Color. Half–hour. Premiered on NBC: September 10, 1977–November 19, 1977.*

Voices:
Archie Andrews: Dallas McKennon, **Jughead Jones:** Howard Morris, **Betty Cooper:** Jane Webb, **Veronica Lodge:** Jane Webb, **Reggie Mantle:** John Erwin, **Big Moose:** Howard Morris, **Big Ethel:** Jane Webb, **Carlos:** Jose Flores, **Mr. Weatherbee:** Dallas McKennon, **Miss Grundy:** Jane Webb, **Sabrina,** the Teenage Witch: Jane Webb

Episodes:
"Archie." (one per show) "Chief Archie," "Me And My Shadow," "There Is No Place Like Outer Space," "A Moving Experience," "Robert Blueford," "Tops In Cops," "Track And Field," "Where There Is Smoke," "Archie's Millions," "Career Day," "The Quixote Caper," "Pirate Key" and "On The 'Q' Tee."
"Surprise Package." (one per show) "French Deception," "Dilton's Invention," "Carlos' Cool Caper," "The Talent Show," "Weatherbee–Fuddled," "TV Witch Watchers," "Chimp Gone Ape," "Talent Test," "All Washed Up," "A Colorful Experience," "The Last Windup," "Bon Appetite" and "Funhouse."

THE NEW CASPER CARTOON SHOW

First appearing in his own theatrical cartoon series, this friendly ghost, who frightened away those he hoped would be his friends, was the star of this half–hour program for Saturday mornings featuring all–new made–for–television episodes of Casper and his supporting cast, Nightmare the Galloping Ghost, Wendy the Good Little Witch and the Ghostly Trio. Twenty–six half–hour programs were made, each consisting of three cartoons. The series was briefly retitled, "The New Adventures of Casper," before ending its network run and entering syndication. Animator Seymour Kneitel, who directed most of the Paramount "Casper" theatrical cartoons, directed the series. *A Harvey Films Production in association with Famous Studios. Color. Half–hour. Premiered on ABC: October 5, 1963–January 30, 1970.*

Voices:
Casper: Ginny Tyler

Additional Voices:
Jack Mercer, Allen Swift

Episodes:
"Visit From Mars," "Be Mice To Cats," "Cane And Able," "Robin Hood," "Bedtime Troubles," "Galaxia," "Abner The Baseball" (Part 1), "Abner The Baseball" (Part 2), "Absent

Minded Robot," "Boss Is Always Right," "Bored Billionaire," "Trick Or Tree," "City Snickers," "Busy Buddies," "Bouncing Benny," "Cape Kidnaveral," "Cool Cat Blues," "Cold Wave," "Enchanted Horse" (The Flying Horse)," "Mike The Masquerader," "Counter Attack," "Crumley Cogwheel," "Enchanted Prince," "Hound About That," "Wendy's Wish," "Top Cat," "Turtle Scoop," "Disquise The Limit," "Funderful Suburbia," "Greedy Giants," "Electronica," "Growing Up," "Fine Feathered Friend," "Fiddle Faddle," "Silly Science," "Heart Of Gold," "Kings Of Toyland," "Giddy Gadgets," "Good And Guilty," "Kid From Mars," "Little Lost Ghost," "Hi–Fi Jinx," "Pick Up Your Own Home," "Lonesome Giant," "Kozmo Goes To School," "Magic Touch," "Lions Busy," "Mother Goose Land," "Micenicks," "Mighty Termite," "Popcorn And Politics," "The Professors Problem," "Red Robbing Hood," "Northern Mites," "Perry Popgun," "The Phantom Moustacher," "Small Spooks," "Scouting For Trouble," "Planet Mousela," "Super Spook," "Shooting Stars," "Shoe Must Go," "Timid Knight," "Turning The Fables," "Terry The Terror," "Twin Troubles," "Weather Or Not," "Without Time Or Reason," "T.V. Or No T.V.," "The Witching Hour," "Monkey Doodles," "Trouble Date," "Goodie The Gremlin" and "Wandering Ghost."

THE NEW FANTASTIC FOUR

Three transformable humans—the stretchable Mr. Fantastic; his wife, Sue (also known as the Invisible Girl); and the rock–like being, The Thing—are joined by a wise–cracking computer, H.E.R.B. (Humanoid Electronic Robot "B" model), in new adventures based on the Fantastic Four comic book series in which they encounter weird machines and villains. *A DePatie–Freleng Production in association with Marvel Comics Group. Color. Half–hour. Premiered on NBC: September 9, 1978–September 1, 1979.*

Voices:

Mr. Fantastic: Mike Road, **Sue,** his wife: Ginny Tyler, **The Thing/Ben Grimm:** Ted Cassidy, **H.E.R.B. the robot:** Frank Welker

Episodes:

"A Monster Among Us!," "The Menace Of Magneto," "Phantom Of Film City," "Medusa And The Inhumans," "The Diamond Of Doom," "The Mole Man," "The Olympics Of Space," "The Frightful Four," "Calamity On Campus!," "The Impossible Man," "The Final Victory Of Doctor Doom!" and "Blastar, the Living Bomb–Burst."

THE NEW FRED AND BARNEY SHOW

America's favorite prehistoric families, the Flintstones and the Rubbles, returned in this half–hour program for Saturday mornings that featured 13 original episodes re–dubbed for broadcast. Teenagers Pebbles and Bamm–Bamm were spotlighted in the series. *A Hanna–Barbera Production. Color. Half–hour. Premiered on NBC: February 3, 1979–September 15, 1979.*

Voices:

Fred Flintstone: Henry Corden, **Wilma Flintstone,** his wife: Jean VanderPyl, **Barney Rubble,** their neighbor: Mel Blanc, **Betty Rubble,** Barney's wife: Gay Autterson, **Pebbles:** Jean VanderPyl, **Bamm–Bamm:** Don Messick, **George Slate,** Fred's boss: John Stephenson

Episodes:

"Sand–Witch," "Haunted Inheritance," "Roughin' It," "C.B. Buddies," "Bedrock Rocks," "Blood Brothers," "Barney's Chickens," "The Butler Did It . . . And Did It Better," "It's Not Their Bag," "Barney's Luck," "The Bad Luck Genie," "Fred And Barney Meet The Frankenstones," "Physical Fitness Fred," "Fred Goes To The Houndasaurs," "Moonlighters," "Dinosaur Country Safari" and "Stone Age Werewolf."

THE NEW PINK PANTHER SHOW

The happy–go–lucky cat and his pantomimic ways provided the entertainment in this half–hour children's series consisting of "Pink Panther," "The Inspector" and "The Ant and the Aardvark" cartoons, each originally released to theaters. Additional network shows followed, among them, "The Pink Panther Laugh And A Half Hour and A Half Show," "Think Pink Panther!" and "The All–New Pink Panther Show." *A DePatie–Freleng Enterprises Production. Color. Half–hour. Premiered on NBC: September 11, 1971–September 4, 1976.*

THE NEW SCOOBY–DOO COMEDY MOVIES

This one–hour cartoon format stars the bashful canine and his pals who are joined weekly by celebrity guests, such as the Three Stooges, Phyllis Diller, Don Knotts, Jonathan Winters, Laurel and Hardy, the Addams Family and Sonny and Cher, all in animated form. *A Hanna–Barbera Production. Color. One hour. Premiered on CBS: September 9, 1972–August 31, 1974.*

Voices:

Scooby-Doo: Don Messick, **Freddy:** Frank Welker, **Daphne:** Heather North, **Shaggy:** Casey Kasem, **Velma:** Nicole Jaffe

Episodes:

1972–1973 "Ghastly Ghost Town" (with the Three Stooges), "Guess Who's Knott Coming To Dinner?" (with Don Knotts), "The Spooky Fog" (with Don Knotts), "The Dynamic Scooby–Doo Affair" (with Batman and Robin), "Scooby–Doo Meets Laurel And Hardy," "Scooby–Doo Meets The Addams Family," "A Good Medium Is Rare" (with Phyllis Diller), "Sandy Duncan's Jekyll And Hydes," "The Frickert Fracas" (with Jonathan Winters), "The Phantom Of The Country Music Hall" (with Jerry Reed), "The Secret Of Shark Island" (with Sonny and Cher), "The Ghostly Creep From The Deep" (with the Harlem Globetrotters), "Ghost Of The Red Baron" (with the Three Stooges), "The Lochness Mess," "The Haunted Horseman In Hagglethorn Hall" (with Davy Jones) and "The Caped Crusader Caper" (with Batman and Robin).
1973–1974 (new shows combined with reruns) "The Haunted Showboat" (with Josie and the Pussycats), "Mystery Of Haunted

Island" (with the Harlem Globetrotters), "Scooby–Doo Meets Jeannie" (with Jeannie and Babu), "The Spirited Spooked Sports Show" (with Tim Conway), "The Exterminator" (with Don Adams), "The Weird Winds Of Winona" (with Speedy Buggy), "The Haunted Candy Factory" (with Cass Elliot) and "Scooby–Doo Meets Dick Van Dyke."

THE NEW SCOOBY–DOO MYSTERIES

Scooby–Doo, Scrappy–Doo, Shaggy and Daphne uncover clues to a series of new mysteries in this half–hour program produced for Saturday morning television. *A Hanna–Barbera Production. Color. Half–hour. Premiered on ABC: September 9, 1984–August 31, 1985.*

Voices:

Scooby–Doo/Scrappy–Doo: Don Messick, **Shaggy:** Casey Kasem, **Daphne:** Heather North

Episodes:

(two per show) "Happy Birthday, Scooby–Doo" (Part 1), "Happy Birthday, Scooby–Doo" (Part 2), "The Hand Of Horror," "Scooby's Peephole Pandemonium," "Doom Service," "Mission: Un–Doo–Able," "Scoo–Be Or Not Scoo–Be," "The Night Of The Living Toys," "The Dooby Dooby Doo Ado," "A Code In The Nose," "South Pole Vault," "The Bee Team," "Showboat Scooby," "The Stoney Glare Scare," "E.I.E.I.O.," "A Night Louse At The White House" (Part 1), "A Night Louse At The White House" (Part 2), "Ghosts Of The Ancient Astronauts" (Part 1), "Ghosts Of The Ancient Astronauts" (Part 2), "A Halloween Hassle At Dracula Castle" (Part 1), "A Halloween Hassle At Dracula Castle" (Part 2), "A Scarcy Duel With A Cartoon Ghoul," "Sherlock Doo" (Part 1), "Sherlock Doo" (Part 2), "The Nutcracker Scoob" (Part 1) and "The Nutcracker Scoob" (Part 2).

THE NEW SHMOO

Al Capp's lovable and trusting comic–strip character uses its ability to change into virtually anything to help three young reporters—Mickey, Nita and Billy Joe—who work for *Mighty Mysteries Comics* and investigate cases of psychic phenomena. *A Hanna–Barbera Production. Color. Half–hour. Premiered on NBC: September 22, 1979–December 1, 1979.*

Voices:

Shmoo: Frank Welker, **Nita:** Delores Cantu–Primo, **Billy Joe:** Chuck McCann, **Mickey:** Bill Idelson

Episodes:

"The Flying Disc Of Doom," "The Beast Of Black Lake," "The Crystal Ball of Crime," "The Wail Of The Banshee," "The Pyramid Of Peril," "Dr. Morton's Monster," "The Warlock Of Voodoo Island," "The Terror Of The Trolls," "The Amazing Captain Mentor," "The Haunting Of Atlantis," "The Valley Where Time Stood Still," "The Return Of Dracula," "The Energy Robbers From Space," "The Ber–Smoo–Da Triangle," "Swamp Of Evil" and "Monster Island."

THE NEW THREE STOOGES

Moe Howard, Larry Fine and Curly–Joe DeRita (the fourth comedian to play the "third stooge" in the long–running comedy act) starred in this series which combined live–action wraparounds and animated segments to tell one complete story. The cartoons reflected the Stooges' style and humor, yet in a less violent manner. Only 40 live–action openings and endings were filmed for this series. (The live segments were rotated throughout the package's 156 cartoon episodes.) Dick Brown, who produced such animated favorites as "Cluth Cargo" and "Space Angel," produced the series in association with Normandy III Productions (the Stooges' own company named after their producer/agent Norman Maurer). *A Cambria Studios Production in association with Normandy III Productions. Color. Half–hour. Premiered: December 20, 1965. Syndicated.*

Voices:

Moe: Moe Howard, **Larry:** Larry Fine, **Curly–Joe:** Joe DeRita

Episodes:

"Little Old Bombmaker," "Woodsman Bear That Tree," "Let's Shoot The Player Piano Player," "Dentist The Menace," "Safari So Good," "Think Of Thwim," "There Auto Be A Law," "That Old Shell Game," "Hold That Lion," "A Flycycle Built For Two," "Three Dizzy Doodlers," "The Classical Clinker," "Movie Scars," "A Bull For Andamo," "The Tree Nuts," "The Tinhorn Dude," "Through Rain, Sleet And Snow," "Goldriggers Of '49," "Ready, Jet Set, Go," "Behind The Eightball Express," "Stop Dragon Around," "To Kill A Clockingbird," "Who's Lion," "Fowl Weather Friend," "Wash My Line," "Little Cheese Chaser," "The Big Windbag," "Babysitters," "Clarence Of Arabia," "Three Jacks And A Beanstalk," "That Was The Wreck That Was," "Three Astronutz," "Peter Panic," "When You Wish Upon A Fish," "A Little Past Noon," "The Hair Of The Bear," "Three Lumps And A Lamp," "Who's For Dessert," "Watts My Lion," "Which Is Witch," "Suture Self," "The Yolk's On You," "Tally Moe, Larry And Joe," "First In Lion," "The Transylvania Railroad," "What's Mew, Pussycat," "It's A Bad, Bad, Bad World," "Bridge On The River Cry," "Hot Shots," "Mel's Angels," "Bee My Honey," "Flag Pole Sitters," "Stone Age Stooges," "Smoke Gets In Your Skies," "Queen Qwong," "Campsite Fright," "Goldibear And The Three Stooges," "The Lyin' Tamers," "The Pen Game," "It's A Small World," "Late For Launch," "Focus In Space," "The Noisy Silent Movie," "Get Outa Town By Sundown Brown," "Table Tennis Tussle," "Phoney Express," "The Best Test Pilots," "The Little Bear," "A Fishy Tale," "The Unhaunted House," "Aloha Ha Ha," "The Rise And Fall Of The Roman Empire," "Deadbeat Street," "Cotton Pickin' Chicken," "Larry And The Pirates," "Trees A Crowd," "Feud For Thought," "Bat And Brawl," "Knight Without End," "Up A Tree," "Turn About Is Bad Play," "Pow, Wow Row," "The Flatheads," "No News Is Good News," "Bully For You Curly," "Free For All," "Goofy Gondoliers," "Bearfoot Fisherman," "Washout Below," "The Three Marketeers," "Follow The White Lion," "One Good Burn Deserves Another," "Curly's Bear," "Land Ho, Ho, Ho," "Surf's You Right," "The Seven Faces Of Tim Bear," "Bear Foot Bandit," "None Butt The Brave," "Three Good Knights," "Call Of The Wile," "Snow Brawl," "Rob N. Hood," "There's

No Mule Like An Old Mule," "Squawk Valley," "Mummy's Boys," "The Plumber's Friends," "Rub A Dub Tub," "Under A Bad, Bad Tree," "Hairbrained Barbers," "Waiter Minute," "Souperman," "The Abominable Showman," "Curly In Wonderland," "Boobs In The Woods," "The Chimney Sweeps," "The Mad Mail Mission," "Out Of Space," "The Three Wizards Of Odds," "Three For The Road," "Feudin', Fussin' Hillbully," "Don't Misbehave, Indian Brave," "You Ain't Lion," "Muscle On The Mind," "Badman Of The Briny," "Furry Fugitive," "How The West Was Once," "Bowling Pinheads," "The Mountain–Ear," "Norse Worst Passage," "Lastest Gun In The West," "Toys Will Be Toys," "First Class Service," "Strictly For The Birds," "Les Stoogenaires," "The Bear Who Came In From The Cold," "The Bigger They Are The Harder They Hit," "Little Red Riding Wolf," "Bell Hop Flops," "Gopher Broke," "Gagsters Dragster," "Just Plane Crazy," "From Bad To Verse," "Droll Weevil," "The Littlest Martian," "The Bear Show–Off," "No Money No Honey," "Get That Snack Shack Off The Track," "Curly's Birthday A Go Go," "The Men From U.C.L.A.," "Super Everybody," "Kangaroo Katchers," "No Smoking Aloud," "The Chicken Delivery Boys," "S'No Ball," "Rug A Bye Baby" and "Dinopoodi."

Twelve–year–old Sandy discovers that Blinky, her favorite stuffed animal, actually becomes a live koala in "Noozles." © Saban Productions

Moe, Larry and Curly–Joe, better known as The Three Stooges, in cartoon form from the live–action/animated series, "The New Three Stooges." © Normandy Productions. All rights reserved. (Courtesy: Muller Media)

NTA CARTOON CARNIVAL LIBRARY

This late 1950s syndicated series was comprised of previously released live–action and cartoon short–subjects originally produced for Paramount Pictures by the following producers: Fleischer Studios, Famous Studios, Jerry Fairbanks Productions and George Pal Productions.

Cartoons that were telecast as part of the package were such highly–acclaimed theatrical series as "Animated Antics," "Color Classics," "Gabby," "Noveltoons," "Screen Songs," "Stone Age Cartoons," "Talkartoons," "Inkwell Imps," plus George Pal's "Puppetoons" and "Speaking of Animals," the Oscar–winning talking animals short–subject series produced by Jerry Fairbanks, who produced the early television versions of "Crusader Rabbit" with "Rocky and Bullwinkle" creator Jay Ward. *A National Television Associates (NTA) Presentation. Black–and–white. Color. Premiered: 1956. Syndicated.*

NOOZLES

It's every child's dream come true as 12–year–old Sandy discovers that Blinky, her favorite stuffed animal, actually becomes a live koala whenever she rubs noses with him. Together, they journey magically throughout the universe in search of fun and excitement. *A Saban International Services Production in association with Fuji Eight Company. Color. Half–hour. Voice credits and episode titles unavailable. Premiered on Nickelodeon: November 8, 1988.*

THE NUTTY SQUIRRELS

Television's forerunners to Ross Bagdasarian's "Alvin and the Chipmunks," this animated series boasted the exploits of another recording group, The Nutty Squirrels, who beat Alvin, Theodore, Simon and David Seville to television screens by one full year. Little else was notable about the series, which even used the same sped–up dialogue and singing style of the Chipmunks, but in less spectacular fashion. *A Transfilm/Wilde Production. Color. Half–hour. Syndicated: 1960.*

THE ODDBALL COUPLE

Adapted from Neil Simon's Broadway and Hollywood film hit and long–running TV series, which mismatched sloppy Oscar Madison and fastidious Felix Unger, this animated spin–off casts the perfectionist cat Spiffy (Unger) and the troublesome dog Fleabag (Madison) in equally funny situations as reporters at large. *A DePatie–Freleng Enterprises Production. Color. Half–hour. Premiered on ABC: September 6, 1975–September 3, 1977.*

Voices:

Spiffy: Frank Nelson, **Fleabag:** Paul Winchell, **Goldie,** the secretary: Joan Gerber

Additional Voices:

Frank Welker, Sarah Kennedy, Joe Besser, Don Messick, Bob Holt, Ginny Tyler

Episodes:

(two per show) "Spiffy's Many Friday," "Who Zoo?," "Fleabag's Mother," "A Day At The Beach," "To Heir Is Human," "Spiffy's Nephew," "A Royal Mixup," "Paper Airplane," "The Bighouse And Garden," "The Talking Plant," "Hotel Boo–More," "Family Album," "Who's Afraid Of Virginia Werewolf?," "Irish Luck," "Dive Bummers," "Do Or Diet," "Klondike Oil Kaper," "Old Bugeyes Is Back," "TV Or Not TV," "Mugsy Bagel," "Ali Kat," "The Joker's Wild," "Momma Fleabag," "Cinderbag," "Roman Daze," "Do It Yourself Fleabag," "Foreign Legion," "Fleabag's Submarine," "Superhound," "Bats In The Belfry," "Talent Scouts" and "Jungle Bungle."

OFFICIAL FILMS CARTOONS

This program featured a recycled package of old Van Beuren Studio cartoons produced in the 1920s and 1930s, first broadcast on "TV Tot's Time" on ABC stations locally and nationally. Making up the package were several notable cartoon stars,

Spiffy is ready to clobber his sloppy roommate, Fleabag, in a scene from the animated version of Neil Simon's The Odd Couple called, "The Oddball Couple." © DePatie–Freleng Enterprises

renamed "Brownie Bear" *(Cubby Bear),* "Dick and Larry" *(Tom and Jerry),* "Jungle Jinks" *(Aesop's Fables),* "Merry Toons" *(Rainbow Parades)* and "The Little King," which remained unchanged. In the early 1950s, the cartoons were also used by local stations on programs hosted by station personalities. *An Official Films Presentation. Black–and– white. Half–hour. Premiered: 1950.*

OSWALD THE RABBIT

The floppy–eared rabbit from Walter Lantz's theatrical sound cartoon series headlined this packaged of formerly released black–and–white cartoons produced by Walter Lantz Studios. Along with Oswald, the packaged included "Meany, Miny and Moe" and "Pooch the Pup," both successful theatrical cartoon series. *A Walter Lantz Production distributed by Revue Productions (MCA–TV). Black–and–white. Half–hour. Premiered: February 28, 1955, KNXT, Los Angeles.*

Voices:

Oswald the Rabbit: Mickey McGuire, Bernice Hansen

OUT OF THE INKWELL

Max Fleischer's innovative silent cartoon series, which combined live–action and animation and featured the comical exploits of Koko the Clown, was among several other successful cartoon series from the early days of cartoon animation which were issued to television in the early 1950s. Initially shown in some television markets in 1952, this series of films was syndicated nationally in 1956 when Paramount sold the cartoons to a television distributor, UM&M–TV (later renamed NTA).

In 1961, Fleischer's creation was revived in all–new color adventures that featured a new supporting cast of regulars. Kokette, Koko's girlfriend; Koko–nut, Koko's dog; and Mean Moe, Koko's primary adversary. Several published reports in the mid–1960s cited Fleischer's disappointment with the series, especially its animation quality. Larry Storch, of TV's "F Troop," did most of the characters' voices. *A Max Fleischer Production (old films). A Video House Incorporated Production (new series). Black–and–white. Color. Premiered: 1952 (old series). Premiered: September 10, 1962 (new series)*

Voices:

Koko: Larry Storch, **Kokette/Mean Moe:** Larry Storch

Episodes:

(four per show) "Achilles Is A Heel," "Arabian Daze," "Arty Party," "Baby Face," "Balloon Blues," "The Big Bank Robbery," "Bluebeard's Treasure," "Blunder Down Under," "Bomb–y Weather," "The Clif Hanger," "Comic Book Capers," "Comic Strip," "A Dog Gone Snooper," "Down To Earth," "The Egg And Me," "Enchanted Prince," "Extra Special Delivery," "The Fan Letter," "Fastest Popgun In The West," "Fearless Female," "A Fishy Story," "Flying Saucery," "Footloose Fox," "Funnyland," "Gigantical," "Gone Hollywood," "Growing Pains," "A Haunting We Will Go," "Having A Hex Of A Time," "The Hillbullies," "In The Army," "The Invisible One," "Irving, The

Indian Nut," "Jungle Bungle," "Knight Work," "Koko Gottum Injun Trouble," "Koko In London Fog," "Koko Meets Barney Beatnik," "Koko Meets Boobnik," "Koko Meets Robin Hood," "Koko Roams In Rome," "Kokonut, Private Eye," "Let George Do It," "A Lot Of Bull," "Love In Bloom," "Mad Scientist Gets Madder," "Make Room For Moe," "Mayor Mean Moe," "Mean Moe And Cleopatra," "Mean Moe Cools Off," "Mean Moe Day," "Mean Moe Means Well," "Mean Moe Rain Maker," "Mean Moe Takes Over," "Mean Moe Tells William Tell," "Mean Moe The Great," "Mean Moe, Lion Tamer," "Mean Moe The Star," "Mean Moe's Fairy Tale," "Mean Moe's Money Mad," "Mean Moe's Side Show," "Medicine Man," "Moe Moves In," "Moving Madness," "Mummy's The Word," "Musketeer Moe," "The Mystery Guest," "No Soap," "Now You See It, Now You Don't," "On With The Show," "Plane Stupid," "Polar Bear Facts," "Pony Express," "Pow—Wow—Wow!," "A Queen For A Day," "Reflection Land," "The Refriger—Raider," "The River Robbers," "Rocket Ranger," "Rodeo," "Romance, Machine Made," "Sahara Today, Gone Tomorrow," "Sing Along With Moe," "The Sleeping Beauty," "So Long Ceylon," "Sold On Manhattan," "Speak For Yourself, Mean Moe," "Station Breaks," "Strictly From Lumber," "Success Story," "TV Or Not TV," "That's Show Biz," "Tic Tac Moe," "The Unwashables," "Whale Of A Story," "Which Witch Is Which?," "Who's Napoleon," "Wild West Story" and "You Are Here."

THE PAC-MAN/RUBIK, THE AMAZING CUBE HOUR

Pac—Man, Ms. Pac, Baby Pac and the rest of the Pac—Land gang returned in all—new adventures in this hour—long fantasy/adventure series which provided equal time to its co-star, Rubik, the Amazing Cube, which made its Saturday—morning television debut. Rubik is discovered by a young boy (Carlos) who brings the colorful cube to life—after he aligns all the cube's sides—and sets out on a magical adventure tour along with his brother and sister, Renaldo and Lisa. (The series was rebroadcast in the spring of 1985 as a mid—season replacement.) Hanna—Barbera Productions (Pac—Man) and Ruby—Spears Enterprises (Rubik) co—produced the series. *A Hanna—Barbera and Ruby—Spears Enterprises Production. Color. One hour. Premiered on ABC: September 10, 1983—September 1, 1984.*

Voices:
Pac—Man: Marty Ingels, **Ms. Pac:** Barbara Minkus, **Baby Pac:** Russi Taylor, **Super—Pac:** Lorenzo Music, **Pac—Junior:** Darryl Hickman, **Chomp Chomp:** Frank Welker, **Sour Puss:** Peter Cullen, **Mezmaron:** Alan Lurie, **Sue Monster:** Susan Silo, **Inky Monster:** Barry Gordon, **Clyde Monster:** Neilson Ross, **Rubik:** Ron Palillo, **Carlos:** Michael Saucedo, **Renaldi,** his brother: Michael Bell, **Lisa,** his sister: Jennifer Fajardo, **Ruby Rodriguez:** Michael Bell, **Marla Rodriguez:** Angela Moya

Episodes:
"Pac—Man" (two 11—minute episodes per show).
"Hey, Hey, Hey . . . It's P. J.," "The Old Pac—Man And The Sea," "Journey Into The Pac—Past," "Pac—A—Thon," "Here's Super—Pac," "The Genii Of Pac—Dad," "Dr. Jekyll And Mr.

Pac—Man," "The Greatest Show In Pac—Land," "Computer Packy," "Around The World In 80 Chomps," "Super—Pac Vs. Pac—Ape," "Pac Van Winkle," "The Super—Pac Bowl," "Public Pac—Enemy #1," "P. J. Goes Pac—Hollywood" and "Happy Pacs—Living."
"Pac—Man Vignettes" (30—second spots per show).
"Clean Sweep," "The Sky's The Limit," "Buffoons—R—Us," "Life Is A Multi—Dimensional Experience," "Shipshape," "Lil' Shrinkers," "Surfs Ooop" and "Mow Me Down."
"Rubik, the Amazing Cube (one 22—minute episode per show).
"Rubik: The Amazing Cube," "Rubik And The Lucky Helmet," "Back Packin' Rubik," "Super Power Lisa," "Rubik And The Mysterious Man," "Rubik And The Pooch—Nappers," "Rubik And The Buried Treasure," "Rubik And The Science Fair," "Honolulu Rubik," "Rubik's First Christmas," "Rubik In Wonderland" and "Saturday Night Rubik."

THE PAC-MAN SHOW

The immensely popular video game character stars in this half—hour series, along with his wife, Ms. Pac, a peppery, liberated lady; the energetic Baby Pac; Chomp Chomp, a lovable dog; and Sour Puss, their sly cat, in fantasy adventures that take place in Pac—Land, a pretty pastel world composed of brightly glowing dots. Their perfect world has one enemy, however: the even—sinister, Mezmaron, who tries to rob the Power Pellet Forest of the power pellets Pac—Land thrives on. (His attempts are always bungled by his comical ghost monsters, Inky, Blinky, Pinky, Clyde and Sue).

In 1983, the series was rebroadcast in combination with Ruby—Spears Enterprises "Rubik, the Amazing Cube" as "The Pac—Man/Rubik, The Amazing Cube Hour." Several new characters were added during the second season to the Pac—Man cartoons. They were Pac—Junior, Pac—Man's fast—talking, free—wheeling cousin, and Super—Pac, a vain and powerful super—hero. *A Hanna—Barbera Production. Color. Half—hour. Premiered on ABC: September 25, 1982—September 3, 1983. Rebroadcast on ABC: September 10, 1983—September 1, 1984 (as "The Pac—Man/Rubik, the Amazing Cube Hour").*

Voices:
Pac—Man: Marty Ingels, **Ms. Pac:** Barbara Minkus, **Baby Pac:** Russi Taylor, **Super—Pac:** Lorenzo Music, **Pac—Junior:** Darryl Hickman, **Chomp Chomp:** Frank Welker, **Sour Puss:** Peter Cullen, **Mezmaron:** Alan Lurie, **Sue Monster:** Susan Silo, **Inky Monster:** Barry Gordon, **Blinky/Pinky Monsters:** Chuck McCann, **Clyde Monster:** Neilson Ross

Episodes:
Pac—Man (two 11—minute episodes per show).
"Presidential Pac—Nappers," "Hocus—Pocus Pac—Man," "The Great Pac—Quake," "Picnic In Pacland," "Southpaw Packy," "Pac—Baby Panic," "The Pac—Man In The Moon," "Neander—Pac—Man," "Super Ghosts," "Invasion Of The Pac—Pups," "Trick Or Chomp," "Pacula," "Once Upon A Chomp," "Journey To The Center Of Pac—Land," "Chomp—Out At The O.K. Corral," "The Bionic Pac—Women," "The Great Power—Pellet Robbery," "Backpackin' Packy," "The Abominable Pac—Man," "Sir Chomp—A—Lot," "Goo—Goo At The Zoo," "Attack Of The

Pac–Mummy," "A Bad Case Of The Chomps," "The Day The Forest Disappeared" and "Nighty Nightmares."
"Pac–Man Vignettes" (30–second spots per show).
"Toot–Toot–Tootsy Goodbye," "Canned Canine," "Gimme A Hand," "Balloon Pie,' "Ghosts Galore," "Stuck Up," "Keep In Step," "Animal Magnetism" "On The Noggin'," "Stacked" and "Hose On First" (title of one spot was not on record).

PADDINGTON BEAR (1981)

Author Michael Bond's child–like honey–bear who can talk was cast in this short–lived series for public television based on chapters from Bond's popular children's books, including his first, *A Bear Called Paddington*. Oscar–winning entertainer Joel Gray introduced each program, featuring five vignettes which blend stop–action animation of a stuffed bear and flat, cut–out figures to tell each story. *A Film Fair Production. Color. Half–hour. Premiered on PBS: April 13, 1981– May 18, 1981.*

Voices:

Narrator/Others: Michael Hordern

Episodes:

"Paddington Goes To The Movies," "Paddington's Birthday Bonanza," "Paddington Goes To School," "Paddington's Christmas," and "Paddington P.I."

PADDINGTON BEAR (1989)

The Brown family discovers a lost little bear at London's Paddington Station, whom they name Paddington and raise as their child in this animated adaptation of the storybook favorite. Paddington never deliberately gets into mischief, but his adventures always snowball in the most alarming, charming and unintentional way to the delight of the Browns' friends: Mrs Bird, their housekeeper; Mr. Gruber, a Hungarian antiques dealer; and David Russell, the Browns' American cousin. Not everyone falls for the innocent bear, however. Next–door neighbor Mr. Curry detests Paddington and plots to take advantage of the bear's trusting nature. The program was broadcast on Sunday mornings as part of "The Funtastic World of Hanna–Barbera." *A Hanna–Barbera Production. Color. Half–hour. Premiered: September, 1989.*

Voices:

Paddington Bear: Charlie Adler, **Mr. Brown:** John Standing, **Mrs. Brown:** B. J. Ward, **Jonathan Brown,** their son: Cody Everett, **Judy Brown,** their daughter: Katie Johnson, **Mrs. Bird:** Georgia Brown, **David Russell:** R. J. Williams, **Mr. Gruber:** Hamilton Camp, **Mr. Curry:** Tim Curry

Episodes:

"Please Look After This Bear," "Calling Dr. Paddington," "Curtain Call For Paddington," "Paddington's Sticky Situation," "Bear–Hugged," "Paddington Meets The Queen," "The Ghost Of Christmas Paddington," "Paddington For Prime Minister," "Goings On At Number 32," "Fishing For Paddington," "Ride 'Em Paddington," "Expedition Paddington" and "The Picture Of Paddington Brown."

PANDAMONIUM

Three talking panda bears (Algernon, Chesty and Timothy) and their teenage human friends (Peter Darrow and his sister Peggy) embark to find the lost pieces of the magical, mystical Pyramid of Power. *A Marvel Production in association with InterMedia Entertainment. Color. Half–hour. Premiered on CBS: September 18, 1982–September 10, 1985.*

Voices:

Julie McWhirter, Jesse White, Cliff Norton, Walker Edmiston, Katie Leigh, Neilson Ross, William Woodson, Rick Dees, Alan Dinehart, David Banks

Episodes:

"The Beginning," "Algernon's Story," "Timothy's Story," "Chesty's Story," "Amanda Panda's Story," "Ice Hastles," "Prehistoric Hysterics," "Once Upon A Time Machine," "The Cybernetic City," "20,000 Laughs Under The Sea," "Itty Bitty City," "Methinks The Sphinx Jinx Stinks" and "The Great Space Chase."

PARTRIDGE FAMILY: 2200 A.D.

Widow Connie Partridge leads an inter–planetary rock and roll group comprising of family members Keith, Laurie, Danny, Tracy and Chris in futuristic adventures on Earth and in outer space, performing their music to new audiences of every kind—alien and otherwise. A spin–off of the popular TV sitcom, "The Partridge Family," the program featured the voices of the original cast members (except Shirley Jones and David Cassidy) and reprised one of the group's most famous songs in each show. Episodes from the series were later syndicated as part of 1977's "Fred Flintstones and Friends." *A Hanna–Barbera Production. Color. Half–hour. Premiered on CBS: September 7, 1974–March 8, 1975.*

Voices:

Connie Partridge: Joan Gerber, **Keith Partridge:** Chuck McClendon, **Laurie Partridge:** Susan Dey, **Danny Partridge:** Danny Bonaduce, **Christopher Partridge:** Brian Forster, **Tracy Partridge:** Suzanne Crough, **Reuben Kinkaid:** David Madden, **Marion:** Julie McWhirter, **Veenie:** Frank Welker

Additional Voices:

Sherry Alberoni, Allan Melvin, Alan Oppenheimer, Mike Road, Hal Smith, John Stephenson, Lennie Weinrib, Frank Welker

Episodes:

"My Son, The Spaceball Star," "Danny And The Invisible Man," "Incredible Shrinking Keith," "If This Is Texas—It Must Be Doomsday," "Cousin Sunspot," "The Dog Catcher," "The Wax Museum," "Laurie's Computer Date," "Movie Madness," "The Pink Letter," "The Cupcake Caper," "Orbit The Genius," "The Switch," "Car Trouble," "The Roobits" and "Let's Stick Together."

THE PAW PAWS

The muffled patter of small tom–toms is the only clue to the whereabouts of the Paw Paws, a tribe of tiny, tenderhearted bearlets who inhabit the enchanted forest where past, present and future are blended in this fantasy/adventure series offered as part of "The Funtastic World of Hanna–Barbera." But all is not rosy for Princess Paw Paw and her tribe, for across the river Dark Paw and his evil tribe, the Meanos, lie waiting for their next chance to conquer the peace–loving Paw Paws. *A Hanna–Barbera Production. Color. Half–hour. Premiered: September, 1985. Syndicated.*

Voices:
Princess Paw Paw: Susan Blu, **Brave Paw:** Thom Pinto, **Mighty Paw:** Bob Ridgely, **Laughing Paw:** Stanley Stoddart, **Wise Paw:** John Ingle, **Trembly Paw:** Howard Morris, **Pupooch:** Don Messick, **Dark Paw:** Stanley Ralph Ross, **Bumble Paw:** Frank Welker, **Aunt Pruney:** Ruth Buzzi

Episodes:
1985–1986 "The Big Spill," "The Wishing Star Crystal," "The Flying Horse Napper," "The Creepy Cave Creature," "Greedy Greenies," "The Rise Of The Evil Spirits," "The Genie–Athalon," "The Golden Falcon," "Honey Of A Robbery," "Tot–Em Termi-Nation," "Waif Goodbye To The Paw Paws," "The Dark Totem Pole Monster," "Dark Paw Under Wraps," "Genie Without A Lamp," "Egging Dark Paw On," "Two Heads Are Better Than One" and "The Great Paw Paw Turnaround."
1986–1987 (new episodes combined with reruns) "The Lost Lake Monster," "Totem Time Trip," "S'No Business" and "The Zip Zap 4–D Trap."

PEBBLES AND BAMM–BAMM

Barney Rubble's muscular son, Bamm–Bamm, and Fred Flintstone's gorgeous daughter, Pebbles, are young adults experiencing tribulations of teenagers—dating, finding work and earning money—but in a prehistoric setting.

Sally Struthers, of TV's "All in the Family" fame, was the voice of Pebbles. (She was replaced by Mickey Stevens when the character was reprised in new adventures on "The Flintstones Comedy Hour.") Episodes later appeared on the syndicated "Fred Flintstones and Friends." *A Hanna–Barbera Production. Color. Half–hour. Premiered on CBS: September 11, 1971–September 2, 1972. Rebroadcast on CBS: February 1974–September 1974; May 1973–September 1973; February 1974–September 1974; March 8, 1975–September 4, 1976.*

Voices:
Pebbles Flintstone: Sally Struthers, **Bamm–Bamm Rubble:** Jay North, **Moonrock:** Lennie Weinrib, **Penny:** Mitzi McCall, **Wiggy:** Gay Hartwig, **Cindy:** Gay Hartwig, **Fabian:** Carl Esser

Episodes:
1971–1972 "Gridiron Girl Trouble," "Putty In Her Hands," "Frog For A Day," "The Golden Voice," "Pebbles Bib Boat," "Focus Foolery," "The Grand Prix Pebbles," "The Terrible Snorkosaurus," "Schleprock's New Image," "Daddy's Little Helper," "Coach Pebbles," "No Cash And Carry," "Woolly The

Great," "Mayor May Not," "They Went That Away" and "The Birthday Present."

THE PERILS OF PENELOPE PITSTOP

In this spoof of the famed silent movie serial, "The Perils of Pauline," villainous Sylvester Sneakly (alias the "Hooded Claw") tries to keep lovely heroine race car driver Penelope Pitstop (formerly of Hanna–Barbera's "The Wacky Races") from winning in international competition using every dirty trick in the book. Penelope is protected by her legal guardians, a bevy of buffoons known as the Ant Hill Mob, who also appeared in "The Wacky Races." (Their car's name was changed from "The Bulletproof Bomb" to "Chug–A–Boom.") Episodes were later syndicated as part of "The Fun World of Hanna–Barbera." *A Hanna–Barbera Production. Color. Half–hour. Premiered on CBS: September 13, 1969–September 5, 1971.*

Voices:
Narrator: Gary Owens, **Penelope Pitstop:** Janet Waldo, **Sylvester Sneakly/The Hooded Claw:** Paul Lynde, **Bully Brothers:** Mel Blanc, **Yak Yak:** Mel Blanc, **Clyde:** Paul Winchell, **Softly:** Paul Winchell, **Zippy:** Don Messick, **Dum Dum:** Don Messick, **Snoozy:** Don Messick, **Pockets:** Don Messick, **Chug–A–Boom:** Mel Blanc

Episodes:
"Jungle Jeopardy," "The Terrible Trolley Trap," "Hair Raising Harness Race," "The Boardwalk Booby Trap," "Wild West Peril," "The Treacherous Movie Lot Plot," "Arabian Desert Danger," "Carnival Calamity," "The Diabolical Department Store Danger," "Tall Timber Treachery," "North Pole Peril," "Cross Country Double Cross," "Big Bagdad Danger," "Bad Fortune In A Chinese Fortune Cookie," "Big Top Trap," "London Town Treachery" and "Game Of Peril."

PETER POTAMUS AND HIS MAGIC FLYING BALLOON

Umbrella title for Hanna–Barbera's sixth syndicated series, whose main star was a purple hippo, Peter Potamus (whose voice sounded like comedian Joe E. Brown), and his sidekick, So So the monkey, who travel back in time and make history in the process. Other series regulars were: "Breezly and Sneezly," the misadventures of a goofy polar bear and smart arctic seal who first debuted on "The Magilla Gorilla Show; and "Yippee, Yappee and Yahooey," tracing the madcap attempts of three palace guard dogs to serve their majesty, the King. Two years after its debut, the program was retitled and rebroadcast on ABC as "The Peter Potamus Show" and again in syndication as "The Magilla Gorilla/Peter Potamus Show." *A Hanna–Barbera Production. Color. Half–hour. Premiered: September 16, 1964. Syndicated.*

Voices:
Peter Potamus: Hal Smith, **So So:** Don Messick, **Breezly:** Howard Morris, **Sneezly:** Mel Blanc, **Colonel:** John Stephenson, **Yippee:** Doug Young, **Yappee:** Hal Smith, **Yahooey:** Daws Butler, **The King:** Hal Smith

Episodes:

"Peter Potamus" (one per show).

1964–1965 "Fee Fi Fo Fun," "Lion Around," "Cleo Trio," "No Rest For A Pest," "Wagon Train Strain," "Monotony On The Bounty," "The Good Hood," "Stars On Mars," "Kookie Spook," "The Island Fling," "Courtin' Trouble," "Big Red Riding Hood," "Hurricane Hippo" and "What A Knight."

1965–1966 "Mask Task," "Pre–Hysterical Pete," "Trite Flite," "Marriage Peter Potamus Style," "Calaboose Caboose," "Eager Ogre" and "The Reform of Clankenstein."

"Breezly and Sneezly" (one per show).

"No Place Like Home," "All Riot On The Northern Front," "Missile Fizzle," "Mass Masquerade," "Furry Furlough," "Bruin Ruin," "Freezing Fleas," "Stars And Gripes," "Armored Amour," "As The Snow Flies," "Snow Biz," "Unseen Trouble," "Nervous In The Service," "Birthday Bonanza" and "Wacky Waikiki."

1965–1966 "General Nuisance," "Rookie Wrecker," "Noodick Of The North," "The Fastest Bear In The North," "Snow Time Show Time" and "Goat A–Go–Go."

"Yippee, Yappee, and Yahooey" (one per show).

1964–1965 "The Volunteers," "Black Bart," "Double Dragon," "Outlaw Inlaw," "Horse Shoo Fly," "Wild Child," "Witch Is Which?," "Wise Quacking," "Nautical Nitwits," "Job Robbed," "Uni–Corn On The Cob," "Mouse–Rout" and "Handy Dandy Lion."

1965–1966 "Sappy Birthday," "Kind Of The Roadhogs," "Palace Pal Picnic," "Sleepy Time King" and "Pie, Pie, Blackbird."

THE PETER POTAMUS SHOW

Network version of the syndicated series which first appeared on television screens nationwide in 1964 under a different title, "Peter Potamus and His Magic Flying Balloon." ABC picked up the series and added the program to its Saturday morning children's lineup in 1966. The cartoon components from the former series remained intact (see entry for voices and episodes), combining new episodes with cartoons which aired previously in syndication. *A Hanna–Barbera Production. Color. Half–hour. Premiered on ABC: January 2, 1966–December 24, 1967.*

Episodes:

(New episodes listed only)

"Peter Potamus" (one per show).

"Debt and Taxes," "Wrong Time No See," "America Or Bust," "Rebel Rumble," "Pilgrims Regress" and "The Crossbow Incident."

"Breezly and Sneezly" (one per show).

"Spy–In The Ointment" and "An Ill Wind."

"Yippee, Yappee and Yahooey" (one per show).

"What The Hex Going On?," "Eviction Capers," "Hero Sandwiched," "Throne For A Loss" and "Royal Rhubarb."

PINK PANTHER AND SONS

The Pink Panther is the father of three sons, Pinky, Panky and Punkin, in all–new misadventures which test his skills at fatherhood in managing the terrorsome trio. As in previous films, the witty panther conveys his message via pantomime. *A DePatie–Freleng Enterprises Production in association*

with Hanna–Barbera Productions. Color. Half–hour. Premiered on NBC: September 15, 1984–September 7, 1985.

Voices:

Pinky: Billy Bowles, **Panky/Punkin:** B. J. Ward, **Chatta:** Sherry Lynn, **Howl:** Marshall Efron, **Anney/Liona:** Jeanine Elias, **Finko/Rocko:** Frank Welker, **Bowlhead:** Gregg Berger, **Buckethead:** Sonny Melendrez, **Murfel:** Shane McCabe

Episodes:

(two per show) "Spinning Wheels," "Pinky At The Bat," "The Great Bumpo," "Take A Hike," "Haunted Howlers," "Traders Of The Lost Bark," "Pink Enemy #1," "Pink Encounters Of The Panky Kind," "Millionaire Murfel," "The Pursuit Of Panky," "Sitter Jitters," "The Fix Up, Foul Up," "Joking Genie," "Panky's Pet," "Punkin's Home Companion," "Insanity Claus," "Rocko's Last Round," "Sleeptalking Chatta," "Pink Shrink," "The Pink Link," "Anney's Invention," "Panky And The Angels," "Arabian Frights," "Brothers Are Special," "A Hard Day's Knight" and "Mister Money."

THE PINK PANTHER LAUGH AND A HALF HOUR AND A HALF SHOW

Following the success of NBC's long–running "The New Pink Panther Show," DePatie–Freleng Enterprises produced this 90–minute version featuring a myriad of old and new cartoon favorites: "The Pink Panther," "The Inspector," "The Ant and the Aardvark," "The Texas Toads" (formerly "The Tijuana Toads," Poncho and Toro, who were redubbed by actors Don Diamond and Tom Holland for television) and "Misterjaws." *A DePatie–Freleng Enterprises Production. Color. One hour and a half. Premiered on NBC: September 11, 1976–September 3, 1977.*

THE PINK PANTHER SHOW

Two madcap adventures of the Academy Award–winning mute feline were presented each week in this half–hour series, hosted by Lenny Shultz and featuring the comical exploits of Paul and Mary Ritts' puppets. Backed by Henry Mancini's popular theme song, the series' episodes were comprised of cartoons from the theatrical cartoon series made in the 1960s.

Other segments included "The Inspector," which was comprised of films originally released theatrically between 1965 and 1969. The program was the first of several Saturday–morning series starring the unflappable feline. Other programs included: "The New Pink Panther Show," "The Pink Panther Laugh And A Half Hour And A Half Show," "Think Pink Panther!" and "The All–New Pink Panther Show." *A DePatie–Freleng Enterprises Production. Color. Half–hour. Premiered on NBC: September 6, 1969–September 4, 1971.*

THE PLASTIC MAN/BABY PLAS SUPER COMEDY SHOW

As if one superhero in the family wasn't enough, Plastic Man and wife Penny give birth to a son, Plastic Baby, who possesses the same fantastic attributes as his famous elastic father, in a series of all–new misadventures. The series also contained 30–second consumer tips by Plastic Man, for which there were no titles. The program was the second in a series of Plastic Man cartoon shows. *A Ruby–Spears Enterprises Production. Color. Half–hour. Premiered on ABC: October 4, 1980–September 5, 1981.*

Voices:

Plastic Man: Michael Bell, **Penny,** his wife: Melindy Britt, **Baby Plas,** their son: Michael Bell, **Chief:** Melindy Britt, **Hula Hula:** Joe Baker

Episodes:

"Plastic Family" (one per show).
"Introducing Baby Plas," "The Abominable Snow Sport," "Baby Plas' Finny Friend," "The Big, Big Crush," "Ali Baba Baby," "Mighty Museum Mess," "Rustlin' Rascals," "Calamity Cruise," "Who Undo The Zoo," "Ozark Family Feud," "Doctor Strangeleaf," "Kewpie Doll Caper" and "Rodeo Ruckus."
"Baby Plas" (one per show).
"Bad Luck Stroll," "Baseball Bully," "Haircut Headache," "Witchin' Worries," "Tiger Trouble," "Clubhouse Calamity," "Babysitter Blues," "Sleepwalking Snafu," "Birthday Blowout," "Movie Mischief," "Tropical Trouble," "Frognapped" and "Mummy Madness."

THE PLASTIC MAN COMEDY– ADVENTURE SHOW

Spawned by the success of competing studios' superhero cartoons, Ruby–Spears Enterprises adapted a comic–book super crimefighter of their own: Plastic Man, whose elasticity enables him to stretch like a rubber band and twist his body into different shapes. Aided by friends Penny and Hula–Hula (whose voice is similar to comedian Lou Costello's), the moldable superhero comes to the rescue wherever evil lurks. Three additional cartoon segments made up this two–hour Saturday morning program: "Mighty Man and Yukk," the adventures of a thimble–sized superhero (Mighty) and the ugliest dog in the world (Yukk); "Fangface and Fangpuss," the exploits of a teenage werewolf and his equally wolfy cousin; and "Rickey Rocket," in which four teenagers (Cosmo, Splashdown, Sunstroke and Venus) with a makeshift rocket head a space detective agency. *A Ruby–Spears Enterprises Production. Color. Two hours. Premiered on ABC: September 22, 1979–September 27, 1980.*

Voices:

Plastic Man: Plastic Man: Michael Bell, **Chief:** Melendy Britt, **Penny:** Melendy Britt, **Hula Hula:** Joe Baker, **Mighty Man and Yukk: Mighty Man/Brandon Brewster:** Peter Cullen, **Yukk:** Frank Welker, **Mayor:** John Stephenson, **Fangface and Fangpuss: Fangface:** Frank Welker, **Fangpuss:** Frank Welker, **Kim,** their friend: Susan Blu, **Biff,** their friend: Jerry Dexter, **Puggsy,** their friend: Bart Braverman, **Rickety Rocket: Rickey Rocket:** Al Fann, **Cosmo:** Bobby Ellerbee, **Splashdown:** Johnny Brown, **Sunstroke:** John Anthony Bailey, **Venus:** Dee Timberlake

Plastic Man coils into action ready to spring forth to wipe out the evildoers of the world in Ruby–Spears' "The Plastic Man Comedy–Adventure Show." © Ruby–Spears Enterprises

Episodes:

"Plastic Man" (two per show).
"Hugefoot," "The Day The Oceans Disappeared," "The Sale Of The Century," "Dr. Irwin And Mr. Meteor," "City Of Ice," "Moonraider," "Honeybee," "The Corruptible Carrot Man," "Dogmaster," "Thunderman," "Toyman," "The Spider Takes A Bride," "Highbrow," "The Hippotist," "The Colossal Crime Of Commodore Peril," "Joggernaut," "Plastic Man Meets Plastic Ape," "The Crime Costume Caper" and "The Royal Gargoyle Foil."
"Mighty Man and Yukk" (two per show).
"Big Mouse And The Bad Mouse," "Magnet Man," "Anthead," "Never Retire With Mr. & Mrs. Van Pire," "Trouble Brews When Glue Man Glues," "Goldteeth's Bad Bite," "Shake Up With Mr. Make–Up," "Baby Man," "The Rooster," "Bad News Snooze," "Coach Crimes Big Play," "The Perils Of Paulette," "The Dangerous Dr. Gadgets," "Bye Bye Biplane," "Rob Around The Clock," "Beach Bums Crime Wave," "The Fiendish Fishface," "Catman," "Kragg The Conqueror," "The Video Villain," "The Menacing Mindreader," "Doctor Icicle," "Copycat," "Dog Gone Days," "The Evil Evo–Ray," "The Malevolent Marble Man," "Krime Klown's Circus Of Evil," "Evil Notions With Evila's Potions," "The Diabolical Dr. Locust," "Sinister Suit Suit," "Where There's A Will—There's A Creep" and "The Glutunous Glop."

"Fangface and Fangpuss" (one per show).

"There Is Nothing Worse Than A Stony Curse," "Evil Guider Of The Giant Spider," "Dr. Lupiter And The Thing From Jupiter," "Who Do The Voodoo," "The Creepy Goon From The Spooky Lagoon," "A Scary Affair In The Skullman's Lair," "A Time–Machine Trip To The Pirate's Ship," "The Ill–Will Of Dr. Chill," "The Romantic Plot Of The She–Wolf Robot," "The Sinister Plan Of Lizard Man," "Royal Trouble With The King's Double," "The Stone–Cold Dragon Of Gold," "The Evil Design Of Vulture–Man's Mind," "The Defiant Casablanca Giant," "The Film Fiasco Of Director Disastro" and "A Goofy Bungle In The Filipano Jungle."

"Rickety Rocket" (one per show).

"The Golden Crystal Caper," "The Case Of The Zombie Monster," "The Spaceship Caper," "The Mysterious Robot Critic Caper," "The Super–Duper Race Case," "The Rickety Robbery," "The Alien Egg Caper," "The Creepy Creature Caper," "The Mad Mummy Mystery," "The Horrible Headless Horseman Caper," "The Mysterious, Serious Circus Caper," "The Mysterious Warnings Of Doom," "The Case Of The Fearsome Phantom," "The Count Draculon Affair," "The Case Of The Vicious Voodoo Villain" and "The Deep Sea Demon Caper."

POLE POSITION

A stunt racing and daredevil family team puts on thrilling automotive acrobatics at the Pole Position Stunt Show, run by Dan Darret and his two sisters, Tess and Daisy, after their parents disappear in an unexplained explosion during a stunt race. The kids carry on their parents' work, along with pet Kuma and two computerized cars, Roadie and Wheels, using the cutting edge technology of their high–tech vehicles to fight crime. Series was based on the popular video arcade game of the same name. *A DIC Enterprises Production. Color. Half–hour. Premiered on CBS: September 15, 1984–August 30, 1985.*

Voices:

Dan Darret: David Coburn, **Tess,** his sister: Lisa Lindgren, **Daisy,** his sister: Kaleena Kiff, **Dr. Zachary,** their uncle: Jack Angel, **Wheels:** Melvin Franklen, **Roadie:** Daryl Hickman, **Kuma:** Marilyn Schreffler, **Teacher:** Helen Minniear

Episodes:

"The Code," "The Canine Vanishes," "The Chicken Who Knew Too Much," "Strangers On The Ice," "The Race," "The Thirty–Nine Stripes," "The Thirty–One Cent Mystery," "Dial M For Magic," "The Bear Affair," "To Clutch A Thief," "The Secret," "Shadow Of A Trout" and "The Trouble With Kuma."

POLICE ACADEMY: THE SERIES

Those wacky defenders of law and order, known for their hijinks in a series of feature–length action/comedies, return to the beat in this first–run series as they attempt to keep the peace while using the most outrageous crime–prevention methods ever seen. Voice work for the series was recorded in Canada. *A Ruby–Spears Enterprises Production. Color. Half–hour. Premiered: September, 1988. Syndicated.*

Those wacky defenders of law and order from feature–film fame keep peace using the most outrageous crime–prevention methods ever seen in television's "Police Academy—The Series." © Ruby–Spears Enterprises, All characters © Warner Brothers, Inc.

Voices:

Mahoney: Ron Rubin, **Hightower:** Charles Gray, Greg Morton, **Hooks/Callahan:** Denise Pidgeon, **Jones:** Greg Morton, **Zed/Tackleberry:** Dan Hennessey, **Sweetchuck/Professor:** Howard Morris, **Proctor:** Greg Swanson, **Lassard:** Gary Krawford, **Harris:** Len Carlson, **House:** Dorian Joe Clark

Episodes:

"The Good, The Bad & The Bogus," "Puttin' On The Dogs," "Phantom Of The Precinct," "Cops & Robots," "Police Academy Blues," "A Blue Knight At The Opera," "Worth Her Weight In Gold," "For Whom The Wedding Bells Toll," "Westward Ho Hooks," "My Mummy Lies Over The Ocean," "Numbskull's Revenge," "Proctor, Call A Doctor!," "Little Red And Big Bertha," "Curses On You!," "Lights, Action, Coppers," "Camp Academy," "The Tell Tale Tooth," "Mr. Sleaze Versus Lockjaw," "Spaced Out Space Cadets," "Sweetchuck's Brother," "Karate Cop," "The Hang Ten Gang," "Nine Cops And A Baby," "Fish And Microchips," "The Precinct Of Wax," "Cop Scouts," "Professor Jekyll And Gangster Hyde," "Operation Big House,"

"Ship Of Jewels," "Zillion Dollar Zed," "The Comic Book Caper," "The Monkey Trial," "Rolling For Dollars," "K–9 Corps And The Peking Pooch," "Santa With A Badge," "Suitable For Framing," "Rock Around The Cops," "Prince And The Copper," "Now You Steal It, Now You Don't," "Mad Maxine," "Trading Disgraces," "Champ," "Wheels Of Fortune," "The Wolf Who Cried Boy," "Snow Job," "A Bad Knight For Tackleberry," "Supercop Sweetchuck," "Deja Voodoo," "Flight Of The Bumbling Blues," "Big Burger," "Fat City," "Elementary, My Dear Coppers," "Dr. Deadstone I Presume," "The Hillbilly Blues," "Survival Of The Fattest," "The Junkman Ransoms The Ozone," "Grads On Tour," "Like Copper Like Son," "Ten Little Coppers," "Big Top Cops," "Alpine K–9s," "The Legend Of Robin Good," "Hawaii Nine–0" and "Thieves Like Us."

POPEYE

The King Features syndicate, which owns the rights to "Popeye," produced this new made–for–television series of 220 episodic adventures reprising the adversarial relationship of spinach–gobbling sailor Popeye and seafaring bully Brutus (whose named was changed to Bluto in the Max Fleischer cartoons), who continue to battle over the affections of fickle Olive Oyl. The rest of the supporting cast from the original Max Fleischer cartoon shorts were also featured, including Wimpy, Swee'pea, Sea Hag and Eugene the Jeep.

The series was animated by Jack Kenney Studios, Paramount Pictures and Rembrandt Films in Italy. *A King Features Production. Color. Half–hour. Premiered: Fall, 1961. Syndicated.*

Voices:
Popeye: Jack Mercer, **Brutus:** Jackson Beck, **Olive Oyl:** Mae Questel, **J. Wellington Wimpy:** Charles Lawrence, Jack Mercer, **Swee'pea:** Mae Questel, **Sea Hag:** Mae Questel, **Eugene the Jeep:** Mae Questel, **Rough House:** Jack Mercer

Episodes:
(four per show) "Hits And Missiles," "Barbecue For Two," "Muskels Shmuskels," "Hoppy Jalopy," "Dead–Eye Popeye," "Mueleer's Mad Monster," "Caveman Capers," "Bullfighter Bully," "Ace Of Space," "College Of Hard Knocks," "Abominable Snowman," "Ski Jump Chump," "Irate Pirate," "Foola-Foola Bird," "Uranium On The Cranium," "Two Faced Paleface," "Childhood Daze," "Sheepich Sheepherder," "Track Meet Cheat," "Crystal Brawl," "Interrupted Lullaby," "See No Evil," "From Way Out," "Seeing Double," "Swee' Pea Soup," "Hag Way Robbery," "The Lost City Of Nubble–On," "There's No Space Like Home," "Potent Lotion," "Astronut," "Where There's A Will," "Take It Easel," "I Bin Sculped," "Fleas A Crowd," "Popeye's Junior Headache," "Egypt Us," "The Big Sneeze," "The Last Resort," "Jeopardy Sheriff," "Baby Phase," "Goon With The Wind," "Insultin' The Sultan," "Dog Gone Dog Catcher," "Voice From The Deep," "Matinee Idol Popeye," "Beaver Or Not," "Battery Up," "Deserted Desert," "Skinned Divers," "Popeye's Service Station," "Coffee House," "Popeye's Pepup Emporium," "Bird Watcher Popeye," "Time Marches Backward," "Popeye's Pet Store," "Ballet De Spinach," "Spinach Shortage," "Popeye And The Dragon," "Popeye And The Fireman," "Popeye's Pizza Palace," "Down The Hatch," "Light-

Seafaring sailor Popeye starred in a new made-for-television series of episodic adventures in 1961. © King Features Entertainment

house Keeping," "Popeye And The Phantom," "Popeye's Picnic," "Out Of This World," "Madame Swiami," "Timber Toppers," "Skyscraper Capers," "Private Eye Popeye," "Li'l Olive Riding Hood," "Hypnotic Glance," "Trojan Horse," "Frozen Feuds," "Popeye's Corn Cherto," "Westward Ho–Ho," "Popeye's Cool Pool," "Jee–Jeep," "Popeye's Museum Piece," "Golf Brawl," "Wimpy's Lunch Wagon," "Weather Watchers," "Popeye And The Magic Hat," "Pest Of The Pecos," "The Blubbering Whale," "Popeye And The Spinach Stalk," "Shoot The Chutes," "Tiger Burger," "Bottom Gun," "Olive Drab And The Swee' Pea," "Blinkin' Beacon," "Aztec Wreck," "The Green Dancin' Shoes," "Spare Dat Tree," "The Glad Gladiator," "The Golden Touch," "Hamburger Fishing," "Popeye The Popular Mechanic," "Popeye's Folly," "Popeye's Used Car," "Spinachonare," "Popeye

And The Polite Dragon," "Popeye And The Ugly Ducklin'," "Popeye's Tea Party," "The Throll That Got Gruff," "Popeye The Lifeguard," "Popeye In The Woods," "After The Ball Went Over," "Popeye And Buddy Brutus," "Popeye's Car Wash," "Camel–Ears," "Plumber's Pipe Dream," "Popeye And The Herring Snatcher," "Invisible Popeye," "The Square Egg," "Old Salt Tale," "Jeep Tale," "The Super–Duper Market," "The Gold Type Fleece," "Popeye And The White Collar Man," "Swee' Pea Thru The Looking Glass," "The Black Knight," "Jingle Jangle Jungle," "The Day Silky Went Blozo," "Rip Van Popeye," "Mississippi Sissy," "Double Cross Country Feet Race," "Fashion Fotography," "I Yam Wet Yamnesia," "Paper Pasting Pandemonium," "Coach Popeye," "Popeyed Columbus," "Popeye Revere," "Popeye In Haweye," "Forever Amgergris," "Popeye De Leon," "Popeye Fisherman," "Popeye In The Grand Steeplechase," "Round The World In 80 Days," "Popeye's Fixit Shop," "Bell Hop Hop Popeye," "The Ghost Host," "Strikes, Spares An' Spinach," "Jeep Is Jeep," "The Spinach Scholar," "Psychiatricks," "Rags To Riches To Rags," "Hair Cut–Ups," "Poppa Popeye," "Quick Change Ollie," "The Valley Of The Goons," "Me Quest For Poopdeck Pappy," "Mopey Hick," "Mirror Magic," "It Only Hurts When They Laugh," "Wimpy The Moocher," "Voo Doo To You Too," "Popeye Goes Soloing," "Popeye's Travels," "Incident At Missile City," "Dog Catcher Popeye," "What's News," "Spinach Greetings," "Baby Contest," "Oil's Well That Ends Well," "Motor Knocks," "Amusement Park," "Duel To The Finish," "Gem Jam," "The Bathing Beasts," "The Rain Breaker," "Messin' Up The Mississippi," "Love Birds," "Sea Serpent," "Boardering On Trouble," "Aladdin's Lamp," "Butler Up," "The Leprechaun," "County Fair," "Hamburgers Aweigh," "Popeye's Double Trouble," "Kiddie Kapers," "The Mark Of Zero," "Myskery Melody," "Scairdy Cat," "Operation Ice–Tickle," "The Cure," "William Won't Tell," "Pop Goes The Whistle," "Autographically Yours," "A Foil For Olive Oyl," "My Fair Olive," "Giddy Gold," "Strange Things Are Happening," "The Medicine Man," "A Mite For Trouble," "Who's Kidding Zoo," "Robot Popeye," "Sneaking Peeking," "Seeing Is Believing," "The Wiffle Bird's Revenge," "Going Going Gone," "Popeye Thumb," "The Billionaire," "Model Muddle," "Which Is Witch?," "Disguise The Limit," "Spoil Sport," "Have Time Will Travel," "Intellectual Interlude," "Partial Post," "Weight For Me," "Canine Caprice," "Roger" and "Tooth Be Or Not Tooth Be."

THE POPEYE AND OLIVE SHOW

In this Saturday–morning series of all–new adventures based on Edgar Segar's popular comic–strip creations, Popeye and Olive shared top–billing in this comedy/adventure show made up of three weekly segments—one ensemble series starred Popeye, Olive and old favorites, Bluto and Wimpy, plus two additional series of short cartoons: "Private Olive Oyl," in which Popeye's stringbean girlfriend stars as a clumsy Army private; and "Prehistoric Popeye," with the muscleman sailor trying to contend with caveman situations before the availability of spinach cans. (The films were mixed in with other modern–day adventures.) *A Hanna–Barbera Production in association with King Features Entertainment. Color. Half–hour. Premiered on CBS: September 12, 1981–November 27, 1982.*

Voices:
Popeye: Jack Mercer, **Olive Oyl:** Marilyn Schreffler, **Bluto:** Allan Melvin, **Wimpy:** Daws Butler, **Sgt. Blast,** Olive's sergeant: Jo Anne Worley, **Alice the Goon:** Marilyn Schreffler, **Colonel Crumb:** Hal Smith

Additional Voices:
Julie Bennett, Richard Erdman, Jackie Joseph, Don Messick, Frank Nelson, John Stephenson, Frank Welker

Episodes:
"The Popeye Show" (two per show).
"Peask And Quiet," "Spa–Ing Partners," "Abject Flying Object," "Top Kick In Boot Camp," "I Wouldn't Take That Mare To The Fair On A Dare," "Popeye Stumps Bluto," "Tough Sledding," "A Good Gone Gooney," "Unidentified Fighting Object," "Olive Goes Dallas," "Merry Madness At The Mardi Gras," "Popeye Of Sherwood Forest," "Bad Company," "Popeye Of The Jungle," "The Great Speckled Whale," "Alpine For You," "Tour Each His Own," "Ships That Past In The Fight," "Pappy Fails In Love," "The Umpire Strikes Back," "Perilous Pursuit Of A Pearl," "Popierre, The Musketeer," "W.O.I.L." and "Popeye's Self–Defense."
"Private Olive Oyl" (one per show).
"Troop Therapy," "Tanks A Lot," "Rocky Rolls," "Mission Improbable," "Infink–Try," "Wreck Room," "Jeep Thrills," "Computer Chaos," "Good Native," "Here Today, Gone Tomorrow," "Alice In Blunderland," "Private Secretaries," "Goon Balloon," "Snow Fooling," "Goon Hollywood" and "Basic Training."
"Prehistoric Popeye" (one per show).
"Olive's Moving Experience," "The Incredible Shrinking Popeye," "So Who's Watching The Bird Watchers," "Winner Window Washer," "Reptile Ranch," "Olive's Devastatink Decorators," "The Midnight Ride Of Popeye Revere," "Hogwash At The Car Wash," "Up A Lizard River," "Would He Come Back, Little Fluffasaurus," "Neanderthal Nuisance," "Vegetable Stew," "Cheap Skate Date," "Bronto Beach," "The First Resort" and "Chilly Con Caveman."

POPEYE AND SON

Updated adventures of strongman sailor, Popeye, and spindly girlfriend, Olive Oyl, who, now married and living in a ramshackle beach house, find they have their hands full with son, Popeye Jr., a feisty, rugged nine–year–old who's a real chip off the old block, except that he hates spinach. Old rival Bluto returns to make trouble, with his own son, Tank, who is more "like father, like son" than Popeye Jr. is to his famous fighting father. *A Hanna–Barbera Production. Color. Half–hour. Premiered on CBS: September 19, 1987–September 10, 1988.*

Voices:
Popeye: Maurice LaMarche, **Olive Oyl:** Marilyn Schreffler, **Popeye Jr.:** Josh Rodine, **Bluto:** Allan Melvin, **Lizzie,** Bluto's wife: Marilyn Schreffler, **Tank,** their son: David Markus, **Woody,** Junior's friend: Penina Segall, **Dee Dee,** Junior's friend: Ka-

leena Kiff, **Rad:** B. J. Ward, **Puggy:** Marilyn Schreffler, **Wimpy:** Allan Melvin, **Eugene the Jeep:** Don Messick

Episodes:

(two per show) "Attack Of The Sea Hag," "Happy Anniversary," "The Sea Monster," "Poopdeck Pappy And The Family Tree," "Bluto's Wave Pool," "Here Today, Goon Tomorrow," "Don't Give Up The Picnic," "The Lost Treasure Of Pirates Cove," "Junior's Genie," "Mighty Olive At The Bat," "Junior Gets A Summer Job," "Surf Movie," "Redbeard," "The Girl From Down Under," "Junior's Birthday Roundup," "Olive's Dinosaur Dilemma," "Dr. Junior And Mr. Hyde," "Popeye's Smurfin' Adventure," "Split Decision," "The Case Of The Burger Burglar," "Orchid You Not," "Ain't Mythbehavin'," "There Goes The Neighborhood," "Olive's Day Off," "Prince Of A Fellow" and "Damsel In Distress."

POPEYE THE SAILOR

One of several early series repackaging old films for television, this series was comprised of the six–minute "Popeye the Sailor" cartoons produced between 1933 to 1954 by Paramount Pictures. In many television markets, the cartoons were screened for young viewers in programs hosted by local television celebrities. (See theatrical series entry for listing of films.) *A Max Fleischer/Famous Studios Production in association with Paramount Pictures. Black–and–white. Color. Half–hour. Premiered: September 10, 1956. Syndicated.*

Voices:

Popeye: William Costello, Jack Mercer, **Olive Oyl:** Mae Questel, **Bluto:** Gus Wickie, Pinto Colvig, William Pennell, **J. Wellington Wimpy:** Jack Mercer, Lou Fleischer, Frank Matalone, **Swee'pea:** Mae Questel, **Poopdeck Pappy:** Jack Mercer, **Pupeye:** Jack Mercer, **Peepeye:** Jack Mercer, **Pipeye:** Jack Mercer, **Shorty:** Arnold Stang

POPPLES

Producing just about anything they need—from a trampoline to a pair of skates—these furry little creatures bring fun and excitement wherever they pop up, living in a world scaled for adults with their human friends, Bonnie and Billy, and always coming up with creative solutions to any obstacles in their way. *A DIC Enterprises Production. Color. Half–hour. Premiered: 1986–1987. Syndicated.*

Voices:

Bonnie: Valerie Bromfield, **Billy:** Valerie Bromfield, **Mike:** Valerie Bromfield, **The Popples: Potato Chip:** Donna Christie, **Penny:** Jeannie Elias, **Punkster/Putter:** Danny Mann, **Pancake:** Sharon Noble, **Party/Punkity/Prize:** Louise Vallance, **Puffball:** Louise Vallance, **Puzzle:** Maurice LaMarche

Episodes:

"Popple Panic At The Library," "Cookin' Up A Storm," "Molars And Biscuspids, And Popples," "Treasure Of Popple Beach," "Poppin' At The Car Wash," "Springtime's A Poppin," "Popples Play Pee Wee Golf," "Popples Flood The Fluff–N–Fold," "Clean Sweep Of Things," "Poppin' Wheelies," "Bonnie's Popple Part,"

"Aisles Of Trouble," "Popples Paint Party," "Pop–Paring For Bed," "Poppolympics," "Sports Shop Pop," "Taking Out The Trash," "A Hair–Raising Experience," "Pop Goes The Radio," "Poppin Pillow Talk," "Where The Pop Flies," "Hurray For Hollywood," "Backyard Bigtop," "Backyard Adventure," "Poppin At The Drive–In," "Poppin' Around The Block," "Moving Day," "Tree House Capers," "No Bizness Like Popple Bizness," "Museum Peace," "Lemonade Stand–Off," "The Popple Fashion Parade," "Cuckoo Choo Choo," "Popple Post Office," "Funhouse Folly," "Fixer–Upper Popples," "Rock Around The Popples," "The College Of Popple Knowledge," "Popple Cheer," "Barn Hoopla," "The Jellybean Jamboree," "Private Eye Popples," "The Repair Shop" and "Decatha–Pop–A–Lon Popples."

THE PORKY PIG SHOW

P–P–Porky Pig was the host of his own Saturday morning series, featuring the cartoons of "Daffy Duck," "Bugs Bunny," "Sylvester and Tweety," "Foghorn Leghorn" and "Pepe Le Pew." In 1971, four years after its network run, the series was syndicated to television under the title of "Porky Pig and His Friends." *A Warner Brothers Production. Color. Half–hour. Premiered on ABC: September 20, 1964–September 2, 1967.*

Voices:

Porky Pig: Mel Blanc

POUND PUPPIES

Inspired by the hit toy from Tonka Corporation, this half–hour adventures series centers on the exploits of a merry band of pooches who lived in the Wagga Wagga Pound. Their goal is to find happy homes for deserving dogs. This pack of determined dogs, led by Cooler, include Bright Eyes, an optimistic cheerleader type; Howler, a zany neurotic dog; Whopper, a toddler with an overactive imagination; and Nose Marie, a vain femme fatale who is convinced she's the Raquel Welch of the dog world. The puppies' human ally is Holly, a pretty 11–year–old, who is in charge of the pound and helps the canines every time she can. Katrina Stoneheart (aided by sister Brattina), who throws roadblocks their way, has other ideas in mind. A second series, "All–New Pound Puppies," also premiered on ABC one season after this original series aired. *A Hanna–Barbera Production. Color. Half–hour. Premiered on ABC: September 13, 1986–September 5, 1987.*

Voices:

Cooler: Dan Gilvezan, **Bright Eyes:** Nancy Cartwright, **Howler:** Bobby Morse, **Whopper:** B. J. Ward, **Nose Marie:** Ruth Buzzi, **Holly:** Ame Foster, **Katrina Stoneheart:** Pat Carroll, **Brattina Stoneheart:** Adrienne Alexander, **Nabbit/Cat Gut:** Frank Welker

Episodes:

(one per show) "Brighteyes Come Home," "How To Found A Pound," "From Wags To Riches," "Snowbound Pound," "The Fairy Dogmother," "Whopper Cries Uncle," "In Pups We Trust," "The Captain And The Cats," "Secret Agent Pup," "Wagga Wagga," "The Star Pup," "Happy Howlidays" and "Ghost Hounders."

PRINCE PLANET

Sent to Earth by the Galactic Council to see if the planet is fit to join the Galactic Union of Worlds, Prince Planet, a member of the Universal Peace Corps, takes on a new identity on Earth (Bobby). Using his awesome powers whose source is a generator on the planet Radion, he battles criminal conspirators and other sinister beings who plan to take over the world. Corps members Hadji and Dynamo join Prince Planet in the fight. The series was among a handful of many Japanese–made cartoons which caught on in the United States via syndication. *A TCJ Animation Center Production. Color. Half–hour. Premiered: September, 1966. Syndicated.*

PUNKY BREWSTER

Based on the short–lived prime–time comedy series, NBC brought back the series in animated form, where it experienced greater success as a Saturday morning vehicle. In this version, stories take place in Punky's neighborhood as well as in exotic locales via her special friend, Glomer, who transports Punky and her friends to the four corners of the earth in the blink of an eye. *A Ruby–Spears Enterprises Production. Color. Half–hour. Premiered on NBC: September 14, 1985–August 22, 1987.*

Voices:

Punky Brewster: Soleil–Moon Frye, **Cherie:** Cherie Johnson, **Margaux:** Ami Foster, **Allen:** Casey Ellison, **Henry:** George Gaynes, **Glomer:** Frank Welker

Episodes:

1985–1986 "Punky To The Rescue," "The Quartersize Quarterback," "Brandon, The Dialogue Dog," "Pretty Ugly," "Winning Isn't Everything," "Growing Pains," "Any Wish Way You Can," "Unidentified Flying Glomer," "Double Your Punky," "The Bermuda Tangle," "Halloween Howlers," "Return To Chaundoon," "Fish Story," "Glomer Punks Out," "A Small

The short–lived prime–time comedy series "Punky Brewster" was given new life in all–new animated adventures for NBC. © Ruby–Spears Enterprises

Mistake," "Glomer's Story," "Punky Wise And Pound Foolish," "The Perils Of Punky," "Spellbound," "The Shoe Must Go On," "Christmas In July," "How The Midwest Was Won," "Louvre Affair," "Switchin' Places," "The Gold Rush" and "Phar Out Pharaoh."

1986–1987 "Little Orphan Punky," "Punky The Heiress," "Punky, Snow White And The Seven Dwarfs," "Punky's Millions," "Be My Glomley," "All In Henry's Family," "Fair Feathered Friend," "Bright Eyes," "Call Me Ms.," "Caught In The Act," "Mississippi Mud," "Punky P.I.," "Camp Confusion," "Punky's Half Acre," "Mother Of The Year" and "Allen Who?"

A PUP NAMED SCOOBY–DOO

Scooby–Doo, the world's favorite chicken–hearted canine, returns as a cute but clumsy puppy along with kid versions of friends Shaggy, Daphne, Velma and Freddy as they solve kid–size mysteries and encounter ghouls, ghosts and goblins in this half–hour series for Saturday mornings. *A Hanna–Barbera Production. Color. Half–hour. Premiered on ABC: September 10, 1988–September 1, 1990.*

Voices:

Scooby-Doo: Don Messick, **Shaggy:** Casey Kasem, **Velma:** Christina Lange, **Daphne:** Kellie Martin, **Freddy:** Carl Stevens, **Red Herring:** Scott Menville

Episodes:

1988–1989 "A Bicycle Built For Boo," "The Sludge Monster From The Earth's Core," "Wanted, Cheddar Alive," "The Schnook Who Took My Comic Book," "For Letter Or Worse," "The Babysitter From Beyond," "Snow Place Like Home," "Now Museum, Now You Don't," "Scooby Dude," "Ghost Who's Coming To Dinner?," "The Story Stick," "Robopup" and "Lights . . . Camera . . . Monster."

1989–1990 (new episodes combined with reruns) "Curse Of The Collar," "The Return Of Commander Cool," "The Spirit Of Rock 'N Roll," "Chickenstein Lives!," "Night Of The Living Burger," "The Computer Walks Among Us," "Dog Gone Scooby" and "Terror, They Name Is Zombo."

PUPPY'S FURTHER ADVENTURES

Joined by his girlfriend, Dolly, and three delightful canine friends, Petey the Pup embarks on a worldwide search for his lost family in this second Saturday morning series which was based on several successful ABC Weekend Specials. The program originally aired as part of the one–hour program block which included Hanna–Barbera Productions' "The All–New Scooby and Scrappy–Doo Show." In January 1984, the program was rebroadcast in its own time slot. *A Ruby–Spears Enterprises Production. Color. Half–hour. Premiered on ABC: September 10, 1983–September 1, 1984. Rebroadcast on ABC: January 12, 1984–September 1, 1984.*

Voices:

Petey the Pup: Billy Jacoby, **Dolly:** Nancy McKeon, **Duke/ Dash:** Michael Bell, **Lucky:** Peter Cullen, **Tommy:** Tony

O'Dell, **Glyder:** Josh Rodine, **Mother:** Janet Waldo, **Father:** John Stephenson

Episodes:
"Glyder, The Misfit Puppy," "Puppy Goes Home," "Puppy And The Badlands," "Puppy In Omega World," "Puppy And The Spies," "Puppy Goes To College," "Puppy And The Brown Eyed Girl" and "Biggest Diamond In The World."

QUICK DRAW McGRAW
Law and order are the name of the game as U. S. Marshall Quick Draw McGraw and his Mexican burro sidekick, Baba Looey, corral cutthroats and other villains in untypical cowboy–hero fashion. (He habitually ignores his pal's advice and strides resolutely into catastrophe.) Additional plotlines feature Quick as notorious crime–fighter El Kabong, a klutzy takeoff of Disney's popular "Zorro" series, and his own romantic entanglements with a frustrated filly named Sagebrush Sal. Snuffles, a "dog biskit" loving dog, was another recurring character in the series. (Once rewarded he gently floated in mid–air symbolizing his ecstasy.)

McGraw's cartoon adventures were the main ingredient of this popular syndicated series, sponsored by Kellogg's and first syndicated in 1959. The program marked Hanna–Barbera's second syndicated series effort made especially for the children's market. It featured two other series regulars: "Snooper and Blabber," a cat (Super Snooper) and mouse (Blabber Mouse) pair of crime investigators who, operating out of the Super Snooper Detective Agency, flush out the city's most–wanted criminals; and "Augie Doggie and Doggie Daddy," starring the ever affectionate father dog, Daddy (who sounds like Jimmy Durante) and his canine son, Augie, who get caught up in various misadventures.

The program was later rebroadcast on CBS as part of its

U. S. Marshall Quick Draw McGraw and sidekick Baba Looey are joined by series stars Blabber, Doggie Daddy, Augie Doggie and Snooper from Hanna–Barbera's "Quick Draw McGraw" series. © Hanna–Barbera Productions

Saturday morning lineup in 1963 before returning to syndication. *A Hanna–Barbera Production. Color. Half–hour. Premiered: September 29, 1959. Syndicated. Rebroadcast on CBS: September 28, 1963–September 3, 1966.*

Voices
Quick Draw McGraw: Daws Butler, **Baba Looey:** Daws Butler, **Injun Joe:** Daws Butler, **Snuffles:** Daws Butler, **Sagebrush Sal:** Julie Bennett, **Snooper:** Daws Butler, **Blabber:** Daws Butler, **Augie Doggie:** Daws Butler, **Doggie Daddy:** Doug Young

Episodes:
"Quick Draw McGraw" (one per show).
1959–1960 "Scary Prairie," "Bad Guys Disguise," "Scat, Scout, Scat," "Choo–Choo Chumps," "Masking For Trouble," "Lamb Chopped," "Double Barrel Double," "Riverboat Shuffled," "Dizzy Desperado," "Sagebrush Brush," "Bow Wow Bandit," "Six Gun Spook," "City Slicker," "Cattle Battle Rattled," "Doggone Prairie Dog," "El Kabong," "Gun Gone Goons," "El Kabong Strikes Again," "Treasure Of El Kabong," "Locomotive Loco," "Bronco Busting Boobs," "The Lyin' Lion," "Chopping Spree," "Elephant Boy Oh Boy," "Bull Leave Me" and "Kabong Kabongs Kabong."
1960–1961 "El Kabong Meets El Kazong," "Bullet Proof Galoot," "Two, Too Much," "Twin Troubles," "Ali Baby Looey," "Shooting Room Only," "Yippee Coyote," "Gun–Shy Girl," "Who Is El Kabong?," "Scooter Rabbit," "Talky Hawky," "Extra Special Extra" and "El Kabong Jr."
1961–1962 "El Kabong Was Wrong," "Dynamite Fright," "Baba Bait," "Big Town El Kabong," "Mine Your Manners" and "The Mark Of El Kabong."
"Snooper and Blabber" (one per show).
1959–1960 "Puss And Booty," "Switch Witch," "Real Gone Ghosts," "Desperate Diamond Dimwits," "Big Diaper Caper," "Flea And Me," "Disappearing Inc.," "Baby Rattled," "Not So Dummy," "Fee Fi Fo Fumble," "Masquerader Raider," "Motor Knows Best," "Slippery Glass Slipper," "Monkey Wrenched," "Gopher Goofers," "Impossible Imposters," "Adventure Is My Hobby," "Cloudy Rowdy," "Snap Happy Saps," "The Lion Is Busy," "Laughing Guess," "Case Of The Purloined Parrot," "Poodle–Toodle–Do," "Doggone Dog, Gone," "Hula Hula Hulabaloo" and "Wild Man, Wild."
1960–61 "Ala–Kazoop," "Hop To It," "Fleas Be Careful," "Observant Servants," "De–Duck–Tives," "Big Shot Blab," "Big Cat Caper," "Scoop Scoop," "Prince Of A Fella," "Flea For All," "Outer Space Case," "Bear–ly Able" and "Surprised Party."
1961–62 "Zoom–Zoom Blabber," "Eenie–Genie Minie–Mo," "Bronco Bluster," "Chilly Chiller," "Gem Jam" and "Person To Prison."
"Augie Doggie and Doggie Daddy" (one per show).
1959–1960 "Fox Hound Hounded Fox," "Augie The Watch Dog," "Skunk You Very Much," "In The Picnic Of Time," "High And Flighty," "Nag! Nag! Nag!," "Talk It Up, Pup," "TV Or Not TV," "Big Top Pop (Circus Daze)," "Million Dollar Robbery," "Pup Plays Pop," "Pop's Nature Pup," "Good Mouse Keeping," "Whatever Goes Pup" "Cat Happy Pappy," "Ro–Butler," "Pipsqueak Pop," "Fan Clubbed," "Crow Cronies,"

"Gone To The Ducks," "Mars Little Precious," "Swat's The Matter," "Snagglepuss," "Hum Sweet Hum," "Peck O' Trouble" and "Fuss N' Feathers."
1960–1961 "Yuk Yuk Duck," "It's A Mice Day," "Bud Brothers," "Pint Giant," "It's A Worm Day," "Patient Pop," "Let's Duck Out," "The Party Lion," "Musket–Tears," "Horse Feathers," "Playmate Pop," "Little Wonder" and "Treasure Jest."
1961–1962 "From Ape To Z," "Growing, Growing Gone," "Dough–Nutty," "Party Pooper Pop," "Hand To Mouse" and "Vacation Tripped."

Q. T. HUSH

This satirical who–dun–it series spotlighted the adventures of a private eye, Q. T. Hush and his "private nose" bloodhound, Shamus, who combine forces to solve baffling crimes and mysteries. Hush succeeds in jailing criminals by transforming himself into a shadow named Quincy, who operated independently in tracking down clues. Ten cliff–hanging segments constituted a complete story. *An Animation Associates Production. Color. Half–hour. Premiered: September 24, 1960. Syndicated. Voice credits unknown.*

Episodes:

(five per show) "The Rhyme Line Caper" (1–10), "The Protection Plan Caper" (11–20), "The Red–Eyed Raven Caper" (21–30), "The Statue Of Liberty Caper" (31–40), "The Magic Mix–Up Caper" (41–50), "The Doomsday Caper" (51–60), "The Goofy Ghost Caper" (61–70), "The Big Masquerade Caper" (71–80), "The Carnival Caper" (81–90) and "The Peeky–Poo Caper" (91–100).

Private eye Q. T. Hush, Shamus, Private Nose, and Quincy look for clues in the popular "whodunit" cartoon series, "Q. T. Hush." © Animation Associates

Bert Raccoon (center), Ralph (left) and Melissa (right) plot their strategy in a scene from the Canadian–produced series, "The Raccoons." © Gillis–Wiseman Productions (Courtesy: Evergreen Productions)

THE RACCOONS

Bert Raccoon is just about the best friend anyone could wish for. He's funny, brave, friendly and slightly crazy. He lives with his good friends Ralph and Melissa in a Raccoondominium. Together they run the forest newspaper, *The Evergreen Standard.* However, Bert is usually more interested in playing detective or flying a hang glider than in writing his news column.

He can also be found right on the tail of Cyril Sneer, the sneakiest and richest resident of the forest. From inside his scary old mansion, Sneer runs a huge financial empire. His moneymaking schemes usually mean trouble for "The Raccoons."

Produced for Canadian television, the series premiered in the United States on the Disney Channel. Previously the characters appeared in several successful animated specials, among them, "The Christmas Raccoons" and "The Raccoons On Ice." *A Gillis–Wiseman Production in association with Atkinson Film–Arts. Color. Half–hour. Premiered on the Disney Channel: October, 1985.*

Voices:

Bert Raccoon: Len Carlson, **Ralph Raccoon:** Bob Dermer, **Melissa Raccoon:** Linda Feige, Susan Roman, **Schaeffer:** Carl Banas, **Cyril Sneer/Snag:** Michael Magee, **Cedric Sneer:** Marvin Goldhar, **Dan the Ranger:** Murray Cruchley, **Julie:** Vanessa Lindores, **Tommy:** Noam Zylberman, **Bear:** Bob Dermer, **Sophia/Broo:** Sharon Lewis, **Pig One:** Nick Nichols, **Pig #2/Pig #3:** Len Carlson, **Narrator:** Geoffrey Winter

Episodes:

1985–1986 "Surprise Attack," "Going It Alone," "A Night To Remember," "Evergreen Grand Prix," "The Runaways," "Buried Treasure," "The Intruders," "Opportunity Knocks," "Cry Wolf," "Rumours" and "Gold Rush."
1987–1988 "Double Play," "The Sweet Smell Of Success," "Blast From The Past," "Power Trip," "Stop The Clock," "The

Artful Dodger," "Last Legs," "Read No Evil," "Courting Disaster" and "Time Trap."

1988–1989 "The Prism Of Zenda," "Paperback Hero," "The Chips Are Down," "Life In The Fast Lane," "Monster Mania," "Mom's The Word," "Picture Perfect," "Strictly By The Book," "Evergreen Express," "Trouble Shooter," "Paper Chase," "Simon Says" and "Games People Play."

1989–1990 "Second Chance," "The Sky's The Limit," "Bully For You," "A Catered Affair," "Search And Rescue," "Spring Fever," "The Family Secret," "The Great Escape," "Making The Grade," "Science Friction," "Stealing The Show," "The Phantom Of Sneer Mansion" and "The Headline Hunter."

RAINBOW BRITE

Rainbow Brite, a courageous, young girl with a special rainbow–making belt, travels the world on rainbow roads to spread happiness and hope to those in need and chase unhappiness away in the form of the miserable and mean Murky and Lurky, who do what they can to take Rainbow's power away. Rainbow is joined in her adventures by her faithful horse, Starlite, and her best friend, Twink. *A DIC Enterprises Production. Color. Half–hour. Premiered: September, 1986. Syndicated.*

Voices:

Rainbow Brite: Bettina Nash, **Starlite,** her horse: Andre Stojka, **Twink,** her best friend: Robbie Lee, **Murky:** Peter Cullen, **Lurky:** Pat Fraley, **Monstromurk/Narrator:** Peter Cullen, **Buddy:** Pat Fraley, **Evil Force:** Pat Fraley, **Brian:** Scott Menville, **Indigo/Violet/Lala/Sprites:** Robbie Lee, **Red/Patty/Canary:** Mona Marshall, **Moonglow/Tickled Pink:** Rhonda Aldrich

Episodes:

"Invasion Of Rainbowland," "Mom," "Beginning Of Rainbowland—Part 1," "Beginning Of Rainbowland—Part 2," "A Horse Of A Different Color," "Queen Of The Sprites," "Star Sprinkled," "Peril In The Pits," "Chasing Rainbows," "Rainbow Night," "Murky's Comet," "Mighty Monstromurk Menace—Part 1" and "Mighty Monstromurk Menace—Part 2."

RAMBO

Rambo, the leader of the specially trained team, "The Force of Freedom," is unofficially assigned by the government to accomplish seemingly impossible missions—his target: the diabolical organization, S.A.V.A.G.E.—in this first–run adventure series based on the character played by Sylvester Stallone in a series of top grossing feature films. *A Ruby–Spears Enterprises Production. Color. Half–hour. Premiered: September, 1985. Syndicated.*

Voices:

Rambo: Neil Ross, **Colonel Trautman:** Alan Oppenheimer, **Kat:** Mona Marshall, **Turbo:** James Avery, **Nomad:** Edmund Gilbert, **General Warhawk:** Michael Ansara, **Gripper:** Lennie Weinrib, **Sgt. Havoc:** Peter Cullen, **Mad Dog:** Frank Welker, **Black Dragon:** Robert Ito

Episodes:

"First Strike," "Angel Of Destruction," "Battlefield Bronx," "Raise The Yamato," "The Taking Of Tierra Libre," "Alpha's Arms And Ambush (Part 1)," Guns Over The Suez," "The Lost City Of Acra," "S.A.V.A.G.E. Island," "Trouble In Tibet," "Subterranean Holdup," "General Warhawk's Curse," "Beneath The Streets," "Deadly Keep," "Fire In The Sky," "Exercise In Terror," "Enter The Black Dragon," "Raid On Las Vegas," "Disaster In Delgado," "The Doomsday Machine," "The Halley Microbe," "When S.A.V.A.G.E. Stole Santa," "Cult Of The Cobra," "Reign Of The Boy King," "Rambo And The White Rhino," "The Konichi," "Children For Peace," "Pirate Peril," "Mephisto's Magic," "Swamp Monster," "Night Of The Voodoo Moon," "Freedom Dancer," "Return Of The Count," "Sepulcher Of Power," "Terror Beneath The Sea," "Texas Inferno," "Target: Supertanker," "The Iron Mask," "Enter The White Dragon," "Alpha's Arms And Ambush (Part 2)," "The Ninja Dog," "Mind Control," "Attack Of El Dorado," "S.A.V.A.G.E. Rustlers," "Death Merchant," "Skyjacked Gold," "Crash," "Masquerade," "Supertrooper," "Blockbuster," "Vote Of Terror," "Horror Of The Highlands," "Mirage," "Robot Raid," "Warhawk's Fortress," "When Black Is White," "Just Say No," "Change Of Face," "S.A.V.A.G.E. Space," "Lagoon Of Death," "Snow Kill," "Monster Island," "Turbo's Dilemma," "Blind Luck" and "Quarterback Sneak."

THE REAL GHOSTBUSTERS

To avoid confusion with Filmation's "Ghostbusters" series based on the previously popular live–action series, the producers of this series, adapted from the hit motion picture, changed the title of their program to make sure that audiences knew the difference.

In this animated update, those three misfits who single-handedly saved New York from supernatural destruction are up to their same old tricks, keeping the city safe from demons, curses, spooks and every other off–the–wall weirdness known (and unknown) to mortal man. Premiering on ABC in 1986, the series was subsequently syndicated with all–new episodes. Ray Parker Jr.'s original hit song is featured as the program's theme song. After two successful seasons on the network, ABC commissioned a third season of shows under the title of "Slimer! The Real Ghostbusters" in 1988. *A DIC Enterprises Production. Color. Half–hour. Premiered on ABC: September 13, 1986–September 3, 1988. Syndicated.*

Voices:

Peter Venkman: Lorenzo Music, Dave Coulier, **Winston Zeddmore:** Arsenio Hall, Edward L. Jones, **Egon Spengler:** Maurice LaMarche, **Janine Melnitz:** Laura Summer, Kathi E. Soucie, **Ray Stantz:** Frank Welker, **Slimer:** Frank Welker

Episodes:

1986–1987 (Network) "Killerwatt," "Ghosts 'R Us," "Look Homeward, Ray," "Mrs. Roger's Neighborhood," "Janine's Genie," "Slimer, Come Home," "Troll Bridge," "The Bogeyman Cometh," "Mr. Sandman, Dream Me a Dream," "When Halloween Was Forever," "Take Two," "Citizen Ghost" and "Xmas Marks The Spot.,"

The hit movie Ghostbusters *was animated for Saturday morning television, featuring the same cast of wacko characters. Added for comic relief: Slimer (center).*
© Columbia Pictures Television, a division of CPT Holdings Inc. All rights reserved. (Courtesy: DIC Enterprises Inc.)

1987–1988 "Baby Spookums," "The Two Faces Of Slimer," "It's A Jungle Out There," "Halloween II–½," "Big Trouble With Little Slimer," "Sticky Business," "The Bogeyman Is Back," "Once Upon A Slime," "The Copycat," "Camping It Up," "The Grundel," "Transylvanian Homesick Blues" and "Loathe Thy Neighbor."
(Syndication) "Knock, Knock," "Station Identification," "Play Them Ragtime Boos," "Sea Fright," "The Spirit Of Aunt Lois," "Cry Uncle," "Adventures In Slime And Peace," "Night Game," "Venkman's Ghost Repellers," "The Old College Spirit," "Aint Nasa–Sarily So," "Who're You Calling Two–Dimensional?," "A Fright At The Opera," "Doctor, Doctor," "Ghost Busted," "Beneath These Streets," "Boo–Dunit?," "Chicken, He Clucked," "Ragnarok And Roll," "Don't Forget The Motor City," "Banshee Bake A Cherry Pie?," "Who's Afraid Of The Big Bad Ghost?," "Hanging By A Thread," "You Can't Take It With You," "No One Comes To Lupusville," "Drool, The Dogfaced Goblin," "The Man Who Never Reached Home," "The Collect Call Of Cthulhu," "Bustman's Holiday," "The Headless Motorcyclist," "The Thing In Mrs. Faversham's Attic," "Egon On A

Rampage," "Lights! Camera! Haunting!," "The Bird Of Kildarby," "Janine Melnitz, Ghostbuster," "Apocalypse—What, Now?," "Lost And Foundry," "Hard Knight's Day," "Cold Cash And Hot Water," "The Scaring Of The Green," "They Call Me Mister Slimer," "Last Train To Oblivion," "Masquerade," "Janine's Day Off," "The Ghostbusters In Paris," "The Devil In The Deep," "Ghost Fight At The O.K. Corral," "Ghostbuster Of The Year," "Deadcon 1," "The Cabinet Of Calimari," "A Ghost Grows In Brooklyn," "The Revenge Of Murray The Mantis," "Roller Ghoster," "I Am The City," "Blood Brothers," "The Long, Long, Long, Long, Etc. Goodbye," "Buster The Ghost," "The Devil To Pay," "Slimer, Is That You?," "Egon's Ghost," "Captain Steel Saves The Day," "Slimer Goes For Broke," "Egon's Dragon," "Dairy Farm Of The Living Dead" and "The Hole In The Wall Gang."

THE RELUCTANT DRAGON AND MR. TOAD

Based on characters and stories in Kenneth Grahame's novel *The Wind in Willows,* the kind–hearted, fire–breathing reluctant dragon and the gadabout Mr. Toad host this half–hour series featuring both characters in their own film segments. (Voice credits were unavailable from the producer.) *A Rankin–Bass Production. Color. Half–hour. Premiered on ABC: September 12, 1970–September 17, 1972.*

Episodes:
Reluctant Dragon (two per show).
"National Daisy Week," "How To Vex A Viking," "Cowardly Herman," "The Robot Dragon," "Saving The Crown," "The Purple Viking," "Tobias The Terror Of The Tournament," "The Campscout Girls," "Taxes Are A Drag On Dragons," "Lights, Camera, Action," "Happy Birthday, Dear Tobias," "Dippy," "Never Count On A Cornflower," "How To Be A Wizard," "Free A Cold, Starve A Viking," "The Kid's Last Flight," "If It's Wednesday, it Must Be Vikingland," "The Flying Flagon," "The Tobias Touch," "Daisies Away," "No Bix Like Show Bix," "Dragon Under Glass," "The Big Break," "A Day At The Fair," "Tobias, The Reluctant Viking," "The Starve Versus Herman, The Atrocious," "The Haunted Castle," "Wretched Robin Hood," "Merlin The Magician, Jr.," "Subway Sabotage," "A Cold Day In Willowmarch" and "Sir Tobias."
Mr. Toad (one per show).
"Jove! What A Day," "Gentlemen's Gentleman," "Ghost Of Toad Hall," "The Demolition Derby," "The Amphibious Mr. Toad," "Casey Tad," "Sail Ho–Ho," "Polo Panic," "Sandhogs," "Micemaster Road," "The Great Motorcycle Race," "The Great Bonfire Contest," "Jack Of All Trades," "Toad's Time Machine," "Movie Maker Toad," "Build A Better Bungalow" and "Twenty Thousand Inches Under The Sea."

RETURN OF THE PLANET OF THE APES

On the futuristic planet Earth a society of apes rule and humans are slaves. Based on the popular film series, *Planet of the Apes,* the brief TV series and the novel by Pierre Boulle.

A DePatie–Freleng Enterprises Production. Color. Half–hour. Premiered on NBC: September 6, 1975–September 4, 1976.

Voices:
Bill Hudson/Dr. Zaius: Richard Blackburn, **Jeff Carter:** Austin Stoker, **Judy Franklin/Nova:** Claudette Nevins, **Cornelius:** Edwin Mills, **Zira:** Phillippa Harris, **General Urko:** Henry Corden

Episodes:
"Flames Of Doom," "Escape From Ape City," "The Unearthly Prophecy," "Tunnel Of Fear," "Lagoon Of Peril," "Terror Of Ice Mountain," "River Of Flames," "Screaming Wings," "Trail To The Unknown," "Attack From The Clouds" "Mission Of Mercy," "Invasion Of The Underdwellers" and "Battle Of The Titans."

THE RICHIE RICH/SCOOBY–DOO HOUR

This hour–long Saturday morning series combined new adventures of Richie Rich, a lucky kid with a $100,000 weekly allowance, who uses his wealth for good causes, and repeat episodes of Scooby–Doo and his crazy cousin, Scrappy–Doo, from 1979's "Scooby and Scrappy–Doo." Richie Rich was based on the popular comic book character owned by Harvey Comics.

Alternating with the misadventures of Scooby–Doo and Scrappy–Doo were several short comical vignettes starring Richie Rich, each running three minutes, seven minutes and 30 seconds long. In the fall of 1982, Richie Rich was re-paired with Hanna–Barbera's cartoon version of the Our Gang kids in "The Little Rascals/Richie Rich Show," in all–new episodes, which ran through the 1983 season. In 1988, the program was repackaged and rebroadcast in syndication as part of "The Funtastic World of Hanna–Barbera." *A Hanna–Barbera Production in association with Harvey Comics. Color. Half–hour. Premiered on ABC: November 8, 1980–September 19, 1982.*

Voices:
Richie Rich: Sparky Marcus, **Freckles,** Richie's friend: Christian Hoff, **Gloria,** Richie's girlfriend: Nancy Cartwright, **Reggie Van Goh,** Richie's friend: Dick Beals, **George Rich,** Richie's father: Stan Jones, **Mrs. Rich,** Richie's mother: Joan Gerber, **Cadbury,** the Rich's butler: Stan Jones, **Irona,** the Rich's maid: Joan Gerber, **Dollar,** the Rich's dog: Frank Welker, **Professor Keenbean:** Bill Callaway, **Scooby–Doo:** Don Messick, **Scrappy–Doo:** Lennie Weinrib, **Shaggy:** Casey Kasem, **Velma:** Pat Stevens, Maria Frumkin, **Freddy:** Frank Welker, **Daphne:** Heather North

Episodes:
"Richie Rich."
(12–minute episodes) "The Robotnappers," "One Of Our Aircraft Carriers Is Missing," "The Shocking Lady Strikes Again," "The Kangaroo Hop," "The Show Bounders," "Who's Afraid Of Big Bad Bug," "Constructo," "Mystery Mountain," "Disaster Master," "Disappearing Dignitaries," "Phantom Of The Movies," "The Great Charity Train Robbery" and "Sinister Sports Spectacular."

Every kid's dreams come true when a rich young boy opens his wallet for fun and adventure in Hanna–Barbera's "Richie Rich," part of "The Richie Rich/Scooby–Doo Hour." © Hanna–Barbera Productions. Based on the character owned and copyrighted by Harvey Cartoons, a partnership

(7–minute episodes) "Piggy Bank Prank," "The Rare Scare," "Spring Cleaning," "The Blur," "Irona Versus Demona," "Counterfeit Dollar," "The Abominable Snowman," "Poor Little Richbillies," "Wiped Out," "It's No Giggling Matter," "Prankster Beware," "The Most Unforgettable Butler" and "Caveboy Richie."
(4–minute episodes) "Muscle Beach," "Kitty Sitter," "Silence Is Golden," "Cur Wash," "Chef's Surprise," "Miss Robot America," "The Greatest Invention In The World," "TV Dollar," "Cowhand," "Welcome Uncle Cautious," "Clothes Make The Butler," "Young Irona" and "Baseball Dollar"
(30–second spots) "Pictures," "Sunlamp," "Diamond," "Computer," "Pillows," "Wishing Well," "Phone Call," "Santi Clause," "Monkey," "Piggie Bank," "Long Distance Call," "Feed The Fish," "Roughing It," "A Box Of Chocolates," "The Telephone," "Stupendous Vehicle," "Tickets," "Big House," "Lunch," "The Vault Leak," "Ordinary Farm," "Name That Person," "Monkey Under Foot," "Rainbow," "Mom's Jewels" and "The Eyes Have It."
"Scooby and Scrappy-Doo" (one per show).
"The Scarab Lives!," "The Night Ghoul Of Wonderworld," "Strange Encounters Of A Scooby Kind," "The Neon Phantom Of The Roller Disco!," "Shiver And Shake, That Demon's A Snake," "The Scary Sky Skeleton," "The Demon Of The Dugout," "The Hairy Scare Of The Devil Bear," "Twenty Thousand Screams Under the Sea," "I Left My Neck In San Francisco," "When You Wish Upon A Star Creature," "The Ghoul, The Bat And The Ugly," "Rocky Mountain Yiiii!," "The Sorcerer's A Menace," "Lock The Door, It's A Minotaur" and "The Ransom Of Scooby Chief."

RING RAIDERS

Led by Ring Commander Victor Vector, a group of heroic aviators from all eras of flight—past, present and future—are brought together to defend the world from the most sinister airborne threat ever known, the evil pilots of the Skull Squadron, in *Top Gun*–styled battles and adventures. *A DIC Enterprises Production. Color. Half–hour. Premiered: 1989*

Voices:

Victor Vector, commander: Dan Gilvezan, **Joe Thundercloud:** Efrain Figueroa, **Hubbub:** Stuart Goetz, **Cub Jones:** Ike Eisenmann, **Kirchov:** Gregory Martin, **Mako:** Jack Angel, **Jenny Gail:** Chris Anthony, **Max Miles:** Roscoe Lee Browne, **Scorch:** Roger Bumpass, **Yasu Yakamura:** Townsend Coleman, **Baron Voin Clawdeitz:** Chuck McCann, **Siren:** Susan Silo

Episodes:

"Ring Fire," "The Best Man For The Job Is A Woman," "Scorch's Revenge," "All The Right Stuff" and "A Pilot's Faith."

THE ROAD RUNNER SHOW

The predictable antics of foxy, fleet–footed Road Runner and his constant pursuer, Wile E. Coyote, were repackaged for television with theatrical cartoons from the Warner Brothers library produced between 1949 and 1966 added to spice up the proceedings. Other Warner characters featured in the series were Daffy Duck, Foghorn Leghorn, Porky Pig and others. The Road Runner/Coyote cartoons were subsequently paired with reruns of Bugs Bunny cartoons as "The Bugs Bunny/Road Runner Hour," which premiered on CBS in 1968. *A Warner Brothers Production. Color. Half–hour. Premiered on CBS: September 10, 1966–September 7, 1968. Rebroadcast on ABC: September 11, 1971–September 2, 1972.*

Voices:

Mel Blanc

ROBOTECH

The planet Earth has been invaded by a fleet of giant alien spaceships capable of destroying the entire planet in a split second. The only hope for survival lies in the secrets of Robotech, an ancient science which has created powerful Robotic weapons systems and interstellar spacecrafts carried out by the Robotech Defense Force, led by Captain Gloval and his troop of newly trained cadets. *A Tatsunoko Production/Harmony Gold U.S.A. Production. Robotech is a registered trademark owned and licensed by Harmony Gold U.S.A. Color. Half–hour. Syndicated: 1985–1986.*

Voices:

Greg Snow, Reba West, Jonathan Alexsander, Drew Thomas, Deanna Morris, Thomas Wyner, Brittany Harlow, Donn Warner, Axel Roberts, Tony Oliver, A. Gregory, Noelle McGraph, Sandra Snow, Guy Garrett, Jimmy Flinders, Anthony Wayne, Eddie Frierson, Leonad Pike, Aline Leslie, Shirley Roberts, Wendee Swan, Larry Abraham, Sam Fontana, Penny Sweet, Mary Cobb, Celena Banas, Chelsea Victoria

Episodes:

"Boobytrap," "Countdown," "Space Fold," "The Long Wait," "Transformation," "Blitzkrieg," "Bye–Bye, Mars," "Sweet Six-teen," "Miss Macross," "Blind Game," "First Contact," "The Big Escape," "Blue Wind," "Gloval's Report," "Homecoming," "Battle Cry," "Phantasm," "Farewell, Big Brother," "Bursting Point," "Paradise Lost," "A New Dawn," "Battle Hymn," "Reckless," "Showdown," "Wedding Bells," "The Messenger," "Force Of Arms," "Reconstruction Blues," "The Robotech Masters," "Viva Miriya," "Khyron's Revenge," "Broken Heart," "A Rainy Night," "Private Time," "Season's Greetings," "To The Stars," "Dana's Story," "False Start," "The Southern Cross," "Volunteers," "Half Moon," "Danger Zone," "Prelude To Battle," "The Trap," "Metal Fire," "Stardust," "Outsiders," "Deja Vu," "A New Recruit," "Triumvirate," "Clone Chamber," "Long Song," "The Hunters," "Mind Game," "Dana In Wonderland," "Crisis Point," "Day Dreamer," "Final Nightmare," "The Invid Connection," "The Lost City," "Lonely Soldier Boy," "Survival," "Curtain Call," "Hard Time," "Paper Hero," "Eulogy," "The Genesis Pit," "Enter Marlene," "The Secret Route," "The Fortress," "Sandstorm," "Annie's Wedding," "Separate Ways," "Metamorphosis," "The Midnight Sun," "Ghost Town," "Frost Bite," "Birthday Blues," "Hired Gunn," "The Big Apple," "Reflex Point," "Dark Finale" and "Symphony Of Light."

ROCKET ROBIN HOOD AND HIS MERRY SPACEMEN

The year is 3000. Headquartered on the floating solar–powered asteroid Sherwood Forest, intergalactic crime–fighter Rocket Robin Hood and his Merry Spacemen—Will Scarlet, Little John, Alan, Jiles and Friar Tuck—team up to battle the universe's top villain, the wicked Sheriff of N.O.T.T. The series' executive producer was veteran animator James "Shamus" Culhane. *A Trillium Production. Color. Half–hour. Premiere: Fall 1969. Syndicated.*

Voices:

Carl Banas, Ed McNamara, Chris Wiggins, Bernard Cowan, Len Birman, Paul Kligman, Gillie Fenwick, John Scott

Episodes:

(three per show) "The Time Machine," "Ye Old Robinhood," "There Is No Time Like The Future," "Giles The Great," "A Meal Fit For A Tyrant," "The Impossible Goal," "The Sad, Sad Sheriff of N.O.T.T.," "The Great Jewel Robbery," "Our Sheriff The Hero," "The Magic Medallion Of Morse," "The Sheriff Cooks Up A Wicked Plot," "Shooting the Works," "Little, Little John," "The Paralyzing Meteor," "Unshrunk," "The Prince Of Plotters," "Warfare Space—Ski Style," "How Merry Can You Get," "Robin Vs. The Robot Knight," "Robin Fights Back," "Space Champion," "Little George," "The Deadly Invasion," "The Secret Weapon," "Goritang!," "Monkey Business On The Planet Lucifer," "Watch Out, Here Comes The Bride," "Marlin The Magician," "Who Do Voo Doo?," "This Trick Will Kill You," "Cleopatra Meet Little John," "Dinosaur Go Home," "The Best Trick Of All," "Wiley Giles," "Double Dealing Giles," "Same Old Giles," "The Maraduke Caper," "Bubble Trouble," "Instant Hero," "Michael Shawn The Leprechaun," "Follow The Leader," "The Spaceman Who Came To Dinner," "Never Trust Your Uncle," "Dr. Mortula," "The Strange Castle," "Bring On The Sun," "The Awful Truce," "Cross And Double Cross,"

Robin Hood rockets out of the past and into the future of deep space in the science–fiction favorite, "Rocket Robin Hood And His Merry Spacemen." (Courtesy: ARP Films Inc.)

"Fleet Of Phantoms," "The Mystery Of The Crown Jewels," "Bovin Caged," "Marvelo Takes A Fall," "Dan Coyote Mc-Pherson," "The Zap Trap," "The Last Laugh," "Jesse James Rides Again," "The Slowest Gun In The Universe," "The Big Heist," "The Orbiting Salesman," "You Gotta Know The Territory," "The First Astral Horse Trade," "Don't Make A Sound," "The Beast Who Came To Dinner," "Barking Beasts Don't Bite," "The Solar Sphynx," "Escape From The Pyramid," "The Tumbling of Tut," "City Beneath The Sea," "Whirlaround The Whirlpool," "Deap Sea Danger," "Catch A Comet By The Tail," "Good King Rocket Robinhood," "The Celestial Joy Ride," "Space Wolf," "Captives In Space," "Partners, On The Loose," "The Emperor Jimmy," "The Making Of An Emperor," "Diamonds Are Prince John's Worst Friend," "Safari," "Tricked Trap," "The Warlord Of Saturn," "A Breath Of Fresh Danger," "Play With Fire And You Get Burned," "The Eternal Planet," "And In This Corner," "Say Ahh . . . Or Hot Tonsils," "Young Dr. Ulysses," "The Death Traps," "The Man Who Turned To Stone," "Dr. Magnet," "Magnetic Meteors," "The Great Gold Robbery," "The Manta Menace," "Welcome To My Parlor," "And The Walls Come Tumbling Down," "The Storm Maker," "Into The Eye," "The Planet Storms," "Who'll Kill Rocket Robin," "The Tomb Of Ice," "The Finger Of Death," "Incredible Gem Of Cosmo Kahn," "Planet–Planet—Who's Got The Planet?," "Escape From Xanador," "The Haunted Asteroid," "The Astro City Of The Dead," "The Cosmic Secret Of Korgor," "The Plot To Destroy N.O.T.T.," "The Saturnian Dungeon," "Runaway Rocket," "Genius In A Bottle," "Three To Make Ready," "Subterranean Captives," "The Tables Turn," "The Three Kingdom Of Caldomar," "The Sword Of Destruction," "Caldomar Ablaze," "Lord Of The Underworld," "Revenge Of The Underworld," "One Minute To Doom," "Space Giant," "Gigantic Doom," "The Black Cloud Of Danger," "Return Trip," "The Beetle's Claw," "Ride Of Death," "Dark Galaxy," "Desent Demons," "Mummies Revolt," "Jaws Of Steel," "Mummy's Host," "The Solar Sphinx," "The Ghost Pirates Of Caribia," "Escape To Caribia," "The Ghost Comes To Life,"

"Dementia 5," "Robin's Precious Cargo," "Escape Into Reality," "Lord Of The Shadows," "Blackout," "Who's Who," "The Living Planet," "And Into The Fire," "The Electric Circle," "Manta Asteroid," "From Menace To Menace" and "Gargoyles, Gators And Gorillas."

ROCKY AND HIS FRIENDS

The flying squirrel Rocky and simple–minded, bristle–haired Bullwinkle Moose (whose voice was reminiscent of Red Skelton's punch–drunk fighter character, Willie Lump–Lump) battle the evil Mr. Big, a midget underworld gangster who hires sinister Boris Badenov and the fetching agent, Natasha Fatale, to foil the duo's activities in cliff–hanging, serialized adventures (narrated by actor William Conrad) that first premiered on ABC in 1959. The series was the second all–new cartoon show to air on network television. It was created by Jay Ward, the father of "Crusader Rabbit."

Other cartoon segments included "Fractured Fairytales," "Aesop and Son," "Peabody's Improbable History" and "Mr Know It All."

In 1961, following its ABC network run, NBC broadcast a new, expanded edition of the series, retitled, "The Bullwinkle Show." (See entry for information.) *A Jay Ward Production. Color. Half–hour. Premiered on ABC: November 19, 1959–September 23, 1961.*

Voices:

Rocky, the flying squirrel: June Foray, **Bullwinkle Moose:** Bill Scott, **Boris Badenov:** Paul Frees, **Natasha Fatale:** June Foray, **Narrator:** William Conrad, **Aesop:** Charles Ruggles, **Aesop's Son:** Daws Butler, **Narrator:** Charles Ruggles, **Mr. Peabody:** Bill Scott, **Sherman,** his adopted son: Walter Tetley, **Narrator** ("Fractured Fairytales"): Edward Everett Horton

Episodes:

"Rocky and Bullwinkle" (two per show).
"Jet Formula (1–40), "Box Top Robbery" (41–52), "Upsidasium" (53–88), "Metal Munching Mice" (89–104), "Greenprint Oogle" (105–116), "Rue Brittania" (117–124), "Buried Treasure" (125–138), "Last Angry Moose" (139–142), "Wailing Whale" (143–156), "Three Mooseketeers" (157–164), "Lazy Jay Ranch" (165–182), "Missouri Mish Mash" (183–208), "Topsy Turvy World" (209–222), "Painting Theft" (223–228), "Guns Of Abalone" (229–232), "Treasure Of Mote Zoom" (233–240), "Goof Gas Attack" (241–248), "Banana Formula" (249–260), (break in production) "Bumbling Brothers Circus" (301–310), "Mucho Loma" (originally "Much Mud"/311–316), "Pottsylvania Creeper" (317–322), "Moosylvania" (323–326), "Ruby Yacht" (327–332), "Bulls Testimonial Dinner" (333–338), "The Weather Lady" (339–344), "Louse on 92nd Street" (345–350), "Wassamotto U" (351–362), and "Moosylvania Saved" (363–366).
"Fractured Fairytales" (one per show).
"Goldilocks," "Fee Fi Fo Fum," "Rapunzel," "Puss And Boots #1," "Enchanted Fish," "Beauty And The Beast," "Brave Little Tailor," "Rumpelstiltskin," "Princess And The Pea," "Sweet Little Beat," "Dick Whittington's Cat," "Cinderella," "Elves

And Shoemaker," "Tom Thumb," "Sir Galahad," "Snow White," "Sleeping Beauty," "Pinocchio," "Little Red Riding Hood," "Androcles And The Lion," "Kind Midas," "Riding Hoods Anonymous," "Ugly Duckling," "Hansel And Gretel," "Dancing Cinderella," "Goose That Laid A Golden Egg," "Three Little Pigs #1," "Slipping Beauty," "Snow White, Inc.," "Rumpelstiltskin Returns," "Leaping Beauty," "Puss And Boots #2," "Jack And The Beanstalk," "Tom Thum #2," "Aladdin," "The Three Bears," "Enchanted Frog," "Pied Piper #2," "Beauty And The Beast," "The Magical Fish," "Prince Darling," "Son Of Beauty And The Beast," "The Frog Prince," "The Golden Goose," "Son Of Rumpelstiltskin," "Elves And The Shoemaker," "Speeding Beauty," "Fisherman And His Wife," "The Princess Of Goblins," "Snow White Meets Rapnuzel," "The Little Princess," "Thom Tum," "Slow White And Nose Red," "Prince Hyacinth And Dear Princess," "The Giant And The Beanstalk," "The Enchanted Fly," "Felicia And The Pot Of Pinks," "Hans Clinker," "The Witches Broom," "Son Of King Midas," "The Magic Chicken," "Aladdin And His Lamp," "The Enchanted Gnat," "The Thirteen Helmets," "The Prince And The Popper," "Booty And The Beast," "Little Red Riding Hood," "Goldilocks And The Three Bears," "The Ugly Almond Duckling," "John's Ogre Wife," "The Absent–Minded King," "The Mysterious Castle," "The Little Tinker," "Sweeping Beauty," "The Teeth Of Baghdad," "The Little Man In The Boat," "Cutie And The Bird," "The Tale Of A King," "Peter And The Three Pennies," "The Wishing Hat," "Son Of Snow White," "Jack B. Nimble," "Potter's Luck," "The Magic Lichee Nut," "The King And The Witch," "The Seven Chickens," and "Sweeping Beauty #2." "Aesop And Son" (one per show).
"The Lion And The Mouse," "The Mice In Council," "The Fox And The Stork," "The Wolf In Sheep's Clothing," "The Hare And The Tortoise," "The Hare And The Hound," "The Hares and The Frog," "The Frogs And The Beaver," "The Lion And The Aardvark," "The Jackrabbits And The Mule," "The Dog And The Shadow," "The Cat And The Fifteen Mice," "The Goldfish And The Bear," "The Vain Cow," "The Canary And The Musical Hares," "The Fox And The Minks," "The Owl And The Wolf," "The Centipede And The Snail," "The Fox And The Owl," "The Hound And The Wolf," "The Fox And The Winking Horse," "The Sick Lion," "The Porcupine And The Tigers," "Son Of The Masked Clock," "The Hen And The Cat," "The Chicken And The Ducks," "The Coyote And The Jackrabbits," "The Rooster And The Five Hens," "The Three Bears," "The Robin, The Pelican, And The Angleworm," "The Eagle And The Beetle," "The Fox And The Hound," "The Bears And The Dragon," "The Fox And The Woodman," "The Country Fog And The City Frog," "The Fox And The Rabbit," "The Hare And The Tortoise," "The French Poodle And the Alley Cat," and "The Fox And the Three Weasels."
"Peabody's Improbable History" (one per show).
"Show Opening," "Napoleon," "Lord Nelson," "Wyatt Earp," "King Arthur," "Franz Schubert," "Lucretia Borgia," "Sir Walter Raleigh," "Robert Fulton," "Annie Oakley," "The Wright Brothers," "George Armstrong Custer," "Alfred Nobel," "Marco Polo," "Richard The Lion Hearted," "Don Juan," "William Tecumseh Sherman," "First Kentucky Derby," "P. T. Barnum," "Stanley And Livingstone," "Louis Pasteur," "Robin Hood," "Robinson Crusoe," "Ponce De Leon," "John L. Sullivan,"

"Rocky and Bullwinkle," starring Rocky the flying squirrel, his friend Bullwinkle Moose and villains Natasha and Boris, marked the second all–cartoon show to air on network television. The series was created by Jay Ward, the father of "Crusader Rabbit." © Jay Ward Productions

"Leonardo Da Vinci," "Paul Revere," "Confucius," "Nero," "Francis Scott Key," "Captain Matthew Clift," "Balboa," "Peter Cooper," "The Battle Of Bunker Hill," "The Pony Express," "Stephen Decatur," "Alexander Graham Bell," "Commander Peary," "Pancho Villa," "Lord Francis Douglas," "Sitting Bull," "Christopher Columbus," "The French Foreign Legion," "Guglielmo Marconi," "Scotland Yard," "John Holland," "Louis XVI," "Francisco Pizzaro," "Daniel Boone," "Jesse James," "Shakespeare," "Zebulon Pike," "The First Golf Match," "William Tell," "James Whistler," "Ferdinand Magellan," "Sir Isaac Newton," "Kit Carson," "The First Caveman," "Johann Gutenberg," "Buffalo Bill," "Hans Christian Oersted," "Leif Ericson," "John Sutter," "Ludwig Van Beethoven," "Calamity Jane," "The Surrender Of Cornwallis," "The First Indian Nickel," "Jules Verne," "Casanova," "Lawrence Of Arabia," "Bonnie Prince Charlie," "Reuter," "Geronimo," "The Great Wall of China," "The Marquis Of Queensbury," "Jim Bowie," "Edgar Allan Poe," "Charge Of The Light Brigade," "The Royal Mounted Police," "The First Bullfight," "The Building Of The Great Pyramid," "James Aubudon," "Mata Hari," "Galileo," "Wellington At Waterloo," "Florence Nigtingale," "Henry The Eighth," "First Indianapolis Auto Race," "Captain Kidd," "The Texas Rangers" and "Cleopatra."
"Mr. Know It All" (one per show).
"How To Train A Doggy," "How To Tame Lions," "How To Cook A Turkey's Goose," "How To Have A Swimming Pool," "How To Sell Vacuum Cleaners," "How To Cure The Hiccups," "How To Open A Jar Of Pickles," "How To Get Into The Movies," "How To Catch A Bee," "How To Be A Cow Puncher," "How To Escape From Devil's Island," "How To Shoot Par Golf," "How To Be A Magician," "A Monstrous Success," "How To Remove A Moustache," "How To Fall Asleep," "Unwanted Guest," "How To Be A Star Reporter," "How To Do Stunts In The Movies," "How To Run A 4–Minute Mile," "How To Be A Big Game Hunter," "How To Be A Barber," "How To Water Ski," "How To Be An Indian," "How To Own A Hi–Fi," "How

To Be Human Fly," "How To Be A Hitch–Hiker," "How To Be A Hobo," "How To Disarm A Live TNT Bomb," "How To Be Beatnik," "How To Conquer Your Fear Of Height," "How To Fix A Flat," "How To Avoid Tipping The Waiter," "Rocky And Bullwinkle Fan Club #1," "How To Buy A Used Car," "How To Be An Archeologist," "How To Travel Through The West," "Rocky and Bullwinkle Fan Club #2," "How To Sell An Encyclopedia," "Rocky And Bullwinkle Fan Club #3," "How To Wash Windows," "Rocky And Bullwinkle Fan Club #4," "Rocky And Bullwinkle Fan Club #5," "Rocky And Bullwinkle Fan Club #6," "Boris' Fan Club," "Rocky And Bullwinkle Fan Club #7," "How To Win Friends," "How To Be A Good Umpire," "How To Interview A Scientist," "Rocky And Bullwinkle Fan Club #8," "Rocky And Bullwinkle Fan Club #9," "Member Of The Peace Corps," "Money Back," "Temperamental Movie Star," "How To Have A Hit Record," "How To Make The Neighbors Quiet," "Tennis Game," "How To Sell Soap," "Top Flight Stock Salesman" and "Bully The Beach."

ROD ROCKET

Entertaining and educational space adventures in serial form of Rod Rocket, his sidekick, Joey, his sister Casey, and their friend Professor Argus. The half–hour series of five–minute cartoons was the first fully animated program produced by Filmation. *A Filmation Production. Color. Half–hour. Premiered: 1963. Syndicated.*

ROGER RAMJET

Daredevil, flying fool and all–round good guy fittingly describe American Eagle Squadron antihero, scientist Roger Ramjet (voiced by famed radio/television personality Gary Owens). A proton energy pill gives Roger the power of 20 atom bombs for a period of 20 seconds. He battles the evil Noodle Romanoff from N.A.S.T.Y., Jacqueline Hyde, Henry Cabbage Patch, Lance Crossfire, the Solenoid Robots, General G. I. Brassbottom, Clara Finork, Lotta Love, the Height Brothers (Cronk, Horse and Gezundt) and other baddies.

Of course, Roger himself has quite a staff of good–doers on the flying squadron: Yank, Doodle, Dan and Dee.

Violent confrontations and undue violence were avoided in the show by inserting the appropriate title cards: "Whack!," "Thunk!," "Hurt!," "Pain!" and "Ouch!" The same technique was later employed on TV's "Batman" series. *A Ken Snyder Production. Color. Half–hour. Premiered: September 1965. Syndicated.*

Voices:

Roger Ramjet: Gary Owens, **Yank/Dan:** Dick Beals, **Doodle/ Noodle Romanoff:** Gene Moss, **Dee/Lotta Love:** Joan Gerber, **General G. I. Brassbottom/Ma Ramjet:** Bob Arbogast, **Lance Crossfire/Red Dog:** Paul Shively, **The Announcer:** Dave Ketchum

Additional Voices:

Jim Thurman, Ken Snyder

Famed "Laugh–In" announcer Gary Owens was the voice of daredevil, flying fool and all–around good guy Roger Ramjet in a series of five–minute color cartoons produced for television in the mid–1960s. © Ken Snyder Productions

Episodes:

(four per show) "Dr. Ivan Evilkisser" (pilot), "The Sheik," "Bat Guy," "The Shaft," "Cowboy," "Kokomo," "Dee Kidnap," "Baseball," "The Pirate," "Miss America," "Drafted," "TV Crisis," "Revolution," "Torture," "The Race," "Jack The Nipper," "Ma Ramjet," "Cockroaches," "Moon," "Hi–Noon," "Bank Robbers," "Sun Clouds," "Football," "Bullfight," "Bathosphere," "Dr. Frank N. Schwein," "Sky Diving," "Monkey," "Martins And Coys," "Planets," "Orbit," "Tennis," "Skateboard," "Scotland Yard," "Werewolf," "Flying Saucers," "Long Joan," "Moonshot," "Treasure In Sierra's Mattress," "Tarzap," "Comics," "Cycles," "Little Roger," "Jet Boots," "Spy In The Sky," "Hollywood," "Air Devil," "Track Meet," "Surf Nuts," "Dry Dock," "Coffee," "Machines," "Assassins," "Stolen," "Genie," "Airplane," "K.O. At The Gun Fight Corral," "Mars," "Puck," "Woodsman," "Pirate Gold," "Doctor What," "Fox," "Super–Mother," "Large Leslie," "Party," "Gamey," "Time Machine," "Pool," "Ancestors," "Horse," "Hoop–De–Doo," "Big Woof," "Robot Plants," "Robot Plot," "Turkey," "Fishing," "Purloined Pinky," "Snow," "Ripley," "Monster Masquerade," "Lompoc Diamond," "School," "Vaudeville," "Coffee House," "Pirate Games," "Missing," "Horse Race," "Dentist," "Desert Ox," "Rip Van Ramjet," "Ad Game," "Lotsa Pizza," "Land Rush," "Show Biz," "The Catnapper," "Opera Phantom," "Pies," "Small World," "Cousin," "Ark," "Sauce," "Whale," "Doodle Legaue," "For The Birds," "Lompoc Cannonball," "Abominable Snowman," "Hero Training," "Tiger," "Rodeo," "Safari," "'Twas The Night Before," "Water Sucker," "Volcano," "Limberlost," "General Kidnap," "Rabbit Man," "The Pill Caper," "Drought," "How's Your Pass," "Three Faces Of Roger," "Espionage Express," "Private Eye," "Winfield Of The Infield," "Branch Office," "Wedding Bells," "Bunny," "Hypno–Chick," "Oil," "Doctor," "Little Monster," "Flying Town," "Daring You Man," "Dry Sea," "Crown Jewels," "April Fool," "Pay Cut," "Killer Doodle," "Polar Bear," "Ruggers," "Hassenfeffer," "Nut," "The Law,"

"Man Hole," "Block Buster," "Sellout," "Scout Outing," "Love," "Blunderosa," "Decorator," "General Doodle," and "Lompoc Lizards."

ROMAN HOLIDAYS

Forum Construction Company engineer Gus Holiday, his wife, Laurie, and their children, Precocia and Happius, struggle with 20th–century lifestyles in Rome, A.D. 63. *A Hanna–Barbera Production. Color. Half–hour. Premiered on NBC: September 9, 1972–September 1, 1973.*

Voices:

Gus Holiday: Dave Willock, **Laurie,** his wife: Shirley Mitchell, **Precocia,** their daughter: Pamelyn Ferdin, **Happius** (Happy), their son: Stanley Livingston, **Mr. Evictus,** the landlord: Dom DeLuise, **Mr. Tycoonius,** Holiday's boss: Hal Smith, **Brutus,** the family lion: Daws butler, **Groovia,** Happy's girlfriend: Judy Strangis, **Herman,** Gus's friend: Hal Peary, **Henrietta,** his wife: Janet Waldo

Episodes:

"Double Date," "The Lion's Share," "Star For A Day," "Hero Sandwich," "The Big Split–Up," "Hectic Holiday," "Switch Is Which," "That's Show Biz," "Double Dilemma," "A Funny Thing Happened On The Way To The Chariot," "Buried Treasure," "Cyrano De Happius," and "Father Of The Year."

RUBIK, THE AMAZING CUBE

In the spring of 1985, ABC rebroadcast the original episodes of this series about the famous multi–colored cube, which comes to life, and engages in a series of magical adventures with three youngsters in this half–hour fantasy series which first premiered as part of "The Pac–Man/Rubik, The Amazing Cube Hour." (See entry for episodic information.) *A Ruby–Spears Enterprises Production. Color. Half–hour. Premiered on ABC: April 27, 1985–August 31, 1985.*

Voices:

Rubik: Ron Palillo, **Carlos:** Michael Saucedo, **Renaldo,** his brother: Michael Bell, **Lisa,** his sister: Jennifer Fajardo, **Ruby Rodriguez:** Michael Bell, **Maria Rodriguez:** Angela Moya

RUDE DOG AND THE DWEEBS

Rude Dog is a cool, "Fonzie–like" dog who drives a pink 1956 Cadillac. The Dweebs are his equally cool gang of canines. Together, they spell problems of every kind in this stylized animated series featuring a whole new color palette for Saturday–morning animation of "hot pinks and neon." *A Marvel Productions in association with Akom Productions Ltd. Color. Half–hour. Premiered on CBS: September 16, 1989–September 8, 1990.*

Voices:

Rude Dog: Rob Paulsen, **Barney:** Dave Coulier, **Winston/ Herman:** Peter Cullen, **Satch:** Jim Cummings, **Kibble/Gloria:** Ellen Gerstell, **Tweek:** Hank Saroyan, **Reggie:** Mendi Segal, **Caboose/Rot/Seymour:** Frank Welker

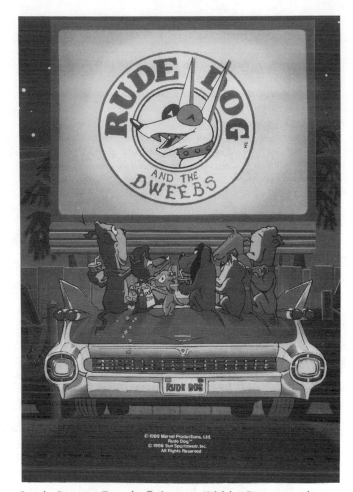

Satch, Reggie, Tweek, Caboose, Kibble, Barney and Winston take in a drive–in movie featuring their Fonzi-like leader in Saturday morning's "Rude Dog And The Dweebs." © Marvel Productions Ltd. Rude Dog is the trademarked property of Sun Sportswear Inc. All rights reserved.

Episodes:

(two episodes per show) "Hello, Mr. Kitty?," "The Fish Who Went Moo," "Dweebiest Dog On The Beach," "Dweeb–illac Dilemma," "No Dweebs Aloud," "Ding–A–Ling Kitty," "War Of The Dweebs," "Dweebs In Space," "Nightmare On Dweeb Street," "Dweebsy Kind'a Love," "Call Of The Dweeb," "Dumbbell Dweeb," "Waiter, There's A Dweeb In My Soup!," "Boardwalk Boss," "To Kibble Or Not To Kibble," "Dweebsday Afternoon," "Dweebochondriacs," "Surprise, You're Itch!," "Leave It To Tweek," "Polly Wanna Dweeb?," "Winston's Family Tree Rot," "Pretty Dweebs All In A Row," "The Hic-cupping Bandit," "Dweeb Your Manners," "Tuesday The 14th, Part Dweeb," and "Home Sweet Dweeb."

THE RUFF AND REDDY SHOW

First telecast in black–and–white until 1959, Hanna–Barbera created this pioneering made–for–television cartoon series which featured the adventures of a talking dog and cat team, Ruff and Reddy, battling sinister forces of evil (Captain Greedy, Scarey Harry Safari, Killer and Diller and others) in serialized stories that were presented in 10 or more six–minute installments in the fashion of Jay Ward's "Crusader Rabbit." The program was hosted by Jimmy Blaine during the first three seasons; Bob Cottle succeeded Blaine as host from 1962–1964. Series episodes concluded production with the 1959–1960 season, so the program repeated stories from earlier broadcasts in programs after that season. *A Hanna–Barbera Production. Black–and–white. Color. Half–hour. Premiered on NBC: December 14, 1957–September 26, 1964.*

Voices:

Ruff: Don Messick, **Reddy:** Daws Butler, **Professor Gizmo:** Don Messick, **Ubble–Ubble:** Don Messick

Episodes:

1957–1958 "Planet Pirates," "Night Flight Fright," "Whama–Bamma–Gamma Gun," "The Master Mind of Muni–Mula," "The Mad Monster Of Muni–Mula," "The Hocus Pocus Focus," "Muni–Mula Mix–Up," "Creepy Creature Feature," "The Creepy Creature," "Surprise In The Skies," "Crowds In The Clouds," "Reddy's Rocket Rescue," "Pinky The Pint–Sized Pachyderm," "Last Trip Of A Ghost Ship," "Irate Pirate," "Dynamite Fright," "Marooned In Typhoon Lagoon," "Scarey Harry Safari," "Jungle Jitters," "Bungle In The Jungle," "A Creep In The Deep," "Hot Shot's Plot," "The Gloom Of Doom," "The Trapped Trap The Trapper," "Westward Ho Ho Ho," "A Slight Fright On A Moonlight Night," "Asleep While A Creep Steals The Deep," "Copped By A Copter," "The Two Terrible Twins From Texas," "Killer And Diller," "A Friend To The End," "Hells On Wheels," "The Whirly Bird Catches The Worms," "The Boss Of Double–Cross," "Ship Shape Sheep," "Rootin' Tootin' Shootin'," "Hot Lead For A Hot Head," "The Treasure of Doubloon Lagoon," "Blunder Down Under," "The Metal Monster Mystery," "The Late Late Pieces Of Eight," "The Goon Of Doubloon Lagoon," "Two Dubs In A Sub," "Big Deal With A Small Seal," "A Real Keen Submarine," "No Hope For A Dope On A Periscope," "Rescue In The Deep Blue," "A Whale Of A Tale Of A Tail Of A Whale," "Welcome Guest In A Treasure Chest" and "Pot Shots Puts Hot Shots On Hot Spot."

1958–1959 "Egg Yeggs," "The Dummy Mummy," "The Chicken–Hearted Chickasaurus Chase," "The Chickasaurus Crack–Up," "The Slick Chickasaurus Chick Trick," "The Chicken Hearted Chickasaurus," "Chickasaurus Choo Choo," "Rumble In The Jungle," "The Sorehead Tyrranosaurus," "Two Eyes Spy On The Guys," "Double–Trouble With Ubble–Ubble," "A Chick In Need Is A Chick Indeed," "A Quick Trick Saves A Slick Chick," "Scary Tale On A Canyon Trail," "Borrowed Burro In A Burrow," "Pint–Size Surprise For The Guys," "Reddy And Me And Pee–Wee Make Three," "Hoss Thief Grief," "Tricked And Trapped By A Tricky Trapper," "Harry Safari And The Pony," "Frantic Antics Of Poco–Loco," "Nag In The Bag," "Bungled Bundle Of Boodle," "Chump's Jumps Bring Bumps And Lumps," "Snow–Biz–Wiz," "The Three Set Pee–Wee Free," "Fantastic Phantom," "Long Gone Leprechaun," "The Goon Of Glocca Morra," "Bungle In Banshee Castle," "Afloat In A Moat With No Boat," "Too Soon The Goon," "Smitten By A Kitten," "Mr. Small Meets Mr. Tall In

The Hall," "Going–Going Goon," "A Scary Chase Thru A Spooky Place," "Bing Bang Boom In A Real Small Room," "Gold Room Doom," "Three See The Princess Free," "Missile Fizzle," "The Missing Missile Mystery," "Never Land In Never–Never Land," "Polar Bear Scare," "A Liking For a Striking Viking," "Bear Hunting Is For The Birds," "Beep–Beep From the Deep–Deep," "Two Friends In A Submarine," "Muscleman Meets Missile Man," "Bull Fight Fright," "Reddy Globbers Robbers," "Machine Gun Fun" and "Bad Guys Meet Good Guys."

1959–1960 "Dizzy Deputies," "Later, Later, Alligator," "Gator Caper," "Chip Off The Ol' Chopper," "La Fitt To Be Tied," "Hide And Seek With A Sneak," "Boom Boom Boom," "Spellbound Fool In A Round Whirlpool," "Fast Chase Through A Spooky Place," "Looks Like The End For a Friend," "No Laugh On Half A Raft," "Gator Thrills And Whooshmobiles," "Trapped And Snapped Sap," "Spooky Meeting At Spooky Rock," "Dig The Big Digger," "The Secret Bizz Of Professor Gizz," "Test Hop Flip Flop," "Sticks And Stones And Aching Bones," "Gun, Gun, Who's Got The Gun?," "Big Papoose On The Loose," "Mine, Mine, All Mine Gold Mine," "The Ghost With The Most," "In The Soup With A Supernatural Snoop," "Sneaky Knaves In The Caves," "Tailspin Twins," "Sky High Fly Guys," "A Tisket A Tasket Who Lost Their Basket," "Three's A Crowd In A Cloud," "Fine Feathered Birds Of A Feather," "A Bird In Hand Is A Handy Bird," "No Laffy Daffy," "Tiff In A Skiff," "Sub A Dub Dub," "Big Break Tweaks Big Sneak," "Off On A Toot With The Loot to Boot," "Thanks A Lot For X Marks The Spot," "Tale Of A Sail In A Whale," "Misguided Missile," "Triple Trouble Trip," "Around The Moon In Eighty Ways," "Button, Button, Who Pushed The Button," "No Traces Of Aces In Spaces," "Lilli Punies Meet Mooney Goonies," "Little Guys Are Big Surprise," "Two Is Company—A Million Is A Little," "Big Bop For Big Flop," "Things Get Tuff For Ruff—Sure 'Nuff," "Whap—Caught In A Trap By A Sap," "Spin, Spin A Web To Catch A Blop In," and "Have Blop—Will Travel."

SABER RIDER AND THE STAR SHERIFFS

In this out–of–this–world futuristic fantasy with a Western twist, Saber Rider, the dashing leader of the Star Sheriffs unit, maintains peace and unity for the settlers of the new frontier by defending against the ghostly "Outrider" foes, mysterious vapor beings who have perfected the technique of "dimension jumping." The program was the first animated strip to incorporate interactive technology, a revolutionary new concept which enables viewers to participate with the program by using specially designed toys. *A World Events Production. Color. Half–hour. Syndicated: September, 1987.*

Voices:

Townsend Coleman, Peter Cullen, Pat Fraley, Pat Musick, Rob Paulsen

Episodes:

"Star Sheriff Round Up," "Cavalry Command," "Jesse's Revenge," "Iguana Get To Know You," "Little Hombre," "Greatest Show On The New Frontier," "Little Pardner," "Brawlin' Is My Calling," "Wild Horses Couldn't Drag Me Away," "The

Castle Of The Mountain Haze," "Oh Boy! Dinosaurs!," "Jesse Blue," "Four Leaf Clover," "What Did You Do On Your Summer Vacation," "The Highlanders," "Show Down At Cimarron Pass," "The Saber And The Tomahawk," "All That Glitters," "Sole Survivor," "Legend Of The Santa Fe Express," "Snake Eyes," "Famous Last Words," "Sharpshooter," "The Monarch Supreme," "Gattler's Last Stand," "Dooley," "The Hole In The Wall Gang," "The All Galaxy Grand Prix," "Snowblind," "Tranquility," "Bad Day At Dry Gulch," "Snowcone," "Sneaky Spies," "Stampede," "The Challenge" (Part 1), "The Challenge" (Part 2), "Born On The Bayou," "April Rides," "The Walls Of Red Wing," "Jessie's Girl," "The Amazing Lazardo," "I Forgot," "Lend Me Your Ears," "Born To Run," "The Legend Of The Lost World," "The Rescue," "Eagle Has Landed," "Cease Fire," "Alamo Moon," "The Nth Degree," "Who Is Nemisis?" and "Happy Trails."

SABRINA AND THE GROOVIE GOOLIES

One year after her debut on "The Archie Comedy Hour," Sabrina, a teenage sorceress, was coupled with The Groovie Goolies, a group of strange monsters (see "The Groovie Goolies"), in this hour–long series of new animated misadventures and humorous vignettes. Sabrina was so well–received that she was given her own series, "Sabrina, the Teenage Witch," which was broadcast for three successful seasons on CBS. *A Filmation Production. Color. One hour. Premiered on CBS: September 12, 1970–September 4, 1971.*

Voices:

Sabrina, the Teenage Witch: Jane Webb, **The Groovie Goolies:** Jane Webb, Howard Morris, Larry Storch, Larry D. Mann

SABRINA, SUPERWITCH

In an attempt to bolster its sagging ratings, NBC repeated 13 episodes of "Sabrina, the Teenage Witch," giving the program a new title, as a last–ditch effort to bring some excitement to their Saturday morning cartoon lineup. Unfortunately, the program failed to cast a spell over its audience and was pulled from the airwaves two months after its debut. The original "Sabrina" was first broadcast on rival network, CBS, in 1971. *A Filmation Production. Color. Half–hour. Premiered on NBC: November 26, 1977–January 28, 1978.*

Voices:

Sabrina: Jane Webb

Episodes:

"Alter Ego," "Goolie Sitter," "Cliche' Castle," "Witch Picnic," "Moose On The Loose," "Pot Luck," "Funny Paper Caper," "Teenage Grundy," "Talking Bird," "Merlin's Story," "Teenie The Terror," "Cartoonie Loonies" and "Party Pooper."

SABRINA, THE TEENAGE WITCH

A 15–year–old apprentice witch works her sorcery on friends Archie Andrews, Jughead, Veronica Lodge, Reggie Mantle,

Riverdale High School principal Mr. Weatherbee and teacher Miss Grundy in this fantasy/comedy series inspired by the success of TV's "Bewitched." The series ran for three successful seasons on CBS.

Sabrina originally debuted as a recurring character on 1969's "The Archie Comedy Hour." The fast–thinking witch was later combined with "The Groovie Goolies" in a one–hour time slot under the series title "Sabrina and the Groovie Goolies," broadcast on CBS in 1970. (The program was later edited into a half–hour for syndication.) *A Filmation Production. Color. Half–hour. Premiered on CBS: September 11, 1971–August 31, 1974.*

Voices:

Sabrina: Jane Webb

Episodes:

(two per show)

1971–1972 "The Fairy Godmother," "Hiccups," "Which Witch Is Which?," "The Basketball Game," "Will The Real Weatherbee Stand Up?," "Caveman," "Paint Story," "Aunt Zelda's Broom," "Cinderella's Story," "What The Hex Going On?," "Wish Bone," "Babysitter," "Carnival," "Stage Fright, (Stage Struck)" "Pet Show," "Funny Bunny," "Hair Today—Gone Tomorrow," "A Witch In Time," "When The Cat's Away," "Costume Party," "Let's Have A Hand For Jughead," "The New Freeway," "Blue Whale," "Football Game," "Town Beautiful," "Horse's Mouth," "Birdman Of Riverdale," "Hoedown Showdown," "Spooky Spokes," "You Oughtta Be In Pictures," "The Generation Flap" and "School Daze."

1972–1973 "Ug At The Bat," "Computerized Moose," "Rose–Colored Glasses," "Living Dolls," "Cake Bake," "Hot Rod Derby," "The Bear Facts," "Child Care," "Witches Gold Open," "Rummage Sale," "High School Drop–Ins," "Big Deal," "Frankie," "Beached," "Ouch," "Smog," "Dirty Pool," "The Grayed Outdoors," "Short Changed," "Mis–Guided Tour," "That Old Track Magic," "Moose's Alter–Falter," "Mortal Terror," "Weather Or Not," "Flying Sorcery," "Too Many Cooks," "Ambrose's Amulet," "Auto–Biography," "Tragic Magic" and "A Nose For News."

SATURDAY SUPERCADE

Five segments made up this series of video game–inspired cartoons which ran for two seasons on CBS. The first season lineup featured: "Donkey Kong," the adventures of a gorilla who escapes from the circus and keeps on the run to avoid captivity; "Donkey Kong Jr.," the misadventures of Donkey Kong Jr. and his friend, Bones, in search of Kong's missing father; "Frogger," the story of a frog and his companions (Fanny Frog and Shelly the Turtle) as reporters for the *Swamp Gazette*; "Pitfall," the exploits of a treasure hunter, his niece and their cowardly pet who travel the world to unearth lost treasures; and "Q*bert," a teenager who battles the evil Coilee Snake and his accomplices (Viper, Ugh and Wrong Way) with the help of his girlfriend, Q*tee.

"Frogger" and "Pitfall Harry" aired only during the first season. For the second season, they were replaced by two new video game–derived segments: "Space Ace," a handsome,

*"Q*bert," one of the video game-inspired cartoons featured in CBS's "Saturday Supercade" series. © Ruby-Spears Enterprises Inc. and D. Gottlieb Company.*

gallant space hero who, with his lovely partner, Kimberly, protects the heavens from the evil Commander Borf, who plots to rule the universe; and "Kangaroo," the misadventures of three youngsters Joey, Katy and Sidney, who run into all sorts of problems at the local zoo, including the Monkey Biz Gang. *A Ruby–Spears Enterprises Production. Color. One hour. Premiered on CBS: September 17, 1983–August 31, 1985.*

Voices:
Donkey Kong: Soupy Sales, **Pauline:** Judy Strangis, **Mario:** Peter Cullen, **Donkey Kong Jr.: Donkey Kong Jr.:** Frank Welker, **Bones,** his friend: Bart Braverman, **Frogger: Frogger:** Bob Sarlatte, **Fanny:** B. J. Ward, **Shellshock:** Marvin Kaplan, **Tex:** Ted Field Sr., **Mac:** Alan Dinehart, **Pitfall: Pitfall Harry:** Bob Ridgely, **Rhonda:** Noelle North, **Quickclaw:** Ken Mars, **Q*bert: Q*bert:** Billy Bowels, **Q*tee/Q*val:** Robbie Lee, **Q*bertha/Q*Mom:** Julie Dees, **Q*bit:** Dick Beals, **Q*mungus/ Q*ball/Q*Dad:** Frank Welker, **Coilee Snake:** Frank Welker, **Viper:** Julie Dees, **Ugg:** Frank Welker, **Wrongway:** Frank Welker, **Sam Slick:** Frank Welker, **Space Ace: Space Ace:** Jim Piper, **Kimberly:** Nancy Cartwright, **Dexter:** Sparky Marcus, **Space Marshall Vaughn:** Peter Renaday, **Commander Borf:** Arthur Burghardt, **Kangaroo: Katy:** Mea Martineau, **Joey:** David Mendenhall, **Mr. Friendly:** Arthur Burghardt, **Sidney:** Marvin Kaplan, **Monkey Biz Gang:** Frank Welker, Pat Fraley

Episodes:
"Donkey Kong."
1983–1984 "Mississippi Madness,," "Gorilla Gangster," "Banana Bikers," "The Incredible Shrinking Ape," "Movie Mania," "Gorilla My Dreams," "Little Orphan Apey," "Circus Daze,"

"The Great Ape Escape," "Apey And The Snowbeast," "How Much Is That Gorilla In The Window," "Private Donkey Kong," and "Get Along, Little Apey."
"Donkey Kong Jr."
"Trucknapper Caper," "Sheep Rustle Hustle," "Rocky Mountain Monkey Business," "Magnificent 7–Year Olds," "The Ventriloquist Caper," "The Great Seal Steal," "The Jungle Boy Ploy," "Junior Meets Kid Dynamo," "Amazing Rollerskate Race," "A Christmas Story," "Gorilla Ghost," "The Teddy Bear Scare," and "Double Or Nothing."
"Frogger."
"The Ms Fortune Story," "Spaced Out Frogs," "The Who–Took–Toadwalker Story," "Hydrofoil & Go Seek," "The Great Scuba Scoop," "The Headline Hunters," "The Legs Croaker Story," "The Blackboard Bungle," "Good Knight, Frogger," "Fake Me Out At The Ballgame," "I Remember Mummy," "Here Today, Pawned Tomorrow" and "Hop–Along Frogger."
"Pitfall."
"Amazon Jungle Bungle," "Raiders Of The Lost Shark," "Tibetan Treasure Trouble," "Mass Menace Mess," "The Sabertooth Goof," "The Pyramid Panic" and "Pitfall's Panda Puzzle."
"Q*bert."
"Disc Derby Fiasco," "The Great Q–Tee Contest," "Q–Bowl Rigamarole," "Crazy Camp Creature," "Thanksgiving For The Memories" and "Dog Day Dilemma."
"Donkey Kong."
1984–1985 "Sir Donkey Kong," "The Pale Whale," "El Donkey Kong," "New Wave Ape," "Greenhouse Gorilla" and "Hairy Parent."
"Q*bert."
"Take Me Out To The Q–Game," "Noser P.I.," "Hook, Line And Mermaid," "Q–Historic Daze," "Q*Bert's Monster Mix–Up," "Game Show Woe," "The Wacky Q–Bot," "Q–Beat It," "Q–Urf's Up," "Little Green Noser," "Rebel Without A Q–Ause," "Looking For Miss Q–Right" and "The Goofy Ghostgetters."
"Space Ace" (one per show).
"Cute Groots," "Cosmic Camp Catastrophe," "Dangerous Decoy," "Moon Missile Madness," "Perilous Partners," "Frozen In Fear," "Age Ray Riot," "Wanted Dexter," "Phantom Shuttle," "Spoiled Sports," "Calamity Kimmie," "Three Ring Rampage" and "Infanto Fury."
"Kangaroo" (one per show).
"Trunkfull Of Trouble," "Zoo For Hire," "Bat's Incredible," "The White Squirrel Of Dover," "The Birthday Party," "Having A Ball," "The Tail Of The Cowardly Lion," "It's Carnival Time," "Lost And Found," "Joey And The Beanstalk," "Zoo's Who?," "The Egg And Us" and "The Runaway Panda."

SCOOBY AND SCRAPPY–DOO

With pals Fred, Shaggy, Daphne and Velma, the mystery–solving Great Dane, Scooby–Doo, stumbles upon solutions to new mysteries involving ghouls and scary monsters, aided by his brave little nephew, Scrappy–Doo. In 1980–1981, episodes repeated as part of "The Richie Rich/Scooby and Scrappy–Doo Show" (see entry for information), also on ABC. *A Hanna–Barbera Production. Color. Half–hour. Premiered on ABC: September 22, 1979–November 1, 1980.*

Voices:

Scooby–Doo: Don Messick, **Scrappy–Doo:** Lennie Weinrib, **Fred:** Frank Welker, **Shaggy:** Casey Kasem, **Daphne:** Heather Storm, **Velma:** Pat Stevens, Maria Frumkin (replaced Pat Stevens)

Episodes:

"The Scarab Lives!," "The Night Ghoul Of Wonderworld," "Strange Encounters Of A Scooby Kind," "The Neon Phantom Of The Roller Disco!," "Shiver And Shake, That Demon's A Snake," "The Scary Sky Skeleton," "The Demon Of The Dugout," "The Hairy Scare Of The Devil Bear," "Twenty Thousand Screams Under The Sea," "I Left My Neck In San Francisco," "When You Wish Upon A Star Creature," "The Ghoul, The Bat And The Ugly," "Rocky Mountain Yiii!," "The Sorcerer's A Menace," "Lock The Door, It's A Minotaur" and "The Ransom Of Scooby Chief."

THE SCOOBY AND SCRAPPY–DOO/PUPPY HOUR

Scooby–Doo, the lovable canine afraid of his own shadow, and his fearless little nephew, Scrappy–Doo, were cast in new comic misadventures in this hour–long series for Saturday morning which featured as its second half "The Puppy's New Adventures," the warm–hearted tale of Petey the Puppy and his human family who was first introduced in a series of "ABC Weekend Specials." The program was co–produced by Hanna–Barbera Productions ("Scooby and Scrappy–Doo") and Ruby–Spears Enterprises ("Puppy's Further Adventures").

In January, 1983, the "Scooby and Scrappy–Doo" cartoons were replaced by reruns of previously run network episodes of Scooby–Doo from various programs starring the popular canine. As a result, the program was retitled," The Scooby–Doo/Puppy Hour." *A Hanna–Barbera Production. Color. One hour. Premiered on ABC: September 25, 1982–January 1, 1983. Rebroadcast on ABC: January 8, 1983–September 3, 1983.*

Voices:

Scooby–Doo: Don Messick, **Scrappy–Doo:** Lennie Weinrib, **Fred:** Frank Welker, **Shaggy:** Casey Kasem, **Daphne:** Heather North, **Velma:** Pat Stevens, **Petey the Pup:** Billy Jacoby, **Dolly:** Nancy McKeon, **Duke/Dash:** Michael Bell, **Tommy:** Tony O'Dell, **Lucky:** Peter Cullen

Episodes:

"Scooby and Scrappy–Doo" (three per show).
"The Maltese Mackerel," "Dumb Waiter Caper," "Yabba's Rustle Hustle," "Catfish Burglar Caper," "The Movie Monster Menace," "Mine Your Own Business," "Super Teen Shaggy," "Basketball Bumblers," "Tragic Magic," "Beauty Contest Caper," "Stakeout At the Takeout," "Runaway Scrappy," "Who's Scooby Doo," "Double Trouble Date," "Slippery Dan The Escape Man," "Cable Car Caper," "Muscle Trouble," "The Low–Down Showdown," "The Comic Book Caper," "The Misfortune Teller," "The Vild Vest Vampire," "A Gem Of A Case," "From Bad To Curse," "Tumbleweed Derby," "Disappearing Car Caper," "Scooby–Doo And Genie Poo," "Law And Disorder," "Close Encounters Of The Worst Kind," "Captain Canine Caper," "Alien Schmalien," "The Incredible Cat Lady Capers," "Go East, Young Pardner," "One Million Years Before Lunch," "Where's The Werewolf," "Up A Crazy River," "The Hoedown Showdown," "Show Job Too Small" and "Bride And Gloom."

"The Puppy's New Adventures" (one per show).
"Treasure Of The Ancient Ruins," "The Puppy's Dangerous Mission," "The American Puppy In Paris," "The Puppy And The Pirates," "The Mystery Of The Wailing Cat," "The Puppy's Australian Adventure," "The Puppy And The Reluctant Bull," "The Puppy's Hong Kong Adventure," "Honolulu Puppy," "The Puppy's Great Escape," "The Puppy's Great Race," "The Puppy's Amazon Adventure" and "Petey And The 101 Seals."

THE SCOOBY–DOO/DYNOMUTT HOUR

Canine detective Scooby–Doo and the superhero dog wonder, Dynomutt, share the spotlight in this one–hour show as they both star in their own half–hour cartoon adventures. The bionic Dynomutt, whose voice recalls Art Carney's, teams up with big–city crime–fighter, the Blue Falcon, to uphold law and order, while Scooby–Doo and the gang (Freddy, Daphne, Shaggy and Velma) undertake cases involving mystery and intrigue which only they can crack. Joining Scooby and his friends was a new character: Scooby–Dum, Scooby–Doo's country cousin, whose voice and actions were reminiscent of Edgar Bergen's Mortimer Snerd. *A Hanna–Barbera Production. Color. One hour. Premiered on ABC: September 11, 1976–November 1976; December 1976–September 3, 1977 (as "The Scooby–Doo/Dynomutt Show").*

Voices:

Scooby–Doo: Don Messick, **Freddy:** Frank Welker, **Daphne:** Heather North, **Shaggy:** Casey Kasem, **Velma:** Nichole Jaffe, **Scooby–Dum:** Daws Butler, **Dynomutt, Dog Wonder:** Frank Welker, **The Blue Falcon:** Gary Owens

Episodes:

"Scooby–Doo" (one per show).
"A Bum Steer For Scooby," "The Gruesome Game Of The Gator Ghoul," "The Spirits of '76," "The Ghost Of The Bad Humor Man," "The No–Face Zombie Chase Case," "Scooby Doo, Where's The Crew?," "The Fiesta Host Is An Aztec Ghost," "Watt A Shocking Ghost," "There's A Demon Shark In The Foggy Dark," "Scared Alot In Camelot," "The Headless Horseman Of Halloween," "The Harum Scarum Sanitarium," "High Rise Hair Raiser," "A Frightened Hound Meets Demons Underground," "The Ghost That Sacked The Quarterback," "Mamba Wamba And The Voodoo Hoodoo," "The Curse Of Viking Lake," "Vampires, Bats and Scaredy–Cats," "Hang In There, Scooby Doo," "The Creepy Heap From The Deep," "The Chiller Diller Movie Thriller," "The Spooky Case Of The Grand Prix Race," "The Ozark Witch Switch" and "The Creepy Cruise."

"Dynomutt" (one per show).
"The Great Brain . . . Train Robbery," "The Day And Night Crawler," "The Harbor Robber," "Everybody Hyde," "What

Now, Lowbrow?," "Sinister Symphony," "Don't Bug Super-mugg," "Factory Recall," "The Queen Hornet," "The Wizard Of Ooze," "Tin Kong," "The Awful Ordeal With The Head Of Steel," "The Blue Falcon Versus The Red Vulture," "The Injustice League Of America," "The Lighter Than Air Raid" and "The Prophet Profits."

SCOOBY–DOO, WHERE ARE YOU?

A cowardly Great Dane, Scooby–Doo, and his four teenage partners—Freddy, Daphne, Velma and Shaggy—tour the country in their "Mystery Machine" mobile van in search of the supernatural. *A Hanna–Barbera Production. Color. Half-hour. Premiered on CBS: September 13, 1969–September 2, 1972; September 8, 1978–November 4, 1978 (new episodes). Rebroadcast on ABC: September 1974–August 1975; September, 1975–August 1976; October 6, 1984–October 13, 1984.*

Voices:

Scooby–Doo: Don Messick, **Freddy:** Frank Welker, **Daphne:** Heather North, **Shaggy:** Casey Kasem, **Velma:** Nichole Jaffe

Additional Voices:

John Stephenson, Henry Corden, Ann Jillian, Joan Gerber, Ted Knight, Olan Soule, Vincent Van Patten, Cindy Putnam, Pat Harrington, Frances Halop, Jim McGeorge, Mike Road

Episodes:

1969–1970 "What A Night For A Knight," "Hassle In The Castle," "A Clue For Scooby Doo," "Mine Your Own Business," "Decoy For A Dognapper," "What The Hex Going On?," "Never Ape An Ape Man," "Foul Play In Funland," "The Backstage Rage," "Bedlam In The Big Top," "A Gaggle Of Galloping Ghosts," "Scooby–Doo And A Mummy, Too," "Which Witch Is Which?," "Spooky Space Kook," "Go Away Ghost Ship," "A Night Of Fright Is No Delight" and "That's Snow Ghost."

1970–1971 (new shows combined with reruns) "Nowhere To Hyde," "Mystery Mask Mix–Up," "Jeepers It's The Cree-per," "Scooby's Night With A Frozen Fright," "Haunted House Hang–Up," "A Tiki Scare Is No Fare," "Who's Afraid Of The Big Bad Werewolf" and "Don't Fool With A Phantom."

1978–1979 "Watch Out! The Willawaw!," "A Creepy Tangle In The Bermuda Triangle," "A Scary Night With A Snow Beast Fright," "To Switch A Witch," "The Tar Monster," "A Highland Fling With A Monstrous Thing," "The Creepy Case Of Old Iron Face," "Jeeper's It's the Jaguaro," "Make A Beeline Away From That Feline," "The Creepy Creature Of Vulture's Claw," "The Diabolical Disc Demon," "Scooby's Chinese Fortune Kooky Caper," "A Menace In Venice," "Don't Go Near The Fortress Of Fear," "The Warlock Of Wimbledon" and "The Beast Is Awake In Bottomless Lake."

SCOOBY'S ALL–STAR LAFF–A–LYMPICS

More than 45 of Hanna–Barbera's favorite cartoon characters participate in track and field competition, spoofing ABC's "Wide World of Sports," in this two–hour Saturday morning series, the first in network history. Assigned to different teams—the Really Rottens, the Scooby Doobys and the Yogi Ya-hooeys—the winner of each event earns the prestigious Laff–A–Lympics Gold Medallion. Snagglepuss and Mildew Wolf serve as the play–by–play announcers.

Other program segments were: "Captain Caveman and the Teen Angels," "Dynomutt, Dog Wonder" (featured in four new two–part episodes under the title of "The Blue Falcon and Dynomutt," plus reruns of old episodes) and "Scooby Doo" (12 episodes repeated from "Scooby–Doo, Where Are You?").

Following the 1977–1978 season, the program returned for a second season under the title of "Scooby's All–Stars." The series aired for three seasons in all, concluding its network run as "Scooby's Laff–A–Lympics," a shortened one–hour version comprised of repeat episodes. *A Hanna Barbera Production. Color. Two hours. Premiered on ABC: September 10, 1977–September 2, 1978; September 9, 1978–September 8, 1979 (as "Scooby's All–Stars"); June 12, 1980–November 1, 1980 (as "Scooby's Laff–A–Lympics").*

Voices:

Announcers: Snagglepuss: Daws Butler, **Mildew Wolf:** John Stephenson, **The Yogi Yahooeys: Yogi Bear/Huckleberry Hound:** Daws Butler, **Hokey Wolf/Snooper/Blabber:** Daws Butler, **Wally Gator/Quick Draw McGraw:** Daws Butler, **Augie Doggie/Dixie/Jinks:** Daws Butler, **Doggie Daddy:** John Stephenson, **Boo Boo/Pixie:** Don Messick, **Grape Ape:** Bob Holt, **Yakky Doodle:** Frank Welker, **Cindy Bear:** Julie Bennett, **The Scooby–Doobys: Scooby–Doo:** Don Messick, **Scooby–Dum:** Daws Butler, **Shaggy:** Casey Kasem, **Hong Kong Phooey:** Scatman Crothers, **Jeannie:** Julie McWhirter, **Babu:** Joe Besser, **Dynomutt/Tinker:** Frank Welker, **Blue Falcon:** Gary Owens, **Captain Caveman/Speed Buggy:** Mel Blanc, **Brenda Chance:** Marilyn Schreffler, **Dee Dee Sykes:** Vernee Watson, **Taffy Dare:** Laurel Page, **The Really Rottens: Mumbly/Dastardly Dalton:** Don Messick, **Daisy May-hem:** Marilyn Schreffler, **Sooey Pig/Magic Rabbit:** Frank Welker, **Dread Baron/The Great Fondoo:** John Stephenson, **Orful Octopus/Dinky Dalton:** Bob Holt, **Dirty Dalton:** Daws Butler, **Mrs. Creepley:** Laurel Page, **Mr. Creepley:** Don Messick

Episodes:

Laff–A–Lympics" (two per show).

1977–1978 "Swiss Alps," "Tokyo," "Florida," "China," "Aca-pulco," "England," "Sahara," "Scotland," "France," "Australia," "Athens," "Ozarks," "Italy," "Kittyhawk, North Carolina," "Egypt," "Sherwood Forest," "Spain," "Himalayas," "India," "Israel," "Africa," "San Francisco," "Grand Canyon," "Ireland," "Ha-waii," "Norway," "North Pole," "Tahiti," "Arizona," "Holland," "Quebec" and "Baghdad."

1978–1979 (new episodes combined with reruns) "Russia," "Caribbean," "New York," "Turkey," "South America," "Tran-sylvania," "French Riviera," "New Zealand," "New Orleans," "Atlantis," "Morocco," "Washington, D. C.," "Canada," "Po-land," "Siam" and "The Moon."

"The Blue Falcon and Dynomutt" (one per show).

"The Glob—Part 1," "The Glob—Part 2," "Madame No Face—

Model sheet for Hanna Barbera's cowardly canine, Scooby–Doo, star of several top–rated shows for Saturday morning. © Hanna–Barbera Productions Inc.

Part 1," "Madame No Face—Part 2," "Beastwoman—Part 1," "Beastwoman—Part 2," "Shadowman—Part 1" and "Shadowman—Part 2."

"Captain Caveman and the Teen Angels" (one per show).

1977–1978 "The Kooky Case Of The Cryptic Keys," "The Mixed Up Mystery Of Deadman's Reef," "What A Flight For A Fight," "The Creepy Case Of The Creaky Charter Boat," "Big Scare In The Big Top," "Double Dribble Riddle," "The Crazy Case Of The Tell–Tale Tape," "The Creepy Claw Caper," "Cavey And The Kabula Clue," "Cavey And The Weirdo Wolfman," "The Disappearing Elephant Mystery," "The Fur Freight Fright," "Ride 'Em Caveman," "The Strange Case Of The Creature From Space," "The Mystery Mansion Mix–Up" and "Playing Footsie With Big Foot."

1978–1979 (new episodes combined with reruns) "Disco Cavey," "Muscle–Bound Cavey," "Cavey's Crazy Car Caper," "Cavey's Mexicali 500," "Wild West Cavey," "Cavey's Winter Carnival Caper," "Cavey's Fashion Fiasco" and "Cavey's Missing Missile Mystery."

"Scooby–Doo." (one per show; no record of titles that aired)

SCOOBY'S MYSTERY FUNHOUSE

Canine detective Scooby-Doo and pals Shaggy and Scrappy-Doo starred in this half-hour collection of classic ghostbusting tales and mysteries originally broadcast on "The Scooby And Scrappy-Doo/Puppy Hour," "The New Scooby and Scrappy-Doo Show," "The Scary Scooby Funnies" and others. *A Hanna-Barbera Production. Color. Half-hour. Premiered on ABC: September 7, 1985–February 22, 1986.*

Voices:

Scooby–Doo: Don Messick, **Scrappy–Doo:** Lennie Weinrib, **Shaggy:** Casey Kasem

Episodes:

(two per show)

"Scoobygeist," "From Bad To Curse," "The Hound Of Scoobyvilles," "Where's The Werewolf?," "Scooby The Barbarian," "Close Encounters Of The Worst Kind," "Who's Minding The Monster," "Captain Canine Cape," "Scooby Of The Jungle,"

"The Incredible Cat Lady," "Scoobsie," "Scooby-Doo And Genie Poo," "No Thanks, Masked Manx," "Basketball Bumblers," "Wizards And Warlocks," "Super Teen Shaggy," "Scooby A La Mode," "The Maltese Mackeral," "Scooby's Gold Medal Gambit," "Hoedown Showdown," "Mission Un-Doo-Able," "Who's Scooby Doo?," "Scoo-Be Or Not Scoo-Be," "Hand Of Horror," "Double Trouble Date," "Scooby Peep-Hole Pandemonium," "The Comic Book Caper," "The 'Dooby Dooby Doo' Ado," "Gem Of A Case," "South Pole Vault," and "Beauty Contest Caper."

SCREEN GEMS CARTOONS

More than 350 black–and–white cartoons produced by Columbia Pictures in the 1930s and 1940s—"Krazy Kat" "Scrappy" and "Phantasies"—were offered in this syndicated package, which also included three previously exhibited Van Beuren series ("Aesop's Fables, "Cubby Bear" and "Tom and Jerry"). Screen Gems, Columbia's television division, purchased the rights to these films in 1956 from Unity Pictures who had distributed the cartoons to television since 1947. *A Screen Gems/Columbia Pictures Television Production. Black–and–white. Half–hour. Premiered: 1956. Syndicated.*

SEABERT

Together with human friends Tommy and Aura, Seabert, a lovable seal, travels the globe protecting his fellow animals. From their home base in a Greenland Eskimo village, the three venture out in snowmobiles that convert into amphibious vehicles to travel across land and sea. *A Sepp International Production. Color. Half–hour. Premiered on HBO: April 5, 1987.*

Voices:
Diana Ellington, Melissa Freeman, Ron Knight, Bruce Robertson, Morgan Upton

Episodes:
"A New Friendship," "The Trio," "Radio Message," "The Professor's Whistle," "The Kidnapping," "Whale Mission," "Poached Turtle Eggs," "Twenty Feet Under Ice," "The Fur Factory," "The Ivory Hunters," "The Hunters' Blues," "The Saboteur," "Leopard Smugglers," "Petnappers In Paris," "Alpine Adventure," "Rock 'N Rescue," "Iceberg Ahead," "The Unicorn," "The Sea Otters," "The Yeti," "Photo Set–Up," "Panda–Monium," "The Land Of The Mayas," "Monkey Business," "Bungle In The Jungle" and "Deadly Plans."

SEALAB 2020

Earth, in A.D. 2020. Dr. Paul Williams leads an underwater expedition to study living conditions while searching for scientific solutions in a domed experimental city operated by 250 inhabitants. Williams is unexpectedly joined on his expedition by Captain Mike Murphy, his niece and nephew, Sallie and Bobby, and radio dispatcher Sparks, who were rescued by three Sealab aquanauts (Hal, Ed and Gail) when their ship ran into trouble. *A Hanna–Barbera Production.*

Color. Half–hour. Premiered on NBC: September 9, 1972–September 1, 1973.

Voices:
Dr. Paul Williams: Ross Martin, **Captain Mike Murphy:** John Stephenson, **Bobby Murphy:** Josh Albee, **Sallie Murphy:** Pamelyn Ferdin, **Sparks:** Bill Callaway, **Hal:** Jerry Dexter, **Gail:** Ann Jillian, **Ed:** Ron Pinckard, **Mrs. Thomas:** Olga James, **Jamie:** Gary Shapiro

Episodes:
"Deep Throat," "Green Fever," "The Singing Whale," "Lost," "The Shark Lover," "Backfire," "The Basking Shark," "Where Dangers Are Many," "The Deepest Dive," "The Challenge," "Collision Of The Aquarius," "The Arctic Story" and "The Capture."

THE SECRET LIVES OF WALDO KITTY

Based on James Thurber's *Walter Mitty* stories, the series stars cowardly Waldo, a day–dreaming cat who imagines himself as the roughriding savior Lone Kitty, the superhero Cat Man and others, fighting swaggering bulldog Tyrone for the honor of his pussycat girlfriend, Felicia. *A Filmation Production. Color. Half–hour. Premiered on NBC: September 6, 1975–September 4, 1976.*

Voices:
Waldo: Howard Morris, **Felicia:** Jane Webb, **Tyrone:** Allan Melvin, **Wetzel/Lone Hench Dog:** Howard Morris, **Pronto/Sparrow:** Jane Webb, **Mr Crock/Ping/Brennan Hench Dog:** Allan Melvin

Episodes:
"Cat Man," "Catzan Of The Apes," "The Lone Kitty," "Robin Cat," "Cat Trek," "Cat Men Meets The Poochquin," "Catzan Or Not Catzan," "The Lone Kitty Rides Again," "Sheriff Or Sherwood," "Cat Man Meets The Puzzler," "Dr. Livingstone, I Perfume?," "Pingo Pongo" and "Chaw The Bullet."

THE SECRET SQUIRREL SHOW

Packaged for two seasons as part of the hour–long "The Atom Ant/Secret Squirrel Show," this buck–toothed private investigator and the supporting elements from his half of the original network series—"Squiddly Diddly" and "Winsome Witch"—were separated into their half–hour time slot in 1967, repeating episodes from the 1965–1966 series which premiered on the same network. The program concluded its network run the way it began, again paired with Atom Ant and company as "The Atom Ant/Secret Squirrel Show" in September, 1967. (See entry for voices and episodes.) *A Hanna–Barbera Production. Color. Half–hour. Premiered on NBC: January 1967–September 2, 1967*

SECTAURS

On a distant planet where inhabitants have taken on the characteristics of insects, a group of telepathically bonded warriors join with their insect companions in the ultimate battle of survival. *A Ruby–Spears Enterprises Production. Color. Half–hour. Premiered: September, 1985. Syndicated.*

Voices:
Dargon/Dragonflyer: Dan Gilvezan, **Pinsor/Battle Beetle:** Peter Renaday, **Mantor/Skito/Toxid:** Peter Cullen, **Zak/Bitaur:** Laurie Faso, **Spidrax/Spiderflyer:** Arthur Burghardt, **Skulk/Trancula/Raplor:** Frank Welker, **Waspax/Wingid:** Neil Ross

Episodes:
"Spidrax Attacks," "Slave City," "Valley Of The Stones," "Trapped In The Acid Desert" and "Battle For The Hyve."

SHAZZAN!

Twins Chuck and Nancy find a broken ancient ring inscribed with the word "Shazzan!" When the two ends of the ring are joined, the youngsters are transported back to the age of the Arabian Nights. The leader of the group, Shazzan, a 60–foot genie, guards the children by working his wizardry on evildoers. *A Hanna–Barbera Production. Color. Half–hour. Premiered on CBS: September 9, 1967–September 6, 1969.*

Voices:
Shazzan: Barney Phillips, **Nancy:** Janet Waldo, **Chuck:** Jerry Dexter, **Kaboobie,** the flying camel: Don Messick

Episodes:
(two per show) "The Living Island," "Valley Of The Giants," "The Underground World," "Demon In The Bottle," "The Black Sultan," "City Of The Tombs," "The Master Wizard Of Mizwa," "Master Of The Thieves," "City Of Brass," "The Flaming Ruby," "The Evil Jester of Masira," "Ring Of Samarra," "Demon In The Bottle Returns," "The Young Rajah Of Kamura," "The Forest Of Fear," "The Sky Pirates Of Basheena," "The Idol Of Turaba," "Lord Of Shadows," "Keys Of The Zodiac," "The Three Horsemen Of Mandragora," "The Diamond Of El Raphir," "The Impossible Quest Of Nazir," "The Land Of Neverwas," "The Circus Of Zahran," "Nastrina Of The Flames," "A Thousand And One Tricks," "Raschild, The Apprentice Sorcerer," "Baharuum, The Befuddled," "A Pound Of Evil Magic," "The Maze Of Mercuraad," "Kahn Of The North Wind," "The Mirage Maker," "The Magical Kingdom Of Centuria," "Quest For The Magic Lamp" and "Mysterio, The Mini-Magi."

SHE–RA: PRINCESS OF POWER

He–Man's twin sister, Adora, who with the power of her magic swords transforms herself into She–Ra, defender of the Crystal Castle, battles the evil forces of Hordak in this companion series to "He–Man: Master of the Universe." *A Filmation Studios Production. Color. Half–hour. Premiered: 1985. Syndicated.*

Voices:
Princess Adora/She–Ra: Melendy Britt, **Hordak:** George DiCenzo

THE SHIRT TALES

A menagerie of lovable little animals, wearing message–bearing T–shirts, use a gigantic oak tree as their base of operation to help others in need around the world after receiving holographic messages of distress on their sophisticated wristwatch communicators. Their sole means of transportation is the S.T.S.S.T. (The Shirt Tales' Super–Sonic Transporter), which can drive, dive or burrow and is loaded with terrific gadgets. For the series' second season, the show featured a new cast member: Kip Kangaroo, a trusting, loving character with powerful hindquarters. The program was based on the popular Hallmark Cards greeting card characters. *A Hanna–Barbera Production. Color. Half–hour. Premiered on NBC: September 18, 1982–September 8, 1984.*

Voices:
TYG Tiger: Steve Schatzberg, **Pammy Panda:** Pat Parris, **Digger Mole:** Bob Ogle, **Bogey Orangutan:** Fred Travalena, **Rick Raccoon:** Ronnie Schell, **Kip Kangaroo:** Nancy Cartwright, **Mr. Dinkel:** Herb Vigram

Episodes:
(two per show)
1982–1983 "The Case Of The Golden Armor," "Crumling's Circus Caper," "Shirt Napped," "Game Masters," "Elephant On The Loose," "Big Foot Incident," "Horsin' Around," "The Humbolt Ghost," "Mission Mutt," "Vacation For Dinkel," "Digger Runs Away," "Wingman," "Figby, The Spoiled Cat," "The Commissioner Is Missing," "The Terrible Termites," "Raiders Of The Lost Shark," "Moving Time," "Back To Nature," "Save The Park," "Pam–Dora's Box," "Hapless Hound," "The Nearsighted Bear," "The Magical Musical Caper," "The Very Buried Treasure," "Dinkel's Ark" and "The Duke Of Dinkel."
1983–1984 "Bogey Goes Ape," "Diggers Three Wishes," "The Rain, The Park, And The Robot," "Digger's Double," "Kip's Dragon," "Taj Mahal Tyg," "Double Exposure," "The Outer Space Connection," "Brass Bogey," "The Forbidden Island," "T. J.'s Visit," "Pleasure Valley," "Saturday Night Shirt Tales," "Kip's To Caper," "Dinkel's Buddy," "The Big Setup," "The Ghost Out West," "Dinkel's Gift," "Mayhem On The Orient Express" and "The Cuckoo Count Caper."

SILVERHAWKS

Music–driven animated series featuring metalic–looking characters—known as The Silverhawks—led by Commander Stargazer, who fight extraterrestrial gangsters and villains, the most prominent being Mon Star and his Mob. Series was a follow–up to the Rankin–Bass first–run cartoon series, "ThunderCats." *A Rankin–Bass Production. Color. Half–hour. Syndicated: September, 1986.*

Voices:
Larry Kenney, Robert McFadden, Earl Hammond, Maggie Jakobson, Peter Newman, Adolph Newman, Adolph Caesar, Doug Preis

Episodes:
"The Origin Story," "Journey To Limbo," "The Planet Eater," "Save The Sun," "Stop Timestopper," "Darkbird," "The Back-

room," "The Threat Of Drift," "Sky–Shadow," "Magnetic Attraction," "Gold Shield," "Zero The Memory Thief," "The Milk Run," "The Hardware Trap " (Part 1), "The Hardware Trap" (Part 2), "Race Against Time," "Operation Big Freeze," "The Ghost Ship," "The Great Galaxy Race," "Fantascreen," "Hotwing Hits Limbo," "The Bounty Hunter," "Zeek's Fumble," "The Fighting Hawks," "The Renegade Hero," "One On One," "No More Mr. Nice Guy," "Music Of The Spheres," "Limbo Gold Rush," "Countdown To Zero," "The Amber Amplifier," "The Saviour Stone," "Smiley," "Gotbucks," "Melodia's Siren Song," "Tally–Hawk Returns," "Undercover," "Eye Of Infinity," "A Piece Of The Action," "Flashback," "Super Birds," "The Blue Door," "The Star Of Bedlama," "The Illusionist," "The Bounty Hunter Returns," "The Chase," "Switch," "Junkyard Dog," "Window In Time," "Gangwar" (Part 1), "Gangwar" (Part 2), "Sneak Attack (Part 1), "Sneak Attack" (Part 2), "Moon*Star," "The Diamond Stick–Pin," "Burnout," "Battle Cruiser," "Small World," "Match–Up," "Stargazer's Refit," "The Invisible Destroyer," "The Harder They Fall," "Uncle Rattler," "Zeek's Power" and "Airshow."

THE SIMPSONS

Cartoonist Matt Groenig ("Life in Hell") created this outlandish series based on the adventures of an exuberantly blue–collar family who are just about everything that most television families are not—crude, loud, obnoxious and sloppily dressed characters, with bizarre hairdos and severe overbites.

Setting examples for the three children (Bart, Lisa and Maggie) are Marge, the relentlessly loving mother who occasionally works as a roller–skating carhop, and Homer, the harried father who insists on being grouchy, due in part to his job at a nuclear power plant. (His passions are eating Pork Rinds Lite and bowling.) The characters were originally featured in brief segments on Fox Network's "The Tracy Ullman Show" before the network spotlighted them in their own weekly series. *A Klasky/Csupo Production. Color. Half–hour. Premiered on Fox Network: January 14, 1990.*

Voices:

Homer J. Simpson: Dan Castellaneta, **Marge Simpson:** Julie Kavner, **Bart Simpson:** Nancy Cartwright, **Lisa Simpson:** Yeardley Smith, **Maggie Simpson:** (no voice)

Additional Voices:

Harry Shearer, Albert Brooks, June Foray, Kelsey Grammar, Penny Marshall, Joanne Harris, Marsha Wallace, Maggie Rosewell, Hank Azaria, Pamela Hayden, Tress MacNeille and Chris Collins.

Episodes:

"Some Enchanted Evening," "Bart The Genius," "Homer's Odyssey," "There's No Disgrace Like Home," "Bart The General," "Moaning Lisa," "The Telltale Head," "Simpson's Roasting On An Open Fire," "Call Off The Simpsons," "Homer's Night Out," "Jacques To Be Wild," "Krusty Gets Busted" and "The Crepes of Wrath."

SINBAD JR., THE SAILOR

Originally called "The Adventures of Sinbad Jr.," the cartoons star the son of the famed sea adventurer, Sinbad, who becomes

Cartoonist Matt Groenig's outlandish blue–collar family from the highly rated Fox Network series, "The Simpsons." © Fox Network

superhuman whenever he draws power from a magic belt. He is assisted in his high–sea adventures by his first mate, Salty, the parrot. *A Hanna–Barbera Production. Sinbad is a trademark of American International Pictures. Color. Half–hour. Premiered: Fall, 1965. Syndicated.*

Voices

Sinbad: Tim Matthieson, **Salty:** Mel Blanc

Episodes:

(four per show) "Rok Around The Roc," "Dragon Drubbers," "Ronstermon," "Caveman Daze," "Circus Hi–Jinks," "Captain Sly," "Look Out, Lookout," "Woodchopper Stopper," "Typical Bad Night," "Arabian Knights," "Size–Mo–Graph Laugh," "Moon Madness," "Big Belt Bungle," "Turnabout Is Foul Play," "Jack And The Giant," "Kooky–Spooky," "Jekyll And Hyde," "Elephant On Ice," "The Gold Must Go Through," "Big Deal Seal," "Belted About," "Birdnapper," "Tiny Tenni–Putians," "Belt, Buckle And Boom," "Big Bully Blubbo Behaves," "Sinbad And The Moon Rocket," "The Menace Of Venice," "Bat Brain," "Sad Gladiator," "Invisible Villain," "About Ben Blubbo," "Hypnotized Guys," "Sizemodoodle Poodle," "Faces From Space," "Mad Mad Movies," "The Truth Hurts," "Bird God," "Evil Wizard," "My Fair Mermaid," "Knight Fright," "Boat Race Ace," "Sinbad And The Mighty Magnet," "Sea–Going Penguin," "Frozen Fracas," "Tin Can Man," "Vulture Culture," "Wild Wax Works," "Trap Happy Trapper," "Wicked Whirlpool," "Whale Of A Tale," "Sinbad And The Counterfeiters," "Irish Stew," "Sea Horse Laughs," "Kooky Spooks," "Dodo A Go–Go," "Sunken Treasure," "Hot Rod Salty," "Gold Mine Muddle," "Paleface Race," "Surfboard Bully," "Magic Belt Factory," "Ride 'Em Sinbad," "Sinbad And the Master Weapon," "Rainmaker Fakers," "Treasure Of The Pyramids," "Fly By Knight," "Railroad Ruckus," "Teahouse Louse," "Killer Diller," "Super–Duper Duplicator," "The Good Deed Steed," "Blubbo Goes Ape," "Blubbo's Goose Goof," "The Monster Mosquito," "Hello Dolphin," "Sea Serpent Secret," "Wacky Walrus," "Cry Sheep," "Cookie Caper," "Daze Of Old," "Way Out Mahout" and "Gaucho Blubbo."

THE SKATEBIRDS

Live–action stars Scooter the Penguin, Satchel the Pelican, Knock Knock the Woodpecker and Scat Cat host this series comprised of wraparounds, comedy skits and animated cartoons, such as "Woofer and Wimper, Dog Detectives" (formerly of "The Club Club"); "The Robonic Stooges," featuring Moe, Larry and Curly as bionic crimefighters; "Wonder Wheels," which pairs two high school journalists and a heroic motorcycle in remarkable adventures; and the film serial, "Mystery Island." The show's poor ratings caused it to be canceled after only four months on the air, and it was replaced by "Speed Buggy" and "The Robonic Stooges," which was retitled "The Three Robonic Stooges." (The cartoon trio received better ratings in "The Skatebirds" than any other segment.) "The Skatebirds" returned after a one–year absence in September, 1979, on Sunday mornings where it completed its network run. *A Hanna–Barbera Production. Color Half–hour. Premiered on CBS: September 10, 1977–January 21, 1978. Rebroadcast on CBS: September 1979–August 1980; September, 1980–January 25, 1981.*

Voices:

Scooter: Don Messick, **Satchel:** Bob Holt, **Knock Knock:** Lennie Weinrib, **Scat Cat:** Scatman Crothers, **Woofer and Wimper: Larry:** David Joliffe, **D. D.:** Bob Hastings, **Pepper:** Patricia Smith, **Dotty:** Tara Talboy, **Woofer:** Paul Winchell, **Wimper:** Jim McGeorge, **Sheriff Bagley:** John Stephenson, **The Robonic Stooges: Moe:** Paul Winchell, **Larry:** Joe Baker, **Curly:** Frank Welker, **Triple–Zero:** Ross Martin, **Wonder Wheels: Willie Sheeler:** Micky Dolenz, **Dooley Lawrence:** Susan Davis

Cast:

Mystery Island: Chuck Kelly: Stephen Parr, **Sue Corwin:** Lynn Marie Johnston, **Sandy Corwin:** Larry Volk, **Dr. Strange:** Michael Kermoyan, **P.A.U.P.S. (voice):** Frank Welker

Episodes:

"Woofer and Wimper, Dog Detectives" (one per show).
"The Paper Shaper Caper," "The Case Of The Lighthouse Mouse," "The Real Gone Gondola," "Who's To Blame For The Empty Frame," "The Weird Seaweed Creature Caper," "The Green Thumb," "The Disappearing Airport Caper," "The Walking House Caper," "The Solar Energy Caper," "The Vanishing Train Caper," "The Dissolving Statue Caper," "The Missing

Pig Caper," "One Of Our Elephants Is Missing," "The Amazing Heist," "The Pre–Historic Monster Caper" and "The Circus Caper."

"The Robonic Stooges" (one per show).

"Invasion Of The Incredible Giant Chickens," "Dimwits And Dinosaurs," "Fish And Drips," "Have Saucer Will Travel," "I Want My Mummy," "The Great Brain Drain," "Flea, Fi, Fo Fum," "Mother Goose On The Loose," "Curly Of The Apes," "Don't Fuel With A Fool," "The Eenie Meanie Genie," "On Your Knees, Hercules," "Rub–A–Dub–Dub," "Three Nuts In A Sub," "There's No Joy In An Evil Toy," "Three Little Pigheads," "The Silliest Show On Earth," "Bye, Bye, Blackbeard," "Mutiny On The Mountie," "Woo Woo Wolfman," "Schoolhouse Louse," "Burgle Gurgle," "Rip Van Wrinkle," "The Three Nutsketeers," "Pest World Ain't The Best World," "Super Kong," "The Three Stooges And The Seven Dwarfs," "Dr. Jekyll And Hide Curly," "Jerk In The Beanstalk," "Blooperman," "Star Flaws" and "Stooges, You're Fired . . . Or The Day The Mirth Stood Still."

"Wonder Wheels" (one per show).

"Wonder Wheels And The Country Fair," "Wonder Wheels And The Rustlers," "Wonder Wheels And The Skycraper," "Wonder Wheels And The Gold Train Robbery," "Wonder Wheels And The Snowmen," "Wonder Wheels And The Vanishing Prince," "Wonder Wheels And The Ghost Town," "Wonder Wheels And His Double Trouble," "Wonder Wheels And The U.F.O.," "Wonder Wheels And The Hermits Hoard," "Wonder Wheels And The Air Race," "Wonder Wheels And The Animals," "Wonder Wheels And The Idol's Eye," "Wonder Wheels And The Race Horse" and "Wonder Wheels And The Studio Steal."

"Mystery Island" (one per show).

"A Matter Of Gravity," "The Mind Blower," "Just Whistle For An Answer," "Sue's Courage," "Valley Of Fire," "Sentinels Of Time," "Who's Whom Here?," "Fate's Just A Dirty Trick," "Golden Birds Of Prey," "Visitors From Falconia," "The Duel," "Kingdom Of The Beasts," "Pops In A Box," "Island Of The Apes," "The Skull's The Clue" and "Home Run."

SKY COMMANDERS

The Sky Commanders, a motley crew of renegade soldiers, battle a world–class villain, the evil General Plague, who is bent on world destruction, in the late 21st century when technology comes face to face with a perilous new wilderness in this half–hour adventure series based on the popular toy line by Kenner Toys. The program aired on Sunday mornings as part of "The Funtastic World of Hanna–Barbera." *A Hanna–Barbera Production in association with Kenner Toys. Color. Half–hour. Premiered: July, 1987. Syndicated.*

Voices:

General Mike Summit, the Sky Commanders' leader: Bob Ridgely, **Cutter Kling,** crew member: William Windom, **R. J. Scott,** crew member: Darryl Hickman, **Books Baxter,** crew member: Richard Doyle, **Jim Stryker,** crew member: Dorian Harewood, **Spider Reilly,** crew member: Triston Rogers, **Kodiak Crane,** crew member: Soon–Teck Oh, **Red McCullough,** crew member: Lauren Tewes, **General Plague:**

Bernard Erhard, **Mordax:** Dick Gautier, **Raider Rath:** Paul Eiding, **Kreeg:** Charlie Adler, **Dr. Erica Slade:** B. J. Ward

Episodes:

"Assault On Raider Stronghold," "Back In The Fold," "Marooned," "Fresh Recruit," "One–On–One," "Divide And Conquer," "Rescuers Need Rescuing," "Terminal Temblor," "S.O.S.," "Turncoat," "Deep Freeze," "Firestorm" and "The Agony Of Defeat."

SKY HAWKS

A former air force colonel, widower Mike Wilson; his children, Steve and Caroline; his World War I flying ace father, Pappy; and Pappy's foster children, Baron Hughes and Little Cindy, head a daredevil air transport rescue service which saves troubled charter planes, helicopter pilots and test pilots. The show was sponsored by Mattel Toys. *A Pantomime Pictures/ Ken Snyder Production. Color. Half–hour. Premiered on ABC: September 6, 1969–September 4, 1971.*

Voices:

Captain Mike Wilson: Michael Rye, **Steve Wilson,** his son: Casey Kasem, **Caroline Wilson,** his daughter: Iris Rainer, **Pappy Wilson,** Mike's father: Dick Curtis, **Baron Hughes,** Pappy's foster child: Dick Curtis, **Cynthia "Mugs" Hughes:** Melinda Casey, **Maggie McNalley:** Joan Gerber, **Buck Devlin:** Bob Arbogast, **Joe Conway:** Casey Kasem

Episodes:

(two per show) "Night Flight," "Flight To Danger" (formerly "Big Wet Bird"), "Untamed Wildcat," "Silent Flight," "The Search," "Mission To Avalanche Wells," "Lobster Pirates," "The Message," "Hidden Valley," "The Snooper," "Bams Away," "Vacation With Danger," "The Radioactive Lake," "Circus Train," "The Sniffers," "Hot Wire On Storm Mountain," "Fire In The Tire," "Runaway Ride," "The Duster," "Animal Airline," "Discover Flying," "Pappy To The Rescue," "The Intruders," "Trouble Times Three," "Operation Slingshot," "Dog Fight," "Quick Frozen," "All At Sea," "Ground Zero," "Devlin's Dilemma," "Barnstormer's Circus," "The Peril Of The Prince," "Carrier Pigeon" and "Mercy Flight."

SLIMER! AND THE REAL GHOSTBUSTERS

Those ghostbusting idiots of the 1984 box–office sensation return for more mysteries and mishaps, joined by their tag-along mascot, Slimer. The first season format featured half-hour adventures of all the characters together. By the second season, the program split its time between two 15–minute episodes every week. *A DIC Enterprises Production in association with Columbia Pictures Television. Color. Half-hour. Premiered on ABC: September 10, 1988–September 1, 1990. Syndicated.*

Voices:

Slimer: Rafael: Charlie Adler, **Professor Dweeb:** Jeff Altman, **Mrs. Van Huego:** Fay De Witt, **Chilly Cooper:** Cree Summer Francks, **Linguini/Bud:** Danny Mann, **Rudy:** Jeff Marder,

Morris Grout: Alan Oppenheimer, **Slimer:** Frank Welker, **The Real Ghostbusters: Peter Venkman:** Dave Coulier, **Winston Zeddmore:** Edward L. Jones, **Egon Spengler:** Maurice LaMarche, **Janine Melnitz:** Kathi E. Soucie, **Ray Stantz:** Frank Welker, **Slimer:** Frank Welker, **Catherine:** April Hong, **Jason:** Katie Liegh, **Donald;** Danny McMurphy

Episodes:

"The Real Ghostbusters."
1988–1989 "Flip Side," "Poultrygeist," "The Joke's On Ray," "Standing Room Only," "Robo–Buster," "Short Stuff," "The Brooklyn Triangle," "Follow That Hearse," "Nothing To Sneeze At," "Doctor Dweeb, I Presume," "A Mouse In The House," "Quickslimer Messenger Service," "Crusin' For A Brusin,'" "Show Dog Showdown," "Slimer For Hire," "Special Delivery," "Go–Pher It," "Cash Or Slime," "Sticky Fingers," "Monkey See, Monkey Don't," "Pigeon–Cooped," "Slimer's Silly Symphony," "Space Case," "Room At The Top," "The Not–So–Great Outdoors," "Dr. Strangedog," "Class Clown," "Unidentified Sliming Object," "Movie Madness," "Little Green Sliming Hood," "Beach Blanket Bruiser," "Rainy Day Slimer," "Tea Without Sympathy," "Dog Days," "Up Close And Too Personal," "Slime And The Beanstalk," "Out With Grout," "The Dirty Half–Dozen," "Sweet Revenge," "Don't Tease The Sleaze" and "Scarface."
1989–1990 (one per show) "Something's Going Around," "Three Men And An Egon," "Elementary My Dear Winston," "If I Were A Witch Man," "Partners In Slime," "Future Tense," "Jailbusters," and "Live! From Al Capone's Tomb!"
"Slimer! And The Real Ghostbusters."
1989–1990 (one per show) "Trading Faces," "Transcendental Tourists," "Surely You Joust," "Kitty–Cornered," "Slimer's Curse," "Til Death Do Us Part," "It's About Time," "The Ransom of Greenspud," "Revenge Of The Ghostmaster," "Loose Screws," "Venk–Man!" and "Slimer Streak."

THE SMOKEY BEAR SHOW

The National Forest Fires Commission folk hero and spokes-bear stars in this animated series, as both a bear and cub, in which he protects the forests and its creatures from fire. Smokey, who made famous the phrase, "Only you can prevent forest fires," provides tips throughout each show on saving nature's wonderland. *A Rankin–Bass Production. Color. Half-hour. Premiered on ABC: September 13, 1969–September 12, 1971.*

Voices:

Smokey the Bear: Jackson Weaver

Additional Voices:

Billie Richards, Paul Soles, Carl Banas

Episodes:

"Founders Day Folly," "Old Club House," "One Born Every Second," "The Outlaws," "Silliest Show On Earth," "Mission Improbable," "Running Wild," "Spooksville," "Saga Of Gas Bag," "Hare Versus Cougar," "High Divin'," "Spit 'N' Polish," "Mighty Minerva," "Ice Frolics," "Hambone Heist," "Casanova Hare," "Great Kite Contest," "Bessie Paints The Town," "Thar

She Blows," "Hobo Jackal," "Sneaky Beaky," "Heroes Are Born," "Winter And Still Champ," "Freddy's Big Date," "Gone Fishin'," "An Apple A Day Keeps," "The Not So Merry Mailman," "An Ill Wind," "The Baby Sitters," "The Fire Fighter's Convention," "End Of The World," "Hizzoner The Admiral," "Invention Is The Mother Of Necessity," "Ancient Caleb Coyote," "Haunted Castle," "The Honorable Freddy Fume," "Gold Medal Grizzly," "Treasure Hunt," "Leave It To Grizzly," "Citizen Fume," "Invisible Benny," "The Battle Of Penny Echo River," "Grizzly Rides Again," "Build A Better Bridge," "Feudin', Fightin' and Fussin'," "Stick 'Em Up," "Goal Line Grizzly," "The Crabtrees Forever," "Hare Of A Thousand Faces," "Whar Fer Art Thou" and "The Celebrity."

THE SMURFS

Tucked away in the middle of the medieval woods is the charming, unique village of the Smurfs. It is populated by a hundred little blue people who are only three apples tall and live in mushrooms for houses. The happy Smurfs are led by Papa Smurf, a wise old magician, who guides the rest of his hyperactive crew—Brainy, Vanity, Hefty, Clumsy, Jokey, Greedy, Lazy, Handy, Grouchy, Harmony and Smurfette, the only female Smurf—through their unfriendly encounters with the inept wizard, Gargamel, and his hencat, Azrael, who want to rid the world of these blue busybodies.

French artist Pierre "Peyo" Culliford created these enchanting characters (called "Schtroumpf" in Flemish) in a Belgian comic strip in 1957, long before they appeared in this Emmy award–winning series. Following its premiere in 1981, the series' first ratings—a 9.5 with a 44 share in Nielsen figures—were the highest for any Saturday morning show in eight years and the highest for an NBC animated series since 1970.

In 1982, NBC responded to the enormous popularity of the Smurfs by expanding the show to an unprecedented 90 minutes. Two new human characters joined the fun that season in cartoon adventures of their own: Johan, a young squire in the swashbuckling Errol Flynn mold, and Peewit, his comical sidekick. 1982 was also the year "Smurfs" won its first Emmy as "Outstanding Children's Entertainment Series," the first of many awards for the series.

During the 1983–1984 season, the series welcomed the arrival of Baby Smurf, and by the 1985–1986 season the series featured a tiny foursome of Smurf kids: the Smurflings (Nat, Slouchy, Snappy and Sassette, the second female). The following season, two new characters, Grandpa Smurf (voiced by comedian Jonathan Winters) and Scruple, were introduced. In 1983, Hanna–Barbera, the series' producers, also broke new ground by introducing the first deaf character in an animated series: Laconia, the mute wood elf who used sign language to communicate.

The Smurfs' format returned to one hour in the 1983–1984 season. The program's locale did not change until the 1989–1990 season when the Smurfs left Smurf Village and their adventures involved them in events and key periods in world history, from the prehistoric days to ancient Egypt. *A Hanna–Barbera Production in association with Sepp International, S. A. Color. One–hour. One–hour and a half. Premiered on NBC: September 12, 1981–September 1, 1990.*

Voices:

Gargamel: Paul Winchell, **Azrael:** Don Messick, **Papa Smurf:** Don Messick, **Brainy Smurf:** Danny Goldman, **Clumsy/Painter Smurf:** Bill Callaway, **Hefty/Poet/Peewit Smurf:** Frank Welker, **Jokey Smurf:** June Foray, **Smurfette:** Lucille Bliss, **Vanity Smurf:** Alan Oppenheimer, **Greedy Smurf:** Hamilton Camp, **Lazy Smurf:** Michael Bell, **Handy Smurf:** Michael Bell, **Grouchy Smurf:** Michael Bell, **Harmony Smurf:** Hamilton Camp, **Johan:** Michael Bell, **King:** Bob Holt, **Dame Barbara:** Linda Gary, **Hominbus:** Alan Oppenheimer, **Tailor:** Kip King, **Sloppy:** Marshall Efron, **Farmer/Scaredy:** Alan Young, **Clockwork Smurf:** Frank Welker, **Baby Smurf:** Julie Dees, **Grandpa Smurf:** Jonathan Winters, **Scruple:** Brenda Vaccaro, **Nanny Smurf:** Susan Blu, **The Smurflings; Snappy:** Pat Musick, **Nat:** Charlie Adler, **Sassette:** Julie Dees, **Puppy:** Frank Welker, **Slouchy:** Noelle North, **Narrator:** Paul Kirby, Kris Stevens

Additional Voices:

Linda Gary, Walker Edmiston, Leon DeLyon, Peter Cullen, William Christopher, Russi Taylor, Phil Proctor, Avery Schreiber, B. J. Ward, John Stephenson, Phil Hartman, Michael Rye, Bob Ridgely, Rene Auberjonois, Marshall Efron, Tress MacNeille, Alexandra Stoddart, Bob Arbogast, Sidney Miller, Dick Erdman, Ronnie Schell, Marvin Kaplan, Les Tremayne, Susan Tolsky, Paul Riding, Clare Peck, Bernard Erhard, Henry Polic, Allan Melvin, Jennifer Darling, Vic Perrin, Peggy Walton Walker, Fred Travalena, Janet Waldo, Bob Holt, Selette Cole, Roger C. Carmel, Norma MacMillan, Peter Brooks, Henry Corden, Sorrell Booke, Ray Walston, Michael Lembeck, Edie McClurg, Lynnanne Zager, Susan Silo, Henry Gibson, Ruth Buzzi, Pat Fraley, Joey Camden, Bernard Behrens, Patti Parris, Mimi Seton, Richard Dysart, Lewis Arquette, Neilson Ross, Keene Curtis, Patti Deutsch, Dick Gautier, Joe Ruskin, Amanda McBroom, Barry Gordon, Cindy McGee, Bever–Leigh Banfield, Peggy Webber, Francine Witkin, Susan Blu, Gregg Berger, Zale Kessler, Victoria Carroll, Andre Stojka, Diane Pershing, Marilyn Schreffler, Dee Stratton, Marlene Aragon, Joy Grdnic, Ed Begley Jr., Kathi Soucie, Mary Jo Catlett, Allen Lurie, Joe Medalis, Tandy Cronyn, Ruta Lee, Patty Maloney, Justin Gocke, William Schallert, Jess Doucettte, Aron Kincaid, Jerry Houser, John Ingle, Will Ryan

Episodes:

1981–1982 (two 12–minute episodes per show) "Vanity Fare," "King Smurf," "Jokey's Medicine," "The Smurf's Apprentice," "Sorcerer Smurf," "The Magical Meanie," "Smurf–Colored Glasses," "Dreamy's Nightmare," "Fuzzle Trouble," "The Hundredth Smurf," "All That Glitters Isn't Smurf," "Smurphony In C," "The Magic Egg," "Paradise Smurfed," "Supersmurf," "The Baby Smurf," "The Fake Smurf," "The Magnifying Mixture," "Foul Weather Smurf," "The Abominable Snowbeast," "Gargamel, The Generous," "Now You Smurf 'Em, Now You Don't," "Spelunking Smurfs" and "The Smurfs And The Honey Tree."

(one 22–minute episode per show) "The Smurfette," "The Astrosmurf," "St. Smurf And The Dragon," "The Smurfs And The Howlibird," "Bewitched, Bothered, And Be–Smurfed," "Soup A La Smurf," "Romeo And Smurfette," "Smurfette' Dancing Shoes," "Sideshow Smurfs," "Sir Hefty," "Poet And Painter," "The Fountain Of Smurf" and "Clockwork Smurf."

1982–1983 "The Smurfs" (two 12–minute episodes per show). "S–Shivering S–Smurfs," "Sister Smurf," "Cormandizing Greedy," "Waste Not, Smurf Not," "It Came From Outer Smurf," "Squeaky," "One Good Smurf Deserves Another," "For The Love Of Gragamel," "The Last Laugh," "The A–maze–ing Smurfs," "Revenge Of The Smurfs," "Smurf Van Winkle," "Turncoat Smurf," "The Sky Is Smurfing! The Sky Is Smurfing!," "Clumsy Smurfs The Future," "Sleepwalking Smurfs," "The Kaplowey Scroll," "Smurf Me No Flowers," "The Stuff Dreams Are Smurfed Of," "Bubble, Bubble, Smurfs In Trouble," "Heavenly Smurfs" and "The Box Of Dirty Tricks."
(one 22–minute episode per show) "The Good, The Bad, And The Smurfy," "The Smurf Who Couldn't Say No," "The Blue Plague," "A Mere Truffles," "Papa's Wedding Day," "The Adventures Of Robin Smurf," "The Three Smurfketeers," "The Lost City Of Yore," "All's Smurfy That Ends Smurfy," "Smurfs At Sea" and "The Littlest Giant."
"Johan and Peewit" (one 22–minute episode per show).
"The Cursed Country," "The Black Hellebore," "The Sorcery Of Malthrochu," "The Goblin Of Boulder Wood," "Johann's Army," "The Magic Fountain," "The Imposter King," "The Haunted Castle," "The Raven Wizard," "The Ring Of Castellac," "Return Of The Clockwork Smurf," "The Prince And The Peewit" and "The Enchanted Baby."
1983–1984 (two 12–minute episodes per show) "The Smurf Fire Brigade," "Hats Off To Smurfs," "The Magic Stick," "Wolf In Peewit's Clothing," "The Winged Wizard," "The First Telesmurf," "April Smurf's Day," "Handy's Kite," "A Little Smurf Confidence," "No Time For Smurfs," "Good Neighbor Smurf," "Hogatha's Heart Throb," "The Chief Record Smurf," "The Magic Earrings," "Born Rotten," A Bell For Azrael," "The Tear Of A Smurf," "How To Smurf A Rainbow," "Smurfette For A Day," "Peewit Meets Bigmouth," "Harmony Steals The Show," "Greedy And The Porridge Pot," "Lumbering Smurfs," "Willpower Smurfs," "A Hovel Is Not A Home," "Baby Smurf Is Missing," "A Chip Off The Old Smurf," "Hefty's Heart," "Speak For Yourself, Farmer Smurf," "Forget–Me–Smurfs," "A Gift For Papa's Day," "The Littlest Witch," "Smurfing In Sign Language," "The Smurfstone Quest," "Clumsy Luck," "The Grumpy Gremlin," "To Smurf A Thief," "Wedding Bells For Gargamel," "Smurfy Acres," "A Hug For Grouchy," "The Magic Rattle," "All Creatures Great And Smurf," "The Smurf Who Would Be King" and "Beauty Is Only Smurf Deep."
(one 22–minute episode per show) "Every Picture Smurfs A Story," "The Golden Smurf Award," "Smurfs' Halloween Special," "Once in A Blue Moon," "The Last Smurfberry," "The Miracle Smurfer," "The Noble Stag," "Handy's Sweetheart," "The Smurfs' Time Capsule," "Baby's First Christmas" and "The Moor's Baby."
1984–1985 (two 12–minute episodes per show) "Symbols Of Wisdom," "The Whole Smurf And Nothing But The Smurf," "Gargamel's Mis–Fortune," "Stop And Smurf The Roses," "Hefty And The Wheelsmurfer," "A Float Full Of Smurfs," "The Secret Of The Village Well," "The Gingerbread Smurfs," The Gargoyle Of Quarrel Castle," "Jokey's Shadow," "Tick Tock Smurfs," "Gargamel's Giant," "Jokey's Funny Side," "The Traveler," "A Pet For Baby Smurf," "The Secret Of Shadow Swamp," "The Man In The Moon," "Smurfette's Sweet Tooth," "Breakfast At

Greedy's," "Smurfette's Golden Tresses," "Monster Smurfs," "Smurf The Other Cheek," "The Trojan Smurf," "The Patchwork Bear," "Tailor's Magic Needle," "Petrified Smurfs," "The Smurfomatic Smurfulator," "Lazy's Slumber Party," "Papa's Worrywarts," "Big Nose Dilemma," "Smurf Box Derby," "Blue Eyes Returns," "Babes In Wartland," "Smurf–Walk Cafe," "The Bad Place," "Bigmouth Smurf," "The Smurfiest Of Friends," "Baby's Enchanted Didey" and "Smurfing For Ghosts."
(new 22–minute episodes combined with reruns) "The Incredible Shrinking Wizard," "Never Smurf Off 'Til Tomorrow," "Hopping Cough Smurfs," "Smurf On Wood," "The Pussywillow Pixes," "A Circus For Baby," "Little Orange Horse With Gold Shoes" and "The Master Smurf."
1985–1986 (two 12–minute episodes per show) "The Masked Pie Smurfer," "Dreamy's Pen Pals," "He Who Smurfs Last," "Stuck On Smurfs," "Papa's Flying Bed," "Mud Wrestling Smurfs," "The Sand–Witch," "Puppy," "Wild And Wooly," "The Smurflings," "Bigmouth's Friend," "Queen Smurfette," "The Grouchiest Game In Town," "Papa's Day Off," "Educating Bigmouth," "Brainy Smurf," "Friend To All The Animals," "Happy Unhappiness Day To You," "The Great Slime Crop Failure," "Papa's Puppy Prescription," "Mutiny On The Smurf," "Poet's Writer's Block," "Love Those Smurfs," "Things That Go Smurf In The Night," "Alarming Smurfs," "Smurfette's Rose," "Brainy's Smarty Party," "The Mr. Smurf Contest," "Have You Smurfed Your Pet Today?," "They're Smurfing Our Song," "Unsound Smurfs," "All Work And No Smurf" and "Gargamel's Time Trip."
(new 22–minute episodes combined with reruns) "Smurf A Mile In My Shoes," "Sassette," "Kow–Tow, We Won't Bow," "The Dark–Ness Monster," "Marco Smurf And The Pepper Pirates," "The Comet Is Coming, The Comet Is Coming," "Papa's Family Album" and "Baby's First Word."
1986–1987 (two 12–minute episodes per show) "Grouchy Makes a Splash," "Farmer's Genii," "The Answer Smurf," "No Smurf Is An Island," "Sassette's Tooth," "The Tallest Smurf," "Smurf Quest" (Part 1), "Smurfette's Gift," "The World According To Smurflings," "Smurf Quest" (Part 3), "Smurfs On Wheels," "All The Smurfs A Stage," "Calling Dr. Smurf," "The Most Popular Smurf," "Reckless Smurfs," "Smurfette's Flower," "Bringing Up Bigfeet," "Can't Smurf The Music," "Papa's Last Spell," "A Myna Problem," "It's A Puppy's Life," "Sweepy Smurf," "Snappy's Way," "The Village Vandal," "Brookworm Smurf," "The Root Of Evil," "Essence Of Brainy," "Jokey's Cloak," "Journey To The Center Of The Smurf," "Handy's Window–Vision," "The Gallant Smurf," "Don Smurfo," "Future Smurfed," "Crying Smurfs," "Dr. Evil And Mr. Nice," "Gargamel's Dummy," "I Smurf To The Trees," "Clumsy's Cloud," "Master Scruple," "Scruple's Sweetheart," "Head Over Hogatha," "Put Upon Puppy," "The Color Smurfy," "The Horn Of Plenty," "Heart Of Gold," "Baby's New Toy," "Smurf On The Run," "The Last Whippoorwill," "The Most Unsmurfy Games" and "Tattle Tail Smurfs."
(new 22–minute episodes combined with reruns) "The Prince And The Hopper," "A Loss Of Smurf," "Smurf Quest" (Part 2), "Smurf Quest" (Part 4), "The Enchanted Quill," "Fire Fighting Smurfs," "Greedy Goes On Strike," "Gargamel's New Job," "The Lure Of The Orb," "Lazy's Nightmare," "The Littlest

Viking," "The Scarlet Croaker," "Papa Smurf, Papa Smurf" and "The Royal Drum."

1987–1988 (two 12–minute episodes per show) "Locomotive Smurfs," "Jokey's Joke Book," "Smurfing For Gold," "Smurfette's Lucky Star," "Timber Smurf," "The Smurfstalker," "Baby's Marvelous Toy," "The Smurflings' Unsmurfy Friend," "All The News That's Fit To Smurf," "Skyscraper Smurfs," "Poet The Know–It–All," "Cut-Up Smurfs," "Sleepless Smurfs," "Crooner Smurf," "Azrael's Brain," "Hefty's Rival," "Flighty's Plight," "Smurf On The Wild Side" (Act IV), "Predictiable Smurfs," "Where The Wild Smurfs Are," "A Hole In Smurf," "Return Of Don Smurfo," "Poet's Storybook," "Little Big Smurf," "Bad Luck Smurfs," "Stop And Go Smurfs," "Polersmurf," "Gargamel's Second Childhood," "The Fastest Wizard In The World," "Sing A Song of Smurfling," "Wild About Smurfette," "Legendary Smurfs," "Gargamel's Last Will," "Dancing Bear," "Smurfing The Unicorns," "Vanity's Wild Adventure," "Smurfing Out Of Time," "Nobody Smurf," "Bouncing Smurf," "Vaniety's Closest Friend," "The Smurf Who Could Do No Wrong," "Castaway Smurfs," "Prince Smurf," "The Smurfy Verdict," "Gargamel's Quest," "I Was A Brainy Weresmurf," "Papa For A Day," "Foul Feather Fiend," "Snappy's Puppet," "Sassette's Bewitching Friend" and "To Coin A Smurf."

(new 22–minute episodes combined with reruns) "Scruple And The Great Book Of Spells," "Smurfette Unmade," "Swapping Smurfs," "A Smurf On The Wide Side" (Act I, II, III), "Sasettes' Hive," "Chlorhydris' Lost Love," "A Long Tale For Grandpa," "Soothsayer Smurfette," "The Magic Sack Of Mr. Nicholas," "Gargamel's Sweetheart," "Peewit's Unscrupulous Adventure" and "Smurf Pet."

1988–1989 (two 12–minute episodes per show) "Stealing Grandpa's Thunder," "A Maze Of Mirrors," "Clockwork's Power Play," "Shutterbug Smurfs," "It's A Smurfy Life," "Smoogle Sings The Blues," "Long Live Brainy," "Smurf The Presses," "Pappy's Puppy," "Bungling Babysitters," "Big Mouth's Roommate," "Nanny's Way," "Denisa's Greedy Doll," "Clusmy In Command," "Don Smurfo's Uninvited Guests" and "Denisa's Slumber Party."

(new 22–minute episodes combined with reruns) "Lost Smurf," "Land Of Lost And Found," "Memory Melons," "Grandpa's Nemesis," "Archives Of Evil," "A Smurf For Denisa," "A House For Nanny" and "Grandpa's Walking Stick."

1989–1990 (two 12–minute episodes per show) "Cave Smurfs," "Hogapatra's Beauty Sleep," "A Fish Called Snappy," "Trojan Smurfs," "Karate Clumsy," "Fortune Cookie," "Shamrock Smurfs," "Smurfs That Time Forgot (Part 1)," "Smurfette's Green Thumb," "Hefty Sees A Serpent," "Like It Or Smurf It," "Scary Smurfs," "Grandpa's Fountain Of Youth," "Jungle Jitterbug," "Sky High Surprise," "The Monumental Grouch," "Greedy's Masterpizza," "No Reflection On Vanity," "G'Day Smoogles," "Papa Loses His Patience," "Big Shot Smurfs," "Small–Minded Smurfs," "Brainy's Beastly Boo–Boo," "Hearts 'N' Smurfs," "Wild Goes Cuckoo" and "Banana's Over Hefty."

(new 22–minute episodes combined with reruns) "Smurfs That Time Forgot" (Part 2), "Mummy Dearest," "Papa's Big Snooze," "The Smurf Odyssey," "Imperial Panda–Monium" "Swashbuckling Smurfs," "Phantom Bagpiper," "The Clumsy Genie," "Curried Smurfs," "Gnoman Holiday," "Painter's Egg–

Cellent Adventure," "The Golden Rhino" and "Smurfs Of The Round Table."

SNIP SNAP

A stop–motion animated series from the English cartoon studio, Halas and Batchelor, featuring the exploits of a dog cut out of paper. The series was syndicated in America along with another Halas and Batchelor cartoon program, "Foo Foo." *A Halas and Batchelor Production. Color. Half–hour. Syndicated: 1961*

Episodes:

"Bagpipes," "Treasure Of Ice Cake Island," "Spring Song," "Snap's Rocket," "Snakes And Ladders," "Lone World Sail," "Thin Ice," "Magic Book," "Circus Star," "Moonstruck," "Snap And The Beanstalk," "Goodwill To All Dogs," "In The Cellar," "The Beggar's Uproar," "The Birthday Cake," "Snap Goes East," "The Hungry Dog" and "Top Dogs."

THE SNORKS

Deep under the sea in the mystical underwater world of Snorkland lives a society of creatures called Snorks, tiny, adorable, snorkel–headed creatures whose adventures center around high school student Allstar and his girlfriend, Casey. The Snorks, created by Freddy Monnickendam, first gained popularity as Belgian comic–book characters. Following its successful network run, the series enjoyed new life as a first–run syndicated program, premiering with all–new episodes. *A Hanna–Barbera/Sepp, S. A. Production. Color. Half–hour. Premiered on NBC: September 15, 1984–September 3, 1988. Syndicated.*

Voices:

Allstar: Michael Bell, **Tooter:** Frank Welker, **Occy:** Frank Welker, **Dimmy:** Brian Cummings, **Governor Wetworth:** Frank Nelson, **Junior Wetworth:** Barry Gordon, **Casey:** B. J. Ward, **Mrs. Wetworth:** Joan Gardner, **Daffney:** Nancy Cartwright, **Mrs. Seaworthy:** Edie McClurg, **Galeo:** Clive Revill, **Elders 1, 2 and 3:** Peter Cullen, **Elder 4:** Michael Bell, **Baby Smallstar:** Gail Matthius, **Willie:** Fredricka Weber, **Mr. Seaworthy:** Bob Holt, **Auntie Marina:** Mitzi McCall, **Mrs. Kelp:** Joan Gerber, **Mr. Kelp:** Bob Ridgley

Episodes:
(two episodes per show)
1984–1985 "Vandal Scandal," "Journey To The Source," "The New Neighbors," "Hooked On A Feeling," "Das Boot," "Which Snork Snitched," "Snorky Mania," "Allstar's All Star Band," "Now You Seahorse, Now You Don't," "A Snorking We Will Go," "Snork Marks The Sport," "Snork Dance," "Junior's Secret," "The Big Scoop," "The Blue Coral Necklace," "Up, Up And Wave," "The Snorkness Monster," "Snorkin' Surf Party," "Allstar's Double Trouble," "A Snork On The Wild Side," "Time Out For Sissies," "Fine Fettered Friends," "Me Jo–Jo, You Daffney," "The Old Shell Game," "Whale Tales" and "The King Of Kelp."

1985–1986 "Snorkitis Is Nothing To Sneeze At," "The Whole Toot And Nothing But The Toot," "Never Cry Wolf–Fish," "Chickens Of The Sea," "Learn To Love Your Snork," "A Hard Day's Snork," "Dr. Strangesnork," "Allstar's Freshwater Adventure," "Water Friends For?," "It's Just A Matter Of Slime," "The Shape Of Snorks To Come," "Junior's Octopuppy," "Casey And The Doubleheader," "The Ugly Yuckling," "Gills Just Want To Have Fun," "Guess What's Coming To Dinner," "A Sign Of The Tides," "The Littlest Mermaid," "The Backwards Snork" and "I Squid You Not."

1987–1988 "All's Whale That Ends Whale," "Allstar's Last Hour," "A Willie Scary Shalloween," "Sea Shore Sideshow," "Snip and Snap," "Freeze Save Our Town," "Junior's Empire," "The Golden Dolphin," "It's Always Darkest Before The Snork," "The Sand Witch," "The Shady Shadow," "Tooter Loves Tadah," "Daffney's Ransom," "Salmon Chanted Evening," "Reefberry Madness," "Casey In Sandland," "Mummy Snorkfest," "A Farewell Of Arms," "Jo–Jo In Control," "The Day The Ocean Stood Still," "Chills, Drills And Spills," "The Longest Shortcut," "Willie And Smallstar's Big Adventure," "Taming Of The Snork," "A Snork In A Gilded Cage" and "The Snorkshire Spooking."

1988–1989 (syndicated) "Daffney's Not So Great Escape," "Willie's Best Friend," "Dr. Strangesnork's Bomb," "Day Of The Juniors," "Ooze Got The Snorks," "A Starfish Is Born," "The Silly Snorkasaurus," "Who's Who?," "Battle Of The Gadgets," "Little Lord Occy," "Junior's Fuelish Kelp Rush," "The Boo Lagoon," "How The Snork Was Won," "In Junior's Image," "Robosnork," "Summer And Snork" "Allstar's Odyssey," "In Greed We Trust," "Jaws Say The Word," "Prehisnorkic," "The Wizard Of Ice," "Rhyme And Punishment," "Big City Snorks," "Nighmare On Snorkstreet," "Snorkerella," "Robin Snork," "The Daring Young Snork On The Flying Trapeze," "Snork Ahoy," "The Story Circle," "Oh Brother!," "The Day They Fixed Junior Wetworth," "I'll Be Senior," "The First Snork In Space," "Wish Or Wish Out," "My Dinner With Allstar" and "All That Glitters Is Not Goldfish."

SPACE ANGEL

This classic animated series follows the intergalactic adventures of Scott McCloud—code name: Space Angel—a one–man Marine Corps for the Earth Bureau of Investigation who, working in utmost secrecy, tackles assignments involving the security of the solar system. McCloud's crew aboard the super–spaceship, Starduster, includes Taurus, an expert pilot and mechanic; Crystal, a specialist in electronics and astro–navigation; and Professor Mace, head of base station Evening Star, who make up the bureau's Interplanetary Space Force. Produced by the creators of "Clutch Cargo" and "Captain Fathom," these serialized science–fiction stories were strung together in 52 weekly half–hour programs. Former National Comics artist Alexander Toth served as art director for the series, which was created by Dik Darley and Dick Brown. Like "Clutch Cargo," films featured the Synchro–Vox process, superimposed human lips speaking over the mouths of the characters. *A Cambria Studios Production. Color. Half–hour. Premiered: February 6, 1962. Syndicated.*

Voices:
Scott McCloud/Space Angel: Ned Lefebver

Scott McCloud is a one–man Marine Corps in the intergalactic adventure series, "Space Angel." © Cambria Studios

Additional Voices:
Margaret Kerry, Hal Smith

Episodes:
(known titles) "Space Hijackers (Solar Mirror)," "The Little People," "Incident Of The Loud Planet," "The Wizard Of Eden," "Cosmic Combat," "Gladiators," "Mission: The LIght Barrier," "The Slave Worked," "The Exiles," "The Saucer Caper," "There Goes Danny," "Visitor From Outer Space," "Rescue Mission," "Space War," "Dragon Fire," "Flight Of The Hot Spots," "The Fugitives," "The Encoder," "Project Hero," "The Frozen Planet," "The Plagued Planet," "The Donivan Plan," "Cosmic Search," "The Plot," "Name, Bank, Serial Number," "Crystal's Anti–Boy Friend," "They Went Thatta' Way," "Power Failure," "Scratch One Chimp," "Red Alert," "The Day The Earth Went Dark," "The Queen Of Three Suns," "Welcome Neighbor," "Space Angel Meets A Devil," "Top Secret," "How To Win A Space Race Without Really Trying," "The Gold City Blues," "The Not So Mythical Beast," "Count Down" and "The Abominable Moon Man."

SPACE GHOST AND DINO BOY

A black–hooded interplanetary crime–fighter who draws powers from his magic belt, Space Ghost counters evil forces, assisted by two teenage wards, Jan and Jace, and their pet space monkey, Blip. The companion cartoon in this series revolved around the adventures of young boy (Tod) who is left in prehistoric times following a time–warp experiment that kills his father. (He earns the name "Dino Boy" from riding on top of a brown–spotted brontosaurus named Bronty.) A caveman (Ugh) saves the boy and the pair become inseparable friends.

Eight years after concluding its normal network run, "Space Ghost" was repackaged as the first half of "The Space Ghost/Frankenstein Jr." show and reappeared in all-new adventures in 1981's "Space Stars" for NBC. *A Hanna–Barbera Production. Color. Half–hour. Premiered on CBS: September 10, 1966–September 7, 1968.*

Voices:
Space Ghost: Gary Owens, **Jan:** Ginny Tyler, **Jace:** Tim Matthieson, **Dino Boy** (Tod): Johnny Carson (not the famed talk–show host), **Ugh:** Mike Road, **Bronty:** Don Messick

Episodes:
"Space Ghost" (two per show).
"The Heat Thing," "Zorak," "The Web," "The Lizard Slavers," "The Sandman," "Creature King," "The Evil Collector," "The Robot Master," "The Drone," "Hi–Jackers," "Homing Device," "The Iceman," "The Energy Monster," "The Lure," "The Schemer," "The Cyclopeds," "Lokar, King Of The Killer Locusts," "Space Sargasso," "Brago," "Revenge Of The Spider Woman," "Space Birds," "Attack Of The Saucer Crab," "Nightmare Planet," "The Time Machine," "Space Armada," "The Challenge," "Jungle Planet," "Ruler Of The Rock Robots," "The Space Ark," "Glasstor," "The Space Pirahnas," "The Sorcerer," "The Ovens Of Moltor," "Transor—The Matter Mover," "The Looters," "Gargoyloids," "The Meeting," "Clutches Of Creature King," "The Deadly Trap," "The Molten Monsters Of Moltar," "Two Faces Of Doom" and "The Final Encounter."
"Dino Boy" (one per show).
"The Sacrifice," "The Treeman," "Marooned," "The Worm People," "The Moss Men," "The Rock Pygmies," "Giant Ants," "The Fire God," "Danger River," "The Vampire Men," "The Wolf People," "Valley Of The Giants," "The Bird Riders," "The Marksman," "The Terrible Chase," "The Mighty Show Creature," "The Spear Warriors" and "The Ant Warriors."

THE SPACE GHOST/ FRANKENSTEIN JR. SHOW

As a replacement for the poorly rated "Land of the Lost" live-action series, NBC tried to bolster ratings of that time slot with this half–hour compendium of two Hanna–Barbera favorites who starred in their own successful network series. (See "Space Ghost" and "Frankenstein Jr." for series and episodic information.) *A Hanna–Barbera Production. Color. Half–hour. Premiered on NBC: November 27, 1976–September 3, 1977.*

Voices:
Space Ghost/Narrator: Gary Owens, **Jan:** Ginny Tyler, **Jayce:** Tim Matthieson, **Frankenstein, Jr.:** Ted Cassidy, **Buzz Conroy:** Dick Beals, **Dr. Conroy:** John Stephenson

SPACE KIDDETTES

Accompanied by their comical pet dog, Pup Star, a group of junior space rangers explore the cosmic world from their space–capsule clubhouse only to become embroiled in battle with creatures and enemies in outer space. The kiddettes' main antagonist was Captain Sky Hook (a parody of Captain

Hook in *Peter Pan*), the meanest pirate in the universe. *A Hanna–Barbera Production. Half–hour. Premiered on NBC: September 10, 1966–September 2, 1967.*

Voices:
Scooter: Chris Allen, **Snoopy:** Lucille Bliss, **Jennie:** Janet Waldo, **Count Down:** Don Messick, **Pup Star:** Don Messick, **Captain Sky Hook:** Daws Butler, **Static:** Daws Butler

Episodes
"Moleman Menace," "Jet–Set–Go," "Space Indians," "Swamped–Swamped," "Space Heroes," "Space Witch," "Tale Of A Whale," "Space Giant," "Space Carnival," "The Laser Breathing Space Dragon," "The Flight Before Christmas," "Beach Brawl," "Dognapped In Space," "Secret Solar Robot," "King Of The Space Pirates," "Planet Of Greeps, "Cosmic Condors," "The Space Mermaid," "Haunted Planet" and "Something Old, Something Guru."

SPACE STARS

Average space citizens and super–powered heroes tackle jet–age problems and cosmic evil in five suspenseful and humorous segments: "Teen Force," three super–teenagers (Kid Comet, Moleculad and Elektra) who fight for freedom in the tradition of Robin Hood and his merry men; "Astro and the Space Mutts," a trio of interstellar police officers—the Jetsons' family pet Astro and two clumsy canines (Cosmo and Dipper)—who fight crime under the direction of their police boss, Space Ace; and "Space Stars Finale," which pits "Space Stars" cast members against a collection of galactic rogues and rascals. The remaining two weekly segments were "Herculoids" and "Space Ghost," back in all–new episodes produced for television. *A Hanna–Barbera Production. Color. One hour. Premiered on NBC: September 12, 1981–September 11, 1982.*

Voices:
Teen Force: Elektra: B. J. Ward, **Moleculad:** David Hubbard, **Kid Comet:** Darryl Hickman, **Plutem/Glax:** Mike Winslow, **Uglor, the terrible:** Allan Lurie, **Narrator:** Keene Curtis, **Astro and the Space Mutts: Astro:** Don Messick, **Cosmo:** Frank Welker, **Dipper:** Lennie Weinrib, **Space Ace:** Mike Bell, **Herculoids: Zandor/Tundro/Zok/Igoo:** Mike Road, **Tara:** Virginia Gregg, **Dorno:** Sparky Marcus, **Gloop/Gleep:** Don Messick, **Narrator:** Keene Curtis, **Space Ghost: Space Ghost:** Gary Owens, **Jan:** Alexandra Stewart, **Jace:** Steve Spears, **Blip:** Frank Welker, **Narrator:** Keene Curtis

Episodes:
"Teen Force "(one per show).
"The Death Ray," "Nebulon," "Decoy Of Doom," "Elektra's Twin," "Uglor's Power Play," "The Ultimate Battle," "Prison Planet," "Trojan Teen Force," "The Space Slime" "Pandora's Warp" and "Wordstar."
"Astro and the Space Mutts" (one per show).
"The Night Of The Crab," "Reverso," "Menace Of The Magnet Maniac," "The Greatest Show Off Earth," "Rock Punk," "Rampage Of The Zodiac Man," "Will The Real Mr. Galaxy Please Stand Up," "Galactic Vac Is Back," "The Education Of Puglor," "Jewlie Newstar" and "Wonder Dog."

"Herculoids" (one per show).

"The Ice Monster," "The Green Menace," "The Firebird," "The Energy Creature," "The Snake Riders," "The Buccaneer," "The Thunderbolt," "Return Of The Ancients," "Space Trappers," "The Invisibles" and "Mindbender."

"Space Ghost" (one per show).

"Attack Of The Space Sharks," "The Haunted Space Station," "The Sorceress," "Planet Of The Space Monkeys," "The Anti-matter Man," "The Space Dragons," "Starfly," "The Big Freeze," "The Toymaker," "Microworld," "Space Spectre," "Web Of The Wizard," "Time Chase," "The Deadly Comet," "The Shadow People," "Time Of The Giants," "City In Space," "Nomads," "Eclipse Woman," "Devilship," "Time Master" and "Spacecube Of Doom."

"Space Star Finale" (one per show).

"Dimension Of Doom," "Worlds In Collision," "Polaris," "Endangered Spacies," "The Olympians," "Magnus," "The Crystal Menace," "The Outworlder," "Mindwitch," "Uglor Conquers The Universe" and "The Cosmic Mousetrap."

SPARTAKUS AND THE SUN BENEATH SEA

Living deep in the center of the Earth are the Arcadians, a primitive civilization whose lives depend on the power of their sun, the Terra. When this once reliable source fails, the children of Arcadia break the law and enter the Forbidden Archives in search of a solution. Using special powers, they create a beautiful messenger—naming her Arkanna—to send above for help. The series' theme song was performed by the teen rock group, Menudo. *A RMC Audio Visual/Monte Carlo Production. Color. Half-hour. Premiered on Nickelodeon: October 11, 1986.*

Episodes:

"The City Of Arkadia," "The Gladiators Of Barkar," "The Emperor Quin And The Eighth Kingdom," "Rebecca: Pirate Of The Sea," "Tada And The Royal Insignia," "The Pirate Convention," "The Capture Of Demosthenes," "Arkana And The Beast," "The Pirate Klub," "Emergency Landing," "Living Crystal," "Out Of Control," "The Law Of The Mogokhs," "Between Two Worlds," "The Drummer," "The Defeat of Gog And Magog," "Children . . . And Mice," "The Dark Hole," "Night Of The Amazons," "Star Healer," "The Icy Web," "The Court Of Miracles," "Dr. Test," "The Prisoners Of Lost Time," "Interstratas War," "The Secret Of The Auracite," "Prophecy Of The Auracite," "The Land Of The Chameleons," "The Floating Casino," "The Most Dangerous Game," "The Tightrope," "The Boy Pharoah," "The Twisted Rainbow," "Cyrano De Borobtrak," "Prince Matt," "The Land Of The Great Spider," "High–Risk Highrise," "The Ransom Of Peace," "The Master Of Tongues," "The Triangle Of The Deep," "Tehrig's Nightmare," "The Token Of Manitou," "Rainbow's End," "Uncle Albert," "Dodo," "The Shadow Of Tehra," "Holiday Fever," "Mama Thot," "The Temple Of The Condor," "Gateway To Dawn," "The Path Of Light" and "The Return Of The Prisoners Of Lost Time."

SPEED RACER

Adventure–loving hero, Speed Racer, a young race–car enthusiast, speeds around the world to fight the forces of evil in his super–charged Mach 5 race car. Speed's efforts are supported by his girlfriend, Trixie, kid brother, Spridal, and pet monkey, Chim Chim. The series was unquestionably one of the most popular Japanese–made cartoon programs to air on American television. *A Tatsunoko Production. Color. Half-hour. Premiered: September 23, 1967. Syndicated.*

Voices:

Speed Racer: Jack Grimes, **Trixie,** Speed's girlfriend: Corinne Orr, **Spridal,** Speed's brother: Corinne Orr, **Racer X,** Speed's older brother: Jack Curtis, **Pops Racer,** Speed's father: Jack Curtis, **Mrs. Racer,** Speed's mother: Corinne Orr

Episodes:

"The Great Plan" (Part 1), "The Great Plan" (Part 2), "Challenge Masked Racer" (Part 1), "Challenge Masked Racer" (Part 2), "The Secret Engine" (Part 1), "The Secret Engine" (Part 2), "Race Vs. Mammoth Car" (Part 1), "Race Vs. Mammoth Car" (Part 2), "Most Dangerous Race" (Part 1), "Most Dangerous Race" (Part 2), "Most Dangerous Race" (Part 3), "Race For Revenge" (Part 1), "Race For Revenge" (Part 2), "Desperate Desert Race" (Part 1), "Desperate Desert Race" (Part 2), "The Fire Race" (Part 1), "The Fire Race" (Part 2), "Girl Daredevil" (Part 1), "Girl Daredevil" (Part 2), "Fastest Car On Earth" (Part 1), "Fastest Car On Earth" (Part 2), "Mach 5

Adventure–loving Speed Racer (center), kid brother Spridal, pet monkey Chim Chim and girlfriend Trixie stand in front of their Mach 5 race car, ready for action, in the Japanese cartoon favorite, "Speed Racer." © Tatsunoko Productions

Vs. Mach 5" (Part 1), "Mach 5 Vs. Mach 5" (Part 2), "The Royal Racer" (Part 1), "The Royal Racer" (Part 2), "The Car Heater," "Race Against Time" (Part 1), "Race Against Time" (Part 2), "The Snake Track," "Man On The Lam," "Gang Of Assassins" (Part 1), "Gang Of Assassins" (Part 2), "Race For Life," "Supersonic Car," "Crash In Jungle" (Part 1), "Crash In Jungle" (Part 2), "Terrifying Gambler," "Secret Invaders" (Part 1), "Secret Invaders" (Part 2), "Man Behind Mask," "Car Destroyer," "Desperate Racer," "Dangerous Witness," "Race/Laser Tank," "Great Car Wrestling," "Motorcycle Apaches," "Car With A Brain," Junk Car Grand Prix," "Car In Sky," "The Trick Race," "Race Around World" (Part 1) and "Race Around World" (Part 2).

SPEEDY BUGGY

Teenagers Debbie, Tinker and Mark, and chugging auto partner, Speedy Buggy, travel throughout the country and to foreign locales finding mystery and adventure, with the sputtering supercar, Speedy, always saving the day. *A Hanna–Barbera Production. Color. Half–hour. Premiered on CBS: September 8, 1973–August 31, 1974.*

Voices:

Speedy Buggy: Mel Blanc, **Debbie:** Arlene Golonka, **Tinker:** Phil Luther, Jr., **Mark:** Mike Bell

Episodes:

"Speed Buggy Went That–A–Away," "Daring Escapades," "Taggert's Trophy," "Speed Buggy Falls In Love," "Kingzilla," "Professor Snow And Madam Ice," "Out Of Sight," "Gold Fever," "Island Of Giant Plants," "The Ringmaster," "The Soundmaster," "The Incredible Changing Man," "Secret Safari," "Oil's Well That Ends Well," "The Hidden Valley Of Amazonia," and "Captain Schemo And The Underwater City."

SPIDER–MAN

College student Peter Parker, reporter for the *New York Daily Bugle,* takes on underground syndicates and other criminals as famed superhero Spider–Man. He encounters such formidable foes as the Phantom from Space, The Sorcerer, One–Eyed Idol, Blotto, Scorpion and others in this half–hour syndicated series based on Stan Lee's "The Amazing Spider–Man" comic adventures.

Executive producers were Robert L. Lawrence and Ralph Bakshi, who also served as story supervisor. Cosmo Anzilotti was assistant director while Martin Taras served as one of the principal animators. Like Bakshi, Anzilotti and Taras were former Terrytoon animators. *A Grantray–Lawrence Animation and Krantz Animation Production in association with Marvel Comics. Color. Half–hour. Premiered on ABC: September 9, 1967–August 30, 1969. Rebroadcast on ABC: March 22, 1970–September 6, 1970. Syndicated.*

Voices:

Peter Parker/Spider Man: Bernard Cowan, Paul Sols, **Betty Brandt,** a reporter: Peg Dixon, **J. Jonah Jameson,** the editor: Paul Kligman

Episodes:

"The Power Of Doctor . . .?," "Where Crawls The . . .," "Menace From Mysterio," "The Sky Is Falling," "Never Step On A . . .," "Diet Of Destruction," "The Kilowatt Kaper," "Armored Car Robbery," "Horn Of The Rhino," "The One–Eyed Idol," "The Revenge of Dr. M," "The Night Of The . . .," "Spider–Man Meets Dr . . .," "Return Of The Flying Dutchman," "The Golden Rhino," "The Spider And The Fly," "Penthouse Robbery," "The Vulture's Prey," "The Terrible Triumph," "Fountain Of Terror," "To Catch A Spider," "Rolleramp," "Sting Of The Scorpion," "The Origin of Spiderman," "King Pinned," "Swing City," "Criminals In The Clouds," "Menace From The Bottom of The World," "Diamond Bust," "Spider–Man Battles The Mole Man," "The Phantom From Depths Of Time," "The Evil Sorcerer," "Vine," "Pardo Presents," "Cloud City Of Gold," "Neptune's Nose Cone," "Home," "Blotto," "Thunder Rumble," "Spider–Man Meets . . .," "Cold Storage," "To Cage A Spider," "The Winged Thing," "Trouble With Snow," "Sky Harbour And The Big Brain Washer," "Vanishing Dr. V. And Scourge of The Scarf," "Super Swami," "Knight Must Fall," "Up From Nowhere," "Rhino," "Revolt In The Fifth Dimension," "Specialist And Slaves," "Down To Earth," "Swing City" and "Trip In Tomorrow."

SPIDER–MAN AND HIS AMAZING FRIENDS

A small suburban town is the setting for this comedy–adventure series about the world's most popular superhero, alias Peter Parker, a shy, 18–year–old science major, who teams up with two superhuman teenagers, Angelica Jones (Firestar—The Girl of Fire) and Bobby Drake (Iceman), in the name of peace and justice. Episodes were later repeated on "The Incredible Hulk/Amazing Spider–Man Hour." (See Series for information.) In 1984, NBC split the program up and Spider–Man returned for one final bow in his own time slot. *A Marvel Production. Color. Half–hour. Premiered on NBC: September 12, 1981–September 11, 1982. Rebroadcast on NBC: September 15, 1984–September 7, 1985.*

Voices:

Anne Lockhart, George DiCenzo, Alan Dinchart, Jerry Dexter, Michael Evans, Walker Edmiston, Alan Young, Dennis Marks, William Woodson, John Hammer, Keye Luke, Allan Melvin, Sally Julian

Episodes:

"The Triumph Of The Green Goblin," "The Crime Of All Centuries," "The Fantastic Mr. Frump!," "Sunfire," "Swarm," "Seven Little Superheroes," "Video Man," "Prison Plot," "Spidey Goes To Hollywood," "The Vengence Of Loki," "Nights And Demons," "Pawns Of The Kingpin," "The Quest of The Red Skull," "The Origin Of Iceman," "Along Came Spidey," "A Fire–Star Is Born," "Spider–Man Unmasked!" (formerly: "Along Came A Sandman"), "The Bride of Dracula!" (formerly: "The Transylvanian Connection"), "The Education Of A Superhero," "Attack of The Arachnoid," "The Origin Of The Spider–Friends" (formerly: "Getting It All Together"), "Spidey Meets

The Girl From Tomorrow" (formerly: "Time Trip To Always"), "The X–Men Adventure" and "Mission: Save The Guardstar!" (formerly: "The Guardstar Affair").

SPIDER–WOMAN

Justice magazine editor–publisher Jessica Drew spins herself into Spider–Woman to fight evil and nab supernatural foes, among them, Tomand, ruler of the Realm of Darkness; the Great Magini; and The Fly, in this half–hour adventure series based on a character created by Stan Lee, creator of Marvel Comics' "The Amazing Spider–Man." *A DePatie–Freleng Enterprises Production in association with Marvel Comics Group. Color. Half–hour. Premiered on ABC: September 22, 1979– March 1, 1980.*

Voices:

Jessica Drew/Spider Woman: Joan Van Ark, **Jeff Hunt,** Jessica's photographer: Bruce Miller, **Billy Drew,** Jessica's nephew: Bryan Scott, **Police Chief:** Lou Krugman, **Detective Miller:** Larry Carroll

Additional Voices:

John Mayer, Vic Perrin, Ilene Latter, Tony Young, Karen Machon, John Milford, Dick Tufeld

Episodes:

"Pyramids of Terror," "Realm Of Darkness," "The Amazon Adventure," "The Ghost Vikings, The Kingpin Strikes Again," "The Lost Continent, The Kongo Spider," "Games of Doom," "Shuttle To Disaster," "Dracula's Revenge," "The Spider Woman And The Fly," "Invasion Of The Black Hole," "The Great Magini," "A Crime In Time," "Return Of The Spider Queen" and "A Deadly Dream."

SPIRAL ZONE

An international super force known as the "5 Zone Riders," headed by Comander Dirk Courage, unite to battle their arch rival, Overlord, a renegade scientist and his band of evil villains, the Black Widows, in order to preserve peace and freedom on Earth. Combining the action and excitement of such hit films as *Star Wars* and *Star Trek,* episodes take place in worldwide locations, including the Florida Everglades, the Austrian Alps, Japan, the Australian Outback and the Soviet Union. *An Atlantic–Kushner Locke Production in association with The Maltese Companies. Color. Half–hour. Premiered: September, 1987. Syndicated.*

Voices:

Dirk Courage: Dan Gilvezan, **Max:** Hal Rayle, **McFarland/ Reaper:** Denny Delk, **Dr. Lawrence/Razorback:** Frank Welker, **Hiro:** Michael Bell, **Duchess Dire:** Mona Marshall, **Katerina/ Mommy:** Mona Marshall, **Overlord:** Neil Ross, **Tank/Bandit:** Neil Ross

Episodes:

"Holographic Zone Battle," "King of The Skies," "Errand Of Mercy," "Mission Into Evil," "Back To The Stone Age," "Small Packages," "Zone Of Darkness," "Gauntlet," "Ride The Whirlwind," "The Unexploded Pod," "Duel In Paradise," "The Im-

poster," "The Hacker," "Overlord's Mystery Woman," "The Sands Of Amaran," "Zone Train," "Breakout," "When The Cat's Away," "Island In The Zone," "The Shuttle Engine," "The Mind Of Gideon Rorshak," "Canal Zone," "Lair Of The Jade Scorpion," "The Man Who Wouldn't Be King," "The Way Of The Samurai," "The Best Fighting Men in The World," "Ultimate Solution," "Hometown Hero," "In The Belly Of The Beast," "The Last One Picked," "So Shall You Reaper," "The Secret of Shadow House," "Zone Of Fear," "Bandit And The Smokies," "Heroes In The Dark," "Zone With Big Shoulders," "Behomoth," "Power Of The Press," "Starship Doom," "Electric Zone Rider," "Australian In Paris," "Enemy Within," "Anti– Matter," "The Siege," "A Little Zone Music," "Elements Of Surprise," "Sea Chase," "Right Man For The Job," "High And Low," "Profiles In Courage," "Darkness Within," "Power Play," "Duchess Treat," "Oversight," "Assault On The Rock," "Zone By Night," "Conflict On Duty," "Final Weapon," "The Face Of The Enemy," "Brother's Keepers," "Little Darlings," "Nightmare On Ice," "Evil Transmissions," "Zone Trap" and "Countdown."

SPORT BILLY

A mascot of major international sports federations is sent to Earth to maintain goodwill and fair play for all those who are involved in sports. Aided by his female companion, Lilly, and pet dog, Willy, Billy and his team crusade together to keep the world of sports on the right track. (Episode titles were unavailable from producer.) *A Filmation Production. Color. Half–hour. Premiered: June, 1982 (Syndicated); NBC: July 31, 1982–September 11, 1982.*

Voices:

Sport Billy: Lane Scheimer, **Sport Lilly:** Joyce Bulifant, **Willie:** Frank Welker, **Queen Vanda:** Joyce Bulifant, **Sporticus XI:** Frank Welker

SPUNKY AND TADPOLE

Investigative, cliff–hangers feature the lanky lad Spunky and friend Tadpole, a real–life teddy bear, in exciting adventures and tall tales in this serialized fantasy series. In most markets, the cartoons were shown on existing children's programs hosted by television station celebrities as well as independently in half–hour time slots. Ten episodes comprised one complete story. *A Beverly Film Corporation Production. Black– and–White. Color. Premiered: September 6, 1958. Syndicated.*

Voices:

Spunky: Joan Gardner, **Tadpole:** Don Messick, Ed Janis

Episodes:

"The Count Of San Francisco" (1–10), "A Message To Marcia" (11–20), "The Smugglers" (21–30), "Lost In Outer Space" (31–40), "Secret Of Cactus Corners" (41–50), "The Frozen Planet" (51–60), "The Private Eyes" (61–70), "Moon Trip" (71–80), "London Mystery" (81–90), "Casbah Capers" (91– 100), "Counterspies In Secret Guise" (101–110), "The Mixed– Up Monster" (111–120), "North Pole Caper" (121–130), "Buried Treasure" (131–140) and "Circus Craze" (141–150).

STAR BLAZERS

Actually Japan's "Space Cruiser Yamato" series dubbed into English, this adventure series—set in the year 2199—chronicles the story of a group of patriots, known as Star Force, whose mission is to save the Earth from an enemy space fleet. heading the Star Force fleet is Captain Avatar, whose crew includes Cadet Derek Wildstar, the second–in–command; Nova, Wildstar's girlfriend and the team's radar operator; Cadet Mark Venture, chief of operations; IQ–9, a robot (nicknamed "Tin–Wit" for his good sense of humor); Sandor, the chief mechanic; and Dr. Sane, the team's physician. Unfortunately, the names of the American actors who voiced the characters are unknown. *An Office Academy/Sunwagon Production in association with Claster Television and Westchester Films Inc. Star Blazers is a registered trademark of Westchester Films Inc. Color. Half–hour. Premiered: September 10, 1979. Syndicated.*

Episodes:

"Quest For Iscandar" (1–26), "The Comet Empire" (27–52) and "The Bolar War" (53–77).

STARCOM

Ultra–sophisticated vehicle and state–of–the–art technology are used by a peacekeeping force in a planetary community where their main foe is the sinister Emperor Dark, assisted by his Shadow Force of evil warriors and robot drones. *A DIC Enterprises Production. Color. Half–hour. Premiered: September, 1987. Syndicated.*

Voices:

Dash: Rob Cowan, **Crowbar:** Robert Cait, **Torvek,** Robert Cait, **Slim:** Phil Aikin, **Dark:** Neil Munro, **Kelsey:** Susan Roman, **Vondar:** Marvin Goldhar, **Malvanna:** Elva May Hoover, **Col. Brickley:** Don Franks, **Klag:** Dan Hennessey, **Romak:** Louis DiBianco

Episodes:

"Nantucket Sleighride," "Trojan Crowbar," "The Long Fall," "The Caverns Of Mars," "Fire And Ice," "Galactic Heartbeat," "The Boys Who Cried Dark," "Dark Harvest," "A Few Bugs In The System," "Turnabout," "Hot Enough For You," "Flash Moskowitz, Space Cadet" and "The Last Star Ranger."

STAR TREK

The indomitable Captain James T. Kirk, his pointy–eared science officer, Spock; chief engineer Scotty; Dr. Leonard McCoy; and the crew of the U.S.S. Enterprise probe outer space where they encounter intelligent aliens and new civilizations, and battle sophisticated forces of evil. The cartoon spin–off from the cult live–action series earned an Emmy Award in 1975, with the stars of the original voicing their own characters. (The character of Ensign Pavel Chekov, played by actor Walter Koenig, did not appear on the animated series.) *A Filmation Production. Color. Half–hour. Premiered on NBC: September 8, 1973–August 30, 1975.*

Voices:

Capt. James T. Kirk: William Shatner, **Science Officer Spock:** Leonard Nimoy, **Dr. Leonard McCoy:** DeForest Kelley, **Chief Engineer Montgomery Scott:** James Doohan, **Nurse Christine Chapel:** Majel Barrett, **Lieutenant Sulu:** George Takei

Episodes:

1973–1974 "More Tribbles, More Tribbles," "The Infinite Vulcan," "Yesteryear," "Beyond The Farthest Star," "The Survivor," "The Lorelei Signal," "One Of Our Planets is Missing," "Mudd's Passion," "The Magic of Megas–Tu," "Time Trap," "Slaver Weapon," "The Ambergis Element," "Jihad," "The Terratin Incident," "The Eye Of The Beholder" and "Once Upon A Planet."
1974–1975 (new episodes combined with reruns) "Bern," "Albatross," "The Pirates of Orion," "The Practical Joker," "How Sharper Than A Serpent's Tooth" and "The Counter Clock Incident."

SUPER FRIENDS

Justice League superheroes Batman, Robin, Superman, Wonder Woman and Aquaman, along with three new members, Marvin, Wendy and Wonder Dog, are called "to fight injustice, right that which is wrong and serve all mankind." In their quest, they contend with supernatural creatures and other powerful forces in this second assemblage of famed crime–fighters from the pages of DC Comics.

Four spin–off series followed—"The All–New Super Friends Hour," "Challenge of the Super Friends," "The World's Greatest Super Friends" and "The Super Friends Hour"—each with new characters added to the cast. *A Hanna–Barbera Production. Color. One hour. Premiered on ABC: September 8, 1973–August 30, 1975. Rebroadcast on ABC: February 1976–September 3, 1977.*

Voices:

Narrator: Ted Knight, **Superman:** Danny Dark, **Batman:** Olan Soule, **Robin:** Casey Kasem, **Aquaman:** Norman Alden, **Wonder Woman:** Shannon Farnon, **Wendy:** Sherry Alberoni, **Marvin:** Frank Welker, **Wonder Dog:** Frank Welker

Episodes:

"The Power Pirate," "The Baffles Puzzle," "Professor Goodfellow's G.E.E.C.," "The Weather Maker," "Dr. Pelagin's War," "The Shamon 'U,'" "Too Hot To Handle," "The Androids," "The Balloon People," "The Fantastic Frerps," "The Ultra Beam," "The Menace Of The White Dwarf," "The Mysterious Moles," "Gulliver's Gigantic Goof," "The Planet Splitter" and "The Watermen."

SUPER FRIENDS: THE LEGENDARY SUPER POWERS SHOW

Comic–book superheroes Wonder Woman, Batman and Robin take on evil forces with assistance from several new superhuman characters in this half–hour fantasy/adventure series for Saturday mornings. *A Hanna–Barbera Production. Color.*

Half–hour. Premiered on ABC: September 8, 1984–August 31, 1985.

Voices:
Superman: Danny Dark, **Wonder Woman:** B. J. Ward, **Batman:** Adam West, **Robin:** Casey Kasem, **Firestorm:** Mark Taylor, **Cyborg:** Ernie Hudson, **Darkseid:** Frank Welker, **Kalibak:** Frank Welker, **Desaad:** Rene Auberjonois

Episodes:
(two per show) "The Bride Of Darkseid" (Part 1), "The Bride Of Darkseid" (Part 2), "The Case Of The Shrinking Super Friends," "The Mask Of Mystery," "Mr. MXYZPTLK And The Magic Lamp," "No Honor Among Super–Thieves," "Super Brat," "The Village Of Lost Souls," "The Royal Ruse," "The Wrath Of Braniac," "The Case Of The Dreadful Dolls," "Darkseid's Golden Trap" (Part 1), "Darkseid's Golden Trap" (Part 2), "Reflections In Crime," "The Curator" and "Island Of The Dinasoids."

THE SUPER GLOBETROTTERS

The Harlem Globetrotters, America's funniest basketball team, are transformed from terrific basketball players to superheroes (Multi–Man, Sphere Man, Gismo Man, Spaghetti Man and Fluid Man), and use their athletic abilities to fight crime throughout the universe. *A Hanna–Barbera Production. Color. Half–hour. Premiered on NBC: September 22, 1979–December 1, 1979.*

Voices:
Curley Neal (Sphere Man): Stu Gilliams, **Geese Ausbie (Multi–Man):** John Williams, **Sweet Lou Dunbar (Gismo Man):** Adam Wade, **Nate Branch (Fluid Man):** Scatman Crothers, **Twiggy Sander (Spaghetti Man):** Buster Jones, **Crime Globe:** Frank Welker, **Announcer:** Mike Rye

Episodes:
"The Super Globetrotters Vs. Museum Man," "The Super Globetrotters Vs. Bwana Bob," "The Super Globetrotters Vs. The Facelift," "The Super Globetrotters Vs. Whaleman," "The Super Globetrotters Vs. Robo And The Globots," "The Super Globetrotters Vs. Tattoo Man," "The Super Globetrotters Vs. Movie Man," "The Super Globetrotters Vs. The Phantom Cowboy," "The Super Globetrotters Vs. The Time Lord," "The Super Globetrotters Vs. Transylvania Terrors," "The Super Globetrotters Vs. Bullmoose," "The Super Globetrotters Vs. Merlo The Magician" and "The Super Globetrotters Vs. Attila The Hun."

SUPERMAN

The famed man of Steel—newspaper reporter Clark Kent of the *Daily Planet* in disguise—keeps the streets of Metropolis safe from the likes of such notorious criminals as Lex Luthor, the Master Shadow and Cybron in this Saturday morning cartoon series revival of the popular comic book character. In addition to featuring new adventures of the fabled crime–fighter, the series also contained a second segment, "Superman Family Album," tracing Superman's youth in separate episodes.

Famed Man of Steel Superman flies into action in the CBS network series, "Superman," based on the popular DC Comics character. © Ruby–Spears Enterprises Inc. Superman ™ and copyright © DC Comics

A Ruby–Spears Enterprises Production in association with DC Comics. Color. Half–hour. Premiered on CBS: September 17, 1988–September 12, 1989.

Voices:
Superman/Clark Kent: Beau Weaver, **Lois Lane:** Ginny McSwain, **Jimmy Olsen:** Mark Taylor, **Perry White:** Stanley Ralph Ross, **Lex Luthor:** Michael Bell, **Jessica Morganberry:** Lynn Marie Stewart, **Ma Kent:** Tress MacNeille, **Pa Kent:** Alan Oppenheimer

Episodes:
"Superman" (one per show).
"Destroy The Defendroids," "Fugitive From Space," "By The Skin Of A Dragon's Teeth," "Cybron Strikes," "The Big Scoop," "The Hunter," "The Triple Play," "Bonechill," "The Beast Beneath These Streets," "Night Of The Living Shadows," "Wildshark," "Superman And Wonder Woman Vs. The Sorceress Of Time" and "The Last Time I Saw Earth."
"Superman Family Album" (one per show).
"The Adoption," "The Supermarket," "At The Babysitter's," "The First Day Of School," "Overnight With The Scouts," "The Circus," "Little Runaway," "The Birthday Party," "The Driver's License," "First Date," "To Play Or Not To Play," "Graduation" and "It's Superman!"

THE SUPERMAN/AQUAMAN HOUR OF ADVENTURE

One year after the debut of his Saturday–morning series, Superman, the Man of Steel, returned in this hour–long fantasy/adventure series which featured the leader of the lost continent of Atlantis, Aquaman, as its co–star. Aided by his son, Aquala, and wife, Mera, Aquaman made the transition to animated cartoon beginning with new episodes produced especially for this series.

Six seven–minute cartoons were rotated during each broadcast. Two episodes each of Superman and Aquaman were shown, along with two episodes of "Superboy" (repeated from "The New Adventures of Superman"), which alternated with "Guest Star" cartoons marking the cartoon debut of "The Atom," "Flash," "The Green Lantern," "Hawkman and Hawkgirl," "The Teen Titans" and "The Justice League of America," each successful comic–book superheroes. (The cartoons were rebroadcast as part of the syndicated "Aquaman" series.) *A Filmation Production. Color. One hour. Premiered on CBS: September 9, 1967–September 7, 1968.*

Voices:
Superman/Clark Kent: Bud Collyer, **Superboy/Aquaman:** Ted Knight, **Aqualad:** Jerry Dexter, **Mera:** Diana Maddox

Episodes:
"Superman" (two per show).

"The Chimp Who Made it Big," "The Saboteurs," "The Imp—Practical Joker," "Luthor Strikes Again," "Superman Meets Braniac," "The Deadly Fish," "The Prankster," "Menace Of The Lava Men," "The Iron Eater," "War Of The Bee Battalion," "The Return Of Braniac," "The Wicked Warlock," "The Image Maker," "Two Faces of Superman," "Merlin's Magic Marbles," "Invisible Raiders," "Malevolent Mummy," "Threat Of The Thrutans," "Tree–Man Of Arbora," "Mission Of Planet Peril," "Mermen Of Emor," "The Lethal Lightening Bug," "Wisp Of Wickedness," "The Prehistoric Pterodactyls," "The Abominable Iceman," "Seed Of Disaster," "Neolithic Nightmare," "Superman Meets His Match—Almost," "The Deadly Icebergs," "The Pernicious Parasite," "The Toys Of Doom," "The Robot Of Riga," "Return Of The Warlock," "Ape Army Of The Amazon," "The Atomic Superman," "The Deadly Super–Doll," "The Fearful Force Phantom," "The Electro–Magnetic Monster," "The Insect Raiders," "The Warlock's Revenge," "The Men From A.P.E.," "The Frightful Fire Phantom," "The Halyah Of The Himalayas," "A.P.E. Strikes Again," "The Bird–Men From Lost Valley," "The Toyman's Super Toy," "Superman's Double–Trouble," "Luthor's Loco Looking Glass," "The Night Of The Octopod," "The Cage Of Glass," "Braniac's Blue Bubbles" and "Luthor's Fatal Fireworks."

"Superboy" (two episodes every other show).

"The Man Who Knew Superboy's Secret," "Operation Counter Invasion," "The Terrible Trio," "Visitor From The Earth's Core," "The Super–Clown Of Smallville," "A Devil of A Time," "Superboy's Super Dilemma," "Krypto, Super–Seeing Eye Dog," "Krypto's Calamitious Capers," "The Deep–Sea Dragon," "Superboy's Strangest Foe," "The Gorilla Gang," "The Spy From Outer Space" (two parts), "Krypto's Capricious Crony," "A Black Knight At Court," "The Beast That Went Berserk," "The Jinxed Circus," "Hurricane Fighters," "The Two Faced Beast," "The Great Space Chase," "The Chameleon Creature," "The Finger Of Doom," "The Revolt Of Robotville," "Krypto—K–9 Detective" and "The Neanderthal Cave Man Caper."

"Aquaman" (two per show).

"Menace Of The Black Manta," "Rampaging Reptile Men," "Return of Nepto," "Fiery Invaders," "Sea Raiders," "War Of The Water Worlds," "Volcanic Monster," "Crimson Monster From Pink Pool," "Ice Dragon," "Deadly Drillers," "Vassa—Queen Of The Mermen," "Microscopic Monster," "Onslaught Of The Octomen," "Treacherous Is The Torpedoman," "Satanic Saturnians," "Brain—Brave And Bold," "Where Lurks

The Fisherman," "Mephistos Marine Marauders," "The Trio Of Terror," "The Torp, The Magneto, And The Claw," "Goliaths Of The Deep–Sea Gorge," "Sinister Sea Scamp," "Devil Fish," "The Sea Scavengers," "In Captain 'Cuda's Clutches," "The Mirror–Man From Planet Imago," "The Sea Sorcerer," "The Sea Snares Of Captain Sly," "The Undersea Trojan Horse," "The Vicious Villainy Of Vassa," "Programmed For Destruction," "The War Of The Quatix And Bimphabs," "The Stickman Of Stygia," "Three Wishes To Trouble," "The Silver Sphere" and "The Old Man Of The Sea (To Catch A Fisherman)."

"Guest Star Segment" (two episodes every other show).

"Between Two Armies" (with Justice League Of America), "Target Earth" (with Justice League of America), "Bad Day On Black Mountain" (with Justice League of America), "Invasion Of The Beetle People" (with The Atom), "The Plant Machine" (with The Atom), "House Of Doom" (with The Atom), "The Monster Machine" (with The Teen Titans), "The Chemo Creature" (with Flash), "Take A Giant Step" (with Flash), "To Catch A Blue Bolt" (with Flash), "Peril From Pluto" (with Hawkman and Hawkgirl), "A Visit To Venus" (with Hawkman and Hawkgirl), "The Twenty–Third Dimension" (with Hawkman and Hawkgirl), "Evil Is As Evil Does" (with The Green Lantern), "The Vanishing World" (with The Green Lantern), and "Sirena—Empress Of Evil" (with The Green Lantern).

SUPER MARIO BROTHERS SUPER SHOW

World famous brother act, Mario and Luigi, play two misfit plumbers from the Italian section of Brooklyn, who suddenly find themselves flushed through a Warp Zone into the exciting and ever–changing landscape of the Mushroom Kingdom where they set out to rescue the perky Princess Toadstool and her factotum Toad from the dastardly King Koopa and his laughable Nintendo minions. The series was derived from the popular Nintendo video game. *A DIC Enterprises Production. Color. Half–hour. Premiered: September, 1989. Syndicated.*

Voices:
Mario: Lou Albano, **Luigi:** Danny Wells, **King Koopa:** Harvey Atkin, **Mushroom Mayor:** Harvey Atkin, **Tryclyde:** Harvey Atkin, **Sniffet:** Harvey Atkin, **Toad:** John Stocker, **Mouser:** John Stocker, **Troopa:** John Stocker, **Beezo:** John Stocker, **Flurry:** John Stocker, **Princess Toadstool:** Jeannie Elias, **Shyguy:** Jeannie Elias

Episodes:
"The Bird! The Bird!," "Butch Mario And The Luigi Kid," "King Mario Of Cramalot," "Mario's Magic Carpet," "Rollin' Down The River," "The Great Gladiator Gig," "Mario And The Beanstalk," "Love 'Em And Leave 'Em," "The Great BMX Race," "Two Plumbers And A Baby," "Stars In Their Eyes," "Pirates Of The Koopa," "Robo Koopa," "Count Koopula," "Jungle Fever," "Mario Of The Deep," "The Fire Of Hercufleas," "Mario Meets Koopzilla," "Mario And Joliet," "Too Hot To Handle," "Brooklyn Bound," "The Adventures Of Sherlock Mario," "Hooded Robin And His Mario Men," "Toad Warrior," "The

Pied Koopa," "Bad Rap," "On Her Majesty's Sewer Service," "Mario And The Red Baron Koopa," "Might McMario And The Pot O' Gold," "Do You Princess Toadstool Take This Koopa . . .?," "The Mark Of Zero," "20,000 Koopas Under The Sea," "The Koopas Are Coming! The Koopas Are Coming!," "Koopenstein," "Quest For Pizza," "The Unzappables," "The Trojan Koopa," "Karate Koopa," "Elvin Lives," "Koopa Claus," "The Ten Koopmandments," "The Provolone Ranger," "The Great Gold Coin Rush," "Mario Of The Apes," "Crocodile Mario," "Plumbers Academy," "Princess, I Shrunk The Mario Brothers," "Flatbush Koopa," "Raiders Of The Lost Mushroom," "Star Koopa," "Escape From Koopatraz" and "Little Red Riding Princess."

SUPER POWERS TEAM: GALACTIC GUARDIANS

The continued adventures of the world's greatest superheroes are featured in this brand–new fantasy/adventure series. *A Hanna–Barbera Production. Color. Half–hour. Premiered on ABC: September 7, 1985–August 30, 1986.*

Voices:

Superman: Danny Dark, **Wonder Woman:** B. J. Ward, **Batman:** Adam West, **Robin:** Casey Kasem, **Firestorm:** Mark Taylor, **Cyborg:** Ernie Hudson, **Darkseid:** Frank Welker, **Kalibak:** Frank Welker, **Desaad:** Rene Auberjonois

Episodes:

(10–minute episodes) "The Bizaro Super Powers Team" and "The Ghost Ship."
(20–minute episodes) "The Case Of The Stolen Powers," "Brainchild," "The Seeds of Doom," "The Wild Cards," "The Darkseid Deception," "The Fear," "Escape From Space City" and "The Death Of Superman."

THE SUPER SIX

Under the organization name of "Super Service Inc.," six superheroes, whose names coincide with their super powers (Granite Man, Super Scuba, Elevator Man, Magnet Man and Captain Zammo), employ their special powers to fight crime. Two additional supporting segments were featured: "Super Bwoing," a guitar–strumming daredevil, and "The Brothers Matzoriley," a pair of Irish–Jewish brothers. This was Depatie–Freleng Enterprises' first production for Saturday morning television. *A DePatie–Freleng Enterprises Production. Color. Half–hour. Premiered on NBC: September 10, 1966–September 6, 1969.*

Voices:

Magnet Man: Daws Butler, **Elevator Man:** Paul Stewart, **Super Scuba:** Arte Johnson, **Granite Man:** Lynn Johnson, **Captain Zammo:** Paul Frees, **Super Bwoing:** Charles Smith, **The Brothers Matzoriley:** Paul Frees, Daws Butler

Episodes:

"Super Service" (one per show).
"Cement Mixup" (with Granite Man), "The Matucci Venus" (with Granite Man), "Who's Watching The Gold?" (with Super

Scuba), "Ship Of Mules" (with Captain Zammo), "The Hessians Are Coming, The Hessians Are Coming" (with Captain Zammo), "One Of Our Missiles is Missing" (with Super Scuba), "A Whale Of A Tale" (with Super Scuba), "Down Please" (with Elevator Man), "Having A Ball" (with Granite Man), "The Right Train On The Wrong Track" (with Granite Man), "The Termite (with Magnet Man), "Will The Real Magnet Man Please Stand Up?" (with Magnet Man), "The Shapoor Caper" (with Elevator man), "London Britches Falling Down" (with Magnet Man), "The Mummy Caper" (with Elevator Man), "The Fly" (with Elevator Man), "Water Water Nowhere" (with Magnet Man), "Smuggler's Cove" (with Super Scuba) and "The Bad Brothers Ride Again" (with Captain Zammo).
"Super Bwoing" (one per show).
"Coldpinky," "Easy Kid Stuff," "Thunder–8–Ball," "Gopher Broke," "The Bomb Glom," "Hag Bag," "Martian Mixup," "Jumping Jack," "Mayor–Go–Round," "Monster Come Home," "Think Little," "Don't Gloat Red Coat," "The Unidentified Floating Object," "The Karate Kid," "A Witch In A Ditch," "Jerk And The Beanstalk," "Topsy–Turvy Time Traveler," "Little Shredded Riding Hood," "The Man From Trash" and "Who Put The Finger On Arnold Hangnail."
"The Brothers Matzoriley" (one per show).
"Ruin And Board," "A Knights Hard Day," "You Go To My Heads," "Dirty Please," "High Moon," "The Jolly Green Gorilla," "Heck's Angels," "Highway Slobbery," "Moby Richard," "Road Scholars," "Heau–Beau Jest," "Window Pains," "The Three Matzoteers," "No Biz Like Schmoe Biz," "A Tree Grows In Matorania," "A Lone Shark," "Hide And Shriek," "Dog Napper," "The Natzonuts" and "Willy Of The Wilderness."

SUPER SUNDAY

The short, cliff–hanging serial, once a popular staple of Saturday morning movie matinees, was revived in this syndicated, animated series featuring three continuing series—"Robotix," "Inhumanoids" and "Bigfoot and the Muscle Machines"—in each half–hour show.

"Robotix" followed the confrontations between two humanoid forces on the planet Skalorr, while "Inhumanoids" traced the adventures of a courageous team of scientists who fight side by side with friendly creatures known as Mutores against vicious monsters who plan on destroying civilization and the world. The third series, "Bigfoot and the Muscle Machines," dealt with a group of powerful land vehicles that assist a young couple in their attempt to escape the evil Mr. Big. *A Marvel Production. Color. Half–hour. Premiered: October 6, 1985. Syndicated.*

Voices:

Charlie Adler, Michael Bell, Susan Blu, Bill Callaway, Nancy Cartwright, Fred Collins, Brad Crandel, Peter Cullen, Linda Gary, Dick Gautier, Ed Gilbert, Chris Latta, Neil Ross, Stanley Ralph Ross, Richard Sanders, Susan Silo, John Stephenson

Episodes:

"Robotix" (one per show).
"Battle Of The Titans," "Paradise Lost," "Traitor In Our Midst," "A Spy Is Born," "Crash Landing," "Firestorm At The Oasis,"

"Captured," "The Lost Cities," "Bront Stands Accused," "The Factory Of Death," "Zarru Takes The Plunge," "Attack Of The Rock Creatures," "All For One," "Battle For Zandon" and "The Final Attack."

"Inhumanoids" (one per show).

"Cyphenoid," "The Surma Plan," "Cult Of Darkness," "Negative Polarity," "The Evil Eye," "Primal Passions," "The Masterson Team" and "Auger For President."

"Big Foot and the Muscle Machines" (one per show).

"Cryptic Cargo," "Mystery Menace," "Deadly Duel," "The Sinister Scroll," "Crooked Cops," "Unleashed Barbarians," "Bigfoot Dead," "Death Race" and "Fountain Of Doom."

THE SYLVANIAN FAMILIES

Young children are transported in time to a warm, wonderful and whimsical forest where they become as tiny as the wee bears, rabbits, raccoons, mice, beavers and foxes who make up the Sylvanian Families, sidestepping danger and others serious troubles by banding together to solve their problems. *A DIC Enterprise Production. Color. Half–hour. Premiered: September, 1987. Syndicated.*

Voices:

The Woodkeeper: Frank Proctor, **Packbat:** Len Carlson, **Gatorpossum:** John Stocker, **Mama Honeysuckle Evergreen:** Jeri Craden, **Papa Ernest Evergreen:** Thick Wilson, **Grandma Primrose Evergreen:** Ellen Ray Hennessey, **Ashley Evergreen:** Pauline Gillis, **Preston Evergreen:** Michael Fantini, **Rusty Wildwood:** Noam Zylberman, **Holly Wildwood:** Catherine Gallant, **Papa Slick Slydale:** Brian Belfry, **Mama Velvetter Slydale:** Diane Fabian, **Buster Slydale:** Jerimiah McCann, **Scarlette Slydale:** Lisa Coristine, **Grandpa Smokey Wildwood:** John Stocker, **Grandma Flora Wildwood:** Diane Fabian, **Papa Herb Wildwood:** Len Carlson, **Mama Ginger Wildwood:** Diane Fabian, **Preston Evergreen:** Michael Fantini, **Buster Slydale:** Jeremiah McCann, **Scarlett Slydale:** Lisa Coristine, **Papa Slick Slydale:** Brian Belfry

Episodes:

"Grace Under Pressure," "Cooking Up Trouble," "Dam Busters," "School Daze," "Double Trouble," "Outfoxing The Foxes," "Know It All," "Beauty And The Beasts," "The Bear Facts," "Fraidy Cats," "Daddy's Little Girl," "Fool's Gold," "The Wheel Thing," "Muddy Waters," "There's No Place Like Home," "Tough Enough," "Hip To Be Bear," "Feud For Thought," "Stand By Your Dad," "My Brother's Keeper," "Really Amelia," "Boy's Intuition," "Here Comes The Brides," "Happily Ever After," "Founders, Keepers" and "Little Ms. Woodkeeper."

TALES OF THE WIZARD OF OZ

L. Frank Baum's "Oz" stories were brought to life in this limited animated series starring Dorothy, Tin Man, Scarecrow and the Cowardly Lion in all–new animated adventures which remained somewhat true to the Baum classic and patterned the cartoon personalities after the MGM classic stars: Judy Garland, Ray Bolger, Jack Haley and Bert Lahr. The program

Gifted jungle man Taro maintains peace in the jungle in the half–hour action/adventure series, "Taro, Giant Of The Jungle." © Global Productions

helped establish its producers, Arthur Rankin Jr. and Jules Bass, who later produced such perennial holiday favorites as "The Little Drummer Boy" and "Frosty the Snowman." *A Videocrafts International Production. Color. Half–hour. Syndicated: 1961.*

TARO, GIANT OF THE JUNGLE

Gifted with a secret power drawn from a radioactive tree, Taro, a jungle–born man, safeguards the peace of the jungle by repelling evil in this half–hour action/adventure series from Japan. *A Global Production. Color. Half–hour. Premiered: 1969. Syndicated.*

TARZAN AND THE SUPER 7

The famous vine–swinging hero, Tarzan, expanded his horizons in this 90–minute show in which he traveled to wherever he could best help others. The program mixed eight new episodes with old episodes from "Tarzan, Lord Of the Jungle," broadcast during the 1976–1977 season. In his new format, Tarzan was joined by several co–stars who appeared in segments of their own: "Web Woman," "The Freedom Force," "Manta and Moray, Monarchs of the Deep," "Superstretch and Microwoman," "Batman and Robin" and "Jason, Of Star Command," a live–action series which ran only during the first season. *A Filmation Production. Color. One hour and a half. Premiered on CBS: September 9, 1978–August 30, 1980.*

Voices:

Tarzan: Robert Ridgely, **Batman:** Adam West, **Robin:** Burt Ward, **Bat Mite:** Lennie Weinrib, **Web Woman:** Linda Gary, **Manta:** Joan Van Ark, **Moray:** Joe Stern, **Superstretch:** Ty Henderson, **Microwoman:** Kim Hamilton, **The Freedom Force: Hercules:** Bob Denison, **Isis:** Diane Pershing, **Toshi:** Mike Bell, **Merlin:** Mike Bell

Episodes:

"Tarzan" (one per show).

1978–1979 "Tarzan And The Spider People," "Tarzan And The Space God," "Tarzan And The Lost World," "Tarzan And The Monkey God," "Tarzan And The Haunted Forest" and "Tarzan And The Island Of Dr. Morphus."

"Web Woman" (one per show).

1978–1979 "The Rainmaker," "The Eye Of The Fly," "The World Within," "Madame Macabre's Calamity Circus," "Red Snails At Sunset," "Send In The Clones," "The Sun Thief," "Dr. Despair And The Mood Machine," "The Perfect Crime" and "The Lady In The Lamp."

"The Freedom Force" (alternated with Manta and Moray).

1978–1979 "The Dragon Riders," "The Scarlet Samurai," "The Planet Soldiers," "Pegasus' Odyssey" and "The Robot."

"Superstretch and Microwoman." (one per show)

1978–1979 "Bad Things Come In Small Packages," "The Ringmaster," "The Toymaker," "Future Tense," "Phantom Of The Sewers," "Shadow Of The Swamp," "The Great Candy Bar Caper," "The Superstretch Bowl," "Superstretch And Magnawoman," "Sugar Spice" and "Gnome Man's Land."

"Manta and Moray" (alternated with The Freedom Force).

1978–1979 "The Waters of Doom," "The Whale Killers," "The Warmakers," "The Souvenir Hunters," "The Freedom Fighters," "The Sunken World" and "Sea of Madness."

"Batman and Robin" (one per show).

1978–1979 "The Pest," "The Mooman," "Trouble Identity," "A Sweet Joke On Gotham City," "The Bermuda Rectangle," "Bite–Sized," "Reading, Writing And Wronging," "The Chameleon," "He Who Laughs Last," "The Deep Freeze," "Dead Ringers," "Curses! Oiled Again!," "Birds Of A Feather Fool Around Together," "Have An Evil Day" (Part 1), "Have An Evil Day" (Part 2) and "This Looks Like A Job For Bat–Mite!"

"Jason, Of Star Command" (one per show).

1978–1979 "The Golden Gryphon Strikes!," "Dragos, Master Of Cosmos," "Escape From Dragos," "Plunge To Destruction," "Star Command Must Be Saved," "Limbo Of The Lost," "Marooned In Time," "Cannons Of Light," "The Adventures Of Peepo And Wicky," "The Invisible Man," "The Mysterious Planet," "Prison Of Light," "The Black Hole," "The Enemy Within," "The Trojan Horse" and "The Final Assault."

1979–1980 "Beyond The Stars," "Secret Of The Ancients," "The Power of The Star Disk," "Through The Stargate," "Mission To The Stars," "Little Girl Lost," "Frozen In Space," "Face To Face," "Web Of The Star Witch," "Phantom Force," "Mimi's Secret" and "Battle For Freedom."

THE TARZAN/LONE RANGER/ ZORRO ADVENTURE HOUR

Zorro, the caped freedom fighter of early California, and famed masked man, the Lone Ranger, join Tarzan, the jungle lord, in separate adventures full of intrigue and cliff–hanging excitement. Episodes of Tarzan were repeated from the previously broadcast network series, "Tarzan, Lord of the Jungle." (See series for episodic information.) *A Filmation Production. Color. One hour. Premiered on CBS: September 12, 1981– September 11, 1982.*

Voices:

Tarzan: Robert Ridgely, **The Lone Ranger:** William Conrad, **Tonto:** Ivan Naranjo, **Don Diego/Zorro:** Henry Darrow, **Maria:** Christine Avila, **Sergeant Gonzales:** Don Diamond, **Ramon:** Eric Mason, **Migel:** Julio Medina, **Frey Gaspar:** East Carlo

Episodes

"Lone Ranger" (two per show).

"Runaway," "Manga The Night Monster," "Yellowstone Conspiracy," "The President Plot," "The Great Balloon Race," The Escape," "The Valley Of Gold," "Tall Timber," "Blow Out," "Abduction Of Tom Sawyer," "The Black Mare," "The Wildest Wild West Show," "The Silver Mine," "The Renegade," "The Great Land Rush," "The Memory Trap," "High And Dry," "Photo Finish," "The Ghost Wagons," "Front Page Cover–Up," "Walk A Tight Rope," "Unnatural Disaster," "Showdown On The Midnight Queen," "The Great Train Treachery," "Blast Out," "The Long Drive," "Renegade Round–Up" and "Banning's Raiders."

"The New Adventures of Zorro" (one per show).

"Three Is A Crowd," "Flash Flood," "The Blockade," "The Frame," "Turnabout," "The Tyrant," "Terremoto," "The Trap," "Fort Ramon," "The Take Over," "Double Trouble," "The Conspiracy" and "The Mysterious Traveler."

TARZAN, LORD OF THE JUNGLE

Edgar Rice Burrough's comic strip and movie character, continues to display his legendary ability of swinging by jungle vines and repulsing attackers and evil game hunters in this animated version of the famed jungle champion of justice. *A Filmation Production. Color. Half–hour. Premiered on CBS: September 11, 1976–September 3, 1977.*

Voices:

Tarzan: Robert Ridgely

Episodes:

"Tarzan And The City Of Gold," "Tarzan And The Vikings," "Tarzan And The Golden Lion," "Tarzan And The Forbidden City," "Tarzan And The Graveyard Of The Elephants," "Tarzan's Return To The City Of Gold," "Tarzan And The Strange Visitors," "Tarzan And The Land Of The Giants," "Tarzan And The Knights Of the Nimmr," "Tarzan's Rival," "Tarzan And The City Of Sorcery," "Tarzan At The Earth's Core," "Tarzan And The Ice Creature," "Tarzan And The Olympiads," "Tarzan's Trial" and "Tarzan, The Hated."

TEENAGE MUTANT NINJA TURTLES

Crime–fighting comes into a new age when a band of turtles (Michaelangelo, Leonardo, Donatello and Raphael), masters of the fine art of Ninja, battle underground criminals and assorted villains using their quick–footed fighting skills to overcome evil.

The program first premiered in 1987 as a five–part mini-series before returning the following fall as a first–run syndicated series. Six episodes for the 1989–1990 season were

The "Teenage Mutant Ninja Turtles" in a scene from their ratings—winning television series. Characters © Mirage Studios Inc. Exclusively licensed by Surge Licensing, Inc. (Courtesy: Murakami-Wolf-Swenson, Inc.)

produced at Murakami—Wolf—Swenson's Dublin, Ireland facility. When the studio's contract with its distributor, Group W, was up for renewal, CBS intervened and secured an agreement to broadcast the series in its Saturday morning lineup in the fall of 1990. The move was timely since a live—action feature based on the characters, released in the spring of 1989, turned out to be one of the biggest box—office hits of the year. *A Murakami—Wolf—Swenson Production in association with Mirage Studios. Color. Half—hour. Premiered: December, 1987 (Syndicated).*

Voices:
Michaelangelo: Townsend Coleman, **Leonardo:** Cam Clarke, **Donatello:** Barry Gordon, **Raphael:** Rob Paulsen

Additional Voices:
James Avery, Pat Fraley, Renae Jacobs, Peter Renaday, Jennifer Darling, Beau Weaver, Thom Pinto, Greg Berg, Jim Cummings, Dorian Harewood, Nicholas Omana, Tress MacNeille, Joan Gerber, Maggie Roswell

Episodes:
1987–1988 "Turtle Tracks," "Enter The Shredder," "A Thing About Rats," "Hot Rodding Teenagers From Dimension X" and "Shredder And Splintered."
1988–1989 "Return Of The Shredder," "Incredible Shrinking Turtles," "It Came From Beneath The Sewers," "The Mean Machines," "Curse Of The Evil Eye," "Case Of The Killer Pizzas," "Enter The Fly," "Invasion Of The Punk Frogs," "Splinter No More," "New York's Shiniest," "Teenagers From Dimension X," "The Catwoman From Channel 6" and "Return Of The Technodrome."
1989–1990 "Beneath These Streets," "April Fool," "Sky Turtles," "Cowabunga Shredhead," "Invasion Of The Turtle Snatchers," "The Old Switcheroo," "Turtles On Trial," "Attack Of The 50—Foot Irma," "The Maltese Hamster," "The Fifth Turtle," "Camera Bugged," "The Ninja Sword of Nowhere," "Green With Jealousy," "Take Me To Your Leader," "Enter The Rat King," "Turtles At The Earth's Core," "Burne's Blues,"

"20,000 Leaks Under The City," "Beware Of The Lotus," "Leatherhead, Terror Of The Swamp," "Recap Story," "Big Mac," "The Turtle Terminator," "The Grybyx," "Mutagen Monster," "Casey Jones—Outlaw Hero," "Michaelangelo's Birthday," "Turtles, Turtles, Turtles," "Return Of The Fly," "The Making of Metalhead," "Four Musketurtles," "Usagi Yojimbo," "Shredderville," "Corporate Raiders From Dimension X," "Usagi Come Home," "Leatherhead Meets The Rat King," "Bye, Bye, Fly," "The Gang's All Here," "The Missing Map," "The Great Bodoni," "Mr. 099 Goes To Town," "The Big Rip Off," "The Big Break In," "The Big Blowout" and "Plan Six From Outer Space."

TEEN WOLF
Based on the hit movie starring Michael J. Fox, an average teenager by day turns into a werewolf by night. *A Southern Star/Atlantic Entertainment Group Production. Color. Half—hour. Premiered on CBS: September 13, 1986–September 5, 1987.*

Voices:
Scott/Teen Wolf: Townsend Coleman

Additional Voices:
Sheryl Bernstein, Jeannie Elias, June Foray, Ellen Gerstell, Frank Welker, James Hampton, Stacy Keach Sr., Donald Most, Will Ryan, Craig Schaffer

TENNESSEE TUXEDO AND HIS TALES
Wisecracking penguin Tennessee Tuxedo (voiced by Don Adams) and walrus Chumley undertake to change the living conditions of the denizens of Megalopolis Zoo. When insoluble situations arise, the pair visit their educator friend, answer man Phineas J. Whoopie, who tackles their problems scientifically and practically. Other recurring characters were Yak, a long—horned steer; and Baldy, a bald American eagle, who portrayed Tennessee's and Chumley's friends.

Also featured were supporting segments of "The King and Odie," "The Hunter" and "Tooter Turtle," each repeated from the NBC series, "King Leonardo and His Short Subjects." (See entry for episodic listings.) The program later added a new segment, seen first on this program, called "The World of Commander McBragg," the tall—tale adventures of a long—winded ex—naval commander with a fantastic imagination. The segment was later repeated on "The Hoppity Hooper Show" and "Underdog." *A Leonardo TV Production with Total TV Productions. Color. Half—hour. Premiered on CBS: September 28, 1963–September 3, 1966. Rebroadcast on ABC: September 10, 1966–December 17, 1966.*

Voices:
Tennessee Tuxedo: Don Adams, **Chumley:** Bradley Bolke, **Professor Phineas J. Whoopie:** Larry Storch, **Yak/Baldy:** Kenny Delmar, **King Leonardo:** Jackson Beck, **Odie Cologne:** Allan Swift, **Itchy Brother:** Allan Swift, **Biggy Brat:** Jackson Beck, **Tooter Turtle:** Allan Swift, **Mr. Wizard:** Frank

Tennessee Tuxedo and Phineas J. Whoopie look on as Chumley encounters a chair–raising experience in the long–running Saturday morning favorite, "Tennessee Tuxedo And His Tales." © Leonardo–TTV

Milano, **The Hunter:** Kenny Delmar, **The Fox:** Ben Stone, **Commander McBragg:** Kenny Delmar

Episodes:

"Tennessee Tuxedo" (one per show).

"Mixed–Up Mechanics," "The Rainmakers," "The Lamplighters," "Telephone Terrors," "The Giant Clam Caper," "Tic–Tock," "Scuttled Sculpture," "Snap That Picture," "Zoo's News," "Aztec Antics," "Coat Minors," "Hot Air Heroes," "Irrigation Irritation," "TV Testers," "By The Plight Of The Moon," "Lever Levity," "The Bridge Builders," "Howl, Howl—The Gang's All Here," "Sail On, Sail On," "Tell–Tale Telegraph," "Rocket Ruckus," "Getting Steamed Up," "Tale Of A Tiger," "Dog Daze," "Brushing Off A Tootache," "Funny Honey," "The Treasure Of Jack And The Joker," "A Wreck Of A Record," "Minor Forty–Niner," "Helicopter Hi–Jinks," "Oil's Well," "Parachuting Pickle," "Wish–Wash," "Private Eye Detectives," "The Eyes Have It," "Madcap Movie–Makers," "Snow Go," "The Big Question," "Brain Strain," "Rocky Road To Diamonds," "Hooray X–Ray," "Food Feud," "How Does Your Garden Grow," "Perils Of Platypuss," "Hail To The Chief," "Physical Fitness," "Playing It Safe," "House Painters," "Admiral Tennessee," "Three Ring Circus," "The Big Drip," "Boning Up On Dinosaurs," "Smilin' Yak's Sky Service," "Teddy

Bear Trouble," "Sword Play," "Phunnie Munnie," "The Romance Of Plymouth Rock," "The Zoolympics," "The Tree Trimmers," "The Goblins Will Get You," "The Cheap Skates," "Going Up," "Monster From Another Park," "Signed And Sealed," "The Barbers," "Catch A Falling Hammock," "Peace And Quiet," "Robot Revenge," "There Auto Be A Law" and "Samantha."

"The World Of Commander McBragg" (one per show).

"Over The Falls," "Fish Story," "The Himalayas," "The North Pole," "Khyber Pass," "The Ace Of Aces," "Niagra Falls," "Dodge City Dodge," "Football By Hex," "Rabelasia," "Okefenokee Swamp," "The Flying Machine," "The Giant Elephant," "The Giant Bird," "Chicago Mobsters," "The Monster Bear," "The Kangaroo," "The Giant Mosquito," "The Black Knight," "The Flying Pond," "The Old Ninety–Two," "Secret Agent In New York," "Oyster Island," "The Steam Car," "Swimming The Atlantic," "Fort Apache," "The Flying Trapeze," "Around The World," "Indianapolis Speedway," "The Rhino Charge," "The Mystifying McBragg," "Mammoth Cavern," "The Astronaut," "Dam Break," "Eclipse," "Ship In The Desert," "Egypt," "The Singing Cowboy," "The Lumber Jack," "Bronco Buster," "Echo Canyon," "Tight Rope," "Lake Tortuga," "Coney Island," "Rainbow Island," "Insect Collector," "Lost Valley" and "The Orient Express."

THESE ARE THE DAYS

In the fashion of TV's dramatic series "The Waltons," this series chronicled the trials and tribulations of the turn–of–the–century Day family, led by Martha, a widow; her children, Ben, Cathy and Danny; and their grandfather, Jeff Day, owner and proprietor of Day General Store, in their hometown of Elmsville. *A Hanna–Barbera Production. Color. Half–hour. Premiered on ABC: September 7, 1974–September 5, 1976.*

Voices:

Martha Day: June Lockhart, **Kay Day:** Pamelyn Ferdin, **Danny Day:** Jack E. Haley, **Grandpa Day:** Henry Jones, **Ben Day:** Andrew Parks, **Homer:** Frank Cady

Additional Voices:

Julie Bennett, Henry Corden, Micky Dolenz, Moosie Drier, Dennis Duggan, Sam Edwards, June Foray, Joan Gerber, Virginia Gregg, Allan Melvin, Don Messick, Vic Perrin, William Schallert, Betsy Slade, John Stephenson, Irene Tedrow, Michele Tobin, Lurene Tuttle, Janet Waldo, Jesse White, Paul Winchell

Episodes:

"Sensible Ben," "The Fire Brigade," "Danny's Musical Dilemma," "Danny Runs Away," "Ben For President," "The Good Luck Charm," "Kathy's Job," "The Runaway Horse," "How Ben Was Cowed," "Grampa And The Great Cyclic Harmonium Swindle," "The Visitor," "The Most Precious Gift Of All," "The Spa," "Hello Mrs. McGivern, Goodbye," "The Balloon" and "The Feud."

THINK PINK PANTHER!

The Pink Panther returned to NBC's Saturday morning lineup with this fourth and final series entry for the network. The program repeated episodes of the non–speaking feline star, "Misterjaws, Supershark," and "The Texas Toads." Each were previously featured in "The Pink Panther Laugh And A Half Hour And A Half Show," which aired on NBC during the 1976–1977 season. For the 1978–1979 season, the character moved over to ABC where he was featured in a new series, "The All–New Pink Panther Show." *A De Patie–Freleng Enterprises Production. Color. Premiered on NBC: February 4, 1978–September 2, 1978.*

Voices:

Misterjaws: Arte Johnson, **Catfish,** his friend: Arnold Stang,, **Fatso:** Tom Holland, **Banjo:** Arte Johnson

---

THE THIRTEEN GHOSTS OF SCOOBY–DOO

In his 16th year on television, Scooby–Doo re–teams with Shaggy, Daphne, Scrappy–Doo and a new sidekick, Flim Flam, a nine–year–old con man, as they track down 13 of the worst ghosts, goblins and monsters scattered in the far corners of the Earth in spine–tingling new adventures narrated by famed movie macabre artist Vincent Price (called Vincent Van Ghoul). *A Hanna–Barbera Production. Color. Half–hour. Premiered on ABC: September 7, 1985–September 6, 1986.*

Voices:

Scooby–Doo: Don Messick, **Scrappy–Doo:** Don Messick, **Shaggy:** Casey Kasem, **Daphne:** Heather North, **Flim Flam:** Susan Blu, **Vincent Van Ghoul:** Vincent Price, **Weerd:** Artie Johnson, **Bogel:** Howard Morris

Episodes:

"To All The Ghouls I've Ever Loved Before," "Scoobra Ca Doobra," "Me And My Shadow Demon," "Reflections In A Ghoulish Eye," "That's Monstertainment," "Ship Of Ghouls," "A Spooky Little Ghoul Like You," "When You Witch Upon A Star," "It's A Wonderful Scoob," "Scooby In Kwackyland," "Coast To Coast," "The Ghouliest Show On Earth" and "Horror Scope."

THE THREE ROBONIC STOOGES

When CBS canceled "The Skatebirds," network executives announced that "The Three Robonic Stooges" (formerly "The Robonic Stooges") would have their own half–hour time slot, because they drew the best ratings in the former show. Norman Maurer, a former Three Stooges producer and son–in–law of Moe Howard, wrote the series which cast the boys as bionic–limbed super stooges who find themselves in typical—and not so typical—Stooge jams to the dismay of their boss, Triple–Zero, whose voice and image is projected from various objects to give them their latest assignment. Sharing the spotlight on the series was another supporting cartoon segment, "Woofer and Wimper, Dog Detectives." In 1979, after its first season, the series was moved to Sunday mornings until concluding its broadcasts two years later. *A Hanna–Barbera Production in association with Norman Maurer Productions. Color. Half–hour. Premiered on CBS: January 28, 1978–September 6, 1981.*

Voices:

Moe: Paul Winchell, **Larry:** Joe Baker, **Curly:** Frank Welker, **Triple–Zero,** their boss: Ross Martin, **Woofer:** Paul Winchell, **Wimper:** Jim McGeorge, **Larry:** David Jolliffe, **D. D.:** Bob Hastings, **Pepper:** Patricia Smith, **Dotty:** Tara Talboy, **Sheriff Bagley:** John Stephenson

Episodes:

"The Three Robonic Stooges" (two per show).
"Invasion Of The Incredible Giant Chickens," "Dimwits And Dinosaurs," "Fish and Drips," "Have Saucer Will Travel," "I Want My Mummy," "The Great Brain Drain," "Flea, Fi, Fo Fum," "Frozen Feud," "Mother Goose On The Loose," "Curly Of The Apes," "Don't Fuel With A Fool," "The Eenie Meanie Genie," "On Your Knees, Hercules," "Rub–A–Dub–Dub, Three Nuts In A Sub," "There's No Joy In An Evil Toy," "Three Little Pigheads," "The Silliest Show On Earth," "Bye, Bye, Blackbeard," "Mutiny On The Mountie," "Woo Woo Wolfman," "Schoolhouse Mouse," "Burgle Gurgle," "Rip Van Wrinkle," "The Three Nutsketeers," "Pest World Ain't The Best World," "Super Kong," "The Three Stooges And The Seven Dwarfs," "Dr. Jeykll And Hide Curly," "Jerk In The Beanstalk," "Blooperman," "Star Flaws" and "Stooges, You're Fired . . . Or The Day The Mirth Stood Still."
"Woofer and Wimper, Dog Detectives" (one per show).
"The Paper Shaper Caper," "The Case Of The Lighthouse Mouse," "Who's To Blame For The Empty Frame," "The Real Gone Gondola," "The Weird Seaweed Creature Caper," "The Green Thumb," "The Disappearing Airport Caper," "The Walking House Caper," "The Solar Energy Caper," "The Vanishing Train Caper," "The Dissolving Statue Caper," "The Missing Pig Caper," "One Of Our Elephants Is Missing," "The Amazing Heist," "The Pre–Historic Monster Caper" and "The Circus Caper."

THUNDARR THE BARBARIAN

When a runaway planet crosses between Earth and the moon, unleashing a cosmic chain reaction that destroys both worlds, the planet is reborn nearly 2,000 years later. But the new world that evolves is unlike the one before: savagery, sorcery and evil beings now rule the universe. One man battles these evil elements: Thundarr, a slave who frees himself and tries to bring justice back into the world by taking on the evil elements that prevail. *A Ruby–Spears Enterprises Production. Color. Half–hour. Premiered on ABC: October 4, 1980–September 12, 1982.*

Voices:

Thundarr the Barbarian: Bob Ridgely, **Princess Ariel,** his aide: Nellie Bellflower, **Ookla,** his aide: Henry Corden

Additional voices:

Rachel Baker, Marilyn Schreffler, Julie McWhirter, Joan Van Ark, Stacy Keach Sr., Alan Dinehart, Shep Menkin, Alan Oppenheimer

Episodes:

1980–1981 "Secret Of The Black Pearl," "Harvest Of Doom," "Mindok The Mind Menace," "Raider Of The Abyss," "Treasure Of The Moks," "Attack Of The Amazon Women," "Brotherhood Of Night," "Challenge Of The Wizards," "Valley Of The Man Apes," "Stalker From The Stars," "Portal Into Time," "Battle Of The Barbarians" and "Den Of The Sleeping Demon." **1981–1982** "Wizard War," "Fortress Of Fear," "Island Of The Body Snatchers," "City Of Evil," "Last Train To Doomsday," "Master Of The Stolen Sunsword," "Trial By Terror" and "Prophecy Of Peril."

THUNDERCATS

Originally action–figure toys, this quintet of muscular heroes battles the sinister Mutants with good always triumphing over evil. Produced two years before the success of "He–Man" and "G. I. Joe," the series did not get released officially until the 1985 season when the rise of first–run syndicated animated series took off in earnest. The series was introduced via a one–hour special in January, 1985, prior to the distribution of 65 half–hour episodes in the fall. In 1986, a two–hour special was made, "ThunderCats Ho!," which was reedited into a five–part adventure for the weekday strip. *A Rankin–Bass Production. Color. Half–hour. Syndicated: September, 1985.*

Voices:

Lion–O–Jackalman: Larry Kenney, **Snarf/S–S–Slithe:** Robert McFadden, **Cheetara/Wilykit:** Lynne Lipton, **Panthro:** Earle Hyman, **Wilykat/Monkian/Ben–Gali/Tygra:** Peter Newman, **Mumm–Ra/Vultureman/Jaga:** Earl Hammond, **Pumyra:** Gerianne Raphael, **Other Voices:** Doug Preis

Episodes:

"Exodus," "The Unholy Alliance," "Ro–Bear–Berbils," "The Slaves Of Castle Plun–Darr," "Trouble With Time," "Pumm–Ra," "The Terror Of Hammerhand," "The Tower Of Traps," "The Garden Of Delights," "Mandor—The Evil Chaser," "The Ghost Warrior," "Doomgaze," "Lord Of The Snows," "The Spaceship Beneath The Sands," "The Time Capsule," "Fireballs Of Plun–Darr," "All That Glitters," "Lion–O's Anointment: Trial Of Strength," "Mongor," "Return To Thundera," "Snarf Takes Up The Challenge," "Mandora And The Pirates," "The Crystal Queen," "Lion–O's Anointment: Trial Of Speed," "Safari Joe," "Return Of The Driller," "Turmagar The Tuska," "Sixth Sense," "Dr. Dometone," "The Astral Prison," "Queen Of 8 Legs," "Dimension Doom," "Lion–O's Anointment: Trial Of Cunning," "The Rock Giant," "The Thunder–Cutter," "Mechanical Plague," "The Demolisher," "Feliner" (Part 1), "Feliner" (Part 2), "Excalibur," "Lion–O's Anointment: Trial Of Mind Power," "The Secret Of The Ice King," "Sword In The Hole," "The Wolfrat," "Good And Ugly," "Divide And Conquer," "Micrits," "Lion–O's Anointment: Trial Of Evil," "The Super Power Potion," "The Evil Harp Of Char–Nin," "Tight Squeeze," "Monkian's Bargain," "Out Of Sight," "Jackalman's Rebellion," "The Mountain," "Eye Of The Beholder," "The Mumm–Ra Berbil," "Trouble With Thunderkittens," "Mumm–Rana," "Trapped," "The Transfer," "The Shifter," "Dream Master," "Fond Memories," "Thundercats Ho!" (five parts), "Mumm–Ra Lives!" (five parts), "Catfight," "Psych Out," "The Mask Of Gorgon," "The Mad Bubbler," "Together We Stand," "Ravage Island," "Time Switch," "Sound Stones," "Day Of The Exlipse,"

"Side Swipe," "Mumm–Rana's Belt," "Hachiman's Honor," "Runaways," "Hair Of The Dog," "Vultureman's Revenge," "Thundercubs!" (five parts), "The Totem Of Dera," "The Chain Of Loyalty," "Crystal Canyon," "Telepathy Beam," "Exile Isle," "Key Of Thundera," "Return Of The Thundercubs," "The Formula," "Locket Of Lies," "Bracelet Of Power," "Wild Workout," "Thunderscope," "The Jade Dragon," "The Circus Train," "The Last Day," "Leah," "Frogman," "The Heritage," "Screw Loose," "Malcar," "Helpless Laughter," "Cracker's Revenge," "The Mossland Monster," "Ma–Mutt's Confusion," "The Shadowmaster," "Swan Song," "The Touch Of Amortus," "The Zaxx Factor," "Well Of Doubt" and "Book Of Omens."

THUNDERBIRDS: 2086

The heroes of this futuristic series are members of International Rescue, an elite corps of daredevil cadets, who fly fantastic fleets of supersonic vehicles as they protect the world from man–made and natural disasters. *An ITC Entertainment Production. Color. Half–hour. Premiered: September, 1988. Syndicated.*

Voices:

Joan Audiberti, Paollo Audiberti, Earl Hammond, Ira Lewis, Keith Mandell, Alexander Marshall, Terry Van Tell

Episodes:

"Firefall," "Computer Madness," "One Of A Kind," "Snowbound," "Space Warriors," "Sunburn," "Fear Factor," "Fault Line," "Shadow Axis," "Starcrusher," "Shock Wave," "Guardian," "Devil's Moon," "Journey Beyond Jupiter," "The Test," "Test Flight," "Droid," "Typhoon," "Kudzilla," "Airport 2086," "Rendezvous With Destiny," "Defenders Of The Deep," "All That Glitters" and "Child's Play."

TIN TIN

A European comic strip favorite, young teenage reporter Tin Tin and his faithful dog, Snowy, engage in rough adventures and mysterious quests in this animated adaptation of Dutch cartoonist Herge's creation. Produced in France, the series was syndicated in the United States, where it was quite popular in its time. *A Tele–Hatchette Production. Black–and–white. Color. Syndicated: 1961–1966.*

THE TOM AND JERRY/GRAPE APE/MUMBLY SHOW

The famous cat–and–mouse team from MGM's cartoon heydays headlined this repackaged hour–long series featuring their own misadventures and those of purple primate, Grape Ape, from 1975–1976's "The New Tom and Jerry/Grape Ape Show," combined with new episodes of the investigating dog, Mumbly, who tracks down criminals with the help of his assistant, Shnooker. In December, 1976, Grape Ape was removed from the cast and the show was shortened to a half–hour under the title of "The Tom and Jerry/Mumbly Show." *A Hanna–Barbera Production. Color. One hour. Premiered on ABC: September 11, 1976–November 27, 1976; December*

4, 1976–September 3, 1977 (as "The Tom and Jerry/Mumbly Show").

Voices:

Grape Ape: Bob Holt, **Beagle,** his canine associate: Marty Ingels, **Mumbly:** Don Messick, **Shnooker:** John Stephenson

THE TOM AND JERRY/GRAPE APE SHOW

When the cartoon humor of Tom and Jerry faded from the silver screen after self–destructing at MGM in 1968, it seemed inevitable that the famed, silent cat–and–mouse team was washed up as cartoon tormentors. After all, how could the destructive duo survive in a new age of anti–violence television codes restricting programming creativity?

Bill Hanna and Joe Barbera, the characters' co–creators, found a way. They produced this less violent series revival for their studio, Hanna–Barbera Productions, featuring the cautious cat and mischevious mouse in brand new misadventures, which, unfortunately, lacked the belly–laughs of the early 1940's film episodes.

The show's co–star was Grape Ape, a 30–foot purple ape (an oversized version of Magilla Gorilla), and his fast–talking canine associate, Beagle, who engaged in fast–paced comedy capers of their own. *A Hanna–Barbera Production in association with Metro–Goldwyn–Mayer. Color. One hour. Premiered on ABC: September 6, 1975–September 4, 1976.*

Voices:

Grape Ape: Bob Holt, **Beagle:** Marty Ingels

Additional Voices:

Henry Corden, Joan Gerber, Bob Holt, Bob Hastings, Virginia Gregg, Cathy Gori, Don Messick, Alan Oppenheimer, Allan Melvin, Hal Smith, Joe E. Ross, John Stephenson, Jean VanderPyl, Janet Waldo, Lurene Tuttle, Paul Winchell, Frank Welker, Lennie Weinrib

Episodes:

"Tom and Jerry" (three per show).

"Stay Awake Or Else," "The Ski Bunny," "No Way Stowaways," "No Bones About It," "An Ill Wind," "Beach Bully," "Mammoth Manhunt," "The Wacky World Of Sports," "Gopher Broke," "Robin Ho Ho," "Super Bowler," "Watch Out, Watch Dog," "Tennis Menace," "Castle Wiz," "Cosmic Cat And Meteor Mouse," "Grim And Bear It," "Towering Fiasco," "Safe But Sorry," "Flying Sorceress," "Tricky McTrout," "Termites Plus Two," "Beanstalk Buddies," "Hypochondriac Lion," "Planet Pest," "The Super Cyclists," "The Sorcerer's Apprentices," "Kitten Sitters," "Police Kitten," "Two Stars Are Born," "Outfoxed Fox," "Give 'Em The Air," "Chickenrella," "Double Trouble Crow," "The Egg And Tom And Jerry," "See Dr. Jackal And Hide," "Triple Trouble," "Lost Duckling," "Hold That Pose," "Son Of Gopher Broke," "It's No Picnic," "The Bull Fighters," "Supercape Caper," "Planet Of The Dogs," "Jerry's Nephew," "Camp Out Cut–Up," "Cruise Kitty," "Big Feet" and "The Great Motor Boat Race."

"Grape Ape" (two per show).

"The All–American Ape," "That Was No Idol, That Was My Ape," "Movie Madness," "Trouble Of Bad Rock," "Flying Saucery," "Thar's No Feud Like An Old Feud," "The Grape Race," "The Big Parade," "A Knight To Remember," "S.P.L.A.T.," "G. I. Ape," "The Purple Avenger," "Grapefinger," "Who's New At The Zoo," "Amazon Ape," "Grape Marks The Spot," "The Incredible Shrinking Grape," "The Invisible Ape," "Public Grape No. 1," "S.P.L.A.T.'s Back" (Part 1), "Return To Baba-boomba," "What's A Nice Prince Like You Doin' In A Duck Like That?," "A Grape Is Born," "The Indian Grape Call," "The First Grape In Space," "S.P.L.A.T.'s Back" (Part 2), "To Sleep Or Not To Sleep," "Olympic Grape," "Ali Beagle And The Forty Grapes," "The Purple Avenger Strikes Again," "Grape Five–O" and "The Grape Connection."

THE TOM AND JERRY SHOW

MGM's top cartoon stars in the 1940s and 1950s, the non-talking Tom the cat and Jerry the mouse made their way to television in this half–hour program which was broadcast on CBS between 1965 and 1972. The series repackaged many of the original theatrical films starring the destructive duo, as well as other cartoons from MGM's cartoon library featuring such animated favorites as Barney Bear and Droopy. MGM later retitled the series, "Tom and Jerry and Friends," for syndication. *A Metro–Goldwyn–Mayer Production. Color. Half–hour. Premiered on CBS: September 25, 1965–September 17, 1972.*

Voices:

Barney Bear: Billy Bletcher, Paul Frees, **Droopy:** Bill Thompson, Don Messick, Daws Butler, **Spike,** the bulldog: Bill Thompson, Daws Butler

Episodes:

(Note: Tom and Jerry cartoons appearing in the series were produced between 1940 and 1967.)

"Tom and Jerry" (two per show).

"Advanced And Be Mechanized," "Ah, Sweet Mouse–Story Of Life," "Atominable Snowman," "Baby Butch," "Baby Puss," "Bad Day At Cat Rock," "Barbecue Brawl," "Blue Cat Blues," "The Bodyguard," "Bowling Alley–Cat," "The Brothers Carry–Mouse–Off," "Buddies Thicker Than Water," "Calypso Cat," "Cannery Rodent," "Casanova Cat," "Carmen Get It," "The Cat Above And The Mouse Below," "The Cat And The Dupli-Cat," "The Cat And The Mermouse," "The Cat Concerto," "Cat Fishin'," "Cat Napping," "The Cat's Me–Ouch," "Catty-Cornered," "City Cousin," "Cruise Cat," "Cueball Cat," "Designs On Jerry," "Dicky Moe," "Dr. Jekyll And Mr. Mouse," "Dog Trouble," "Down And Outing," "The Duck Doctor," "Duel Personality," "Filet Meow" and "Fine Feathered Friends."

(Note: Barney Bear cartoons appearing in the series were produced between 1948 and 1954.)

"Barney Bear."

"Barney's Hungry Cousin," "Bird Brain Bird Dog," "Busy Body Bear," "Cobs And Robbers," "Goggle Fishing Bear," "Half–Pint Palomino," "Heir Bear," "The Impossible Possum," "Little Wise Quacker," "Rock–A–Bye Bear," "Sleepy–Time Squirrel" and "Wee Willie Wildcat."

(Note: Droopy cartoons appearing in the series were produced between 1949 and 1958.)

"Droopy."

"Blackboard Jumble," "Billy Boy," "Caballero Droopy," "Chump Champ," "Daredevil Droopy," "Deputy Droopy," "Dixieland Droopy," "Drag–A–Long Droopy," "Droopy Leprechaun," "Droopy's Double Trouble," "Droopy's Good Deed," "Field And Scream," "The First Bad Man," "The Flea Circus," "Grin And Share It," "Homesteader Droopy," "Mutts About Racing," "One Droopy Knight," "Outfoxed," "Senor Droopy," "Sheep Wrecked," "Three Little Pups" and "Wags To Riches."

"Miscellaneous MGM Cartoons."

"Bad Luck Blackie," "Car Of Tomorrow," "The Cat That Hated People," "Cellbound," "Cock–A–Doodle Dog," "Counterfeit Cat," "The Cuckoo Murder Case," "Dog Tired," "The Dot And The Line," "Farm Of Tomorrow," "Garden Gopher," "Give And Tyke," "The House Of Tomorrow," "Little Johnny Jet," "Little Rural Riding Hood," "Lucky Ducky," "The Magical Maestro," "One Cab's Family," "The Peachy Cobbler," "Scat Cats," "A Symphony In Slang," "T.V. Of Tomorrow" and "Ventriloquist Cat."

TOMFOOLERY

Patterned after NBC's comedy–variety series "Rowan and Martin's Laugh–In" but aimed at children, this half–hour series consisted of riddles, stories, limmericks and jokes based upon the characters and events portrayed by Edward Lear in *The Nonsense Books*. The purpose of the program was to entertain and enlighten young viewers on elements of children's literature, but most viewers found the show to be somewhat disjointed and difficult to follow. *A Halas and Batchelor Production for Rankin–Bass Productions. Color. Half–hour. Premiered on NBC: September 12, 1970–September 4, 1971.*

Voices:
Peter Hawkins, Bernard Spear, The Maury Laws Singers

TOM TERRIFIC

The world's smallest superhero, this curly–haired boy derived his super powers from his funnel–hat, which enabled him to assume any shape or figure and become anything he wanted—a bird, a rock or a locomotive—to apprehend culprits with the help of his reluctant, droopy–eyed canine, Mighty Manfred the Wonder Dog. He and Manfred's main nemesis: the infamous Crabby Appleton, who was "rotten to the core."

Each story lasted five episodes and was initially presented as a daily cliff–hanger on "The Captain Kangaroo Show," Monday through Friday. Foreign cartoon producer Gene Deitch created "Tom Terrific" in late 1956 along with his fellow artists at Terrytoons, one year after the studio was sold to CBS. (It became a division of CBS Films.) Following its serialization on "Captain Kangaroo," the episodes were edited into 26 half–hour adventures and syndicated nationwide. *A Terrytoons Production in association with CBS Films. Black–and–white. Half–hour. Premiered on CBS: June 10, 1957–September 21, 1961. Syndicated.*

Voices:
Tom Terrific/Mighty Manfred: Lionel Wilson

Episodes:
1957–1958 "Nasty Knight," "The Pill Of Smartness" (with Crabby Appleton), "Sweet Tooth Sam," "Snowy Picture," "Crabby Appleton Dragon," "Captain Kidney Bean," "The Gravity Maker," "Scrambled Dinosaur Eggs," "Who Stole The North Pole," (with Crabby Appleton), "Instant Tantrums," "Track Meet Well Done," "Great Calendar Mystery" (with Crabby Appleton) and "Elephants Stew."
1958–1959 "Missing Mail Mystery" (with Crabby Appleton), "The Prince Frog," "Isotope Feeney's Foolish Fog," "Moon Over Manfred," "The Silly Sandman," "Crabby Park" (with Crabby Appleton), "The Million Manfred Mystery," "The Flying Sorcerer," "Big Dog Show–Off" (with Crabby Appleton), "The End Of Rainbows," "Robin's Nest Crusoe" and "The Everlasting Birthday Party."

TOP CAT

Near the outskirts of the 13th Precinct police station in New York City, Top Cat—T. C. for short—is a sly con artist and leader of a pack of Broadway alley cats, who do everything possible to outswindle and outsmart the cop on the beat, Officer Dibble, in madcap situations. *A Hanna–Barbera Production. Color. Half–hour. Premiered on ABC: September 27, 1961–September, 1962. Rebroadcast on ABC: October 1962–March, 1963; NBC: April, 1965–September, 1965; October, 1965–September, 1966; September 1966–December, 1966; September, 1967–August, 1968; September, 1968–May 10, 1969.*

Voices:
Top Cat (T. C.): Arnold Stang, **Choo Choo:** Marvin Kaplan, **Benny the Ball:** Maurice Gosfield, **Spook:** Leo de Lyon, **The Brain:** Leo de Lyon, **Goldie:** Jean VanderPyl, **Fancy Fancy:** John Stephenson, **Pierre:** John Stephenson, **Officer Dibble:** Allen Jenkins

Episodes:
"Hawaii—Here We Come," "The Maharajah Of Pookajee," "All That Jazz," "The $1,000,000 Derby," "The Violin Player," "The Missing Player," "The Missing Heir," "Top Cat Falls In Love," "A Visit From Mother," "Naked Town," "Sargent Top Cat," "Choo Choo's Romance," "The Unscratchables," "Rafeefleas," "The Tycoon," "The Long Hot Winter," "The Case Of The Absent Ant Eater," "T. C. Minds The Baby," "Farewell Mr. Dibble," "The Grand Tour," "The Golden Fleecing," "Space Monkey," "The Late T. C.," "Dibble's Birthday," "Choo Choo Goes Ga Ga," "King For A Day," "The Con Men," "Dibble Breaks The Record," "Dibble Sings Again," "Griswald" and "Dibble's Double."

TOUCHÉ TURTLE

Brandishing his trusty sword, knightly Touché Turtle and his simpleminded assistant, Dum Dum, heroically save queens, maidens and other people in distress in a series of five–minute cartoon adventures which were first distributed to television stations as part of a trilogy series called, "The Hanna–Barbera New Cartoon Series." Along with the series' two other components—"Wally Gator" and "Lippy the Lion"—stations either programmed the cartoons back–to–back, in separate time slots, or as elements of children's programs hosted by local television station personalities.

One of the Touché Turtle cartoons offered the character actually produced in 1960, two years before the character appeared in this series. The episode was called, "Whale Of A Tale."

Bill Thompson, who created the voice of MGM's sorrowful basset–hound Droopy, supplied the voice of Touché Turtle. *A Hanna–Barbera Production. Color. Half–hour. Premiered: September 3, 1962. Syndicated.*

Voices:
Touché Turtle: Bill Thompson, **Dum Dum:** Alan Reed

Episodes:
(four per show) "Whale Of A Tale," "Zero–Hero," "Dilly Of A Lilly," "Missing Missile," "Lake Serpent," "You Bug Me," "Roll–A–Ghoster," "Giant Double Header," "Loser Take All," "Takes Two To Tangle," "Mr. Robots," "Touché At Bat," "Billy The Cad," "Dog Daze," "Ant And Bungle," "Black Is The Knight," "Dragon Along," "Satellite Fright," "Sheepy Time Pal," "Hex Marks The Spot," "Catch As Cat Can," "Sea For Two," "High Goon," "Grandma Outlaw," "Duel Control," "Rapid Rabbit," "Thumb Hero," "Kat–Napped," "Romeo, Touché And Juliet," "The Big Bite," "Flying Saucer Sorcerer," "Aladdin's Lampoon," "Haunting License," "The Phoney Phantom," "Touché's Last Stand," "Whale Of A Tale," "Chief Beef," "Like Wild, Man," "Dum–De–Dum–Dum," "Et Tu, Touché?," "Dragon Feat," "Red Riding Hoodlum," "Dough Nuts," "Save The Last Trance For Me," "Waterloo For Two," "Robin Hoodlum," "The Shoe Must Go On," "Quack Hero," "Aliblabber And The Forty Thieves," "Out Of This Whirl," "Hero On The Half Shell," "Tenderfoot Turtle" and "Peace And Riot."

THE TRANSFORMERS

The Autobots, residents of the planet Zobitron, attempt to stop the Deceptitrons, a race of deadly robots who want to control the universe in this futuristic battle of good over evil. *A Marvel Production. Color. Half–hour. Premiered: September, 1984. Syndicated.*

Voices:
Astro Train: Jack Angel, **Prowl/Scrapper/Swoop/Junkion:** Michael Bell, **Grimlock:** Greg Berger, **Arcee:** Susan Blu, **Devastator:** Arthur Burghardt, **Spike/Brawn/Shockwave:** Corey Burton, **Cyclonus:** Roger Carmel, **Optimus/Prime/Ironhide:** Peter Cullen, **Jazz:** Scatman Crothers, **Dirge:** Brad Davis, **Inferno:** Walker Edmiston, **Perceptor:** Paul Eiding, **Blitzwing:** Ed Gilbert, **Bumblebee:** Dan Gilvezan, **Blaster:** Buster Jones, **Scourge:** Stan Jones, **Cliffjumper:** Casey Kasem, **Star Scream/Cobra Comm:** Chris Latta, **Daniel:** David Mendenhall, **Gears:** Don Messick, **Blurr:** John Moshitta, **Hot Road/Rodimus:** Judd Nelson, **Shrapnel:** Hal Rayle, **Kickback:** Clive Revill, **Bone Crusher/Hook/Springer/Slag:** Neil Ross, **Soundwave/Megatron/Galatron/Rumble/Frenzy/Wheelie:** Frank Welker

Additional Voices:
John Stephenson, Ken Samson, Victor Caroli

Episodes:
"Transport To Oblivion," "Roll For It," "Divide And Conquer," "Fire In The Sky," "S.O.S. Dinobots," "Fire On The Mountain," "War Of The Dinobots," "The Ultimate Doom" (Part 1: "Brainwash"), "The Ultimate Doom" (Part 2: "Search"), "The Ultimate Doom" (Part 3: "Revival"), "A Plague Of Insecticons," "The Heavey–Metal War," "Autobot Spike," "Changing Gears," "City Of Steel," "Attack Of The Autobots," "Traitor," "The Immobilizer," "The Autobot Run," "Atlantis Arise," "The Machine Rebellion," "Enter The Ninja," "Prime Problem," "The Core," "The Insecticon Syndrome," "Dinobot Island" (Part 1), "Dinobot Island" (Part 2), "The Master Builders," "Auto Berserk," "Microbots," "Megatron's Master Plan" (Part 1), "Megatron's Master Plan" (Part 2), "Desertion Of The Dinobots" (Part 1), "Desertion Of The Dinobots" (Part 2), "Blaster Blues," "A Deception Raider In King Arthur's Court," "The Golden Lagoon," "The God Gambit," "Makes Tracks," "Child's Play," "The Secret Of Omega Su," "The Gambler," "Kremzeek," "Sea Change," "Triple Takeover," "Prime Target," "Auto–Bop," "The Search For Alphatrion," "The Girl Who Loved Powerglide," "Hoist Goes Hollywood," "Key To Vector Sigma" (Part 1), "Key To Victor Sigma" (Part 2), "Aerial Assault," "War Dawn," "Trans–Europe Express," "Cosmic Rust," "Starscream's Brigade," "The Revenge Of Bruticus," "Masquerade," "B.O.T.," "Five Faces Of Darkness" (five parts), "The Killing Jar," "Chaos," "Dark Awakening," "Forever Is A Long Time Coming," "Starscream's Ghost," "Thief In The Night," "Surprise Party," "Madman's Paradise," "Nightmare Planet," "Ghost In The Machine," "Webworld," "Carnage In C–Minor," "The Quintesson Journal," "The Ultimate Weapon," "The Big Broadcast Of 2006," "Fight Or Flee," "The Dweller In The Depths," "Only Human," "Grimlock's New Brain," "Money Is Everything," "Call Of The Primitives," "The Face Of Nijika," "The Burden Hardest To Bear" and "The Rebirth" (three parts).

TRANZOR Z

The evil Dr. Demon and his army of powerful robot beasts continue in their eternal quest to take control of the world, but encounter a protector of peace more powerful than all of them combined: Tranzor Z, a super robot ("the mightiest of machines") created by the great Dr. Wells. *A 3 B Production in association with Toei Animation. Color. Half–hour. Premiered: September, 1985. Syndicated.*

Voices:
Gregg Berger, Mona Marshall, Paul Ross, Willard Jenkins, Robert A. Gaston, James Hodson, William Lloyd Davis

THE TROLLKINS

A mini–civilization of wee playful folks with purple, blue and green faces find modern living possible by fashioning 20th century devices out of glow worms, spider threads and other natural wonders in the magical community of Trolltown. *A Hanna–Barbera Production. Color. Half–hour. Premiered on CBS: September 12, 1981–September 4, 1982.*

Voices:
Sheriff Pudge Trollsom: Allan Oppenheimer, **Pixlee Trollsom:** Jennifer Darling, **Blitz Plumkin:** Steve Spears, **Flooky:** Frank Welker, **Grubb Trollmaine:** Michael Bell, **DepuTroll Dolly Durkle:** Jennifer Darling, **DepuTroll Flake:** Marshall Efron, **Mayor Lumpkin:** Paul Winchell, **Bogg:** Frank Welker, **Afid:** Hank Saroyan, **Slug:** Bill Callaway, **Top Troll:** Frank Welker

Episodes:
"Trolltown Goes Trollywood," "Trolltown Meets Kling Klong," "The Case Of The Missing Trollosaurus," "The Trollerbear Scare," "Escape From Alcatroll," "The Trollness Monster," "The Trollchoppers Meet Frogzilla," "Robotroll," "The Trollyapolis 500," "Trollin The Magician," "The Great Troll Train Wreck," "Trolltown Goes Ga–Ga," "Treasure Of Troll Island," "Mirror, Mirror On The Troll," "The Empire Strikes Trolltown," "Raiders Of The Lost Troll," "The Moth That Ate Trolltown," "Fine, Feathered Lumpkin," "Bermuda Trollangle," "Supertroll," "Flooky And The Troll Burglar," "Dr. Frankentroll, I Presume," "The Abominable Trollman," "The Trollcat In The Trollhat" and "Agent Double–O–Troll."

TURBO TEEN

A top–secret government experiment goes awry when a high school journalism student, Bret Matthews, accidentally crashes his sports car through the walls of the test laboratory and is struck by a ray from a machine that causes him to become one with his car. As a result of this freak accident, Matthews is able to transform himself into a car whenever his temperature rises. He then uses his unique ability to solve mysteries and fight crime, assisted by his friends, Pattie and Alex, who share his secret. *A Ruby–Spears Enterprises Production. Color. Half–hour. Premiered on ABC: September 8, 1984–August 31, 1985.*

Voices:
Brett Matthews: Michael Mish, **Pattie,** his girlfriend: Pamela Hayden, **Alex,** his friend: T. K. Carter, **Eddie:** Pat Fraley, **Flip/Rusty:** Frank Welker

Episodes:
"Dark Rider," "Mystery Of Fantasy Park," "No Show U.F.O.," "Micro–Teen," "The Sinister Souped–Up Seven," "Video Venger," "Dark Rider And The Wolves Of Doom," "The Curse Of The Twisted Claw," "Daredevil Run," "The Amazon Adventure," "Fright Friday" and "The Mystery Of Dark Rider."

TV TOTS TIME

One of the first network cartoon shows, ABC aired this 15–minute program on weekdays and Sundays, presenting a variety of black–and–white films, including animated cartoons originally produced by Van Beuren Studios (retitled under Official Films) and early Paul Terry cartoons (called "Terryland" films) from the 1920s. Before making its network debut, the series was broadcast by local ABC stations (February 4, 1950–April 22, 1950) in several major markets. *Black–and–white. Fifteen minutes. Premiered on ABC: December 30, 1951–March 2, 1952.*

UNCLE CROCK'S BLOCK

Charles Nelson Reilly, in live segments, hosted this spoof of local children's shows presenting skits and jokes along with his buffoonish assistant, Mr. Rabbit Ears. (He also occasionally engaged in some lighthearted bickering with his program's director, Basil Bitterbottom, played by Jonathan Harris.) Between shticks, Reilly introduced several animated cartoons to round out the program. They were: "Fraidy Cat," a cowardly cat who is haunted by his eight ghostly selves; "M*U*S*H*," a satirical takeoff of the television sitcom M*A*S*H; and "Wacky and Packy," a pair of Stone Age characters who become misplaced—in New York, of all places—and learn to deal with modern civilization. *A Filmation Production. Color. One hour. Premiered on ABC: September 6, 1975–February 14, 1976.*

Cast:
Uncle Croc: Charles Nelson Reilly, **Mr. Rabbit Ears:** Alfie Wise, **Basil Bitterbottom:** Jonathan Harris

Voices:
Fraidy Cat: Alan Oppenheimer, **Tinker/Dog/Mouse/Hokey:** Alan Oppenheimer, **Tonka/Wizard/Captain Kitt/Sir Walter Cat/Winston:** Lennie Weinrib, **M*U*S*H:** **Bullseye/Tricky John/Sonar/Hilda:** Robert Ridgely, **Sideburns/Coldlips/Colonel Flake/General Upheaval:** Ken Mars, **Wacky/Packy:** Allan Melvin

Episodes:
"Fraidy Cat" (one per show).
"The Not So Nice Mice," "Cupid And The Cat," "Over The Wall And Havin' A Ball," "Feline Fortune," "Puss 'N' Boots," "A Scaredy Fraidy," "Meaner Than A Junkyard Cat," "Fraidy Goes Fishin'," "Fraidy Come Home," "Double Trouble," "Love Is A Many Feathered Thing," "It's A Dog's Life," "Unlucky Fraidy," "This Cat For Hire," "Choo–Choo Fraidy," "Magic Numbers," "A Semi–Star Is Born" and "Culture Shock."
"M*U*S*H" (two per show).
"I Am The Commanding Officer," "The Camp Show," "Cat On A Cold Tin Roof," "The Big Budget Car," "The Moose Who Came To Dinner," "Make Room For Candi," "The Crash Diet," "Man Cannot Live On Ice Alone," "Home Sweet Haunt," "Hi-Brow Menace," "No Talent Show," "Major Mynah," "More Power To Ya," "Cowering In This Corner," "The Iceman Melteth," "The Great Gold Rush," "Sideburns' Surprise Party," "The Mushiest Athlete," "Love Makes The World Go Round," "Will The Real Sidcburns Please Stand Up?," "Sleep Can Be Hazardous To Your Health," "I'm O.K., You're Nuts," "Toying Around With The General," "Room And Bored," "Cinema Weirdate," "The Six Zillion Dollar Dog," "Gridiron Grief," "3–D TV," "To Flea Or Not To Flea" and "The Calumso Caper."
"Wacky and Packy" (one per show).
"The New York Sweats," "In The Zoo," "Wacky's Fractured Romance," "Packy Come Home," "Let's Make A Bundle," "All In A Day's Work," "The Party Crushers," "Magic Mayhem," "The Bad News Cruise," "The Fender Benders," "Uncle Sam

Wants You?," "No Place Like Home," "One Of Your Missing Links Is Missing," "The Shopping Spree," "Getting A Piece Of The Rock" and "Is This Any Way To Run An Airline?"

UNCLE WALDO

In 1965, this syndicated series, a retitled version of "The Adventures of Hoppity Hooper," first appeared. The show was designed for weekday programming. Two episodes of "Hoppity Hooper" were featured daily, along with one episode each of "Fractured Fairytales" and "Peabody's Improbable History." (See "The Adventures of Hoppity Hooper" for voice and episodic information.) *A Jay Ward Production. Color. Half–hour. Premiered: 1965.*

UNDERDOG

From his guise of humble, lovable canine Shoeshine Boy, superhero Underdog (voiced by "Mr. Peppers" TV series star Wally Cox) emerges to overpower criminals in Washington, D. C., chiefly mad scientist Simon Bar Sinister and underworld boss Riff Raff.

Two adventures were featured each week, along with repeat episodes of several rotating components: "The Hunter," which was first seen on "King Leonardo and His Short Subjects" and "The World of Commander McBragg," which first appeared on "Tennessee Tuxedo and His Tales." (See these two series for voice and episodic information.)

In the fall of 1966, after the series' initial run on NBC, the program was restructured. The original components were replaced by "Go Go Gophers." The cartoons starred Running Board and Ruffled Feathers, a pair of renegade, buck–toothed gopher Indians, who are rebuffed by Colonel Kit Coyote, a blustering Teddy Roosevelt type, in their continuous scheme to seize the U. S. calvary fort near Gopher Gulch. In 1968, CBS repeated episodes of the characters along with reruns of "Klondike Kat" in their own series, "Go Go Gophers." That same year, NBC began rebroadcasting the "Underdog" series, which lasted three more seasons. *A Total TV Production with Leonardo TV Productions. Color. Half–hour. Premiered on NBC: October 3, 1964–September 3, 1966; Premiered on CBS: September 10, 1966–September 2, 1967. Rebroadcast on NBC: September 7, 1968–September 1, 1973.*

Voices:
Underdog: Wally Cox, **Sweet Polly Purebred,** reporter: Norma McMillan, **Colonel Kit Coyote:** Kenny Delmar, **The Sergeant:** Sandy Becker, **Ruffled Feathers:** Running Board

Episodes:
"Underdog" (two per show).
"Safe Waif," "March Of The Monsters," "Simon Says," (the following are in four parts unless otherwise noted), "Go Snow," "Zot," "The Great Gold Robbery," "Fearo," "Shrinking Water," "The Bubble Heads," "From Hopeless To Helpless," "Tricky Trap By Tap Tap" (one part), "The Wicked Witch Of Pickyoon," "Weathering The Storm," "The Gold Bricks," "Pain Strikes Underdog," "The Molemen," "The Flying Sorcerers," "The Forget–Me–Not," "Guerilla Warfare," "Simon Says 'No

An artist's rough conception of feeble shoeshine boy, Underdog, from the popular network series of the same name. © Leonardo–TTV

Thanksgiving,' " "The Silver Thieves," "Raffaffville," "The Tickle Feather Machine," "Underdog Vs. Overcoat," "The Big Dipper," "Just In Case," "The Marblehead," "Simon Says 'Be My Valentine,' " "Round And Round," "A New Villain," "Batty Man" and "Vacuum Gun."
"Go Go Gophers" (one per show).
"Moon Zoom," "The Trojan Totem," "Introducing General Nuisance," "Gatling Gophers," "Cleveland Indians," "Medicine Men," "A Mesa Mess," "Termite Trainers," "Who's A Dummy," "Tapping The Telegraph," "Bold As Gold," "Up In The Air," "The Big Banger," "He's For The Berries," "Swamped," "Tanks To The Gophers," "Indian Treasure," "The Horseless Carriage Trade," "Honey Fun," "The Colonel Cleans Up," "The Raw Recruits," "Tenshun!," "Cuckoo Combat," "The Unsinkable Iron Clad," "Amusement Park," "Losing Weight," "Wild Wild Flowers," "Lookout, Here Comes Aunt Flora," "Root Beer Riot," "Tricky Tepee Trap," "3–Ring Circus," "Don't Fence Me In," "Locked Out," "Hotel Headaches," "Choo Choo Chase," "Rocket Ruckus," "Go Go Gamblers," "Radio Raid," "Steam Roller," "Mutiny A Go–Go," "Marooned On Cannibal Island," "The Indian Giver," "The Big Pow–Wow," "Back To The Indians" and "California Here We Come."

UNITY PICTURES THEATRICAL CARTOON PACKAGE

In March, 1947, this package of Van Beuren–RKO theatrical cartoons—"Aesop's Fables" and "Tom and Jerry" (not the famous cat–and–mouse)—were broadcast on the first children's television series, "Movies for Small Fry," hosted by Big Brother Bob Emery of WABD–TV, New York. The program was telecast weekdays on the DuMont Television Network. In 1948, "Cubby the Bear" was added to the package for television viewing. *A Van Beuren–RKO Production for Unity Pictures. Black–and–white. One hour. Premiered: March 11, 1947.*

THE UPA CARTOON SHOW

This series is a repackaged version of "The Gerald McBoing Boing Show," which was first shown on CBS in December, 1956. The program was then repeated in 1957, and then syndicated in the late 1960s (under the title of "UPA Cartoon Parade") by UPA. In 1989, the series was packaged as part of the "Mr. Magoo and Friends" show and broadcast on USA Network.

Hosted by Gerald McBoing Boing, the series features cartoon segments starring the Twirlinger Twins, Dusty of the Circus, among others, as well as 130 five–minute Mr. Magoo cartoons produced in the 1960s and episodes from "What's New Mr. Magoo?," produced in 1977 by DePatie–Freleng Enterprises in association with UPA. (See "The Gerald McBoing Boing Show" for voice and episodic information.) *A UPA Production. Color. Half–hour. Rebroadcast on USA Network: September 1989–September 1990 (as part of "Mr Magoo and Friends"). Syndicated.*

U. S. OF ARCHIE

Timed with the country's bicentennial, Archie, Jughead and Veronica recreate the accomplishments of America's forefathers in this half–hour Saturday morning series which was a major ratings failure for CBS. By mid–season, the program was moved to Sunday mornings where it completed its network run. *A Filmation Production. Color. Half–hour. Premiered on CBS: September 7, 1974–September 5, 1976.*

Voices:

Dal McKennon, Howard Morris, John Erwin, Jane Webb

Episodes:

"The Underground Railroad," "Gold," "The Day Of The Ladies," "The Star–Spangled Banner," "The Wright Brothers," "The Roughrider," "The Golden Spike," "Flame Of Freedom," "There She Blows," "Ben Franklin And The Post Office," "The Giver," "Mr. Watson, Come Here," "The Crime Of Ignorance," "The Great Divide," "Fulton's Folly" and "Wizard Of Menlo Park."

VALLEY OF THE DINOSAURS

A modern–day family gets caught up in a whirlpool while exploring an uncharted river in the Amazon and is transported back in time to the world of prehistoric animals and cave people. *A Hanna–Barbera Production. Color. Half–hour. Premiered on CBS: September 7, 1974–September 4, 1976.*

Voices:

John Butler, the father: Mike Road, **Kim Butler,** his wife: Shannon Farnon, **Katie Butler,** their daughter: Margene Fudenna, **Greg Butler,** their son: Jackie Earle Haley, **Gorak,** the prehistoric father: Alan Oppenheimer, **Gera,** his wife: Joan Gardner, **Tana,** their daughter: Melanie Baker

Episodes:

"Forbidden Fruit," "What Goes Up," "A Turned Turtle," "The Volcano," "Smoke Screen," "The Saber–Tooth Kids," "After Shock," "Top Cave, Please," "S.O.S.," "Fire," "Rain Of Meteors," "To Fly A Kite," "Test Flight," "The Big Toothache" and "Torch."

VISIONAIRIES

On the planet Prysmos, the age of technology has come to an end and a new age of magic has begun under the great wizard, Merklyn, who transforms knights into warriors with spectacular capabilities. Calling themselves "The Spectral Knights," they protect the citizens from the evil forces of the Darkling Lord. *A TMS Entertainment Production in association with Sunbow Productions. Visionairies are trademarks of Hasbro, all rights reserved. Color. Half–hour. Premiered: Fall 1987. Syndicated.*

Voices:

Spectral Knights: Leoric: Neil Ross, **Ectar:** Michael McConnohie, **Cyrotek:** Bernard Erhard, **Witterquick:** Jim Cummings, **Arzon:** Hal Rayle, **Feryl:** Beau Weaver, **Galadria:** Sue Blu, **Darkling Lords: Darkstorm:** Chris Latta, **Cravex:** Chris Latta, **Mortredd:** Jonathan Harris, **Cindarr:** Peter Cullen, **Lexor:** Michael McConnohie, **Reekon:** Roscoe Lee Browne, **Virulina:** Jennifer Darling, **Narrator:** Malachi Throne, **Wisdom Owl:** Hal Rayle, **Bearer of Knowledge:** Jim Cummings

Episodes:

"The Age Of Magic Begins," "The Dark Hand Of Treachery," "Quest For The Dragon's Eye," "The Price Of Freedom," "Feryl Steps Out," "Lion Hunt," "The Overthrow Of Merklyn," "The Power Of The Wise," "Horn Of Unicorn/Claw Of Dragon," "Trail Of Three Wizards," "Sorcery Squared," "Honor Among Thieves" and "Dawn Of The Sun Imps."

VOLTRON: DEFENDER OF THE UNIVERSE

Set in the 25th century, a team of young, dauntless space explorers seek and recover five fierce robot lions who unite to form "Voltron," the most incredible robot warrior ever. Once united, the voltron force protects the Planet Arus and neighboring galaxies and establishes peace in the universe. *A World Events Production. Color. Half–hour. Syndicated: 1984.*

Voices:

Jack Angel, Michael Bell, Peter Cullen, Neil Ross, Lennie Weinrib

Episodes:

"In Search Of New Worlds," "First Day On A New World," "Building A New World," "Goodbye, New World," "Try This World For Size," "A Storm Of Meteors," "Help Not Wanted," "Ghost Fleet From Another Planet," "A Very Short Vacation," "Planet Of The Bats," "A Temporary Truce," "Wolo's Lost World," "Planet Stop For Repairs," "A Curious Comet," "In The Enemy Camp," "Who's On First," "No, Who's On Second," "What's On First," "Great Stone Space Faces," "Defend The New World," "Meanwhile Back At Galaxy Garrison," "Nerok Scores Big," "Hazar On The Carpet," "Hazar Is Demoted," "Just Like Earth," "The Planet Trap," "Save The Space Station,"

"Planet Of The Amazons," "Revolt Of The Slaves," "Raid On Galaxy Garrison," "Smashing The Meteor Barrier," "A Man Made Sun," "Captain Newley Returns," "Hazar Bucks The Empire," "Letters From Home," "Peace—A Fish Story!," "The Red Moon People," "This World's For The Birds!," "That's The Old Ball Game," "Red Moon Rises Again," "Another Solar System," "Whose World Is It," "It's Anybody's World," "Frozen Assets," "Coconuts," "It Could Be A Long War," "Color Me Invisible," "Time Running Out," "Zero Hour Approaches," "The Drules World Cracks Up," "The Drules Surrender," "The End Of Hazar's World," "Space Explorers Captured," "Escape To Another Planet," "A Ghost And Four Keys," "The Missing Key," "The Princess Joins Up," "The Right Arm Of Voltron," "The Lion Has New Claws," "The Stolen Lion," "A Pretty Spy," "Secret Of The White Lion," "Surrender," "Bad Birthday Party," "The Witch Gets A Facelift," "Yurak Gets His Pink Slip," "Give Me Your Princess," "Bridge Over The River Chozzerai," "My Brother Is A Robeast," "Zarkon Is Dying," "The Burried Castle," "Pidge's Home Planet," "It'll Be A Cold Day," "The Deadly Flowers," "It Takes Real Lions," "Raid Of The Alien Mice," "Short Run Of The Centipede Express," "The Invisible Robeast," "The Green Medusa," "The Treasure Of Planet Tyrus," "Magnetic Attraction," "The Sleeping Princess," "The Sincerest Form Of Flattery," "A Transplant For The Blue Lion," "Attack Of The Fierce Frogs," "Lotor Traps Pidge," "Doom Boycotts The Space Olympics," "Lotor's Clone," "Lotor's New Hit Man," "Raid Of The Red Berets," "The Captive Comet," "The Little Prince," "There Will Be A Royal Wedding," "The Sand People," "Voltron Frees The Slaves," "Voltron Vs. Voltron," "One Princess To Another," "Mighty Space Mouse," "Summit Meeting," "Return Of Coran's Son" (Part 1), "Coran's Son Runs Amuck" (Part 2), "Zarkon Becomes A Robeast," "Lotor The King," "Final Victory," "Dinner And A Show," "Envoy From Galaxy Garrison," "Mousemania," "The Shell Game," "The Traitor," "Voltron Meets Jungle Woman," "Little Buddies," "Who Was That Masked Man?," "Take A Robot To Lunch," "War And Peace . . . And Doom!," "Who's Flyin' Blue Lion? The Return Of Sven!," "Enter Merla: Queen Of Darkness," "A Ghost Of A Chance," "To Sooth The Savage Robeast," "Doom Girls On The Prowl," "With Friends Like You . . .," "Lotor—My Hero . . .?," "No Muse Is Good Muse," "The Alliance Strikes Back" and "Breaking Up Is Hard To Doom."

THE VOYAGES OF DR. DOLITTLE

With his helpers Tommy and Maggie, the world's most famous doctor sets sail around the world to exotic lands full of fantasy and excitement and meets among others, the Monkey King, the Whiskered Rat and Pushmi–Pullyu, the two–headed creature, in this adaptation of Hugh Lofting's classic tales in which the good doctor and his patients converse in animal talk. *A Knack Television Production in association with 20th Century Fox Television. Color. Half–hour. Premiered: 1984. Syndicated.*

Voices:

Dr. Dolittle: John Stephenson, **Tommy Stubbins:** B. J. Ward, **Maggie Thompson:** Jeannie Elias

Additional Voices:

G. Stanley Jones, William Callaway, Ralph James, Jerry Dexter, Linda Gary

Episodes:

"The Strange Doctor," "First Step To The Sea," "Luke The Hermit," "Voyage To Africa," "To Save 10,000 Monkeys," "Chee–Chee, Don't Die," "The King Of The Beasts," "The Sun God," "The Dragon Of Barbary," "Save My Uncle!," "Aboard The Ghost Ship," "Our Town, Puddleby" and "Our Friend, Pushmi–Pullyu."

VYTOR, THE STARFIRE CHAMPION

This program highlights the adventures of the teenage hero, Vytor, and his female co–star, Skyla, who work together to recapture the Starfire Orb, the world's most powerful energy source, and create peace and unity in the world. The program aired via syndication as a one–week mini–series. *A World Events/Calico Productions presentation. Half–hour. Color. Syndicated: January, 1989.*

Voices:

Vytor: Michael Horton, **Skyla:** Liz Georges, **Lyria:** Liz Georges, **Myzor:** Peter Cullen, **Eldor:** Peter Cullen, **Targil:** Neil Ross, **Baboose:** Allison Argo, **Windchaser:** Patrick Fraley, **Mutoids:** Patrick Fraley

Episodes:

"Vytor—The Starfire Champion," "Aerion," "The Spirit Tree" and "Wilderland."

THE WACKY RACES

Zany race car drivers and their equally daffy turbine–driven contraptions enter international competitions, with the single goal of winning the coveted title "The World's Wackiest Racer." Their efforts are endangered by the devious activities of evildoer Dick Dastardly and his snickering dog, Muttley. Competitors include Pat Pendig, Rufus Ruffcut, Sawtooth, Penelope Pitstop, The Slag Brothers (Rock and Gravel), the Ant Hill Mob, the Red Max, the Gruesome Twosome, Luke and Blubber Bear. *A Hanna–Barbera Production. Color. Half–hour. Premiered on CBS: September 14, 1968–September 5, 1970.*

Voices:

Dick Dastardly: Paul Winchell, **Penelope Pitstop:** Janet Waldo, **Red Max:** Daws Butler, **Rufus Ruffcut:** Daws Butler, **Rock:** Daws Butler, **Peter Perfect:** Daws Butler, **Rock:** Don Messick, **Luke and Blubber Bear:** John Stephenson, **The General:** John Stephenson, **Muttley:** Don Messick, **Ring–A–Ding:** Don Messick, **Big Gruesome:** Daws Butler, **Little Gruesome:** Don Messick, **The Ant Hill Mob:** Mel Blanc, **Professor Pat Pending:** Don Messick, **Narrator:** Dave Willock

Episodes:

(two 10–minute episodes per show) "See Saw To Arkansas," "Creepy Trip To Lemon Twist," "Why Oh Why Wyoming," "Beat The Clock To Yellow Rock," "Idaho A Go–Go," "Mish–

Mash Missouri Dash," "Scout Scatter," "Real Gone Ape," "By Roller Coasters To Upsans–Downs," "Free Wheeling To Wheeling," "The Baja–Ha–Ha Race," "The Speedy Arkansas Travelers," "The Great Cold Rush Race," "Eeny Meeny Missouri Go," "Zippy–Mississippi Race," "Hot Race To Chillicothe," "Traffic Jambalayan," "Wrong Lumber Race," "Rhode Island Road Race," "Wacky Race To Rip Saw," "Oil's Well That Ends Well Race," "Whizzing To Washington," "The Super Silly Swamp Sprint," "The Dipsy–Doodle Desert Derby," "Race Rally To Raleigh," "Dash To Delaware," "Dopey Dakota Derby," "Speeding For Smogland," "Fast Track To Hackensack," "Ball Point, Penn., Or Bust," "Racing To Racine," "The Carlsbad Or Bust Bash," "The Ski Resort Road Race" and "Overseas Hi–Way Race."

WAIT TILL YOUR FATHER GETS HOME

Cast in the mold of TV's long–running sitcom, "All in the Family," this wildly funny first–run animated series illustrated the generation gap between an old–fashioned father (Harry Boyle, president of Boyle Restaurant Supply Company) and his modern–day children (Chet, Alice and Jamie) who have difficulty accepting their father's timeworn methods and philosophies of life. Broadcast between 1972 and 1974, the series appeared in prime–time in many major markets across the United States. *A Hanna–Barbera Production. Color. Half–hour. Premiered: September 12, 1972. Syndicated.*

Voices:

Harry Boyle: Tom Bosley, **Irma Boyle,** his wife: Joan Gerber, **Alice Boyle,** the daughter: Kristina Holland, **Chet Boyle,** the son: David Hayward, **Jamie Boyle,** the youngest son: Jackie Haley, **Ralph,** their neighbor: Jack Burns

Episodes:
1972–1973 "The Fling," "Alice's Dress," "The Hippie," "The Beach Vacation," "Help Wanted," "Love Story," "The Victim," "Chet's Job," "Chet's Fiancee," "The Mouse," "Duty Calls," "Expectant Papa," "The New Car," "The New House," "The Prowler," "Mama's Identity," "The Patient," "The Swimming Pool," "Sweet Sixteen," "The Commune," "The Music Tycoon," "Accidents Will Happen," "Papa In New York" and "The Neighbors."
1973–1974 "Bringing Up Jamie," "The Lady Detective" (with Phyllis Diller), "Permissive Papa," "The Boyles On TV," "My Wife, The Secretary," "Papa, The Housewife," "Jamie's Project," "Don For The Defense" (with Don Adams), "Alice's Diet," "Mama Loves Monty" (with Monty Hall), "Alice's Crush," "Papa's Big Check," "Mama's Charity," "Chet's Pad," "Papa, The Coach," "Birdman Chet," "Back To Nature," "Alice's Freedom," "Don Knotts, The Beekeeper" (with Don Knotts), "Maude Loves Papa" (with Jonathan Winters), "Rich Little, Supersleuth" (with Rich Little), "Model Alice," "Marriage Counselor" and "Car 54."

WALLY GATOR

Giddy alligator Wally, who speaks like comedian Ed Wynn, yearns for freedom from the confines of his zoo cage in five-minute cartoon adventures which were first offered to television stations as a component of "The Hanna–Barbera New Cartoon Series," also featuring "Touché Turtle" and "Lippy the Lion" in their own individual series. Local television programmers broadcast the cartoons in consecutive or individual time slots and as part of daily children's programs hosted by local television personalities. *A Hanna–Barbera Production. Color. Half–hour. Premiered: September 3, 1962. Syndicated.*

Voices:
Wally Gator: Bob Holt, **Mr. Twiddle,** his friend: Don Messick

Episodes:
"Droopy Dragon," "Gator–Napper," "Swamp Fever," "White Tie And Frails," "Escape Artist," "California Or Bust," "Frame And Fortune," "Tantalizin' Turnips," "Over The Fence Is Out," "Bear With Me," "Outside Looking In," "Bachelor Buttons," "Which Is Which Witch?," "Pen–Striped Suit," "Ship Shape Escape," "Semi Seminole," "Little Red Riding Gator," "Ice Cube Boob," "The Forest Prime Evil," "Snoopy Snowzer," "Unconscious Conscience," "Gator–Baitor," "False Alarm," "Phantom Alligator," "Puddle Hopper," "Baby Cheese," "Gosh Zilla," "Camera Shy Guy," "Rebel Rabble," "No More Mower," "Knight Nut," "Ape Scrape," "Gator–Imitator," "Safe At Home," "Balloon Baffoon," "Rassle Dazzle," "Sea Sick Pals," "Accidentally On Purpose," "Whistle Stopper," "Birthday Grievings," "Medicine Avenue," "Marshall Wally," "One Round Trip," "Gopher Broke," "Gladiator Gator," "Bubble Trouble," "Ice Charades," "Creature Feature," "Squatter's Rights," "The Big Drip," "Gourmet Gator" and "Carpet Baggers."

WHAT'S NEW, MR. MAGOO?

The near–sighted, Academy Award–winning Mr. Magoo is joined by an equally myopic canine companion, McBarker, in further adventures marked by mistaken identity gags and other improbable situations reminiscent of previous productions featuring the querulous and sometimes irritable character. *A DePatie–Freleng Enterprises Production in association with UPA Productions. Color. Half–hour. Premiered on CBS: September 10, 1977–September 9, 1979.*

Voices:
Mr. Magoo: Jim Backus, **McBarker,** his bulldog: Robert Ogle, **Waldo:** Frank Welker

Episodes:
(two per show) "Mr. Magoo's Concert," "Baby Sitter Magoo," "Who's Zoo Magoo?," "Motorcycle Magoo," "Unglued Magoo," "Lion Around Magoo," "Caveman Magoo," "Tut Tut Magoo," "A Magoo Bagatelle," "For The Birds Magoo," "Choo, Choo, Magoo," "Good Neighbor Magoo," "Magoo's Kidnap Kaper," "Boo, Magoo!," "Magoo's Yacht Party," "Magoo's Pizza," "Come Back Little McBarker," "Magoo's Fountain Of Youth," "Gold Rush Magoo," "Miniature Magoo," "Roamin's Magoo," "Spaceman Magoo," "McBarker, The Wonder Dog," "Jungle Man Magoo," "Millionaire Magoo," "Shutterbug Magoo," "Magoo's Driving Test," "Secret Agent Magoo," and "Rip Van Magoo."

WHEELIE AND THE CHOPPER BUNCH

The world's greatest stunt–racing car, Wheelie, a souped–up Volkswagen, takes on the Chopper Bunch motorcycle gang, whose leader tries to win the affections of the "bug" girlfriend, Rota Ree, in situations that involve other rotary–engined characters with distinct personalities. *A Hanna–Barbera Production. Color. Half–hour. Premiered on NBC: September 7, 1974–August 30, 1975.*

Voices:

Wheelie: Frank Welker, **Rota Ree:** Judy Strangis, **Chopper:** Frank Welker, **Scrambles:** Don Messick, **Revs:** Paul Winchell, **High Riser:** Lennie Weinrib

Other Voices:

Rolina Wolk

Episodes:

(three per show) "Get A Doctor," "A Day At The Beach," "Ghost Riders," "Double Cross Country," "The Stunt Show," "Razzle–Dazzle Paint Job," "The Autolympics," "The Delivery Service," "The Infiltraitor," "The Big Bumper," "Surprise Party," "On The Town," "Black Belt Fuji," "Our Hero," "Wheelie Goes Hawaiian," "The Inspection," "The Old Timer," "The Copter Caper," "Dr. Crankenstein," "Bulldozer Buddy," "Happy Birthday Wheelie," "Wheelie, The Super Star," "Down On The Farm," "Roadeo," "Carfucious Says," "Mighty Wheelie," "Camping With Go–Go," "Lennie Van Limousine," "Snow Foolin'," "Wheelie In Paris," "Dragster Net," "Dragula," "Boot Camp," "Dr. Cykll And Mr. Ryde," "Johnny Crash," "Wheelie And The Smoke Eater," "Friday The Thirteenth," "Wings Of Wheelie" and "Wheelie's Clean Sweep."

WHEN FUNNIES WERE FUNNY

Series of original black–and–white silent cartoon favorites— the Little King, Mutt and Jeff, Felix the Cat and others—newly colorized with soundtracks (music and sound effects) added and packaged for syndication. *A Radio and Television Packagers Production. Color. Half–hour. Premiered: 1974. Syndicated.*

Episodes:

"Accidents Won't Happen" (with Mutt and Jeff), "Dog Missing" (with Mutt and Jeff), "Egyptian Daze" (with Mutt and Jeff), "The Invisible Revenge" (with Mutt and Jeff), "Mixing In Mexico" (with Mutt and Jeff), "Oceans Of Trouble" (with Mutt and Jeff), "Soda Jerks" (with Mutt and Jeff), "They Shall Not Pass" (with Mutt and Jeff), "When Hell Froze Over" (with Mutt and Jeff), "Where Am I?" (with Mutt and Jeff), "The Adventures Of Mutt And Jeff And Bugoff," "Art For Art's Sake" (with the Little King), "The Steadfast Tin Solder" (Cartoon Classics), "The Villain Pursues Her" (Cartoon Classics), "Toy Shop" (Cartoon Classics), "Ain't Nature Grand" (Cartoon Classics), "Barnyard Frolic" (Cartoon Classics), "Batter Up" (Cartoon Classics), "Big City" (Cartoon Classics), "Bosco's Woodland Daze" (Cartoon Classics), "Chinese Lanterns" (Cartoon Classics), "Cinderella" (Cartoon Classics), "Country Boy Rabbit" (Cartoon Classics), "Jack Frost" (Cartoon Classics), "Love

Bugs" (Cartoon Classics), "Lumberjack" (Cartoon Classics), "Magazine Rack" (Cartoon Classics), "Music And Charm" (Cartoon Classics), "Off To The Races" (Cartoon Classics), "On Duty" (Cartoon Classics), "Puss 'N' Boots" (Cartoon Classics), "Mr. Do–All" (with Felix the Cat), "Sunken Treasure" (with Felix the Cat), "The Inventor" (with Felix the Cat), "Misses His Swiss" (with Felix the Cat), "Tuning In," "Double Performance," "The Under Dog," "Spring Cleaning" and "The Dancing Bear."

WHERE'S HUDDLES?

Originally a summer replacement, the show revolves around a fumbling football quarterback, Ed Huddles, and his next–door neighbor, team center Bubba McCoy, who are members of the Rhinos, a disorganized pro team that Huddles somehow manages to lead to victory. The program was broadcast for two consecutive summers. *A Hanna–Barbera Production. Color. Half–hour. Premiered on CBS: July 1, 1970–September 10, 1970. Rebroadcast on CBS: July 1971–September 5, 1971.*

Voices:

Ed Huddles: Cliff Norton, **Bubba McCoy:** Mel Blanc, **Marge Huddles,** Ed's wife: Marie Wilson, **Claude Pertwee,** perfectionist neighbor: Paul Lynde, **Rhinos' Coach:** Alan Reed, **Freight Train:** Herb Jeffries, **Sports Announcer:** Dick Enberg

Episodes:

"The Old Swimming Hole," "A Weighty Problem," "The Ramblin' Wreck," "The Offensives," "Hot Dog Hannah," "To Catch A Thief," "Get That Letter Back," "The Old Trio," "A Sticky Affair" and "One Man's Family."

WILDFIRE

This half–hour adventure series tells the story of Princess Sara of the planet Dar–Shan who, as an infant, is spirited away from the clutches of an evil sorceress, Diabolyn, by the mystically powerful stallion, Wildfire. Wildfire carries the baby princess to the safety of the mortal world where, now grown up, she reunites with the great stallion to defeat Diabolyn and rescue Dar–Shan for the forces of goodness. She is joined by a motley band of companions (Dorin, Brutus and Alvinar) who help her on every step of her perilous quest. Grammy Award–winning composer Jimmy Webb created the series' music. *A Hanna–Barbera Production. Color. Half–hour. Premiered on CBS: September 13, 1986–September 5, 1987.*

Voices:

Princess Sara: Georgi Irene, **Wildfire,** the stallion: John Vernon, **Dorin,** a young boy: Bobby Jacoby, **Brutus,** his clumsy horse: Susan Blu, **Alvinar,** a loyal farmer: Rene Auberjoinois, **John,** Sara's father: David Ackroyd, **Ellen,** John's best friend: Lilly Moon, **Diabolyn,** wicked sorceress: Jessica Walter, **Dweedle,** her hapless servant: Billy Barty, **Mrs. Ashworth:** Vicky Carroll

Episodes:

"The Once And Future Queen," "A Visit To Wonderland," "The Ogre's Bride," "Secret Of The Sinti Magic," "A Meeting

In Time," "The Highwayman," "The Pixie Pirates," "The Name Is The Game," "Strangers In The Night," "Dragons Of Dar-Shan," "King For A Day," "Where Dreams Come From" and "Wildfire: King Of The Horses."

WILL THE REAL JERRY LEWIS PLEASE SIT DOWN?

Comedian Jerry Lewis created this half–hour series in which his animated self, a bumbling janitor for the Odd Job Employ-ment Agency, becomes a last–minute substitute and is reluc-tantly given several temporary assignments by the agency's owner, Mr. Blunderbuss. Lewis did not voice his own char-acter in the series (David L. Lander, who played Squiggy on TV's "Laverne and Shirley," provided the voice characteriza-tion), but he did contribute to several stories which were based on his roles in features including *The Caddy* (1958) and *The Errand Boy* (1962). Other series regulars included his girlfriend, Rhonda; his sister, Geraldine: and Spot, her pet frog. *A Filmation Production. Color. Half–hour. Premiered on ABC: September 12, 1970–September 2, 1972.*

Voices:
Jerry Lewis: David L. Lander

Episodes:
"To Beep Or Not To Beep," "Computer Suitor," "Movie Mad-ness," "Crash Course," "Jerry Goes Ape," "2–½ Ring Circus," "Haunted House Guest," "Good Luck Charm," "Penthouse," "Out To Launch," "Shipboard Romance," "Watch Of The Rhino," "Hokus Pokus," "How Green Was My Valet," "Double Trouble," "Rainmaker" and "Double Oh–Oh."

WINKY DINK AND YOU

Children were given the chance to participate in this unique series, featuring the adventures of Winky, a little boy, and his dog, Woofer. By attaching a transparent sheet to the television screen, kids were able to assist their cartoon friends in escap-ing from danger by drawing on the sheet outlets and other imaginery pathways with ordinary crayons. The program orig-inally aired on CBS between 1953 and 1957, hosted by Jack Barry, who co–created the series with Dan Enright. (Barry and Enright later gained prominence as producers of such top–rated game shows as "The Joker's Wild.") CBS Films syndicated the old black–and–white series through the mid–1960s before it was given this color revival in 1969. *An Ariel Productions in association with Barry and Enright Produc-tions. Color. Half–hour. Syndicated.*

Voices:
Winky Dink: Mae Questel, **Woofer:** Dayton Allen

Episodes:
(four per show) "Follow The Notes," "The Rambling Brook," "Dig We Must," "Canine Cantata," "No Laughing Matter," "The Long–Eared Grant," "Waggin' Dragon," "Handsome Ransom," "Woofer's Draw–In," "Water, Water, Everywhere," "Damsel In Distress," "Fair And Squaw," "U–Boat In The Moat," "The Vacation Draw–In," "The Missing Color Mystery," "Hot Fid-

The imagination of young viewers enabled stars Winky and his dog Woofer to escape trouble in the innovative children's series, "Winky Dink And You." (Courtesy: Mark Kausler)

dle," "Wizard Of The Opera," "Dynamic Ceramics," "Moon Balloon," "The Way Out Watercolor," "Twinkle, Little Star," "Dependence Day," "The Chocolate Cookie Caper," The Ver-nalite Crystal," "Simple Scarum," "The Boisterous Oyster," "A Stitch In Time," "Plane Mayhem," "Over A Barrel," "The Igneosaur," "A Lot Of Hot Air," "The Kindly Defender," "Farm Versus Freeway," "Winged Woofer," "What's The Big Idea?," "Speedy Saucer," "Gone Fission," "The Zip Code Zipper," "Witch's Stew," "Woofer For The Defense," "Pilfered Pump-kins," "Witch's Switch," "Golden Fraud," "Harm On The Range," "Ace High Scarum," "Et Tu Wooder," "Circus Draw In," "Winky Dink And The Whale," "Fastest Gum In The West," "Romance Of The Nose," "All Squared Away" and "Prince Or Frog."

WOLF ROCK TV

Famous radio disc jockey Wolfman Jack hires three teenagers, Sara, Ricky and Sunny, to run his rock and roll television station. Along with their pet bird, Bopper, they keep the station manager, Mr. Morris, on the edge of his seat worrying about the next broadcast. *A DIC Enterprises Production. Color. Half–hour. Premiered on ABC: September 8, 1984– September 30, 1984.*

Voices:
Wolfman Jack: Himself, **Sara:** Siu Ming Carson, **Sunny:** Noelle North, **Bopper:** Frank Welker, **Mr. Morris:** Jason Bernard, **Ricardo:** Robert Vega

Episodes:
"The Video Nappers," "Bad News Birds," "Bopper Goes Ape," "The Nerds Who Fell To Earth," "No Time For Sarge," "Rockin Robot" and "Wolfman's Granny."

THE WONDERFUL STORIES OF PROFESSOR KITZEL

Historic and cultural events are related by Professor Kitzel, an electronic wizard, combining film clips, commentary and animation in this half–hour educational series produced by veteran animator James "Shamus" Culhane. The series, which was originally produced for classroom instruction, was syndicated between 1972 and 1976. *A M.G. Animation Production. Color. Half–hour. Premiered: 1972. Syndicated.*

THE WONDERFUL WIZARD OF OZ

The land of Oz is revisited in this animated series featuring Dorothy, the Scarecrow, the Tin Woodman, the Lion, Mombi, Tip and all the favorite Oz characters in the Emerald City. The series was narrated by actress Margot Kidder of *Superman* fame. *A Cinar Films Production. Color. Half–hour. Premiered: 1987–1988. Syndicated.*

Voices:
Dorothy: Morgan Hallett, **Tinman:** George Morris, **The Lion:** Neil Shee, **The Scarecrow:** Richard Dumont, **Narrator:** Margot Kidder

Additional Voices:
Steven Bednarski, Harvey Berger, Maria Bircuer, Mark Denis, Kathleen Fee, Carol Ann Francis, Gayle Garfinkle, Susan Glover, Arthur Grosser, Dean Hagopian, A. J. Henderson, Adrian Knight, Terrence Labrosse, Linda Lonn, Liz Macrae, Bronwen Massey, Gordon Masten, Steve Michaels, Carla Napier, Linda O'Dwyer, Barbara Pogemiller, Rob Roy, Michael Rudder, Howard Ryshphan, Vlasta Vrana, Tim Webber, Jane Woods

Episodes:
"Dorothy Meets The Munchkins," "Dorothy Finds A Friend," "Adventures Along The Yellow Brick Road," "The Journey To Emerald City," "Saved By The Mouse Queen," "The Emerald City, At Last," "The Wicked Witch Of The West," "Dorothy's Magic Powers," "Freedom From The Witch," "Mombi, Tip And The Golden Cap," "Back To Emerald City," "The Wizard's Disappointing Secret," "The Wizard Tries To Help," "Journey To The South," "Glinda, The Good Witch," "Home Sweet Home Again," "Dorothy Meets The Wizard, Again," "Back To Oz," "General Jinjur Attacks," "Escape From The Emerald City," "Tinman To The Rescue," "Mombi's Terrible Magic," "Trapped In The Palace," "The Magical Escape," "Glinda Agrees To Help," "The Emerald City, Captured," "Mombi's Attempt To Trick Glinda," "Ozma, Princess Of Oz," "Tik, Tok, The Mechanical Man," "The Kidnapped Prince," "The Deadly Desert," "The Talking Hen," "Monsters Of Stone," "The Underground Country Of Gnomes," "The Deadly Guessing Game," "Dorothy Outsmarts The King," "The Secret Fear Of The Nomes," "The Nome King Sets A Trap," "Saved By The Sun," "The Nome King Plans Revenge," "Princess Ozma's Secret," "Miss Cuttenclip And Mister Fuddle," "The Growleywog Joins The Nomes," "The Water Of Oblivion," "Nomes On The March," "A Winky Helps His King," "The Crowning Of Ozma," "The Nomes Attack," "Dorothy And Her Friends Defend The Palace" and "A Very Happy Ending."

WOODY WOODPECKER AND HIS FRIENDS

Cartoon favorite Woody Woodpecker appeared in this syndicated series of popular cartoon shorts, combined with additional episodes of creator Walter Lantz's "Inspector Willoughby," "Chilly Willy," "Maw and Paw," "The Beary Family" and others, in this half–hour weekday program for first–run syndication. *A Walter Lantz Production. Color. Half–hour. Premiered: 1958–1966; 1972. Syndicated.*

THE WOODY WOODPECKER SHOW

Walter Lantz's high–strung woodpecker, whose staccato laugh ("Ha- ha–ha–ha–ha!") was his trademark, headlined this series of theatrical one–reelers starring himself and other characters from Lantz's studio—Oswald the Rabbit, Wally Walrus, Andy Panda, Chilly Willy, Inspector Willoughby and others. The series was first broadcast on ABC in 1957. Creator Walter Lantz initially hosted the program in live–action wraparounds introducing the cartoons. In 1970, the series shifted to NBC, which broadcast 26 additional half hours of episodes from Lantz's post–1948 cartoon classics. The program was later syndicated as "Woody Woodpecker and Friends." *A Walter Lantz Production. Black–and–white. Color. Premiered on ABC: October 3, 1957–September, 1958; premiered on NBC: September, 1970–September, 1971 (new episodes). Rebroadcast on NBC: September, 1971–September, 1972; September, 1976–September 3, 1977.*

THE WORLD OF DAVID THE GNOME

Based on the world–famous children's books *The Gnomes* and *The Secret of the Gnomes* by Rien Poortvliet and Wil Huygen, this half–hour series narrates the life and circumstances of a Gnome named David; his wife, Lisa; his fox, Swift; and other characters that compose the ordinary life of a Gnome family, including their enemies, the Trolls. The program is narrated by actor Christopher Plummer. *A Cinar Films Production in association with Miramax Films and B.R.B.*

Internacional, S. A. Color. Half–hour. Premiered on Nicke-lodeon: January 4, 1988.

Voices:

David: Tom Bosley, **Lisa:** Jane Woods, **Holler:** A. J. Hender-son, **Susan:** Barbera Pogemiller, **King:** Richard Dumont, **Pit:** Adrian Knight, **Pat:** Rob Roy, **Pot:** Marc Denis, **Narrator:** Christopher Plummer

Episodes:

"Good Medicine," "Witch Way Out," "David To The Rescue," "The Baby Troll," "Little Houses For Little People," "The Wedding That Almost Wasn't," "To Grandfather's House We Go," "Ghost Of Black Lake," "Kingdom Of The Elves," "The Magic Knife," "Young Dr. Gnome," "Happy Birthday To You," "The Siberian Bear," "Foxy Dilemma," "Three Wishes," "Ivan The Terrible," "Rabbits, Rabbits Everywhere," "Any Milk To-day," "The Shadowless Stone," "Friends In Trouble," "Airlift," "Big Bad Tom," "Kangaroo Adventure," "The Careless Cub," "The Gift" and "The Mountains Of Beyond."

THE WORLD'S GREATEST SUPER FRIENDS

The success of Hanna–Barbera's 1978 superheroes series, "The All–New Super Friends," spurred network interest in another show based on the comic book stories of the League of Justice. As before, the new series featured such popular superheroes as Superman and Wonder Woman in animated form. *A Hanna–Barbera Production. Color. One hour. Premiered on ABC: September 22, 1979–September 27, 1980.*

Voices:

Wonder Woman: Shannon Farnon, **Superman:** Danny Dark, **Batman:** Olan Soule, **Robin:** Casey Kasem, **Aquaman:** Bill Callaway, **Zan:** Mike Bell, **Jayna:** Liberty Williams, **Gleek:** Mike Bell, **Narrator:** Bill Woodson

Episodes:

"Rub Three Times For Disaster," "Lex Luthor Strikes Back," "Space Knights Of Camelon," "The Lord Of Middle Earth," "Universe Of Evil," "Terror At 20,000 Fathoms," "The Super-friends Meet Frankenstein" and "The Planet Of Oz."

THE WUZZLES

The Wuzzles (Bumblelion, Eleroo, Hoppotamus, Moosel, Rhi-nokey and Butterbear) are two creatures in one (i.e., a duck/fox, a pig/chicken, etc.) who live on the island of Wuz. The furry creatures never leave the island, so they never encounter any being that is not born of Wuzzle convention, nor are they even aware of other such beings in this fantasy/adventure series originally produced for Saturday–morning television. The program was rebroadcast on the Disney Channel follow-ing its network run. *A Walt Disney Television Production. Color. Half–hour. Premiered on CBS: September 14, 1985–September 6, 1986. Rebroadcast on ABC: September 13, 1986–September 5, 1987.*

Voices:

Bumblelion/Flizard: Brian Cummings, **Eleroo/Girafbra:** Henry Gibson, **Hoppopotamus:** Jo Anne Worley, **Moosel/Brat:** Bill Scott, **Rhinokey/Croc/Pack–Cat:** Alan Oppenheimer, **Butterbear:** Kathy Helppie, **Mrs. Pedigree:** Tress MacNeille, **Narrator:** Stan Freberg

Episodes:

"Bulls Of A Feather," "Hooray For Hollywuz," "In The Money," "Croc Around The Cloc," "Moosel's Monster," "Klutz On The Clutch," "Bumblelion And The Terrified Forest," "Eleroo's Wishday," "Ghostrustlers," "A Pest Of A Pet," "The Main Course," "Class Dismissed" and "What's Up, Stox?"

YOGI AND HIS FRIENDS

The picnic–basket stealing Yogi and best friend, Boo Boo, enjoyed new life in syndication via this half–hour series of old Hanna–Barbera favorites, including "Hokey Wolf," "Huck-leberry Hound," "Pixie and Dixie," "Snagglepuss" and "Yakky Doodle." *A Hanna–Barbera Production. Color. Half–hour. Premiered: 1967.*

THE YOGI BEAR SHOW

After making his debut on "The Huckleberry Hound Show" in 1958, shrewd Yogi ("Smarter than the average bear") and his shy sidekick, Boo Boo, quickly elevated to stardom and were given their own half–hour series two years later, spon-sored by Kellogg's Cereals and syndicated by Screen Gems, a subsidiary of Columbia Pictures. The program contained mad-cap adventures of the picnic–stealing bears who cause trouble for vacationers at Jellystone Park, plus individual episodes of two other Hanna–Barbera favorites: Snagglepuss, the calam-ity–stricken lion ("Exit stage left . . .") and Yakky Doodle, a dwarf duckling protected by his friend, Chopper the bulldog (who affectionately calls Yakky "Little Fella").

In 1988, Hanna–Barbera resurrected the series, featuring Yogi and Boo Boo in all–new adventures, in a half–hour program for first–run syndication. *A Hanna–Barbera Pro-duction. Color. Half–hour. Premiered: January 30, 1961. Syndicated.*

Voices:

Yogi Bear: Daws Butler, **Boo Boo,** the bear cub: Don Messick, **John Smith,** park ranger: Don Messick, **Snagglepuss:** Daws Butler, **Yakky Doodle:** Jimmy Weldon, **Chopper,** the bull-dog: Vance Colvig, **Fibber Fox:** Daws Butler, **Major Minor:** Don Messick, **Alfy Gator:** Daws Butler

Episodes:

"Yogi Bear" (one per show).
1960–1961 "Oinks and Boinks," "Booby Trapped Bear," "A Bear Pair," "Spy Guy," "Do Or Diet," "Bears And Bees," "Biggest Show–Off On Earth," "Genial Genie," "Cub Scout Boo Boo," "Home, Sweet, Jellystone," "Love–Bugged Bear," "Bearfaced Disguise," "Slaphappy Birthday," "A Bear Living," "Disguise And Gals," "Touch and Go–Go–Go," "Acrobatty Yogi," "Iron Hand Jones," "Yogi's Pest Guest," "Missile Bound

Yogi Bear welcomes visitors to Jellystone Park in Hanna–Barbera's classic cartoon series, "The Yogi Bear Show." © Hanna–Barbera Productions Inc.

Yogi," "Locomotive Loco," "Missile Bound Bear," "A Wooin' Bruin," "Yogi In The City," "Queen Bee For A Day," "Batty Bear" and "Droop–A–Long Yogi."

1961–1962 "Threadbare Bear," "Ice Box Raider," "Bear Foot Soldiers," "Birthday Show Segment #1," "Birthday Show Segment #2" and "Birthday Show Segment #3."

"Snagglepuss" (one per show).

1960–1961 "Major Operation," "Fixed For Thought," "Live And Lion," "Fraidy–Cat Lion," "Lion's Share Sheriff," "Cagey Lion," "Charge That Lion," "Royal Ruckus," "The Roaring Lion," "Paws For Applause," "Knights And Daze," "The Gangsters All Here," "Having A Bawl," "Diaper Desperado," "Arrow Error," "Twice Shy," "Cloak And Stagger," "Remember Your Lions," "Remember The Daze," "Express Trained Lion," "Jangled Jungle," "Lion Tracks" and "Fight Fright."

1961–1962 "Spring Hits A Snag," "Legal–Eagle Lion," "Don't Know It Pest," "Wail Wag Snag," "Rent And Rave," "Footlight Fright," "One, Two, Many" and "Royal Rodent."

"Yakky Doodle" (one per show).

1960–1961 "Out Of Luck Duck," "Hope, Duck And Listen," "Dog Fight," "Easter Duck," "Foxy Duck," "Railroaded Duck," "Duck Hunting," "Whistle Stop And Go," "Duck The Music," "School Fool," "Oh, Duck–Ter," "It's A Duck's Life," "Happy Birthdaze," "Horse Collared," "Ha–Choo To You," "Foxy Proxy," "Count To Tenant," "Shrunken Headache," "The Most Ghost," "Stamp Scamp," "All's Well That Eats Well," "Foxy Friends," "Mad Mix–Up" and "Beach Brawl."

1961–1962 "Duck Seasoning," "Hasty Tasty," "Nobody Home Duck," "Dog Pounded," "Witch Duck–Ter," "Full Course Meal," "Baddie Buddies" and "Judo Ex–Expert."

"Yogi Bear" (new) (three per show).

1988–1989 "Kahuna Yogi," "Grin And Bear It," "Board Silly," "Shine On Silver Screen," "Buffalo'D Bear," "The Yolk's On Yogi," "Yogi De Beargeac," "Bearly Sick," "Bear Exchange," "To Bear Is Human," "Slim And Bear It," "Old Biter," "Pokey

The Bear," "Shadrak Yogi," "Bruise Cruise," "Bear Obedience," "Come Back Little Boo Boo," "La Bamba Bear," "Clucking Crazy," "Misguided Missle," "Double Trouble," "Attack Of The Ninja Racoon," "Biker Bear," "Bearly Buddies," "Predaterminator," "Little Lord Boo Boo," "Yogi The Cave Bear," "Little Big Foot," "Top Gun Yogi," "The Hopeful Diamond," "Real Bears Don't Eat Quiche," "Slippery Smith," "In Search Of The Ninja Racoon," "Balloonatics," "The Big Bear Bullet," "Blast Off Bears," "Battle Of The Bears," "Bringing up Yogi," "Unbearable," "Banjo Bear," "Boxcar Pop," Yogi Meets The Mummy," "Ninja Showdown," "The Not So Great Escape" and "My Buddy Blubber."

YOGI'S GANG

Yogi Bear, Boo Boo, Snagglepuss, Wally Gator and other cartoon pals traverse the world in a flying ark, battling environmental pollution and other hazards along the way. *A Hanna–Barbera Production. Color. Half–hour. Premiered on ABC: September 8, 1973–August 30, 1975.*

Voices:

Yogi Bear: Daws Butler, **Boo Boo:** Don Messick, **Paw Rugg:** Henry Corden, **Doggie Daddy:** John Stephenson, **Huckleberry Hound:** Daws Butler, **Snagglepuss:** Daws Butler, **Quick Draw McGraw:** Daws Butler, **Augie Doggie:** Daws Butler, **Wally Gator:** Daws Butler, **Touché Turtle:** Don Messick, **Squiddly Diddly:** Don Messick, **Ranger Smith:** Don Messick, **Magilla Gorilla:** Allan Melvin, **Atom Ant:** Don Messick, **Secret Squirrel:** Mel Blanc, **Peter Potamus:** Daws Butler, **So–So:** Don Messick

Episodes:

"Mr. Bigot," "The Greedy Genie," "Mr. Prankster," "Mr. Fibber," "Gossipy Witch," "Mr. Sloppy," "Mr. Cheater," "Mr. Waste," Mr. Vandal," "The Sheik Of Selfishness," "Mr. Smog," "Lotta Litter," "The Envy Brothers," "Captain Swipe," "Mr. Hothead," "Yogi's Ark Lark" (Part 1) and "Yogi's Ark Lark" (Part 2).

YOGI'S SPACE RACE

The theatrical release of *Star Wars* spawned several science–fiction spoofs. Hanna–Barbera followed suit by teaming the irrepressible Yogi Bear and his pals in a space race to different galactic planetoids. Along the way they battle space guardian Captain Good, Clean Cat (alias Phantom Phink) and Sinister Sludge, who try to prevent Yogi and friends from crossing the finish line.

Yogi's TV return was minus his cherubic cub partner, Boo Boo, who had co–starred in early adventures in the late 1950s and early 1960s. Instead, Hanna–Barbera's animators created a new sidekick, Scarebear (voiced by former Three Stooges member Joe Besser) for the "Space Race" and "The Galaxy Goof–Ups" segments.

In November, 1978, NBC gave "The Galaxy Goof–Ups" its own half–hour time slot after shuffling the Saturday morning kidvid network lineup. It was the most popular segment of the entire "Space Race" show, featuring Yogi Bear, Scarebear, Huckleberry Hound and Quack–Up (a modern version of Daffy Duck) as purveyors of justice—under the command of Captain Snerdley (a Joe Flynn prototype)—who find more time for disco dancing then completing missions.

Other weekly segments of "Yogi's Space Race" were: "The Buford Files," a crime–solving dog and his teenage companions, Woody and Cindy Mae; and "Galloping Ghost," the adventures of a wild and woolly cowboy ghost, Nugget Nose. *A Hanna–Barbera Production. Color. One hour and a half. Premiered on NBC: September 9, 1978–March 3, 1979.*

Voices:

Yogi Bear: Daws Butler, **Scarebear:** Joe Besser, **Huckleberry Hound:** Daws Butler, **Quack–Up:** Mel Blanc, **Captain Snerdley:** John Stephenson, **Jabberjaw:** Frank Welker, **Buford,** dog detective: Frank Welker, **Woody:** Dave Landsburg, **Cindy Mae:** Pat Parris, **Sheriff:** Henry Corden, **Goofer,** his deputy: Roger Pelz, **Nugget Nose:** Frank Welker, **Rita:** Pat Paris, **Wendy:** Marilyn Schreffler, **Mr. Fuddy:** Hal Peary

Episodes:

"Yogi's Space Race" (one per show).
"The Saturn 500," "The Neptune 9000," "The Pongo Tongo Classic," "Nebuloc—The Prehistoric Planet," "The Spartikan Spectacular," "The Mizar Marathon," "The Lost Planet Of Atlantis," "Race Through Oz," "Race Through Wet Galoshes," "The Borealis Triangle," "Race To The Center Of The Universe," "Race Through The Planet Of The Monsters" and "Franzia."
"The Buford Files" (one per show).
"The Demon Of Ur," "The Vanishing Stallion," "The Swamp Hermit," "Man With The Orange Hair," "The Missing Bank," "Swamp Saucer," "Scare In The Air," "Buford And The Beauty," "Peril In The Park," "The Magic Whammy," "The Haunting Of Swamp Manor," "The Case Of The Missing Gator" and "Don't Monkey With Buford."
"Galloping Ghost" (one per show).
"Phantom Of The Horse Opera," "Too Many Crooks," "Sagebrush Sergeant," "The Bad News Bear," "Robot Round–Up," "Pests In The West," "Rock Star Nuggie," "Frontier Fortune Teller," "I Want My Mummy," "Mr. Sunshine's Eclipse," "Klondike's Kate," "A Ghost Of A Chance" and "Elmo The Great."
"The Galaxy Goof–Ups." (one per show)
"The Purloined Princess," "Defective Protectives," "Whose Zoo?," "The Space Pirates," "The Clone Ranger," "The Dopey Defenders," "Tacky Cat Strikes Again," "Space Station USA," "Hail, King Yogi!," "Dyno–Mite," "Vampire Of Space," "The Treasure Of Congo–Bongo" and "Captain Snerdley Goes Bananas."

YOGI'S TREASURE HUNT

Yogi Bear captains a crew of classic Hanna–Barbera characters, who set sail aboard the magical *S.S. Jelly Roger* in search of treasures which they donate to charitable causes. He is joined in his adventures by co–captain Ranger Smith, first–mate Boo Boo, treasure master Top Cat, ship's mechanic Huckleberry Hound, ship's security crew Super Snooper and Blabbermouse, head chef Snagglepuss and navigators Augie

Young superhero Zoran and his pet, Space Squirrel, travel to Earth only to find action and adventure in the Japanese cartoon series, "Zoran, Space Boy." © Global Productions

Doggie and Doggie Daddy. Episodes were produced for first–run syndication as part of "The Funtastic World of Hanna–Barbera." *A Hanna–Barbera Production. Color. Half–hour. Premiered: September, 1985. Syndicated.*

Voices:

Yogi Bear: Daws Butler, **Boo Boo:** Don Messick, **Huckleberry Hound:** Daws Butler, **Top Cat:** Arnold Stang, **Quick Draw McGraw:** Daws Butler, **Snooper/Blabbermouse:** Daws Butler, **Augie Doggie:** Daws Butler, **Doggie Daddy:** John Stephenson, **Snagglepuss:** Daws Butler, **Ranger Smith:** Don Messick, **Dastardly:** Paul Winchell, **Muttley:** Don Messick

Episodes:

1985–86 "The Riddle In The Middle Of The Earth," "Bungle In The Jungle," "Count Down Drag," "The Return Of El Kabong," "Ole The Red Nosed Viking," "The Curse Of Tutti Frutti," "Yogi And The Unicorn," "The Case Of The Hopeless Diamond," "Merlin's Lost Book Of Magic," "Beverly Hills Flop," "Follow The Yellow Brick Gold," "To Bee Or Not To Bee, That Is Treasure," "Heavens To Planetoid," "Beswitched, Buddha'd And Bewildered," "There's No Place Like Nome," "The Great American Treasure" and "Huckle Hero."
1986–1987 (new episodes combined with reruns) "The Search For The Moaning Lisa," "Snow White And The Seven Treasure Hunters," "Yogi's Heroes" and "Attack Of Treasure Hunters From Mars."
1987–1988 (new episodes combined with reruns) "20,000 Leaks Under The Sea," "Goodbye, Mr. Chump," "Yogi Bear On The Air," "Yogi And The Beanstalk," "The Greed Monster" and "Secret Agent Bear."

ZORAN, SPACE BOY

Accompanied by his pet Space Squirrel, Zoran, who is a superhero from outer space, travels to Earth looking for his sister only to find action and adventure in this Japanese cartoon import for first–run syndication. *A Global Production. Color. Half–hour. Premiered: 1966. Syndicated.*

AWARDS AND HONORS

ACADEMY AWARDS

The Academy of Motion Picture Arts and Science first began recognizing animated cartoons in its annual Oscars derby in the 1931–1932 season. Initially, the films were nominated under one category—Best Short Subject—along with live–action comedy and novelty short–subjects. (The category underwent several changes throughout its history, and is now called Best Short Films.) Over the years, animated films have garnered nominations in other major categories, including Best Musical Score, Best Song and many others.

The following is a complete listing of the winners and runners–up in the respective categories for each year. Winners are preceded by an asterisk.

1931–1932
* Flowers and Trees, Walt Disney
Mickey's Orphans, Walt Disney
It's Got Me Again, Warner Brothers

1932–1933
Building A Building, Walt Disney
The Merry Old Soul, Walter Lantz
* The Three Little Pigs, Walt Disney

1934
Holiday Land, Charles Mintz/Columbia
Jolly Little Elves, Walter Lantz
* The Tortoise And The Hare, Walt Disney

1935
The Calico Dragon, MGM
* Three Orphan Kittens, Walt Disney
Who Killed Cock Robin?, Walt Disney

1936
* Country Cousin, Walt Disney
Old Mill Pond, MGM
Sinbad The Sailor, Max Fleischer

1937
Educated Fish, Max Fleischer
The Little Match Girl, Charles Mintz/Columbia
* The Old Mill, Walt Disney

1938
Brave Little Tailor, Walt Disney
Mother Goose Goes Hollywood, Walt Disney
* Ferdinand The Bull, Walt Disney
Good Scouts, Walt Disney
Hunky And Spunky, Max Fleischer

1939
Detouring America, Warner Brothers
Peace On Earth, MGM
The Pointer, Walt Disney
* The Ugly Duckling, Walt Disney

1940
* Milky Way, MGM
Puss Gets The Boot, MGM
A Wild Hare, Warner Brothers
* Best Original Score: Pinocchio (Leigh Harline, Paul J. Smith, Ned Washington)
* Best Song: "When You Wish Upon Star" from Pinocchio (Leigh Harline, Ned Washington)

1941
Boogie Woogie Bugle Boy Of Company B, Walter Lantz
Hiawatha's Rabbit Hunt, Warner Brothers
How War Came, Columbia
* Lend A Paw, Walt Disney
The Night Before Christmas, MGM
Rhapsody In Rivets, Warner Brothers
The Rookie Bear, MGM
Rhythm In The Ranks, George Pal Puppetoon
Superman No. 1, Max Fleischer
Truant Officer Donald, Walt Disney
* Best Scoring of a Musical Picture: Dumbo (Frank Churchill, Oliver Wallace)
Best Song: "Baby Mine" from Dumbo (Frank Churchill, Ned Washington)
* Special Award: Walt Disney, William Garity, John N. A. Hawkins, and the RCA Manufacturing Company for their outstanding contribution in the advancement of sound in motion pictures through the production of Fantasia (Certificate)

* Special Award: Leopold Stokowski and his associates for their innovative achievement in the creation of a new form of visualized music in *Fantasia*
* Irving Thalberg National Award for Consistent High–Quality Production: Walt Disney

1942

All Out For V, Terrytoons
The Blitz Wolf, MGM
* *Der Fuehrer's Face,* Walt Disney
Juke Box Jamboree, Walter Lantz
Pigs In A Polka, Warner Brothers
Tulips Shall Grow, George Pal Puppetoons
Best Documentary: *The New Spirit* (Donald Duck), Walt Disney
Best Documentary: *The Grain That Built A Hemisphere,* Walt Disney
Best Song: "Love Is A Song" from *Bambi* (Frank Churchill, Larry Morey), Walt Disney
Best Score: *Bambi* (Frank Churchill, Edward Plumb), Walt Disney
Best Sound Recording: *Bambi* (C. O. Slyfield), Walt Disney

1943

The Dizzy Acrobat, Walter Lantz
The Five Hundred Hats Of Bartholomew Cubbins, George Pal Puppetoon
Greetings Bait, Warner Brothers
Imagination, Columbia
Reason And Emotion, Walt Disney
* *Yankee Doodle Mouse,* MGM
Best Song: "Saludos Amigos" from *Saludos Amigos* (Charles Wolcott, Ned Washington), Walt Disney
Best Sound Recording: *Saludos Amigos* (C. O. Slyfield), Walt Disney
Best Scoring of a Musical Picture: *Saludos Amigos* (Edward H. Plumb, Paul J. Smith, Charles Wolcott), Walt Disney
Best Scoring of a Dramatic or Comedy Picture: *Victory Through Air Power* (Edward H. Plumb, Paul J. Smith, Oliver G. Wallace), Walt Disney
* Special Award: George Pal for the development of novel methods and technique in the production of short–subjects known as Puppetoons (Plaque)

1944

And To Think I Saw It On Mulberry Street, George Pal Puppetoon
The Dog, Cat And Canary, Columbia
Fish Fry, Walter Lantz
How To Play Football, Walt Disney
* *Mouse Trouble,* MGM
My Boy, Johnny, Terrytoons
Swooner Crooner, Warner Brothers

1945

Donald's Crime, Walt Disney
Jasper And The Beanstalk, George Pal Puppetoons
Life With Feathers, Warner Brothers
Mighty Mouse In Gypsy Life, Terrytoons
Poet And Peasant, Walter Lantz
* *Quiet Please,* MGM

Rippling Romance, Columbia
Best Scoring of a Musical Picture: *The Three Caballeros* (Edward H. Plumb, Paul J. Smith, Charles Wolcott), Walt Disney
Best Sound Recording: *The Three Caballeros* (C. O. Slyfield), Walt Disney
Best Picture: *Anchors Aweigh,* MGM (has animated sequence with Jerry the Mouse)
Best Song: "I Fall in Love Too Easily," from *Anchors Aweigh* (Jules Styne, Sammy Cahn), MGM
Best Scoring of a Musical Picture: *Anchors Aweigh* (Georgie Stoll), MGM

1946

* *The Cat Concerto,* MGM
Chopin's Musical Moments, Walter Lantz
John Henry And The Inky Doo, George Pal Puppetoons
Squatter's Rights, Walt Disney
Walky Talky Hawky, Warner Brothers
* Special Scientific or Technical Award: Arthur F. Blinn, Robert O. Cook, C. O. Slyfield and the Walt Disney Studio Sound Department for the design and development of an audio finder and track viewer for checking location noise in sound tracks (Certificate)

1947

Chip 'An Dale, Walt Disney
Dr. Jekyll And Mr. Mouse, MGM
Pluto's Blue Note, Walt Disney
Tubby The Tuba, George Puppetoon
* *Tweetie Pie,* Warner Brothers
Best Scoring of a Musical Picture: *Song Of The South* (Daniele Amfitheatrof, Paul J. Smith, Charles Wolcott), Walt Disney
* Best Song: "Zip–A–Dee–Doo–Dah" from *Song Of The South* (Allie Wrubel, Ray Gilbert), Walt Disney
* Special Award: James Baskette for his able and heartwarming characterizations of Uncle Remus, friend and storyteller to the children of the world (Statuette)

1948

* *The Little Orphan,* MGM
Mickey And The Seal, Walt Disney
Mouse Wreckers, Warner Brothers
Robin Hoodlum, UPA
Tea For Two Hundred, Walt Disney
* Best Two–Reel Subject: *Seal Island,* Walt Disney
Best Song: "The Woody Woodpecker Song" from *Wet Blanket Policy* (Ramey Idriss, George Tibbles), Walter Lantz

1949

* *For Scent–Imental Reasons,* Warner Brothers
Hatch Up Your Troubles, MGM
Magic Fluke, UPA
Toy Tinkers, Walt Disney
Best Song: "Lavender Blue" from *So Dear To My Heart* (Eliot Daniel, Larry Morey), Walt Disney (has animated sequence)
* Special Award: Bobby Driscoll as the outstanding juvenile actor of 1949 for *So Dear To My Heart,* Walt Disney (Miniature Statuette)
* Best Documentary Short: *So Much For So Little* (cartoon), Warner Brothers

1950

* *Gerald McBoing Boing*, UPA

Jerry's Cousin, MGM

Trouble Indemnity, UPA

Best Scoring of a Musical Picture: *Cinderella* (Oliver Wallace, Paul J. Smith), Walt Disney

Best Song: "Bibbidy–Bobbidy–Boo" from *Cinderella* (Mack David, Al Hoffman, Jerry Livingston), Walt Disney

1951

Lambert, The Sheepish Lion, Walt Disney

Rooty Toot Toot, UPA

* *Two Mouseketeers*, MGM

Best Scoring of a Musical Picture: *Alice In Wonderland* (Oliver Wallace), Walt Disney

1952

* *Johann Mouse*, MGM

Little Johnny Jet, MGM

Madeline, UPA

Pink And Blue Blues, UPA

Romance Of Transportation, National Film Board of Canada

Best One–Reel Subject: *Neighbors*, National Film Board of Canada/Norman McLaren

* Best Documentary Short: *Neighbors*, National Film Board of Canada/Norman McLaren

1953

Christopher Crumpet, UPA

From A To Z–Z–Z–Z, Warner Brothers

Rugged Bear, Walt Disney

The Tell–Tale Heart, UPA

* *Toot, Whistle, Plunk And Boom*, Walt Disney

Best Two–Reel Subject: *Ben And Me*, Walt Disney

1954

Crazy Mixed–Up Pup, Walter Lantz

Pigs Is Pigs, Walt Disney

Sandy Claws, Warner Brothers

Touché, Pussy Cat, MGM

* *When Magoo Flew*, UPA

1955

Good Will To Men, MGM

The Legend Of Rock–A–Bye Point, Walter Lantz

No Hunting, Walt Disney

* *Speedy Gonzales*, Warner Brothers

1956

Gerald McBoing Boing On Planet Moo, UPA

The Jaywalker, UPA

* *Mr. Magoo's Puddle Jumper*, UPA

Best Documentary Short: *Man In Space*, Walt Disney

1957

* *Birds Anonymous*, Warner Brothers

One Droopy Knight, MGM

Tabasco Road, Warner Brothers

Trees And Jamaica Daddy, UPA

The Truth About Mother Goose, Walt Disney

1958

* *Knighty Knight Bugs*, Warner Brothers

Paul Bunyan, Walt Disney

Sidney's Family Tree, Terrytoons

1959

Mexicali Shmoes, Warner Brothers

* *Moonbird*, Storyboard Inc.

Noah's Ark, Walt Disney

The Violinist, Pintoff Productions

Best Documentary Short: *Donald In Mathemagic Land*, Walt Disney

* Special Scientific or Technical Award: Ub Iwerks of Walt Disney Productions for the design of an improved optical printer for special effects and matte shots

1960

Goliath II, Walt Disney

High Note, Warner Brothers

Mouse And Garden, Warner Brothers

* *Munro*, Rembrandt Films (released by Paramount)

A Place In The Sun, George K. Arthur–Go Pictures Inc.

1961

Aquamania, Walt Disney

Beep Prepared, Warner Brothers

* *Ersatz (The Substitute)*, Zagreb Film

Nelly's Folly, Warner Brothers

The Pied Piper Of Guadalupe, Warner Brothers

1962

* *The Hole*, Storyboard Inc.

Icarus Montgolfier Wright, Format Films

Now Hear This, Warner Brothers

Self Defense—For Cowards, Rembrandt Films

Symposium On Popular Songs, Walt Disney

1963

Automania 2000, Halas and Batchelor Productions

* *The Critic*, Pintoff–Crossbow Productions

The Game, Zagreb Film

My Financial Career, National Film Board of Canada

Pianissimo, Cinema 16

Best Scoring of Music—Adaptation or Treatment: *The Sword In The Stone* (George Bruns), Walt Disney

1964

Christmas Cracker, National Film Board of Canada

How To Avoid Friendship, Rembrandt Films

Nudnik No. 2, Rembrandt Films

* *The Pink Phink*, DePatie–Freleng

1965

Clay Or The Origin Of Species, Eliot Noyes

* *The Dot And The Line*, MGM

The Thieving Magpie, Giulio Gianini–Emanuele Luzzati

1966

The Drag, National Film Board of Canada

* *Herb Alpert And The Tijuana Brass Double Feature*, Hubley Studio (released by Paramount)

The Pink Blueprint, DePatie–Freleng

1967
* The Box, Murakami–Wolf Films
Hypothese Beta, Films Orzeaux
What On Earth!, National Film Board of Canada

1968
The House That Jack Built, National Film Board of Canada
The Magic Pear Tree, Murakami–Wolf Productions
Windy Day, Hubley Studio (released by Paramount)
* Winnie The Pooh And The Blustery Day, Walt Disney

1969
* It's Tough To Be A Bird, Walt Disney
Of Men And Demons, Hubley Studio (released by Paramount)
Walking, National Film Board of Canada

1970
The Further Adventures of Uncle Sam: Part Two, The Haboush Company
* Is It Always Right To Be Right?, Stephen Bosustow Productions
The Shepherd, Cameron Guess and Associates
Best Original Song Score: "A Boy Named Charlie Brown" (Music by Rod McKuen and John Scott Trotter; Lyrics by Rod McKuen, Bill Melendez, and Al Shean; Adapted by Vince Guardaldi)

1971
* The Crunch Bird, Maxwell–Petok–Petrovich Productions
Evolution, National Film Board of Canada
The Selfish Giant, Potterton Productions

1972
* The Christmas Carol, Richard Williams
Kama Sutra Rides Again, Bob Godfrey Films
Tup Tup, Zagreb Film

1973
* Frank Film, Frank Mouris
The Legend of John Henry, Stephen Bosustow–Pyramid Film Production
Pulcinella, Luzzati–Gianini
Best Song: "Love" from Robin Hood (Music by George Bruns; Lyrics by Floyd Huddleston), Walt Disney

1974
* Closed Mondays, Lighthouse Productions
The Family That Dwelt Apart, National Film Board of Canada
Hunger, National Film Board of Canada
Voyage To Next, Hubley Studio
Winnie The Pooh And Tigger Too, Walt Disney

1975
* Great, British Lion Films Ltd.
Kick Me, Swarthe Productions
Monsieur Pointu, National Film Board of Canada
Sisyphus, Hungarofilms

1976
Dedalo, Cinetaeam Realizzazioni
* Leisure, Film Australia
The Street, National Film Board of Canada

1977
The Bead Game, National Film Board of Canada
The Doonesbury Special, Hubley Studio
Jimmy The C, Motionpicker Productions
* Sand Castle, National Film Board of Canada

1978
Oh My Darling, Nico Crama Productions
Rip Van Winkle, Will Vinton/Billy Budd
* Special Delivery, National Board of Canada
Honorary Award: Walter Lantz, for bringing joy and laughter to every part of the world through his unique animated motion pictures (statuette)

1979
Dream Doll, Godfrey Films/Zagreb Films/Halas and Batchelor
* Every Child, National Film Board of Canada
It's So Nice To Have A Wolf Around The House, AR&T Productions for Learning Corporation of America

1980
All Nothing, National Film Board of Canada
* The Fly, Pannonia Film
History Of The World In Three Minutes, Michael Mills Productions Ltd.

1981
* Crac, Societ Radio–Canada
The Creation, Will Vinton Productions
The Tender Tale Of Cinderella Penguin, National Film Board of Canada

1982
The Great Cognito, Will Vinton Productions
The Snowman, Snowman Enterprises Ltd.
* Tango, Film Polski

1983
Mickey's Christmas Carol, Walt Disney Productions
Sound Of Sunshine—Sound Of Rain, Hallinan Plus
* Sundae In New York, Motionpicker Productions

1984
* Charade, Sheridan College
Doctor Desoto, Sporn Animation
Paradise, National Film Board of Canada

1985
* Anna & Bella, The Netherlands
The Big Snit, National Film Board of Canada
Second Class Mail, National Film & Television School

1986
The Frog, The Dog And The Devil, New Zealand National Film Unit
* A Greek Tragedy, CineTe pvba
Luxo Jr., Pixar Productions
Best Song: "Somewhere Out There" from An American Tail, Universal; music by James Horner and Barry Mann. Lyrics by Cynthia Well

1987

George And Rosemary, National Film Board of Canada
* *The Man Who Planted Trees,* Societe Radio–Canada
Your Face, Bill Plympton

1988

The Cat Came Back, National Film Board of Canada
Technological Threat, Kroyer Films, Inc.
* *Tin Toy,* Pixar

1989

* *Balance,* A Laurenstein Production
The Cow, The Pilot, Co-op Animated Film Studio with VPTO
  Videofilm
The Hill Farm, National Film & Television School

EMMY AWARDS

In 1949, following the formation of the National Academy of Television Arts and Sciences, the annual presentation of the Emmy Awards was born. Local and national awards shows were organized to honor local television station programming and prime–time entertainment programming that aired on the three major networks. The awards presentation became an annual event in 1957. Animated cartoons have been the recipient of Emmys throughout the history of the awards. A complete listing of Emmy nominated cartoon series and prime–time animated specials follows. Winners are designated by an asterisk.

1959–1960
Outstanding Achievement in the Field of Children's Programming:
* "Huckleberry Hound" (Syndicated)
"Quick Draw McGraw" (Syndicated)

1960–1961
Outstanding Achievement in the Field of Children's Programming:
* "Huckleberry Hound" (Syndicated)

1965–1966
Outstanding Children's Program:
* "A Charlie Brown Christmas" (CBS)

1966–1967
Outstanding Children's Program:
"Charlie Brown's All–Stars" (CBS)
"It's The Great Pumpkin, Charlie Brown" (CBS)

1973–1974
Outstanding Children's Special:
"A Charlie Brown Thanksgiving" (CBS)

1974–1975
Outstanding Children's Special:
* "Yes, Virginia There Is A Santa Claus" (CBS)
"Be My Valentine, Charlie Brown" (CBS)
"Dr. Seuss' The Hoober–Bloob Highway" (CBS)
"It's The Easter Beagle, Charlie Brown" (CBS)
Outstanding Entertainment Children's Series:

* "Star Trek" (NBC)
"The Pink Panther" (NBC)

1975–1976
Outstanding Children's Special:
* "You're A Good Sport, Charlie Brown" (CBS)
Outstanding Informational Children's Special:
* "Happy Anniversary, Charlie Brown" (CBS)

1976–1977
Outstanding Children's Special:
"It's Arbor Day, Charlie Brown" (CBS)
"The Little Drummer Boy, Book II" (NBC)

1977–1978
Outstanding Children's Special:
* "Halloween Is Grinch Night" (ABC)
"A Connecticut Yankee In King Arthur's Court" (CBS)
"The Fat Albert Christmas Special" (CBS)

1978–1979
Outstanding Animated Program:
* "The Lion, The Witch And The Wardrobe" (CBS)
"You're The Greatest, Charlie Brown" (CBS)
"Happy Brithday, Charlie Brown" (CBS)

1979–1980
Outstanding Animated Program:
* "Carlton Your Doorman" (CBS)
"Dr. Seuss' Pontoffel Rock, Where Are You?" (ABC)
"Pink Panther In Olym–Pinks" (ABC)
"She's A Good Skate, Charlie Brown" (CBS)

1980–1981
Outstanding Children's Program:
"Paddington Bear" (PBS)
Outstanding Animated Program:
* "Life Is A Circus, Charlie Brown" (CBS)
"Bugs Bunny: All American Hero" (CBS)
"Faeries" (CBS)
"Gnomes" (CBS)
"It's Magic, Charlie Brown" (CBS)

1981–1982
Outstanding Animated Program:
* "The Grinch Grinches The Cat In The Hat" (ABC)
"A Charlie Brown Celebration" (CBS)
"The Smurf Springtime Special" (NBC)
"Smurfs" (NBC)
"Someday You'll Find Her, Charlie Brown" (CBS)

1982–1983
Outstanding Animated Program:
* "Ziggy's Gift" (CBS)
"Here Comes Garfield" (CBS)
"Is This Goodbye, Charlie Brown?" (CBS)
"The Smurfs Christmas Special" (NBC)
"What Have We Learned, Charlie Brown?" (CBS)

1983–1984
Outstanding Animated Program:
* "Garfield On The Town" (CBS)

"A Disney Christmas Gift" (NBC)
"It's Flashbeagle, Charlie Brown" (CBS)
"The Smurfic Games" (NBC)

1984–1985
Outstanding Animated Program (Daytime):
* "Jim Henson's Muppet Babies" (CBS)
"Alvin And The Chipmunks" (NBC)
"Fat Albert And The Cosby Kids" (Syndicated)
"Smurfs" (NBC)
Outstanding Animated Program (Nighttime):
* "Garfield In The Rough" (CBS)
"Donald Duck's 50th Birthday" (CBS)
"Snoopy's Getting Married" (CBS)

1985–1986
Outstanding Animated Program (Daytime):
* "Jim Henson's Muppet Babies" (CBS)
"CBS Storybreak" (CBS)
"The Charlie Brown And Snoopy Show" (CBS)
"Fat Albert And The Cosby Kids" (Syndicated)
"The Smurfs" (NBC)
Outstanding Animated Program (Nighttime):
* "Garfield's Halloween Special" (CBS)
"Garfield In Paradise" (CBS)

1986–1987
Outstanding Animated Program (Daytime):
* "Jim Henson's Muppet Babies" (CBS)
"Alvin And The Chipmunks" (NBC)
"Disney's Adventures Of The Gummi Bears" (NBC)
"Punky Brewster" (NBC)
"The Smurfs" (NBC)
Outstanding Animated Program (Nighttime):
* "Cathy" (CBS)
"Garfield Goes Hollywood" (CBS)

1987–1988
Outstanding Animated Program (Daytime):
* "Jim Henson's Muppet Babies" (CBS)

"Alvin And The Chipmunks" (NBC)
"CBS Storybreak" (CBS)
"Disney's DuckTales" (Syndicated)
"The Smurfs" (NBC)
Outstanding Animated Program (Nighttime):
* "A Claymation Christmas Celebration" (CBS)
"Brave Little Toaster" (Disney)
"A Garfield Christmas Special" (CBS)

1988–1989
Outstanding Animated Program (Daytime):
* "The New Adventures Of Winnie The Pooh" (ABC)
"DuckTales" (Syndicated)
"Jim Henson's Muppet Babies" (CBS)
"A Pup Named Scooby–Doo" (ABC)
"The Smurfs" (NBC)
Outstanding Animated Program—For Programming More Than
    One Hour (Nighttime):
"Disney's DuckTales: Super DuckTales" (NBC)
Outstanding Animated Progarm—For Programming Less Than
    One Hour (Nighttime):
* "Garfield: Babes And Bullets" (CBS)
"Abel's Island" (PBS)
"Garfield: His Nine Lives" (CBS)
"Madeline" (HBO)
"Meet The Raisins" (CBS)

1989–1990
Outstanding Animated Program (Daytime):
* "The New Adventures of Winnie the Pooh" (ABC)
* "Beetlejuice" (ABC)
Outstanding Animated Program—One Hour or Less (Nighttime)
* "The Simpsons"
"Garfield's Feline Fantasies"
"Garfield's Thanksgiving"
"Why, Charlie Brown, Why?"
"The Simpsons Christmas Special"

SELECTED BIBLIOGRAPHY

Adamson, Joe. *Tex Avery: King of Cartoons*. New York: Popular Film Library, 1975.

———. *The Walter Lantz Story*. New York: Putnam, 1985.

Bakshi, Ralph. *The Animated Art of Ralph Bakshi*. Norfolk, VA: Donning Company Publishers, 1989.

Beck, Jerry, and Friedwald, Will. *Looney Tunes and Merrie Melodies: A Complete Illustrated Guide to the Warner Bros. Cartoons*. New York: Henry Holt, 1989.

Blanc, Mel, and Bashe, Phillip. *That's Not All Folks!: My Life in the Golden Age of Cartoons and Radio*. New York: Warner Books, 1988.

Brooks, Tim, and Marsh, Earle. *The Complete Guide to Prime Time Network TV Shows: 1946–Present*. New York: Ballantine Books, 1988.

Cabarga, Leslie. *The Fleischer Story*. New York: DaCapo Press, 1988.

Canemaker, John. *Felix: The Twisted Tale of the World's Most Famous Cat*. New York: Pantheon Books, 1991.

———. *Winsor McCay: His Life & Art*. New York: Abbeville Press, 1987.

Crafton, Donald. *Before Mickey: The Animated Film 1898–1928*. Cambridge, Massachusetts: MIT Press, 1982.

Culhane, Shamus. *Animation from Script to Screen*. New York: St. Martin's Press, 1990.

———. *Talking Animals and Other People*. New York: St. Martin's Press, 1986.

Edera, Bruno. *Full Length Animated Feature Films*. New York: Hastings House, 1977.

Erickson, Hal. *Syndicated Television: The First Forty Years, 1947–1987*. Jefferson, North Carolina: McFarland & Company, 1989.

Fischer, Stuart. *Kids' TV: The First 25 Years*. New York: Facts On File, 1983.

Gifford, Denis. *American Animated Films: the Silent Era, 1897–1929*. New York: McFarland & Company, Incorporated, Publishers, 1990.

Grant, John. *Walt Disney's Encyclopedia of Animated Characters*. New York: Harper & Row, 1987.

Grossman, Gary H. *Saturday Morning TV*. New York: Arlington House, 1987.

Jones, Chuck. *Chuck Amuck: The Life & Times of an Animated Cartoonist*. New York: Farrar Straus & Giroux, Inc., 1989.

Lenburg, Jeff. *The Great Cartoon Directors*. Jefferson, North Carolina: McFarland & Company, 1983.

Maltin, Leonard. *Of Mice and Magic*. New York: McGraw-Hill, 1980.

McNeil, Alex. *Total Television: A Comprehensive Guide to Programming from 1948 to 1980*. New York, Penguin, 1980.

Peary, Danny, and Peary, Gerald. *The American Animated Cartoon: A Critical Anthology*. New York: E. P. Dutton, 1980.

Schneider, Steve. *That's All Folks!: The Art of Warner Bros. Animation*. New York: Henry Holt, 1988.

Sennett, Ted. *The Art of Hanna-Barbera: Fifty Years of Creativity*. New York: Viking, 1989.

Terrace, Vincent. *Encyclopedia of Television Series, Pilots and Specials: 1937–1973*. New York: New York Zoetrope.

———. *Encyclopedia of Television Series, Pilots and Specials: 1974–1984*. New York: New York Zoetrope.

Woolery, George. *Children's Television: The First Thirty-Five Years, 1946–1981* (Part I: Animated Cartoon Series) Metuchen, New Jersey: Scarecrow Press, 1983.

INDEX